Mastering
SolidWorks

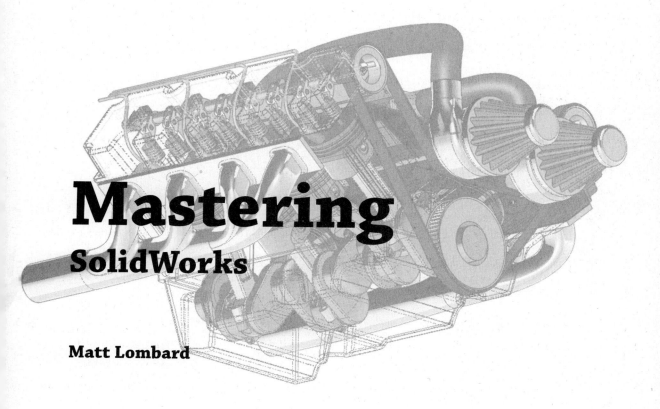

Mastering
SolidWorks

Matt Lombard

SYBEX®

A Wiley Brand

Development Editor: Mary Ellen Schutz

Technical Editor: Alin Vargatu

Production Editor: Athiyappan Lalith Kumar

Copy Editor: Kathy Carlyle

Content Enablement and Operations Manager: Pete Gaughan

Production Manager: Kathleen Wisor

Executive Editor: Jim Minatel

Proofreader: Kathryn Duggan

Indexer: Johnna VanHoose Dinse

Project Coordinator, Cover: Brent Savage

Cover Designer: Wiley

Cover Image: © Matt Lombard, 2018

I dedicate this book to the memory of those of my friends and family who have gone before. Hard work and integrity are important, but who you are is more important than what you have done.

Acknowledgments

I would like to acknowledge three individuals who have together inspired me and pushed me to be my best whatever I'm doing.

Alin Vargatu of Javelin Technologies (located in Oakville, Ontario, Canada) was the technical editor for this book, and is responsible for improving the thoroughness and accuracy of the entire book. Alin has a drive and integrity that is truly an example for us all. His dedication to helping his own customers as well as those who aren't his customers coupled with the boggling amount of energy he must put into this endeavor is really inspiring.

Imre Szuc is Alin's equivalent in the Solid Edge world, as a Solid Edge reseller in Hungary. Imre's enthusiasm for what he does and for technical excellence and sheer drive to help others in highly technical tasks have helped me see what's possible with some dedication.

Arthur Patrick is a Siemens PLM employee who shows real dedication to those who use the product of his efforts. He's responsible for many of the best enhancements to his software over the last several years. He's able to develop and communicate highly productive techniques, and does it all while keeping a sense of humor and not taking himself too seriously. I wish that I could get some of the brilliance from these people to rub off on me a little.

Thanks also to Kim and Zoey, who help with the details in life, allowing me to do this kind of work.

About the Author

Matt Lombard is an independent engineering consultant specializing in design, CAD Management, and product development process consulting. He also writes a blog on product development and related technology, which you can find at www.dezignstuff.com. Matt lives in the picturesque Shenandoah Valley of Virginia, where he enjoys reading the classics and fishing.

Contents

Introduction

SolidWorks is an immense topic, especially if you are new to the software. There is a lot to know and a lot to write about. While I have made every effort to be complete in this book, I'm sure there are some niche topics that have gone untreated. In this edition, I rely more on video introductions for each chapter to demonstrate some of the basic concepts.

Who Should Read This Book

This book is primarily meant as an encyclopedic desk reference for SolidWorks Standard users who want a more thorough understanding of the software and process than can be found in other available documentation. As such, it is not necessarily intended to be a guide for beginners, although it has elements of that. Nor is it necessarily intended as a classroom guide, but it could be used for that as well. This book will take you into areas of technical application where training classes don't go—and into best practices you won't find anywhere else.

What You Will Learn

To keep the size of the book down, I have tried to avoid topics found only in SolidWorks Professional or Premium, although some discussion of these topics was unavoidable at times.

While the book does point out limitations, bugs, and conceptual errors in the software, in every case this is meant to give the reader a more thorough understanding of the software and how it is applied in the context of everyday design or engineering practice. I believe that you don't know how much you can do until you find the boundary—so I frequently push past the limits of the software.

The overall goal of this book is not to fill your head with facts, but to help you think like the software, so that you can use the tool as an intuitive extension of your own process. As your modeling projects get more complex, you will need to have more troubleshooting and workaround skills available to you. Along with best practice recommendations, these are the most compelling reasons to study this book.

This is not a book about machine design, nor industrial design, nor even engineering. This is a book about how to use SolidWorks as a CAD design documentation tool. There is some assumption that you are familiar with general design and engineering practice and terminology.

Thank you for your interest.

What You Need

Make sure that your computer meets the minimum system requirements listed on the SolidWorks website. If your computer doesn't match up to these requirements, you may have a problem using the contents of the download site.

You need to be somewhat familiar with engineering principles (a first-year college engineering curriculum would certainly suffice) and have some experience with engineering documentation practices. Spatial reasoning skills are very helpful to visualize some 3D concepts, and a basic understanding of logic or programming will help you understand the typical workings of a history-based modeler.

WINDOWS VERSIONS

These requirements apply to Windows 7 and Windows 10:

- Intel and AMD processors, single, dual, or quad cores

- 1 GB RAM minimum (2 GB recommended)

- Virtual memory twice the amount of RAM (recommended)

- A certified OpenGL workstation graphics card and driver (Check the SolidWorks website for details: www.solidworks.com.)

- A mouse or other pointing device

- Microsoft Internet Explorer 6 minimum (IE 7 recommended)

- A CD drive minimum (DVD drive recommended)

For more details about the system requirements for SolidWorks 2018 and a list of certified graphics cards and drivers, visit www.solidworks.com.

SOLIDWORKS VERSIONS

Files created in SolidWorks 2018 are not compatible with older versions of SolidWorks. So, if you have a version of SolidWorks older than 2018, you will have difficulty reading most of the accompanying downloaded files. You may find some files that came from older versions in the downloaded data, but this will happen only where the files have not been updated for new versions. If you have any questions, you should contact your SolidWorks reseller. The author of this book does not have the ability to save 2018 files to previous versions.

This book was written using the SolidWorks 2018 version software, and while some of it may be applicable to previous versions, some of it may not be due to annual changes that happen in the course of software development.

TROUBLESHOOTING

If you have difficulty installing or using any of the material from the download data, try the following solutions:

- Turn off any antivirus software that you may have running. Installers sometimes mimic virus activity and can make your computer incorrectly believe that it is being infected by a virus. (Be sure to turn the antivirus software back on later.)

- Close all running programs. The more programs you're running, the less memory is available to other programs. Installers also typically update files and programs; if you keep other programs running, installation may not work properly.

- See the ReadMe file. Refer to the ReadMe file located at the root of the download website for the latest product information at the time of publication.

If you are having trouble viewing the downloaded videos, please install the TechSmith video codec.

The *Mastering* Series

The *Mastering* series from Sybex provides outstanding instruction for readers with intermediate and advanced skills, in the form of top-notch training and development for those already working in their field, and clear, serious education for those aspiring to become pros. Every *Mastering* book features the following:

- The Sybex "by professionals for professionals" commitment. *Mastering* authors are themselves practitioners, with plenty of credentials in their areas of specialty.

- A practical perspective for a reader who already knows the basics—someone who needs solutions, not a primer.

- Skill-based instruction, with chapters organized around real tasks rather than abstract concepts or subjects.

- Self-review tests with "The Bottom Line" problems and questions, so you can be certain you're equipped to do the job right.

What Is Covered in This Book

You will find enough information here that the book can grow with your SolidWorks needs. I wrote the tutorials for most of the chapters with newer users in mind, because for them, it is most helpful to see how things are done in SolidWorks step by step. The longer narrative examples give more in-depth information about features and functions, as well as the results of various settings and options.

This book includes many details that come from practical usage and is focused on the needs of professional users, not on student learners. My preference is to teach concepts rather than button pushes, because if you understand what is going on, you can find the button pushes for yourself.

This book is divided into five parts. You will find that some topics are visited multiple times, such as sketching, mates, templates, and so on. When a topic is visited more than once, it is because there are many aspects to that topic. One such example is sketching, which includes simple sketches, sketch relations, sketch editing, troubleshooting, 3D sketches, shared sketches, and more. Sketch information is found in at least 10 different chapters. It cannot be consolidated because shared sketches are an advanced technique, while simple sketching is not.

Part I: Introducing SolidWorks Basics

This part explores the basic concepts and terminology used in SolidWorks. You need to read this section if you are new to the software and especially if you are new to 3D modeling or parametric history-based design.

Part II: Building Intelligence into Your Parts

This part takes a deeper look at creating parametric relations to automate changes.

Part III: Working with Assemblies

This part examines the tools available to users within SolidWorks assemblies. Assemblies enable you to put parts together in different ways. You can create motion and animations, check for interference and clearance, and look at the data in many different ways.

Part IV: Creating Drawings

This part goes through the tools and techniques for creating drawings from your SolidWorks parts and assemblies. Drawings are the industry-standard way of communicating designs, inspection requirements, and manufacturing processes. Part IV examines several types of advanced techniques, such as surface modeling and multibody modeling. This is information you won't find in other SolidWorks books, explained here by someone who uses the functionality daily.

Part V: Using Advanced and Specialized Techniques

Specialized functionality, such as sheet metal and plastics, requires detailed information. Part V includes these topics because they are key to unlocking all the power available in SolidWorks. Part V examines several types of advanced techniques, such as surface modeling and multibody modeling. This part also contains information you won't find in other SolidWorks books, explained here by someone who uses the functionality daily.

Appendixes

The appendixes in this book contain information that was not appropriate for the main body of the text, such as the contents of the download material and other sources of help.

NOTE   The companion download site (www.wiley.com/go/mastersolid) is home to all the demo files, samples, and resources mentioned in the book. See Appendix B, "Finding Help," for more details on the contents and how to access them.

How to Contact the Author

You might want to contact me for some reason. Maybe you found an error in the book, or you have a suggestion about something that you think would improve it. It is always good to hear what real users think about the material, whether you like it or think it could be improved.

The best way to contact me is either through e-mail or through my blog. My e-mail address is matt@dezignstuff.com. You will find my blog at www.dezignstuff.com. On the blog, you can leave comments and read other things I have written about the SolidWorks software, CAD, and engineering or computer topics in general. If you want to contact me for commercial help with a modeling project, my e-mail address is the best place to start that type of conversation.

Thank you very much for buying and reading this book. I hope the ideas and information within its pages help you accomplish your professional goals.

Wiley strives to keep you supplied with the latest tools and information you need for your work. Please check their website at www.wiley.com/go/mastersolid, where we'll post the download materials for each chapter, additional content, and updates that supplement this book if the need arises.

Part I

Introducing SolidWorks Basics

Chapter 1

Introducing SolidWorks

In SolidWorks, you build 3D parts from a series of simple 2D sketches and features such as extrude, revolve, fillets, cuts, and holes, among others. You can put the parts together into assemblies. You can then create 2D drawings from the 3D parts and assemblies.

This chapter will familiarize you with some of the basic concepts employed by SolidWorks.

IN THIS CHAPTER, YOU WILL LEARN TO:

- ◆ Install SolidWorks
- ◆ Get started with SolidWorks
- ◆ Identify different types of SolidWorks documents
- ◆ Understand feature-based modeling
- ◆ Understand history-based modeling
- ◆ Sketch with parametrics
- ◆ Control changes with design intent
- ◆ Modify design intent
- ◆ Work with links between documents

> **VIDEO**
>
> You can view videos for every chapter on the Wiley website and download sample files. View the Chapter 1 Introduction video to get started.

Installing SolidWorks for the First Time

Some of you will have SolidWorks installed for you by people in your company or by SolidWorks reseller experts, and some of you will need to perform the installation on your own. Regardless, it is best to make sure that your hardware and software are compatible with the SolidWorks system requirements, which are available on the SolidWorks website at www.solidworks.com/sw/support/SystemRequirements.html.

SolidWorks installs natively only on 64-bit operating systems. It is supported only for Windows 7, 8.1, and 10. In all cases, the professional-level OS is recommended, as opposed to the Home edition. Excel and Word 2016 are also recommended. Although it is possible to install and run SolidWorks under emulators on Apple hardware, that configuration is not supported or tested by SolidWorks Corporation or its resellers.

You can find graphics card requirements at the previously mentioned link for system requirements. The main concern with a graphics card for SolidWorks is that it must be compatible with OpenGL and be SolidWorks certified. Hardware changes too rapidly for me to give specific recommendations here.

In addition to having the correct hardware installed, you also must have a compatible driver version installed. Again, refer to the SolidWorks system requirements website.

Alternatively, you might not want to get that involved at first. You can install the software with all the defaults just to get started, using the first attempt as a practice installation, especially if you intend to learn as much as you can about SolidWorks, and then come back and do a more thorough job of implementing it later.

You should count on the installation requiring about 16 GB of space on your hard drive, depending on the options you select to install. The locations of files on your computer will vary by SolidWorks version, by your operating system, and by your own installation choices, but the bulk of the files will be placed into two separate folders: the Program Files folder (`C:\Program Files\SolidWorks Corp\SolidWorks`) and the Toolbox Data folder (`C:\SolidWorks Data`).

Before installing any software, be sure to exit out of all other software first, turn off antivirus software, make sure you have enough hard drive space, and verify that the system meets the requirements outlined on the SolidWorks System Requirements web page.

Installations generally begin from a download of an installer application named `SolidWorksSetup.exe`, which is about 30 MB. You may need a login to access this area of the site. Find the download area at `http://www.solidworks.com/sw/support/downloads.htm`, shown in Figure 1.1.

FIGURE 1.1

The Downloads area of the SolidWorks website

Once you download and execute the installer, you will be prompted to unzip the installation files, and the installation will begin, as shown in Figure 1.2.

FIGURE 1.2
The SolidWorks 2018
Installation Manager

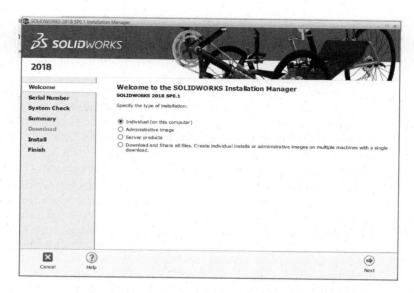

The next screen asks for your serial number, which is a 24-character code. After the installation, you will be required to activate your SolidWorks license. Figure 1.3 shows the Activation page of the installation process. If you have difficulty with this, you may want to contact your support organization.

FIGURE 1.3
SolidWorks 2018
Activation

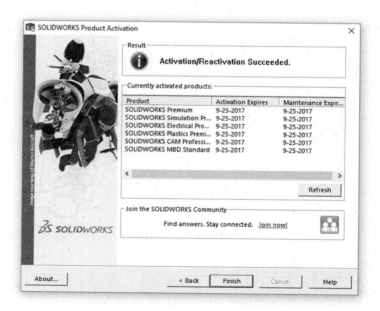

When the installation is complete, reboot the system.

Starting SolidWorks for the First Time

SolidWorks has many tools that are available for beginning users when the software is installed. A default installation presents you with several options when the software is started the first time. This section includes a description of these options and how you can most benefit from them. If you plan to go to formal SolidWorks reseller-based training classes, be sure to go through some of the tutorials mentioned in this section first, so you will be prepared to ask educated questions and have a leg up on the rest of the class. You will get more out of the training with the instructor if you have already seen the material.

Examining the SolidWorks License Agreement

Becoming familiar with the license agreement can be useful, but the agreement does not have any bearing on learning how to use the software other than the fact that it allows you to reactivate as needed. This ability enables you to use your license on different computers—for example, at work and at home. To use your license at home, make sure the software is installed at both locations and both locations are connected to the Internet, and then activate it at work. When you are done at work, deactivate the license and reactivate it at home using the same serial number. It would be a good idea to consult your CAD administrator before you do this. You can access the Activation options in the Help menu, as shown in Figure 1.4. Network licenses may work differently. When you are done at home, you can deactivate the license at home and reactivate at work. It is like a floating license, where the server is at a SolidWorks facility. Again, contact your support organization with questions about any specific details.

FIGURE 1.4
Activation options on
the Help menu

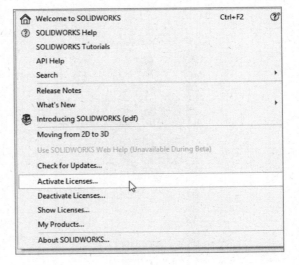

Using the Help Menu

You can access the Help menu in two ways. A question mark in the upper right has a drop-down arrow next to it that enables you to access all the Help options. Help is also on the flyout menu next to the SolidWorks logo in the upper left. You will find that SolidWorks offers multiple ways to access many commands. You should become comfortable with at least one method for accessing the tools you need to use. It isn't necessary to know all the ways unless you are teaching others (or writing a book).

VIEWING THE WELCOME TO SOLIDWORKS DIALOG

The Welcome to SolidWorks screen, shown in Figure 1.5, is the first thing to greet you when you open the software. This helps you open recent files, browse for existing data, or create a new document. The Advanced button gives you access to all available templates (templates will be covered later in this chapter), and you can look inside the folders for each of the recent documents by hovering the mouse cursor over the preview.

FIGURE 1.5
The Welcome to
SolidWorks screen

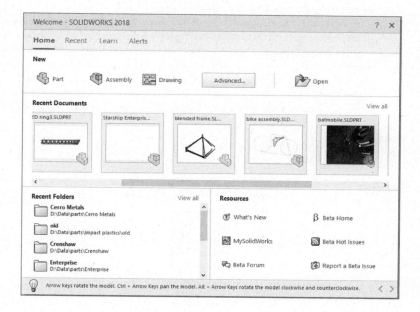

The tabs at the top of the dialog (Home, Recent, Learn, and Alerts) will reconfigure the Welcome dialog to show various topics. The Learn tab has links to various training and tutorial material, sample parts, and assemblies. The Alerts tab shows SolidWorks news such as the release of a Beta or special notices about problems or fixes in the software.

Also notice at the bottom of the Welcome dialog is the Tip of the Day. You can cycle through these tips when you have a few spare moments.

ACCESSING WHAT'S NEW

You can find the What's New documentation in the Help menu, as shown in Figure 1.4. You can also enable interactive What's New options (Help ➤ What's New ➤ Interactive). This adds a question mark with an asterisk symbol next to menu items that are new and have special Help file entries. You will find more information about setting up the SolidWorks interface in Chapter 2, "Navigating the SolidWorks Interface."

ACCESSING OTHER RESOURCES

Between the Help and the Welcome dialogs, SolidWorks offers several options for help, including tutorials, What's New, and the SolidWorks forums.

Creating a New Document

New...

To start a new SolidWorks document, click the New icon in the title bar of the SolidWorks application. With standard functions such as creating a new document, SolidWorks works just like a Microsoft Office application, and the icons even look the same.

SolidWorks has three basic types of documents: parts, assemblies, and drawings. *Parts* are the basic 3D file type. You put parts together to create *assemblies,* and *drawings* are the 2D file type for documenting parts and assemblies.

When you create a new SolidWorks document, you will see the screen shown in Figure 1.6. By default, this dialog box contains templates for parts and assemblies. You can make your own customized templates to add to them or share templates with other users on a network. Templates have several already-established settings, most importantly units. You can change the units of a document after it is created, but most people find it easier to start with the correct units. You can mix units in parts, and used parts with different units in assemblies, but this can get confusing when editing parts with mixed units in the context of an assembly.

FIGURE 1.6

Selecting a template in the New SolidWorks Document dialog

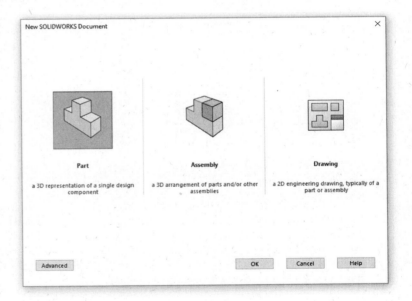

Templates also control the drafting standard used with the document. ANSI and ISO are the two primary standards, although others are available. One option you need to be aware of with the ISO standard is that some locations that use the ISO standard also use First Angle Projection, while ANSI users and some ISO users use the Third Angle Projection system.

The Drafting Standard setting is found under Tools ➢ Options ➢ Document Properties ➢ Drafting Standard, as shown in Figure 1.7. The projection angle can be specified both in drawings and in parts/assemblies. You can find the drawing setting by clicking the right mouse button (RMB), clicking on the Sheet entry in the FeatureManager on the left of the drawing document window, and selecting Sheet Properties.

FIGURE 1.7
Drafting
Standard setting

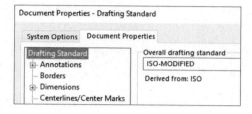

The projection type for 3D parts and assemblies becomes important when you set up viewports within the SolidWorks window. The setting for this is located under Tools ➢ Options ➢ Display/Selection ➢ Projection type (at the bottom of the list). This does not follow the drafting standard selected for the default templates or the country in which the software is installed.

For more information on first- and third-angle projections, refer to this Wikipedia article: `http://en.wikipedia.org/wiki/Multiview_orthographic_projection`.

Be sure to get the option correct. If someone else, such as a computer specialist who is not familiar with mechanical drafting standards, initially sets up SolidWorks on your computer, verify that the default templates use the correct standards, units, and projection method. The projection angle setting is shown in Figure 1.8.

FIGURE 1.8
Projection Angle setting

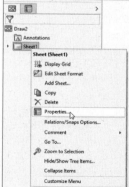

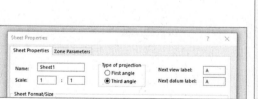

Identifying SolidWorks Documents

SolidWorks has three main data type files: parts, assemblies, and drawings; however, if you are concerned with customizing and creating implementation standards, you may want to become familiar with some additional supporting types. Table 1.1 outlines the document types.

TABLE 1.1:   Document Types

DESIGN DOCUMENTS	DESCRIPTION
.sldasm	SolidWorks assembly file type
.slddrw	SolidWorks drawing file type
.sldprt	SolidWorks part file type
Templates and Formats	**Description**
.asmdot	Assembly template
.asmprp	Assembly custom properties tab template
.drwdot	Drawing template
.drwprp	Drawing custom properties tab template
journal.doc	Design journal template
.prtdot	Part template
.prtprp	Part custom properties tab template
.sldbombt	BOM template (table-based)
.sldtbt	General table template
.slddrt	Drawing sheet format
.sldholtbt	Hole table template
.sldrevtbt	Revision table template
.sldwldtbt	Weldment cutlist template
.xls	BOM template (Excel-based)
Library Files	**Description**
.sldblk	Blocks
.sldlfp	Library part file
Styles	**Description**
.sldgtolfvt	Geometric tolerance style
.sldsffvt	Surface finish style
.sldweldfvt	Weld style

TABLE 1.1   Document Types *(CONTINUED)*

DESIGN DOCUMENTS	DESCRIPTION
Symbol Files	**Description**
gtol.sym	A symbol file that enables you to create custom symbols
swlines.lin	A line-style definition file that enables you to create new line styles
Others	**Description**
.btl	Sheet metal bend table
calloutformat.txt	Hole-callout format file
.sldclr	Color palette file
.sldreg	SolidWorks settings file
.sldmat	Material database
.sldstd	Drafting standard
.swb, .swp	Macros, macro features
.txt	Custom property file, sheet-metal-bend-line note file
.xls	Sheet metal gauge table

Unlike some other CAD programs, SolidWorks does not use separate file types for sheet metal and weldment parts; they are all just `*.sldprt`. The features within the parts distinguish them as either sheet metal or weldment parts.

Also unlike other CAD programs, SolidWorks' templates have a special file type (for example, part templates are `*.prtdot`) and are not just "start parts."

Saving Your Setup

If you need to reinstall SolidWorks, move to another computer, or duplicate the setup for another user, you need to copy the files you have used or customized. By default, all these files are located in different folders within the SolidWorks installation directory. Chapter 2 deals with interface settings and creating a Registry Settings file to copy to other computers or use as a backup.

BEST PRACTICE

When you are performing complex implementations that include templates of various types of tables or customized symbol files, it is especially important to have copies of any customized templates or library files in a location other than the default installation folder. Uninstalling SolidWorks or installing a new version could wipe out all your hard work. Choose Tools ➤ Options ➤ File Location to establish separate library folders on the local hard drive or on a network location.

Using Templates

I have included some of my part and assembly templates with the download materials for this book. After you have downloaded the zip files for each chapter, extract and copy them to the folder specified at Tools ➢ Options ➢ File Locations ➢ Document Templates.

ON THE WEBSITE

Wiley has established a website for the material in this book. You can download files for each chapter from www.wiley.com/go/mastersolid

---

When you begin to create a new document, and the New SolidWorks Document dialog box gives you the option to select one of several files to start from, those files are templates. Think of templates as "start parts" that contain all the document-specific settings for a part (Tools ➢ Options ➢ Document Properties). The same concept applies to assemblies and drawings. Templates generally do not have any geometry in them (although it is possible).

As shown in Figure 1.6, several tabs can be displayed on the Advanced interface. Each of these tabs results from creating a folder in the template directory specified in the Options dialog box (Tool ➢ Options ➢ File Locations ➢ Document Templates). To switch from the Novice interface to the Advanced interface, click the Advanced button. To switch from Advanced to Novice, click the Novice button shown in Figure 1.9.

MULTIPLE DOCUMENT TEMPLATES

When starting a new document, you will be given many options if you have multiple templates available. This offers an advantage in many situations, including the following:

◆ Standardization for a large number of users

◆ Work produced in various units

◆ Preset materials

◆ Preset custom properties

◆ Parts with special requirements, such as sheet metal or weldments

◆ Parts and assemblies with standardized background colors

◆ Drawings of various sizes with formats (borders) already applied

◆ Drawings with special notes already on the sheet

Drawing templates and formats are so complex that I devote an entire chapter to them. Chapter 24, "Automating Drawings: The Basics," discusses the differences between drawing templates and formats, and how to use them to your advantage. This chapter addresses part and assembly templates.

Depending on your needs, it might be reasonable to have templates for metric parts and assemblies and Imperial parts and assemblies, templates for steel and aluminum, and templates for sheet metal parts and weldments, if you design these types of parts. If your firm has different

FIGURE 1.9

The Novice and Advanced interfaces for the New SolidWorks Document dialog box

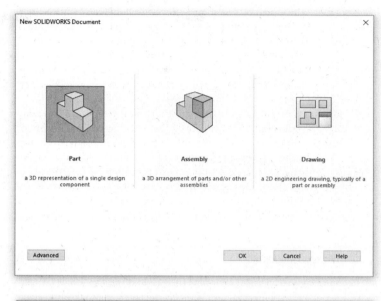

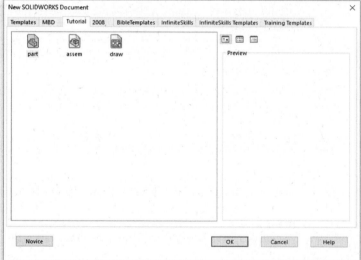

customers with different requirements, you might consider using separate templates for each customer. Over time, you will discover the types of templates you need, because you will find yourself repeatedly making the same changes to new parts.

To create a template, open a document of the appropriate type (part, assembly, or drawing), delete all features. (Although it is possible to use templates with pre-created geometry, it is unusual.) Make the settings you want the template to have. For example, units are one of the most common reasons to make a separate template, although any Document Property setting is fair game, from the dimensioning standard used to the image quality settings. You can find these settings through the menus at Tools ➤ Options➤ Document Properties.

Some document-specific settings do not appear in the Document Properties dialog box, such as the names of standard planes or the use of axes as reference geometry. Still, these settings are saved with the template. Settings that fall into this category are the View menu's entity-type Visibility option and the Tools ➤ Sketch Settings menu options.

Custom properties are another piece of the template puzzle. If you use or plan to use BOMs (Bills of Materials), PDM (Product Data Management), or linked notes on drawings, you need to take advantage of the automation options available with custom properties.

Two Default Template options are available: "Always use these default document templates" and "Prompt user to select document template." The Default Template options apply to situations when a template is required by an automatic feature in the software, such as an imported part or a mirrored part. In this situation, depending on the option selected, the system automatically uses the default template or the user is prompted to select a template.

PERFORMANCE

Allowing the software to apply the default template automatically can speed up the process dramatically. This is especially true in the case of imported assemblies, which require you to select templates manually for each imported part in the assembly if the "Prompt user to select document template" option is selected.

SHARING TEMPLATES

If you are administering an installation of a large number of users, or even if just a couple of users are working on similar designs, shared templates are necessary. If every user does what he or she thinks is best, you may get an adverse combination of conflicting ideas, and the consistency of the company's documentation may suffer. Standardized templates cannot make users model, assemble, and detail in exactly the same way, but they do help users start on the same foot.

To share templates among several users, create a folder for templates on a commonly accessible network location, preferably with read-only access for users and read-write permissions for administrators. Then point each user's File Locations and Default templates to that location. Access problems due to multiple users accessing the same files do not arise in this situation, because users copy templates to create new documents and do not use them directly.

CAUTION   One of the downfalls of this arrangement is that if the network goes down, users no longer have access to their templates. This can be averted by also putting copies of the templates on the local computers; however, this has the tendency to undermine the goal of consistent documentation. Users may tend to use and customize the local templates rather than use the standardized network copies.

Understanding Feature-Based Modeling

Before diving into building models with SolidWorks, you need to be familiar with some terminology. Notice that I talk about modeling rather than drawing or even design. Whether you are building an assembly line for automotive parts or designing decorative perfume bottles, SolidWorks can help you visualize your geometrical production data in the most realistic way possible without actually having it in your hand. This is more akin to making a physical model in the shop than drawing on paper.

Feature-based modeling means that you build the model by creating 2D sketches and applying processes (features) to create the 3D shape. For example, you can create a simple box by using the Extrude process, and you can create a sphere using the Revolve process. However, you can make a cylinder using either process, by revolving a rectangle or extruding a circle. Figure 1.10 shows images of simple feature types along with the 2D sketches from which they were created.

FIGURE 1.10
Simple extruded and
revolved features

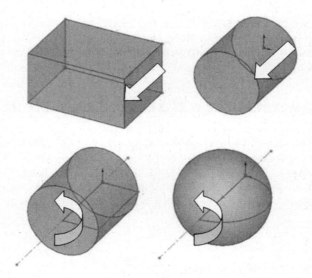

Many different feature types in SolidWorks enable you to create everything from the simplest geometry shown in Figure 1.10 to more complex shapes. In general, when I talk about modeling in this book, I am talking about *solid* modeling, although SolidWorks also has a complete complement of surfacing tools. I discuss the distinction between solid and surface modeling in Chapter 32, "Working with Surfaces."

Table 1.2 lists some of the most common features in SolidWorks and classifies them according to whether they always require a sketch, a sketch is optional, or they never require a sketch. As an example of a sketch optional feature, a sweep can use a model edge as a sweep path.

TABLE 1.2:   Feature Types

SKETCH REQUIRED	SKETCH OPTIONAL (USES FACES OR EDGES)	NO SKETCH (APPLIED FEATURES)
Extrude	Loft	Fillet
Revolve	Sweep	Chamfer
Rib	Dome	Draft
Hole Wizard	Boundary	Shell
Wrap	Deform	Flex

In addition to these features, other types of features create reference geometry, such as curves, planes, axes, and surface features (Chapter 32); specialty features for techniques like sheet metal (Chapter 34, "Using SolidWorks Sheet Metal Tools"); and plastics/mold tools (Chapter 38, "Using Plastic Features," and Chapter 39, "Using Mold Tools").

Understanding History-Based Modeling

In addition to being feature-based, SolidWorks is also *history-based*. The process history is shown in a panel to the left side of the SolidWorks window called the *FeatureManager*. The FeatureManager keeps a list of the features in the order in which you have added them. It also enables you to reorder items in the tree (in effect, to change history). Because of this, the order in which you perform operations is important. For example, consider Figure 1.11. This model was created by the following process, left to right starting with the top row:

1. Create a sketch.
2. Extrude the sketch.
3. Create a second sketch.
4. Extrude the second sketch.
5. Create a third sketch.
6. Extrude Cut the third sketch.
7. Apply fillets.
8. Shell the model.

If the operations used in the previous part were slightly reordered (by putting the shell and fillet features before Step 6), the resulting part would look slightly different, as shown in Figure 1.12. You can find this part in the download materials for this chapter.

FIGURE 1.11
Features used to create a simple part

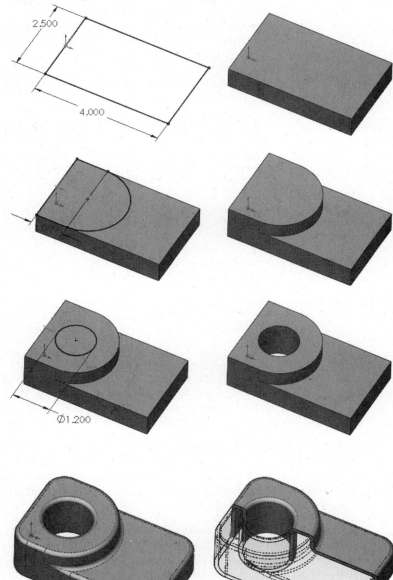

FIGURE 1.12
Using a different order of features for the same part

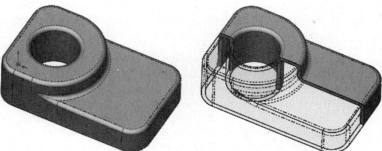

Figure 1.13 shows a comparison of the FeatureManager design trees for the two different feature orders. You can reorder features by dragging them up or down the tree. However, relationships between features can prevent them from being reordered; for example, the fillets are dependent on the second extruded feature and cannot be reordered before it. This is referred to as a *parent/child relationship*.

Reordering and parent/child relationships are discussed in more detail in Chapter 12, "Editing, Evaluating, and Troubleshooting."

FIGURE 1.13
Comparing the FeatureManager design trees for the parts shown in Figure 1.11 and Figure 1.12, respectively

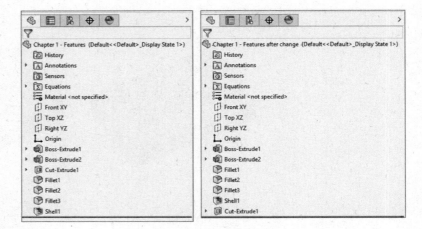

The order of operations, or *history*, is important to the final state of the part. For example, if you change the order so that the shell comes before the extruded cut, the geometry of the model changes, removing the sleeve inside instead of the hole on top. You can try this for yourself by opening the part indicated previously, dragging the Shell1 feature in the FeatureManager and dropping it just above the Cut-Extrude1 feature.

NOTE You can drag only one item at a time in the FeatureManager. If you try to drag more than one, only the last selected item is dragged. Therefore, you may drag the shell and then drag each of two fillets, or you could just drag the cut feature down the tree. Alternatively, you can put the shell and fillets in a folder and drag the folder to a new location. Reordering is limited by parent/child relationships between dependent features.

You can read more about reordering folders in Chapter 12.

In some cases, reordering the features in the FeatureManager can have a result that does not make any sense; for example, if the fillets are applied after the shell, they might break through to the inside of the part. In these cases, SolidWorks gives an error that will help you fix the problem.

Features are really just like steps in building a part; the steps can add material, remove it, or both. However, when you make a part on a mill or lathe, you are only removing material. Some people choose to model following manufacturing methods, so they start from a piece of stock and apply features that remove material, as you would on a mill. This approach works best for machining, but doesn't work well for molding, casting, sheet metal, or progressive dies. The FeatureManager is like an instruction sheet to build the part. When you reorder and revise the list of features, you change the order of operations and thus the final result. Some people look at the FeatureManager as a recipe for cooking.

Sketching with Parametrics

Sketching is the foundation that underlies the most common feature types. You will find that sketching in parametric software is vastly different from drawing lines in 2D CAD.

Dictionary.com defines the word *parameter* as "one of a set of measurable factors . . . that define a system and determine its behavior and [that] are varied in an experiment." SolidWorks sketches are parametric. What this means is that you can create sketches that change according to certain rules and maintain relationships through those changes. Creating sketches and features with intelligence is the basis of the concept of *design intent,* which I cover in more detail later in this chapter.

In addition to 2D sketching, SolidWorks also makes 3D sketching possible. Of the two methods, 2D sketches are by far more widely used. You create 2D sketches on a selected plane or planar face and then use them to establish shapes for features such as Extrude, Revolve, and others. Relations in 2D sketches often are created between sketch entities and other model edges that may or may not be in the sketch plane. In situations where other entities are not in the sketch plane, the out-of-plane entity is projected into the sketch plane in a direction that is normal to the sketch plane. This does not happen for 3D sketches.

You can use 3D sketches for the Hole Wizard, routing, weldments, and complex shape creation, among other applications.

For more information on 3D sketching, refer to Chapter 6, "Getting More from Your Sketches."

For a simple example of working with sketch relations in a 2D sketch, consider the sketch shown in Figure 1.14. The only relationships among the four lines are that they form a closed loop that is touching end-to-end and one of the corners is coincident to the part origin. The small square icon near the origin shows the symbol for a *coincident* sketch relation. These sketch relations are persistent through changes and enable you to dynamically move sketch elements with the cursor on the screen. The setting to enable or disable displaying the sketch relation symbols is found at View ➤ Sketch Relations.

FIGURE 1.14
A sketch of four lines changes as relationships and dimensions are added.

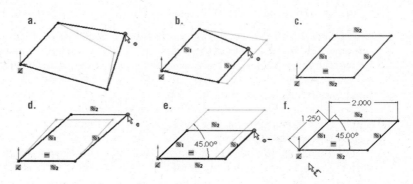

If you drag any of the unconstrained corners (except for the corner that is coincident to the origin), the two neighboring lines follow the dragged endpoint, as shown in Figure 1.14. Notice the ghosted image left by the original position of the sketch. This is helpful when you're experimenting with changes to the sketch because you can see both the new and the old states of the sketch. The setting to enable or disable this ghosted position is found at Tools ➤ Options ➤ Sketch ➤ Ghost Image On Drag.

If you add a parallel relation between opposing lines, they now act differently, as shown in Figure 1.14. You add a parallel relation by selecting the two lines (Ctrl + Select) to make parallel and selecting Parallel from the context toolbar or the PropertyManager panel.

You can read more about the PropertyManager in Chapter 2.

Next, add a second parallel and a horizontal relation, as shown in Figure 1.14. If you are following along by re-creating the sketch on your computer, you will notice that one line has turned from blue to black.

The line colors represent sketch states. It may be impossible to see this in the black-and-white printing of this book, but if you are following along on your own computer, you should see one black line and three blue lines. Sketch states include Underdefined, Overdefined, Fully Defined, Unsolvable, Zero Length, and Dangling, and they are described as follows:

Blue: Underdefined   The sketch entity is not completely defined. You can drag a portion of it to change size, position, or orientation.

Black: Fully Defined   The sketch entity is fully defined by a combination of sketch relations and dimensions. A sketch cannot be fully defined without being connected in some way to something external to the sketch, such as the part origin or an edge. (The exception to this rule is the use of the Fix constraint, which, although effective, is not a recommended practice.)

Red: Overdefined—Not Solved   When a sketch entity has two or more relations and one of them cannot be satisfied, the unsatisfied relation will be red. For example, if a line has both Horizontal and Vertical relations, and the line is actually vertical, the Vertical relation will be yellow (because it is conflicting but satisfied), and the Horizontal will be red (because it is conflicting and not satisfied).

Yellow: Overdefined—Conflicts   Solving the sketch relations would result in a zero-length entity. For example, this can occur where an arc is tangent to a line, and the centerpoint of the arc is also coincident to the line.

Brown: Dangling   The relation has lost track of the entity to which it was connected.

Entities with different states can exist within a single sketch. In addition, endpoints of lines can have a different state than the rest of the sketched entity. For example, a line that is sketched horizontally from the origin has a *coincident* at one endpoint to the origin, and the line itself is *horizontal*. As a result, the line and first endpoint are black, but the other endpoint is underdefined because the length of the line is not defined. Sketch states are indicated in the lower-right corner of the graphics window and in the status bar. You can see that dragging one corner allows only the lines to move in certain ways, as shown in Figure 1.14.

In addition to sketch relations, dimensions applied using the Smart Dimension tool are also part of the parametric scheme. If you apply an angle dimension (by clicking the two angled lines with the Smart Dimension tool) about the origin and try dragging again, as shown in Figure 1.14, you see that the only aspect that is not locked down is the length of the sides. Notice also that when the angle dimension is added, another line turns black.

Finally, adding length dimensions for the unequal sides completes the definition of the sketch, as shown in Figure 1.14. At this point, all lines have turned black. This state is called "fully defined." Between the dimensions and sketch relations, there is enough information to re-create this sketch exactly.

BEST PRACTICE

It is widely considered best practice to fully define all sketches to control how the sketch reacts to potential changes.

Parametric relations within a sketch control how the sketch reacts to changes from dimensions or relations within the sketch or by some other factor from outside the sketch. Other factors can drive the sketch as well, such as equations, other model geometry that is external to the sketch, and even geometry from another part in an assembly, as you'll see later.

Understanding Design Intent

Design intent is a phrase that you will hear often among SolidWorks users. I like to think of it as "design for change." Design intent means that when you put the parametric sketch relations and dimensions together with the feature intelligence, you can build models that react to change in predictable ways. This gives you a great deal of control over changes.

An example of design intent could be a statement that describes general aspects that help define the design of a part, such as "This part is symmetrical, with holes that line up with Part A and thick enough to be flush with Part B." From this description, and the surrounding parts, it is possible to re-create the part in such a way that if Part A or Part B changes, the part being described updates to match.

Some types of changes can cause features to fail or sketch relations to conflict. In most situations, SolidWorks has ample tools for troubleshooting and editing that you can use to repair or change the model. In these situations, it is often the design intent itself that is changing.

BEST PRACTICE

It is considered best practice to edit existing entities rather than delete. Deleting often causes problems with items that have relations to the entities deleted. Many users find it tempting to delete anything that has an error on it, but you should avoid this practice.

Editing Design Intent

One of the most prominent aspects of design in general is change. I have often heard it said that you may design something once, but you will change it a dozen times. You will find this to be true with both sketching and 3D modeling. Design intent is sometimes thought of as a static concept that controls changing geometry. However, design intent itself often changes, thus requiring the way in which the model reacts to geometric changes to also change. Fortunately, SolidWorks has many tools to help you deal with changing requirements.

Choosing Sketch Relations

The sketch relation symbols are the most helpful tools for visualizing design intent. You can show or hide icons that represent the relations by choosing View Sketch Relations from the Heads-Up View toolbar (or through the menus at View ➤ Hide/Show ➤ Sketch Relations). When shown, these relations appear as an icon in a small colored box in the graphics area next to the sketch entity. Clicking the icon highlights the sketch elements involved in that relation. Refer to Figure 1.15 for examples of these relations.

FIGURE 1.15
Turn on or turn off the display of sketch relations.

TIP   The View Sketch Relations option is an excellent candidate for use with a hotkey, thereby enabling you to easily toggle it on and off. For more information on creating and managing hotkeys, see Chapter 2.

You can use the sketch relation icons on the screen to delete relations by selecting the icon in the graphics area and pressing Delete on the keyboard. You also can use them to quickly determine the status of sketch relations by referring to the colors defined earlier.

Selecting Display/Delete Relations

The Display/Delete Relations tool enables you to list, sort, delete, and repair sketch relations. You can find the Display/Delete Relations tool on the Sketch toolbar. The sketch status colors defined earlier also apply here, with the relations appearing in the appropriate color. (Relations are not shown in blue or black, only the colors that show errors, such as red, yellow, and brown.) This tool also enables you to group relations by several categories:

◆   All In This Sketch

◆   Dangling

◆ Overdefining/Not Solved

◆ External

◆ Defined In Context

◆ Locked

◆ Broken

◆ Selected Entities

In the lower Entities panel of the Display/Delete Relations PropertyManager, shown in Figure 1.16, you can replace one entity with another or repair dangling relations.

FIGURE 1.16
The Display/Delete Relations PropertyManager enables you to repair broken relations and replace entities.

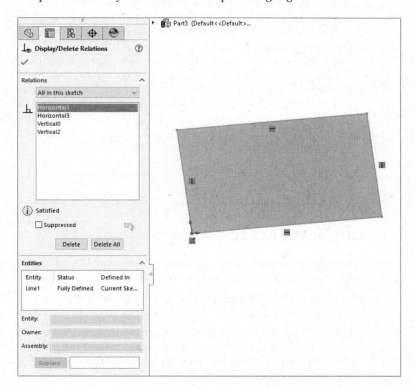

You can read more about repairing dangling entities in Chapter 6.

Using Suppressed Sketch Relations

Suppressing a sketch relation means that the relation is turned off and not used to compute the position of sketch entities. Suppressed relations generally are used in conjunction with configurations. You can also suppress relations temporarily to resolve problems.

Configurations are discussed in detail in Chapter 11, "Working with Part Configurations."

Working with Associativity

In SolidWorks, *associativity* refers to links between documents, such as a part that has an associative link to a drawing. If the part changes, the drawing updates as well. *Bidirectional associativity* means that the part can be changed from the part or the drawing document window. One of the implications of this is that you do not edit a SolidWorks drawing by simply moving lines on the drawing; you must change the 3D model, which causes all drawing views of the part or assembly to update correctly.

Other associative links include using *inserted* parts (also called *base* or *derived* parts), where one part is inserted as the first feature in another part. This might be the case when you build a casting. If the part is designed in its "as cast" state, it is then inserted into another part where machining operations are performed by cut features and the part is transformed into its "as machined" state. This technique is also used for plastic parts where a single shape spans multiple plastic pieces. A "master part" is created and split into multiple parts. An example would be a mouse cover and buttons.

One of the most important aspects of associativity is file management. Associated files stay connected by filenames. If a document name is changed and one of the associated files is not updated appropriately, the association between the files can become broken. For this reason, you should use either SolidWorks or SolidWorks Explorer to change the names of associated files.

> **BEST PRACTICE**
>
> It is considered best practice to use SolidWorks or SolidWorks Explorer to rename associated parts. Avoid using Windows Explorer.

The Bottom Line

Easy access to your tools   cuts just seconds out of your work time every day, but a good habit will cut minutes, and several good habits can cut hours.

> **Master It**   After SolidWorks has been installed as shown in this chapter, find the desktop icon, and put it on your taskbar or other easy-to-access interface element.

File organization is one of   the keys to a successful SolidWorks implementation. While I don't expect you to have everything figured out at this stage in your learning, you need to start thinking about how to manage your SolidWorks libraries of templates and key features as well as your project data.

> **Master It**   Make sure you know where the settings in Tools ➤ Options are located for identifying the locations for templates, and change this location if necessary.

One of the key concepts   of managing SolidWorks is associativity. Data created in one file can be shown in another file. For example, part data is shown in both assemblies and drawings.

> **Master It**   Open a SolidWorks drawing (*.slddrw) and drag a SolidWorks part (*.sldprt) onto it. Make a change to the part and watch it update on the drawing.

Chapter 2

Navigating the SolidWorks Interface

The SolidWorks interface offers a wide range of tools. You'll find more than one way to do almost everything. There is no single best way to use the interface; this book generally shows the most standardized and quickest methods.

In this chapter, I start by displaying the entire default interface, but in the rest of the book, I will show only a reduced interface, mainly to save space and keep the focus on the graphics window.

After you have mastered the various interface elements and customized your SolidWorks installation, working with the software will become much more efficient and satisfying.

IN THIS CHAPTER, YOU WILL LEARN TO:

- ◆ Recognize elements of the SolidWorks interface
- ◆ Find what you need in the interface
- ◆ Customize the interface to work for you

Identifying Elements of the SolidWorks Interface

The major elements of the SolidWorks interface are the graphics window, where all the geometry is shown; the FeatureManager, which is the list of all the features in the part; the PropertyManager, where most of the data input happens; and the CommandManager and toolbars, where you access most of the commands in the software.

Each interface element identified in Figure 2.1 is explained in detail in this chapter.

You might want to bookmark the next page and refer to Figure 2.1 often, because much of the interface discussion refers to elements illustrated in this figure. You'll never see all the interface elements shown in Figure 2.1 on the screen at the same time; this image has been composited for illustration purposes. It shows the default interface with a couple of exceptions. First, I pinned the title bar menu in place. Second, I detached the PropertyManager.

Using the CommandManager and Toolbars

In some respects, the CommandManager resembles the Microsoft (MS) Ribbon interface, but it is not a strict implementation, because SolidWorks wanted to add more customizability. In this section, I show you how to make the CommandManager work for you and how to use regular or flyout toolbars to replace it effectively.

FIGURE 2.1
Elements of the SolidWorks interface

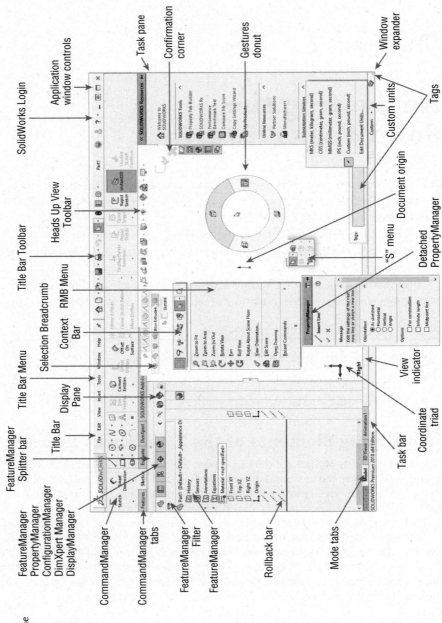

EXPLORING THE COMMANDMANAGER

The CommandManager is an area of the interface that you can use to flip between sets of related commands. The main purpose of the CommandManager is to give you easy access to commands without cluttering the entire screen with toolbars.

The CommandManager accomplishes this by providing small tabs under the left end of the toolbar area to enable you to switch the collection of tools that appears. Figure 2.2 shows the CommandManager in Customize mode, showing all the tabs available in a default setup. To get the CommandManager into Customize mode, right-click one of the CommandManager tabs and select Customize CommandManager.

NOTE   To access the pull-down menus in a default setup, place the cursor over the SolidWorks logo or the small flyout triangle to the right of it in the upper-left corner of the SolidWorks window. Figure 2.2 shows the flyout for pull-down menus pinned in place. To keep the menu in that position, click the pushpin on the right end of the flyout menu bar.

FIGURE 2.2
Customizing the
CommandManager

Customizing the CommandManager

The best way to get the most efficiency from the SolidWorks interface is to customize it. Notice the last tab along the bottom of the CommandManager on the right. If you want to add another tab, you can right-click this tab and select the tab you want to add. You also can select to add a blank tab and then rename it and populate it with individual buttons. Figure 2.3 shows a detail of the Add Tab menu options that opens after you right-click the right-most tab.

FIGURE 2.3
Adding or removing
tabs from the
CommandManager

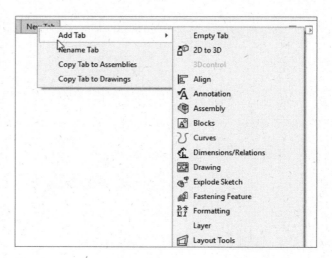

To add individual buttons to the CommandManager, follow these steps:

1. Choose Tools ➤ Customize from the menu bar.

2. When the Customize dialog box opens, find the button you want to add.

3. Click the Commands tab in the Customize dialog box, and then switch the CommandManager to the tab to which you want to add the button.

4. Drag the button from the Customize dialog box to the CommandManager.

You can remove buttons from the CommandManager by dragging them into the blank graphics window area.

Docking the CommandManager

In SolidWorks, you can undock the CommandManager and leave it undocked, pull it to a second monitor, or dock it vertically to the left or right. To undock it, click and drag on any tab of the CommandManager. To redock an undocked CommandManager double-click the title area. To change its docking location, drag it onto one of the docking stations around the screen. Figure 2.4 shows the CommandManager undocked. You can also double-click on the command manager title in order to dock it back in the last parking position.

FIGURE 2.4
The undocked
CommandManager
with text labels

Using Auto Collapse

The small box with the arrows in it in the upper-right corner of the undocked CommandManager and the undocked PropertyManager is the Auto Collapse option. When the option is active, the PropertyManager expands and collapses automatically when your mouse goes over it. This can be very handy because it saves lots of space on the screen, but at the same time, it requires additional mouse movement to open it up. This is the common trade-off in this interface: You can trade screen space for additional mouse movement or clicks.

Mixing the CommandManager with Toolbars

To put a toolbar inline with the CommandManager, drag the toolbar close to the right end of the CommandManager. A space on that row or column opens up. The amount of space that opens up depends on the CommandManager tab with the longest set of icons, even if that tab is not showing.

Basing Tabs on Document Types

SolidWorks remembers which tabs to show on a per-document-type basis. This means that when you are working on a part document, you have one set of tabs. When you switch to an assembly document, you see a different set of tabs. The same goes for drawings. Notice that in Figure 2.3, in the right mouse button (RMB) menu, the Copy Tab To Assemblies option and the Copy Tab To Drawings option appear. These options make it easier to set up customizations that apply for all document types.

Changing the Appearance of the CommandManager

You can turn off the text in one of two ways. The easiest way to do this is to right-click in the CommandManager and deselect the Use Large Buttons With Text option, as shown in Figure 2.5.

FIGURE 2.5
Adding or removing text from the CommandManager buttons

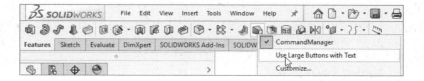

I will use the interface with the hidden text for the rest of the book, primarily to save space on the printed page. Remember that if you need help with the name of an icon, you can hover the cursor over the icon to see a tool tip that tells you what it is.

You can scroll through the tabs of the CommandManager by pressing Ctrl+PageUp or Ctrl+PageDown. These key combinations can be controlled at Tools ➢ Customize ➢ Keyboard.

The most streamlined and space-efficient way to set up the CommandManager is to remove the text. Notice that the CommandManager without text takes up the same amount of height as a normal toolbar, with the added room for the tabs at the bottom. The text can be useful for new users or features that you do not commonly use.

The final setting for the CommandManager's appearance is the size of the icons. You have control over the size of the icon images in the CommandManager. You can find this setting in the Options flyout on the Title Bar toolbar shown in Figure 2.6. The difference between large and small icons is shown in the lower part of the figure.

FIGURE 2.6
Setting large icons

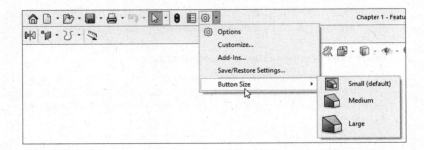

This setting applies to all the toolbar icons except the menu bar, RMB menu, and context bar icons. The setting may not take full effect until you restart SolidWorks. Large icons can be useful on displays with very high resolution; in particular, on laptops where the screen itself may be small but the resolution is very high. All the screenshots in this book are taken with the Large Icons option turned on for improved visibility.

Recognizing the Limitations of the CommandManager

If you undock the CommandManager, you cannot reorient the tabs horizontally. They remain vertical. In addition, you cannot place multiple rows of toolbars on the same row as a CommandManager using large buttons with text. You cannot dock the CommandManager to the bottom of the SolidWorks window. Another minor limitation is that although SolidWorks allows you to place toolbars at the right end of the CommandManager and above the CommandManager when the CommandManager is docked at the top, it does not allow you to place them to the left of the CommandManager or below it.

USING TOOLBARS

Interface setup is frequently about compromise or balancing conflicting concerns. In the case of the CommandManager, the compromise is between screen space, mouse travel, and clicks. You may find yourself clicking frequently back and forth between the Sketch and Features tabs. For this reason, you may find it valuable to put the Sketch toolbar vertically on the right side of the graphics window and remove it from the CommandManager. This enables you to see the Sketch and Features toolbars at the same time and greatly reduces clicking back and forth between the CommandManager tabs.

The SolidWorks interface performs best with some customization. No two people set it up exactly the same, but everyone needs some adjustment because he or she might be working on specialized functionality (such as molds or surfacing) or might work with limited functionality (such as predominantly revolved features). Of course, customization can accommodate personal preferences—for example, if one user prefers to use hotkeys and another uses menus, gestures, or the S key.

To enable or disable a toolbar, you can right-click in a toolbar area and choose the toolbar you are interested in enabling from a list of all the toolbars in SolidWorks. Another way to do this is to use the Customize dialog box by choosing Tools ➤ Customize, or the Customize option near the bottom of the RMB toolbar list. Yet another way is to choose View ➤ Toolbars.

Exploring the Heads-Up View Toolbar

The Heads-Up View toolbar appears along the middle of the top edge of the graphics window. Figure 2.7 shows the default arrangement of the Heads-Up View toolbar, and it is shown in relation to the rest of the interface in Figure 2.1.

FIGURE 2.7
The Heads-Up View toolbar

You can customize the Heads-Up View toolbar by using the Toolbars dialog box (Tools ➤ Customize ➤ Toolbars). Customization includes turning the Heads-Up View toolbar on or off and adding or removing buttons. If you have multiple document windows or multiple view ports showing, the Heads-Up View toolbar shows only in the active window or view port. This toolbar often overlaps with other interface elements when the active window is small.

Exploring the Title Bar Toolbar and Menu

The Title Bar toolbar is found just to the right of the SolidWorks logo on the title bar in the top-left corner of the SolidWorks window. By default, it contains most of the elements of the standard toolbar, and it is available even when no documents are open. It uses mostly flyout toolbar icons, so again it follows the trend of saving space at the expense of an extra click. This toolbar can be customized in the same way as other toolbars in the Customize dialog box in the Commands tab. This toolbar cannot be turned off, but you can remove all the icons from it.

NOTE You can run the SolidWorks interface from just the CommandManager without any additional toolbars. You can do the same with just the Title Bar toolbar, customizing it with all flyout toolbars. The main advantages of the Title Bar toolbar are that it is visible when no documents are open and that it utilizes otherwise wasted space in the title bar. You might set up the interface for a 12-inch normal-aspect-display laptop very differently from that of a desktop unit with a 24-inch-wide screen.

There is also a Title Bar menu, which is hidden by default. The SolidWorks logo in the upper left of the SolidWorks window or the small triangle next to the logo serve as a flyout to expand the main SolidWorks menus. You can pin the menus in place using the pushpin.

Notice that on low-resolution or non-maximized SolidWorks windows, you can run into some space problems if the Menu Bar menu is pinned open. You need to examine customizations to the SolidWorks interface with display size in mind. You might consider having different sets of settings for using a laptop at a docking station with a large monitor, using the laptop with a small monitor, and using the computer with a low-resolution digital projector.

A setting exists to help you control the display for these situations. Figure 2.8 shows the View ➤ Workspace menu. This gives you the options of Default, Widescreen, and Dual Monitor. With dual monitors, you can put some elements of the interface on the second monitor to save graphics space. You will also see a Touch Mode option in the View menu, which will help you set up the display for touch screens and tablets.

FIGURE 2.8
The Workspace and
Touch Mode interface
settings

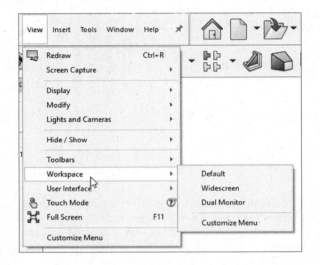

Looking at the Flyout Toolbar Buttons

SolidWorks saves space by putting several related icons on flyout toolbars. For example, the Rectangle tool has a button for each of the several different ways to make a rectangle, and they are all on the rectangle flyout. To see all available flyouts, choose Tools ➤ Customize ➤ Commands ➤ Flyouts.

Flyouts primarily save toolbar space when several tools are closely related. SolidWorks has set up flyouts in two configurations: flyouts that always maintain the same image for the front button image (such as the Smart Dimension flyout) and flyouts that use the last-used button image (such as the Rectangle flyout).

Exploring the Context Toolbars

Context toolbars are toolbars that appear in the graphics window and in the FeatureManager when you right-click or left-click something. When you right-click, a context toolbar appears at the top of the RMB menu and shows the functions that SolidWorks deems the most commonly used functions. The advantage of this block of tools is that because they are more commonly used, you should be familiar with the icons, so they don't need supporting text titles, as do the less commonly used tools on the RMB menu. Figure 2.9 shows the RMB menu with context bar.

FIGURE 2.9

The right-click menu and context toolbar

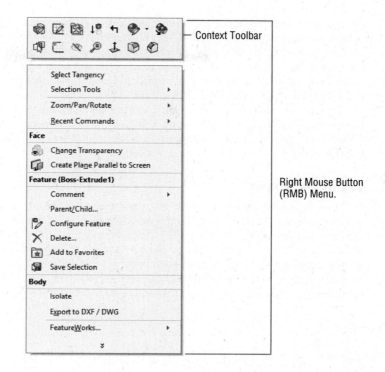

Context Toolbar

Right Mouse Button (RMB) Menu.

When you left-click an item, the context toolbar appears by itself; the rest of the RMB menu does not appear. If you do not recognize an icon on the context toolbar, you can refer to its tool tip. Context toolbars are editable in two ways. First, you can turn them off and restore the RMB menu to its complete configuration. To turn off the context toolbars, click the context toolbar and choose Tools ➤ Customize. Use the options on the right side of the main Toolbars tab. (refer to upper right corner of Figure 2.10) Second, you can add or remove icons on specific context toolbars by right-clicking the toolbar itself and selecting Customize.

The purpose of the context toolbars is to save space by condensing some commands into a toolbar without text instead of a menu with icons and text. The left-click and right-click context toolbars are the same, but they work differently. The left-click context toolbar fades as you move the cursor away from it and becomes darker as you move the cursor toward it. After it fades completely, you cannot get it back without reselecting the item.

Exploring the Shortcut (S) Toolbar

The Shortcut toolbar is also known as the S toolbar because, by default, you access it by pressing the S key. You can customize this toolbar so it has different content for sketches, parts, assemblies, and drawings. To customize the S toolbar, right-click it when it is active and click Customize from the RMB menu.

Users claim to have customized the S toolbar to such an extent that they have been able to remove the CommandManager and all other toolbars from their interface or if the Shortcut Toolbar is used in conjunction with well-customized Context Toolbars. This is possibly true if you use a limited number of sketch entities, sketch relations, and feature types, or if you make extensive use of flyouts on the S toolbar. However, if you work with a wide range of tools (say, surfacing, sheet metal, and plastic parts), you may need some additional toolbar space. It is completely believable to have access to most of the software's functions with the S toolbar and either the Menu Bar toolbar or the CommandManager. CommandManager by far gives you the most flexibility, but it also requires the most space.

The S key shortcut may conflict with another keyboard customization. To change the S toolbar key to another character or to reassign it, follow the directions for creating and maintaining hotkeys later in this chapter in the section on customization. It is referenced as the shortcut bar in the Keyboard list (Tools ➤ Customize ➤ Keyboard).

USING TOOL TIPS

Tool tips come in two varieties: large and small. Large tool tips show the names of the tools and available shortcut keys, along with brief descriptions of what they do. Small tool tips show only the tools' names and shortcut keys. To change the tool tip display from large to small, or to deselect the tool tip display altogether, choose Tools ➤ Customize. The options for sizing tool tips and showing tool tips appear in the upper-right corner. In addition to the tool tip balloons, tips also appear in the status bar at the bottom of the screen when the cursor is over an icon. Figure 2.10 provides the options for tooltips and shows a comparison between large, medium, and icons.

FIGURE 2.10
SolidWorks uses large tool tips by default.

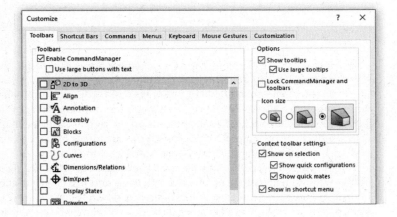

NOTE The Customize option (Tools ➤ Customize) is inactive unless a SolidWorks document is open. To access the Customize dialog box, first open a SolidWorks part, assembly, or drawing, and then choose Tools ➤ Customize from the menu. Customize is different from the Customize Menu option found in all SolidWorks menus. The Customize Menu option is discussed later in this chapter.

In addition to the tool tips, this area of the Customize dialog also controls icon size and the setting to show or hide context toolbars.

MANAGING TOOLBARS

After all that, if you still feel you need to work with standard toolbars, it is easy to move, select and deselect, and add icons to toolbars. It is important to remember that different document types retain different toolbar settings; for example, the toolbars that you see with a part open are different from the toolbars that you see for drawings. For this reason, when you change from a part document to a drawing document, you may see your display adjust because the changing toolbars increase or decrease the amount of space that is required.

> ### BEST PRACTICE
>
> A best practice is to set up the toolbars for each document type so they take up similar amounts of space—for example, two rows on top and one column to the right. This way, when changing between document types, the graphics area does not need to resize.

Moving Toolbars

To move a toolbar, you can click with the cursor at the dotted bar on the left-most or top edge of the toolbar. Figure 2.11 shows the dotted bar on the top edge of a toolbar. When the cursor changes to a four-way arrow, you can drag the toolbar where you want it. Toolbars dock either vertically or horizontally. You can resize undocked toolbars so they have rows and columns. This arrangement is typically used with the Selection Filter toolbar, which is often left undocked and compressed into a block that is three or four columns wide.

FIGURE 2.11
Dotted bars enable you
to move toolbars.

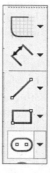

Using Flyout Toolbars

You can use any toolbar as a flyout toolbar. Figure 2.12 shows the list of all flyout toolbars; it is the same as the list of *all* toolbars. To use a toolbar as a flyout, select it from the flyout toolbars list and drag it onto an existing toolbar. It displays with an arrow to the right. Clicking the arrow causes all the tools to scroll out temporarily until you click a toolbar icon or anything else.

FIGURE 2.12

The flyout toolbars are on the Commands tab in the Customize dialog box.

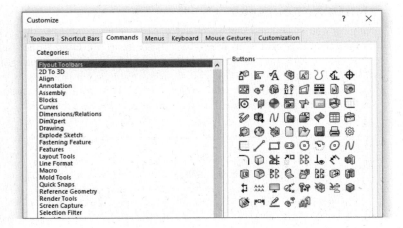

To add icons to a flyout toolbar, temporarily show the regular toolbar that corresponds to the flyout toolbar and add icons to the regular toolbar. When you are finished adding or removing icons, turn off the regular toolbar; the changes will be applied to the flyout. Some flyout toolbars are not available, such as the Rectangle flyout, but you can use this technique on toolbars that are used as flyouts, such as the Reference Geometry toolbar.

TIP If you want to create a separate toolbar, you can commandeer an existing one for your own purposes. For example, because I do not use the Tools toolbar, I have removed all the regular icons from it and replaced them with relevant flyout toolbars, which I do use extensively. This enables me to consolidate space and not have unused icons on my toolbars. Alternatively, creating a custom CommandManager tab and putting on it what you like is much easier.

Working in Various Screen Configurations

Full Screen mode enables you to toggle quickly to the display so that only the graphics window and the Task pane appear. The FeatureManager, menus, toolbars, and status bar are all hidden. Alternatively, you can hide just the FeatureManager or the toolbars.

In Full Screen mode, you can still access the menus by clicking with the cursor along the top border of the window:

- F8 toggles the DisplayPane.

- F9 toggles the FeatureManager.

- F10 toggles the toolbars.

- F11 toggles Full Screen mode.

Under View ➢ Workspace, you find other screen setups, including Widescreen and Dual Monitors. Widescreen puts the CommandManager to the left of the FeatureManager, and Dual Monitors puts the CommandManager and PropertyManager on the second screen.

Controlling Menus

Everyone has his or her own style of working. For example, some people like to use menus, and others do not. Some like to use hotkeys, and others like the mouse.

Most users avoid menus because they seem like an old way of working. However, some commands, such as Modify Section View, are available only through the drop-down menus. Also, SolidWorks users who use a wide range of features wind up using the menus more often than users who use a more limited set of tools.

The most frequently used menu items are in the View, Insert, and Tools menus. All the menus shown in this section have all the possible options shown. Customizing menus is rarely done, although it is possible. To customize a menu, activate the menu and select Customize Menu from the bottom of the menu, as shown in Figure 2.13.

FIGURE 2.13

Access to customize a menu

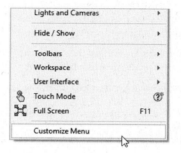

You use the View menu primarily for turning visibility on or off for entity types such as planes, sketches, or temporary axes. You can also do this by using hotkeys or via the Heads-Up View toolbar.

The Insert menu is used mostly for creating feature types for which you do not have a toolbar icon on the screen. For example, although the Move Face tool is on the Mold Tools toolbar, you can also find the Move Face tool on the Direct Editing toolbar. Move Face has many uses aside from mold design. You can find the Move Face tool by choosing Insert ➤ Face.

You can customize menus by adding or omitting items. By using the Customize Menu option at the bottom of any menu—including shortcut (RMB) menus—you can remove items from any menu by clearing the check boxes next to tools you do not use. To bring back the removed items, you can go back to Customize Menu or choose Tools ➤ Customize ➤ Options and click the Reset to Defaults buttons for menu and shortcut customization.

While omitting items may not sound like much of a benefit, some of these menus are so long that they may not fit on your monitor—even a large monitor—and they may include tools that you never use. So, sometimes trimming down a menu to make it fit the interface better is a good choice for your particular situation. You may also find administrative reasons to remove certain commands from the available list (to prevent users from adding certain features to the tree).

NOTE Be careful not to confuse this Customize Menu selection with the Customize Menu selection on the Tools menu. Figure 2.13 shows the Tools menu being customized. In addition, I do not recommend removing items from the menus. At some point, someone may need one of those items and no one will remember where it was or how to get it back.

INTERPRETING THE USE OF THE WORD "SHORTCUT" IN SOLIDWORKS

Between the SolidWorks and Microsoft interfaces, the word *shortcut* is used in several overlapping and confusing ways. The following list describes where SolidWorks and Microsoft users might encounter the word *shortcut* as a formal name for interface functionality and how they might understand it.

◆ A Windows **shortcut** is a link to another file or folder. Most users still refer to this link as a *shortcut* or *desktop shortcut*.

◆ **Shortcuts** (as identified in the SolidWorks Help under Shortcut ➤ Keys) are either accelerator keys or keyboard shortcuts. Users refer to accelerator keys as *Alt keys* and to keyboard shortcuts as *hotkeys*.

◆ SolidWorks **shortcut menus** are commonly called the right mouse button (RMB) menus. They have detached toolbars called context bars for both right-click and left-click options. These are commonly known as the *RMB bar* and the *LMB bar*.

◆ **Shortcut tabs** (found as the "shortcut" entry in the SolidWorks Help) presumably refer to DriveWorksXpress functionality, although there is no direct mention of that in the Help entry.

◆ **Shortcut bars** are commonly known as the *S key toolbar*.

If you use the alternative terminology offered here, it will be clear to all users what you are talking about.

Changing Cursors

SolidWorks cursors are context-sensitive and change their appearance and function depending on the situation. Sketching cursors display a pencil and the type of sketch entity that you are presently sketching. Sketch cursors also display some dimensional information about the entity that you are sketching, such as its length or radius. Sketch cursor feedback is necessary for fast and accurate sketching.

To learn more about sketch cursor feedback, see Chapter 3, "Working with Sketches and Reference Geometry."

The select cursor changes depending on the item over which it is positioned. Cursor symbols also help remind you when selection filters are active. Figure 2.14 shows various cursors and their significance.

FIGURE 2.14
Various SolidWorks
cursors

Working with Models in the FeatureManager and PropertyManager Windows

The FeatureManager and PropertyManager are windows in the interface where you will spend much of your time. You can manipulate the content inside the windows in various ways.

USING THE FEATUREMANAGER

The FeatureManager window is the panel to the left of the screen; it shows the features describing how the part was built. SolidWorks users spend a fair amount of time using the FeatureManager to edit or inspect models. You can use the tree (as it is known informally) to see items in the order in which they were created or to search for specific items. You can put parts or features in folders for organization. Using the Display pane, you can turn visibility on or off for bodies, parts, reference geometry, and other items. You can use it to display names, descriptions, and other metadata.

Figure 2.15 names the various parts of the FeatureManager interface.

FIGURE 2.15
The parts of the
FeatureManager

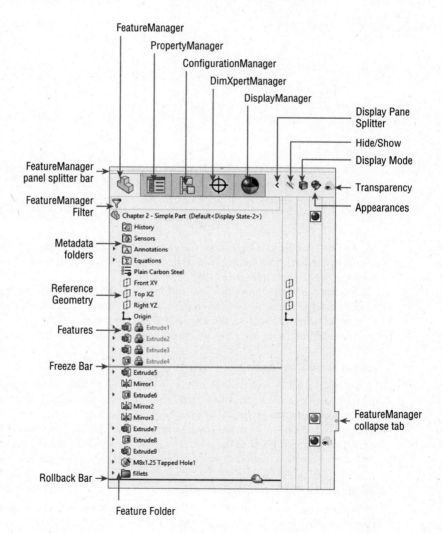

Feature Folder

Figure 2.16 again shows the FeatureManager for a simple model, this time using the options for Dynamic Reference Visualization (DRV). Parent features are typically above the selected feature, and are indicated by the blue DRV arrows. Child features are typically below the selected feature and are indicated by purple DRV arrows. (Child features can sometimes be found below the selected feature due to SolidWorks method of putting sketches below the feature. Using the shortcut Ctrl+T will switch the FeatureManager to a more literal representation of the feature order where all child features come after the parents.) You will learn more about this in Chapter 12, "Editing, Evaluating, and Troubleshooting."

FIGURE 2.16
Dynamic Reference
Visualization

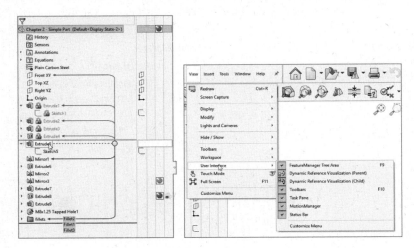

The DRV enables you to instantly understand the parent/child relations between the various features in the part. The setting to enable or disable DRV is at View ➤ User Interface, as shown in the image to the right in Figure 2.16.

A splitter bar at the top of the FeatureManager (see Figure 2.15) enables you to split the FeatureManager window into two windows. This enables you to display the FeatureManager and another window, such as the PropertyManager (refer to Figure 2.17). The tab on the right of the FeatureManager (or the F9 key) can collapse the FeatureManager to save space.

Looking at the Display Pane

You can open the Display pane flyout from the FeatureManager by using the arrow at the top-right corner of the FeatureManager. The Display pane helps you to visualize where appearances (colors), display styles, or hidden bodies have been applied in a part document and additional functions in an assembly document. The Display pane is helpful when you're looking for colors that are applied to the model at some level other than the part level.

Appearances are covered in more detail in Chapter 5, "Using Visualization Techniques."

Looking at the Rollback and Freeze Bars

The Rollback bar at the bottom of the FeatureManager enables you to see the part in various states of history. Features can be added while the rollback bar is at any location. The model also can be saved while rolled back.

A bar at the top of the FeatureManager is called the Freeze bar (refer to Figure 2.15), and it locks the features that are above it from being rebuilt or edited. To enable it, go to Tools ➤ Options ➤ General. You can position it just like the Rollback bar.

FIGURE 2.17
Split FeatureManager with PropertyManager on the bottom

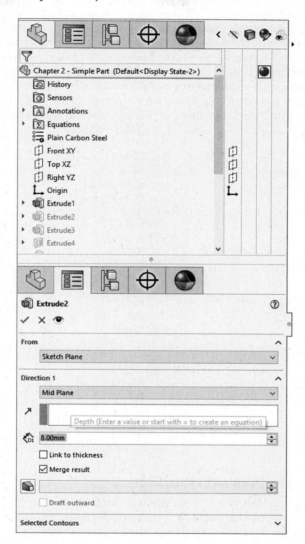

Looking at the FeatureManager Filter

One of the most useful elements of the FeatureManager is the FeatureManager filter. The filter resides at the top of the FeatureManager. If you type text in the filter, SolidWorks searches feature names, descriptions, comments, tags, and dimension names for text matching the string, and it shows only matching features in the window. This also works in assemblies, where you can filter for part names or document properties. The filter is very useful for quickly finding parts, features, mates, or anything else that shows up in the part or assembly FeatureManager.

Looking at Folders

The FeatureManager allows a couple of different types of folders. One type enables you to group features together, which is especially useful when you have long feature trees and you want to put all the fillets together into one folder. It is also useful in assemblies when you want to group certain types of parts together, such as fasteners.

Another type of folder is the special-use folders at the top of the FeatureManager for things such as solid bodies, surface bodies, sensors, and Favorites. You can add features to the Favorites folders by right-clicking the feature and selecting Add to Favorites.

These special-use folders are not all turned on by default. To turn them on or off (or allow them to be turned on only if they have content), go to Tools ➢ Options ➢ FeatureManager, where you will find a list of tree items, including these special-use folders. Figure 2.18 shows a FeatureManager with several kinds of folders in use.

FIGURE 2.18
FeatureManager folders
of various types in use

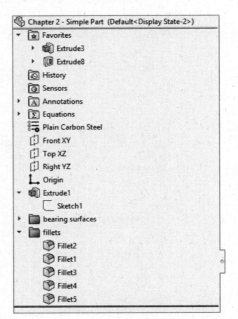

USING THE PROPERTYMANAGER

The PropertyManager is where you set most of the feature parameters and where you edit the properties of selected items such as sketch elements. You can manually switch to the PropertyManager using the tabs on the top of the Display pane or allow it to pop up automatically when your input is needed.

One of the benefits of putting all the data entry into the PropertyManager is that it saves lots of space on the screen. On the other hand, you will often need to make a selection from the FeatureManager at the same time the PropertyManager pops up and takes its place. You can disable this automatic pop-up behavior by choosing Tools ➢ Options ➢ System Options ➢ General and selecting the Auto-show PropertyManager setting.

My favorite option for dealing with the PropertyManager is to detach it from the FeatureManager so I can see the two side by side instead of one or the other. To detach the

PropertyManager, drag its icon from the tabs out into the graphics area and release. You can see the detached PropertyManager in Figure 2.1. After the PropertyManager is detached, you can move it to a second monitor, float it within the SolidWorks window, dock it, or reattach it. To put it back in its place under the FeatureManager, just drag it back on top of the FeatureManager using one of the docking station symbols on the screen, allow it to snap into place, and release it.

You can also use the splitter bars (shown in Figure 2.1 in the upper-left corner) to put the FeatureManager on top and the PropertyManager beneath, or you can use the flyout FeatureManager. When creating or editing a feature, you can access the flyout FeatureManager by double-clicking the name of the feature at the top of the PropertyManager. The flyout FeatureManager is displayed just to the right of the regular FeatureManager, in the main graphics window; it's transparent to enable you to see the model through it. The various ways of combining the FeatureManager and PropertyManager are shown in Figure 2.19.

Introducing the DisplayManager

The DisplayManager helps you understand the various display-related items applied to your part or assembly. This includes lights, scenes, backgrounds, appearances, colors, textures, and decals. Figure 2.20 shows the DisplayManager with the Appearances active. Chapter 5 discusses the DisplayManager in more depth.

Getting Around the Task Pane

By default, the Task pane sits to the right of the SolidWorks screen, although you can undock it entirely. If you want to keep it open, click the pushpin in the upper-right corner of the pane. The Task pane is shown in Figure 2.21. If you cannot see the Task pane, it may be turned off. You can turn it and other interface elements on or off using the View menu (refer to Figure 2.16).

The Task pane is the home for several panels:

Home Tab: This tab enables access to the Welcome screen as well as several miscellaneous SolidWorks tools. You can also access the Subscription Services from here.

Design Library: This includes locally stored libraries, Toolbox, and 3D Content Central. It also contains "SolidWorks Content," which can be downloaded directly from the Task pane.

File Explorer: You can use this Windows Explorer interface to browse for files.

View Palette: This palette enables you to visually select views and drag them onto a drawing sheet.

Appearances, Scenes, and Decals: This panel enables you to select appearances and scenes for your SolidWorks documents. SolidWorks has also moved decals into the SolidWorks Standard level of the software instead of being part of the rendering software.

Custom Properties: The Custom Property tab in the Task pane enables you to create a custom interface that goes inside this Task pane tab, which will help you enter custom property data quickly, easily, and accurately.

SolidWorks Forum: This tab shows some of the latest comments on the SolidWorks forums. Clicking a link in this panel launches a web browser window for more convenient access.

Recovered Documents: After a crash, auto-recovered documents are listed in this special-purpose Task pane tab.

FIGURE 2.19
The detached
PropertyManager, the
split FeatureManager,
and the flyout
FeatureManager

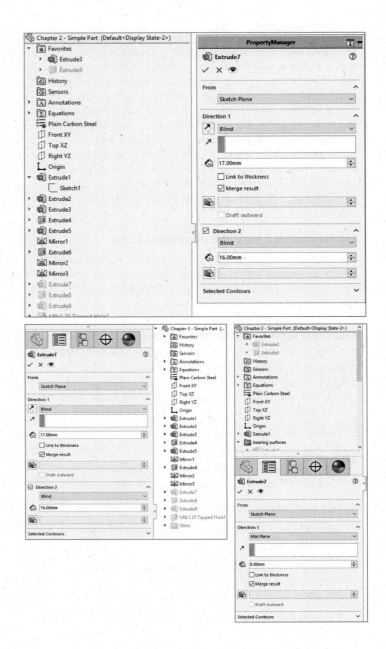

FIGURE 2.20
The DisplayManager helps you sort through everything that affects how the model looks.

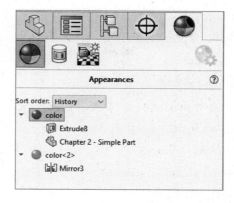

FIGURE 2.21
The Task pane, Home tab

Getting Familiar with the Status Bar

The status bar nonintrusively communicates SolidWorks information back to users, and it contains some interactive options. It is located at the bottom of the screen, and you can enable it from the View menu. Figure 2.22 shows the status bar in action.

FIGURE 2.22
The status bar showing sketch information

The status bar can display the following information, indicators, and icons:

◆ Progress as parts, assemblies, or drawings load

◆ Change units

◆ Tool tips feedback for commands

◆ Measurement results

◆ The sketch status for an active sketch

◆ In-context editing

◆ Suspend automatic rebuilds

◆ Quick Tips toggle

◆ Tags data-entry window toggle

◆ The sheet scale for drawings

◆ The cursor position for drawings and sketches

◆ Whether you are editing the sheet, sheet format, or view of a drawing

◆ Window expander when SolidWorks is not maximized

ASSIGNING TAGS

Tags work like document keywords. Tags can be searched using either SolidWorks Explorer or the FeatureManager Filter. You can assign tags by clicking the tag icon in the lower-right corner of the SolidWorks status bar. (Refer to Figure 2.1.)

Using SolidWorks Search

You can find SolidWorks Search in the upper-right corner of the SolidWorks application window, on the title bar, as shown in Figure 2.23. This is different from the FeatureManager Filter, which enables you to search within a part, assembly, or drawing for feature names or other types of data.

FIGURE 2.23
SolidWorks Search
options

SolidWorks Search enables you to search the SolidWorks Help, Knowledge Base, commands, or community forums for information (some of these require an Internet connection and login) and to look for SolidWorks models on your local or network drives.

SEARCHING FOR FILES

The file searches include 3D ContentCentral, SolidWorks Explorer, and SolidWorks PDM, if it is installed.

To configure where SolidWorks is going to search for files, you can use the options at Tools ➢ Options ➢ File Locations ➢ Search Paths. Remember that SolidWorks follows search rules that force it to look in directories that may not be obvious to you, including recent folders where you have saved documents and other directories.

You also can select custom properties to search from the drop-down list.

Making the Interface Work for You

As engineers and designers, we all like to tinker with things to optimize efficiency and to apply our personal stamp. When the SolidWorks software is installed, the interface is functional, but not optimal. Earlier in this chapter, I discussed managing and customizing toolbars and menus. In the remainder of this chapter, I will focus more on customizing the interface and suggest some strategies that you might use to help customize your work environment.

Customizing Colors

Before you change the standard colors in the SolidWorks interface, you need to be aware of a few things. The first is that SolidWorks does not automatically alter text color to contrast with your background. As a result, if you set the background to black and the text is black, you won't be able to see the text. This may seem obvious to some people, but AutoCAD automatically changes text color to contrast with the view port background, so AutoCAD users may take this function-ality for granted.

Also, be aware that the colors in the SolidWorks interface have been chosen carefully to offer good contrast between elements that may be adjacent or superimposed on one another. In most cases, colorblindness has been factored in to the selections, so you probably won't see blue and green right next to one another where it matters in the interface.

EXPLORING DEFAULT SELECTION COLORS

All the interface colors are controlled in the Systems Options Colors dialog box. You can access the dialog box by choosing Tools ➢ Options ➢ Colors, as shown in Figure 2.24.

NOTE   Systems Options includes a search box. It has hundreds of settings, and even if you know them well, finding what you are looking for is sometimes difficult.

Notice that you can set a color scheme. If you want to change the colors used in the interface, I recommend that you save the settings as a color scheme so the scheme can be re-created easily later or copied to another computer. Color schemes are stored in the Windows Registry, not as separate files. To transfer color settings to another computer, you need to either use the Copy Settings Wizard or manually copy data from the Windows Registry.

FIGURE 2.24
Controlling interface
colors

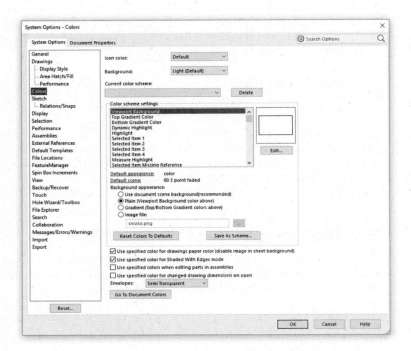

Before making changes, you might consider saving your initial settings as a separate scheme so you can get back to them if necessary.

CAUTION   Making changes to the Windows Registry can adversely affect software installation and hardware performance. You should not attempt changes to the Registry unless you know exactly what you are doing.

SELECTING BACKGROUND OPTIONS WISELY

You should avoid some colors for the background, or you should make some changes if you choose these colors. Black is used with fully defined sketches, dimensions, FeatureManager text, and annotations. Blue can mask the underdefined sketch color and some dimensions. Bright green can cause problems with seeing selected items. Bright red, aside from being a terrible color to stare at all day, also does not contrast well with some of the red highlights and error colors. Even gray masks reference dimensions.

You might think that no matter which color background you select, aside from the default, something will become difficult to see. For this reason, many users choose a gradient or image background, which enables them to pick colors where items are always visible on one half of the screen. Staring at a white screen all day can be uncomfortable for your eyes, so pick colors that enable you to see everything with "reasonable" contrast, yet are not glaringly bright. Very high contrast is hard on the eyes, and low contrast may make it difficult to distinguish items on the screen.

You have to consider the purpose of the background. Some people doing presentations may want the background to be attractive while otherwise staying out of the way. Others may need the background only to contrast with whatever is in front of it in a way that does not strain the eyes. For writing a book, the background generally needs to be white to match the page. No one scheme will suit all needs.

In addition to colors and gradients, you can use an image as the graphics window background. This gives you a wider range of customization capabilities, and several sample images are already available in the default settings. Also, be aware that document scene backgrounds are document-specific but can be overridden by system options.

RealView also adds some capabilities with *scenes*. Scenes can be applied from the Appearances, Scenes, And Decals tab on the Task pane. Most of the display settings work in conjunction with RealView, which is an advanced display mode. Depending on your graphics card, your computer may or may not be capable of using RealView. SolidWorks offers three different types of scenes: Basic, Studio, and Presentation. Of these, I find the Studio scenes to be the best when I need a reflective floor with shadows; otherwise, I stick with the Basic scenes. I find it distracting to use either reflections or shadows in models while working. However, adding a nice, shiny RealView appearance to the part is often useful, especially for visualizing curvature on curvy parts.

I describe RealView, along with scenes, in more detail in Chapter 5.

Customizing Strategies

You can easily customize many aspects of the SolidWorks interface, including the following:

- Toolbars

- Menus

- Background colors or images

- Task pane location

- Hotkeys

- Macros

- Custom application programming

Whether you should customize each of these items depends partially on how much time and energy you have to spend, how much you work with others, whether you share your workstation with other users, and how much money you are ready to dedicate in the case of custom programming.

Considering Hotkey Approaches

Any command that you use more than a few times an hour is worth assigning to a hotkey. I like to use alliteration when assigning keys to help with my faulty memory. The most frequently used commands are assigned single-letter hotkeys, and the less frequently used commands are assigned combinations. Thus, Tools Options is linked to O, Measure to M, Select Vertex to Shift+V, and Curve Projected to Ctrl+J. (Ctrl+P is the Windows standard for the Print command.) Some of the settings I like to use conflict with the default settings. SolidWorks has a nice mechanism to deal with entering conflicts—it will warn you of the conflict, and you can choose to proceed with the change or not. Other people like to group keys into easy-to-reach combinations; this is why the Q, W, A, S, Z, and X keys are often assigned first for right-handed mouse users.

ORGANIZING HOTKEYS

Hotkeys are assigned and organized in the Keyboard dialog box (Tools ➤ Customize ➤ Keyboard), as shown in Figure 2.25. This interface enables you to see all the hotkeys (called *shortcuts* in the list) easily. If you try to enter an existing hotkey, SolidWorks issues a prompt, telling you that the key is assigned to another command and its name. The prompt asks whether you want to clear the other instance of the hotkey and make the new one active. You can print or copy to the Clipboard a list of commands that use hotkeys.

Because the list of commands is so long, a Search function is available, and a drop-down arrow makes visible only the commands from a selected menu. The list of commands is organized by menu name, and the menus are listed as they occur in the interface. Fortunately, you can use the Keyboard tab to sort and list menus, commands, or hotkeys in alphabetical order just by clicking the corresponding column header. This is a highly usable interface and one of my favorite interface changes in the last several releases.

FIGURE 2.25
The Keyboard dialog box
(Tools ➤ Customize ➤
Keyboard)

Hotkeys for menu items are listed on the right side of the regular drop-down menus. They serve more as learning aids than interface elements.

I have included a spreadsheet of the default hotkeys in SolidWorks 2018 with the download materials for Chapter 2. You can save the list of settings by using the Copy List button in the dialog shown in Figure 2.25. If you do a lot of customizations, it might be handy to print them out and tape them to the side of your monitor. It is a little pointless to have to refer to a chart to remember shortcuts, but you might think of it more as a training aid or a means to allow other people to use your workstation effectively.

Using Mouse Gestures

You can customize and use a mouse-gestures interface, shown in Figure 2.26. To make the interface appear, just drag the RMB slightly, about ¼ inch. After you get used to the interface, a drag of about ¾ inch in a single motion activates the commands.

FIGURE 2.26
The mouse-gestures interface

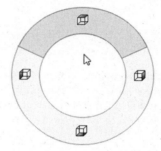

NOTE I have found that this interface works best when you have memorized the commands available at various positions around the donut. You can set it to use 2, 4, 8, or 12 divisions. Accuracy is more difficult with the larger number of divisions.

You can establish the donut in four or eight segments; it comes set to four by default. You can also do the customization in the Customize dialog box (Tools ➤ Customize) using the Mouse Gestures tab. The advantage of this interface is that it is very easy to invoke. I like the way you can use the default setup to control views. The mouse moving in a particular direction is easily associated with a view direction, so it should be easy to remember.

Mouse gestures will probably not replace hotkeys or the S toolbar, but they do add effective quick access for a few functions.

Using the Keyboard

Moving between the mouse and the keyboard can be bothersome and time-consuming. In addition to the hotkey approach, you can use another keyboard method to save time. Many users become adept at using the Alt-key combinations to invoke menu items. Most menu items in Windows applications contain a single underlined letter.

To access a top-level menu, you can hold down the Alt key, press the underlined letter for that menu, and then just press an underlined letter in the menu to access specific commands. This decidedly old-school technique enables you to navigate most of the interface without using the mouse. For example, to exit SolidWorks, instead of using the mouse to click the red X in the upper-right corner, you could press Alt+F, X. In Figure 2.27, you can see that the F in File is underlined, as is the X in Exit.

FIGURE 2.27
Alt keys in the Window menu

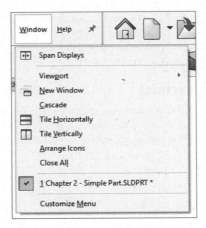

You may potentially run into conflicts when using Alt keys for menu functions. A combination of Alt plus another keyboard key is valid for use as a hotkey combination. If you use any Alt-hotkey combinations, it is likely that you have seen a conflict like this. In cases of conflict, the hotkey combination seems to gain priority over the Alt-key accelerator.

MINIMIZING ICONS

In order to maximize valuable space on the monitor, many SolidWorks users strive to minimize the number of toolbar icons on the screen or confine them to two rows of toolbars. You can do this by using the CommandManager, flyout toolbars, the S toolbar, right-click and left-click toolbars, and hotkeys, and by removing unused icons, as well as the other techniques discussed here.

Having an uncluttered workspace is definitely a plus, but having easy access to commands is the real purpose of an interface in the first place. You need to strike a balance between too much and not enough. The more kinds of work you do in SolidWorks, the more tools you will need to have available. If you create only relatively simple, machined parts and drawings, you will need fewer tools available than someone who creates complex plastic part assemblies with rendering and animation.

CONTEMPLATING DEVICE APPROACHES

If you have never used a 3D mouse or equivalent view-manipulation device, you should consider it. They are wonderful devices and do far more than just spin the view. Most of the devices also have several programmable buttons that you can link to menu items. They can move drawing views, move parts within assemblies, and even manipulate selected objects in other Office applications and Web browsers. You can, from time to time, find these devices on auction sites. Be careful, however, since the older devices use serial ports rather than USB connectors.

Mice are the standard input device, and many of them are recommended for CAD work, but you might also consider a trackball. I've been using a Kensington Slimblade trackball for several years in CAD and normal office computing, and it takes up a lot less space on the desk. It does take some time to get used to it. It is wired, but it doesn't move around.

Using Touch and Multi-Touch Support

I have written portions of this book on a tablet PC. A tablet might not be ideal for long periods of SolidWorks usage, but I use it regularly for presentations and even modeling when I really want to get the feel of drawing a line by hand. The stylus is not quite as intuitive as a pencil, but it is less of an impediment to the tactile feel of actual drawings than a clunky mouse. Tablets are a great option when used in combination with the touch functions in SolidWorks, such as mouse gestures.

The mouse-gestures functionality is considered a tool well-suited to a tablet interface, where flicking the stylus is easier than mouse clicking. This is a single-touch technique, because the stylus typically adds only a single point of contact with the screen.

SolidWorks 2018 has added a new Touch mode, enabled via View ➤ Touch Mode. Touch mode changes the size of interface elements to make them easier to select, and it also adds a Touch Mode toolbar, as shown in Figure 2.28. The tools on the toolbar are Escape, Shortcut to the S menu, Multi-select (like pressing Ctrl), Delete, and Lock 3D Rotate, to prevent view rotations while sketching.

Figure 2.28
The Touch Mode toolbar

Multi-touch devices are becoming more widely available in CAD-worthy configurations, including the Microsoft Surface Studio, a full-size touch display that can be set up horizontally like an old drafting board or used vertically like a large monitor. In preparation for this future functionality that seems ideally suited to visual applications such as CAD and 3D, SolidWorks has added functionality to take advantage of these tools. Multi-touch Action Mappings, as the SolidWorks Help refers to them, are intuitive two-finger motions that enable you to control the view for actions such as these:

◆ Zoom in or out

◆ Rotate

- ◆ Pan
- ◆ Roll
- ◆ Zoom to fit
- ◆ Right-click

Accessing the Pen and Touch Interfaces

The Pen tool is found on the Sketch Ink toolbar. It enables you to create freeform strokes as a feature within a sketch. Pen is used in conjunction with the Pen Sketch and Touch tools on the Sketch toolbar.

This topic will be covered in more depth in Chapter 6, "Getting More from Your Sketches."

ACCESSING MACROS

A *macro* is a short snippet of programming code that has a particular function. Most macros are small and intended for simple tasks that are repeated many times, such as changing selected dimensions to four decimal places or zooming the screen so it is sized 1:1 (actual size). Macros may be recorded, be written from scratch, or be a combination where you record a particular action for use as a starting point and then embellish it manually from there. Recorded macros may not always record the parts of the action that you want to make into a macro, but you can edit them manually to include anything that you can program with the SolidWorks API (application programming interface), which is included with the base SolidWorks package at no extra cost.

To access macros by using hotkeys, follow these steps:

1. Make a folder in your SolidWorks installation directory called "macros."

2. Copy macros into this folder.

3. Start (or restart) SolidWorks.

4. Choose Tools ➤ Customize ➤ Keyboard.

5. Scroll to the bottom of the list under the Macros category, and assign hotkeys as you would for standard SolidWorks commands.

Whether you are skilled at writing or recording macros, or you are just using macros collected from other people, they can be huge time-savers and offer functionality that you would not otherwise be able to access. You might want to consider joining the SolidWorks Community to share macros and other work with other users. The SolidWorks Community can be accessed through the Task pane within the SolidWorks software or via the SolidWorks website.

SAVING CUSTOM INTERFACE SETTINGS

After you have set up your menus and toolbars, worked out all the custom colors, figured out your hotkey usage, and connected your macros, you won't want to lose these settings when you reinstall the software or move to a different computer. Another user may want to share your settings, or you may want to transfer them to your home computer (for modeling the new deck or the doghouse, of course). Fortunately, these settings are very portable.

You can use the Copy Settings Wizard to save these settings to a file. Access the wizard by choosing Start ➤ SolidWorks 2018 Tools ➤ Copy Settings Wizard. This creates a file with a `sldreg` file extension. You can restore settings by double-clicking this file on a computer that has SolidWorks installed on it.

NOTE   You may need to have administrator access to your computer to apply a SolidWorks Registry file. Changing Registry files is kind of dangerous, and I don't really encourage novices to do it unless they have access to someone who understands the Windows Registry.

The SolidWorks settings are actually Windows Registry settings. The file that is saved by the wizard is just a Registry file that has a different extension to prevent it from being applied too easily. Saved Windows Registry files have a `reg` file extension, and you can integrate them into the Registry by simply double-clicking them. If you are not familiar with the Windows Registry, you should not make direct changes, because even small changes can cause serious problems with your operating system, installed software, or even hardware. The settings that are saved by the Copy Settings Wizard are safe to transfer between computers. In order for the Copy Settings Wizard to work, you need to have Administrator-level access to your computer. The Copy Settings Wizard is shown in Figure 2.29.

FIGURE 2.29
The Copy Settings
Wizard

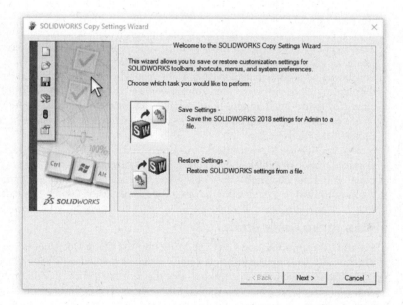

Working with Multiple Document Windows

You may sometimes have the luxury of working on a single part at a time, but more often, you will find yourself with several documents open at once. This is a common situation for most users. Fortunately, SolidWorks has several methods for dealing with "information overload" to help you sort through it all.

GETTING THE MOST FROM THE OPEN COMMAND

The Open dialog box presents some options that you will learn more about in later chapters. Figure 2.30 shows this interface.

FIGURE 2.30
The Open command interface

You can use the Open dialog box just as you would use an open Windows Explorer window. That means you can copy, paste, rename, delete, and move files while you are deciding which one to open. You can also show a preview window and control the size of the icons. The SolidWorks-specific controls you may use most are the Quick Filter controls to narrow the display to just the types of files you're seeking. The icon to the far right of the Quick Filter list shows only top-level assemblies (assemblies that are not a subassembly in another assembly).

If you have other types of files to open, you can use the Custom button for the traditional SolidWorks file type list.

Also notice the Mode button. This button allows you to open a part in Resolved (normal, editable) mode or Quick View (view only). Configurations and Display State buttons are topics covered in later chapters—they allow you to more quickly access the information you are looking for rather than having to open the file and then switch to a different configuration.

MANAGING OPEN FILES

Pressing the combination Ctrl+Tab brings up the Open Documents window, shown in Figure 2.31. To keep the window open, continue to hold down the Ctrl key. Press Tab again to cycle through the open documents. Use the mouse to click an X in any of the thumbnails to close that document. You also can click a link to show that document in its own folder. To close the preview without changing documents, you can press Esc; however, Ctrl+Esc opens the Windows Start menu.

MANAGING RECENT DOCUMENTS

The list of recently used documents is available from the File menu or by pressing the R hotkey. This is actually just a tab in the Welcome dialog, which is also available by pressing Ctrl+F2. The Recent file list can also be accessed using File ➤ Open Recent, which gives a text-based list.

FIGURE 2.31
Ctrl+Tab displays all the
open documents.

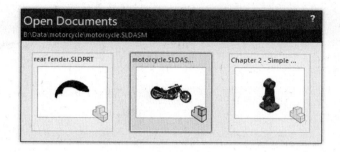

The documents within the window can be opened or pinned in place so they always remain on
the Recent Documents list. Figure 2.32 shows this dialog box.

FIGURE 2.32
Pressing R accesses the
Recent Documents tab
of the Welcome dialog.

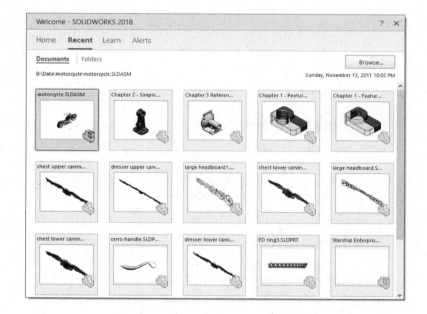

The Folders option at the top gives you a view of the paths to all of the recent documents, and
the Browse button takes you to a Windows Explorer view of the folder.

If you hover over an icon in the Documents list, a small double arrow appears in the lower-
right corner of the icon. Clicking on that double arrow displays certain information and allows
you to open that document in particular configurations, particular display states, open as
read-only, or access the references. This is shown in Figure 2.33. A lot of capability is packed into
this Welcome box.

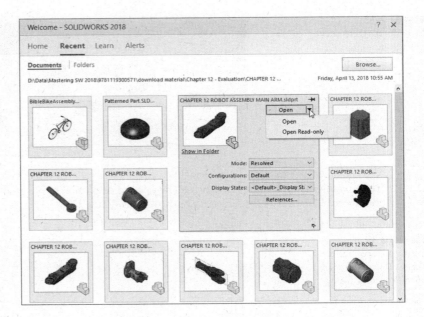

FIGURE 2.33
More functionality behind the Recent Files list icons

MANAGING WINDOWS

Like most Windows applications, SolidWorks can arrange the open document windows in one of several ways that are available through the Window menu:

New Window: Opens a new window of the active document. Dynamic highlights and selections in one window appear in both.

Cascade: This is most useful for accessing documents that are to be edited one-by-one.

Tile Horizontally: This is most useful for comparing wide and short parts side-by-side.

Tile Vertically: This is most useful for tall, narrow parts or documents where you want to compare items in the FeatureManager.

Arrange Icons: When windows are minimized to icons, this menu selection arranges the icons neatly, starting in the lower-left corner of the window.

Close All: Closes all open windows. This option may prompt you to save modified documents.

SPANNING MULTIPLE MONITORS

SolidWorks has tools to help you manage the display across multiple monitors. Figure 2.34 shows the document and application window control buttons in the upper-right corner of the SolidWorks window. In addition to the usual Minimize, Maximize, and Close, the application window controls add the Span Displays tool, which makes the SolidWorks window use both displays in a dual display arrangement.

Figure 2.34
Multiple monitor
controls

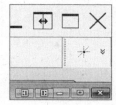

The document window controls add Tile Left and Tile Right, which force the current document window onto the left or right monitor, respectively. When accessing the Tile Left/Right icons on a single monitor, the documents will be sent to the left or right half of the screen. Multiple monitors work best if they have the same vertical resolution; for example, a 1920 × 1200 wide screen and a 1600 × 1200 normal aspect-ratio monitor would work well side by side, but mixing with a 1024 × 768 screen would not. When monitors of different vertical resolutions are used, SolidWorks sizes to the lowest resolution monitor (the second number listed is the vertical resolution).

The Bottom Line

Learn the different parts.   The SolidWorks interface has many elements because SolidWorks has so much functionality. You can access most elements multiple ways, which can be liberating because it offers options, but it can also add to the confusion because there is so much to know. You do not need to know every way to do everything; you only need to know the best way for you.

   Master It   Identify each area around the SolidWorks window.

Customization is key.   Customization opportunities in SolidWorks are vast. Everyone has different tastes and preferences when it comes to running the interface. Some prefer the keyboard, some the mouse. Some prefer the touch interface. There are different strategies that depend on your specific situation—for example, saving space, saving mouse travel, or saving mouse/keyboard clicks. SolidWorks has touch interface options, as well as various accessibility tools intended to accommodate special needs, such as different input devices or color blindness.

   Master It   Create some simple keyboard shortcuts (hotkeys) for the functions you think you will use the most.

Manipulate multiple windows.   Manipulating multiple windows is important in all computer use, but especially in CAD, where you work with enormous amounts of data and numbers of documents that surpass other types of programs.

   Master It   Open several sample documents from the Wiley download data and practice manipulating the windows.

Chapter 3

Working with Sketches and Reference Geometry

The first step to learning how to create models in SolidWorks is to learn how to sketch. If you are coming from another history-based modeling program, many of your skills are transferable to SolidWorks. If you have never used CAD before, think of the sketch-feature relationship as creating a simplified 2D drawing that represents a portion of the part that you can make with some sort of process such as extruding or revolving.

So far in this book, you have looked mainly at concepts, settings, and setup, which are necessary but mundane. In this chapter, you'll begin to learn how to control parametric relationships in sketches. Then in later chapters, you'll begin to build models—simple at first, but gaining in complexity and always demonstrating new techniques and features that build your modeling vocabulary. Beyond this, you'll use the parts to create assemblies and drawings.

This chapter deals entirely with sketches in parts. However, you can apply many of the topics covered here to sketches in assemblies and drawings. Some related topics, such as layout sketches, have functionality that is exclusive to assemblies, and these topics will be covered in later chapters.

IN THIS CHAPTER, YOU WILL LEARN TO:

◆ Begin a sketch

◆ Distinguish sketch entities

◆ Create relationships in sketches

◆ Examine sketch settings

◆ Use sketch blocks in parts, assemblies, and drawings

◆ Create and use reference geometry

Creating a New Part

Before you can create a sketch, you must create a new part. To create a new part, you must follow these two simple steps:

1. Click the New tool.

2. Select a part template from the list. The part template will have the units and drafting standards already set.

Each new part will start with some basic items. The items you need to focus on about right now are the base planes and the origin (shown in Figure 3.1 in the FeatureManager of a brand new blank part made from a template). The planes can be named anything you want: X, Y, and Z; Front, Top, and Right; Larry, Moe, and Curly; or whatever. The naming scheme is determined by the person who saved the template.

FIGURE 3.1
The FeatureManager of
a new part

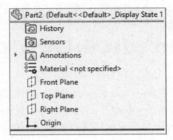

Chapter 1, "Introducing SolidWorks," has more detailed information on part templates and setting up SolidWorks to use existing templates. Several templates are included with the downloadable materials for this book.

Creating a Sketch

Best practice for sketching in SolidWorks dictates that you should keep a few things in mind while creating and editing sketches:

♦ Sketches need to be clean and precise, with no gaps or overlaps and no stray sketch entities.

♦ It is best to keep each sketch simple. Complex sketches tend to fail or cause problems later.

♦ You should create sketches with the general "design intent" (for example, a horizontal rectangle) and then add the details later (for example, precise dimensions).

♦ It is best if you can pick up the desired automatic relationships as you sketch rather than waiting to create them manually later. At the same time, you need to be able to avoid extraneous and unwanted automatic relationships you may get from careless sketching.

♦ The use of reference geometry can save you from unwanted parent/child relationships between features.

SolidWorks allows several workflows you can use to create a sketch. To try to simplify it, think of it this way. You have the Sketch tool that opens a sketch, and you have tools such as Line, Arc, Circle, and so on. You also have planes and planar faces, straight line segments, and straight edges. To create a new sketch, you have to make two selections. One selection must be a tool that tells SolidWorks you want to make a sketch, such as the Sketch tool, or Line, Arc, Circle, etc. The second selection has to be where you want the sketch to be located, such as a plane, a planar face, or an edge on which a perpendicular plane will be created.

Here's one way to create a new sketch:

1. Click the Sketch tool. Notice the prompts in the FeatureManager area.

2. Click the Front plane in the FeatureManager.

Here's another way:

1. Right-click on a plane (either in the FeatureManager or in the graphics window if they are shown). As an alternative, you can click a plane to call the context-sensitive toolbar.

2. Select Sketch from the context bar (on top of the RMB menu).

Here is yet another way:

1. Click the Line tool. Notice the FeatureManager disappears and the PropertyManager shows up in its place. The flyout FeatureManager has actually moved over into the graphics window and has collapsed.

2. Click the down arrow next to the Part1 symbol.

3. Click a plane in the tree.

   Clicking a straight edge creates a plane perpendicular to the end of the edge closest to where you clicked. The plane will show up in the FeatureManager automatically. (This is an obscure trick that a lot of existing users have forgotten.)

When you create a sketch, several tools become available, specifically all the sketch entities and tools. Open sketches and selection filters are two very common sources of frustration for new users. If you are having difficulty selecting items that you want because the software won't allow you to select specific items or because items are grayed out, you could have an open sketch. Several indicators will let you know when you are in Sketch mode:

◆ The title bar of the SolidWorks window displays the text "Sketch X of Part Y."

◆ The lower-right corner of the status bar displays the text "Editing Sketch X."

◆ The Confirmation Corner displays a Sketch icon in the upper-right corner of the graphics window.

◆ The Sketch toolbar button displays the text "Exit Sketch."

◆ The red sketch origin is displayed.

◆ If you are using the grid, is displayed only in Sketch mode.

While most users find the sketch grid annoying or distracting, some new users use it as a reminder that they are in Sketch mode. If you tend to forget or would like a visual cue, the sketch grid is a useful option. You can find the settings for displaying the grid in Sketch mode at Tools ➤ Options ➤ Document Properties ➤ Grid/Snap.

A sketch can be edited only when it is open (unless Instant 3D is off—I recommend you turn it off, except when you intend to use it). You can have only one sketch open at a time. SolidWorks uses many indicators to show the state of a sketch, including the Confirmation Corner and the taskbar.

Just as you can create sketches in several ways, you can also open existing sketches several ways:

◆ Right-click a sketch in the FeatureManager or graphics window and select Sketch.

◆ Select a sketch from the FeatureManager or graphics window, and click the Sketch icon on the Sketch toolbar.

◆ Left-click a sketch or feature and click the Sketch icon from the context toolbar.

◆ Double-click a sketch with the Instant 3D tool active.

TIP   The 3D view can be at any angle while you are sketching. If you prefer to always show the sketch in the plane of the display, use the setting at Tools ➢ Options ➢ Sketch ➢ Auto-rotate View Normal To Sketch Plane On Sketch Creation And Sketch Edit.

Identifying Sketch Entities

SolidWorks sketching tools include many types of entities. Some you will use all the time, and others you may never use, even if you spend years working with the software. In this section, I offer tips for using each entity.

Using the Sketch Toolbar

In the following section, I first identify the default buttons on the Sketch toolbar, followed by the rest of the entities that you can access by choosing Tools ➢ Customize ➢ Commands ➢ Sketch.

Take a minute and hover your cursor over the buttons on the Sketch toolbar. Let the tooltips come up. When a button has a triangle to the right of it, the triangle is a flyout button that provides access to additional tools. For example the Line flyout allows you to also select the centerline (also used as construction line) and the midpoint line. As shown in Figure 3.2.

FIGURE 3.2
Options with the Line
flyout toolbar

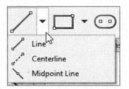

TIP   I personally like to turn off the Sketch toolbar in the CommandManager and use a separate Sketch toolbar vertically on the right side. This is because switching back and forth between Sketch and Features in the CommandManager becomes a little tedious. I find it more efficient to have both toolbars showing at the same time.

The Sketch tool opens and closes sketches. You may notice that the name of the button changes depending on whether the sketch is open or closed. If you preselect a plane or planar face and then click the Sketch button, SolidWorks opens a new sketch on the plane or face. If you preselect a sketch before clicking the Sketch button, SolidWorks opens this sketch. If you preselect an edge or curve feature before clicking the Sketch button, SolidWorks automatically makes a plane perpendicular to the nearest end of the curve. If you do not use preselection and click the Sketch tool with nothing selected, SolidWorks prompts you to select a plane or planar face on which you want to put a new sketch, or an existing sketch to edit.

The 3D Sketch tool opens and closes 3D sketches with no preselection required. 3D Sketch is covered in more detail in Chapter 6, "Getting More from Your Sketches."

The Smart Dimension tool can create all types of dimensions used in SolidWorks, such as horizontal, vertical, aligned, radial, diameter, angle, and arc length. You can create dimensions several ways, as shown in Figure 3.3. The dimensions shown were created by selecting the line itself and moving the cursor to different locations to get horizontal, vertical, or aligned dimensions

We will return to smart dimensions later in this chapter.

The Line tool creates straight lines using one of two methods. You should practice these two methods to determine which one you prefer. If you have used other CAD products, you probably already have a preference.

Click+click: This method is used for drawing multiple connected end-to-end lines. Click and release the left mouse button to start the line; each click and release ends the previous line and starts a new one. Double-click (to cancel the first click point but remain in the Line command), press Esc (to exit the Line command altogether), or deselect the Line tool to end.

Click-and-drag: This method is used to draw individual or unconnected lines. Click, drag, and drop. The first click initiates the line, and the drop ends it.

TIP   Some functions, such as Enable On-Screen Numeric Input, seem to function better with Click+click than with click-and-drag.

Alternative methods exist for drawing lines that include horizontal, vertical, angle, and infinite lines. The interface for these options appears in the PropertyManager, as shown in Figure 3.3.

FIGURE 3.3
The Insert Line
PropertyManager
interface

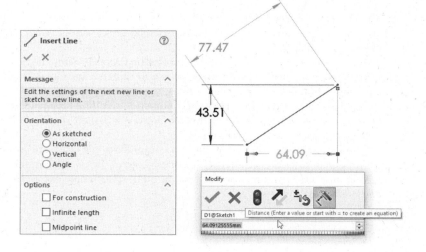

Horizontal, Vertical: These settings require you to select a starting point and an ending vertical or horizontal position. I see no compelling reason to use this setting instead of the regular Line command. It is useful in a strictly 2D world, but I can't see what I would use it for here.

Angle: This setting enables you to specify an angle and drag a line at this angle. Again, I can find no compelling reason to use this tool.

Infinite Length: SolidWorks parts have a working space limited to 1000 meters on a side, centered on the origin. Infinite lines extend well beyond this, although you cannot draw or dimension a regular line outside of this box. This feature would be most useful if you are working with parts with vastly divergent scales of features (some very large, some very small).

TIP   The Add Dimensions option exists in several sketch-entity PropertyManagers and adds Smart Dimensions to newly sketched entities. The option appears in the sketch-entity PropertyManager only if the setting at Tools ➤ Options ➤ Sketch ➤ Enable On-Screen Numeric Input On Entity Creation is selected.

The On-Screen Numeric Input option is not the same as the Input Dimension Value function; in fact, it overrides that option. You cannot input dimension values when using the Add Dimensions in conjunction with click-and-drag sketching. It appears to be intended for Click+click sketching only, so that you can enter values between clicks.

When you select the Corner Rectangle tool, you can create a rectangle by clicking one corner and dragging to the diagonal corner. This action creates four lines with Horizontal and Vertical sketch relations, as appropriate. The Corner Rectangle is also available as a flyout icon with a Corner Rectangle, Center Rectangle, 3 Point Corner Rectangle (rectangle at an angle), 3 Point Center Rectangle, and Parallelogram. Figure 3.4 shows the flyout and flyout icons, as well as the PropertyManager for the Rectangle, which also enables you to switch types of rectangles easily. Remember that the shortcut shown on the right cycles through all of the rectangle options in the PropertyManager.

If you have activated any of the items under the Rectangle flyout, you can press the A key to cycle through the rest of the items. If you have already started sketching the rectangle but haven't yet finished, pressing the A key will cancel out of the current rectangle and cycle to the next type. This may be faster than actually using the flyout; just click the first icon and cycle to the one you want. The cursor icon changes to show which type of rectangle it will presently sketch.

Notice the Add Dimensions check box in the PropertyManager. Selecting this box while creating a rectangle causes the software to add dimensions aligned with the sides of the rectangle. This option is also available for lines, arcs, and circles.

Note that if you use this option in conjunction with the Enable On-Screen Numeric Input On Entity Creation setting, found at Tools ➤ Options ➤ Sketch, it makes creating sketch entities to the correct size immediately much easier.

The Parallelogram tool is used to draw a *parallelogram* (adjacent sides are not perpendicular, and opposite sides are parallel). Click one corner of the parallelogram, and then click the second and third corners. It works like the 3 Point Rectangle except that adjacent sides are not perpendicular.

FIGURE 3.4
The Rectangle flyout with associated icons

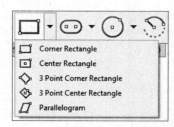

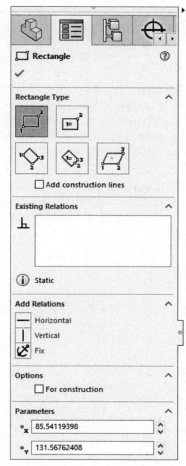

NOTE   The Shaded Sketch Contours option is turned on by default. This option adds shading to any sketch area where entities enclose an area end-to-end. The lines or arcs (or whatever) have to touch at their end points and not cross in the middle of the line. Circles enclose an area and are therefore shaded. This option is partly a diagnostic tool and is useful for one-click selection of the contour entities. You will also find it useful when you want to use a subset of a sketch to create a single feature. (Note that you cannot create multiple features using contours from one large sketch.) You can turn off the option from the Sketch toolbar or through the menus at Tools ➤ Sketch Settings ➤ Shaded Sketch Contours.

The Circle tool creates a circle using one of two methods, which are available from either the flyout icon or the Circle PropertyManager:

Center Creation: Click the center of the circle and drag the radius. The Circle PropertyManager calls this function *center creation*.

Perimeter Creation: To create a circle using this technique, you must select the Perimeter Creation option from the Circle PropertyManager window after clicking the Circle tool. There is also a separate Perimeter Creation toolbar button and a menu selection for Tools ➤ Sketch Entities ➤ Perimeter Circle. This creates only tangent relations with other entities in the current sketch; if you are building a circle from model edges or entities in other sketches, you need to apply the relations manually. SolidWorks calls these functions *perimeter creation*.

Tangent to Two Entities: Start the circle with the cursor near one line in the sketch. A Tangent symbol appears by the cursor with a yellow background. Click and drag the diameter to the second tangent entity, where a similar cursor symbol should appear. Release the mouse button and right-click the green checkmark icon. This process is shown in Figure 3.5.

Tangent to Three Entities: Use the same process used for Tangent to Two Entities, but omit the right-click of the green checkmark icon. After dropping on the second tangent, drag again to the third tangent entity.

FIGURE 3.5
Creating a circle

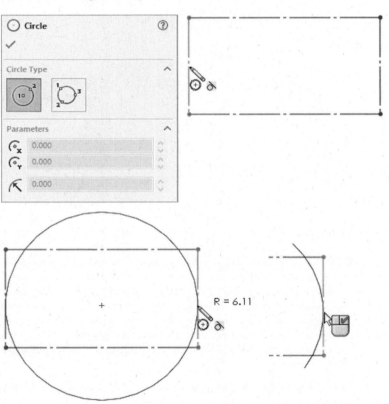

When you select the Centerpoint Arc tool, you can create arc by clicking the center, dragging the radius, and then clicking and dragging the included angle of the arc. The first two steps are exactly like those for the Center-Radius circle.

The Tangent Arc tool creates an arc tangent to an existing sketch entity. Depending on how you move the cursor away from the end of the existing sketch entity, the arc can be tangent, reverse tangent, or perpendicular, as shown in Figure 3.6.

FIGURE 3.6
Using the Tangent
Arc feature

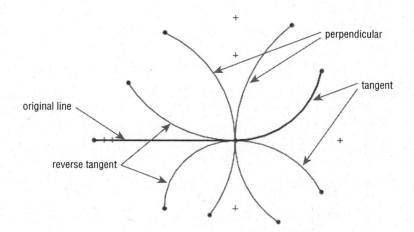

Another way to create a tangent arc (called auto-transitioning) is to start drawing a line from the end of another sketch entity, and while holding down the left mouse button, press the A key; or return the cursor to the starting point and drag it out again. This second method can be difficult to master, but it saves time compared to any of the techniques for switching sketch tools.

The 3 Point Arc tool creates an arc by first establishing endpoints and then establishing the included arc, as shown in Figure 3.7. Again, this tool also works using the Click+click or click-and-drag methods.

FIGURE 3.7
Creating a
three-point arc

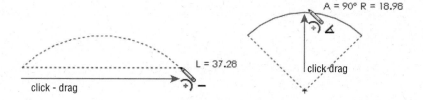

The Sketch Fillet tool creates a sketch fillet in two ways. Either you can select the endpoint where the sketch entities intersect, or you can select the lines themselves, selecting the portion that you want to keep. Figure 3.8 illustrates both techniques.

The Sketch Chamfer tool is on the same flyout as the Sketch Fillet by default. Sketch Chamfer does not have a list selection box the way that fillet does, and it does not use a preview like the fillet.

FIGURE 3.8
Creating a sketch fillet

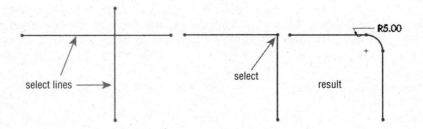

select lines →

select

result

R5.00

SKETCH FILLETS

Although the Sketch Fillet tool is easy to use and may align with your way of working in a 2D program, it is not considered best practice to use sketch fillets extensively. Some of the reasons for this include:

◆ Large changes in the size or shape of the rest of the sketch can cause the feature built from the sketch to fail.

◆ SolidWorks (and other parametric programs as well) often has difficulty solving tangent arcs in some situations. You may see fillets flip tangency or go around 270 degrees instead of just 90 degrees. Using many fillets in a sketch can often cause trouble.

◆ If you want to remove the fillets temporarily, there is no good way to do this if you have used sketch fillets.

◆ Sometimes feature order requires that other features, such as draft, come before the fillet, which is difficult to do if they are part of the sketch.

◆ Sometimes a 2D fillet simply cannot create the required 3D geometry.

Fillet features are the preferred method for creating rounds and fillets. The same can be said for chamfers. Still, sometimes you need to use tangent arcs in sketches. You will have to decide which way works best for you in each situation.

The Centerline tool follows the same methods as regular lines and is called a *construction line* in some cases. Other construction entities, such as construction circles, are not available directly, but you can create them by selecting the For Construction option in the PropertyManager for any entity.

The Spline tool draws a freeform curve. Splines may form either a single closed loop or an open loop. In either case, the spline is not allowed to cross itself. You can draw a spline by clicking each location where you want to add a control point. Figure 3.9 identifies the elements of a spline. The detail image shows the structure of a spline handle.

Splines are used mainly for freeform complex shapes in 2D and 3D sketches, although you can also use them for anything in which you would use other sketch elements. If you need more information on splines and complex shape modeling, refer to the *SolidWorks Surfacing and Complex Shape Modeling Bible* (Wiley, 2008).

FIGURE 3.9
The structure of a spline
and spline handles

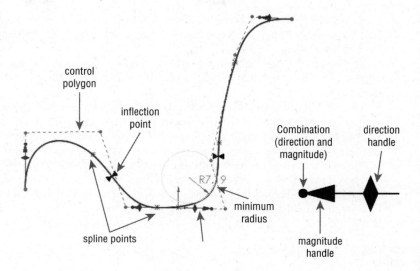

control
polygon

inflection
point

Combination
(direction and
magnitude)

direction
handle

R7.9

minimum
radius

spline points

magnitude
handle

The Point tool creates a sketch point. Aside from limited cases of lofting to a point or using a point as a constraint sketch in a Fill feature, sketch points are usually used for reference, in patterns, or for the location of the centerpoint of Hole Wizard features.

You can also use the sketch point as a virtual sharp. If two sketch entities do not actually intersect because of a fillet or chamfer, selecting the two entities and clicking the Point tool creates a point at the location where they would intersect if they were extended. This is useful for dimensioning to the sharp. Virtual sharp display is controlled by a Document Property setting.

The 3D Sketch Plane tool creates a plane in a 3D sketch. I discuss 3D sketches in more detail in Chapter 6. By sketching on planes within a 3D sketch, you get most of the benefits and usage of 2D sketches, and you do not have to deal with history between sketches. Before committing too much work to this course, you should look into some of the shortcomings of 3D planes. The planes are treated just like any other entity in the 3D sketch, which means you can assign sketch relations to them, but it also means that they can move around within the sketch the way sketch entities do.

The Add Relation tool displays a PropertyManager window that enables you to apply sketch relations. This interface appears to be obsolete, because it is easier to simply select sketch items and apply relations via the context toolbar or in the PropertyManager window that appears automatically when you select them; however, there are some subtle workflow-related reasons for using this tool.

Using the Add Relations dialog box has two advantages over simply selecting sketch entities and adding relations. When the Add Relation PropertyManager is active, you do not need to use the Ctrl key to select multiple entities. You also do not need to clear a selection before making a new selection for the next relation. These two reasons sound minor, but if you have a large number of sketch relations to apply, the workflow goes much more smoothly using this tool than the default method.

The Display/Delete Relations tool enables you to look through the relations in a sketch and sort them according to several categories. From this window, you can delete or suppress relations and replace entities in relations.

The Quick Snaps flyout enables you to quickly filter types of entities that sketch elements will snap to when you move or create them. To access the tools, click the drop-down arrow to the right of the toolbar button.

The Mirror Entities tool mirrors selected sketch entities about a single selected centerline and applies a Symmetric sketch relation. In addition, a Dynamic Mirror function is described later in this chapter.

The Convert Entities tool converts edges, curves, and sketch elements from other sketches into entities in the current sketch. When edges are not parallel to the sketch plane, the Convert Entities feature projects them into the sketch plane. Some elements may be impossible to convert—for example, a helix, which would produce a projection that overlaps itself. Sketch entities created using Convert Entities get an On-Edge sketch relation.

The Offset Entities command works like the Convert Entities feature, except that it offsets the sketch to one side or the other of the projection of the original edge, sketch, or curve, and Offset Entities doesn't have a selection box. Figure 3.10 shows the PropertyManager interface for this command.

FIGURE 3.10
The Offset
Entities interface

The options available in the Offset Entities interface are as follows:

Add Dimensions: This option constrains offset sketch entities. Instead of the On-Edge relations, Offset Entities creates an Offset sketch relation that cannot be re-created manually.

Reverse: This option changes the direction of the offset.

Select Chain: This option selects continuous end-to-end sketch entities.

Bi-directional: This option offsets to both sides simultaneously.

Cap Ends: This is available only when you have selected the Bi-directional option. Capping the ends with arcs is an easy way to create a slot from a sketch of the centerline. This function works with all sketch entities; it is not limited to straight slots. Figure 3.11 shows examples of the Cap ends option.

Construction Geometry: This option enables you to select which geometry (if any) you would like to make into construction geometry—the original selection, or the entities that are offset.

FIGURE 3.11
The Offset
Entities interface

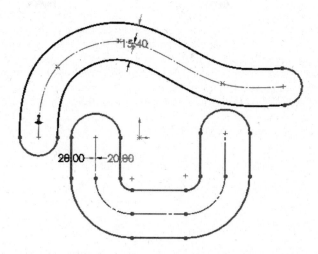

FIGURE 3.11
The Offset
Entities interface

CAUTION   The Offset Entities command may fail if the offset distance is greater than the smallest radius of curvature and you are attempting to offset to the inside of the arc.

In addition to the bidirectional offset with capped ends, SolidWorks also has slot sketch entities for straight and curved slots, which are covered later in this chapter. Composite slots (made of a combination of straight and curved sections) still require the offset method.

 The Trim tool is actually several functions rolled into one, including extending and deleting sketch entities. Figure 3.12 shows the PropertyManager interface for this function.

FIGURE 3.12
The Trim interface

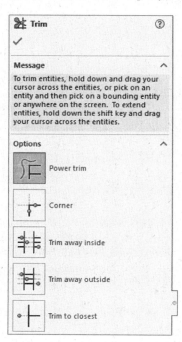

Power Trim: This trims by dragging a cursor trail over multiple entities. The entities that you drag the cursor over are trimmed back to (or extend up to, when using the Shift key) the next intersecting sketch entity. Each time you trim an entity, a red box remains until you trim the next entity. If you backtrack with the cursor and touch the red box, this trim is undone. This option is best used when you need to trim a large number of entities that are easy to hit with a moving cursor. Figure 3.13 shows the Power Trim feature in action. You can also use Power Trim to extend sketch entities along their paths by dragging the endpoints. Regular dragging can also change the position or orientation of the rest of the entity, but by using the Power Trim feature, you affect only the length.

FIGURE 3.13
Power Trim in action

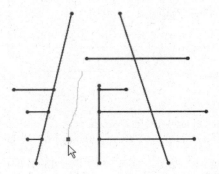

Corner: This trims or extends two selected entities to their next intersection. When you use the Corner option to trim, the selected portion of the sketch entities is kept, and anything on the other side of the corner is discarded. Figure 3.14 shows two ways that the Corner option can work.

FIGURE 3.14
Using the Corner option

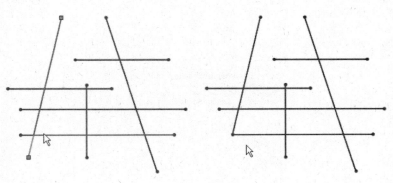

Trim Away Inside: This trims away selected entities inside a selected boundary. The boundary may consist of a pair of sketch entities or a model face (edges of the face are used as the boundary). Only entities that cross both selected boundaries (or cross the closed loop of the face boundary twice) can be trimmed. This option does not trim a closed loop such as a circle, an ellipse, or a closed spline.

Trim Away Outside: This functions exactly like the Trim Away Inside option, except that sketch entities outside of the boundary are discarded. The Trim Away Inside and Trim Away Outside options are illustrated in Figure 3.15.

FIGURE 3.15
Using the Trim Away
Inside and Trim Away
Outside options

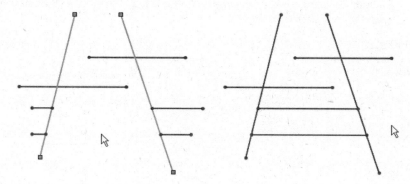

Trim To Closest: This is the default setting. Clicking a sketch entity:

◆ Trims it back to the next entity if there is only one crossing entity.

◆ Trims between two crossing entities if there is more than one.

◆ Deletes the entity if there are no crossing entities.

◆ In all cases, the selected section of the entity is removed. The Trim To Closest option can also extend when you drag one entity to another; if an intersection is possible, the first entity is extended to the second entity. Figure 3.16 illustrates how the Trim To Closest option functions.

FIGURE 3.16
Using Trim To
Closest to extend

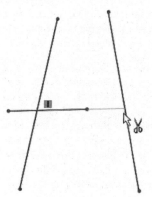

The Construction Geometry tool toggles between regular sketch entities and construction entities. Construction sketch entities are not used to create solid or surface faces directly; they are used only for reference—for example, revolve centerlines, extrude and pattern directions, and so forth. Be careful with the icon for this function, because it looks almost identical to the No Solve Move icon, especially as printed here in grayscale.

The Stretch sketch tool is intended for use in sketches where there are enough dimensions to make a particular change difficult by changing dimensions only. Stretch enables you to specify a change that will change several dimensions simultaneously. Figure 3.17 shows the sketch being stretched. Notice one of the lines is not selected at the top, so the top vertical line becomes angled and loses its vertical relation.

FIGURE 3.17
Using the Stretch sketch tool

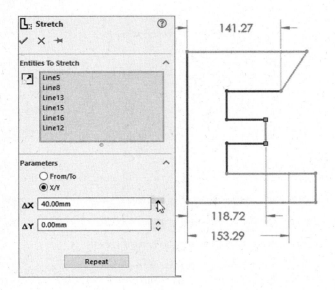

TIP The main ideas to remember with the Stretch tool are that it is used to stretch dimensioned lines and that you need to select the lines that will lengthen or shorten as well as the lines that will move. Because of this, selecting entities for Stretch is best done with the right-to-left window selection or the lasso, which also selects any items that the selection box crosses. (Left-to-right window selection selects only items that are completely within the selection box.)

The Move, Rotate, Copy, and Scale sketch tools operate on selections within a sketch. You can use these tools with pre- or post-selection methods. These tools delete existing sketch relations when necessary to accomplish the task. For example, if you want to move a rectangle connected to the origin, the Move tool deletes the coincident relation between the sketch endpoint and the origin. If you want to rotate a rectangle, the Rotate tool deletes all the horizontal and vertical relations on the entities being rotated. This operation may result in a completely underdefined sketch. SolidWorks does not warn you that sketch relations are being deleted.

If you use the Scale tool on a fully defined sketch, SolidWorks scales the position of the selected entities, deleting sketch relations if necessary to do so, but no dimensions are scaled or deleted.

CAUTION Be careful when using these sketch tools. They can delete sketch relations without warning. Some of the tools have a check box for Keep Relations.

These sketch tools were originally put in the software to avoid some of the complexities and limitations of the Modify Sketch tool, which can also move, copy, rotate, and scale sketches.

Figure 3.18 shows the simple interface for the Move Entities command. Select the entities to move in the upper box and the method to move them from the Parameters box.

FIGURE 3.18
The Move
Entities interface

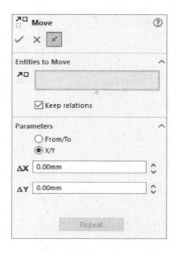

The Select tool is usually used to turn off the previous command and return the cursor to its default state. It is not found on toolbars in the default interface.

The Grid/Snap tool is used to open the Grid/Snap section of Tools ➤ Options ➤ Document Properties.

The Polygon tool creates a regular *n*-sided polygon in the same way as a circle. Click the center and drag the radius. You need to set the number of sides in the PropertyManager before clicking in the graphics window.

An ellipse is created by clicking the center, dragging one axis, and then dragging the other axis.

A partial ellipse is created by clicking the center, dragging one axis, dragging the other axis, and then clicking and dragging the included angle of the partial ellipse. The Partial Ellipse feature works like the Centerpoint Arc command.

A parabola is created by clicking the location for the focus and then dragging the position of the apex. You then click and drag the included angle of the parabola. This is a rarely used sketch entity and is often difficult to control with sketch relations or dimensions.

A *conic* is a special curve that is used to create smooth shapes that are limited to convexity on one side. A spline can have a point of inflection, but a conic cannot. It is similar to a partial ellipse, but it has an additional point called a *top vertex* in the PropertyManager. To create a conic, place the two end points, then place the top vertex, and finally place the shoulder. (See Figure 3.19.) If you are familiar with systems that use a rho (ρ) value, you can specify the value in the PropertyManager.

The Spline On Surface tool is used in 3D sketches to draw a freeform spline on any 3D surface. The Spline On Surface feature can cross face boundaries as long as the faces are at least tangent (ideally curvature continuous) across the edge. Spline On Surface can be used to trim surfaces or create split lines.

FIGURE 3.19
Drawing a conic

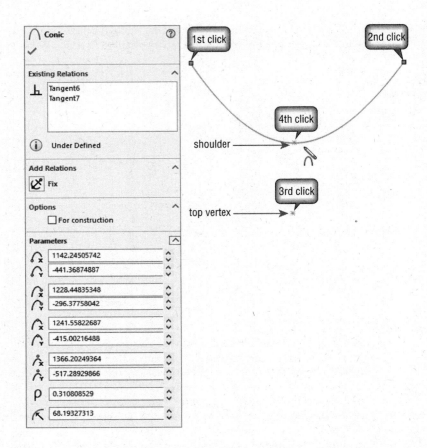

The Sketch Text tool creates editable text in sketches using TrueType fonts installed in your Windows Fonts folder. Some fonts produce sketches that are unusable for solid features, due to violating sketch rules with overlapping or zero thickness. You need to be careful which fonts you select, but I have had success with a wide variety of fonts I have found on the Internet. Sketch Text may be dissolved into lines and arcs so that you can edit them manually. Dissolve is available on the RMB menu. Figure 3.20 points out the key elements of the Sketch Text interface.

For some machine scribing functions, you will want single line or stick fonts. In SolidWorks, the default for that functionality would be OLF SimpleSansOC.

NOTE   Note that the Link To Property icon enables you to link sketch text to a custom property or to a configuration-specific custom property. Using configurations and properties to drive sketch text can be a valuable function.

The Intersection Curve tool creates sketch entities in 2D sketches, where the sketch plane intersects selected faces. In 3D sketches, the Intersection Curve sketch tool creates sketch entities where any types of selected faces intersect. This can be an extremely useful tool in many situations.

FIGURE 3.20
The text has been attached to a curve, created within the current sketch.

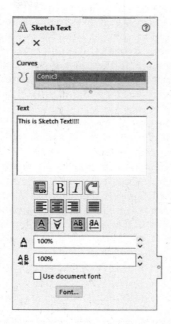

 The Face Curves tool applies the underlying U-V isoparameter mesh to a selected face. It is most commonly used as an evaluation tool for complex surfaces, but you can also use it to create curves to rebuild faces. Accepting the results by clicking OK creates a separate 3D sketch for each spline (unless you have a 3D sketch open before clicking Face Curves, in which case you get a single 3D sketch with all of the curves). Figure 3.21 shows the original surface and the results of using face curves on a complex lofted surface.

FIGURE 3.21
Using face curves on a complex surface

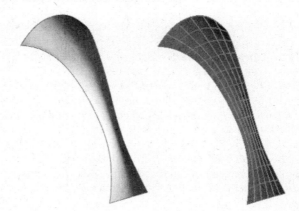

The Extend tool extends a sketch entity up to its next intersection with another sketch entity. This is not to be confused with the Extend for surface entities. The Power Trim tool mentioned earlier can be used to extend if you hold down the Shift key while dragging the cursor over sketch entities to be extended.

The Split Entities tool splits a sketch entity into two segments, automatically adding appropriate sketch relations and automatically adding colinear, coradial, or tangent relations for lines, arcs, and splines. You can also delete it later to rejoin the entity back into a single segment. You should be aware that the rejoining works only if there is a colinear relation between line segments, a coradial relation between arcs, or a tangent or Equal Curvature relation between splines. If you split the entity and delete these relations, they cannot be rejoined. Closed-loop entities require at least two split points.

The Dynamic Mirror command can be used when you preselect a centerline and Dynamic Mirror is turned on. Any new sketch entity that you draw is automatically mirrored to the other side of the centerline. The ends of the mirror line have hatch marks on them to remind you that you have mirroring turned on. A word of caution: If a line is drawn normal to the centerline with the endpoint on the centerline, it will just be doubled in size.

The Segment tool either places equally spaced sketch points along an existing sketch entity or breaks the entity up into a number of equal length segments. It acts as a pattern along a curve. The resulting segment is editable, so you can delete or add points, and they will autospace dynamically. This is an excellent tool for the Hole Wizard or for Sketch Driven Patterns.

The Linear Sketch Pattern tool creates a one- or two-directional pattern of sketch entities. You can define spacing and angles.

The Circular Sketch Pattern tool creates a circular pattern of sketch entities.

BEST PRACTICE

You should use sketch patterns as little as possible. For many of the same reasons that fillet features are preferred over sketch fillets, pattern features are preferred over sketch patterns. Sketch patterns are not as editable or as flexible as feature patterns. They solve slowly, especially when you pattern many entities. Best practice is to avoid sketch patterns unless there is no alternative.

The Make Path function is intended to help create machine-design motion in sketches, in particular, cam-type motion. Although it is helpful, you do not need to make a block of the cam first. You can then right-click the block and select Make Path. A tangent relation to a path enables a follower to roll around the entire perimeter.

The Modify Sketch tool is one of the few remaining dialog box interfaces in the software that doesn't use the PropertyManager. It enables you to move, rotate, and scale the sketch, as well as mirror about a horizontal or vertical axis or about both axes simultaneously. Figure 3.22 shows the interface, which consists of a dialog box, a special origin-like symbol, and a context-sensitive cursor.

Both the left and right mouse buttons have special functions, which change when the cursor is moved over the three knots on the special Modify Sketch origin. The RMB enables you to mirror or rotate the sketch, and the left mouse button (LMB) enables you to move the origin or move the sketch.

This function has some limitations when you use it with sketches that have external relations. Certain functions may be disabled or a warning message may appear, saying that you need to remove external relations to get a particular function to work correctly. It is best used for controlling the orientation of Derived Sketches that by default cannot have internal relations.

The No Solve Move option enables the moving of sketch entities without solving any relations in the sketch. If you select this option and you move an entity with relations that

FIGURE 3.22
The Modify
Sketch interface

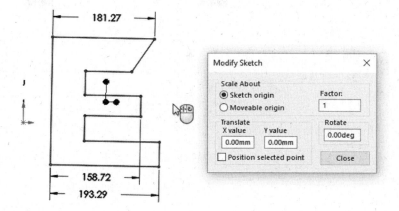

would otherwise not allow it to be dragged (such as a collinear relation), you are prompted with a choice to delete the existing relation and continue or copy the entity without the relation.

A *sketch picture* is a picture that is placed in the sketch, lies on the sketch plane, and is listed in the FeatureManager indented under the sketch as a child. The sketch picture may be suppressed independently from the rest of the sketch, and when the sketch is hidden, the picture is not visible. You can easily move, resize, and rotate sketch pictures, as well as apply a transparent background color to them. Sketch pictures are usually used for tracing over or as a planar decal without the need for rendering.

The Equation Driven Curve tool creates a sketch spline driven by either an explicit or a parametric equation, as shown in Figure 3.23. An explicit equation is in the form $y = f(x)$, while a parametric equation uses multiple equations driven by a common parameter value of the form, such as

$x = cos(t)$

$y = sin(t)$

$0 > t > pi$

where t is a number in radians.

The result is a proportional spline in a sketch, not a curve feature as the name suggests. You can drag the spline itself, or its endpoints, in 2D or 3D, and SolidWorks calculates the new transformation. To reposition a sketch, use sketch relations and dimensions.

If you start an equation-driven curve in a 2D sketch, you get the form for a 2D curve equation. If you start in a 3D sketch, you get the form for a 3D curve. After these splines are created, you cannot remove the relation to the equation and manually edit the spline; they are tied to the equation until you delete the entire spline.

One way to get around this limitation would be to create an equation-driven curve in one sketch and then open another sketch and use Convert Entities to copy the spline, delete the On Edge relation, and use Simplify Spline to add control points to it. This is a technique commonly used with other types of curves; it does not enable you to update the overall size or shape of the spline through the equation, but you can manually adjust sections of a curve originally created from equations. Examples of where this might be useful would be a lead-in or lead-out on a cut thread, a special attachment loop in the middle of a spring, or a flare around the edge of a lens or reflector dish for mounting.

FIGURE 3.23
The Equation Driven
Curve
PropertyManager

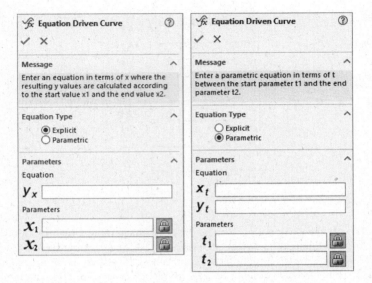

The Straight Slot and Curved Slot tools draw slots of a given width and length with full rounds on the ends. All the Slot sketch entities can be seen in the PropertyManager shown in Figure 3.24. If you need to draw a composite slot or a slot with multiple entities, you need to use the bidirectional sketch offset with capped ends mentioned earlier.

FIGURE 3.24
The PropertyManager
for the Slot
sketch entities

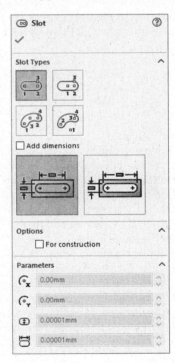

Driving Sketches with Smart Dimensions

All dimensions in SolidWorks sketches can be created with a single tool, the Smart Dimension.
Dimensions are half of what you can use to drive changes in sketches with precision, the other
half being sketch relations.

The Smart Dimension tool can be used to create length, point to point, aligned, angular, radial,
diameter, arc length dimensions, and even reference (nondriving) dimensions.

 By default, SolidWorks installs with a setting called Instant2D activated. Instant2D is relatively new and has some advantages and disadvantages. One of the advantages is that it enables
you to drag dimensions by the handle as shown in Figure 3.25. One disadvantage is that it
disables the Modify box, shown in Figure 3.26.

FIGURE 3.25

Dragging a dimension
with Instant2D activated

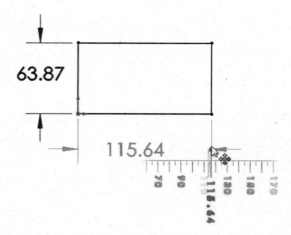

SolidWorks sometimes forces you to use new functionality by activating it by default, instead
of allowing you to decide. This is done in order for you to quickly discover new functionality.
Then if you like the new functionality, you keep it; if not, you can turn it off. The downside can
be a bit of initial confusion. I think in the case of Instant2D, they should allow users to turn it on
if they want. The new setting adds ease-of-use at the expense of precision dimensions. If you
wanted to drag type precision, you wouldn't have put a dimension on it. You can turn off
Instant2D by deselecting the Instant2D tool on the Sketch CommandManager tab. The rest of the
book will assume that this option is turned off.

When you place a dimension you just created, SolidWorks automatically puts you into the
Modify box, which enables you to edit the dimension in several ways. You can disable this option
by removing the check from the setting at Tools ➤ Options ➤ General ➤ Input Dimension Value.
With that setting off, when you place the dimension, it will not display the Modify box.

You can change Smart Dimension values in several ways using the Modify box, shown in
Figure 3.25. The most direct method is to key in a value such as **4.052**. The software assumes
document units unless you key in something specific. You can also key in an expression, even
with mixed units, such as 8.5 mm/2+.125 or 25.4+.625 in. You can also key in negative dimensions, which function the same as the Change Dimension Direction button in the Modify box.

To the right of the drop-down arrow is a pair of up and down spin arrows that enable you
to change the value in the Modify box by a set increment amount. You set the increment in

FIGURE 3.26
Using the Modify
Dimension box

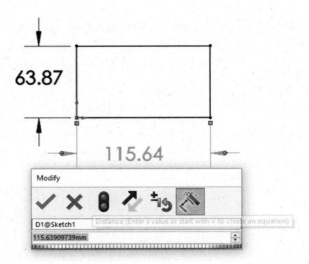

Tools ➤ Options ➤ System Options ➤ Spin Box Increments. You can also store multiple increment values within the Increment Value icon on the Modify box.

The final way to change the value in the Modify box is by using the wheel underneath the
value field. The wheel uses the default increment value. Pressing Ctrl while using the wheel
multiplies the increment by 10, and pressing Alt while using the wheel divides the increment by
10. Once you have created the dimension and determined that you do not need the Modify box
again, you can click on an existing dimension, and the Modify box will reappear with the value
of the new selected dimension. Sketch dimensions can be displayed in dual units (for example,
inch and millimeter), using the Dual Dimension panel of the Dimension PropertyManager.
Here's a look at the Dimension Properties interface (Figure 3.27).

Radial: You create the dimension by selecting an arc and placing the dimension. If you want a
radial dimension of a complete circle, you must right-click the dimension after you create it,
select Display Options, and select the Display As Radius/Display As Diameter toggle.
Alternatively, you could use the Radius or Diameter leader display options on the Leaders tab
of the Dimension PropertyManager.

Diameter: You can create the dimension by selecting a complete circle and placing the
dimension. If you want a diameter dimension for an arc, use the RMB menu or Dimension
Properties dialog box and select the Diameter Dimension option.

NOTE   Along with the Radial and Diameter dimensions, you may also want to dimension between
arcs or circles, from tangent or nearest points. To do this, press the Shift key and select the Smart
Dimension tool to select the arcs near the tangent points. Alternatively, to change a dimension from
a center-to-center dimension to a max-to-max dimension, you can drag dimension attachment points
to tangent points or use the dimension properties.

Angle: You can create the angle dimension in two ways. If the angle to be driven is between
two straight lines, simply select the two straight lines and place the dimension. If you are
creating an included angle dimension for an arc where there are not necessarily any straight

FIGURE 3.27
The Dimension
PropertyManager tabs

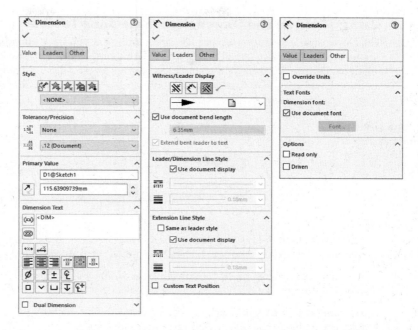

lines drawn, then make the Smart Dimension tool active, select the vertex of the angle, and then select the two outlying points, as shown in Figure 3.28. You can also create an angle dimension between a line and an orthogonal direction. To do this, with the Smart Dimension tool active, click on the line, and then click on the end point of a line. Four orthogonal arrows will appear. Click one of these arrows as a direction to complete the angle dimension.

FIGURE 3.28
Dimensioning an
included angle
without lines

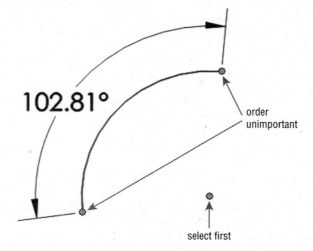

Arc Length: You can create the dimension by selecting an arc and its endpoints with the Smart Dimension tool. This displays the actual linear length of the arc.

Using Tools on the Dimensions/Relations Toolbar

The Dimensions/Relations toolbar has a few tools that you have already seen; but as the name suggests, it also contains tools that help you to either create or investigate dimensions and sketch relations. Figure 3.29 shows the default toolbar; but in the following pages, you'll look at all the tools available at Tools ➤ Customize ➤ Commands ➤ Dimensions/Relations. These tools are available on the Dimensions/Relations toolbar:

FIGURE 3.29
The Dimensions/
Relations toolbar

Smart Dimension: Lets you dimension the sketch entity and combines several dimensioning methods into a single tool, such as horizontal, vertical, aligned, radial, diameter, and so on.

Auto Insert Dimension: Automatically adds dimensions appropriate for selected sketch entities.

Horizontal Dimension: Applies a dimension to a sketch entity that drives the horizontal distance between the selected points or parallel lines.

Vertical Dimension: Works like a horizontal dimension but vertically.

Baseline Dimensions: Creates dimensions in *drawing* documents only. The Baseline Dimensions tool is different from most of the dimension tools that you find on the Dimensions/Relations toolbar in that it can create driven dimensions on view geometry or driving dimensions on sketch geometry in a drawing, but the dimensions cannot be used on sketch geometry in parts. Baseline dimensions originate from a single reference; then as you select additional references, their dimensions are stacked, as shown in Figure 3.30.

FIGURE 3.30
Baseline dimension
on a drawing

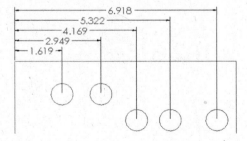

Ordinate Dimensions: Drives dimensions where a set of ordinate dimensions originate from a common zero point. To use these dimensions, simply click a zero location, place the zero dimension, and then click additional points. The dimensions are placed and are automatically aligned to the rest of the dimensions.

NOTE If a line is *not* selected as the zero reference entity, the Ordinate Dimension feature defaults to a horizontal ordinate.

◆ You can remove ordinate dimensions from the common alignment by right-clicking the dimension and selecting Break Alignment. Ordinate dimensions jog automatically if SolidWorks senses that the dimensions are getting too close to one another. You can also jog them manually. After you create the Ordinate Dimension set, you can add to it by accessing the Add To Ordinate command through the RMB menu. All the options for ordinate dimensions are shown in Figure 3.31.

◆ Not all the listed options are available in the model sketch environment; some are available only in drawings.

FIGURE 3.31
Options for baseline dimension

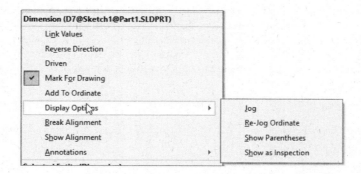

A *chamfer dimension* is another type of dimension that is only driven and only applied in drawing documents. It works by first selecting the chamfered edge and then selecting the angle reference edge.

However, there is a Sketch Chamfer tool that adds dimensions to the chamfer in the sketch when the chamfer is created.

The Automatic Relations toggle enables and disables the automatic creation of sketch relations while sketching. This toggle is also available through Tools ➤ Sketch Settings ➤ Automatic Relations. Automatic relations help you to create intelligent sketches with less manual intervention. Although using them takes a little practice, it is well worth the effort.

CAUTION As with any automatic function, there are times when automatic relations will do things that you do not expect or want. While you are sketching, I recommend that you watch the cursor and the relations that it automatically applies.

While sketching, symbols appear on the cursor to show that a relation will automatically be created. These symbols have a yellow background and apply horizontal, vertical, coincident, tangent, parallel, and perpendicular relations. Figure 3.32 shows two situations where automatic relations are applied: a horizontal and a tangent relation.

Fully Define Sketch is a tool that can add relations and dimensions to lock down any open degrees of freedom in a sketch when the option for All Entities In Sketch is enabled. This sounds like a better idea than it is. Although you can control how the sketch and even portions of the sketch are defined, this tool is used mainly to overcome a fear of underdefined sketches. Sketches that are just randomly fully defined are worse to work with than undefined sketches. You are

FIGURE 3.32
Automatic relations
appear on the cursor.

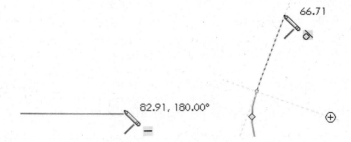

better off to fully define a sketch manually. Although it may seem odd for someone in my position to say this, you are better off with a fully undefined sketch than a large sketch that is fully defined with random dimensions in it. (See Figure 3.33.) Troubleshooting something that goes wrong with a very large sketch can take a lot of time, while a fully undefined sketch can never go wrong unless you move it with the cursor. If your sketch is large, consider breaking it up in multiple features. If it has a lot of small entities, try using sketch relations, which are more flexible than dimensions.

FIGURE 3.33
Fully defining a sketch
automatically can
make a mess.

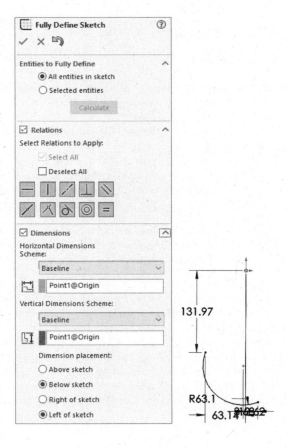

The Add Relations tool is for those times when you have to manually add relations to sketch elements. It is generally better to use the Automatic Sketch Relations tool; but when you're editing, this is not always possible. (See Figure 3.34.) Select the sketch entity and pick the relation.

FIGURE 3.34
Manually adding sketch
relations to
selected entities

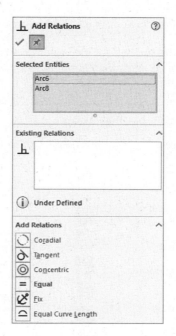

Automatic Relations is a setting that is turned on by default. When you are sketching, it displays relations that are suggested by the sketch (such as tangent or coincident) as small yellow icons attached to the cursor (inferences are separate and are covered in the next section of this chapter) and adds those relations to the current sketch entity. Some relations displayed as small icons on the cursor do not have the yellow background, and they are not added as relations to the sketch. Figure 3.32 shows examples of automatic relations being added as sketch entities are created.

The Scan Equal tool searches an active drawing sketch for entities of equal length or radius. It will then set Equal sketch relations for those entities.

Again, the Isolate Changed Dimensions tool is used only in drawings. This identifies any dimensions that have changed since the drawing was last saved. This will be covered in a later chapter.

Inferencing in Sketch

Inferencing refers to the blue dotted lines that display in Sketch mode when the cursor aligns with endpoints, centerpoints, or the origin. Inferencing creates sketch relations only when the symbol shown on the sketch cursor has a yellow background.

When the cursor displays a small sketch-relation symbol with a yellow background, an automatic relation will be applied. If the relation symbol has a white background, the relation is inferenced, but not applied, as an actual sketch relation. The symbols with the blue background are relations that have been applied to existing sketch entities. Be aware that differences in versions and differences in color schemes can cause these colors to be different on your system. (The color may be green in SolidWorks 2008 or later. The symbols look the same, regardless of background color.)

Table 3.1 shows the symbols for the various inferences, automatic relation cursors, and applied sketch relations. The difference among the three types is simply the background colors: white, yellow, and blue, respectively.

TABLE 3.1:　　Symbols and Their Meanings

SYMBOL	MEANING	SYMBOL	MEANING	SYMBOL	MEANING
	Along X		Along Y		Along Z
	At Intersection of Two Faces		Coincident		Collinear
	Concentric		Coradial		Equal
	Equal Curvature		Fix		Horizontal
	Intersection		Midpoint		Offset
	On Edge		On Surface		Parallel
	Perpendicular		Pierce		Symmetric
	Tangent		Vertical		Display/ Delete Relations
	Fully Define Sketch				

Exploring Sketch Settings

In addition to sketch tools, sketch settings also control sketches. Sketch settings are found in two locations. The first location is at Tools ➢ Options ➢ Sketch. In this chapter, I cover the settings found at the second location, Tools ➢ Sketch Settings, shown in Figure 3.35. These settings mainly affect sketch relations.

Automatic Relations: As described earlier, it is on by default. It adds relations to newly sketched entities.

Automatic Solve: It is also turned on by default. As you make changes to a sketch by adding relations or changing dimensions, SolidWorks automatically and immediately updates the sketch to reflect the changes. When the Automatic Solve setting is turned off, these changes are deferred until you exit the sketch or turn the Automatic Solve setting back on. The setting

FIGURE 3.35
Tools ➤ Sketch Settings

can be useful to prevent intermediate solutions (for example, when half of the changes are made) that may cause problems with the sketch. It can also be useful when you are confident that the outcome will be correct. It is a rarely used option, and you could probably exist just fine without even knowing this option was there at all.

If you import a large drawing from the DXF or DWG format, these drawings import as sketch entities into either a SolidWorks sketch or a drawing. SolidWorks may automatically turn off the Automatic Solve setting for performance (speed) reasons on files of this type.

Enable Snapping: It is also turned on by default. It enables the cursor to snap to the end-points of existing sketch entities to help you make cleaner sketches. When you turn this setting off, Automatic Relations is also disabled (although the icon for the setting remains depressed; Automatic Relations are not created). Holding down the Ctrl key while sketching disables snapping. Holding down the Ctrl key while dragging sketch entities functions like copying sketch geometry. No Solve Move is discussed in the Sketch toolbar section.

Shaded Sketch Contours: As described earlier, it is turned on by default. It adds shading inside of enclosed sketch areas. It enables one-click selection of all entities in the contour and moving of the contour just by dragging the shaded area.

No Solve Move: It is also turned off by default. This rarely used option is mainly useful when moving entities within a large sketch where there are a lot of existing relations that prevent moving.

Detach Segment On Drag: This setting is also turned off by default. When you turn it on, the Detach Segment on Drag feature enables you to pull a single sketch element away from a chain of elements. For example, if you had a rectangle and you wanted to detach one of the lines from the rest of the rectangle without using this setting, you would have to draw extra geometry and then trim and delete lines in order to release the endpoints.

Override Dims On Drag: This setting is off by default. When you turn it on, it enables you to drag fully defined sketch geometry, and the dimensions update to match the dragged size. This is another setting that you should use sparingly. It can be useful for doing concept work, but you should leave it off when working with production data for obvious reasons.

Pen Settings: These are covered later in this chapter in the section "Sketching with Touch Interface."

NOTE Combining Override Dims On Drag with Instant3D can be very handy for concept work, enabling you to drag sketches, model faces, and edges easily.

Using Sketch Blocks

Sketch blocks are collections of sketch entities that can be treated as a single entity and can be reused within a single document or shared between documents. You can use sketch blocks in parts, assemblies, and drawings. To create a sketch block, select a group of sketch entities and click the Make Block button on the Blocks toolbar, or select Tools ➤ Blocks ➤ Make. Preselection is not necessary; you also can select the entities after you invoke the command.

Blocks may be internal to a particular document, or they may be saved as an external file. The externally saved block may be linked to each document where it is used so that if the block is changed, it updates in the documents where it is used.

You can use blocks in conjunction with the Make Path function mentioned earlier in this chapter to create functional layouts for mechanisms. You also can use blocks in an assembly to build parts in context.

Refer to Chapter 16, "Working with Assembly Sketches and Layouts," for a more in-depth examination of the assemblies aspects of blocks in SolidWorks and to Chapter 26, "Using Annotations and Symbols," for the use of blocks in 2D drawings.

These tools are available on the Blocks toolbar:

Make Block: Creates a sketch block from selected sketch entities. You can position a manipulator to denote the insertion point for the block. Blocks may attach at any entity endpoint, but the insertion point follows the cursor.

Edit Block: Enables you to edit an existing block as if it were a regular sketch.

Insert Block: Enables you to select from a list of open blocks or browse to a location where blocks are stored. You can edit the insertion point by using the Edit Block function.

Add/Remove: Enables you to add or remove sketch entities from the block without deleting them from the sketch while editing a block.

Rebuild Block: Allows changes to a block to be reflected in any external relations without exiting the block. For example, if you have a block in a sketch and a sketch line is coincident to one of the endpoints in the block, you may edit the block such that the referenced endpoint moves. As a result, the line in the sketch will not move until you exit the block or use the Rebuild Block function.

Save Block/Save Sketch As Block: Saves a selected block to an external file (with the *.sldblk extension) or saves the selected sketch as a block.

Explode Block: Removes all the sketch entities from a block and brings them into the current sketch.

Belt/Chain: Enables you to make a belt or chain around a set of pulleys. Each pulley must be a block. After activating the command (by right-clicking a sketch or block), you can select each pulley and use the arrow on the pulley to switch the side of the pulley to which the belt goes. You can also compensate for the thickness of the belt (this is important when both sides of the belt are in contact with pulleys) and drive the pulley arrangement using the length of the belt.

Working with Reference Geometry

Reference geometry in SolidWorks is used to help establish locations for geometry that you can't physically touch, such as planes, axes, coordinate systems, and points. (See Figure 3.36.) You often use reference geometry to establish a characteristic of the finished solid model before the model is created or to include an item that you may want to mate another part to in an assembly later. *Mate references* are also classified as reference geometry and are dealt with in the assembly chapters.

FIGURE 3.36
The Reference
Geometry toolbar

The importance of working with reference geometry becomes obvious in situations where you need to create geometry that doesn't line up with the standard planes. You might use planes to represent faces and axes to represent the centers of holes. Axes are often used to establish a direction, such as in plastic parts where, because of draft, you never truly have any vertical edges; an axis is frequently used to establish the direction of pull for the mold.

Coordinate systems come in handy, especially when translating a part from one system to another for the purpose of machining or some type of analysis. SolidWorks users usually model in such a way that the modeling work is made simpler by the choice of how the part origin is positioned relative to features of the part; however, rapid prototyping, machining, mold building, and sheet metal manufacturing applications may have different requirements. As a part modeler, you cannot account for the needs of all downstream applications with your initial choice of origin placement, but you can always create a reference coordinate system for those downstream applications to use. Coordinate systems are fantastic as input for mates (especially for defining smart mates). They have the same functionality as origins, offering the option to define the location and the orientation with only one mate.

Creating Planes

Planes are the most commonly used type of reference geometry because they are used for sketching and cutting, as extrude end conditions, and more. The Plane PropertyManager is shown in Figure 3.37. You start by selecting model items (faces, edges, points, vertices, or other sketch or reference geometry) that you want to have some relationship to the new plane. The new plane uses constraints like sketch relations from the selected references. For example, in Figure 3.37, the new plane is tangent to the selected First Reference cylindrical face and at an angle to the selected Second Reference of a plane.

The good news about this method is that there are a lot more options for creating planes than in the previous method; the bad news is that the options are not all spelled out anywhere. You have to make a selection before it shows you the available constraints. You may need to experiment with this interface to see what works best for the type of modeling you do.

One of the options in the Plane PropertyManager is Flip Normal. This option has little application until you start getting into heavy parametric editing. Keep the existence of this option in the back of your head, because you will someday run into a situation where you make a change and a sketch or feature flips in an unexpected way. That will be the time to use this option.

FIGURE 3.37
Creating a new plane
from a set of selections
and constraints

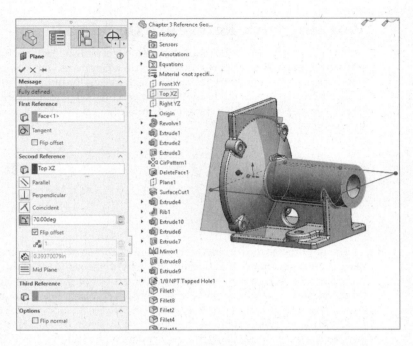

A newer function of the Plane feature is that it will allow you to make a plane parallel to the display at a selected point. This is a somewhat hidden functionality. To enable it, you have to start the Plane command; and select a point, origin, or vertex; and then click the Parallel To Screen option.

TIP   Because most planes are created from an existing plane or planar face, you should customize the context toolbar to include the Plane command. Then, when you select a face from the graphic area, you will find the Plane command next to your cursor.

Working with Axes

You can use axes to create pivot points in a part where you do not have any hole-type geometry for mating with other parts. You can also use them as a direction of pull for plastic parts or molds. Axes are frequently used to establish direction for rotation, draft, or a number of other things. Figure 3.38 shows that the first three features in a plastic part are axes established from the standard planes.

Consider using axes set up in this way as standard features in your template files (X-, Y-, and Z-direction axes). They can be effective in assemblies for moving parts in orthogonal directions and in parts for pattern or draft directions.

Using Coordinate Systems

Coordinate systems in SolidWorks are primarily used for import and export, but they also can be used for mates, mass properties, and other purposes. Coordinate systems are usually positioned by selecting a point or a set of edges to determine direction. Figure 3.39 shows the

FIGURE 3.38
Creating an axis to
establish direction

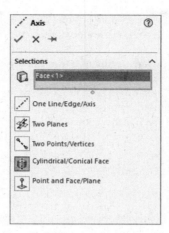

FIGURE 3.39
Use Coordinate Systems
to export parts and
assemblies with a new
origin location.

PropertyManager for assigning a coordinate system, along with the Export Options dialog box, which you can access from the Save As dialog box when the Files of Type dropdown is set to an export format.

To use the coordinate system when saving as a translated file type such as IGES or Parasolid, click the Options button (in the Save As dialog box, after setting the translation file type). At the bottom of the Export Options dialog box, a selection box for the Output coordinate system appears.

To use the coordinate system with mass properties, choose Tools ➢ Evaluate ➢ Mass Properties from the menu, and then select the Output coordinate system, as shown in Figure 3.40.

FIGURE 3.40
Assigning the coordinate system for mass properties

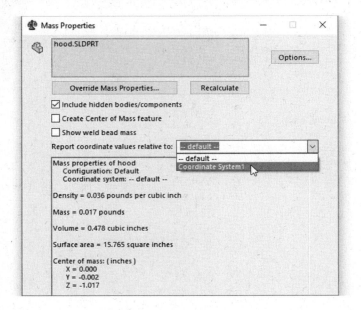

Using Points as Reference Geometry

The Point reference geometry feature is infrequently used; however, in some situations, nothing else does the job quite as well. This is not the same as a sketch point and does not require a sketch to be open. It is just a reference point that you can place in space. Figure 3.41 shows the PropertyManager for the Point reference geometry feature. An excellent use of this capability is to mark the center of a face.

The reference point and the sketch point are somewhat different in that you can use sketch points in 2D or 3D sketches, and they can be dragged or driven by dimensions and sketch relations.

Sketching with Touch Interface

Sketching with the touch interface is limited to hardware specifically developed for that purpose. You can use small Wacom tablets for the touch input, but I'm referring to large touch monitors in this case. In some cases, the touch display is able to distinguish between the use of a pen (stylus) for input and your finger. Typically, fingers are used for manipulating the view, rotation, and zoom.

FIGURE 3.41
The Point reference geometry feature has several modes of point creation you won't find elsewhere.

The pen is used for tasks that require more precision, such as selecting interface elements and sketching.

You can find special settings for Touch interface in Tools ➤ Options ➤ Touch, as shown in Figure 3.42.

FIGURE 3.42
The settings for Touch interface

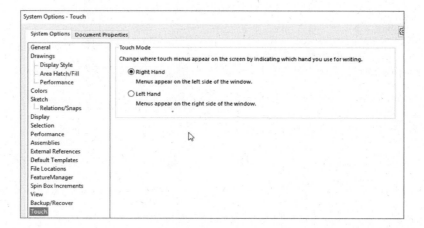

Beyond the settings, SolidWorks also makes available a Sketch Ink toolbar specifically for use with the pen. This is automatically available on the CommandManager of a touch-enabled device. The Sketch Ink toolbar is shown in Figure 3.43.

The Pen tool enables you to change color and width of what is shown on the screen. If you have Auto Sketch Entities turned on, it will take your pen sketch and convert it into lines or arcs, and add an entry called Pen Sketch under the regular sketch feature in the FeatureManager. If Auto Sketch Entities is not turned on, then you will get on the screen whatever squiggle you entered with your pen. The Pen Sketch and squiggle are shown in Figure 3.44.

FIGURE 3.43
The Sketch Ink tab of the
CommandManager

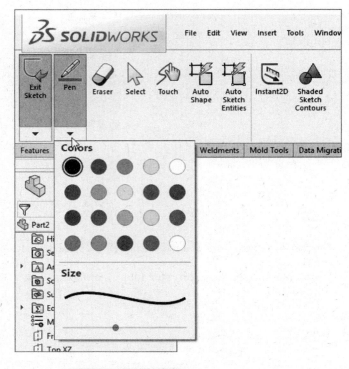

FIGURE 3.44
Pen Sketch entry in the
FeatureManager and a
pen-drawn squiggle on
the screen

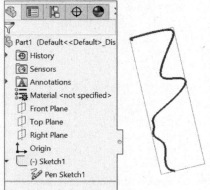

Tutorial: Learning to Use Sketch Relations

This tutorial makes sure that you get to know all the major functions in SolidWorks sketches. Almost every part that you build will start with a sketch, so this is a skill worth mastering. Follow these steps to learn about sketch relations:

ON THE WEBSITE

The BibleInchTemplate.prtdot template used in this tutorial is in the Chapter 3 folder in the materials you can download for this chapter from the Wiley website.

1. Create a folder on your hard drive called D:\Library\BibleTemplates. You can put it where you like, but I recommend a nonsystem drive in a location where it is unlikely to be overwritten or lost.

2. Go to Tools ➤ Options ➤ File Locations and add a path to the Document Templates list for the location of the templates folder you just created.

3. Click the New icon. In the New SolidWorks Document dialog box, make sure you see the Advanced interface. (The button in the lower-left corner should say Novice. If the button is labeled Advanced, click it to open the Advanced interface.) Click the tab in the interface that has the name of the new templates folder you just created.

4. Open a new part using the template you just set up.

5. If the planes are showing in the graphics window, turn them off. Go to View ➤ Hide/ Show ➤ Planes. This turns off all planes. If you want to turn off a single plane, right-click the plane in the graphics window or in the FeatureManager, and select Hide.

6. Select the Front plane in the FeatureManager, and click the Sketch button on the Sketch tab of the CommandManager (or right-click the plane and select Insert Sketch). Click the Line tool from the Sketch tab of the CommandManager.

7. Move the cursor near the origin untill the yellow Coincident symbol appears.

8. Draw a line horizontal from the origin. Remember that you can sketch the line in two ways: Click+click or click-and-drag. Make sure that the line snaps to the horizontal and that there is a yellow Horizontal relation symbol. The PropertyManager for the line should show that the line has a Horizontal relation. Also notice that the line is black, but the free endpoint is blue (after you press Esc to clear the tool). This means that the line is fully defined except for its length. You can test this by dragging the blue endpoint.

9. Click the Smart Dimension tool on the Sketch toolbar; use it to click the line that you just drew, and place the dimension. If you are prompted for a dimension, type **1.000**. If not, then double-click the dimension; the Modify dialog box will appear, enabling you to change the dimension. The setting to prompt for a dimension is found at Tools ➤ Options ➤ General, Input Dimension Value.

10. Draw two more lines to create a right triangle to look like Figure 3.45. If the sketch relations symbols do not show in the display, turn them on by clicking View ➤ Sketch Relations. You may want to set up a hotkey for this, because sketch relations are useful but often get in the way. When you enclose the triangular area, SolidWorks will shade the triangle if the Shade Sketch Contours is active. This tool is by default on the right end of the Sketch CommandManager tab.

FIGURE 3.45
Draw a right triangle.

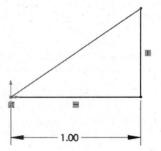

1.00

11. Drag the blue endpoint of the triangle. Dragging endpoints is the most direct way to change the geometry. Dragging the line directly will also work by causing the angle of the line to change. The sketch leaves a ghost when dragging so that you can see where you started. Note that the setting for leaving a ghost when dragging a sketch is found at Tools ➤ Options ➤ Sketch, Ghost Image On Drag.

12. Click the Smart Dimension tool, and then click the horizontal line and the angled line. This produces an angle dimension. Place the angle dimension and give it a value of 30 degrees.

13. Click the Sketch Fillet tool, set the radius value to 0.10 inches, and click each of the three corner points. Press OK in the PropertyManager, OK in the RMB menu, or Enter on the keyboard to accept the preview of the fillet. SolidWorks creates a *virtual sharp* at the ends of the horizontal line to preserve the connection points for the 1.00 dimension. Figure 3.46 shows the sketch at this point. You may now want to turn off the Sketch Relations display because the screen is getting pretty busy. You can find this setting at View ➤ Hide/Show ➤ Sketch Relations, or use the Heads Up View toolbar for quicker access.

14. Draw a line starting from the midpoint of the angled line. The midpoint should highlight when you move the cursor close to it. Draw the line perpendicular to the angled line. A dotted yellow line appears, showing where the perpendicular lies. When you follow this line, the yellow perpendicular symbol appears on the cursor. Make this line approximately 0.12 inches long. Feedback on the cursor also shows the length of the line as you draw it.

15. Draw two more lines ending at the endpoint of the sketch fillet, as shown in Figure 3.47. Use the Inferencing lines to line up the second angled line with the end of the arc.

16. Click the Trim tool from the Sketch toolbar. Make sure that the Trim option is set to Closest. Click the angled line of the triangle between the two lines sketched in step 15. This trims out that section and makes the sketch a single closed loop. A warning may appear because you have a midpoint relation to the line being trimmed; you no longer want this relation, but you want the lines to intersect at their endpoints. Select Yes at the prompt.

17. Add a sketch relation. Click on one of the two parallel lines and then Ctrl+click on the other. Now click Equal in the PropertyManager to make these two lines equal length.

FIGURE 3.46
Add a sketch fillet.

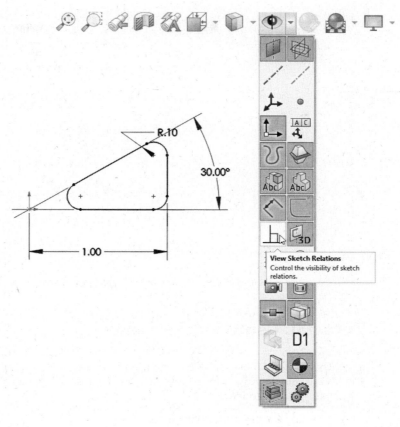

FIGURE 3.47
Add some lines.

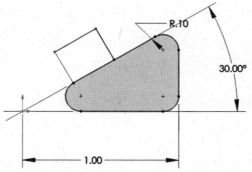

18. Add smart dimensions. Click the Smart Dimension tool and add an aligned dimension to one of the lines just set as Equal. Make this line 0.125 inches. This turns one line black, so add a dimension to the black line to make it 0.25 inches. The result is a fully defined sketch, as shown in Figure 3.48.

FIGURE 3.48
A fully defined sketch

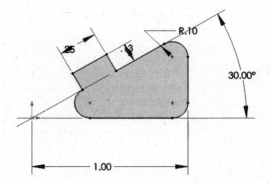

19. Save the part with the name `Sketch Relations Tutorial1.sldprt`. Close the part.

Tutorial: Using Blocks and Belts

Sometimes I am amazed at the things that can be done in SolidWorks, even with fairly simple tools. This is one of those times. If you design machines, this tutorial has some extra meaning for you. Blocks and Belts are a valuable toolset for various situations. Follow these steps to learn about using Blocks and Belts.

1. Open a new part with inches as the units.

2. Draw and dimension a sketch on the Front plane connected to the origin as shown in Figure 3.49. Exit the sketch and rename it Layout Sketch, either by clicking twice (slow double-click) on the name of the sketch in the FeatureManager or by selecting it and pressing F2.

FIGURE 3.49
The layout sketch

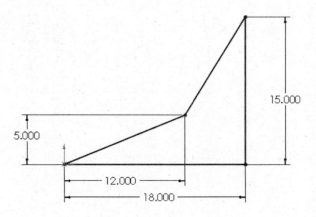

3. Exit the sketch by clicking the Confirmation Corner Exit Sketch symbol in the upper-right corner of the graphics window (not the red X).

4. Open a second sketch on the Front plane and draw a circle with a 6-inch diameter centered on the origin. This needs to be a second sketch, not just reopening the first sketch.

5. Inside the circle, draw a Centerpoint rectangle centered on the origin.

6. Select two adjacent sides of the rectangle and make an Equal sketch relation between them. This makes the rectangle into a square, but still doesn't define its size.

 New...

7. Click the Smart Dimension tool and apply a 1.000-inch dimension to one side of the square. Turn off the Smart Dimension tool by clicking it again on the toolbar or pressing Esc.

8. If the Blocks toolbar is not active, activate it and then select Make Block. You also can access this command through Tools ➤ Block ➤ Make.

9. Window select the circle and the square by clicking and dragging a box that includes all the items in the sketch. The PropertyManager to the left displays a circle and six lines that are to be made into a block. SolidWorks by default forces you into using the Lasso selection. You can switch to Box selection in the Tools menu, or in Tools ➤ Options ➤ Selection, Box. This would be a good tool to put on a hotkey.

10. Expand the Insertion Point panel in the PropertyManager. This causes a blue manipulator origin to appear in the graphics window. Click this origin and drag it onto the center of the circle. Then click the green checkmark icon to exit the Make Block dialog box, as shown in Figure 3.50.

FIGURE 3.50
Making a block

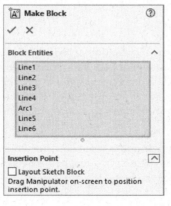

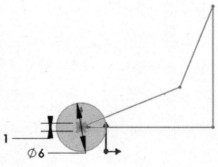

11. The items in the block now turn gray. Click anywhere on the block and drag it out of the way. Then drag the center of the circle and drop it on the part origin.

12. Click the Insert Block tool on the Blocks toolbar. There should be only a single block named Block1 in the Open Blocks box. Place the block on the opposite sharp corner of the layout sketch.

13. Create another block that is identical to the first one, except with a diameter of 3 inches instead of 6 inches. You can do this by selecting the first block, clicking Edit Block from the toolbar, and copying (Window select and Ctrl+C). Then exit the Edit Block and paste (Ctrl+V) in the regular sketch. Make sure to also change the insertion point for this second block to the center of the circle

14. Insert a second instance of this second block, and make sure that both of them have the center of the circle at the two remaining intersection points of the four-sided shape of the layout sketch. At this point, your sketch should look like Figure 3.51.

FIGURE 3.51
Block placement

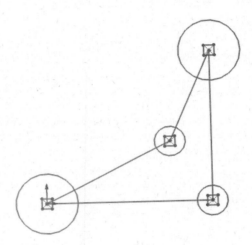

15. Click the Belt/Chain tool on the Blocks toolbar. Select the blocks in counterclockwise order, starting at the top pulley so that they go in the Belt Members selection box, as shown in Figure 3.52. On the last pulley, you will have to click the Flip Bent Side arrow to get the belt to go the correct way around the pulley. If this doesn't work for you, clear the selection box and try to select the pulleys in a different order. Press F on the keyboard to get the display to Zoom to Fit.

16. Make sure that the Engage Belt option is selected. This will enable you to make the pulleys move in the same way that they would in a real belt-driven mechanism. This will help you calculate the required length of the belt.

17. Click the Use Belt Thickness option and assign 0.25 inches for the thickness. The belt should be offset from the pulleys.

18. Click the green checkmark icon.

19. Click and drag one of the corners of the square in a pulley. All the pulleys should turn as if they were real mechanisms. The ratios are also observed because the small pulleys rotate faster than the large ones.

20. Save this part as **Blocks and Belts Tutorial.sldprt**. Exit the part.

FIGURE 3.52
Belt placement

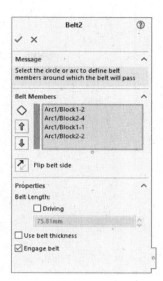

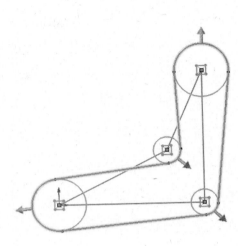

Tutorial: Creating Reference Geometry

This tutorial steps you through creating reference geometry on an existing part in preparation for locating 3D features.

ON THE WEBSITE

The Chapter 3 Reference Geometry- start.SLDPRT file used in this tutorial is in the Chapter 3 folder in the data downloaded from the Wiley website.

---

1. Open the file from the download materials in the Chapter 3 folder called Chapter 3 Reference Geometry - start.sldprt.

2. In the FeatureManager filter, type **plane1**. Double-click Plane1 in the FeatureManager. Double-click the 3.25-inch dimension on the screen and change it to 3.35 inches. Click the rebuild symbol (traffic light) and watch the update. This plane locates the mounting base of the part. Click the green check mark to accept the change and exit the Modify box.

3. Click the Axis toolbar button from the Reference Geometry flyout menu (on the Features tab of the CommandManager in a default install).

4. Select the inside face of a hole on the part, as shown in Figure 3.53. This creates an axis on the centerline of the hole. You should note that temporary axes are automatically created for all cylindrical faces, but making a true axis feature helps this one stand out as different from the other holes on the part.

   The selection of the Cylindrical/Conical Face option is automatically activated by your selection of the cylindrical face of the hole. Accept the result with the green check mark when the selections and settings are complete.

FIGURE 3.53
Creating an axis

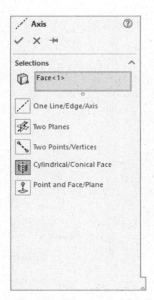

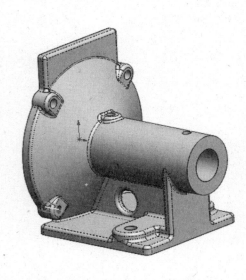

5. Click the Plane toolbar button from the Reference Geometry flyout on the Features tab of the CommandManager.

6. Select the large cylindrical face of the part as the First Reference and the axis you just created as the Second Reference. (Go to View ➤ Hide/Show ➤ Axes if you cannot see the axis.) Make sure the First Reference uses the Tangent constraint and the Second Reference uses the Coincident constraint. This makes a plane tangent to the main cylinder in the part that goes through the patterned hole, as shown in Figure 3.54.

FIGURE 3.54
Creating a plane

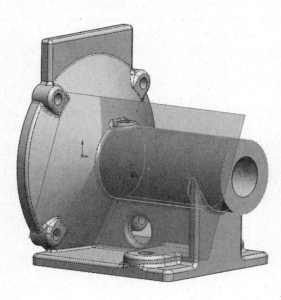

Click the green check mark to accept the result.

7. Open a new sketch on the new plane.

8. Click the View ➤ Hide/Show menu and activate the Temporary Axes option. You should now see blue axes (without names) appear along the centerlines of every conical or cylindrical face on the model (except for faces created by fillet or chamfer features).

NOTE The View Orientation toolbar appears when you press the spacebar; it is also available from the Heads Up View toolbar. You can also use Ctrl+spacebar to access the View Selector cube. If the view is already normal to the selected plane and you double-click Normal To, the view switches to 180 degrees opposite. The setting to auto-rotate the view normal to the sketch plane when a new sketch is opened is located at Tools ➤ Options ➤ Sketch.

9. Select the sketch plane either from the graphics window or the FeatureManager. Press the spacebar on the keyboard and double-click Normal To. You can click the pushpin to keep this box available. There are other ways to access this command, but this is the method that works regardless of your interface setup.

10. Use the Centerpoint Rectangle to create a rectangle centered around the temporary axis of the large cylindrical face. Make sure that the centerpoint, which is the first click you make, picks up a coincident automatic relation with the temporary axis. Make sure the second click to place the corner of the rectangle does not pick up any automatic relations. This is shown in Figure 3.55.

FIGURE 3.55
Creating a rectangle centered on the temporary axis

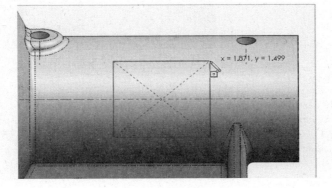

You can tell if any relations have been applied if you go to the View ➤ Hide/Show menu and activate Sketch Relations. Make sure the centerpoint has a coincident relation and that none of the corners has any relations.

NOTE The temporary axis is not on the same plane as the sketch plane, so if the view is not normal to the sketch plane, picking up an automatic relation between the centerpoint of the rectangle and the temporary axis will be difficult.

11. Use the Smart Dimension tool to apply dimensions, as shown in Figure 3.56. Note that the 3.450-inch dimension goes to the part origin on the left. You can select this from either the graphics window or the FeatureManager.

FIGURE 3.56
Creating a rectangle centered on the temporary axis

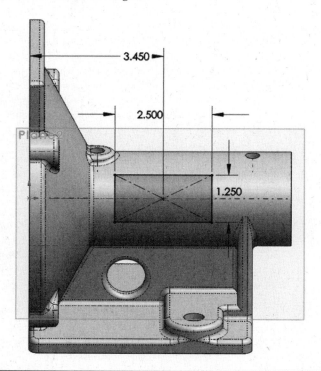

BEST PRACTICE

It is best practice to dimension or create sketch relations to items that have the fewest other relations. You should try to use the part origin and standard planes when possible. Dimensioning to reference geometry is better than dimensioning to model edges, although this is not always possible. Use the Dynamic Reference Visualization under View ➤ User Interface to get visual cues regarding parent/child links.

12. Click the Extrude toolbar button on the Features tab of the CommandManager. Rotate the model (by dragging with the mouse wheel depressed) slightly so you can see the side of the extrusion preview, as shown in Figure 3.57.

You may have to adjust the direction of the extrude using the icon with the arrows just below the Direction1 heading in the Boss-Extrude PropertyManager.

FIGURE 3.57
Creating the extrusion

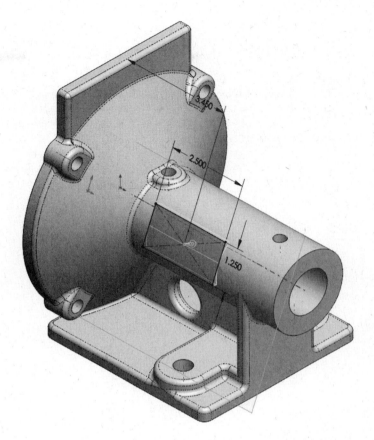

13. Use the Up To Next end condition, which makes the extruded solid go up to the next solid that it encounters.

14. Use the View menu to turn off the display of Axes, Temporary Axes, and Planes.

The Bottom Line

Create new sketches and edit existing ones.   In SolidWorks, each sketch is named and must be on a plane or planar face. You can edit only one sketch at a time, and there are things you cannot do while in a sketch.

Master It   Practice creating new sketches and using the various sketch entities on the Sketch toolbar to familiarize yourself with the range of tools that are available and how they work.

Create new reference geometry and use the planes to create new sketches.   As you get deeper into this book, you will learn more uses for the Reference Geometry tools. For now, the primary function is to establish planes for sketches without relying on adding relationships to solid geometry.

Master It   Practice moving or redefining planes to see how the change affects the resulting 3D geometry. Also build your skills by creating planes using the available options. If you can imagine a way to define a plane, use the three selection boxes and available constraints to see how many different types you can create.

Use a range of sketch entities.   While you can often get by using just lines and arcs, there are times when more advanced sketch entities are more appropriate. Ellipses, parabolas, conics, splines, even slots, polygons, and sketch text are all valid sketch entities that are very useful in certain situations.

Master It   Practice using some of the more advanced sketch entities on the Sketch toolbar.

Chapter 4

Creating Simple Parts and Drawings

Good modeling practice is based on robust design intent. This just means that you should try to build parts that can adapt easily to changes. This section of the book begins with things you need to know in order to make good models—models that react predictably in drawings and that update properly with changes. A robust design intent will make downstream operations easier.

Creating simple parts will help you understand the techniques used in more complex modeling projects. Learning on simple tools and then expanding your skills will help you understand best-practice issues, which will make you a better contributor to a team environment.

IN THIS CHAPTER, YOU WILL LEARN TO:

◆   Establish design intent

◆   Build a simple part

◆   Create a simple assembly tutorial

◆   Make a simple drawing tutorial

Discovering Design Intent

By knowing the right information about the part's function before you start modeling or design-ing, you can create a model that will be easier to edit, easier to properly place into an assembly, easier to detail in drawings, and easier for other SolidWorks users to understand when someone else has to work on your models. *Design intent* is a statement of how the part functions, the major features of the part, and how the model reacts to modeling changes.

It may help if you try to put the design intent into words to help you focus on what is important in the design. An example of a statement of design intent is "This part is symmetric about two planes, is used to support a 1.00 inch (diametral pitch) diameter shaft with a constant downward load of 150 pounds using a bronze bushing, and is bolted to a plate below it." This does not give you enough information to design the part, but it does give you information about two surfaces that are important (a hole for the bushing and the bottom that touches the mounting plate), as well as some general size and load requirements.

Using Symmetry

Symmetry is an important aspect of design intent. Taking advantage of symmetry can significantly reduce the time needed to model the part. Symmetry can exist on several levels:

◆   Sketch symmetry

◆   Individual feature symmetry

◆   Whole-part symmetry

◆   Axial symmetry (a revolved part)

◆   "Almost" symmetry (the whole part is symmetrical, except for a few features)

◆   Left and right opposite hand (symmetrical) versions of the part

◆   Assembly symmetry

Determining Primary or Functional Features

This is probably the most important information to know. Primary or functional features include how the part mounts or connects to other parts, motion that it needs to accommodate, and additional structure to support loads.

Often, it is a good idea to create a special sketch as the first feature in the part that lays out the functional features. This could be as simple as a straight line to denote the bottom and a circle to represent the position and size of a mating part, or as complex as full outlines of parts and features from all three standard planes. This technique is called creating a layout sketch, and it is an important technique in both simple and complex parts. You can use layout sketches for anything from simply drawing a size-reference bounding box to creating the one point of reference for all sketched features in the part. You can use multiple layout sketches if a single sketch on one plane is not sufficient.

Predicting Change

When the marketing department gets out of a meeting at 4:45 P.M., what changes do you need to be prepared for so that you can still be out the door by 5:00 P.M.? No one expects you to be able to tell the future, but you do need to model in such a way that your model easily adapts to future changes. As you gain experience with the software and engineering design processes, keep this idea in mind: you will develop some instincts for the type of modeling that you do.

I've talked a lot about what success looks like with a good design intent model, but let's talk a little bit about failure. Failure will turn out to be more motivating in practice. When design intent fails, you get a feature tree full of errors, and you have to go through each feature, investigate what's wrong, and then fix it. The failures are generally due to errors in the parent/child dependencies following the original change. Fixing errors like this can take up much more time than creating a model in the first place. This is, in essence, the big weakness of history-based modeling. There are a few ways to solve it:

◆   Be really careful. When this method fails, it is mostly due to the fact that you can't predict the future. (How will change happen?)

◆   Use a method like Resilient Modeling. This is a structured method where you keep track of the parent/child connections, and only start new sketches on reference geometry with a direct link back to something that will not change (origin or base planes).

◆ Use a method other than history-based design. This would require a different software package, such as Solid Edge. SolidWorks, in fact, cannot do what is known as "direct modeling," although the company will tell you otherwise.

I discuss this issue again in Chapter 12, "Editing, Evaluating, and Troubleshooting."

Creating a Simple Part

Chapter 2, "Navigating the SolidWorks Interface," introduced the tools and features you will use to create simple parts, and this chapter teaches you how to string the simple features together intelligently. In this section, I'll show you how to build the simple part shown in Figure 4.1. Although the shape is simple, the techniques used and discussed here are applicable to a wide variety of real-world parts. The discussion on how to model the part contains information on some of the topics you must understand in order to do the work.

FIGURE 4.1
A simple machined part

Deciding Where to Start

Deciding where to start can be more difficult than it sounds, especially for new users. For this reason, I'll go through some sample parts and discuss possible starting points. Figure 4.2 shows the first part. For reference, all of these parts can be found www.wiley.com/go/mastersolid.

As you decide how to model geometry in SolidWorks, you should be thinking of a 2D shape and a process. You typically create prismatic shapes by using an Extrude feature and round shapes by using a Revolve feature. Features can also add material (boss) or remove material (cut). Obviously, your first feature must add material.

If you look at the 3D geometry and see it as a series of 2D drawing views arranged in 3D space (as shown in Figure 4.2), you are on your way to deciding where to start.

FIGURE 4.2
Which starting sketch
is the best?

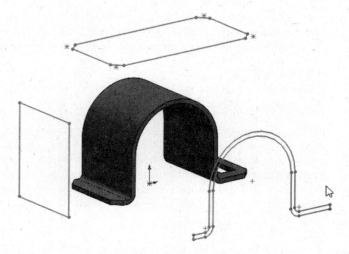

The part in Figure 4.2 has flat and round faces, but if you examine it, you can create the overall shape using a single extrude. The best option in this case would be to start with a sketch like the one in the lower-right corner and extrude it. This is a good beginning. Although you can make the same part starting from any of the three sketches, the one in the lower-right corner gets you closest to the final shape.

Also realize that you don't need to make all the geometry in a single feature. It is often best to use multiple features for elements such as holes, fillets, chamfers, and other groups of geometry that can be separated out from the main shape.

You might look at the part and see many ways to create it, but the most straightforward way is to extrude the U shape, a rectangular cutout, and four chamfers, as shown in Figure 4.3.

FIGURE 4.3
Breaking down the
features in this part

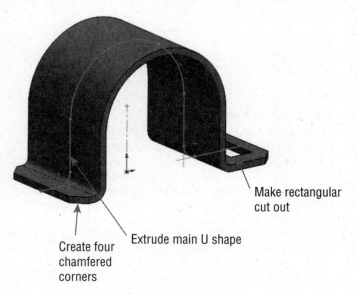

Make rectangular
cut out

Extrude main U shape

Create four
chamfered
corners

Notice where the part is placed in relation to the origin. Different people might do this differently, and the same person might even do it differently depending on the function of the part. In this case, the origin is aligned with the center of the round shape and at the bottom of the flat face. The placement of the origin suggests that this part sits on the flat face of another part and may hold a cylindrical face of another part.

If you open the part from www.wiley.com/go/mastersolid, you will notice that the origin is also placed in the middle of the extrusion depth. This suggests that the part is symmetrical from front to back.

If you are new to 3D modeling, this might be too much to take in all at once, but you should try to keep the ideas presented here in mind as you work through your first several parts and when you examine SolidWorks parts made by more-experienced users.

Figure 4.4 shows another part with other features. Again, you can choose from several ways to make this part.

FIGURE 4.4
Identify the best starting point for this part.

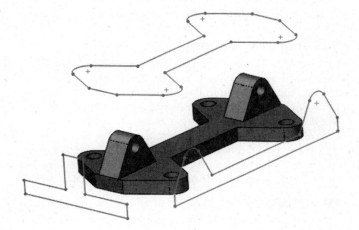

In this case, the best option is to use the one on top. (The other two profiles would add geometry that you would have to remove later.) Notice that the holes in the part are not represented in any of the profiles. This is because holes are often added as separate features later. This gives you control over whether the holes are there or not, as well as the size and placement of the holes.

Returning to the part in Figure 4.1, it should be clear enough that this part would be best started from a rectangle, although the rectangle could come from any of the three directions. I personally try to use the biggest sketch that will create a solid that requires the fewest number of additional features. The first feature that you create should also be positioned relative to the origin. Whether a corner of a rectangle is coincident to the origin, the rectangle is centered on the origin, or dimensions are used to stand the rectangle off from the origin at some distance, you need to lock the first feature to the origin with every part you build.

Many people ask how to move the origin, and this is perhaps one of the first things you need to understand about working in SolidWorks. You *don't move* the origin in SolidWorks. You move everything else in relation to the origin. If you have a part built with the origin in a certain place and want to move it, depending on how the part was built, this might be a very big job. If every feature was created dimensioned from the origin, you will have to move every feature. If features were created dimensioned from an edge of the first feature, you only need to move the first feature. It is also possible to move the entire body, but that is a more complex operation that will be addressed later.

When working with a simple part, the entire part can sometimes be described as rectangular or cylindrical. In cases like these, it is easy to know where to start: You simply draw a rectangle or a circle, respectively. On complex parts, it may not be obvious where to start, and the overall part cannot be said to have any simple shape. In cases like these, it may be best to select *the* (or *a*) prominent feature, mounting location, functional shape, or focus of the mechanism. For example, if you were to design an automobile, what would you designate as the 0,0,0 origin? The ground might be a reasonable location, as would the plane of the centers of the wheels. The end of the crankshaft in the engine is often used as the assembly origin in automotive modeling. As long as everyone working on the project agrees, many different reference points could work. With that in mind, it seems logical to start the rectangular part by sketching a rectangle. Select the Top plane, and sketch a centerpoint rectangle centered on the part origin.

Building in Symmetry

Your next decision is about part symmetry. The part in Figure 4.1 is not completely symmetrical. Modeling a quarter of it and mirroring the entire model twice is not the most effective technique. Instead, you should build the complete part around the origin and mirror individual features as appropriate. To start this type of symmetry, you need to sketch a rectangle centered on the origin. Again, to some extent, this is personal judgment.

Sketch a center rectangle where the first point, the *centerpoint*, is created at the origin. Drag or click the second point (one of the corners) to an approximate size. This creates symmetry in both directions. You can use additional construction geometry and sketch relations to make the rectangle symmetrical side-to-side only.

TIP   To make a rectangle work like a square, use an Equal sketch relation on two adjacent sides. This requires only a single dimension to drive the size of the square.

Beginning with the rectangle you sketched in the preceding section, apply one horizontal dimension by clicking the Smart Dimension tool on a single horizontal line, placing the horizontal dimension (4.00 inches), and clicking a vertical line, placing the vertical dimension (6.00 inches). The sketch is fully defined at this point because both the size and position of the rectangle have been established. Figure 4.5 shows the sketch at this point.

FIGURE 4.5
Sketch and dimension a center rectangle.

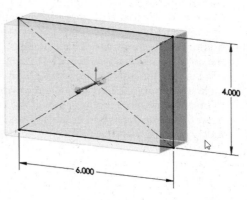

Making It Solid

The Extrude feature is one of the staples of SolidWorks modeling. Depending on the type of modeling you do, the Extrude feature may be one of your main tools. This section describes some of the available Extrude options.

EXTRUDING FROM A SELECTION

The From panel establishes where the Extrude feature starts. By default, SolidWorks extrudes from the sketch plane. These other options are available:

Surface/Face/Plane: The extrusion begins from a surface body, a face of a solid, or a reference plane as shown in Figure 4.6. Surface features are discussed in detail in Chapter 32, "Working with Surfaces."

FIGURE 4.6

Extruding from a surface

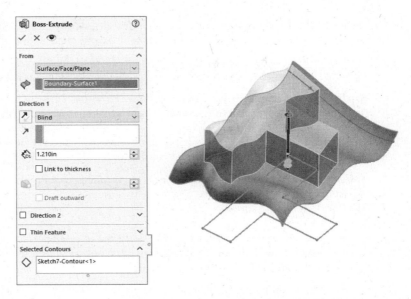

Vertex: The distance from the sketch plane to the selected vertex is treated as an offset distance.

Offset: You can enter an explicit offset distance, and you can change the direction of the offset.

UNDERSTANDING DIRECTION 1 AND DIRECTION 2

Direction 1 is always in the direction of the plane normal. The plane normal for the face of a solid is always away from the solid. For a reference plane, the interface will show you the normal direction with an arrow when creating or editing.

Direction 1 and Direction 2 are always opposite one another. Direction 2 becomes inactive if you select Mid Plane for the end condition of Direction 1. In the graphics window, you will see a single arrowhead for Direction 1 and a double arrowhead for Direction 2. For the Blind end condition, which is described next, dragging the arrows determines the distance of the extrusion.

Each of the end conditions is affected by the Reverse Direction toggle. This toggle simply changes the default direction by 180 degrees. You need to be careful when using this feature, particularly when using the Up To end conditions, because if the entity that you are extruding up to is not in the selected direction, an error results.

Ending an Extrusion

Following is a brief description of each of the available end conditions for the Extrude feature:

Blind: In this case, Blind means an explicit distance. The term is usually used in conjunction with holes of a specific depth, although here it is associated with a boss rather than a hole.

Up To Vertex: In effect, Up To Vertex works just like the Blind end condition, except that the distance is parametrically controlled by a model vertex, edge, or sketch point.

Up To Surface: Up To Surface could probably be better named Up To Face, because the end does not necessarily have to be an actual surface feature or body. This end condition may display a warning if the projection of the sketch onto the selected face extends beyond the boundary of the face. In that case, it is advisable to knit several faces together into a surface body and to use the Up To Body end condition.

Offset From Surface: By default, Offset From Surface extrudes until it reaches a specified distance from a selected surface. There are two methods for determining the type of offset and one for determining direction.

- The default offset method behaves as if the selected surface were offset radially, so that a surface with a 4-inch radius and a 1-inch offset would give a curvature on the end of the extrude of a 3-inch radius (Figure 4.7).

- The second method, called Translate Surface, behaves as if the surface were *moved* by the offset distance (Figure 4.8).

- Reverse Offset refers to specifying whether the offset stops short of the selected face (Figure 4.9 top) or goes past it (Figure 4.9 bottom).

Up To Body: The Up To Body end condition is very useful in many situations, especially when you receive the error message, "The end face cannot terminate the extrusion," from the Up To Surface end condition.

Mid Plane: The Mid Plane end condition eliminates the Direction 2 options and divides the extrude distance equally in both directions. For example, if you specify a 1.00-inch Mid Plane, SolidWorks extrudes .50 inches in one direction and .50 inches in the other direction. This is a useful option for ensuring symmetry in a direction normal to the sketch plane.

FIGURE 4.7
Offset From Surface
using the default

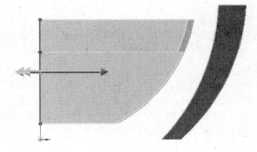

FIGURE 4.8
Offset From Surface
using Translate
Surface options

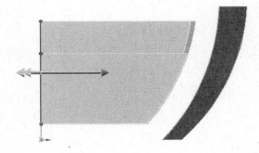

FIGURE 4.9
The Reverse
Offset option

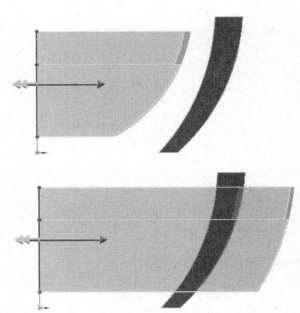

Through All: The Through All end condition is available only when solid geometry already exists in the part. When used for an extruded boss (which adds material), it extrudes to the distance of the farthest point of the solid model in a direction perpendicular to the sketch plane. When used for a cut, it simply cuts through everything.

Up To Next: Up To Next extrudes the feature until it runs into a solid face that completely intercepts the entire sketch profile. If a portion of the sketch hangs over the edge of the face, the extrude feature keeps going until it runs into a condition that matches that description, which may be the outer face of the part in the direction of the extrusion. Figure 4.10 shows the Up To Next end condition used with a Cut extrude.

FIGURE 4.10
Up To Next
end condition

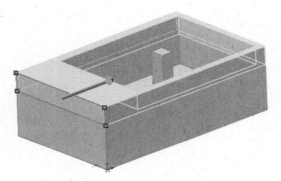

By default, the Direction Of Extrusion is normal to the sketch plane, but you can also select a linear entity such as an edge, planar face, face, plane, or axis as the direction. All the end-condition options are still available when you manually define the Direction Of Extrusion as something other than the default.

You can also assign a draft option to an extrusion as it is created, and you can control the draft separately for Direction 1 and Direction 2.

BEST PRACTICE

Arranging draft, fillet, and shell features in the correct order so the model is efficient and achieves the desired results is challenging. It is usually best to apply the draft as a separate feature rather than using it in the definition of the Extrude feature. It is also best to apply the draft after most of the modeling is done, but before you apply the cosmetic fillets and before you use the shell feature.

USING THE THIN FEATURE PANEL

The Thin Feature panel is activated by default when you try to extrude an open-loop sketch (a sketch that does not fully enclose an area). The end-condition options remain the same. What changes is that the feature applies a thickness to the sketch elements in the manner of a sheet metal part, thin-walled plastic part, or rib. The Thin Feature panel of the Extrude PropertyManager, along with a representative thin feature extrusion, are shown in Figure 4.11.

FIGURE 4.11
The Thin Feature panel
and a thin feature
extrusion

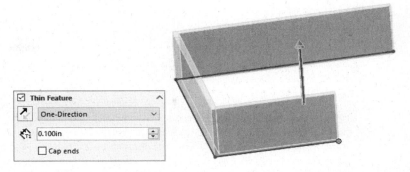

The Cap Ends option is available only when you specify a Thin Feature to be created from a closed-loop sketch. This creates a hollow, solid body in a single step. You can also use Thin Features with cuts, and they are very useful for creating slots or grooves.

USING CONTOUR SELECTION

SolidWorks sketches are easiest to control when the sketches are neat and clean, when nothing overlaps, and when no extra entities exist. However, when you need to use a sketch that does not meet these criteria, you can use contour selection as an alternative method. Contour selection enables you to select areas completely bounded by sketch entities for use with features such as Extrude. For example, you could use a sketch like the number sign (#) where lines do not connect at end points. You can use contour selection to select the box in the center, which is completely bound by sketch elements. Figure 4.12 shows an extrude feature making use of contour selection in a sketch.

FIGURE 4.12
Using contour selection

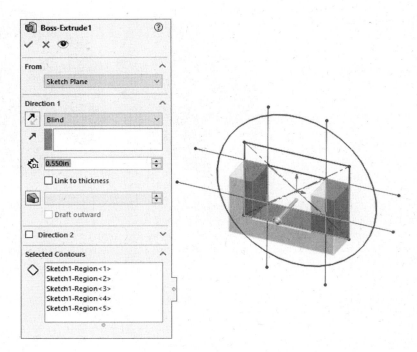

NOTE The part used in the image shown in Figure 4.12 is available from www.wiley.com/go/ mastersolid and is called Chapter 4 – Contour Selection.sldprt.

BEST PRACTICE

I believe contour selection was introduced into SolidWorks only to keep up with other CAD packages, not because it is a great feature. I do not recommend using contour selection on production models. It is useful for creating quick models, but the selection is too unstable for data that you may want to rely on in the future. The main problem is that if the sketch changes, the selected area may also change, or SolidWorks may lose track of it entirely.

Using Instant 3D

Instant 3D enables you to pull handles to create extrusions and to drag model faces to change the size and location of features. Several feature types enable you to use arrows to adjust elements visually of parametric features and sketches. Figure 4.13 shows the ruler added by Instant 3D shows the arrows added by Instant 3D, which are the handles that you pull on to create a solid from a sketch or edit an existing feature. Notice also that you can make cut features with Instant 3D. In fact, you can change a boss feature into a cut. I'm sure this is a neat sales demo trick, but I'm not aware of any practical application of changing a boss into a cut. Figure 4.13 shows the interface for Instant 3D.

FIGURE 4.13
Using Instant 3D and
Live Section

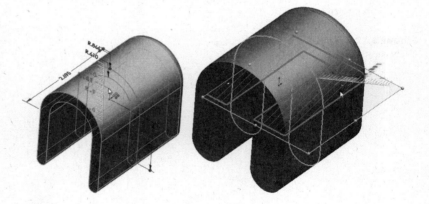

The intent is for this functionality to look and feel like direct modeling, but it is not direct modeling. What you can do is still limited by the features in the history tree and the sketches and dimensions driving the design intent. While this may be handy for making quick visual changes to a model, it is not a great method for precise modeling. Instant 3D can also be an effective tool when used in conjunction with the direct editing type of tools such as Move Face. Instant 3D mimics some of the direct edit type of functionality found in applications such as Solid Edge, SketchUp, and SpaceClaim.

NOTE   When combined with the sketch setting Override Dims On Drag (found at Tools ➤ Options ➤ Sketch ➤ Override Dimensions On Drag/Move), Instant 3D can be a powerful concepting tool, even on fully dimensioned sketches.

Instant 3D also offers a tool called Live Section, which enables you to section a part with a plane or drag the edges of the section regardless of the features to which the edges belong. To activate Live Section, right-click a plane that intersects the part and select Live Section Plane. Live Section is shown in Figure 4.13.

Chapter 37, "Using Imported Geometry," discusses the direct edit theme in more detail and revisits the Instant 3D manipulators in that light.

Making the First Extrude Feature

Going back to the sketch in Figure 4.5, I will show you how to continue building the part using the newly learned tools. By centering the sketch on the origin and extruding using a Mid Plane end condition, the initial block is built symmetrically about all three standard planes, with the part origin at the center. In many parts, this is a desirable situation. It enables you to create mirrored features using the standard planes and helps you put parts together later, when parts must be centered and do not have a hard face-to-face connection with other parts. Figure 4.14 shows the initial feature with the standard planes.

FIGURE 4.14
An initial extruded feature centered on the standard planes

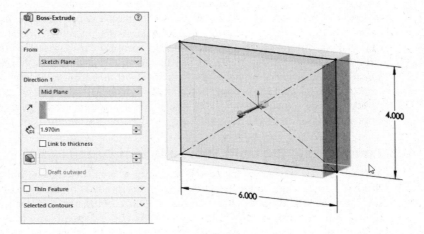

NOTE   When you create a feature from a sketch, SolidWorks by default hides and absorbs (consumes) the sketch under the feature in the FeatureManager. So, unless the tree is in Flat Tree View mode, you need to click the plus sign (+) next to the feature to see the sketch in the tree. You can right-click the sketch in the FeatureManager to show it in the graphics window.

The next modeling step is to create a groove on the back of the part. How is this feature going to be made? You can use several techniques to create this geometry. List as many techniques as you can think of, whether or not you know how to use them.

Figure 4.15 shows multiple methods for creating the groove. From left to right, the methods are a thin feature cut, a swept cut, and a nested-loop sketch.

FIGURE 4.15
Methods for creating
the groove

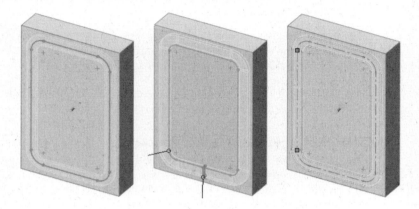

With a thin feature cut (shown on the left), you sketch the centerline of the groove and in the Cut-Extrude feature, select the Thin Feature option and assign a width and depth. The option on the right is what is called a *nested loop,* because it has a loop around the outside of the slot and another around the inside. Only the material between the loops is cut away. The method in the center is a sweep where the cross section of the slot is swept around a path to make the cut.

Another potential option could include a large pocket being cut out, with a boss adding material back in the middle. Each option is appropriate for a specific situation. The thin feature cut is probably the fastest to create, but also the least commonly used technique for a feature of this type. (Many users are not even aware of the thin feature unless they attended specific training or read about it in some of my other books.) Most users tend to use the nested-loop option (one loop inside another) because it enables you to specify geometry more directly, as opposed to specifying the geometry indirectly using the combination sketch and feature settings.

CONTROLLING RELATIVE SIZE OR DIRECT DIMENSIONS

You can control the size of the groove as an offset from the edges of the existing part, or you can drive the dimensions independently. Again, this depends on the type of changes you anticipate. If the groove will always depend on the outer size of the part, the decision is easy—go with the offset from the outside edges. If the groove changes independently from the part, you need to re-create dimensions and relations within the sketch to reflect a different design intent.

The decision of how to control the size of the slot is something I've been putting in the context of design intent, but there is another way of looking at it. Some SolidWorks users, like me, are focused on the 3D model. Many users, however, need to focus on the 2D drawing. If that's your situation, the decision of how to control the 3D model comes down to what dimensions you want on the 2D drawing. You can take the dimensions from the 3D model and put them directly onto the 2D drawing. If you can do this, it saves you a lot of time. Sometimes, though, the way you create a 3D part is going to be different from how you want to show that part on your drawings. Both methods work. You have to decide how you want to create your parts and how you want to create your drawings.

SolidWorks includes tools for *Model-Based Definition (MBD).* This is a method where you document the 3D part separate from a 2D drawing. Chapter 41, "Facilities Design Tools," covers MBD methods in detail, and drawings start in Chapter 24, "Automating Drawings: The Basics."

CREATING THE OFFSET

You need to consider one more thing before you create the groove sketch. What should you use to create the offset—the actual block edges or the original sketch? The answer to this is a Best Practice issue.

BEST PRACTICE

When creating relations that need to adapt to the largest range of changes to the model, it is best to go as far back in the model history as you can to pick up those relations. In most cases, this means creating relations to sketches or reference geometry rather than to edges of the model. Model edges can be fickle, especially with the use of fillets, chamfers, and drafts. The technique of relating features to driving layout sketches helps you create models that do not fail through the widest range of changes.

One tool to help you easily see the parent/child relations between features is the Dynamic Reference Visualization, found at View ➤ User Interface ➤ Dynamic Reference Visualization.

Much of the SolidWorks software was created with initial ease of use in mind. Sometimes doing what's easy initially creates complications later in the design process. The easiest way to create the slot is to open a sketch on the back face, and offset a sketch from the edges of the face, and then apply sketch fillets. This method is very fast, but it is not very robust, meaning that there are several ways in which errors can happen. In the end, there is no truly bullet-proof way to create a model. Each method has its benefits and potential problems.

VIDEO   Watch the video tutorial `www.wiley.com/go/mastersolid` for a demonstration of making a simple part. You can follow along if you like. The finished part is also supplied in the downloadable materials.

Creating a Simple Assembly

An assembly is a special document type in SolidWorks that allows you to position multiple parts with respect to one another using geometrical mate relationships (such as coincident and concentric) or distance relationships (such as dimensions). The simple assemblies you begin creating here start with a single part that is located with respect to the assembly's origin and standard planes. This is very much like orienting the first sketch of a part to the part's origin.

Parts can be added to the assembly in a number of ways and mated together using reference geometry or faces. It is best if you can use reference geometry, because items like planes and axes tend to be more stable than edges and faces. If you make a change later that removes a face that an assembly mate depends on, that mate fails or does something unexpected.

SolidWorks assembly documents can become extremely complex, with patterns, layouts, in-context, virtual parts, subassemblies, flexible subassemblies, configurations, assembly features, exploded views, in-context features, special Toolbox features, and an assortment of other assembly-only tools available. For the purposes of this chapter, we'll just talk about putting parts together with mates.

When creating an assembly, give careful thought to the selection of the first part. The first part or component of an assembly should always be the key component. In an assembly for a bicycle, the frame would be added first and locked in place using the assembly planes. Similarly, an assembly of an engine would be started with the block, where the block is fixed at the assembly origin.

Like other document types, SolidWorks assemblies start from templates. Before you get started making lots of assemblies, you should make sure you have at least one custom template that you intend to use. Special settings common for assembly templates are units, plane names, drafting standard, custom properties, and other items.

Assemblies have a FeatureManager arrangement of their own. In the assembly FeatureManager, you will find parts and subassemblies, special folders for mates, component patterns, assembly features, Toolbox parts and features, and other assembly-specific items.

Creating the Assembly

To get started with an assembly, click New, find an assembly template, and double-click it. The settings that come up in the PropertyManager will be the topic of later chapters, starting with Chapter 13, "Building Efficient Assemblies." You can insert any of the currently open parts or assemblies shown in the Browse window by double-clicking the filename and then clicking in the graphics window to place the part or assembly (Figure 4.16).

Notice that the assembly has some folders and reference geometry just like part documents. As you add parts to the assembly, they will be listed in the FeatureManager. Very large assemblies require some special techniques to manage all the data, but for now we are starting simple.

Populating the Assembly

You can use one of several methods for putting a part into an assembly:

◆ Click Make Assembly from Part/Assembly from the Title Bar toolbar.

◆ Choose Insert ➤ Component.

◆ Drag the part from another SolidWorks window.

◆ Drag the part from Windows Explorer.

◆ Use the Library in the Task pane.

◆ Use the Begin Assembly PropertyManager.

◆ Ctrl+drag to make a copy; Ctrl+C and Ctrl+V to copy and paste parts.

FIGURE 4.16

Creating a new assembly

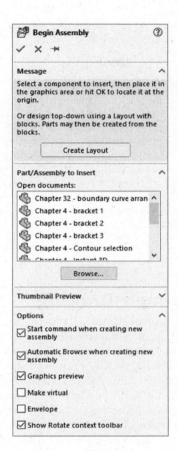

FIGURE 4.16

Creating a new assembly

The first part you put into an assembly is always automatically fixed, meaning it does not move. Any other parts you put in have no constraints or mates, unless you add them using Smart Mates or Mate References, as explained in more detail in Chapter 14, "Getting More from Mates."

Examining Mates

Mates work very much like sketch relations, but they work in 3D space, and they relate edges, faces, vertices, or different types of reference geometry to one another. They do this in order to position and orient parts with respect to one another, but also to allow for motion when a part is dragged with the cursor. Common mates are coincident and concentric—again, just like sketch relations.

Mates are not just for positioning parts, but are also used to establish design intent in the assembly.

Figure 4.17 shows the assembly FeatureManager with several components and some mates.

FIGURE 4.17
A simple assembly

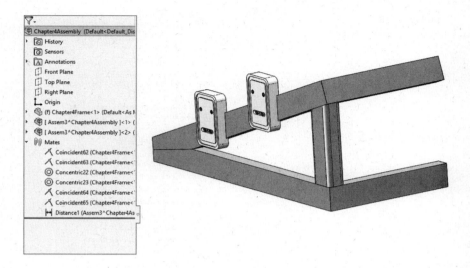

Creating a Simple Drawing

CAD salesmen have been telling us for 30 years that 2D paper drawings are going away. 2D drawings may never go away, but what is happening less is drawing three views with individual lines and arcs. Although AutoCAD is still a popular product, it is tedious for view creation.

Drawings in SolidWorks are really just automated snapshots of the model from various views. Any change to the model automatically updates all the views. You can make section views, auxiliary views, cutaway views, and other specialized views quickly when you are working from a 3D model. There are some exceptions to the automatic updates, including when models aren't loaded and a setting called Detached Drawings, when they are intentionally not updated.

To create a new drawing, you again start with a drawing template, which contains the document-specific settings such as units, drafting standard, and so on. You also might use a *format*, which determines the paper size and has the drawing border with the title block and other items. So, the *template* is the drawing file with overall settings, and the *format* is the drawing border. Usually, templates are saved with the format within it, so the blank drawing already has a sheet size and a border.

You can make drawings of individual parts or assemblies, and you can make multi-sheet drawings with an assembly on the front and all the detail parts on subsequent sheets. Drawings can also contain tables such as bills of materials, general tables, hole charts, and other types of annotated charts.

You can also make drawing views from simple sketches. This is useful for layouts, schematics, and items that might not have a physical representation.

Figure 4.18 shows a drawing with some simple views, dimensions, and annotations.

Tutorial: Creating a Simple Part

To create the simple part for this chapter from scratch, follow these steps:

1. Click the New icon from the Title Bar toolbar, and select an inch part template. (I have included an inch part template with the download materials.)

2. Open a sketch on the Front plane.

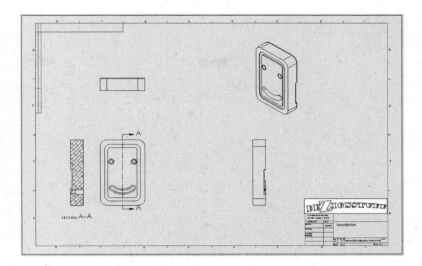

3. Sketch a center rectangle that is 6-inches tall and 4-inches wide, starting from the origin.

4. Create an Extrude feature, using the Direction 1 option for Mid Plane, with a depth of 1 inch. Before you accept the Extrude.

To create the groove, follow these steps:

1. Open a sketch on a face of the part that's parallel to the Front plane. To create the offset, expand the Extrude feature by clicking the plus icon (+) next to it in the FeatureManager so you can see the sketch. Regardless of how it displays here, this sketch appears before the extrude in the part history. Right-click the sketch and select Show (or expand the DisplayManager and click the icon in the first column, in the row of the sketch you want to show).

TIP   You can view individual sketches and reference geometry entities such as planes from the RMB menu. The global settings for the visibility of these items are found in the View menu. You can access these items faster by using the View toolbar or by linking the commands to hotkeys.

2. Right-click the sketch in the graphics window, and click Select Chain. This selects any nonconstruction, end-to-end sketch entities. Click Offset Entities on the Sketch toolbar. Offset to the inside by .400 inches. Apply .500-inch sketch fillets to each of the corners. Exit out of the Fillet command using the green check when the fillets have been applied to the sketch.

3. Click Extruded Cut on the Feature toolbar. By default, the extruded cut will cut away everything inside the closed profile of the sketch. Look down the PropertyManager window, and select the check box on the top bar of the Thin Feature panel. Make the cut settings under Direction 1 Blind, .100 inch. The Thin Feature type should be set to Mid Plane with a width of .400 inches. The PropertyManager and graphics window should look like Figure 4.19.

FIGURE 4.19
Creating the groove with a thin feature cut

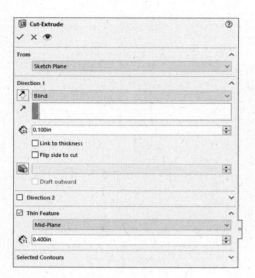

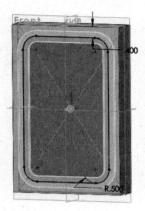

USING SKETCH TECHNIQUES

Continue with the part from the previous section, and follow these steps:

1. Open a new sketch on the large face opposite from the groove. Draw an angled line across the part, as shown in Figure 4.20. Sketch1 should be visible. Click on the Extrude button, and you will be prompted to close the sketch loop. Use the yellow arrow to select the smaller loop.

TIP If you want to continue using the recommended best practice of making relations to sketches rather than model edges, here are a few tips. In some situations (such as the current one), the sketch plane is offset from the sketch that you want to make relations to, and the best bet is to use the Normal To view. The next obstacle is making sure that automatic relations pick up the sketch rather than the edge, so you can use the Selection Filter to select sketch entities only.

2. Extrude the sketch to add 0.25-inch material.

3. Choose Tools ➤ Options ➤ Sketch and ensure that Prompt To Close Sketch is turned on; then click OK to close the dialog box.

4. Open another new sketch on the same face that was used by the last extrusion. Begin drawing another angled line, but before placing the second endpoint, hover the cursor over the angled edge created by the previous feature, and it will highlight orange. Now position the cursor approximately to make a parallel line, and a dotted yellow inference will appear. Draw the angled line using all the automatic relationships that are appropriate, as shown in Figure 4.21.

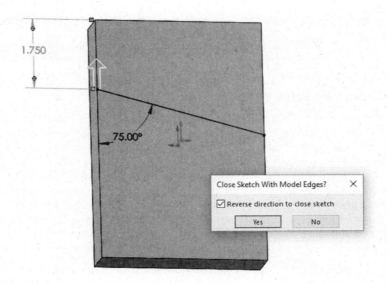

FIGURE 4.20
Closed loop with
angled side

NOTE The parallel relation will not be applied automatically, as shown in Figure 4.21. The line will be parallel to the slanted edge, but a relation might need to be applied manually after the line is created. Time relations are applied automatically based on inference lines only when the mouse hovers over a sketch entity, not an edge. In this particular case, the relation will be replaced by the dimension between two parallel lines from step 5, so no redundant parallel relation is needed.

FIGURE 4.21
Using automatic
relationships

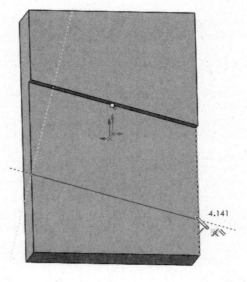

5. Dimension the angled line such that it is 2.025 inches from the first line.

6. Use the same technique as in step 1 to make a closed loop, and extrude the feature using the Through All end condition so that it will always match the previous extrusion.

USING THE HOLE WIZARD

The next features that you will apply are a pair of counterbored holes. SolidWorks has a special tool called the Hole Wizard that you can use to create common hole types. The Hole Wizard helps you create standard hole types using standard or custom sizes. You can place holes on any face of a 3D model or constrain them to a single 2D plane or face. A single feature created by the Hole Wizard may create a single hole or multiple holes, and a feature that is not constrained to a single plane can create individual holes originating from multiple faces, nonparallel faces, and even nonplanar faces (holes may go in different directions). All holes in a single feature that you create by using the Hole Wizard must be the same type and size. If you want multiple sizes or types, you must create multiple Hole Wizard features.

To apply counterbored holes to your part, follow these steps:

1. Select the face that the groove feature was created on, and click the Hole Wizard tool on the Features toolbar. Then set the hole to Counterbored, the Standard to ANSI Inch, the type to Socket Head Cap Screw, the size to one-quarter, and the end condition to Through All, as shown in Figure 4.22.

2. Click to select the Positions tab at the top of the PropertyManager. This is where you place the centerpoints of the holes using sketch points. It is often useful to create construction geometry to help line up and place the sketch points. Make sure the plane or face that the holes originate from is selected in the Positions tab.

3. Draw two colinear construction lines, horizontally across the part, with Coincident relations to each side. Select both lines, and give them an Equal relation. The point of this step is to use parametric relations to evenly space holes across the part without dimensions or equations. Refer to Figure 4.23.

TIP Although several methods exist to make multiple selections, a box or window selection technique may be useful in this situation. If the box is dragged from left to right, only the items completely within the box are selected. If the box is dragged from right to left, any item that is at least partially in the box is selected. Selecting the common point of the two lines applies an equal relation.

4. Place sketch points at the midpoint of each of the construction lines. If there is a sketch point other than the two that you want to make into actual holes, delete the extra points. Dimension one of the lines down from the top of the part, as shown in Figure 4.23. All the sketch relation icons are displayed for reference. Click OK to accept the feature after you are happy with all the settings, locations, relations, and dimensions.

FIGURE 4.22
The Hole Wizard Hole
Specification interface

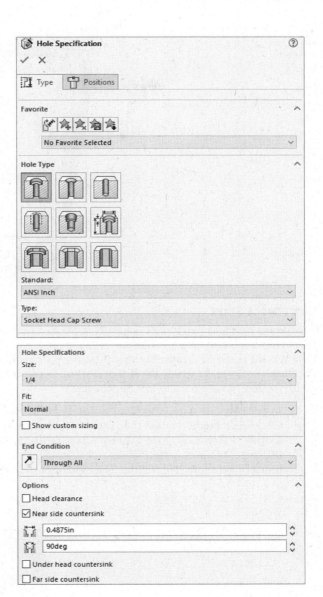

FIGURE 4.23
Placing the center-
points of holes

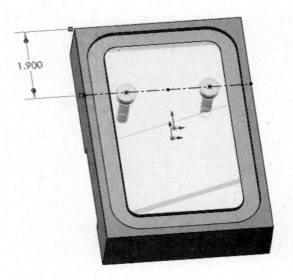

CUTTING A SLOT

SolidWorks provides two types of slots: Hole Wizard slots and sketched slots. Fancier slots with the counterbores and countersinks can be made more quickly using the Hole Wizard, but the Hole Wizard is able to create only straight slots. For curved slots, you will need to use the curved slot sketch entity and extrude the sketch as a cut. In this tutorial, we create a curved slot.

To cut slots in your part, follow these steps:

1. In this case, use the Centerpoint Arc Slot option. Slots are easiest to create with the Click+click method rather than click-and-drag. Make sure the Sketch 1 under Boss-Extrude 1 is shown. Open a sketch on the face with the groove. Click near where you want the center of the curvature of the slot. Click again for the center of one end; click a third time for the width/end radius. The Slot PropertyManager is shown in Figure 4.24.

FIGURE 4.24
Creating a slot

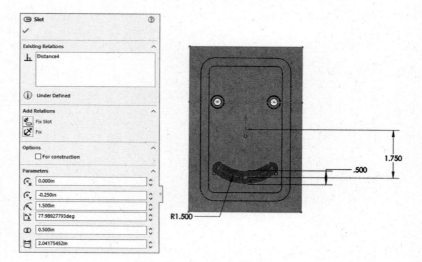

Create a vertical sketch relation between the origin and the centerpoint of the slot. Make the slot 0.500 inches wide. One way to do this is to place a 0.25 inches radial dimension on one of the end arcs, but a more interesting way to do it is to hold down the Shift key and click both of the big arcs with the Smart Dimension tool. This will give you the difference between the arcs. Continue to dimension as shown in Figure 4.24.

NOTE Using the Add dimensions option in the Slot PropertyManager can help you size the slot more quickly. This does not require the Enable onscreen numeric-input option to be turned on.

2. From this sketch, create an extruded cut .75" deep.

3. Open a sketch on the bottom of the previous slot, and offset the slot to the inside by 0.110". Create a cut using the Through All end condition.

Creating Fillets and Chamfers

As mentioned earlier, it is considered a best practice to avoid using sketch fillets when possible and use feature fillets instead. Another best-practice guideline is to put fillets at the bottom of the design tree or at least after all the functional features. You should not dimension sketches to model edges created by fillets unless no better methods are available. Several chapters could be written just about fillet types, techniques, and strategies in SolidWorks. Chapter 7, "Modeling with Primary Features," deals with more complex fillet types.

Best Practice

Do not dimension sketches to model edges that are created by fillets. Although the previous best practice about relations to sketch entities instead of model edges was a mild warning, you must heed this one more carefully.

To add fillets and chamfers to your part, follow these steps:

1. Initiate a Fillet feature, and select the four short edges on the part. Set the radius value to .600 inches. Click OK to accept the Fillet feature. You can use the first icon on the left of the pop-up toolbar, as shown in Figure 4.25, to help you select all four edges around the part quickly.

TIP When selecting edges around a four-sided part, the first three edges are usually visible and the fourth edge is not. You can select invisible edges by expanding the Fillet Options panel of the Fillet PropertyManager and selecting the Select Through Faces option. When you have a complex part with many hidden edges, this setting can be bothersome, but in simple cases like this, it is useful.

FIGURE 4.25
Selecting edges using the
context toolbar

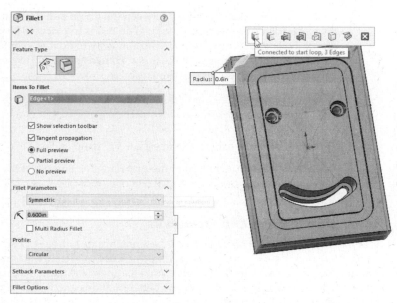

FIGURE 4.25
Selecting edges using the
context toolbar

2. Apply chamfers to the edges of the angled slot through the part, as indicated in
   Figure 4.26. Make the chamfers .050 inches by 45 degrees.

   Chamfers observe many of the same best practices as fillets.

TIP Feature order is important with features like chamfers and fillets because of how they both tend
to propagate around tangent edges. Although you can turn this setting off for both types of features,
it is best to get the correct geometry by applying the features in order.

FIGURE 4.26
Edges for fillet and
chamfer features

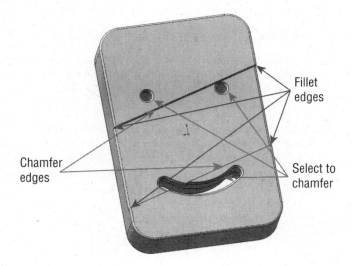

3. Select the four edges that are indicated for fillets in Figure 4.26. Apply .050-inch-
   radius fillets.

4. Apply a last set of .050-inch chamfers to the backside of the counterbores and slot.

5. Save the part, as **Chapter4SimpleMachinedPart** and then close it.

The finished part is simple, but you have learned many useful techniques along the way.

Tutorial: Making a Simple Drawing

In SolidWorks, drawing views are created from the 3D model. Even the most complex section views are almost free, because they are simply projected from the 3D model. When you make changes to the 3D model, all 2D views update. You can handle dimensions in a couple of ways, either using the dimensions that you used to create the model or placing new dimensions on the drawing. (Best practice for modeling is not necessarily the same as best practice for manufacturing drawings.) Model-Based Definition (MBD) is covered in Chapter 40, "Using Model-Based Design."

To make a simple drawing of a SolidWorks native part, follow these steps:

1. Click the New button from the standard toolbar, or choose File ➤ New. From the New SolidWorks Document window, select the Blank Drawing template. The template contains all the document-specific settings.

2. After selecting the drawing template, the Sheet Format/Size dialog box appears, as shown in Figure 4.27. This only appears if the format is not already in the template. If your template comes up with the border around it, you can change the border/format by right-clicking on the Sheet1 in the FeatureManager and selecting Properties.

   Select the D-Landscape sheet size, as well as the format that automatically associates with that sheet size, and click OK. If the Model View PropertyManager appears, click the red X icon to exit. (If the template you selected already has a format, you can skip this step.)

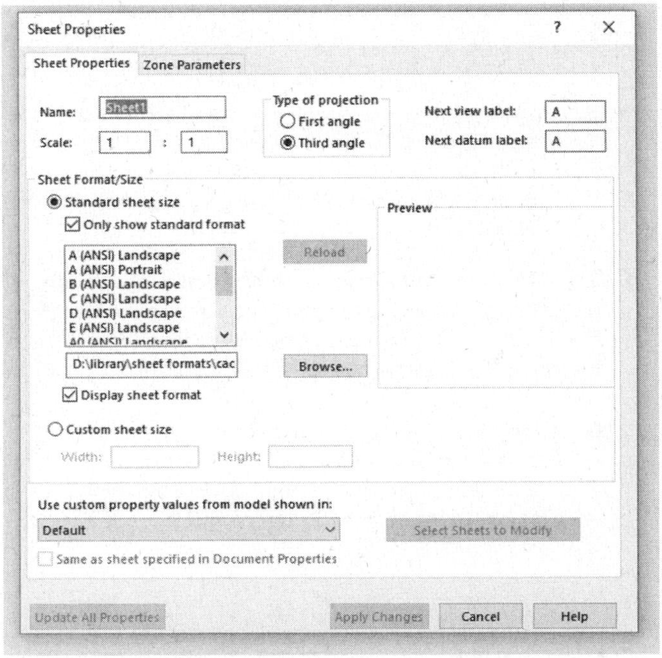

FIGURE 4.27
The Sheet Properties
dialog box

3. From the Drawings toolbar, click the Standard 3 View button, or through the menus, choose Insert ➤ Drawing View ➤ Standard 3 View. If the Chapter4 SimpleMachinedPart document does not appear in the list box in the PropertyManager, then use the Browse button to select it. When you click the OK button, the three drawing views are created.

4. After creating views on the drawing, set up some fields in the format to be filled out automatically when you bring the part into the drawing. Right-click anywhere on the drawing sheet (on the paper) and select Edit Sheet Format.

5. Zoom in to the lower-right corner of the drawing. Notice that there are several variables with the format $PRPSHEET:{Description}. These annotations are linked to custom properties. Some of them have properties with values (such as the Scale note), and some of the properties do not have values (such as the Description).

6. Add an annotation in the Drawn row, in the Date column. You can add annotations by choosing Insert ➤ Annotations ➤ Note, or by activating the Annotations toolbar in the CommandManager and clicking the Note button. Type today's date as the text of the note.

CAUTION If you are using a SolidWorks default template and a circle appears around your note, use the Text Format PropertyManager that appears when you are creating a note, expand the Border panel, and change the Circle option to None.

7. Add another note, this time to the Name column. Do not type anything in the note, but click the Link to Properties button in the Note PropertyManager to create a link to a custom property. In the Link To Property dialog box, click the Model In Drawing View Specified option in Sheet Properties. Type **user** in the drop-down text box below the option. This now accesses a custom property in a part or assembly that is put onto this drawing and called "user," and it puts the value where the note is placed.

8. To return to Edit Sheet mode (out of Edit Format mode), select Edit Sheet from the RMB menu. A little text reminder message appears in the lower-right corner on the status bar to indicate whether you are editing the Sheet or the Format.

9. Drawing views can be sized individually or for each sheet. The Sheet Properties dialog box in Figure 4.27 shows the sheet scale. If this is changed, all the views on the sheet that use the sheet scale are updated. If you select a view and activate the Drawing View PropertyManager, you can use the Scale panel to toggle from Use Sheet Scale to Use Custom Scale.

CAUTION Sometimes, in the United States, the SolidWorks software installs with ISO standard templates. ISO drawing templates project views using First Angle Projection. To check the projection method of a drawing, right-click the drawing sheet and select Sheet Properties. The Type Of Projection setting appears in the top middle of the dialog box, as shown in Figure 4.27.

10. To create an Isometric view, activate the Drawings toolbar in the CommandManager and click the Projected View button. Then select one of the existing views, and move the cursor at a 45-degree angle. If you cannot place the view where you would like it to go, press the Ctrl key to break the alignment and place the view where you want it.

11. You can change the appearance of the drawing view in several ways:

♦ View ➤ Display ➤ Tangent Edges With Font uses the phantom line type for any edge between tangent faces.

♦ View ➤ Display ➤ Tangent Edges Removed completely removes any tangent edges. This is not recommended, especially for parts with many filleted edges, because it generally displays just the outline of the part.

♦ Shaded or Wireframe modes can be used on drawings and are accessed from the View toolbar.

♦ Perspective views must be saved in the model as a named view and placed in the drawing using the view name.

♦ RealView drawing views can be placed on the drawing. RealView can be shown in drawings using Shaded or Shaded With Edges and RealView turned on.

12. Look at the custom properties that you created in the title block. The date is there because you entered a specific value for it, but the Name field is not filled in. This is because there is no User property in the part. Right-click the part in one of the views, and select Open Part. In the part window, choose File ➤ Properties, and in the Property Name column, type the property name **user**, with a value of your initials, or however your company identifies people on drawings. The Properties dialog box, also called Summary Information, is shown in part in Figure 4.28.

NOTE When used in models and formats, Custom Properties are an extremely powerful combination, especially when you want to fill in data automatically in the format, in a BOM (Bill of Materials), or a PDM (Product Data Management) product. These topics are discussed in more detail in Chapter 13.

FIGURE 4.28
The Custom Properties entry table

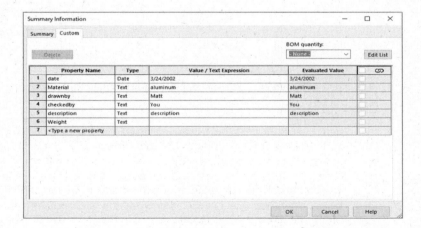

13. When you flip back to the drawing (using Ctrl+Tab), the Name column now contains the value of your initials.

14. Click the Section View button on the Drawings toolbar. This activates the Section View Assist command so you can place a section line in a view. If you need a cutting line other than a single straight line, the PropertyManager has some options, and other options will be presented after you place the line to allow you to edit it.

15. Bring the cursor down to the midpoint of the top edge of the part. When the midpoint is active, you can use the dotted inference lines to ensure that you are lined up with the center. Another option is to manually create sketch relations. Turning on temporary axes displays center marks in the centers of arcs and circles. Figure 4.29 shows the technique with the inference lines being used.

FIGURE 4.29
Creating a section view with the Section View Assist

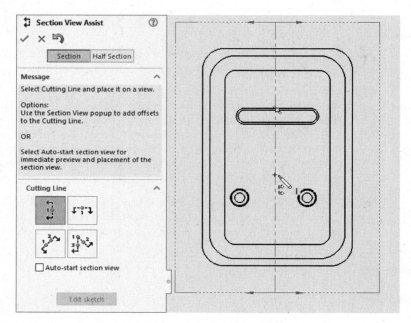

16. As mentioned earlier, you can use two fundamentally different methods for dimensioning drawings:

Model Items imports the dimensions used to build the SolidWorks model and uses them on the drawing. These dimensions are *bidirectionally associative*, meaning that changing them on the drawing updates the model and changing them on the model updates them in the drawing. On the surface of things, this sounds too good to be true, and it is. The potential problems is that you might not model things the way you would dimension them for the shop. You have to answer several questions for yourself, such as "Do the leader lines go to the right locations or can they be moved?" The dimensions usually come in such a way that they need to be moved around quite a bit.

Reference (driven) Dimensions can be applied to the drawing view directly. These are only associative in one direction, meaning that they measure what is there, but they do not drive the size or position of the geometry. All changes must be made from the model. Again, on the face of things, this appears to be redundant and a waste of time; but in my personal estimation, by the time you finish rearranging dimensions, checking to ensure that you have everything you need, and hiding the extraneous dimensions, you are usually far better off using reference dimensions.

BEST PRACTICE

Users have strong opinions on both sides of the issue of dimensioning drawings. The best thing for you to do is to use both methods and decide for yourself.

---

17. If you choose to use the Model Items approach, you can do this by choosing Insert ➤ Model Items. Specify whether the dimensions should come from the entire model or just a selected feature. You also need to ask whether the dimensions should come into all views or just the selected one, and whether you want just a certain type of dimension, annotation, or reference geometry.

18. After the dimensions are brought in, you need to move some of them from one view to another, which you can do by Shift+dragging the dimension from the old location to the new location. Ctrl+dragging predictably copies the dimension. You can move views by dragging an edge in the view.

SHEET VS. SHEET FORMAT

With new and even experienced users, there is some confusion around the Sheet versus Sheet Format issue. Part of the confusion is due to SolidWorks terminology. SolidWorks names the two items Sheet and Sheet Format. In this book, I simply use the terms *Sheet* and *Format* to avoid linking the two items with a common first name. It would be better yet if *Format* were changed to *Border* or *Title Block* so that the name more closely matched the function. Just be aware that Title Block has a precise meaning in SolidWorks; there are commands associated with it.

In a SolidWorks drawing, you are editing a view, the sheet, or the format. When editing the sheet, you can perform actions such as view, move, and create views, but you cannot select, move, or edit the lines and text of the drawing border. When editing the format, you can edit the lines and text that make up the drawing border, but the drawing views disappear. Also, you can edit annotations in the format from the sheet layer.

Often, users save a template that already contains a format to save themselves some time every time they create a new drawing. Chapter 24 covers setting up automation of drawing creation.

The Bottom Line

SolidWorks data is made of parts, assemblies, and drawings. In this chapter, you learned how to create simple examples of each type.

Master It   Create a simple block with holes in it, where every item is dimensioned fully. Use an existing SolidWorks template.

Master It   Create a simple assembly where you bring together some of the parts that you created or worked with in this chapter, and use mates to locate them with respect to one another.

Master It   Create a simple drawing of a single part you made earlier in this chapter. Fill in some custom properties, and make sure the properties propagate over to fill out the title block on the drawing. Use various types of views, annotations, symbols, and dimensions.

Chapter 5

Using Visualization Techniques

Part of the overall mission of SolidWorks software is to visualize geometry. Visualizing 3D CAD data is more than seeing shaded solids or shiny surfaces; it includes being able to see the interior and exterior at the same time and using sections, transparency, wireframe, and other tools or techniques. SolidWorks takes it so much further than just being able to see things in 3D; you can look at some parts of an assembly in wireframe while others are transparent and others are opaque. You can see a part with a reflective appearance. You can create section views in parts and assemblies to visualize internal details. This chapter will show you important capabilities that will expand how you can use SolidWorks and maybe even change the way you use the tools or look at modeling tasks.

IN THIS CHAPTER, YOU WILL LEARN TO:

◆ Customize the view

◆ Use View tools to view parts and assemblies

◆ Make the best use of RealView

◆ Use Display States in parts and assemblies

◆ Apply edge settings to display features clearly

◆ Sort items in an assembly

Manipulating the View

One of the most important skills in SolidWorks is manipulating the view. (Figure 5.1 shows the Heads-Up View toolbar, an easy way to access most visualization tools.) This is something you'll do more frequently than any other function in SolidWorks, so learning to do it efficiently and effectively is very important, whether you look at it as rotating the model or rotating the point of view around the model. The easiest way to rotate the part is to hold down the middle mouse button (MMB) or the scroll wheel and move the mouse. If your mouse does not have a middle button or a scroll wheel that you can use as a MMB, you can use the Rotate View tool in the menus at View ➤ Modify ➤ Rotate or via the RMB menu.

The Heads-Up View toolbar can be customized and disabled using the same method you use for all the other toolbars, through the Tools ➤ Customize dialog box.

FIGURE 5.1
Use the Heads-Up View toolbar to easily access most visualization tools.

TIP Some mouse drivers change the middle-button or scroll-wheel settings to do other things. Often, you can disable the special settings for a particular application if you want SolidWorks to work correctly and still use the other functionality. For example, the most common problem with mouse drivers is that when the model gets close to the sides of the graphics window and the scroll bars engage, the middle mouse button suddenly changes its function. If this happens to you, you should change the function of the MMB to Middle Mouse Button from its present setting.

For visualization, you cannot buy any hardware that's quite as nice as a spaceball (3D mouse). It allows you to rotate with one hand and select with the other hand. It is also great for customizing buttons; depending on the model you get, it may even have some keyboard buttons such as Alt, Esc, and Ctrl right there on the device.

Using Arrow Keys

You can use the arrow keys on the keyboard to manipulate the view in predictable and controllable ways. You can use the Shift, Ctrl, and Alt keys to add to the behavior. The arrow keys enable you to rotate to the following views:

Arrow: Rotate 15 degrees (to customize this setting, choose Tools ➤ Options ➤ View)

Shift+arrow: Rotate 90 degrees

Alt+arrow: Rotate in a plane flat to the screen

Ctrl+arrow: Pan

Using the Middle Mouse Button

Most, if not all, mice sold today have middle mouse buttons (MMBs), usually in the form of a clickable scroll wheel. The MMB or scroll wheel has several uses in view manipulation:

MMB alone: Rotate

Click or hover: Work on an edge, a face, or a vertex with MMB and then drag MMB: Rotate around selected entity

Ctrl+MMB: Pan

Shift+MMB: Zoom

Double-click MMB: Zoom to fit

Scroll with wheel: Zoom in or out (to reverse direction of the zoom setting, choose Tools ➤ Options ➤ View)

Alt+MMB: Rotate in a plane flat to the screen

When you're rotating the model view with the MMB, the view can easily get into a state where it's hard to see. Using the Rotate About Scene Floor option, however, makes this easier. Figure 5.2 shows this option in the RMB menu. You may see documentation that describes this as "lock vertical axis," but it does not do that. "Lock vertical axis" would be if the model were sitting on a turntable going around. The Rotate About Scene Floor option seems to understand which way is "up," and it doesn't allow the view to proceed in such a way that the model gets turned upside down easily. It's possibly more difficult to describe in writing than to just try it—so just try it. You may agree that this should have been the default method for rotation.

FIGURE 5.2
Using the Rotate About
Scene Floor option

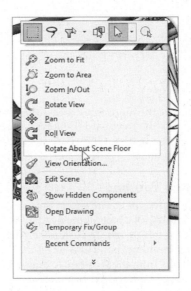

To change the floor position or orientation, go to the DisplayManager tab of the FeatureManager area, right-click Scene, and select Edit Scene. In the Floor panel, change the setting in the Align Floor With selection box and select the appropriate plane or Bottom View Plane.

As a caution, you may be prevented from accessing the Edit Scene PropertyManager if you are using the Plain Viewport Background color (Tools ➤ Options ➤ Colors ➤ Background Appearance). This uses System Options to determine the background for each document rather than allowing each document to control its own background. To access the Scene options, you have to change to Use Document Scene.

Using Mouse Gestures

Mouse gestures are an interface method that you can customize to do anything a SolidWorks toolbar button can do, but by default, it controls view orientation. Figure 5.3 shows the default configuration of the mouse gesture donut.

It may take a little time for you to get used to the mouse-gestures interface. It works best when you understand what the commands are before you use them, so you can invoke the Top View command in a single motion, without pausing to see where each command is located on the donut. For this reason, it might be better to limit the donut to four commands rather than eight or 12 and to set it up intuitively such that the top view is an RMB stroke up, a right view is an RMB stroke to the right, and so on.

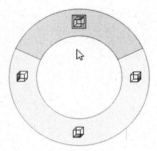

FIGURE 5.3
Click+drag the right mouse button (RMB) to access the commands on the donut.

You can customize the mouse-gestures donut in the Tools ➤ Customize ➤ Mouse Gestures. This works much like the Keyboard (hotkey) customization, where you can turn gestures on or off, set the mouse gesture donut to two, four, eight, or 12 sections, and set any gesture direction to any available command.

Using the View Toolbar

The View toolbar, shown in its entirety in Figure 5.4, contains the tools that you need to manipulate the view in SolidWorks. Not all the available tools are on the toolbar by default, but I have added them here for this image. To customize your own View toolbar, you must use choose Tools ➤ Customize from the menu and select the Commands tab. Then click the View toolbar, and either drag items from the Customize dialog box to the View toolbar to add them or from the View toolbar into the empty graphics area to remove them. You can use all these tools with part and assembly models, but only a few of them with drawings.

The toolbar that holds tools for direct access to standard named views such as Front, Top, and Normal To is called the Standard Views toolbar and is described later in this chapter. The Add Walk-through tool is discussed more in Chapter 22, "Working with Large Scale Design," and Chapter 23, "Animating with the MotionManager." This is a means of creating an animation for a large-scale design. The Ambient Occlusion option is covered in this chapter, and it simply adds self-cast shadows to a model to make it look more realistic.

The Take Snapshot option works like the combination of a custom-named view and a display state. It allows you to return to a particular view of an assembly with parts hidden or shown as they were when you took the snapshot. You remain "in" the snapshot until you click the button to exit it, much like Isolate. You can find the saved snapshots in the DisplayManager on the Scene, Lights, And Cameras tab. The Filter Modified Components option makes any parts that have not been modified transparent, so that what you see as opaque are the parts that have been changed.

FIGURE 5.4
The View toolbar tools

Adding Scrollbars and Splitters

An option exists to add scrollbars and view pane splitters to the graphics window. To use it, choose Tools ➤ Options ➤ Display/Selection, Display Scrollbars in graphics view. This selection is grayed out if any SolidWorks documents are open (so you must close all SolidWorks documents to change it). When you zoom in such that the part, assembly, or drawing is partially off the screen, the scrollbars activate on the right side and bottom of the SolidWorks window, enabling you to scroll up and down as well as left and right to pan the view. Scrollbars and splitters are turned off by default. You cannot turn off one or the other; scrollbars and splitters come as a package deal.

Figure 5.5 shows a detail of the bottom-right corner of the SolidWorks graphics window, where you find the scrollbars and splitters. Notice the cursor in the lower right, over one of the splitters. The splitters can be easy to miss if you do not know what they look like.

FIGURE 5.5
Scrollbar and splitter
controls can be turned
on or off.

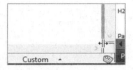

The splitters enable you to split the main graphics window into multiple view ports. The options are two ports horizontally, two ports vertically and four ports, two horizontal and two vertical for a total of four view ports per document. The splitter bars are located at the intersection of the scrollbars in the lower-right corner of the graphics window. Of course, you can also use the icons on the View Orientation box for splitting the view into two vertical ports, two horizontal ports, or four ports.

After a viewport has been split, you can remove the split with the toolbar icons, either by dragging the border back to the edge of the display window or by double-clicking the split border. If the view has been split into four, you can set it back to a single viewport by double-clicking the intersection of the horizontal and vertical port borders.

Using the Magnifying Glass

You can invoke the Magnifying Glass by pressing G and dismiss it when you select something or when you press Esc. To change the hotkey it is associated with, choose Tools ➤ Customize ➤ Keyboard. Magnifying Glass is listed in the Other category. The Magnifying Glass is intended to magnify a small area of the view to enable you to make a more precise selection without zooming.

The magnified area follows your cursor as it moves, and you can zoom in and out by scrolling the MMB. Ctrl+dragging the MMB keeps the Magnifying Glass centered on the cursor. Pressing Alt creates a section view parallel to the view current, and scrolling the wheel with the Alt key pressed moves the section plane farther away or closer. Figure 5.6 shows the Magnifying Glass in operation, cutting a section view through a part.

FIGURE 5.6
Using the Magnifying
Glass with the
section view

Clicking the Triad Axes

The Triad is the multicolored coordinate axis in the lower-left corner of the SolidWorks graphics window. You generally use it passively to see how the view is oriented and to get X, Y, Z reference directions for features that need them. To use the Triad to actively control the view orientation, try the following:

Click an axis: The view rotates to point this axis out of the screen.

Click an axis a second time: This axis points into the screen.

Shift+click an axis: This view spins 90 degrees about that axis (using the right-hand rule).

Alt+click an axis: This view spins 15 degrees (or the default view rotation angle) around the axis.

When you are in a named view, the name of the view is shown in the lower-left corner under the Triad. This includes standard named views and custom named views. Anything that shows up in the View Orientation box (accessed by the spacebar) displays a name in the corner. Figure 5.7 shows the Triad and the named view in the lower-left corner.

By Shift+clicking an axis of the Triad, the view is rotated 90 degrees from the original

FIGURE 5.7
The Triad, named view, and View Orientation box

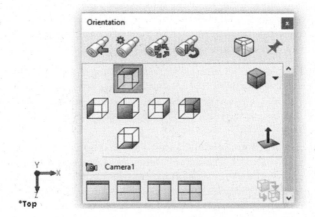

orientation about that axis. Alt+clicking rotates the view around the clicked axis by the view rotation increment set in Tools ➤ Options ➤ View, which is 15 degrees by default. Pressing Ctrl in conjunction with any of these causes the view to rotate in the opposite direction. Therefore, if pressing Shift+click makes the view rotate against the right-hand rule about the clicked axis, pressing Ctrl+Shift+click makes the view rotate with the right-hand rule.

Using the View Tools

SolidWorks has many additional tools for managing the view, and you can easily access them through the Heads-Up View toolbar, hotkeys, RMB menu, View Orientation box, or the normal toolbars and menus.

The tools in this section help you to control how you view parts and assemblies. The following tools are mainly found in the View, View ➤ Display, and View ➤ Modify menu areas.

 Zoom To Fit: This resizes the contents of the graphics window to include everything that is shown in the model. You can also access this command by pressing the F key or double-clicking with the MMB.

Zoom To Area: When you drag the diagonal of a rectangle in the display area, the display zooms to fit it to the current window. The border size around the fit area is fixed and cannot be adjusted. This only zooms in, not out.

Zoom In/Out: Drag the mouse up or down to zoom in or out, respectively. You can also access this command by holding down the Shift key and dragging up or down with the MMB. The hotkey Z and Shift+Z work for Zoom Out and Zoom In, respectively. The percentage of the zoom is a fixed amount and cannot be adjusted. You can also use the scroll wheel to zoom in and out, and if you are accustomed to using a different CAD product where the scroll works the opposite way, a setting exists at Tools ➤ Options ➤ View that allows you to reverse the function of the scroll wheel.

Zoom To Selection: This resizes the screen to fit the selection. You can also access this command by right-clicking or left-clicking a feature in the FeatureManager. For example, if you select a sketch from the FeatureManager and right-click and select Zoom To Selection, the view positions the sketch in the middle of the screen and resizes the sketch to match the display. The view does not rotate with Zoom To Selection.

TIP A reciprocal function to Zoom To Selection enables you to find an item in the tree from graphics window geometry. If you right-click a face of the model, then you can select Go To Feature In Tree, which highlights the parent feature. This function has been relegated to the expanded menu, so you may have to click the double arrow at the bottom of the RMB menu to see it.

Zoom About Screen Center: This enables you to zoom straight in and straight out. This tool is off by default. The default behavior is that zooming with the scroll wheel works around the cursor. If the cursor is off to one side, zooming in and out can cause the view to "walk" away from that side. Turning on Zoom About Screen Center is not dependent on the location of the cursor. If you are frustrated with how zooming with the scroll wheel works, try this setting and see if you like it better. This command is found only in the menus at View ➤ Modify and does not have an icon.

Rotate View: This enables you to orbit around the part or assembly using the left mouse button (LMB). You can also access this command by using the MMB without the toolbar icon.

Roll View: This spins the view on the plane of the screen, similar to Rotate View with the Alt key.

Pan: This scrolls the view flat to the screen by dragging the mouse. You can also access this command by holding down the Ctrl key and dragging the MMB without using the toolbar icon; another way to access it is with Ctrl+arrow.

3D Drawing View: This enables you to rotate the model within a drawing view to make selections that would otherwise be difficult or impossible. This is available only in drawing documents.

View Orientation (Standard Views flyout) toolbar: View Orientation is discussed later in this chapter. The flyout enables you to access all the Standard Views tools. This button is also called the View Orientation flyout, depending on where you see it.

Wireframe: This displays the model edges without the shaded faces. No edges are hidden.

Hidden Lines Visible (HLV): This displays the model edges without the shaded faces. Edges that would be hidden are displayed in a font.

Hidden Lines Removed (HLR): This displays the model edges without the shaded faces. Edges that are hidden by the part are removed from the display.

Shaded With Edges: The model is displayed with shading, and edges are shown using HLR. Edges can all be a single color that you set in Tools ➤ Options ➤ Colors (typically black), or they can match the shaded color of the part. Tools ➤ Options ➤ Document Properties ➤ Colors is where you find the document-specific setting to use the same color for shaded and wire-frame display, which becomes very useful in an assembly when all the parts shown in wireframe are the same color as they are when they are shaded, instead of all being black.

Shaded: The model is displayed with shading, and edges are not shown.

Shadows In Shaded Mode: When the model is displayed shaded, a shadow displays on a plane parallel to the floor as established in the scene. The shadow is not necessarily on the floor, but on the plane at the furthest extent of the model parallel to the floor.

Section View: This sections the display of the model. Figure 5.8 shows the Section View command at work. You can use up to three section planes at once. Solid and surface models, as well as assemblies, can be sectioned. You can use the spin boxes, enter numbers manually, or drag the arrows that are attached to the section planes to move the section through the model. Section planes can also be rotated by dragging the border of the plane. Parts can be omitted from the cut, or the cut parts can be transparent. You can show the cut caps or leave the cuts looking hollow.

FIGURE 5.8
Sectioning a 3D model

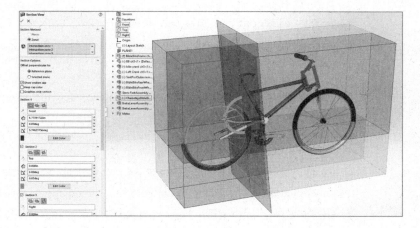

◆ Clicking the checkmark icon in the Section View PropertyManager enables you to continue working with the sectioned model, although you may not be able to reference edges or faces that are created by the section view. It is only a displayed section; the actual geometry is not cut.

◆ Section views can be saved either to the View Orientation box or to the Annotation View folder, which enables 3D section views to be reused on the drawing. When you are working in a section view, if you want to alter it, you can access Modify Section View through the menus at View ➤ Modify ➤ Section View. You should notice that no toolbar icon exists for modifying a section view. You have to access this command through the menus or by turning off the Section View tool and then turning it back on. You might also notice that Modify Section View is available in the hotkey assignment area, Tools ➤ Customize ➤ Keyboard.

◆ The orange interface elements allow you to move or rotate the section, which can also be done in the PropertyManager. Notice the many options in the PropertyManager.

◆ You can section by 2D planes (act as cutting planes) or by 3D zones (bounding box segmented into solid zones by section planes)

I encourage you to experiment with this tool to see what it can do.

 RealView: This creates a more realistic reflective or textured display for advanced material selections. This feature does not work with all graphics hardware, so check the SolidWorks system requirements website to see if it supports your hardware. An entire section of this chapter is devoted to the various tools available with RealView graphics.

 Cartoon: This applies a cartoonish, less realistic appearance to the model. It creates a harsh lighting and a different type of shadow that doesn't rely on shadow settings. It is an effect you may want to experiment with, especially when using the edge and silhouette edge display options.

 Ambient Occlusion: This option displays shadows that the part casts on itself. It is particularly useful when a part or assembly has an interior area that can be seen from outside the model. The interior area will be shown in shadows with this setting on. The setting may affect performance especially on large assemblies.

 View Bounding Box: This option enables you to turn on the display of the bounding box (Insert ➤ Reference Geometry ➤ Bounding Box). The bounding box encloses the entire model (parts only) and looks like the edges of a cube created in a phantom-line 3D sketch.

 Apply Scene: This enables you to apply a scene to your document background. It may also turn off the system background color you are using.

 Edit Appearance: This enables you to apply and edit colors, textures, and materials to faces, bodies, features, parts, and components.

 Copy Appearance: This enables you to copy an appearance from the model to the Clipboard.

 Paste Appearance: This enables you to paste a copied appearance onto a model.

  Draft, Undercut, and Parting Line Analysis: These display options enable you to evaluate the manufacturability of plastic and cast parts. These three types of geometric analysis are discussed in more detail in Chapter 12, "Editing, Evaluating, and Troubleshooting."

 Simulation Display: If your model contains results from a stress analysis, this button will allow you to display those results on your model.

Walkthrough: The Walkthrough helps you create an animation that records a movie as if you were walking through a part or assembly.

Change Display States: Display states help you retain visual or display settings for a document, and this tool enables you to switch between stored states.

Hide All Types: Any of the icons with a picture of an eye on them can be used to show or hide the entity depicted in the icon. This includes planes, axes, sketches, curves, relations, parting lines, decals, and so on. You can access these icons quickly from the Heads-Up View toolbar. The eye icon on its own is Hide All Types, and it toggles each of these individual settings.

Zebra Stripes and Curvature

Zebra Stripes, another geometrical analysis tool that helps you visualize the quality of transitions between faces across edges, simulates putting a perfectly reflective part in a spherical room where the walls are painted with black-and-white stripes. In high-end shape design, surface quality is measured qualitatively using light reflections from the surface. Reflecting stripes make it easier to visualize when a transition between faces across an edge is not smooth. Zebra Stripes can help you identify these three cases (see Figure 5.9):

Contact: Faces intersect at an edge but are not tangent across the edge, such as at the edges of a cube. This condition exists when stripes do not line up across the edge.

Tangency: Faces are tangent across an edge but have different radii of curvature on either side of the edge (noncurvature continuous), such as between a fillet face and an adjacent face. This condition exists when stripes line up across an edge, but the stripe is not tangent to itself across the edge.

Curvature continuity: Faces on either side of an edge are tangent and match in radius of curvature. Zebra Stripes are smooth and tangent across the edge.

FIGURE 5.9
Zebra Stripes help you visualize the qualities of curvature.

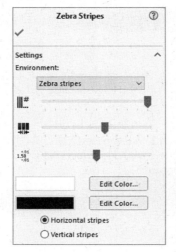

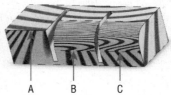

In Figure 5.9, the Zebra Stripes in example A do not match across the edge labeled A at all. This is clearly the nontangent, contact-only case. Example B shows that the stripes match in position going across the indicated edge, but they change direction immediately. This is the tangent case. Example C shows the stripes flowing smoothly across the edge. This is the curvature continuous case.

You can use the remaining icons in the View toolbar to toggle the display of various types of entities from reference geometry to sketches.

Curvature colors the model with various colors depending on the local surface curvature. Mathematically, curvature is the inverse of radius, so $c = 1/r$. A large radius is a small curvature and vice versa. Generally, on models where you are looking at curvature, you are looking for sudden changes, flat spots, constant radius, or inflections. Figure 5.10 shows a model of a cricket bat with the curvature displayed.

FIGURE 5.10
The Curvature display
helps you evaluate
properties of
smooth models.

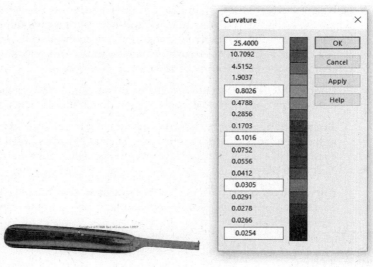

You can control the colors for various curvature values at Tools ➤ Options ➤ Document Properties ➤ Model Display ➤ Curvature using the table shown in Figure 5.10.

View Orientation

The View Orientation dialog box and the Standard Views toolbar are very similar to one another. View Orientation is the more modern of the interfaces. The View Orientation dialog box and the View Selector are shown in Figure 5.11.

FIGURE 5.11
The View Orientation
dialog box and the
View Selector

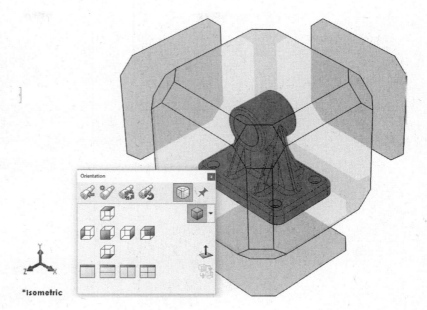

*Isometric

You can access the View Selector independently from the View Orientation dialog box by pressing Ctrl+spacebar or by accessing it from the Standard Views toolbar. The View Selector graphic enables selection of various angled unnamed views, giving you a visual preview for selection. The View Orientation dialog box contains the following controls:

Pushpin: This keeps the dialog box active.

New View: This creates a new custom-named view.

Update Standard Views: This sets the current view to be the new Front view; all other views update relative to this change. This also updates any associated drawing views but does not move any geometry or change plane orientation.

Reset Standard Views: This resets the standard views so that the Front view looks normal to the Front plane (Plane1, XY plane).

Previous View (undo view change): You can access this tool by pressing the default hotkey Shift+Ctrl+Z.

The Normal To option has four modes of operation:

First Mode: With nothing selected, Normal To will find the nearest orthogonal view.

Second Mode: Click a plane, planar face, or 2D sketch. When you click Normal To, the view reorients normal to the selected plane, face, or sketch and zooms to fit the model in the view. This method is shown in Figure 5.12.

FIGURE 5.12
Using Normal To on an
angled face

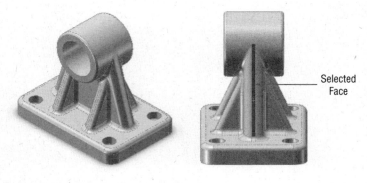

FIGURE 5.13
Using Normal To with a
second selection to
define the top

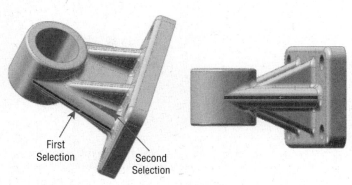

Third Mode: Click Normal To a second time. The view rotates 180 degrees to display the opposite direction.

Fourth Mode: After making the first selection, Ctrl+select another planar entity. The view is normal to the first selection, and the second selection is rotated to the top. This method is shown in Figure 5.13.

Annotation Views

Annotation views enable you to group annotations that were made in a 3D model into views that will be used on the drawing. They are collected under the Annotations folder in the FeatureManager for parts and assemblies. Annotation views can be created automatically when 3D annotations are added or created manually. An Unassigned Items annotation view acts as a catchall for annotations that are not assigned to any particular views. In the 3D model, you can use the views to reorient the model and display annotations. As mentioned earlier, annotation views can also capture a model section view to be shown in a drawing view.

Annotation views are listed in the Annotations folder in the FeatureManager of the document where they are created. Right-clicking the Annotations folder provides all the options for Annotation views. The Annotation views are shown for the Chapter5SampleCasting part in Figure 5.14.

FIGURE 5.14
Annotation views for
`Chapter5SampleCasting`
`.sldprt`

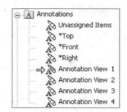

Using the DisplayManager

The DisplayManager organizes all the display and visual information into a form that makes it easier to understand and control. The DisplayManager lists Appearances, Decals, Scenes, Lights, and Cameras. You can find the DisplayManager as a tab in the FeatureManager window area. Figure 5.15 shows the Appearances data for a part with a material and color applied to two faces and a feature.

FIGURE 5.15
Using the Display-
Manager to manage
appearances

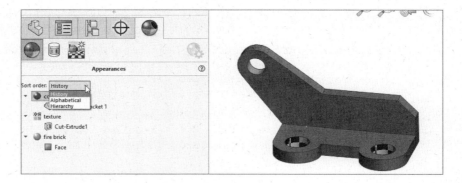

Appearances in SolidWorks are a combination of color and texture. In order to have appearances display and sort in the DisplayManager, you have to first apply appearances. Most of the appearances are meant to look like idealized materials in real life. Remember that materials are applied separately and control physical properties such as density, strength, and so on. Appearances deal with cosmetic properties. Polished, cast, knurled, machined, sand-blasted, and other surface finish types are available to add realism to your models.

Applying Appearances

You can apply appearances to faces, bodies, features, parts, assembly components, or even the top-level assembly. Even if you don't apply an appearance, every part and assembly template starts with a default appearance (except very old templates), which is white, glossy plastic.

You can apply appearances in several ways:

Double-click: Double-clicking an appearance in the Appearances panel of the Task pane applies the appearance to the document (part or assembly).

Drag-and-drop: Dragging an appearance from the Appearances panel of the Task pane enables you to drop it on geometry in the graphics window. When you do this, the appearance palette pops up and presents you with several options. Figure 5.16 shows this toolbar with the options for Face, Feature, Body, and Part.

FIGURE 5.16
Determining a target for the appearances after drag-and-drop

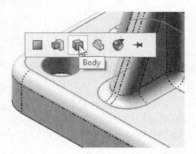

Appearance palette: If you pin the Appearance palette, the workflow reverses. Select the type of entity to which you want to apply the appearance and select model faces.

Appearance filter: The Appearance filter enables you to change all items of a given appearance to a new appearance. Just drag the new appearance onto any face with the old appearance, and click the Appearance filter when it appears. All other items with that particular appearance are changed to the new appearance.

Context toolbar: You can also invoke the Appearance function from the context bars (left-click or right-click). You can do this with preselection or no selection. This method also gives you options for the target to which to apply the appearance, face, feature, body, or part. Figure 5.17 shows this method.

FIGURE 5.17
Determining a target for the appearances after drag-and-drop

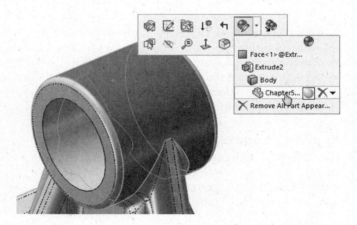

You can copy and paste appearances from the DisplayManager (or the model) onto the model. To distinguish between copying geometry and copying appearances, the appearance copy shortcut is Ctrl+Shift+C, and the appearance paste shortcut is Ctrl+Shift+V.

DIFFERENTIATING APPEARANCES AND MATERIALS

It is easy to confuse appearances and materials. The biggest reason for this is that, in many cases, appearances have the same names as materials, and the texture associated with the appearance typically also has the name of a material. SolidWorks has appearances with names such as high-gloss plastic, wrought iron, and chromium plate. It may become even more confusing because materials (which you can assign from the FeatureManager on the left) have appearances (which you assign from the Task pane on the right) assigned to them. For example, you could assign an appearance called polished aluminum to a material called AISI 304.

You cannot use appearances to assign mass properties (such as density or stiffness) to a part, but you can use materials to assign an appearance as well as mass properties to a part. Figure 5.18 shows the RMB menu for editing material, which you invoke from the Material folder in the FeatureManager.

FIGURE 5.18

Editing a material

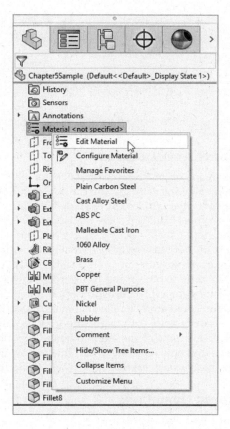

Materials assign properties to your parts for drawing hatch and mass properties, as well as simulation. Notice in Figure 5.19 that the second tab allows you to assign an appearance to the material. You can use this interface to create your own custom materials, which automatically apply appearances to your parts.

FIGURE 5.19
Editing or creating
custom materials

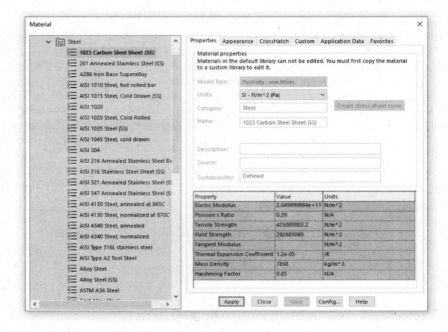

UNDERSTANDING APPEARANCES

Appearances are made up of a combination of color, illumination properties, a surface finish image, and image-mapping settings. You can control all these options in the Advanced interface of the Appearances PropertyManager, as shown in Figure 5.20. To access this interface, click the Appearance icon in the Heads-Up View toolbar, and click the Advanced button at the top of the PropertyManager.

You can adjust the default appearances that install with SolidWorks when you apply them to your models. For example, you can apply a shiny, reflective appearance such as Stainless Steel and then adjust its color to blue or red. You could apply a cast-iron appearance and then increase the roughness. You might apply a brushed-aluminum appearance and change the direction of the brush lines. You could apply a reflective-glass appearance and then reduce the reflectivity and increase the transparency. You might apply a knurled-steel appearance to a cylindrical part and adjust the mapping so the knurled image does not smear improperly across a face. Figure 5.21 shows the contents of the Color/Image, Mapping, Illumination, and Surface Finish tabs of the Appearances PropertyManager, where you can adjust all these settings and more.

UNDERSTANDING OVERRIDES

Keeping track of colors and appearances in SolidWorks can be difficult. Many users have difficulty understanding when one color overrides another color and how to remove layers of applied colors or appearances. This functionality is called Overrides.

Here is the hierarchy that SolidWorks uses when applying colors (appearances), listed from lowest priority to highest:

◆ Default

◆ Part

FIGURE 5.20
Controlling the
components of
appearance

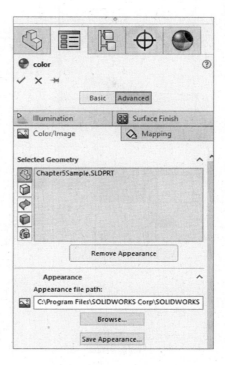

- Body

- Feature

- Face

- Component

- Assembly

You should read this list with the words ". . .is overridden by. . ." between the items. As you can see, the default appearance is overridden by anything else, and an appearance that you apply to the assembly overrides everything else.

In Figure 5.15, the DisplayManager shows the colors and appearances listed by history, which refers to the order in which they were added to the model. Figure 5.22 shows the appearances sorted by hierarchy, using the order established by Overrides. The Sort Order drop-down list allows you to select from History, Hierarchy, and Alphabetical sorting.

Appearances can be difficult to understand, but the best way to visualize them is to use the View Appearances tab of the DisplayManager, shown previously. The DisplayPane flyout from the FeatureManager is tempting, but it is incomplete. It does not show appearances applied to faces, because individual faces are not listed in the FeatureManager unless they are also bodies or features. It sounds complicated, right? Just use the View Appearances tab of the DisplayManager, and you will have access to appearances applied to your parts and assemblies.

FIGURE 5.21
Adjusting the display
properties in the
Appearances
PropertyManager

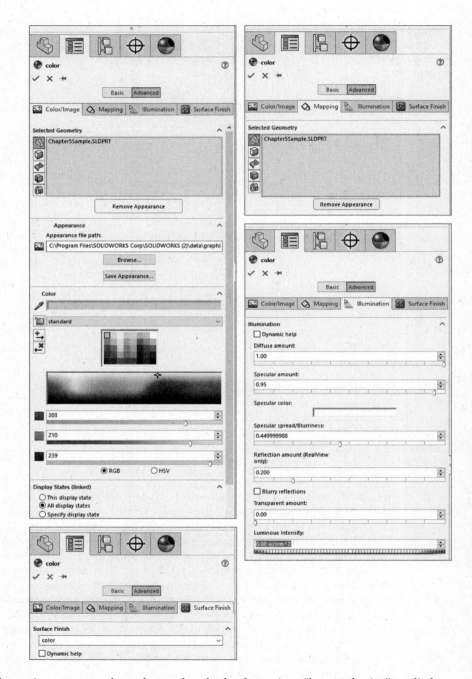

As an alternative, you can select a face and probe for the various "layers of paint" applied to it. You can do that by clicking the "beachball" icon on the context toolbar. You get a clear picture of the various "layers of paint" applied on the face you selected.

FIGURE 5.22
Sorting appearances and colors by hierarchy

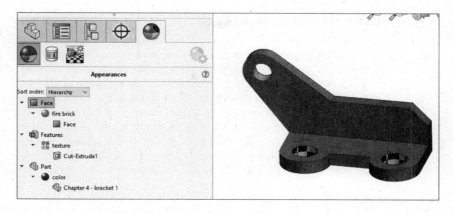

USING APPEARANCES WITH DISPLAY STATES

Display States allow you to have named sets of display settings for parts and assembliesl; which are covered in detail in this chapter. You also need to understand configurations (see Chapter 11, "Working with Part Configurations") to completely grasp the use of appearances with Display States. You can assign appearances to apply to all Display States or just to the current Display State. Display States, in turn, can be linked or unlinked to configurations, and some display properties, such as color, can be controlled by configurations. The control of appearances and colors for Display States and configurations is convoluted at best. This is a warning that mixing changes to these four items can result in colors that you can neither remove nor apply. It is difficult to say how much of this is due to bugs and how much is due to convoluted logic and too many sources of control. You can control the setting for the Display State to which an appearance change applies. You do this in the Display States panel at the very bottom of the Appearances PropertyManager.

FIGURE 5.23
Controlling appearances with Display States

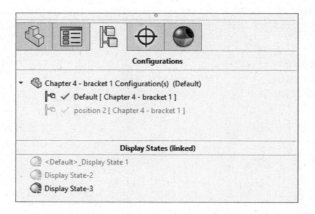

You can find the Display States interface at the bottom of the ConfigurationManager, as shown in Figure 5.23.

REMOVING APPEARANCES

You can think of multiple appearances applied as overrides within the part as an old chair with many layers of paint. In this case, you can remove those layers of paint one by one until you get down to the base material, which in this case is the default material: white plastic.

Look at Figure 5.24. Notice the red X to the right of each entity—face, feature, body, and part—and another one at the bottom. Each red X enables you to remove one or more layers of paint from this part. You can remove any appearance applied at any level just by clicking the red X. Clicking the bottom red X removes all the overrides (all the face, feature, body, part, and other colors that have been applied) and assigns the default appearance for that part. You may want to open this part from www.wiley.com/go/mastersolid, because the book is in black and white, and does not convey color well. The part name is Chapter 5 - bracket override.sldprt.

FIGURE 5.24
Removing appearances
from a part

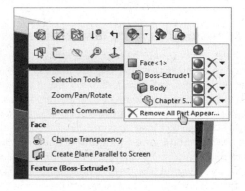

You can assign the default appearance in a part or assembly template by saving it with a name reflecting the material. As an alternative, you can reassign it in an existing part. To assign or reassign the appearance, open the Appearances, Scenes, And Decals tab in the Task pane, find an appearance that you like, and right-click it. Figure 5.25 shows the menu that appears.

FIGURE 5.25
Assigning a default
appearance

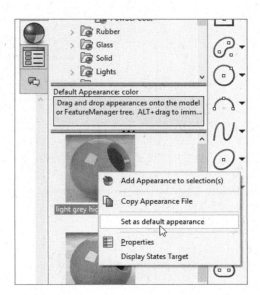

To save this appearance to a part template, assign the default appearance in an empty part document with settings that you want to use, set the default appearance, and save the empty part as a part template with a name indicating the appearance. You may also want to assign a corresponding material.

Using Decals

Decals are images applied to a part without rendering software. All decals used in a model are listed in the Decal area of the DisplayManager. To apply a decal, you can use the Appearances, Scenes, And Decals tab of the Task pane to access the stock or sample images, or you can right-click in the open area of the Decals DisplayManager and select Add Decal. This brings up the Decals PropertyManager, shown in Figure 5.26.

FIGURE 5.26

Working with the Decals PropertyManager

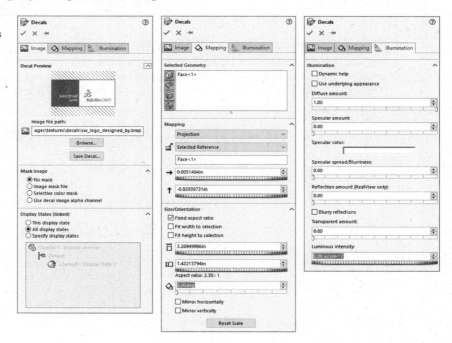

You can use *.bmp, *.jpg, *.tif, and *.png images as decals in SolidWorks. The images can be mapped onto flat, cylindrical, or spherical surfaces. You can use masks or images with an alpha channel to create transparent parts of the decal. You can also select a color of the image to set to transparent. Only *.tif and *.png images can use alpha channel transparency.

You can size, position, and rotate the decal on the screen with handles, as shown in Figure 5.27. You can use any of the corner nodes on the image to resize the decal. Dragging anywhere inside the image border moves the decal, and dragging the orange ring around the image rotates it. Decals can also emit light.

FIGURE 5.27
Sizing and positioning
the decal

Using Scenes, Lights, and Cameras

Scenes, lights, and cameras are important for visualing and rendering. Rendering is not covered in this book, because PhotoView 360 and SolidWorks Visualize are not part of the SolidWorks Standard package. The Scene, Lights, And Cameras DisplayManager is shown in Figure 5.28.

FIGURE 5.28
Using the Scene, Lights,
And Cameras
DisplayManager

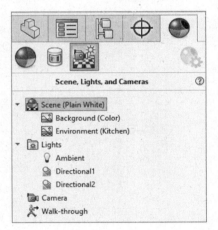

CONTROLLING SCENES

In SolidWorks, a scene is composed of three things: a background, which may be an image, a gradient, or a color; a floor, on which shadows and reflections are cast; and an environment, which is a wraparound 3D image (*.hdr or *.hdri—high dynamic-range image) that provides light to the model in a rendering and will reflect on the model if the model is a highly reflective material. If the environment is hidden, you see only the background. You can also hide the floor so there are no shadows or reflections, and the model will appear to hang in space.

Be aware that the small, square image shown for each scene in the Task pane is a thumbnail rendering of the scene and does not reflect how the scene will look in the graphics window. For most of this book, I have used the Plain White scene.

Floors and environments appear only when you do a rendering. If you want to remove shadows from the modeling window while you work, use the View Settings icon in the Heads-Up View toolbar to do this. This is shown in Figure 5.29.

FIGURE 5.29
Turning off shadows in
the modeling window

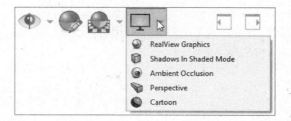

RealView Graphics

Shadows In Shaded Mode

Ambient Occlusion

Perspective

Cartoon

When you are using Real View Display, you can take advantage of a special setting called
Ambient Occlusion. With this combination, the SolidWorks model can throw shadows on itself,
and holes in the model appear in shadow. It gives some of the effect of a rendering, but it is just
the RealView display.

Ambient Occlusion has some limitations; for example, it does not show shadows on the part
while rotating, only when you stop rotating the view (unless you use Draft Quality Ambient
Occlusion, found at Tools ➤ Options ➤ Display). It also only works when in Shaded mode (with
or without edges).

Figure 5.30 shows a part with the various Ambient Occlusion settings. Ambient occlusion
does slow down the graphics performance of SolidWorks, but it can also help a part look more
realistic without you having to take the time to do a rendering. Depending on your graphics card
and workstation, Real View, Ambient Occlusion, and other advanced graphics settings may or
may not noticeably affect display calculation time. It is best practice, of course, to work without
these advance settings, unless they do not affect performance.

FIGURE 5.30
This Ambient Occlusion
scene gives more
realistic shadows
without rendering.

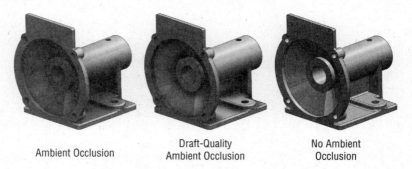

Ambient Occlusion

Draft-Quality
Ambient Occlusion

No Ambient
Occlusion

If you want to turn off reflections on the floor while modeling, you can apply a Basic scene or
turn off the reflective floor in the Scene PropertyManager, as shown in Figure 5.31. From here
you can also perform other common tasks, such as aligning the floor with a different plane,
offsetting the floor, and adjusting the brightness of the scene.

To apply a scene to a document, you can use the Appearances, Scenes, And Decals tab of the
Task pane; expand the Scenes heading; choose from Basic, Studio, or Presentation scenes; and
double-click or drag the scene into the graphics area. Note these differences between Basic,
Studio, and Presentation scenes:

◆ Basic scenes use only a background color.

◆ Studio scenes use a gradient background.

◆ Presentation scenes use an HDRI image, so the image rotates with the part as you rotate the view.

FIGURE 5.31
The Scene
PropertyManager
allows you to turn off
the reflective floor
while modeling.

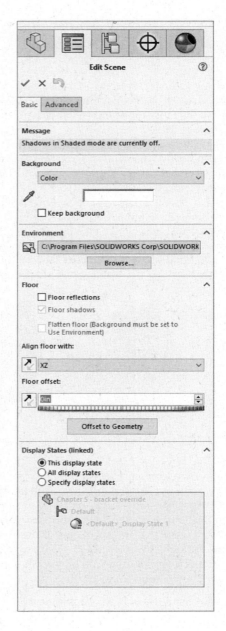

SolidWorks scenes can be either document or system property. Document property is the default. This means that each document can have a different scene, and the scene will travel with the document when opened by different users. You can override the default with a system option, Tools ➤ Options ➤ Colors, and change the Background Appearance setting to Plain, Gradient, or Image, which gives control of the scene to the local computer. When a document that has been saved with a document scene is opened on a computer set to use system scenes, the system setting overrides the document setting.

If you right-click on the Scene folder in the SceneManager, SolidWorks will prompt you with a message to change any system scene setting to the document scene.

TURNING ON THE LIGHTS

All models have ambient light. (If there were no light, you wouldn't be able to see the model.) Additional light types are Directional, Point, Spot, and Sunlight. You can add lights by right-clicking the Lights folder in the DisplayManager and selecting one of the new light options shown in Figure 5.32.

FIGURE 5.32
Adding lights
to the scene

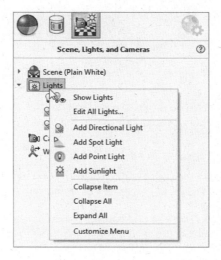

The light appears as an icon in 3D space, which you can drag around. You can also use the PropertyManager for editing the light to key in a specific XYZ location for the light source or direction. Lights added to the scene can be turned on or off in SolidWorks.

TIP   To use a combination of rotating the view and moving the light icon in 3D space, you can use the Lock To Model option so that the light moves with the model when you rotate the model.

The Ambient setting raises the overall brightness of the part, the Brightness setting refers to just the light, and the Specularity slider controls how lights shine or create "hot spots" on curved faces of models. You can even edit the color of a light to give a part a two-tone effect.

Lighting effects are most dramatic on curved parts. This is why adding even small fillets to a rectangular model can help make the part look more realistic for presentation purposes. Figure 5.33 compares a model with filleted edges to a model with perfectly sharp edges. The model with the fillets is also displayed with Real View and Ambient Occlusion to help it look more realistic.

FIGURE 5.33
Demonstrating the difference between the appearance of a part with fillets and a part with sharp corners

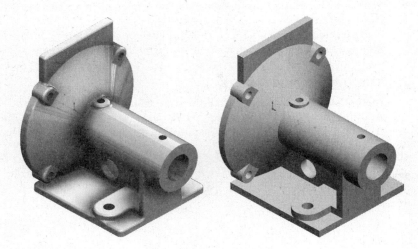

Materials can also be set up to emit light, for the situations where you might want to have a light bulb, LED panel, or a car taillight in the model.

WORKING WITH CAMERAS

You create cameras through the RMB menu on the Scene, Lights, And Cameras DisplayManager, as shown in Figure 5.34. When you add a camera, an interface displays in the PropertyManager, as shown in Figure 5.35.

In this interface, you can position the Camera object by dragging the Triad. To resize the Field Of View box, use the controls in the Field Af View panel in the PropertyManager. In the graphics window, you can use the left panel to target and position the camera, while the right panel shows the view through the camera.

You get the most lifelike perspective from a lens setting of about 50 mm. Shorter distances produce wide-angle or fish-eye lens effects. Larger settings make it look like a telephoto lens. It should be noted that perspective within SolidWorks works much differently. Within SolidWorks, the perspective setting is based on how many object lengths you are away from the model. For example, if a model is approximately 2 feet tall, you would set your perspective as multiples of 2, so three model lengths would be 6 feet.

The Depth of Field panel of the Camera PropertyManager is not shown, because it requires that PhotoView be installed. Depth of field can make objects outside of the focus area slightly out of focus, which can greatly add to the realism of renders.

FIGURE 5.34
Adding a new camera
with the Camera
PropertyManager

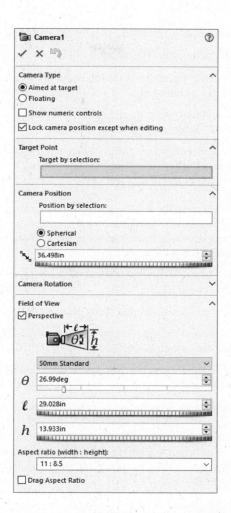

FIGURE 5.35
Positioning a camera
with split windows

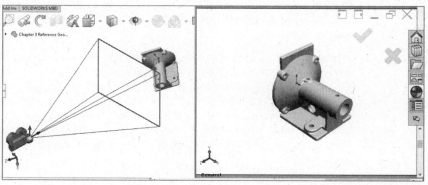

You can use three methods to switch the graphics window to the Camera view:

◆ Access the View Orientation dialog box by pressing the spacebar.

◆ The View Orientation dialog has a Camera View icon. The icon appears only if there is a camera in the model.

◆ As an alternative, go through the RMB menu on the camera in the Lights, Cameras, And Scene folder in the FeatureManager.

Be aware that there are two separate tools: Camera View and View Cameras. They look almost identical, except that View Cameras has a small eye in one corner of the icon. View Cameras allows you to see the placement of the camera; Camera View allows you to see what the camera sees.

When you switch the view to the Camera view, the regular Rotate View command does not function. Rotating the view means moving the camera. You can move the camera by editing the Camera properties, you can reposition the camera by dragging the Triad, or you can rotate the view while looking through the camera using the Turn Camera tool.

Camera View: This views the model through a camera. You can use cameras for these purposes:

◆ View the model from a particular point of view.

◆ Create renderings with perspective and depth-of-field (focus) blur. This feature is available only when PhotoView 360 is installed.

◆ Animate the position and target of the point of view in an animation. This feature is available only when a Motion Study is active.

◆ Create a view inside a cavity or other occluded area.

Turn Camera: This enables you to rotate the camera view when looking through the camera without editing the Camera properties. You must be looking through the camera and it must be unlocked for this to work. Dragging with the MMB does the same thing if the camera is unlocked.

Draft Quality HLR/HLV: This toggles between low-quality (draft) and high-quality edge Hidden Lines Removed (HLR) or Hidden Lines Visible (HLV) display. This setting affects display speed for complex parts or large assemblies. When in Draft Quality mode, edge display may be inaccurate.

Perspective: This displays the model in perspective view without using a camera. If you want to create a perspective view on a drawing, you must create a custom view in the View Orientation dialog box with Perspective selected. You can adjust perspective through View ➤ Modify ➤ Perspective by adjusting the relative distance from the model to the point of view. Relative distance is measured by the size of the bounding box of the model; therefore, if the model fits into a box roughly 12 inches on a side and the perspective is set to 1.1, the point of view is roughly 13 inches from the model. For more accurate perspective, you can use a camera.

CAUTION   Perspective view and sketching do not work well together. Sketches and dimensions look distorted and incorrect with Perspective turned on. I recommend disabling perspective view when sketching.

USING REALVIEW

RealView is the display technology behind the fancy appearances of SolidWorks models, such as ambient occlusion, reflective materials, and shadows. The reflections and lighting depend on RealView. If you turn off RealView or if you don't have hardware that supports it, you can't get the great displays. RealView does not affect rendering, just the live display. Check the system requirements listed on the SolidWorks website for information about whether your video card supports RealView.

You can even use RealView as a diagnostic tool for smooth transitions between surfaces because RealView appearances apply a reflective surface to a part and then apply a reflective background. This is essentially what the Zebra Stripes functionality is doing, but Zebra Stripes applies a specific reflective background to make examining curvature continuity across edges more straightforward.

You can turn RealView on or off by using the shiny sphere icon in the View Settings of the Heads-Up View toolbar. If this icon is grayed out, your system is not equipped with an appropriate RealView-capable graphics card.

The Display Pane

The Display pane flies out from the right side of the FeatureManager and displays a quick list of which entities have appearances, transparency, shown/hidden assigned. It also shows hidden parts or bodies for assemblies and multibody parts. The Display pane is shown in Figure 5.36.

FIGURE 5.36
The Display pane allows you to control display elements of your SolidWorks model.

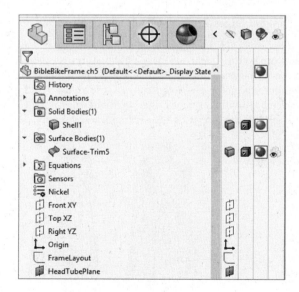

This tool to some extent duplicates the DisplayManager, but it also provides a quick summary of most of the display information, including Wireframe/Shaded display mode, transparency, hide/show state, and color. It works in both parts and assemblies, and it's a highly valuable tool. Between the DisplayManager and the Display pane, you can easily manage one of the most confusing areas of the SolidWorks software: Appearances.

Applying Color Automatically to Features

You can use the settings found at Tools ➢ Options ➢ Document Properties ➢ Model Display to automatically color certain types of features with specific colors. For example, you can color all Shell features red as you create them.

This function has worked intermittently for many years. For example, you can assign Boss features to always be red, and that works. You can assign surface features to always be yellow, and it works for Extrude, Revolve, Planar, Offset, Loft, and Sweep surfaces, but not for Boundary, Fill, or Ruled.

Using Edge Display Settings

Earlier in this chapter, I discussed the Shaded With Edges display style. Sometimes this method is useful to see the breaks between faces, especially fillets. It is especially useful in assemblies when parts are different colors.

Taking this one step further, you can also utilize the tangent edge settings. These settings are found in the View➢ Display menu and also in the Heads-Up View toolbar. These are the settings:

Tangent Edges Visible: This setting displays tangent edges as solid lines, just like all other edges.

Tangent Edges As Phantom: This setting displays tangent edges in a phantom line font.

Tangent Edges Removed: This setting displays only nontangent edges.

The Tangent Edges Removed setting leaves parts looking like a silhouette. I prefer the Phantom setting because I can easily distinguish between edges that will actually look like edges on the actual part and edges that serve only to break up faces on the model. The Tangent Edges Visible setting conveys no additional information and is the default setting. Figure 5.37 shows a sample part with Tangent Edges as Phantom, Tangent Edges Visible, Tangent Edges Removed, and Shaded (no tangent edge settings), respectively.

FIGURE 5.37
Samples of the tangent edge settings

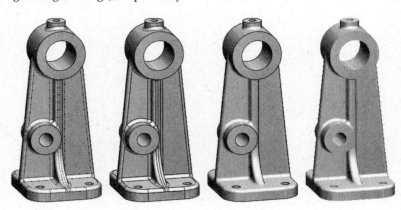

Tutorial: Applying Visualization Techniques

Visualization is a key factor when you're working with SolidWorks software. Whether you are presenting a design to customers or management, or you are simply checking a design, being able to see the model in various ways is important. This tutorial guides you through using several tools and techniques.

1. If the part named Chapter5Sample.sldprt is not already open, open it from the download materials for this chapter. If it is open and changes have been made to it, choose File ➤ Reload ➤ OK.

2. Practice using some of the controls for rotating and zooming the part. In addition to the View Toolbar buttons, you should also use Z and Shift+Z (Zoom Out and Zoom In, respectively), the arrow keys, and the Ctrl+arrow, Shift+arrow, and Alt+arrow combinations.

3. Use the MMB to select a straight edge on the part, and then drag it with the MMB. This rotates the part about the selected entity. Also apply this technique when selecting a vertex and a flat face.

NOTE The technique described in step 3 works only when Rotate About Scene Floor is disabled.

4. Select the name of the part at the top of the FeatureManager.

5. Click the Edit Appearance button from the Heads-Up View toolbar at the top of the graphics window.

6. Click the color you want in the Favorite panel. The model should change color. If you click and drag the cursor over the colors, the model changes color as you drag over each new color. You can also drag appearances from the Task pane. Figure 5.38 shows interfaces for both methods.

7. If the Color panel is not expanded, click the double arrows to the right to expand it. Select the colors you want from the continuous color map. Again, click and drag the cursor to watch the part change color continuously.

8. Create a swatch. In the Favorites panel, select the Create New Swatch button and call the new swatch color file **BibleColors**.

9. Select a color from the Color Properties continuous map; the Add Selected Color button becomes active. Clicking the button adds the color to the swatch palette. You can add several colors to the palette to use as favorites later.

TIP You can access these colors again later by selecting BibleColors from the drop-down list in the Favorites panel. You can transfer the colors to other computers or SolidWorks installations by copying the file BibleColors.slddclr from the <SolidWorks installation directory>\ lang\<english or your installed language> folder.

10. In the Appearance panel, move the Transparency slider to the right and watch the part become transparent.

FIGURE 5.38
Color PropertyManager
and the Appearances
Task pane

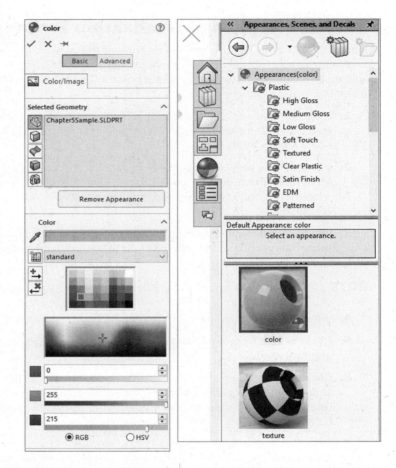

11. To prevent the Appearance window from closing after every change, click the pushpin at the top of the window.

12. Click the green checkmark icon to accept the changes. Note that with the pushpin icon selected, the window remains available.

13. Expand the flyout FeatureManager in the upper-left corner of the graphics window, as shown in Figure 5.39, so all the features in the part are visible.

14. Select the features Extrude1, Fillet7, and Fillet6 from the FeatureManager so they are displayed in the Selection list of the Color FeatureManager. Select a color from the BibleColors swatch palette that you just created.

15. Click the checkmark icon to accept the changes and clear the Selection list.

16. Select the inside face of the large cylindrical hole through the part, and assign a separate color to the face.

FIGURE 5.39
The Flyout
FeatureManager

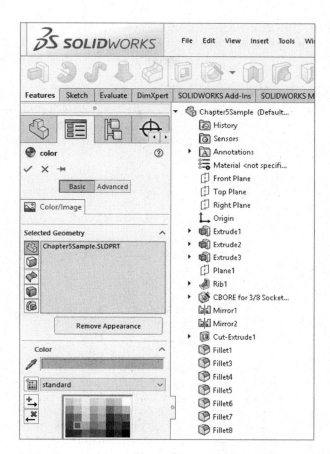

17. Click the checkmark icon to accept the changes, and click the red X icon to exit the command.

18. Expand the Display pane (the upper-right area of the FeatureManager). You should see color and transparency symbols for the overall part and color symbols for three features. There is no indication of the face color that is applied.

19. Remove the colors. Open the Appearances window again, reselect the three features (Extrude1, Fillet7, and Fillet6), and click the Remove Color button below the Selection list. Do the same with the colored face of the cylindrical hole. Return the part transparency to fully opaque.

20. Click the checkmark icon to accept the changes.

21. Change the edge display to Shaded (without edges). Then change to a Wireframe mode. Finally, change back to Shaded With Edges.

22. Use the Display Style drop-down in the Heads-Up View toolbar to cycle through the edge display options.

TIP   Using the Tangent Edges as Phantom setting is a quick and easy way to look at a model to determine whether face transitions are tangent. It does not help to distinguish between tangency and curvature continuity; you need to use Zebra Stripes for that.

23. Switch back to Shaded display.

24. If you do not have a RealView-capable computer, skip this step. Ensure that the RealView button in the View toolbar is depressed. Click the Appearances/Scenes tab on the Task pane to the right of the graphics window. Expand Appearances ➤ Metal ➤ Steel; in the lower pane, scroll down to the Cast Carbon Steel appearance.

25. Turn the part over, select the bottom face, and drag and drop the appearance from the Task pane. Apply the appearance just to the bottom face using the pop-up toolbar that appears. The rest of the part should retain the semireflective surface, as shown in Figure 5.40. Click the checkmark icon to accept the change.

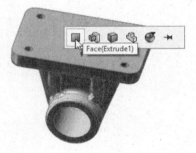

FIGURE 5.40
Applying an appearance
to a face

26. Click the Section View button on the View toolbar. Drag the arrows in the middle of the section plane back and forth with the cursor to move the section dynamically through the part, as shown in Figure 5.41. You can also rotate the section along various axes. Play around with this to get a feel for the capabilities of the command.

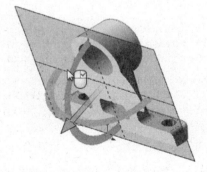

FIGURE 5.41
Applying a section view
to a model

27. Select the check box next to the Section 2 panel name, and create a second section that is perpendicular to the first.

28. Click the green checkmark icon to accept the section. Notice that while in the Section View PropertyManager, the RealView material does not display, but after you close the dialog box, RealView returns.

VIDEO   For more tutorial-based information on working with visualization tools, see the video tutorials included with the download data from Wiley for this chapter.

The Bottom Line

Visualization is one of the most important tools in SolidWorks. Visualization is a key function of the SolidWorks software. You will use these tools multiple times an hour and, in some cases, constantly throughout the day. Visualization can be an end to itself if you are showing a design to a vendor or client, or it can be a means to an end if you are using visualization techniques to analyze or evaluate the model. In both cases, SolidWorks presents you with an astounding list of tools to accomplish the task. The tools range from the analytical to the cosmetic, and some of the tools have multiple uses.

Master It   Practice using the keyboard and mouse display controls, including the arrows and modifier keys. Access the Orientation box with Ctrl+spacebar and manipulate the view using each of these tools.

To become acquainted with the names of all the tools on toolbar, use the mouse to hover over the Heads-Up View toolbar. Make sure to look at all the drop-downs and flyouts.

Master It   Use the DisplayManager and the Task pane to access all of the information and tools to apply appearances and visual properties to your model. Make sure to use the DisplayPane flyout from the FeatureManger to have quick access to appearances applied to your part.

Master It   Acquaint yourself with all of the settings available in Tools ➢ Options ➢ Colors and ➢ Display. Don't forget the settings under Tools ➢ Options ➢ Document Properties ➢ Model Display. Create templates with the background and visual properties you want to use.

Part II

Building Intelligence into Your Parts

Chapter 6

Getting More from Your Sketches

Previous chapters described the basic tools for sketching. This chapter takes you to the next level and teaches you about more advanced sketch tools, as well as how to edit and manipulate sketches, and how to work with sketch text, sketch pictures, and sketch colors. By the end of this chapter (with a little practice to reinforce the tools and techniques), you should feel like you have mastered the topic of SolidWorks sketching and can handle almost any problem that is thrown at you.

IN THIS CHAPTER, YOU WILL LEARN TO:

◆   Edit sketch relations

◆   Copy and move sketch entities

◆   Use sketch pictures

◆   Use sketch text

◆   Use colors and line styles with sketches

◆   Use other sketch tools

◆   Sketch 3D

Editing Sketch Relations

Delete is not an editing option. In time, you'll find that this is good advice, even if you don't agree with it now. There are times to delete instead of editing, but you should delete only when it is necessary. Especially while learning, you should strive to at least know how to repair instead of delete in every situation. In my own work, I sometimes go to extreme lengths to avoid deleting sketch entities, in part to stay in practice, but also because when you delete sketch entities, dependent features may lose their references or *go dangling*. Because of this, even when you can use the Delete command instead of making edits, it is still good practice to edit instead. Deleting relations is not as critical as deleting sketch entities, unless the relations are referenced by equations or design tables.

Using Display/Delete Relations

Display/Delete Relations is the primary tool for dealing with sketch relations. It is particularly useful for sorting relations by the various categories shown in Figure 6.1. The capability to show sketch relations in the graphics window is nice; sorting them in a list according to their state makes this feature even more useful. To show the sketch relation symbols on the screen beside the sketch entities, use the View ➤ Sketch Relations menu selection.

FIGURE 6.1
The Display/Delete
Relations
PropertyManager

The sketch relations in the Display/Delete Relations dialog box can be divided into the following categories:

All In This Sketch: This shows all the relations in the active sketch.

Dangling: This shows only the dangling relations. Dangling relations appear in a brownish-green or olive color and represent relations that have lost one of the entities that drives the relation. You can repair dangling relations by selecting the entity with the dangling relation and then dragging the red dot onto the entity to which it should have the relation.

Overdefining/Not Solved: Overdefined relations are any set of conflicting instructions that are given to a sketch entity; they appear in red or yellow. If a line has conflicting relations, but it can still meet the requirements, it turns yellow. If the sketch relations cannot be solved, it turns red.

◆ When an overdefined situation exists as shown in Figure 6.2, all the relations and dimensions in a sketch often become overdefined. This can look like a daunting task to repair, especially when the entire problem is caused by a single relation. Do not automatically delete everything. Instead, try deleting or suppressing the last dimension or relation that was added, or any single relation that looks suspect. You can suppress a dimension by setting it to Driven in the right mouse button (RMB) menu, and you can suppress relations in the Display/Delete Relations PropertyManager.

FIGURE 6.2
An overdefined sketch

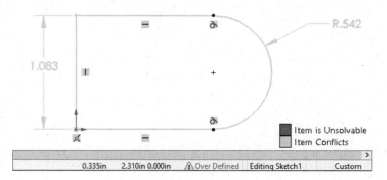

External: External relations connect with an entity outside the active sketch. This includes the part origin or any model edges. The term *external relations* can also signify any relations outside of the part.

Defined In Context: Any relation between features in one part in an assembly and another part is considered an in-context relation.

Locked (Broken): External relations (outside the part) may be locked or broken to increase speed and to lock out parametric changes. There is no advantage to breaking relations rather than locking them. Both are ignored, but locked relations can be unlocked; broken relations can only be deleted.

Selected Entities: Sketch relations are shown only for the selected sketch entities.

In-context design, also called *top-down*, as well as locked and broken relations are covered in detail in Chapter 20, "Modeling in Context."

CAUTION   Some of the relations listed in the Display/Delete Relations dialog box may be colored to signify the state of the relation. Unfortunately, colored relations are typically placed at the top of the list to attract attention; however, when you select them, they are always gray, and so the advantage of color-coding is always defeated for the first relation in the list. The only way around this is to select a relation other than the first one in the list. If there is only one relation in the list, you cannot see the state color.

A setting in Tool ➤ Options controls the display of errors. You can choose Tools ➤ Options ➤ FeatureManager to find an option called Display Warnings. There you can choose Always, Never, and All But Top Level. When a sketch contains sketch relations with errors, they display as warning signs on the sketch and will propagate to the top level of a part or assembly if you have selected the Always option.

Using Replace Entity

The Replace Entity tool enables you to swap out a particular sketch entity with all of the associated references further down the tree reconnected. When you extrude a rectangle into a solid, for example, all of the faces and edges that are created are given specific names so that the software can internally keep track of what references what. If you were to change one of the lines of the rectangle to an arc by making the line a construction line and drawing a new arc, then rebuilding the solid, any faces or edges that were built from the original line would now be different; and if any features like a fillet referenced the original edge, they would fail. Using Replace Entity makes sure that everything updates properly. It is easy to do, but in order for it to work, you have to actually use it. Here is a step-by-step procedure to help you see how the tool works:

1. Open a new part.

2. Sketch a rectangle on any standard plane, making sure one corner references the origin.

3. Extrude the rectangle to some depth.

4. Apply a Fillet feature to an edge parallel to one of the sketch lines, as shown in Figure 6.3.

FIGURE 6.3
Filleting an edge

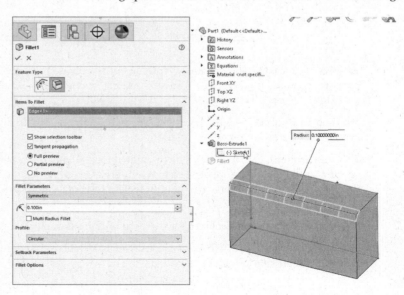

5. Expand the Boss-Extrude1 feature in the FeatureManager so you can see the Sketch1 underneath it.

6. Right-click Sketch1 and select Edit Sketch.

7. Sketch a three-point arc across the line that is parallel to the filleted edge, as shown in Figure 6.4. Notice the new arc is displayed as a thinner line than the lines of the rectangle.

FIGURE 6.4
Sketching the arc

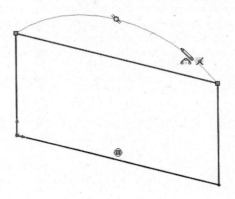

8. Manually convert the line under the arc to construction.

9. Use the Confirmation Corner to close the sketch. Notice that the Fillet feature fails.

10. Right-click Sketch1 and select Edit Sketch.

11. Convert the construction line back to a regular line.

12. In the menu, select Tools ➤ Sketch Tools ➤ Replace Entity.

13. Make sure the line is in the top box and the arc is in the bottom box, with the settings as shown in Figure 6.5.

FIGURE 6.5
Replacing a line
with an arc

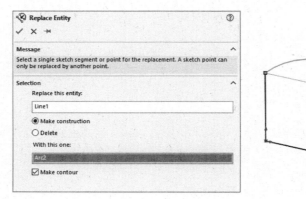

14. Exit the Replace Entity command and exit the sketch. Notice that the Fillet feature now rebuilds properly.

Using SketchXpert

The SketchXpert, shown in Figure 6.6, can help you to diagnose and repair complex sketch-relation problems. The Diagnose button at the top creates several possible solutions that you can toggle through using the forward and backward arrow buttons in the Results panel. The Manual Repair button displays all the relations with errors in a window where you can delete them manually.

By selecting the option at the very bottom of the dialog box—always open this dialog when a sketch error occurs—you can make the SketchXpert appear whenever a sketch error occurs. To display the SketchXpert manually instead of automatically, you can access it by right-clicking in any sketch or clicking in the Over Defined warning on the right end of the status bar.

FIGURE 6.6
The SketchXpert
dialog box

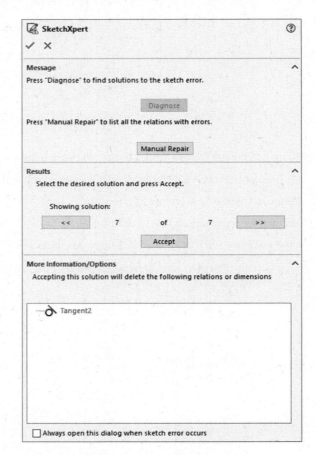

Getting More from Dimensions

Dimensions have some workflow enhancements that might not be obvious if you don't know about them. One of my favorites is dimensioning from centerlines.

Dimensioning from Centerlines

In Figure 6.7, I have dimensioned from a centerline. Notice that the cursor changes and displays an R, which indicates that the next dimension will be radial and will be made with respect to the centerline. This means that if I select the center of one of the holes, it will be dimensioned from the centerline. When placing the dimension that originally went to the centerline, if I had placed it on the other side of the centerline, SolidWorks would have given me a diameter dimension on the cursor displayed with a D (for diameter). Selecting the circle itself cancels the function because that implies a diameter, not a distance from something.

FIGURE 6.7
Dimensioning from centerlines

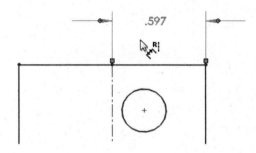

If you want to get out of the Radial or Diameter Dimension mode, press Esc on the keyboard to revert to normal dimensioning. This feature works like automatic baseline dimensioning.

Sketching with Numeric Input

To use the numeric input, first enable it with Tools ➤ Options ➤ Sketch ➤ Enable On Screen Numeric Input On Entity Creation.

With the Create Dimension Only When Value Is Entered setting turned on, when you sketch a rectangle, for example, SolidWorks automatically dimensions the length and height of the rectangle. The catch here is that you must use click+click sketching. Click-and-drag cannot be used with this technique. After you click the first corner of the rectangle, SolidWorks will put up a numeric entry field; and if you enter a number, it will automatically put dimensions on the rectangle and prompt you to edit one of them. You can then key in another dimension for the other side of the rectangle.

Working with Sketch Entities

SolidWorks offers several different tools to help you move sketch entities around in a sketch. In SolidWorks, I recommend keeping the sketch as simple as you can and creating patterns using feature patterns rather than sketch patterns. This section discusses the main tools for moving and copying sketch entities.

Moving, Rotating, Copying, and Scaling Entities

Move Entities Tool   The Move Entities tool enables you to move selected sketch entities by either selecting From and To points or by entering XY coordinates for the move. When the Keep Relations Option is unselected, the Move tool automatically detaches sketch segments whose endpoints are merged, as shown in Figure 6.8. If Keep Relations is selected, SolidWorks moves the entities and tries to maintain the sketch relations and merged points. All the tools have a pushpin icon in the interface. You can use the tool multiple times in succession when the pushpin icon is pushed in; tools with the pushpin are deactivated after one use if the pushpin icon is not pushed in.

FIGURE 6.8
Using the Move tool

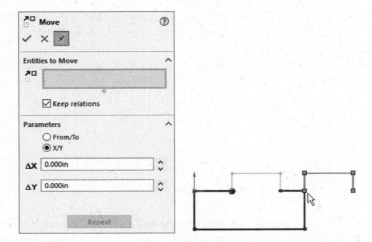

Rotate Entities Tool   The Rotate Entities tool rotates selected entities in a sketch in the same way that Move Entities works. You can drag the angle or enter it manually. The green check-mark icon is on the RMB, as shown in the cursor display in Figure 6.9.

FIGURE 6.9
Using the Rotate tool

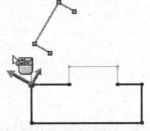

Keep Relations Option   The Keep Relations option does not actually keep any relations—it deletes the Horizontal and Vertical relations in the sketch, as shown on the left in Figure 6.8—but it does keep the merged endpoints, as shown on the right in Figure 6.8. This can be useful, especially considering how many sketch relations it would take to make a sketch move like this naturally.

Copy Entities Tool   The Copy Entities tool works exactly like the Move Entities tool, except that it copies instead of moving. The Copy Entities tool enables you to copy selected sketch entities by either selecting From and To points or by entering XY coordinates to place the copy. SolidWorks copies the entities and tries to maintain the sketch relations and merged points.

Scale Entities Tool   Scale Entities is one of those functions probably best left alone. This is because the results are erratic and unpredictable, particularly if there are dimensions on the sketch. This tool works on a selection of entities, particularly on an isolated selection that is not connected to other entities in the sketch. The PropertyManager for the Scale Entities tool is shown in Figure 6.10.

FIGURE 6.10
The Scale
PropertyManager

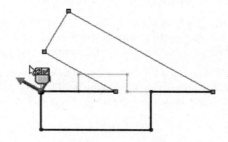

Modifying a Sketch

The Modify Sketch tool has been available in SolidWorks for a long time, but it has been superseded by some of the newer tools, such as Move Entities. However, it still has some unique functionality that is not covered by any other sketch tool. Modify Sketch works on the entire sketch rather than on selections within the sketch. It works best if there are no external relations between sketch entities and anything outside the sketch. It can also work on a sketch without the sketch being active. While most feature and tool interfaces have been moved to the PropertyManager, Modify Sketch still uses a dialog box (shown in Figure 6.11) that floats in the graphics window.

FIGURE 6.11
The Modify Sketch
dialog box

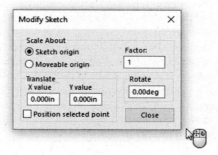

The Modify Sketch dialog box enables you to perform the following functions:

Scale About: The Scaling function in the Modify Sketch tool enables you to scale about either the part origin or the movable origin. The movable origin is shown with a black origin symbol with knobs on the ends of the axes and at the intersection. The movable origin can be moved and even snapped to entities that are internal or external to the sketch.

Translate: The Translate function of the Modify Sketch tool enables you to click and drag to move the entire sketch or to select a point and move it to a specific set of coordinates that you enter. If the sketch is dragged onto an external entity and picks up an automatic relation, then a message may appear saying that you can now use Modify Sketch only for rotating the sketch because there is an external relation.

Rotate: The Rotate function of the Modify Sketch tool enables you to position the movable origin to act as the center of rotation. You can rotate either by entering a rotation angle or by dragging with the right mouse button to rotate, as indicated by the cursor.

When you place the cursor over the knobs on the movable origin, the cursor symbols change to indicate the functionality of the RMB. These cursors are shown in action in Figure 6.12. The cursors enable rotation, mirroring about X, Y, or both simultaneously.

FIGURE 6.12
The Modify Sketch
tool's cursors

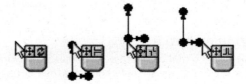

Copying and Pasting Sketch Entities

Probably the simplest way to copy sketch entities in a sketch is to select the entities and use Ctrl+C, Ctrl+V, or one of the many other methods available for this purpose (such as the RMB button menu, the Edit menu, or Ctrl+dragging). Copying with box dragging, lasso, Ctrl+A, or contour selection are all useful methods.

In addition to copying selected entities within an active sketch, you can also select a sketch from the FeatureManager and then copy and paste it to a selected plane or planar face (if you are not in a sketch to begin with). This creates a new sketch feature in the FeatureManager that is not related to the original, although it does maintain internal dimensions and relations. (External relations are not copied with the sketch.) This is particularly useful when setting up certain types of lofts that use several profiles that can be created from a single copied profile. Copying and pasting is a fast and effective method of putting sketches on planes.

A copied sketch is similar to a derived sketch (addressed later in this chapter), except that with a copied sketch, there is no link or internal relations; and with the derived sketch, the new and old sketches remain identical through changes to the original sketch.

Dragging Entities

If a selected set of sketch entities has no external relations, you can select it as a group and move it without distorting or resizing the sketch. For the best results with this technique, avoid dragging endpoints; drag an actual line.

Creating a Derived Sketch

A *derived sketch* is a parametrically linked copy. The original parent and derived sketches do not need to have any geometrical relation to one another, but when the parent sketch is changed, the dependent derived copy is updated to stay in sync.

To create a derived sketch, you can select a plane or planar face, Ctrl+select the sketch you want to copy, and then choose Insert ➤ Derived Sketch.

Once you create a derived sketch, you cannot change its shape or size; it works like a block of a fixed shape driven by the parent. However, you can change the position and orientation of the derived sketch. Figure 6.13 shows a derived sketch and its parent. Modify Sketch is a great tool to use for manipulating derived sketches that are not related to things outside the sketch, especially for mirroring or rotating.

FIGURE 6.13
A derived sketch and its parent

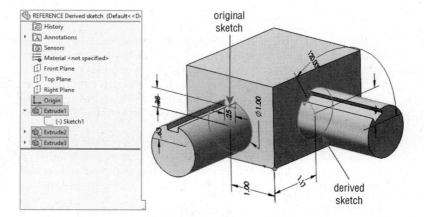

Using Sketch Pictures

Sketch pictures are images that are placed in a sketch. You can resize and rotate the images, give them a transparent background, trace over them, and suppress them. They display as children of the sketch in the FeatureManager. You can use these image types as sketch pictures: BMP, GIF, JPEG, TIFF, PNG, PSD, and WMF.

To bring a picture into a sketch, the sketch must first be active. Click Sketch Picture on the Sketch toolbar (it is not there by default, so you may need to drag it onto the Sketch toolbar from the Tools ➤ Customize ➤ Commands dialog box). You can also access this command by choosing Tools ➤ Sketch Tools ➤ Sketch Picture from the menu. You cannot use sketch pictures in assembly sketches, but you can use them in a part sketch in an assembly.

To change the size of a sketch picture, you can double-click it and drag one of the handles around the outside of the image. Refer to Figure 6.14 for the Sketch Picture PropertyManager. When the picture comes into the sketch, it is usually too big, having been sized at a ratio of 1 pixel to 1 mm. To size a picture accurately, you should include a ruler or an object of a known size in the image. If you cannot do this, the next best thing is to guess the size. Draw a line in your sketch and dimension it to approximately the size of something that is recognizable in the image, and then move the image by clicking and dragging it to lay the dimensioned sketch entity as close over the object in the image as possible.

FIGURE 6.14
The Sketch Picture
PropertyManager
with a scaling
tool enabled

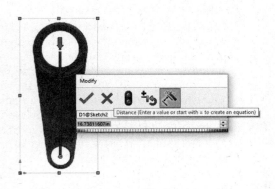

SolidWorks has also included scaling functionality. When you insert the picture, you will see a pink dot and a pink arrow connected by a blue line. Position the dot first and then the arrow; SolidWorks will provide a Modify box to allow you to specify how long the blue line should be.

You can rotate and mirror images using the Sketch Picture PropertyManager. Images are opaque, and you cannot see the model through them, but at the same time, you also cannot see the images through the model. They are like flat pieces of paper that are pasted to the model or hanging in space.

You can add transparency to images, either by selecting a color or by using the built-in transparency in the image file (alpha channels are available only in certain types of image files). When you select a color to be transparent, you also need to increase both the Matching Tolerance and the Transparency sliders, which are by default set to their minimum values.

CAUTION If a sketch picture has had user-defined transparency applied to it, and you double-click the picture, SolidWorks will automatically bump you into Eyedropper mode, which selects a color to be transparent. A single extra click in this mode can make a mess of your Sketch Picture transparency settings by changing the selected transparency color.

TIP Although the most common use for the sketch picture is as a tracing guide, you can use it for a variety of other purposes. For example, any sort of logo, decal, or display that is on a flat surface can be shown as a sketch picture.

BEST PRACTICE

Best practice for using sketch pictures is to put them in the Favorites folder or into a separate sketch near or at the top of the FeatureManager. Even though you can have sketch entities in a Sketch Picture sketch, I recommend keeping them in separate sketches. This is because when you use the sketch entities for an extrude or a loft guide curve, this sketch will be consumed under that feature, meaning the image will become buried somewhere in your model rather than being easily accessible at the top of the FeatureManager. Promoting these sketches to the Favorites folder will also ensure that they are always available right on the top of the tree

Using Three Views

When you're building a model from images, it is often helpful to have three or more images from orthogonal views, similar to re-creating a part from a 2D drawing. If you have a left view and a right view, it may be a good idea to put them on planes that are slightly separated so the images are not exactly on top of one another, which makes them both hard to see. Putting them on slightly offset planes means that one will be clearly visible from one direction and the other visible from the other direction.

Each sketch picture must be in a separate sketch. Figure 6.15 demonstrates the use of multiple sketch pictures to trace the outline of a vehicle, with the partially complete model shown with the images.

FIGURE 6.15
Using multiple
sketch pictures

Additionally, you can put multiple sketch pictures inside a single sketch. Both images will show up in the FeatureManager, and both can be displayed at the same time, although you may have difficulty if you want to put them on top of one another.

Compensating for Perspective

When taking digital photographs to be used as sketch pictures in SolidWorks, you have to consider how perspective affects the image. Perspective can make it difficult to size items in the foreground or background. If you are taking the pictures that will be used as sketch pictures, you can minimize the effects of perspective by standing farther away from the object and using zoom on the camera if possible.

Estimating Sharp Edges

When you are sketching an object, you usually draw theoretically sharp corners of the model. Real parts usually have rounded corners, so you may have to use your imagination to project where the 3D surfaces would intersect at an edge minus the fillets.

Reverse-modeling a part from images is not an exact science. It is better than not being able to put pictures into the sketch, but there is nothing about it that can be considered precise. Often, putting a ruler or size gauge in the image somewhere is useful.

Using Auto Trace

Auto Trace is an add-in that you can select by choosing the Tools ➤ Add-ins menu. Auto Trace is intended to trace between areas of contrast in sketch pictures, creating sketch entities. Activating the Auto Trace add-in activates a set of arrows at the top of the Sketch Picture PropertyManager. There is nothing to identify the functionality with the Auto Trace name.

Auto Trace works best with solid blocks of black and white in the sketch pictures. To achieve this, you may need to use image-processing software and reduce your picture to a two-color (black and white) bitmap, TIF, or PNG image. Even if this preprocessing gives perfect results, don't expect much from Auto Trace.

Using Stick Fonts

SolidWorks makes available the OLFSimpleSansOC Regular font for those times when you need a stick font in your sketch to drive CNC machinery.

Using Sketch Text

Sketch text uses TrueType fonts to create text inside a SolidWorks sketch. This means that any TrueType font you have can be converted to text in solid geometry; this includes Wingdings and symbol fonts. Keep in mind that some characters in certain fonts do not convert cleanly into SolidWorks sketches. Sketch text must still follow the rules for sketching and creating features such as closed contours. You cannot mix open and closed contours.

You can make sketch text follow a sketch curve. To space the text evenly along the curve, you can control character width and spacing, as well as overall size, by specifying points or actual dimensions. Sketch text can also be justified right, left, centered, and evenly, as well as reversed, rotated, and flipped upside down. Figure 6.16 shows the Sketch Text PropertyManager and some examples of sketch text options.

FIGURE 6.16
Examples of sketch text

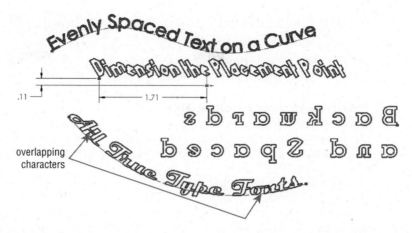

The icons in the Sketch Text PropertyManager are self-explanatory, other than the Rotated Text option; Rotated Text rotates individual letters (as shown in the *Dimension the Placement Point* text in Figure 6.16) and not the whole string of text.

You can use the Sketch Text tool multiple times in a single sketch to make pieces of text with different properties. Each string of text has a placement point located at the lower left of the text. This point can be given sketch relations or dimensions to locate the text.

If the text overlaps in places, as shown in Figure 6.16, you can correct this in a couple of ways. First, you can extrude it with the Merge option unselected, so each letter is created as a separate solid body and then manually merged later. You can also explode sketch text so it becomes simply lines and arcs in a sketch, which you can edit the same as any other sketch (not recommended). You can also adjust the Width Factor and Spacing settings. Or, you can extrude some letters in a separate feature so that if the features overlap, at least the characters don't overlap in a single sketch.

You can link the text to a custom property. This means that sketch text can be changed with configurations. (Configurations are covered in a later chapter.) The text used to extrude a feature can come from custom properties, which can be driven by a design table or directly through the Sketch Text PropertyManager.

PERFORMANCE

Sketch text can dramatically slow down the performance of your SolidWorks part. If you write an entire paragraph of text in a sketch and use that text to extrude a solid feature, you will likely notice that the part runs much more slowly. One way to avoid this is to suppress the feature and turn it on only when needed.

Using Colors and Line Styles with Sketches

Custom colors and line styles are usually associated with drawings, not sketches; in fact, they are most valuable when used for drawings. In sketches, this functionality is little known or used, but it's still of value in certain situations.

Working in Color Display Mode

The Color Display Mode button is found on the Line Format toolbar. In drawings, you can use the Color Display Mode button to switch sketch entities on the drawing between displaying the assigned line or layer color and displaying the sketch status color. It has exactly the same effect in part and assembly sketches.

When you select the button, the sketch state colors are used. When the button is not selected, any custom colors that you have applied to the sketch entities appear. If the button is not selected and you have not applied colors to the entities, the default sketch state colors are used.

You can use sketch colors for emphasis, to make selected sketch entities stand out, or to make sketches with various functions immediately distinguishable. Color Display mode has an effect only on an active sketch. Once a sketch is closed, it returns to the gray default color for inactive sketch entities.

Assigning Line Color

Line color enables you to assign color to entities in an active sketch. The Color Display Mode tool determines whether the assigned color or the default sketch status colors are used. Chapter 28, "Using Layers, Line Fonts, and Color," has more information on this functionality, especially related to drawings.

Using the Edit Sketch or Curve Color Tool

The Edit Sketch Or Curve Color tool can be found on the View toolbar. You can use the Edit Sketch Or Curve Color tool to assign color to an inactive sketch or to a sketch block to replace the default gray color. The color that you assign to sketches in this way displays only when the sketch is inactive. The sketches also follow the toggle state of the Color Display Mode button. For example, if the Color Display Mode button is selected, then inactive sketches display as gray. When the Color Display Mode button is not selected, then inactive sketches display in any color that you have assigned by using the Edit Color tool.

When you use this tool to color a sketch block, the block displays the color inside the active sketch. You cannot use the Line Color tool mentioned earlier to assign color to a block.

Assigning Line Thickness and Line Style

The Line Thickness and Line Style tools function independently from the Color Display Mode button, but they are still used only when the sketch is active. As soon as a sketch that contains entities with edited thickness and style is closed, the display goes back to the normal line weight and font.

To assign a thickness or a style, you can select the sketch entities to be changed, click the button, and then select the thickness or style. Although a single sketch entity may have only a single thickness or style, you can use multiple thicknesses or styles within a single sketch. Figure 6.17 shows a sketch with the thickness and style edited.

Line thickness and line styles are covered in more detail in the discussion of drawings in Chapter 30, "Creating Assembly Drawings."

FIGURE 6.17
A sketch with edited line thickness and line style

Using Other Sketch Tools

SolidWorks has lots of functionality that overlaps between multiple topics. The following tools could appear in other sections of the book, but I include them here because they will help you work with and control 2D sketches in SolidWorks.

Working with RapidSketch

RapidSketch is meant to help you easily change sketch planes. As you move a sketch cursor over flat faces of a model, the faces highlight to indicate that you can start a new sketch there. Each new sketch appears in the FeatureManager.

The workflow with this tool is that you start in one sketch with RapidSketch activated. Activate a sketch tool, move the cursor over a plane or face, and a dark plane will appear to indicate you can start sketching on that plane. To move to another plane, the sketch tool must still be active, but not be in-progress on an entity (nothing attached to the cursor). This option makes SolidWorks sketching work more like Solid Edge, where it's easier to change to a new sketch.

Adding Sensors

You can add sensors in the SolidWorks FeatureManager for parts and assemblies by right-clicking the Sensors folder and selecting Add Sensor. You can find the Sensors folder at the top of the FeatureManager. If you cannot find the Sensors folder, make it visible by choosing Tools ➤ Options ➤ FeatureManager, and make sure the Sensor folder is set to Show.

You are not limited to using sensors only when working with sketches; you can use them outside of sketches in parts and assemblies to warn you when various types of parameters meet various types of criteria.

Figure 6.18 shows the Sensor PropertyManager. You can create sensors for measurements, simulation data, or mass properties. I included sensors in this chapter due to the measurement options, which enable you to select a dimension and set a range of values or criteria for which you want to be notified. The dimension can be a driving (black) sketch dimension, a driven (gray) dimension on a sketch, or even a driven dimension placed directly on solid geometry.

FIGURE 6.18
The Sensor
PropertyManager

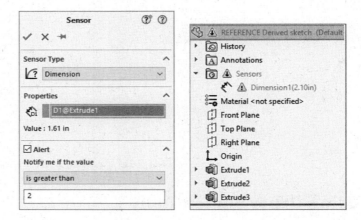

Figure 6.18 shows what happens when a sensor finds a condition that you asked it to notify you about.

In addition to turning sensor alarms on or off, you can suppress sensors when they are no longer needed or to improve performance.

Sensors are a great way to keep an eye on particular values, such as wall thickness or clearance between parts. You can use a sensor to monitor any value you want to monitor but don't drive directly.

Using Metadata for Sketches

Metadata in SolidWorks is nongeometrical text information attached to geometrical data. Metadata is particularly helpful as keywords in searches, in Product Data Management (PDM) applications, or as custom properties in drawing and tables. If you don't use metadata within your CAD documents, it can be easy to forget that it is there at all.

You can use the following items as metadata in SolidWorks files:

◆ Sketch and feature names

◆ Sketch and feature comments (access comments via the RMB menu)

◆ Custom properties

◆ Design Binder documents

◆ Tags for features (located in the lower-right corner of the status bar)

Metadata searches can be particularly useful in large assemblies or parts with long lists of features that you need to find or search through. You can conduct searches for metadata through the FeatureManager Filter at the top of the FeatureManager. The Advanced Search function in assemblies can also search metadata sources. SolidWorks Explorer is a good first-level data management solution that can search, display, and edit metadata and previews. Windows Explorer can also search properties and tags.

Creating Construction Geometry

In SolidWorks, the only construction geometry that can be created directly is the *construction line*. All other sketch entities can be converted to construction geometry by selecting the Construction Geometry option within the sketch entity's PropertyManager or by using the Construction Geometry toggle toolbar button.

SolidWorks terminology is inconsistent, because it sometimes refers to construction lines as centerlines. The two are really the same thing. *Centerlines* are used for revolved sketches and mirroring, but there is no difference between a centerline and a construction line in SolidWorks.

Construction geometry is useful for many different types of situations. I use it frequently for reference sketch data. You can make sketch relations to construction geometry, to create symmetry, and you can use it for layout sketches or many other purposes.

Sketching in 3D

The 3D sketch is an important tool for creating weldments (and many other features) in SolidWorks. 3D sketches can be challenging, but they are certainly manageable if you know what to expect from them.

Earlier chapters discussed the tools that are available for 2D sketches; next, I cover techniques for 3D sketching.

Navigating in Space

To start a 3D sketch, activate the 3D Sketch icon on the flyout under the 2D sketch icon; or, in the menus, go to Insert ➤ 3D Sketch. When drawing a line in a 3D sketch, the cursor and origin initially look like those shown in Figure 6.18. The large red origin is called the *space handle*, with the red legs indicating the active sketching plane. Any sketch entities that you draw lie on this plane. The cursor also indicates the plane to which the active sketching plane is parallel. In the XY graphic shown in Figure 6.19, the sketch is not required to be *on* the XY plane, just on an imaginary plane parallel to it.

FIGURE 6.19
The space handle and the
3D sketch cursor

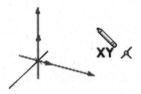

Pressing the Tab key causes the active sketching plane to toggle between XY, YZ, and ZX. The active sketching plane indication does not create any sketch relations; it just lets you know the orientation of the sketch entities that are being placed. If you want to create a skew line that is not parallel to any standard plane, you can do this by sketching to available endpoints, vertices, origins, and so on. If there are no entities to snap to, you will need to accept the planar placement, turn off the sketch tool, rotate the view, and move one end of the sketch entity.

The biggest challenge with 3D sketches is visualization. It can be tough to see if a line is coming out of the screen or is just a short line in another plane. An excellent tool to help you visualize what is happening in a 3D sketch is the Four Viewport view. This divides the screen into four quadrants, displaying the front, top, and right views in addition to the trimetric or isometric view. You can sketch or edit in any of the viewports, and the sketch will update live in all the viewports simultaneously. This arrangement is shown in Figure 6.20. You can easily access the divided viewport screen by using buttons on the Standard Views toolbar. You can also manually split the screen by using the splitter bars at the lower-left and upper-right ends of the scroll bar areas around the graphics window. These window elements are also described in Chapter 2, "Navigating the SolidWorks Interface."

FIGURE 6.20
The Four Viewport view

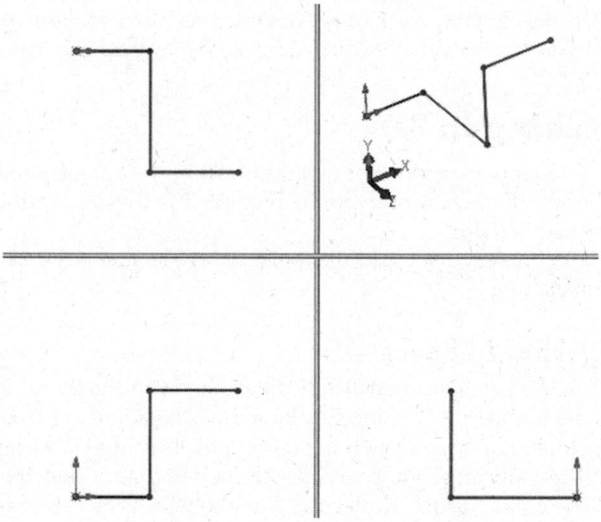

When unconstrained entities in a 3D sketch are moved, they move in the plane of the screen. This can lead to unexpected results when viewing something at an angle, moving it, and then rotating the view, which shows that it has shot off into deep interplanetary space. This is another reason to use the Four Viewport view, which enables you to see what is going on from all points of view at once.

Exploring Sketch Relations in 3D Sketches

Sketch relations in 3D sketches are not exactly the same as in 2D sketches. Relations are not projected into a plane in a 3D sketch the way they are in 2D. For example, an entity in a 2D sketch can be made coincident to an entity that is out of plane. This is because, to make the relation, the out-of-plane entity is projected into the sketch plane, and the relation is made to the projection. In a 3D sketch, coincident means coincident, with no projection.

Several relations are available in 3D sketches that are not found in 2D sketches, such as AlongX, AlongY, AlongZ, and OnSurface.

As a general caution, keep in mind that solving sketches in 3D is more difficult than it is in 2D. You will see more situations where sketch relations fail or they flip in the wrong direction. Angle dimensions in particular are notorious in 3D sketches for flipping direction if they change and go across the 180-degree mark. When possible, it is advisable to work with fully defined sketches and to be careful (and conservative) with sketch relations.

Using Planes in Space

It is possible to create planes directly in 3D sketches. These planes work like regular planes initially. Having planes in the sketch also enables planar sketch entities such as arcs and circles in 3D sketches. Sketches can be created on these planes, and the sketch will move with the plane, but the plane will also move with the sketch. Planes within 3D sketches can be confusing if you expect them to work like 2D sketches and planes.

Figure 6.21 shows the PropertyManager interface for creating 3D planes.

FIGURE 6.21
The 3D Planes
PropertyManager

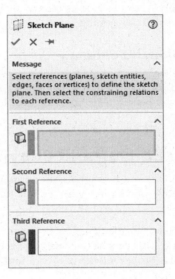

The confusing part is this: Say you create a vertical line on a plane in a 3D sketch. You can then angle the line, and the plane will rotate with it. There is no way to rotate the plane on its own unless you have some sketch geometry on the plane and cause that to rotate.

To open a sketch on a plane in a 3D sketch, double-click on the sketch or use the 3D Sketch on Plane tool. The plane is activated when it displays a grid. You can double-click an empty space to return to regular 3D Sketch mode. The main thing you give up with abandoning 3D sketch planes is the simplification of certain sketch entities such as arcs and relations.

The advantage of using planes within a 3D sketch is that you abandon the parent/child concept that you would otherwise embrace if you used a series of 2D sketches and 2D planes. In my opinion, 3D sketches are an incredibly useful tool; however, the 3D planes concept is not very well developed. I'm not ready to say it's dangerous, but it certainly is not fully thought out.

Using Planar Path Segments

Some path segments that are allowed in 3D sketches can be used only if they are sketched on a plane. These entities include circles and arcs and can include splines, although splines are not required to be on a plane. I've already mentioned that to sketch on a 3D plane (a plane created within the 3D sketch), you can simply double-click the plane.

To sketch on a standard plane or reference geometry plane, you can double-click the plane or Ctrl+click the border of the plane with the Sketch Entity icon active. The space handle moves, indicating that newly created sketch entities will lie in the selected plane.

Defining Dimensions

Dimensions in 2D sketches can represent the distance between two points, or they can represent the horizontal or vertical distance between objects. In 3D sketches, dimensions between points are *always* the straight-line distance. If you want to get a dimension that is horizontal or vertical, you should create the dimension between a plane and a point (the dimension is always measured normal to the plane) or between a line and a point (the dimension is always measured perpendicular to the line). For this reason, reference sketch geometry is often used freely in 3D sketches, in part to support dimensioning.

Using 3D Sketch Summary

Three-dimensional sketches are extremely powerful for many different applications. The problem is that they are also limited in some of their capabilities, and they do not work exactly like 2D sketches. You will benefit from knowing how to use 3D sketches at some point, even if it isn't every day.

Tutorial: Editing and Copying

This tutorial guides you through some common sketch-relation editing scenarios and using some of the Copy, Move, and Derive tools. Follow these steps to learn about editing and copying sketches:

1. Open the part named Chapter6 Tutorial1.sldprt from the download materials for Chapter 6. This part has several error flags on sketches. In cases where there are many errors, it is best to roll the part back and go through the errors one by one.

2. Right-click the name of the file at the top of the FeatureManager, click the Tree Display option, and select Show Flat Tree (Ctrl+T). This is a function that allows you to show the features in a straight history list, without features consuming sketches.

3. Drag the Rollback bar from just after the last fillet feature to just after Sketch3. Figure 6.22 shows before and after views for the rollback.

FIGURE 6.22
Rolling the part back
to Extrude3

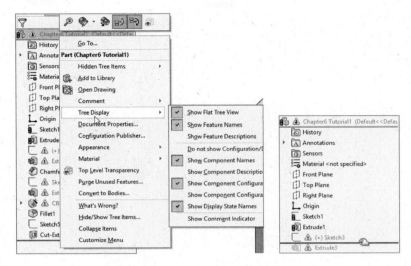

4. Edit Sketch3, and then Right-click in the white space and select Display/Delete Relations. Notice that all the relations conflict, but only one is unsolvable: the Equal Radius relation. This appears to be a mistake because the two arcs cannot be equal.

5. Delete the Equal Radius relation. Select the relation in red and click the Delete button in the PropertyManager. (You can also press the Delete key on the keyboard.) The sketch is still not repaired.

6. Click the green checkmark icon to close the Display/Delete Relations PropertyManager.

7. Right-click the graphics window and select SketchXpert (toward the bottom); then click Diagnose.

8. Using the double arrows in the Results panel, toggle through the available solutions. All the solutions except one remove sketch relations and leave the sketch underdefined. Accept the one solution that removes the dimension. This is shown in Figure 6.23. The sketch no longer shows errors in the graphics window, but it still does in the FeatureManager.

9. Close the sketch. Notice that the error flag does not disappear until the sketch has been repaired and closed.

10. Use the Rollback bar to roll forward to after Extrude2 and Sketch2. Figure 6.24 shows the tool-tip message that appears if you place the cursor over the sketch with the error. This message tells you that there is a *dangling* relation—a relation that has lost one of the entities.

11. Edit the sketch (see Figure 6.25). If you show the Sketch Relation icons again, the errors will be easier to identify. When you use Display/Delete Relations (Tools ➢ Relations ➢ Display/Delete Relations), the first two Coincident relations appear to be dangling. Clicking the relation in the Relations panel of the Display/Delete Relations PropertyManager shows that one point was coincident to a line and the other point was coincident to a point.

FIGURE 6.23
Using the SketchXpert
to resolve an overde-
fined sketch

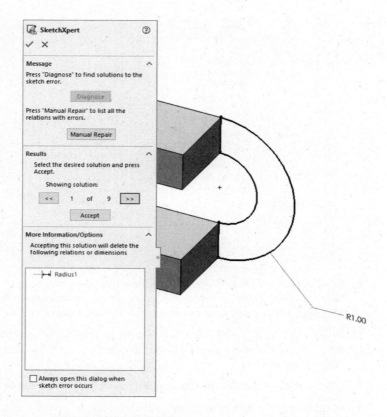

FIGURE 6.24
A tool tip provides a
description of
the error.

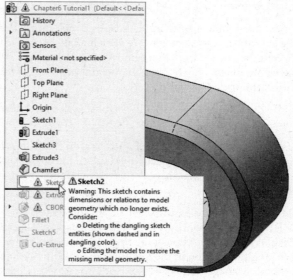

FIGURE 6.25
Fixing dangling errors

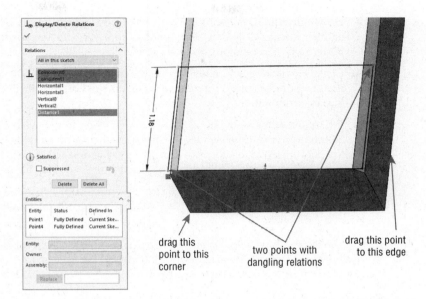

12. Click the name of the dangling entity in the Entities panel of the PropertyManager; then click the vertex indicated in Figure 6.25 in the Replace box at the bottom. When you have fixed the errors, exit the sketch and confirm that the flag is no longer on Sketch2.

An easier way to repair the dangling relation is to click the dangling sketch point once. It will turn red. Next, drag the red handle onto an entity to which you want to reattach the relation.

13. Exit the sketch.

14. Drag the Rollback bar to just before CutExtrude1 and expand the CBore feature. (This should be already flattened, but the Flat Tree view does not apply consistently to all types of features, which is a bug.) Edit 3DSketch1. This sketch is overdefined.

TIP Because selecting and deselecting the display of the sketch relations in the graphics window is a task that you will perform many times, this is a good opportunity to set up a hotkey for this function. As a reminder, to set up a hotkey, choose Tools ➤ Customize ➤ Keyboard, and in the Search box, type **relations**. In the Shortcut column for this command, select a hotkey to use.

15. Double-click any of the relation icons; the Display/Delete Relations PropertyManager will appear. Notice that one of the sketch relations is a Fixed relation. Delete the Fixed relation and exit the sketch.

16. Right-click anywhere in the FeatureManager and select Roll To End.

17. Click CutExtrude1 in the FeatureManager so you can see it in the graphics window, and then click a blank space to deselect the feature.

18. Ensure Instant 3D is disabled, then Ctrl+drag any face of the Cut feature, and drop it onto another flat face. The Ctrl+drag function copies the feature and the sketch, but the external dimensions and relations become detached.

19. Click Dangle in response to the prompt. This means that you have to reattach some dangling dimensions rather than re-create them. Edit the newly created sketch, which now has an error on it.

20. Two of the dimensions that went to external edges now have the olive dangling color. Select one of the dimensions; a red handle will appear. Drag the red handle and attach it to a model edge. Do this for both dimensions. The dimensions will update to reflect their new locations. Exit the sketch and verify that the error flag has disappeared.

21. Select Sketch5. Ctrl+select a flat face on the model other than the one that Sketch5 is on. In the menu, choose Insert ➤ Derived Sketch. You are now in a sketch editing the derived sketch.

TIP The sketch is blue, so you should be able to resize it, right? No, it doesn't work that way for derived sketches. Derived sketches are driven by their parent sketches. You can test this by dragging the large circle; it repositions the entire sketch as a unit.

22. Dimension the center of the large circle to two perpendicular edges of the model. Move the sketch over the solid geometry if necessary.

23. Drag the smaller circle and observe that it swivels around the larger circle. Create an angle dimension between the construction line between the circle centers and one of the model edges. Notice that the sketch is now fully defined.

24. Exit the sketch and look at the name of the derived sketch in the FeatureManager. The term Derived appears after the name, and the sketch appears as fully defined.

25. Right-click the sketch and select Underive Sketch. Notice that the sketch is now underdefined. The Underive command removes the associative link between the two sketches.

26. Close the file.

Tutorial: Controlling Pictures, Text, Colors, and Styles

This tutorial guides you through some of the miscellaneous functions in sketches. It also shows you what they are used for and how they are used. Follow these steps to learn how to control these items:

1. Open a new part using a template with inches as units. Open a sketch on the front plane and draw a construction line starting from the origin 12 inches down (negative Y), away from the origin.

2. Insert a sketch picture in this sketch. Use `Sketch Picture 1.tif` from the download material for Chapter 6. Use Tools ➤ Sketch Tools ➤ Sketch Picture.

3. Resize and reposition the image so the endpoints of the construction line are near the centers of the holes on the ends of the part. To move the image, just double-click it first and then drag it. To resize it, drag the corners—or use the Scale tool in the Sketch Picture PropertyManager if you prefer.

4. In the Transparency panel of the Sketch Picture PropertyManager, select the User Defined option, select the Eyedropper tool, and then click in the white background of the image. Make sure that the color field next to the Eyedropper tool changes to white.

5. Slide the Transparency and Matching Tolerance sliders all the way to the right, or type **1.00** in the number boxes.

6. Close the sketch and rename it **Sketch Image Front View**.

7. Insert the image `Sketch Picture 2.tif`, also from the website download, in a sketch on the right plane, and resize it to fit with the first image. Center it symmetrically about the origin. Also, set the transparency to the same setting as the first image.

8. Open a new sketch, also on the front plane, and draw two circles to match the features on the ends. Extrude them using a Mid Plane extrusion to match the image in the other direction (about 2.5 inches), as shown in Figure 6.26.

FIGURE 6.26
Using sketch pictures

9. Open another new sketch on the front plane and draw the tangent lines to form the web in the middle of the part. Use the automatic relations to draw the lines tangent to the two cylinders. It is easiest if you use the front view for this. Close the sketch to make a solid extrusion. Extrude this part 0.5 inches Mid Plane.

10. Open a new sketch on the face of the large flat web that you created in the previous step, and offset the arc edge of the larger circular boss by 2.10 inches.

11. Change the arc to a construction arc and drag its endpoints to approximately the position shown in Figure 6.27. The endpoints of the arc will be blue after you drag them. Give them a Horizontal relation and then dimension them.

    To create the 2.10 dimension as shown, select the arc and circle with the Dimension cursor while pressing down the Shift key.

FIGURE 6.27
Creating an offset arc

12. Choose File ➤ Properties. Make sure the Custom tab is active, and type **Sketch Text** in the first open box of the Property Name column. Make sure the Type is set to Text, and in the Value field, type **SolidWorks**. Click OK when you are finished.

13. Choose Tools ➤ Sketch Entities ➤ Text to initiate the creation of sketch text.

14. Select the construction arc to go into the Curves window.

15. Below the Text window, click the Link To Property button. Select Sketch Text from the Property Name drop-down list, then click OK. Select the Full Justify option and click the green checkmark icon to accept it.

16. Deselect the Use Document Font option, click the Font button, and then set the Units to 0.50 inches. Click the Bold button to make the text thicker. Click OK to exit the dialog box. Click the green checkmark icon to exit the sketch text, and then exit the sketch.

17. Extrude the text to a depth of .050 inches with 3 degrees of draft. The part at this point resembles Figure 6.28.

FIGURE 6.28
Creating extruded text

PERFORMANCE

Sketch text is a real performance killer. The more text that you use, the longer it takes to extrude. Draft on the extrusion adds to the time required.

18. Select the flat face on the other side of the part from where you just extruded the text, and open a sketch.

19. Select the face and click the Offset button to make a set of sketch entities offset to the inside of the face by .50 inches. Remember that you may have to reverse the offset to get it to work properly.

20. Open the Line Format toolbar (right-click any toolbar other than the CommandManager and select Line Format).

21. Select all the sketch lines, and change their color using the Line Color tool. Change the line thickness and the line style using the appropriate tools. The sketch should look something like Figure 6.29.

FIGURE 6.29
Using line thickness and
line style

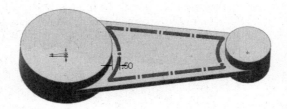

22. When you click the Color Display Mode tool, the colors will return to regular sketch colors. When you exit the sketch, the line weight and style will also return to normal.

Tutorial: Using Metadata

If you integrate the use of metadata into your company's modeling process, your SolidWorks models can be a resource for much more than just geometrical data. In this tutorial, discover the hidden treasure of extra information stored as metadata in this model.

1. Open the part from the downloaded material called `Chapter 6 - Dials Cover.sldprt`.

2. Check the Custom Properties in this file by choosing File ➢ Properties. Notice the Thickness and Process properties in particular.

3. Add a custom property called **Material**, type **Text**, and value **ABS**. The Custom Property interface is located at File ➢ Properties.

4. Check the comments in this part. Notice that a Comments folder exists near the top of the FeatureManager. Inside it is a list of the features for which I have written comments.

5. Add a comment by right-clicking the VarFillet3 feature, selecting the Comment flyout arrow, and clicking the Add Comment option. Click the Date/Time Stamp button and add a comment that includes the word Blend.

6. Check the tags for the part by clicking the small yellow tag in the lower-right corner of the status bar, click any feature, and then double-click in the Tags interface box.

7. Add a tag by selecting the Cut-Extrude1 feature and adding the tag **pilar**.

8. Right-click any item in the FeatureManager and select Go To from the options.

9. Type **37** in the box and click the Find Next button. The FeatureManager should highlight a feature near the bottom of the tree named Fillet37.

10. Click Fillet37 in the Feature Manager and select the Zoom To Selection tool. Zoom To Selection is a magnifying glass with an equal sign in it. The display zooms and pans to a fillet on one end of the part.

11. Right-click a face of Fillet37 on the model and select Go To Feature (In Tree), which selects the FeatureManager if necessary and scrolls to show Fillet37. This sequence of tools shows the importance and interdependence of feature names and the actual geometry.

12. Type the word **Thickness** in the filter at the top of the FeatureManager. Figure 6.30 shows the result. Notice how quickly the results appear. Notice also that the metadata item that caused the feature to show in the list can be shown in a tool tip by hovering the mouse over the feature.

FIGURE 6.30
Using the FeatureManager filter to search for metadata

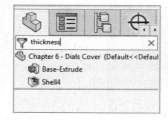

13. Click the X at the right end of the filter to restore the FeatureManager to its original state, and type the word **Pilar** instead. Now filter for Thermoform.

Tutorial: Sketching Calculator

Sketches can be used as geometrical calculators. Parametrics can be extremely powerful when you can define relationships between geometry. In this tutorial, you will set up a sketch to calculate the complex size and location relationships between the rings of a child's stacking toy.

1. Open a new part document with inch units.

2. Draw a triangle with a rounded top with the base centered on the origin, as shown in Figure 6.31. Do not use dimensions; use sketch relations and construction geometry to enable it to change symmetrically.

3. Draw three circles to the right of the pyramid. The bottom circle should be tangent to the bottom and the angled side of the pyramid. The middle and top circles should be tangent to the lower circle and the angled side of the pyramid, respectively. Figure 6.32 shows this process partially completed.

FIGURE 6.31
Build a triangle with a rounded top without dimensions.

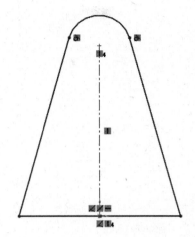

FIGURE 6.32
Sketching stacking rings

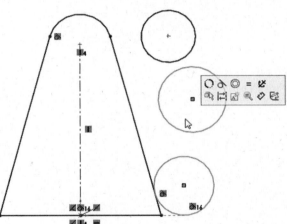

4. Put a diameter dimension on each circle. In the PropertyManager for each dimension, rename the dimension for `ring1dia@Sketch1`, `ring2dia`, and so on. This is shown in Figure 6.33.

5. Place a dimension from the center of the bottom circle to the construction line, and place the dimension on the far side of the construction line from the circle. This creates a diameter dimension.

6. Place a dimension for the middle circle in the same way as the bottom circle, but this time, make the dimension value about 75 percent of the first diameter.

7. Complete the sketch as shown in Figure 6.34, with all the dimensions and sketch relations.

FIGURE 6.33
Naming dimensions

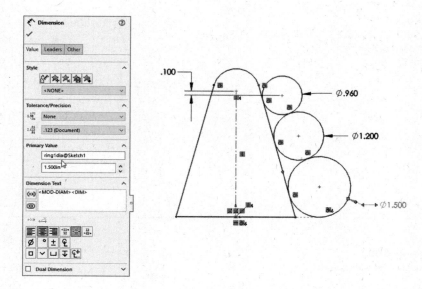

FIGURE 6.34
The finished sketch

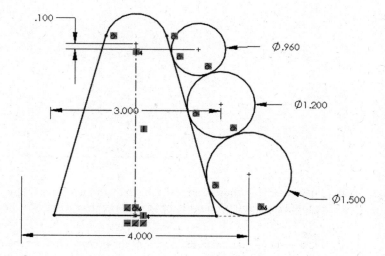

8. Make changes to the sketch to see which changes it allows and which it does not. Double-click dimensions and use the wheel in the middle of the Modify dialog box to apply changes smoothly. Try changing each dimension.

The Bottom Line

Edit sketch relations. Effectively using sketch relations is a fundamental skill that you need to have to be successful with SolidWorks. You will use them constantly to make sure your models behave predictably to change.

Master It   Open one of the sample parts from this chapter, show the flat tree, and edit each sketch. Make sure you understand what each sketch relation is doing.

Reverse engineer a simple part using digital images.   Take pictures from at least two sides of a simple object you can model using simple extrude features, trying to make the photos look like drawing views. Use the images as sketch pictures, align the edges on the photo with the X and Y of the sketch, and sketch over them.

Master It   Insert the photos into sketches and model with the image as a reference.

Create a wireframe representation of a chair from 3D sketches.   3D sketches are frequently used in many types of design. Getting some practice drawing lines in 3D space will help you gain command of these tools.

Master It   Start by creating the centerlines of the square members of a simple wooden chair.

Chapter 7

Modeling with Primary Features

This chapter helps you identify which features to use in which situations—and in some cases, which features to avoid. It also helps you evaluate which feature is best to use for a particular job. With some features, it is clear when to use them, but not for others. This chapter guides you through the decision-making process. I have split the list of SolidWorks features into two groups: primary features and secondary features. Primary features are, of course, the ones you use most frequently.

IN THIS CHAPTER, YOU WILL LEARN TO:

- ◆ Understand the details for extrudes

- ◆ Understand the details for revolves

- ◆ Understand some complex solid features

- ◆ Understand the different fillet types

Identifying When to Use Which Tool

I always try to think of alternative ways to do things. It is important to have a backup plan—or sometimes multiple backup plans—in case a feature doesn't perform exactly the way you want it to perform. As an exercise, I often try to see how many different ways a particular shape might be modeled and how each modeling method relates to manufacturing methods, costs, editability, efficiency, and so on. You may also want to try this approach for fun or for education. If you are familiar only with the standard half dozen or so most-used features, your options are limited. Sometimes, simple features truly are the correct ones to use, but using them because they are the only things you know is not always the best approach.

Using the Extrude Feature

Extruded features can be grouped into several categories, with extruded Boss and Cut features at the highest level. You can extrude closed-loop sketches, regions, and, in some cases, faces. You can extrude from a face, an offset, or a plane. Extrude features can also be made in one direction, two directions, or as a midplane. Draft is also an option with Extrude features.

CREATING A SOLID FEATURE

In this case, the term *solid feature* is used as an opposite of *thin feature*. A solid feature is the default when you extrude a closed-loop sketch. A closed-loop sketch fully encloses an area without gaps or overlaps at the sketch entity endpoints. Figure 7.1 shows a closed-loop sketch creating an extruded solid feature.

FIGURE 7.1
A closed-loop sketch and an extruded solid feature

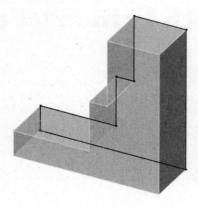

CREATING A THIN FEATURE

The Thin Feature option is available in several features, but it's most commonly used with Extruded Boss features. Thin features are created by default when you use open-loop sketches, but you can also select the Thin Feature option for closed-loop sketches or sketches with mixed types. Thin features are commonly used for ribs, thin walls, hollow bosses, and many other types of features that are common to plastic parts, castings, or sheet metal.

Even experienced users tend to forget that thin features are not just for bosses, but that they can also be used for cuts. For example, you can easily create grooves and slots with Thin Feature cuts.

Figure 7.2 shows thin features. In addition to the default options that are available for the Extrude feature, the Thin feature adds a *thickness* dimension, as well as three options to direct the thickness relative to the sketch: One-Direction, Mid-Plane, and Two-Direction. The Two-Direction option requires two dimensions.

You can create a cube from a single sketch line and a Thin Feature extrude. However, because they are more specialized in some respects, thin features may not be as flexible when the design intent changes. For example, if a part is going to change from a constant width to a tapered or stepped shape, thin features will not handle this kind of change. Figure 7.2 shows different types of geometry that are typically created from thin features.

FIGURE 7.2
Different types of
geometry created from
Thin Feature extrudes

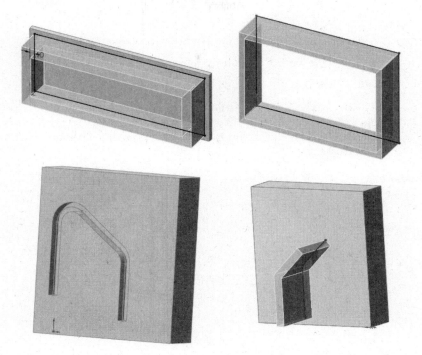

UNDERSTANDING THE WORKFLOW

SolidWorks offers multiple ways to do things in most functions. Most of the time, there is no one way that is better than the others. Having a lot of ways to do things makes remembering ways to do things easy, but sometimes it is hard to teach or learn because the options get overwhelming quickly. My suggestion is to find a way that works for you and use it. Learn other ways if something stops working for you. Here's an example.

The Extrude Feature workflow offers several options:

1. From within an active sketch with appropriate geometry, click the Extrude toolbar icon.

2. Set the Extrude Feature options.

3. Click OK.

Or:

1. With no sketch active, click the Extrude toolbar icon.

2. Select an existing sketch with appropriate geometry.

3. Set the Extrude Feature options.

4. Click OK.

Or:

1. With no sketch active, click the Extrude toolbar icon.

2. Select a plane on which to create a sketch to extrude.

3. Create your sketch.

4. Exit the sketch using the Confirmation Corner icon.

5. Set the Extrude Feature options.

6. Click OK.

Different types of features and geometry require different types of sketches, as shown in Figure 7.3. Some sketch types can't be used directly for making features at all, but may be used as reference. Closed, Open, and Nested contours are the types you will probably use the most in SolidWorks.

FIGURE 7.3
Sketch types

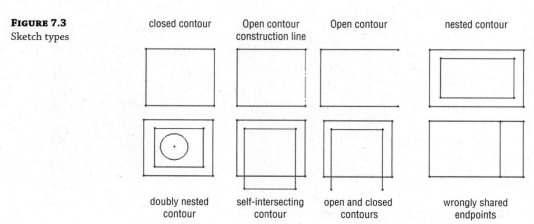

In addition to extruding 2D sketches, SolidWorks can also extrude 3D sketches. SolidWorks will automatically fill in the 3D sketch to form a solid face. You need to define a direction such as a plane (the plane normal is used as direction) or an edge, line, or axis, as shown in Figure 7.4.

FIGURE 7.4
Extruding from a 3D sketch

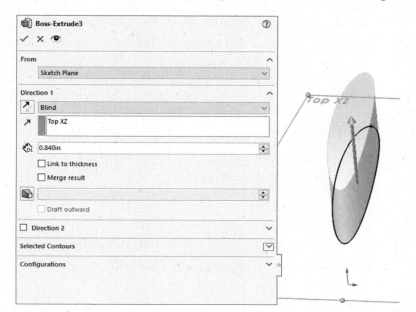

USING END CONDITIONS

End conditions control how the extrude starts and stops. In most situations, the extrude starts from a sketch plane and goes a specified distance, but there are other options.

Start conditions

- From sketch plane
- From offset distance/vertex
- From selected plane
- From 3D sketch
- From selected face

End conditions

- Distance (blind)
- Through all (up to the furthest face)
- Up to a selected vertex
- Up to a selected surface
- Offset from surface (either near or far offset, and either offset or translated)
- Up to a selected body
- Midplane (divides distance in half about start plane)

Direction

- In addition to the start and end conditions, you can control the direction of the extrude.
- If you want to push a profile along a curve, you can use either a revolve or a sweep, as appropriate, which are both covered later in this chapter.

Understanding Instant 3D

Instant 3D is the tool that enables you to use the mouse to pull arrows or handles on the screen to change various dimension parameters for features such as Extrude, Revolve, Fillet, and even Move Face. Not every dimension parameter is editable in this way. In some cases, Instant 3D offers you convenient ways to edit geometry without needing to figure out which feature is responsible for which faces. With Instant 3D, you simply pull on handles on the screen to move and resize sketches and features including fillets.

To me, Instant 3D is a gimmick that tries to imitate direct-edit software without the actual benefits of direct-edit software. If you want direct-edit software, you will need to get different software. The usefulness of Instant3D is probably limited to concept modeling, or quick looks-like models. I just want to make sure that no one confuses Instant3D with actual direct editing, as the SolidWorks marketing seems to try to do.

Working with the Revolve Feature

Like all other features, Revolve features have some rules that you must observe when choosing sketches to create a revolve:

◆ You can use any type of line or model edge for the centerline, not just the centerline/construction line type.

◆ If there is only one actual center/construction line in the sketch, it will automatically be used as the axis of revolution.

◆ Draw only half of the revolve profile. Draw the section to one side of the centerline.

◆ The profile must not cross the centerline.

◆ The profile must not touch the centerline at a single point. It can touch along a line but not at a point. Revolving a sketch that touched the centerline at a single point would create a point of zero thickness in the part.

UNDERSTANDING END CONDITIONS

There are five Revolve end conditions:

◆ Blind

◆ Up To Vertex

◆ Up To Surface

◆ Offset From Surface

◆ Midplane

There is no equivalent for Up To Next or Up To Body with the Revolve feature. Figure 7.5 shows the Revolve PropertyManager.

FIGURE 7.5
Using the Revolve
PropertyManager

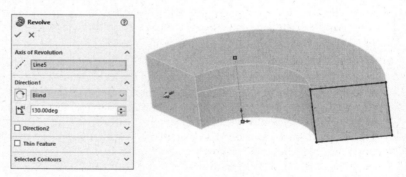

WORKFLOW

This is the workflow for the Revolve feature:

1. Create a sketch.

2. Invoke the Revolve feature.

3. Select an axis (typically a construction line).

4. Set the end conditions.

5. Click OK.

Using Contour Selection

Like Extrude features, Revolve features can also use contour selection, and as with the Extrude features, I recommend that you avoid using contours for production work.

Introducing Loft, Boundary, and Sweep

Sweep, loft, and boundary are known as *interpolated* features. This means that you can create profiles for the feature at certain points, and the software interpolates the shape between the profiles. You can use additional controls with loft, such as guide curves or centerlines, and establish end conditions to help direct the shape. A loft with just two profiles is a straight-line transition. If you have more than two profiles, the transition from one profile to another works more like a spline.

Many users struggle when faced with the option to create a loft, boundary, or sweep. Some overlap exists among the three features, but as you gain some experience, it becomes easier to choose among them. Generally, if you can create the cross section of the feature by manipulating the dimensions of a single sketch, a sweep might be the best feature. If the cross section changes character or severely changes shape, loft or boundary may be best. If you need a very definite shape at both ends and/or in the middle, loft and boundary are better choices because they enable you to explicitly define the cross section at any point. However, if the outline is more important than the cross section, you should choose a sweep. In addition, if the path between ends is important, choose a sweep.

Both types of features are extremely powerful, but the sweep has a tendency to be fussier about details, setup, and rules, although the loft and boundary can be surprisingly flexible. I am not trying to dissuade you from using sweeps, because they are useful in many situations. However, in my own modeling, I probably use about 10 lofts or boundary features for every sweep. For example, although you would use a loft or combination of Loft features to create the outer faces of a complex laundry detergent bottle, you would use the sweep to create a raised border around the label area or the cap thread.

A good example of the interpolated nature of a loft is to put a circle on one plane and a rectangle on an offset plane and then loft them together. This arrangement is shown in Figure 7.6.

Figure 7.6
Interpolation inside a loft

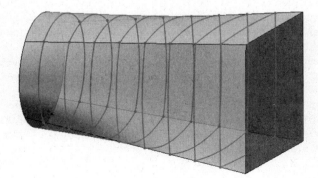

The transition between shapes is the defining characteristic of a loft and is the reason for choosing a loft instead of another feature type. Lofts can create both Boss features and Cut features.

Notice how the cross-sectional shape of the loft transitions from the circle to the rectangle. The default setting (refer to Figure 7.6) is for the interpolated transition to happen evenly across the loft, but the distribution of change from one end to the other could be altered, which might result in the transitions shown in Figure 7.7.

FIGURE 7.7
Adding end conditions to a loft alters how the interpolation is distributed.

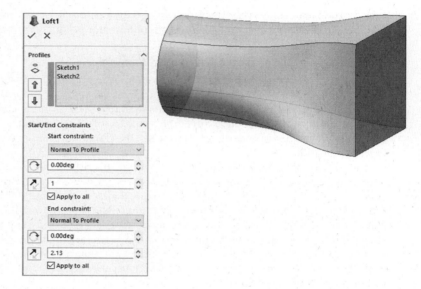

Both shapes are two-profile lofts. The two-profile loft with default end conditions always creates a straight transition, which is shown in the Figure 7.6. A two-point spline with no end tangency creates a straight line in exactly the same way. By applying end conditions to either or both of the loft profiles, the loft's shape is made more interesting, as shown in Figure 7.7. Again, the same thing happens when applying end tangency conditions to a two-point spline: It goes from being a straight line to being more curvaceous, with continuously variable curvature.

COMPARING THE LOFT AND BOUNDARY FEATURES

An important difference between boundary and loft is that there are more options for setting up Boundary features in terms of the geometrical layout of profiles and guide curves. A second major difference is that there are no profiles and guide curves in boundary—the two directions are treated equally, and they are simply called Direction 1 and Direction 2. In the Loft feature, you don't have as much continuity control across the guide curve direction. This is less meaningful with solid features than with surfaces. In fact, the Boundary feature is used far less often than its surfacing-related cousin, the Boundary Surface.

The geometrical layout of profiles is the most important difference between boundary and loft. With loft, you must have a profile at the beginning and end of the feature. With boundary, you can lay out the profile sketch planes like an X. You could also lay the feature out like a T, which would act like a sweep. Using a layout shaped like an F actually combines the functionality of a loft with that of a sweep. Boundary is a very powerful feature, with options for creating interpolated solid shapes. Face-by-face control, however, still must come from using surfacing features.

Figure 7.8 shows the features made with F and X layouts of sketches. The F layout resembles the letter F, and the sketches lie on the planes Right YZ, FrontXY, and Plane1. The X layout uses sketches on RightYZ and Plane2. These two features represent sketch layouts that you can't use with the Loft feature.

FIGURE 7.8
Using different profile arrangements for Boundary solid features

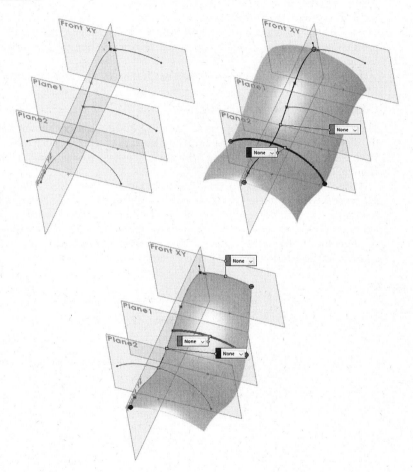

Loft does have two conditions that Boundary cannot answer:

Centerline loft: All boundary profiles must intersect.

Closed loop loft without Direction 2 (guide) curves: To make a closed-loop boundary, you must have Direction 2 curves that intersect Direction 1 curves.

Using Entities in a Loft

For solid lofts, you can select faces, closed-loop 2D or 3D sketches, and surface bodies. You can use sketch points as a profile on the end of a loft that comes to a point or rounded end. For surface lofts, you can use open sketches and edges in addition to the entities that are used by solid lofts, but you cannot combine open and closed contours.

Some special functionality becomes available to you if you put all the profiles and guide curves together in a single 3D sketch. In order to select profiles made in this way, you must use the SelectionManager, which is discussed later in this chapter.

The Sketch Tools panel of the Loft PropertyManager enables you to drag sketch entities of any profile made in this way while you are editing or creating the Loft feature, without needing to exit and edit a sketch.

I discuss 3D sketches in more detail in Chapter 6, "Getting More from Your Sketches."

Comparing Lofts and Splines

The words *loft* and *spline* come from the shipbuilding trade. The word *spline* is actually defined as the slats of wood that cover the ship, and the ribs of the hull very much resemble loft sections. With the splines or slats bending at each rib, it is easy to see how the modern CAD analogy came to be.

Lofts and splines are also governed by similar mathematics. You have seen how the two-point spline and two-profile loft both create a straight-line transition. Next, a third profile is added to the loft and a third point to the spline, which demonstrates how the math that governs splines and lofts is also related to bending in elastic materials. Figure 7.9 shows how lofts and splines react geometrically in the same way that bending a flexible steel rod would react (except that the spline and the loft do not have a fixed length).

FIGURE 7.9
Splines, lofts, and bending

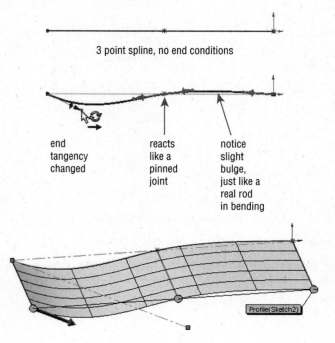

3 point spline, no end conditions

end tangency changed

reacts like a pinned joint

notice slight bulge, just like a real rod in bending

Profile(Sketch2)

With this bit of background, it is time to move forward and talk about a few of the major aspects of Loft features in SolidWorks. In this single chapter, I do not have the space to cover the topic exhaustively, but coverage of the major concepts will be enough to point you in the right direction.

Controlling Sweep Features

The Sweep feature generally uses multiple sketches. A sweep is made from a profile (cross section) and a path, and it can create a Boss or a Cut feature. If you want, you can also use guide curves. Sweeps can run the gamut from simple to complex. Typical simple sweeps are used to create wire, tubing, or hose. Sweeps that are more complex are used for creating objects such as bottles, involutes, springs, and corkscrews.

The main criterion for selecting a sweep to create a feature is that you must be able to identify a cross section and a path. The profile (cross section) can change along the path, but the overall shape must remain the same. The profile is typically perpendicular to the path, although this is not a requirement.

A recent addition to the software includes an option in the Sweep PropertyManager for a Circular Profile. This is for simple sweeps with a circle driven along a path by its center, maintaining a constant diameter (such as wire, hose, pipe, and so on). To use this function, specify the diameter of the circle in the PropertyManager.

USING A SIMPLE SWEEP

An example of a simple sweep is shown in Figure 7.10. The paper clip uses a circle as the profile and the coiled lines and arcs as the path. Simple sweeps keep the same size and shape profile along the entire path. This sweep could use the previously mentioned option for Circular Profile, also shown in Figure 7.10.

FIGURE 7.10
The Sweep Profile follows the path.

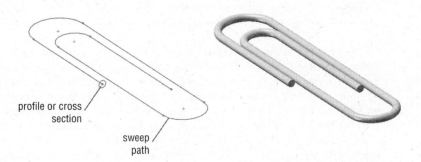

profile or cross section

sweep path

USING A SWEEP WITH GUIDE CURVES

Sweeps that are more complex begin to control the size, orientation, and position of the cross section as it travels through the sweep. When you use a guide curve, several analogies can be used to visualize how the sweep works. The cross section/profile is solved at several intermediate positions along the path. If the guide curve does not follow the path, the difference between the two is made up by adjusting the profile. Consider the following example. In this case, the profile is an ellipse, the path is a straight line, and there are guide curves that give the feature its outer shape. Figure 7.11 shows all these elements and the finished feature.

FIGURE 7.11
The sweep profile follows the path and is controlled parametrically by guide curves.

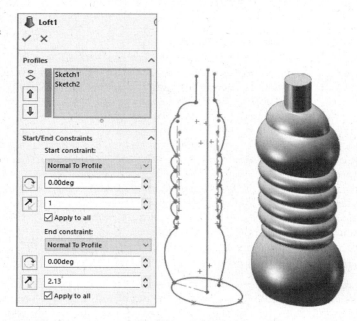

ON THE WEBSITE

The part shown in Figure 7.11 is in the download materials from the Wiley website for this chapter under the filename Chapter7 Bottle.sldprt.

The PropertyManager for the Sweep function includes an option for Show Sections, which in this case creates almost 200 intermediate cross sections. These sections are used behind the scenes to create a loft. You can think of complex sweeps with guide curves or centerlines as an automated setup for an even more complex loft. It is helpful to envision features such as this when you are troubleshooting or setting up sweeps that are more complex. Once you open the Chapter7 Bottle.sldprt part, you can edit the Sweep feature to examine the sections for yourself.

In most other published SolidWorks materials that cover these topics, sweeps are covered before lofts because many people consider lofts the more advanced topic. However, I have put lofts first because understanding them is necessary before you can understand complex sweeps, because complex sweeps really are just lofts.

USING A PIERCE RELATION

The Pierce sketch relation is the only sketch relation that applies to a 3D out-of-plane edge or curve without projecting the edge or curve into the sketch plane. It acts as if the 3D curve is a length of string and the sketch point is the hole in the center of a bead. The Pierce relation is most important in the Sweep feature when it is applied in the profile sketch between endpoints, centerpoints, or sketch points and the out-of-plane guide curves. This is because the Pierce relation determines how the profile sketch will be solved when it is moved down the sweep path to create intermediate profiles.

Figure 7.12 illustrates the function of the Pierce relation in a sweep with guide curves. The dark section on the left is the sweep section that is sketched. The lighter sketches to the right represent the intermediate profiles that are automatically created behind the scenes and are used internally to create the loft.

FIGURE 7.12
The effects of the Pierce relation

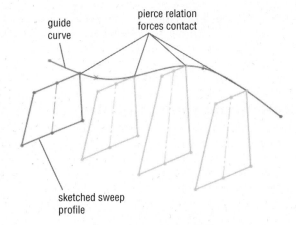

Figure 7.12 shows what is happening behind the scenes in a Sweep feature. The sweep re-creates the original profile at various points along the path. The guide curve in this case forces the profile to rebuild with a different shape. Pierce constraints are not required in simple sweeps, but when you start using guide curves, you should also use a Pierce.

TIP   If you feel that you need more profile control, but still want to create a sweep-like feature, try a centerline loft. The centerline acts like a sweep path that doesn't touch the profiles—but unlike a sweep, you can use multiple profiles with it.

Figure 7.13 shows a more complicated 3D sweep, where both the path and the guide curve are 3D curves. I cover 3D curves in Chapter 8, "Selecting Secondary Features"; you can refer to these sections to understand how this part is made.

FIGURE 7.13
A 3D sweep

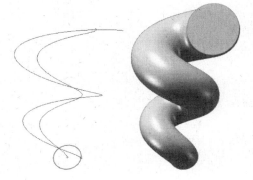

> **ON THE WEBSITE**
>
> The part shown in Figure 7.13 is in the download material from the Wiley website for this chapter under the filename Chapter 7 3D Sweep.sldprt.

This part is created by making a pair of tapered helices, with the profile sketch plane perpendicular to the end of one of the curves. The taper on the outer helix is greater than on the inner one, which causes the twist to become larger in diameter as it goes up.

To make the circle follow both helices, you must create two Pierce relations, one between the center of the circle and a helix, and the other between a sketch point that is placed on the circumference of the circle and the other helix. This means that the difference in taper angles between the two helices is what drives the change in diameter of the sweep.

USING A CUT SWEEP WITH A SOLID PROFILE

The Cut Sweep feature has an option to use a solid sweep profile. This kind of functionality has many uses, but it's primarily intended for simulating complex cuts made by a mill or lathe. Figure 7.14 shows a couple of examples of cuts you can make with this feature. The part used for this screen shot, called Chapter 7 - cut sweep solid profile.sldprt, is also in the website download material.

FIGURE 7.14
Cuts you can make with the Cut Sweep feature using a solid profile

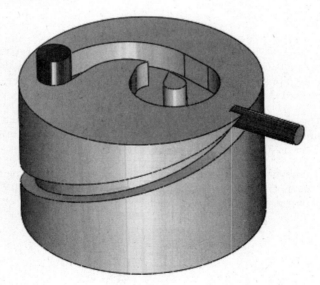

The solid profile cut sweep has a few limitations that I need to mention:

◆ It requires two bodies: the target and a cutting tool.

◆ The path must start at a point where it intersects the solid cutting tool body (path starts inside or on the surface of the cutting tool).

◆ The path must be tangent within itself (no sharp corners).

◆ The cutting tool must be definable with a revolved feature.

◆ The cutting tool must be made of simple analytical faces (sphere, torus, cylinder, and cone; no splines).

◆ You cannot use a guide curve with a solid profile cut (because you cannot control alignment).

◆ The cut can intersect itself, but the path cannot cross itself.

You can create many useful shapes with the solid-profile-cut sweep, but because of some of the limitations I've listed, some shapes are more difficult to create than others. For these shapes, you might choose to use regular Cut Sweep features.

WORKFLOW

Use the following general steps to create Sweep features:

1. Create the path first. It may be tempting to create the profile first, but as a general rule, things work out better if you make the path first.

2. Create guide curves. Again, these work out better if you create them before the profile.

3. Create the profile (sweep cross section) and relate it to the path with a Pierce sketch relation. Select a point in the sweep profile that you want to be driven down the path, as a bead follows a string.

4. Make sure that, as the profile is driven down the path (with the profile sketch plane maintaining its original relationship with the path), the profile has the flexibility to change the way it needs to change. The sketch is reevaluated at each point along the path. Use relative relations (parallel, perpendicular, and so on) instead of absolute ones (horizontal, vertical, or fixed).

5. Start the Sweep feature from the toolbar or menu. All sketches must be closed.

6. Select the profile first and then the path. SolidWorks automatically toggles from the profile selection box to the path selection box as soon as a profile is selected, so take advantage of this automation to help you work quickly. Note that for circular profiles centered on the path, there is no longer a need to create a sketch.

CAUTION   Pay attention to any tool tip warnings or error messages that come up. If you are unable to select something, it is usually because something about that entity is inappropriate for the purpose you are trying to assign to it.

7. Use the preview to check that it is performing the way you want. Click OK when you are satisfied with the result.

Understanding Fillet Types

SolidWorks offers very powerful filleting functions. The Fillet feature comprises various types of fillets and blends. Simple fillets on straight and round edges are handled differently from variable-radius fillets, which are handled differently from the single or double hold-line fillet or setback fillets. After you click the OK button to create a fillet as a certain type, you cannot switch it to another type. You can switch types only before you actually create the feature.

Many filleting options are available, but most of them are seldom used or even known. In fact, most users confine themselves to the constant-radius or variable-radius fillets. This section describes all the available fillet types and options:

- ◆ Constant-size fillet
  - ◆ Symmetric fillet
    - ◆ Circular
    - ◆ Conic rho
    - ◆ Conic radius
    - ◆ Curvature continuous
  - ◆ Asymmetric fillet
    - ◆ Elliptic
    - ◆ Conic rho
    - ◆ Curvature continuous
  - ◆ Multiple-radius fillet
  - ◆ Round corners
  - ◆ Keep edge/Keep surface
  - ◆ Keep feature

- ◆ Variable-size fillet
- ◆ Face fillet
  - ◆ Curvature-continuous fillet
  - ◆ Face fillet with Help Point
  - ◆ Single hold-line fillet
  - ◆ Double hold-line fillet
  - ◆ Constant-width fillet

- ◆ Full round fillet
- ◆ Setback fillet
- ◆ Setback fillet with variable radius

Figure 7.15 shows the Fillet PropertyManager.

Note that SolidWorks does not distinguish between fillets and rounds, and even two edges that are selected for use with the same Fillet feature can have opposite functions—for example, both adding and removing material in a single feature.

FIGURE 7.15
The Fillet
PropertyManager

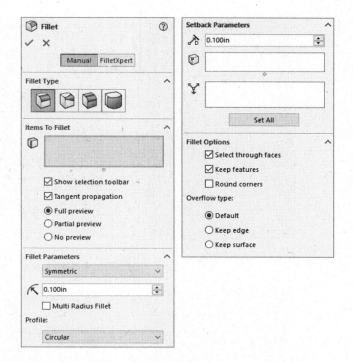

Creating a Constant-Size Fillet

Constant-size fillets are the most common type that are created if you select only edges, features, or faces without changing any settings. When you select features or faces that cause large numbers of fillets to be applied, you should consider several best-practice guidelines and other recommendations that come later in this chapter.

SELECTING ENTITIES TO FILLET

You can create fillets from several selections, including edges, faces, features, and loops. Edges offer the most direct method and are the easiest to control. Figure 7.16 shows how you can use each of these selections to create fillets on parts more intelligently.

TIP You must select features for filleting from the FeatureManager. The Selection Filter filters only edges and faces for fillet selection. You can select loops in two ways: through the right-click Select Loop option or by selecting a face and Ctrl+selecting an edge on the face.

TIP Another option for selecting edges in the Fillet command is the Select Through Faces option, which appears on the Fillet Options panel. This option enables you to select edges that are hidden by the model. This can be a useful option on a part with few hidden edges, or it can be a detrimental option on a part where there are many edges due to patterns, ribs, vents, or existing fillets. You can control a similar option globally for features other than fillets by choosing Tools ➤ Options ➤ Display/Selection, Allow Selection In HLR [Hidden Lines Removed] And Shaded Modes.

FIGURE 7.16
Selection options
for fillets

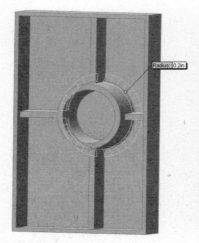

Select individual edges

Selecting a face fillets all
edges around the face

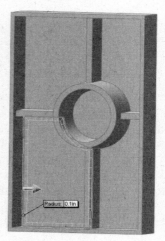

Selecting a feature fillets all
the edges that touch the feature

Selecting a loop is just a
shortcut to selecting several
edges

Faces and features selections are useful when you are creating fillets where you want the selections to update. In Figure 7.16, the ribs that intersect the circular boss are also being filleted. If the rib did not exist when the fillet was applied but was added later and reordered so it came before the Fillet feature, then the fillet selection automatically considers the rib. If the fillet used edge selection, this automatic selection updating would not take place.

USING TANGENT PROPAGATION

By default, fillets have the Tangent Propagation option turned on. This is usually a good choice, although there may be times when you want to experiment with turning it off. Tangent propagation simply means that if you select an edge to fillet, and this edge is tangent to other edges, then the fillet keeps going along tangent edges until it forms a closed loop, the tangent edges stop, or the fillet fails.

If you deselect Tangent Propagation, but there are still tangent edges, you may see different results. One possible result is that it could fail. One of the tricks with Fillet features is to try to envision what you are asking the software to do. For example, if one edge is filleted and the next edge is not, then how is the fillet going to end? Figure 7.17 shows two of the potential results when fillets are asked not to propagate. The fillet face may continue along its path until it runs off the part or until the feature fails.

FIGURE 7.17
Deselecting the Tangent Propagation option

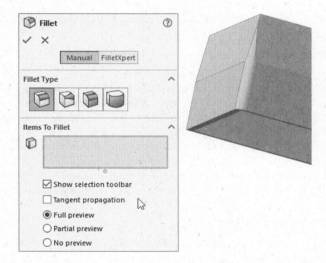

TIP   This may sound counterintuitive, but sometimes when Fillet features fail, it may be useful to deselect propagation and make the fillet in multiple features. There are times when creating two fillets like the one shown in Figure 7.17 will work and times when making the same geometry as a single feature will not. This may be due to geometry problems where the sharp edges come together and are eliminated by the fillet.

BEST PRACTICE

In general, fillets should be the last features applied to a model, particularly the small cosmetic or edge break fillets. Larger fillets that contribute to the structure or overall shape of the part may be applied earlier.

Be careful of the rock-paper-scissors game that you inevitably are caught up in when modeling plastic parts and deciding on the feature order of fillets, draft, and shell. Most fillets should come after draft, and large fillets should come before the shell. Draft may come either before or after the shell, depending on the needs of the area that you are dealing with on the part. In short, there is no single set of rules that you can consistently apply and that works best in all situations.

Dealing with a Large Number of Fillets

Figure 7.18 shows a model with a bit of a filleting nightmare. This large plastic tray requires many ribs underneath for strength. Because the ribs may be touched by the user, the sharp edges need to be rounded. Interior edges also need to be rounded for strength and plastic flow through the ribs. Literally, hundreds of edges will need to be selected to create the fillets if you do not use an advanced technique.

Figure 7.18
A plastic tray with a large number of fillets

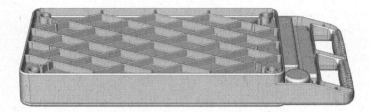

Selecting Entities

Some of the techniques outlined previously, such as face and feature selection, can be useful for quickly filleting a large number of edges that all meet the same criteria. Another method is window selection of the edges. To use this option effectively, you may want to first position the model into a view where only the correct edges will be selected, turn off the Select Through Faces option, and use the Edges selection filter.

The first option in the Fillet PropertyManager is the Selection toolbar. This toolbar highlights several selection options based on types of selections similar to your initial selection. For example, if you selected an edge, the Selection toolbar might highlight edges parallel to the selected edge, faces that touch the selected edge, or edges tangent to the selected edge.

Using the FilletXpert

The FilletXpert automatically finds solutions to complex fillet problems, particularly the problems that can arise when you have several fillets of different sizes coming together. It also allows you to select multiple edges. A part like the one shown in Figure 7.18 is ideal for this tool.

To use the FilletXpert, click the FilletXpert button in the Fillet PropertyManager (Figure 7.19). When you select an edge, the FilletXpert presents a pop-up toolbar, giving you several selection options. Notice that Figure 7.19 shows the majority of the edges selected that are needed for this fillet. This is the same type of functionality you will find in the Selection toolbar, in fact; the Selection Toolbar toggle is found in the FilletXpert PropertyManager shown in Figure 7.19.

The Corner tab of the FilletXpert enables you to select from different corner options, which are usually the result of different fillet orders. To use the CornerXpert, make sure the FilletXpert is active, then click the corner face, and toggle through the options.

Using Preview

I like to use the fillet preview. It helps to see what the fillet will look like, and perhaps more important, the presence of a preview usually (but not always) means that the fillet will work.

Unfortunately, when you have a large number of fillets to create, the preview can cause a significant slowdown. Deselecting and using the partial preview are both possible options. Partial preview shows the fillet on only one edge in the selection and is much faster when you are creating a large number of fillets.

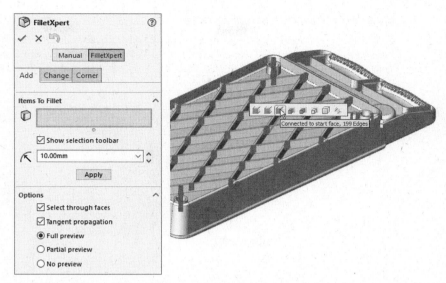

PERFORMANCE

For rebuild speed efficiency, you should make fillets with a minimum number of features. For example, if you have 100 edges to fillet, it is better for performance to do it with a single Fillet feature that has 100 edges selected rather than 100 Fillet features that have one edge selected. This is the one case where creating the feature and rebuilding the feature are both faster by choosing a particular technique. (Usually, if it is faster to create; it rebuilds more slowly.)

BEST PRACTICE

Although creation and rebuild speed are in sync when you use the minimum number of features to create the maximum number of fillets, this is not usually the case. (There had to be a downside.) When a single feature has a large selection, any one of these edges that fails to fillet will cause the entire feature to fail. As a result, a feature with 100 edges selected is 100 times more likely to fail than a feature with a single edge. Large selection sets are also far more difficult to troubleshoot when they fail than small selection sets that fail.

USING FOLDERS

When you have a large number of Fillet features, it can be tedious to navigate the FeatureManager. Therefore, it is useful to place groups of fillets into folders. This makes it easy to suppress or unsuppress all the fillets in the folder at once. Separate folders can be particularly useful if the fillets have different uses, such as fillets that are used for PhotoWorks models and fillets that are removed for FEA (Finite Element Analysis) or drawings. Folders also allow the bulk-selection of such features if they were saved in selection sets.

MAKING MULTIPLE FILLET SIZES

The Multiple Radius Fillet option in the Fillet PropertyManager enables you to make multiple fillet sizes within a single Fillet feature. Figure 7.20 shows how the Multiple Radius Fillet feature looks when you are working with it. You can change values in the callout flags or in the PropertyManager.

FIGURE 7.20
Using the Multiple
Radius Fillet option

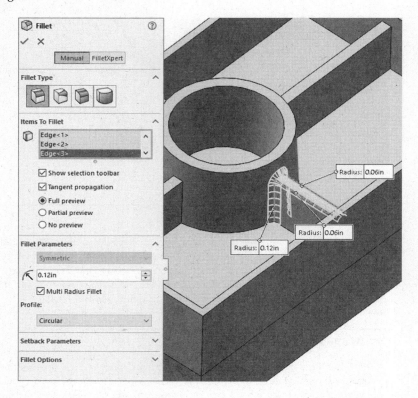

Although you may see a small performance benefit when condensing several features into one, many more downsides adversely affect performance:

◆ You lose control of feature order.

◆ A single failed fillet causes the whole feature, and therefore all the fillets, to fail.

◆ Troubleshooting is far more difficult.

◆ Smaller groups of fillets cannot be suppressed without suppressing everything.

◆ You cannot change the size of a group of fillets together.

BEST PRACTICE

Although this may be more personal opinion than best practice, I believe that there are good reasons to consider using techniques other than single features that contain many fillets or single features that drive fillets of various sizes. Best practice would lean more toward grouping fillets that have a similar use and the same size. For example, you may want to separate fillets that break corners on ribs from fillets that round the outer shape of a large plastic part.

Another consideration is feature order when it comes to the fillet's relationship to draft and shell features. If the fillets are all grouped into a single feature, then controlling this relationship becomes impossible.

ROUNDING CORNERS

The Round Corners option refers to how SolidWorks handles fillets that go around sharp corners. By default, this setting is off, which leaves fillets around sharp corners looking like mitered picture frames. If you turn this setting on, the corner looks like a marble has rolled around it. Figure 7.21 shows the resulting geometry from both settings.

FIGURE 7.21
The Round Corners option, both on and off

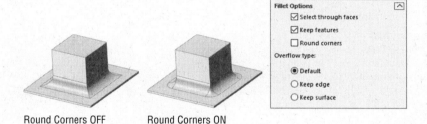

Round Corners OFF   Round Corners ON

USING THE KEEP EDGE/KEEP SURFACE TOGGLE

The Keep Edge/Keep Surface toggle determines what SolidWorks should do if a fillet is too big to fit in an area. The Keep Edge option keeps the edge where it is and tweaks the position (not the radius) of the fillet to make it meet the edge. The Keep Surface option keeps the surfaces of the fillet and the end face clean; however, to do this, it has to tweak the edge. There is often a tradeoff when you try to place fillets into a space that is too small. Sometimes, it is useful to visualize what you think the result should look like. Figure 7.22 shows how the fillet would look in a perfect world, followed by how the fillet looks when cramped with the Keep Edge option and how it looks when cramped with the Keep Surface option.

The Default option chooses the best option for a particular situation. As a result, it seems to use the Keep Edge option unless it does not work, in which case it changes to the Keep Surface option.

USING THE KEEP FEATURE OPTION

The Keep Feature option appears on the Fillet Options panel of the Fillet PropertyManager. By default, this option is turned on. If a fillet surrounds a feature such as a hole (as long as it is not a through hole) or a boss, then deselecting the Keep Feature option removes the hole or boss. When Keep Feature is selected, the faces of the feature trim or extend to match the fillet, as shown in Figure 7.23.

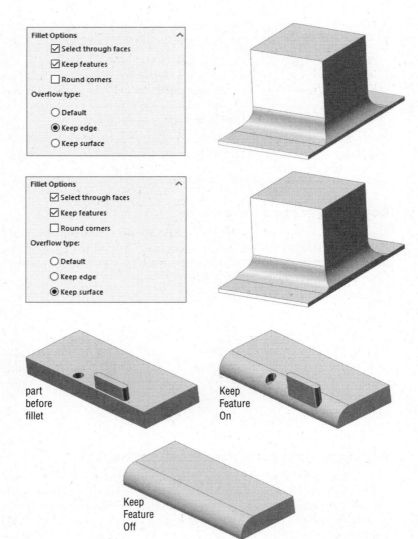

FIGURE 7.22
The Keep Edge option and the Keep Surface option

FIGURE 7.23
The Keep Feature option, both selected and unselected

USING SYMMETRIC OR ASYMMETRIC FILLETS

Standard fillets are symmetrical on either side of the selected edge. An asymmetrical fillet can have a different radius on either side of the selected edge. This makes for a more complex-looking fillet and may also complicate troubleshooting in complex parts. Figure 7.24 illustrates the concept of asymmetrical fillets, along with the Fillet Parameters panel of the Fillet PropertyManager associated with specifying this type of fillet.

Asymmetrical fillets can also be used in variable-radius fillets, described later in this chapter. In addition to specifying the two radius values, you can also flip the sides of the values using the opposing arrows icon.

FIGURE 7.24
Asymmetrical fillets

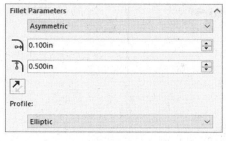

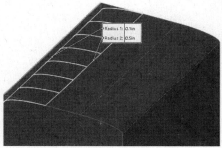

SELECTING A FILLET PROFILE

Within the Symmetric and Asymmetric fillets, you also have some profile options:

◆ Circular (only symmetric)

◆ Elliptic (only asymmetric)

◆ Conic rho (symmetric and asymmetric)

◆ Conic radius (only symmetric)

◆ Curvature continuous (symmetric and asymmetric)

You can think of these profiles as being the fillet cross sections. Circular cross sections can be defined with a single radius. This should make intuitive sense. You should also be familiar with the shape of an ellipse, although this is not directly specifiable with a radius value, SolidWorks uses the radius value to approximate. The cross sections are shown in Figure 7.25.

FIGURE 7.25
Fillet profiles change the
shapes of the fil-
leted edges.

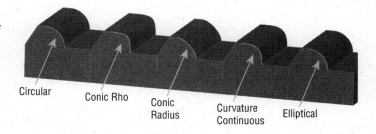

The Circular profile is the normal type of fillet specified with a single radius. This is what we think of as a default fillet.

The Elliptic profile is available only when specifying asymmetric fillets. The two radius values determine an ellipse, which is used to round the selected edge instead of the usual arc.

The Conic rho profile is driven by rho (ρ). Conic in the name refers to the conic sections from classical geometry–circle, ellipse, hyperbola, parabola—but as driven by the parameter rho in many other CAD systems. Rho runs between 0 and 1. Figure 7.26 shows the effect of the range of

FIGURE 7.26
The effect of parameter
rho on Conic rho
profile fillets

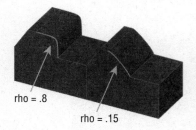

rho = .8

rho = .15

rho values on the profile of the fillet. If you want to experiment with this, the file used to create this screen capture is in the download materials under the filename `Conic rho fillet.sldprt`.

The Conic radius profile is specified by the main radius value and a conic radius value, which can be any positive number. The Conic radius value is the radius of the conic section curve at the *shoulder*, which in this case means the middle of the curve. This works in a way similar to the rho value, and the range of effects is similar to what you see in Figure 7.26.

Curvature Continuous profile is available on edge-selected fillets. This is new. Previously, curvature continuity was available only on face fillets, as discussed next. Curvature Continuity (c2) is a spline-based profile that matches the curvature of the faces on either side of the selected edge. This edge-selected c2 fillet is a big convenience over needing to select faces. Any old c2 face fillets you have should still work, but going forward in most cases, the edge-selected fillets will be easier to create.

USING CONTINUOUS CURVATURE FACE FILLETS

Curvature continuity refers to the quality of a transition between two curves or faces, where the curvature is the same or continuous at and around the transition. The best way to convey this concept is with simple 2D sketch elements. When a line transitions to an arc, you have noncontinuous curvature. The line has no curvature, and there is an abrupt change because the arc has a specific radius.

NOTE   Radius is the inverse of curvature, so $r = \frac{1}{c}$. For a straight line, $r = \infty$—in which case, $c = 0$.

To make the transition from $r = \infty$ to $r = 2$ smoothly, you would need to use a variable-radius arc if such a thing existed. There are several types of sketch geometry that have variable curvature, such as ellipses, parabolas, and splines. Ellipses and parabolas follow specific mathematical formulas to create the shape, but the spline is a general curve that can take on any shape you want, and you can control its curvature to change smoothly or continuously. Splines, by their very definition, have continuous curvature within the spline, although you cannot control the specific curvature or radius values directly.

All this means that continuous curvature fillets use a spline-based profile for the fillet, rather than circular or elliptical. Figure 7.27 illustrates the difference between continuous curvature and constant curvature. The spikes on top of the curves represent the curvature ($\frac{1}{r}$, so the smaller the radius, the taller the spike). These spikes are called a *curvature comb*.

FIGURE 7.27
Using curvature combs to evaluate transitions

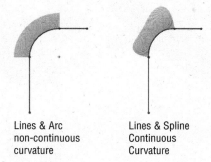

Lines & Arc
non-continuous
curvature

Lines & Spline
Continuous
Curvature

Some of these fillet profile options may seem esoteric to you, but there are people who are glad to have these options, and the options are available in some other CAD programs.

Creating Variable-Radius Fillets

Variable-radius fillets are another powerful weapon in the fight against boring designs; they also double as a useful tool to solve certain filleting problems that arise.

> **BEST PRACTICE**
>
> It may be easier to identify when *not* to use a variable-radius fillet. Fillets are generally used to round or break edges, not to sculpt a part. If you are using fillets to sculpt blocky parts and are not actively trying to make blocky parts with big fillets, you may want to consider another approach and use complex modeling, which gives the part a better shape and makes it more controllable. Other options exist that give you a different type of control, such as the double hold-line fillet.

APPLYING THE VALUES

When you first select an edge for the variable-radius fillet, the endpoints are identified by callout flags with the value *unassigned*. A preview does not display until at least one of the points has a radius value in the box. You can also apply radius values in the PropertyManager, but they are easier to keep track of using the callouts. Figure 7.28 shows a variable-radius fillet after the edge selection, after one value has been applied, and after three values have been applied. To apply a radius value that is not at the endpoint of an edge, you can select one of the three colored dots along the selected edge. The preview should show you how the fillet will look in wire-frame display.

By default, the variable-radius fillet puts five points on an edge, one at each endpoint, one at the midpoint, and one each halfway between the ends and middle. If you want to create an additional control point, there are three ways to do it:

◆ Ctrl+drag an existing point.

◆ Select the callout of an existing point and change the P (percentage) value.

◆ Change the Number Of Instances value in the Variable Radius Parameters panel of the PropertyManager.

FIGURE 7.28
Assigning values to a
variable-radius fillet

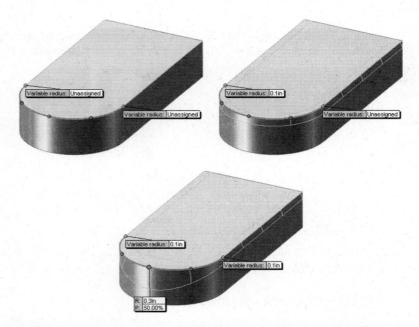

FIGURE 7.28
Assigning values to a
variable-radius fillet

If you have selected several edges, and several unassigned values are on the screen, you can use the Set Unassigned option in the PropertyManager to set them all to the same value. The Set All option sets all radius values to the same number, including any values that you may have changed to be different from the rest. Figure 7.29 shows the Variable Radius Parameters panel.

FIGURE 7.29
The Variable Radius
Parameters panel of
the Fillet
PropertyManager

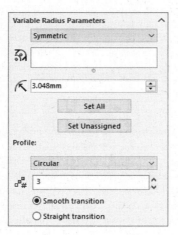

You can set an end of a variable-radius fillet to a value of zero, but you need to be careful because it is likely to cause downstream problems with other fillets, shells, offsets, and even machining operations. You cannot assign a zero radius in the middle of an edge, only at the end. If you need to end a fillet at a particular location, you can use a split line to split the edge and apply a zero radius at that point. (Chapter 8, "Selecting Secondary Features," covers split lines.) Figure 7.30 shows a part with two zero-radius values.

FIGURE 7.30
Zero-radius values in the variable-radius fillet

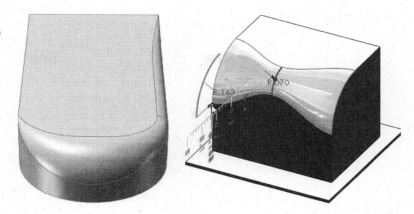

The image on the right shows Instant3D being used to edit a variable-radius fillet. Select the face of the fillet with Instant3D turned on, and blue dots appear wherever radius values are assigned. You can move these dots to dynamically edit the corresponding value of the variable radius.

USING STRAIGHT VS. SMOOTH TRANSITIONS

Variable-radius fillets have an option for either a straight transition or a smooth transition. This works like the two-profile lofts that were mentioned earlier in this chapter. The names may be somewhat misleading because both transitions are smooth. The straight transition goes in a straight line, from one size to the next, and the smooth transition takes a swooping S-shaped path between the sizes. The difference between these two transitions is demonstrated in Figure 7.31.

FIGURE 7.31
Straight versus smooth transitions of a variable-radius fillet

smooth transition

straight transition

RECOGNIZING OTHER USES FOR VARIABLE-RADIUS FILLETS

Variable-radius fillets use a different method to create the fillet geometry than the default constant-radius fillet. Sometimes, using a variable-radius fillet can make a difference where a constant-radius fillet does not work. This is sometimes true even when the variable-radius fillet uses constant-radius values. It is just another tool in the toolbox.

Using Face Fillets

Face fillets may be the most flexible type of fillet because of the range of what they can do. Face fillets start simply as an alternative selection technique for a constant-radius fillet and extend to the extremely flexible double hold-line face fillet, which is more of a blend than a fillet.

Under normal circumstances, the default fillet type uses the selection of an edge to create the fillet. An edge is used because it represents the intersection between two faces. However, sometimes there can be a problem with the edge not being clean, being broken into smaller pieces, or any number of other reasons causing a constant-radius fillet using an edge selection to fail. In cases like this, SolidWorks displays the error message, "Failed to create fillet. Please check the input geometry and radius values or try using the 'Face Fillet' option."

Users almost universally ignore these messages. In the situation shown in Figure 7.32, the Face Fillet option suggested in the error message is exactly the one you should use. Here the face fillet covers over all the junk on the edge that prevents the fillet from executing.

FIGURE 7.32
A face fillet covering a bad corner

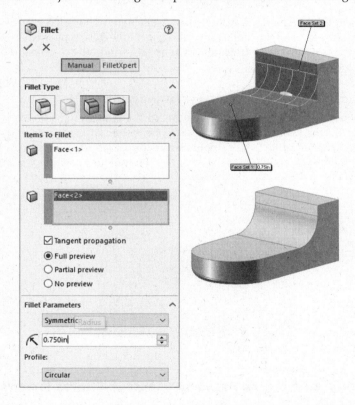

Face fillets are sometimes amazing at covering over a mess of geometry that you might think you could never fillet. The main limitation on fillets of this type is that the fillet must be *big* enough to bridge the gap. That's right, I said *big* enough. Face fillets can fail if they are either too small or too large. Figure 7.33 shows a complex fillet situation that is completely covered by a face fillet.

FIGURE 7.33
A face fillet covering geometry

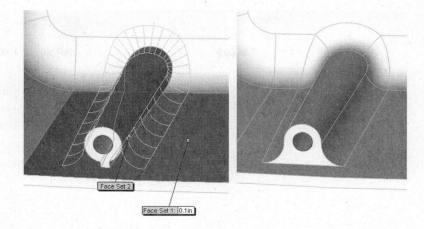

Face Set 2

Face Set 1: 0.1in

ON THE WEBSITE

The model used for this image can be found in the download materials from the Wiley website for this chapter; look for the filename `Chapter 7 Plastic Cover Fillets.sldprt`.

USING FACE FILLETS WITH THE HELP POINT

The Help Point in the Face Fillet PropertyManager is a fairly obscure option. However, it is useful in cases where the selection of two faces does not uniquely identify an edge to fillet. For example, Figure 7.34 shows a situation where the selection of two faces could result in either one edge or the other being filleted (normally, I would hope that both edges would be filleted). The fillet will default to one edge or the other, but you can force it to a definite edge using the Help Point.

In some cases, the Help Point is ignored altogether. For example, if you have a simple box, and select both ends of the box as Selection Set 1, and the top of the box as Selection Set 2, then the fillet could go to either end. Consequently, assigning a Help Point will not do anything, because multiple faces have been selected. The determining factor is which of the multiple faces is selected first. If this were a more commonly used feature, the interface for it might be made a little less cryptic; but because this feature is rarely, if ever, used, it just becomes a quirky piece of trivia.

APPLYING A SINGLE HOLD-LINE FILLET

A single hold-line fillet is a form of variable-radius fillet. Rather than the radius being driven by specific numerical values, it is driven by a *hold line,* or edge, on the model. The hold line can be an existing edge, forcing the fillet right up to the edge of the part, or it can be created by a split line, which enables you to drive the fillet however you like. Figure 7.35 shows these two options, before and after the fillets. Notice that these fillets are still arc-based fillets; if you were to take a cross section perpendicular to the edge between filleted faces, it would be an arc cross section with a distinct radius. However, in the other direction, hold-line fillets do not necessarily have a constant radius, although they may if the hold line is parallel to the edge between faces.

FIGURE 7.34
Using a Help Point with a face fillet

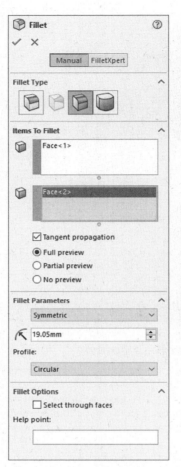

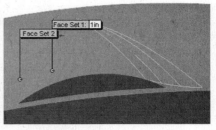

Face Fillet defaults to the right side

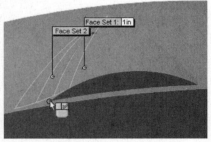

Selecting the Help Point forces it to the other side

FIGURE 7.35
Single hold-line fillets

Hold line (edge)   Hold line (split line)

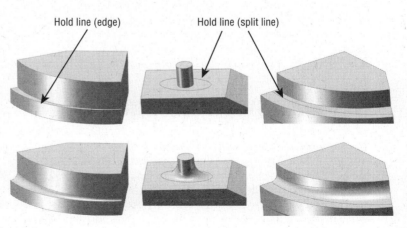

You can select the hold line in the Fillet Options panel of the Face Fillet PropertyManager. The top panel, Fillet Type, is available only when the feature is first created. When you edit it after it has been created, the Fillet Type panel does not appear. As a result, you cannot change from one top-level type of fillet to another after it has been initially created.

USING A DOUBLE HOLD-LINE FILLET

Sometimes, a single hold line does not meet your needs. The single hold line controls only one side of the fillet, and in order to control both sides of the fillet, you must use a double hold-line fillet. SolidWorks software does not specifically differentiate between the single and double hold-line fillets, but they are radically different in how they create the geometry. When both sides of the fillet are controlled, it is not possible to span between the hold lines with an arc that is tangent to both sides unless you were careful about setting up the hold lines so that they are equidistant from the edge where the faces intersect. This means that the double hold-line fillet must use a spline to span between hold lines, as shown in Figure 7.36.

FIGURE 7.36

A double hold line uses a spline cross section, not an arc.

Arc tangent on both ends does not fit both edges

Spline tangent on both ends fits

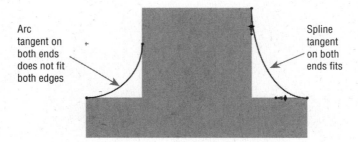

To get this feature to work, you need to use the Curvature Continuous option in the Fillet Options panel. Remember that this option creates a spline-based fillet rather than an arc-based fillet, which is exactly what you need for a double hold-line fillet. This makes the double hold-line fillet more of a blend than a true fillet. This requirement is not obvious to most users and may not even be documented in the SolidWorks Help, nor is it exactly intuitive. To get the double hold-line fillet to work, you must use the Curvature Continuous option. Figure 7.37 shows examples of the double hold-line fillet.

USING A CONSTANT-WIDTH FILLET

The Constant Width option of the Face Fillet PropertyManager drives a fillet by its width rather than by its radius. This is most helpful on parts where the angle of the faces between which you are filleting is changing dramatically. Figure 7.38 illustrates two situations where this is particularly useful. The setting for constant width is found in the Options panel of the Face Fillet PropertyManager. The part shown in the images can be found in the download material as `Chapter 7 Constant Width.sldprt`.

FIGURE 7.37
Examples of the double hold-line fillet

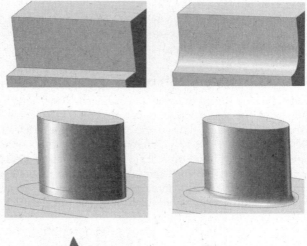

FIGURE 7.38
The constant-width fillet

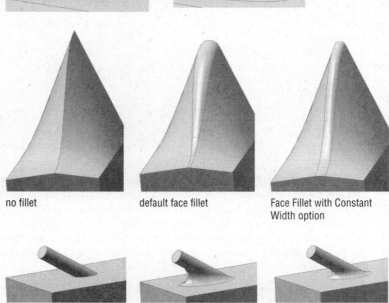

no fillet

default face fillet

Face Fillet with Constant Width option

Applying a Full Round Fillet

To create a full round fillet, you must select three sets of faces. Usually, one face in each set is sufficient. The fillet is tangent to all three sets of faces, but the middle set is on the end and that face is completely eliminated. Figure 7.39 shows several applications of the full round fillet. Notice that it is not limited to faces of a square block, but it also propagates around tangent entities and can create a variable-radius fillet over irregular lofted geometry.

FIGURE 7.39
A full round fillet

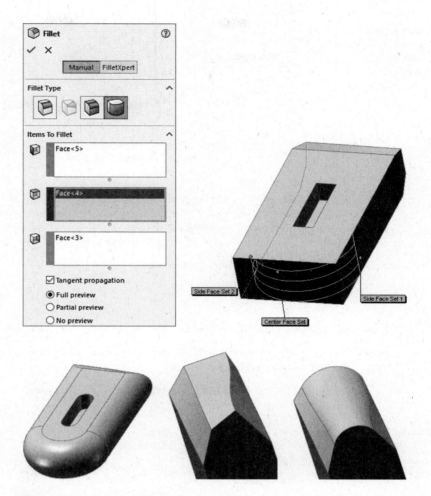

NOTE Be aware that special workflow-assisting options exist for the full round fillet. After selecting a face, you can right-click to advance to the next selection box. If you are already at the last selection box, you can click OK and finish the feature. You might instinctively reach for the Tab key, but remember to look at the cursor to find that backward green L-shaped arrow or the check mark.

Building a Setback Fillet

The setback fillet is the most complex of the fillet options. You can use the Setback option in conjunction with constant-radius, multiple-radius, and variable-radius fillet types. A setback fillet blends several fillets together at a single vertex, starting the blend at some "setback" distance along each filleted edge from the vertex. At least three, and often more, edges come together at the setback vertex. Figure 7.40 shows the PropertyManager interface and what a finished setback fillet looks like. The following steps demonstrate how to use the setback fillet.

FIGURE 7.40
The Setback Fillet interface and a finished fillet

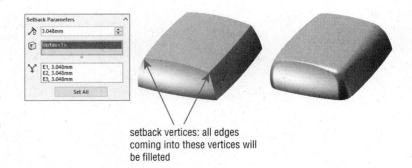

setback vertices: all edges coming into these vertices will be filleted

Setting up a setback fillet can take some time, especially if you are just learning about this feature. You must specify values for fillet radiuses, select edges, and vertices, and specify three setback distances for every vertex. If you are using multiple-radius fillets or variable-radius fillets, this becomes an even larger task. These are the steps:

1. Determine the type of fillet to be used:

    ◆ Constant-radius fillet

    ◆ Multiple-radius fillet

    ◆ Variable-radius fillet

2. Select the edges to be filleted. Selected edges must all touch one of the setback vertices that will be selected in a later step.

3. Assign radius values for the filleted items. Figure 7.41 shows a sample part that illustrates this step.

FIGURE 7.41
The setback fillet setup for steps 1 through 3

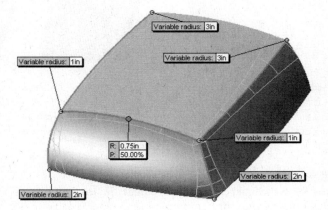

4. Select the setback vertices. In the Setback Parameters panel of the PropertyManager, with the second box from the top highlighted, select the vertices. Although this box looks as if it is only big enough for a single selection, it can accept multiple selections.

5. Enter setback values. As shown in Figure 7.42, the setback callout flags have leaders that point from a specific value to a specific edge. Alternatively, you could use the Set All or Set Unassigned options in a similar way to how they are used with the variable-radius fillet interface. The dimensions refer to distances, as shown in the right-most image in Figure 7.42. The *setback distance* is the distance over which the fillet will blend from the corner to the fillet.

FIGURE 7.42
Entering setback values

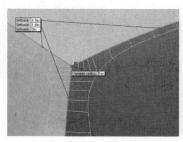 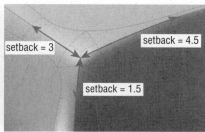

CAUTION   When you select multiple vertices, the preview arrows that indicate which edge you are currently setting the setback value for may be incorrect. The arrows can be shown only on one vertex, so you may want to rely on the leaders from the callouts to determine which setback distance you are currently setting.

6. Repeat the process for all selected setback vertices. If you are using a preview, you may notice that the preview goes away when starting a second set of setback values. Don't worry. This is probably not because the feature is going to fail. After you finish typing the values, the preview returns. When you have spent as much time setting up a feature as you will spend on this, seeing the preview disappear can be frustrating; however, persevere and it will return.

Using Chamfers

Chamfers in SolidWorks are not as flashy as fillets. Some similarities exist, such as the propagation to tangent edges, selecting faces to select the loop of edges around the face, and the ability to see full, partial, or no preview of the finished feature. Many of the best-practice ideas you can apply to fillets also apply to chamfers. Figure 7.43 shows the PropertyManager for chamfers.

You can specify a chamfer using either an angle and a distance or two distance values. For most common situations, these methods are adequate. The situation becomes less definite if you are creating a chamfer between faces that are not at right angles to one another or may not even be planar. These situations require some experimentation to find the correct geometry.

FIGURE 7.43
Working with
Chamfer features

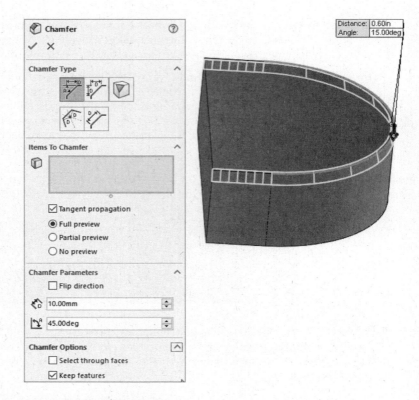

Creating Asymmetrical Chamfers

When you create chamfers at angles other than 45 degrees, you can use the Flip Direction option to control the feature. It is important to note the difference between having *direct control* (angle the chamfer from *this* face) and *indirect control* (angle the chamfer from *the other* face). Indirect control is essentially trial and error. If you don't like what you are given automatically, you can try the other option.

The Flip Direction option flips the direction of all the chamfers being created by a particular feature. This is obviously important only when you have chamfers made at an angle that is not 45 degrees, or unequal distances in the case of a distance-distance chamfer. So in some situations, where the default directions of more than a single edge are going in opposite directions, your only recourse is to create multiple Chamfer features and control them independently.

One of the most interesting functions of the Chamfer tool is the vertex chamfer, shown in Figure 7.44. You can chamfer a corner with equal distances or distances along each edge. This feature can be used only at corners where three edges come together—standard block corners.

ON THE WEBSITE

Check the download material from the Wiley website for video tutorials and sample parts for this chapter.

FIGURE 7.44
Applying a cor-
ner chamfer

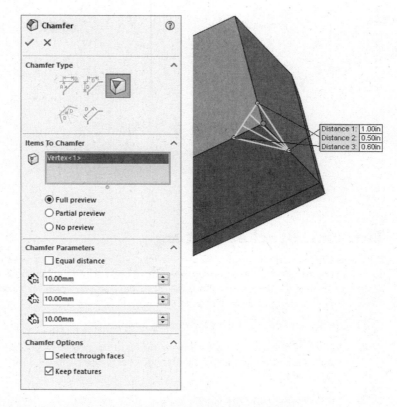

Switching Between Fillet and Chamfer Features

Switching features from fillets to chamfers is now possible, although it has a lot of limitations. You can still start the two features from different icons in the interface, but you can only switch a feature started as a fillet to a chamfer; you cannot change a feature started as a chamfer into a fillet. You can, however, change a fillet to a chamfer back to a fillet.

You may notice that you can't make the change from fillet to chamfer until the Fillet feature has been finished and then edited. So you have to create a fillet, click the green checkmark icon to finish the feature, then right-click and edit the feature, and only then will you be presented with the Chamfer icon at the top of the PropertyManager as shown in Figure 7.45.

This may seem odd, because you still can't switch from a constant-size fillet to a variable-size fillet, but you can change from a constant-size fillet to a chamfer. You also cannot change from a variable size fillet to a chamfer. Another change is the terminology from "constant radius" to "constant size," probably because the fillet profile itself can have multiple radii.

Fillets changed to chamfers retain the automatically assigned Fillet name, but they get a Chamfer icon. You may surmise from this that SolidWorks is preparing to merge Fillet and Chamfer into a new feature called Edge Break, but this is just conjecture and may be incorrect. Because of the unpredictable nature of this change, it will be better for you if you just continue working with separate Fillet and Chamfer features as you have been and try to ignore what appear to be incomplete changes to the Fillet and Chamfer tools.

FIGURE 7.45
Changing from a fillet
to a chamfer

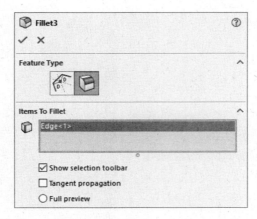

Tutorial: Bracket Casting

When you follow this tutorial, you are encouraged to follow the directions the first time to make sure that you understand the concepts involved, and then to go through it again, this time deviating from the instructions to see if you can expand your understanding by experimentation. To try bracket casting, follow these steps:

1. Open a new part using an inch-based template.

2. On the Right plane, draw a circle centered at the origin with a diameter of 1.50 inches, and draw a second circle placed 4.000 inches vertically from the first, with a diameter of 2.250 inches.

3. Exit the sketch, and make sure Instant 3D is selected. The Instant 3D icon is on the Features toolbar and looks like a ruler with an arrow. Click the sketch in the graphics window and pull the Instant 3D arrow to create a solid. Edit the feature (right-click or left-click the feature either in the graphics window or in the FeatureManager, and click the Edit Feature icon, which is the yellow and green block with a hand pointing to it). Now enter numbers by hand so you extrude the sketch 1.000 inch using a From condition of Offset by 1.000 inch, such that the offset and the extrude depth are in the same direction. Rename this feature **Bosses** in the FeatureManager. Figure 7.46 shows the results of these steps.

NOTE   These steps produce multiple bodies that will be merged in a later step. Multi-body parts are covered in more detail in Chapter 31, "Modeling Multibodies." You can tell that there are multiple bodies by looking at the Solid Bodies folder near the top of the tree and expanding the folder.

FIGURE 7.46
The results of
steps 1 to 3

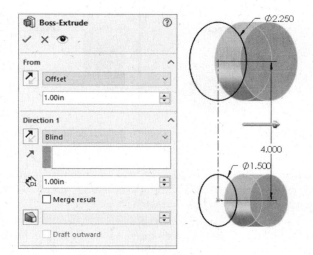

4. On the Top plane in the Top view, open a new sketch and draw a horizontal construction line across the cylinder, from the midpoint of one side to the midpoint of the other side. To pick up the automatic relations for the midpoints more easily, I recommend that you orient the view, normal to the sketch, or use the Top view. It does not matter if you make the relations to the top or bottom cylinder, because the midpoints of the sides are in the same place when they are projected into the sketch plane.

5. Draw an ellipse (Tools ➤ Sketch Tools ➤ Ellipse) that is centered at the midpoint of the construction line and that measures 0.700 inches horizontally and 1.375 inches vertically. Remember that horizontal is along the short sketch origin arrow and vertical is along the long sketch origin arrow. You may want to assign a relation between the center of the ellipse and one of the control points to prevent the ellipse from rotating and fully define the sketch. Exit the sketch when you are satisfied with the result.

6. Show the sketch for the Bosses feature. Click the plus icon next to the Bosses extrude to show the sketch, and then right-click the sketch and select Show.

7. Create a plane parallel to the Top plane at the center of the larger circle. You can access the Plane Creation interface by choosing Insert ➤ Reference Geometry ➤ Plane. If you prese-lect the Top plane from the flyout FeatureManager and the center of the larger sketch circle from the graphics window, the interface automatically creates the correct plane. Click OK to create the plane. Rename this plane **Top Boss Plane**.

8. Draw a second ellipse on the Top Boss Plane. Do not draw a construction line as you did for the first ellipse; instead, just make the centerpoint of the second ellipse directly on top of the first ellipse's centerpoint. Use the Top view again. The dimensions should be 1.000 inch horizontal by 1.750 inches vertical. Figure 7.47 shows the results up to this point.

FIGURE 7.47
The results up to step 8

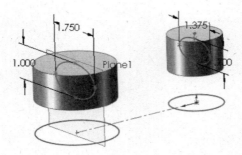

TIP   When you are sketching on parallel planes that are separated by some distance and trying to pick up automatic relations, it is often very helpful to be looking "normal to" the sketch, so you can see how other entities are projected into the sketch plane.

9. Use the Loft feature to loft between the two ellipses. Be sure to select the ellipses in approximately the same location so they do not twist. If the loft preview accidentally twists, use the connectors (light-blue square dots on the sketches that are connected by a straight line) to straighten out the loft.

NOTE   Notice that this feature joined together the other two disjoint bodies with the body that was created by the loft. This is a result of selecting the Merge Result option in the Options panel.

TIP   If you want to experiment, expand the Start/End Constraints panel and apply end conditions for the loft. This causes the loft to change from a straight loft to a curved loft.

10. Right-click all sketches that are displaying and select Hide. Do the same for the Top Boss Plane. This cleans up the display to prevent it from becoming confusing. However, if you prefer to see the sketches, then you can leave them displayed.

TIP   You can either hide or display different types of entities in groups by using the Hide/Show menu. Hide All Types hides everything and disables the options for individual entity types to be used.

11. Open a sketch on the Right plane. Sketch an ellipse such that the center is oriented 1.750 inches vertically from the origin, and the ellipse measures 0.750 inches horizontally and 1.500 inches vertically.

12. Extrude this ellipse using the Up To Next end condition. If Up To Next does not appear in the list, change the direction of the extrude and try it again.

13. Show the sketch of the Bosses feature by expanding the feature (click the "+" next to it), right-clicking or left-clicking the Sketch icon, and clicking the Hide/Show icon (eye-glasses). Next, open a sketch on the Right plane. Sketch two circles that are concentric with the original circles, with the dimensions of .875 inches and 1.250 inches. Exit the sketch.

14. Use Instant 3D to create an extruded cut that goes through the large circular bosses. This feature will look like a boss extrusion at first, so when you have finished dragging its depth, a small toolbar with two icons appears. One of the icons enables you to add draft; the other enables you to turn the boss into a cut. Figure 7.48 shows the state of the model up to this step.

FIGURE 7.48
The results up to step 14

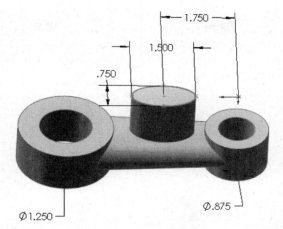

15. Start a Fillet feature and select the face of the Loft feature. Assign a radius of 0.200 inches.

NOTE Although this fillet is created by selecting a face, it is not a face fillet. Selecting a face for a regular constant-radius fillet simply fillets any edge that is on the face.

16. Create a Mirror feature, using the Right plane as the mirror plane. In the Mirror PropertyManager, expand the Bodies To Mirror panel, and select anywhere on the part. Make sure that the Merge Solids option is selected. Click OK to accept the mirror.

17. Orient the view to the Front view, and then turn the view on its side (hold down Alt and press the left-arrow key or right-arrow key six times).

18. Open a new sketch on the Front plane. From the Heads Up View menu, make sure that Hide All Types is not selected and show Temporary Axes. Draw and dimension a horizontal construction line, as shown in Figure 7.49.

FIGURE 7.49
The results up to step 20

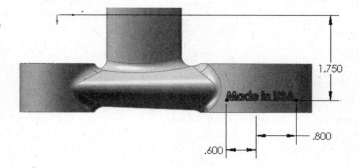

19. With the construction line selected, start the Sketch Text command (Tools ➤ Sketch Entities ➤ Text). Make sure the line appears in the Curves selection box.

20. Click in the text box, and type **Made in USA** (or your name or company name). Select the text and click the Bold button. Deselect the Use Document Font option, change the font to use units, and set the height to 0.175 inches.

21. Click OK to exit the Sketch Text PropertyManager, and click OK again to exit the sketch. You can turn off the Temporary Axis display.

22. Choose Insert ➤ Features ➤ Wrap. You should be prompted to select a plane or a sketch. Use the flyout FeatureManager to select the sketch that you just created with the sketch text in it. Next, select the cylindrical face of the boss to see a preview of the text wrapped onto the face. If the text appears backward, select the Reverse Direction option in the Wrap PropertyManager.

23. Select the Emboss option and assign a thickness of 0.025 inches. Click in the Pull Direction selection box and select the Front plane. Click OK to accept the feature.

24. Save the part and close it. If you would like to examine the reference part, you can find it in the download materials under the filename Chapter 7 Tutorial Bracket Casting. sldprt. The finished part is shown in Figure 7.50.

FIGURE 7.50
The finished part

The Bottom Line

SolidWorks has a wide selection of feature types to choose from, ranging from simple extrudes and revolves to more complex lofts and sweeps. Some features have so many options that it may be difficult to take them all in at once. You should browse through the models from the downloads for this chapter and use the Rollback bar (described in detail in Chapter 2, "Navigating the SolidWorks Interface") to examine how the parts were built. Then you can try to create a few on your own. The best way to learn these features is to use them on practice parts and through experimentation. Curiosity is your greatest teacher.

Master It Copy the part (remodel it from scratch) called LowerLinkBibleBike ch7.sldprt from the download material. Use the Measure tool under Tools ➤ Evaluate ➤ Measure. Depending on the type of work you do, Fillet features can be an important part of your job. Work through this exercise to get some practice with fillets.

Master It Open the part Chapter 7 fillet example.sldprt from the download materials for this chapter. Add fillets to all edges except the outer edges on the Top plane. Remove existing fillets where necessary.

Whether you create a lot of complex shapes or do machine design at your job, sweeps can be important features to master. Open the part Chapter 7 Curves.sldprt and examine how each feature was made. Use the Rollback bar, expand all features, and use the Flatten Tree option (RMB on name of part in FeatureManager, or use Ctrl+T) to try to understand as much as you can about how it was made.

Master It The curves are the tricky part to this one. You have a 3D sketch, a helix, a projected curve (one sketch projected onto another), and a composite curve (two curves added together end to end). Re-create Chapter 7 Curves.sldprt using your own dimensions.

Chapter 8

Selecting Secondary Features

When you need to create features that are somewhat outside the mainstream, you may need to reach deeper into SolidWorks. SolidWorks has lots of functionality that lies out of the public eye that may be just what you are looking for in certain situations. You probably will not use the tools you find in this chapter every day, but knowing about them may mean the difference between having the capability and not having it.

IN THIS CHAPTER, YOU WILL LEARN TO:

◆ Define and create curves in SolidWorks

◆ Choose an occasional specialty feature

Creating Curve Features

Curves in SolidWorks are often used to help define sweeps and lofts, as well as other features. Curves differ from sketches in that curves are defined using sketches or a dialog box, and you cannot manipulate them directly or dimension them in the same way that you can sketches. Functions that you are accustomed to using with sketches often do not work on curves.

These curve features are covered in this chapter:

◆ Projected Curve

◆ Helix and Spiral

◆ Curve Through XYZ Points

◆ Curve Through Reference Points

◆ Composite Curve

◆ Imported Curve

Several features that carry the curve name are actually sketch-based features:

◆ 3D Sketch

◆ Equation-Driven Curve

◆ Intersection Curve

◆ Face Curve

Split Line is another feature that can create edges on faces that can be used like curve features. Split Lines can function as curves in some situations, so this section discusses the Split Line along with the rest of the curve and other curve-like features.

Of these, the Projected and Helix curves are by far the most frequently used, but the others may be important from time to time. Curve functions do not receive much attention from SolidWorks. Updates to curve features are few, and in some cases the functions are buggy. The usefulness of curve features is limited in the software, but in some cases there is no other good way to achieve the same result.

TIP When you come across a function that does not work using a curve entity, but it works on a sketch (for example, making a tangent spline), it may help to use the Convert Entities function. Converting a helix into a 3D sketch creates a spline that lies directly on top of the helix and enables you to make another spline that is tangent to the new spline.

You can find all the curve functions on the Curves toolbar or by choosing Insert ➤ Curve from the menu. Curve features, in general, have several limitations; some of them are serious. You often have to be prepared with workaround techniques when using them.

Manipulating Curves

Curves cannot be mirrored, moved, patterned, or manipulated in any way. (A workaround for this may be to use Convert Entities to create a sketch from the curve, or to create a surface using the curve, and pattern or mirror the surface, using the edge of the surface in place of the curve feature.)

Working with Helix Curve Features

The Helix curve types are all created from a sketch circle. The circle represents the starting plane, center, and diameter of the helix. Figure 8.1 shows the PropertyManagers of the Constant Pitch and Variable Pitch helix types.

You can create all the helical curve types by specifying some combination of total height, pitch, and the number of revolutions. The start angle depends on the relation of the sketch plane to the origin. The start angle can be controlled outside of the PropertyManager through dimensions, design tables, equations, and so forth. The term *pitch* refers to the straight-line distance along the axis between the rings of the helix. Pitch for the spiral is different and is described later.

USING THE TAPER HELIX PANEL

The Taper Helix panel in the Helix PropertyManager enables you to specify a taper angle for the helix. The taper angle does not affect the pitch. If you need to affect both the taper and the pitch, you can use a Variable Pitch helix. Figure 8.2 shows how the taper angle relates to the resulting geometry.

USING THE VARIABLE PITCH HELIX

You can specify a Variable Pitch helix either in the chart or in the callouts that are shown in Figure 8.3. Both the pitch and the diameter are variable. The diameter number in the first row cannot be changed but is driven by the sketch. In the chart shown, the transition between 4 and 4.5 revolutions is where the pitch and diameter both change.

FIGURE 8.1
The Helix/Spiral
PropertyManager

FIGURE 8.2
The Taper Helix panel

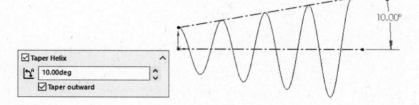

FIGURE 8.3
The Variable Pitch helix

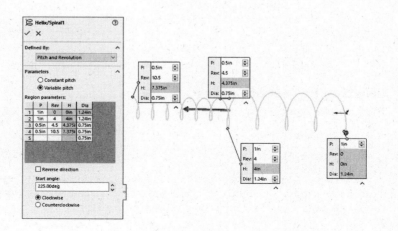

When you double-click a helix feature, SolidWorks displays the dimensions on the screen, which you can then double-click and change. The dimensions displayed this way aren't as organized as when using the PropertyManager, but it may be more convenient.

ESTABLISHING A WORKFLOW

One workflow for all the Helix-type curves is as follows:

1. Draw a circle or select an existing circle.

2. Start the Helix command.

3. Set the options.

4. Click the green checkmark icon to accept the feature.

USING THE SPIRAL

A *spiral* is a flattened (planar) tapered helix. The pitch value on a spiral is the radial distance between revolutions of the curve. (See Figure 8.4.)

FIGURE 8.4
The Spiral option of the Helix feature

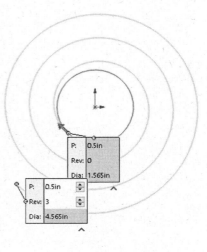

Creating Projected Curves

There are two types of projected curves:

◆ Sketch On Faces

◆ Sketch On Sketch

These names can be misleading if you do not already know what they mean. In both cases, the word *sketch* is used as a noun, not a verb, so you are not actively sketching on a surface; instead, you are creating a curve by projecting a sketch onto a face.

USING SKETCH ON FACES

With this option set, the projected curve is created by projecting a 2D sketch onto a face. The sketch is projected normal (perpendicular) to the sketch plane. The sketch can be an open loop or a closed loop, but it may not be multiple open or closed loops, nor can it be self-intersecting. Figure 8.5 shows an example of projecting a sketch onto a face to create a projected curve.

FIGURE 8.5
A projected curve using the Sketch On Faces option

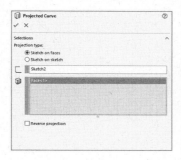 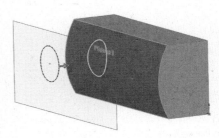

USING SKETCH ON SKETCH

The easiest method to use for visualizing Sketch On Sketch projected curves is the Intersecting Surfaces method. In this method, you can see the curve being created at the intersection of two surfaces that are created by extruding each of the sketches. This method is shown in Figure 8.6.

FIGURE 8.6
Using intersecting surfaces to visualize a Sketch On Sketch projected curve

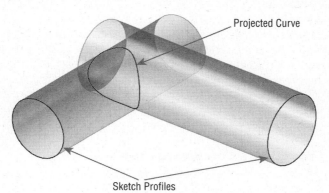

Projected Curve

Sketch Profiles

Using the Curve Through XYZ Points Feature

The Curve Through XYZ Points feature enables you to either type or import a text file with coordinates for points on a curve. The text file can be generated by any program that makes lists of numbers, including Excel. The curve reacts like a default spline, so the teeter-tottering effect may be noticeable, especially because you cannot set end conditions or tangency. To avoid this effect, it may be a good idea to overbuild the curve by a few points on each end or to have a higher density of points.

If you import a text file, the file can have an extension of either `*.txt` or `*.sldcrv`. The sample data file `Chapter 8 - Curve File.sldcrv` is in the download material. The data that it contains must be formatted as three columns of X-, Y-, and Z-coordinates using the document units (inch, mm, and so on), and the coordinates must be separated by a comma, space, or tab. Figure 8.7 shows both the Curve File dialog box displaying a table of the curve through X, Y, and Z points, and the `*.sldcrv` Notepad file. You can read the file from the Curve File dialog box by clicking the Browse button; but if you manually type the points, then you can also save the data out directly from the dialog box. Just like any type of sketch, this type of curve cannot intersect itself.

FIGURE 8.7
The Curve File dialog box showing a table of the curve through X, Y, and Z points, and a Notepad text file with the same information

Using the Curve Through Reference Points Feature

The Curve Through Reference Points feature creates a curve entity from selected sketch points or vertices. The curve can be an open loop or a closed loop, but a closed loop requires that you select at least three points. You cannot set end conditions of the curve, so this feature works like a default spline in the same way as the XYZ curve.

The most common application of this feature is to create a wire from selected points along a wire path. Another common application is a simple two-point curve to close the opening of a surface feature such as Fill, Boundary, or Loft. One drawback in that regard is that the end tangency directions cannot be controlled on curve features. If a 3D sketch spline is used, end tangency direction is controlled easily through the use of spline handles and tangency to construction geometry. Curve Through Reference Points is largely unused, probably because 3D sketch splines are so much more powerful.

Putting Together a Composite Curve

A *composite curve* joins multiple curves, edges, or sketches into a single curve entity. The spring shown in Figure 8.8 was created by using a composite curve to join a 3D sketch, Variable Pitch helix, and projected curve. You can also use model edges with a composite curve. The curve is shown on half of the part; the rest of the part is mirrored. Curves cannot be mirrored, but solid/surface geometry can.

Composite curves overlap in functionality with the Selection Manager to some extent. In some ways, the composite curve is nicer because you can save a selection in case the creation of the feature that uses the Selection Manager fails. (If you can't create the feature, you can't save the selection.) On the other hand, composite curves don't function the same way as a selection of model edges for settings like tangency and curvature.

FIGURE 8.8
A part created from a
composite curve

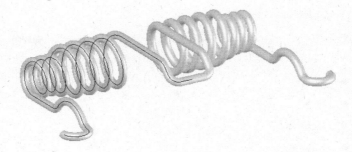

Using Split Lines

Split lines are not exactly curves; they are just edges that split faces into multiple faces. Split lines are used for several purposes, but they are primarily intended to split faces so that draft can be added. They are also used for creating a broken-out face for a color break or to create an edge for a hold-line fillet, as discussed in Chapter 7, "Modeling with Primary Features."

There are some limitations to using split lines. First, they must split a face into at least two fully enclosed areas. You cannot have a split line with an open-loop sketch where the ends of the loop are on the face that is to be split; they must either hang off the face to be split or be coincident with the edges. If you think you need a split line from an open loop, try using a projected curve instead.

CAUTION   A word of caution is needed when using split lines, especially if you plan to add or remove split lines from an existing model. The split lines should go as far down the tree as possible. Split lines change the face IDs of the faces that they split, and often the edges as well. If you roll back and apply a split line before existing features, you may have a significant number of feature references to fix. Similarly, if you remove a split line that already has several dependent features, many other features may also be deleted or simply lose their references.

Using the Equation-Driven Curve

An equation-driven curve is not really a curve feature; it is a sketch entity. It specifies a spline inside a 2D sketch with an actual equation. Even though this is a spline-based sketch entity, it can be controlled only through the equation and not by using spline controls. This feature is covered in more detail in Chapter 3, "Working with Sketches and Reference Geometry," with other sketch entities.

Selecting a Specialty Feature

SolidWorks contains several specialty features that perform tasks that you will use less often than some of the standard features mentioned in Chapter 7, "Modeling with Primary Features." Although you will not use these features as frequently as others, you should still be aware of them and what they do—you never know when you will need them.

These features include:

◆ Scale

◆ Dome

◆ Wrap

◆ Flex

◆ Deform

◆ Indent

Other types of less commonly used features fall into specialty categories such as sheet metal, multibodies, surfacing, plastics, and mold design. This includes features such as Freeform, Combine, Cavity, Scale, and several others. I placed the discussion about these features in chapters devoted to those specialized topics. The features discussed in this chapter are more general-use features.

Using Scale

 The Scale feature, found at Insert ➤ Feature ➤ Scale, is mainly used for preparing models of plastic parts to make mold cavity geometry; however, it can be used for any purpose on solid or surface geometry. Scale does not act by scaling up dimensions for individual sketches and features; rather, it scales the entire body at the point in the FeatureManager history at which it is applied. The Scale PropertyManager is shown in Figure 8.9.

FIGURE 8.9
Applying the
Scale feature

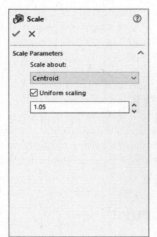

The Scale feature becomes available only when the part contains at least one solid or surface body. You can scale multiple bodies at once and select from one of three options for the Scale About setting or fixed reference: the part origin, the geometry centroid, or a custom coordinate system. Of these, it is generally preferable to select the part origin because you most often want the standard planes moving with respect to the rest of the part as little as possible. If you needed to scale about a specific point on the geometry, you would need to create a custom coordinate system at that point and use that as the reference.

The Scale Factor works like a multiplier, so if you want to double the length, you would enter the Scale Factor 2. This does not work like the Scale function in the Cavity feature, which is less commonly used. Scale within Cavity uses a scale factor that is shown as a percentage increase, so to double the linear dimensions of a part would require a scale factor of 100 percent. The Cavity feature is available only in the context of an assembly and has fallen out of favor with most mold designers.

Scale is also configurable, meaning that different configurations can use different scale factors. Configurations are covered in Chapter 11, "Working with Part Configurations."

An interesting aspect of the Scale feature is that you can disable the Uniform Scaling option. This allows you to apply separate scale factors for the X, Y, and Z directions. In mold making, this can be used if you have a fiber-filled material and the mold requires differential shrink compensation based on the direction of plastic flow, and thus of fiber alignment (the part will shrink less in the direction of fiber alignment). But you could also use it to size any general part. Just remember that if you apply differential scale, circles may be distorted. To get around this, you may be able to reorder the features to apply the Scale feature before the circular features are added.

Because Scale is simply applied to the body rather than to features and sketches, it can be applied to imported parts as well as SolidWorks native parts. Sometimes, people use the Scale feature to compensate for improper imported units. For example, if a part was originally built in inches and translated in millimeters, you might want to scale the part by a factor of 25.4. You can also enter an expression in the Scale Factor box so that if the import units error went the other way, you could scale a part down by 1/25.4. The limitation to the Scale feature is that the SolidWorks modeling space for a single part is a box that's approximately 500 to 700 meters centered about the origin. There appears to be some difference between sketching limits and 3D solid limits.

An implication of the Scale feature that is not stated outright is that it does not scale features, sketches, or dimensions. It is a history-based feature, so the size difference only applies after the Scale feature in the tree.

Using the Dome Feature

The Dome feature in SolidWorks is generally applied to give some shape to flat faces or an area of a flat face. A great example of where a dome fits well is the cupped bottom of a plastic bottle or a slight arch on top of buttons for electronic devices. Domes can add or remove material.

Until SolidWorks 2010, another very similar feature existed, which was called Shape. You can no longer make Shape features, but you may run into one from time to time in old parts. If you find a Shape feature on an old part, it will continue to function unless any of its parent geometry changes. Shape features do not update in SolidWorks 2010 or later. SolidWorks recommends you re-create the geometry as another feature, possibly a Dome or Freeform feature. Included in the sample parts for Chapter 8 is a part called Chapter 8 Domes.sldprt; this part is shown in Figure 8.10. Opening this part will allow you to see the error that appears when you open a part with a Shape feature. The part also demonstrates several ways in which Dome features can be used.

The Dome feature has several attributes that either help it qualify for a given task or disqualify it. These attributes can help you decide if it will be useful in situations you encounter:

◆ The Dome feature can create multiple domes on multiple selected faces in a single feature, although it creates only a single dome for each face.

◆ Using the Elliptical Dome setting, Dome can create a feature that is tangent to the vertical.

◆ Dome can use a constraint sketch to limit its shape.

◆ Dome works on nonplanar faces.

◆ Dome cannot establish a tangent relationship to faces bordering the selected face.

◆ Dome cannot span multiple faces.

◆ Dome displays a temporary untrimmed four-sided patch that extends beyond the selected face when you use it on a non-four-sided face.

◆ Dome functions only on solids, not on surfaces.

The Dome feature has two notable settings: Elliptical Dome and Continuous Dome.

The Elliptical Dome is available only on flat faces where the boundary is either a complete circle or an ellipse. The cross section of the dome is elliptical and does not account for draft, which means that it is always tangent to the perpendicular from the selected flat face.

Continuous Dome is a setting for any noncircular or elliptical face, including polygons and closed-loop splines. The setting results in a single unbroken face. If you deselect the Continuous Dome setting, it functions like the Elliptical Dome setting. Figure 8.10 shows the most useful settings for the Dome feature.

FIGURE 8.10
Examples of various types of domes

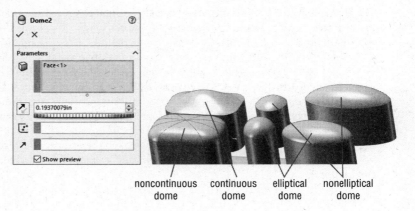

noncontinuous dome   continuous dome   elliptical dome   nonelliptical dome

The workflow for the Dome feature is as follows:

1. Select an area to be domed, or use a split line to create an area to be domed on an existing face.

2. Initiate the Dome feature, set a height, tell it to add or remove material, and set the other settings including the constraint sketch.

3. Accept the feature with the green checkmark icon.

Using the Wrap Feature

The Wrap feature enables you to wrap 2D sketches around analytical or complex faces. Trying to wrap around 360 degrees can cause some difficulties, so you might try that sort of thing in two steps, either with two wraps or a combination of features.

The Wrap feature works by flattening the face, relating the sketch to the flat pattern of the face, and then mapping the face boundaries and sketching back onto the 3D face. It is not a simple projection; it actually does wrap the sketch onto curved faces. Figure 8.11 shows the Wrap PropertyManager interface along with a Wrap onto a cylinder and a Wrap onto a complex shape. The complex wrap is available in the download materials for this chapter (see `Complex Wrap.sldprt`).

FIGURE 8.11
The Wrap Property-Manager interface

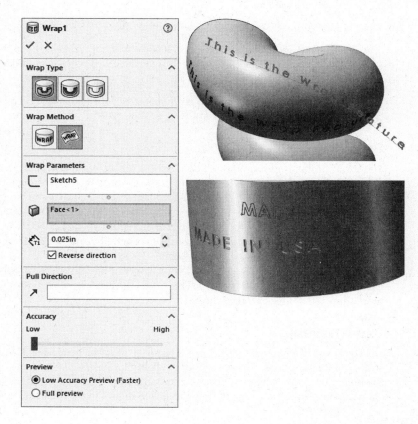

The Wrap feature has three main options:

◆ Emboss

◆ Deboss

◆ Scribe

Wrap can be placed on analytical (cylindrical, conical, and the like) or complex spline surfaces (lofts, sweeps, etc.).

USING SCRIBE

Scribe is the simplest of the options to explain, and understanding it can help you understand the other options. Scribe creates a split line–like an edge on the face.

Several requirements must be met in order to make a wrap feature work:

◆ The face must be a cylindrical or conical face.

◆ The loop must be a closed-loop or nested-closed-loop 2D sketch.

◆ The sketch must be on a plane that is either tangent to or parallel to another plane that is tangent to the face.

◆ Wrap supports wrapping onto multiple faces.

◆ The wrap should not be self-intersecting when it wraps around the part. (Self-intersection will not cause the feature to fail, but on the other types, Emboss and Deboss, it may produce unexpected results.)

Scribes can be created on solid or surface faces. Scribed surfaces are frequently thickened to create a boss or a cut. Figure 8.12 shows a scribed wrap.

USING EMBOSS

The Wrap Emboss option works much like the scribe, but it adds material inside the closed-loop sketch, at the thickness that you specify in the Emboss PropertyManager. Embossing can be done only on solid geometry. If the feature self-intersects, then the intersecting area is simply not embossed and is left at the level of the original face. One result is that creating a full wraparound feature, such as the geometry for a barrel cam, requires a secondary feature. This is because the Wrap feature always leaves a gap, regardless of whether the sketch to be wrapped is under or over the diameter-multiplied-by-pi length.

When you use the Emboss option, you can set up the direction of pull and assign draft so that the feature can be injection molded. This limits the size of the emboss so that it must not wrap more than 180 degrees around the part.

USING DEBOSS

Deboss is just like emboss, except that it removes material instead of adding it. Figure 8.12 demonstrates all these options. The part shown in the images is available in the download material under the filename `Chapter 8 Wrap.sldprt`. For each of the demonstrated cases, the original flat sketch is shown to give you some idea of how the sketch relates to the finished geometry.

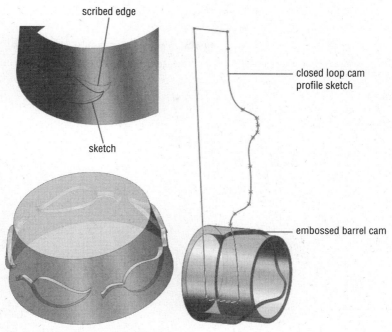

scribed edge

closed loop cam
profile sketch

sketch

embossed barrel cam

Scribed surface feature thickened into
a solid and patterned

Keep in mind that this feature is not like the projected sketch. A projected sketch is projected normal from the sketch plane. A sketch that is 1-inch long when flat will measure 1 inch when wrapped along the curvature of the surface, and it will measure less than 1 inch linearly from end to end.

The embossed cam employed a workaround with a Revolve feature to close the gap that is always created when wrapping all the way around a part.

The example with the debossed text employs a direction of pull and draft so that the geometry can be molded. Sample models are available in the download material for Chapter 8 for Deboss, Emboss, and Scribe.

Using the Flex Feature

The Flex feature is different from most of the other features in SolidWorks. Most of them create new geometry, but Flex (and Deform, which follows) takes existing geometry and changes its shape. Flex can affect the entire part or just a portion of it. Flex works on both solid and surface bodies, as well as imported and native geometry as shown in Figure 8.13.

Flex has four main options and many settings. The four main options are as follows:

Bending: This option establishes two trim planes to denote the ends of the bent area and specifies an angle or radius for the bend.

Twisting: This option establishes two trim planes to limit the area of the twist and enters the number of degrees through which to twist.

Tapering: This option establishes two trim planes to limit the area of the taper. The body is larger toward one end and smaller toward the other end.

Stretching: This option establishes two trim planes to limit the area to be stretched. You can stretch the entire body by moving the trim planes outside of the body.

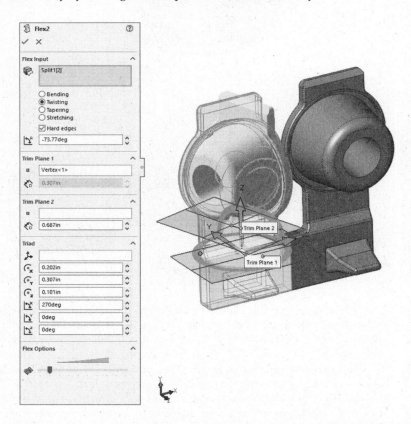

FIGURE 8.13
The Flex feature creating a twist

BEST PRACTICE

Flex is not the kind of feature that you should use to actually *design* parts, but it can be extremely valuable when you need to show a flexible part in an "in use" state. A simple example would be a rubber strap that stretches over something when it is used, but it's designed and manufactured in its free state. The geometry that you can create by using the flex functions is not generally production-model quality, but it is usually adequate for a looks-like model.

The part shown in the figure can be found in the download material under the filename `Chapter 8 Flex.sldprt`.

In some cases, the Triad and trim planes are slightly disoriented. The best thing to do in situations like this is to simply reorient the Triad using the angle numbers in the Triad panel of the PropertyManager. This is also a solution if the planes are turned in such a way that the axis of bending is not oriented to the bend that the part requires.

The Flex feature is very conscious of separate bodies. In some cases this can be helpful, but in default situations when there is only one body in the part, it can be annoying. Remember to select the body to be affected in the very first selection box at the top of the PropertyManager.

TIP   If you want to bend only one of the tabs on the grommet, the best solution is to split the single body into two bodies and flex only one of the bodies. (Splitting a single body into multiple bodies is covered in Chapter 31, "Modeling Multibodies.") The examples shown for twisting and stretching use this technique.

You can place the trim planes by selecting a model vertex, by dragging the arrow on the plane, or by typing in a number. Be careful when dragging the plane arrows because dragging the border of the plane drags the flex value for the feature. (Dragging the plane in a bending operation is like changing the angle or radius for the bend.)

Using the Triad can be very tricky. Moving the Triad in the Bending option moves the axis of the bend, so it determines whether the bend compresses or stretches the material. The position of the Triad also determines which side of the bent body moves or stays stationary, or if both sides move. Placing the Triad directly on a trim plane causes the material outside the bend on that side of the trim plane to remain stationary.

I highly recommend looking at the models provided with this chapter to examine the various functions of the Flex feature more carefully. The model uses configurations, which are covered in Chapter 11, "Working with Part Configurations."

Applying the Deform Feature

Like the Flex feature, the Deform feature changes the shape of the entire model without regard to parametrics, features, history, or dimensions. Some software packages call this technique *global shape modeling*. Also like Flex, Deform works on surface bodies as well as solids. Deform can also handle imported geometry as well as SolidWorks native parts. Model complexity is not an issue unless the part runs into itself during deformation.

The Deform feature is another feature type that you may not use to actually design anything, but you may use to show a model in a deformed state.

BEST PRACTICE

Typically, if you want a model to have a certain shape, you need to intentionally and precisely model it with that shape. The problem with using deform and flex geometry for actual design data is that they both create fairly approximate geometry, and this process yields a result that is not completely intentional. The shape that you finally achieve is the result of an arbitrary uncontrolled function of the feature, not necessarily creating a shape that you had clearly envisioned beforehand.

Deform has three types:

Point: This type deforms a portion of the model by pushing a point and the geometry around it.

Curve To Curve: The most precise and useful deform type. This type selects an existing edge and forces the edge to match a curve.

Surface Push: This type of deform, while conceptually a very interesting function, is nearly unusable in practice. The part is deformed into a shape vaguely resembling an intermediate shape between the existing state of the part and a "tool" body.

Figure 8.14 shows the PropertyManager interface for the Deform feature. The interface is different for each of the three main types, and it changes depending on selections within the individual types. The interface shown is for the Curve To Curve type because I believe this to be the most useful type.

FIGURE 8.14
Using Deform to shape the chair back

LOOKING AT POINT DEFORM

The Point deform option enables you to push a point on the model, and the model deforms as if it were rubber. The key to using this feature is to ensure that the Deform Region option is unselected. Aside from that, you just have to use trial and error when applying the Point deform option. The depth, diameter, and shape of the deformation are not very precise. Also, you cannot specify the precise location for the point to be deformed. Again, this is best used for "looks-like" models, not production data.

LOOKING AT CURVE TO CURVE DEFORM

Because the Curve To Curve deform uses curve, sketch, or edge data, it is a more precise method than the other deform types. The main concept here is to transform a curve on the original model to a new curve, thereby deforming the body to achieve the new geometry.

The model shown in Figure 8.15 has been created using the Curve To Curve deform. The part starts as a simple sweep (sweep an arc along an arc), and then a split line is created to limit the deform to a specific area of the model. The model is in the downloaded files under the filename `Chapter 8 Deform Curve to Curve.sldprt`.

FIGURE 8.15
Using the Curve To Curve deform option

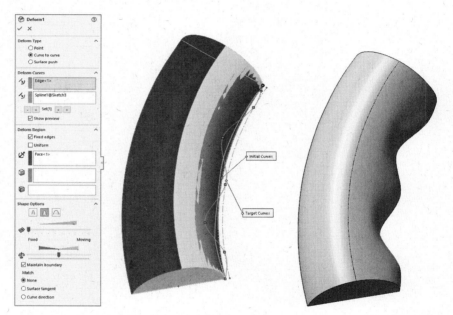

LOOKING AT SURFACE PUSH DEFORM

I don't go into much detail on the Surface Push deform type because it's not one of the more useful functions in SolidWorks. In order to use it, you must have the body of the part that you are modeling and a tool body that you will use to shape the part that you are modeling. The finished shape doesn't fit the tool body directly, but looks about halfway between the model and the tool body, blended together in an abstract sort of way. It looks like the dent that would result from an object being thrown very hard at a car fender, in that neither the thrown part nor the fender is immediately recognizable from the result.

Using the Indent Feature

Indent uses the same ingredients as the Surface Push, but it produces a result that is more useful. For example, if you are building a plastic housing around a small electric motor, the Indent feature shapes the housing and creates a gap between the housing and the motor.

Figure 8.16 shows the PropertyManager interface for the Indent feature, as well as what the indent looks like before and after using the feature.

In this case, the small motor is placed where it needs to be, but there is a wall in the way. Indent is used to create an indentation in the wall by using the same wall thickness and placing a gap of 0.010 inches around the motor. The motor is brought into the wall part using the Insert ➤ Part command. This is a multibody technique. Multibodies are examined in detail in Chapter 31, "Modeling Multibodies."

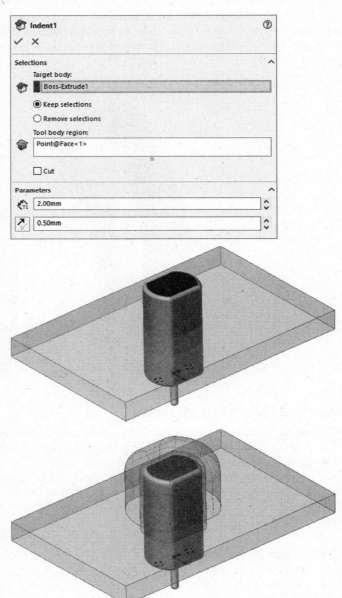

It is possible to use Indent in mold applications; however, most mold designers will prefer to use the shrink percentage that you can get with the Scale/Cavity/Boolean operations rather than the discreet offset that Indent provides.

Using Intersect

Intersect combines the functionality of general solids Boolean operations, Trim Surface, Knit Surface, Split, Replace Face, and Cut With Surface. The tool does not appear to have any exclusive functionality, but it reduces the work to complete some tasks that used to take many steps with a combination of different tools. It is useful for determining the volume of "open" cavities. For example, the part file shown in Figure 8.17 is a multibody with solids and surfaces. The small part in the center is a knob. The big block around it is a mold block, currently a single piece. The four cylinders are surfaces representing alignment pins, and the cylinder in the center is an ejector sleeve. The Top plane goes through the center and represents the parting line of the mold. You can find this part file in the download material for Chapter 8 under the filename `Chapter 8 - Intersect Example.sldprt`.

FIGURE 8.17
Creating a mold from representative solids and surfaces using Intersect: starting point

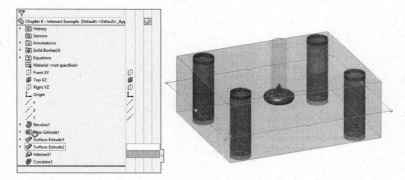

The first step is to select all the entities involved. This is much like the Mutual Trim feature. In the Selections panel of the Intersect PropertyManager, select every solid, surface, and plane that will take part in the operation.

You have the option to cap open surfaces while doing this, but this example does not require it. If one of the holes was a blind hole, but the surface body was open inside the solid, that situation would require a capped surface.

In this example, the only thing about the feature that is not very elegant is that the Merge result is not selective. Perhaps you can think of it as being the split function that is not selective. Notice that the final feature in the tree is a Combine. This was necessary because the original part was split into pieces. You may argue that the original part should be consumed—in which case, I wouldn't have allowed the pieces to remain—but this kind of decision should be up to the individual user, not the programmer.

The Consume Surfaces option simply removes any surface bodies used in the operation.

Tutorial: Creating a Wire-Formed Part

Follow these steps to create a wire-formed part:

1. Open a new part using an inch-based template.

2. Open a sketch on the Right (or Side) plane, and sketch a circle that is centered on the origin with a diameter of 1.500 inches.

3. Create a Helix, Constant Pitch, Pitch, and Revolution, where Pitch = .250 inches, Revolutions = 5.15, and Start Angle = 0. The Helix command is found at Insert ➤ Curve ➤ Helix/Spiral.

4. Create a sketch on the Front plane, as shown in Figure 8.18. Pay careful attention when adding the construction line, as shown. This line is used in the next step to reference the end of the arc.

FIGURE 8.18
The results up to step 4

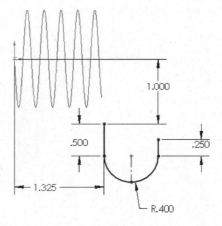

5. Open a sketch on the Right plane, and use the information from Figure 8.19 to add the correct relations and dimensions. Be aware that the two sketches shown are on different sketch planes, which makes it difficult to depict in 2D. You can also open the part from the download materials for reference.

FIGURE 8.19
The sketch for step 5

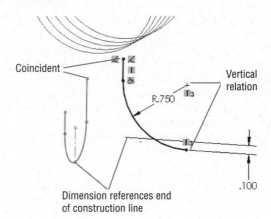

6. Exit the sketch and create a projected curve. The Projected Curve function is found at Insert ➤ Curve ➤ Projected Curve. Use the Sketch On Sketch option.

7. Open a 3D sketch. You can access a 3D sketch from the Insert menu. Select the helix and click Convert Entities on the Sketch toolbar. Then select the projected curve, and click Convert Entities again. You now have two sections of a 3D sketch that are not connected in space.

8. Draw a two-point spline to join the ends of the 3D sketch entities that are closest to one another. Assign tangent relations to the ends to make the transition smooth. Figure 8.20 illustrates what the model should look like at this point.

FIGURE 8.20
The results up to step 8

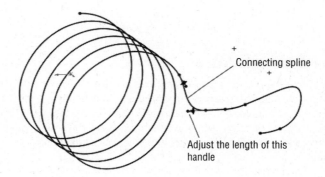

Connecting spline

Adjust the length of this handle

> **TIP** You may have to adjust the length of one of the spline tangency length arrows to keep the spline from remaining inside the cylinder of the helix.

9. Open a sketch on the Right plane, and draw an arc that is centered on the origin and coincident with the end of the 3D sketch helix. The 185-degree angle is created by activating the Dimension tool and clicking first the center of the arc and then the two endpoints of the arc. Now place the dimension. This type of dimensioning allows you to get an angle dimension without dimensioning to angled lines. Exit the sketch.

10. Create a composite curve (Insert ➤ Curve ➤ Composite) consisting of the 3D sketch and the new 2D sketch.

11. Create a new plane using the Normal To Curve option, selecting one end of the composite curve.

12. On the new plane, draw a circle that is centered on the end of the curve with a diameter of 0.120 inches. You need to create a Pierce relation between the center of the circle and the composite curve.

13. Create a Sweep feature using the circle as the profile and the composite curve as the path. To create the sweep, you must first exit the sketch.

14. Hide any curves that still display.

15. Choose Insert ➤ Cut ➤ With Surface. From the flyout FeatureManager, select the Right plane. Make sure the arrow is pointing to the side of the plane with the least amount of material. Click OK to accept the cut. The finished part is shown in Figure 8.21.

FIGURE 8.21
The finished part

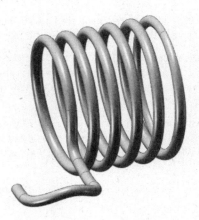

FIGURE 8.21
The finished part

The Bottom Line

SolidWorks has a wide range of features beyond the basic extrudes and revolves. You saw the depth of the standard features in Chapter 7 "Modeling with Primary Features"; now in Chapter 8, you have seen the breadth of some of the less-used, but still useful operations. You won't use each of these secondary features every day, but it is nice to know that if you need to show a model in a flexed in-use state, you at least don't have to directly model the deformed part manually.

The need to custom-design springs in the design of small mechanisms is quite common. Having the ability to create such designs is a valuable skill.

Master It   Use a Helix and a 3D sketch to create a sweep path for a spring with elongated ends for use in a light mechanism.

Packaging and fixturing are additional types of design and modeling that are important for an engineer to master. Create a cavity such that the file named Chapter 8 Bottle.sldprt can nest into it.

Master It   Use the Indent feature to create the cavity in a thin sheet of material.

Text often has to go on irregular surfaces. Work through this example to gain some experience putting it there.

Master It   In the downloadable file Chapter 8 Tutorial Bracket Casting.sldprt, some text is wrapped onto one of the cylindrical bosses. Put a model number on the second boss using the same process.

Chapter 9

Patterning and Mirroring

Patterning and mirroring in SolidWorks are great tools to help you improve your efficiency. SolidWorks software provides many powerful pattern types that also help you accomplish design tasks. In addition to the different types of patterns, some options enable functionality that you may not have considered.

IN THIS CHAPTER, YOU WILL LEARN TO:

- ◆ Use the Pattern function in Sketch mode
- ◆ Use the Mirror function in Sketch mode
- ◆ Use the Geometry Pattern option
- ◆ Pattern or mirror as bodies
- ◆ Understand Pattern Faces
- ◆ Pattern fillets with their parent geometry
- ◆ Use pattern types
- ◆ Create the appearance of geometry with Cosmetic Patterns
- ◆ Discover 3D mirroring techniques

Patterning in a Sketch

You can use both pattern and mirror functions in Sketch mode, although sketch patterns are not a preferred choice because 3D patterning is generally more efficient. The distinction between patterning and mirroring in Sketch mode is important when it comes to sketch performance.

PERFORMANCE

Although there are many metrics for how software performs, in SolidWorks the word *performance* is synonymous with speed. Sketch patterns have a very adverse effect on speed and do not offer the same level of control as feature patterns.

You might hear a lot of conflicting information about which features are better to use in different situations. Users coming from a 2D background often use a function such as sketch patterning because it's familiar, without questioning whether a better approach is available, and often without having a way of measuring how it performs. When in doubt, you can perform a test to determine which features work best for a given situation.

To compare the performances of various types of patterns, I made a series of 20 × 20 patterns using circles, squares, and hexagons. The patterns are both sketch patterns and feature patterns, and I created them with both Verification On Rebuild and Geometry Pattern turned on and off. Verification On Rebuild is an error-checking setting that you can access through Tools ➤ Options ➤ Performance. Geometry Pattern is a setting that is applicable only to feature patterns, and it disables the intelligence in patterned features.

Table 9.1 shows the rebuild times (in seconds) of solid geometry created from various types of patterns as measured by Performance Evaluation. (It is found at Tools ➤ Evaluate ➤ Performance Evaluation; this was formerly called Feature Statistics.) Sketch patterns are far slower than feature patterns, by a factor of about 10. The biggest speed reduction occurs when you use sketch patterns in conjunction with the Verification On Rebuild setting, especially as the number of sketch entities being patterned increases.

VERIFICATION ON REBUILD

When the Verification On Rebuild (VOR) setting is turned off, a given face is tested against each of its neighbors (for example, to see if the model is self-intersecting). When it is turned on, VOR tests each face against every other face in the model. On a simple cube, the difference between on and off is four tests versus five tests. On a larger model, it could well be the difference between four tests and a thousand tests. The type of error this would catch would be, for example, if you had a box and shelled it out, removing one face, and then you put a large fillet on an outer edge. You would see the inside of the shell break through the outside of the fillet. If VOR were turned on, this would cause an error. If VOR were turned off, SolidWorks would allow this, and you would have invalid geometry with no error. To examine this in more detail, open the sample model `Chapter 9 - VOR.sldprt`. Of course, having VOR turned on for large models is very costly from a performance point of view.

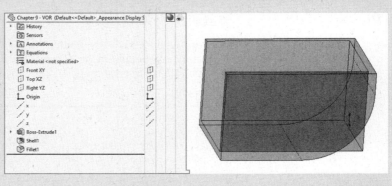

Generally, the number of faces and sketch relations being patterned has a significant effect on the speed of the pattern. The sketch pattern times are taken for the entire finished model, including the sketch pattern and a single Extrude feature, using the sketch with the pattern to do an extruded cut. The sample parts are in the download materials for this chapter for reference. Look for the filenames beginning with Reference1 through Reference7.

The most shocking data here is the difference between a sketch pattern of a hex when a patterned sketch cuts into a flat plate compared to a feature pattern of a single extruded hex with each using the Verification on Rebuild option—0.36 seconds compared to 126 seconds.

TABLE 9.1:   Pattern Rebuild Times in Seconds

PATTERN TYPE	DEFAULT	GEOMETRY PATTERN	VERIFICATION ON REBUILD
20 × 20 sketch circle	.87	n/a	5.52
20 × 20 sketch square	4.5	n/a	60
20 × 20 sketch hex	9.6	n/a	126
20 × 20 feature circle	0.06	0.53	0.08
20 × 20 feature square	0.23	0.53	0.23
20 × 20 feature hex	0.36	0.55	0.36

NOTE   It is true that using a multicontour sketch for the cut is a slow process, but that might not be because of the pattern. Delete the sketch pattern relation, do a Ctrl+Q, and check the statistics. In my test, the results were very close. A big feature (with many resulting faces) will be slow, regardless what relations are in the sketch, sketch patterns or not.

Always keep this general information about sketch patterns in mind:

◆   Sketch patterns are bad for rebuild speed.

◆   The more faces created by any pattern, the longer it takes to rebuild.

◆   The more sketch relations a sketch pattern has, the longer it takes to rebuild.

◆   Geometry Pattern does not improve rebuild speed unless a special end condition like Up To Surface has been used.

◆   Verification On Rebuild dramatically increases rebuild time with the number of faces but is far less affected by feature patterns than extruded sketch patterns.

Figure 9.1 shows one of the parts used for this simple test.

One interesting finding of this test was that if a patterned extruded feature creates a situation where the end faces of the extruded features have to merge into a single face, the feature could take 10 times the amount of time to rebuild as a pattern with unmerged end faces. This was an inadvertent discovery. I'm sure you will make your own discoveries if you investigate rebuild speeds for end conditions for cuts such as Through All, Up To Face, Up To Next, and so on, as well as the difference between cuts and boss features. Further, using Instant 3D can be an impediment when you're editing very large sketches simply due to the effects of the preview.

FIGURE 9.1
A pattern part used
for the test

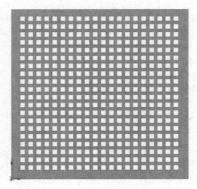

You should also note that the situation this simple test covers is very limited in scope. Because the plate is a constant thickness, the Geometry Pattern option actually works, which it wouldn't if the plate varied in thickness (with the through holes). It also tests only the Through All end condition, and the Geometry Pattern is best used to simply disable intelligent end conditions. I believe that many people use it as a random toggle trying to get patterns to work that SolidWorks would otherwise not allow to work.

I discuss the Geometry Pattern option in more detail later in this chapter. I wanted to start the chapter with a discussion that called attention to the common misperception that sketch patterns are somehow better than feature patterns.

Debunking More Sketch Myths

People often say that it is best practice to define your sketches fully. I completely agree with this statement. However, I have heard people say that fully defined sketches solve faster, with the rationale being that SolidWorks must figure out how to solve the under-defined sketch, but the fully defined sketch is already spelled out. Let's find out.

FIGURE 9.2
Comparing the rebuild
times of a fully defined
sketch to a completely
undefined sketch

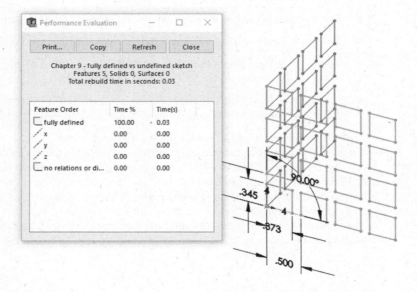

In this example, I created a sketch pattern of 4 × 4 rectangles and used the Fully Define Sketch tool to add dimensions. Then I copied and pasted the sketch and removed all the dimensions and relations. Figure 9.2 shows the Feature Statistic results.

Fully defined sketches are best practice, but it is not due to rebuild speed. Sketch relations are costly from a rebuild-time point of view. Patterning sketch relations are even more costly. The rebuild time does not even come close to the time that it takes the Fully Define Sketch tool to create all the dimensions and relations in the first place. This combination of geometry, software, and hardware took about 30 seconds of CPU time to add the relations and dimensions.

For most models that have fewer than 50 features, you may never notice this rebuild time, and the price you pay is certainly worth the peace of mind you get from having the stability of a fully defined sketch. For large models where you have hundreds of features, or features that use lots of very busy sketches, you should pay attention to how much information you put into the sketch and try to limit sketch patterns and even elements such as sketch fillets, using feature fillets instead where possible.

Patterning a Sketch

Sketch patterns are an available tool—they are valid, and in a few cases, they are truly necessary. It is best to preselect the sketch entities that you want to pattern before using the Sketch Pattern tool. If you do not preselect, then after the PropertyManager is open, you can only select entities to pattern one by one, because the window select is not available for this function. The RMB selection options, such as Select Chain, are also not available in this interface, reinforcing the need to treat sketch patterns as a preselection feature.

TIP　When creating a linear sketch pattern, be sure to select the Add Spacing Dimension check boxes. If these dimensions are not added, then editing the pattern becomes more difficult.

USING THE LINEAR SKETCH PATTERN

The Linear Pattern PropertyManager is shown in Figure 9.3.

Unlike other PropertyManagers, the selected entities for the sketch pattern functions are found at the bottom of the PropertyManager instead of at the top. This is a little confusing. Sketch tool PropertyManagers, such as Convert Entities and Mirror, place the selection box at the top.

The Direction 1 panel works predictably by establishing the direction and spacing and then the number. The Angle setting enables you to specify a direction that does not rely on anything outside of the sketch.

The Direction 2 panel works a little differently. You must first specify how many instances you want, and then the other information will become available. The spacing is grayed out until you tell it you want more than one instance in Direction 2.

FIGURE 9.3
The Linear Pattern
PropertyManager

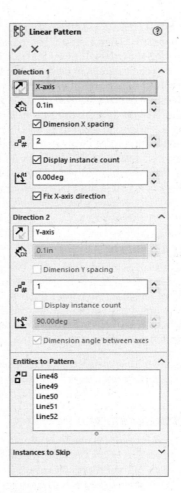

USING THE CIRCULAR SKETCH PATTERN

The Circular Sketch Pattern option defaults to the sketch origin as the center of the pattern. You can move and position this point using the numbers in the PropertyManager, but you cannot dimension it until after the pattern is created. Again, this is another feature where you need to preselect because window selection is not available (patterned sketch entities must be selected one by one to go into the Entities to Pattern panel). Figure 9.4 shows the Circular Pattern PropertyManager.

FIGURE 9.4
The Circular Pattern
PropertyManager

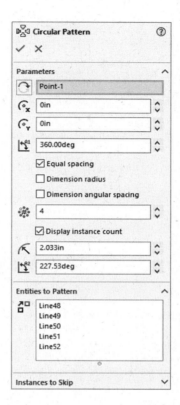

FIGURE 9.4
The Circular Pattern
PropertyManager

Mirroring in a Sketch

Mirroring in a sketch is a completely different matter from patterning in a sketch. It offers superior performance, and the interface is better developed. Mirrored entities in a sketch are instrumental parts of establishing design intent.

Two methods of mirroring items in a sketch are discussed here, along with a method to make entities work as if they have been mirrored when in fact they were manually drawn.

Using Mirror Entities

You can use the Mirror Entities tool in two ways: with the interface or without the interface.

Figure 9.5 shows the Mirror Entities PropertyManager.

If you preselect the entities to be mirrored along with a single centerline and then click the Mirror Entities icon, you will never see the PropertyManager interface, and the regular sketch entities will be mirrored about the single centerline.

FIGURE 9.5
Selecting items in the
Mirror Entities
PropertyManager

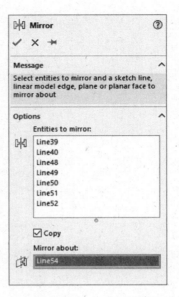

If you prefer to use the interface, just click the Mirror icon first and then select entities. If you use this method, you can mirror centerlines as well as regular lines, and you can select a regular line, an edge, or a plane in the Mirror About box. Also, you can turn off the Copy option to remove the original entities when creating the mirror. Using the interface allows you much more flexibility; avoiding the interface has some special requirements, but it's much faster.

Using Dynamic Mirror

As the name suggests, Dynamic Mirror mirrors sketch entities as they are created. You can activate it by selecting a centerline and clicking the Dynamic Mirror button on the Sketch toolbar. Dynamic Mirror is not on the toolbar by default; you need to choose Tools ➤ Customize ➤ Commands to add it to the toolbar. You can also access Dynamic Mirror by choosing Tools ➤ Sketch Tools ➤ Dynamic Mirror from the menu.

When you activate this function, there is no PropertyManager interface. The centerline displays with hatch marks on the ends and remains active until you turn off or exit the sketch. Figure 9.6 shows the centerline with hatch marks.

FIGURE 9.6
The Dynamic Mirror
centerline with
hatch marks

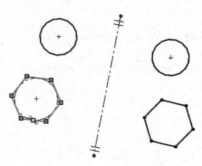

Using Symmetry Sketch Relation

In some editing situations, you may not want to create new geometry, but will use existing entities with new relations driving them. To create the Symmetry sketch relation, you must have two similar items (such as lines or endpoints) and a centerline selected.

To add the symmetry relation after you have made the proper selection, use the pop-up toolbar interface or the Add Relation toolbar button. These two options are shown in Figure 9.7.

You can find more information on manipulating sketch relations in Chapter 3, "Working with Sketches and Reference Geometry."

FIGURE 9.7
Two ways to add a symmetric sketch constraint

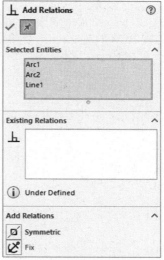

Using Mirroring in 3D Sketches

Chapter 6, "Getting More from Your Sketches," deals with 3D sketches in more detail, but I discuss the mirror functionality here to connect it with the rest of the mirroring and patterning topics. You can mirror sketch entities in 3D sketches, when sketching in 3D space or on 2D planes. Mirroring in 3D space requires a plane to mirror about; then you can use the regular Mirror Entities tool that you use in 2D sketches.

Sketch patterns are unavailable in the 3D sketch, but you can use the Move, Rotate, and Copy sketch tools on planes in 3D sketches.

Working with 3D Patterns

Patterning 3D geometry—whether components, bodies, features, or faces—is extremely powerful. It saves design time, as well as compute time, when used correctly. Selecting the right type of entities to serve as the seed for the pattern can determine your success with this function.

One of the basic functions in patterns is determining the original instance (*seed*) from the patterned instances. These are determined by color when you select the pattern feature in the FeatureManager using the Selected Item 1 and 2 determined by the settings at Tools ➤ Options ➤ Colors. This coloring does not follow the same scheme that you see when editing or creating the feature, but at those times the seed should be obvious, as patterned instances are not shown shaded.

To be able to visualize the seed without selecting the feature, some users manually change the color of the seed.

Exploring the Geometry Pattern Option

The SolidWorks Help file says that the Geometry Pattern option in feature patterns results in a faster pattern because it does not pattern the parametric relations. This claim is valid only when there is an end condition on the patterned feature such that the feature will actually pattern the end condition's parametric behavior. The part shown in Figure 9.8 falls into this category. After you turn on the Geometry Pattern option, the improved rebuild time goes from 0.30 to 0.11 seconds. Although a 60-percent reduction is significant, the most compelling argument for the use of the Geometry Pattern has nothing to do with rebuild time. It is to avoid the effect of patterning the start- and end-condition parametrics. It ignores all settings in the feature definition. In effect, Geometry Pattern has much of the same effect as patterning faces, but with some differences.

FIGURE 9.8
A Geometry Pattern test

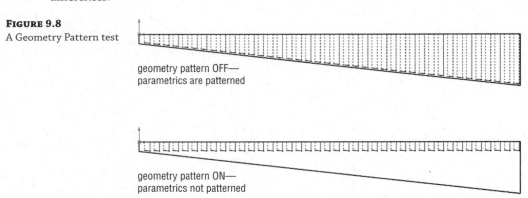

geometry pattern OFF—
parametrics are patterned

geometry pattern ON—
parametrics not patterned

In fact, the Geometry Pattern option is intended to pattern existing geometry without the parametric intelligence. Geometry Pattern was not designed to improve rebuild speed.

Under some conditions, Geometry Pattern does not work. One example is any time a patterned face merges with a face that cannot be patterned. Figure 9.9 shows two patterns, one that can use Geometry Pattern and one that cannot.

FIGURE 9.9
Merged faces

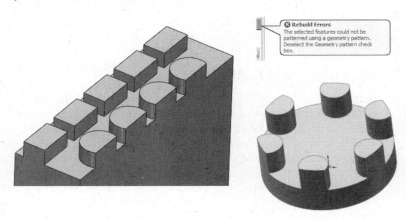

The pattern of the rectangular bosses cannot use Geometry Pattern because the face that is merged is not merged in all pattern instances. The pattern of truncated cylinders shown on the same part as the pattern of rectangular bosses can use Geometry Pattern because the flat face is merged in every pattern instance. The circular pattern in the image to the right in Figure 9.9 also allows Geometry Pattern for the same reason.

In some situations, SolidWorks error messages may send you in a loop. As shown in Figure 9.10, one message may tell you that the pattern cannot be created with the Geometry Pattern turned on, so you should try to turn it off.

When you do that, you may get another message that says the pattern will not work and that you should try to use the Geometry Pattern setting. In cases like this, you may try to use a different end condition for the feature that you want to pattern or change the selection of features patterned along with the feature, such as fillets. You may also try to pattern bodies or even faces rather than features. These last two options are covered in the following sections.

FIGURE 9.10
Geometry Pattern
error message

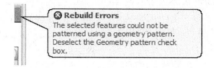

Patterning Bodies

I cover multibodies in depth in Chapter 31, "Modeling Multibodies," but I will briefly discuss the topic here. No discussion of patterning is complete without a discussion of bodies.

SolidWorks parts can contain multiple *solid* or *surface* bodies. A solid body is a solid that comprises a single contiguous volume. A surface body is different—think of it as a sheet knitted together from several faces that does not have the requirement to enclose a volume—but it can also be patterned and mirrored as a body.

There are both advantages and disadvantages to mirroring and patterning bodies instead of features. The advantages can include the simplicity of selecting a single body for mirroring or patterning. In cases where the geometry to be patterned is complex or there is a large number of features, patterning bodies also can be much faster. However, in the example used earlier (Table 9.1) with patterning features in a 20 × 20 grid of holes, when done by patterning a single body of 1″ × 1″ × 0.5″ with a 0.5″ diameter hole, patterning bodies gives a rebuild time of about 60 seconds with or without Verification on Rebuild. The function that combines the resulting bodies into a single body takes most of the time. This means that for large patterns of simple features, patterning bodies is *not* an efficient technique. Although I do not have an experiment in this chapter to prove it, it seems intuitive that creating a pattern of a smaller number of complex bodies using a large number of features in the patterned body would show a performance improvement over patterning the features.

Another disadvantage of patterning or mirroring bodies is that it does not allow you to be selective. You cannot mirror the body minus a couple of features without doing some shuffling of feature order in the FeatureManager. In addition, the Merge Bodies option within the mirror feature does not work in the same way that it works for other features. It merges only those bodies that are part of the mirror to other bodies that are part of the mirror. Pattern Bodies does not even have an option to merge bodies. Both of these functions often require an additional combine feature (for solid bodies) or knit (for surface bodies) to put the final results together.

Some of these details may seem obscure when you're reading about them, but when you begin to work patterning bodies and begin trying to merge them into a single body, read over this section again. The inconsistency between the Merge option existing in Mirror but not in Pattern, as well as the functional discrepancy between the Merge in Mirror and the Merge Result in, for example, Extrude is unexplainable and is a possible opportunity for an enhancement request.

Patterning Faces

Most of the pattern types have an option for Pattern Faces. This option has a few restrictions, the main limitation being that all instances of the pattern must be created within the boundaries of the same face as the original. Figure 9.11 shows an example of the Pattern Faces option working with a Circular Pattern feature.

FIGURE 9.11
A circular pattern using the Pattern Faces option

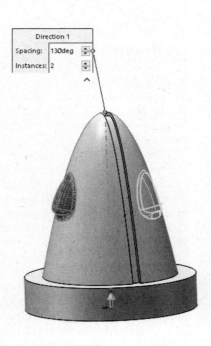

To get around the same face limitation, you can knit faces together and pattern the resulting surface body, as shown in Figure 9.12.

FIGURE 9.12
Patterning a
surface body

A split in the face means faces
from the feature on the side
cannot be patterned all
the way around.

Patterning faces is another way of patterning geometry within SolidWorks without patterning the feature intelligence that was built into the original. It is also a way to make patterns on imported parts from existing geometry. Chapter 37, "Using Imported Geometry and Direct Editing Techniques," addresses this topic briefly in the discussion on imported geometry and direct edit techniques.

Patterning faces is not a widely used technique; however, it should be somewhere in your toolbox of tricks. Although it may be lurking near the bottom of the pile, it is still useful in special circumstances.

Patterning Fillets

You may hear people argue that you cannot pattern fillets. This is only partially true. It is true that fillets as individual features cannot be patterned. For example, if you have a symmetrical box and a fillet on one edge and want to pattern only the fillet to other edges, this does not work. However, when a fillet is patterned with its parent geometry, it is a perfectly acceptable candidate for patterning. This is also true for the more complex fillet types, such as variable radius and full radius fillets. You may need to use the Geometry Pattern option, and you may need to select all the fillets affecting a feature, but it certainly does work.

Understanding Pattern Types

Up to now, I have discussed patterns in general; differentiated sketch patterns from feature patterns, face patterns, and body patterns; and looked at some other factors that affect patterning and mirroring. In this section, I will discuss each individual type of pattern to give you an idea of what options are available.

When we discuss component patterns in assemblies, keep in mind that component pattern types are limited, but you can use a feature pattern from a part to drive a component pattern in an assembly.

Using the Linear Pattern

The Linear Pattern feature has several available options:

Single Direction or Two Directions   Directions can be established by edge, plane, planar face, sketch entity, axis, or linear dimension. If two directions are used, the directions do not need to be perpendicular to one another.

Spacing   The spacing represents the center-to-center distance between pattern instances. It can be driven by discreet spacing dimension or by an Up To Reference where the software automatically figures the spacing when you input the end reference, minimum end offset distance, and the required spacing.

The reference for spacing can be figured on the feature centroid or on a selected reference, such as a vertex, an edge, or a plane. This is most important to get the correct relationship between the last instance and the "up to" or end reference.

Number of Instances   This number represents the total number of features in a pattern, which includes the original seed feature. It can also be driven by an equation. Equations are covered in detail in Chapter 10, "Using Equations."

These options are shown in Figure 9.13.

FIGURE 9.13
The Direction 1 panel of the Linear Pattern driving an Up To Reference pattern

Direction 2   The second direction works just like the first, with the one exception of the Pattern Seed Only option. Figure 9.14 shows the difference between a default two-direction pattern and one using the Pattern Seed Only option.

FIGURE 9.14
Using the default
two-direction pattern
and the Pattern Seed
Only option

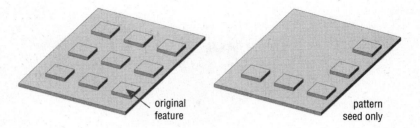

Instances To Skip   This option enables you to select instances (individually or with a box or lasso) that you would like to leave out of the final pattern. On your monitor, the pink dots are the instances that remain, and the red dots are the ones that have been removed. Figure 9.15 shows the interface for skipping instances. Pink is used for the instances to be created and gray for the instances to be skipped.

FIGURE 9.15
Using the Instances To
Skip option

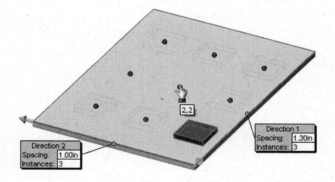

Propagate Visual Properties   This option patterns the color, texture, or cosmetic thread display, along with the feature to which it is attached.

Vary Sketch   This option in patterns is often overlooked and not widely used or understood. Although it may have a niche application, it is a powerful option that can save you lots of time and open up design possibilities you may not have considered previously.

Vary Sketch allows the sketch of the patterned feature to maintain its parametric relations in each instance of the pattern. It is analogous to Geometry Pattern. Where Geometry Pattern disables the parametric end condition for a feature, Vary Sketch enables the parametric sketch relations for a pattern.

To activate the Vary Sketch option, the Linear Pattern must use a linear dimension for its Pattern Direction. The dimension must measure in the direction of the pattern, and adding the spacing for the pattern to the direction dimension must result in a valid feature.

The sketch relations must hold for the entire length of the pattern. Figure 9.16 shows the sketch relations and the resulting pattern. This feature does not have a preview function.

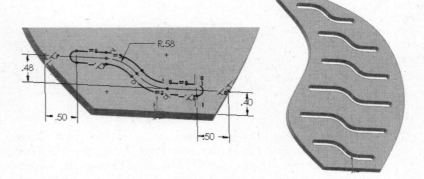

FIGURE 9.16
Using the Vary
Sketch option

ON THE WEBSITE

To better understand how this feature works, open the sample file called `Chapter 9 Vary Sketch .sldprt` from the materials downloaded and edit Sketch2.

Edit the 0.40-inch dimension. Double-click it, and use the scroll arrow to increase the dimension; watch the effect on the sketch. If a sketch does not react to changes properly, it cannot be used with the Vary Sketch option. In this case, the 0.40-inch dimension is used as the direction, because that is the dimension that will drive the sketch down the pattern. When using this option, the feature sketch must be driven by a single dimension. If the 0.48-inch dimension were anchored to the origin or the edge of the part like the 0.40-inch dimension, the pattern would not work properly. The direction dimension must be able to drive the sketch in the same way that this one does. These dimensions cannot pass through the Zero value and cannot flip directions or move into negative values. The whole operation is being driven by the construction lines and arcs at the centerline of the slot. Sketch points along the model edges are kept at a certain distance from the ends of the slots using the 0.50-inch dimensions. The arcs are controlled by an Equal Radius relation and a single 0.58-inch radius dimension. The straight lines at the ends of the slots are controlled by an Equal Length relation.

This type of dimensioning and relation creation is really what parametric design is all about. The Vary Sketch option takes what is otherwise a static linear pattern and makes it react parametrically in a way that would otherwise require lots of setup to create individual features. If you model everything with the level of care that you need to put into a Vary Sketch Pattern feature sketch, then your models will react very well to change.

Instances To Vary   Instances To Vary is different from Instances To Skip and Vary Sketch. It allows you to make various edits to the pattern. This is extremely powerful stuff for patterning. Refer to Figure 9.17 to see the Instances To Vary PropertyManager panel of the Linear Pattern feature.

Direction 1 Increments   Direction 1 Increments controls the pattern spacing for the current direction. So the first spacing is X, the second spacing is X + Y, then X + 2Y, and so on. Using this option, the spacing between pattern instances can either grow or shrink, because the increment can be positive or negative.

In the table below the Direction 1 Spacing Increments box, you can select additional dimensions from the patterned feature to increment in the same way. In Figure 9.17, you see the patterned feature gets further apart, narrower, taller, and moved to one side with each instance.

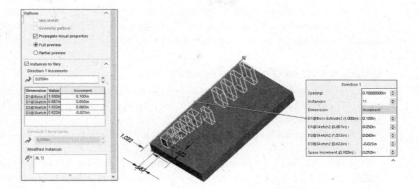

The preview does not show the final variation of the instances unless you use the Full Preview toggle in the Options panel. The advantage of using the Partial Preview is the preview calculation speed for large or complex patterns.

Modified Instances   Modified Instances controls any further modifications you want to make to an individual instance. For example, in Figure 9.17, you can see that one instance has been pushed to the side, and one instance has been skipped. The familiar pink dots usually used for Instances To Skip are also used here, whereas the gray dot still means the instance has been skipped, but the green dot means that the instance has been modified. I recommend that you edit the part from the downloaded example files for this chapter named Up to Reference pattern. sldprt and edit the LPattern1 feature to see the colors and the previews fully on your monitor.

Using the Circular Pattern

The Circular Pattern feature requires a circular edge or sketch, a cylindrical face, a revolved face, a straight edge, an axis, or a temporary axis to act as the Pattern Axis of the pattern. All the other options are the same as for the Linear Pattern—except that the Equal Spacing option works differently.

Equal Spacing takes the total angle and evenly divides the number of instances into that angle. The name *equal spacing* is a bit misleading because all Circular Patterns create equal spacing between the instances, but somehow everyone knows what they mean.

Without using the Equal Spacing option, the Angle setting represents the angular spacing between instances.

The Vary Sketch option is available in Circular Pattern, as well. The principles for setup are the same, but you must select an angular dimension for the direction. The part shown in Figure 9.18 was created using this technique.

FIGURE 9.18
A Circular Pattern
vary sketch

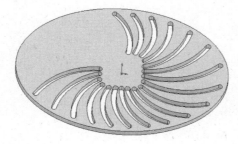

If you are creative with the sketch relations you apply to a sketch, you can obtain some pretty exotic results from patterns using the Vary Sketch option. Instances To Vary also is available in the Circular Pattern, with comparable functionality to the Linear Pattern described earlier.

Using a Curve-Driven Pattern

The Curve Driven Pattern command does just what it sounds like: It drives a pattern along a curve. The curve could be a line, an arc, or a spline. It can be an edge, a loop, a 2D or 3D sketch, or even a real curve feature. An interesting thing about a curve-driven pattern is that it can have a Direction 2—and Direction 2 can be a curve. This pattern type is one of the most interesting and has many options.

For an entire sketch to be used as a curve, the sketch must not have any sharp corners: all the entities must be tangent. This could mean using sketch fillets or a fit spline. The example shown in Figure 9.19 was created using sketch fillets. This pattern uses the Equal Spacing option, which spaces the number of instances evenly around the curve. It also uses the Offset Curve option, which maintains the patterned feature's relationship to the curve throughout the pattern, as if an offset of the curve goes through the centroids of each patterned instance. The Align To Seed option is also used, which keeps all the pattern instances aligned in the same direction.

FIGURE 9.19
A curve-driven pattern using sketch fillets

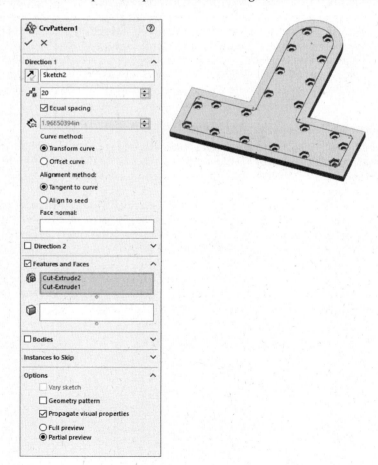

Figure 9.20 shows the same part using the Transform Curve positioning option and Tangent To Curve alignment option.

Instead of an offset of the curve going through the centroids of each patterned feature instance, in the Transform Curve, the entire curve is moved rather than offset. On this particular part, this causes a messy pattern. The Tangent to Curve option gives every patterned instance the same orientation relative to the curve as the original.

FIGURE 9.20

Using the Transform Curve and Tangent To Curve options

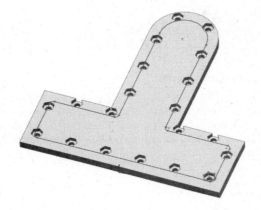

The Face Normal option is used for a 3D pattern, as shown in Figure 9.21. Although this functionality seems a little obscure, it is useful if you need a 3D Curve Driven Pattern on a complex surface. If you are curious about this example, it is in the material from the download with the filename `Reference 3d Curve Driven.sldprt`.

FIGURE 9.21

Using a 3D curve-driven pattern

Using a Direction 2 for a curve-driven pattern creates a result that's similar to what is shown in Figure 9.22. This is another situation that, although rare, is good to know about.

The rest of the Curve Driven Pattern command works like the other pattern features that have already been demonstrated.

FIGURE 9.22
Using Direction 2 with a
curve-driven pattern

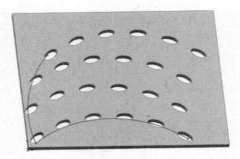

Using a Sketch-Driven Pattern

Sketch-driven patterns use a set of sketch points to drive the locations of features. The Hole
Wizard drives the locations of multiple holes using sketch points in a similar way. However, the
Sketch Driven Pattern command does not create a 3D pattern in the same way that the Hole
Wizard does. Figure 9.23 shows a two-directional sketch-driven pattern. A reference point is not
necessary for the first feature.

FIGURE 9.23
Using a sketch-
driven pattern

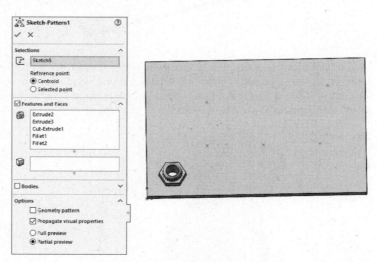

The Centroid option in the Reference Point section is fine for symmetrical and other easily
definable shapes such as circles and rectangles, where you can find the centroid just by looking at
it; but on more complex shapes, you may want to use the Selected Point option.

Using a Table-Driven Pattern

A table-driven pattern drives a set of feature locations, most commonly holes, from a table. The
table may be imported from any source with two columns of data (X and Y) that are separated by
a space, tab, or comma. Extraneous data will cause the import to fail.

The X, Y origin for the table is determined by a Coordinate System Reference Geometry feature. The XY plane of the coordinate system is the plane to which the XY data in the table refers.

You can access the Coordinate System command by choosing Insert ➤ Reference Geometry ➤ Coordinate System from the menu. You can create the coordinate system by selecting a combination of a vertex for the origin and edges to align the axes. Like the Sketch Driven Pattern command, this feature can use either the centroid or a selected point on the feature to act as the reference point.

The fact that this feature is still in a floating dialog box points to its relatively low usage and priority on the SolidWorks upgrade schedule. The interface for the feature is rather crude in comparison to some of the more frequently used features. This interface is shown in Figure 9.24.

FIGURE 9.24
The Table Driven Pattern dialog box

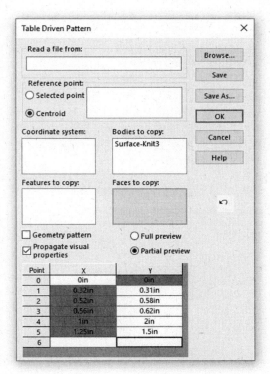

Using the Fill Pattern

The Fill Pattern feature fills a face or area enclosed by a sketch with the pattern of a selected feature or a seed cut. The type of pattern used to fill the area is limited to one of four preset patterns that are commonly used in gratings and electronics ventilation in plastics and sheet metal. These patterns and other options for the Fill Pattern feature are shown in Figure 9.25.

FIGURE 9.25
Using the Fill
Pattern feature

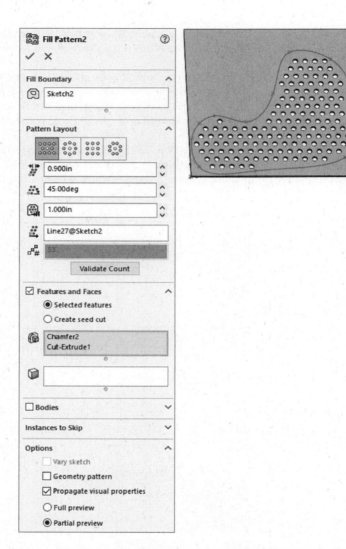

The Pattern Layout panel enables you to control spacing and other geometrical aspects of the selected pattern layout, as well as the minimum gap from the fill boundary. This is most useful for patterns of regularly spaced features with an irregular boundary.

Using a Variable Pattern

The Variable Pattern command combines techniques from the table-driven pattern with design tables. You control all the parameters of multiple instances of a table-patterned feature. The name might be misleading, because there is no actual pattern. The command just places a parametric copy of features wherever you want them.

One of the biggest distinguishing characteristics of the Variable Pattern command is that it records failed instances. The alternative is for the entire feature to fail rather than just a single instance, as will happen with other pattern features.

As you might expect with anything so powerful, there are limitations. For example, it will not allow you to pattern Hole Wizard holes or other patterns. Also, it will not accept a 3D sketch as reference geometry. Being such a highly parametric feature, the Variable Pattern command tends to be susceptible to some long-standing difficulties in SolidWorks, such as getting directions confused when spinning an angle.

Most of the examples of this function you will see around the Internet are simplistic, 2D, and don't really capture its unique capabilities, nor do they offer any compelling reasons to use it. I have two examples for you here. One is rather abstract and presented to show the concept. The other shows a slightly more plausible application. The difficulty with spinning angles is the reason most of the examples you see involve XY-grid sort of parametrics. You can get it to work, but it may be easier to do a different way. Let's start with a simple example.

Figure 9.26 shows an arrow-shaped feature, which is placed on the curvy surface at random points and rotated at various angles. The feature is always extruded normal to the surface. The Variable Pattern function enables you to simply create multiple instances of the feature, and apply different dimensions to it. It's like a design table where you have all the possible configurations at the same time.

FIGURE 9.26
A simple, variable-
pattern Waffle
Mat.sldprt

Here is how this particular feature is set up:

◆ Section Plane a plane that is offset from the end of the solid by a certain dimension, D1@ Section Plane.

◆ Intersection Sketch is a sketch with an intersection curve between Section Plane and the curvy surface, so as Section Plane moves, Intersection Sketch will undulate.

◆ There is a sketch point in Intersection Plane some distance (D5@Intersection Sketch) from the left edge of the solid.

◆ Tangent Plane is a plane that is tangent to the curvy surface at the sketch point.

◆ Arrow Sketch is a sketch on the Tangent Plane of an arrow that can rotate and change length, driven by an angle and a length dimension.

◆ Variable Pattern is a feature that can place multiple Arrow features simultaneously with various values for the following dimensions/parameters:

D1@Section Plane (position of intersection sketch)

D1@Arrow Sketch (rotation of arrow)

D3@Arrow Sketch (length of arrow)

D5@Intersection Sketch (position of tangent point)

The name Variable Pattern may be somewhat misleading, because technically, it's not really a pattern, in that there is no discernable recurring pattern; it's just a collection of several versions of a single feature in different positions and orientations.

Let's move on to a more complex but less abstract example. I will set it up the same way: several parametrically driven entities that enabled me to position, size, and orient one or more features, which are placed in any way that the parametric scheme allows. In this case, I patterned a flower around an irregularly shaped bottle.

The first try at this didn't work. Well, it worked all except getting the feature to pattern all the way around the bottle; it only worked on the front half, as shown in Figure 9.27. The error here says that "Some instances were disjoint," which to me suggests that the Extrude features are pointing off into space instead of toward the bottle. So I simplified it by applying the same pattern to a cylinder, which could more easily be done with a circular pattern. I got the cylinder to work, as shown in Figure 9.28.

FIGURE 9.27
Patterning around an irregular shape works only on the front half, `Variable Pattern Bottle3.sldprt`.

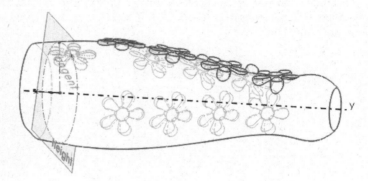

FIGURE 9.28
Variable Pattern around a cylinder works all the way around, `Variable Pattern cylinder .sldprt`.

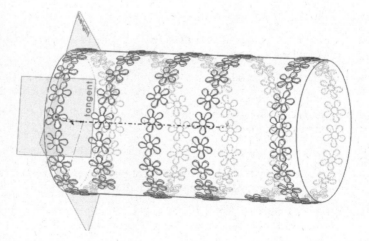

In the end, I was not able to get this to work 100 percent on complex geometry, and the matter has been forwarded to SolidWorks as a technical support issue. I got one row to go around the part all the way, but other rows would project the back side features onto the front, so there were no back features and double the front features. This is shown in Figure 9.29, and you can look at the file named `Variable Pattern Bottle4.sldprt`. I have a feeling this has to do with the overall propensity in SolidWorks to flip planes as they rotate.

FIGURE 9.29
Variable Pattern flips
when driving a
sketch plane.

The reason all of the Internet examples of this function are simplistic seems to be that it is not really capable of full 3D function, and this appears to expose underlying weaknesses in the SolidWorks parametric function that have been there all along. If you need to do more complex patterning, you will need to make copies of your features manually or use mirroring or more conventional patterning.

Cosmetic Patterns

Cosmetic Patterns are not patterns in the same sense as all the other pattern types in SolidWorks. The Cosmetic Patterns feature does not actually create any geometry, just the appearance of geometry. Cosmetic Pattern features are applied using RealView functionality, which may or may not be available to you depending on your hardware, in particular your video card.

NOTE   More information is available on RealView-capable video cards from the SolidWorks corporate website at: `www.solidworks.com/sw/support/videocardtesting.html`.

Cosmetic Patterns are appropriate if your manufacturing method does not require actual geometry. For example, rapid prototyping requires explicit geometry in order to build a part, but a perforated sheet metal panel or a knurled cylindrical handle may require only a note on a drawing for the shop to set up a manufacturing process to create the geometry.

To apply a Cosmetic Pattern to a face, feature, body, or entire part, click the Appearances, Scenes, And Decals tab from the Task pane, and choose Appearances ➢ Miscellaneous ➢ Pattern Or Appearances ➢ Miscellaneous ➢ RealView Only Appearances. Drag and drop the desired pattern onto the model, and use the pop-up menu to apply it to a face, feature, body, or the entire part. Figure 9.30 shows the Appearances, Scenes, And Decals tab of the Task Manager with some of the Cosmetic Pattern options.

FIGURE 9.30
Cosmetic Pattern options in the Appearances, Scenes, And Decals tab of the Task Manager and the Cosmetic Pattern PropertyManager

Mirroring 3D Solids

Because symmetry is an important aspect of modeling parts in SolidWorks, mirror functions are a commonly used feature. This is true whether you work on machine, sheet metal, injection-molded, cast, or forged parts. I discussed sketch-mirroring techniques earlier in this chapter, and now I will discuss 3D mirroring techniques.

Mirroring Bodies

Earlier in this chapter, I discussed patterning bodies. I mentioned that the patterning and mirroring tools in SolidWorks do not have adequate functionality when it comes to body management (specifically the merge options). Neither tool allows the patterned or mirrored bodies to be merged with the main body if the main body is not being patterned or mirrored. Here you can see that the Pattern function has no provision whatsoever for merging bodies. The Mirror appears to have the functionality, but it applies only to bodies that are used or created by the mirror feature and ignores any other bodies that may exist in the part.

BEST PRACTICE

Mirroring bodies is the fastest and simplest method when a part has complete symmetry. However, this may not be an option if the part is not completely symmetrical. In addition, the decision to mirror must often be made when you are creating the first feature. If the first feature is modeled as a sketch that is built symmetrically around the origin, then you may need to cut the part in half to mirror it. This is an adequate modeling technique, although it is not very efficient.

Mirroring Features

Features can be mirrored across planes or flat faces used as the plane of symmetry. If you are mirroring many features, then it is best to mirror them all with a single mirror feature rather than to make several mirror features. You may have to do this by moving the mirror feature down the tree as you add new features. Depending on your part and what you are trying to accomplish, it may be better to mirror bodies than to mirror features, but you should not go too far out of your way or model in a contrived manner to make this happen.

Mirroring Entire Parts

Often when modeling, you are required to have a left-handed part and a right-handed part. For this, you need to use a method other than body or feature mirroring. The Mirror Part command creates a brand-new part by mirroring an existing part. The new part does not inherit all the features of the original, so any changes must be created in the original part. There is an external link (remember the → symbol) that links the parts, but they must both be open to update changes. If you want different versions of the two parts, you need to use Configurations.

You can use the Mirror Part command by preselecting a plane or planar face. You should be careful when choosing the plane because the new part will have a relationship to the part origin, based on the plane on which it was mirrored. The Mirror Part command is one of the few remaining features that relies completely on preselection techniques.

The Mirror Part command is found in the Insert menu, but it is not highlighted unless a mirror plane is selected. When mirroring a part, you can bring several entity types from the original file to the mirrored part. These include axes, planes, sketches, cosmetic threads, and surface bodies. You can also bring over features and even break the link to the original file.

Mirror Part invokes the Insert Part feature, which is covered in more detail in Chapter 31, Modeling Multibodies, and Chapter 33, "Employing Master Model Techniques."

One of the options available when you make a mirrored part is to break the link to the original part. This option brings forward all the sketches and features of the original part, and then adds a Move/Copy Body feature at the end of the tree that simply mirrors the body. Figure 9.31 shows the PropertyManager for the Insert Part feature.

NOTE   Under normal circumstances, you cannot get the Move/Copy Body feature to mirror a body. SolidWorks has applied some magic pixie dust behind the scenes to make this happen.

FIGURE 9.31
Selecting items to bring
into the mirrored part

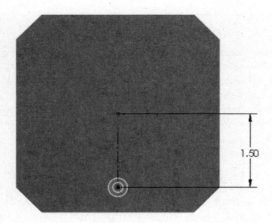

1.50

Tutorial: Creating a Circular Pattern

Follow these steps to get practice and create Circular Pattern features:

1. Draw a square block on the Top plane centered on the origin, 4 inches on each side,
   .5-inch-thick extruded Mid Plane with .5-inch chamfers on the four corners.

2. Preselect the top face of the block, and start the Hole Wizard. Select a counterbored hole
   for a 10-32 socket-head cap screw, and place it as shown in Figure 9.32.

FIGURE 9.32
Start drawing a plate
with holes.

Axis1

3. Create an axis using the Front and Right planes. Choose Insert ➤ Reference
   Geometry ➤ Axis. Select the Two Planes option, and then select Front and Right planes
   from the flyout FeatureManager. (Click the bar that says Axis at the top of the
   PropertyManager to access the flyout FeatureManager.) This creates an axis in the
   center of the rectangular part.

4. Click the Circular Pattern tool on the Features toolbar. Select the new Axis in the top Pattern Axis selection box in the Circular Pattern PropertyManager. Select the Equal Spacing option, and make sure that the angle is set to 360 degrees. Set the number of instances to 8.

5. In the Features To Pattern panel, select the counterbored hole. Make sure that Geometry Pattern is turned off.

6. Click OK to finish the part. The result should be as shown in Figure 9.33.

FIGURE 9.33
The finished circular pattern

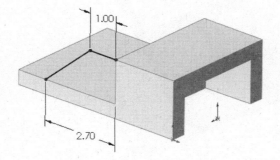

Tutorial: Mirroring Features

Follow these steps to get some practice and create mirror features:

1. Open the Chapter9 Tutorial2.sldprt file from the download material.

2. Open a sketch on the side of the part, as shown in Figure 9.34. The straight line on top is 1.00-inch long, and the angled line ends 2.70 inches from the edge, as shown.

FIGURE 9.34
The sketch for the Rib feature

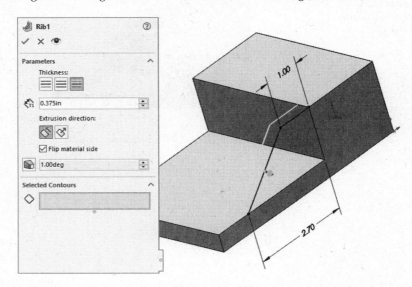

3. Click the Rib tool on the Features toolbar, or select it from the menu at Insert ➤ Features ➤ Rib. Set the material arrow to go down toward the block and the thickness setting to go to the inside by .375 inches. The PropertyManager and the preview should look like Figure 9.35.

FIGURE 9.35
Applying the Rib feature

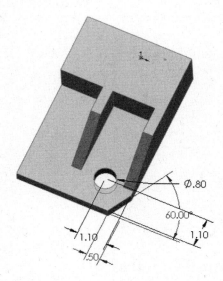

4. Create a linear pattern using the rib, making the pattern reach 2 inches into the part.

5. Create a chamfer on the same side of the part as the original rib, as shown in Figure 9.36. The chamfer is an Angle-Distance using 60 degrees and 0.5 inches.

FIGURE 9.36
Additional features
on the part

6. Create a round hole, sized and positioned as shown.

7. Mirror the hole and the chamfer about the Right plane. The parametrics of the chamfer will have difficulty patterning, so you need to use the Geometry Pattern option. The finished part is shown in Figure 9.37.

FIGURE 9.37
The finished part

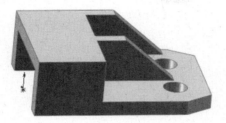

Tutorial: Applying a Cosmetic Pattern

Follow these steps to practice creating a cosmetic pattern:

1. Open the `Chapter 9 – tutorial – cosmetic pattern.sldprt` file from the download materials for Chapter 9.

2. Click the Appearances tab in the Task pane. These steps work whether or not you have RealView selected.

3. Expand the Appearances heading, then the Metal heading, then Steel, and then drag the Sandblasted Steel icon from the lower panel onto the part. When the pop-up menu appears, select the Part icon to apply the appearance to the entire part. Figure 9.38 shows the Task pane and the pop-up menu.

FIGURE 9.38
Applying an appearance to a part

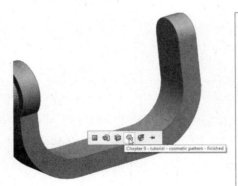

4. Expand the Miscellaneous listing (under Appearances) and the Pattern heading. Drag the Waffle Pattern onto the large cylindrical face of the part, and then Alt+click the Face icon in the pop-up toolbar. Using the Alt key while dragging or to select face, feature, body, or part automatically activates the PropertyManager to edit the appearance. Figure 9.39 shows the Appearances PropertyManager.

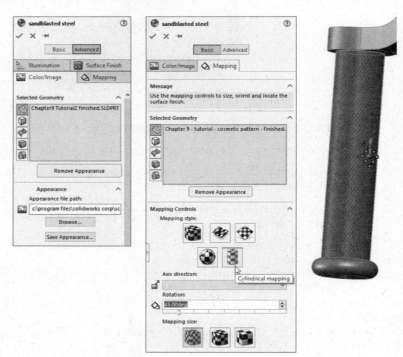

5. In the Mapping tab of the Appearances PropertyManager, select the cylindrical mapping under the Mapping Style section of the Mapping Controls panel.

6. Change the Rotation to 45 degrees, and choose the smallest Mapping Size.

The Bottom Line

Feature patterns and mirrors are powerful tools, but you must have some discipline to benefit from their usefulness. Patterns in particular are extremely flexible, with many types of functions and options available. You should avoid sketch patterns if possible, not only because of performance considerations, but also because complex sketches (sketches with lots of entities and relations) tend to fail more often than simple sketches.

Master It   Create an irregular sketch region on a flat face of a solid part of your choosing, add a hole inside the irregular region, and then use the Fill Pattern feature to fill the region with patterned holes.

Master It   Create a two directional linear pattern where the directions are not perpendicular to one another.

Master It   Create a pattern feature and use the Instances to Skip to remove a couple of instances of the patterned feature.

Chapter 10

Using Equations

Parametric sketch relations are not the only way to drive dimensions with intelligence. You can also use equations and variables. Equations help you create simple or complex mathematical relationships between dimensions. Global variables can be used in equations just as other dimension names can.

IN THIS CHAPTER, YOU WILL LEARN TO:

- ◆ Use equations to create relationships between dimensions
- ◆ Link dimensions together
- ◆ Assign global variables
- ◆ Enter expressions
- ◆ Control suppression states of features and components
- ◆ Link to an existing equation from a SolidWorks model

Understanding Equations

Σ

You can gain access to the Equations dialog box by using the Tools toolbar or by choosing Tools ➤ Equations from the menu. Equations are stored in a folder at the top of the FeatureManager. Figure 10.1 shows the Equations interface.

Using the Equations interface, you can suppress individual equations temporarily by deselecting the Active check box to the left of the equation. Equations can also be deactivated by a design table. I discuss design tables in more detail in Chapter 11, "Working with Part Configurations," where I also discuss configurations.

CAUTION Although I do not cover configurations until Chapter 11, I mention part of the relationship between equations and configurations here. Equations and configurations (particularly those that are driven by a design table) should probably not be mixed. This is not because they do not work together; it's more for the sake of organization. Add to this the fact that global variables are configurable, and it certainly opens up new possibilities—but it also creates potential problems for users, because they can control dimensions from both configurations and equations. Also, equations in Excel are far more powerful than the comparatively limited equation functionality offered in SolidWorks. Of course, every user has different reasons for working one way or another; I am just offering a warning about a potential source of conflict.

FIGURE 10.1
The Equations interface

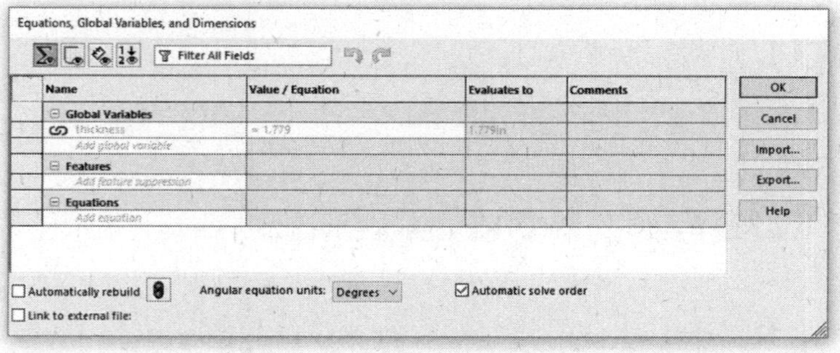

The Equations interface offers four ways to view the equations:

Equation View Lists the global variables, features suppressed by equation, and all equations in the part or assembly.

Sketch Equation View Lists all equations and variables used in sketches.

Dimension View Lists all global variables, features suppressed by equation, and dimensions in the part or assembly that can be used in equations.

Ordered View The simplest view. It lists the driven variable, the equation itself, the value of the equation, and any available comments.

Creating Equations

Let's take a look at a part with a variable hole pattern. Equations can be used to space holes along the length of a bar. To prepare for this, we need to name some dimensions that will be used in the equations.

NAMING DIMENSIONS

It is not necessary to name every entity in every SolidWorks document, but you should get in the habit of naming important features, sketches, and even dimensions. Named dimensions become particularly important when you use them in equations, configurations, and design tables. Under most circumstances, you do not use or even see dimension names, but with equations, you do.

Named dimensions make a huge difference when you want to recognize the function of an equation by simply reading it. A most obvious example would be the difference between D3@ Sketch6 and Length@WindowExtrusionSketch. The first name means nothing, but the second one is descriptive if you are familiar with the part.

To name a dimension, click the dimension and type the new name in the top of the Modify box—or you can go to the Dimension PropertyManager and, in the Primary Value panel shown in Figure 10.2, type the new name for the dimension in the Name text box. You cannot use the symbol @ in dimension names, because it is used as a delimiter between the name of the dimension and the feature or sketch to which it applies. Also, be aware that even though the software appears to allow you to change the name of the sketch or feature in the Dimension

PropertyManager, it will not accept this change. You can't change the sketch or feature name from the Dimension PropertyManager.

FIGURE 10.2

Renaming a dimension

Other ways also exist to change dimension names, including using Configuration Table View and the Equation Manager/Dimension view.

BEST PRACTICE

You should keep dimension names as short as possible while still making them unique and descriptive. This is because space in the interface is often limited, and when combined with sketch or feature names (and even part names when used in an assembly), the names can become difficult to display in a readable fashion. Also, keep in mind that spaces in dimension names can be misinterpreted by Excel, so don't use spaces in the names you assign.

TIP   You can show dimension names as a part of the actual dimension by using the Hide/Show All Types dropdown in the Heads-Up View toolbar. It's also helpful to know that the FeatureManager Filter filters dimension names, which makes named dimensions easy to find. Figure 10.3 shows the filter displaying features and sketches that include a dimension containing the filtered word "height." Other filtered words display in tool tips, but dimension names don't.

You can use the FeatureManager Filter to find features with specific dimension names. In Figure 10.3, the filter finds Sketch1, which has the HeightEnd dimension. The model view is shown just to illustrate the dimension. The filter did not display the dimension on the model, but clicking a feature found by the filter displays the value.

FIGURE 10.3
Using the Feature-
Manager Filter to filter
dimension names

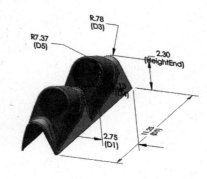

BUILDING THE EQUATION

When creating an equation in SolidWorks, it is often a good idea to write it out on paper first to make sure that the concept is correct. Examine the part shown in Figure 10.4, where the relevant dimensions have been named and displayed. (The part shown in Figure 10.4 is included with the download material for this chapter. The filename is `Chapter 10 Equations.sldprt`.) The number of holes—called Instances here—is the driving variable. From that number, the spacing of the holes is calculated over the length of the part. There is also a gap on each end of the pattern of holes. This gap (measured between the center of the last hole and the end of the part) always needs to be half of the spacing between the holes. The sigma symbols (Σ) to the left of the dimensions indicate that an equation is driving it. Dimensions driven by equations cannot be directly edited.

FIGURE 10.4
Variables for the
hole pattern

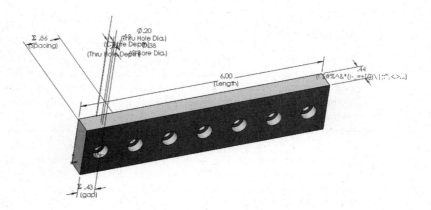

TIP Dimensions—and text in general—can be difficult to read when foreshortened on a 3D display. To make text easier to read, there is a setting to show all dimensions flat to the screen; it can be found at Tools ➤ Options ➤ Display.

In this case, a more sophisticated equation has not been implemented to account for the diameter of the holes possibly interfering with one another when there are a large number of holes. In other words, because there are two values that need to be calculated (the spacing and the gap), you need to create two equations. Because the gap dimension is always half of the spacing, the spacing needs to be calculated first, as follows:

$$Spacing = \frac{Length}{\left(\left(Instances - 1\right) + 1\right)}$$

The *Instances* –1 term stands for the number of spacings. If you have two holes, then there is only one spacing. The +1 term stands for the two half-spacings for the two ends. The second equation is simpler and looks like this:

$$Gap = \frac{Spacing}{2}$$

The order of the equations is important. The SolidWorks Equations interface figures out if there is a necessary order to the equations and puts them in that order. Because the gap is dependent on the spacing, the spacing must be calculated before the gap. SolidWorks also automatically figures out if the equations need to be solved multiple times in order to stabilize. Figure 10.5 shows the resulting set of equations. Notice that the Equations interface this time is being shown in Ordered view, as opposed to Equation view in Figure 10.1.

FIGURE 10.5
Equations for the hole pattern

Before beginning to build the equation, you should first display the dimensions that you need to use to create the equation. You can add dimensions to the equation by clicking them from the graphics window. To do this, right-click the Annotations folder at the top of the FeatureManager and select Show Feature Dimensions. You also should select the Display Annotations (Heads-Up View toolbar ➤ Hide/Show All Types ➤ View Component Annotations) option if it is not already selected as shown in Figure 10.6. When you have done this, all the dimensions that you need to create every feature are displayed. Also, be sure to turn on the Show Dimension Names option; you will find it on the Heads-Up View toolbar.

FIGURE 10.6
Showing all the
dimensions in a part

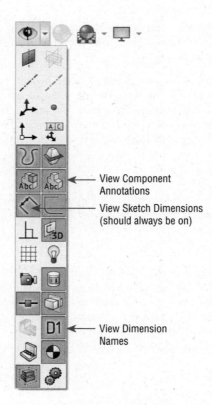

View Component
Annotations

View Sketch Dimensions
(should always be on)

View Dimension
Names

TIP For models that have more than a few features, showing all the dimensions in the entire model may overload the screen with information. In this case, you can double-click a feature from the Fea-tureManager to show all the dimensions on that feature.

To build the equation, go to Tools ➤ Equations. (As an alternative, you can click Equations on the Tools toolbar or right-click the Equations folder in the FeatureManager and select Manage Equations.) Make sure you have the Ordered or Equation view activated (in the upper-left corner, sigma (Σ) is Equation view, dimension is Dimension view, and 123 is Ordered view).

Next, click in the Add Equation box (at the bottom of the list), and then click the dimension you want to drive. SolidWorks adds the name of the dimension and automatically switches focus to the Value/Equation column where you enter the body of the equation. Click the driving dimensions shown in the view as needed, type as needed, or select from lists of functions or properties.

You can also measure right here in the Equations dialog box. Any measurement you make is saved as a reference dimension and entered into the equation as such. When you have a valid equation, SolidWorks fills out the Evaluates To column for you. Notice also that if your equation is valid, a green check appears in the box. If it is not valid, the syntax that makes it invalid is displayed in red, and the check mark is shown in gray.

Using Comments

Notice the comment to the right of the Evaluates To column in Figure 10.5. Comments can be very useful for annotating equations for yourself or others. Two important reasons to annotate are to remember the significance of variables or dimensions and to add special notes about the logic of the equation that may not be obvious.

TIP   You can make general comments for the model in the Design Journal, a Microsoft Word document that is embedded into the SolidWorks file. The Design Journal is found in the Design Binder folder near the top of the FeatureManager.

Using Driven Dimensions

Sometimes it is necessary to use a driven (reference) dimension in an equation. Reference dimensions are displayed in gray. This is particularly true when the best way to calculate a number is to use existing 3D geometry. For example, if you are manufacturing a helical auger in 90-degree sections from flat steel stock, you need to design the auger in 3D but begin to manufacture it in 2D.

What is the shape of the auger when flat? The best way to figure this out (aside from lofted bends, which are discussed in Chapter 34, "Using SolidWorks Sheet Metal Tools") is to use a little high-school geometry, a construction sketch, and some simple equations.

Figure 10.7 shows a 90-degree section of an auger blade. The outside diameter is 12 inches, and the blade width is 3 inches. (The part shown in Figure 10.7 is included with the download material for this chapter and is in the file named Chapter 10 Auger.sldprt). The overall height is 4 inches. In this case, the auger is represented as a surface because the thickness is ignored. Surface features can be useful in situations like this (used as construction geometry) and are discussed in Chapter 32, "Working with Surfaces."

FIGURE 10.7
A representation
of the auger

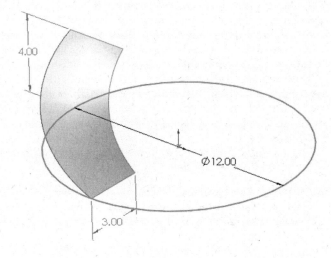

With this information, you can calculate the lengths of the 3D edges using a sketch and a simple equation. In Figure 10.8, the hypotenuses of the triangles represent the helical edges of the inside and outside of the auger. By making the triangles the same height as the auger section, and by making the horizontal side of the triangle the same length as a quarter of the inside or outside diameter by using simple equations, the geometry and sketch relations automatically calculate the flat lengths of the inside and outside edges of the auger $\left(length\_of\_triangle\_side = \dfrac{diameter\_of\_circle \times pi}{4} \right)$. In this way, the triangle is used to simplify the calculation and give it a visual result.

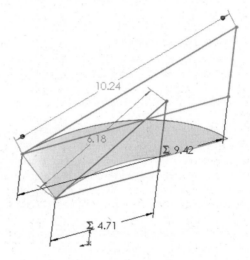

From this point, you can calculate the flat pattern again, using the SolidWorks sketch-solving capabilities as the calculator. Think of the auger as being the cardboard tube inside a roll of paper towels. If you examine one of these tubes closely, you will see that it is simply a straight and flat strip of cardboard that has been wound around a cylinder. What was the flat, straight edge of the original board is wound into a helix. This method simply reverses that process.

This example requires the little-used arc-length dimension to drive the size of the arc. The hypotenuse dimensions are shown by driven dimensions or reference dimensions, which are used to drive the arc-length dimensions, as shown in Figure 10.9. Remember that you can create arc length dimensions by using the Smart Dimension tool to click both endpoints of the arc and then the arc itself.

The reasoning behind this example may be a little difficult to grasp, but the equations and the sketches are certainly simple.

CAUTION   Using reference dimensions on the driving (independent or right) side of the equation can, in some situations, require more than one rebuild to arrive at a *stable value* (meaning a value that does not change with the next rebuild). SolidWorks detects this and can adjust for it.

FIGURE 10.9
Figuring the flat pattern
of the auger

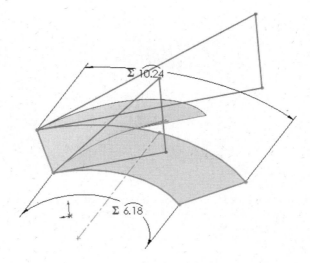

Using Equation Tricks

SolidWorks equations allow several mathematical operators, such as sine, cosine, tangent, and others. SolidWorks also allows IF statements, conditional operators (=, <, >, < >, =>, <=), and file properties.

USING *IF* STATEMENTS

In words, this is how an IF statement is used:

If some relationship is fulfilled, then the IF function returns a value. If the relationship is not fulfilled, then it returns a different value.

A more technical description is

IF(*expression, value if true, value if false*)

In practice, you could use it like this:

IF(*x* > 5, *x*-1, *x*+1)

which reads, "if *x* is greater than 5, then subtract 1 from *x*; if not, then add 1 to *x*." One of the reasons why this is considered a parlor trick is that this function causes the value of *x* to oscillate between two numbers (depending on the number that it starts with) with each rebuild. SolidWorks also identifies this as a circular reference because the same value is on both sides of the equation. It may be difficult to imagine an application where this sort of behavior would be desirable, but when you combine it with a macro that simply rebuilds a model a number of times, you can use it to create a certain animation effect. Figure 10.10 shows an equation using the IF function.

FIGURE 10.10
An equation using IF

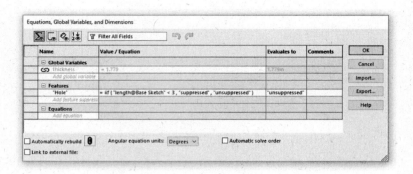

You can use an IF statement—or any other VBA (Visual Basic for Applications) function—to control the suppression state of features and components. This function is described in detail later in this chapter.

Using Global Variables

A *global variable* (supersedes pre-2012 link value) is just a name assigned to a dimension, a reference measurement, or an entire equation. *Linked values* are still extremely powerful tools. The fastest way to link multiple dimensions in bulk is by using a link value.

Global variables are assigned in the Equations dialog box or in the Modify dimension box as simply the variable name equaling an expression or a value. Figure 10.11 shows a list of equations and global variables. When you type a variable name, you do not need to add the quotation marks; they are added automatically. The global variable named "multiplier" uses an expression to calculate its value. The global variable shown in Figure 10.11 called "global variable" is simply assigned a value directly.

FIGURE 10.11
Equations and global variables

You can use custom and file properties to drive equations. If you right-click your Equations folder and select Show File Properties, you will see that the default file properties already exist in the list, as shown in Figure 10.12.

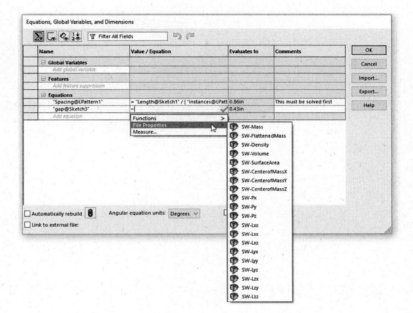

In the Equation Editor shown in Figure 10.12, you can expand the list of functions and custom properties for easy selection and placement into equations. Any custom properties you add that are of the type "number" are automatically added to this list and can be used in equations.

Note that you can assign both a custom property and a global variable with the same name. The global variable takes precedence over the custom property when evaluating an equation.

Global variables are configurable. Chapter 11, "Working with Part Configurations," covers this feature in more detail, but the syntax for using a design table to drive a global variable is as follows:

$VALUE@*global_variable_name*@equations

Using the Modify Box

The Modify dimension box can accept equations. You can also use it to create on-the-fly global variables.

To start an equation in the Modify box, first replace the numeric value with an equal sign (=) in the value box. When you do this, you will see a dropdown for functions and file properties, as shown in Figure 10.13. You can also change the name of the dimension right there. To add other dimensions to the equation, just click them.

FIGURE 10.13
Starting an equation in
the Modify box

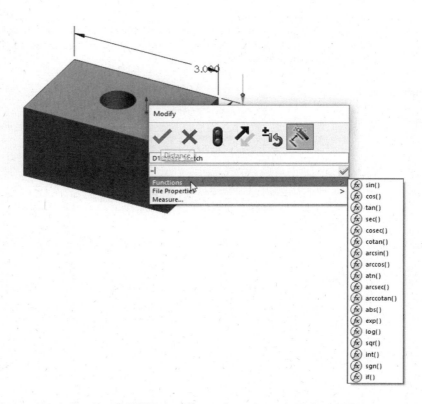

If you key in a numerical value, SolidWorks offers a drop-down list of possible units, properties, or operators. If you don't select anything, then the document units setting is used.

Additionally, you can use dimension-entry boxes in PropertyManager windows in the same
way, as shown in Figure 10.14.

FIGURE 10.14
Using the
PropertyManager
dimension-entry box to
write an equation

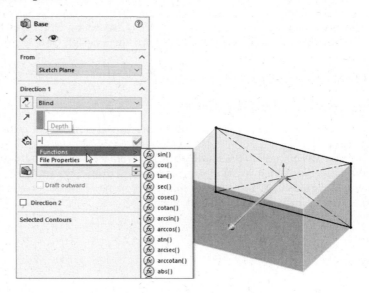

Using Expressions

Expressions can also be entered directly into Dimension dialog boxes in the Modify dialog box and PropertyManager value boxes. The expressions must be composed of numbers and mathematical operators. An expression such as

2.375+(4.8/3)-1.1

is perfectly acceptable, as is

1+1/2

or

1 1/2

In the second case in this example, the plus symbol is understood.

Other types of operations are also available, such as ones for changing units in a dimension box. For example, if you are editing a part in inches and enter 40mm, then SolidWorks performs the conversion for you. You can even mix units in a single expression such as 4.875+3.5mm, where the inch part is assumed as the document units.

Unlike equations, SolidWorks does not remember the expression itself, only the final value. The difference between an expression and an equation is the presence of dimension or variable names. Expressions can be entered into any place where you enter dimensions for SolidWorks features.

Controlling Suppression States of Features

You can use the IF statement described earlier in this chapter to control suppression states of features and components. An example of the syntax is

<feature name> = if(*expression, value if true, value if false*)

Figure 10.15 shows this type of equation in use. In this case, the features area is in the middle of the chart in Equations view. To get the feature into the cell, make sure the cell is selected and click the feature in the FeatureManager or graphics window. Anything in quotes can be selected, so you don't have to worry about spelling or syntax. The IF statement reads in English, "If the spacing is greater than 0.5, then do not suppress. If not, then do suppress." There's a little double-negative thing going on here, but it is the suppression state, not the existence of the feature itself that you are controlling.

FIGURE 10.15
Using IF to control suppression states

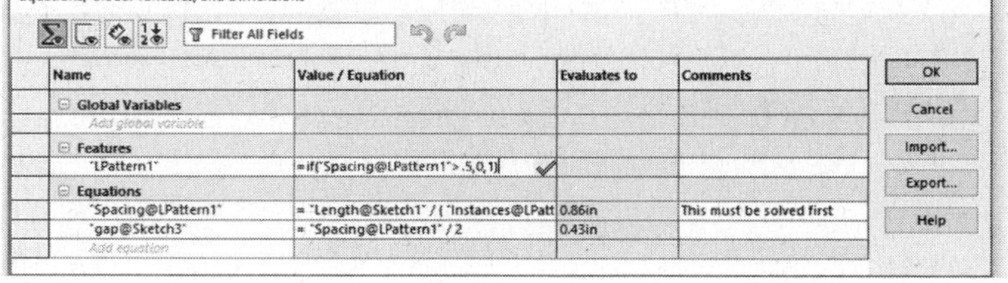

You can also use this equation in assemblies to control suppression states of components (parts and subassemblies).

Linking to External Equations

You can use externally saved equations to share equations between models. To export an equation, click the Export button on the right side of the Equations dialog box, as shown in Figure 10.15. To link the current model to the externally saved equation, make sure the Link To External File option is checked at the bottom left of the Equation Export dialog box, as shown in Figure 10.16.

FIGURE 10.16

Saving an equation to an external file

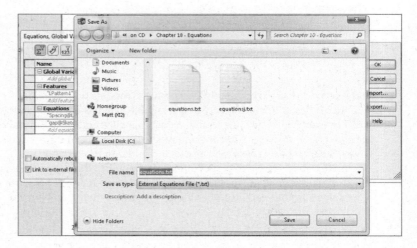

The equation is saved to a simple *.txt file. The default name for the external equation text file is equations.txt. You can change the name if you like, but remember that if you use Windows Explorer to change the name or change it with the referencing file closed, SolidWorks will not know that the filename has been changed. At the bottom of the Equations dialog box is a path for a linked equation file. You can link to only one equation file at a time.

To link to an existing equation from a SolidWorks model, use the Import button in the Equations dialog box. Also be aware that only equations and global variables can be shared in this way.

TIP   Having the equations in multiple parts linked by an external text file is a nice technique for creating families of parts without the need of an assembly or a configuration table.

Tutorial: Using Equations

Get some practice with using equations by following these steps:

1. Start from the part with the filename Chapter10 Tutorial Start.sldprt in the download materials, shown in Figure 10.17.

FIGURE 10.17

Starting the
Equations tutorial

2. Show the dimension names. Use the Heads-Up View toolbar to find this setting.

3. Double-click the Circular Pattern feature to display the angle and number of instances of the feet and related features. You may have to move the angle dimension to see the pattern instance number.

4. Click the instance number. Change the name of the dimension to # (pound or number sign) in the Dimension PropertyManager. Make sure that the Instant3D option is deselected when you do this.

5. Double-click the first feature in the FeatureManager, which is the revolve, and rename the 3.60-inch dimension **CapRad**, again by selecting it and using the PropertyManager.

6. Write an equation that drives the number of legs by CapRad/7.

   a. Open the Equations dialog box by choosing Tools ➤ Equations.

   b. Click Add to add an equation.

   c. Double-click the Circular Pattern, and click the # dimension. Make sure that the name of the dimension is listed in the equation box, and type an equal sign (=).

   d. Double-click the Revolve feature, and select the CapRad dimension; then type **/1.5**.

   e. Add a comment to the equation to identify the driving dimension.

7. Click Rebuild, press Ctrl+B or Ctrl+Q to rebuild the model, and observe whether any update takes place.

8. Rename the 6.00-inch dimension for the height of the revolved feature to **DomeHt**.

9. Create a second equation that drives the DomeHt dimension at the current ratio of the height to the radius.

   a. In the Equations dialog box, create a global variable called **Ratio = 6/3.6 (1.66667)**.

   b. Create the equation. The equation takes the form of DomeHt = (Ratio) × CapRad. You can use the drop-down list under the calculator pad to select the Ratio variable from the list.

10. Use a variable to make the radii of Fillet1 and Fillet2 the same.

11. Double-click the Revolve feature. Change the CapRad dimension to **5** and rebuild. You should observe three feet. Change it again to **6**, and you should see four feet.

12. Give the part a new name, including your initials or the date, and save and close it. See Figure 10.18.

FIGURE 10.18
The finished part

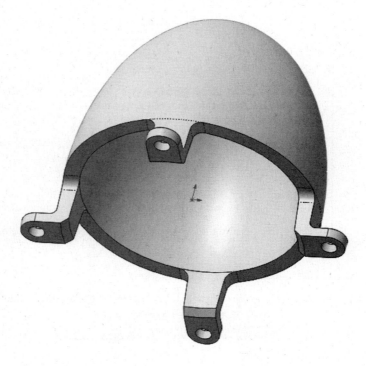

The Bottom Line

SolidWorks equations and related dimension-management tools are powerful. In the last several releases, they have been vastly updated. Even if you're not a huge equation user, the ability to build equations in the Modify and PropertyManager dimension boxes is a great convenience for such a powerful function.

Be careful about crossing SolidWorks native equation functionality with configurations; you may end up with dimensions that are controlled by both tools. Remember that the calculation capability of Excel is far greater than what is found in SolidWorks equations.

Master It Equations and variables are keys to parametric design. Start simple by creating a rectangle with sides made equal by using the same variable name for vertical and horizontal dimensions.

Master It After you have created the rectangular sketch with equal sides, make the extrusion depth also equal so that no matter what size it is, the solid will always be a cube.

Master It One of the most common situations in design is needing to spread out holes. Equations are a great way to do this. Study the part named `Chapter 10 Equations.sldprt` and re-create it on your own.

Chapter 11

Working with Part Configurations

Configurations, also known as simply *configs*, are variations of a part in which dimensions are changed, features are suppressed (turned off), and other items such as color or custom properties may be controlled. Configurations enable you to have these variations within a single part file, which is both convenient and efficient.

This chapter deals only with part configurations, but assemblies can also have configurations. Assembly configurations can use different part configurations, among other things. This will mean more to you as you learn about part configurations. Assembly configurations are discussed in Chapter 19, "Controlling Assembly Configurations and Display States".

One example of configurations is having many sizes of a fastener within a single part file. For example, socket-head cap screws can come in thousands of sizes, and you can very efficiently reuse the same sketches and features to create all of those sizes based on a table. Configured parts can also have features that you can turn off and on (suppress and unsuppress, respectively), such as a cross drive or a slotted drive. Changing dimensions and suppressing or unsuppressing features are the most commonly used techniques available through configurations.

There is some overlap between the topics of configurations and display states, with colors and hide/show states being controlled by both methods. When you have the option, always control visual properties using display states, because they require fewer resources, which means they'll be faster. Display states for part documents are covered in more detail in Chapter 5, "Using Visualization Techniques," and Chapter 19, "Controlling Assembly Configurations and Display States."

IN THIS CHAPTER, YOU WILL LEARN TO:

◆ Control part configurations

◆ Explore design tables

◆ Create a design table

◆ Examine the benefits of using the Configuration Publisher

Controlling Items with Configurations

With every new release of SolidWorks software, it seems that more items become "configurable"—that is, able to be driven by configurations. Configurable items for parts include the following:

- Feature dimensions, tolerances, and driving/driven state
- Suppression of features, equations, sketch relations, and feature start and end conditions
- Sketch planes used by a sketch
- Materials
- Configuration-specific custom properties
- Parts, bodies, features, and face colors
- Derived configurations
- Properties that can be assigned, such as mass and center of gravity
- Base or split parts
- Sketch pattern instances
- Sketch text
- Scale feature sizes
- Cosmetic threads
- Equations
- Global variables
- Helix feature parameters
- Size of Hole Wizard holes

You can control configurations in several ways:

- Making changes manually to dimensions and features
- Using the Configure Feature/Modify Configurations table
- Using an Excel-based design table
- Using the Configuration Publisher

Finding Configurations

SolidWorks configurations are listed in the ConfigurationManager. This is a tab at the top of the FeatureManager area, shown in Figure 11.1.

TIP You can split the FeatureManager interface into two by dragging the splitter bar at the top of the panel. This very useful function is shown in Figure 11.1, and it enables you to see the Configuration-Manager in the upper panel and the FeatureManager in the lower panel. Also remember that you can detach the PropertyManager from the left-side panel area.

FIGURE 11.1

Locating the Configuration-Manager tab

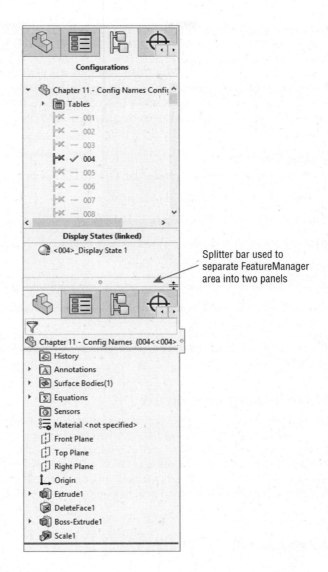

Splitter bar used to separate FeatureManager area into two panels

Deleting Configs

When you're using a standard template, each part has a default config named "Default." There is nothing special about this config; you can rename it and even delete it. At least one config must always remain in the tree, and you cannot delete the configuration that is currently active. If you want to remove a config, switch to another config (by double-clicking the other configuration in the ConfigurationManager) and then delete the one you want to remove.

If you try to delete a part configuration being used by an open assembly, SolidWorks will simply issue the message "None of the selected entities could be deleted" without explanation.

If you delete a configuration of a part that is used in an assembly, but the assembly is not currently open, the next time the assembly is opened, it will issue the message "The following component configurations could not be found [component configuration name]. If the configuration was renamed the same configuration will be used, otherwise the last active configuration will be substituted for each instance."

You can delete groups of configs using Windows select tools (Shift+select or Ctrl+select) in the ConfigurationManager. You can also use the right mouse button (RMB) menu, much like regular features in the FeatureManager. None of the configurations selected for deletion may be active or referenced by other open and resolved documents.

Sorting Configs

In the ConfigurationManager, configs can be listed in one of five ways:

Numeric: Sorts in ascending numeric order

Literal: Sorts ascending alphabetical order

Manual: Allows you to determine the order by drag-and-drop

History-based: Sorts by creation date

Design Table: Sorts by the order in which they are found in the design table

To control which sorting option is used, right-click on the name of the part in the ConfigurationManager tab and select Tree Order.

TIP   If you work in Excel and drive the configurations with a table, all of Excel's sorting options will be available to you.

ENHANCING ALPHABETIZATION

This alphabetized order is significant because many other sections of the SolidWorks interface are not alphabetized, which causes problems when you are browsing for items in larger lists. Sections that are not alphabetized include Help/Contents, Files Of Type lists in Open and Save dialog boxes, the File Locations settings (Tools ➤ Options ➤ File Locations), Entity Color lists, and several others. If you are inclined to submit an Enhancement Request to SolidWorks, alphabetization of lists is one topic that would benefit everyone and should be easy for SolidWorks to implement.

NAMING CONFIGS

In order for this sorting and alphabetizing to work, you must first properly name the configs. For example, if you have a list of sizes or config names from 1 to 100, then you should use 001, 002 . . . 100 as your syntax. This makes it easier to browse the config names. Syntax becomes most important when you place a part with many configs into an assembly, because you must select a config from the list, and typing the first few numbers is often faster and easier than scrolling to it.

To understand this technique better, you can open the part called Chapter 11 Config Names.sldprt from the download files, split the FeatureManager area, and change one of the panes to display the ConfigurationManager. Click one of the configuration names and type a number between 001 and 100. The highlight will scroll to the number that you typed.

By thoughtfully selecting the configuration names, you can save yourself and your coworkers lots of time when inserting select configs into an assembly.

Activating Configurations

Within a part file, to change the display from one configuration to another, you must first switch to the ConfigurationManager panel, and then either double-click the desired config or right-click it and select Show Configuration.

Alternatively, you can right-click the config in the ConfigurationManager and select Show Preview, as shown in Figure 11.2. A small preview thumbnail will display in the PropertyManager panel. However, not all configurations have previews. For example, in a part with many configs that have been generated automatically by a design table, the configurations may not have previews because the config itself has never actually been rebuilt. Previews exist only when the configuration has been activated at least once, the image on the screen generated, and the part saved. SolidWorks stores both the body (geometry) and the preview image of the part so that next time you access the configuration, the software does not have to rebuild everything again. Storage space is cheaper than rebuild time.

FIGURE 11.2
Showing a configuration preview

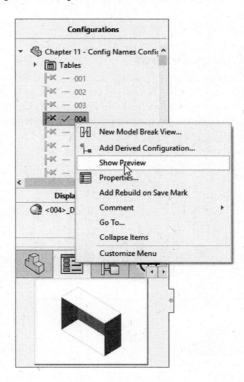

You can even select a configuration while opening a file. By doing this, you will save time by not needing to rebuild the model. To take advantage of this option, you must use the File ➤ Open interface, which is shown in Figure 11.3. You can select the config from the lower-left drop-down Configurations list.

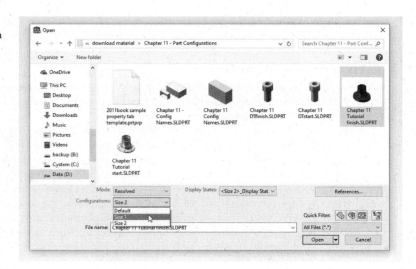

Creating Configurations

You can create configs manually using the Modify dialog box, using the Configure Feature/
Modify Configurations table (shown in Figure 11.4), or through Excel-driven design tables.
Design tables are extremely useful for situations where more than a few configs or more than a
few items are being controlled, and as always, the more people who will be working with the
data, the more tightly you need to control it. It would be a safe best practice to say that any time
you use configurations, and the items being controlled can be handled by a design table, you
should use the design table.

FIGURE 11.4
Selecting a configuration
from the Modify
dialog box

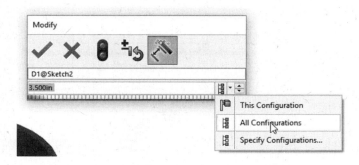

For now, I'm going to focus on creating and manipulating configs manually so you can
become familiar with them without also worrying about Excel and design-table syntax. I will talk
about design tables near the end of this chapter.

CREATING A NEW CONFIG

To make a new config, you can right-click the top-level icon in the ConfigurationManager, which displays a part symbol and the name of the part, and select Add Configuration. New configurations copy the currently active configuration. If you right-click an existing configuration, SolidWorks makes a derived config, which I will discuss later in this chapter. Figure 11.5 shows the RMB menu and the Properties dialog box that you can use to set up the new config.

FIGURE 11.5

Creating a new configuration

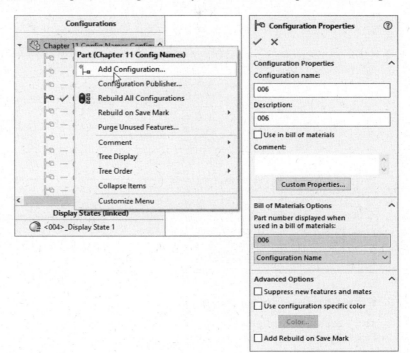

USING CONFIGURATION PROPERTIES AND OPTIONS

The name of the config is important mainly for quick access and organizational purposes. The configuration description is also important, because it can display in the ConfigurationManager and even in the Assembly tree. (You can also use the FeatureManager filter to search configuration descriptions.) This is important when the name of the config is numerical rather than descriptive, and you want to also have a description but not include it in the name. The config description can also appear in place of the filename in the Assembly tree display. Config descriptions can be driven manually through the Configuration Properties dialog box or through a design table if you have very many configs to manage. You can display config descriptions through the RMB menu, as shown in Figure 11.6.

The Bill Of Materials (BOM) option is set in the Configuration Properties to use the filename, the configuration name, or a custom name that the user specifies. You can save this setting with a template. You achieve control over configurations through the combination of the Configuration Properties and the Advanced Options, which I discuss next.

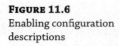

FIGURE 11.6
Enabling configuration
descriptions

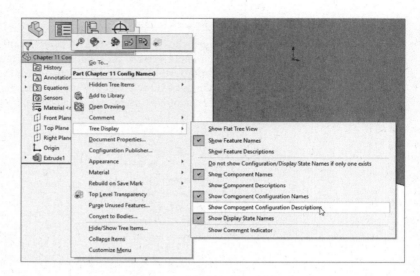

BEST PRACTICE

Although you can change the preferred settings at any time, a best practice is to make a template early on when you are using SolidWorks to model parts. SolidWorks remembers the BOM options and Advanced options that you set for the Default configuration and uses them in document templates. This is true for both part and assembly templates.

USING ADVANCED OPTIONS

Three advanced configuration options are found in the bottom panel of the Configuration Properties PropertyManager and are shown in Figure 11.5:

Suppress New Features And Mates The Suppress option suppresses any new features that are added to other configurations of this part while this option is active. It also suppresses any assembly mates that are added to another active configuration in an assembly. Relying on these options, regardless of the setting, can create problems if you are not using design tables. Manually controlling options in large numbers of configurations can be very error-prone. I personally wish the features and mates options were separated because I like the Suppress Features option to be on, while I would prefer the Suppress Mates option to be off.

Use Configuration Specific Color Colors are actually driven by display states. Display states in turn can be linked to configurations. If you are driving colors in configured models, you should get into the habit of using display states and just linking them to configurations.

Add Rebuild On Save Mark When the Add Rebuild On Save Mark option is enabled, the next time your model rebuilds, this configuration will be rebuilt whether it is active or not. Generally, we think of rebuilds as being good thing, because they keep all the relationships and the geometry up-to-date. But the one problem with rebuilds is that they can take a lot of time. This is especially true if you have a lot of configurations that need to be rebuilt. Be careful how you use this switch. It also can increase the file size. Very often there is a trade-off between options like this and some other variable. You must decide for yourself what is most valuable to you.

USING THE MODIFY DIALOG BOX

The Modify dialog box enables you to change dimensions by just double-clicking the dimension and changing the value. When you change a dimension using the Modify dialog box in a part that has more than one configuration, an additional button, shown in Figure 11.7, appears in the Modify dialog box.

FIGURE 11.7
The Modify dialog box

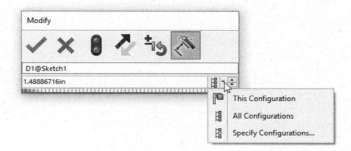

Modify has three options for configuring dimensions: This Configuration, All Configurations, and Specify Configurations. All Configurations is the default option. Choosing the Specify Configurations option opens a dialog box, which is shown in Figure 11.8.

FIGURE 11.8
Using the Specify Configurations dialog box to change a dimension in multiple configurations

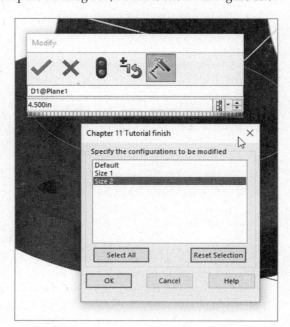

USING NEGATIVE DIMENSIONS

A negative dimension serves only to change the direction of the dimension, and then the negative dimension is discarded; it does not stay with the dimension. An equation that results in a negative dimension flips the sense of the dimension every time it is rebuilt. This may be a useful trick, but in most modeling situations, it's an annoyance. When you put a negative dimension in a Modify dialog box, the dimension changes sense (direction) and the negative sign disappears after one rebuild. If you put a negative dimension into a Modify Configurations dialog box, it also disappears and changes the direction of the dimension for all configurations. When you enter a negative dimension into a design table, the negative is retained (until the next time you open the design table), and the sense of the dimension is retained only for the configs to which you assigned negative dimension values.

NOTE   This design-table functionality is something that arouses my suspicion. I would not build a design-intent scenario based on negative dimensions in design tables. The functionality seems unintentional, unstable, or otherwise subject to change.

Negative dimensions can be assigned only to sketch dimensions, not to feature dimensions. You cannot change the extrusion direction by making the blind depth negative. Be careful if you use Instant 3D to change the direction of an extrude, because this may change a boss to a cut in addition to making it go in the other direction.

Using the Modify Configurations Dialog Box

The Modify Configurations dialog box, shown in Figure 11.9, enables you to create and modify configured features and dimensions in a more organized way than by using the simple manual methods described earlier, but without getting involved in an Excel-based design table, described later in this chapter. Do not confuse the Modify Configurations dialog box with the Modify dialog box, which is used to change dimensions.

FIGURE 11.9
Using the Modify Configurations dialog box to configure a feature

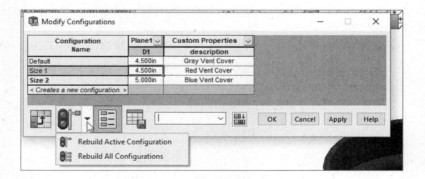

You can access the Modify Configurations dialog box by right-clicking a dimension or feature you want to drive via configurations and selecting Configure Dimension or Configure Feature.

With the Modify Configurations dialog box active, double-click a dimension to add it to the configured features list. You can add configurations on the fly by typing in the appropriate box, and you can change values or states of features by double-clicking and entering numbers or selecting the check box in the appropriate column (suppressed features will use a check box to define whether the feature is suppressed or not).

I tend to use either the manual or Excel-based techniques. Modify Configurations is valuable for people who want to configure a couple of features without getting involved in a big spreadsheet. It might also be valuable to people who do not have Excel available on their computers but want to create a more structured way to manage configuration data. You can also use it to rename dimensions by following these steps:

1. Turn on the Show Feature Dimensions setting in the Annotations folder.

2. Select a dimension.

3. Use Ctrl+A to select all dimensions.

4. Select Configure Dimension from the RMB menu

5. Use the Modify Configurations dialog to rename multiple dimensions.

In addition, I should mention that much folklore exists surrounding what is perceived as a problematic relationship between Excel and SolidWorks. Some users claim that Excel often causes SolidWorks to crash. Beyond that, many workplaces may not have Excel available to them, either because of the cost or because they use a non-Microsoft solution for spreadsheet applications. These users still want the functionality of design tables even if Excel is not installed on their machines.

The icons in the lower left of the Modify Configurations dialog box enable you to use the dialog box for more than just dimensions and feature suppression, including custom properties.

The Modify Configurations dialog box does not give you control over everything. Some things, such as part color, Some things that you can configure, such a part color, cannot be driven from this dialog box. Design tables are still the most powerful way to go, but Modify Configurations offers lots of flexibility and immediacy.

Using Table Views

The Modify Configurations dialog box adds significantly to your options for creating and editing configurations. Two very nice tools that add to the convenience and power of SolidWorks configurations are called Table Views and Hide/Show Custom Properties.

The Table Views tool enables you to keep a small table of only the parameters you want to show. The Parameters drop-down list enables you to select which table view you want to display or to create a new one. Using drop-down lists on the parameter headings, you can suppress the display of any parameter in a new table view.

Dividing what might otherwise be a large design table into several table views helps to keep your data organized and easy to access. Figure 11.10 shows the ConfigurationManager of a part with configurations managed with table views.

FIGURE 11.10
Displaying table views in the Configuration-Manager of a con-figured part

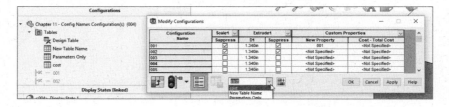

ADDING CUSTOM PROPERTIES WITH THE MODIFY CONFIGURATIONS DIALOG BOX

The second nice option in the Modify Configurations dialog box is the Hide/Show Custom Properties option. When this button is depressed, the Modify Configurations dialog box shows columns for existing custom properties, as well as a drop-down list that enables you to add more custom property columns. This makes it very easy to control configuration-specific custom properties within a configured part. You might also try the All Parameters toggle at the bottom of the box to automatically pick up all of the differences between configurations.

Using Custom Property Managers

The Property Tab Builder enables an administrator to create special Task pane tabs that are used to control custom properties and configuration-specific custom properties. Configuration-specific custom properties can be controlled through design tables, Custom Property tabs, or the regular SolidWorks configuration-specific custom property interface. Select the method that works best for the way you and your company use the software.

Figure 11.11 shows the Property Tab Builder interface. You can access the Property Tab Builder by clicking the Windows Start button and choosing SolidWorks ➤ SolidWorks Tools from the menu. This is the place where you actually construct the interface that shows up in the Properties tab of the Task pane on the right side of the SolidWorks graphics window.

FIGURE 11.11

Using the Property Tab Builder to construct a Custom Properties tab for the Task pane

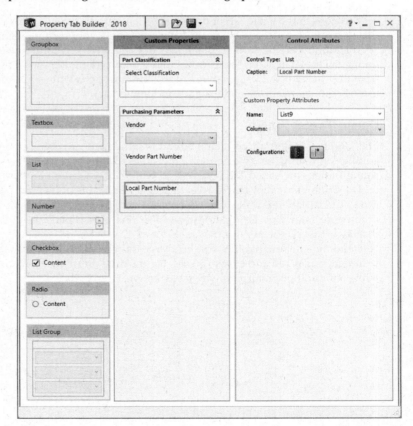

Using this type of interface enables the administrator to standardize custom properties values due to spelling or differences in interpretation. The Task Pane interface is easy to use and highly customizable. Notice that you can create regular custom properties or configure custom properties, and that option can be set independently for each property value entered using this interface.

After you create a Property Tab file (called a *template*), save it to the location indicated at Tools ➤ Options ➤ File Locations ➤ Custom Property Files. If you have only one template for a document type (part, assembly, or drawing), it automatically appears when you display the Custom Properties tab of the Task pane. If you have multiple templates established, the Custom Properties tab lets you choose which one to use. Figure 11.12 shows a Custom Properties tab in use within the SolidWorks Task Pane interface.

FIGURE 11.12
Using the Custom Properties tab to assign custom properties

Using Derived Configurations

Derived configurations are configs that are dependent on other configs. You can create them from the RMB menu on a configuration, and they appear indented underneath the parent config. Figure 11.13 shows the RMB menu and the position of the derived config in the tree.

Derived configurations maintain the same values and properties of the parent config unless you break the link to the child (derived) config by explicitly changing a value in the child config. For all other configurable items, the child config value changes when the parent config value changes.

One very nice application of derived configs is to use them for simplified configurations and to set the properties so that any features added to the parent config are also added to the derived config. You can do this by deselecting the Advanced Option Suppress Features (turn it off) in the PropertyManager for the configuration. This causes the derived config to inherit *only* features that are added to the parent, not to other configs. You can use the simplified configs for Finite Element Analysis (FEA), making drawings of models where all the edge breaks have actually been modeled, or simplified large assemblies. You can also use them for the reverse (a complex config rather than a simple one) to have a config that includes fillets for rendering purposes that are otherwise not used in the manufacturing or documentation processes. In addition, you can create and maintain derived configs using design tables, which are discussed in the next section.

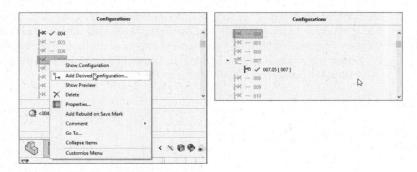

Understanding How File Size Affects Speed

A long-standing dispute has raged over the effects of file size on speed. Here are the facts: When SolidWorks creates a configuration, it can store information about the 3D geometry and a preview thumbnail of the configuration inside the part file. While this is not the default (sometimes only the active configuration data is saved), it can make it faster to access the configuration the next time because it has only to read the stored display data, rather than read parameters and then recalculate new display data. As a result, saving the stored data makes the file larger but also enables you to avoid recalculating.

Many people assign more importance to file size than I do, and they use it as a criterion on which to base decisions about which features or techniques to use or not use. If I have a choice between using a single file instead of multiple files by using configurations, I prefer the single-file technique, even though it is guaranteed to produce larger files—and in some cases, *much* larger files. This is true especially when the choice is between larger files or longer calculation time. Libraries of parts can often be made more manageable by using configured parts rather than many individual parts. Storage space is cheaper and easier to upgrade than processors. In the end, reading stored data rather than recalculating it is faster, hence cheaper. This is why when SolidWorks can store data that will probably be needed again at some point, it's a good idea to take advantage of the storage. It is useful to take advantage of the single-file technique. Storage space is cheaper than rebuild time. The result is that configurations definitely increase file size. While SolidWorks never loads all of the data by default, larger files take longer to open, save, move, and perform just about any operation.

Fortunately, SolidWorks can work with very large data sets. There are a couple of options that can tip the balance in your favor between saved data and recalculated data. In the ConfigurationManager, right-click the name of the part and select Add Rebuild On Save Mark. Figure 11.14 shows the options available.

Add Mark For This Configuration means that a Rebuild On Save Mark will be added to the current configuration. The next time the part is saved, that configuration (the active one) will be rebuilt and the data saved.

FIGURE 11.14
Purging or saving
configuration data

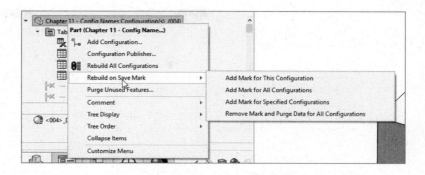

Add Mark For All Configurations will force the software to rebuild and update all configurations the next time the part is saved. Be aware of the time required for an operation like this. It will vary depending on the complexity of your part (the number of features versus the number of configurations).

Add Mark For Specified Configurations presents you with a dialog box to select which configurations to rebuild and for which to save data.

Remove Mark And Purge Data For All Configurations reduces the size of the file by purging all the configuration data. This is great for file size, but it has an adverse effect on performance when SolidWorks must rebuild configurations.

These four options give you the choice of and control over what is important to you. Figure 11.15 shows what happens when you just right-click on a specific configuration. Notice that some of the configs have a floppy disk symbol. These individual configurations have been marked to be rebuilt and saved. The RMB menu shown reflects that the selected configuration is currently marked with the disk symbol, but it can be unmarked.

FIGURE 11.15
Marking and unmarking
configurations to be
rebuilt and saved

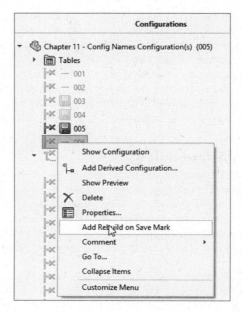

To use these options on a larger scale, a new system option purges all cached configuration data. You can find this setting at Tools ➤ Options ➤ Performance ➤ Purge Cached Configuration Data.

PERFORMANCE

File size has a negative effect on speed when you are sending data across the Internet or working across a network. If the data is on your hard drive, then storing data instead of calculating it offers a big benefit. If you are sending data across a slow network connection, you should take measures to decrease the size of the file before sending it, such as using a zip or other compression utility.

Controlling Dimensions

Controlling dimensions with configurations is simple. You need only three things to start: one dimension and two configurations. Because you already know how to create these elements, you are ready to start. Configurations require that you spend some time developing "design intent" for parts. Configurations drive changes in models; if they are properly modeled, you can avoid feature or sketch failures due to dimension changes—or at least you can understand the limits that each dimension needs to remain within.

I will start with the example of a simple block. A fully dimensioned block has three dimensions. Make sure that you have manually created at least two configurations. Double-clicking a model face opens all the dimensions, and double-clicking one of the dimensions opens the familiar Modify dialog box. Figure 11.7 shows that there is a small difference in the Modify dialog box. It now has a drop-down list where you can specify whether this change applies only to this config, to all configs, or to specified configs. If you select specified configs, then a dialog box listing the existing configurations will allow you to select which configurations get the change.

After you're finished, you can toggle back and forth between the configs by double-clicking each of the configs in the ConfigurationManager. Although this is simple, if you forget to change the drop-down list from the All Configurations setting to either the This Configuration or the Specify Configurations setting, you will apply the change to all the configurations. Building a configuration manually is fine for a few simple changes, but it can become unwieldy if you are changing more than a few dimensions or handling only a few configurations in this way. You would then have to remember which dimensions were changed to what in which configurations. As you can see, using design tables is a better method for multiple dimensions.

Controlling Suppression

Suppressing a feature is just like turning it off; the feature appears as grayed-out text in the FeatureManager. With configurations, you can suppress a feature in one config and unsuppress it in another. Also, while a feature may be suppressed, the sketch associated with it is not necessarily suppressed. When you're dealing with manual configuration techniques, there are two methods for controlling suppression: manually suppressing features and creating configurations with the appropriate options for the inclusion of new features, which I discussed previously in this chapter.

In addition to the Suppress toolbar button, you can also use the Unsuppress and Unsuppress With Dependents functions. When you suppress a feature, any feature that is dependent on it is also suppressed. If you then use the Unsuppress feature, it unsuppresses only the feature itself. However, Unsuppress With Dependents brings back all the dependent features as well.

Generally, SolidWorks users employ a combination of these methods, mainly because configurations are not usually started on a complete model; they are often added when the model is still in progress, so features are added after the users create the configurations.

On the left side of Figure 11.16, you can see a feature that is alternately unsuppressed and suppressed in the tree. The text and icon for the suppressed feature are grayed out. You can suppress features from the RMB menu on the feature, from the Edit menu, or through a tool on a toolbar. The Suppress button is not on a toolbar by default, but you can find it in the Commands dialog box (Tools ➤ Customize ➤ Commands), along with the other buttons for the Features toolbar. Only the Edit menu offers the options of Unsuppress With Dependents and This Configuration, All Configurations, Specify Configurations options for each of the Suppress, Unsuppress, Unsuppress With Dependents functions.

FIGURE 11.16
Suppressing a feature

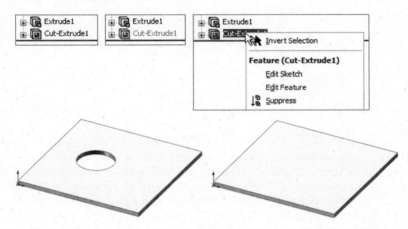

Using Unsuppress With Dependents can save you lots of time or the hassle of looking for all the features dependent upon a feature that has been suppressed. Because it is not available on the RMB menus, this function is used less than it might otherwise be.

You may also need more control than the use of the simple suppress and unsuppress features. All three options (Suppress, Unsuppress, and Unsuppress With Dependents) have three options: This Configuration, All Configurations, and Specified Configurations. This is a case where the drop-down menu options (Edit ➤ Suppress) offer more detailed functionality than you can find in the RMB menus.

Controlling Custom Properties

Several reasons may compel you to use custom properties, including integration with searches for a Product Data Management system, automatically filling out drawing title blocks, or adding information to the BOM.

When you use custom properties with configurations, you must use the Configuration Specific Custom Properties interface (or an appropriately configured custom property tab or the Modify Configurations dialog box), which enables you to have custom properties that change with each configuration. Standard custom properties apply to the top-level part and keep the same value for all configurations. The configuration-specific functionality is useful for situations such as different part numbers for configurations and many other situations that are limited mostly by your use of configs. The Custom tab of the Summary Information dialog box still applies custom properties that do not change with the configurations to the part.

The interface for managing custom properties manually is shown in Figure 11.17. You can access this dialog box by choosing File ➤ Properties from the menu.

FIGURE 11.17
The Configuration Specific tab in the Summary Information dialog box

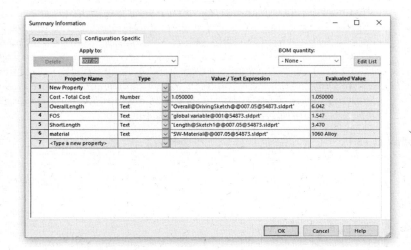

You can also link custom properties to mass properties, model dimensions, link values, sketch text, and global variables by selecting from the drop-down list under the Value/Text Expression column, which appears when you select a cell in the column. To link a custom property to a model dimension, simply activate the Value/Text Expression box in the Summary Information interface that you want to populate and click a dimension in the graphics window. Again, managing this data for a single config or only a few configs is easy enough; however, it can quickly become unwieldy, which is where using design tables can make a huge difference.

Controlling Sketch Relations

You can individually suppress or unsuppress sketch relations using configurations. Figure 11.18 shows the Display/Delete Relations PropertyManager interface, at the bottom of which is the Configurations panel. To suppress a relation, select it from the list and select the Suppressed option in the Relations section above the Delete buttons.

Remember that Display/Delete Relations can be located through the menus at Tools ➤ Relations ➤ Display/Delete, or by double-clicking a sketch relation symbol within a sketch.

FIGURE 11.18
The Display/Delete
Relations dialog box
for configuring
sketch relations

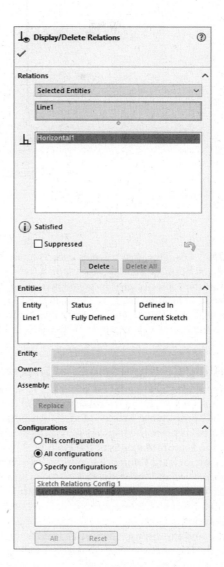

Controlling Sketch Planes

You can configure the Offset distance in the From option for extrudes, and you *can* configure the sketch plane for the sketch that is used in the feature. The Sketch Plane PropertyManager interface expands when configurations are present, as shown in Figure 11.19. To access the Sketch Plane PropertyManager, right-click on a closed sketch and select the Edit Sketch Plane option.

TIP Another way to change the sketch plane is to put the sketch on an offset plane or a plane that can otherwise be driven by a dimension (for example, using reference sketch geometry). Actually moving a sketch to another plane can cause the sketch to rotate or flip. Moving the plane it is on is a better option that does not cause the sketch to rotate or flip.

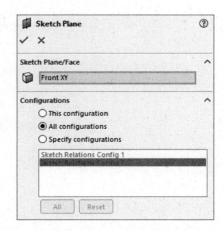

CAUTION   Changing sketch planes indiscriminately can have serious consequences for your model. "Face/Plane Normals" sometimes point in different directions and can cause a sketch to flip, rotate, or mirror when you change it from one plane to another. One strange result is that changing it back to the original location can cause the sketch to flip again, but in a different way so that it does not go back to its original location and orientation. As a result, every time you change the configuration, the sketch could appear in a new and unexpected location or orientation.

Controlling Configurations of Inserted Parts

Inserted parts may also be called *derived* or *base* parts. However, both of these terms are obsolete. Inserted parts are discussed in detail in Chapter 31, "Modeling Multibodies," and Chapter 33, "Employing Master Model Techniques".

Inserted parts place the features for one part inside another part. The inserted part becomes a feature in the FeatureManager of the child part. You can insert just the body geometry itself, or you can bring forward reference geometry, sketch data, features, and configuration-specific custom properties and break the link to the original part if you like.

The role of configurations with inserted parts is that the configuration of the inserted part can be controlled from the child component. For example, you may have designed an engine block for an automobile. This engine block is a casting, and using configurations, you have both the six-cylinder and the eight-cylinder blocks in a single-part file. This model represents the "as-cast" engine block. The next step is to make the block with all the secondary machining operations, such as facing mating surfaces, boring cylinders, drilling and tapping holes for threaded connec-tions, and so on. As a result, the as-cast part is inserted into the as-machined part, and the configuration is selected before you add the cut features. As the name suggests, you add inserted parts by choosing Insert ➤ Part from the menu.

The interface for assigning the configuration is shown in Figure 11.20. Simply right-click the inserted part feature, and select List External References. It would seem to make more sense if the configuration could be selected when the part is first inserted, but it does not work this way; you must select the configuration after the part is inserted.

FIGURE 11.20
Assigning the configuration of an inserted part

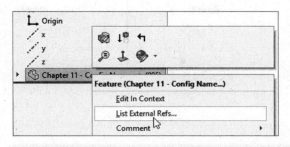

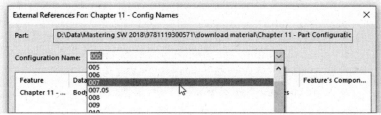

Using Library Features

Library features can have configurations, and they carry those configurations with them into the part in which they are placed. Unfortunately, part configs cannot reference different library-feature configs. Although library features can be configured, after you drop them into a part and click OK, the configurations will no longer be accessible (unless you have selected Link To Library Part), so a part's configurations cannot select the configuration of a library feature. A part's configurations can change the dimensions of a library feature.

Configurations for library features are created in exactly the same ways that configurations are created for other parts. The technique for saving the configs to the library feature is discussed in Chapter 18, "Using Libraries, Assembly Features, and Hole Wizard."

Using Design Tables

In addition to describing some of the basic concepts involved with configurations, the first part of this chapter presented reasons for using design tables. For example, while manual configuration management can be haphazard and highly prone to mistakes, design tables lay everything out in an Excel spreadsheet. Although many new users ask whether they can use a different replacement spreadsheet program, you must use Excel for design tables.

NOTE   Excel is a format that is easy to read and print out, and even non-SolidWorks users can understand and work with it. Although there is some special syntax that you must use with design tables, for most uses, SolidWorks can create the syntax automatically for you; therefore, there is minimal manual data entry. If you are careful to name dimensions, features, and configurations properly, design tables should be easy to understand and manage. In Excel, you can also color cells, rows, and columns in such a way that large amounts of tabulated data are easier to sort through. In addition, because design tables use Excel, they can also use all of Excel's calculation capabilities.

> **BEST PRACTICE**
>
> When using equations and design tables, be sure to name dimensions, sketches, features, and other configured items, but don't mix design tables with SolidWorks equations. Besides the fact that Excel equations are far more sophisticated than those of SolidWorks, driving dimensions from too many locations can be confusing when you edit the part after you have forgotten the details of how the part was built.
>
> You should document design intent using comments in the features or the design journal. You should also add comments to design tables as needed.

Identifying What Can Be Driven by a Design Table

Just because something can be configured does not necessarily mean that it can also be driven by a design table. Here is a small list of items that fit into this category:

♦   Sketch plane configuration

♦   Suppressed sketch relations

♦   Suppressed dimensions (Suppressed dimensions become driven dimensions.)

However, the good news is that many items can be driven by a design table. Table 11.1 lists these items, along with their associated syntax. For the most up-to-date list, check the SolidWorks Help documentation.

TABLE 11.1:   Items That Can Be Driven by a Design Table

ITEM	SYNTAX (GOES IN COLUMN HEADER)	POSSIBLE VALUES (GOES IN FIELD CELL)	DEFAULT VALUE IF FIELD IS BLANK
Configs of Inserted Parts	$configuration@<part name>	<config name>	not evaluated
Configs of Split Parts	$configuration@<split feature name>	<config name>	not evaluated
Comment Column	$comment	comment text	blank
Configuration Description	$description	description text	<config name>
BOM Part No.	$partnumber	$d, $document = document name $p, $parent = parent config name $c, $configuration = config name <text> = custom name	config name

TABLE 11.1:   Items That Can Be Driven by a Design Table   *(CONTINUED)*

ITEM	SYNTAX (GOES IN COLUMN HEADER)	POSSIBLE VALUES (GOES IN FIELD CELL)	DEFAULT VALUE IF FIELD IS BLANK
Feature Suppression State	`$state@`*`<feature name>`*	suppressed, s unsuppressed, u	present suppression state
Dimension Value	`dimension@`*`<feature name>`* `dimension@`*`<sketch name>`*	allowed numerical values	not evaluated
Parent Config (creates a derived config)	`$parent`	parent config name text	not evaluated
Config Specific Custom Property	`$prp@`*`<property name>`*	property name text	not evaluated
Equation State	`$state@`*`<equation number>`*`@equations`	suppressed, s unsuppressed, u	unsuppressed
Light Suppression State	`$state@`*`<light name>`*	suppressed, s unsuppressed, u	unsuppressed
Sketch Relation Suppression	`$state@`*`<relation name>`*`@`*`<sketch name>`*	suppressed, s unsuppressed, u	unsuppressed
User Notes (same as comment)	`$user_notes`	text	blank
Part or Feature Color	`$color` `$color@`*`<feature name>`*	See SolidWorks Help, Colors, Parameters in design tables.	0, black
Assigned Mass	`$sw-mass`	allowed numerical values	value from Mass properties
Assigned Center of Gravity X, Y, Z Coordinates	`$sw-cog`	allowed numerical values in the format of *x, y, z*	value from Mass properties
Dimension Tolerance	`$tolerance@` *`<dimension name>`*	See SolidWorks Help, Tolerance Keywords, and Syntax in Design Tables.	none

Creating a Simple Design Table

When you prepare to create a design table, you generally need to give appropriate names to dimensions, sketches, and features. Remember that although the feature is the most visible item and the easiest to rename, most of the dimensions probably belong to the sketch, which you may also need, or want, to rename. Names should reflect the function or location of the item. It is a good idea to show dimension names when renaming items. (Remember that you can show dimension names by selecting the Dimension Names option by choosing View ➢ Dimension Names.) Figure 11.21 shows the result of renaming the feature and dimension.

FIGURE 11.21
Renamed features and dimensions

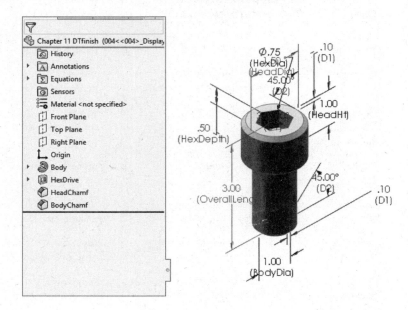

You can use one of the following three techniques to add a design table to a SolidWorks part by choosing Insert ➢ Tables ➢ Design Tables from the menus:

Insert Blank Design Table: This method starts from a blank template that contains the underlying framework, but no values.

Auto-Create Design Table: This method populates the new design table with any existing configurations and items that are different between the configs.

From File: This method enables you to create a design table externally and then import it.

Although I prefer the Auto-Create method, it is most appropriate when you have existing configurations. The From File method is best when a design table has been exported from another part, saved externally, and brought into the current part. For the following example, I used the Insert Blank Design Table method.

ON THE WEBSITE

If you want to follow along with creating the design table, you can use the part from the download materials for this chapter with the filename Chapter 11 DTstart.sldprt.

Figure 11.22 shows the results of starting with the new blank design table. You may notice that the window title bar at the top says SolidWorks, but the toolbars look very much like the

Excel interface. This is because Excel is actually running inside of SolidWorks. Clicking outside of the Excel window can cause the Excel window to close; however, there are several items outside of the Excel window that you can select without the window closing, such as features in the FeatureManager and dimensions in the graphics window. You can also rotate and pan the view in the graphics window without closing the Design Table window. If you are very careful, you can also drag the thin hatched border of the Excel window to adjust its size or location.

FIGURE 11.22
The interface to create the design table and the resulting blank design table

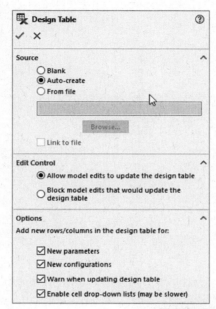

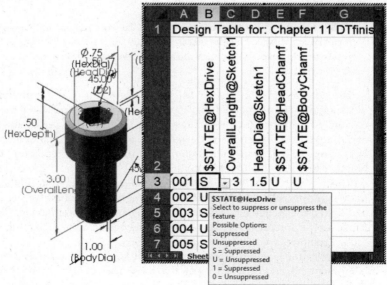

You can also edit design tables in a separate window, which makes editing easier but makes adding dimension and feature names more difficult. To edit the table in its own window, right-click the design table in the FeatureManager and select Edit Table In New Window.

Figure 11.23 shows a fully developed design table, with some complexity. Although your first design table doesn't need to be this complex, this example demonstrates what you can do with this feature.

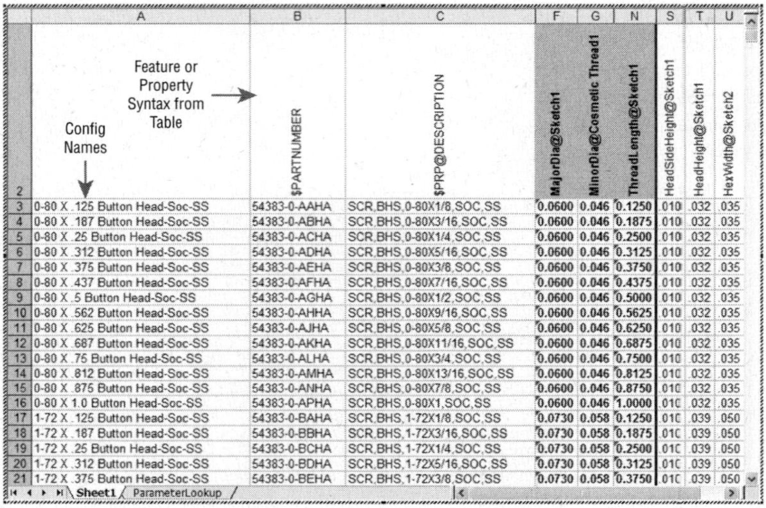

FIGURE 11.23

A fully populated design table

	A	B	C	F	G	N	S	T	U
	Config Names / Feature or Property Syntax from Table	$PARTNUMBER	$PRP@DESCRIPTION	MajorDia@Sketch1	MinorDia@Cosmetic Thread1	ThreadLength@Sketch1	HeadSideHeight@Sketch1	HeadHeight@Sketch1	HexWidth@Sketch2
3	0-80 X .125 Button Head-Soc-SS	54383-0-AAHA	SCR,BHS,0-80X1/8,SOC,SS	0.0600	0.046	0.1250	.010	.032	.035
4	0-80 X .187 Button Head-Soc-SS	54383-0-ABHA	SCR,BHS,0-80X3/16,SOC,SS	0.0600	0.046	0.1875	.010	.032	.035
5	0-80 X .25 Button Head-Soc-SS	54383-0-ACHA	SCR,BHS,0-80X1/4,SOC,SS	0.0600	0.046	0.2500	.010	.032	.035
6	0-80 X .312 Button Head-Soc-SS	54383-0-ADHA	SCR,BHS,0-80X5/16,SOC,SS	0.0600	0.046	0.3125	.010	.032	.035
7	0-80 X .375 Button Head-Soc-SS	54383-0-AEHA	SCR,BHS,0-80X3/8,SOC,SS	0.0600	0.046	0.3750	.010	.032	.035
8	0-80 X .437 Button Head-Soc-SS	54383-0-AFHA	SCR,BHS,0-80X7/16,SOC,SS	0.0600	0.046	0.4375	.010	.032	.035
9	0-80 X .5 Button Head-Soc-SS	54383-0-AGHA	SCR,BHS,0-80X1/2,SOC,SS	0.0600	0.046	0.5000	.010	.032	.035
10	0-80 X .562 Button Head-Soc-SS	54383-0-AHHA	SCR,BHS,0-80X9/16,SOC,SS	0.0600	0.046	0.5625	.010	.032	.035
11	0-80 X .625 Button Head-Soc-SS	54383-0-AJHA	SCR,BHS,0-80X5/8,SOC,SS	0.0600	0.046	0.6250	.010	.032	.035
12	0-80 X .687 Button Head-Soc-SS	54383-0-AKHA	SCR,BHS,0-80X11/16,SOC,SS	0.0600	0.046	0.6875	.010	.032	.035
13	0-80 X .75 Button Head-Soc-SS	54383-0-ALHA	SCR,BHS,0-80X3/4,SOC,SS	0.0600	0.046	0.7500	.010	.032	.035
14	0-80 X .812 Button Head-Soc-SS	54383-0-AMHA	SCR,BHS,0-80X13/16,SOC,SS	0.0600	0.046	0.8125	.010	.032	.035
15	0-80 X .875 Button Head-Soc-SS	54383-0-ANHA	SCR,BHS,0-80X7/8,SOC,SS	0.0600	0.046	0.8750	.010	.032	.035
16	0-80 X 1.0 Button Head-Soc-SS	54383-0-APHA	SCR,BHS,0-80X1,SOC,SS	0.0600	0.046	1.0000	.010	.032	.035
17	1-72 X .125 Button Head-Soc-SS	54383-0-BAHA	SCR,BHS,1-72X1/8,SOC,SS	0.0730	0.058	0.1250	.010	.039	.050
18	1-72 X .187 Button Head-Soc-SS	54383-0-BBHA	SCR,BHS,1-72X3/16,SOC,SS	0.0730	0.058	0.1875	.010	.039	.050
19	1-72 X .25 Button Head-Soc-SS	54383-0-BCHA	SCR,BHS,1-72X1/4,SOC,SS	0.0730	0.058	0.2500	.010	.039	.050
20	1-72 X .312 Button Head-Soc-SS	54383-0-BDHA	SCR,BHS,1-72X5/16,SOC,SS	0.0730	0.058	0.3125	.010	.039	.050
21	1-72 X .375 Button Head-Soc-SS	54383-0-BEHA	SCR,BHS,1-72X3/8,SOC,SS	0.0730	0.058	0.3750	.010	.039	.050

Sheet1 / ParameterLookup

The config names go in the first column, and the feature or property names go in the second row. The first row is reserved for the name of the table. All of this is automatically set up by SolidWorks.

NOTE   Because you are actually working in Excel when working with design tables, you can use Excel formatting, which is how the text in Figure 11.23 is rotated 90 degrees for the column headers. (To rotate text in a table, right-click the cell, group of cells, or row; select Format Cells; and then select the Alignment tab.)

In a new design table, the next step is to type some configuration names. Because you are working in Excel, all the fill functionality is available. To populate the configuration names column, I typed the first three values of 001, 002, and 003, and then window-selected the cells and dragged the fill handle on the selection window to fill the number pattern to populate a larger area. To find more information about this technique, look for "Fill" or "Automatically Number Rows" in the Excel Help files.

The next step is to fill in some feature and dimension names in the second row. The first thing to do is suppress the HexDrive feature. To make this the first feature in the list, click in cell B2 and then double-click the HexDrive feature in the FeatureManager. The name of the feature and its current suppression state are added to the design table with all the necessary syntax and correct spelling.

To rotate the text in this row vertically, right-click row number 2, select Format Cells, click the Alignment tab, and turn the orientation to 90 degrees. The word *UNSUPPRESSED* displays in all capitals and is fully spelled out, although all you need is a *U* or an *S*. Replace the word with an *S*, and double-click the line between the column heading letters *B* and *C* at the top of the Excel window to condense column B as much as possible. Alternate the rest of the rows between *U*s and *S*s to either suppress or unsuppress the HexDrive feature in various configurations. Figure 11.24 shows the current state of the design table.

FIGURE 11.24
Building the design table

	A	B	C
1	Design Table for: Chapter 10 (		
2		$STATE@HexDrive	
3	001	s	
4	002	u	
5	003	s	
6	004	u	
7	005	s	
8	006	u	
9	007	s	
10	008	u	
11	009	s	
12	010	u	
13	011	s	
14	012	u	
15	013	s	

Close the Design Table window, and click OK on the message box that lists the new configurations created by the design table. Now split the FeatureManager, set the lower pane to the ConfigurationManager, and double-click some configurations. Notice that in the configs where you specified an *S*, the HexDrive is suppressed and no longer appears in the model.

You can now add a dimension to the design table. When you're adding a dimension, it is most convenient to display the dimensions on the screen at all times. To show all the dimensions in the part, right-click the Annotations folder in the FeatureManager and select Display Annotations. If the dimensions do not display, you may have to go back and select Show Feature Dimensions. Arrange the dimensions so you can clearly see them all, as shown in Figure 11.25.

FIGURE 11.25
Dimension and annotation display settings

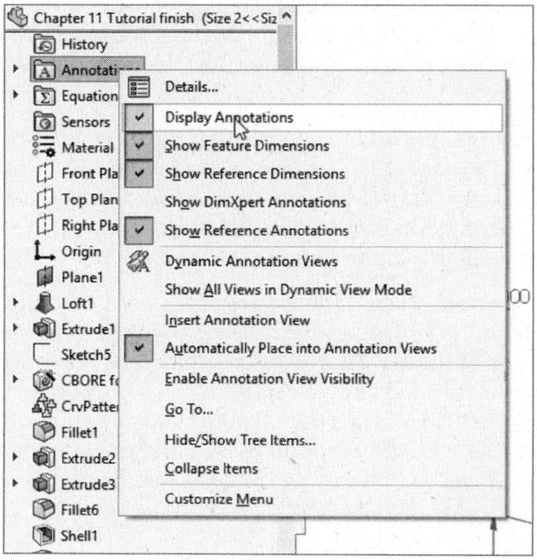

To display the design table again, locate it in the ConfigurationManager, right-click it, and select Edit Table. Editing the feature changes the settings used for the design table. Edit Table in New Window is an option that you will use later because it simplifies many things; however, for now, using the Edit Table option is the easy way to add new items to the design table.

NOTE   If a window appears with the name "Add Rows and Columns," just click OK for now. In its lower pane, this window lists parameters that have changed, and it is asking if you want to add any of the changed parameters to the design table. If you want to add them, just select the parameter in the lower pane and click OK. If not, just click OK.

If the design table displays on top of your model, you can either move the model or move the design table. Moving the design table is a bit tricky and involves dragging the striped-line border of the Excel window; remember not to grab it at the corners or midpoints, because this simply resizes it. If you click inside the border, nothing will happen. If you click outside of the border, the Excel window will close. Moving the model may be easier. To do this, Ctrl+drag in a blank space in the graphics window; it will pan the display so you can see the part dimensions.

With cell C2 selected, or whatever the next available cell is in the second row, double-click the OverallLength dimension in the graphics window. SolidWorks will add the proper syntax to the design table, along with the current value for the first configuration in the list. Fill in values for the rest of the configurations. Now you can calculate these values in Excel using any of the available techniques.

Exit the design table, and toggle through the various configurations to see their different lengths. These examples should get you started on more complex configurations and design tables. Any dimensions that are controlled by the design table (and therefore locked) display in pink on the screen.

A row with special function can be added between the second and third rows. This row can be used to identify column headings with user-assigned names. If you use this method, you may want to hide the second row. The second row cannot be deleted.

Editing Design Table Settings

Figure 11.22 shows the PropertyManager for design tables. After you have created the table, you can edit the table settings by right-clicking the table and selecting Edit Feature. Edit Feature enables you to edit the settings for the table only; it does not enable you to edit values within the table.

Linked Design Table   By selecting the From File source option, you can create a design table from an external file; you can also link the table to the external file. When you use the other two options, Blank and Auto-Create, SolidWorks stores the Excel file within the SolidWorks document. Linking to an external file may be useful if you have a non-SolidWorks user who is entering data into the design table or if a single table controls multiple parts.

Edit Control   The Edit Control panel has two options, which act as a toggle. The Allow Model Edits To Update The Design Table option is self-explanatory, as is its opposite, the Block Model Edits That Would Update The Design Table option. If the Allow Model Edits option is selected and you make a manual change to the model, the next time you open the design table, SolidWorks will warn you about the change and that it will update the design table. Likewise, if you try to make a manual change and the Block Model Edits option is selected, you will receive a warning that the value cannot be changed.

Options   The Options settings determine the behavior when you are using the Allow Model Edits option and a new item has been configured. For example, the design table may already exist, and you manually add a configuration and suppress a feature.

Configurations that have been added manually are displayed somewhat differently from configs that are being managed by the design table. Figure 11.26 shows the two configurations at the bottom of the tree with square symbols, while the design table configs have X (Excel) symbols.

FIGURE 11.26
Manually created configs versus design-table-created configs

After you manually add the config and suppress the feature, the next time you open the design table, the Add Rows And Columns dialog box appears. Many users are simply annoyed by this, but that may be because they don't understand what it does or why it appears. In the example shown in Figure 11.27, a new configuration has been manually added; it appears in the Configurations box as ManuallyAddedConfig, and in the Parameters box, it looks like a feature named BodyChamfer has been either suppressed or unsuppressed manually. The appearance of this dialog box means that SolidWorks is asking if you want to include these items in the design table. If so, simply select the items you want to add to the design table and click OK. If you do not want to include the items in the design table, simply click OK or Cancel. If you click OK, you will not be offered these choices again; if you click Cancel, the next time you open the table, the dialog box with the same choices will reappear. If you never want to see this dialog box again, make sure that all the options in the Options panel shown in Figure 11.22 are deselected.

FIGURE 11.27
The Add Rows And Columns dialog box

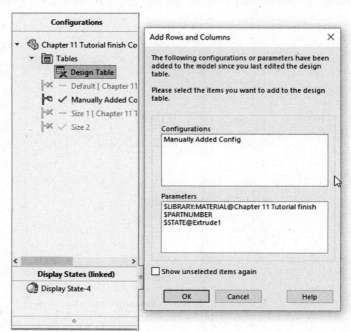

Editing the Design Table

As I mentioned earlier, working with a design table opened inside the SolidWorks window can sometimes be difficult. One way to handle this problem is to edit the design table inside SolidWorks only when you want to add new features to the column headers; when adding new configurations or editing the field values, edit the table in a separate window. This option appears on the RMB menu as Edit Table In New Window. It gives you much more flexibility in resizing the Excel window, changing the zoom scale, and other operations, but it doesn't enable you to double-click a dimension so it is added automatically to the column header.

CAUTION   When working on design tables, avoid conflicts with other sessions of Excel by closing any other Excel windows. The combination of operating Excel spreadsheets inside both SolidWorks and Excel has been known to cause crashes or trigger the "Server Busy" warning message. If you are diligent about having only one session of Excel active at a time when you are working on design tables (or Excel BOMs), there is less likelihood of a crash or conflict.

Using the Configuration Publisher

The Configuration Publisher enables you to create an interface that creates configurations on the fly based on rules that you establish. The interface that you create appears when you put the part into an assembly, enabling you to create a custom size and a new configuration to go with it. This is similar to putting a Toolbox part into an assembly and getting a special interface to specify sizes and create new configurations if necessary. In order to create a Configuration Publisher for a part, the part must contain a design table with at least a single row. You can use an auto-created design table if needed.

You access the Configuration Publisher by right-clicking the name of the part at the top line of the ConfigurationManager and selecting Configuration Publisher from the menu.

Figure 11.28 shows the Configuration Publisher interface. It is like the Property Tab Builder in that you use it to place interface controls on a PropertyManager that will pop up when the part is placed into an assembly.

FIGURE 11.28
The Configuration Publisher helps you build an interface to create configurations as you place a part into an assembly.

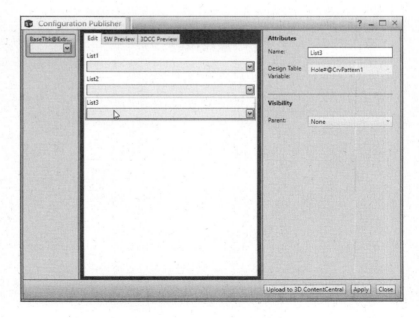

Aside from users putting parts into assemblies, the interface you create using the Configuration Publisher can also be used in 3D Content Central to specify a new component size. If you are a supplier and make parts in a wide variety of sizes, instead of creating all the sizes and uploading to 3D Content Central, you can just create the rules in the Configuration Publisher interface and allow the configurations to be created automatically according to the rules.

When the interface has been created, a PropertyManager entry will show up under the name of the part in the ConfigurationManager, as shown in Figure 11.29.

FIGURE 11.29

The PropertyManager entry in the ConfigurationManager

When the part is placed into an assembly, the PropertyManager, which is the one created in the Configuration Publisher, will appear and enable you to access options to size and configure the new instance. A similar interface is also used if you have uploaded the part to 3D Content Central to allow other people to download the part.

Tutorial: Working with Configurations and Design Tables

Throughout this book, the parts that I use for one purpose may also be useful for other purposes. For example, the part used in this tutorial uses a loft with guide curves where both guide curves are created in the same sketch. The guide curve sketch is made from symmetrical splines where I have used the spline handles to change the shape smoothly and in a controlled way. I have also used a curve-driven pattern to go around an elliptical shape. This demonstrates that configurations can be applied to different types of parts, and some of the more loosely defined shape tools are often used in parts where cosmetic issues are not a design concern.

TIP   If at some point you decide that you have made mistakes from which you cannot recover, or you simply want to start over, you can choose File ➢ Reload. This is the same as exiting the part without saving and then reopening the part to start from the beginning.

To start working with configurations and design tables, follow these steps:

1. From the download materials for this chapter, open the part called Chapter 11 Tutorial start.sldprt. Take a moment to become familiar with this part by using the rollback bar and then editing each feature in turn to see how it was made. In particular, look at the two patterns, which must be parametrically linked. Figure 11.30 shows the part.

2. Manually create a configuration for the part called Size 1. Remember that to create a configuration, you must show the ConfigurationManager tab in the FeatureManager area and right-click the name of the part at the top level. Do this by splitting the FeatureManager window and setting the lower pane to the ConfigurationManager.

3. Set the Advanced option by selecting both Suppress Features and Use Configuration Specific Color.

4. Before closing the Add Configuration PropertyManager, click the Color button on the Advanced Options panel of the Configuration PropertyManager and select a different color for the Size 1 configuration. The color doesn't change immediately. It will change after you close the PropertyManager.

5. Choose View ➤ Dimension Names.

6. Double-click the feature CrvPattern1 in the FeatureManager. A numeral 6 with a D1 under it appears on one of the holes in the pattern. If you have changed your part to a blue color, it may be difficult to see because the text is also blue.

7. Change the name of the dimension to Hole# by clicking the dimension and using the PropertyManager.

8. Change the value of the number to 8, and also change the drop-down setting to This Configuration Only instead of All Configurations. If you forget to do this, you must go to the other configuration and set it back to 6.

9. Click the Rebuild symbol (which resembles a traffic light) to show the changes before exiting the Modify dialog box. Notice that the CrvPattern2 fails after rebuilding CrvPattern1 with eight instances. Click the green checkmark icon to exit the Modify dialog box, and then make the same changes to the CrvPattern2: change the dimension name and the number of patterned instances to 8 (remember to use the This Configuration Only setting). The part should look like Figure 11.31.

10. When you double-click to change configurations, the SolidWorks interface displays a part with a different color and a different number of holes and ribs. After the first change between configurations, the changes should happen quickly because SolidWorks has stored the geometry.

FIGURE 11.31
The model after step 9

11. Choose File ➤ Properties and select the Configuration Specific tab. Set the Apply To drop-down list to Default, and type a Property Name of **description** and a Value of **Gray Vent Cover**. Now change the Apply To drop-down setting to Size 1, and type a description for the new configuration using the name of the color that you applied to this config.

12. Exit the Custom Properties dialog box. Now that you have made a few changes manually, the following steps will guide you through bringing these changes into a design table and using the design table to make additional changes.

13. Choose Insert ➤ Tables ➤ Design Table from the menus. Use Auto-Create as the Source, allow model edits, and select all three options in the Option panel. Click OK to create the design table. Figure 11.32 shows the design table you automatically created.

FIGURE 11.32
The automatically created design table

	A	B	C	D	E	F	G
1	Design Table for: Chapter 10 Tutorial start						
2		$DESCRIPTION	$COLOR		$PRP@description	Hole#@CrvPattern1	Rib#@CrvPattern2	BaseThk@Extrude1
3	Default	Default	12632256	Gray Vent Cover	6	6	0.5
4	Size 1	Size 1	255	Red Vent Cover	8	8	0.8
5	Size 2	Size 2	16711680	Blue Vent Cover	10	10	1
6							

14. Use the striped border to move the window without closing it. This may take some practice. If the window closes, right-click the design table in the FeatureManager and select Edit Table. Move the window to a place where you can see the model clearly.

15. If a cell in the second row of the design table is selected, select a different empty cell that is not in the second row (this prevents data from automatically populating cells until you have the correct data). Now double-click the Extrude1 feature in the FeatureManager. Find the 0.500"(D1) dimension on the screen. Right-click the dimension, and rename it **BaseThk**.

16. Click the next open cell in the second row, and double-click the 0.500″ dimension that you just renamed. You may have to use the handles at the corners and side midpoints to resize the Excel window to see everything. Add another configuration row and the additional values in the cells, as shown in Figure 11.32. The color number is determined by a formula that you can find in the help section under the topic Color Parameter.

17. Remember that this part must have the number of ribs always equal to the number of holes. This is simple to do in Excel. Click in the first row value for the Rib# number. (This is cell F3 in Figure 11.32.) Type the equal sign, and then click in the cell to the left, E3. You can also simply type **=E3** in this cell. This links the Rib# cell to the Hole# cell.

18. Use the Window Fill feature by selecting the dot at the lower-right corner of the selected F3 cell and dragging it down to include cells F4 and F5, as shown in Figure 11.33.

19. Click in a blank space to exit the design table. Double-click through the configurations in the ConfigurationManager to see the results of your efforts.

FIGURE 11.33
Copying the equation to other cells

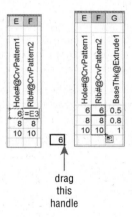

The Bottom Line

Configurations are a powerful way to control variations of a design within a single part file. Many aspects of a part can be configured, although a few cannot. Manually created configurations are useful for making a small number of variations and a small number of configurations, but they become unwieldy when you need to make more than a few variations of either type.

Using design tables to control design variations is recommended because you will be able to see more clearly all the changes you have made to all the configurations. Additionally, by having the power of Excel available, you will be able to access many functions that are not shown here, such as using lookup tables and Concatenate functions to build descriptions or configuration names.

Master It Create a simple block from a fully dimensioned sketch, name all of the dimensions, and create three configurations such that each configuration changes one of the dimensions. Show all the dimensions on the screen.

Master It   Take the part from the previous exercise and auto-create a design table, add 10 more configurations, with different dimensions in each, and configure a custom property called Vendor to have a different value in each configuration.

Master It   Take the part from the previous exercise and add a feature to it. Use the design table to turn the feature on or off (unsuppressed or suppressed) in each configuration. Also change the part color in several configurations.

Chapter 12

Editing, Evaluating, and Troubleshooting

When you use CAD programs, you typically create a part once but edit it many times. *Design for change,* also known as *design intent,* is at the core of most of the modeling work that you will do in SolidWorks.

This chapter starts with some very basic editing concepts, which you may already have picked up if you have been reading this book from the beginning. It also contains a summary of best practice techniques for modeling parts and a set of model evaluation tools that can help you evaluate parts. I placed these evaluation tools in a chapter devoted to editing because the create-evaluate-edit-evaluate cycle is one of the most familiar in modeling and design practice.

IN THIS CHAPTER, YOU WILL LEARN TO:

◆   Use Rollback to look at the results of the design tree

◆   Reorder features in the design tree

◆   Reorder all features as a folder

◆   Select items using the flyout FeatureManager

◆   Summarize best practices for modeling parts

◆   Apply evaluation techniques to plastic parts and complex shapes

Using Rollback

Rolling back a model is one of the first and simplest things you will do when examining a model. It simply means using the Rollback bar to look at the results of the design tree up to a selected point in the model history. The order in which you create features is recorded, and if you change this order, you will get a different geometric result.

You can use several methods to put the model in this rolled-back state:

◆   Drag the Rollback bar with the cursor.

◆   Click the right mouse button (RMB) and select one of the Rollback options.

◆   Edit a feature other than the last one in the design tree. (SolidWorks rolls back the model automatically.)

◆ Choose Tools ➤ Options ➤ FeatureManager ➤ Arrow Key Navigation to control the Rollback bar with the arrow keys.

◆ Save the model while editing a feature or sketch and then exit the model. When the part is opened again, it is rolled back to the location of the sketch that was being edited.

◆ Press Esc during a long model rebuild. This method is supposed to roll you back to the last feature that was rebuilt when you pressed Esc. However, in practice, I have rarely seen it do this; it usually rebuilds the entire model.

◆ Select a face of the model, and from the pop-up menu, select the Rollback icon. The FeatureManager will roll back to the point in the feature list just before that feature was created.

◆ Select a face on the graphic area and select the Rollback icon. The model will roll back to just before the feature that created that face. This is a great technique for quickly rolling back before a specific fillet has been applied.

Using the Rollback Bar

The Rollback bar, which typically appears at the bottom of the FeatureManager in SolidWorks part documents, enables you to put the part into almost any state in the model history. Rollback is not the same as the Undo command; it's the equivalent of going back in time to change your actions at a particular point and then replaying everything that you did after that point. Figure 12.1 shows the Rollback bar in use. Notice how the cursor changes into a hand icon when you move it over the bar.

UNDERSTANDING CONSUMED FEATURES

When you use a sketch for a feature such as the Sketch Driven Pattern command, the sketch is left in the design tree, in the place where it was created. However, most of the other features—such as extrudes—*consume* the sketch, meaning that the sketch disappears from its natural order in the FeatureManager and appears indented under the feature that was created from it. Consumed sketches are sometimes also referred to as *absorbed* sketches.

To show features in their natural order instead of their consumed order, use the Show Flat Tree option (use Ctrl+T shortcut), accessed by right-clicking on the name of the part at the top of the FeatureManager, under the Tree Display selection, as shown in Figure 12.2.

EXAMINING THE PARENT-CHILD RELATIONSHIP

In genealogical family tree diagrams, the parent-child relationship is represented with the parents at the top and the children branched below the parents. In SolidWorks, parent-child relationships are tracked differently. Figure 12.3 shows the difference between a genealogical family tree and the SolidWorks design tree.

You can display the parent-child relationships between SolidWorks features, as shown in Figure 12.4, by right-clicking any feature and selecting Parent/Child. This helps you determine relationships before you make any edits or deletions, because you can see which features will be removed or go dangling (lose their references). Also, the Dynamic Reference Visualization (DRV) is helpful in showing both parent and child relationships (however, as shown in Figure 12.4,

FIGURE 12.1
Using the Rollback bar

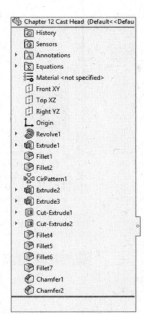

FIGURE 12.2
Selecting the Show Flat Tree option

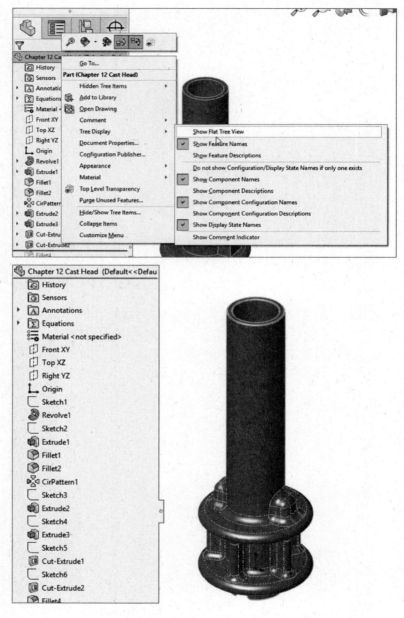

FIGURE 12.3
Different interpretations of the structure of parent-child relationships

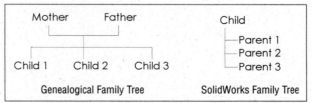

it does not indicate that Sketch6 is a parent of Cut-Extrude2). You can turn on the DRV through the menus at View ➤ User Interface ➤ Dynamic Reference Visualization.

FIGURE 12.4
SolidWorks Parent/Child Relationships panel and the Dynamic Reference Visualization

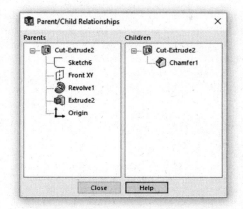

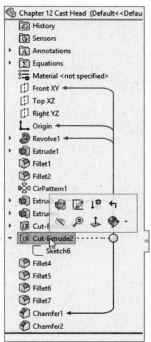

When SolidWorks puts the child feature at the top, it is, in effect, turning the relationship upside down. In the SolidWorks FeatureManager, the earliest point in history is at the top of the tree, but the children are listed before the parents. The SolidWorks method stresses the importance of solid features over other types of sketch or curve features.

For example, you create an extrude from a sketch, so the sketch exists before the extrude in the FeatureManager. However, SolidWorks places the sketch underneath the extrude. This restructuring can become more apparent when a sketch (for example, Sketch1) is created early in the part history and then not used to create a feature (for example, Extrude5) until much later. If you roll down the FeatureManager feature by feature, you arrive at a point at the end of the design tree where Extrude5 appears and Sketch1 suddenly moves from its location at the top of the tree to under Extrude5 at the bottom of the tree.

This scenario may cause a situation where many sketches and other features that are created between Sketch1 and Extrude5 are dependent on Sketch1, but where Sketch1 suddenly appears after all these other features. This can be difficult to understand, but it's key to effectively editing parts, especially parts that someone else created.

The main point here is that SolidWorks displays many relationships upside down. You need to understand how to navigate and manage these history-bound relationships.

To get around difficulties in understanding the chronological order of features when compared against the relationship order of features, roll back a model tree item by item or to work with the Flat Tree option.

ROLLING BACK FEATURES WITH MULTIPLE PARENTS

Take an example such as a loft with guide curves. If you create the guide curves first, and then you create the loft profiles by referencing the guide curves, the loft automatically reorders these sketches when they display under the Loft feature such that the profiles are listed in the order in which they were selected, followed by the guide curves in the order in which they were selected. This is shown in Figure 12.5. This restructuring can be confusing if you want to go back and edit any of the relationships between the sketches. The order in which the sketches are displayed is not the order in which you created them. You can find this example in the downloaded files for this chapter under the filename Chapter 12 Loftwgc.sldprt.

FIGURE 12.5
Multiple parents and sketch reordering

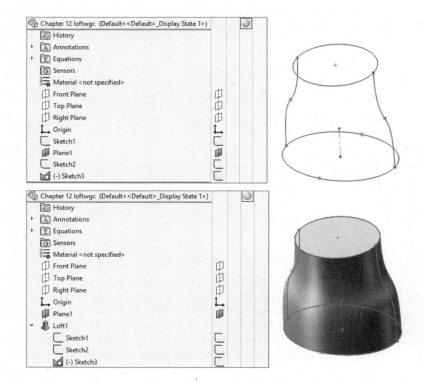

Using Other Rollback Techniques

The Rollback tool is located on the RMB menu. Simply right-click a feature, and select either Rollback or Roll To Previous. If you are already rolled back and you right-click below the Rollback bar, you can access additional options to Roll Forward and Roll To End.

Editing any feature other than the last feature also serves to roll back the model while you are in Edit mode. As soon as you rebuild the feature or sketch, SolidWorks rebuilds the entire design tree.

The Tools ➢ Options ➢ View setting for Arrow Key Navigation enables you to use the up- and down-arrow keys to manipulate the Rollback bar. Under normal circumstances, the arrow keys control the view orientation, but after you have moved the Rollback bar once using the cursor, the up- and down-arrow keys control the Rollback bar. The left- and right-arrow keys have no effect on the Rollback bar.

CAUTION The one situation where this technique does not work as expected is when you are working on a part in the context of the assembly, with the design tree rolled back. The down arrow simply causes the Rollback bar to roll immediately to the end of the design tree.

Using Part Reviewer

Part Reviewer is a tool within SolidWorks that helps you examine the feature history of a part. You can find the Part Reviewer under Tools ➤ SolidWorks Applications ➤ Part Reviewer, or as one of the icons in the Task pane on the right side of the SolidWorks window, as shown in Figure 12.6.

FIGURE 12.6
Using the Part Reviewer

The controls at the top of the Part Reviewer window are, from left to right:

Jump to Beginning: Roll back to the first feature.

Step Back: Roll back one feature.

Step Forward: Roll ahead one feature.

Jump Forward: Unroll the entire tree.

Show Sketch Details: When a feature is being examined, show the sketch and any dimensions as well.

Show Only Feature With Comments: Only features to which comments have been added will be examined.

The small window under the controls is for the feature name that is currently under review. The pencil icon enables you to edit that feature, and the eye icon will hide the feature.

The large window under that is for comments. Comments can be added to each feature or sketch to help anyone who has to work on the part after you to understand anything that might need to be explained about the feature.

Reordering Features

Feature order can make a big difference in the final shape of a part. For example, this order:

Extrude

Cut

Fillet

Shell

gives you a very different part from this order:

Extrude

Shell

Cut

Fillet

The results of these different orders are shown in Figure 12.7. (The part is split and partially transparent for demonstration purposes only.) You can view this part in the download material for this chapter, under the filename Chapter 12 Reorder.sldprt.

On the part in the example shown in Figure 12.7, it is fairly simple to reorder the Shell feature by dragging it up the design tree. As a result, the well created by the Cut feature is not shelled around (to create a tube) if the cut comes after the shell. Also, notice the effect of applying the fillets after the shell rather than before it. The corners inside the box are sharp, while the outside corners have been filleted. When you apply the fillet before the shell, fillets that have a radius larger than the shell thickness are transferred to the inside of the shell.

When you are reordering the features, a symbol may appear on the reorder cursor that says that you cannot reorder the selected feature to the location you want. In this case, you may want to check the parent/child relationships to investigate. Sketch relationships, sketch planes, feature end conditions, and faces or edges selected for features such as shell, patterns, and mirror can cause relationships that prevent reordering. Also, remember that the Flat Tree display can be used to overcome some of these issues.

If two adjacent features are to swap places, it generally does not matter whether you move one feature up the design tree or move the other one down. However, there are isolated situations that are usually created by the nested, absorbed features discussed earlier, where one feature cannot go in one direction, but the other feature can go in the opposite direction, achieving the same result. If you run into a situation where you cannot reorder a feature in one direction even though it appears you should be able to, try moving another feature in the other direction.

Figure 12.7
How feature order
changes a part

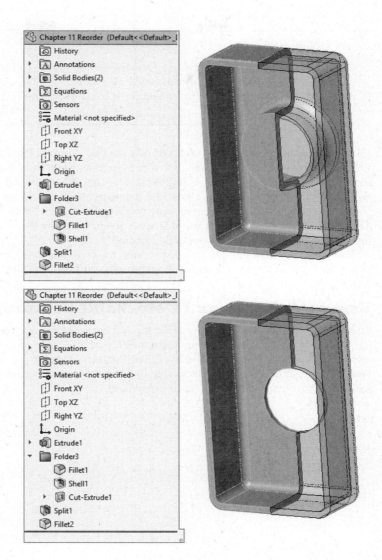

Reordering Folders

There are times when, regardless of which features you choose to move and which direction you choose to move them in, you are faced with the task of moving many features. This can be time-consuming and tedious, not to mention having the potential to introduce errors. To simplify this process, you can put all the features to be moved into a single folder and then reorder the folder. Keep in mind that you cannot skip parent features, and you can reorder the folder only if each individual feature within the folder can be reordered.

BEST PRACTICE

Folders are frequently used for groups of features that go together and that may be suppressed or unsuppressed in groups. You can also use folders in assemblies. Folders are frequently used to group cosmetic fillet features that are often found at the end of design trees for plastic parts or for groups of whole features.

To create a folder, right-click a feature, or a selected group of features, and select Add To New Folder. Folders should be renamed with a name that helps identify their contents. You can reorder folders in the same way as individual features. When you delete a folder, the contents are removed from the folder and put back into the main tree; the contents are not deleted.

You can add features to or remove features from the folders by dragging them in or out. If a folder is the last item in the FeatureManager, the next feature that is created is not put into the folder; you must place it in the folder manually.

The combination of the Flat Tree display and the Dynamic Reference Visualization can help you quickly answer many questions about parent/child relationships within a part.

Using the Flyout and Detachable FeatureManagers

The flyout FeatureManager resides at the top-left corner of the graphics window and is automatically displayed if something like the PropertyManager covers over the space where the FeatureManager is usually displayed. The PropertyManager goes in the same space as the FeatureManager and is sometimes too big to allow this area to accommodate both managers in a split window. Figure 12.8 shows this arrangement.

FIGURE 12.8
The flyout
FeatureManager and
the PropertyManager

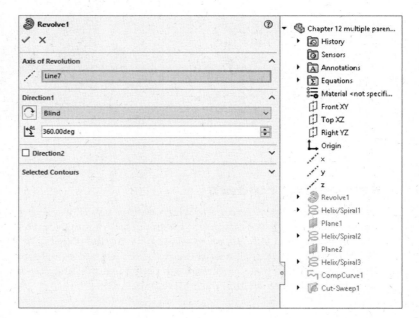

The flyout FeatureManager enables you to select items from the design tree when the regular FeatureManager is not available because it is covered by the PropertyManager. It usually appears collapsed, so that you can see only the name of the part and the part symbol. To expand it, click the plus icon next to the name of the part in the flyout FeatureManager.

You can use the flyout FeatureManager in parts or assemblies. However, you cannot use the flyout FeatureManager to suppress or roll back the tree.

You can access the settings for the flyout FeatureManager by choosing Tools ➤ Options ➤ FeatureManager ➤ Use Transparent Flyout FeatureManager In Parts/Assemblies.

You may prefer not to work with the flyout FeatureManager because it interrupts your workflow by covering the regular FeatureManager with a PropertyManager; this inhibits your access to items you may have to select from the FeatureManager, such as features and reference planes. If this is the case, you can use the detachable PropertyManager instead. Detaching the PropertyManager removes the need for the flyout. I often dock the detachable PropertyManager where the flyout FeatureManager would go or even use it undocked on a second monitor. The main advantage of using the detachable PropertyManager instead of the flyout FeatureManager is that with the detachable PropertyManager, you don't have to relocate features in the FeatureManager that were already in view.

Displaying the FeatureManager and PropertyManager

Figure 12.9 shows the difference between the flyout FeatureManager on the left and the detachable PropertyManager on the right. My preference is clearly the detachable PropertyManager. When you use the PropertyManager, you don't have to go hunting for features that are listed right in front of you when you do something that opens a PropertyManager. You can put the PropertyManager on a second monitor, in the graphics area, or outside the SolidWorks window. This works best on a wide-aspect monitor or multiple monitors.

You may ask, "What's the difference?" The difference is that when you do something like edit a sketch plane, the current state of the FeatureManager is covered and replaced by the PropertyManager. You may have had the new plane you wanted to use in view. Especially with long FeatureManagers, in both parts and assemblies, when the flyout appears, you have to again scroll to find the plane that was right in view. However, if you use the detachable PropertyManager, I think you will find it an improvement over the flyout.

To detach the PropertyManager, just display it by editing a feature, then pull the PropertyManager tab out of the FeatureManager area into the graphics window and release it. You can allow it to float or dock it with one of the available docking icons.

Following Selection Breadcrumbs

Selection Breadcrumbs is a tool that helps you see what you have selected. Any particular item may be characterized in many ways. For example, if you select a face, it is possible that you are selecting a top-level assembly, a subassembly, an individual part, a body, a feature, a face, and so on. The Selection Breadcrumb identifies exactly what is selected. It will display whether you have made a selection from the graphics window or the FeatureManager. If you have selected multiple items, the Selection Breadcrumb displays only the first item selected. It may display parents and children of the selected item, and the selected item is always highlighted in light blue within the breadcrumb. Breadcrumbs are displayed in the part document, but have more utility in assemblies where mates are involved. We will revisit breadcrumbs when we start working with assemblies in more depth.

FIGURE 12.9
Comparing the flyout
FeatureManager with
the detachable
PropertyManager

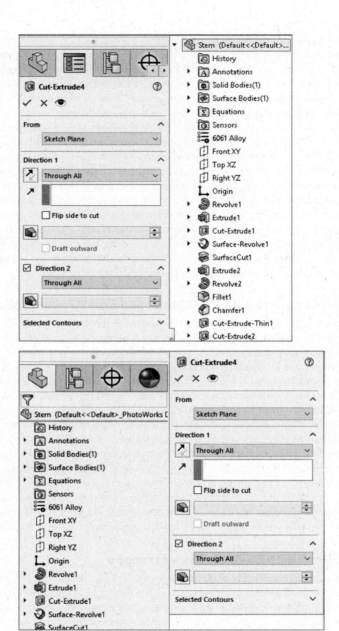

NOTE   The word "breadcrumb" is derived from the children's story where a child leaves a trail of breadcrumbs as she walks so she knows how to get back home.

The breadcrumb itself is displayed in the same area as the flyout FeatureManager, and is shown in Figure 12.10.

FIGURE 12.10
Selection Breadcrumbs show the detail of selection.

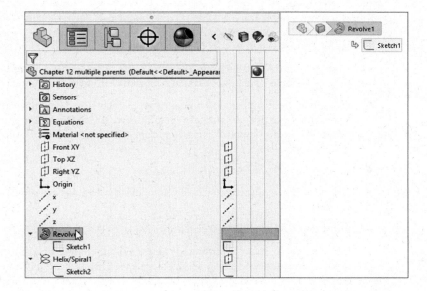

The display of Selection Breadcrumbs can be controlled at Tools ➤ Options ➤ Display ➤ Show Breadcrumbs On Selection.

Breadcrumbs not only show information; you can select individual breadcrumbs to make sure you have the proper level of entities selected. For example, if you have selected a face of a fillet, but you want to select the Fillet feature, first select the face. When the breadcrumb appears, you can select the feature name. Breadcrumbs also display child features, such as sketches or planes. Pressing the D key will move the display of the breadcrumbs to the location of the cursor.

Summarizing Part Modeling Best Practices

This section summarizes the best practices for modeling parts. Best practice lists are important because they lay the groundwork for using the software, which is helpful for new users and users who are trying to experiment with the limits of the software.

Only after you respect the rules and understand why they are so important will you know enough to break them. However, best practice lists should not be taken either too lightly nor too seriously. They are not inflexible rules, but conservative starting places; they are concepts that you can default to, but they can be broken if you have good reasons.

To a great extent, best practice rules are a function of CAD administration, but if you are a CAD user, you need to be aware of these suggested rules as implemented by the company for which you work. The purpose of best practices is to standardize procedures so that everyone at your company can work on the same models without needing to reinvent methods or guess how something was done. If all users at your company are CAD experts and never create models others can't edit, then you don't need best practices. If you have a mixture of users with high and low skill levels, then everybody needs to be trained up to a defined level and model according to your best practices. Best practices need to be defined most for the most difficult tasks. It can be tempting to try to define everything with best practices, but in the long run, you will find it more practical to limit your best practices to only what's necessary and make sure everything else is covered in training.

Following is a list of suggested best practices:

◆ Always use unique filenames for your parts. SolidWorks assemblies and drawings may pick up incorrect references if you use parts with identical names.

◆ Using Custom Properties is a great way to enter text-based information into your parts. Users can view this information from outside the file by using applications such as Windows Explorer, SolidWorks Explorer, eDrawings, and Product Data Management (PDM) applications.

◆ Learn to sketch using automatic relations.

◆ Use fully dimensioned sketches when possible. Splines are often impractical to fully dimension.

◆ Limit your use of the Fixed constraint.

◆ When possible, make relations to sketches or stable reference geometry, such as the origin or standard planes, instead of edges or faces. Sketches are far more stable than faces, edges, or model vertices, which change their internal ID at the slightest change and may disappear entirely with fillets, chamfers, split lines, and so on.

◆ Do not dimension to edges created by fillets or other cosmetic or temporary features.

◆ Apply names to features, sketches, and dimensions that help to make their functions clear.

◆ When possible, use feature fillets and feature patterns rather than sketch fillets and sketch patterns.

◆ Combine fillets into as few fillet features as possible; this also enables you to control fillets that need to be controlled separately—such as fillets to be removed for Finite Element Analysis (FEA), drawings, and simplified configurations—or added for rendering. The trade-off is that troubleshooting is more difficult with fillets that use more edges.

◆ Create a simplified configuration when building very complex parts or working with large assemblies.

◆ Model with symmetry in mind. Use feature patterns and mirroring when possible.

◆ Use link values or global variables or custom properties to control commonly used dimensions.

◆ Do not be afraid of configurations. Control them with design tables when you have more than a few configs, and document any custom programming or automated features in the spreadsheet for other users.

◆ Use display states when possible instead of configurations.

◆ Use multibody modeling for various techniques within parts; it is not intended as a means to create assemblies within a single part file.

◆ Cosmetic features—fillets, in particular—should be saved for the bottom of the design tree. It is also a good idea to put them all together into a folder.

◆ Use the Tools ➤ Options ➤ Performance ➤ Verification On Rebuild setting in combination with the Ctrl+Q command to check models periodically and before calling them "finished." The more complex the model, or the more questionable some of the geometry or techniques might be, the more important it is to check the part.

◆ Always fix errors in your part as soon as you can. Errors increase the time it takes to rebuild, and if you wait until more errors exist, troubleshooting may become more difficult.

◆ Troubleshoot feature and sketch errors from the top of the tree down.

◆ Do not add unnecessary detail. For example, it is not important to actually model a knurled surface on a round steel part. This additional detail is difficult to model in SolidWorks, it slows down the rebuild speed of your part, and there is no advantage to actually having it modeled (unless you are using the model for rapid prototype or to machine a mold for a plastic part where knurling cannot be added as a secondary process). This is better accomplished by a drawing with a note. The same concept applies to thread, extruded text, very large patterns, and other features that introduce complex details.

◆ Do not rely heavily on niche features. For example, if you find yourself creating helices by using Flex/Twist or Wrap instead of Sweep, you may want to rethink your approach. In fact, if you find yourself creating lots of unnecessary helices, you may want to rethink this approach as well, unless there is a good reason for doing so.

◆ File size is not necessarily a measure of inefficiency.

◆ Be cautious about accepting advice or information from Internet forums. You can get both great and terrible advice from people you don't know, along with everything in between. Sometimes, even groups of people can be dead wrong. Get someone you trust to verify ideas, and as always, test your ideas on copied data to determine if they're effective.

If you're the CAD administrator for a group of users, you may want to incorporate some best practice tips into standard operating procedures for them. The more users that you manage, the more you need to standardize your system.

Using Design for Change

SolidWorks users have traditionally been taught to build each feature linearly, on top of the one that came previously. It turns out that this is not a great idea, especially as the parts become more complex. When each feature is dependent on the one before it, all the features must be solved in a particular order, and if one feature fails, so do all the features that come after it. This also slows down the rebuilding process.

Rather than using a linear daisy-chain modeling scenario, you should base features on entities that are less likely to fail or change in such a way that dependent downstream features also fail. In earlier chapters, I suggested that you make sketch relations to other sketches when possible instead of model edges for this very reason.

Keeping Track of References

The aim of these techniques is to help you organize the references between features in a part (and eventually in assemblies) such that you can make changes that you didn't plan on originally without breaking references, causing errors, and requiring a lot of model repair.

The underlying problem here is the dirty laundry that the history-based modeling paradigm has swept under the rug for decades: it doesn't handle changes in design intent very well. Experienced users are familiar with the scenario of making a seemingly simple change and seeing the FeatureManager light up with red Xs and exclamation marks (a lot of errors)—or trying to delete one little feature, and the software insists it must also take 15 other more important features with it.

In essence, you need to keep track of your references. If you sketch on a face, the feature that created the face becomes a reference. If a corner of your rectangle picks up an edge created by a fillet, then that fillet is part of the parent/child arrangement for the sketch. As your individual parts become more complex, the way these models react to change becomes more and more important because each change can potentially cost you more and more time. You will learn about the consequences of being too free with in-context relations in Chapter 20, "Modeling in Context".

It's one thing to make models quickly the first time. Edits should take less time and not require a lot of rework. So how do you avoid this apocalyptic scenario with design for change?

Visualizing Horizontal Modeling

This better approach has been visualized in different ways. One technique calls it *horizontal modeling* or a "wide tree" approach, where instead of a long chain of features, you have a list of features all based on the initial planes and sketches such that there are only a couple of parents (and no grandparents). The rules for this type of modeling are such that no references to 3D geometry are allowed—only references to the stable reference geometry and initial sketches are allowed. To learn more about this technique, you can begin by reading Evan Yares's article on 3D CAD World:

    http://www.3dcadworld.com/going-horizontal/

Understanding Resilient Modeling

Another approach is called *resilient modeling*, where there is a specific method for different types of features. Features that require parents (such as non-sketch fillets or extruded text) come at the end of the tree. Resilient modeling was created by Richard Gebhard, and he has a set of training videos and other information at his web presence at:

    http://learnrms.com/

Using Skeleton Sketches

What if a handful of sketch and plane features were used to centralize control of all the rest of the features? What if every feature, to the extent possible, related back to these "skeleton" features? Features such as fillets, shell, and draft by design require selections from solid geometry—but other features, such as any feature created from sketches, could be made with only reference to those original skeleton sketches and planes. The parent/child relationship would look very different for a model made in this way. Instead of looking like a long staircase, this tree would look more like a tree that gets wide very quickly. There would be fewer "generations," but each generation would be more populated. The main upshot of this is that if any feature fails, the dependent features that fail should be minimized.

The first thing to notice is that errors in features at the top of the tree do not cascade down the tree as they do in the "stairstep" model. Second, it is always much easier to find how a model is constructed, because all the reference geometry used to build it is set up in the first few features. This scenario also has the potential to make better use of multithreaded processing because the logic is less linear and more parallel.

Proper design for change is a discipline that you need to make sure you follow with every model, every day. It is easy to get sloppy and take the easy way out, referencing model edges, sketching on 3D faces, but unless you are making very simple parts and get everything right the first time, this will come back to get you at some point.

Using Evaluation Techniques

You can use evaluation techniques to evaluate geometry errors, demonstrate the manufacturability of a given part, or to some degree quantify the aesthetic qualities of a given part or section of a part. I discuss evaluation techniques here because the design cycle involves iterations around the combination of create-evaluate-edit-evaluate functions. I discuss the following techniques in this section:

- Verification On Rebuild
- Check
- Zebra Stripes/RealView/Lights and Specularity
- Curvature Display
- Deviation Analysis
- Tangent Edges As Phantom
- Geometry Analysis
- Feature Statistics
- Curvature Comb

Many of these techniques apply specifically to plastic parts and complex shapes, but even if you do not become involved in these areas of design or modeling, these tools may help you to find answers on other types of models as well.

A special tab called Evaluate appears in the CommandManager; this tab has much of the functionality that is discussed in this chapter. Plus, the Tools menu has conveniently located several evaluation tools under the Evaluate option, as shown in Figure 12.11. You can use the commands on this tab to evaluate parts in several ways. Some focus on plastic parts or thin-walled parts or symmetric parts, and so on. Most of these tools are from the Tools toolbar and are also are found on the Evaluate tab in the CommandManager.

FIGURE 12.11
The Evaluate tab and the Tools ➤ Evaluate menu

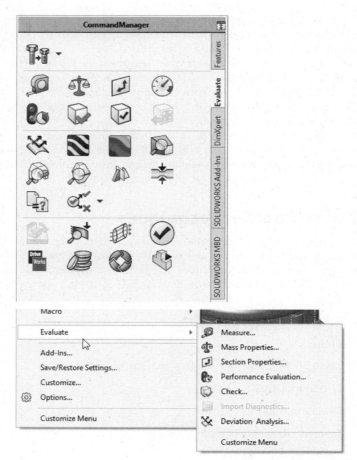

Using Verification On Rebuild

Verification On Rebuild is an option that you can access by choosing Tools ➤ Options ➤ Performance ➤ Verification On Rebuild. Under normal circumstances (with this setting turned off), SolidWorks checks each face to ensure that it does not overlap or intersect improperly with every adjacent face. Each face can have several neighbors. This option is shown in Figure 12.12.

FIGURE 12.12
The Verification On
Rebuild option

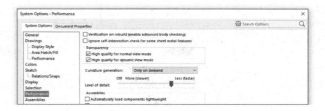

With the setting selected, SolidWorks checks each face with every other face in the model. This is a better check than with the setting off, but it greatly increases the workload. The switch is deselected by default to prevent rebuild times from getting out of control. For most parts, the default setting is sufficient; however, when parts become complex, you may need to select the more advanced setting.

If you are having geometry or rebuild error problems with a part and cannot understand why, try turning on the Verification On Rebuild option and pressing Ctrl+Q. Ctrl+Q applies the Forced Rebuild command and rebuilds the entire design tree. Ctrl+B, or the Rebuild command, rebuilds only what SolidWorks determines needs to be rebuilt.

If you see additional errors in the design tree that were not there before, then the combination of Verification On Rebuild and Forced Rebuild has identified problem areas of the model, and the features that caused the errors failed. If not, then your problem may be elsewhere. You still need to fix any errors found this way.

PERFORMANCE

For speed reasons, it is normal practice to turn off Verification On Rebuild and to use it selectively to check models with potential errors. The type of speed degradation that you can see is dependent on the number of faces and bodies in the model. Some of the performance degradation that relates to patterns is documented in Chapter 9, "Patterning and Mirroring."

Using the Check Tool

Check is a tool that checks geometry for invalid faces and other similar geometry errors. It is also often used to find open edges of surface bodies, short edges, and the minimum radius on a face or entity. I usually apply the Check tool before selecting the Verification On Rebuild option. The Check tool points to the specific face or edge geometry (not features or sketches) that is the cause of the problem. When the Check tool finds general faults, the locations it points to may or may not have something obvious to do with a possible fix.

Much of the time, the best tool for tracking down geometry errors is the combination of experience and intuition. It is not very scientific, but you will come to recognize where potential problems are likely to arise, such as those that occur when you attempt to intersect complex faces at complex edges, sharp or pointy geometry, and geometry or faces that vary significantly from rectangular with 90-degree corners. Figure 12.13 shows the Check Entity dialog box.

FIGURE 12.13
The Check Entity
dialog box

Evaluating Geometry with Reflective Techniques

Evaluating complex shapes can be difficult. A subjective evaluation requires an eye for the type of work you are doing. An objective evaluation requires some sort of measurable criteria for determining a pass or fail, or a way for you to assign a score somewhere in the middle.

One way to subjectively evaluate complex surfaces, and in particular the transitions between surfaces around common edges, is to use reflective techniques. If you look at an automobile's fender, you can tell whether it has been dented or if a dent has been badly repaired by seeing how the light reflects off the surface. The same principle applies when evaluating solid or surface models. Bad transitions appear as a crease or an unwanted bulge or indentation. The goal is to turn off the edge display and not be able to identify where the edge is between surfaces for the transition to be as smooth as if the whole area were made from a single surface.

With all the RealView functionality in SolidWorks that emphasizes reflective finishes and backgrounds that emphasize the reflections, sometimes the RealView Appearances and Scenes are all you need to employ reflective evaluation techniques. Chapter 5, "Using Visualization Techniques," covers all the display information you need to make the most of RealView Appearances and Scenes.

USING ZEBRA STRIPES

Zebra Stripes can be activated in three ways: by choosing View ➤ Display ➤ Zebra Stripes from the menus or by clicking a toolbar button on the View toolbar, or via the context/RMB menus. Zebra Stripes place the part in a room that is either spherical or cubic, where the walls are painted with alternating black and white stripes (although you can change the colors and the spacing of the stripes). The part is made to be perfectly reflective, and the way the stripes transition over edges tells you something about the qualities of the faces on either side of the edge. Four conditions are of particular interest:

$c0$ = Faces contact at edge

$c1$ = Faces are tangent at edge

$c2$ = Curvature of each face is equal at the edge and the transition is smooth

$c3$ = Rate of change of curvature of each face is equal at the edge

The Zebra Stripes tool can only help you identify $c0$, $c1$, and $c2$, and only subjectively. This feature is of most value between complex faces. Figure 12.14 illustrates how the Zebra Stripes tool shows the differences between these three conditions.

Notice how, on the Contact-only model, the Zebra Stripe lines do not line up across the edge. On the Tangent example, the stripes line up across the edges, but the stripes themselves are not smooth. On the Curvature Continuous example, the stripes are smooth across the edges. The part shown in Figure 12.14 is a surface model and can be found in the download materials under the filename `Chapter 12 Zebra Stripes.sldprt`.

FIGURE 12.14
Contact, tangency, and curvature continuity

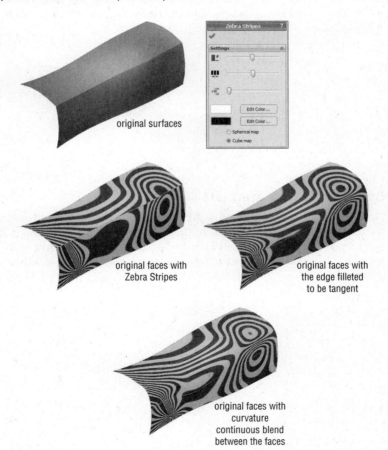

original surfaces

original faces with
Zebra Stripes

original faces with
the edge filleted
to be tangent

original faces with
curvature
continuous blend
between the faces

TIP You should rotate the model often when using the Zebra Stripes tool. Changing the density of the lines can also help, as can increasing the image quality (Tools ➤ Options ➤ Document Properties ➤ Image Quality). Turning off the edge display may also help.

You can also use HDR images instead of Zebra Stripes (use the From File option). The ones with one line are the most useful for local inspections

USING REALVIEW

The RealView Graphics display is available only to users with certain types of video cards. To see whether your card supports RealView, consult the system requirements on the SolidWorks website.

RealView causes reflections that can be used in a way similar to the reflections in Zebra Stripes. Rotate the part slowly, and watch how the reflections flow across edges. Instead of black and white stripes, it uses the reflective background that is applied as part of the RealView Scene.

USING CURVATURE DISPLAY

Model curvature can be plotted onto the model face using colors, as shown in Figure 12.15. The accuracy of this display leaves a bit to be desired, but it does help you identify areas of very tight curvature on your part. Areas of tight curvature can cause features such as fillets and shells to fail.

FIGURE 12.15
Curvature display

USING DEVIATION ANALYSIS

Deviation Analysis measures how far from tangent the surfaces on either side of a selected edge actually are. For example, the edges shown in Figure 12.16 are found to be fair, but not very good. I prefer deviations of less than 0.5 degrees. Often, with some of the advanced surface types such as Fill and Boundary, SolidWorks can achieve edges with less than 0.05 degree maximum deviation.

FIGURE 12.16
An example of
Deviation Analysis

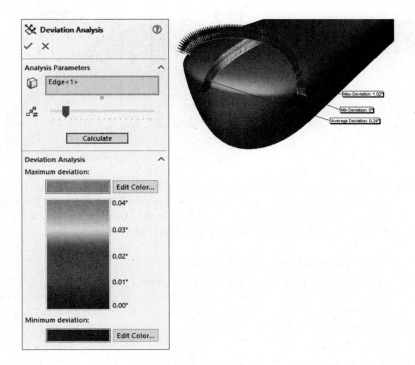

Although Deviation Analysis helps to quantitatively measure how close to tangent the faces on either side of the selected edge are, it doesn't tell you anything about curvature, so you must still run Zebra Stripes to get the complete picture of the flow between faces. Both tests must return good results to have an acceptable face transition.

USING THE TANGENT EDGES AS PHANTOM SETTING

Using the Tangent Edges As Phantom setting is an easy way to evaluate a large number of edges visually. This function does not do what the Zebra Stripes tool does, but it gives you a good indication of the tangency across a large number of edges very quickly. Again, it represents only tangency and tells you nothing about curvature continuity, nor does it give you as detailed information as the Deviation Analysis; it only tells you whether SolidWorks considers the faces to be tangent across the edge. Several releases ago, SolidWorks widened the tolerance of what it considers to be tangent, which is both good and bad news. It's good because features that require tangency will work more frequently, and it's bad because if fractional tangency degrees matter to you, "close" is not close enough. If you use Tangent Edges As Phantom as an analysis technique, you should follow it up with Deviation Analysis to find out how close you actually are.

I have never seen this function deliver false positives (edges displayed as tangent when in fact they were not), but I have seen many false negatives (edges that display as nontangent when in fact they were). Figure 12.17 shows a situation where the edges are displayed with solid edges, but Deviation Analysis shows them to have a zero-degree maximum deviation.

FIGURE 12.17
Using the Tangent Edges
As Phantom setting

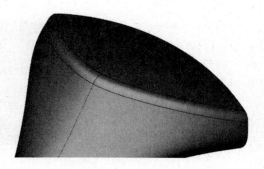

FIGURE 12.17
Using the Tangent Edges
As Phantom setting

The measure of tangency has some tolerance. Users cannot control the tolerance, nor does the documentation say what it is. If SolidWorks says two faces are *not* tangent at an edge, you can believe that, but if SolidWorks says that the faces *are* tangent, you still have to ask *how* tangent. That is the question that Deviation Analysis can answer.

USING GEOMETRY ANALYSIS

Another tool that is fairly new is the Geometry Analysis tool. You can find it in the Tools menu or the new Evaluate tab in the CommandManager. It's an extremely useful tool for troubleshooting problematic geometry. The PropertyManager, shown in Figure 12.18, allows you to look for several specific items:

- ◆ Short edges
- ◆ Small faces
- ◆ Sliver faces
- ◆ Knife edges/vertices
- ◆ Discontinuous faces or edges

FIGURE 12.18
Using Geometry
Analysis to find typical
problem spots

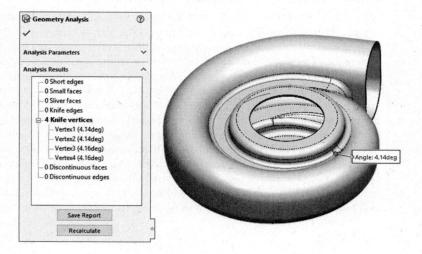

These specific types of geometry typically cause problems with other features, such as shells or fillets. If you are having difficulty with a feature failing for a reason that you can't explain, use the Geometry Analysis tool to point out potential problem spots. This is not a tool that will do your job for you, but it will give you useful information to help you do your job better with less guesswork.

The Geometry Analysis tool is available only with SolidWorks Professional and higher.

USING PERFORMANCE EVALUATION

The Performance Evaluation tool (formerly called Feature Statistics) has been used previously in this book to measure rebuild times for individual features in parts. You can find it either in the Tools menu or the Evaluate tab of the CommandManager.

Performance Evaluation lists the rebuild times of each individual feature in a part. This is useful for researching features, benchmarking hardware or versions of SolidWorks, and developing best practice recommendations for different tools and techniques. Figure 12.19 shows the Performance Evaluation interface.

FIGURE 12.19
Performance Evaluation
helps you analyze
rebuild times
for features.

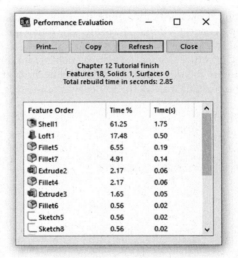

Overall, I don't recommend relying heavily on the data the Performance Evaluation tool provides, not because it's inaccurate, but because rebuild time is not always the best way to evaluate a model. You can certainly use the information, but you also need to keep it in perspective. A feature that takes a long time to rebuild but gives the correct result is always better than any feature that doesn't give the correct result, regardless of rebuild time.

USING THE CURVATURE COMB

The Curvature Comb is a graphical tool that you can apply to a spline, circle, arc, ellipse, or parabola to indicate the curvature along the length of the curve. You cannot apply a Curvature Comb to a straight line, because a straight line has no curvature. The height of the comb indicates the curvature. *Curvature* is defined as the inverse of radius ($c = 1/r$), so that as the radius gets smaller, the curvature gets bigger.

Figure 12.20 shows a Curvature Comb applied to a spline. Notice that the spline continuously changes curvature. An arc has constant curvature.

FIGURE 12.20
A Curvature Comb shows the constantly changing curvature of the spline.

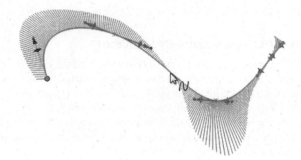

When the comb crosses the spline, it means that the direction of curvature has changed (concave up to concave down, for example). When the comb intersects the spline, it means that the spline at that point has no curvature.

Surface Curvature Combs are also available from the RMB menu over a surface (although you may need to use the double-arrow expander at the bottom of the menu to see it). This helps you visualize the curvature along the UV curves of the face, as shown in Figure 12.21.

FIGURE 12.21
Surface Curvature Combs help you visualize curvature on curved faces.

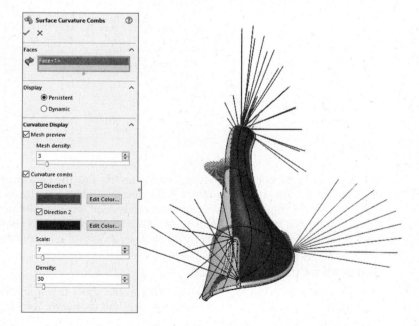

Troubleshooting Errors

You will encounter many types of errors in SolidWorks. Improper installation and even bad computer hygiene can cause errors that might look like bugs in the software. Software bugs can cause errors that look like training issues. Operator errors can cause problems that are very difficult to sort out. I don't have the space in this book to go into all the possible errors and how to work around or fix them, but I will focus on feature-related errors that happen in the course of working on models.

When you get an error in SolidWorks, figuring out what caused the error and how to fix it is the goal of troubleshooting. Error messages appear in several places, including in message boxes in the graphics window, in the taskbar, in tooltip bubbles next to the PropertyManager, and in small symbols within the FeatureManager window.

Interpreting Rebuild Errors

Chapter 3, "Working with Sketches and Reference Geometry," discussed sketch colors and troubleshooting errors in sketches. You can apply much of what you learned from troubleshooting sketches to troubleshooting features in parts. The FeatureManager displays yellow triangles with black exclamation marks that point out some sort of warnings. A warning means there's a problem, but the feature hasn't failed. The red circle with an X in it is a failure symbol, and it means that the feature doesn't create any geometry.

Figure 12.22 shows a portion of a feature tree of a part from which a feature in the middle of the tree was deleted. Unless you are very careful about how you set up your part, a deletion of this kind will result in lots of errors.

FIGURE 12.22
Deleting a feature in the middle of a tree can cause many errors.

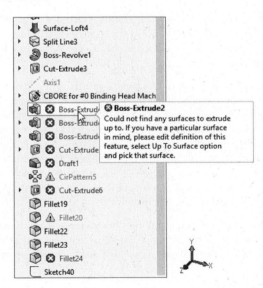

Notice the tooltip balloon in Figure 12.22. Many users get into the habit of clicking out of any sort of warning or error message. You shouldn't be afraid of errors. After you know how to deal with them, you will think of errors as a tool to help you investigate your model. The first thing you should do with an error message is read it. Eventually, you'll be able to recognize error messages and their meanings very quickly.

This error message says, "Could not find any surfaces to extrude up to. . . ." This means that you have lost the "top to surface" end condition on an Extrude feature. This is because the feature was deleted or possibly renamed in a Trim or Knit command. You may know the cause of errors, or you may not. If you inherited this part from someone who did not explain the state of the model to you, you might have to figure it out yourself. Most of the time, it's not difficult to figure out what's going on, especially with a little practice. If there's one thing I can guarantee you, it's that you are going to get a lot of practice evaluating errors.

When you inherit a model with errors, the first thing you should do is look for the error highest in the tree. Because of the nature of the history-based feature tree, errors always cascade down. When you make a change that causes errors, these errors will be lower in the tree than the change. Special situations can arise where a change causes an error up the tree, but they are rare. Again, the Flat Tree display and Dynamic Relationship Visualization should help you understand these situations.

Identifying Common Errors

Here are some common error messages and what they are really trying to tell you:

Some Items are no longer in the model. You can reselect the items using the Edit Definition in the FeatureManager design tree. The first thing to know here is that Edit Definition has been gone for several releases now. The name of the command to look for is Edit Feature. You can get this message when an edge or a face for a selected feature no longer exists. A number of things can cause it, but the culprit is usually changed to the model upstream. As a result, if you roll back the model and make changes (especially if you delete something, but adding features can also cause errors of this sort), you can expect some problems when you unroll the model.

Operation failed due to geometric condition. This is one that frustrates lots of users, because "geometric condition" is vague and could mean just about anything related to geometry. It can sometimes mean that a selection set is incomplete—the feature requires another face or another edge to be selected in order to work, or a fillet cannot work because an edge flips convexity, or a sketch line does not cut all the way across a solid body. There are too many possibilities to list, but this clue indicates that you need to check either the selections for the feature or the body on which the feature is operating. In more complex cases, it might mean that the part has some geometrical errors that you need to figure out by using the Check tool or Verification On Rebuild.

Warning: This sketch contains dimensions or relations to model geometry which no longer exists. This is one of the better messages that SolidWorks provides. It is fairly self-explanatory and goes on to give you a couple of useful suggestions as to how you might fix the problem.

Some filleted items are no longer in the model. Edit the feature to reselect the items. When all the edges selected in a Fillet feature are suddenly not there, the entire Fillet feature fails because there's nothing to do. This warning displays the red circle with the X in it. Some edges may remain selected, and the Fillet feature can still work. In these cases, you will get the next message, which is just a warning rather than an error.

Warning: Edge for fillet/chamfer does not exist. In this case, you see the yellow triangle warning, and the fillet still creates some fillets, but one of the selected edges is missing, and the feature can't create all the fillets it created originally. The fastest way to fix this warning is to right-click it, select Edit Feature, and then immediately click the green checkmark icon. SolidWorks displays a message to make sure you want to just remove the references to the missing edge, but it continues to create fillets on the selected edges. Another option is to find the missing edge in the selection box and reselect an edge to take its place.

Many more types of errors exist, and rather than going through an exhaustive list, which would require another book of its own, I would like to impart to you some guidelines to help you find a useful answer. I hope you only have to figure out an error once, and you will remember it the next time you see it. Here are some general guidelines for troubleshooting errors with causes that aren't obvious:

CAD doesn't like line-on-line geometry. In SolidWorks, you don't get extra points for being close. Most features require you to be exact. It is often a good idea to "overbuild" geometry so it's bigger than it needs to be if it's going to merge with other geometry.

Zero thickness errors are difficult to diagnose. Zero thickness errors can be some of the most difficult errors for users who are new to 3D to diagnose. Much in the same way that CAD doesn't like line-on-line geometry, it doesn't like edges that create a section of a single body where there is air on two sides of an edge. If you were to extrude two rectangles that touch at a point, SolidWorks would create two separate bodies from that point, because it physically would fall apart if it were a single body. If the two touching rectangles were also trying to merge with an existing solid body, you would get an error.

Planar means planar. If you click a face and it just won't let you open a sketch, maybe the face is not planar. Errors of this sort can happen in surfacing applications and imported geometry quite often. I use the Sketch icon as a quick test for whether a face is planar. SolidWorks doesn't really give you another way to measure this. Nonplanar faces can also cause lots of trouble with assembly mates.

Even if it's planar, is it square to the coordinate system? If you work with plastic parts or castings, or anything else that requires draft, you can (and probably do) have faces that are not perpendicular or parallel to the standard reference planes. This can cause problems with projections and extrusion directions. For example, a circle projected at an angle becomes an ellipse, and an ellipse projected at an angle becomes a spline.

If SolidWorks doesn't like one method, try another that produces similar results. One common example of this is when a constant radius fillet won't work, and you think it should work. In this case, try to use a variable radius fillet with all the same radius values.

For most errors, a rational reason exists. Belief in supernatural forces is not likely to be useful when troubleshooting errors in SolidWorks. If you're using very common features such as extrudes and cuts, and you run into errors, it's very unlikely that you've found a bug (although bugs in sketches are quite common). Generally speaking, the more traffic a feature sees, the less likely you are to find bugs with it. Sometimes, just determining whether the problem is with the software or with something you're doing is the toughest thing to troubleshoot. In general, users are far too eager to assign blame to the software.

Dismissing Errors

Some errors have the Don't Show This Again box. Don't get in the habit of checking that box unless you are very familiar with the cause of the error and how to fix it. Missing an existing error is much more costly than acknowledging redundant errors.

The What's Wrong box shown in Figure 12.23 gives you a list of the errors in the existing model. Some people find it embarrassing to be reminded about errors, especially if people have the habit of looking over your shoulder while you're working. Errors are in red; warnings are in yellow. The difference is between a feature that fails (red) and a feature that may just partially fail, such as a fillet that is missing a selected edge, but the rest of the edges have been filleted.

FIGURE 12.23
The What's Wrong box gives you a summary of all the errors and warnings in the current model.

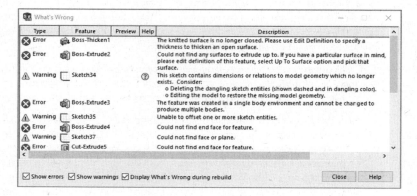

The What's Wrong box can be turned off so it isn't displayed each time the model is rebuilt. You have this option with many of the error or warning messages. Each time a message is turned off in this way, it is added to a list of dismissed messages in System Options, shown in Figure 12.24. You may come up against a situation where you want to change how you respond to a repeating warning message. This box can fill up with a lot of messages, so think twice and make sure you understand the issue before you dismiss a warning message.

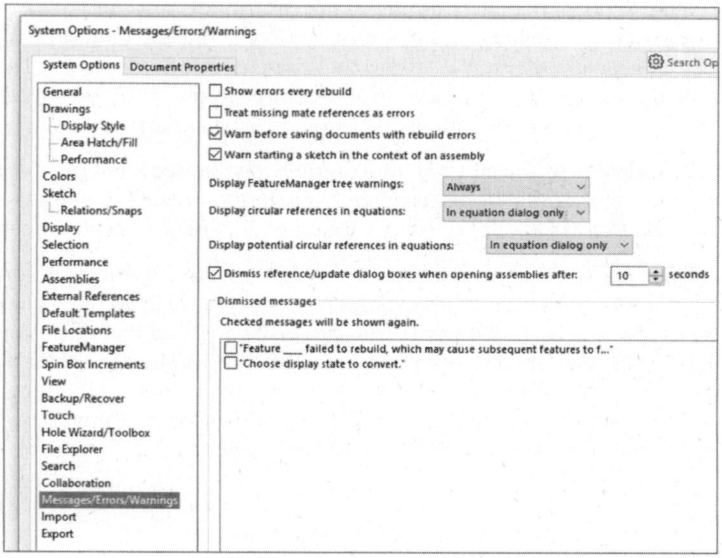

FIGURE 12.24
The list of dismissed messages is found in System Options.

Using SolidWorks RX and Performance Benchmark

SolidWorks provides a couple of automated troubleshooting tools: SolidWorks RX and Performance Benchmark. SolidWorks RX troubleshoots your system, or at least records facts about your system so someone trained in how to view the results can diagnose the problem.

USING SOLIDWORKS RX

SolidWorks RX is a diagnostic tool that SolidWorks provides to help support techs solve your problem or to help you solve it yourself. You can access SolidWorks RX through the Windows Start menu ➤ All Programs ➤ SolidWorks 2018 ➤ SolidWorks 2018 Tools ➤ SolidWorks RX. Figure 12.25 shows the Home page of the interface.

FIGURE 12.25
Using SolidWorks RX

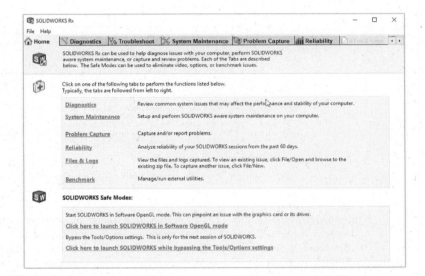

Diagnostics Tab

The first tab in the SolidWorks RX interface is a self-help diagnostics list, shown in Figure 12.26. This points out that my computer is compatible with my video card and that the driver is out of date (it gives me the option to download the correct driver); it also lists other information related to system maintenance.

The items in the Diagnostics tab are things that a support tech might ask you about if you were to call with a crash problem or some other problem that might be related to general system issues. Running SolidWorks RX before calling tech support could save you time and make you more self-reliant.

Troubleshoot Tab   The Troubleshoot tab contains mostly links to the SolidWorks Knowledge Base. (You'll need a subscription login.) These links are useful, and it is a good idea to check them out before calling tech support.

FIGURE 12.26
Using the SolidWorks RX
Diagnostics tab

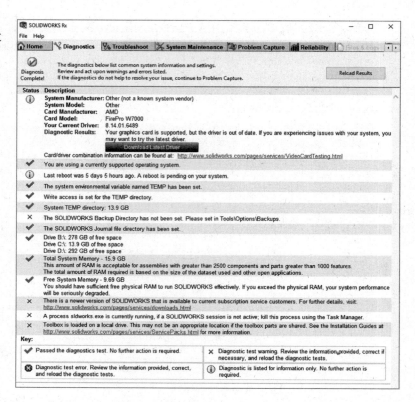

FIGURE 12.26
Using the SolidWorks RX
Diagnostics tab

System Maintenance Tab   The System Maintenance tab contains paths to critical SolidWorks and system folders. If you click the Start Maintenance button in the upper-right corner, SolidWorks RX clears all the files from the listed paths. If you use the Browse buttons, you can clear paths individually. These are generally temporary and backup folders, so make sure you don't need any of the files before clearing them. Figure 12.27 shows the System Maintenance tab.

Problem Capture Tab   Often, when you call your reseller tech support asking for help with some sort of difficulty that isn't readily explained, the technician asks you to submit a SolidWorks RX log file. This log file includes the information from the other tabs, along with an optional description of the problem, SolidWorks files that were in use when the problem occurred, and a video of the problem actually happening. Figure 12.28 shows the Problem Capture tab.

Reliability Tab   The Reliability tab in SolidWorks Rx shows a history of your SolidWorks sessions over the last two weeks. This history helps your tech support people and your CAD administrator see how much trouble you've been having with crashes (the red dots denote abnormal terminations). The Reliability tab is shown in Figure 12.29.

Files & Logs Tab   The Files & Logs tab shows a summary of the issue and a list of all the files included in the RX package. You can click the files that have been added to view their contents before sending the package. The Files & Logs tab is shown in Figure 12.30.

FIGURE 12.27
Clearing temp files with the System Maintenance tab

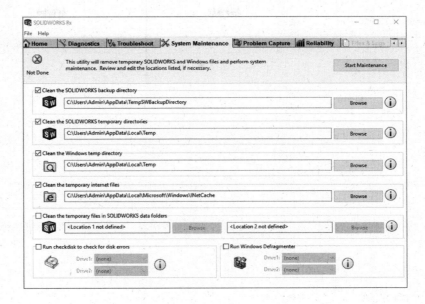

FIGURE 12.28
Collecting information in the Problem Capture tab

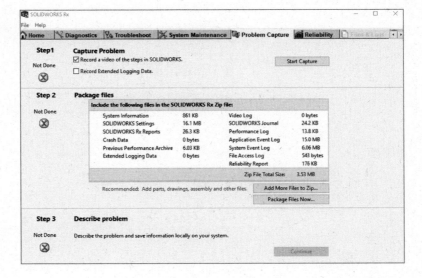

USING PERFORMANCE BENCHMARK

SolidWorks RX has an Add-in tab that allows add-ins to be developed to extend the RX functionality. The Performance Benchmark runs your installation of SolidWorks through some automated display and rebuild exercises, and it measures the time for various operations such as zoom, rotate, and rebuild for a part and an assembly. Figure 12.31 shows the interface for the Performance Benchmark test.

FIGURE 12.29
The Reliability tab gives you a record of sessions and crashes.

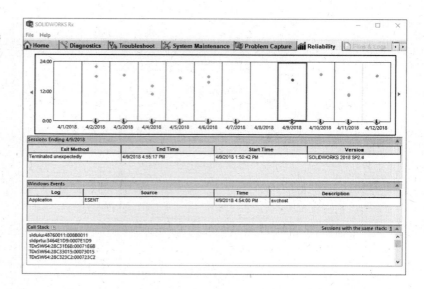

FIGURE 12.30
Listing the files to be sent in the RX package

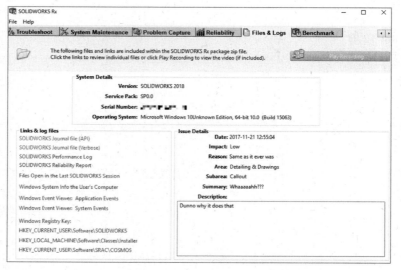

This benchmark is similar to the SPECapc benchmark, which can be used across several different CAD systems. SPECapc still exists (and is available at www.spec.org), and the SolidWorks specific portion of the benchmark was last updated in 2015. The point of benchmarks like this is to measure hardware capabilities.

The models for the SolidWorks RX Performance Benchmark are a small, stamped part and an injection-mold die set. Figure 12.32 shows the benchmark in action.

You can also submit your results to the SolidWorks website, where they are posted immediately for comparison. This is used to help people make decisions about what hardware to buy.

FIGURE 12.31
Running Performance
Benchmark

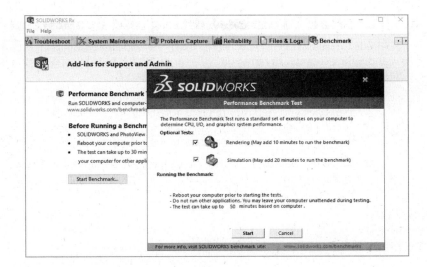

FIGURE 12.32
Putting the computer
through its paces with
Performance Benchmark

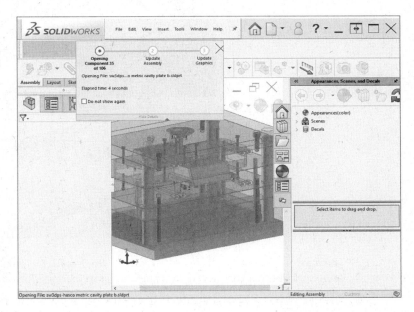

You can check out the compared scores at www.solidworks.com/sw/support/
shareyourscore.htm. Look through the list to see which kind of hardware receives a
consistently high score and which is not represented in the top results.

You can find more information on benchmarking and SolidWorks at www.solidworks.com/
sw/support/benchmarks.htm.

Tutorial: Utilizing Editing and Evaluation Techniques

In this tutorial, you will make some major edits to an existing part. You will use some simple Loft and Spline commands, and you will work with the rollback states and feature order, as well as some evaluation techniques. Follow these steps:

1. Open the existing part with the filename Chapter 12 Tutorial Start.sldprt. Roll the part back and step through it feature by feature to see how it was made. Edit the Loft feature to create it to help you understand how the part was built. Exit the Loft command, and move the Rollback bar back to the bottom of the tree.

2. Open the Deviation Analysis tool (Tools ➢ Evaluate ➢ Deviation Analysis). Select the edges, as shown in Figure 12.33.

FIGURE 12.33

Deviation Analysis of an existing part

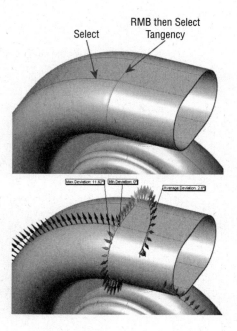

The maximum deviation is over 10 degrees, which is far too much. This part needs to be smoothed out, which you can do using splines in place of lines and arcs.

3. The first step is to make the outlet all one piece with the spiral. You can do this with a fit spline. You need to create the fit spline before the loft profiles and after the spiral.

   Expand the loft, and roll back between the Loft feature and the first sketch. Click OK in response to the prompt, and then roll back to just after the spiral, as shown in Figure 12.34. You could also use the Flat Tree view by right-clicking on the name of the part at the top of the tree, and selecting Tree Display ➢ Flat Tree View.

4. Right-click the spiral in the FeatureManager and show it. Open a new sketch on the Top plane.

5. Draw a tangent line from the outer end of the spiral. You will notice that you cannot reference the end of the spiral.

TIP Working with curves that are absorbed into other features is notoriously difficult. Generally, you need to select the curves from the FeatureManager to do anything at all with them. Also, if you need to reference an end of an absorbed curve, you are better off using Convert Entities to make it into a sketch entity.

6. Notice that you cannot select the spiral from the graphics window. Even when selected from the FeatureManager, it appears not to be selected in the graphics window. Ensure that it is selected in the FeatureManager, and then click the Convert Entities button on the Sketch toolbar.

7. Draw a tangent line from the outer end of the spiral, and dimension it to be 3-inches long, as shown in Figure 12.35. This will be slightly angled up to the right.

FIGURE 12.35
Preparing for the
fit spline

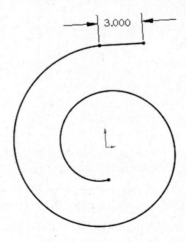

8. Select both the converted spiral and the line, and select Tools ➤ Spline Tools ➤ Fit Spline. Set the Tolerance to .1 inch and make sure that only the Constrained option is selected. Click OK to accept the fit spline. Test to make sure that a single spline is created by moving your cursor over the sketch to see whether the whole length is highlighted. The goal is to make sure the Curvature Comb that automatically appears shows as smooth a transition as possible between the converted spiral and the straight line.

NOTE The Fit Spline feature fits a spline to a set of sketch entities within the specified tolerance. It can be a useful tool for smoothing out sketch geometry.

9. Exit the sketch, and create a new plane. Choose Insert ➤ Reference Geometry ➤ Plane from the menus. Select the fit spline as the first reference and the outer end of the fit spline as the second reference. Click OK to accept the new plane. This is illustrated in Figure 12.36.

FIGURE 12.36
Creating a new plane

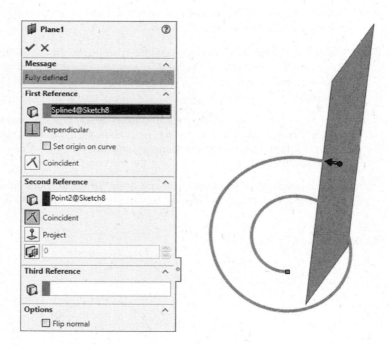

10. Drag the Rollback bar down between Sketch3 and Loft1. If it goes beyond Loft1, then you need to navigate back to this position again.

11. Right-click Sketch3 and select Edit Sketch Plane. Select the newly created Plane1 from the flyout FeatureManager, and click OK to accept the change.

12. Notice that the loft profile has moved to a place where it does not belong. This is because the sketch has a Pierce constraint to the spiral, and there are multiple places where the spiral pierces the sketch plane.

Edit Sketch3, and delete the Pierce constraint on the sketch point in the middle of the construction line. Create a Coincident relation between the sketch point and the outer end of the fit spline, as shown in Figure 12.37 (most easily done by dragging the point in the sketch onto the point of the fit spline). Do not exit the sketch.

FIGURE 12.37
Sketch3 in its
new location

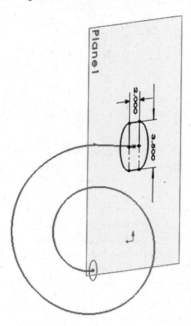

13. One of the goals of these edits is to smooth out the part. Remember that the Deviation Analysis tool told you that the edges created between the lines and arcs in Sketch3 were not very tangent. For this reason, it would be a good idea to replace the lines and arcs in Sketch3 with another fit spline.

Right-click one of the solid sketch entities in Sketch3, and click Select Chain.

14. Create another fit spline using the same technique as in step 8. Again, keep an eye on the Curvature Comb to make sure the curvature around the connections between lines and arcs doesn't vary too much. Exit the sketch.

15. Drag the Rollback bar down one feature so it's below the loft. Notice that the Loft feature has failed. If you hold the cursor over the Feature icon, the tool tip confirms this by displaying the message, "The Loft Feature Failed to Complete."

16. Edit the Loft feature. Expand the Centerline Parameters panel if it isn't already expanded, and delete the spiral from the selection box. In its place, select the Spiral fit spline.

17. If the loft does not preview, check to ensure that the Show Preview option is selected in the Options panel at the bottom.

18. If it still doesn't preview, right-click in the graphics window and select Show All Connectors. Position the blue dots on the connector so it looks like Figure 12.38.

FIGURE 12.38
Positioning the
connectors

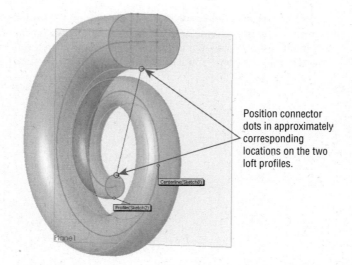

Position connector
dots in approximately
corresponding
locations on the two
loft profiles.

19. Click OK to accept the loft. The loft should be much smoother now than it was before. To check this, right-click on the surface and select Surface Curvature Combs (remember you may have to expand the RMB menu). In addition, the Spiral feature should no longer be under the loft; it should now be the first item in the design tree. (If there are any irregularities in the loft, edit the Number Of Sections slider in the Centerline Parameters panel so the slider is in the middle instead of all the way to the right.)

20. Drag the Rollback bar down to just before the Shell feature. Notice that Fillet5 has failed. Move the mouse cursor over Fillet5. The tool tip tells you that some references are missing. Edit Fillet5, and select edges in order to create fillets, as shown in Figure 12.39.

FIGURE 12.39
Repairing Fillet5

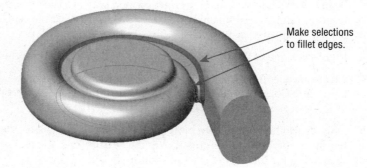

Make selections
to fillet edges.

21. Right-click in the design tree and select Roll To End. This causes the FeatureManager to become unrolled all the way to the end.

22. The outlet of the involute is now longer than it should be. This is because the original extrude was never deleted from the end. Right-click the Extrude1 feature and select Parent/Child. The feature needs to be deleted, but you need to know what will be deleted with it.

23. The Shell is listed as a child of the extrude because the end face of the extrude was chosen to be removed by the Shell. Edit the Shell feature, and remove the reference to the face. (A Shell feature with no faces to remove is still hollowed out.)

24. Right-click Extrude1 and select Parent/Child again to verify that the Shell feature is no longer listed as a child.

25. Delete Extrude1, and when the dialog box appears, press Alt+F to select Also Delete Absorbed Features.

26. Edit the Shell feature, and select the large end of the loft. Exit the Shell feature. The results up to this step are shown in Figure 12.40.

FIGURE 12.40
The results up to step 26

27. Drag a window in the design tree to select the four Fillet features. Then right-click and select Add to New Folder. Rename the new folder **Fillet Folder**.

28. Click the Section View tool, and create a section view using the Front plane.

29. Reorder the Fillet folder to after the Shell feature.

30. At this point, you should notice that something doesn't look right. This is because creating the fillets after the Shell causes the outside fillets to break through some of the inside corners. The fillets should have failed, but have not, as shown in Figure 12.41.

FIGURE 12.41
Fillets that should
have failed

31. Choose Tools ➢ Options ➢ Performance, and select Verification On Rebuild. Then click OK to exit the Performance menu, and press Ctrl+Q. The fillets should now fail.

32. Click Undo to return the feature order to the way it was. Make sure to turn off the Verification On Rebuild option, because this unnecessarily slows down rebuild times.

33. Save the part.

The Bottom Line

Working effectively with feature history, even in complex models, is a requirement for working with parts that others have created. When I get a part from someone else, I usually look first at the FeatureManager and roll it back if possible to get an idea of how the part was modeled. Looking at sketches, relations, feature order, symmetry, redundancy, sketch reuse, and so on are important steps in being able to repair or edit any part. Using modeling best practice techniques helps to ensure that when edits have to be done, they are easy to accomplish, even if they are done by someone who did not build the part.

Evaluation techniques are really the heart of editing, as you should not make too many changes without a basic evaluation of the strengths and weaknesses of the current model. SolidWorks provides a wide array of evaluation tools. Time spent learning how to use the tools and interpret the results is time well spent.

Master It Set and test the following ease-of-use settings. Set and test the following settings to make sure you know where to find them and what they do:

◆ Arrow Key Navigation for the FeatureManager

◆ Flyout FeatureManager

◆ Selection Breadcrumbs

◆ Dynamic Reference Visualization

◆ Show Flat Tree

Master It Use the part from the download material called Horizontal.sldprt. This part uses several sketches to drive the entire part. Take a look through this part, and try to re-create one that is similar.

Master It Edit the previous part to see if you can make features fail. In particular, reorder some fillets. Next, try the same thing with the part called Vertical.sldprt, which is provided with the download material. Examine the Vertical part and try to figure out why reordering the fillets causes so many failures.

Part III

Working with Assemblies

Chapter 13

Building Efficient Assemblies

This chapter introduces you to techniques you can use to manage performance issues as well as general-use issues, efficiency, browse-worthiness, and searchability in assemblies.

IN THIS CHAPTER, YOU WILL LEARN TO:

◆ Set apart the elements of an assembly

◆ Increase performance by using SpeedPaks

◆ Organize assemblies by using subassemblies

◆ Group parts and mates by using folders

◆ Show names and descriptions with Tree Display options

◆ Employ helpful assembly tools

Understanding the Purpose of Assemblies

In the physical world, assemblies exist for several reasons:

◆ Separating materials

◆ Allowing relative motion

◆ Reducing material

◆ Allowing for different manufacturing techniques

◆ Allowing for disassembly or repair

Independent of the reasons stemming from physical-world requirements, CAD assemblies might have some unique reasons for existing:

◆ Depicting an assembly process such as order of operations

◆ Specifying dimensional assembly relationships and tolerances

◆ Establishing clearances and limits of motion

◆ Visualizing motion and spatial relationships between parts

◆ Designing parts in-context

- Creating a parts list for assembly (Bill of Material, or BOM)

- Creating a parts list for purchasing

- Automating data entry through product data management (PDM)

- Staging renderings

- Creating data for downstream applications such as animation or motion analysis

You can probably come up with a number of additional reasons for making CAD assemblies. In fact, almost as many reasons exist for making assemblies as there are people making those assemblies.

If you are trying to drive product development with a single top-level assembly, you might run into situations where the various functions of the assembly start conflicting with one another. For example, you might have an assembly where a part flexes. It is difficult or impossible to make flexible parts work effectively in SolidWorks with dynamic assembly motion. Another situation might be in-context relationships where the parent and child components move relative to one another—or maybe you need an assembly for a rendering and the assembly must have multiple instances of in-context components, which can be tricky to manage. You get the picture. You can't always do everything with a single assembly.

You can certainly have multiple assembly files for a single product. In fact, in some cases, this may be necessary. Rendering is probably one of the most common reasons to create a new assembly. Conflicts between external references and motion are another common reason to create a new assembly document.

Identifying Types of Assemblies

The average SolidWorks user thinks an assembly is a collection of parts put together with mates that position parts and may also allow motion. In this kind of assembly, you might use patterns, configurations, in-context techniques, and so on. The goal of the assembly is probably to simulate reality in the way the product looks and moves.

DRIVING AN ASSEMBLY WITH A BASE PART AND MATES (BOTTOM-UP WITH MATES)

This is considered "orthodox" SolidWorks assembly usage and is the way the SolidWorks training materials describe creating assemblies. Insert a part or subassembly at the origin, which becomes fixed in place automatically, and then start mating parts and subassemblies to the base component and add on from there.

It's difficult to criticize an assembly modeling method that has been used for so long by so many people, but the high failure rate of mates attached to edges and faces speaks for itself. SolidWorks has tried to solve this problem for many releases of the software, but the failure rate hasn't changed much, if at all. You may find that the software even tries to hide certain types of mate errors to make them easier to ignore.

If you read Chapter 12, "Editing, Evaluating, and Troubleshooting," you know that the most common methods for part modeling are also the easiest and most error prone. I ask you to consider that the same is true in assembly modeling. To make truly robust assemblies, a little more forethought is required. In Chapter 12, we used reference geometry to build the bones of the part because that is a more stable approach. Here with assemblies I will recommend the same.

The bottom line for the method of mating to base parts is that it is unreliable through changes. Of the methods that are presented in this book, this is the most common yet least reliable method. This is not the fault of the software, but of the method. This faulty method is popular because it's the easiest and requires the least planning.

An example of where you might use this kind of assembly is a robotic arm. Figure 13.1 shows an assembly that was created with bottom-up techniques (parts made individually) and assembled with face-to-face mates.

FIGURE 13.1
Mechanical parts using mates to locate and enable motion

But if you were to create, say, a scale model of a car, as shown in Figure 13.2, the method of independently designing each component, especially something like body panels, and then mating them together wouldn't make much sense. Methods in the other types of assemblies shown later in this chapter will help with this type of design.

FIGURE 13.2
Considering how you would design the parts of a scale model car

Using the "bottom-up with mates" method to design the body panels of the car so that they fit together well and looked smooth next to one another would be difficult or impossible.

Driving an Assembly with Sketches and Planes (Bottom-Up with Skeleton)

One way to avoid the potential pitfalls of mating to a base part is to replace the changeable faces and edges with items that are more stable. The stability hierarchy listing items from the most to the least stable looks like this:

- Assembly or part origin
- Assembly or part standard planes
- Reference geometry (plane, axis, point)
- Reference geometry from inserted parts (from using the Insert ➢ Part command)
- Sketch lines and midpoints
- Sketch endpoints
- Surface model faces
- Solid model faces
- Edges and vertex points
- In-context items
    - Reference geometry
    - Faces
    - Edges

An easier way to remember this without memorizing the list is that the more parents something has, the less reliable it is as a reference. This becomes more applicable if external references are involved, such as inserted parts or an in-context situation. Edges created by fillets or chamfers are lower on the list of stable references than other edges.

There is no clear answer to the question, "Is this reference stable enough?" It is entirely possible for you to be completely successful using in-context edges for all your model references. In order for that to happen, you have to plan your model very well and avoid any big topological changes (changes to the number or function of faces) to the model.

When you are building a part, selecting references from near the top of the previous list can be challenging, especially when faces and edges are so easy to use. You need to evaluate how much editing and rework you think you will generate when you must make changes for which you haven't necessarily planned.

Now consider the two examples mentioned in the previous assembly modeling method—the robot arm and the model car. You could design the robot easily with the sketch layout, but simulating the motion in 3D would be difficult if you did it in conjunction with the sketch. The model car would still be difficult to assemble, and if you were simply using sketches as the references between parts, it would be difficult to design the body panels such that they fit together smoothly.

MODELING PARTS IN PLACE (IN-CONTEXT DESIGN)

In-context design is discussed in more detail in Chapter 20, "Modeling in Context," but here you will get some idea of what to expect. Modeling parts in the context of an assembly that contains other parts enables you to make relationships between the parts. Those relationships are managed by the assembly. The parts have to be arranged spatially with respect to one another, and the references to the files must also be managed.

When you see a sales demonstration, the technique of using edges of other parts from the assembly to make a new part looks very compelling, especially when you make a change to the other part and the new part updates as well. It's hard to argue with that kind of functionality. But the price you pay for that sort of associativity is that you must manage the relationships between three files: the parent part, the child part, and the assembly. Furthermore, within the assembly, the relationships are made between specific instances of the parts, so if you have multiple instances of each, you must do something to remember which pair of parts is the driving pair.

Also, model history with parts doesn't work the same with assemblies. The relationship between the parts doesn't have any memory, so if you started the in-context relationships before the parent part was complete, and then put fillets over the edges that you had referenced, your in-context references would fail.

Take another look at the robot arm and the model car examples. Using in-context methods, you could certainly design the robot arm, but again you might run into some problems with getting it to move correctly while maintaining the references. However, with the model car, getting the parts in the right place wouldn't be any problem, because you would be modeling the parts in-place. On the other hand, you might be able to get the shape to flow smoothly, but it's still doubtful. In-context modeling can copy 3D surfaces between parts, but for an improved workflow for this type of work, you must read further into this chapter.

An example of a part where modeling in-context works well is a table with legs, as well as a fixture that sits on the table, as shown in Figure 13.3. The in-context work lines up the holes between the parts. There is no relative movement between the parts, and the individual parts aren't likely to be used in other assemblies.

The ideal situation in which to use in-context techniques is when two parts are assembled face-on-face, the shape of the contact faces are the same or offset, and holes are used for fasteners. The main requirement is that there is no relative motion between the two parts.

MODELING PARTS AS MULTIBODIES

Another method you can use to model parts is to start the models in a multibody part. I don't recommend this method for creating finished parts as multibodies, but getting some of the major parts on an assembly started as single parts and then breaking them out into individual parts for details can be a very effective method.

Suppose you're modeling a riding lawn mower, and you need to create the plastic cowling on the front of the mower. The cowling is made up of multiple pieces because some of them are different colors and some are transparent. The complex shapes of the cowling encompass multiple parts. If you were to model one part and then try to model another part independently that shared some of the same shape, it would be very difficult or impossible to get the shapes to match acceptably.

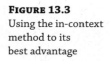

FIGURE 13.3
Using the in-context
method to its
best advantage

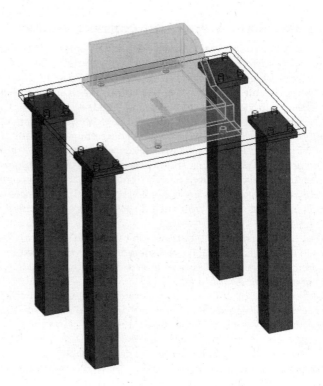

One answer to this problem is to create the shape in a single part, then break the single part into individual bodies, and then save the bodies external to the original part. When you put these parts back together into the assembly, each part can be placed so its origin matches with the assembly origin. Because all the parts started from the same part, they will share the same origin. This makes putting the parts back together much simpler. It makes assembly for motion more difficult, but parts that have a shape in common are more likely to be fixed with respect to one another.

Multibody modeling has advantages over in-context modeling in that it reduces external references (although saving bodies out as parts creates an external reference), but it also has some drawbacks. If you were to take all the features of individual parts and stack them into a single feature tree in a single part, you would probably be unhappy with the result. By making all the features for all parts within a single part file, you make troubleshooting much more difficult, and rebuild times are dramatically increased. Add to this the inability to reuse parts, do individual revision management, or perform simple assembly operations such as dynamic motion, exploded views, or BOMs, and following the multibody method through to finished parts becomes very unattractive.

The best option for using multibodies to create parts for an assembly is to start the parts in Multi-body mode, and then as soon as the interbody references are no longer needed, transition the bodies to separate parts.

Multibody modeling may not do so well when parts are repeated or where purchased components represent a large percentage of the total parts. Although you do have mate-like functionality for placing bodies within a multibody part, it is probably not the best use of this method. Figure 13.4 shows a product that's designed as a multibody part, but it involves many difficulties because of reused parts and hardware.

FIGURE 13.4

Reusing parts is not a strength of multi-body methods.

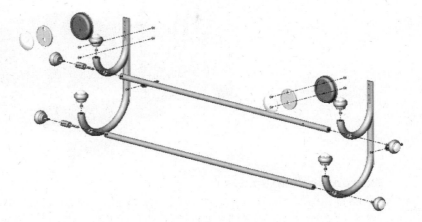

Revisiting the test for each method, you would find that the robot arm is well suited to being designed as a multibody part and then reassembled with mates in an assembly. In fact, the multibody method is probably the best method for this type of work, because it maintains references between parts and then assembles the parts into an assembly mechanism with motion.

The model car, with its shape that flows between parts, would still be awkward, although it could be done as individual parts. Let's look at the last method to see if this helps with the car model.

INSERTING A MASTER MODEL

You will learn about the master model technique in Chapter 33, "Employing Master Model Techniques." In a nutshell, a *master model* is a single part where you place sketches, reference geometry, surfaces, and maybe some solids, and then you insert that part into other parts to use a reference to build each individual part. Using this technique makes in-context work unnecessary, and it eliminates some of the dangers of creating too many features in a multibody part.

You assemble parts in this manner the same as with the multibody part method, and then you drop each part into the FeatureManager of the assembly. This aligns the part origin with the assembly origin, and because each part was built from the same master model, all parts share the same origin.

Take another look at the robot arm and model car examples. The robot arm may be a little awkward using this method, but it works. The multibody method is probably best for this type of design.

On the other hand, the master model method brings real power to projects such as the model car. You can design the entire outside of the car as if it were a single part and then break it into individual parts. In Figure 13.5, notice how some parts that will be manufactured as a single part can be easily pulled off the master model. Sketches within the master model can help define breaks between parts and can help determine if there is relative motion—for example, with the doors.

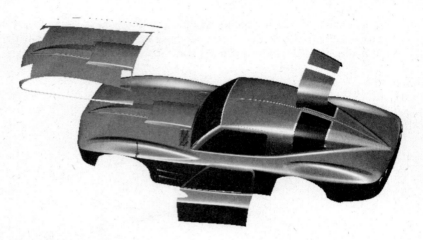

EXCLUDING SOME PARTS

Methods such as those mentioned previously are great for any part that is unique to an assembly, but should not be used for library-type parts. If you have a part that will be used in more than one assembly, it should not have any external references. All these methods create external references except *bottom-up assembly* (where parts are modeled individually and then assembled to one another or to a skeleton).

Any library parts that you have—and standard hardware such as nuts, bolts, washers, and so on—should be modeled without references. You should not create them as a part of multi-body parts.

Some SolidWorks users think that eliminating the distinction between assemblies and parts would be a good thing. That point of view works only for the simplest small assemblies with simple parts. It's easy to come up with situations in which the tree management tools required to maintain models built using that philosophy through changes do not even exist in the software.

Creating an Alternative to Multiple Assemblies

Re-creating or copying assemblies for different uses may seem very inefficient. In Chapter 19, "Controlling Assembly Configurations and Display States," you will learn about another way: using assembly configurations. Assembly configurations are a great tool with lots of theoretical benefits and practical limitations. As with most other functions in SolidWorks, when you need to create assemblies for multiple purposes, you may find that assembly configurations meet your needs. Or you may find it easier to just save a copy of the assembly, knowing that changes for the sake of rendering do not diminish the usefulness of the data for something like exploded views or managing external in-context references.

Identifying the Elements of an Assembly

As the number of parts and design requirements for an assembly grows, you may need to add some of the following types of assembly elements:

- Assembly equations
- Assembly Layout feature
- Assembly layout technique
- Assembly reference geometry (plane, axis, point, coordinate system)
- Parts
- Subassemblies
- Folders for parts
- Folders for mates
- Mates
- Assembly features (cuts that are made after the parts are assembled)
- Component patterns
- Mirror components

- In-context reference placeholders
- Smart Fasteners
- Smart Components
- Virtual components
- Envelopes
- Assembly configurations
- SpeedPaks
- Display states
- Assembly Design Tables
- Assembly Bill of Materials (BOM)
- Hidden/Suppressed/ Lightweight/SpeedPak performance techniques
- Sensors
- Hole Series

You may already be familiar with some of these elements from having worked with part documents. They are shown in Figure 13. 6 and described in detail throughout this book.

FIGURE 13.6
Elements of an assembly

Working with Assembly Equations

Assembly equations work like part equations, but with some additional complications and considerations. For example, one of the additional features of assembly equations is the ability to drive the dimensions of one part from another part. The syntax is slightly different for assemblies, as shown in Figure 13.7.

FIGURE 13.7
An assembly equation driving one part from another

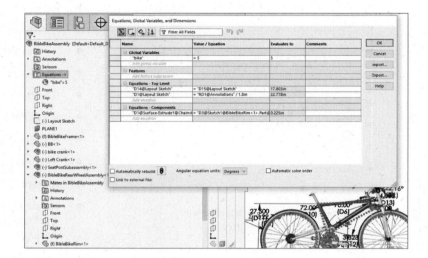

Solving External References

Notice the arrow symbol (→) after the Equations folder in the assembly FeatureManager. This means that there is an external or in-context reference. An *external reference* means that an aspect of one part is dependent on something outside of the part. This has file management implications because you must maintain the names of the files so they always recognize the other file involved in the external relation. *In-context* means that one part has a relationship to another part in a position determined by an assembly. In this case, the in-context external reference can be solved only if the original part, the referenced part, and the assembly where the relationship was created are all open at the same time.

Understanding Global Variables

Global variables also work in assemblies, but they don't work between parts. Local assembly sketches can use these functions, and the parts can use them when edited in the context of the assembly.

Renaming

Equations update with new part names regardless of how you rename the parts. Names of subassemblies also update when you rename assembly files. This includes renaming a document using the Save As command, using SolidWorks Explorer, or using Windows Explorer. It also includes redirecting the assembly to the new part name, as well as renaming the assembly using each of these techniques. If the assembly can find the part and recognizes the part as the one it's looking for, then the equation will work.

Some of the methods mentioned previously for renaming parts are not recommended. SolidWorks Explorer and the Save As methods can be effective when used properly. References between files are a different issue from an equation's references to local filenames.

RECOMMENDATIONS

Although assembly equations are certainly a valid way to control part sizes, you should use assembly or part configurations, possibly with design tables, to accomplish something similar. Equations and configurations don't mix well, because the two methods conflict over which one controls the dimensions. Configurations with design tables are recommended over equations.

CAUTION   You may have unexpected results if a single dimension is controlled from more than one location. For example, if you have a part-level equation and an assembly-level equation, then one of the equations will be automatically set to Read Only and will not be used.

SOLIDWORKS EXPLORER

SolidWorks Explorer is a simple file-management tool that you can use with or without SolidWorks. You can access it through the menus at Tools ➤ SolidWorks Applications ➤ SolidWorks Explorer. When initially opened, it looks like a search function, but you can expand it into a Windows Explorer–type window with specific SolidWorks functionality such as adding tags to parts, properties, References, Where Used, Configurations, and more. (See Figure 13.8.)

FIGURE 13.8
SolidWorks Explorer helps you manage several aspects of files and assembly references.

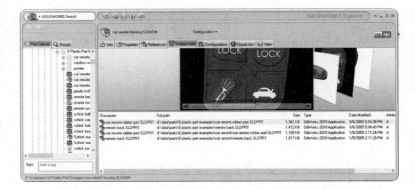

SOLIDWORKS TREEHOUSE

SolidWorks Treehouse enables you to create the framework for a product assembly using empty part, assembly, and drawing files. You can then use SolidWorks to build actual geometry within the files created by Treehouse. A lead engineer or manager would use Treehouse to set up the structure of the assembly—complete with subassemblies, parts, and drawings—and then plan the work to document the complete design. (See Figure 13.9.)

In Treehouse, you can:

- Create and organize assembly structure
- Create files using SolidWorks document templates
- Name files
- Create and edit properties

◆ Create and edit configurations

◆ Include existing documents from Windows Explorer

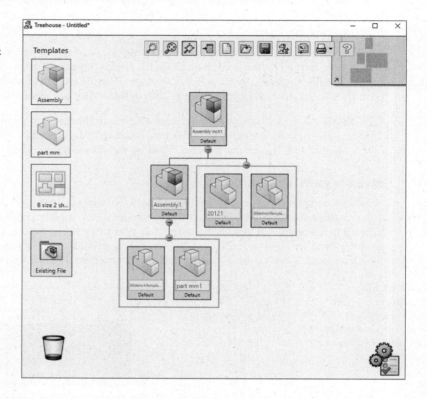

To start working on a new assembly, put your cursor over the Assembly icon, and then drag an assembly template into the work area. To put a part into an assembly, put your cursor over the Part icon, and drag a part template onto the Assembly icon placed earlier.

Using an Assembly Layout Sketch

SolidWorks has an assembly feature called Layout that uses a 3D sketch to lay out the major functions of an assembly and even details of parts. The word *layout* also refers to a long-standing technique using 2D sketches in an assembly to do exactly the same thing. The distinction between the technique and the formal assembly feature is bound to be confusing. The Layout feature is relatively new and works only in assemblies, but layout techniques have been used in parts as well as assemblies for many years. This is simply a case of the unfortunate naming of a specific function with a name already used by a general technique. Let's just acknowledge this is confusing and move on.

When you look at the two functionalities, the feature is definitely intended to be used as an in-context tool, although you can more easily use the technique as a reference for controlling part position (through mating) rather than as a way to directly control the sizes and shapes of the parts. So when you see a reference to a *Layout* (capitalized), this refers to the formal feature. When you see a reference to a *layout* or *layout sketch* (lowercased), this refers to a technique where a sketch is used at the part or assembly level to control geometry or part placement in some way.

The layout sketch is a very useful tool for laying out a mechanism in an assembly or even details on parts within the assembly. Sketches in the assembly have the same characteristics as

FIGURE 13.10
An assembly layout sketch controls the geometry of the frame and the overall bicycle assembly.

they do in the part environment. In Figure 13.10, the assembly layout sketch is indicated with a heavy, dashed line for emphasis.

When combined with in-context techniques, assembly layout sketches can help to determine the shape of parts or the location, size, or shape of features within the parts. You also can use layout sketches to mate assembly components to far more robust and dependable mates, rather than mating part to part. The sketch shown in Figure 13.10 is used for both of these techniques. The shape of the frame and the major pivot points are established in the 2D sketch. The wheels also are mated to the sketch.

When you use an assembly layout sketch for either the in-context part building or simply part positioning, its main advantage is that it gives you a single driving sketch that enables you to change the size, shape, and position of the parts. You can use as many layout sketches as you want, and you can make them on different sketch planes. This enables you to control parts in all directions.

CAUTION When using layout sketches, it is assumed that the relationships are created such that the sketch drives the parts. However, nothing prevents you from using other elements in the assembly to drive the sketch. You should avoid this type of conflict, called a *circular reference*. It can create sketches that change with every rebuild and can seriously impact rebuild times. When using any type of *in-context relations* (relationships between items in an assembly), you need to be careful to establish one or more driving entities, which are not in turn driven by other entities.

To take this a step further, it is best to avoid *daisy chaining*, where A drives B, B drives C, and so on. A better practice is to make A drive both B and C directly. This saves on rebuild times and trouble-shooting and reduces future problems with lost references.

One of the drawbacks of this technique is that you give up dynamic assembly motion. To move the parts, you have to move the sketch and rebuild. The part does not move until the sketch is updated. If you need to combine layout functionality with dynamic assembly motion, refer to the discussion of the Layout feature in Chapter 16, "Working with Assembly Sketches and Layouts."

Working with Virtual Components

Virtual components are parts that are saved so they are internal to the assembly. You can save them out so they are external to the assembly and can be reused in other assemblies. You also can convert external components to virtual components. *Virtual components,* as the name suggests, can be either parts or subassemblies.

You may consider using virtual components for certain types of parts that need to be in the assembly but might not require drawings, such as glue, paint, oil, and so on. You may even use virtual components to model purchased subassemblies that flex; for example, you could create a hinge, and use the hinge assembly as a part in a library. However, if you choose to use virtual components, make sure that they won't cause you any difficulties downstream in file management, data sharing, or other requirements.

Creating Assembly Reference Geometry

Planes and axes are frequently created within assemblies to drive symmetry or placement of parts. You can use assembly layout sketches to create the reference geometry entities. When you create reference geometry within the assembly in this way, be aware that the normal parent/child relationships are still followed. The familiar icons for reference geometry entities are also used in the assembly tree.

Comparing History-Based and Non-History-Based Portions of the Assembly Tree

Because features such as sketches and reference geometry are history-based and found in the assembly tree, at least a portion of the assembly FeatureManager is history-based. However, not all of it is. For example, the list of parts and subassemblies is not history-based—the order does not matter at all to the software.

Sketches and reference geometry may appear before or after the list of parts, subassemblies, and mates. All the remaining entity types that can be found in the assembly FeatureManager are also history-based features, and you can reorder them in the tree. However, several situations can disrupt the process. Under normal circumstances, sketches and reference geometry at the top of the assembly FeatureManager are solved, then the parts are rebuilt if required, and then the mates are rebuilt. This ensures that the sketches and reference geometry are in the correct locations so that if parts are mated to them, all the components end up being the correct size and in the right position.

Assembly-level reference geometry can be created that references component geometry instead of layout sketches. This creates a dependency that changes the usual order. For example, the planes are usually solved before the part locations, but when the plane is *dependent* on the part location, the plane must be solved *after* the part. If a part is then mated to the plane, you will begin to create a dependency loop, such that the plane is solved, followed by the part, then the plane again because the part has moved, and then the mate that goes to the plane must resolve the part.

BEST PRACTICE

If you are a bit confused by all this, don't worry. You can simply follow this rule: Do not mate to anything that comes after the mates in the assembly FeatureManager tree. This includes assembly planes or sketches that are dependent on part geometry, as well as assembly features such as cuts, in-context features, component pattern instances, Hole Series, or Smart Fasteners.

This is probably a lot of information to absorb if you are a new user, but if you remember this rule, you can avoid creating models with circular references, where A is dependent on B, which is dependent on A—a never-ending loop that causes major problems for large assembly rebuild times.

Understanding Parts and Subassemblies

Parts and subassemblies are shown with their familiar icons in the design tree. You can reorder and group them in folders (covered in the next section) and edit the hierarchy of parts and subassemblies within an upper-level assembly.

The primary task of parts and assemblies is to help you organize your data. Information that relates to the geometry of a single manufacturable item is put into a part. Information that relates to the relationships between the parts is put into an assembly.

You may hear some people argue that parts and assemblies don't need to have different file types—that a part file should be able to handle both the geometric data and the relations between items. Organizing the data into different file types is necessary because it helps your computer know when to calculate which data. For example, if your computer had to rebuild all the features in every part as well as all the mates, rebuild times would suffer greatly.

In addition, parts in an assembly are different from bodies within a part. If you have bodies within a part, all your features are in one big list, rather than segmented into individual lists for each part. This is important for three reasons: rebuild times, troubleshooting errors, and reusing data. Part features that are in a big list with other part features cannot be organized or separated easily for other purposes.

Organizing Mates

The Mates area remains a constant, single folder, but you can organize it by reordering the mates and grouping them into folders. Each mate is shown with a symbol corresponding to the type of mate it is, but the Mates folder is shown as a pair of paper clips.

TIP In previous versions, the Mates folder was broken up into various mate groups when the model had a mate that caused a history-imposed rebuild. Therefore, mates in each group were rebuilt as folders. This had the effect of confusing a lot of people, so SolidWorks combined them all into one. Combining all the mates into a single folder allows you to ignore when you make a mistake and mate to a history-based item in the tree, thereby causing another mate group to be created. This is an example of SolidWorks trading ease-of-use for lack of control.

Mates are typically shown at the bottom of the assembly FeatureManager in their own area, but they are also organized in a folder underneath each individual part, so you can see the mates that each part is involved in, as shown in Figure 13.11.

FIGURE 13.11

Mates organized in a folder under parts in an assembly

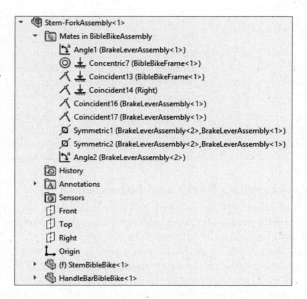

The symbols that look like ground next to the mate symbols help you identify the mates that connect the part to ground, or another fixed part that prevents the mated part from moving.

Another way of organizing mates is to change the way the assembly FeatureManager is displayed. There is a pair of settings that work together. One is the Show Hierarchy/Feature Detail toggle, and the other is the View Features/Mates And Dependencies toggle. If you choose the Hierarchy and the Mates And Dependencies options, you can get a tree where the mates are shown under the part or assembly names, as shown in Figure 13.12.

The Show Hierarchy/Feature Detail toggle is found in the top-level assembly RMB menu. The View Features/Mates And Dependencies toggle is found in the same RMB menu, under Tree Display, which is shown in Figure 13.13.

Applying Assembly Features

In manufacturing, after parts are assembled, secondary machining operations are sometimes applied to them to ensure that holes line up properly, or for other purposes. For example, assembly features can be cut extrudes, cut revolves, or hole features. These features appear only in the parts at the assembly level, not in the features of the individual parts.

You should not confuse assembly features with in-context features. *In-context features* are created when you are editing a part in the assembly with a reference between parts, but the sketch and feature definition are in the actual part.

Assembly features still cause additional assembly complexity, and if you mate to an assembly feature, you cause another hitch in the assembly rebuild cycle (and formerly would have created another mate group). If you need this kind of feature, that's fine; make it, but be extra careful not to mate to it or create in-context references to it.

If functionality in SolidWorks seems powerful, it probably is. But there is always a price to be paid for power, and the cost is usually in rebuild speed or more complex troubleshooting if you have problems.

FIGURE 13.12
Showing Hierarchy and
Mates And
Dependencies

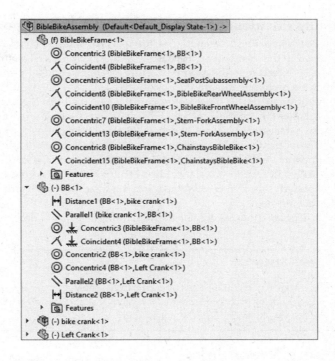

FIGURE 13.13
Settings for organizing
the display of mates

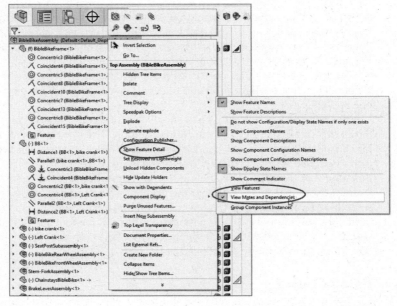

Using Component Patterns and Mirror Components

Component patterns can pattern either parts or subassemblies by creating either a pattern defined in the assembly or a pattern that follows a pattern feature created in a part. The pattern is listed as a feature in the assembly FeatureManager, and all the instance parts appear indented from the pattern feature in the design tree. You can hide or suppress each instance, change its configuration, and in most ways control it as if it were a regular part in the design tree.

Because the options for locally defined patterns are comparatively limited, users generally like to use part feature patterns to drive the component patterns when possible.

Component patterns are listed at the bottom of the assembly FeatureManager with a set of components under a LocalPattern icon. The component instances under the LocalPattern can be controlled in several ways, including through assigned configurations, colors, and display states. The pattern can even be dissolved, leaving the components but removing the intelligent pattern that places them.

Mirror components are listed under a special MirrorComponent icon after the mates.

> **PERFORMANCE**
>
> To improve performance, you should pattern subassemblies if possible. If it's not possible, patterning a group of parts is the next best option. Making multiple patterns, one for each part, is an inefficient way to accomplish the same thing.

Using SpeedPaks

A SpeedPak is a derived configuration of an assembly that keeps only selected solid bodies and faces but can represent the rest of the assembly with nonselectable display data. You can use a SpeedPak to represent an entire subassembly within an upper-level assembly. SpeedPaks are intended to increase performance with very large assemblies and drawings.

Figure 13.14 shows the SpeedPak PropertyManager on the left, which you access by right-clicking an active configuration and selecting Add SpeedPak. Each configuration can have only one SpeedPak.

The center image in Figure 13.14 shows the configuration list with the SpeedPak indented under the Default config, and the entire assembly. The right image shows the SpeedPak inserted into an assembly document, consisting of a single face and two solid bodies. Notice the special icon associated with SpeedPaks. You can change a part in an assembly from or to a SpeedPak in the same way that you would change a configuration using Component Properties.

Remember that this is a tool for increasing assembly speed, and you must always give up something to increase speed. A SpeedPak is similar to Lightweight assemblies and components in that it's display-only data. If your expectations of the tool match its actual functionality, you will be very satisfied with what the SpeedPak offers. For this reason, it's important to understand the abilities and limitations of SpeedPaks.

Using Ghosts

You can use any faces or bodies that you select in the Include lists either manually or through the Quick Include sliders (which automatically select bodies and faces based on size) in assemblies to mate to or in drawings to dimension to. Any geometry that isn't selected is included as a ghost: It displays, but you cannot select it. When you move the cursor near ghost geometry, the ghost fades away, revealing only selectable geometry. Notice at the bottom of the SpeedPak

PropertyManager that you can also choose to remove the ghost data and further increase the memory savings.

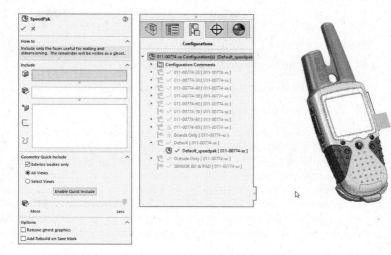

Sharing Self-Contained Data

The SpeedPak is self-contained. All the selected face and body geometry is saved inside the assembly. If you want to send someone a visual representation of an assembly, you can make a SpeedPak configuration and send only the assembly file; no parts are required. This is the equivalent of being able to put an eDrawing file into an assembly.

Using SpeedPaks with Drawings

You can even use SpeedPaks with drawings. Just remember that only edges created by the faces or bodies in the Include lists can be dimensioned to. Some functionality exists for the ghost data, such as BOM inclusion and numbered balloons. Ghost data displays as gray on the drawing, while geometry in the Include list is black.

Using Subassemblies

The primary tool for organizing assemblies is the subassembly. A *subassembly* is just a regular assembly that is used as a component in another assembly.

BEST PRACTICE

You are not limited to a specific number of levels of subassemblies, although for different sizes and types of assemblies, you should establish a best practice for your company. For example, you might establish a guideline that suggests that assemblies of 100 parts or fewer go no deeper than three levels.

You can use several criteria to determine how subassemblies are assigned:

◆ Performance

◆ BOM

◆ Relative motion

◆ Prefabricated, off-the-shelf considerations

◆ According to assembly steps for a process drawing

◆ To simplify patterning

The underlying question here is based on the multiple functions of your SolidWorks assembly model. Is the assembly intended primarily for design? For visualization? For documentation? For process documentation? When used primarily for design, the assembly is used to determine fits, tolerances, mechanisms, and many other things. As a visualization tool, it simply has to look good and possibly move properly if that's part of the design. As a documentation tool, how the model relates to the BOM is important, and so is the order in which subassemblies are added. When you are using a subassembly as a process tool, you need to be able to show the assembly in various intermediate states of being assembled, likely with configurations.

Creating Subassemblies from Existing Parts

You can create subassemblies from parts that already exist in an assembly. To do this, select the parts you want to add to the subassembly by pressing and holding the Shift or Ctrl key, or using box selection techniques, and then selecting Form New Subassembly Here from the right mouse button (RMB) menu. You will prompted to assign a name or possibly select a template for the new subassembly.

CAUTION   When you're creating a new subassembly from existing parts or moving parts into or out of a subassembly from the upper-level assembly, some things may be lost. For example, mates are moved from the upper level to the subassembly. If you have in-context relationships, they may be removed. You cannot easily undo operations that create subassemblies.

After you have created the subassembly, you can add or remove components using the drag-and-drop method. For example, Figure 13.15 shows two different actions with two different cursors. On the left is the cursor that indicates that the part named BB is being moved into the subassembly named bike crank. On the right is the cursor that indicates BB is being reordered after the bike crank. To move a part out of a subassembly, you can simply drag the part into the upper-level assembly.

FIGURE 13.15
Moving parts into a
subassembly

NOTE   When you are dragging a part out of an assembly and into another one, you may again see the cursor symbol that appears in Figure 13.10. If you do not want this to happen, press and hold the Alt key while dragging. The cursor symbol will change to the Reorder cursor (a reversed, L-shaped arrow), and the part will be placed after the subassembly rather than within it.

Inserting a New Subassembly

Along with the RMB menu option Form New Subassembly Here, which takes existing parts and puts them into a newly created subassembly, you can use another option called Insert New Subassembly. The names of these functions don't adequately describe their different functions. Insert New Subassembly inserts a blank subassembly at the point in the design tree that you indicate by right-clicking it. You can place components into the subassembly by dragging and dropping them from the main assembly, or you can open the assembly in its own window and insert parts by using the usual methods, such as drag-and-drop, or the Insert ➤ Component tool.

Dissolving Subassemblies

If you want to get rid of a subassembly but want to keep its parts, you can use the Dissolve Subassembly option through the RMB menu. This option has some of the same consequences of the Form New Subassembly Here option in that mates are moved from the subassembly to the upper-level assembly, and you may lose in-context relations and assembly features.

Organizing for Performance

In SolidWorks, performance refers to speed. Subassemblies can contribute to speed-saving modeling techniques by segmenting the work that the software needs to do at any one time.

Solving Mates

The mates that contribute to putting the pieces of an assembly together are solved at the top assembly level. Under normal circumstances, subassemblies are treated as static selections of parts that are welded together, and their mates are not solved at the same time the top-level assemblies' mates are solved. This segmenting of the mates leads to improved performance by solving only one set of mates at a time.

Mates are usually solved as a single group unless there is a special situation, such as mates to in-context features, component pattern instances, or an assembly feature, all of which have already been described in this chapter. When one of these situations occurs, the mates must be divided into separate groups or solved multiple times. This is done behind the scenes so the user doesn't have to worry about it. Multiple rebuilds affect the user only in terms of rebuild times.

Using Flexible Subassemblies

When you put a subassembly into an upper-level assembly, the mates for the parts of the subassembly are not solved in the upper-level assembly. This means that if a subassembly is a mechanism, the mechanism does not allow dynamic assembly motion in the upper-level assembly, and it is considered rigid. For example, in Figure 13.16, the front fork is a linkage mechanism, but it's also a subassembly. Without reassembling the parts of the fork in the upper-level assembly, you can allow the mates from the fork subassembly to be solved in the upper-level assembly by using the Solve As option in the Component Properties dialog box, shown in Figure 13.16. When you select the Flexible option, you enable the mates of this subassembly to be solved in the upper-level assembly, which allows the parts of the subassembly to move in the upper-level assembly. To access the Component Properties dialog box, right-click the subassembly and select Component Properties from the menu.

FIGURE 13.16
Creating a flexible subassembly

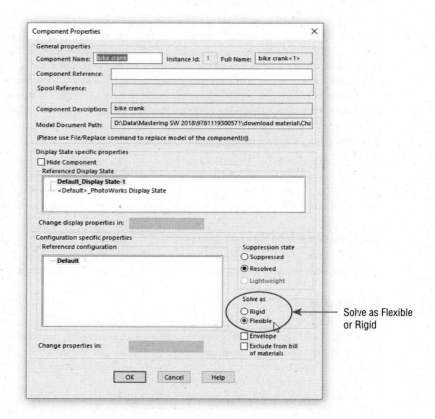

Flexible subassemblies have become more reliable and easier to use. You should work with them or do some experimentation to see if they assist your modeling process. If you find they cause trouble in some situations, they are easy enough to deactivate.

Organizing for the Bill of Materials

The Bill of Materials (BOM) is a table that is placed either into a drawing of an assembly or in an actual assembly. This table shows the parts used in the assembly and includes other information, such as part numbers, quantities, descriptions, and custom property data.

Businesses often represent assemblies and subassemblies in various ways by using Manufacturing Resource Planning (MRP) or Enterprise Resource Planning (ERP) software. The methods that accountants and manufacturers use to organize assemblies are not always the same as those that engineers or designers might choose, but some companies require the BOM on the drawing to match the MRP or ERP Bill of Materials.

BEST PRACTICE

When you are forced to model something in an unnatural way to satisfy an outside demand such as special BOM requirements, it might be best to detach the unnatural part and model normally. In the situation mentioned here—where MRP is forcing how the assembly is put together by requiring the BOM to match MRP—you should separate the BOM from the assembly structure rather than build an assembly that makes other SolidWorks functions difficult. This ensures that the BOM becomes a manually maintained document. Alternatives to this approach would be to make configurations or entirely new assembly documents to drive the BOM.

Grouping Subassemblies by Relative Motion

A more natural way to group subassemblies is by considering relative motion. In the bicycle example, each wheel is a separate subassembly because it moves as a unit relative to the rest of the assembly.

Grouping subassemblies by relative motion is great for assembly modeling, but it doesn't usually reflect product reality very well. Using this method, you often end up with parts in the subassembly that must be disassembled in order to actually put the physical parts together. However, if your only consideration is ease of modeling, then you should probably use this method.

Organizing Groups of Purchased Components

If you are modeling a product that is created from a shopping list of purchased components, then it may make the most sense to organize your subassemblies into groups of parts that are purchased together. In fact, purchased subassemblies are often modeled as single parts, except when relative motion is required in the purchased assembly.

For example, in the bicycle assembly, the sprockets on the rear wheel are purchased as a separate unit, but the part that mounts onto the wheel moves relative to the sprockets that are driven by the chain. This is an example of a purchased part that would be modeled as a subassembly to show relative motion. The bicycle chain, another purchased subassembly, has not yet been added to this assembly and is a more complex model. The desire to show all the individual links moving through the path may override both the complexity of assembling it and the performance considerations of exercising all the mates.

Although the BOM method of organizing assemblies sometimes leads to unnatural solutions, you should not discard it altogether. If you can devise concessions in order to make the BOM work automatically, then you should do this.

Depicting an Assembly Process

Manufacturing and assembly processes need to be documented as well as individual part design. You often need to create exploded-view assembly instructions for manufacturing or service documentation at each step of a multistep assembly process. Figure 13.17 shows an example of this type of process documentation.

FIGURE 13.17
Assembly process
documentation

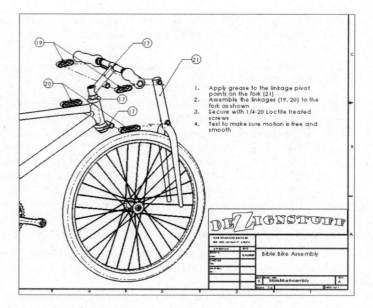

This task is certainly different from the initial design or modeling of the assembly, and it may require an entirely separate assembly model. Generally, you can perform the different steps by using a separate configuration for each process step, with exploded views for each configuration.

INFLUENCING ITEM NUMBERING

Balloons number the parts according to the item number used in the BOM, but of course, you don't know the item numbers until the BOM is created. You can influence the item numbers by reordering the parts in the assembly (which is discussed later in this chapter), by manually editing item numbers, or by manually numbering the balloons.

SEPARATING STEPS

Each step corresponds to an assembly configuration (discussed in Chapter 19, "Controlling Assembly Configurations and Display States"), and you can place them on a separate sheet of the drawing (discussed in Chapter 30, "Creating Assembly Drawings"). Each configuration can have multiple exploded views, if necessary, to show all the steps.

Patterning Considerations

The most efficient way to pattern large numbers of components in an assembly is to pattern a single subassembly with all the components to be patterned in it. Although this may not be easily combined with some of the other considerations mentioned previously, it's another option that you can use to organize assemblies.

Using Folders

Folders are primarily used in the assembly FeatureManager for grouping parts and mates into special classifications for easy browsing, or groups that you can easily hide and show, or suppress and unsuppress, as appropriate. Figure 13.18 shows some examples of these folders.

FIGURE 13.18

Folders that are used to organize components and mates

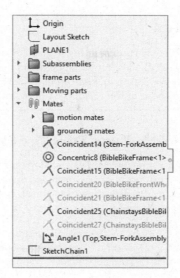

Creating Folders in the FeatureManager

You can add folders to the assembly FeatureManager in two ways:

- By adding existing components to a new folder
- By creating an empty new folder

USING ADD TO NEW FOLDER

To use the Add To New Folder tool, right-click a component or mate (or selection of components or mates) and select Add To New Folder from the menu. This moves the component or mate into the folder. Folders don't affect the assembly in any functional way; they are simply for organization, to speed browsing and selection.

USING CREATE NEW FOLDER

To simply create a new folder without putting anything into it right away, right-click either the Mates area or the Components list and select Create New Folder from the menu.

Reordering Items in the Tree

Sometimes, you may want to reorder items in the assembly tree. For example, you may want to place items close to one another in the tree, or you may be preparing to put items that are next to one another into a single folder. You also may want to reorganize components for the BOM display.

You can reorder mates simply by dragging them. Mates display in the order in which they are created, but the order is not significant. You can reorder them however you like.

Components also display in the order in which they are added to the assembly, and you can reorder them in any way you like.

BEST PRACTICE

It is often useful to have an ordering strategy that helps you work with the model. For example, you should try to keep the biggest parts, the parts that everything else is mated to, or the part that is treated as "ground" as the first part(s) in the assembly. Then put the fasteners and other cosmetic or BOM-driving parts at the end of the tree, usually in a descriptively named folder.

Working with Tree Display Options

Display options for items in the FeatureManager are often overlooked but can be useful for displaying data about parts, subassemblies, mates, and features. Figure 13.13 shows the RMB options. You must right-click the top-level assembly name in the FeatureManager, and click Tree Display to access this menu.

NOTE   All these options are available for parts and drawings as well, except for the View Features option and the View Mates And Dependencies option, which are related to assemblies.

Showing Feature Names and Descriptions

If you are so thorough that you have added descriptions to your features, then you are doing well. Figure 13.13 shows the options for displaying feature names and descriptions in the FeatureManager. Generally feature names are sufficient, but descriptions can add to search and filtering options in long feature trees.

Showing Component and Config Names and Descriptions

By default, SolidWorks uses the filename of a part or assembly as the component name. If you want to use some other name in the assembly FeatureManager, you must change a couple of settings.

First, go to Tools ➤ Options ➤ External References, and turn off Update Component Names When Documents Are Replaced. This enables you to keep the same component name even if you replace that component (you have to use the Replace Component functionality—as opposed to simply deleting and reinserting—in order for this to work).

Second, right-click on the component with the name you want to change and go to Component Properties, shown in Figure 13.19. Now you can change the Component Name (if you didn't do the first step, you will get a lengthy warning message). Notice the difference between the Component Name, which I changed manually, and the Model Document Path, which is filled in automatically. This dialog even has a handy hint on how to replace the component if you want to, with File ➤ Replace.

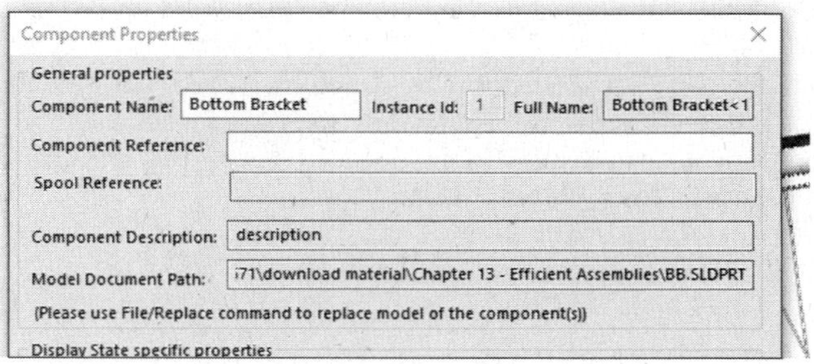

FIGURE 13.19
Changing a component name in Component Properties

Component Properties				
General properties				
Component Name:	Bottom Bracket	Instance Id: 1	Full Name:	Bottom Bracket<1
Component Reference:				
Spool Reference:				
Component Description:	description			
Model Document Path:	i71\download material\Chapter 13 - Efficient Assemblies\BB.SLDPRT			
(Please use File/Replace command to replace model of the component(s))				
Display State specific properties				

Don't stop reading now; this gets slightly more complex. If you want to rename the component in the assembly FeatureManager without the Component Properties dialog, you would probably try the slow double-click or F2 Windows methods. But that wouldn't work unless you have selected. Go to Tools ➤ Options ➤ FeatureManager and turn on the setting "Allow component files to be renamed from FeatureManager tree." Then when you try to rename it from the FeatureManager, you get another SolidWorks warning as shown in Figure 13.20. At least here you can choose the Don't Show Again option.

FIGURE 13.20
Renaming from the
FeatureManager

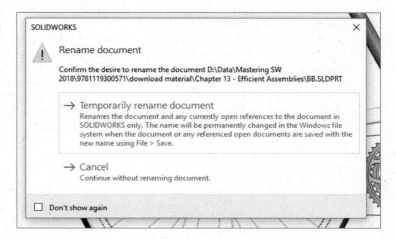

Using Component Reference per Instance

In the Component Properties dialog box (refer to Figure 13.19), enables you to enter Component Reference information. This capability is typically used in electrical diagrams for similar components with different values, such as power ratings, capacitance, or resistance. Instances of the same component in a SolidWorks assembly that have the same Component Reference can be listed together on a BOM. Instances with different Component References are listed separately on the BOM. Figure 13.21 shows parts listed in a pattern with Component References listed for each instance.

FIGURE 13.21
Listing parts in an
assembly containing
Component Reference
information

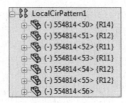

In order for Component References to be used in balloons on an assembly drawing, the drawing must have a BOM with a Component Reference column. BOMs are handled in detail in Chapter 31, "Modeling Multibodies," where the topic of Component References will be revisited.

Viewing Features, Mates, and Dependencies

The set of options shown in Figure 13.13 determines whether you see the part features or the assembly mates after the name of each component in the assembly tree. The default setting is for the part's features or the subassembly's components to display, just as if the part or subassembly were open in its own window.

The View Mates And Dependencies option can also show the features, but they are placed into a separate folder. This option makes it very easy to see the mates that are assigned to an individual component. For example, in Figure 13.22, the image to the right shows the mates directly under the BibleBikeFrame part. This often makes troubleshooting much easier because it isolates the mates for a single part. Notice also that the first folder under the part name in the image to the left in Figure 13.22 is the Mates folder. This indicates that, regardless of whether you choose to display mates or features, you always have easy access to the other type.

FIGURE 13.22

You can view features, as well as mates and dependencies.

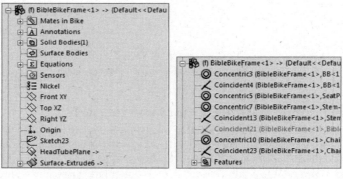

View Features   View Mates

The View Mates tool is extremely valuable for looking at how an assembly is held together with mates. When you right-click a component in the assembly and choose View Mates from the RMB menu, SolidWorks highlights the component you clicked and makes all parts that mate to that component transparent. Any parts that are not related are hidden. SolidWorks also displays a small dialog box with the list of mates touching the component you clicked.

Figure 13.23 shows this arrangement using the Bible Bike assembly. This is a big help in mate visualization.

If you Ctrl+select multiple components before starting the View Mates tool, SolidWorks no longer displays the common mates in bold format; it just lists them at the top of the dialog box.

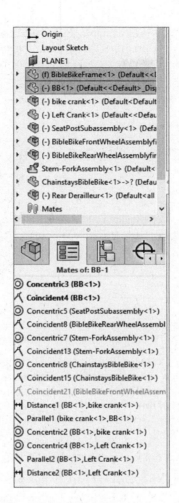

FIGURE 13.23
Showing mates in the
PropertyManager pane

Tutorial: Arranging Assemblies

In this tutorial, you will take an assembly that is already put together, group its components into subassemblies, and then convert one subassembly into a flexible subassembly. Note that some of the commands and RMB options you are asked to select may not be shown on the truncated RMB menus. To remedy this, click the double-arrow at the bottom of the RMB menu or choose Tools ➤ Customize ➤ Options from the menu, and click the Show All button for both shortcuts and menu customization.

Follow these steps to learn how to effectively arrange items in an assembly:

1. Start by opening the Robot Assembly .sldasm file from the download material for this chapter.

   Notice that the filenames are long and somewhat difficult to read. This would also apply for files that use sequential numbers for the filename instead of a descriptive name.

2. To display a more readable name, right-click the name of the assembly at the top of the FeatureManager, select Tree Display from the menu, and then turn on Show Component Descriptions. Repeat these steps, and this time turn off Show Component Names.

Figure 13.24 shows the display of the FeatureManager after the change. Even the top-level assembly uses its description rather than its filename.

FIGURE 13.24
Simplifying the
FeatureManager display
to include descriptions

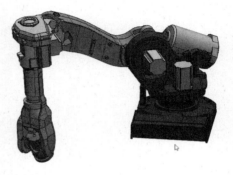

Notice that two components still use their clumsy filenames rather than easy-to-read descriptions. This is because descriptions were never entered for those two components.

3. Open the Large Cylinder Piston part by clicking the part in the FeatureManager and then clicking the Open icon. Choose File ➤ Properties from the menu, and make sure the Custom tab is active. Create a new property called **description**, assign a type of text, and then enter **large cylinder piston** for the value. Save the part (Ctrl+S is a fast way to do that), and then flip back to the assembly (the fastest way to do that is to press and hold Ctrl and press Tab).

If the display has not yet updated, press Ctrl+Q to force the tree to rebuild.

4. Open the Large Cylinder Body part. In this part, choose File ➤ Save As from the menu, and select Save As when prompted. Leave the name as is, but where it says Description, enter **large cylinder body**, as shown in Figure 13.25. Click Yes when asked if you want to replace the document of the same name. Flip back to the assembly when you are finished. You may have to rebuild to see the change update.

5. Press and hold Ctrl, and select the large cylinder piston and the large cylinder body parts from the FeatureManager. Then right-click and select Form New Assembly from the menu. If your assembly template has a description, it will appear in the FeatureManager. If not, the filename will appear.

You have just created an assembly as a virtual component while the parts are external documents. There is no actual file corresponding to this entry in the assembly FeatureManager. If you switch the Tree Display to show filenames, you will see what is shown in Figure 13.26; the name of the assembly is Assem1^Robot Assembly. So the virtual component gets a default name (Assem1) followed by the name of the parent assembly (Robot Assembly) to ensure that it has a unique name, if there are other virtual components in other assemblies.

FIGURE 13.25
Adding a description in
the Save As dialog box

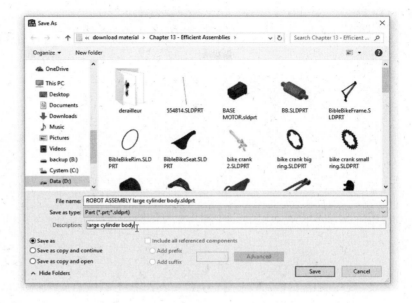

FIGURE 13.26
The newly created virtual
component subassem-
bly and its
external parts

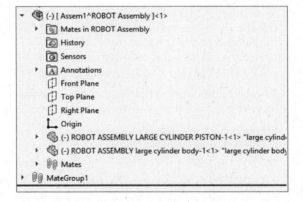

6. Press and hold Ctrl; select the Base Motor, the Main Arm Motor, and the Cradle; and make
another new subassembly. After you create this subassembly, right-click it and select Save
Assembly (In External File) from the menu (and select "Save only the subassembly to an
external file"). Change the name of the assembly from Assem2 to **Cradle**. Save it in the
same path as the rest of the parts.

After a virtual component is saved externally, you cannot use the Undo command to
reverse it, but you can right-click the external file in the FeatureManager and select Make
Virtual from the menu.

In Figure 13.27, notice that several of the mates came along into the new subassembly.
These are the mates between the motors and the cradle. The mates that locate the cradle to
the other parts in the assembly have remained in the upper-level assembly.

FIGURE 13.27
The cradle assembly
brings along
internal mates.

FIGURE 13.27
The cradle assembly
brings along
internal mates.

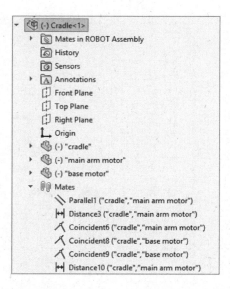

Note that you cannot undo the subassembly operations. If you need to remove the assembly but keep the parts, right-click the assembly and select Dissolve Subassembly from the menu.

If you try to move the parts in the assembly, you should notice that all parts work as they should, except that the Main Arm does not move up and down. This is because you turned the cylinder and piston into a subassembly, and the subassembly mates are not solved in the top level, which means the subassembly cannot move within itself.

To get around this, you need to make the subassembly into a flexible subassembly, which solves the subassembly's mates in the top-level assembly.

7. Right-click the cylinder subassembly in the FeatureManager, and select Component Properties from the menu. In the lower-right corner of the dialog box, there is the option to Solve As Rigid or Flexible. Change this setting to Flexible.

After you click OK and return to the assembly, the main arm will move as it did originally, and the piston will move in and out of the cylinder. Notice that the symbol for the assembly changes when it is changed to a flexible subassembly.

Tutorial: Managing the FeatureManager

This tutorial uses the `BibleBikeAssembly.sldasm` file located in the Chapter 13 folder in the download material from the Wiley website. Open the file and follow these steps to learn about managing the FeatureManager:

1. Create a new subassembly within the existing assembly using the parts BibleBikeFrame and ChainstayBibleBike. Name this new assembly **FrameAssembly.SLDASM**.

2. Reorder the new FrameAssembly to the top of the design tree.

3. Reorder the other parts and assemblies so the bigger assemblies appear higher on the list and the parts appear at the bottom. (Remember that Alt+dragging a component prevents it from being placed into a subassembly.)

4. Drag the part called BB (for Bottom Bracket) into the Frame Assembly (drag without using the Alt key). The assembly FeatureManager at this point is shown in Figure 13.28.

FIGURE 13.28
The starting state and the state as of step 4

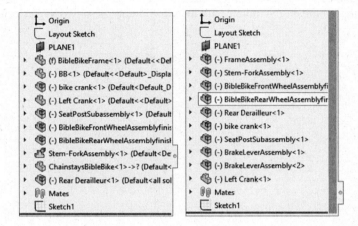

5. Select both wheels, and then select Add To New Folder from the RMB menu. Name the new folder **Wheels**, and move it to the bottom of the tree.

6. Expand the Mates folder, select the first four mates, and put them in a new folder (select Add To New Folder from the RMB menu). Name the new folder **Centering Mates**.

Remember that if you make a mistake, you can go to File ➤ Reload to reload the assembly and parts in the last saved state.

The Bottom Line

Assemblies are more than simply parts and subassemblies put together with mate relationships; several other types of features and placeholders can also exist in the assembly FeatureManager. Organizing assembly components is fairly straightforward and can offer benefits for finding parts as well as controlling suppression and display states globally.

The assembly FeatureManager contains several options for the data to display for subassemblies, parts, configurations, metadata, and features within. Remember that all the data that you include in your SolidWorks documents can be accessed and reused later, so it's worth the effort to name it properly. Descriptions can be very important, both at the part level and also for features and configs.

Master It   Use SolidWorks Treehouse to establish the framework for a simple product with two layers of subassemblies. Add some custom properties to the documents that you might want to use to fill in a BOM. Use appropriate templates and save the documents to a special folder.

Master It   Speed is a huge part of building an efficient assembly. You measure speed with the Tools ➤ Evaluate ➤ Performance Evaluation tool. Open the Performance Evaluation tool while looking at an assembly (for example, the Bike Finished.sldasm) and learn what you can about what types of features and techniques cost you the most rebuild or display regeneration time.

Master It   Use the Assembly Visualization tool to sort the parts according to various criteria, and become more familiar with the information presented by Performance Evaluation.

Chapter 14

Getting More from Mates

Mates provide the glue that holds SolidWorks assemblies together. When properly handled, mates enable your assembly to react predictably to changes in parts in exactly the same way that sketch relations drive changes in part features. As a result, mates and sketch relations often have the same function and even the same weaknesses.

This chapter goes one step further with mates, by not simply putting parts together with Coincident and Concentric mates, but also mating parts when real-life situations such as tolerances, gaps, and symmetry become issues. You will also learn about the more advanced mate types that may be useful for special situations.

One of the assumptions made in this chapter is that assembly mates are not just used for positioning parts, but also for motion. Making motion work takes a little more than just establishing the right spatial relationship between parts; it usually also involves analyzing the open degrees of freedom.

IN THIS CHAPTER, YOU WILL LEARN HOW TO:

◆ Implement efficient mating strategies

◆ Perform degrees-of-freedom analysis

◆ Use Advanced and Mechanical mate types

◆ Edit and troubleshoot assembly mates

◆ Choose mate options

◆ Examine mate best practices

Applying Mates

An average assembly of 100 parts is likely to have almost 300 individual mates. If you created these parts one at a time, taking perhaps 30 seconds for each mate, you would spend two and a half hours just applying mates. In this section, you will learn efficient mating strategies, as well as speedy techniques.

As you apply mates to parts in your assembly, keep in mind that SolidWorks has high-risk and low-risk mating schemes. High-risk schemes generally involve mate techniques that are easier but more likely to have problems later in the evolution of your model, such as lost references or conflicts with other mates. More stable mating schemes favor reference geometry (such as planes and axes, and possibly sketches) over model faces and edges.

Mating Through the Mate PropertyManager

The Mate PropertyManager is the default method for applying mates, and you used it briefly in Chapter 4, "Creating Simple Parts and Drawings," while creating the simple assembly. The Mate PropertyManager interface is shown in Figure 14.1. You can create mates by preselecting entities before applying the Mate command or by selecting them after you open the Mate PropertyManager. The three types of mates are Standard, Advanced, and Mechanical.

FIGURE 14.1
The Mate PropertyManager interface

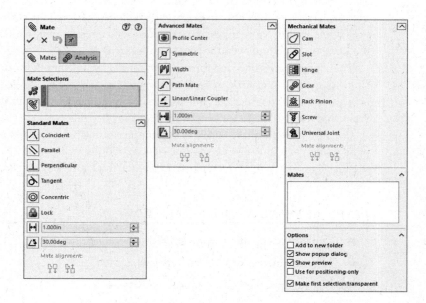

UNDERSTANDING THE MATE WORKFLOW

There are several different ways of making mates, and I'll get around to showing them all at one time or another in the course of this book. If you make lots of mates, you must have an efficient rhythm when working with the interface. Assuming you have the Mate PropertyManager already active, the most efficient way to use the Mate interface is as follows:

1. Click the first geometric entity.

2. Click the second geometric entity.

3. Click OK on the right mouse button (RMB) cursor icon to accept the default mate selection or select another from the pop-up list that appears.

    Alternatively, if the automatic default mate type is not the mate you want to apply, select the mate you want from the pop-up list, shown in Figure 14.2, and use the Mate PropertyManager to set additional options.

FIGURE 14.2
The Mate Selection
context bar

4. Click the green checkmark icon on the pop-up list.

5. Repeat steps 1 to 4.

6. After the last mate, press Esc, the green checkmark icon, or the red X icon in either the PropertyManager or the confirmation corner (located in the upper-right corner of the graphics area).

CHANGING THE VIEW AND MODEL POSITION

Sometimes, you will have to rotate the model to achieve the correct view in order to select faces or edges. Other times, you will want to *pre-position* parts so the model snaps into the correct position automatically. You can rotate individual parts in an assembly by clicking and dragging with the RMB. (Dragging the RMB over a part rotates that part.) You rotate the view by dragging with the middle mouse button (MMB). You can move parts by dragging them with the left mouse button (LMB). You can pan the view by pressing Ctrl and dragging with the MMB. When you drag a part with the LMB while the Mate PropertyManager is active, SolidWorks does not add the selected entity to the Mate Selections list. 3D spaceballs can both manipulate the view and rotate and/or translate parts within an assembly.

To summarize these actions:

- To rotate an individual component in an assembly, click and drag with the RMB.

- To move an individual component in an assembly, drag with the LMB.

- To rotate an assembly view, drag with the MMB.

- To pan an assembly view, Ctrl+drag with the MMB.

Also, be aware of the view manipulation tools, available by clicking the Triad in the lower-left corner:

- To rotate normal to an axis, click the Triad axis in that direction.

- To rotate by 15 degrees about an axis (you can specify the angle at Tools ➤ Options ➤ View), Alt+click the Triad axis in that direction.

- To rotate by 90 degrees about an axis, Shift+click the Triad axis in that direction.

- To activate the mouse gesture wheel, drag the RMB in blank space (dragging the RMB over a part rotates the part).

- To zoom to fit, double-click the MMB in the graphics window (same as using the F hotkey).

TIP   If you have a spaceball or other 3D motion controller, you can perform all these actions easily and simultaneously using one hand for view rotations and the other hand for selections. You can also use a spaceball to move parts.

APPLYING THE SELECT OTHER COMMAND

The Select Other command enables you to select items that are hidden by other items. It is often used to select faces that are hidden behind other faces without rotating the part. You can apply the Select Other command through the RMB menu. Right-click where the face would be if you could see it. A list of entities displays. You can select the entity you want from this list or from the graphics window.

Moving your mouse over an entity in the list highlights the entity in the graphics window. Pressing Tab or scrolling the mouse wheel cycles through the entities one by one. Clicking faces with the RMB hides them, which enables you to see farther down into the part or assembly. Clicking with the LMB in either the graphics window or the selection list box selects the item. Figure 14.3 shows the Select Other cursor and dialog box.

FIGURE 14.3
The Select Other cursor and dialog box

Another aid in the selection of mate entities in the assembly is an option shown in Figure 14.1, in the box on the right. At the very bottom of the PropertyManager is the option Make First Selection Transparent. Not only does this make the first part you select in the process of mating temporarily transparent visually, but it is also transparent to the cursor, so you can pick items behind the transparency.

HIDING FACES DURING MATE SELECTION

Sometimes it is useful to select through faces without using the Select Other tools. The Alt key will temporarily hide the top face when you are making mate selections. This works when you are using Insert Mates, Edit Mates, Copy With Mates, or when viewing Mated Entities.

This technique is particularly useful any time you find yourself tempted to rotate the assembly so you can see the bottom of something to mate—for example, when you mate the underside of a bolt head to a plate, you might rotate the assembly to see the underside of the bolt head. Instead of doing that, just hold the cursor over the face you can't see but want to select, and press Alt. The face obscuring the one you want to select will be hidden, allowing you to select the one behind it. Again, this is like Select Other, but somewhat less cumbersome. You can hide multiple faces, which will be shown again after you make a second mate selection, press Shift+Alt over a single face, or select Ctrl+Shift+Alt to show all hidden faces.

For this functionality to work, the parts must be displayed in a Shaded mode. The hidden face becomes visible again after the selection. This function is shown in action in Figure 14.4.

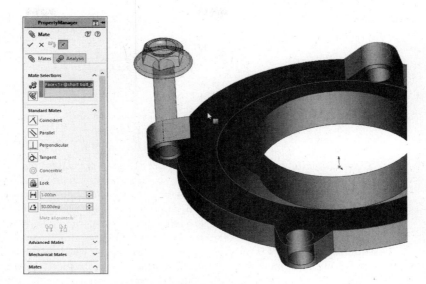

FIGURE 14.4
Using the Alt key to hide
faces during
mate selection

TEMPORARILY HIDING FACES WHEN SELECTING MATES

Use the Alt key to temporarily hide a face when you need to select an obscured face for mates. Be aware, however, that this keyboard shortcut works only with the following Mate commands:

◆ Insert Mates

◆ Edit Mates

◆ Copy With Mates

◆ Mated Entities

The components must be displayed in Shaded or Shaded With Edges modes.
After you select a mate, the hidden faces become visible.
To temporarily hide a face:

1. Click Mate (Assembly toolbar) or select Insert ➢ Mate.

2. With focus in the graphics area, hover over a face and press Alt. The face will be temporarily hidden.

3. To show the temporarily hidden face, press Shift+Alt.

4. To show all temporarily hidden faces in a semitransparent state, press Ctrl+Shift+Alt.

USING MULTIPLE MATE MODE

Multiple Mate mode enables you to select one face in order to mate multiple parts to it.
Figure 14.5 shows the interface for this mode, which you can toggle to from the Mate PropertyManager interface. The Multiple Mate mode icon looks like a paper clip with a lightning bolt running through it. This function works only with the Standard Mate types, not with any of the Advanced mates, which are discussed later in this chapter.

FIGURE 14.5
The Multiple Mate
mode interface

You can tell the software to automatically create a special folder for all the multiple mates by selecting the Create Multi-Mate Folder check box in the Mate Selections PropertyManager. You can also automatically link the values for distance and angle mates with link values by selecting the Link Dimensions check box. When you use the Link Dimensions check box, distance or angle values for mates made in Multiple Mate mode will be set equal with link values.

If you're a fan of preselection for mates (a technique sometimes used with mate macros), Multiple Mate mode is induced by preselecting three cylindrical faces or five planar faces. When you select three planar faces, Symetrical Mate mode is induced. With four planar faces or a cylindrical or conical face selected along with two planar faces, Width Mate mode is activated.

Taking Advantage of SmartMates

SmartMates are mates that you can create automatically by dragging one part onto another without invoking the Mate command. There are three different methods that you can use to apply SmartMates:

◆ Alt+dragging the part

◆ Dragging the part from one window to another

◆ Using Mate references

ALT+DRAGGING A SMARTMATE

Probably the easiest way to create a SmartMate quickly is by Alt+dragging. One, two, or even three mates can be applied at once by holding down the Alt key while dragging a face or edge from one part onto a face or edge on another part.

When you are dragging a part while pressing the Alt key, the part is made transparent to enable you to see other part faces to which you may want to mate it. A special cursor appears when a SmartMate is about to be applied. Figure 14.6 shows the cursors that appear for adding Concentric and Coincident mates.

When you drop the face or edge onto the mating face or edge to complete the mate, you must use the pop-up Mate toolbar to accept or alter the mate. In the examples in Figure 14.6, a face is being dragged onto another face. However, you can also drag edges and vertices. Mates are limited to being either Coincident or Concentric.

FIGURE 14.6
Applying a SmartMate

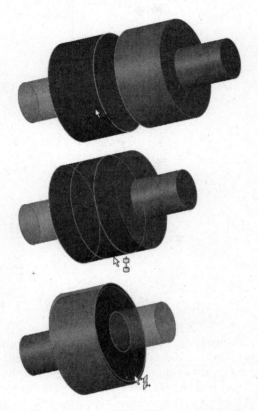

The *Peg-in-Hole* mate is the combination of a Concentric mate and a Coincident mate. This is the type of mate that is created between a screw and a hole, and it's the result of Alt+dragging a circular edge onto a circular edge. When the circular edges are created by the intersection of a cylindrical face and a flat face, the Concentric mate goes between the two cylindrical faces, and the Coincident mate goes between the flat faces. The Peg-in-Hole mate is illustrated in Figure 14.7. The top two images show the state of the parts before the SmartMate. The image in the lower left shows the SmartMate orienting the part in the wrong way so the two parts interfere. In the image in the lower right, the part to which the SmartMate is applied has been reoriented by the Tab being pressed before the SmartMate is accepted by the part being dropped.

TIP   If a SmartMate tries to put parts together in the wrong way, you can press the Tab key to flip the alignment. If you are in the process of Alt+dragging, make sure to release the Alt key before pressing Tab. The Alt+Tab combination is a Windows shortcut to show a list of open applications.

FIGURE 14.7
Using the SmartMate to create the Peg-in-Hole mate combination

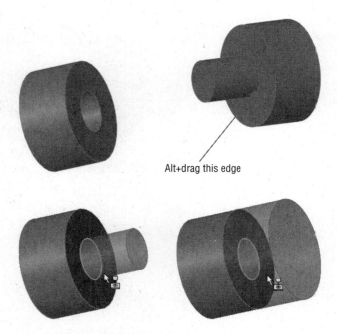

Alt+drag this edge

You can also Alt+drag a SmartMate to mate origins and coordinate systems. When you Alt+drag one origin onto another, you get the special cursor shown to the left, and when you release the mouse button, the pop-up option box shown in Figure 14.8 appears. If you only want the origin points mated Coincident, turn off the Align Axes option. With the Align Axes option on, the origin points will be Coincident, and the X, Y, and Z directions will be parallel to the same directions in the counterpart origin.

FIGURE 14.8
Using the Align Axes option on the pop-up option box for origin-to-origin SmartMates

Dragging Between Windows

You can simply Ctrl+drag a face of the part to the face of another part in a different SolidWorks window. It is probably most useful to tile windows before creating this kind of SmartMate. Be aware that the Tab functionality changes where three mates are applied simultaneously and a flange mating is created.

Using Mate References

Mate references are model faces, edges, or vertices that are preselected and used in a SmartMate-like fashion when you drag a part in from Windows Explorer or from a library window. Mate references are discussed in Chapter 18, "Using Libraries, Assembly Features, and the Hole Wizard," in the course of discussing library parts. They are a great way to automate common mates with commonly used parts, such as library parts.

Using the Component Preview Window

The Component Preview window splits the display, and opens up to the right of the main graphics window. It allows you to inspect, rotate, zoom, select, and perform other tasks. To open the window, click on a component in an assembly, and use the Preview Component tool in the context menu, or through the drop-down menu under Tools ➤ Component ➤ Preview Window. The display of the component in the main graphics window turns transparent. You can select from the main window and the Preview window for mate selections, for example. When the Preview window is open, a small toolbar is displayed with an Exit Preview button, as shown in Figure 14.9.

FIGURE 14.9
The Component Preview window is shown to the right.

Using Copy With Mates

Copy With Mates enables you to copy a component from one instance that is mated in place to multiple instances, also mated in place. This is not a pattern; it is more of a shortcut for inserting and mating in place one component multiple times. The time it saves you is in re-creating all the mates and making copies of the component. Remember, a component can be a single part or a subassembly.

The Copy With Mates icon can be found on the RMB menu and on the main Assembly toolbar, although it may not be there by default.

To use the Copy With Mates tool, you must start with a component mated in place. The workflow for Copy With Mates is as follows:

1. Start with the component you want to copy mated to another part.

2. RMB on the component to copy, and select Copy With Mates.

3. In the Copy With Mates PropertyManager, make sure the component to be copied is selected, and then click the right arrow to move to the next step

4. Note that the second page of the PropertyManager contains the mates associated with the selected part to be copied, as shown in Figure 14.10.

5. If a face will be selected for multiple mates, check the Repeat box and select the face—for example, a single face to which several bolt heads will mate.

6. Select other faces that mate to the copied part, clicking the green check mark after each selection to place the copied part.

You can practice with the `Copy with Mates.sldasm` assembly from the downloaded materials for this chapter.

FIGURE 14.10
Using Copy With Mates
to place bolts in holes

Mating with Macros

If you are just applying simple mates, and you'd prefer not to have to deal with all the the confirmations and extra mouse-clicks just to open and close windows, you may want to use macros to mate parts. Macros won't give you the same flexibility; but for simple and predictable mates, they will greatly increase your speed. You must have the parts ready to go when you press the Macro button, or you will create the wrong mate.

You can find macros for Coincident, Concentric, Parallel, Perpendicular, and Tangent mates in the download material for this chapter. For example, to use the Concentric macro, you need to pre-position the parts so they are within 90 degrees of the proper alignment, have one of the parts mated in place such that only one part will move, select the two cylindrical faces, and then run the macro. Ideally, the macro should be connected to a hotkey, so the workflow for this process will be extraordinarily fast. You can click one face, click the other face, and press the hotkey—and the parts will fly together.

NOTE To connect a macro to a hotkey, first put the macro in a folder identified at Tools ➤ Options ➤ File Locations ➤ Macros, and then restart SolidWorks. Then use the Keyboard dialog box (Tools ➤ Customize ➤ Keyboard) to assign hotkeys to the macros in the list.

Like SmartMates, macros work best for the simpler mate types where you do not need to select any options. The workflow with macros can be very fast, but you must have the parts pre-positioned and be very sure of what you want and what you will get.

Mating for Motion

Dynamic Assembly Motion is a powerful tool for visualizing the motion of mechanisms in SolidWorks. It works best if there is a single *open degree of freedom*. Assemblies with more open degrees of freedom can do some unexpected things when you try to move them. If there are multiple possible positions, the parts could jump between those positions. If the assembly has parts with unrelated open degrees of freedom, such as fasteners not constrained rotationally on an articulating arm, you may have some difficulty getting the motion you want.

Keep in mind that not all assemblies can function in multiple roles. For example, if you are trying to use a single assembly for an accurate BOM drawing, an exploded view, Dynamic Assembly Motion, setting up in-context references, and a rendering, you may find that even if you are using configurations (covered in Chapter 8, "Selecting Secondary Features") to divide the types, they still might interfere with one another.

For these reasons, you may want to consider separate assemblies for types of data that are most likely to interfere with other purposes, such as anything to do with moving parts around—Dynamic Assembly Motion, animation, rendering, or others.

Another question you need to ask yourself is whether the Dynamic Assembly Motion is actually necessary. Often, people set it up just because they can, and they may have unnecessary difficulties. For example, parts with in-context references should not have motion between the parts involved. If a referenced part moves, a hole or boss on the referencing part may also move. This sort of thing can be managed, but it requires discipline, and there is an element of risk to the integrity of your data if an untrained or forgetful user gains access to it.

Analyzing Degree of Freedom

When working with motion in SolidWorks, you need to be comfortable with the concept of *degrees of freedom*. When inserted into an assembly, each component after the first one inserted (which is fixed in place) begins with six degrees of freedom:

- Translation in X (tX)
- Translation in Y (tY)
- Translation in Z (tZ)
- Rotation about X (rX)
- Rotation about Y (rY)
- Rotation about Z (rZ)

When applying mates, and especially when troubleshooting motion or over-definition problems, you must look at how each mate translates into degrees of freedom being tied down. For example, a Coincident mate, planar face to planar face, ties down one translation degree of freedom (in the direction perpendicular to the faces) and two rotational degrees of freedom (about directions which lie in the plane of the faces). What remains are two translational degrees of freedom in the plane of the faces and one rotational degree of freedom about an axis perpendicular to the planar faces.

A point-to-point Coincident mate ties down three translational degrees of freedom, and the part can only rotate.

An edge-to-edge Coincident mate ties down two translational and two rotational degrees of freedom. As a result, a part that you mate in this way can only slide along the mated edge and rotate around the mated edge.

TIP   When you're using face-to-face Coincident mates, it takes three mates to define a block type part fully. When you're using edge-to-edge Coincident mates, it takes only two mates.

Something to be careful about is that a degree-of-freedom analysis frequently predicts an over-defined mate scenario when SolidWorks does not in fact display any errors or warnings. For example, if one block is mated to another with the simple case of three face-to-face Coincident mates, and each Coincident mate ties down one translational and two rotational degrees of freedom, then the mating scenario ties down nine degrees of freedom, so the part is over-constrained by three rotational degrees of freedom. However, SolidWorks has lots of forgiveness built in, so it commonly allows situations like this, where parts are severely over-constrained. When troubleshooting any over-constrained situation, you should not take this forgiveness for granted. If SolidWorks reports an assembly as over-constrained and the reason is not intuitively obvious, try reducing some of the degrees of freedom constrained. For example, instead of making two faces coincident, consider making them simply parallel or mating a point to a face instead of two faces.

BEST PRACTICE

This may be an overly cautious approach, but it can mean the difference between an assembly that works and one where errors are frustratingly persistent. If you are careful to approach all parts with the degree-of-freedom analysis in mind such that any newly added mate does not duplicate any of the degrees of freedom that are already tied down, you will have fewer assembly mate errors and fewer problems with assembly motion.

This means that instead of having the traditional three face-to-face Coincident mates, you would have one face-to-face Coincident mate (which locks down one translational degree of freedom and two rotational degrees of freedom), one edge-to-face Coincident mate (which locks down one translational degree of freedom and one rotational degree of freedom), and one point-to-face Coincident mate (which locks down one translational degree of freedom). This accounts for locking down all three translational and three rotational degrees of freedom without over-defining any of them. It is true that SolidWorks internally compensates for over-defined degrees of freedom, but relying on it to do so—and then tempting fate by methodically over-defining all assemblies—is a risk that you do not have to take, even though it is common practice.

Setting Up Successful Motion

The best bet for creating motion in a SolidWorks assembly is to leave open a single degree of freedom. This means that there is only one way the part can move: back and forth, by translation or rotation. Computers in general do not respond well to ambiguity. Dragging an item that might move in several ways is more likely to cause jerky or hesitant motion.

A good example of this kind of problem with motion can be found in one of the sample assemblies that installs with SolidWorks. This example is included in the download material for

your convenience and is shown in Figure 14.11. The filename for the assembly is
`Plunger.sldasm`.

FIGURE 14.11
An assembly displaying
the best bet
for motion

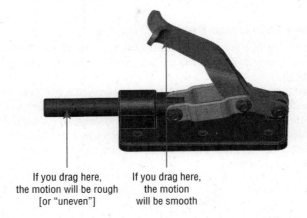

If you drag here,
the motion will be rough
[or "uneven"]

If you drag here,
the motion
will be smooth

If you drag the assembly parts from the location shown in Figure 14.11, the performance
varies. This is because when you drag the handle parts, for every position of the handle, there is
only one solution for the rest of the parts. However, when you drag the plunger bar, for every
position of the plunger bar, there are two possible positions for both the links and the handle
(one possibility is as shown, and the other would be with the handle interfering with the base of
the assembly). This kind of ambiguity causes problems in SolidWorks assemblies such as
assemblies that have open degrees of freedom but will not move or move only in a jerky fashion.

Another example of difficulties related to open degrees of freedom and motion is shown in
Figure 14.12. The grippers at the end of the arm move when the rest of the arm moves, but the
grippers cannot be independently controlled by dragging. To fix this problem, you may want to
use the Fix/Float option (available through the RMB menu) or use configurations with mates
suppressed or unsuppressed. Fix the part that you want to remain stationary closest to the part
you want to move. Remember to float the part when you are finished. Also, be aware that fixing
a part may over-define some mates. You can open this assembly from the download materials in
the filename called `Robot Assembly.sldasm`.

FIGURE 14.12
A robot arm assembly
with degree-of-
freedom conflicts

Sometimes dragging parts more slowly can help you get the results you expect more easily. Also, moving parts in a more controlled manner—for example, using Move With Triad or Move Along XYZ—can help the software resolve ambiguity.

Using Reference Entities

Reference entities are particularly useful in Angle mates. The best reference entity is a plane or face perpendicular to both of the angled entities. You can think of this like a section plane that defines the angle.

SolidWorks never really mentions it, but when you place (or measure) an angle between two faces, it takes the minimum angle; but depending on how you measure the angle, there are infinite options. This sometimes leads to confusion for users and ambiguity for the software.

The easiest way to use this function is to click the Auto Fill Reference Entity button, to the left of the box in the PropertyManager, as shown in Figure 14.13. SolidWorks will select something appropriate for you.

FIGURE 14.13
Using Reference Entity
and Dimension Selector

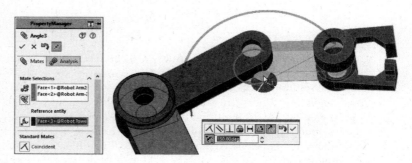

The Dimension Selector is the disk under the cursor in Figure 14.13. The disk is broken into blue and yellow quandrants at the angle pivot axis.

Working with Advanced and Mechanical Mate Types

Advanced and Mechanical mate types greatly expand the number of ways you can put parts together into assemblies and the kinds of motion you can create. Advanced mate types include Symmetric, Width, Path Mate, Linear/Linear Coupler, and Limit. Mechanical mate types include Cam, Hinge, Gear, Rack and Pinion, Screw, and Universal Joint. You can access Advanced and Mechanical mates by expanding the corresponding panels on the Mate PropertyManager (refer to Figure 14.1).

If you understand sketch relations, the standard mate relations fall into place easily. One exception is the Lock mate. Lock is different from Fix, which pins a part to the background. The Lock mate locks two parts to one another, so they always maintain the same relationship to one another, regardless of how they move with respect to other parts. This section goes into some detail about the Advanced and Mechanical mates, with a brief example of each.

Profile Center Mate

The Profile Center mate aligns the center-of-area of two selected faces (or sketches) for rectangular, regular polygons, and circular shapes. For example, a rectangular face and a circular sketch will mate, but if you substitute a rectangular or a "+" or "T" shape, you'll get a warning message "Selected entity is not valid for current mate type." It also accepts inner holes in the face, chamfers, and fillets. This is demonstrated in Figure 14.14.

You get the options to offset the selected faces, lock rotation, or select the orientation.

This mate type is still new; you can be forgiven for hoping that SolidWorks might in the future include other profile shapes in addition to rectangular and circular. (Hint: use the Enhancement Request process: `https://forum.solidworks.com/thread/39406`.)

FIGURE 14.14
Setting up a Profile
Center mate

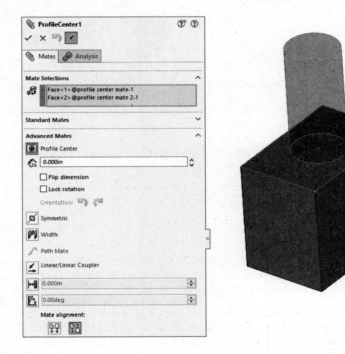

Symmetric Mate

The Symmetric mate works much like the Symmetry relation in sketches, except that a plane is used as the plane of symmetry instead of a construction line. Figure 14.15 shows a Symmetric mate being applied to the gripper jaws. The Symmetric mate is listed in the Advanced Mates pane of the Mate PropertyManager.

FIGURE 14.15
Applying a
Symmetric mate

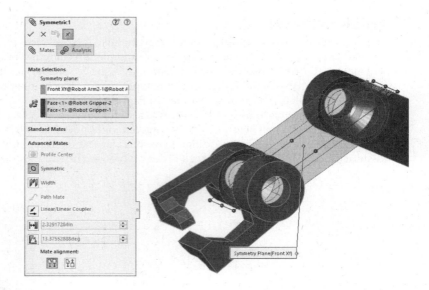

Cam Mate

The Cam mate creates a special instance of either the Coincident or Tangent mate. Four conditions exist with the Cam mate:

Coincident: The vertex on the follower mated to a cam that is created from a single closed-loop face (spline, circle, and ellipse).

Tangent: The cylindrical or planar face mated to a cam that is created from a single closed-loop face.

CamMateCoincident: The vertex on the follower mated to a cam that is created from multiple faces. This condition enables the follower to go all the way around the cam, without stopping at the broken faces or following the extension of a single face.

CamMateTangent: The cylindrical or planar face mated to a cam that is created from multiple faces. This condition enables the follower to go all the way around the cam, without stopping at the broken faces or following the extension of a single face.

Figure 14.16 shows a multi-face cam setup, along with the Cam Mate interface. The example files are available from the download material for this chapter in the file named Cam.sldasm.

If you open the assemblies and spin the cam plate, you will notice that in both cases, the flat follower does not work very well. In fact, in the single-face cam assembly, it does not work at all, because a planar face is considered an infinite plane for the purpose of mating. For more information, take a look at https://forum.solidworks.com/thread/203350.

NOTE   Barrel (cylindrical) cams cannot use the Cam mate to create cam motion, but they do work with the Path mate. Path mates are covered in more detail later in this section.

FIGURE 14.16
Using Cam mates

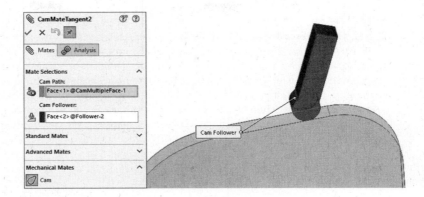

Width Mate

The Width mate is often used as a replacement for the Symmetric mate in situations where parts are modeled with some tolerance and have a gap rather than touching face to face. The Width mate requires two pairs of faces to be selected, and it works particularly well when a part must be spaced evenly (or at some percentage to one side) between two faces and there is no mid-plane—for example, when a square key is placed in a square keyway that is somewhat larger than the key. Dovetail keyways are another good application for this mate. If a mid-plane is available, the Symmetric mate may be a better option—or at least a faster one to mate, given that the Symmetric mate requires only two faces and a plane. Figure 14.17 shows a good application for a Width mate as well as the PropertyManager interface for the mate.

FIGURE 14.17
Centering one part on others with a Width mate

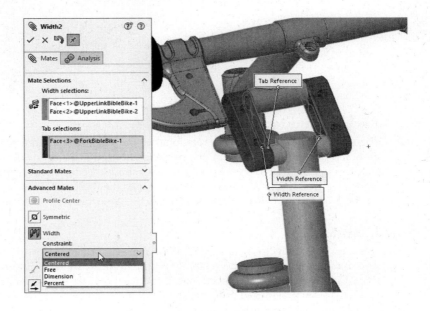

Gear Mate

The Gear mate enables you to establish gear type relations between parts without making the parts physically mesh. You can also apply gear ratios and directions without physical connections, so you can have a shaft in and a shaft out of a black-box transmission without requiring the detail of the gear profiles. You can open the assembly shown in Figure 14.18 from the download material in the file named Gear Mate.sldasm. To see the effect of the mate, open the assembly and rotate the parts. Then edit the mate, and change the ratio and direction. The selection for the Gear mate is just two cylindrical faces or circular edges. Sketches of pitch diameters are also used.

FIGURE 14.18

Applying a Gear mate

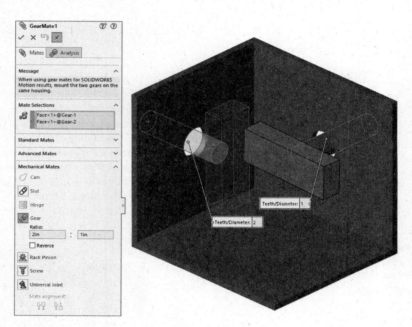

Rack and Pinion Mate

The Rack and Pinion mate takes rotational motion of one part and turns it into translational motion for a second part. Again, the parts do not need to be physically connected and can be simple representations of the actual geometry that is needed to drive the motion in the real world. Figure 14.19 shows an assembly that uses the Rack and Pinion mate. You can find this assembly in the download material with the filename RackPinionMate.sldasm.

Limit Mates

You can apply limits to Distance and Angle mates in order to allow the parts to move within a certain range of values. Figure 14.20 shows the PropertyManager interface for the Limit Angle mate. Limit mates accept zero and negative values that are not normally accepted for dimensions in SolidWorks. When used properly, the Limit mate can be an extremely powerful tool for creating more realistic motion in assemblies.

FIGURE 14.19
Applying a Rack and
Pinion mate

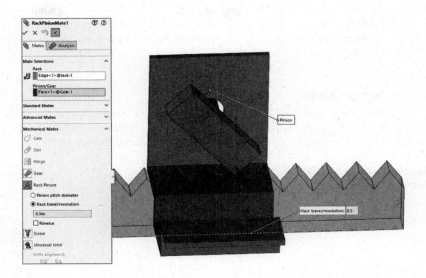

FIGURE 14.20
The LimitAngle
PropertyManager

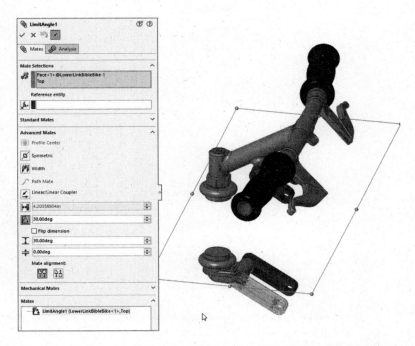

In the download material for this chapter, open the assembly named Robot Limit Mate .sldasm. Drag the Robot Tower part. Notice that it rotates only within a limited angle. LimitAngle2 is the mate that is driving this motion.

NOTE For Angle Limit mates and for Angle mates, I strongly suggest using the new Reference Entity option to define the reference quadrant for the angle. Otherwise, there is the danger of flipping mates.

Screw Mate

The Screw mate functions just the way the name suggests. For every revolution of a part relative to another part, the part moves in a linear direction by a specified amount. This mate requires two cylindrical faces and a pitch value, as shown in Figure 14.21.

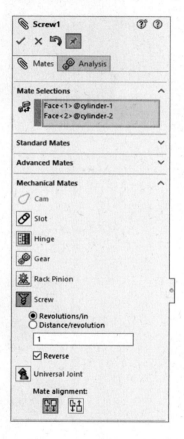

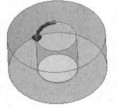

Screw mates can be handy for lead screw animations. Although they are not recommended general modeling; however, if you are working with animations, they are a fantastic addition to the mate toolbox.

Path Mate

The Path mate is the one that makes complex barrel-cam motion possible, as well as other types of path-driven motion. Another application for this mate type beyond barrel cams is for the motion of a camera in a fly-through animation. The Path mate requires a point or vertex on one part and a curve selection on a second part. If the path selection is not just a single sketch or curve entity, it requires the use of the SelectionManager, which enables you to select multiple end-to-end entities to form closed or open paths. Figure 14.22 shows the setup for a Path mate. The `Barrel Cam.sldasm` file from the download material demonstrates the selections necessary to make this work.

The Path Mate includes some controls for keeping the follower properly oriented. One of these is the Roll Control, which enables you to specify an Up vector. The second of these is the Pitch/Yaw Control, which can be free, or controlled by the path.

FIGURE 14.22
Setting up a Path mate

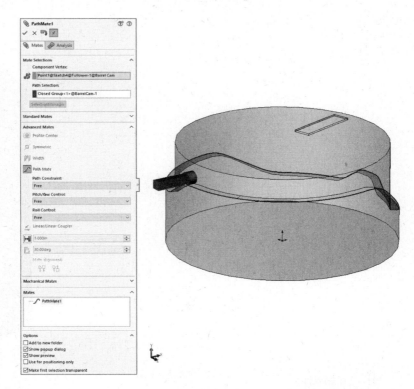

NOTE   On the barrel cam in Figure 14.22, notice that a sketch point is being driven along the path. In reality, this does not exactly reflect the motion of the follower around the cam surface. The Path mate does not take into account the tangent contact point between the surfaces; it simply drives the point along the curve. There is a slight amount of error in this scenario, such that the leading or trailing surface of the follower will interfere with the cam on angled slopes, depending on the angle of the cam surface. Also note that the Path sketch entity has nothing to do with the Path mate; it is not required to make the Path mate work.

You may find that this works better for controlled motion using Animation or motors than for simple dynamic assembly motion driven by the mouse.

Linear Coupler Mate

The Linear Coupler mate relates the motion of one part in one direction to another part in either the same or a different direction. It also enables you to apply a ratio between the motions. The directions do not have to be parallel or anti-parallel; they can be at right angles, or at any angle. The mate controls motion only in one direction, so other directions are free to move.

You can use this mate to simulate symmetric motion or geared motion without modeling the rest of the detailed mechanism. Figure 14.23 shows the setup for this mate.

FIGURE 14.23
Setting up a Linear
Coupler mate

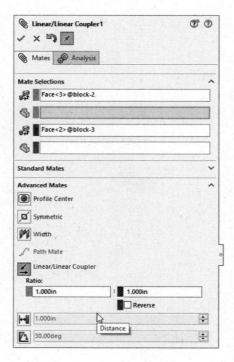

Hinge Mate

The Hinge mate is just a shortcut for making a Concentric mate and a Coincident mate combined with an Angle and Limit mate, but it does it all in a single feature and a single interface. Figure 14.24 shows the PropertyManager interface for the Hinge mate.

Belt/Chain

The Belt/Chain assembly feature is not technically a stand-alone mate type, but it uses mates to accomplish its task. You can use the Belt/Chain feature in two ways: to create relationships between sketch blocks and to create relations between parts. This feature also creates a sketch and a solid part representing the belt or chain. You can initiate the Belt/Chain function from a toolbar button on the Assembly toolbar or through the menus by choosing Insert ➤ Assembly Feature ➤ Belt/Chain.

FIGURE 14.24
Setting up a Hinge mate

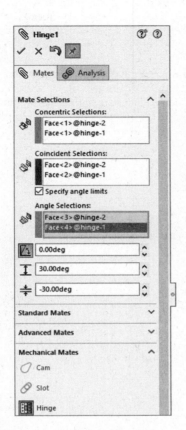

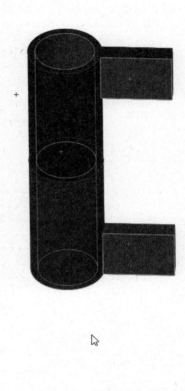

Editing and Troubleshooting

You should become proficient with editing and troubleshooting assembly mates, because you are going to spend a fair amount of time editing assemblies. After you master the techniques, you will be more confident and willing to experiment with assembly changes. Assemblies with errors run more slowly and are unpredictable. Others who use those assemblies may be confused about the assembly design intent if you leave errors in the model. It is always good practice to leave your assemblies error-free for the next user.

Editing Existing Mates

If you are editing just one mate, you can simply right-click it and select Edit Feature (or if you are using context toolbars, left-click it and click the Edit Feature button). Remember that you can find mates in places other than the Mates folder at the bottom of the assembly FeatureManager; most notably, you can find them in folders under the parts they are mating together.

You can also select View Mates from the RMB or LMB menu for a part in an assembly, and for multiple selections of parts. This brings up a small window containing all the mates that involve the selected parts.

Mates are also listed in the breadcrumbs, and you can bring the breadcrumb to your cursor with the D hotkey. Breadcrumbs can be very handy to quickly find items related to whatever you have selected at the time.

You can make several types of changes to mates, including changing the selections, the mate types, and the mate alignment. These types of changes are all shown in Figure 14.25, which displays a mate being edited. The selected faces are highlighted in the graphics window.

FIGURE 14.25
Editing a mate

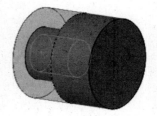

To edit multiple mates consecutively without exiting the Mate PropertyManager, you should preselect the mates. Preselected mates are shown in the Mates panel (refer to Figure 14.21). You can switch from editing one mate to another by simply selecting the new mate in the Mates panel. If you select only one mate before clicking Edit Feature, but realize later that you want to edit multiple mates, you can select more mates through the FeatureManager.

When mate entities are lost, the mate appears grayed out. You can repair the missing reference problem by selecting the invalid reference in the Mate Selections window and then selecting the correct item from the graphics window. When multiple mates are missing the same reference, and it is repaired in one of them, SolidWorks gives you the option to replace the new reference in the rest of the broken mates.

A yellow triangle symbol in front of a mate is satisfied, but it is in conflict with another mate that is not satisfied.

To repair the mate shown in Figure 14.25, select the Missing Face entry in the PropertyManager, and then select the correct face in the graphics window using any of the selection options available in SolidWorks. When a missing reference used by multiple mates is repaired, you have the option to repair all the mates using it. Also, it is important to know, that when you attempt to apply a mate that would contradict existing mates, there are three options: cancel the application of the new mate, break the new mate, or break the other mates.

Troubleshooting Assembly Mates

It is best to troubleshoot an assembly mate problem as soon as it appears, not after it has become complicated by other issues. Failed mates also cause performance problems because SolidWorks keeps trying to solve the mates that are in conflict with one another.

Assembly problems often appear to be far larger than they actually are. For example, the entire tree may light up with warnings and error symbols when one extra mate is applied. You can use several approaches to troubleshoot situations like this. For example, you can purposely over-define mates just to locate a leftover mate or a mate that is not supposed to be there.

Two types of symbols may help you distinguish the kinds of errors that are present in different mate features. A yellow triangle that contains an exclamation point is not an *error*; it is actually more of a *warning*. It tells you that this mate is in conflict with other mates (this symbol is used for a variety of warnings), but that the mate is still satisfied geometrically. One of the other mates with which it conflicts is probably not valid, so this type of warning is usually accompanied by an actual error symbol where the mate is not satisfied.

A red circle containing an X is a failed mate. This mate is in conflict *and* is invalid. If it is also a Coincident mate, then the two Coincident entities are not coincident.

To make it easy to find problem mates, if you click on the top-level assembly name in the AssemblyManager, SolidWorks displays all of the mates under warning and error messages, as shown in Figure 14.26.

FIGURE 14.26
SolidWorks shows the mate errors and warnings at the top level.

Troubleshooting Warnings and Errors

SolidWorks distinguishes between errors and warnings. Errors are situations where a condition is not satisfied, such as a Coincident mate where the selected entities are not coincident. Errors are marked with a red symbol. Warnings mark situations where a conflict exists, but otherwise all conditions are met, with a yellow triangle and an exclamation point. For example, both a Coincident and a Perpendicular mate use the same faces. One mate will have an error and the other a warning, because one can be satisfied, but not both.

You can use the following troubleshooting techniques to work with assemblies where errors or warnings exist:

Last In First Out   When a mate is added that causes warning and error signs to appear throughout the design tree, you can usually correct the problem by removing this last mate.

Single Elimination   If you are sure that the last mate added is correct, then you may want to go backward up the tree, starting at the bottom and suppressing individual mates until you find one that causes the warning and error signs to disappear from the tree.

Single Addition   It may be easier to take the opposite approach, by suppressing all but the mates that you are sure of and then gradually unsuppressing mates until the conflict reappears.

Suppress a Part   With all the mates active, try suppressing an individual part to see whether this makes a difference. If it does, then unsuppress the part and look at the mates for that part in the Mates folder under the part.

MateXpert   The MateXpert is an automated routine that creates subsets of groups of conflicting mates. Each subset of mates has one mate that is not satisfied because of the conflict. This may help you to find the cause of the conflict. Figure 14.27 shows the MateXpert interface. You can access the MateXpert from the RMB menu on mates with errors, or through the main menus at Tools ➤ Evaluate.

Examining Mate Options

The Options pane of the Mate PropertyManager is shown in Figure 14.28. These options control actions taken with newly created mates.

Add To New Folder puts any newly created mate in its own new folder. When it is turned off, new mates are put at the top level after the last folder.

Show Popup Dialog shows the pop-up list in Figure 14.2 when a mate is being created. The pop-up list is displayed in the graphics area next to the geometry selections for the mate.

Show Preview pre-positions the mated parts before exiting the command.

Use For Positioning Only positions a part but does not apply or remember the mate. Some users select this option often for various applications where they need the part located precisely, but they do not need or want a mate feature in the tree. One example of using this option is to position a part for animations where the part does not move according to a mate.

Make First Selection Transparent was mentioned earlier in this chapter. It turns the first part you select for the mate transparent to the user and to the cursor, so you can select whatever is behind it.

FIGURE 14.27
The MateXpert interface

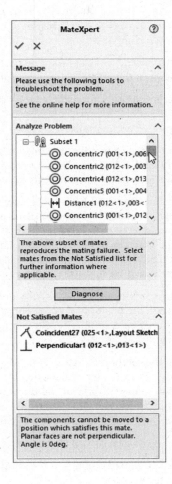

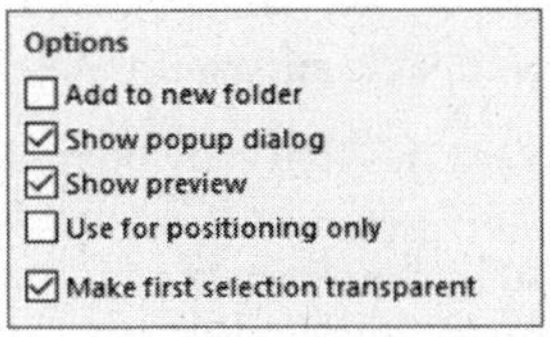

FIGURE 14.28
The Options pane
of the Mate
PropertyManager

Options
☐ Add to new folder
☑ Show popup dialog
☑ Show preview
☐ Use for positioning only
☑ Make first selection transparent

Reviewing Mate Best Practices

Sometimes, best practice recommendations can contradict one another, and for each best practice recommendation you find, there are likely several specific situations where the recommendation is invalid or even a bad idea. As a result, you should apply the following recommendations carefully. Don't take best practices too seriously, but you should not disregard them altogether. Some companies use best practice recommendations as modeling standards. The less experience your SolidWorks team has, the more you need standards of this sort. Every situation has a different need for best practice—and maybe even a need for a set of rules that are different from the ones laid out here. You can think of this set of mate best practices as a starting point for the discussion at your own company.

- Each assembly should have at least one part that is either fixed or fully mated to the standard planes of the assembly so it cannot move relative to the assembly.

- Use fixed parts sparingly. One part that serves as a "ground" for the assembly should be fixed. Other than that, the parts of imported assemblies are sometimes fixed to keep them from being moved accidentally.

- Do not mate to time-dependent features in the assembly tree, to patterned components, or to in-context features in parts. This can create circular references where the assembly must be rebuilt multiple times to fully resolve the positions of all parts and sketches.

- When possible, mate all parts to the "ground" part. Creating *daisy-chain* mates (where A mates to B, which mates to C, and so on) forces the mates to be solved in a particular order, which may take more time to solve. If all the mates relate to established assembly references, the mates may be more stable. Chapter 13, "Building Efficient Assemblies," describes using a skeleton in a part to make sketch and feature relations. You can apply a similar concept in an assembly by mating parts to an assembly sketch.

- When possible, leave part positions fully defined, especially when other geometry is dependent upon the position of parts. Some examples include in-context features, assembly features, or assembly-level reference geometry, which are dependent on part geometry.

- Constraining the rotational degree of freedom for components such as screws, washers, and nuts is usually considered excessive. At times, too many open degrees of freedom may cause problems with complex motion, such as a gripper on the end of a robotic arm. SolidWorks functions well when there is a single, well-defined path between two points; but when there are multiple options, the software may become confused.

- Do not leave errors unresolved in the tree.

- Remember to use subassemblies to break up the number of mates that are solved in the top-level assembly.

- Limit the use of flexible subassemblies.

- Do not mate to entities that may be removed later by suppressing or unsuppressing features, especially edges or faces that are created by features such as fillets. For this reason, it is usually best to wait until parts are complete before you use them to create an assembly, although this is rarely practical.

- Use a degree-of-freedom analysis to prevent mates from becoming over-defined.

- Mate the hardware (nuts, bolts) to the main components, not the other way around. If the hardware is suppressed, the assembly motion should be unaffected.

Tutorial: Mating for Success

In this tutorial, you will put together a model of a robotic arm to better understand some of the mate issues discussed in this chapter. Follow these steps to mate for success:

1. Open the part named `Robot Base.sldprt` from the download website.

2. In the part document window, click the Make Assembly From Part icon, and click the cursor on the origin of the assembly to place the part origin at the assembly origin. The part is automatically fixed in place.

3. Choose Insert ➤ Component ➤ Existing Part/Assembly. Click the Browse button in the PropertyManager, and find the part called `Robot Tower.sldprt`. This part contains a Mate reference to help you mount it to the base. If you bring the cursor near the big circular hole in the base, you can see the preview of the tower snap into place. Click to accept this placement. Figure 14.29 shows this placement in progress. Notice the Rotate context toolbar option and the bar itself in the graphics window. This helps you get the newly placed part oriented correctly. Also notice that the cursor appears as a SmartMate cursor for the Peg-in-Hole mate. When the part is dropped, check the mate list to confirm that a Concentric mate and a Coincident mate have been applied by the Mate reference.

FIGURE 14.29
A Mate reference being used to SmartMate a component

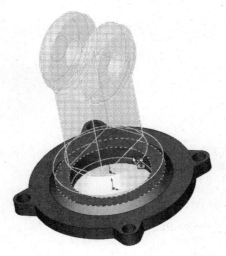

4. Open the part with the filename `Robot Arm.sldprt`, the default configuration, in its own window, and choose Window ➤ Tile Vertically. The part and the assembly should be open in adjacent windows.

5. Click the face inside the hole without the chamfer around it in the Arm part, as shown in Figure 14.30. Then drag it into the assembly to the cylindrical face inside the hole at the top of the Robot Tower part. The concentric SmartMate symbol should appear on the cursor.

FIGURE 14.30
Displaying a SmartMate
when dragging
between windows

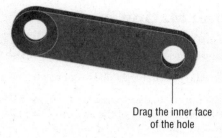

Drag the inner face
of the hole

6. Click the green checkmark icon to accept the Concentric mate. Move the part to test that the mates are correct.

7. Click the Mate tool on the Assembly toolbar. Expand the Advanced Mates panel, and click the Width mate.

8. In the Width Selections box, select the two inner faces of the Robot Tower part, and in the Tab Selections box, select the outer faces of the Arm part. The selection should look as shown in Figure 14.31.

9. Open a Windows Explorer window, and select the following parts: Robot Arm2 and Robot Gripper. Drag these parts into the SolidWorks assembly window, and drop them in a blank space.

10. Select the chamfered faces of the Arm and Arm2 parts, and create a Coincident mate between them. You can make Coincident mates between conical faces as long as the cones are the same angle. This special case acts like a combination of Concentric and Coincident mates. Figure 14.32 shows the selections and the result.

FIGURE 14.31
Creating a Width mate

FIGURE 14.32
Making conical faces
coincident

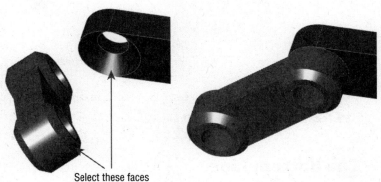

Select these faces

11. Create a copy of the gripper part so there are two instances of it in the assembly. You can do this by Ctrl+dragging the part within the assembly window with the Mate PropertyManager closed.

12. Mate both of the grippers to the Arm2 end using the same mating technique that you used for the previous conical face Coincident part.

13. After you have applied these parts, try moving the various joints of the assembly. Notice that it is difficult, if not impossible, to isolate the motion of just a single part. This is because there are too many open degrees of freedom and lots of ambiguity.

14. Fix Arm2 to allow you to move the gripper parts as you want. Create a Symmetric mate between the indicated faces of the grippers and the Front plane of the Arm2 part, as shown in Figure 14.33.

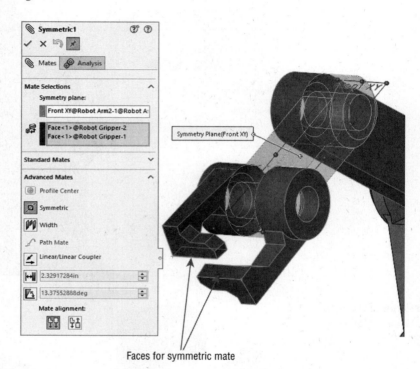

FIGURE 14.33
Creating a
Symmetric mate

Faces for symmetric mate

15. Practice making angle mates, suppressing mates, and fixing parts to limit motion.

16. Save the assembly and exit the file.

The Bottom Line

A thorough understanding of mates (and their editing and troubleshooting techniques in particular) makes the difference between a real assembly artist and a user who struggles through or avoids certain tasks. Much about mates is not straightforward, but with practice, you can understand and master them. You can put assemblies together quickly, with a focus on rebuild performance and Dynamic Assembly Motion.

Although best practice concepts should not dominate your designs, they are great guidelines from which to start. To avoid making big mistakes, watch out for the pitfalls outlined in page 27, Reviewing Mate Best Practices section in this chapter that summarizes mate best practices to follow.

Master It   SmartMates are a key to putting assemblies together quickly in SolidWorks. Practice using SmartMates in a single assembly window, and also between a part and assembly in tiled windows. Practice using the Tab key to flip the orientation of the mate.

Master It   Make sure you understand the function of mates. Go through a sample assembly and sort through the mates that prevent motion and the mates that enable motion. Put these mates into separate folders.

Master It   Work through several of the specialized mechanical mates and make sure you can use the sample assemblies to re-create the motion. Use the parts from the sample assemblies for each of the mates and reassemble the parts to have the intended motion.

Chapter 15

Patterning and Mirroring Components

In SolidWorks assemblies, the word *component* can refer to either parts or subassemblies. Component patterns can be patterns of parts, subassemblies, or combinations of parts and subassemblies.

IN THIS CHAPTER, YOU WILL LEARN TO:

◆ Create local component patterns

◆ Place the initial components for feature-driven component patterns

◆ Examine other pattern options

Component Patterns

Component patterns come in several varieties, as shown in Figure 15.1. Of these, only the Linear and Circular patterns do not require references outside of the assembly, which is to say that most component patterns are going to require some sort of external (in-context) reference. These references can be sketches or pattern features from parts.

FIGURE 15.1
Types of component patterns in SolidWorks

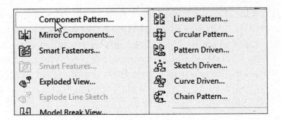

Mirroring components in assemblies is far more complex than mirroring features in parts. SolidWorks provides options for mirrored parts, mirrored positions, left-hand and right-hand versions of parts, and mirroring parts and subassemblies within top-level assemblies.

Using Local Component Patterns

Local component patterns are limited to Linear and Circular patterns; SolidWorks assemblies do not offer all the options available for patterning features in a part, such as table-driven and fill pattern. The Linear pattern directions work just like the Linear Pattern feature in parts and must reference a line, axis, edge, plane, planar face, and so on to establish the direction. Remember, it is best if possible to reference items close to home in the local assembly file rather than select something external from part geometry. In an assembly, this means that the pattern feature uses either local reference geometry from the assembly (such as axes, planes, or assembly sketches) or model geometry from a part (such as solid or surface edges, sketches, or reference geometry). Keep this in mind if you are concerned about external or circular references. By using references belonging to the assembly rather than to parts, you avoid some common referencing pitfalls.

BEST PRACTICE

If you have a feature pattern in a part, you should take advantage of it and use a feature-driven pattern instead of a local pattern. The rebuild time may be longer, but associativity between the part and assembly helps maintain design intent.

Creating Local Pattern References

It is best to use references that are not dependent on part geometry. Remember that when part geometry is used as an assembly pattern reference, the parts must be solved first (sketches and features rebuilt), then the mates must be solved (to position the parts), then any in-context references must be solved (which may change the part geometry), and then any assembly features or component patterns must be solved. As a result, it is best practice to use assembly reference geometry or assembly sketches without references as pattern direction references. The assembly sketches should sit at the top of the assembly FeatureManager to ensure that they do not pick up references from the history-based features in the design tree (mated components, patterns, assembly features, and so on).

When a local pattern really requires a reference from a part, you have no alternative. However, if you can avoid this situation by using a sketch assembly skeleton to which the parts are mated and used for the pattern references, then you should do so. At all costs, you should avoid using in-context features, assembly reference geometry that is dependent on part geometry, and assembly features (other than sketches) for the local pattern reference.

USING THE INSTANCES TO SKIP OPTION

The Instances To Skip option for component patterns, shown in Figure 15.2, works just like the equivalent option for features. Click the dots in the graphics window to toggle each instance of the pattern. On the screen, the instances to keep use pink dots and the instances to skip use orange dots. The colors are almost indistinguishable at a relatively wide spacing.

FIGURE 15.2

The Instances to Skip option

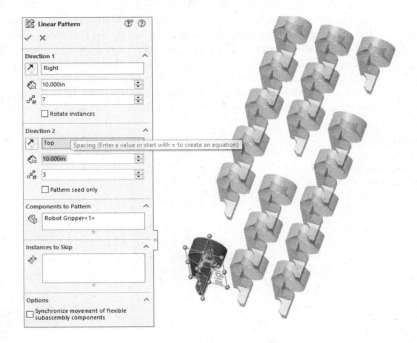

PERFORMANCE

For best pattern performance, you should use subassemblies as the patterned unit as much as is practical. Multiple patterns of individual components are not as efficient as a single pattern of multiple components. A single pattern of a single component, where the single component is itself a subassembly, is the best choice, if available.

Another performance issue is the fact that component patterns require external references (for the direction or center of the pattern). These external references have the potential to increase rebuild times if you do not choose them carefully. Reference geometry internal to the assembly would be the best choice.

Although you may experience performance problems with patterns, they can also significantly decrease the number of mates in an assembly, which always improves performance.

PATTERNING THE SEED ONLY

All the aspects of the interface should be familiar to you, such as the direction, instances, and spacing. The Pattern Seed Only option is used in feature patterns.

This option is designed to allow you to create a single pattern in two directions that are separated by 180 degrees, where the internal instances do not overlap one another. For example, if you take a basic two-directional pattern and change the angle between the directions so that they are *antiparallel* (parallel but going in opposite directions), then all the component instances that were between the two legs of the L created by the two directions will overlap one another. One flaw in this feature is that it will not allow you to select the same linear entity (for example, an axis) for both directions, so that, as in the example in Figure 15.3, you have to find two separate entities (in this case, an axis and an edge) that are parallel. The assembly used for this image is available in the download material for Chapter 15 as `Pattern Seed Only.sldasm`. The assembly template with the axes in it is in the MBD folder and is named `AxesAssembly.asmdot`.

FIGURE 15.3
Use the Pattern Seed Only option for two-directional patterns.

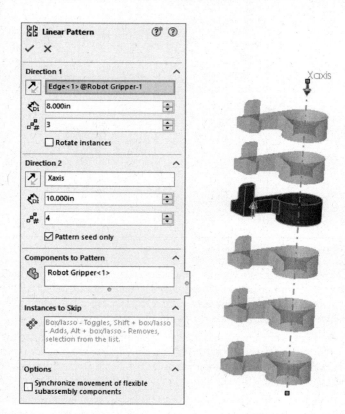

Using Mirror Components

The Mirror Components tool leaves a feature in the assembly tree just as pattern features do. It gives you the option to align each mirrored part and decide which parts require opposite-handed versions and which can just use the original in a mirrored location. Figure 15.4 shows the

PropertyManager for this assembly feature. Notice that the mechanism linkages require only the identical part in a mirrored position. The brake lever assembly, however, requires opposite-handed parts in a mirrored position. To examine this assembly more closely, open `Mirrored Components.sldasm`.

FIGURE 15.4

Mirroring components of an assembly with the Mirror Components tool

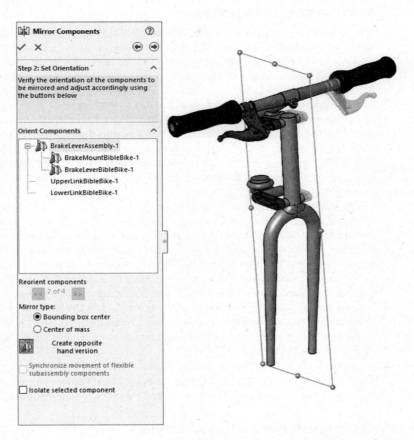

The workflow to mirror components in the assembly has three steps, the second of which is shown in Figure 15.4:

1. Selections. Select the parts and subassemblies that you want to mirror, along with the plane about which you want to mirror the components.

2. Set Orientation. Identify the components that must have opposite-hand versions; for the others, you can toggle through the available options for placement.

3. Opposite-Hand Versions. For the parts that need opposite-hand versions, you can assign them to use new parts or derived configurations.

The first step should be self-explanatory. Just select the parts and plane as you would in other situations. You move between the steps by clicking the arrows in blue circles in the upper-right corner of the Mirror Components PropertyManager.

SETTING THE ORIENTATION

The second step requires some explanation. In the PropertyManager labeled Step 2: Set Orientation (refer to Figure 15.4), notice that there are some mirror symbols in front of the BrakeLeverAssembly and BrakeMountBibleBike selections in the Orient Components panel. This means that these documents must have mirrored instances. You control this option by selecting the part or assembly in the Orient Components list box and then clicking the Create Opposite Hand Version button at the bottom of the PropertyManager.

Another thing you need to do in this second step is correctly orient parts that do not require an opposite-hand version. To do this, select a part in the Orient Components list box, such as the GripsBibleBike part, and click through the double-arrows just below the selection box. In Figure 15.4, the message "2 of 4" is grayed out because a part that requires an opposite hand is selected. When you click the arrows, the part repositions in another possible mirrored position and orientation.

The Mirror Type options Bounding Box Center and Center Of Mass determine how the mirrored component is positioned. If you create an opposite-hand version, the position is automatically determined, so the options do not make any difference.

When you mirror a component, you first have to consider the mirror plane, and then you have to consider the pivot orientation of the component once its position is determined. The Reorient Components control in this case gives you four different options for the pivot orientation. Notice that some of the options change if you use Bounding Box rather than Center of Mass. Essentially, two mirrors are occurring. The first is the mirror about the selected mirror plane, and the second is the mirror about either the Bounding Box Center or the Center Of Mass. It's not critical, as long as the components wind up in the correct position and orientation. Use the Reorient Components options to determine that.

Figure 15.5 shows all of the combinations of the Reorient Components 1 through 4 for both Bounding Box Center (left) and Center Of Mass (right) mirror types.

The correct result should be obvious, but there could be more than one correct result.

CREATING OPPOSITE-HAND VERSIONS

In the third step, in the Opposite Hand Versions panel of the PropertyManager, only the documents that must be changed are listed. In this case, the brake lever assembly is made of two parts: the lever part can be used in both left-hand and right-hand versions, but the mount must have two different versions of the part. This means the assembly must also have two versions.

This Mirror Components functionality is fantastic, involving a well-thought-out process. To make the mirrored versions, you have the option to create new files or to create a derived configuration within the existing files.

As you are setting up these options, SolidWorks displays a preview of the result in the graphics window. The preview parts are transparent and may be a pale yellow. (You may want to change them to a darker orange color at Tools ➤ Options ➤ Colors ➤ Temporary Graphics, Shaded.) You can see how the parts are oriented and can immediately fix any problems that arise.

FIGURE 15.5
The mirror results of the Bounding Box Center and Center Of Mass options

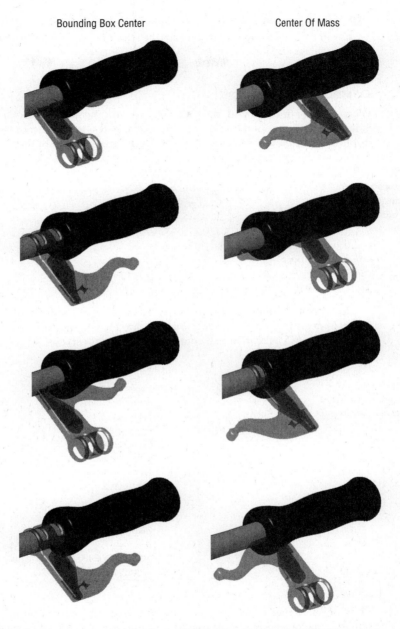

Bounding Box Center   Center Of Mass

With larger assemblies and larger sets of mirrored components, the visualization may be more difficult, but the process demonstrated here on these parts works and gives a complete set of options as you work through the process of mirroring parts and assemblies within the top-level assembly.

TIP   The Isolate Selected Component option turns off the display of all of the other components being mirrored while you work on options for the selected component. This can be useful when mirroring many things at once.

COMPLETING THE TASK

When you are finished with the task, you can click the green checkmark icon. In this case, SolidWorks displays a message that one of the mates in the mirrored assembly could not be duplicated, as shown in Figure 15.6. After testing the motion of the fork linkage, this missing mate does not appear to affect the assembly.

FIGURE 15.6
A mate is not created as the mirroring task is completed.

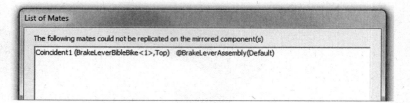

The Mirror Component feature leaves a marker in the assembly FeatureManager after the Mates folder. In Figure 15.7, notice that the BrakeLeverAssembly and BrakeMountBibleBike documents use a MirrorDefault configuration, as was established while mirroring the assembly and parts.

FIGURE 15.7
Examining the list of mirrored components

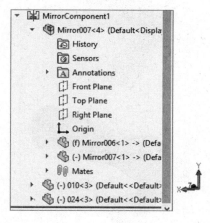

TIP   If you happen to be mirroring a flexible subassembly and you want the mirrored subassemblies to move simultaneously, you can use the Synchronize Movement Of Flexible Subassembly Components option. This option links the mates of the subassemblies.

Using Feature-Driven Component Patterns

By their very nature, feature-driven component patterns defy some of the best practice sugges-tions in this book. This is because the pattern is driven by part geometry, and the part must first be solved (by solving features internal to the part) and then placed (by solving mates); only then can the feature-driven pattern be solved. Nevertheless, you should use feature-driven patterns instead of local patterns when available because of the parametric link. Parametric associativity is, after all, one of the main benefits that SolidWorks offers.

NOTE For the feature-driven component patterns, the location of the initial component is important. You need to match the placement of the initial component with the position of the original feature from which the pattern was created, not one of the patterned instances. You can get around this requirement if you use the Select Seed Position option. When you do this, the pattern instances all appear with dots, and you can select which instance to use as the seed. Again, the selected dot is blue and unselected dots are purple; they are nearly indistinguishable at the size and spacing of the dots.

Figure 15.8 shows the PropertyManager interface for a feature-driven component pattern. This sample file is with the download material for this chapter under the name `Feature Driven Pattern.sldasm`.

FIGURE 15.8
The feature-driven Component Pattern interface

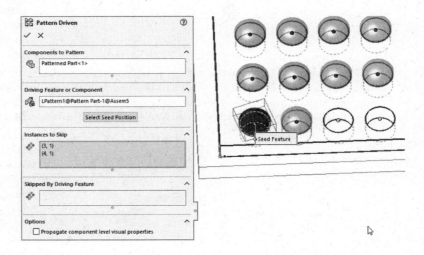

You can nest feature-driven component patterns such that one component pattern is patterned by another component pattern, just as you do using feature patterns. The second pattern can be a local pattern or a feature-driven pattern.

In the case shown in Figure 15.8, I used the Instances To Skip option, selecting multiple adjacent instances with a box or lasso.

Creating a Chain Pattern

We have been using a bicycle as an example file for much of this book, so using the Chain Pattern feature seems appropriate here.

Start with a sketch of the chain line, which SolidWorks refers to as the *path*. The chain of a real bicycle would flex; but for SolidWorks purposes, your chain line must be planar. The sketch must also be clean, with no gaps or overlaps, and it must be a single continuous loop where all the entities are tangent end-to-end. Also, in this case, you may notice that the chain interferes with the drive-side chain stay when in the highest gear, but this is left for you to work out as a design exercise. Figure 15.9 shows the sketch for the chain path.

FIGURE 15.9
Create a sketch for the chain line.

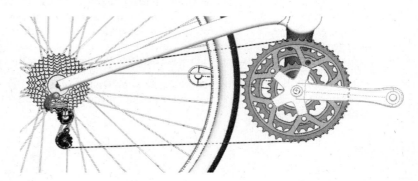

Next, you need to create the links in your chain. Bicycle chains are made of inner and outer links. Other types of chain may have just one element. You may choose to model the chain links another way because of the way the chain is manufactured or assembled, but Figure 15.10 shows how I chose to model the chain to work best with the SolidWorks Chain Pattern feature.

FIGURE 15.10
Chain links are made of separate parts.

Next, the links need to be placed in the assembly. You may choose to have a separate assembly for the chain. The chain shows up in the assembly where it is created as a feature, with several part instances under it, just like a pattern. The links will be placed on the chain path sketch by the Chain Pattern feature, so you don't need to mate them there yourself. The Chain Pattern interface walks you through the process, shown in Figure 15.11.

FIGURE 15.11
The Chain Pattern
PropertyManager
interface

If you choose the third option in the Pitch Method, which is Connected Links, you need to have two separate link parts, or at least a single link with alternating position. The Connected Links Pitch Method activates the second chain group. Use the Path Alignment Plane to make sure the correct faces of the links are mated.

To get a chain pattern to be perfectly end-to-end, you have to work with the path sketch length and adjust it until the first and last links connect.

The chain pattern can help you get an idea of how long your actual chain needs to be, as well as produce a looks-like visual for your drawings. For situations where your chain needs to be nonplanar, such as the actual application of a bicycle chain, that is something you can't simulate with this tool. The chain pattern helps you identify that the design of the chain stay on this bike needs to be altered to avoid rubbing on the chain in the highest gears.

The Dynamic and Static options allow or disallow motion, respectively. The advantage of disallowing motion would be that you would avoid calculating all the associated mates.

Once the pattern is created, all the necessary links components are kept under the Chain Pattern feature, as partially shown in Figure 15.12.

FIGURE 15.12
The Chain Pattern feature in the assembly FeatureManager tree

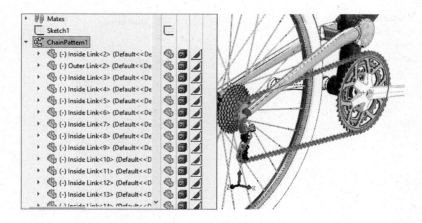

Understanding Other Pattern Options

SolidWorks provides additional options to help you work with patterns. These options can help you with component organization and visualization, which are always key elements when you are working in an assembly.

Figure 15.13 shows the RMB menu for a component pattern. The selections relevant to patterns available on the RMB menu are as follows:

Dissolve Pattern: The Dissolve Pattern option removes the component instances from the pattern feature and puts them in the main part of the assembly FeatureManager. The components just become normal components in the assembly without the intelligence of the pattern feature placing them. The components are left in the assembly without any mates and are simply floating in position.

Add To New Folder: You can add patterns to folders. If you have a list of patterns at the end of an assembly, it may make sense to group them into related folders for the purpose of organization. This is the same as using folders for features, mates, or components.

Component pattern display options: You can change the appearance of individual component pattern instances either individually or collectively as a pattern feature using the Display pane, shown in the four columns to the right of the FeatureManager in Figure 15.11. Remember you can access the Display pane quickly by pressing the F8 key.

Component patterns and configurations: Individual instances of the component pattern also enable you to control configurations. After you create the pattern, you can select individual instances and change their configurations. This can be extremely useful if you have a mechanism subassembly shown in various positions—for example, patterned around an indexing dial.

FIGURE 15.13
The component
RMB menu

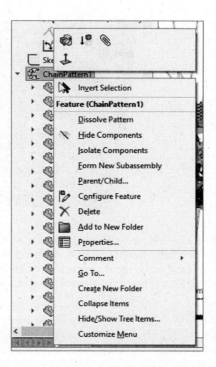

Tutorial: Creating Component Patterns

To learn how to create component patterns, follow these steps:

1. Open a new assembly. Create a new 3D sketch, and draw three lines from the origin out at odd angles so that they do not pick up horizontal or vertical automatic relations. Draw two of the lines; then rotate the view, press the Tab key, and draw the third line.

2. Apply sketch relations such that each line lies on a plane: one line on the Front, one on the Top, and one on the Right. Make sure none of the lines overlap.

3. Click Close to exit the sketch when you are finished.

4. Open the Pattern Part.sldprt part from the download materials. This part already contains several features that you can use to practice working with feature-driven component patterns.

5. Insert the part into the new assembly created in step 1. Locate the part at the assembly origin such that the part origin matches the assembly origin.

6. Place the part called Patterned Part.sldprt in the assembly.

7. Place the small part on the original feature of the rectangular pattern of round holes near the origin, as shown in Figure 15.14. All the original features are colored red. Remember that Alt+dragging the circular edge on the flat side of the part enables you to SmartMate the part to the round holes. SmartMate cannot help you with the rectangular or hex holes. For them, it may be best to show the sketch for the holes and place the part with respect to the sketch entities.

FIGURE 15.14
Placing the pat-
terned part

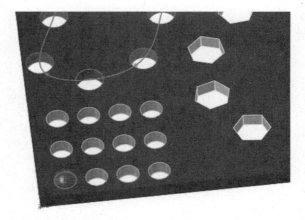

8. Create feature-driven patterns (Insert ➤ Component Pattern ➤ Feature Driven). Try to use each of the patterns from the pattern part. For each new pattern, make a copy of the patterned part and place it in one of the holes. Remember to use the Select Seed Position option to pick a feature-pattern instance instead of the original feature.

9. After you have created a few feature-driven patterns and have a better understanding of how it is done, right-click the top level of the assembly FeatureManager and select Collapse Items (near the bottom of the menu). The point of this example is simply to practice placing a part and patterning it with an existing feature pattern. The assembly will look like Figure 15.15 when you are done.

FIGURE 15.15
Several feature-
driven patterns

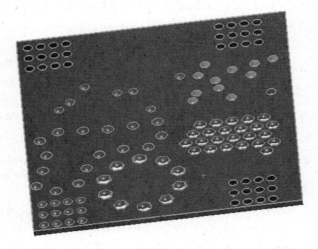

10. Create a local pattern (Insert ➤ Component Pattern ➤ Linear Pattern). Select one of the 3D sketch lines drawn in step 1 as a pattern direction.

11. Highlight the Components To Pattern selection box. Select the first part in the FeatureManager and then Shift+select the last pattern feature. This patterns everything in the assembly.

12. Make the spacing 4 inches with three instances.

13. Create a second direction using another of the sketch lines with 6-inch spacing and four instances.

14. Notice how the preview shows 12 instances of the patterned assembly. Select the option for Pattern Seed Only, and see how the preview changes to seven instances. Figure 15.16 shows this difference. Click OK to accept the feature.

FIGURE 15.16
Two direction patterns, one with and one without the Pattern Seed Only option

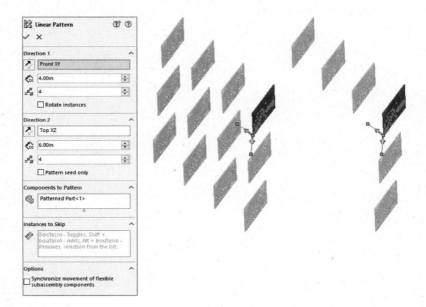

The Bottom Line

Performance and best practice are both issues that require compromise. Patterns can cause a performance reduction because of the nature of the references. However, they can also improve performance because the need for extra mates is reduced, and it is easier to simplify the assembly by suppressing the pattern feature.

Feature-driven patterns are driven by feature patterns and transgress best practice suggestions, but they also add a parametric link, which updates the component pattern automatically. In addition, they offer many more options that are driven by the pattern options available to features in a part.

Master It   Create a new part with multiple features, one of them being a hole of a 0.2" diameter. Make a pattern of the hole feature. Put this new part into an assembly with the part called Patterned Part.sldprt. Use the Patterned Part.sldprt in a pattern driven pattern, using the pattern of holes from the new part you just created.

Master It   Create a new assembly from a template that uses axes for the main X-, Y- and Z-directions. There is one called AxesAssembly.asldot in the MBD template folder. Insert an assembly such as one of the sample bicycle wheel assemblies, and pattern it in three directions.

Master It   Create a new assembly, and open a new sketch in the assembly. Create a closed-loop sketch that is bigger than 6 inches on a side where all of the elements are tangent (no small fillets or tangent arcs between lines).

Create a curve-driven pattern that uses the Patterned Part.sldprt to be patterned in two directions based on elements in the sketch.

Copy the sketch to a perpendicular plane in the assembly and create a chain pattern using the same part and the Distance Pitch method in the Chain Pattern PropertyManager.

Chapter 16

Working with Assembly Sketches and Layouts

When you're working on parts or assemblies, design work will often begin with 2D sketches. In the previous chapter, we used assembly sketches to drive patterns. You can follow through to 3D with data created in this phase by laying out the design as a sketch in the assembly before you start making actual 3D parts. When you use a single sketch or multiple sketches either as a visual guide or as a functional framework for a model, the visual guide is called a *layout*. Two-dimensional sketches are easy to produce and easy to use as the first step in design or modeling work. SolidWorks provides both formal and informal techniques for achieving this sort of effect.

The topic of layout sketches involves other topics, such as in-context modeling and master model techniques, which are covered in more detail later in this book. These topics are introduced here at a conceptual level to prepare you for the detailed information later.

In-context modeling involves the creation of relationships between parts in an assembly such that one part drives features on another part. Layout concepts apply to in-context modeling because you can use an assembly-level sketch to drive geometry within individual parts.

IN THIS CHAPTER, YOU WILL LEARN TO:

◆ Understand layout techniques

◆ Apply special treatment within an assembly

Looking at the Techniques

An informal technique called an *assembly layout sketch* has existed since early versions of SolidWorks. This technique has been included in the SolidWorks official training materials for many years, and it simply allows an assembly-level sketch. You can do one of several things with the sketch: build parts in place on it, use it to drive component patterns, mate parts to it, or use it to cut up a single part into multiple pieces. You can also adapt the assembly layout sketch technique for use as a single point of reference when you need to change multiple features within a single, highly complex part.

The formal assembly feature is called the Layout. The *Layout* is an assembly-level 3D sketch that displays a specific icon and has some special properties. Although the formal feature and the informal technique have similar names, they have very different functions.

In this book, the word *layout* is used with a lowercase "l" to refer to the informal assembly-based sketch layout method. The formal assembly-based 3D sketch with special properties is referred to with a capital "L" as a *Layout*. The Layout icon from SolidWorks may also accompany the formal feature.

Using the Assembly Layout Sketch

In SolidWorks, layout sketches are a great way to simulate mechanisms or to locate the major components of an assembly. Figure 16.1 shows three examples of assemblies created with the assistance of an assembly layout sketch.

FIGURE 16.1
Assembly layout sketches can be used in a wide range of applications.

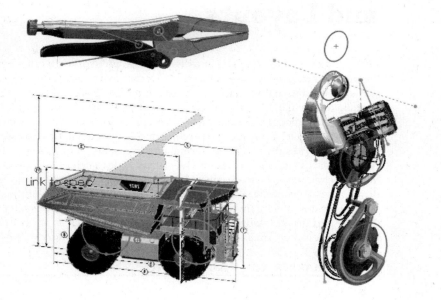

The bicycle example is used throughout this book, and the layout sketch was instrumental in establishing the geometry of the frame, wheels, and fork. Most of the components of a bicycle are purchased as off-the-shelf items that may come in different sizes but are not custom-created for individual bikes. The only parts that are generally custom-built for a particular size are the frame and possibly the fork. Therefore, to design the frame, you must lay out all the data that you are given for the individual components, such as wheels, stem, crank set, and seat. When you put everything together, additional pieces of information determine the frame geometry before the detail design of the frame can be started. You need to know the following:

◆ The size of the wheels

◆ The wheelbase (distance between the wheel centers)

◆ The length of the pedal arm

◆ The necessary clearance between the bottom of the pedal and the ground

◆ The head angle (effective pivot angle of the front fork)

◆ The distance between the center of the crank and the center of the rear wheel

The workflow for using an assembly layout sketch is as follows:

1. Open a new assembly.

2. Create sketches on the standard planes, or create new reference planes (you cannot use sketch pictures in assembly sketches).

3. Mate existing parts to the sketch and reference geometry (bottom-up method).

As previously mentioned, the assembly-level sketches from Chapter 15, "Patterning and Mirroring Components," that we used to create chain patterns were assembly layout sketches used in a slightly different way. Alternatively, you can build parts in place using the layout sketches as references (top-down or in-context method).

First, you start with the wheels. In this example, you want to design an urban utility bike based on mountain bike components, with dual suspension, but using narrow tires, and that means 26-inch wheels. You need a certain amount of ground clearance as the pedals rotate, and you need clearance between the rider's toes and the back side of the front wheel. You will design the frame to fit a rider who is about 5-feet, 8-inches tall.

The size information is important because the distance between the wheel centers (*wheelbase*) creates certain characteristics for riders of different heights. A longer wheelbase generally means a more stable and comfortable ride, but the bike is less maneuverable and heavier. In this case, based on other research, you want the wheelbase to be 41 inches.

Those specifications allow you to create the sketch shown in Figure 16.2.

FIGURE 16.2
Starting the bicycle
layout sketch

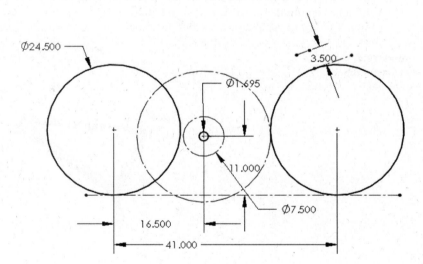

The next set of information you can put into the sketch has to do with the height of the top bar (which is important when you stand over the bike with your feet on the ground) and clearance between the frame and front wheel for the travel of the front suspension fork. This establishes most of what you need to know to design the frame, but you still have to work out the rear suspension arm.

With this information, the layout sketch looks like Figure 16.3.

FIGURE 16.3
Adding information to
the layout sketch

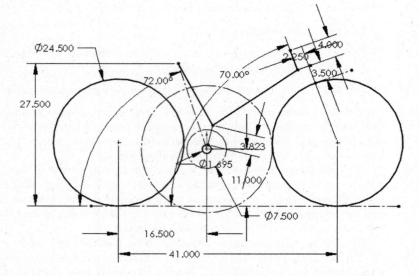

With this data, you have all the critical point locations to design the actual frame. The first step in creating the frame is to place reference geometry (sketch planes) from which to make sketches for the individual tubes of the frame. The frame will be a carbon fiber monocoque, but it still relies on tubular geometry, with smooth blends between the tubes to reduce stress concentrations. The layout with the planes and the initial tubes is shown in Figure 16.4.

FIGURE 16.4
Building the tubes
for the frame

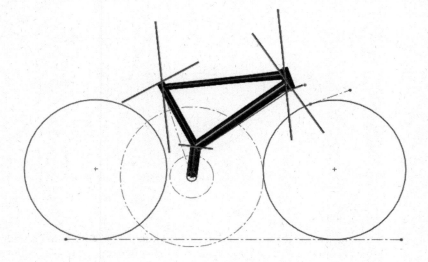

When all the tubes are created in-place in the assembly from the assembly layout sketch, the top of the assembly FeatureManager looks like Figure 16.5.

FIGURE 16.5

Examining the features built from the assembly layout sketch

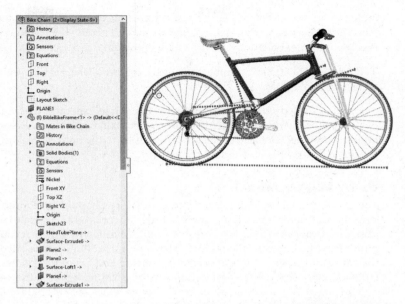

The arrow symbol (→) indicates that there is an external reference from the part to the assembly sketch. (External references are covered in more detail in Chapter 21, "Editing, Evaluating, and Troubleshooting Assemblies.") Using the assembly layout sketch technique, an external reference is made every time a relationship is made from the part to the assembly sketch. Many users prefer to avoid external references, mainly because of the file management issues they cause, the difficulty in repairing them when broken, and rebuild speed performance issues. However, references to an assembly sketch are more stable than references between two parts in an assembly.

When you use an assembly layout sketch for either the in-context part building or simply part positioning, the main advantage that it offers is to give you a single driving sketch that enables you to change the size, shape, and position of the parts. You can use as many layout sketches as you want, and you can make them on different sketch planes. This enables you to control parts in all directions.

CAUTION   When you use layout sketches, you may assume that the relationships are created such that the sketch drives everything else. However, nothing prevents you from using other things in the assembly to drive the sketch. You should avoid this type of conflict, called a *circular reference*. It can create sketches that change with every rebuild and can seriously impact rebuild times. When using any type of in-context relations, be careful to establish one or more driving entities, which are not in turn driven by other entities.

To take this a step further, avoid *daisy chaining*, where A drives B, B drives C, and so on. A better practice is to make A drive both B and C directly. This saves on rebuild times and troubleshooting.

One of the drawbacks of this technique is that you give up dynamic assembly motion. When you create the parts in the context of the assembly and create relationships between sketches or features and the assembly sketch, you cannot move the parts by just dragging them with the cursor. To move the parts, you must move the sketch and rebuild. The part does not move until the sketch is updated. If you need to combine layout functionality with dynamic assembly motion, you can add more instances of the in-context parts that are mated in the traditional way. However, when using this method, be very careful about which instance you make your edits to, because in-context relations are driven by the original instance.

TIP   I suggest defining the initial component as an envelope and using only copies of it for movement, drawings, and BOM.

Another drawback of the assembly-level sketch in general is that you cannot use a sketch picture inside the sketch. Sketch pictures can contain important reference information for building a model. The lack of this capability is certainly noticeable. You can put your sketch picture in a part or even a virtual component.

Using Master Model

The master model technique is covered in depth in Chapter 33, "Employing Master Model Techniques," but it is mentioned here because it works as an alternative method with the layout idea. The term *master model* can mean a couple of different things: It could be a single part where multiple bodies are created and then later split into multiple parts. Also, it is sometimes used as the name for inserting a single part with sketches and reference geometry into one or more other parts to have a single reference without creating that reference in the assembly.

This still creates an external reference, but it creates only a single external reference instead of possibly dozens, and updates of the inserted part can be locked. Performance problems with this technique are less serious. Also, if the file management fails and SolidWorks cannot find the inserted part, you can still keep working. SolidWorks keeps enough data in the child part that it does not need to constantly access the parent part.

The master model technique seems to have more advantages and fewer disadvantages than the methods that use assemblies. The dynamic assembly motion problem doesn't exist in a master model arrangement, nor does the lack of sketch picture functionality.

An example of this kind of work is shown in the derailleur assembly in Figure 16.6.

FIGURE 16.6

Using a master model to drive the individual parts of an assembly

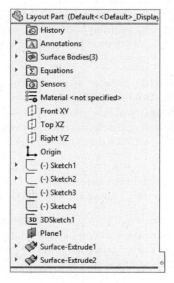
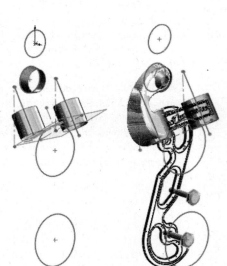

The part shown on the left is the master model. Notice that it contains sketch, plane, and surface data. The image on the right shows some parts superimposed on the master model part.

Using the Layout Feature

Due to some quirky behavior, the Layout feature is not generally employed by users. Most people who have been using the layout techniques described earlier in this chapter haven't switched to that method, even though it has replaced older methods in the official SolidWorks assemblies training manuals.

The Layout feature is a 3D sketch that is given special treatment within an assembly. It works best with sketch blocks. These are the special properties of the Layout feature when compared to a 2D assembly sketch:

- Uses a 3D sketch

- Works best when actively sketching on a plane

- Works best when the sketch making up a part is made into a sketch block

- Enables you to extrude the first feature of a part directly from the sketch block

- Enables sketch relations between blocks to turn into mates

- Permits unlimited dynamic assembly motion—parts move with the motion of blocks in the Layout

To initiate a Layout, click the Layout button on the Layout tab of the assembly CommandManager or activate it from the Insert menu. After you are in a Layout, SolidWorks puts you into a 3D sketch with the Front (XY) plane activated, so it displays a small grid.

For now, you should treat the 3D sketch as much like a set of 2D sketches as possible. The main difference is that you can double-click a different plane to start sketching on the new plane, and you always see this small grid when a plane is active.

You may find that 3D sketches have some limitations when you are working with Layouts. For example, they lack the capabilities to use sketch patterns and sketch pictures.

Using the Layout Workflow

With most functions in software of any type, you tend to get better results when you can use the software in the way it was intended. Generally, developers have a workflow in mind when they design the function itself and the interface. Working with the software is usually easier than working against the software.

Here is the general workflow for using the Layout feature:

1. Open a new or existing assembly.

2. Click the Layout toolbar button on the Layout tab of the CommandManager.

3. Sketch on the plane in the 3D sketch to create 2D sketches representing parts of a mechanism or other assembly.

4. Make selections of the sketch into blocks representing individual parts.

5. Insert multiple instances of the blocks to represent multiple instances of the parts.

6. Use sketch relations to put the blocks together like mating parts in an assembly.

7. Test the mechanism by dragging sketches. (Blocks function as a single sketch entity, so you can drag them within the sketch like parts in an assembly.)

8. Right-click the block (from inside or outside the Layout), and select Make Part From Block (also a button on the Layout toolbar).

NOTE The Make Part From Block command uses large and small icons that are slightly different. The large icon was shown at the beginning of this "Using the Layout Feature" section.

Working with Virtual Components

Virtual components always exist with in-context workflows and frequently with the Layout workflow. *Virtual components* are parts or subassemblies that are created within the assembly. You can save a virtual component externally, and you can make an externally saved part into a virtual component. The advantages of virtual components are that you don't have to worry about saving out additional files and that the assembly will never lose track of any virtual component.

Some SolidWorks users use virtual components to represent non-geometric parts such as glue or paint. Anytime you choose Insert ➤ Component ➤ New Part from the menus and select a template and a plane to put the part on, the part is placed immediately into the assembly, and you can start working without worrying about having to save the assembly and the part. This saves lots of time initially. Later, when you save the assembly, SolidWorks will prompt you to save the parts externally and name them as well, or you may choose to leave the parts internal to the assembly.

Virtual components are named `Part1 Assem1`, where `Part1` and `Assem1` are default names. You can easily rename the part by clicking the RMB menu and selecting Rename Part. You cannot do this for external parts (unless this option is enabled). If you make an external part virtual, the name in the assembly becomes `Copy of filename Assem1`, where `filename` is the name of the external file. The name of the assembly is always included (and cannot be removed) to ensure that if you have subassemblies that also have virtual components, you always have unique filenames for all the parts.

Virtual components can also be accessed in their own window, which makes them easier to edit for some purposes. Bills of Materials (BOMs) and numbered balloons work correctly with virtual components, but they cannot have their own drawings.

BEST PRACTICE

A best practice is to save any parts that will be a permanent part of the assembly as external files. Virtual components should be limited to temporary parts or possibly non-geometrical parts, like BOM-only parts such as glue or paint. A good general rule is that if you need to have a drawing of it, don't leave it as a virtual component.

Balancing Advantages and Limitations

In theory, the Layout feature has several advantages:

- You can make parts from blocks within the Layout.

- You can move parts by moving blocks in the Layout.

- It is a great way to structure your relations within an assembly.

- A single 3D sketch doesn't have the history concerns that multiple 2D sketches have.

- It is useful for motion analysis studies in 2D, using stick sketches, before any 3D components are created.

In practice, this feature needs some enhancements before it is ready for use on real assemblies. Using 2D sketches as assembly layout sketches may still be a better idea than trying to avoid the following limitations of the formal Layout feature:

- The 3D sketch used for Layout has all the limitations that come with 3D sketches.

- Sketch relations are listed in the Mates folder.

- Gaining access to edit the Layout after it has been closed requires a method you don't expect from a sketch: You click the Layout button on the toolbar rather than right-click and edit an icon in the FeatureManager.

- It requires that you use blocks to access all the functionality.

- A fully defined 3D sketch with blocks is very unstable.

- Part creation from blocks doesn't save time.

- You cannot paste copied sketch entities from a 2D sketch into the Layout.

- You cannot use sketch pictures in the Layout.

- You cannot use auto-dimension (or polygons or ellipses) in the Layout.

Although the formal Layout feature has serious advantages over regular layout sketches, at this time, the limitations outweigh the advantages. The rest of the discussion on layouts addresses the generic layout technique rather than the formal feature.

Tutorial: Working with a Layout

In this tutorial, you will use regular assembly sketches to lay out and build a tooling die.

1. Open the `Chapter 16 tutorial layout start.sldasm` assembly from the download material. Notice that three layout sketches and some of the parts have been added already. The existing parts are virtual components, saved inside the assembly, so there are no referenced part files.

2. Click Add New Part under the Insert Components dropdown on the Assembly tab. The cursor appears with a green check mark; in the lower-left corner, the taskbar prompts you

to select a plane on which to place the Front plane of the part. A sketch automatically opens on that plane. Click the Front plane of the assembly in the FeatureManager.

3. Click the Corner Rectangle sketch tool from the Sketch toolbar. Create a rectangle from the two corners indicated in Figure 16.7. It may be helpful to switch to the Front view before drawing.

FIGURE 16.7
Creating a new plate in the context of an assembly with layout sketches

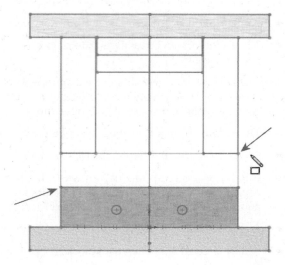

4. Extrude the rectangle using the Up To Vertex end condition for both Direction 1 and Direction 2. Select sketch endpoints in the Plane Depth Layout sketch for both directions so the new plate matches the other existing plates. You will need to rotate cut of the Front view to make these selections.

   Be careful not to click model faces, edges, or vertices when creating these depth references. Make sure that all your selections are sketch entities, and not solid geometry.

5. Click the Exit Edit Part icon in the Confirmation Corner (the upper-right corner of the SolidWorks graphics window). Right-click the new part in the FeatureManager, and select Rename Part. Rename it **Plate4**. You can also use the Windows standard method of slowly double-clicking (or pressing F2) to rename parts. The "Chapter 16 tutorial layout start" part of the name is automatically added because this is still a virtual part. Assign a material from the Appearances tab for the new plate.

6. Follow the procedure outlined in steps 2 through 5 for the four remaining plates, as shown in Figure 16.8. To summarize the steps again, you add the new part, create a sketch, and extrude the block.

NOTE   Be careful with the plates labeled 5, 6, 7, and 8. There is a clearance gap between the sides of the 7 and 8 plates and the vertical plates 5 and 6.

FIGURE 16.8
All the plates controlled
by the layout sketches

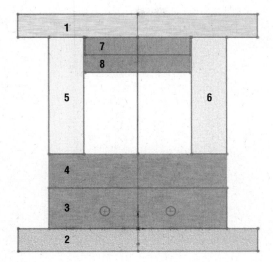

7. Reorient the view to the Top view (Ctrl+5), and make sure you can see the Pin Layout sketch.

8. Select the top face of Plate 1, and click the Hole Series toolbar. The Hole Series may be hidden under the Assembly Features flyout on the Assembly tab of the CommandManager.

9. Place two sketch points at the centers of the circles, as shown in Figure 16.9. Make sure that the two points are both over the same plate, 5 or 6. You cannot cut both plate 5 and plate 6 in the same Hole Series feature. Use the settings shown in Figure 16.9.

   Make sure the holes are Counterbored, ANSI Metric, Socket Head Cap Screw, M10, with a head clearance of 0.10 inch. All other conditions should follow Figure 16.9.

10. Place two more new holes on the other side. Make the parts transparent so that you can see how the holes have been placed.

11. Create a Plane feature. Make the new plane parallel to the Top plane of the assembly, and coincident to the line indicated in the Plate Depth Layout sketch in Figure 16.10 (best displayed in Right view). Rename the new plane **Sprue Bushing Seat**.

12. Create a new part on the Sprue Bushing Seat plane.

13. Activate the Convert Entities sketch tool, select the large (approximately 4-inch diameter) circle from the Pin Layout sketch, and convert it into the sketch plane of the new part.

14. Draw a ½-inch circle in the center (at the origin). Extrude the sketch 0.875 inch so it protrudes from Plate 2.

15. Exit the Edit Part mode (using the Confirmation Corner). Rename the new part **Sprue Bushing**.

16. Click Plate2, and select Edit Part from the shortcut toolbar.

17. Open a new sketch on the Sprue Bushing Seat plane (which is part of the assembly, not part of the part).

FIGURE 16.9
Placing screw holes through multiple parts in the die

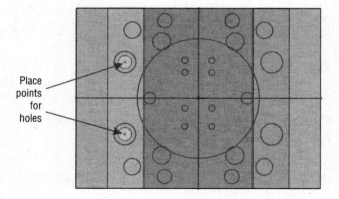

Place points for holes

FIGURE 16.10
Creating a plane in
the assembly driven
by the layout sketch

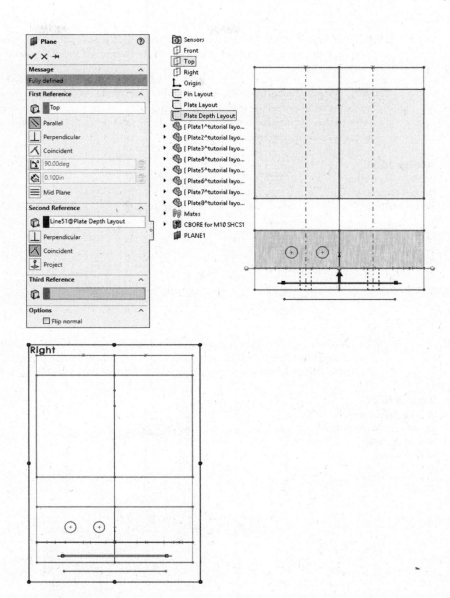

18. Select the large circle used in step 13, and use the Offset sketch tool to offset the circle 0.005 inch to the outside. Create a Through All cut that comes out the exposed side of Plate2, clearing an area for the Sprue Bushing. You may need to switch to Wireframe display to accomplish this.

19. Apply a chamfer to the outer edge of the new cut, 0.010 inch.

20. Exit Edit Part mode, and save the assembly to a new folder by choosing File ➤ Save As. Click the Save All button, and then select the Save Externally option, as shown in Figure 16.11.

NOTE When you start working with in-context relations, the file management issues become more important. Simply saving the assembly in step 20 to a new name will disconnect all of the relationships between the parts and the assembly. Refer to Chapter 20, "Modeling in Context," for more in-context file management information.

FIGURE 16.11
Saving the internal virtual components to external parts

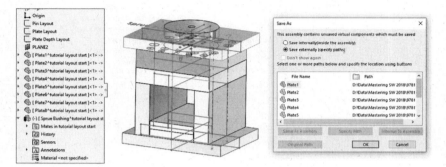

21. Double-click the Plate Layout sketch, and change the 5.836-inch dimension to **6** inches. Change the 7.244-inch dimension to **7** inches. Make sure the model rebuilds, and watch the individual parts update. Figure 16.12 shows these dimensions for reference.

FIGURE 16.12
Editing layout sketch dimensions to drive the size of the individual parts

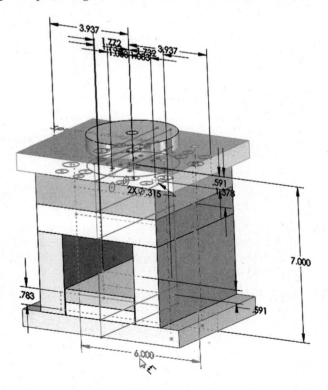

The Bottom Line

Laying out an assembly with reference sketches is a more disciplined way of working that can help you avoid some of the complications of external references and in-context design work. It is up to you to decide whether the informal 2D layout sketches are preferable to the formal 3D sketch-based Layout feature. Both offer tools to control positions of parts and even features of parts within an assembly.

Traditional assembly-modeling methods where each part is located by mates from another part do not stand up well against changes in the parts themselves. The main goals of the layout methods are centralization of control and stability of changes. I invite you to explore some of these methods using the tools you have learned in this chapter.

Master It   Use an assembly Layout to create a four-bar link and assign parts to the blocks in the Layout sketch. To remind you, the workflow for Layout is like this:

1. Open the assembly.

2. Click the Layout tool.

3. Sketch three bars of differing lengths.

4. Create three separate sketch blocks, one using each bar.

5. Assemble the bars to create a four-bar link mechanism. (Yes, a four-bar link can have only three bars, the fourth bar is ground.) If you cannot see how to do this in a 3D sketch, refer to the downloaded example for this chapter for hints.

6. Test the motion of the assembled link blocks.

7. Exit the Layout.

8. Create parts on each of the blocks.

9. Use the sketches in the parts to create solid geometry for the bars.

10. In the assembly, test the motion using dynamic assembly motion (dragging parts).

Master It   Use the assembly you created (or the downloaded example named 4-bar Link Layout solution.sldasm) to first rename and then save out the internal virtual parts so they are external, stand-alone parts.

Master It   Edit the Layout from the previous exercise. Change the length of one of the Links. This will involve first clicking the Layout tool, and then editing one of the blocks. When you exit the block, the layout sketch and then the solid geometry should both update. Perform a test by exiting the layout and making sure the motion is still correct.

Chapter 17

Using Assembly Tools

SolidWorks assemblies enable you to take advantage of several tools in addition to the standard and best known functionality. The tools covered in this chapter are general tools that have wide application throughout assembly topics.

IN THIS CHAPTER, YOU WILL LEARN TO:

- ◆ Assemble without mates
- ◆ Use interfering options
- ◆ Use Performance Evaluation
- ◆ Defeature in assemblies
- ◆ Use sensors
- ◆ Align holes

Placing Parts without Mates

Assembly mates are great tools, but they aren't the only tools for placing parts in an assembly. Sometimes, you might need to place parts without applying a mate, such as when you are setting up an animation and the mate would prevent the animation from working correctly. You might also want to place a part and allow motion of the part it is placed relative to while making sure the part itself remains stationary.

In a perfect world, assembly mates are well controlled and easy to understand. But in reality, sometimes things happen that you cannot explain. If you build an assembly without mates (with the parts simply positioned in space using any technique that works), the parts are guaranteed not to move unless you accidentally move one.

NOTE   A setting found at Tools ➤ Assemblies enables you to turn off the click-and-drag method to move parts. It requires you to click a toolbar button to enable the cursor to move parts. If you have parts in your assembly that are placed with nothing holding their location, If you have a 3D mouse device, one of the options available is for the 3D mouse to move parts in the assembly when one is selected. When this method is used to move a part, the SolidWorks Undo command cannot undo moves made in this way.

On the other hand, if your design changes and you want a set of parts to move together, they will not. You have to change their positions by whatever means you used to get them to their current positions.

As a final touch for an assembly of parts that have nothing holding them in place, you might consider fixing the parts in place. Using the Fix and Float commands with parts is easy, and knowing that parts will not move brings peace of mind.

There is also a Locked mate, which creates a relationship between selected parts, but allows those parts to move relative to other parts.

Using the Move Component Options

The Move Component tool has several options for locating parts without using mates. These options are shown in Figure 17.1.

FIGURE 17.1
Selecting a positioning option with
Move Component

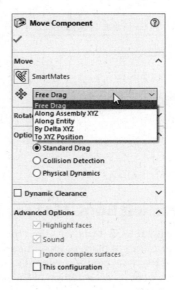

This section describes how to use the Free Drag, Along Assembly XYZ, and Along Entity methods with the Move Component command, but these methods are also available in the Rotate section of the Move Component PropertyManager interface.

Both Move and Rotate enable you to select Standard Drag, Collision Detection, or Physical Dynamics under the Options section. Collision Detection and Physical Dynamics are described in a later section of this chapter. The methods described in this section for moving components assume the use of the Standard Drag option.

USING FREE DRAG

The Free Drag option of Move Component enables you to simply move the part around the screen by dragging with the cursor. This is the same as the default function of the cursor when in an assembly. Click a part and drag. The part follows any existing mates and moves the part in 3D space. For a part that is completely unconstrained, it moves in a plane parallel to the screen. If you are viewing the assembly such that the screen isn't parallel to any standard plane, the part you are moving may be moving in and out of the assembly or in some other unexpected manner. If you have some mates applied to the part, it is less likely to do something odd. You might consider using the Four View option to move parts using this method.

Free Drag is not a great method to precisely position parts, but it is okay if you are just trying to position something visually as a prop for a rendering.

Moving Along Assembly XYZ

When you drag a part in an assembly with the Along Assembly XYZ option enabled, the part can move only along the X-axis, the Y-axis, or the Z-axis at one time. It can't move at an angle. To use this option properly, you should use an orthogonal view so it's easier for you to get the part going in the correct direction and easier to see which direction it's heading. Again, using the Four View display option would also be helpful.

If you want to change directions, you must stop dragging and then restart the drag, getting the initial direction of the drag in the direction you want to move the part.

Moving Along Entity

The Along Entity option for Move Component is similar to the Along Assembly XYZ option except that you select a custom direction and the part can move only back and forth along that direction. The custom direction must be either linear or planar, and it can be an edge, axis, face, plane, sketch line, and so forth.

Moving By Delta XYZ

The By Delta XYZ method is the first that offers direct numerical input for moving parts. *Delta* means *change*, so the numbers you enter change the position of the part along the specified axis. Figure 17.2 shows the PropertyManager interface for this part-moving option.

Because this is the first move option that uses an Apply button, shown in Figure 17.2, you can move a selection of parts multiple times just by entering a number in one of the boxes and clicking Apply multiple times. Each time you click Apply, it moves by the amounts listed in the three boxes ΔX, ΔY, or ΔZ. Remember that you can create selection sets—which can include parts and subassemlbies—to save in the FeatureManager, which include parts in an assembly.

This does not work the same way as the Modify dialog box for dimensions, where if you change the number and click the check mark, the dimension changes from, say, 3 inches to 5 inches. If you have 3 in the ΔX box, and click Apply, it moves 3 inches. If you then change ΔX to 5 and click Apply again, it moves 5 inches for a total of 8 inches. If the second time you used –5 instead of 5, the total movement would be 2 inches in the opposite direction from the original 3 inches.

Also notice that the interface does not have a selection box to tell it which parts you want to move. To select a part to move, you can select a face from the graphics window, or select a part or subassembly in the FeatureManager. Clicking Apply moves all the parts selected.

You can even change selections while the command is active. So you can move one selection of parts and then move a different selection.

FIGURE 17.2
Using the By Delta XYZ
option to move parts

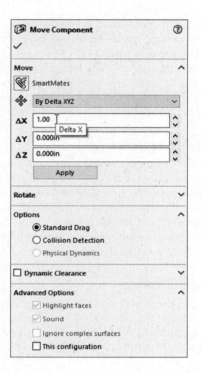

USING TO XYZ POSITION

Using the To XYZ Position option is also different from the By Delta XYZ option. You may find that this option has a few quirks. First, it is intended to move the selected point of the selected part to the XYZ location you keyed into the X, Y, and Z boxes.

Again, this PropertyManager does not have a selection box to list parts to move or points to move to the specified XYZ location. That makes this interface a little more limited than some of the other options.

If you do not select a point, SolidWorks assumes you want to move the origin of the part. If you have multiple parts selected, it assumes you want to move the center of gravity (CG) of the combined parts.

If, in a previous move, you did have a point selected on an instance of the part and you then moved a different instance, SolidWorks assumes you wanted to position the same point on the second instance of the part.

The rules for which point gets positioned are not spelled out and are too difficult to follow. If I were to use this option, I would position only origins or points, and if I were to change between origins and points, I would cancel the command and restart it.

You can select multiple parts by selecting them from the assembly FeatureManager; however, it does not appear to allow you to select points to position anymore.

If you select a point on a part and then want to change to a different point on the same part, you can't do that. You have to first select a point on another part, and then select a different point on the original part.

In general, this option appears to be underdeveloped. This means that it may not have all the flexibility you are looking for, or it might appear to have quirks if you don't follow the perfect workflow process every time.

USING MOVE WITH TRIAD

The Move With Triad tool is different from the Move/Copy Bodies feature. Move/Copy Bodies is found in the part environment and is intended to help move individual solid and surface bodies by using a Triad with arrows, wings, and rings, shown in Figure 17.3. Another difference between Move/Copy Bodies and Move With Triad is that Move/Copy Bodies creates a feature in the tree, but Move Component does not.

FIGURE 17.3
The Triad for Move Bodies works the same as it does for Move With Triad.

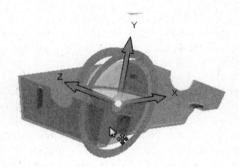

Move With Triad, unlike Move Component, is available only from the RMB menu on parts and subassemblies in the graphics window and the FeatureManager. On some menus (such as RMB in the FeatureManager, but not RMB in a graphics window), you will have to expand the menu if you are using truncated menus.

Move With Triad enables you to move components by dragging along the orange axes, on the wings (transparent planes), or around the rings of a Triad symbol in the display. To select which entity is being used to move or rotate the part, move the cursor around the Triad, and various elements will turn blue. You can reposition the Triad itself (to rotate around a different center) by dragging and dropping the white ball at the origin of the Triad.

Using the For Positioning Only Option

The Mate PropertyManager has an option called Use For Positioning Only, which is shown in Figure 17.4.

This option has been in the software for a long time, but it may not be taught in the standard SolidWorks reseller class or demonstrated in most tutorials on the market. This option essentially allows you to go through the motions of creating a mate; however, when you are finished, the part you are positioning will be in place, but it will have no mate.

The result is similar to using any of the tools described in the preceding section of this chapter, but you don't have to calculate a position or movement amount; the new position is driven by geometry on another part.

FIGURE 17.4
Using the Use For
Positioning
Only option

The people I have talked to who use this option tend to use it for visualization—to help see the part in position before they commit to a method of attaching it. Usually, people who use the positioning-only option wind up mating the part completely later, but they may consider multiple mate strategies that achieve the desired goal more efficiently or cleanly.

Why would you want to go through all the work of creating a mate and then not have a mate to show for it? Possibly to avoid deleting it later or to avoid conflicts that it might cause later. For example, when trying to define the initial position between a chain link and a sprocket, you want the link to be concentric to the sprocket tooth gap, but a concentric mate would block the movement of the chain when you are using a Rack and Pinion mate. If you use a concentric mate for positioning and then add a rack and pinion, everything is peachy. If you are working in reverse, the part you are placing without the mate should be the fixed part, so you place it, fix it, and mate other parts to it. Sometimes with animations, you want parts placed correctly without a mate to interfere with the animated motion of the part.

So why wouldn't you create the mate and then just suppress it? Configurations can be complicated enough without adding a configuration just to remove a mate. One case in which the position-only option might be used is with packaging design. You could place the packaging around the product without mates so you can use in-context techniques without ill effects later.

Building Parts in Place

Building parts in place, like the method shown in Chapter 16, "Working with Assembly Sketches and Layouts," is a relatively easy way to place parts without mating them. This technique might be called *top-down*, or in-context, and is dealt with in other chapters of this book. I mention it here to introduce the method while pointing to other chapters for the details.

Using Proximity Tools

SolidWorks has several tools that are meant to detect proximity between parts in an assembly:

◆ Interference Detection

◆ Clearance Verification

◆ Collision Detection

◆ Physical Dynamics

◆ Sensors

Using Interference Detection

Interference Detection is available through the menus at Tools ➤ Evaluate ➤ Interference Detection. You can also find it in the Evaluate tab of the CommandManager. It is a stand-alone tool that finds existing interferences in an assembly. The PropertyManager for Interference Detection is shown in Figure 17.5, after detecting interferences in an assembly.

FIGURE 17.5
Finding interferences in an assembly

You can use two different types of selections for Interference Detection. The first type is to simply select the top-level assembly from the assembly FeatureManager. This checks all the parts in the assembly for interference. The second method is to select individual components (parts or subassemblies) from the assembly FeatureManager. In either case, click the Calculate button when you are finished with the selection and ready to see the interferences.

DISPLAYING THE RESULTS

The default result display (shown in Figure 17.6) shows each interference with the pair of interfering components underneath the interference. Interferences are listed with the size (volume) of the interferences.

FIGURE 17.6
Displaying interference results with the Component View option

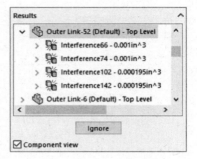

Remember that you cannot judge the size of a number just by looking at the left-most digit. The numbers are listed in scientific notation, so 1.05e-005in^3 means 1.05×10^{-5} cubic inches (read that as 1.05 times 10 to the negative 5 power), or 0.0000105 cubic inches. Interferences are not listed in any order, but can be sorted by size.

As you click each interference, the interfering volume highlights in red in the graphics window. You can also right-click an interference and select Zoom To Selection if the interference is very small.

IGNORING INTERFERENCES

You can ignore an interference by right-clicking the interference in the Results panel and selecting Ignore from the menu or by clicking the Ignore button in the Results panel. You can also ignore interferences Smaller Than. After an interference is ignored, it is simply removed from the list. You can Shift+select or Ctrl+select to ignore multiple interferences at once. A counter immediately under the Results list keeps track of how many ignored interferences there are. After an interference is ignored, you can get it back into the Results panel by enabling the Show Ignored Interferences option in the Options panel. Ignored interferences are displayed as grayed out. After the grayed-out interferences are shown, you can select them in the list and use the Un-ignore button or select them from the RMB menu.

USING COMPONENT VIEW

The Component View option at the bottom of the Results panel toggles from the default display, where components are listed under each interference, to the component view in which all components are listed. The interference volumes are listed under the component, and under the interference is listed the other interfering part, as shown in Figure 17.6.

SELECTING OPTIONS

The Options panel is shown in Figure 17.5. Most of the options are self-explanatory. There are, however, a couple of items to note: You cannot do body interference checks in multibody parts, but you can include multibodies in the assembly interference detection.

In addition, when the Make Interfering Parts Transparent option is used with the display option in the Non-interfering Components panel, the entire assembly is shown as transparent except the interfering volume, which is displayed opaque. The Make Interfering Parts Transparent option is turned on by default, and the noninterfering-components default option is Use Current.

DISPLAY OPTIONS FOR NONINTERFERING COMPONENTS

The final panel of the Interference Detection PropertyManager controls the display of noninterfering components. You have the option of making them wireframe, hidden, or transparent, or you can leave the display properties alone. I personally prefer the Hidden option because it offers the most contrast with the interfering parts to make the interferences stand out.

You can also eliminate fasteners and cosmetic threads that can create false or unwanted interferences. Note that the software does not give the option to distinguish between screw heads and threads. Interferences from threads may not be significant, while head interferences are.

Using Clearance Verification

Clearance Verification enables you to check that clearances between parts in an assembly or model faces are at least a certain amount. The tool lists any clearances that are less than the clearance you specify, which means it identifies interferences as well as clearances. This is for clearances between static parts, not between moving parts. For clearances between moving parts, use the Dynamic Clearance option in the Move Component PropertyManager described later in this chapter.

You can find the Clearance Verification tool in the menus at Tools ➤ Clearance Verification or on the Evaluate tab of the CommandManager. The Clearance Verification PropertyManager is shown in Figure 17.7.

The secret to using Clearance Verification is to understand what it measures. Clearance Verification is concerned only with clearances *less* than the distance you specify. This means that parts that touch or interfere are listed as "Clearances" in the Results box.

If you want to find the minimum clearance between two parts in an assembly, this tool can do that, but you must enter a value in the Minimum Acceptable Clearance box that is larger than the clearance you are looking for. A value of zero will return all interferences. If you are looking for the minimum clearance between two parts, you may get a more intuitive result using the Dynamic Clearance options, which are part of the Move Component tool.

The Clearance Verification PropertyManager shown in Figure 17.7 is in many ways similar or identical to the Interference Detection PropertyManager (refer to Figure 17.5). The results can be fairly similar as well.

TIP You can use the Measure tool to find the clearance between part components. Just select two part components from the tree and start the Measure tool.

FIGURE 17.7
Using the Clearance
Verification
PropertyManager

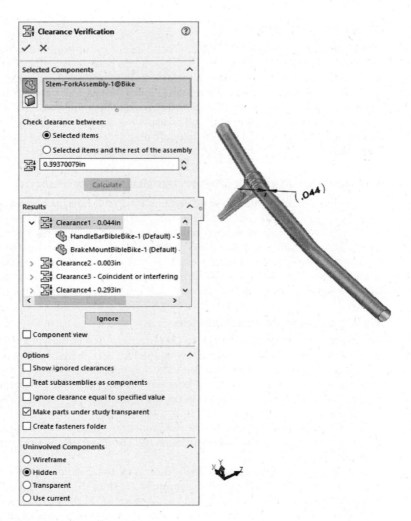

Using Dynamic Clearance

The Dynamic Clearance options are part of the Move Component tool. Move Component is on the Assembly toolbar. Dynamic Clearance has a panel of its own in the middle of the Move Component PropertyManager.

To use Dynamic Clearance, activate the selection box shown in Figure 17.8 and pick two parts that can move relative to one another. In this case, I'm using the fork assembly from the Bike model in the download files, selecting the fork and the stem.

The Dynamic Clearance panel has an icon that looks exactly like the Clearance Verification icon, described earlier in this chapter. Clicking the icon enables you to enter a Clearance value. This Clearance value is the minimum clearance that the tool allows when you move the parts around. If the clearance reaches that value, the motion will stop.

Notice the dimension in parentheses (1.347) in Figure 17.8. This is the minimum clearance between the stem and the fork, and it changes dynamically as you move one of the parts. If you specify a minimum clearance value, SolidWorks stops the motion of the part you are dragging when the clearance between the parts reaches that number.

FIGURE 17.8
Using the Dynamic
Clearance options in
Move Component

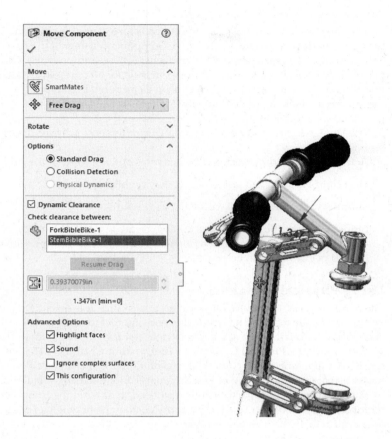

Using Collision Detection

Collision Detection is another tool available in the Move Component PropertyManager, and it
can be used at the same time as Dynamic Clearance. You turn on Collision Detection in the
Options panel of the Move Component PropertyManager. When you activate it, you get several
additional options, shown in Figure 17.9.

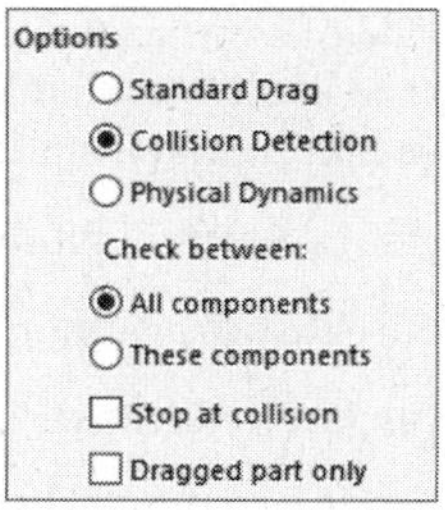

FIGURE 17.9
The Collision Detection
option activates
other options.

You can use Collision Detection to find collisions caused by dynamic assembly motion (dragging parts on the screen with Move Component) using all the parts in the assembly (All Components) or just selected components (These Components). Obviously, there is a performance (speed) cost to calculating collisions for all parts, so especially for larger assemblies, you should limit the parts used in Collision Detection if possible.

You can also set an option that will stop motion at a collision, which will help you visualize more realistic motion of the mechanism.

The Dragged Part Only option calculates interferences only for the dragged part with those around it.

Activating Collision Detection also activates other options in the Advanced Options panel:

Highlight Faces: When faces collide, they highlight.

Sound: When parts collide, you will hear a sound.

Ignore Complex Surfaces: Faces that are created by loft, boundary, or other complex methods are more time-consuming when calculating interferences. To prevent diminished performance these types of faces can be ignored.

Using Physical Dynamics

The name Physical Dynamics may be a bit misleading. It is essentially unconstrained, free motion, and collision of parts where the parts interact to some extent. It is not any sort of real analytical dynamics. Physical Dynamics does not take into account initial velocity or momentum.

You cannot use Physical Dynamics with Dynamic Clearance. The only adjustment with it is a sensitivity adjustment that controls the resolution of the reactions. Because it is a live tool (all the reactions happen in real time as you drag parts on the screen), calculation speed is a factor.

Physical Dynamics is very useful if you need to find out if a component can be installed in or removed from a confined space. One of my customers modeled an engine in place and wondered if it could actually be installed through the narrow window on-site. I used Physical Dynamics to test the route and guide the engine out.

Using Sensors

Sensors in SolidWorks keep track of several measurable values and notify you when a value deviates from high and low limits you can specify. You can use sensors in both parts and assemblies. The types of sensors available in assemblies are

Simulation Data: Select one of a number of common simulation results to act as a trigger. (A simulation study must be available, so this sensor type is not available in SolidWorks Standard—you must have Simulation installed, licensed, and running for this to work.)

Mass: When the mass satisfies a certain relation, the sensor displays a flag.

Volume: When the volume satisfies a certain relation, the sensor displays a flag.

Surface Area: When the surface area satisfies a certain relation, the sensor displays a flag.

Dimension: You can use reference dimensions or driving dimensions, including dimensions calculated by equations.

Interference Detection: SolidWorks looks for the interference of static parts in assemblies.

Measurement: Any value you would normally take from the Measure tool can be tracked.

Proximity: If you establish a sensor location, direction, and acting distance, the sensor returns a True value if a selected part passes through that sensor.

To add a sensor to an assembly, you must first have the Sensors folder in the assembly FeatureManager, as shown in Figure 17.10. FeatureManager If it is not there, you can activate it at Tools ➤ Options ➤ FeatureManager and make sure the Sensors folder is set to Show.

FIGURE 17.10
Activating the Sensors folder in the FeatureManager

To add a sensor, right-click the Sensor folder at the top of the assembly FeatureManager and select Add Sensor. Sensors can also be added through the Measure Tool interface. The Sensor PropertyManager is shown in Figure 17.11, with the sensor-type drop-down list expanded.

FIGURE 17.11
Adding a sensor to an assembly

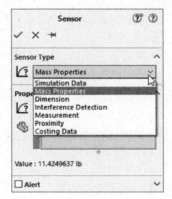

After you have selected a type of sensor to add to the assembly, you then select the parts affected, set the options, and set the alert. The alert shows a notification balloon if the value returned by the sensor matches the expression you establish in the Alert panel of the Sensor PropertyManager.

For example, when the reference dimension shown in Figure 17.12 changes and becomes less than a certain value, SolidWorks displays an alert on the Sensors folder.

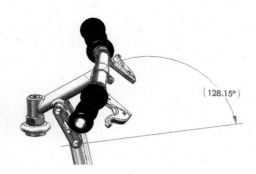

Selecting Components

In the SolidWorks Tools menu for assemblies, in addition to the normal selection methods such as Box, Lasso, Select All, there is an entry called Component Selection that offers a wide range of methods, as shown in Figure 17.13. You can also access these tools by expanding the flyout toolbar from the Select icon in the standard toolbar or other places it is used, such as the Title Bar toolbar.

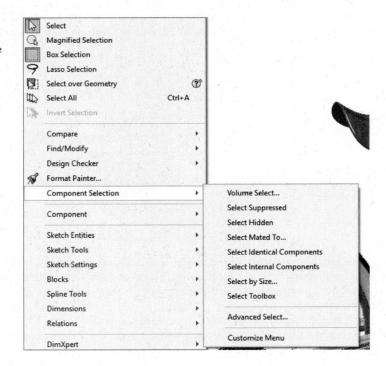

SolidWorks does not have icon-driven activations for these tools, but they are available in the Customize ➤ Keyboard interface so you can make hotkey shortcuts to them.

Selecting with a Volume

The Volume Select option has no dialog box or PropertyManager interface. The workflow for this command goes like this:

1. Put the assembly into a view orthogonal to a rectangular volume that you would like to create to select parts of the assembly.

2. Preselect items to determine where the rectangular volume starts. Preselecting a point makes the face of volume go through the point; preselecting a plane makes the face of the volume coincident with that face.

3. Initiate the Volume Selection command through the menus at Tools ➤ Component Selection ➤ Volume Select. Then go on to step 4 even though nothing appears to happen— no interface, no change to the screen, no special cursor.

4. With the cursor, drag a rectangle on the screen (as you would to box select items in a sketch). After you drag the rectangle, SolidWorks will display a temporary volume and change to an isometric view. If you draw the original rectangle in an isometric view, the rectangular volume will line up with the screen (not the standard planes), and SolidWorks will rotate the view somewhat to give you access to all three dimensions of the temporary volume. SolidWorks will display arrows on the volume so you can tug and pull the faces to position it to select parts.

5. Use the arrows to resize the resulting volume on the screen, as shown in Figure 17.14. SolidWorks will select any part that is completely within the volume. The selection is made when the volume contains the part; you don't have to do anything to activate the selection. Clicking outside the volume will dismiss the temporary display of the volume, but it will retain the selection. While the selection is active, you can use the commands from the RMB menus as usual.

FIGURE 17.14
Sizing the selec-
tion volume

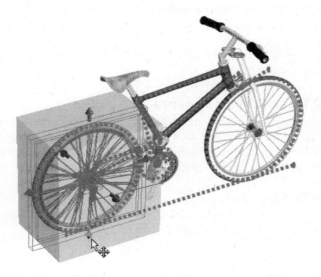

Selecting Suppressed Components

To select all the parts in an assembly that are currently suppressed, you can use the command available at Tools ➤ Component Selection ➤ Select Suppressed. This command does not have a toolbar button, but you can assign a hotkey to it through the Tools ➤ Customize ➤ Keyboard interface.

The only indication that parts have been selected is in the FeatureManager. After the parts are selected, you can use RMB options with the selection.

Selecting Hidden Components

You can select hidden components just as you would select suppressed components. Again, this command has no interface or toolbar icon, but it can be linked to a hotkey. Remember that to hide a part quickly, put the cursor over it and press Tab. To show the part, put the cursor where the part should be and press Shift+Tab.

Selecting Subassemblies

The easiest and most traditional way to select a subassembly is to select it from the FeatureManager. You can also right-click any component in the graphics area and select the Select Subassembly option, and SolidWorks will display the assembly context toolbar. Subassemblies can also be selected through the Breadcrumbs interface because the current selection, such as a face, is identified by breadcrumbs as being part of a feature, body, part, subassembly, and so on in the current assembly.

Selecting Parts Mated to Another Part

The Tools ➤ Component Selection ➤ Select Mated To command, as the name suggests, selects any part mated to the part you select after you execute the command. There is no interface and no indication of what to do after you select the Select Mated To menu option, but for whatever part you click next, SolidWorks selects all the parts mated to it.

Selecting Identical Components

Select Identical Components can be activated with either preselection or post-selection methods. With post-selection, it uses a PropertyManager to prompt you to select a component. With preselection, there is no PropertyManager. The identical components are highlighted in the FeatureManager without a count.

Selecting Internal Components

The criteria for what SolidWorks means by "internal components" are not well spelled out. If you run this selection method on the Bike model, it selects a couple of parts that I would not consider to be strictly internal parts (parts under the seat and the small chain-ring on the crank). You may have to experiment with this tool to get the results you expect.

Selecting Toolbox Parts

The tool found at Tools ➤ Component Selection ➤ Select Toolbox selects all the Toolbox parts in an assembly, including parts at different levels in subassemblies.

Using the Advanced Select Options

Advanced Select has been around for a very long time in the software, but it has seen only limited use. It used to stand alone as the only advanced selection method, but now with all the options under the Component Selection heading, it has lots of company.

The interface used for Advanced Select is very old dialog-box style rather than the newer PropertyManager type of interface to which the more commonly used tools have been updated. Figure 17.15 shows the Advanced Component Selection dialog box.

FIGURE 17.15

Using the Advanced Component Selection dialog box

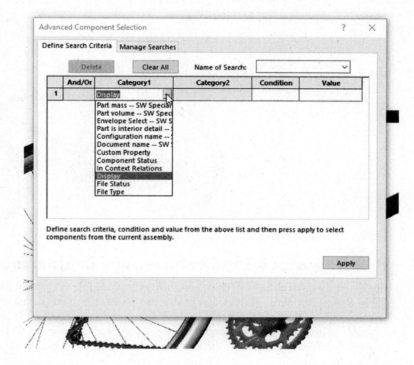

You can use the criteria in the Advanced Component Selection dialog box to set up, save, and reuse queries (searches) based on special categories, conditions, and values. Figure 17.15 shows an example of setting up a search where the display is Shaded With Edges. Clicking the Apply button runs the search and selects the appropriate parts in the FeatureManager.

In this example, Category 2 would be used if Category 1 were File Status; Category 2 could be Read Only, Write Access, User With Write Access, Needs Save, or Out Of Date. The Condition options would be Is, Is Not, Contains, Does Not Contain, and so on.

Selections can be reused by using the Save Selection option, which is available through the RMB, which adds an entry to a folder in the FeatureManager.

Selecting by Size

The Select By Size option allows you to dynamically move the slider and see the parts that are under a certain percentage of the overall assembly size. Figure 17.16 shows the interface used to facilitate this selection. Components that meet the requirement are shaded blue. The dialog also tallies how many parts meet the criterion. Clicking OK leaves the components selected for whatever you choose to do next.

FIGURE 17.16
Selecting components by size

Reading Assembly Performance Evaluation Results

The Assembly Performance Evaluation (formerly AssemblyXpert) tool provides information about assemblies. It gives statistics about parts, mates, resolved and lightweight components, subassembly depth, and other information. It may offer suggestions for things you might consider to improve assembly performance. The AssemblyXpert presents information in three status categories, displayed on the left side of the AssemblyXpert window:

◆   Passed

◆   Warning

◆   Information Only

A sample Assembly Performance Evaluation result window is shown in Figure 17.17.

Assembly Performance Evaluation results are meant to help you speed up the performance of your assemblies by combining them with your knowledge of best practices. Assembly Performance Evaluation will never simply tell you what to do, but it might suggest you use Large Assembly mode, or it might tell you that 386 mates are evaluated when the assembly is rebuilt (which, along with performance problems and best practice knowledge should tell you that you might want to do something to minimize mates at this level of the assembly).

You should also consider using Assembly Performance Evaluation in conjunction with SolidWorks Rx, which can point out many system-level issues.

FIGURE 17.17
Assembly Performance
Evaluation results can
help you discover
issues with slow
assembly
performance.

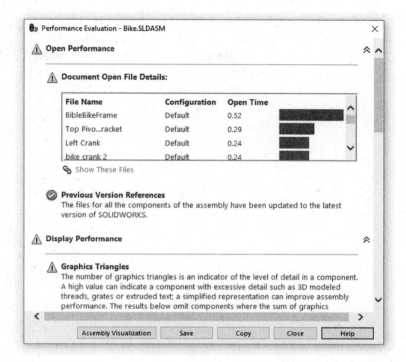

Using Defeature

Defeature works in both parts and assemblies. It also works on both imported and native data. The purpose of this tool is to remove geometrical detail to improve performance and security when sharing data. The output of this function can be internally stored simplified geometry or simplified geometry sent to an external file or to 3D Content Central. (3DCC.com is the SolidWorks online sharing library for commonly used data.)

In parts, Defeature removes small features, or selected features, and leaves a folder at the top of the FeatureManager, as shown in Figure 17.18. The Defeature folder is associated with a "dumb" featureless, imported body stored in the file as a separate body. You can save these from the RMB menu for the Defeature folder in the FeatureManager.

Defeature in the assembly uses a PropertyManager that has several steps:

1. The Components step enables you to remove components, simplifying the defeatured assembly. You can allow SolidWorks to use an automatic method, or you can make the selections yourself.

2. The Motion step enables you to group the remaining parts into groups that work like subassemblies for the purpose of motion.

3. The To Keep step defeatures individual parts, filling in holes, removing small features, and so on.

4. The Removing Features step of the process waits for SolidWorks to make all the changes you have asked it to do. This may take some time, depending on your computer and the assembly you are defeaturing.

FIGURE 17.18
Defeature in parts

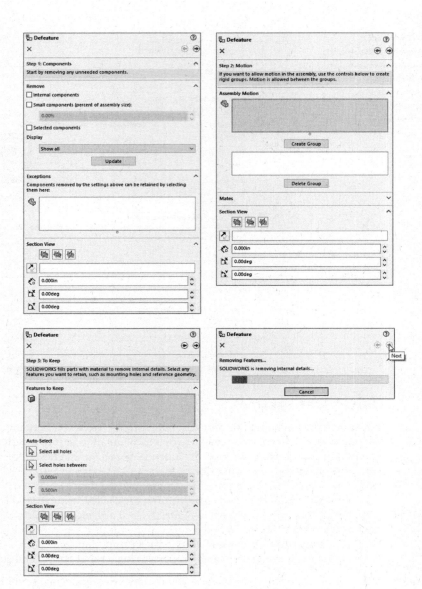

Using the Hole Alignment Tool

You can find the Hole Alignment tool through the menus at Tools ➤ Hole Alignment or on the Evaluate tab of the CommandManager. Hole Alignment is a feature-based evaluation tool. It detects misalignment (defined as centerlines that are more than a given distance from one another that you specify yourself) of Hole Wizard holes, simple holes, and extruded cylindrical holes. Figure 17.19 gives a look at the interface of the Hole Alignment tool.

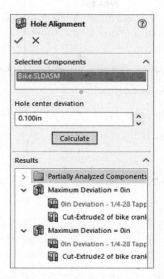

FIGURE 17.19
Using the Hole
Alignment
PropertyManager

This tool does have some limitations, which are mostly in the kinds of holes for which it can detect misalignment. The unsupported hole types are as follows:

- Multiboundary extrudes (multiple circles in a single sketch used for an extruded cut)
- Imported geometry
- Geometry created with any of the following:
  - Move Face
  - Move/Copy Body
  - Split Part
  - Mirror Body
  - Mirror Part
  - Mirror Component
  - Pattern Body
  - Insert Part

This list excludes many potential sources for error, and it doesn't leave many items of consequence. If you misalign holes using sketches or Hole Wizard holes, you have other problems.

The Bottom Line

SolidWorks packs lots of powerful and useful tools into the assemblies environment. Even if you are an experienced user, it pays to look through the list now and then because new functions are added frequently, or you may have a new use for an old tool.

Master It   Open the assembly called `Bike.sldasm` from the downloaded materials for this chapter. Use each of the tools in the Tools ➤ Component Selection list to practice selecting parts in the assembly:

◆ Volume Select—Drag a rectangle and then drag it to create a solid volume.

◆ Select Suppressed

◆ Select Hidden

◆ Select Mated To

◆ Select Identical Components

◆ Select Internal Components

◆ Select By Size

Master It   Use Advanced Select to select any components where the configuration name is *not* Default. Then invert the selection (RMB on a highlighted item, and it should be the first selection in the list), and then suppress all of the nonconfigured items.

Master It   Use one of the selection methods to select multiple components. Save the selection as a Selection Set.

Chapter 18

Using Libraries, Assembly Features, and Hole Wizard

Libraries help you make more efficient use of data that you will reuse frequently. Some features can be made to be very flexible so you can apply them in a wide range of situations. Some libraries, such as the Hole Wizard, are premade and can be combined with automation to create tools like Smart Components, which are library parts that can use library features and resize as necessary.

Shared libraries in multiuser environments require additional setup, including Windows permissions settings and SolidWorks File Location settings.

IN THIS CHAPTER, YOU WILL LEARN TO:

- ◆ Use library features
- ◆ Create library features
- ◆ Use the Hole Wizard
- ◆ Create assembly features
- ◆ Use envelopes
- ◆ Use Smart Components

Using Library Features

Library features are intended to be parametrically flexible to fit into many types of geometry, but they can also be of a fixed size and shape. In this chapter, you will use the information you have learned in previous chapters about designing for change and design intent, and you will learn how to create, use, and store library features.

Library features reside in the Design Library, which is located in the Task pane to the right of the graphics window.

TIP You can detach the Task pane from its docking location and move it wherever you want, leave it undocked, or move it to a second monitor.

One very useful aspect of library features is that they can be driven by configurations and design tables. After the feature is in the part, the configurations are still available, so you can change the config of an applied library feature at any time.

You can also link a library feature to an external file. This enables you to change a feature or a set of features in several parts at once if they are all externally linked to the file.

Getting Started with Library Features

Library features are simple to use and only slightly less simple to set up. For that reason, I will discuss using them first, so you know what kind of behavior you are trying to create when you go to make your own features.

To use a library feature, drag and drop it from the Design Library onto the appropriate geometry. You will then be prompted to select references in the new part that match the base geometry to which the library feature is attached. You can be fairly creative with references, but one of the goals when creating the feature is to make it work with as few references as possible. Fewer references make the feature easy, fast, and reliable to use.

SolidWorks software installs with several sample library features in the Design Library. The following demonstration uses some of these standard library features. Later, you can add library features from the download files to your Design Library.

Applying the Library Feature Interface

Library features work best if they go from a certain type of base geometry to a similar type of base geometry—for example, from rectangular to rectangular or from circular to circular. This is because the relations or dimensions that link the feature to the rest of the part tend to be dimensions from straight edges or concentric sketch relations. Of course, there are other ways of applying library features, but these are the most prevalent. Library features can be applied unconstrained and then constrained or moved later, but the process is cleanest when it all falls together correctly the first time.

Using the Task Pane

You don't have to save the part or do anything special before applying a library feature. You simply need to find the Task pane. The Task pane is the window that flies out from the right when you open SolidWorks. You may have turned it off and forgotten about it, in which case you can turn it on by choosing View ➤ Task Pane from the menu.

The Task pane automatically closes when you click outside of it unless you pin it open using the pushpin icon in the upper-right corner of the window. When you do this, any toolbars that appeared on the right side of the Task pane control tabs are moved out and positioned between the graphics window and the Task pane, which now remains open by default.

You can also detach the Task pane by dragging the bar at the top of the pane. Figure 18.1 shows the Task pane docked to the right side of the SolidWorks window.

Using the Design Library

The Design Library tab displays an image of a stack of books. It is the overall library area for all sorts of elements in SolidWorks. The part of the Design Library to be concerned with now is the Features folder. If you expand this folder, you can see that it is populated with some sample features.

FIGURE 18.1
The Task pane docked to
right side of the
SolidWorks window

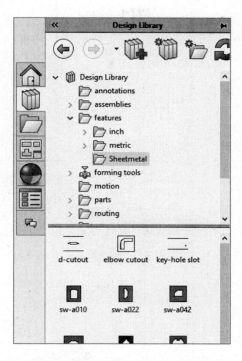

Open a new part, and create a cylinder using any method you want (for example, extrude or revolve). Make the diameter 3 inches and the length a little more than 1 inch.

In the Expand the Features ➤ Inch subfolder and select O-Ring Grooves. The first feature in the list is called *face static – gas*. Drag and drop this feature onto the end flat face of the cylinder.

The next step is to select the configuration, as shown in Figure 18.2. Not all library features have multiple size configurations. The configs in this case are driven by design tables. Select configuration 330.

When you select the configuration, the interface changes. In this case, only a sketch relation locates the feature; it is not located by dimensions. Notice that in the References panel, there is an Edge entry with a question mark, which becomes a check mark after you select the edge. This means that the library feature needs a circular edge to locate it. A small window appears, displaying the library feature. You need to select an edge that has the same relation to the library feature as the highlighted edge. Pick the circular edge of the part on the end of the cylinder where you want to place the library feature.

Next, create a new part from a rectangle 1.5 inches by 2 inches and extrude it to about 2 inches in depth.

In the Design Library, browse to Features, then Inch, and then the Fluid Power Ports folder, and drag the SAE J1926-1 feature onto the end of the extruded rectangle. Select the 38-24 size from the configurations list. A window appears, prompting you for reference selections, as shown in Figure 18.3.

FIGURE 18.2
Placing the feature and
selecting the
configuration

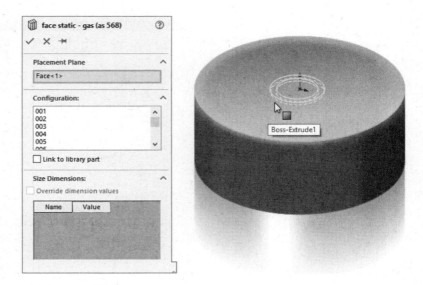

FIGURE 18.3
Placing a library feature
with dimensions

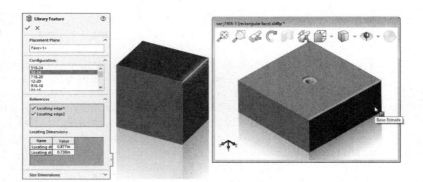

After the locating edges have been identified, the Locating Dimensions box becomes active and you can change the values of the dimensions to locate the feature. Further, in the Size Dimensions pane at the bottom of the PropertyManager, selecting the Override dimension values option enables you to change dimensions of the feature itself.

When you use a library feature with a design table, the design table is not brought into the part with the library feature. If the part already had a design table, this would cause multiple tables, which is not currently possible in SolidWorks. The configurations in the design table are brought forward, however.

If you override the feature dimensions using the Override Dimension Values option in the Size Dimensions panel of the Library Feature PropertyManager when feature configurations already exist, then a new configuration called Custom Configuration will be created in the list of feature configurations. It appears that multiple custom configurations are not allowed, so if you must make changes, you must ensure that they are right before you use the library feature in a part.

Exploring Other Design Library Functions

The Design Library has other functions besides library features. For example, you can use it as a repository for other items that you use frequently.

STORING ANNOTATIONS

You can store commonly used annotations in the Design Library. If you look at the Annotations folder with the default sample annotations, you see a combination of symbols and blocks. You can use symbols and notes in 3D models, but you can use blocks only in sketches or 2D drawings. Keep in mind that not all annotation types can be used in all places.

Annotations can be stored in the library as favorites or blocks. Many file extensions are used for different types of favorites, but they typically begin with `*.sld` and end with `fvt`, as in `*.sldweldfvt`. Figure 18.4 shows the default location of the Design Library and the thumbnail view of the favorites and blocks in the Annotations folder.

FIGURE 18.4
The Annotations folder in Windows Explorer

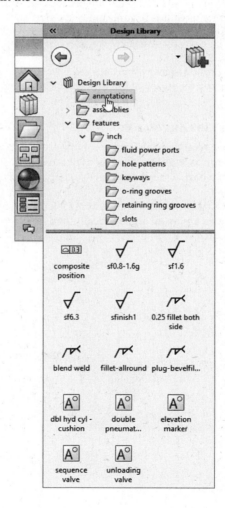

LOCATION OF THE DESIGN LIBRARY FOLDER

If you frequently work with different types of annotations, you should organize the library into subfolders to separate symbols, annotations, and blocks, and move these folders to a different location. By default, the Design Library folders are found at C:\ProgramData\SolidWorks\ SolidWorks 2018\design library\. You should store them in another location, not in the SolidWorks installation directory, but in an area that you have selected to maintain SolidWorks data between releases. For example, I have a folder at D:\Library that contains folders for macros, templates, library features, library parts, favorites, and so on. You can easily back up or copy these files from one computer to another, although you must quit SolidWorks before making these changes. Keeping the data off the operating system drive is also a good idea because if you ever have to reinstall the OS, you won't lose your SolidWorks library data.

After moving the library, you must point SolidWorks to the new location. To do this, choose Tools ➤ Options ➤ File Locations ➤ Design Library (or access it through the Add File Location icon in the Library pane). Delete the old location and browse to the new location. You should move other items in this list and redirect any items that you use, such as the templates and any other items you use frequently. After you have specified the settings, they should be retained when you install service pack upgrades or future versions.

TIP You can add as many shortcuts to folders in the Design Library as you want. Just use the Add File Location icon on the top of the Task pane. There is no need to go through the options.

STORING LIBRARY PARTS

The Design Library can also store commonly used library parts. One of the advantages of using the library for parts is that placement of the library part into the assembly, if configurations are available in a part, a window pops up, enabling you to select which configuration to place into the assembly.

Figure 18.5 shows the Configuration selection window for library parts. Note that the configurations are listed alphabetically, and you can type in the box to go to the configuration you want.

FIGURE 18.5
Selecting a Library Part
Configuration

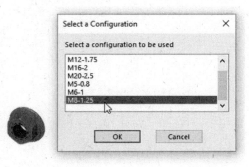

Parts inserted from the Library Parts folder can also take advantage of the Mate References functionality in the same way as the Toolbox, by allowing parts to snap into place.

USING SHEET METAL FORMING TOOLS

I only mention sheet-metal-forming tools here as a part of the library. They work much the same as other library features, but they do so within the specialized functions of sheet metal parts in SolidWorks. I discuss sheet-metal-forming tools in Chapter 35, "Creating Sheet Metal Drawings." Forming Tools folders have special properties. If you want to use the parts in a folder as forming tools, you must right-click the folder in the Design Library and choose Forming Tool Folder. The only other library type that needs a special folder is the one for library assemblies.

USING ASSEMBLIES

You can use library assemblies in SolidWorks in the same ways that you use library parts because they are inserted into the top-level assembly as a subassembly. For subassemblies that require motion, such as universal joint subassemblies, you can set the subassembly to solve as flexible or simply dissolve the subassembly into the upper-level assembly.

TIP When you're saving assemblies to the library, I recommend that you put the parts in a separate folder to segregate the parts of different assemblies.

ROUTING

SolidWorks Routing-Electric is a separately purchased add-in that is included with SolidWorks Office Premium. It includes piping, tubing (rigid and flexible), and wiring. Routing makes extensive use of libraries and automation, but it isn't part of the scope of this book.

USING SMART COMPONENTS

Smart Components are components that resize by automatically selecting configurations, depending on the size of the geometry onto which they are being dropped. They do this from a design table—such as the interface that you set up to enable it to automatically select part configurations based on mating part sizes. For example, a clamp with many sizes driven by configurations would select the correct config when it is dropped onto different sizes of cylinders.

Smart Components are covered more thoroughly later in this chapter.

Creating Library Features

When you save library features to the library, they use the file extension `*.sldlfp` (library feature part). They must contain some base geometry, which simulates the part onto which the feature will be dropped. The base geometry isn't transferred to the new part; only features that are marked with the "L" (for Library) in the FeatureManager are transferred to the new part. Figure 18.6 shows the FeatureManager of a library feature part.

Creating a Library Feature

When you are creating a library feature, the first problem you need to solve is how the feature will be located on a new part. Does it need to be placed on cylindrical parts, rectangular parts, other types of shapes, or does this matter at all? Will the feature be located by using dimensions or sketch relations, or will it be placed underdefined and later fully defined manually rather than automatically?

You may have noticed in one of the earlier examples that the sample fluid power ports had two versions of the same feature. One version is intended for the feature to be placed on the flat end of a cylinder, and the other version is intended for the feature to be placed on a rectangular face.

UNDERSTANDING LIBRARY LIMITATIONS

Library features can contain multiple features of different types. They may add and remove material, even within a single library feature. However, a few limitations exist. For example, they require a base feature, and external references are not allowed, nor are surfaces, sheet metal, weldments, or molds-related features. In addition, you cannot add a scale feature (a feature that affects the entire body) to the library, nor can you apply library features to an assembly.

CREATING A NEW LIBRARY FEATURE

For this example, I use a rectangular base. The library feature that I want to create consists of two boss extrudes, a cut extrude, and several fillets.

First, you need to create a rectangular extrusion. The size should be bigger than the feature that goes on it and representative of the face of the end part onto which this feature will typically be placed.

Next, in creating the features that you want to reuse, you must pay attention to any references outside the sketch; these include absolutely *anything* outside the active sketch, such as the sketch plane, references to edges, the origin, other planes, other sketches, and axes. Each reference to anything that isn't already part of the library feature must be reconnected when you place the feature on a new part. The ideal situation is obviously a single drag-and-drop, but generally speaking, at least one other step is usually needed. The initial drag-and-drop determines the starting face for the feature, and from there, you usually need to locate features, either by using relations or dimensions. A concentric relation locates the feature in a single reference selection of a circular edge (although it may also need to be rotated), and dimensions typically require one dimension in the X dimension and another one in the Y dimension.

Figure 18.7 shows the base feature and the first feature of the library feature. The only relations between the sketch of the library feature and the base feature are the sketch plane and the two dimensions.

FIGURE 18.7

Creating a library feature

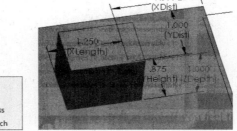

You should ensure that subsequent features after the first one reference only the first feature of the library feature (which is the second feature in the part). This is not a mandatory requirement, but a helpful guideline. You can make additional references, but they should be limited to the same items that were already referenced if possible. Users who model carelessly or do not pay attention to what they are doing typically have trouble making library features that function and are easy to use. Successfully modeling library features is like planning a strategy in a game of chess.

Now you can add the second extruded feature, being careful to reference only geometry that's going to move with the library feature. Figure 18.8 shows the newly added feature. To follow along as I detail how this feature is built, open the part from the download materials under the filename Chapter 18 First Library Feature.sldlfp.

Notice that a plane has been added. The plane is made to reference only geometry that is internal to the library feature; it's perpendicular to an edge at the midpoint, which simultaneously locates and orients the plane correctly to enable it to be used to mirror the Ear feature.

Also, notice that the EarSketch uses the same face reference from the base feature. This will appear in the Reference list as a single reference.

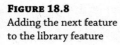

FIGURE 18.8
Adding the next feature
to the library feature

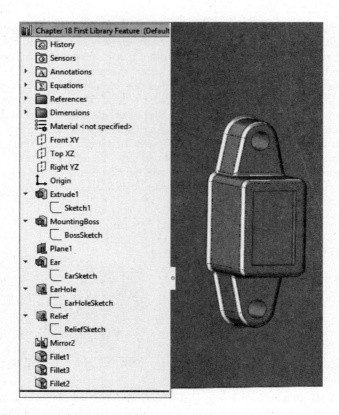

SAVING THE LIBRARY FEATURE

You can use three methods to save a library feature. You can either drag and drop it into a Design Library folder, use the Save As method, or use the Add To Library button in the Task pane. Because Save As is a little more common, I will describe it first.

The first step in saving the library feature is to select all the features in the FeatureManager that are intended to be a part of the library feature. Collapse the features first so the sketches belonging to features aren't selected. If the sketches are selected, you may get a warning message saying that no selected features can be used in the library feature. Don't worry; the sketches still will be included.

TIP   Remember that you can Ctrl+select individual features, Shift+select a range, or click and drag a selection box in the FeatureManager to select multiple features. Also keep in mind that if you don't select a feature (other than the base feature), then it won't be placed into the part when you insert the library feature. If there are any relations to the omitted feature, they may display as errors or warnings when you place the feature.

With the features selected, click File, click Save As, and in the Files of Type drop-down list, select the *.sldlfp file type. Browse to the Design Library folder and save the part. Figure 18.9 shows the FeatureManager of the finished library feature.

FIGURE 18.9
The finished library
feature part

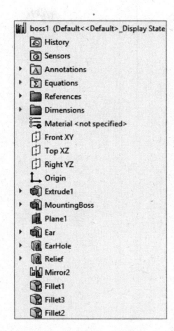 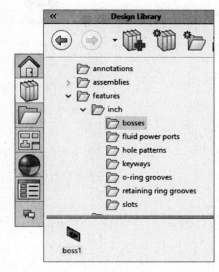

FIGURE 18.9
The finished library
feature part

CHANGING THE DISPLAY OF THE LIBRARY FEATURE THUMBNAIL

During the Save As process, a new folder called Bosses was added to the Design Library, as shown in Figure 18.9. Notice the new icon for the library feature in the lower window. You may notice that some of the default library features saved in the Design Library have a bluish background, as shown in Figure 18.10. This occurs because of the SolidWorks viewport background color, which you can set by choosing Tools ➢ Options ➢ Colors. Even if you never see that color because you are using a gradient background or a scene, SolidWorks still uses the color specified by that setting as the background when saving thumbnails and previews. I always set this color to white, so document backgrounds in previews do not have the blue color.

You may want to orient and zoom the library feature before saving it so it displays clearly in the panel. I like to make the base feature a different color from the library feature itself; this technique helps me to more easily determine the geometry that will be transferred and what is just dummy material. You can also fill out the Description field for the library feature, which pops up when your cursor hovers over the icon.

The real test for a library feature comes when you actually use it. This feature is re-created perfectly on the new part, but I have noticed one problem. When the feature was placed, it was 90 degrees away from the orientation that I wanted it to be in. It seems that the only way to make the feature rotatable is to create it with parallel and perpendicular relations rather than horizontal and vertical ones, so that one of the references can act as a rotation reference. Figure 18.11 shows the completed library feature placed on a part.

FIGURE 18.10
Display modes for the
Design Library

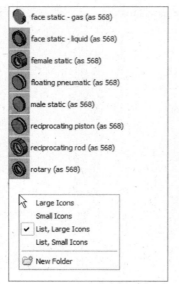

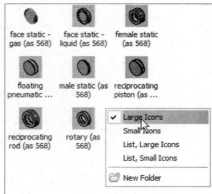

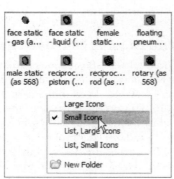

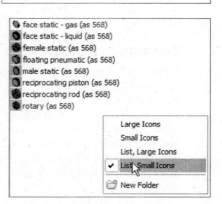

After you place a library feature on a part, it can be edited unless you select the Link to Library Part option in the Configuration pane, in which case the feature is driven externally from the *.sldlfp file. The Link To Library Part option is available only when the feature is first placed; it isn't available when you edit an existing library feature in a part, although the Dissolve Library Feature option will break the link. This option also causes all the constituent features to become regular features in the main part. Doing this on a configured library feature destroys the configurations.

FIGURE 18.11
The completed library
feature placed on a part

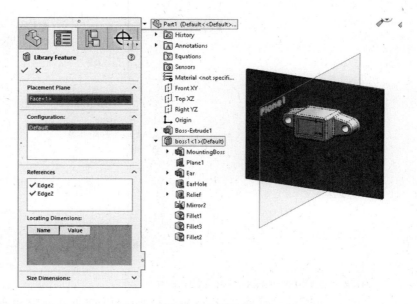

Creating a Library Feature from an Existing Part

When creating a library feature from an existing part, you use essentially the same process, but it is somewhat more difficult to achieve the correct results. It is best to remove all the features that don't either form the base feature or go into the library feature itself. This can cause many broken references, so it may be best to work from a saved copy of the original part. Most parts aren't modeled with creating a library feature in mind, and creating library features with effective references, as I mentioned earlier, is like a chess match that requires some forethought. It may be better to use a different technique, such as creating a new part with only the base feature. You can then Ctrl+drag the desired features from the existing part to the new part, set up the rest of the library feature, and save it with a *.sldlfp extension.

You can also create a library feature by dragging and dropping, although there are some limitations with this technique that seem to override the convenience. However, there is a workaround for the biggest limitation. If you select faces from features and drag them into the lower Design Library window, an Add To Library PropertyManager interface will appear that will enable you to start creating a library feature. The Add To Library PropertyManager interface is shown in Figure 18.12. You must select the features from the flyout FeatureManager. This is the source of one of the limitations. In the example, the plane cannot be selected by this method. The workaround for this is to complete the feature without the plane, right-click the icon in the Design Library window, and then select Open. With the library feature open in its own window, right-click the plane feature and select Add To Library; that individual feature is then added.

In addition to the Add To Library option, there is also an option to Remove From Library any selected features currently part of a library feature. Ordinarily, you wouldn't see both options in the RMB menu at the same time, but I forced the issue by Ctrl+selecting both library and nonlibrary features before right-clicking.

FIGURE 18.12
The RMB options for
Add To Library and
Remove From Library

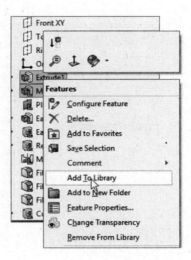

FIGURE 18.12
The RMB options for
Add To Library and
Remove From Library

Adding Folders to the Library

You can add folders to the library in three ways: by right-clicking in the Design Library window and selecting New Folder, by using the Windows Explorer interface, or by using the Add File Location button at the top of the Task pane. Another RMB menu option is Add Existing Folder, which enables you to add a folder from another location to the library. The folder is not moved or copied, but a shortcut is added to the Design Library and the contents appear in the lower pane.

TIP After a library feature has been edited, or folders or documents have been added to the library using Windows Explorer, you can press F5 in either the lower or the upper window to update the display for that window or use the Refresh icon located at the top of the Task pane.

Locating Dimensions and Internal Dimensions

When you create a library feature, SolidWorks adds two folders to the FeatureManager: the References folder and the Dimensions folder. In turn, the Dimensions folder has two subfolders: Locating Dimensions and Internal Dimensions. All these folders are shown in Figure 18.13.

The References folder shows the entities you used to reference the library feature. These are the features you are prompted to select upon placing the library feature in a new part. No additional work on your part is required with this folder.

The Dimensions folder lists all the dimensions in the library feature. Some of these dimensions are used to locate the feature to the dummy block, and some are meant to size the feature itself. When you make a library feature, I recommend that you separate the locating features from internal features by dragging the dimensions into the separate folders. The Locating Dimensions can be changed while placing the library feature, but the Internal Dimensions cannot be accessed. You may want to limit user access to some dimensions if you have standard tooling for the library feature that you are creating. Also be aware that the interface for moving the dimensions to the folders does not allow more than one dimension to be moved at a time.

FIGURE 18.13
References, Locating
Dimensions, and
Internal Dimensions in a
library feature

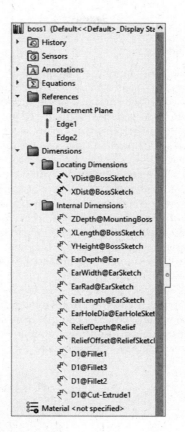

Creating Assembly Cuts

Several types of design require various cuts to be made after the product is assembled. For example, plates may be stacked, clamped, and then drilled to make sure the holes line up perfectly. Cast parts may be assembled and then given a final grinding cut to remove the cast surface finish.

Some assembly cuts can also be created visually by using section views. If you do not need a physical cut to your finished assembly, you should look into using sections, which will cost you less rebuild time and cause fewer complications.

To access the cut features to make an assembly cut, you can use the Assembly Features toolbar icon on the Assembly tab of the CommandManager, or you can choose Insert ➤ Assembly Feature ➤ Cut ➤ Extrude.

Because removing material in the assembly is the most commonly used technique, I will discuss it first. Some additive processes exist, such as welding and techniques such as adhesives and putty fillers, and they will be discussed later in this chapter.

SolidWorks allows only certain types of features to be used as assembly cuts:

- Extruded cuts
- Revolved cuts

◆ Swept cuts

◆ Hole features

For example, you cannot use a lofted cut as an assembly feature, but you can use a lofted solid in a cavity feature (which is an in-context feature, not an assembly feature). You can also do a lofted cut of a combined solid in a single part, then split the part into multiple bodies, and then split into multiple parts (which is discussed in Chapter 33, "Employing Master Model Techniques"). SolidWorks provides many ways to do almost anything you can imagine. Your job is to determine which methods give you the most flexibility, cost you the least time, and give the most accurate results.

When you set up an assembly cut, you do it in the same way that you would set up a cut in the part environment, but with a couple of exceptions.

First, it's best to sketch on an assembly plane rather than a part face or plane that belongs to a part. This is not a requirement; it's just a best practice suggestion.

Second, you must use the Feature Scope to tell SolidWorks if you want to cut through all possible components or just selected components. Further, you can have SolidWorks automatically select parts for you. For the most stable results, it's probably best to manually select the parts that you want to cut.

Sometimes assembly cuts are created for documentation purposes rather than design purposes. For example, if you want to cut a model section and display it in an isometric view or an exploded section view, you must do that using an assembly cut, probably in conjunction with a configuration so you can also show the assembly without the section. For example, Figure 18.14 shows an isometric cutaway view created by an assembly feature, Cut Extrude.

FIGURE 18.14
Using an assembly feature to cut away a model for illustration purposes

When you place a feature in the assembly like this, the cut exists only in the context of the assembly. If you open any individual part in its own window, the part isn't cut. If you open the part in another assembly, the part isn't cut there either. The cut exists only within the assembly in which it was made.

Figure 18.15 shows the PropertyManager of the cut. The Cut-Extrude1 feature is displayed in the FeatureManager of the assembly, after the Mate folder, local patterns, and even after an assembly sketch.

Using the Feature Scope

You can access the Feature Scope in the PropertyManager. In this example, all the parts were cut because the cut went through the entire assembly. In reality, some of the parts may not have needed to be cut, but in this case, it would have taken longer to find them than it did to just cut all the parts. You can partially cut the assembly in a couple of different ways. One way is to orient the feature such that you can control the depth of the cut by the sketch, and then sketch to suit your needs. Another way is to use the blind cut depth to control the depth. Finally, of course, you can use the Feature Scope to avoid cutting certain parts.

Propagating Features to Parts

One of the common mistakes SolidWorks users make is sketching in the assembly when they mean to sketch in a part in order to create a feature in the part. For example, you may not be paying attention to what you are doing, and you may forget to click the Edit Part button before starting a sketch.

In addition to that common mistake, sometimes features are simply easier to draw at the assembly level, especially if they affect multiple parts. The Feature Scope panel of the assembly feature Cut-Extrude PropertyManager contains an option called Propagate Feature To Parts. You draw the sketch in the assembly, create an assembly feature, and then select the Propagate Feature To Parts option, making sure you have the correct parts selected in the Feature Scope selection box. After you click the green checkmark icon, SolidWorks propagates the sketch and the feature to each of the selected Feature Scope parts, so the sketch and the feature reside in the FeatureManager of the individual parts.

The assembly feature cut Feature Scope is shown in Figure 18.15.

FIGURE 18.15
The Feature Scope controls which parts are cut.

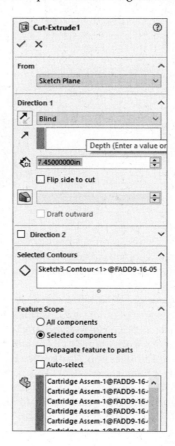

Next, you select the Propagate Feature To Parts option in the Feature Scope box to enable it. When you do this, the assembly still displays the Cut-Extrude feature at the bottom of the assembly FeatureManager, but now each part included in the Feature Scope also gets an in-context Cut-Extrude feature. If you delete the assembly-level feature, the feature will also be deleted from each of the individual parts.

Although this is a nice shortcut, it's not something you should do on a regular basis. In this particular assembly, it caused errors with about a dozen mates.

This kind of functionality also exists with the assembly fillets, chamfers, and the Hole Series functionality with Hole Wizard holes, where you specify hole locations in the assembly, and the holes show up as features in the individual parts. You can read more about the Hole Series feature later in this chapter.

Making Fillets and Chamfers in Assemblies

After parts are assembled, the corners are sometimes filed, sanded, or machined to round them. Figure 18.16 shows a stack of plates that have been filleted and chamfered in the assembly.

FIGURE 18.16
An example showing fillets on an assembly of stacked plates

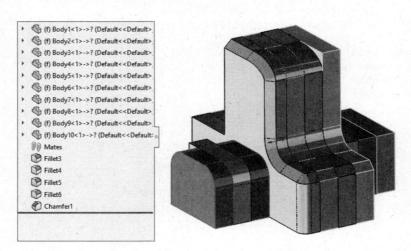

This book sometimes uses more abstract examples so you can learn about the limitations of a feature from simplified geometry. The first thing you can learn from this particular example is that large fillets started on one part do not carry over (overflow) to other parts where you have not made a selection.

A second thing to notice is that when you are creating these fillets, they don't automatically propagate to tangent edges of other parts, as fillets in parts do. If you want to fillet a string of edges, you have to select each edge individually.

A third thing to notice is that you can use assembly fillets to add material as well as remove material. Therefore, this goes beyond the intention that assembly fillets will be used just for filing, sanding, or machining sharp edges. This is the realm of body filler putty. SolidWorks gives you capabilities here that you may not have in the real world, and what you model in the end is your own responsibility (in other words, pay attention to what you are doing).

Notice that here you also have the option to propagate the fillets to the parts.

Assembly fillets do not give you all the capabilities you have with individual part fillets. You cannot create setback, hold line, or curvature continuous fillets in this way.

Not everyone will find a use for this feature, but it does offer an alternative to the workaround options that users had to rely on in the past.

Using the Hole Wizard

The Hole Wizard uses the Toolbox database for standardized hole types and sizes. Toolbox isn't covered in this book, because it isn't part of SolidWorks Standard. Toolbox is a hardware configurator that most experienced users don't use in the intended method. Toolbox implementation, if not done correctly, can cause problems when sharing data, especially when you're upgrading the version of your SolidWorks installation.

The Hole Wizard is mainly used in parts, but it can also be used in assemblies. It makes sense to use the Hole Wizard in the assembly to make sure that holes between parts are properly aligned and parametrically linked.

Smart Fasteners works with the Hole Wizard to automatically fill the holes created by the wizard with hardware. Hole Series is another assembly-based automated tool that links counterbored, clearance, and threaded holes in different parts in a fastened stack.

The Hole Wizard enables you to place holes for many types of screws with normal, loose, or close fits. With the Hole Wizard, you can create holes as assembly features in an assembly or as features in individual parts that are built in the context of an assembly using the Series Hole functionality. This tool is called a *wizard* because it guides you through the process step by step. A summary of the process of using the Hole Wizard to create a hole is as follows:

1. Preselecting a face to start holes before initiating the Hole Wizard command enables you to eliminate the possibility of getting a 3D sketch for the hole centers sketch. If you want holes starting from different planes, you need a 3D sketch, so select the 3D Sketch button in step 9.

2. Select the type of hole—for example, counterbored, countersunk, drilled hole, tapped hole, pipe tap, or legacy. If you have favorites set up, you can select the appropriate favorite and skip to step 9.

3. Set the standard to be used, such as ANSI (American National Standards Institute) inch, ANSI metric, or ISO (International Organization For Standardization).

4. Select the type of screw. For example, a counterbored hole can accommodate a socket head cap screw or a hex head screw, among others.

5. Select the size of the screw.

6. Select the fit of the screw into the hole, such as normal, loose, or close.

7. Select the end condition of the hole.

8. Select the options for clearance and countersinks or edge breaks.

   Alternatively, you can use or assign a favorite. A *favorite* is a hole with settings that you use frequently and want to save. I will discuss these later in this chapter.

   You can use Custom Sizing when you need a hole with nonstandard dimensions.

9. Switch to the Positions tab. If you have preselected a face, you will get a 2D sketch. If the 3D Sketch button is visible, you will also have a 2D sketch. If you click the 3D Sketch button, you will be placing sketch points in a 3D sketch. In either case, the point of this step is to place sketch points at the center of each hole you want to create. If you want holes on multiple levels, or holes on nonplanar surfaces, use the 3D sketch; otherwise, use 2D because it is simpler and faster.

10. Click OK to accept the type, size, and placement of the hole. Figure 18.17 shows the Hole Wizard PropertyManager interface.

FIGURE 18.17
The Hole Wizard PropertyManager interface

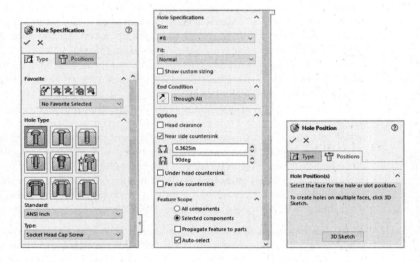

Using the Hole Series

The Hole Series enables you to make a series of in-context hole features in individual parts that are connected by a Hole Series assembly-level feature. It is intended for a stack of parts where, for example, the top part has a counterbored hole, the middle part has a clearance through hole, and the final part has a blind threaded hole.

HOLE SERIES INTERFACE

The Hole Series is a four-step, wizard-based feature, unless you have the Toolbox add-in turned on, in which case it is a five-step process. The final step added by Toolbox involves populating the new hole with a parametrically linked fastener using Smart Fasteners functionality. Figure 18.18 shows the interface for the various steps.

FIGURE 18.18
The Hole Series interface

BASIC HOLE SERIES STEPS

When using the Hole Series feature, you must follow these basic steps:

1. Have an assembly open with two or more parts that need to be fastened together.

2. Initiate the Hole Series tool by choosing Insert ➤ Assembly Features ➤ Hole ➤ Hole Series. It's also available as a toolbar button, but it isn't on the toolbar by default.

3. If the Hole Series is to be started from an existing hole, select it in the Hole Position panel. If not, use sketch points, construction geometry, dimensions, and sketch relations to locate the hole centerpoints.

4. Use the tabs at the top of the PropertyManager to advance from one panel to the next.

   ◆ The Start Hole Specification refers to the part where the series of holes starts.

   ◆ The Middle Hole Specification is for all parts between the first part and the last part.

   ◆ The End Hole Specification is the last part and is either a through clearance hole or a threaded hole.

The finished feature leaves an in-context feature in each part, with the Hole Series part in the assembly, as shown in Figure 18.19.

FIGURE 18.19
The finished Hole Series

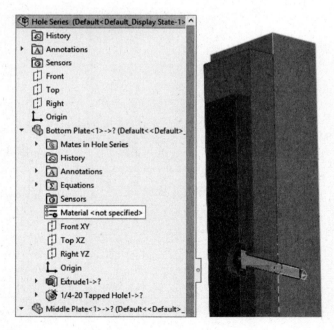

Creating Weld Beads

Weld beads are covered in Chapter 36, "Creating Weldments and Weldment Drawings," but the assembly feature side of weld beads is covered here from a slightly different perspective. Although the SolidWorks Help refers to a Fillet Weld Bead feature, there is actually a difference between the Fillet Bead tool and the Weld Bead tool. The icons are similar, but the one with the bigger weld is the Fillet Bead. Both can be found on the Weldments toolbar, but only the Weld Bead can be found on the Assembly Features menu or flyout toolbar.

When comparing the functionality in the Weld Bead and Fillet Bead features, even the SolidWorks Help for the Fillet Bead recommends using the Weld Bead tool instead of Fillet Bead to insert weld beads.

The Weld Bead feature offers some advantages over the Fillet Bead feature:

◆ The same interface is available in parts and assemblies.

◆ It has a minimal effect on the performance of even a large number of weld beads.

◆ A basic weld symbol is created and applied automatically.

◆ It works with weldable gaps.

◆ The Smart Weld Selection tool speeds up selection significantly.

◆ Weld properties serve to evaluate mass, production time, and cost.

◆ Weld information can be pulled onto drawings.

To be clear, the Fillet Bead feature is only for weldment parts, and it creates a body with additional volume. The Weld Bead feature is for weldments and general assemblies, and it creates a cosmetic display body, not something that affects mass properties.

The workflow to create a weld bead is as follows:

1. Select the weld path(s). The weld path can be a set of edges (they must be between two bodies or parts) or a set of faces (they must be from adjacent parts).

You can select multiple weld paths, and the paths don't need to touch. The weld path appears as bright pink for an active path or orange for an existing path listed in the PropertyManager.

The Smart Weld Selection tool creates new weld paths automatically based on your selections, and it greatly simplifies face or edge selection for weld bead creation. Just roughly sketch with the pencil where you want the weld to go, and SolidWorks will automatically select the faces or edges to make that weld happen.

2. Set the size of the weld.

3. Define the weld symbol that includes all the details about the weld for the welder on the drawing.

4. Set the length limit of the weld.

5. Establish requirements for an intermittent weld from the options given.

The PropertyManager for a weld bead made in a multibody part is shown in Figure 18.20.

Notice that the welds are organized by size and type within the Weld folder. Fillet Weld is the default weld type if you don't specify another type.

The PropertyManager looks the same for the weld bead done in a multibody part as it does in an assembly. The results also look the same. Aside from the duplicate names, none of this has anything to do with the Fillet Bead feature that is available only in weldment parts.

To edit the weld bead, you must right-click the Weld Bead item listed under the size of the Fillet Weld in the Weld folder. This brings you back to the original Weld Bead PropertyManager.

FIGURE 18.20
Creating a weld bead

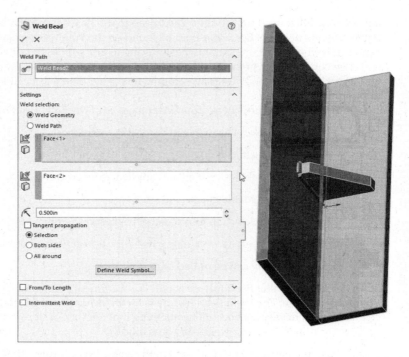

FIGURE 18.20
Creating a weld bead

You can manage other weld properties by right-clicking the size of the weld and selecting the Properties option. The Weld Bead Properties dialog box appears, as shown in Figure 18.21.

FIGURE 18.21
The Weld Bead Properties dialog box enables you to set many options.

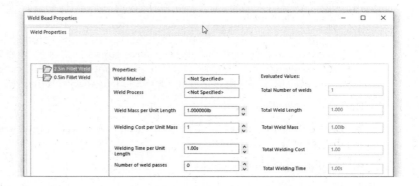

Working with Envelopes

Envelopes in SolidWorks are regular parts or subassemblies that are used for selection or for reference. They are display-only items. You can make selections based on whether other parts are inside, outside, or crossing the envelope boundary. You can make an envelope in place in the assembly, or you can make an envelope from an existing part. Envelope parts don't count toward BOM part counts or material properties.

To insert an envelope, you must first insert a regular part and then designate it as an envelope. The two places to do this are in the Insert Component PropertyManager and the Component Properties dialog box, as shown in Figure 18.22.

FIGURE 18.22

Inserting a new envelope into an assembly

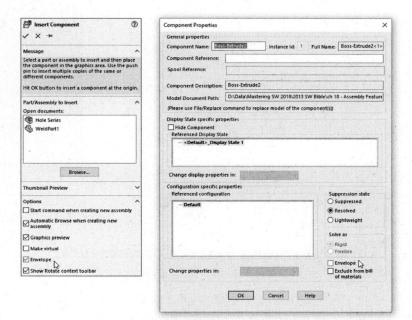

Once in the assembly, the envelope displays in the graphics window as a transparent light-blue part and in the assembly FeatureManager as an Envelope folder.

The two options that the Envelope function was meant to work with—Select Using Envelope and Show/Hide Using Envelope—are shown in Figure 18.23. You can access these options by right-clicking the Envelope from the FeatureManager or the graphics window and then selecting Envelope.

Component selection also includes a Volume Select function that enables you to create a rectangular volume on the fly that works very much like an envelope.

Envelopes can be external or virtual components.

Envelopes can also be shown in a drawing view, from the View Properties interface. They show up as phantom lines by default, although there are easier ways to show parts as phantom on a drawing, simply use the Component Line Font tool.

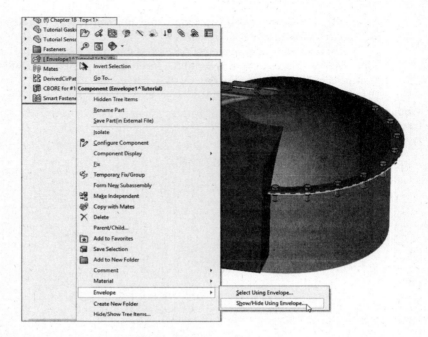

Understanding Smart Components

A Smart Component can comprise several elements:

- ◆ A single part or an assembly that may use size configurations

- ◆ A configurable library feature that usually serves as mounting holes or an opening for the Smart Component

- ◆ Associated hardware that may also be driven by size configurations

- ◆ A training assembly that is used to define the Smart Component

As you might expect, some minor limitations exist:

- ◆ A Smart Component part cannot have references that are external to the Smart Component group of which it is a member.

- ◆ When placed in the assembly, the associated library feature can affect only one component.

- ◆ The associated library feature is limited to these feature types:

  - ◆ Extruded or revolved cuts or bosses

  - ◆ Hole Wizard holes

  - ◆ Simple hole features

The setup time for Smart Components can be significant for the first one or two that you create, especially if you use the auto-size option. The complexity of the setup depends mainly on the number of configurations and configured parts that you use. The auto-sizing function takes the most time to set up because it requires matching configurations, and the auto-size table takes a while to manage, especially for multiple parts. Still, if you end up placing a given part with associated features and other components many times manually, or if there are others in your group that do, this technique can save you and your team lots of time.

Using Smart Components

A *Smart Component* is a library part or set of parts that needs to mate to features in another part. The Smart Component brings those features with it when it is placed in the assembly. You can access the Make Smart Component command in the Tools menu or in the toolbars; it is with the Assembly tools, although it may not be on the Assembly toolbar by default.

Figure 18.24 shows a simple assembly. It took approximately 20 minutes to model all the parts, set up the Smart Component, and test it in an assembly. This example doesn't use auto-sizing, but it does use a library part, an in-context feature, and two instances of a single hardware piece. This is an excellent example of Smart Component functionality because it is fast to create and apply, and it saves you time whenever you use it.

FIGURE 18.24
A simple
Smart Component

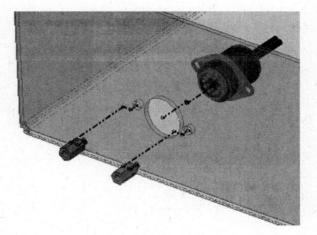

Getting Started with a Simple Smart Component

In this assembly, you first place the electrical connector part in the assembly, mate it in place, and then apply Smart Components. You can apply Smart Components by clicking the Smart Component icon that appears on the part in the graphics window when you select it. SolidWorks then prompts you to select the inside and outside faces of the sheet metal part (the hardware references the outside, and the cutout feature references the inside). SolidWorks then creates the cutout as an in-context feature that it places in the sheet metal part.

When you create the Smart Component, a new folder is added to the FeatureManager of the component. This folder contains all the required information about the other elements, such as the in-context feature, any other parts that go with the Smart Component, the "training assembly" location, and the face references to locate everything. The left image in Figure 18.25 shows this folder in the connector part that is used in this example. The right image shows what is added to the assembly FeatureManager when you add a Smart Component. The only thing that existed in the design tree shown in Figure 18.25 before the Smart Component was the Test Box sheet metal part.

FIGURE 18.25

The Smart Component folder in the connector part

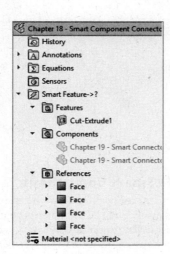

Feature Tree of Smart
Component

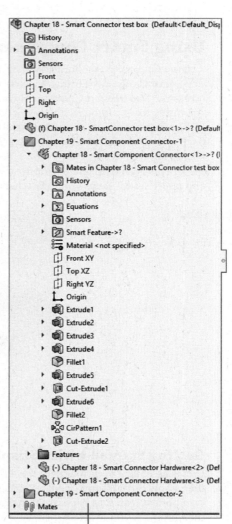

Feature tree of assembly where a
Smart Component has been used

A thunderbolt appears on the part symbol at the top of the FeatureManager, indicating that the part is a Smart Component. You can place this Smart Component by following these steps:

1. Create an assembly and add the target part to it. The target part is the one that the Smart Component will be mated to and the one that will have the in-context cutout inserted into it. In this case, the target part is a sheet metal box.

CAUTION   It is a good idea to save the assembly *before* you add the Smart Component to it. If the Smart Component is placed before the assembly is saved, the assembly has a tendency to forget that it hasn't been saved, and it bumps the in-context feature to out-of-context when the name is changed from whatever the default name is (for example, Assem1.sldasm) to the name that you assign to it.

2. Put the Smart Component into the assembly. You can do this in the same way that you would add any normal part, including one from the Design Library. If you use a part frequently enough to make it into a Smart Component, then you may want it in the Design Library for quick access. In fact, you can add a Smart Component to an assembly without using any of the Smart Component options.

3. Mate the Smart Component in the assembly. In this case, it's done with a face-to-face coincident mate and a pair of distance mates.

4. Apply Smart Components by clicking the Smart Component symbol on the part. Select the part in the FeatureManager to make a small lightning bolt appear on the part, as shown in Figure 18.26. Alternatively, you can select Insert Smart Features from the RMB. If you insert many instances of a Smart Component, then each instance will have the option to apply the Smart Component features and associated components.

FIGURE 18.26
The Smart Component
symbol on a part

At this point, an interface similar to that of the Library Feature interface appears, with the small prompt window and a box for selecting references, as shown in Figure 18.27.

FIGURE 18.27
The interface for adding the Smart Feature and additional components of the Smart Component

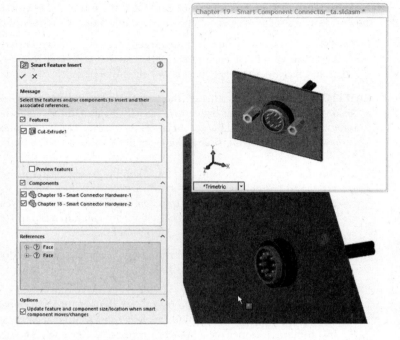

5. Select the references and click the green checkmark icon. Then place the Smart Component, as well as the Smart Feature (in-context feature) and associated hardware components, to complete the job. You can rotate the part in the small preview window to get a better look at the part.

Auto-Sizing Smart Components

Auto-sizing is the capability of a Smart Component to automatically select a size from a list of configurations based on the size of the geometry onto which it is being dropped. At this time, the only shape that can be auto-sized is the cylindrical shape.

Figure 18.28 shows the effects of auto-sizing. Notice the two shaft holders. These are two instances of the same part, using different size configurations. When you drag the Smart Component over the small end of the stepped shaft, the configuration corresponding to that shaft size appears. As you drag the part along the shaft and the shaft diameter increases, the next-larger Smart Component configuration appears. This is part of the functionality of Smart Components. Each configuration of the Smart Component is set up to fit onto a range of shaft diameters. If the diameter of the shaft is outside of the range or between sizes, then the Smart Component is not applied.

FIGURE 18.28
A Smart Component with auto-sizing

Sizes are governed by a configurator table, which looks similar to a design table but works somewhat differently. The configurator table relates the configurations of the Smart Component to configurations of the individual parts, which may also change size with the Smart Component. This serves as a subset of the function of a design table in an assembly, assigning part configurations to assembly configurations. Figure 18.29 shows a sample configurator table made for the assembly shown in Figure 18.28.

FIGURE 18.29
A configurator table

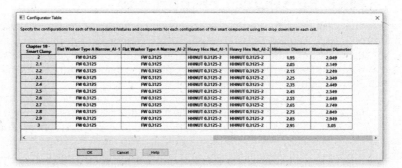

Chapter 18 - Smart Clamp	Flat Washer Type A Narrow_Al-1	Flat Washer Type A Narrow_Al-2	Heavy Hex Nut_Al-1	Heavy Hex Nut_Al-2	Minimum Diameter	Maximum Diameter
2	FW 0.3125	FW 0.3125	HHNUT 0.3125-2	HHNUT 0.3125-2	1.95	2.049
2.1	FW 0.3125	FW 0.3125	HHNUT 0.3125-2	HHNUT 0.3125-2	2.05	2.149
2.2	FW 0.3125	FW 0.3125	HHNUT 0.3125-2	HHNUT 0.3125-2	2.15	2.249
2.3	FW 0.3125	FW 0.3125	HHNUT 0.3125-2	HHNUT 0.3125-2	2.25	2.349
2.4	FW 0.3125	FW 0.3125	HHNUT 0.3125-2	HHNUT 0.3125-2	2.35	2.449
2.5	FW 0.3125	FW 0.3125	HHNUT 0.3125-2	HHNUT 0.3125-2	2.45	2.549
2.6	FW 0.3125	FW 0.3125	HHNUT 0.3125-2	HHNUT 0.3125-2	2.55	2.649
2.7	FW 0.3125	FW 0.3125	HHNUT 0.3125-2	HHNUT 0.3125-2	2.65	2.749
2.8	FW 0.3125	FW 0.3125	HHNUT 0.3125-2	HHNUT 0.3125-2	2.75	2.849
2.9	FW 0.3125	FW 0.3125	HHNUT 0.3125-2	HHNUT 0.3125-2	2.85	2.949
3	FW 0.3125	FW 0.3125	HHNUT 0.3125-2	HHNUT 0.3125-2	2.95	3.05

When you look at this table, you can begin to understand why creating auto-sizing Smart Components is much more involved than the first example in this chapter. The configurations of the Smart Component are listed to the left, and you can select the individual part configurations in each cell from a drop-down list of all available configurations for that part. There's no way to set the configurations for multiple components at once, nor is there a copy-and-paste function. These shortcomings combine to make this format less user-friendly than an Excel-based design table.

Most notable are the Minimum Diameter and Maximum Diameter columns to the right. These columns supply the parameters that make the auto-size function work. SolidWorks understands that mating sizes are not always exactly equal, and the ability to use a range rather than exact values (minimum and maximum diameter columns) accommodates this limitation very nicely, although it can be tedious to set up.

Another aspect of the setup shown here is that it uses Toolbox parts. If you want to use the auto-size functionality, then you need to be using configurations for Toolbox parts. You should prebuild all the needed configurations and ensure that they are always available.

The Auto Size capability, as well as the creation of the configurator table, is triggered by the Auto Size panel in the Smart Component PropertyManager. To access the PropertyManager, click the Make Smart Component icon in the Assembly Command Manager or use the Tools menu in an open assembly document.

To edit the Smart Component, follow these steps:

1. Open a Smart Component in its own window.

2. Right-click on the Smart Feature folder.

3. Select the Edit In Defining Assembly option.

4. (At the upper-right of the graphics window, there will be a small box with a button that says Edit Definition.) Click Edit Definition.

5. This will bring up the Smart Component PropertyManager from which you can access the configurator table and other defining features.

Making Smart Components

The most important point to remember about Smart Component setup is that you need to do it only once for each Smart Component. The second most important point is that the first setup is the most difficult. After that, subsequent setups become much easier to create. Adding components to the Smart Component isn't so time-consuming unless the additional components are also configured and auto-sized.

Smart Components must contain at least one associated component and one in-context feature, or the configurator table must be filled out and functional. If you try to create a Smart Component from a stand-alone part, nothing happens; the Smart Component interface simply closes because there's nothing for it to do. You may combine all three elements (associated component, in-context feature, and auto-size), but you must have at least one element.

Getting Started with a Simple Smart Component

Because the electrical connector shown in Figure 18.27 was already used to demonstrate the insertion of a Smart Component, it's used here to demonstrate how to create one.

All that you need to make a Smart Component with an associated Smart Feature (in this case, a cutout and mounting holes) and mounting hardware (in this case, two stand-off screws) is the actual part. The part can even be imported (a Smart Component made from dumb geometry). This example uses the file named `Chapter 18 - Connector Start.sldprt` from the Chapter 18 folder.

There's nothing special about this part. It's modeled in SolidWorks using standard features, and there are no configurations or special features. It could have been downloaded from 3D Content Central. It represents an electrical connector that may be mounted in a sheet metal electrical enclosure.

The first step in setting it up is to create a mock assembly with a dummy part representing the sheet metal box. The part doesn't need to be complex—or even sheet metal for that matter; it just needs to be close to the thickness to which you would expect the Smart Component to be mounted. The assembly is called a *training* assembly, not because you are learning how to make a Smart Component, but because you are training the Smart Component to be *smart*.

1. Open the part `Chapter 18 - Connector Start.sldprt` from the materials downloaded from the Wiley website.

2. Make a simple rectangular part, approximately 4 inches square and about .06 inch thick. Save the part to your hard drive. Give a name to the part so it's clear that it belongs to this training assembly.

3. Place the rectangular dummy part into a new assembly, with a name that is both unique and identifiable.

4. Put the connector into the assembly. Mate the part so the flange is flush with the rectangular piece. Also use distance mates to locate the connector planes from the edges of the part, similar to Figure 18.30 in the image to the left.

FIGURE 18.30

Placing the connector on
the dummy part

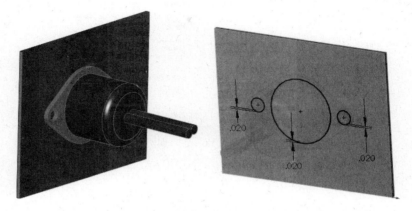

5. Edit the dummy part in context (right-click the dummy part in the assembly and select Edit Part), and offset edges of the connector part to extrude a cut, as shown in the image to the right in Figure 18.30. Offset the two mounting holes and the area around where the connector will stick through the sheet metal by about .02 inch.

6. Exit Edit Component mode and add two instances of the part named Chapter 18 – Smart Connector Hardware.sldprt to the assembly. Mate the hardware part to the in-context hole, making sure that it goes to the outside thickness of the dummy sheet metal part.

NOTE Although it is generally a best practice to *avoid* mating parts to in-context features, in this example you are doing exactly that. Keep in mind that best practice suggestions are more like guidelines. If you are having performance problems with an assembly, this may not be the best technique to use. However, sometimes there is a price to pay for sophisticated functionality; if you think that your design can afford the price and will benefit from this functionality, then you should use it.

7. Now that everything is in place, click the Make Smart Component tool on the Assembly toolbar. If the button is not there, you can add it to the Assembly toolbar by choosing Tools ➤ Customize Menu or by choosing Tools ➤ Make Smart Component. The resulting interface is shown in Figure 18.31.

8. In the Smart Component selection box, select the connector part.

9. In the Components selection box, select the two hardware components.

10. In the Features selection box, select the in-context feature from the dummy part. You are now finished setting up the Smart Component.

11. Click the green checkmark icon to accept the changes, exit out of the PropertyManager, and save the file.

FIGURE 18.31
The Smart Component
PropertyManager
interface

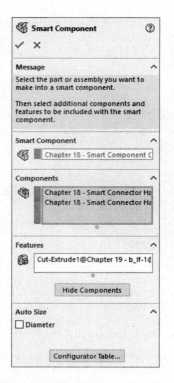

FIGURE 18.31
The Smart Component
PropertyManager
interface

Creating an Auto-Sizing Smart Component

The simple Smart Component took about 20 minutes to model and set up. That's not too bad for a feature that you will probably use often. The benefits are somewhat modest, placing three components and a feature.

However, when it comes to the auto-sizing example that is shown next, the benefits are more extensive. A total of seven individual parts are placed (including Toolbox parts)—three of which are automatically sized, depending on the geometry into which the Smart Component is dropped—and an in-context feature is added.

To begin, open the part from the website download materials named Chapter 18 - Clamp Start.sldprt. Notice that this is a multibody part. You don't need any special knowledge about multibody parts to complete this task. Multiple bodies are discussed in detail in Chapter 31, "Modeling Multibodies."

1. With the Clamp Start part open, click through the configurations or examine the design table in the part; you can see that various dimensions change. Notice that several configurations already exist. The primary dimension that changes is the diameter of the hole, and this change drives the diameter of, and distance between, the mounting holes.

NOTE   You can only drive auto-sizing by cylindrical geometry.

Part of the Smart Component definition includes applying a Mate Reference to the part so that the big hole automatically snaps to cylindrical geometry. Another aspect is that it adds in-context holes that match the mounting holes to the plate. Figure 18.28 shows the assembly into which this part is meant to go. The clamp snaps onto the stepped shaft and adds holes to the plate.

2. Open the file named `Chapter 18 Autosize Training Assembly.sldasm`. This has been prepared to help you get started with the Smart Component training.

NOTE   The shaft isn't necessary in the training assembly. The training assembly is intended to create the in-context Smart Feature and to create the configurator table. The shaft part has been added here for visualization only.

3. Insert the clamp part into the assembly, and mate it concentric to the shaft and coincident to the blue plate. It does not matter where the clamp sits along the shaft, but it should be fully mated into the location so it doesn't slide back and forth. A distance mate from a plane or planar face would be a good choice.

4. Edit the plate in the context of the assembly, and convert entities from the mounting holes in the clamp to create holes in the plate that align with the holes in the clamp.

5. Exit Edit Component mode.

6. Activate Toolbox, select the four holes, as shown in Figure 18.32, and insert Socket Head Cap Screws $\left(\frac{3}{8} \times 24 \times \frac{5}{8}\right)$ inch. If you do not have Toolbox or choose not to use it, then you can use the part with the correct name and correctly sized configurations that is provided in the website download material.

FIGURE 18.32
Inserting four screws at
once using Toolbox

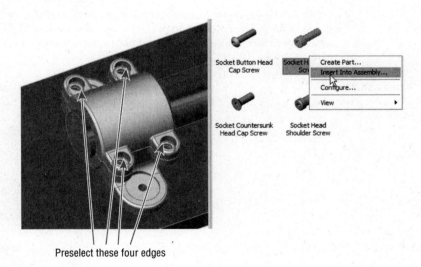

Preselect these four edges

7. Use the same fastener to place in the mounting holes, using the correct size for the holes. You will set the length later. Use a default length of 2.25 inches for both mounting holes.

NOTE   Working with the length of the fasteners is not a clean operation in Smart Components. The length is dependent on the thickness of the plate, which isn't controlled by the Smart Fastener, and the Smart Fastener can't account for it, except through mates. (Remember that auto-sizing is driven only by a diameter.) Later in this chapter, you will see how the washers and nuts are put in place on the underside of the plate, but the screw length cannot be automatically calculated (unless the actual screw had an in-context relation to the nut, which is not possible if you're using Toolbox).

8. Place washers and nuts on the screws on the backside of the plate.

9. When the shaft diameter changes, the hole in the clamp changes to match (within the ranges that you will establish). As the clamp becomes larger, bigger screws are needed to secure the clamp and the holes grow farther apart. Bigger screws mean additional configurations for the screw, washer, and nut parts. Remember that the configurations do not necessarily exist. You should not count on a Smart Component working if this means that Toolbox must create new configurations.

In this example, the Toolbox parts are prepopulated with all the configurations needed for the range of sizes involved with this Smart Component. When you make your own Smart Components, you must do the same thing if you intend to use auto-sizing with Toolbox parts. The difficulty here is that the configurations include the diameter size of the screw as well as the length, which is unknown until you place the part.

For this step, you must make sure the configurations are available and the screws are placed properly.

Up to this step, you have just assembled the parts as if this were the only time you were going to do it. The automation of the process comes next. Figure 18.33 shows the training assembly to this point. The shaft and plate are shown in wireframe because they are external to the Smart Component.

FIGURE 18.33
The training assembly
up to step 9

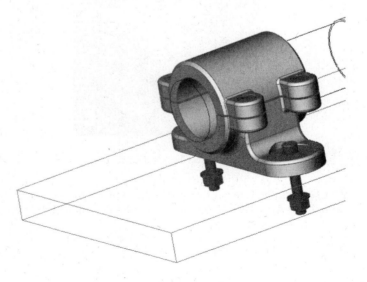

10. Click the Make Smart Component tool on the Assembly toolbar. In the previous example, this was the point where the Make Smart Component command was used, and it's no different here.

11. Activate the Smart Component selection box and pick the clamp part. Figure 18.34 shows the filled-in Smart Component PropertyManager.

In the Components selection box, select the six screw instances, the two washers, and the two nuts.

In the Features selection box, select the in-context feature or features that are associated with the Smart Component.

FIGURE 18.34
The Smart Component
PropertyManager

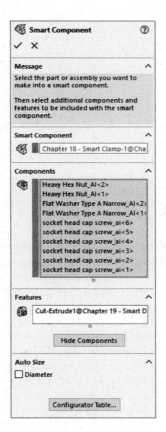

NOTE Although the in-context feature can affect only a single part, this doesn't mean that you're limited to a single in-context feature. In most cases, only one feature is needed, but there are probably situations where more than one would be useful. Also remember that the in-context features are limited to extruded and revolved bosses and cuts, Hole Wizard holes, and simple hole features.

The configurator table is simply a table that enables you to select which component configurations are to be used with which Smart Component configuration. It looks and works very much like an assembly design table, but it is not Excel-based, and every cell must be set explicitly rather than using techniques for mass population or assigning properties to a range of configurations, as you can do with a real design table.

Each cell has a drop-down list of all the available configurations for that component. If you have four instances of a single component, then you must set each instance of each component. Figure 18.35 shows the configurator table for this example.

FIGURE 18.35
The configurator table
for the Clamp
Smart component

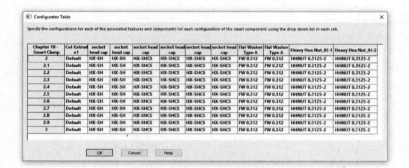

12. Click OK. You are now done creating the auto-sizing Smart Component.

Managing Files with Smart Components

You might expect that with the training assembly, there's an extra burden of file management with Smart Components. This may seem counterintuitive, but in fact, the only file you need to worry about is the actual Smart Component.

Although this isn't explained very well in any of the documentation, the Help and reseller demonstrations on the topic generally recommend that you simply *delete* the training assembly after you're done with it because it's not needed any more. It turns out that all the information to re-create the training assembly is stored in the Smart Component. This includes the in-context feature (which is stored as a library feature) and the locations of any associated components, as well as the configurator table. Figure 18.36 shows a part of the FeatureManager of a Smart Component. As you can see, the in-context feature, the associated components, and the face references are all listed there.

FIGURE 18.36
Part of the
FeatureManager of a
Smart Component

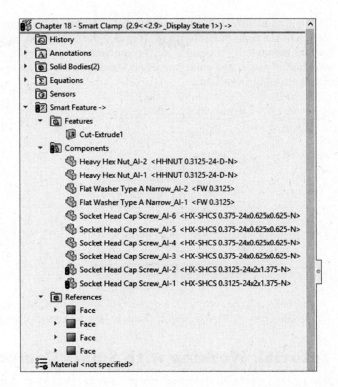

FIGURE 18.36
Part of the
FeatureManager of a
Smart Component

Deleting the training assembly does not cause any data to be lost; you will delete an assembly in the following section.

Editing Smart Components

Expanding on the discussion about whether to keep the training assembly file, here's a little exercise that you can try. Make a Smart Component by going through the preceding steps, using the following tutorial or creating one of your own. Just make a simple Smart Component with perhaps one associated component and an in-context feature. Then delete the training assembly.

With the defining assembly gone, there appears to be no way to edit the setup of the Smart Component. Right-click the Smart Feature folder in the FeatureManager of the Smart Component, and select Edit In Defining Assembly, as shown in Figure 18.37. SolidWorks re-creates the defining assembly from the data that is stored in the Smart Component. This assembly is saved in a system `temp` folder using the name `<Smart Component name>_ta .sldasm`. If the Smart Component uses an in-context feature, it's saved to the `temp` directory as a library feature file using the name of the dummy part and appending `_lf` to the filename (for example, `Dummy_lf.sldlfp`).

The Edit Definition button appears in the upper-right corner of the graphics window and is shown to the right in Figure 18.37. It covers the Close Document X. If you click this button, the Smart Component PropertyManager interface appears again, enabling you to change the selection of associated components and in-context features, to change the auto-size setting, or edit the configurator table.

FIGURE 18.37
Selecting the Edit in Defining Assembly command

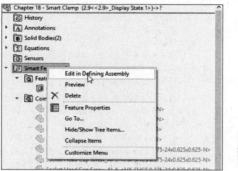

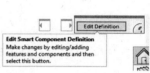

Therefore, all the settings are preserved, and the training assembly exists only as a phantom in a temp directory. Although this appears to be counterintuitive, it works.

Tutorial: Working with Smart Components

This tutorial guides you through the process of creating a Smart Component that uses only the auto-sizing feature. This enables you to manually create parts that snap to size like Toolbox parts, but without using Toolbox functionality. Follow these steps:

1. Open the part from the website download materials that has the filename Chapter 18 – Tutorial Start.sldprt. This part originally came from Toolbox and already contains a few configurations.

2. Make an assembly that contains only this part.

3. Make the part into a Smart Component (Tools ➤ Make Smart Component) and turn on the option to auto-size.

4. Select the small diameter of the part as the concentric Mate Reference. Figure 18.38 shows the selection.

FIGURE 18.38
Selecting the concentric
Mate Reference face

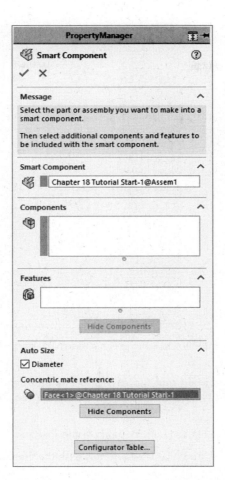

5. Click the Configurator Table button and fill in the table so it looks like Figure 18.39. Some configurations are blank. This is because only the rows that have minimum and maximum values are used by the auto-size function. The rest are overlooked.

FIGURE 18.39
Filling in the configu-
rator table

Chapter 19 Tutor	Minimum Diameter	Maximum Diameter
Default		
HX-SHCS 0.138-3		
HX-SHCS 0.19-32		
HX-SHCS 0.19-32		
HX-SHCS 0.19-32	0.1	0.199
HX-SHCS 0.25-20		
HX-SHCS 0.25-20		
HX-SHCS 0.25-28	0.2	0.249
HX-SHCS 0.3125-		
HX-SHCS 0.3125-		
HX-SHCS 0.3125-		
HX-SHCS 0.3125-		
HX-SHCS 0.375-2		
HX-SHCS 0.375-2		
HX-SHCS 0.375-2		
HX-SHCS 0.375-2		
HX-SHCS 0.375-2	0.25	0.449
HX-SHCS 0.4375-	0.45	0.469
HX-SHCS 0.4375-	0.47	0.479
HX-SHCS 0.4375-	0.48	0.499
HX-SHCS 0.5-20x	0.5	0.529
HX-SHCS 0.5-20x	0.53	0.549
HX-SHCS 0.5-20x	0.55	0.579
HX-SHCS 0.5-20x	0.58	0.599
HX-SHCS 0.625-1	0.6	0.629
HX-SHCS 0.625-1	0.63	0.659
HX-SHCS 0.625-1	0.66	0.699
HX-SHCS 0.75-16	0.7	0.8
HX-SHCS 0.875-1	0.801	1.109
HX-SHCS 1.25-12	1.11	2
PreviewCfg	0.801	1

6. Close the configurator table, click the green checkmark icon to exit the feature, and save the assembly.

7. Exit the assembly, and in the part file, save it to a folder in your Design Library. If you do not know where your Design Library is located, choose Tools ➤ Options ➤ File Locations ➤ Design Library.

8. Display the part in the Design Library panel of the Task pane.

9. Open the part from the downloaded materials with the filename Chapter 18 Tutorial Plate.sldprt. Place this part into a new assembly.

10. Drag the Tutorial Start (Smart Component) from the Design Library into the assembly and move the part over the holes in the plate. As you drag the part up and down the row of holes, the part changes size to match each hole. Figure 18.40 shows all the holes that are populated with the matching Smart Component sizes, as driven by the configurator table. Place the part over one of the diameters.

FIGURE 18.40
Smart Component parts
match holes
in the part.

11. To edit the configurator table, open the Smart Component part in its own window. Then right-click the Smart Feature folder and select Open In Defining Assembly. An assembly that was created from the data stored in the part opens.

12. Click the Edit Definition button that appears in the upper-right corner of the graphics window.

13. Reassign the minimum and maximum diameter values for the $\frac{3}{16}$-inch and $\frac{1}{4}$-inch configurations to the shortest lengths. For example, the chart shows the $\frac{3}{16-32} \times 0.75$-inch configuration to be assigned to a minimum of .1 and a maximum of .199. Move the .1 and .199 values up two cells to the $\frac{3}{16-32} \times \frac{1}{4}$-inch configuration. Do something similar for the $\frac{1}{4} - 28 \times 1$-inch configuration. The edited part of the chart now looks like Figure 18.41.

FIGURE 18.41
The edited configurator table

Chapter 19 Tutor Default	Minimum Diameter	Maximum Diameter
HX-SHCS 0.138-32x0.5x0. 5-N	0.1	.199
HX-SHCS 0.19-32x0.25x0. 25-N		
HX-SHCS 0.19-32x0.4375x 0.4375-N		
HX-SHCS 0.19-32x0.75x0. 75-N		
HX-SHCS 0.25-20x0.625x0 .625-N	.2	.249
HX-SHCS 0.25-20x1.375x1 .375-N		
HX-SHCS		

TIP You may have difficulty expanding the width of the column that contains the configuration names, thereby making it difficult or impossible to read the ends of the long configuration names. However, as with Excel, you can expand the height of the rows, which causes the configuration names to wrap, as shown in Figure 18.41.

Tutorial: Working with Library Features

This tutorial guides you through the process of customizing a Hole Wizard hole to use as a specialty library feature, storing it in the library, editing it, and placing it in a part. Follow these steps:

1. Open a new part, and create a rectangular base feature, about 3 inches high by 3 inches wide and 3 inches deep.

2. Preselect a flat face and start the Hole Wizard.

3. Create a counterbored hole for a Heavy Hex Bolt, 1/2-inch, Normal Fit, Blind, 1.2 inches deep. Locate the hole with dimensions from two perpendicular edges, as shown in Figure 18.42. Click the green checkmark icon twice to accept the hole settings.

FIGURE 18.42
Placing a hole

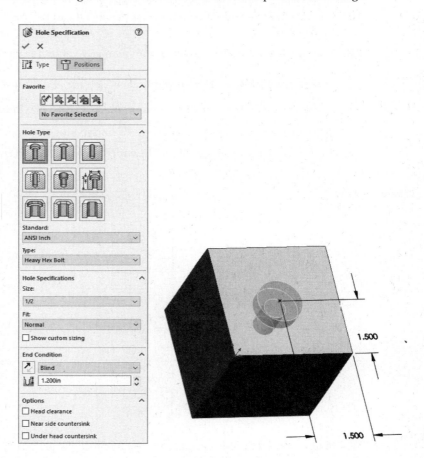

4. Turn on the setting at View ➤ Dimension Names.

5. Double-click the counterbored hole feature in the FeatureManager to show the dimensions. Make sure Instant3D is unselected for the next step.

6. Click one of the dimensions that you created to locate the center of the hole and rename the dimension in the Dimension PropertyManager (Primary Value panel) using names that will have meaning when you place the dimension, such as XDir or YDir. Do this for both dimensions.

7. Edit the second sketch of the hole. Figure 18.43 shows what the sketch should look like before and after the edit.

FIGURE 18.43

Reconfiguring the hole

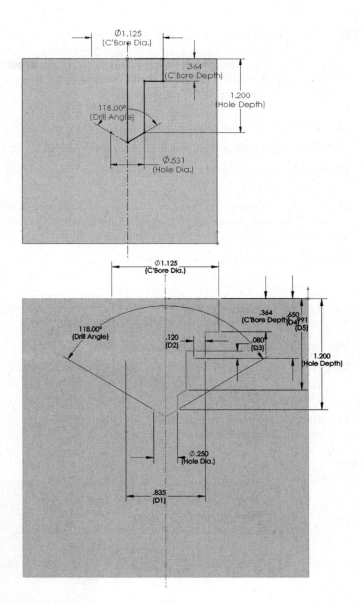

CAUTION   Don't delete any of the named dimensions in a normal or revised Hole Wizard hole. SolidWorks has a checking mechanism that looks for these names and displays an error if any of the named dimensions are not there. If there's no use for the dimension, it still must be there, although it doesn't need to be used for its original use. You could rename another dimension with the same name or simply dimension the length of the centerline or an otherwise unused construction line. It doesn't matter about the function of the dimension, as long as there's a dimension with that name in the sketch.

TIP Remember that to get the diameter dimensions shown in Figure 18.43 (instead of radius dimensions), you must use the Dimension tool to select the centerline (construction line) and the line or endpoint on one side, and then move the cursor to the other side of the centerline to place the dimension (the order of selection doesn't matter). When the cursor crosses the centerline, the dimension displays as a diameter instead of a radius.

8. When you are finished editing the sketch and renaming the dimensions, exit the sketch.

9. Click the CBORE feature twice, or click it once and press F2 to rename it as **SpecialHole**.

10. Preselect the same flat face that the first hole feature was placed on, and start the Hole Wizard again.

11. Place a #8-32 tapped hole, accept the default depth, and specify a center-to-center distance of .75 inches between it and the SpecialHole in the Horizontal or Vertical direction. Rename the radial dimension as **MountRad**.

12. Using a cylindrical face of the SpecialHole, make a circular pattern of the new tapped hole, creating a total of four instances of the tapped hole. Make the SpecialHole Feature red and the tapped hole and pattern yellow.

13. Split the FeatureManager window into two by using the splitter bar at the top. Change the lower panel to the ConfigurationManager.

14. Rename the Default configuration **Size1**.

15. Create a new configuration called **Size2**. Double-click the SpecialHole feature, and change the dimension named C'Bore Dia to 1.5 inches. Be sure to change to This Configuration Only using the drop-down menu.

16. Make a dimension change for the MountRad dimension to 1 inch. The results up to this step are shown in Figure 18.44.

FIGURE 18.44
The results after step 16

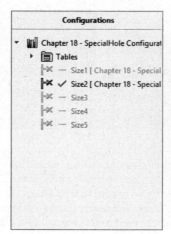

17. Auto-create a design table by choosing Insert ➤ Design Table and then selecting the Auto-Create option. Edit the design table to look like Figure 18.45. Hide or delete extra columns that don't match the data shown.

FIGURE 18.45
The design table for the SpecialHole feature

	$DESCRIPTION	$COLOR	C'Bore Dia.@Sketch3	MountRad@Sketch5
Size1	Size1	8289918	1.125	0.81
Size2	Size2	8289918	1.5	1
Size3	Size3		1.625	1.06
Size4	Size4		1.75	1.13
Size5	Size5		1.875	1.19

TIP Remember that to fill the first two columns up to Size5, you can make the two-by-two selection of the Size1 and Size2 entries in the first two columns and pull down the handle in the lower-right corner of the selection box until the appropriate boxes are filled.

18. Manually fill in the C'Bore Dia values, but in cell D3, type the equation **=C3/2 + 0.25**. Then use the same Fill technique to populate cells D3 to D7. Click outside of the design table to close it.

19. Test the configurations to make sure they all work.

20. In the Design Library, browse to a folder where you would like to put this library feature. (Make sure it's not used by any assemblies or sheet metal forming tools.) Click a face created by the SpecialHole feature, and drag the feature into the lower pane of the Design Library. The Add to Library PropertyManager should appear on the left.

21. Although you selected a feature and dragged it into the library, the Items To Add field appears blank, so you must select the SpecialHole, tapped hole, and circular pattern features using Ctrl+select for multiple selections, either through the detachable PropertyManager, the split FeatureManager, or the flyout FeatureManager. Selecting the features from the graphics window won't work.

22. Position and zoom the view of the part so that when it is saved, you see a good preview of the library feature. Also, if you have not changed your background color from blue to white, this would be a good time to do so.

23. In the Save To pane, make sure you select the correct folder, and then fill in a filename and click OK. Figure 18.46 shows the completed PropertyManager interface for this function.

FIGURE 18.46
Saving the
library feature

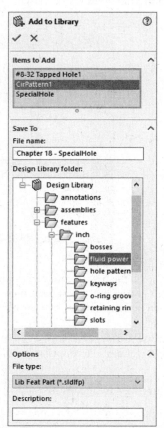

TIP   You may notice that there are two library entries in the window. This is because an additional path has been added in Tools ➤ Options ➤ File Locations ➤ Design Library.

24. If the new library feature does not appear in the Design Library, then click in the Design Library and press F5. If you don't like the way it displays, right-click in a blank space inside the lower library window and select one of the other three options.

25. To edit the preview image of the feature, right-click the feature in the Design Library window, select Open, reposition or zoom the view, and save it. Click in the Design Library and press F5 again.

26. From the download materials, open the part called `Chapter 18 Tutorial Blank .sldprt`. If you would like to examine the version of the SpecialHole part that I created, it's saved as `Chapter 18 - SpecialHole.sldlfp`. Notice that this is a library feature part file, not a regular SolidWorks part file.

27. Drag the SpecialHole library feature from the Design Library onto the face of the blank part. Place the feature near the squared-off end. Select a configuration from the list in the PropertyManager.

TIP Although there's no prompt, when the Library Feature interface hesitates and there are configurations in the library feature, it's waiting for you to select a configuration. A prompt actually does exist, but it appears in the lower-left corner of the screen on the status bar in a tiny font, and most users probably don't notice it.

28. Try to orient the part in the same way that it appears in the preview window, as shown in Figure 18.47.

FIGURE 18.47
Orienting the part and selecting references

29. On the blank part, select edges that correspond to the preview window. Click OK to accept the placement of the feature.

30. Double-click the SpecialHole feature, and change the X and Y placement dimensions to place it 1 inch from the edges in both directions.

31. Place another library feature onto the blank part. Select a configuration and click the green checkmark icon without selecting edges for the references.

32. Notice that the feature in the FeatureManager appears with an exclamation mark. If you investigate the cause of this, you will see that the two dimensions that should be attached to edges are dangling because you didn't select the references while placing the library feature. This was done on purpose to show a different technique.

33. Expand the library feature and the SpecialHole feature, and edit the first sketch in the Special Hole. This is the placement sketch. Delete the two dimensions that appear in dangling colors.

34. Add a concentric sketch relation between the placement point and the arc edge of the blank part, and exit the sketch. The error message should now be gone, and the hole should now be placed in the center of the arc.

35. Right-click the second library feature and select Dissolve Library Feature. Figure 18.48 shows the finished part and FeatureManager. Good job!

FIGURE 18.48
The finished part

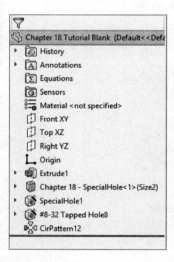

NOTE When you dissolve a library feature, you lose any access to any configurations. This technique may also be useful if you want to reorder some of the individual features within the library feature.

The Bottom Line

Assembly features can be quirky and are often used for specialized or niche applications. Having this functionality available gives you another tool in your toolbox for solving design and documentation problems.

The Hole Wizard can be a useful tool for placing machined holes through multiple parts. Automation is a great thing, and you should utilize it where it helps your process.

Master It   The most basic step in reusing data in the form of libraries is establishing the location of your libraries. Use the settings at Tools ➢ Options ➢ File Locations to do this. First, determine if you need local (on your computer) or network locations for these libraries.

Master It   Make sure you know where in your interface to find the Design Library and how to navigate its various elements.

Master It   Toolbox can be an integral part of using libraries with SolidWorks. Learning to manage Toolbox, however, may drive you to make the decision to create and manage your own library of standard parts. Make sure you have learned where the weaknesses of Toolbox are and how to work around those weaknesses.

Chapter 19

Controlling Assembly Configurations and Display States

Assembly configurations enable you to control many things, including part configurations, suppression, visibility, color, assembly feature sizes, assembly layout sketch dimensions, mate values, and suppression states. In this chapter, you will learn about related topics such as design tables, SpeedPak, derived configurations, and display states.

Display states are a better performance alternative than configurations for controlling visibility and display styles in assemblies. Display state options are discussed at length in this chapter.

IN THIS CHAPTER, YOU WILL LEARN TO:

- ◆ Change visual properties by using display states

- ◆ Use assembly configurations to manage large assemblies

- ◆ Work with the assembly configurations tutorial

Using Display States

Display states enable you to change visual properties more quickly and efficiently than configurations in assemblies and drawings. Configurations can be slow to change from one configuration to another, whereas you can change between display states almost instantaneously.

Assembly display states can also control part display states, and different instances of a part in an assembly can use different display states. Display states can be used in parts, assemblies, and drawings. They can have a great impact on assembly and drawing work.

Assembly display states also have a huge impact on drawing performance. Whenever a drawing references multiple configurations of the same assembly, it rebuilds all the referred configurations and loads all the resulting models into RAM. So, for two configurations, two assemblies load, for three configurations, three assemblies load, and so on. Display states are much more efficient, because only one set of model data is loaded, with simple flags controlling the component visibility and appearance.

Controlling Display States and Configurations

Display states can be either independent of configurations or linked to them, depending on your settings. To control the display, you can use the Display pane that pops out when you click the double-arrow icon in the upper-right corner of the FeatureManager (or you can press F8). Figure 19.1 shows the Display pane in action, along with an assembly showing parts in different display states.

FIGURE 19.1
The Display pane and an assembly with parts in different display states

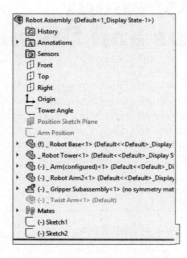

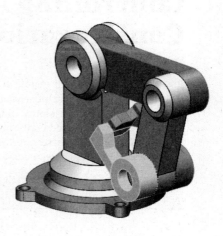

The column symbols for the Display pane are as follows:

- ◆ Hide or show state of the part
- ◆ Display Mode options for each component:
- ◆ Appearances
- ◆ Transparency
- ◆ Default Display
- ◆ Component/Part Color

Appearance overrides are settings that apply color to different aspects of model geometry. There is a hierarchy in which the appearances are applied, so an appearance applied to a feature may override or be overridden by another appearance applied to the part or an individual face. The appearance override hierarchy is summarized here, showing the highest priority at the top:

- ◆ Assembly
- ◆ Component
- ◆ Face
- ◆ Feature
- ◆ Body
- ◆ Part

So, you can read into this that the part appearance is overridden by every other type of appearance, and the appearance applied to the assembly overrides everything else.

If you override the appearance or display mode for a component in a subassembly, and the upper-left triangle appears in the Display pane, you can remove the override through the left mouse button (LMB) or the right mouse button (RMB) menu. Figure 19.2 shows the LMB menu from a component of a subassembly with overrides.

FIGURE 19.2
You can remove overrides in the assembly Display pane.

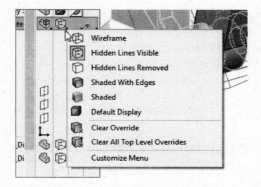

When you select Clear Override, SolidWorks clears any overrides for the currently selected component. Clear All Top Level Overrides clears all overrides in all the subassemblies in the entire top-level assembly. There is no intermediate option to clear all top-level overrides for a particular subassembly; if you want to distinguish between overrides at that level, you need to clear several individual overrides. The options to remove overrides do not affect top-level components.

The active display state appears in angle brackets after the configuration name and the filename at the top of the FeatureManager, as shown in the image on the left in Figure 19.3. Display states are created and managed in a panel at the bottom of the ConfigurationManager, as shown in the image on the right in Figure 19.3. To create a new display state, simply right-click in the Display pane and choose Add Display State. As an alternative, you can isolate the components you need to show and then click the Save icon on the Isolate tab to create a new display state.

FIGURE 19.3
Display states shown in the Feature-Manager and the ConfigurationManager

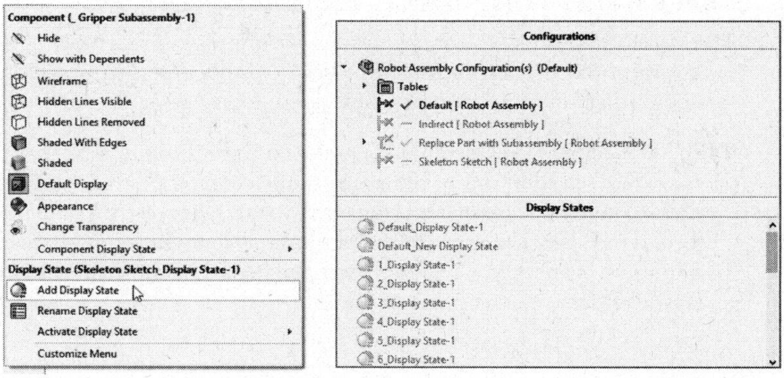

SolidWorks also allows you to open display states right from the Open dialog. This can be a big time-saver when you're opening very large assemblies that make good use of display states.

Using Display States with Drawings

Display states can be shown on drawings. If you only show or hide parts in display states, you can still use display states on drawings. For display states that change the display mode (Wireframe, Shaded, and so on) to work properly, you must set the view to the desired display mode and then select the display state from the PropertyManager for the view.

Using Part Display States in Parts

Parts can also have display states, including separate bodies within parts. You can control the part display state for specific instances of a part within an assembly in the Component Properties dialog box. Using part display states offers the same advantages as using assembly display states (mainly display speed), especially when compared to configurations.

Understanding Assembly Configurations

Assembly configurations are used for many different purposes, including assembly performance, simplified assemblies, variations of assemblies, assemblies in different positions or states, manufacturing assembly processes, and many others. Like part configurations, assembly configurations also have a few best-practice suggestions. Configuration settings for assemblies control how an assembly appears in a Bill of Materials (BOM), and what happens to parts, features, or mates that are added to other configurations, and so on. All these uses of assembly configurations are discussed in this section.

Applying Configurations for Performance

Assembly configurations are some of the best tools to make working with large assemblies easier. You can use several techniques to improve the speed of working with assemblies. Selecting a method that is appropriate to the situation is important because each method has its strengths and weaknesses.

SUPPRESSING COMPONENTS AND FEATURES

The most obvious use of configurations for improving assembly speed is to have a configuration or several configurations with suppressed components. Suppressed components are not loaded or displayed, so memory and video power are conserved.

TIP   Remember that you can use a folder for parts and suppress that folder. As an alternative, you can create selection sets of components and compress those sets. If you are just using configurations to hide parts, consider using display states, because they are more efficient for that purpose. Also, remember that a SpeedPak is a subset of configurations. A SpeedPak is a simplified representation, enabling you to select faces and bodies to represent the entire subassembly for performance reasons.

Schemes that you may want to use for suppressing parts need to have one of the following:

◆ Configurations that isolate functional areas of an assembly

◆ Configurations that remove the fasteners or purchased components

◆ Configurations that remove complex parts

◆ Configurations that leave only the parts used in in-context relations

◆ Configurations that suppress patterns and assembly features

◆ Assembly configurations that use simplified part configurations

◆ Configurations that show the assembly in different positions

◆ Variations of the assembly using different part configurations

If you suppress the "ground" part or any part that connects groups of parts, keep in mind that this can cause other parts to float in space unattached. Obviously, this is not a good situation, and you should avoid it if possible. One way to avoid it is to use an assembly layout sketch and mate the parts to the sketch instead of to the ground part.

Aside from components, other items can also be suppressed to improve performance, such as assembly features and component patterns. Do you really need to see all those parts patterned around the assembly to work on it in a simplified representation? You may be able to suppress the parts. If you feel that you cannot suppress parts, then at least consider using display states to hide parts that are needed to complete the parametrics but do not need to display.

CONFIGURING SPEEDPAKS

A SpeedPak is a configuration that uses only display data for selected faces and bodies to represent an entire subassembly, instead of opening all the parts in the assembly. In fact, a SpeedPak stores the geometry in the assembly file so it doesn't have to open any part files at all. Further, it stores all the graphic data (graphics-triangles) for all components and the body data for the selected faces or bodies.

SpeedPaks are mentioned here because they are a form of configuration, essentially a derived configuration. As a result, you can have top-level assembly configurations that call on subassemblies to use their SpeedPaks. That can be extremely helpful with very large assembly and drawing performance.

USING PART CONFIGURATIONS FOR SPEED

Simplified part configurations can consist of configurations with cosmetic features such as small fillets and extruded text, or other cosmetic details that are suppressed. Assembly configurations can use different part configurations, which, for example, would enable you to make an assembly configuration called "Simplified" and in it reference all the "Simplified" part configurations.

Other special operations for assembly configurations in the Open dialog box include creating a new configuration that has all the components suppressed. This enables you to see the structure of the assembly without fully resolving all the components. Another option is to open the assembly with a new configuration, where all the components are resolved. Beyond that, the

Open dialog box also enables you to select a specific configuration to open so that you don't have to wait for the last saved configuration to load and then make the change.

GETTING FAMILIAR WITH THE ADVANCED COMPONENT SELECTION

The Advanced Component Selection dialog box, shown in Figure 19.4, was formerly called Advanced Show/Hide Components. You can access this dialog box by right-clicking the configuration name in the ConfigurationManager and selecting Advance Select.

FIGURE 19.4

The Advanced Component Selection dialog box

This tool enables you to establish search criteria and show or hide parts based on the criteria. Multiple criteria can be used, stored, and retrieved. This tool is generally underused, and people are often surprised to find it in the software. The Category 1 options enable you to search on things such as document name, in-context status, part mass, and other standard SolidWorks information. Category 2 can be either custom property information or structured options for Category 1, such as specific in-context conditions.

LOOKING AT THE ISOLATE FUNCTION

Isolate works like the inverse of the Hide command. If you select multiple parts and click Isolate from the RMB menu, the selected parts remain shown, and everything else becomes hidden. A little pop-up menu gives you the option to show the removed components in a Wireframe or Transparent display mode, or to save the current display as a new display state. This is a very useful function, as shown in Figure 19.5.

CONTROLLING DISPLAY PERFORMANCE

Overall, SolidWorks performance is split into two categories: CPU processing and GPU (graphics processing unit) processing. Which of these functions your computer performs better depends on your hardware, drivers, and system maintenance, among other factors.

When trying to speed up the performance of an assembly, you can make the biggest impact by reducing the load on both the CPU and the GPU. You can do this by suppressing a part. When a part is suppressed, it is neither calculated nor displayed; this means the load on each processor for that part is zero.

When you hide a part, its parametric features are still calculated by the CPU; however, because the part is hidden, it does not create a load on the GPU. If you have a good main processor and a questionable video card, then you will achieve a greater benefit from removing graphics load from your display. Simply unload the hidden component from RAM.

FIGURE 19.5
The Isolate function can create display states.

Using Lightweight Parts Settings

If you want to show a part, but not calculate any of its parametric relations, you can use lightweight parts. You can access the Lightweight default settings by choosing Tools ➤ Options on both the Assemblies and Performance pages. You can make parts lightweight through the RMB menu. The opposite of lightweight is resolved. *Resolved* means that the part is fully loaded, its parametrics are loaded and calculated by the CPU, and its graphics display data is calculated and shown by the GPU. In lightweight, the body data is loaded, along with the reference geometry features and the mates for the top-level components. The graphics data will always be computed in the current session in both Resolved and Lightweight modes. The LDR mode is the only mode where the graphics data is read from the file and not computed in the session.

Working with SpeedPak

There is some confusion about where the SpeedPak functionality falls in this scheme of things. With a SpeedPak, the parametrics are not loaded, but the graphics are. In addition, some of the geometry is selectable, as if it were imported geometry (actual geometry but without rebuildable parametrics). However, a SpeedPak applies only to subassemblies, where the need for improvement is much higher.

There is a five-way relationship among the Resolved, SpeedPak, Lightweight, Hidden, and Suppressed states, as shown in Figure 19.6.

Comparing Resolved to Unsuppressed

The terminology becomes a little convoluted here because of the relationships between the five different states. In parts, the feature states are easy to remember because features can be either suppressed or unsuppressed. However, in assemblies, there are five states instead of two, so *unsuppressed* could mean anything that is not suppressed, which still leaves three states. For this reason, *resolved* is used instead of *unsuppressed* when dealing with components in an assembly.

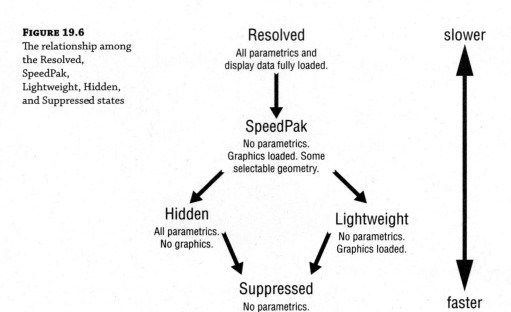

FIGURE 19.6
The relationship among
the Resolved,
SpeedPak,
Lightweight, Hidden,
and Suppressed states

Using Configurations for Positions

When you use configurations to display an assembly in various positions, you can do it either by changing mates or by changing a layout sketch. Mates are configurable in two ways: Mates can be suppressed and unsuppressed, and angle and distance mate values can be configured in the same way that sketch dimensions can be configured. Although creating a mate scheme that enables you to reposition the assembly using mate suppression states and values is essential to this method, it may not be the best approach. When mates are suppressed, the components move, and if the mates are later unsuppressed, the assembly may not return to the original position. Mates can often be solved in different orientations and may flip if turned on and off in this way.

Using a skeleton or layout sketch to mate parts may be a better approach, although this also has drawbacks. If you mate to a layout sketch, you cannot use Dynamic Assembly Motion. If you use the mate scheme discussed previously, this generally means having a fully defined assembly, and this doesn't allow for Dynamic Assembly Motion.

As a compromise, a good way to handle this is by using one configuration for Dynamic Assembly Motion, with one or more open degrees of freedom. You can use other configurations to fully define the mechanism and show it in particular positions using either method. Probably the best way to demonstrate this idea is with an example using the robot arm assembly.

POSITIONING WITH MATES

First, look at positioning with mates. On an assembly such as this one, the goal is to position the grippers. You can do this a couple of ways, both directly and indirectly. In the assembly used for this chapter, the grippers have been rebuilt as a subassembly, which allows different types of control. Notice that the subassembly has a configuration for the closed position and one that allows Dynamic Assembly Motion. In addition, the subassembly is being solved as Flexible. Figure 19.7 shows the assembly and the FeatureManager.

FIGURE 19.7

The assembly used for this example

Driving the Position Directly

A sketch point has been added to the subassembly to identify the precise point on the gripper that is to be positioned. Sketch points have also been added to the main assembly to represent parts that need to be picked up by the robotic arm.

Check the derived configurations under the default configuration. Notice that when you switch between certain configurations, the parts seem to separate. Moving one of the links causes the parts to snap back together again. This is probably because there are so many options when moving between configurations that the software has difficulty choosing a final position. This is definitely one of the potential problems when using configured mates to show an assembly in various positions.

Notice also that although the grippers are positioned correctly, the arm is still allowed to swivel around the intended target point. You can correct this by defining an orientation for the grippers for each location. If an additional pivot were added to the assembly, then fully defining the parts would become more difficult. The arm would not be able to reach any additional points, but it would not be so limited in orienting the grippers at each point.

Driving the Position Indirectly

You can also use mates to drive configured positions of the assembly using a series of angle mates. This makes it more difficult because to get to a particular location, you have to do some calculations, but the angle mates are more stable than simply relying on moving parts to uncon-strained positions.

If you cycle through the derived configurations under the Indirect top-level configuration, you will notice that mates are not suppressed and unsuppressed; instead, the values are changed. This makes it more difficult to position the grippers precisely, but because it is specific about the positions of the individual parts, there is no ambiguity.

POSITIONING WITH SKETCHES

Although this technique still uses mates to position the parts and to change the position, you change sketch dimensions rather than mate values. Sketches used to drive parts from an assem-bly are sometimes called *layout sketches* or *skeletons*. They are also discussed in Chapter 16, "Working with Assembly Sketches and Layouts," for in-context or top-down assembly tech-niques. Figure 19.8 shows the assembly that is used for the rest of this chapter.

FIGURE 19.8
Positioning assembly
components
with sketches

This particular assembly is driven by two sketches on different planes to govern the position of the parts. Keep in mind that this assembly has been used for all the other techniques as well; this means that all these techniques can exist together simultaneously and are controlled by configurations.

Examine the assembly to see how the parts are mated to the sketches. This is important. The first time you create a part such as this, you may be tempted to mate part planes to the sketch lines.

CAUTION   Be aware that mating planes to sketch lines has a very serious drawback. Unlike other types of mates, which have an alignment that you can control, plane-to-sketch line mates cannot be aligned. This means that the software may not align elements correctly on any plane-to-line mate.

BEST PRACTICE

A better way to mate part planes to sketch lines is to mate the Temporary Axes through the joints with the sketch endpoints. This solves the alignment problem.

Applying Configurations for Product Variations

In this case, *product variations* are variations in size or part replacement. Some examples are a 4-foot cabinet and an 8-foot cabinet, or a two-button mouse and a three-button mouse.

As a simple example, Figure 19.9 shows the familiar robotic arm assembly, but with a variation: one of the arms has been replaced with a subassembly. The subassembly is made of the original replaced part using configurations, and there are configurations of the subassembly, which is again being used as a flexible subassembly.

FIGURE 19.9
A part that is replaced by
a subassembly

Through the course of this chapter, the robot arm assembly has greatly increased in complexity, but it has retained the original information that was in the first version. Maintaining valid assembly data through manually managed configurations is difficult, and all it takes is a simple mistake to wipe out lots of assembly configuration data. Appropriately, the next section discusses assembly design tables.

Using Design Tables for Assembly Configurations

This chapter augments information that you need to know to use design tables effectively in assemblies. Assembly design tables can do everything that part design tables can do, except for selecting configurations of base parts and split parts, which are not valid assembly functions. Assembly design tables can also do some things that a part design table cannot, including the following:

◆ Suppressing the state of a part (R for Resolved or S for Suppressed)

◆ Assigning the component configuration for the assembly configuration

◆ Enabling you to activate the Never Expand In BOM option

Figure 19.10 shows the design table results from auto-creation using the robot arm assembly. Some columns have been hidden to make it small enough to fit on the page. If you want to see the entire table, you must open the assembly. If you edit the design table, you will probably want to use the Open In Separate Window option, which is easier to navigate and control.

FIGURE 19.10
A design table automatically created from the robot arm assembly

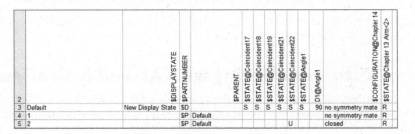

Working with Modify Configurations and the Configuration Publisher

The Modify Configuration interface is a dialog box where you can create configurations to configure dimensions, features, and custom properties in parts; you can use it in assemblies as well. It is sometimes used in place of design tables when you do not need the advanced functionality of Excel.

The Configuration Publisher is used to create a PropertyManager that pops up when the part is placed into an assembly. The PropertyManager enables you to select a configuration to go into the assembly. You can also create new configurations on demand, inside the constraints defined in the Configuration Publisher. It is a great tool for assemblies with zillions of possible variations (for example, the catalog of a crane vendor). The Configuration Publisher is also available in assemblies; this means you can use a pop-up PropertyManager when assemblies are placed into other assemblies as well. Library subassemblies may be less common than library parts, where the pop-up PropertyManager would be used to best effect.

Both tools are useful for managing assembly configurations. Design tables offer the most complete control, but they also have some drawbacks associated with being tied to Microsoft Excel. Both Modify Configurations and the Configuration Publisher are internal to SolidWorks, regardless of the level of the software you have purchased, so if you use one of them, you can be sure that whomever you send data to can access all the functionality.

Looking at Assembly Configuration Dos and Don'ts

Assembly configurations have some potential pitfalls that you can avoid if you pay attention to some of these dos and don'ts.

♦ Avoid using Delete as an editing option when working with configurations. Delete is forever and removes items from all configurations.

♦ Avoid the use of in-context relations to size parts when you are also using configurations to size parts. A nonconfigured part driven by a configured part only causes confusion.

♦ Avoid using configurations to represent document control-type revisions. When people attempt to do this, it ultimately limits the kinds of edits they can make to their parts and assemblies, and it is far too easy to make a mistake that wipes out all their work. In the end, this is not a viable technique.

♦ If you are working with manually created configurations, you should create a new configuration and activate it before making the changes. Otherwise, you will end up trying to set the original configuration back to the way it was.

♦ Remember to select the This Configuration Only option for changed dimensions instead of leaving it at the default All Configurations setting.

Tutorial: Working with Assembly Configurations

To begin this tutorial, open the assembly named Chapter 19 -Bike start tutorial.sldasm. This file contains all the aspects that you need to work with in this chapter, including subassemblies, motion configurations, and part configurations.

To learn how to work with assembly configurations, follow these steps:

1. Prepare to use configurations by splitting the FeatureManager window into upper and lower panes. Place the FeatureManager on the top and the ConfigurationManager on the bottom.

2. Before starting to make changes to this assembly, add the top-level configurations that you will need, as follows:

♦ Small Tires

♦ Motion Configuration

♦ Skeleton Driven Positions

♦ Mate Driven Positions

The configurations will list alphabetically.

3. Make sure the Advanced options for each configuration are set to suppress new features and mates and suppress new components.

4. Activate the Small Tires configuration. Figure 19.11 shows the FeatureManager up to this point.

FIGURE 19.11
The FeatureManager and ConfigurationManager up to step 4

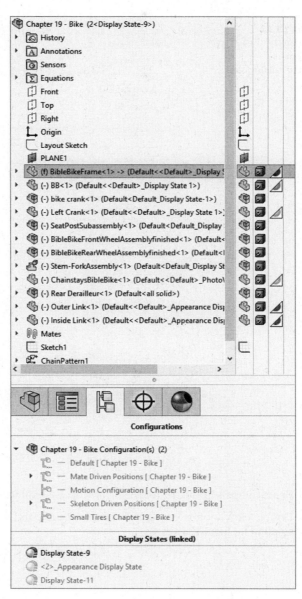

5. Open the Front Wheel Assembly in its own window, and switch to the ConfigurationManager. Add a configuration called Small Tires, and change the tire to the configuration called Small Tires, which has already been created.

6. Switch back to the main assembly window (Ctrl+Tab), right-click the Front Wheel Assembly in the FeatureManager, and select Component Properties. Select the Small Tires configuration for the Front Wheel assembly, as shown in Figure 19.12.

FIGURE 19.12
Changing the tires in the Component Properties dialog box

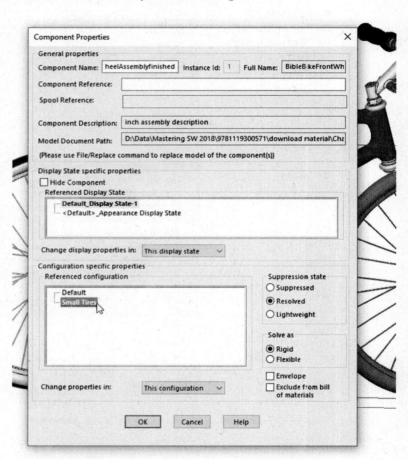

7. Repeat steps 4 through 6 for the Rear Wheel assembly.

8. Double-click another configuration from the list, and watch the assembly change from small to fat tires.

9. Change to the Motion configuration. Right-click the Stem-Fork assembly, select Component Properties, and set the assembly to be solved as Flexible.

10. Exit the dialog box, and check to see that the fork linkage mechanism moves by dragging the fork. Notice that the fork works but the front wheel does not move with it. The bike design is not yet complete, so you do not need to worry about that at this point. Putting the front wheel in the fork assembly could be used to make the wheel move with the fork.

11. Switch to the Skeleton Driven Positions configuration.

12. Display the assembly layout sketch at the top of the FeatureManager.

13. Create two new derived configurations under the Skeleton Driven Positions configuration, one called Default Position and the other called Compressed Position.

14. Activate the Default Position configuration, and make a coincident mate between the Top plane of the Chainstay part and the sketch line indicated in Figure 19.13. Again, the wheel does not move at this time.

FIGURE 19.13
Positioning the rear
of the bike

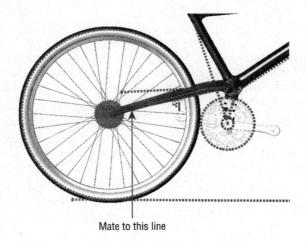

Mate to this line

15. Activate the Compressed Position configuration, and make a coincident mate between the same plane and the line that is angled up at 10 degrees.

NOTE For these configurations, you also need to set the Advanced options just as you set the top-level configurations in step 3. If you do not do this, you may need to suppress the unwanted mates manually in the appropriate configurations.

16. Switch to the Mate Driven Position configuration. Change the stem-fork assembly to a flexible subassembly (right-click and choose Component Properties ➤ Solve As Flexible).

17. Add new derived configurations called 1, 2, and 3. While creating the new configurations, ensure that the Suppress New Features And Mates and the Suppress New Components options are selected. Leave the 1 configuration activated.

18. Make an angle mate between the Bike assembly Top plane and the face of the link, as shown in Figure 19.14.

FIGURE 19.14
Using angles to position the fork

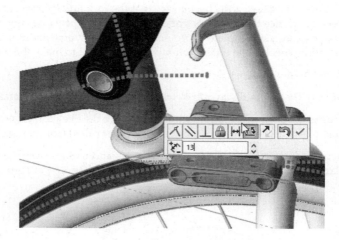

19. After the mate is complete, double-click the angle dimension (you may have to double-click the angle mate to get it to display and then zoom out to see it), and change the value to 18 degrees. Again, with the change, the fork may fly to an unexpected location. Pressing Ctrl+Q brings it back.

20. Switch to the configuration 2, unsuppress the angle mate that you made in step 18 and change the value to 25 degrees. You may have to change the configuration 2 to Flexible, although it should inherit this property from the parent configuration.

NOTE   You need to set the Fork assembly to solve as Flexible for each configuration. You may also need to control the alignment for the angle mate manually for each configuration.

The Bottom Line

Display states in the assembly can save you lots of time because they change faster than configurations and offer more options for visualization, including mixed display modes. Assembly design tables can select display states and drive many other parameters in assemblies. Remember also that Modify Configurations and the Configuration Publisher work in assemblies as well as in parts. Assembly configurations are very powerful tools for product variations and performance, especially when combined with a SpeedPak.

Master It   List at least three of the reasons or conditions under which to use display states instead of configurations.

Master It   List at least three reasons to use design tables when you're working with assembly configurations.

Master It   Explain the difference between Hidden and Lightweight model states.

Chapter 20

Modeling in Context

This chapter provides the information you need to make informed decisions about whether or not to use and how to use this powerful tool. In-context modeling is a topic worthy of some investigation before you combine production data with external references. Almost anything you can do with in-context modeling can also be done another way, but in-context is the traditional way of using the geometry of one part to drive another.

In-context modeling extends parametric design from individual parts to top-level assemblies. With this power comes the potential for unexpected results. If you are not careful, in-context modeling can lead to difficulties with file management and loss of control over changes.

IN THIS CHAPTER, YOU WILL LEARN TO:

- ◆ Understand external references in sketches and features
- ◆ Evaluate in-context modeling pros and cons
- ◆ Understand inserted, split, and mirror parts

Understanding In-Context Modeling

In-context modeling is also known as *top-down* or *in-place* modeling. This technique is used to create relationships between parts in the context of an assembly in which the geometry of one of the parts is controlled by both the other part and the mates that position them relative to one another. In contrast, *bottom-up* modeling involves making the parts in their own individual windows and assembling the finished parts into an assembly with mates.

In its simplest form, in-context modeling involves a sketch in one part in an assembly that is related to an edge in another part in the assembly. The relationship is specific to that particular assembly and is relevant only *in the context of* that assembly. For example, you may create a box and put it into an assembly. You must then create a lid that is parametrically linked to the size and shape of the box. You can create a lid part in the context of the assembly such that the lid always matches the box regardless of how the box changes. Sketch relationships, dimensions, and feature end conditions from the lid can reference the box. This in-context relationship is also known as an external relationship, where one part has a relationship to something external to itself. When the box changes, the lid also changes *if the assembly and both parts are open*. This arrangement creates another type of parent/child relationship, where the box is the parent (driving), the lid is the child (driven), and the assembly is the context. As you can see, getting used to the terminology will be one of the first hurdles. As you begin to use the techniques, you will understand why the relationship metaphors make sense.

The assembly maintains a record of each in-context reference. If the box is changed with both the assembly and the top open, then the top updates, but if the box is changed without the assembly being open, then the lid won't update until the assembly is opened. The record of the reference that the assembly maintains is held in what is called an *update holder*. SolidWorks has arranged things such that the update holder is all but forgotten and difficult to find. One update holder is created for every sketch or feature that contains references to other entities within that particular assembly. To show update holders, right-click the top-level assembly name in the FeatureManager and select Show Update Holders.

Working Through a Simple In-Context Example

Rather than continuing to discuss this topic theoretically, I'll demonstrate some in-context modeling situations, starting with a simple rectangular block. This example starts with a simple rectangular block. You have multiple options to get an in-context part into an assembly, but this example demonstrates just one. The following steps are general, because you should already be familiar with the basics of assemblies and part modeling.

STARTING A NEW ASSEMBLY

Open a new assembly, using the template of your choice. When modeling in-context, it's especially important that the parts and the assembly use the same units. If the assembly units are different from the part units, and you edit the part in the context of the assembly, then you may be presented with one type of unit while editing the part in the assembly and another type of unit while editing the part in its own window.

The next step is to save the assembly. SolidWorks doesn't force you to save it before adding the part, but it's a good idea to save the assembly (and any file, actually) after creating it.

CAUTION   SolidWorks Help says that virtual components are particularly useful with in-context modeling. This may be true, but there's more to the story. If you create parts in-context in an assembly that has not yet been saved, you may lose all your references when you save the assembly. To be safe, avoid creating in-context relations in an unsaved assembly.

What's more, you can fall into the "multiple contexts" trap where the original unsaved assembly and the new saved assembly represent separate "contexts" into which you have created features. Working in multiple contexts requires a special setting, the use of which should be reserved for special situations where you know what you are doing and why (in other words, don't create multiple contexts; it's a very bad idea).

With Virtual Parts, SolidWorks has allowed ease-of-use to create a nightmare scenario that sets up the unwary for disaster, or frustration at minimum. Is this overstated? I don't think so. Just like Toolbox and File Management, Virtual Parts and in-context are areas you need to explore using throw-away data with an experienced guide before you're ready to risk production data.

INSERTING A NEW PART

To insert a new part in the new assembly, choose Insert ➤ Component ➤ New Part and select the toolbar icon for New Part from the Insert Component flyout toolbar.

After you click the New Part command, SolidWorks will add the new part to the FeatureManager of the new assembly. Note the default naming convention shown in Figure 20.1.

Also, note the cursor with the green check mark on it. This check mark tells you (in conjunction with the text in the message bar at the bottom of the screen) that you need to select a plane or planar face to place the Front (or first, or XY) plane on the Front plane of the assembly. Remember that every template may have the standard planes renamed to anything you choose, so the first standard plane may not be called the Front plane.

FIGURE 20.1

Inserting a new blank part into a new assembly

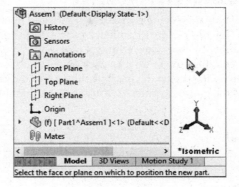

When you click the cursor with the green check mark on a plane or planar face, the Front plane of the part becomes fixed to the Front plane of the assembly, with the origins of the two files aligned, and SolidWorks automatically opens a new sketch on the Front plane of the part. The part name also turns blue. This color means that you are editing the part in the context of the assembly. Whatever you do in this state changes the part document rather than the assembly document. A new sketch, for example, is added to the part rather than the assembly.

TIP   If you simply click on the empty area of the screen, instead of selecting a plane or a face, the new part will be Fixed, with its origin and major planes sharing the origin and the planes of the assemblies. It is a great way to ensure that all the new parts share the same origin. This way, you do not need mates and you avoid having to manage the dangerous InPlace mates.

INTRODUCING VIRTUAL COMPONENTS

The part you have just added to the new assembly is called a *virtual component*. It is called "virtual" because the part is not saved yet; it's still just inside the assembly. This is why the name appears as shown in Figure 20.1. When you save the part to an external file, it loses the part of the name that's associated with the current assembly. The "components" part of the name means that both parts and subassemblies can be virtual or they can exist only within the top-level assembly. You will find more information on virtual components later in this chapter.

NOTE   A virtual component cannot have a drawing.

If you want to save the part to an external file by default, SolidWorks has an option for that. You can find the option at Tools ➤ Options ➤ Assemblies ➤ Save New Components To External Files. Without this setting, you will get a reminder to save virtual parts external to the assembly the next time you save the assembly, unless you have clicked the Do Not Show Again option for that reminder. You can get the reminder back by going to Tools ➤ Options ➤ Messages/Errors/ Warnings and deleting it from the list. If you have difficulty keeping track of all these options, the SolidWorks search bar allows you to search options, or you can use the search bar inside the Tools ➤ Options dialog box.

CREATING THE PART GEOMETRY

Sketch a centered rectangle from the origin, and give it dimensions of 4 inches (100 mm) tall by 5 inches (125 mm) wide. Extrude it 2 inches (50 mm). You can find the Extrude Command icon on the Assembly toolbar when editing a part in the context of the assembly.

Now exit the part. To do this, click the Edit Component icon in one of the places where it shows up on the screen. Figure 20.2 shows it in the Confirmation Corner in the upper-right corner of the graphics window. You can also find it on the Assembly toolbar.

FIGURE 20.2
Using the Confirmation
Corner to exit Edit
Component mode

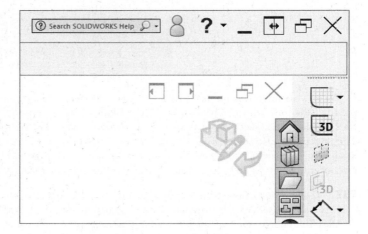

UNDERSTANDING IN-CONTEXT

You have to be really careful about what you do in the context of an assembly. For example, when you sketched your rectangle in-context, did you make any references that went outside of the part? Of course not, how could you? There is nothing outside the part. Are you sure about that?

The tell-tale sign of an in-context relation is the arrow symbol (->) after a sketch, feature, or part in the FeatureManager. Look to see if you have a symbol like that after your sketch. You probably do. If you have this in-context symbol and haven't saved your assembly, you're primed to fall into the "multiple contexts" trap mentioned earlier. Here's how

First, your centerpoint of the rectangle has probably referenced the assembly origin rather than the part origin. This qualifies as an external reference; therefore, it gets an arrow symbol (->). You could get another one by sketching on an assembly plane instead of the part plane. I told you, you have to be careful in assemblies.

To see these relationships in more detail, while editing the assembly (not the part), right-click on the top-level assembly name in the FeatureManager and select Show Update Holders.

Figure 20.3 shows an update holder at the bottom of the new assembly tree, along with the arrow symbol (->) after the sketch.

FIGURE 20.3

Update holders indicate in-context relations.

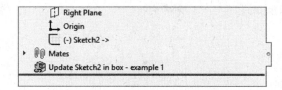

If you've created this situation, it's easy enough to repair. Edit the sketch, delete the relation between the sketch point and the assembly origin, and re-create it to the part origin. As a hint, select items from the FeatureManager (or from the Select Other dialog) when you're unsure about what the cursor is selecting when multiple items are stacked on top of one another.

SAVING A VIRTUAL COMPONENT

Next, right-click the name of the part you just added and select Save Part (in External File), as shown in Figure 20.4. Give the part the name Box (by slowly double-clicking the default name in the Save As dialog box that appears), and save it to your desktop (by clicking the Specify Path button in the Save As dialog box) or another place where it will be easy to find and delete later. This part is just for practice in this chapter.

FIGURE 20.4

Saving the virtual components to an external file

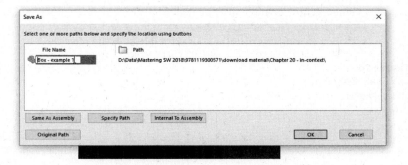

Notice that the name of the part in the assembly FeatureManager has changed, and the name is no longer surrounded by brackets or followed by the assembly name.

CREATING AN IN-CONTEXT PART

To create another new part in the assembly, and use the first part to drive this one, you must again click the New Part icon. When you see the cursor with the green check mark, click the 5 × 4 end face that you created using the Extrude feature.

When you do this, the first part you created turns transparent. This helps you identify which part is being worked on (the nontransparent part is current). You can find the settings controlling this behavior at Tools ➤ Options ➤ Colors. Toward the bottom of that page is a setting called Use Specified Colors When Editing Parts In Assemblies. You can find a related setting at Tools ➤

Options ➤ Display. Under the heading for Assembly Transparency For In Context Edit is a drop-down list with three options: Opaque Assembly, Maintain Assembly Transparency, and Force Assembly Transparency. The default is Force Assembly Transparency. These options are shown in Figure 20.5.

FIGURE 20.5
Establishing assembly transparency while editing in-context parts

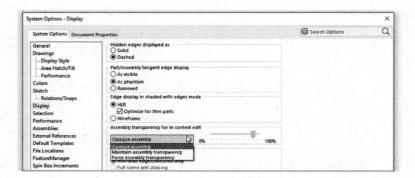

To create the sketch for the first feature of the in-context part, click the same face that you just clicked to place the second part, and use the Offset Entities to make a sketch loop offset by 0.25 inch (5 mm) to the outside.

To contrast two methods of selection, after using the face selection to offset to the outside, right-click one of the edges of the face of the Box part and choose Select Loop from the menu. A small yellow arrow will indicate the side to which the offset will be created. Then use the Offset Entities to offset sketch lines from the selected loop of edges toward the inside again by 0.25 inch (5 mm). Figure 20.6 shows the result of the offset.

FIGURE 20.6
Using two methods to offset sketches in context

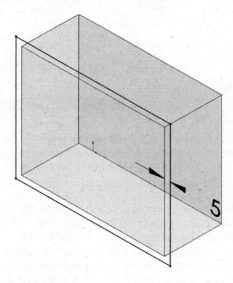

With this single sketch containing a nested loop, use the Extrude feature to extrude 0.5 inch (10 mm). When complete, use the Confirmation Corner again to exit the part. You should now have an assembly that is not saved, a part that is saved with the name Box, and a second part that is just a virtual component.

After exiting Edit Component mode, you should also see that the two parts are the same color. Click a face of the newly created part, click the Appearance drop-down menu, and select the indicator for the part. Figure 20.7 shows the cursor pointing to this indicator. Change the part color using the panel that appears in the PropertyManager (don't change the entire appearance, just the color).

FIGURE 20.7
Changing the color of a virtual component

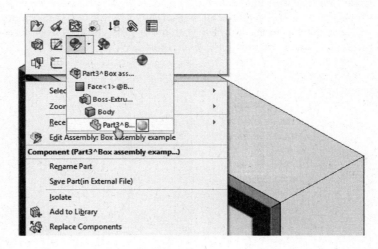

Another thing to notice about the creation of an in-context part is that SolidWorks adds InPlace mates to the Mates folder that lock the new part in place. Motion can cause in-context features to move unexpectedly, so parts that have in-context features are usually recommended to be locked down in one way or another. This is one way that SolidWorks is looking out for you in the in-context scheme. Figure 20.8 shows InPlace mates and update holders.

FIGURE 20.8
SolidWorks creates InPlace mates for parts started in the assembly and update holders for in-context features.

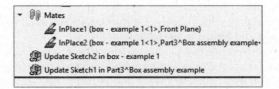

EDITING THE DRIVING PART OF AN IN-CONTEXT REFERENCE

Now comes the tricky part. You are going to change the overall shape of the Box part and observe the effect on the virtual component. In order to do this, click the sketch under the Extrude feature in the Box part and select Edit Sketch from the pop-up toolbar.

NOTE   Notice that there's a difference between using Save As from the menu and the Save button from the Title Bar toolbar. Save As allows you to save only the assembly file, while the Save command enables you to save both the assembly and the virtual component.

After this is complete, you will be ready to edit the sketch of the Extrude feature in the Box part. If necessary, expand the Box part in the FeatureManager by clicking the plus symbol (+) to the left of the name and clicking the plus symbol next to the Extrude feature. Now you can click the sketch and select Edit Sketch from the pop-up list.

While editing the sketch of the box, right-click one line of the rectangle and choose Select Chain. With all four lines selected, click the Construction Geometry toggle in the PropertyManager. This turns all lines of the rectangle into construction lines.

Next, draw a circle concentric with the origin, with the circumference on one corner of the rectangle. The sketch now looks like Figure 20.9.

FIGURE 20.9
Replacing a rectangle
with a circle

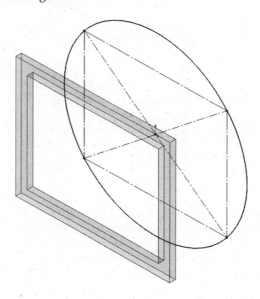

After you make this change, exit the sketch. The in-context references won't update until you exit the part and return to the assembly.

Just to get you prepared, what do you expect to see? Remember that one set of referenced edges was referenced by selecting a face, and the other set was referenced by selecting edges.

When you leave Edit Part mode and return to Edit Assembly mode, you'll find that the outer lines have updated to the circle (because the face you selected is circular instead of rectangular), but the edges you selected will still be rectangular and display a warning symbol. This is because the edges referenced by those lines no longer exist. If you hover your cursor over one of the errors shown in Figure 20.10, the message "Warning: Unable to offset one or more sketch entities" will appear. You can avoid this error by using the same technique to select the inner lines as the outer lines (or just using the outer lines and making a Thin feature).

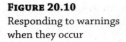

Figure 20.10

Responding to warnings when they occur

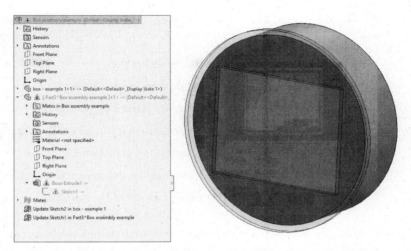

Go ahead and fix this error by editing the sketch in the Virtual Part (box lid), deleting the lines causing the problem, and remaking them by offsetting from the selected face. Offset sketch relations cannot be repaired or edited in the way you need to repair the existing relations. In general, you should avoid using Delete as an editing technique, but there's no other way in SolidWorks to repair this kind of issue.

This demonstration points out some of the strengths and weaknesses of in-context modeling, but not all of them. The rest of the chapter will help you get a better idea of how to evaluate this technique for yourself.

Weighing the Advantages of In-Context Modeling

The advantages of in-context modeling are obvious. In-context modeling is just an extension of parametric techniques to include parts in the context of an assembly. Making a change to one part and having all related parts update offers indisputable advantages. When it works correctly, all the parts of an assembly can be updated from a single change. Changes propagate all the way through to the part drawings.

Some users approach modeling haphazardly—and if it works, it's "good enough." For some types of work, this is acceptable and really may be good enough. For example, it usually works when you create something that will never be changed or if you are working on initial concept models that won't be given to other users.

On the other hand, users who need to build models that will be reused frequently, changed often, or given to other users to work on must approach the decisions they make during modeling as if they were playing chess. Each decision has consequences. You rarely know exactly how things are going to turn out, but you need to prepare for the most likely contingencies, assessing potential risks along the way.

Anticipating Problems with In-Context Modeling

The overall concept of in-context modeling is a great idea; the problems occur with the practical application of the technique and the management of the results through changes. In particular, the biggest problems seem to arise when in-context techniques are combined with other techniques. You must be very careful about things such as file management, assembly motion, multiple instances of parts in assemblies, configurations, and related issues when in-context references exist in your assembly.

Major potential problems include the following:

◆ Lost references due to renamed parts or assemblies

◆ Convoluted (multiple) references causing long rebuild times

◆ Circular (self-referring) references causing changes with each rebuild

◆ External references causing conflicts with motion

◆ Serious difficulties between in-context techniques and configurations

◆ Frustrated users who don't understand how to manage changes or references in an in-context scheme

For users who prefer to use model items in drawings, in-context techniques offer some challenges. Model items are either unavailable or limited in availability for features created in-context. This is because if you have used Convert Entities to copy edges of one part to another, no dimensions have been used, so none will show up in inserted model items. In-context model items would show up when you use offset edges or dimension sketch elements to in-context edges. Aside from these, the only model item drawings you can create are in an assembly drawing. For this reason, the majority of dimensions on drawings are driven dimensions.

Identifying Alternatives to In-Context Modeling

One of the most frequent problems with in-context modeling is related to file management. Inexperienced users may move or rename a file or a folder in Windows Explorer and unknowingly break links, or they may try to use an in-context part in some assembly other than where the in-context relation was created. As a result, they may not be able to make changes that they want to make, or changes may happen when they do not want them.

Sometimes these problems are the result of users simply not understanding what to expect from the tool, and sometimes it is because the tool is not capable of doing what they want. Right or wrong, many users have developed an irrational fear of references that can control a part from outside of the part. In-context modeling in itself is not a bad technique, but sometimes it is not the best option, depending on the particular situation. You need to understand in-context and all related techniques first before passing judgment on any of the techniques.

It's always important to identify alternative techniques because one tool never solves all possible problems. In-context modeling is powerful, but in some situations, other techniques are more appropriate. The following sections introduce a couple of techniques that share with in-context the ability to control individual parts from a centralized location, but they achieve that in ways that are somewhat different: assembly layout and multibody modeling. *Assembly layout modeling* enables you to control individual parts not from other parts but from an assembly-level sketch. *Multibody modeling* enables you to control several parts from a single part without worrying about the file management issues of having another assembly as the middle agent.

USING ASSEMBLY LAYOUT MODELING

Assembly layouts are powerful tools that remove much of what some people object to in in-context modeling. Relationships in this technique are controlled by top-level sketches, where a single sketch or multiple sketches can control most of the features on all parts through relationships between part sketches or features and the assembly sketch. This still creates an external reference that requires the existence of an assembly to update the relationships, but it is not a direct link between different parts in the context of the assembly.

Assembly layouts do not lend themselves well to dynamic assembly motion, but they are great if you want to have a single location to drive an entire assembly. Assembly layouts come in two types: the generic layout, which is simply done using sketches in an assembly; and the formal Layout feature, which is essentially a 3D sketch in the assembly with special properties. The Layout feature is described in more detail later in this chapter. Assembly layout sketches are covered in more detail in Chapter 3, "Working with Sketches and Reference Geometry."

Using Multibody Modeling

Multibody modeling, like in-context modeling, is a powerful technique with strengths and weaknesses. If you model something that later will be separate parts together in a single part, you can avoid in-context modeling altogether. You should not replace assemblies with multibody modeling for a number of reasons, such as limitations of multibody techniques for common assembly operations such as dynamic assembly motion and interference detection. Used judiciously, multibody modeling can help you save time making models that hold up well to changes. Master model techniques are discussed at length in Chapter 33, "Employing Master Model Techniques."

Dealing with the Practical Details of In-Context Modeling

Figure 20.11 shows a simple box with the sketch of a simple top for the box. Notice in the FeatureManager that two parts are listed as the top and base. The .050-inch offset is creating a sketch in the top part that is driven by the edges of the base part. This simple assembly demonstrates the in-context process in the sections that follow.

FIGURE 20.11
The top of the box being built in-context

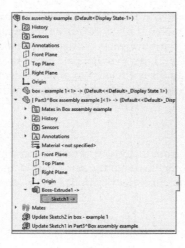

Understanding the In-Context Process

You can perform in-context modeling using one of two basic schemes. You can build parts from the very beginning in the context of the assembly (using the Insert ➤ Component ➤ New Part menu option), or you can start them using bottom-up techniques, creating the parts in a separate part window, adding them to the assembly, and then adding additional in-context features later.

STARTING IN CONTEXT

To start a new part in the context of an assembly, you first assume that the assembly contains another part. Creating a new part in a blank assembly isn't very interesting. This example uses the assembly shown in Figure 20.11. To create the new part, choose Insert ➤ Component ➤ New Part. This command is also available through a toolbar button (shown to the left) that you can place on the Assembly toolbar. At this point, SolidWorks prompts you to select a face or plane on which to locate the new part. When you select the face or plane to place, SolidWorks places the Front plane of the new part on it, opens a new sketch, and adds an InPlace mate to the assembly. In-context parts start as virtual parts, saved inside the assembly; you can choose to save them as external or internal parts the next time you save the assembly. Virtual part functionality will be discussed later in this chapter.

InPlace Mate

The mate that SolidWorks automatically adds when a part is created in-context is called an *InPlace* mate. It works like the Fixed option, although it is actually a mate that is listed with the other mates and may be deleted but not edited.

The InPlace mate clamps the part down to any face or plane where it is applied. It is meant to prevent the in-context part from moving. Later in this chapter, you will learn why it is so important for in-context parts not to move.

Alternative Technique

Instead of using the Insert ➤ Component ➤ New Part command, you can simply create a blank part in its own window and save it to the desired location. Then you can insert the blank part into the assembly and mate the origins coincident. You can then edit the part in-context, the same as if you had created it in-context from the beginning. The only differences between parts developed this way and parts created in-context are the InPlace mate and the fact that the in-context part starts as a virtual part while the existing part does not. The InPlace mate cannot be edited and is not related to other geometry in the usual sense. Many users feel more secure with real mates to real geometry, which they can identify and change if necessary.

Valid Relations

Sketches, vertices, edges, and faces from the other parts in the assembly can be referenced from the in-context part as if they were in the same part as the sketch. Most common relations are concentric for holes and coincident for hole centers. Converted entities

(On-Edge relations) make a line-on-edge relation between the parts, and Offset sketch relations are also often used.

Other types of valid in-context relations include in-context sketch planes and end conditions for Extrude features such as Up To Face and Up To Body. Beyond that, you can copy surfaces from one part using the Knit Surface feature or the Offset Surface feature.

WORKING IN-CONTEXT

When you are working in-context or using in-context data, visual cues offer information about the part on which you are working. The following topics will help you understand what is going on while you are working in-context.

Text Color

When you are working in-context, the FeatureManager text of the part you are working on turns blue. This should make two things immediately obvious: first, that you are working in-context, and second, which part is being edited.

Part Color and Transparency

You can control the color and transparency behavior of parts in the assembly where a part is being edited in-context by choosing Tools ➤ Options ➤ Colors Page. Figure 20.12 shows a detail of this page. The option at the bottom of the dialog box determines whether the colors specified in the list at the top are used or ignored. If they are ignored, the parts are the same colors they would be if you were not using in-context techniques.

FIGURE 20.12
Part-color settings for
in-context control

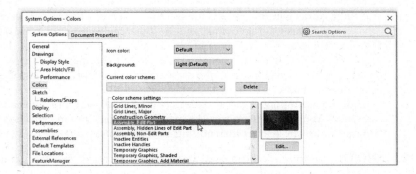

The Tools ➤ Options ➤ Display/Selection Assembly Transparency For In Context Edit setting controls the transparency of the parts not being edited. Figure 20.5 shows this setting. Forcing the nonedited parts to become transparent helps you keep focus on the part you are editing in the assembly.

These are the options in the Assembly Transparency for In Context Edit drop-down list:

Opaque Assembly: All parts that are not being edited when an assembly component is being edited in-context turn opaque, even if they are otherwise transparent.

Maintain Assembly Transparency: This option leaves all assembly components in their default transparency state.

Force Assembly Transparency: This option forces all the parts, except for the one being edited in the assembly, to become transparent.

These options reflect personal preference more than anything else does, but it's useful to have a reminder as to whether a part is being edited in the assembly or the assembly document is being edited in its own window.

TIP The color selected in the box shown in Figure 20.12 controls both the text color and the color of the part shown in the graphics window.

Edit Component Button

You can use the Edit Component button in three ways. First, after you have created a part in-context, seeing the Edit Component button depressed reminds you that you are editing the part rather than editing the assembly. Along with the part color and transparency displays, this is important feedback because assembly functions such as mates, exploded views, and others are not available when you are editing the part.

Second, you can use the Edit Component button to begin or finish editing a part that is already in an assembly. When you are editing a part in the context of an assembly, the title bar of the SolidWorks window reflects the fact that you are editing a part in an assembly, the toolbar changes to a part-editing toolbar, and the lower-right corner of the taskbar displays the words *Editing Part*, as shown in Figure 20.13.

Third, a Confirmation Corner image exists in the upper-right corner of the graphics window when you are editing a part in the context of the assembly. This makes it easier to leave Edit Component mode.

Editing a component can also mean editing a subassembly in the context of the top-level assembly. You can create in-context assembly features and mates if necessary; however, you will do this far less frequently than editing parts in-context.

NOTE Creating in-context relations is not the only reason to edit a part or subassembly in the context of the top-level assembly. Sometimes it is simply more convenient to do normal editing when you are in the top-level assembly; this way, you can see how the part relates to other parts after making changes in the assembly without making relations between the parts.

Editing a subassembly in the context of the upper-level assembly is often useful as well, to see how changing subassembly mates affects the top level.

FIGURE 20.13
Indicators that you are
editing a part in-context

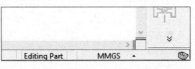

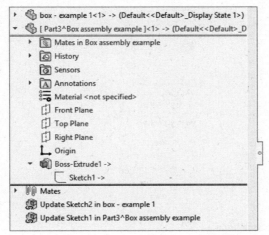

Probably the most common mistake you can make with in-context editing has to do with editing the part versus editing the assembly when you add a sketch. If you intend to add a sketched feature to a part in the context of an assembly, but you fail to switch to Edit Part mode before creating the sketch, then the sketch ends up in the assembly rather than the part. You can do only limited things with a sketch in an assembly. Likewise, if you intend to make an assembly layout sketch, but you do not switch out of Edit Part mode, you end up with a sketch in a part that cannot do what you want it to do.

Fortunately, SolidWorks has added a remedy for the first situation. When you make a sketch in the assembly but need to make a feature in the part, you can choose the Propagate Feature To Parts option in the Feature Scope area of the PropertyManager for the feature, as shown in Figure 20.14.

Notice in the image on the right that the last sketch in the part appears as derived. This means that the sketch and the feature are still driven from the assembly, but they have been propagated to the part enough to allow the feature to be edited in the part. You may not want to go this route just because you made a mistake and it's simpler to do this than to move the sketch to the part, but it's a valid option in some situations. Interestingly, this feature cannot be deleted from the part (unless you RMB on the feature in the part and select Make Independent); you must delete it from the assembly.

FIGURE 20.14
Propagating an assembly
feature to the part

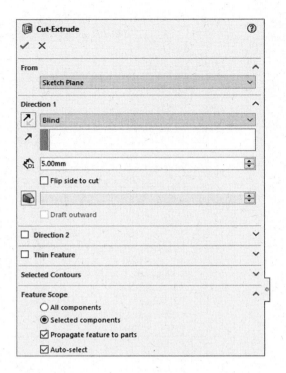

External Reference Symbols

I have already discussed the external reference symbol (->). But there are more variations of the symbol that I haven't mentioned. External references can have four states, as shown in Figure 20.15. These are in-context (->), out-of-context (-> ?), locked reference (-> *), and broken reference (-> x):

In-context (->): The in-context symbol signifies that the relation created between two parts within the current assembly is fully resolved. Both parts involved in the relationship and the assembly where the relationship that was created are open and available.

Out-of-context (-> ?): Out-of-context means that the document—usually but not necessarily an assembly—where the reference was created is not open at the time. You can open the document where the reference was created by clicking the right mouse button (RMB) and selecting the Edit In Context option from the menu. Edit In Context opens either the parent part of an inserted part or the assembly where the reference was created for an in-context reference. When you open the referencing document, the out-of-context symbol changes to the in-context symbol.

Locked reference (-> *): You can lock external references so the model does not change, even if the parent document changes. Other features of the part may be changed, but any external reference within the part remains the way it is until the reference is either unlocked or removed. In the top and base example mentioned earlier, this means that if the Bottom part is changed, and the external reference on the Top is locked, then the Top no longer fits the Bottom.

One of the best things about locked references is that you can unlock them. They are also flexible and give you control over when updates take place to parts with locked references.

Broken reference (-> x): The broken reference is another source of controversy. Some users believe that if you make in-context references, the best way to respond to them is to break them immediately. However, one could argue that using the Break References function is *never* a good thing to do. You should remove the reference by editing the feature or the sketch or change it to make it useful.

The problem with a broken reference is that it has absolutely no advantage over a locked reference. For example, while locked references can at least be unlocked, broken references cannot be repaired. The only thing that you can do with a broken reference is to use Display/Delete Relations or to edit features manually to completely remove the external reference.

NOTE Some users employ Break References when they want to push features from the parent parts into the children parts. This is a limited case, though, employed mostly for mirrored parts.

There exists an option in Tools ➢ Options that can eliminate the "x" for broken external references. This doesn't actually remove the reference, it just removes the marker. To reassign any sort of reference, you would still have to edit the reference and remove the broken portion. This is just another example where ease-of-use (or in this case laziness) trumps information, especially where the information is actually bad news. Avoid breaking references. It's lazy, sloppy, and bad practice. Instead, edit the reference and remove it completely.

FIGURE 20.15
External reference symbol variations

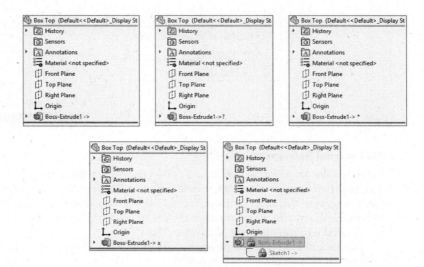

Frozen reference (??): Freezing is a technique that is not necessarily intended for external references, but it can be used on them. To freeze any feature, including external references, use the yellow Freeze bar at the top of the FeatureManager to pull down the tree. It works just like the Rollback bar, but instead of undoing features temporarily, it freezes their parametrics, so that a portion of the tree from the top to where ever you put the Freeze bar acts like imported data until it is thawed by rolling the Freeze bar back up the tree.

Best Practice

The best practice is to avoid placing yourself in a situation where you are using broken references. Parametric relations should not change if the driving geometry does not change.

You cannot selectively lock or break external relations. For example, all the external relations in the part can be locked or broken, or none of them can be locked or broken. If you need to disable relations selectively, you should consider suppressing features, sketch relations, end conditions, or sketch planes.

List External References

You can access the locked and broken references through the List External References option on the RMB menu of any feature with an external reference symbol. Figure 20.16 shows the name and path of the assembly where the external reference was created, as well as the part names and entity types.

Figure 20.16
The External References
dialog box

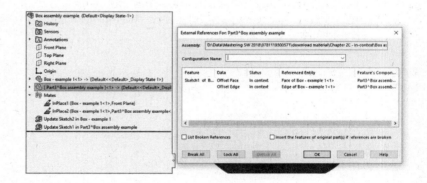

No External References

To access the No External References button on the Assembly toolbar, choose Tools ➤ Options ➤ External References ➤ Do Not Create References External To The Model from the menus. As its name suggests, this setting prevents external relations from being created between parts in an assembly. When you offset in-context edges or use Convert Entities, the resulting sketch entities are created without relations of any type.

This lack of references includes the InPlace mate, which is not created when a part is created in-context. As a result, when you add the part to the assembly, if you exit and later reenter Edit Part mode, SolidWorks reminds you that the part is not fixed in space by displaying the warning shown in Figure 20.17.

FIGURE 20.17
The dialog box that
warns you about adding
in-context relations
to an under-
defined part

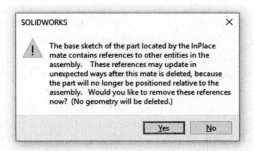

This message should remind you that in-context features should be used only on parts that are fully positioned in the assembly.

External Reference Settings in Tools ➤ Options

The Tools ➤ Options ➤ External References pane of settings controls many aspects of the behavior of external references. One of these options (No External References) was discussed earlier, and the other option (Multiple Contexts) is discussed in the next section. This pane in the Tools ➤ Options dialog box is shown in Figure 20.18.

FIGURE 20.18
The Tools ➤ Options ➤
External
References pane

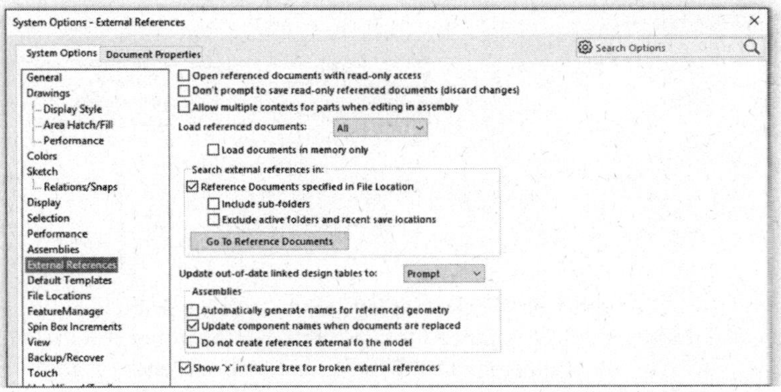

Managing References

SolidWorks offers several ways to handle missing or broken references:

◆ Break all external references in an assembly. Access this tool by right-clicking the top-level assembly name in the FeatureManager, selecting List External References, and choosing Break All or Lock All. You can also access this tool for each individual assembly component.

◆ The new functionality in 2018 is that you can do this at the top level. Previously, you could do it only for individual components.

◆ Hide the Broken Reference indicator (-> x) through the setting at Tools ➤ Options ➤ External References ➤ Show "x" in Feature Tree for Broken External References. This option is not recommended. If something is wrong, you need to know it, not ignore it.

◆ In the Open dialog box, when you open an assembly, select the References button to see the parts and subassemblies referenced by the assembly.

Looking at In-Context Best Practices

This technique requires a fair amount of discipline, restraint, foresight, and judgment. The potential problems associated with overuse or misuse of in-context techniques primarily include performance problems (speed) and lost references due to file management issues. Users may also experience problems with features or sketches that change with each rebuild. The following section contains best practice suggestions that can help you avoid these situations.

WORKING WITH MULTIPLE CONTEXTS

Multiple contexts occur when a part has references that are created in multiple assemblies. By default, multiple contexts are prevented from happening. If you place a part that already has external references into a different assembly, a warning appears, as shown in Figure 20.19.

FIGURE 20.19
The warning message that appears about multiple contexts

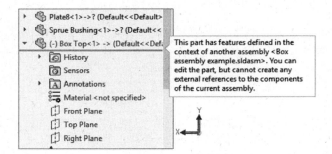

Although SolidWorks displays many warnings about multiple contexts, you may still run into situations where you need to use them. For example, you may have a subassembly where a part, such as a top plate of a stand, has in-context references to locate a set of mounting holes for legs of the stand. When you place the subassembly into the top-level assembly and mount another assembly to the top plate, another set of in-context holes is required in the top plate.

Figure 20.20 shows the first table and points out the update holders. The large bracket appears for the machine that is mounted to the tabletop using more in-context relations. If you examine the External References dialogs for the two in-context features in the table top, you will notice that the Assembly fields at the top of the External References dialog boxes are different. You can achieve this only by selecting the Allow Multiple Contexts for Parts When Editing in Assembly option shown in Figure 20.18.

NOTE   The Tools ➤ Options setting for multiple contexts is a system option. This means that this option is either on or off for every document on a single machine, but when the assembly is used on another machine, the option may be off.

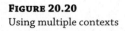

FIGURE 20.20
Using multiple contexts

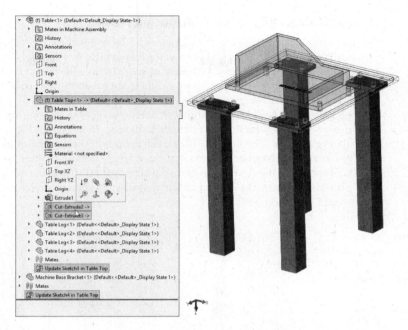

Multiple-context modeling should be the exception rather than standard practice. If you do not have all the assemblies open where the in-context references were created, then you will have some out-of-context references. This can make for a troubleshooting nightmare if someone ever has to try to reconstruct how the assembly is driven.

> **BEST PRACTICE**
>
> The best practice is to avoid creating multiple-context references. If you need to do this, then be very careful about naming files, and remember to turn off the multiple-context option when you have finished creating the reference.

If you receive a multiple-context part from someone else, the first thing to do is to determine whether you have all the files required to make it work. Right-click the external reference symbol and select Edit In Context to determine whether SolidWorks can find the right files. Also, looking for an out-of-context symbol will tell you if any of the necessary files are not currently open.

Aside from doing some programming, the only way to find out whether a part was created as a multiple-context part is to examine the External References list for each in-context feature. This can be very time-consuming. Although multiple-context parts should be very rare, it is impossible to determine ahead of time whether a part that you have received is a multiple-context part, at least without programming. The one exception to this is when some features are in-context and some are out-of-context.

USING IN-CONTEXT WITH CONFIGURATIONS

On the surface, mixing in-context references with configurations sounds as if it combines two powerful techniques that should offer you great control over models. Although this may sometimes be true, you need to be aware of some of the effects that combining these two techniques may cause. In particular, you should be careful about part configurations, particularly configurations of the *referenced* part.

If you are using in-context relations to parts with configurations, then you may want to consider a few things. First, look at the door-hinge part shown in Figure 20.21. One plate has three configurations. The second hinge plate is built in the context of the assembly so it will always match the first plate; therefore, it has a single default configuration. The figure shows the results of changing the first hinge-plate part configuration in the assembly. This looks like an ideal situation because the second hinge plate always changes to match the first hinge plate. What could be wrong with this?

FIGURE 20.21
Combining in-context references with configurations

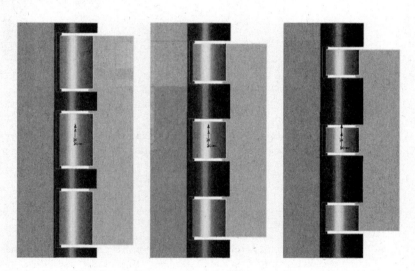

The problem here is that you can show only the size of the second hinge plate that corresponds to the configuration of the first plate that is active in the assembly. If you had two instances of the hinge assembly in a top-level assembly, you would be able to show only one size for the second plate.

A second situation where combining in-context references and configurations can cause you trouble is if you have referenced the edges of a part from another part, and a configuration of the referenced part either adds or removes fillets or chamfers, thereby breaking the edges. Both of these situations can cause either the in-context sketches or other features to fail. This may be a reason to reference the underlying sketches, rather than the actual model edges or faces.

In some situations, configurations work well with in-context relations. One example of this would be when an assembly has many configurations used for positioning parts. In this case, you would use one configuration for the sole purpose of creating in-context relations.

USING IN-CONTEXT WITH MOTION

You should make in-context references between parts where there is no relative motion. The parts themselves can move relative to the rest of the assembly, but they should remain stationary relative to one another. The parts should also be fully defined to ensure that they won't move; you should not simply assume that you would avoid dragging underdefined parts. This is because if one part drives a feature on another part, and the parts move relative to one another, the in-context feature is also likely to move within its parent part.

In some cases, such as an assembly of imported parts, it may make sense to fix parts in bulk rather than to mate them. When you are using in-context relations, you need to take extra care to ensure that the parts do not move around. When parts move around, in-context features also move.

Obviously, if the motion is around a circular hole and the in-context feature is circular and is not affected by the rotation of the referenced part, then it makes less difference; however, if there is a keyway, that may change things. You need to pay attention when combining underdefined parts and in-context features.

BEST PRACTICE

As a best practice, you should avoid in-context relations between parts when relative motion is allowed between those parts.

WORKING WITH IN-CONTEXT WITH MULTIPLE INSTANCES

Another situation that can cause problems is when multiple instances of an in-context part are being used in the assembly. In cases like this, you need to be careful and consistent, by always using the same instance to create the in-context relations. You can do this by putting parts into folders or by giving the in-context part a special component color.

One trick is to use one instance of an in-context part for the in-context relation and a second instance of the part to allow motion. In-context relations are tied to one specific instance of a part, regardless of how many of those parts are in the assembly. You might want to set the driving in-context part aside by putting it in a folder, changing its color, or hiding it.

USING IN-CONTEXT AND FILE MANAGEMENT

Understanding what you are doing with file management is imperative when working with parts that depend on in-context features. Because the references are stored in both the part that is doing the referencing and the assembly where the reference is created, improperly changing the name of either document or even the referenced document is bound to cause problems. For example, if you rename an in-context part using Windows Explorer, the assembly won't recognize the part. This also means that any in-context references won't update. The part will show the out-of-context symbol.

BEST PRACTICE

As a best practice, you should use either the SolidWorks Save As command or SolidWorks Explorer to rename parts and assemblies. This applies to all parts and assemblies, but even more to in-context documents.

USING IN-CONTEXT AND MATES

A section on in-context best practices wouldn't be complete without issuing the warning against mating to in-context features. Mating parts to in-context features creates a parametric daisy chain, thereby establishing an order in which assembly features and mates must be solved. This always creates performance problems in assemblies, especially large ones. The SolidWorks Performance Evaluation looks for this condition when examining assemblies.

IDENTIFYING CIRCULAR REFERENCES

Circular references in assemblies are a bigger problem than most people realize. In fact, most people do not realize that circular references *are* a problem, or for that matter, that they even exist.

A circular reference takes the form of "Part A references Part B, which references Part A." It creates a circular loop that really disrupts assembly rebuild times by requiring multiple rebuilds. Part feature design trees aren't susceptible to this sort of looping, because the part FeatureManager operates in a linear fashion (at least when it comes to applying relations between sketches or features).

The assembly FeatureManager is solved in this order—or an order that is very similar:

1. Solve reference geometry and sketches that are listed before parts in order, at the top of the design tree.

2. Rebuild individual parts as necessary.

3. Solve the mates and locate the parts.

4. Solve the in-context features in parts.

5. Solve reference geometry and sketches listed after the mates.

6. Solve the assembly features and component patterns.

7. Loop to step 3 to solve mates that are connected to anything that was solved after the first round on the mates.

8. Continue to loop until complete. SolidWorks breaks the loop after the second evaluation of the mates matrix to avoid an infinite loop. Any feature not rebuilt at the end of the loop will get the traffic light Rebuild symbol.

Even if you do not have a reference such as "Part A references Part B, which references Part A," it is still possible to get a highly convoluted, if not entirely circular, loop. Many users with smaller assemblies in the hundreds of parts complain about very poor performance.

USING SKELETONS AND LAYOUTS

When you are making in-context references, a technique that can help you avoid circular references is to always create references to parts that are higher in the design tree. You can expand on this idea until a single entity is at the top of the design tree, to which all in-context references are made. This could take the form of a layout sketch or a skeleton. These concepts are discussed in Chapter 16, "Working with Assembly Sketches and Layouts," and Chapter 13, "Building Efficient Assemblies." The Layout feature, which is different from the layout sketch, is discussed later in this chapter as an additional in-context tool.

Remember that the layout sketch consists of a single or even multiple sketches that control the overall layout of the assembly, as well as all the relationships between parts. When you refer all the relations to a single entity that does not change with part configurations, or lose or gain filleted edges, the intra-part parametrics become much stronger and more stable.

When you are building a mold for plastic injection molding, a single sketch can control the size and position of the plates, pins, and so on. If all the 3D parts are mated to the 2D sketch, or use the 2D sketch by converted entities, then the parts will move with the sketch. This same technique is important and useful for any type of die or punch design, along with many other types of design.

Using In-Context in Libraries

Library parts should never contain in-context references, especially if the in-context references are out of context. Small library assemblies may have in-context references between the parts, but a single part should not have features created in-context. External references may be unavoidable in the form of mirrored or inserted parts, but in-context references are completely avoidable.

Removing Relations

The correct way to remove in-context sketch relations is by using the Display/Delete Relations tool. you can select the option in the "all in this sketch" selection box as shown in Figure 20.22.

FIGURE 20.22
Sorting sketch relations by type

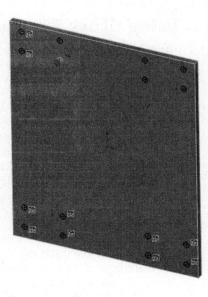

If you are considering using the Break Relations tool, then I encourage you to either reconsider and use Lock Relations instead or simply remove all the in-context relations altogether.

Other types of in-context references are not as easy to remove as sketch relations are. When you see the External Reference symbol on a sketch, it could be the sketch relations or it could be the sketch plane that was in-context. In order to remove the reference from an in-context sketch plane, you must redefine the plane locally in the part.

Don't forget end conditions such as Up To Surface, Offset From Surface, or even From Surface. If an external reference symbol remains on a feature, you can use the Parent/Child option on the RMB menu to locate it. Remember that using an edge or vertex for a plane definition can cause an in-context relation.

DECIDING WHETHER TO USE MATING OR IN-CONTEXT

In-context is initially so fast and easy to use that it can be addictive, but you need to think before you use it because of the speed and file management implications these relations will have on your design process.

COMMUNICATING DESIGN INTENT

If someone else needs to use your model after you are done with it and possibly edit it, you should leave some clues to help this person understand how the model works and how it is best changed. For example, you can use descriptive feature and sketch names, comments that are associated with features, the Design Binder to add documentation, and the Design Journal to write notes. You can even put HTML (Hypertext Markup Language) links in notes that display in the graphics window.

In-context design intent may not always be obvious, and an impatient user may find it more expedient to delete the in-context references and replace them with either local relations or no relations at all. The more you document your intent, the more likely others will be to follow it.

Using Other Types of External References

The external reference symbol (->) indicates in-context features that have been created in the context of an assembly, but it also indicates three other types of external references: inserted parts, split parts, and mirrored parts.

In the past, inserted parts have also been called base parts and derived parts, and some users and even SolidWorks sometimes still use those names.

An inserted part is simply an entire part that has been inserted into another part. This is sometimes referred to as a *pull* operation because the data is pulled from the original part into the child part. The part may be inserted at any point in the history of the design tree, and it may create an additional body within the part or be added to the existing one. Additional features also can be added to the inserted part.

Items that can be brought along with the inserted part are solid bodies, surface bodies, planes, axes, sketches, cosmetic threads, and even features. You can also use a particular configuration of the inserted part.

You can use inserted parts for many modeling applications, such as cast parts and secondary operations. You first insert the original cast part into a new blank part. Then you add cut and hole features until the part resembles the finished part. Also, sometimes purchased parts are altered to create a special part number.

Another application for inserted parts is a single part that has been built from several models. An example might be a large, rather complicated plastic basket, where the basket is modeled as three individual parts and then reassembled into a single part. Another application may be to insert a part as a body into a mold block to create a mold cavity. To insert a part into another part, you can choose Insert ➤ Part.

Working with Split Parts

Inserted and split parts are both master model techniques, as are a few more techniques that are discussed in Chapter 33. Some people also include in-context techniques with the master model tools because this is a way of making several parts update together.

Split parts are sometimes called a *push* operation because the data is pushed from the original multibody part to the individual child parts. The *split* function takes a single body and splits it into several bodies, optionally saving the bodies out as individual parts. This is done for various reasons, such as creating a single, smooth shape out of several different parts—for example, automobile body panels or the various covers and buttons on a computer mouse. You can use the split parts technique for other applications as well. Sometimes, a product is designed as a single solid to keep the modeling simple and because it is not known how the parts will be assembled or manufactured. When the manufacturing decisions are made, the part can be split into several models that have the engineering details added to them.

Using Mirror Parts

You can mirror a right-handed part to create a left-handed part. To activate the Mirror Part command, you must select a plane or planar face. Then choose Insert ➤ Mirror Part to initiate the Mirror Part command. Mirror parts can also use configurations, so if you have one of those "mirrored exactly except for . . ." parts, you can select the configuration of the parent from the child document.

Tutorial: Working In-Context

Follow these steps to get a feel for working with parts in the context of an assembly:

1. Open the assembly from the download materials named `Tutorial Table.sldasm`.

2. Set the colors that are to be used during in-context editing. Remember that two settings control this—one at Tools ➤ Options ➤ Colors, and the other at Tools ➤ Options ➤ Display—as shown in Figure 20.23.

   Set the Assembly Edit Part color to a shade of blue and the Assembly Non-Edit Parts to a shade of gray.

   Also set the Assembly Transparency For In Context Edit setting to Force Assembly Transparency, with the slider at around 90%. Now you are ready to begin.

3. Select the Table Top part and click the Edit Component button on the Assembly toolbar. This command is also available through both the RMB menu and the drop-down menu as Edit Part. (If you right-click a subassembly, the Edit Subassembly option becomes available.) Notice that the Table Top part and the FeatureManager text turn the same color.

4. Expand the Table Top part in the assembly FeatureManager, select the Front plane, and open a new sketch on it. Notice that you cannot select the edges of the transparent parts through the transparency, even if the Select Through Transparency option is selected (Tools ➤ Options ➤ Selection). This setting applies only to faces, not to edges. Instead, change the display mode for the entire assembly to Wireframe.

FIGURE 20.23
Setting in-context colors

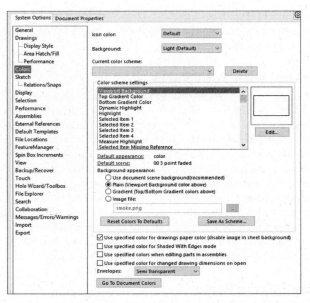

5. Now select the 16 hole edges on the legs. It doesn't matter whether you select the top edges or the bottom, or even a combination of top and bottom. Use the Convert Entities command to project the edges into the sketch plane as circles, as shown in Figure 20.24.

FIGURE 20.24
Converting entities in-context

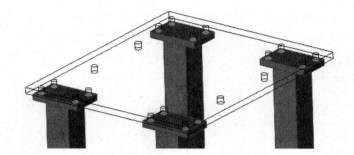

6. Create a cut that goes Through All. You may have to change the direction of the extrude to get it to work. Leave Edit Component mode using the Confirmation Corner and save the tutorial assembly.

7. Now open the file named `Tutorial Machine Assembly.sldasm`. Notice that the Table Top part in this assembly is using the Wireframe display state, which is assigned in the Display pane.

8. Right-click the part and select Edit Part from the list, or select the part and click the Edit Component button on the toolbar. A warning displays that the part has features that were created in the context of another assembly. You can edit the part, but you cannot add any more external references (in-context features) to it.

9. Toggle off the Edit Component button on the Assembly toolbar to leave Edit Part mode.

10. Choose Tools ➤ Options ➤ External References and select the Allow Multiple Contexts For Parts When Editing In Assembly option. Now try to edit the Table Top part again in the context of the assembly. This time, no warning message displays.

11. Make sure you are editing the Table Top part. It does not change colors as specified in the Tools ➤ Options ➤ Colors settings because it is using the Wireframe display mode. Ensure that the status bar in the lower-right corner displays *Editing Part* rather than *Editing Assembly.*

12. Open a sketch on the Front plane, and convert the four edges of the holes, as shown in Figure 20.25.

FIGURE 20.25
Creating holes in-context

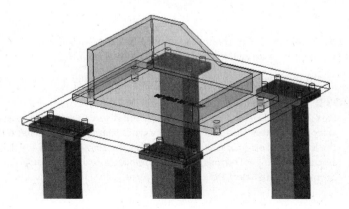

13. Cut the holes using the Through All setting. Again, be aware of the direction of the cuts. Toggle out of Edit Component mode and press Ctrl+S to save the assembly. Figure 20.26 shows the finished assembly.

FIGURE 20.26
The assembly as of step 13

14. Open the Machine Base Bracket part in its own window by selecting Open Part from the RMB menu. The part is shown in Figure 20.27.

FIGURE 20.27
The Machine Base Bracket part, ready for mirroring

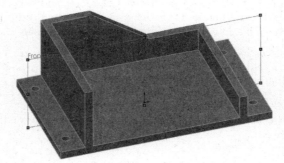

15. Select the Front plane and choose Insert ➤ Mirror Part. This creates a new part and opens a new PropertyManager interface, as shown in Figure 20.28.

In this case, select Solid Bodies and click the green checkmark icon.

NOTE   Notice that you used the Insert ➤ Mirror Part command, but the PropertyManager says Insert Part. The Mirror Part functionality uses the Insert Part function but adds a feature to mirror the body after it's inserted. Notice all the entity types that you can transfer and the fact that you can break the link to the original part. Also note that the template used for this part was chosen based on the settings at Tools ➤ Options ➤ Default Templates ➤ Always Use These Default Document Templates or Prompt User To Select Document Template.

FIGURE 20.28
The Mirror Part
PropertyManager

16. Notice that the new part is indeed a mirrored copy of the original. You can see that the "MADE IN USA" text on the bottom is backward. Fortunately, a configuration exists specifically for this purpose. Change the configuration by selecting For Mirroring in the Configuration Name drop-down list in the External References dialog box (from the RMB selection, List External References). Notice that this configuration removes the extruded text from the model.

17. Add your own "MADE IN . . ." extruded text to the bottom of the part. Save the part.

The Bottom Line

Although in-context functions are powerful and seductive, you should use them sparingly. In particular, be careful about file management issues such as renaming parts and assemblies. The best approach is to use SolidWorks Explorer or the Save As command with both the parts and assemblies open.

In-context techniques, including the Layout feature, are the pinnacle of true parametric practice and enable you to take the concepts of design intent and design for change to an entirely new level.

Master It   The first step in being able to work fluently with external references is to be able to recognize, identify, and edit them. Select a part from the download materials for this chapter with external references, and use the skills you developed in this chapter and others to remove all of the external references without deleting sketches or features.

Master It   Sometimes mixing advanced techniques can lead to undesirable results. Name a couple of advanced techniques you need to be careful of when combining with in-context.

Master It   Describe the differences and similarities between a broken reference and a frozen reference.

Chapter 21

Editing, Evaluating, and Troubleshooting Assemblies

This chapter goes through the essential tools you need to get real-world work done—and do it in a way that shows you understand what you are doing. Editing, evaluating, and troubleshooting skills are tools that will help you deal with the reality of working with SolidWorks assemblies. These tasks can be dauntingly tedious unless you have a working knowledge of the available tools.

IN THIS CHAPTER, YOU WILL LEARN TO:

- ◆ Manipulate existing mates
- ◆ Change filenames and locations
- ◆ Evaluate assembly changes

Working with Mates

When you think of editing in assemblies, the main task that comes to mind is editing mates—and probably editing broken mates. Although you can do several other kinds of editing in assemblies—such as changing subassembly structure, replacing components, and managing files—mates really are the biggest item you face when you are talking about editing assemblies.

Chapter 4, "Creating Simple Parts and Drawings," and Chapter 13, "Building Efficient Assemblies," introduced you to the world of creating mates between parts and other items in assemblies. This chapter is more concerned with manipulating mates that already exist.

In assemblies, you can find mates in two different locations and display them in two different modes. The first place you'll find them is in the Mates folder at the bottom of the assembly FeatureManager, as shown in Figure 21.1.

Listing Mates in the Mates Folder

The Mates folder can contain other folders that also contain mates to help you organize them. The mates can be renamed, reordered, deleted, suppressed, and edited from this list. By default, the mates are listed in the order in which they were created, and the name of each mate is followed by the names of the parts or assembly features between which the mate was made.

FIGURE 21.1

All the mates in an assembly are shown in the Mates folder at the bottom of the assembly FeatureManager.

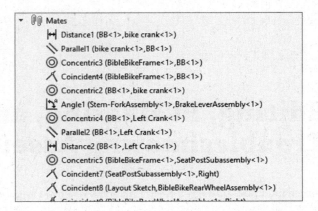

Mates can fail, have warning markers, or be suppressed like other features inside parts. A red octagon with an X in it means that the mate does not meet the geometric conditions. A yellow triangle with an exclamation point means that the mate is in conflict with another mate. Grayed-out mates are suppressed. A small (f) means a mate is suppressed because its part is fixed. A concentric mate with the center filled in means that rotation is locked for that mate. Figure 21.2 shows examples of these errors.

FIGURE 21.2

Know the difference between a warning and an error.

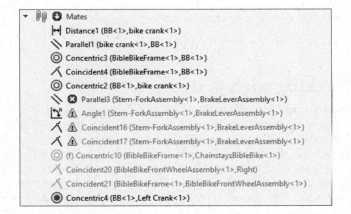

You can see from the mates in the list that there is one error and some warnings. Other mates are also in conflict, and this is one of the biggest difficulties when troubleshooting mates in an assembly. Although several mates are in conflict, only one mate may be causing the problem. A good general rule is to troubleshoot the list of mates from the bottom to the top. This is based on the expectation that more recently added mates are the ones causing trouble. The MateXpert, which is discussed later in this chapter, is a good tool for troubleshooting mates.

Listing Mates Under the Component

Mates are also listed under the component in the FeatureManager. These are the same mates as those listed in the Mates folder at the bottom; however, under the component, only the mates relating to that particular component are listed. Figure 21.3 shows mates listed in this way.

FIGURE 21.3
Mates are also listed in a folder under the component and in breadcrumbs.

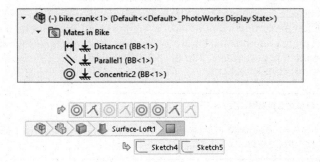

This is a very convenient way to list the mates, making them easy to find and nicely organized. One of the drawbacks of listing them this way is that when a mate is causing an error, the error shows up in the Mates folder at the bottom of the FeatureManager, and an error flag appears on each of the parts containing the bad mate.

If you're a fan of using the Breadcrumb display, mates are listed in that as well, with a list of mate symbols showing the state of each mate.

Additionally, subassemblies have mate folders of their own, and parts from the subassembly can be mated to parts or features in the top-level assembly. Ideally, you should mate only a limited number of parts between a subassembly and the upper level, but this is not always possible.

Displaying Mates Instead of Features

Another method of displaying mates under the components enables you to see the mates of more parts at once. In the previous method shown in Figure 21.3, the mates were shown along with the features of the part.

To show the mates associated with each part without the features, right-click the top-level assembly, select Tree Display, and then select View Mates And Dependencies. This option is shown in Figure 21.4.

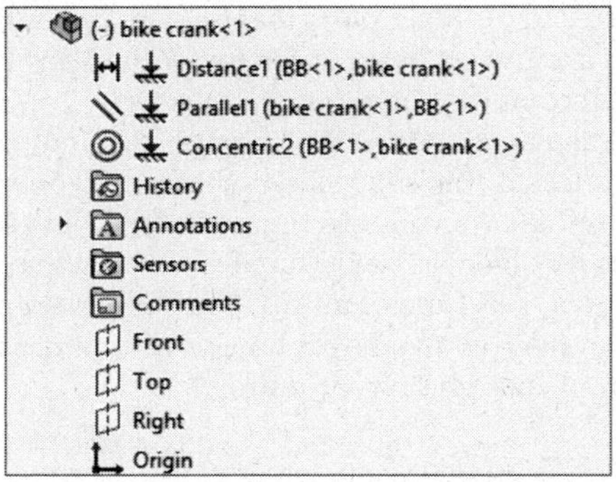

FIGURE 21.4
Displaying the mates without part features

Notice that you can still access the features if you want. They are in a collapsed folder at the bottom of the list of mates. This is a more convenient option for looking at the mates of several parts at one time.

Working with the View Mates Tool

As its name implies, View Mates is a special tool just for viewing mates. You can access it from the RMB menu when you select a single assembly component (part or subassembly) or multiple assembly components. Figure 21.5 shows the View Mates window when the frame and stem-fork subassembly are selected in the bike assembly located in the materials available for download from the Wiley website.

ON THE WEBSITE

To view this example, open the file `bike.sldasm`, located in the folder of material downloaded for Chapter 21.

FIGURE 21.5
The View Mates window shows the mates for selected components.

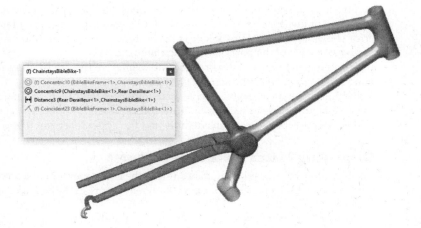

The icon shown to the left of Distance1 in Figure 21.4 indicates that mate is in the "path to ground," which means that it is part of the link from the part that is either fixed or mated to assembly planes to outlying parts that depend on other parts for their location. The Path to Ground parts are always listed at the top of the View Mates window. The rest of the mates in the window are all from the parts that are selected.

The parts displayed in blue in the graphics window are the parts mated together from the components selected (the entire fork subassembly is not shown, just the stem part that is actually mated to the frame). As you select mates in the View Mates window, SolidWorks highlights the faces or edges involved, as well as mate names in the graphics window.

View Mates is a useful tool for investigating mating relationships between parts, especially in assemblies that have evolved over time or assemblies that someone else built and that you must understand well enough to work with.

Using the View Mate Errors Window

The View Mate Errors window looks identical to the View Mate window, but it shows only mates that have error or warning flags. It shows all the mates with errors in the entire top-level assembly, not just for the selected component. The View Mate Errors window is available only from the RMB menu and only on components where there are mate errors. It is available only for single selections, never for multiple components. Figure 21.6 shows this window.

FIGURE 21.6
Using the View Mate Errors window to troubleshoot mate problems

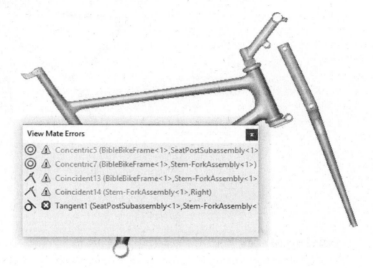

Using the MateXpert

The MateXpert tool helps you troubleshoot assembly problems. You can access the MateXpert by right-clicking a mate with an error, or you can access it from the Tools menu. Don't confuse the MateXpert with the AssemblyXpert; the MateXpert doesn't have an icon, and it deals only with mates.

This example intentionally creates a problem in the bike assembly, so you can see how the MateXpert deals with issues that arise. The problem created here is the same as the one earlier in this chapter, which forced the seat post to be concentric with the stem. After clicking the Diagnose button in the MateXpert, you will see the result shown in Figure 21.7.

The MateXpert returns one possible problem in the Analyze Problem panel of the PropertyManager. In this case, the only mate in the assembly that is causing trouble is Tangent1; the rest of the mates display the yellow warning triangle. Notice at the bottom that SolidWorks correctly identifies the one red marker mate as a mate that is not satisfied.

This tool returns lots of information; you may need to sort through it to find the most relevant. When troubleshooting assemblies, you should use whatever set of tools you feel give you the best information for fixing the problem. If you are working through a tangle of mate errors, you may want to use other troubleshooting methods before you rely too heavily on the MateXpert—or you may want to give the MateXpert a glance to see if it points out something you missed before you try a more robust method.

FIGURE 21.7
Using the MateXpert to
diagnose problems

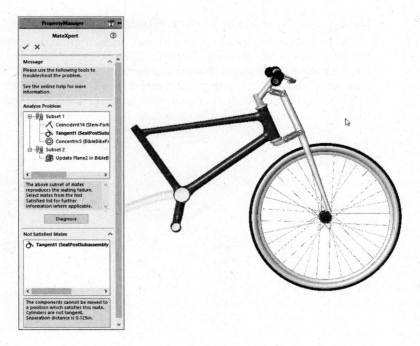

Editing Mates

You can edit mates using the same Mate PropertyManager that you used to create the mates. You access this PropertyManager by right-clicking a mate and selecting Edit Feature from the menu. You can also select multiple mates. Using Edit Feature causes the list of selected mates to show in the Mates window of the Mate PropertyManager. Move from editing one mate to another by just selecting another mate in the window. The Mate PropertyManager for an existing mate is shown in Figure 21.8.

One of the advantages of using this method to edit mates is that you can change the type of mate simply by selecting it in the PropertyManager. This is different from features such as the Fillet. After you select a fillet type and create the feature with Fillet, you cannot edit it later and change the type of fillet.

If you want to replace the mated entities, you can delete the one you want to change from the Mate Selections selection box and choose a new one. You can even select an entity from a different part if necessary.

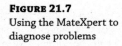

Another feature for replacing mate entities that is more tailored to the specific task is the Replace Mate Entities tool. You can also find this in the RMB menu for a mate (as well as in the LMB menu, but you must be able to recognize it by its icon or its tooltip). Figure 21.9 shows where you can access both the Edit Feature and the Replace Mate Entities tools from the RMB menu.

Selecting Replace Mate Entities displays a PropertyManager called Mated Entities. This interface shows which entities from which parts are used together in the mate. To replace an entity, select it from the Mate Entities selection box; it will appear in the small selection box below. Then simply select the new entity.

FIGURE 21.8
Editing a mate with the
original Mate
PropertyManager

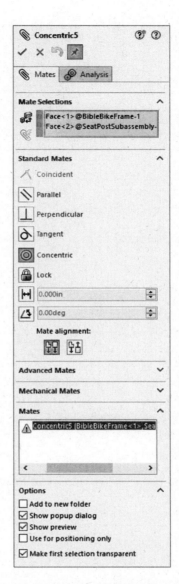

When you open this PropertyManager, the Isolate toolbar will also automatically appear. Isolate is a tool that hides parts that are not involved in the current operation. The Mated Entities PropertyManager and the Isolate toolbar are shown in Figure 21.10.

One of the nice features of the Replace Mate Entities tool is that you can select multiple mates before activating the tool from the RMB menu, and all the mate entities will appear in the PropertyManager. This makes changing several mates in one step relatively easy.

FIGURE 21.9
Accessing the Edit
Feature and the Replace
Mate Entities from
the RMB menu

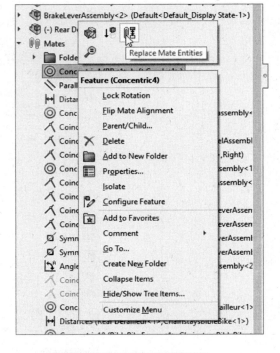

FIGURE 21.10
Changing mated entities
using the Mated Entities
PropertyManager and
the Isolate toolbar

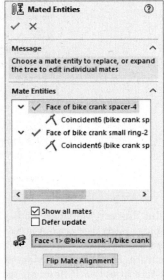

You can also select multiple mates to edit in this way using the Mate PropertyManager. The multiple-selected mates will appear in the Mates panel toward the bottom of the PropertyManager (refer to Figure 21.8 where the Concentric 5 mate is shown).

Editing File Management Issues

File management in SolidWorks assemblies requires a certain amount of attention. You must be careful when changing filenames and locations, and you must use the correct tools, or SolidWorks may lose track of where to find necessary data. The best tools to use for SolidWorks file management are, of course, PDM (product data management) tools such as PDM Standard and PDM Professional. After that, SolidWorks and SolidWorks Explorer are good tools for users who don't have access to PDM tools, but these tools require more expertise to keep the references intact.

Using Save Options and Pack And Go

When making changes to the files involved in SolidWorks assemblies, understanding the Save options will serve you well. Whenever you want to change a name, change a location, or make a copy of a particular SolidWorks document, you should use some combination of the Save, Save As, and Save As Copy tools, as well as Pack And Go. (The icon to the left is shown in the File menu, but the icon shown on the Pack And Go window header is different).

The Save command displays only a dialog box the first time you save a document. If you are saving an assembly with virtual components, it may ask you to save the assembly with a name in addition to asking you to name and save virtual components externally. Typically, Save isn't an option for anything other than initially placing and naming your files.

Save As is the tool to use when you want to save the current document to a new name. When you do this, SolidWorks leaves the last saved version of the previous part behind, and going forward, the new name and location you used in Save As will be the one that remains in the assembly.

For example, if you have Assembly 1 and it's made up of Part 1 and Part 2, and these files are already saved to your local hard drive, but you want to rename Part 1 as **875003 base structure.sldprt**, then you can use the Save As command to do this. First, you *must* have the assembly and parts open. Then you can open Part 1 in its own window and use Save As from there. You will get a dialog that helps you sort out what you want to happen, as shown in Figure 21.11. This is one case where you really shouldn't click the Don't Show Again box.

You can also rename parts in the FeatureManager, but you must set a Tools ➤ Options setting first. Go to the FeatureManager page in System Options and make sure the setting called "Allow component files to be renamed from FeatureManager tree" is on. Then to rename, just right-click on the component and select Rename.

If you make the name change using Windows Explorer, SolidWorks won't know anything about the name change, and the next time you open the assembly, it will tell you it can't find Part 1.sldprt and will ask you to find it.

FIGURE 21.11
The options you get before the Save As dialog appears

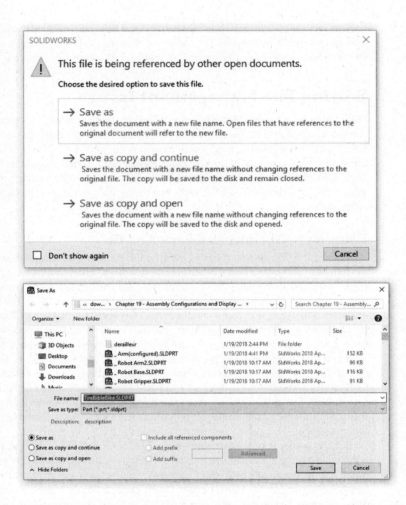

The More Options section in the Save As With References dialog box enables you to add a prefix or suffix, as well as to use a simple Find/Replace function to rename files in the list. Remember that this makes a copy of the assembly and all the parts with new names or locations.

SolidWorks users frequently use the Pack And Go tool to make a copy of an entire assembly in a new location or to a zip file used to transfer an assembly with all parts to someone who does not have access to the local network. Pack And Go has all the functionality of Save As With References, as well as some additional options. You can also replace files, include drawings and simulation results, and get a quick summary on the number of parts, assemblies, and drawings that are being included. If you aren't using a formal PDM application, Pack And Go can at least serve as a main copy, archive, and renaming utility. The Pack And Go window is shown in Figure 21.12.

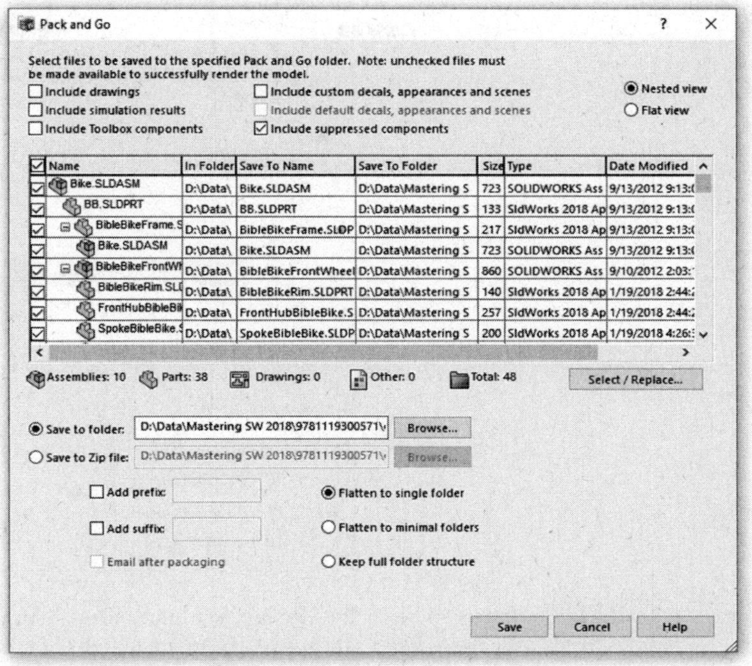

FIGURE 21.12

Pack And Go contains most of your file management needs outside of PDM.

Replacing Components

Following the philosophy that "delete is not an editing method," SolidWorks includes a tool to replace components that is an improvement over the less graceful delete-and-add technique. When you delete a component, you lose lots of information that you could otherwise keep. Whether you delete a sketch line, a mate, or a part in an assembly, deleting more than doubles the work you have to do. You have to do lots of repair work after you make a deletion. The deeper into a design you are, the more data you lose when you delete something from it. Each piece of information in SolidWorks has some other piece of information attached to it. That associativity is supposed to help rather than hinder you. Learning to use the tools in the way you were meant to use them is one way to improve your efficiency with the software—so you work *with* the software rather than *against* it.

The Replace Components tool is available from the RMB menu of any top-level component in the assembly (not components in subassemblies), although you may have to expand a truncated RMB menu to see it (click the double arrow at the bottom of the RMB menu). Figure 21.13 shows the PropertyManager for the Replace command.

The All Instances option is an important one. Sometimes, you need to replace only one instance of a particular component with some other part. The All Instances option makes it easy and convenient to replace just what you need.

Other important options have to do with configurations and mates. If the replacement part will use the same configuration name as the original part, you can use the Match Name option. If not, you can use the Manually Select option.

FIGURE 21.13
Replacing a component
in an assembly with
another component

Reattaching mates can be tricky. The more similar parts are in their topology (general layout of model faces), the more likely the automatic reattachment of mates will work. If the mates cannot be reattached automatically, you will be presented with the interface shown in Figure 21.14. This interface shows each of the mates that cannot be reattached automatically, with a small window showing the equivalent face on the old part. It asks you to select a face on the new part that matches the highlighted face on the old part to repair each mate.

FIGURE 21.14
Reattaching mates by
selecting indicated faces
on the replacement part

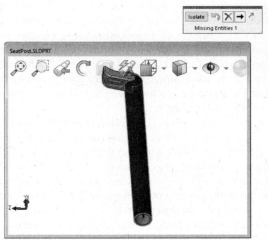

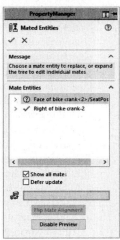

This is a fairly easy process, and it's certainly better than deleting the original part, reinserting the part, and re-creating mates.

Forming and Dissolving Subassemblies

When you initially create an assembly, you may not always know exactly how you want to organize it. Assemblies can serve many purposes, such as for motion, analysis, rendering, assembly instructions, inspection, or a BOM. The structure of each type of assembly with subassemblies might be very different. Therefore, SolidWorks must be flexible in allowing you to change the structure on the fly, again without the wasted effort of deleting and re-creating data.

To create a new subassembly within an existing top-level assembly, select a set of components through appropriate selection methods (advanced select, Ctrl+select, window select, and so on), and then right-click and select Form New Subassembly Here. When the new subassembly is first created, SolidWorks just moves the selected components into the subassembly without any fanfare. The new subassembly is created as a virtual component, so it's just saved within the top-level assembly. If you want to immediately save the new subassembly (named in a format similar to [Assem1^Bike], where Bike is the name of the top-level assembly), right-click the new assembly and select Save Assembly (In External File) from the menu.

TIP   When forming and dissolving subassemblies, you have to be careful about things like mates, patterns, and in-context relations. Each of these can be deleted when the structure changes. Be careful to understand your inter-assembly relationships when making structural changes of this sort.

USING TREEHOUSE

SolidWorks Treehouse is a tool installed with SolidWorks that you can access through the Windows Start menu, under SolidWorks Tools. It enables you to establish the basic assembly structure of a product including subassemblies, parts, and even drawings. You can use any templates available to your SolidWorks installation to establish the structure, name the files, add configurations, establish custom properties, and save them to a location where individual SolidWorks users can begin working on the detailed geometrical data to go into the file. You can even add existing files if you are reusing data or part of the design is already created when you start mapping the structure.

Treehouse enables you to have a CAD manager establish the structure, an intern add custom properties, engineers or designers create the detailed design, and then drafters create 2D drawings. A sample structure is shown in a Treehouse window in Figure 21.15.

You can also edit existing assemblies by dragging the assembly file into the Treehouse window. You can add an existing subassembly to an existing top-level assembly by dragging a file from Windows Explorer onto the assembly in Treehouse.

MOVING PARTS IN AND OUT OF SUBASSEMBLIES

Back in the SolidWorks interface, without Treehouse, if you have an existing subassembly, and you want to add to it or remove parts from it, you can drag the component name in the FeatureManager to accomplish this. To drag a part into the subassembly, drag the filename onto the name of the subassembly. You will see the special cursor shown in Figure 21.16. Be sure to pay attention to the text tips being displayed, especially if you're not familiar with the icons.

FIGURE 21.15
Using Treehouse to establish a product assembly structure

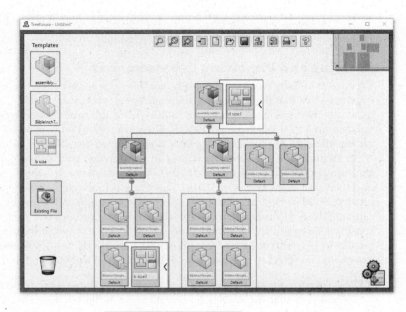

FIGURE 21.16
Adding the BB part to the subassembly Bike Crank

In the example shown in Figure 21.16, the Bottom Bracket part (BB) is being added to the subassembly Bike Crank.

If you want to move a part out of a subassembly into an upper-level assembly, you have to drag the filename from its spot in the subassembly onto the name of the top-level assembly. If you just drag the part above the subassembly, SolidWorks might think you are trying to reorder the display of the name within the assembly FeatureManager. Remember that different symbols exist for moving parts up or down the subassembly hierarchy and reordering parts in the FeatureManager. Undo works for this type of assembly operation.

MOVING MATES FROM AN ASSEMBLY TO A SUBASSEMBLY

Sometimes when you move a part into or out of an assembly, SolidWorks requires that you move mates or destroy certain in-context relationships. If SolidWorks displays a message that it must move mates to another level or break some external references, you must read the message carefully and try to determine whether you can accept the conditions mentioned in the message. You may not be able to easily undo some actions after they are complete. A typical message is shown in Figure 21.17. Losing all the in-context relations in a particular sketch could mean lots of repair work, so you must consider these things carefully.

FIGURE 21.17
Read warning boxes
when they are displayed;
they could be
important.

When a mate is moved from a top-level assembly to a subassembly, the mate is no longer solved in the top level, which means you may not be able to use Dynamic Assembly Motion on the parts you just moved from the top level to the subassembly level. You may need to employ a flexible subassembly, which solves the subassembly's mates in the top level. The drawback of this technique is that more mates to solve means more time to rebuild the assembly document and, therefore, a slower working environment. Assembly editing actions often have consequences that you may not anticipate, so be sure to pay attention to warnings from the SolidWorks software.

Evaluating Assemblies

Evaluation tools help you to gain a better understanding of what your starting point is so you can be more efficient with your changes. In the sections that follow, you will learn some new ways to look at and evaluate your SolidWorks assemblies.

Using the Performance Evaluation Tool

The SolidWorks Performance Evaluation tool is described in Chapter 12, "Editing, Evaluating, and Troubleshooting," but it's reviewed here as well to keep related information together. Performance Evaluation is an informational tool that offers statistics about how many parts, subassemblies, lightweight parts, and so on are in the assembly. It also offers some advice about assembly performance and various settings. Figure 21.18 shows the Performance Evaluation window.

FIGURE 21.18

Using the Performance
Evaluation tool to
gain information and
important statistics
about your assembly

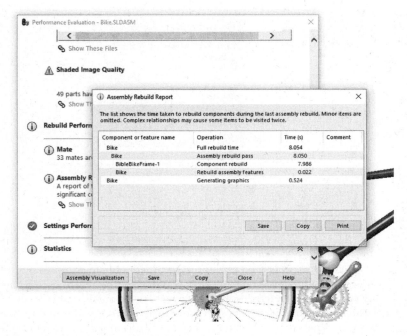

Identifying FeatureManager Symbols

You may be wondering what certain rarely seen symbols in the FeatureManager signify. This list
includes some of the ones that users often ask about.

 Flexible subassembly

 Lightweight (blue feather)

 Out-of-date lightweight (red feather)

 Path to ground is a mate that is between the part and the fully defined part

 Part made in the academic version of the software

 Toolbox part

Following are some additional symbols in the FeatureManager that are part of the text name.

(f) This indicates the part is Fixed. The opposite of Fixed is Float.

(-) This indicates the part is underdefined, that there are not enough mates to lock its position.

(+) This indicates the part location is overdefined. Overdefined parts typically must have one
or more mates removed. This is a situation you should fix in any case.

-> This indicates an External Reference to a file outside of the current document.

-> ? This indicates an Out of Context reference, which means it isn't currently loaded
in memory.

-> * This means the External Reference is Locked. You can unlock locked references.

-> x This means the External Reference is Broken. You cannot repair broken external
references.

Using the Isolate Function

Isolate is a tool that enables you to display only selected components. If you right-click a subassembly and select Isolate, you can have it set so that all the other parts are shown as wireframe, transparent, or hidden. This is a nice method to draw attention to a couple of parts or a subassembly while still being able to see the rest of the assembly for reference.

Figure 21.19 shows the Isolate tool in use. To activate Isolate, right-click a part or a selection of parts and click Isolate in the menu.

FIGURE 21.19
Using Isolate in an assembly

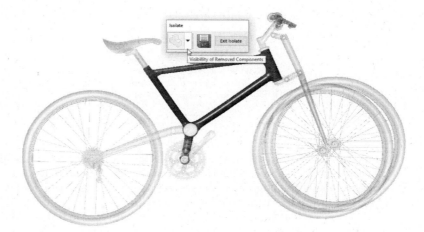

When you use Isolate, the small toolbar shown in Figure 21.19 appears and gives you the option to show the rest of the parts in the assembly in one of three modes: Wireframe, Transparent, or Hidden. As long as you have the part or parts isolated, the Isolate toolbar will remain on the screen.

The Save icon on the Isolate toolbar enables you to save the current display as a Display State. This lets you get back to that particular combination of display settings for parts. To return to the previous display, click the Exit Isolate button.

If you want to show another component while in Isolate mode, right-click and select Show Hidden Components, then select the one you want to show, and exit the Show dialog. The Isolate display will be updated to show this newly selected component.

Using Reload

For people who try things that don't always work out, Reload is one of the most useful commands in SolidWorks. It acts as a shortcut for exiting the current document without saving and then reopening. Reload is available for parts and assemblies, but not for drawings. You can find Reload in the File menu or add it to your toolbars from the Standard category in Tools ➤ Customize ➤ Commands.

Figure 21.20 shows the dialog box that appears when you invoke the Reload command. Notice that this dialog box gives you the option to load Read Only if available, and it includes other file management options that you need to be aware of, especially if you are working on an assembly with other SolidWorks users.

FIGURE 21.20
Reloading an assembly
to discard changes

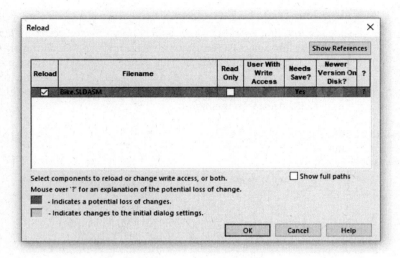

Reload is very handy when you make a change to your part or assembly that you don't want to keep, but you cannot use the Undo command to get rid of it. Reload is useful if you are trying out a technique and don't want to save the results. Just be careful that you don't wind up discarding work that you should keep. Save often.

 A command that you can use in conjunction with Reload is the Check Read-only Files command. This command is available only from a toolbar icon that isn't on the standard toolbar by default, but it's listed in the Tools ➤ Customize ➤ Commands List.

The Check Read-only Files tool checks to see if any read-only files have been changed or if new versions exist in the folder in which you are working. If new versions exist, this tool brings up the Reload tool.

The Bottom Line

You might create your work once in SolidWorks, but you are almost guaranteed to spend more time editing it than you did creating it. Because of that, you need to be even more adept at editing and evaluating your SolidWorks assembly than you are at creating it. SolidWorks has lots of tools to help you do this.

Master It   File management is one skill that doesn't relate to engineering or design, but all CAD operators must be experts. Mismanaging the file can mean you lose a lot of work—or worse yet, by mismanaging, you can create problems with the work that you don't realize until it's too late.

As an exercise, use the SolidWorks Pack And Go to make a zipped copy of an assembly that has in-context references. If possible, take the zip file to another computer with SolidWorks on it and open it up. Check to make sure all of the in-context references are still in-context (and not out of context).

Master It   Sometimes it's easier to look at the big picture and the small detail separately. When you are working on getting Fillet34 to work just right, it's not always a convenient time to also be changing the overall structure of your product's assemblies and subassemblies.

To get some practice, use the SolidWorks Treehouse tool to create the assembly structure for one of your company's products or an automobile if you need a different idea. Get as detailed with it as you can with the time you have available.

Master It   Efficiency is one of the most important qualities of processes, workers, and tools. Use the SolidWorks Performance Evaluation tools to look at the Bike assembly to evaluate which parts are costing you the most to open on your computer. Cost is often measured by rebuild time. Make a set of recommendations for remodeling the bike so that the design costs are lower.

Chapter 22

Working with Large Scale Design

According to SolidWorks marketing materials, "Large Scale Design brings together the tools you need to effectively design machinery, heavy equipment, plants, small ships, and other large objects."

Large Scale Design encompasses topics exclusively covered in this chapter: Walk-through animation, GridSystem, IFC export, Large Design Review, and Facility Layout. Although Large Scale Design also uses standard SolidWorks functionality such as sketching, part modeling, assembly modeling, weldments, and drawings, these latter topics don't have Large Scale Design–specific capabilities at this time.

IN THIS CHAPTER, YOU WILL LEARN TO:

◆ Understand Large Scale Design

◆ Use Walk-through

◆ Export to IFC

◆ Create a grid structure

◆ Lay out a facility

◆ Use Large Design Review

Using Large Design Review

Large Design Review is a view-only mode that enables you to perform design review activities with large assemblies. You have access to the following features of SolidWorks:

◆ FeatureManager

◆ Measure tool

◆ Section tool

◆ Hide/Show

◆ Assembly Xpert

◆ Walk-through

◆ The Large Design Review tab on the CommandManager

In Large Design Review, you don't have access to these features:

◆   Part features

◆   Assembly features

◆   Component patterns

◆   Mates

◆   Dynamic assembly motion

◆   The Assembly tab of the CommandManager

◆   Change component properties

◆   Change configurations in LDR mode

To open an assembly in Large Design Review, use the Open dialog box, and in the Mode drop-down box, select Large Design Review (LDR), as shown in Figure 22.1.

FIGURE 22.1
Using the Open dialog to open an assembly in Large Design Review mode

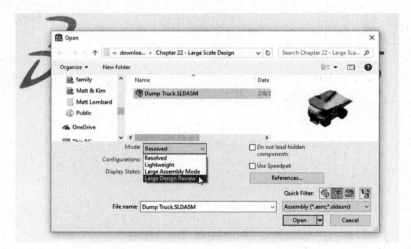

Figure 22.2 shows the dialog box that welcomes you to LDR on the left and the LDR FeatureManager and toolbar on the right.

One of the things that has been removed from this window is a list of some of the limitations. When working with a new tool, it is important to know how far you can expect it to go. The window does suggest that you have a look at the Help for more information on limitations. However, the linked Help page does not directly list limitations; per the typical SolidWorks method of handling such things, you are on your own to discover the boundaries of what can and cannot be done.

For example, Large Design Review is a stripped-down interface, built to help you look at a simplified data set. For this reason, it does not enable you to do everything you can do in the full SolidWorks interface, so some tools will be missing. You cannot see assembly features or mates. Some of the fancy visual effects such as RealView, shadows, reflections, and some materials will also be missing. Also, things like rebuild or forced rebuild will not have any effect.

FIGURE 22.2
Large Design Review
enables you to review
large assemblies
more quickly.

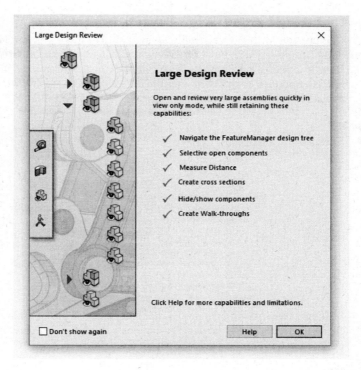

The Large Design Review interface appears as shown in Figure 22.3.

FIGURE 22.3
The Large Design
Review interface

Updating Large Design Review

Components within an assembly opened in LDR mode can become out-of-date due to changes to other components. To be notified when parts become out-of-date, you can use a system option at Tools ➤ Options ➤ Assemblies ➤ Automatic Check and update all the components. You may also need to update a component after the assembly has been opened in LDR. Options to do this are available from the RMB menu within an LDR assembly. Figure 22.4 shows some of these options.

FIGURE 22.4
An out-of-date
component and how
to update it

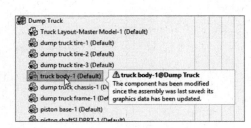

If you are working on a model that someone else has open in LDR and you make and save a change, you will get a message that warns you of the situation and gives you the option to update the LDR graphics, as shown in Figure 22.5.

FIGURE 22.5
When making a change
to a model open in LDR,
SolidWorks gives
you the option to update
the graphics.

Resolving Components

Because LDR is a lightweight mode, gaining full edit capabilities to parts within an assembly requires resolving that component. To do this, you can use one of the Selective Open or Set All options shown in Figure 22.2.

Taking Snapshots

Snapshots save a custom named view as a Snap feature in the Scene, Lights, And Cameras tab of the DisplayManager. One difference between a snapshot and a custom named view is that hidden parts remain hidden in a snapshot.

You can access the Snapshot tool from the View toolbar, through the menus at View ➤ Lights And Cameras ➤ Take Snapshot, or though the default hotkey Alt+spacebar. When you take the snapshot, SolidWorks asks you to name it, just as with a custom named view. Figure 22.6 shows snapshots saved in the DisplayManager.

FIGURE 22.6
Snapshots are saved in
the DisplayManager.

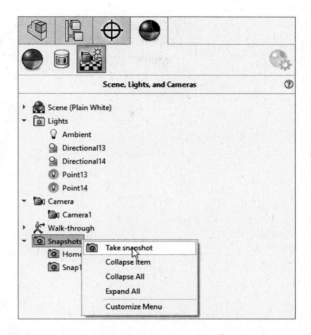

The Home Snapshot is like the Default configuration. It is automatically created if you open an assembly in Large Design Review.

Creating a Walk-Through

Walk-through is a method to create an animation simulating what a person would see as he walks through a large-scale design. This chapter looks at the example of the very large dump truck. This turns out to be a good example of equipment design where a walk-through could be useful. Figure 22.7 shows the walk-through area of the DisplayManager along with the model used for this example. You can do walk-throughs using an interface to direct an *avatar* (virtual mannequin), or you can drive the camera along a sketched path. The sketched path method has some overlap with MotionManager animation, which is covered in Chapter 23, "Animating with the MotionManager."

The interface for the walk-through consists of two elements. The initial setup is controlled by the Walk-through PropertyManager, shown in Figure 22.8.

In the PropertyManager, you select a base plane, which acts as a floor, and then you establish a camera height to simulate the height of your eyes off the floor. If you intend to drive the walk-through using a sketch, you can select the sketch elements in the Motion Constraints selection box. For the most fluid motion, use splines. You can use 2D or 3D sketches.

To start the walk-though, click the Start Walk-through button on the PropertyManager, and the interface shown in Figure 22.9 will appear.

FIGURE 22.7
Using the
DisplayManager to
manage a walk-through

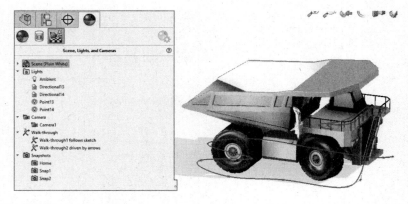

FIGURE 22.8
Using the Walk-through
PropertyManager for
the initial setup.

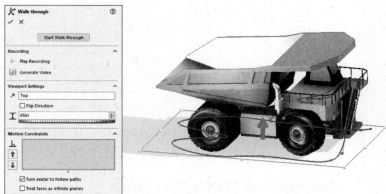

FIGURE 22.9
The Walk-through
interface helps you
manipulate the view
and the motion of
the camera.

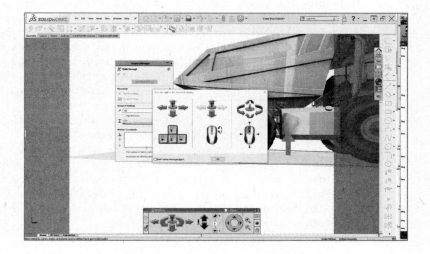

Capturing the walk-through requires an interface that's significantly different from other SolidWorks tools, shown in Figure 22.9. Although the interface and documentation refer to an "avatar," you won't notice any sort of virtual manikin walking through the model, except in SolidWorks sales demonstrations.

When you're in this mode, the scroll wheel on your mouse works backward from standard SolidWorks functionality for zooming. You also cannot turn and walk at the same time. The feel is very much like an early 1990s primitive video game.

The workflow to create a walk-through goes like this:

1. Select a suitable model, preferably something with an interior that you want to virtually wander around inside. It works best with models on the scale of buildings.

2. Click the DisplayManager tab in the FeatureManager area.

3. Click the Scene, Lights, And Cameras button.

4. Right-click the Walk-through entry in the list and select Add Walk-through.

5. Establish a floor or vertical direction and tell it which end is up (literally). Also establish the height of your eyes above the floor.

6. If you are using a sketch path, select the sketch segments in the Motion Constraints selection box.

7. Begin the capture of your walk-through. If you are using sketches to drive the motion, just press the Forward button on the interface, and the camera will walk along the path. If you are not using sketches, use the arrows on the interface to make the camera (called an "avatar" in this interface) move.

8. Generate and save the video.

The Dump Truck files I used for this example are in the download materials from the Wiley website. This is a good model to use for practice.

Creating a GridSystem

In SolidWorks, a GridSystem is a 3D sketch that repeats a 2D sketch on every level of a structure. You start by creating a 2D sketch where lines represent structural members for that level. SolidWorks uses derived sketches on planes. The 3D sketch itself contains only columns. The structure could be bolted together from fabricated I-beams, a welded tubing structure, or an assembled scaffolding, for example.

The GridSystem can help you identify interior and exterior walls, structural columns, and beams. Figure 22.10 shows a complete GridSystem.

Here is the basic workflow for creating a GridSystem:

1. Click the GridSystem button on the Feature toolbar or in the Insert ➤ Reference Geometry menu selection.

2. Draw a sketch that represents the outer shape of the structure, as well as inner structural members.

3. Use the GridSystem PropertyManager to establish the number of levels (floors), the default height for levels, and the specific height for each level.

4. Click OK in the PropertyManager, and watch SolidWorks build the GridSystem.

Each step includes some detail and requires more explanation to make it work.

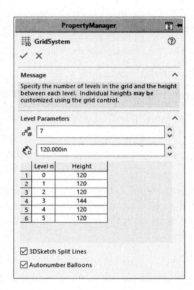

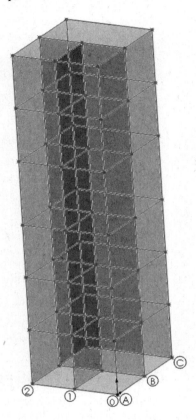

Starting the GridSystem Feature

The GridSystem toolbar icon is listed as part of the Feature toolbar, although it's not there by default. If you want to add the GridSystem icon to any toolbar, use Tools ➤ Customize ➤ Commands, and select it from the end of the list of icons for the Feature toolbar.

You can access GridSystem through the menus by default, but it's in a different location. Through the menus, click Insert ➤ Reference Geometry ➤ GridSystem.

Creating the Sketch

When you start the GridSystem feature, SolidWorks puts you into a 2D sketch on the Top (XZ) plane, but it provides no other explanation. The software is waiting for you to create a sketch with some specific properties. This sketch essentially represents the layout of the structural members forming one level of the structure. Figure 22.11 shows a sample sketch.

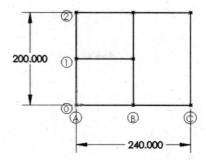

The sketch is dimensioned in inches, but you also can use more appropriate units, such as feet or meters.

Notice also that annotations label the intersections of the lines with letters for the X direction and numbers for the Z direction. Structural engineers use this method to identify the columns in the structure. The column in the center of the sketch shown in Figure 22.11 would be called 1B. These column line labels are automatically generated by SolidWorks when the Autonumber Balloons option at the bottom of the GridSystem PropertyManager is turned on.

Several rules for the sketch are not obvious. First, all the lines are planar and either horizontal or vertical within the sketch. You cannot make a circular structure or use the sketch to lay out something like a power line tower. You might be able to add diagonal members later, but you cannot use them as part of the initial layout for the GridSystem.

Using the GridSystem PropertyManager

When you are finished creating the sketch, exit the sketch using the Sketch icon in the Confirmation Corner (in the upper-right of the graphics window). This brings up the GridSystem PropertyManager, shown in Figure 22.11.

Everything in the GridSystem PropertyManager seems self-explanatory. The default level height of 118.11023622 inches is a conversion of the default 3-meter height that SolidWorks uses.

Notice that you can customize the height of each level. For example, if Level 3 has some specialized equipment that needs more room than the standard-level height, you can easily specify this as part of the design.

The setting for 3DSketch Split Lines controls whether the columns that extend through all levels of the grid will be continuous from top to bottom or whether they will be split at each level. Which option you select mainly depends on what you plan to do with the GridSystem. If you plan to use it to create a weldment, you may want to split the lines. If you plan to simply extrude shapes the entire height of the structure, you may prefer to not split them.

Understanding the GridSystem Output

The GridSystem creates a single feature in the FeatureManager with a number of derived sketches and planes, as shown in Figure 22.12.

The additional features are listed as parents of the GridSystem, indented below it in the FeatureManager.

FIGURE 22.12
Listing the
GridSystem output

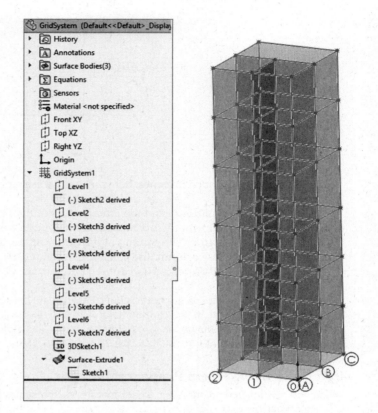

I already noted the derived sketches and planes, one each per level, created at the appropriate heights. A derived sketch is simply a parametric copy of the original sketch, placed on a different plane. If the original sketch changes, the derived copies also are updated. Derived sketches can be moved or rotated only. They cannot be edited; all changes must be performed at the parent sketch.

The 3D sketch in the FeatureManager contains lines forming the columns (Y-direction lines between the levels). This sketch is hidden by default.

You also may notice that the GridSystem uses transparent surfaces to represent interior and exterior walls. These are hidden by default. Depending on your structure, you may or may not have any use for information about walls, or you may care only about the exterior walls.

When you're using the GridSystem, your interaction with surfaces is limited to showing and hiding them. You can use the Display pane or RMB menus to do this.

Viewing the Grid Components

If you right-click the GridSystem feature in the FeatureManager, you'll see a selection named View Grid Components. This is useful if you create a weldment from the grid and want to see a list of the features that comprise the grid itself, rather than all the weldment features. The View Grid Components dialog box is shown in Figure 22.13.

FIGURE 22.13
Isolating the grid components in a separate window

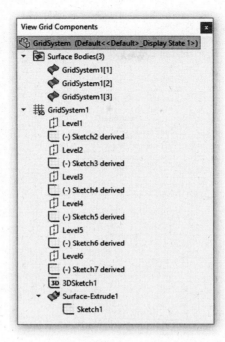

Transferring Data with the IFC File Type

IFC stands for Industry Foundation Classes, which was developed by the IAI (International Alliance for Interoperability) as an open data-exchange format. It's meant to be used to transfer data on building models between BIM (building information model) software packages. ArchiCAD and Revit are two examples of BIM modelers that might use this type of information.

The IFC file type includes geometry, but it also includes nongeometrical information about the function and occupant spaces within the building. You could think of this as the ability to transfer SolidWorks custom property information along with a STEP file transfer.

Although the use of SolidWorks in the AEC realm is limited, SolidWorks is firmly established in equipment design, which is closely related to the design of plants and industrial steel-framed structures.

To save a GridSystem as an IFC file, go to File ➤ Save As, and in the drop-down list, select the *.IFC file type.

You can also select the Options button in the Save As dialog box to set the units and OmniClass, as shown in Figure 22.14.

The OmniClass classifications give you a detailed structure for classifying the data prior to importing it into a building model. Software such as SolidWorks would be useful for small components in buildings rather than for the building itself, but the equipment produced in SolidWorks could still be used in the BIM model. Air conditioning equipment, windows, plumbing, and other component hardware would be commonly created in SolidWorks.

If you want to learn more about the IFC standard, refer to the following website, which has a detailed description of the structure, purpose, and history of the file type:

`http://www.aecbytes.com/feature/2004/IFC.html`

FIGURE 22.14
Saving data as an IFC file

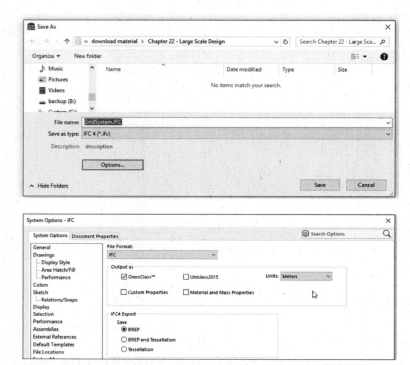

The Bottom Line

SolidWorks has long been used for the design of equipment and components that go into buildings. With Large Scale Design, the software also works for the design of small plants and gridded structures. Walk-through capabilities give Large Scale Design users some animation capabilities, and the *.IFC export options allow users to share SolidWorks Large Scale Designs with other BIM software users.

Master It Use Large Design Review to examine the dump truck.sldasm model that is included with the download materials for this chapter. Also open the same model in standard SolidWorks and familiarize yourself with the differences between the two.

Master It Again, use the dump truck model to make a walk-through. Use either the manual controls or the 3D sketch path to direct the walk-through.

Master It Start a new part and open a new GridSystem feature. Lay out a three-story structure to hold processing equipment, where the spacing between the first two floors is 10 feet and the spacing between Floors 2 and 3 is 12 feet.

Chapter 23

Animating with the MotionManager

The MotionManager is an interface that enables you to create animations showing the motion of parts and assemblies based on a timeline. These animations can range from a simple rotating part to complex moving machinery, involving motion constrained by assembly mates or motion driven by motors, springs, gravity, and contact. You can render the animations using PhotoView 360 or show them in a SolidWorks display mode, including RealView.

Collectively, the results of any of the motion capabilities in SolidWorks are called *motion studies*. Some of the capabilities are more focused on analysis (also called *simulation*), while others involve simple *animation,* but all can create movie output.

IN THIS CHAPTER, YOU WILL LEARN TO:

- ◆ Use the MotionManager

- ◆ Create rotating and exploded view animations

- ◆ Animate view changes in the MotionManager

- ◆ Use key points

- ◆ Work with Basic Motion

- ◆ Animate exploded views

SolidWorks has three primary methods and two ancillary methods of creating motion in assemblies:

Animation: This creates simple motion driven by the Animation Wizard, key frames, mates, and motors.

Basic Motion: This includes motors, springs, friction, and standard mates.

SolidWorks Motion (analysis): This includes Basic Motion as well as forces and dampers, and it will calculate loads, velocities, and accelerations. This isn't covered here because it's not part of SolidWorks Standard. It's available only with SolidWorks Premium or SolidWorks Simulation Professional.

There are two ancillary methods of capturing movies:

Walk-through: This is a summary of preexisting tools paired with a simplified interface for architectural-type walk-through animations.

Record Screen: This records simple view rotation and dynamic assembly model motion.

Exploded View: This is used to animate the steps in exploded views.

Mate Controller: The Mate Controller is an interface for controlling mates toward the goal of creating an animation without first creating configurations.

Familiarizing Yourself with the MotionManager

To get usable results from these tools, you need to be comfortable with the limits of the technology that SolidWorks provides. Your success with the tools depends heavily on having realistic expectations of their capabilities.

Understanding the Terminology

Here's an overview of the terminology used in conjunction with motion in SolidWorks:

MotionManager: The MotionManager interface gives you access to the Animation, Basic Motion, and SolidWorks Motion tools. This single interface controls all the tools.

Animation: Animation uses the *key frame* method, where the software interpolates between positions established by mates, free-hand drag, or positioning via the Triad or XYZ values. Don't confuse animation with *dynamic assembly motion*, which is simply dragging parts in an assembly with the cursor to create motion.

Basic Motion: Basic Motion uses motors, springs, gravity, and so on; it doesn't use key frames. It includes the Physical Dynamics feature, which deals with the calculation of motion due to collisions.

SolidWorks Motion: If you need detailed input and output including graphed functions, SolidWorks Motion is the best choice. This option isn't available in the SolidWorks Standard level of the software, so it's not covered here in detail.

If you need a function that's only allowed in another type of motion study, you need to change the motion study type in the drop-down selection box in the upper-left corner of the MotionManager. The default option is Animation, and the other two available options are Basic Motion and Motion Analysis. Motion Analysis is available only if you have SolidWorks Motion turned on in the Tools ➤ Add-ins dialog box, and that's available only if you have SolidWorks Premium or SolidWorks Simulation Professional. You can see the Study Type box in the interface shown in Figure 23.1.

Another method that you can use to capture screen motion to a movie file is by using the Record Video tool (View ➤ Screen Capture ➤ Record Video). The Record Video tool also appears as a toolbar button on the Screen Capture toolbar. You can use Record Video to record whatever happens in the graphics window, from using the Rollback bar to dynamic assembly motion dragging parts with the cursor.

NOTE The videos that accompany this book were recorded using a third-party screen capture and video-editing software called Camtasia by TechSmith.

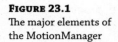

FIGURE 23.1

The major elements of the MotionManager

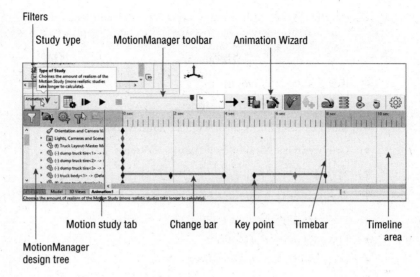

Driving an Animation

You can animate the following:

- Distance mates
- Angle mates
- Part appearance (including display modes—Shaded, Wireframe, and so on)
- Part transparency
- Part visibility
- Part position
- View/zoom state
- Camera position and properties

When you animate colors and appearances, simple colors can fade from one to another, but appearances with a texture do not fade; it will simply snap to the next texture at the appropriate time. For example, you can fade red to blue, but you cannot fade marble to fabric. This is also true with fading transparency in an animation that is rendered using PhotoView 360.

You cannot animate the following:

- Changing part dimensions
- Changing PhotoView 360 materials
- Configurations

Although you can't animate the changing of part dimensions directly, with some creativity, you can animate in-context changes driven by changing mates. You will see an example of creating a part that is flexible later in this chapter.

You can use these items to drive an animation:

◆   Key points (Animation)

◆   Mates (Animation, Basic Motion, SolidWorks Motion)

◆   Motors (Animation, Basic Motion, SolidWorks Motion)

◆   Gravity (Basic Motion, SolidWorks Motion)

◆   Springs (Basic Motion, SolidWorks Motion)

◆   Contact (Basic Motion, SolidWorks Motion)

◆   Friction (Basic Motion, SolidWorks Motion)

◆   Force (SolidWorks Motion)

◆   Dampers (SolidWorks Motion)

These types of motion are available:

◆   Kinematic (mates and motors—Animation, Basic Motion, SolidWorks Motion)

◆   Dynamic (physics based—Basic Motion, SolidWorks Motion)

◆   Free motion (motion based only on key points—Animation)

When you think of "physics" in SolidWorks, you may need to adjust some of your expectations; some of the tools don't follow real physics concepts very rigorously. For example, a motor applied to a part in an assembly creates a constant velocity instantly, without regard for inertia. Friction has only a single component rather than the static and kinetic, which exist in real engineering problems. You can simulate static friction with a force and an equation, but it isn't available as a function of friction.

Planning an Animation

It is often useful to plan an animation that's more involved than just a few moves on the screen. You can do this in a couple of different ways. The easiest way is to write out a list of moves or positions you want to display, with the approximate time of each action or position.

Another way is to use the storyboard technique employed by professional videographers. In this method, you create a series of images to represent the state of the animation at specific points in time. You can use static screen captures from SolidWorks or hand sketches to do this, depending on the complexity of the geometry and animation.

In general, even for simple animations, the better you plan, the better the final product will be. The animation tools in SolidWorks tend to perform much better when you follow a clean workflow, without lots of major editing. This is something you could probably say about almost any process, but the animation tools seem to be particularly sensitive to editing.

Identifying Elements of the MotionManager

The parts of the interface that you will use the most are the key points, the design tree, and the timebar. The filters help you select or view limited sets of items, and the tabs at the bottom enable you to set up alternative studies. Playback speed enables you to change the rate of playback to either view a long animation more quickly or see motion in one area in more detail. The timeline zoom tools enable you to rescale the time interval on the timeline. Figure 23.1 identifies the major elements of the MotionManager.

Using Display Options

When recording an animation to a movie file or a series of still images, you can choose from several types of display output. The first and easiest type is the default SolidWorks display, without RealView. This is most appropriate for fast, technical presentations. You might want to use this to demonstrate the function of a particular mechanism or to simply rotate around a model to demonstrate the model in 3D rather than as a flat image or an eDrawing.

You can also turn on RealView and record the animation. If you do this, you should have appropriate appearances in use for individual parts. RealView appearances enable you to use reflective or textured materials on your parts.

The highest-quality images come through the PhotoView 360 renderer. Using PhotoView 360 takes much more time than the other options because each individual frame must be rendered just like a normal PhotoView 360 rendering. PhotoView 360 is beyond the scope of this book because it is not an add-in for SolidWorks Standard.

SolidWorks Visualize is another SolidWorks rendering product. Visualize is a separate stand-alone renderer and is not included in the scope of this book.

Using the MotionManager Interface

You can access the MotionManager interface in the lower-left corner of the graphics window. The Model, 3D Views, and Animation1 tabs enable you to toggle the interface on and off. The Model tab shows the normal SolidWorks interface. The 3D Views tab enables you to capture 3D Views for 3D pdf, Step w/PMI, or eDrawings.

You can add tabs to create multiple motion studies. If you cannot see this interface, you may need to turn on the MotionManager. To do this, right-click a toolbar and select MotionManager from the list of toolbars.

Motion Study Properties within the MotionManager, shown in Figure 23.2, enable you to establish the accuracy or frame rate of the display. Use the gear symbol on the MotionManager toolbar.

Formatting Output

The MotionManager enables you to create animations within SolidWorks and output movies as `*.avi` files or a series of `*.bmp` or `*.tga` still images. You can use it with the default (OpenGL) SolidWorks display, RealView display, or in conjunction with PhotoView 360 to create more realistically rendered animations.

You can control the pixel size and frame rate of the recorded animation to help control finished file size, movie quality, and the amount of time it takes to record the animation. You can rotate or fly through single parts or assemblies. You can also make assembly mechanisms move through animating mates, driving them with motors or manually positioning the parts in space.

FIGURE 23.2
Motion Study Properties
enable you to set
frame rates and other
display qual-
ity settings.

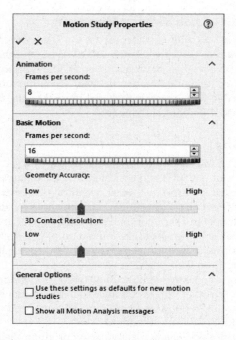

One of the beautiful things about SolidWorks animations is that you can save them to an
eDrawings file. You can send eDrawings to non-SolidWorks users for review, and because the file
format is small, you can easily send animations over the Internet.

Using the Animation Wizard

You can use the Animation Wizard to create simple animations. The Animation Wizard accommodates two types of animations: The first is where a part or assembly is simply rotated on the
screen (or camera revolves around part or assembly), and the second uses an existing exploded
view from an assembly. You can combine, reorder, reverse, copy, or move both types of animation
sequences within a larger animation.

Creating a Rotating Animation

A simple rotating animation is the simplest animation you can create. To create a rotating
animation, first click the Animation1 tab at the bottom-left corner of the graphics window. This
opens the MotionManager interface. Remember that you can turn the MotionManager on or off
in the list of toolbars. (Choose Tools ➢ Customize or View ➢ Toolbars, or right-click any toolbar to
access the setting for the MotionManager.)

Click the Animation Wizard icon in the toolbar on top of the MotionManager. Figure 23.3
shows the dialog box that appears, where you can choose options that include Rotate Model,
Explode, Collapse, Import Motion From Basic Motion, and Import Motion From Motion
Analysis. In this example, all options are grayed out except for Rotate Model. The model that is
loaded does not have an exploded view, Basic Motion, or SolidWorks Motion data.

After you select the appropriate type of animation and click Next, you select an axis of
rotation, the number of rotations, and the direction. An important thing to note here is that the
X-, Y-, and Z-axes do not refer to axes of the part; they refer to axes on the screen. Rotating about
the X-axis is like holding down the right-arrow key on the keyboard. The sample animation that
appears in the upper-left corner of the Animation Wizard, shows what you can expect. It changes
direction if you change the option (see Figure 23.4).

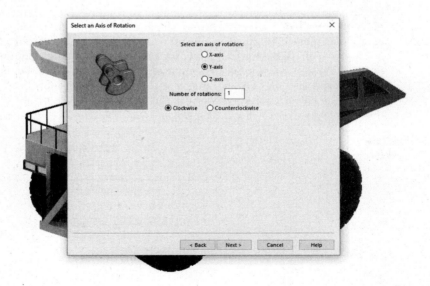

The final step in creating the rotating animation is to determine how long the animation will last and at what point in the overall animation it should start. Figure 23.5 shows the Animation Wizard page where you can set these options.

NOTE Looping is controlled only during playback. The actual animation has a beginning and an end; so if you want to play the finished movie with smooth looping, you should make sure that the start point and the end point of the animation are the same.

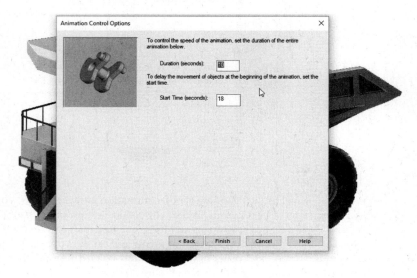

FIGURE 23.5
The third page of the Animation Wizard: Animation Control Options

After you click Finish, the MotionManager will populate the timeline with key points for the Orientation and Camera Views. Instead of rotating the part, the software will rotate the view. It seems like a semantic difference, but when you start working with moving parts in assemblies while changing the view, the difference becomes important. Notice the heavy black line with diamonds in the row for the Orientation and Camera Views in Figure 23.6. Each diamond is a key point that represents a view angle, and the line between the diamonds indicates that MotionManager will interpolate the view between the key points, making the view transition smoothly. You will learn how to create key points later in this chapter.

FIGURE 23.6
Change bars in the MotionManager

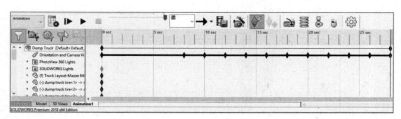

To play the animation, click the Play From Start button or the Play button in the MotionManager toolbar. Note also that you can run the Animation Wizard multiple times to create various sequences within a single animation. You can control the start time and duration, which are added to the timeline. You can also edit the key points and even mirror the path.

Creating an Exploded View Animation

The sample assembly in the Animations folder of the download materials is named Robot Assembly.sldasm, and it's saved with an exploded view. You can use this assembly or create your own. If you use this file, you must first create a new motion study for practicing. To do that, right-click on the Animation1 tab at the bottom and select Create New Motion Study.

To use the Animation Wizard to create an animated explode and collapse, first start with an assembly that has an exploded view and activate the Animation Wizard. Remember that exploded views are kept under a configuration in the Configuration Manager. Figure 23.3 shows the first page of the Animation Wizard where you select the animation type. Select the Explode option and click Next. Figure 23.7 shows the second page. (Explode animations skip the second step, which is used by rotate animations.)

FIGURE 23.7

The second page of the Explode Animation Wizard

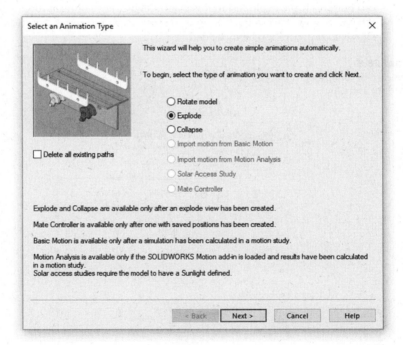

If you add the explode animation at the end of the rotate animation, the resulting animation does both: rotates then explodes, each in sequence. Later you will learn how to copy and reverse the key points for the explode to make it collapse, and how to adjust key points to make parts move faster, slower, or simultaneously.

You can also edit the animation created by the explode or collapse in the same way you would edit the rotate animation created by the wizard. If you have multiple parts moving at different times, you can edit the sequence so that certain parts move at the same time by marquee selecting (or Ctrl+selecting) a group of key points and moving them along the timeline.

Animating an Assembly

Here's an example of using the Animation Wizard to first rotate a model and then explode and collapse it, along with some simple editing. If you want to follow along with this example, open the Yoke Link.sldasm assembly from the download materials for Chapter 23. Note that this assembly already has a complete animation, so you need to create a second motion study when you want to try to make your own animation with this assembly.

CREATING AN EXPLODE

The first step in creating this animation is to have an explode in place before starting the animation. To do this, start by switching to the ConfigurationManager and then activating the configuration in which you want to create the explode or create a new configuration. Each configuration can hold multiple explodes. In this example, the new configuration is called Example (right-click the name of the part in the ConfigurationManager and select Add Configuration). Figure 23.8 shows a configuration being added.

FIGURE 23.8
Adding a new configuration to the assembly

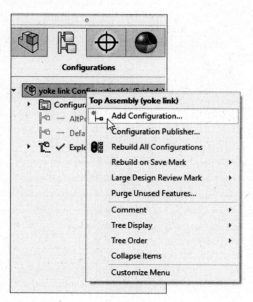

To add the new explode, right-click the new configuration name and select New Exploded View, as shown in Figure 23.9.

Adding the explode brings up the PropertyManager shown in Figure 23.10. In this PropertyManager, you can create the individual explode steps.

FIGURE 23.9
Adding a new explode

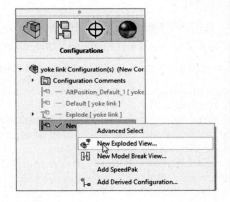

FIGURE 23.10
Detailing the explode
steps for this example

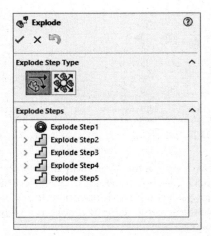

Without reviewing the material for explodes in Chapter 13, "Building Efficient Assemblies," in detail, the general workflow for creating the individual explode steps is as follows:

1. Select a part.

2. Select Regular Step (translate or rotate) or Radial Step.

3. Use the Triad to move the part. You may have to set the explode direction for parts not aligned with the assembly axes.

4. Repeat steps 1, 2, and 3 for each explode you want to add.

This example uses six explode steps (step 1 creates two different explode steps):

1. Explode the nut and the bolt to opposite sides (radially). Select a flat face of the nut and a cylindrical face of the bolt; then tug the orange arrow to pull them to opposite sides.

2. Explode the strap straight up.

3. Explode the Head and the Bushing straight down together.

4. Explode the Bushing to one side. You must establish a direction.

5. Explode the Tie Rod down half the distance of the Head and Bushing explode.

Now that the explode is complete, make sure the assembly is in its collapsed state (right-click ExplView1 under the configuration name).

Before displaying the MotionManager interface, change the assembly view to the proper orientation. Press the spacebar to display the View Orientation dialog box and select the Animation 1 view. Then close the View Orientation dialog box.

Next, right-click the Animation 1 tab at the bottom-left corner of the SolidWorks window to display the MotionManager interface and select Create New Motion Study. This gives you a fresh start with a new animation timeline. Figure 23.11 shows how to create the new motion study.

FIGURE 23.11
Creating a new
motion study

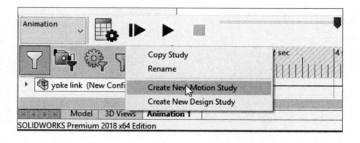

Next, click the Animation Wizard icon in the MotionManager toolbar. The Select An Animation Type window will appear, as shown in Figure 23.3. Select the Rotate Model option and click Next. In the next window, select the Y-axis option and click Next. Remember, in this case, "Y-axis" means the Y-axis of the screen, not of the model. If it were the Y-axis of the model, the assembly would simply spin in place.

PUTTING THE ROTATE INTO AN ANIMATION TIMELINE

In the Animation Control Options window, set the rotation to last 3 seconds and the start time to 0. You'll change these settings later to get some practice making edits to timelines and key points. When you click Finish, you should get the result shown in Figure 23.12.

FIGURE 23.12
Using the Animation Wizard to add key points to the animation timeline

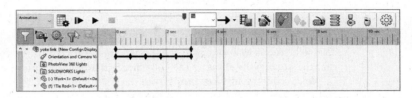

When you're making an animation, it's nice to have a gap between the start of the movie and the motion of the parts, to give the viewer some time to adjust to what he's seeing on the screen. Of course, if you're making a movie that you want to use as a continuous loop, the gap might interrupt the motion. You could also insert a gap between the end of the motion and the end of the movie, which might make the gap seem more natural.

In any case, you want to add a gap of a second or one-half second at the beginning of this animation. To do this, drag a selection window around the heavy black line and black key points in the Orientation And Camera View row, and then drag them to the right by slightly less than 1 second.

ADDING THE EXPLODE TO THE ANIMATION

You can now add the explode to the animation. To do this, follow these steps:

1. Start the Animation Wizard again, but this time, select the Explode option and click Next.

2. In the Animation Control Options window, set the duration again to 3 seconds, with the start time at 6.25 seconds, and click Finish. The result is shown in Figure 23.13.

FIGURE 23.13
Bringing the explode steps into the Motion-Manager timeline

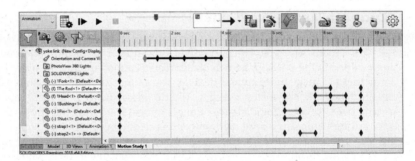

COLLAPSING THE EXPLODED ASSEMBLY

Now you will add the collapse, but this time without running the wizard. To accomplish this, follow these steps:

1. Drag a rectangle around all the key points created by the explode.

2. Ctrl+drag them so the first copied step lands at about ½ second after the last original key point.

3. With the block of key points still selected, right-click one of the copied key points and select Reverse Path. The copied explode now becomes a collapse.

4. Change the order of the explode by dragging key points or pairs of key points. For example, the Bushing has three key points in its path. You can delete the middle key point and shorten its motion to match the Head.

ANIMATING A ZOOM

The next step is to zoom in to the looped area of the strap. To do this, you have to first make sure that the view is the same as the last change made to the orientation.

Next, copy the last key point from the rotate motion (Ctrl+drag) to the same time that the collapse finishes. Then move the timebar forward a couple seconds, zoom in so you can see the fork and the looped section of the strap, right-click the timebar in the row for orientation, and select Place Key, as shown in Figure 23.14.

FIGURE 23.14
Zooming in to the
flexible area of the strap

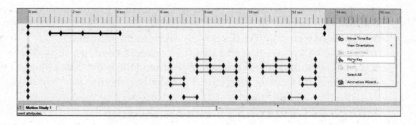

There are other ways to place this View Orientation key, such as by enabling the Orientation and Camera Views item. If you enable the Orientation, the MotionManager records every view change you make, so it's cleaner and safer if you just use the RMB ➤ Place Key method instead of enabling the orientation.

MAKING A PART LOOK FLEXIBLE

Click the Calculate button on the MotionManager toolbar. Notice that when the strap moves up, the part actually shortens. The part will also twist later in the animation when you change the angle of one of the parts. In general, SolidWorks cannot animate flexible parts, but you can use some tricks to make parts appear flexible. You cannot animate part dimension changes, but you can animate mate dimension changes. You do this by using in-context relations and driving mating parts by changing distance or angle mates. Therefore, the appearance of flexibility comes only through animating parts with in-context relations, and maybe some well-thought-out features.

Animating through in-context relations is not available in Basic Motion.

ANIMATING A CHANGING MATE

The next item that this movie will animate is the Angle1 mate. If you expand the Mates folder in the FeatureManager, you'll find that it has two folders. One folder is for model mates, and the other is for mates that drive the animation. The only mate in the Animation Mates folder is Angle1.

Start by copying the initial key point for Angle1 from 0 seconds to slightly after the view change just made. Next, move the timebar one more second past the copied key point; you can do this precisely by right-clicking the timebar, selecting Move Time Bar, and then typing in the time to which you want to move it. Then double-click the Angle1 mate and change its value from 45 to 180.

Make the angle mate change from 45 to 180, back to 45, then 0, and then 45 again, with about one-half second for each change. Remember, you can use copied key points to make the multiple 45-degree values. Finish the animation by returning to the original view. To do this, copy the first key point of the orientation and then the last key point (at about 10.25 seconds). Figure 23.15 shows the final result.

FIGURE 23.15

The finished timeline for this animation

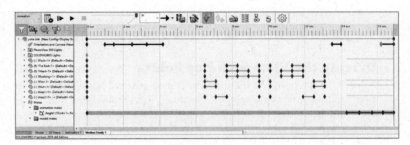

This example serves as a demonstration of the overall workflow, while the rest of this chapter offers a detailed discussion of the functions that are available.

Animating the View

This section reintroduces some of the view animation items that you saw earlier in this chapter—that is, tools involved in changing the point of view from which the animation is recorded. The first part of the chapter mostly offered a practical overview of the animation workflow. This section gives you a more thorough knowledge of individual tools for changing and controlling the view. You already understand how the tools combine to make an animation; now you just need to know what tools are available and how they work.

View Animation is an important and even reusable function. For example, you can save an animation where the only things that are animated are the view changes in an assembly, and then you can put any part or other assembly that you want into this pre-created animation. If your PhotoView 360 settings are established (except materials and appearances for the individual parts), you can even create a rendered animation very quickly by reusing existing data.

A great example is when you want to show an assembly spinning on its axis, like a turntable (instead of on the axis of the screen as shown in the Animation Wizard); in this case, you can record a camera following a path focused on a particular point. This is a great animation to set up as a template, so you can reuse it as a quick-and-easy animation boilerplate. This technique is covered later in this chapter.

You can animate view changes in the MotionManager in the following ways:

◆ Orientation And Camera Views (must be enabled)

◆ Using key points (move timebar, rotate model)

◆ Using key points (move timebar, rotate model, right-click and select Place Key)

◆ Using the Animation Wizard to rotate a model

◆ Using any of the above techniques with a camera

◆ Attaching a camera to a part that moves

◆ Attaching a camera to a path (use an animation or a walk-through)

◆ Using a screen capture to record the screen

Driving the View with Key Points

A *key point* is a point on the timeline where you tell SolidWorks what state something will be in at a specific time. For example, at 9 seconds, the view will be a front view; this is represented by a diamond along the timeline that contains the information. You can use key points to animate assembly motion, the view, or even properties such as color, transparency, or mate values. We've already done some work with key points in this chapter.

USING THE ORIENTATION AND CAMERA VIEWS FEATURE

An important fact about using view and camera key points is that the Orientation And Camera Views feature in the MotionManager is locked by default. This means that you cannot change the view in an animation by accident. To unlock it, right-click the Orientation And Camera Views entry, and deselect the Disable View Key Creation option.

If you don't understand why this setting is turned off by default, try working with it turned on for a while as you are learning the software. You may find that, unless you are extraordinarily well organized, you will make many unwanted changes to the view, because you are unconsciously rotating the view to see it better and forgetting that the change is being recorded. This is a very common mistake among users when creating an animation.

> **BEST PRACTICE**
>
> The best way to handle the Orientation and Camera Views feature is to keep it locked and use the RMB option Place/Replace Key when you want.

DISABLING PLAYBACK OF VIEW KEYS

You can play back the assembly animation and disable the view changes. To do this, right-click the Orientation And Camera Views item in the MotionManager and select Disable Playback Of View Keys from the menu. Very often when you're dealing with assembly motion, it helps to see the assembly from a particular point of view. You can't do that if your animation is always changing the view. Remember to deselect this setting before recording the animation to a file.

INTRODUCING THE TIMEBAR

The timebar is the vertical gray line in the timeline area that denotes the current time that you are editing in the animation. Refer to Figure 23.1, which identifies the major parts of the MotionManager interface. When you make a change to any element that can be animated, that change is applied at the time denoted by the timebar. To make a key point-driven animation, the workflow usually involves moving the timebar, making a set of changes, moving the timebar, making another set of changes, and so on.

To try this out on an assembly, open the Robot Assembly in the Robot Arm folder from the download materials. You can follow along with the existing motion study or create a new one and experiment on your own. Start by making sure the timebar is set to 0 (all the way to the left), and then position the view to start the animation. In this case, display the View Orientation dialog box (press the spacebar) and double-click the view named 1.

Because the Orientation And Camera Views item is disabled, this view change is not recorded. In order to record it, right-click the key point to the right of Orientation And Camera Views, and select Replace Key, as shown in Figure 23.16. This replaces the existing key with the new view orientation.

FIGURE 23.16
Selecting Replace Key to change the view at a View Orientation key point

The view should remain static for a brief time when the animation starts; it might be too confusing to start the animation immediately with the view changing. To create this pause, copy the first key point from the 0-second mark to the 1-second mark. It is as easy as it sounds. Click the key point in the same row as the Orientation And Camera Views, and then Ctrl+drag it to the right to the 1-second mark. This causes the first second of the view to be static.

CREATING KEY POINTS

Next, move the timebar to the 3-second mark, display the View Orientation dialog box again, activate View 2; then right-click where the Orientation row intersects the 3-second column, and select Place Key to make a new key point for the view orientation. The black bar between the 1-second key point and the 3-second key point indicates that the animation will interpolate the view orientation between the two defined points. The MotionManager now looks like Figure 23.17.

FIGURE 23.17
The timeline at the
2-second mark

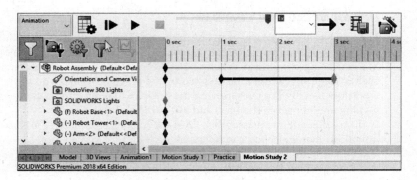

Remember that the View Orientation dialog box stores both the Orientation and Zoom factor, so when you use View 2, it may be zoomed at a different state; therefore, when the view changes from 1 to 2, it may rotate and zoom in or out slightly. If you want to measure rotation more precisely, it may be a good idea to use the arrow keys rather than something like a 3D mouse.

ZOOMING AND FREE VIEW MANIPULATION

The next step is to zoom in to the grippers and simultaneously turn the view slightly to give a better view. Before changing the view, though, it would be nice to have another pause to give the viewer the chance to see what's there. To create the pause, click the last key point in the Orientation And Camera Views row and then Ctrl+drag it to the 5-second mark. Then move the timebar to the 7-second mark. Remember that the workflow for copying a particular key is to select and then Ctrl+drag, not just Ctrl+drag. If you Ctrl+drag without making the initial selection, you may be copying other key points that were also selected at the time. The select operation serves two functions: to deselect anything else and to select only the key point that interests you.

After you have the timebar moved to the 7-second mark, use the View Orientation (press the spacebar) to move to View 3. After doing this, zoom in on the grippers using whatever method you use to zoom: Shift+Z, middle mouse button (MMB) scroll, Zoom To Area, Zoom To Selection, Zoom In/Out, or a 3D mouse. After you have made both changes, add the key point to the Orientation change bar in the same way you have done it previously. The rotate and zoom will happen at the same time. The idea is to get a good partial side view of the grippers, such as the view shown in Figure 23.18. Play the animation to see what you have created.

FIGURE 23.18
The timeline at the
7-second mark

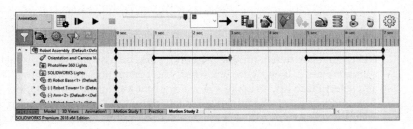

USING INTERPOLATION MODES

When you play the animation, it may appear somewhat jerky. When the MotionManager interpolates between key points, for changing either views or part positions, the default interpolation mode is Linear. This means that it changes between points at a constant speed. This creates the jerkiness because the motion starts and stops abruptly.

To remedy this, the MotionManager offers several interpolation modes. Right-click one of the key points that you have created and select Interpolation Mode at the bottom of the list that appears. Another menu will fly out, as shown in Figure 23.19.

FIGURE 23.19
Selecting
Interpolation Mode

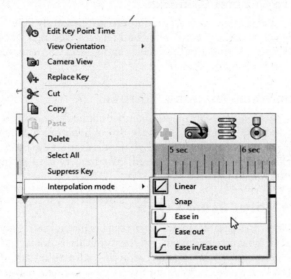

The icons for the modes signify how the motion increases or decreases between key points. In any case, curves make smoother motion than lines. Ease In/Ease Out creates the smoothest motion; Ease In works best at the beginning of a change, and Ease Out works best at the end of a change. Snap causes an abrupt change in position from one place the part will move immediately to another location at the next key point. The Linear option causes the part to move at a constant velocity from one point to another.

The default mode is Linear, so if you want to change all four of the key points, you must go through this selection four times, right? No, there's an easier way. You can box-select all four key points, right-click any of the selected key points, and change them all to the Ease In/Ease Out mode. Now play the animation again. Notice how much smoother the view changes are.

CORRECTING MISTAKES

When you start to use the MotionManager, you'll probably make mistakes. Don't feel bad; this happens even to seasoned veterans. The difference between you and experienced users is that they know how to deal with mistakes and not panic. The MotionManager does you the favor of recording all your mistakes in the form of adding key points to the change line for either the part position or view orientation. One way to troubleshoot these types of mistakes is to drag the timeline through the key points and identify which key points need to be edited or removed.

To edit a key point, you can use options from the RMB menu such as Replace Key, Edit Key Time, select a different view orientation, and so on. To remove a key point, just click it and press Delete.

If you are making an animation that covers a long period of time—say, more than 30 seconds—the key points may be close together and difficult to distinguish from one another. You can use the zoom tools in the lower-right corner of the timeline area to zoom the timeline in or out. Zooming in makes the key points appear farther away from one another, enabling you to select one that might be right on top of another.

Using Paths to Control Cameras

The main camera controls you need for animations are Target By Selection, Position By Selection, and Set Roll By Selection, in addition to the Field Of View settings. These settings are available if you click the RMB on the Camera in the Scene, Lights, And Cameras pane of the DisplayManager, and select Edit Camera.

Recalling the Walk-Through Feature

Walk-through is a stand-alone feature, but its functionality is borrowed from the MotionManager for animating a camera along a path. The Walk-through feature is somewhat simplified and intended for large structures where you can go in and around the object. Remember that Chapter 22, "Working with Large Scale Design," used a very large dump truck with a staircase and an observation platform.

Rotating the Model Using a Path

The main weakness of the Rotate Animation Wizard is that it rotates about the screen axis, which appears to make it wobble on the screen, and this typically is not what users have in mind when they ask to rotate the model. Most users envision the "turntable" sort of rotation, where the model rotates about its own axis. Changing the rotation to rotate about the part axis isn't as easy as it probably ought to be, but after you understand the process, you can simplify it. This example involves making the camera revolve around the axis of a part, regardless of the orientation of the part, to show you how to drive a camera along a path. This exercise starts simple and gradually becomes more complex.

The best way to spin the view around the part axis is to make a looped path on a plane perpendicular to the axis. The plane should in most cases be slightly elevated from the base of the model and probably should be circular or at least a smooth, closed-loop spline.

Starting with the robot assembly from the download material (Robot Assembly.sldasm), move to a top view and open a 3D sketch. When doing prep work like this, it's better to work using the Model tab instead of the MotionManager. This prevents you from creating any unnecessary key points for animatable items.

In the 3D sketch, from the top view, draw a four-point closed-loop spline, as shown in Figure 23.20. This is in a 3D sketch, so you can change the path to nonplanar if you desire.

The path doesn't have to be perfectly circular; in fact, it might be better if it gets closer to the assembly on one side, making it rather kidney-shaped. You can use a circle, ellipse, or closed-loop spline for the path.

Next, press Shift+down arrow to rotate the view 90 degrees, and drag the entire spline up a little bit. Finally, tweak a couple of spline points so the spline goes higher and lower. This will give you a more interesting result than just a straight turntable-rotation animation.

FIGURE 23.20
Creating a camera path

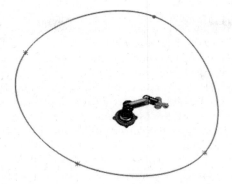

NOTE   To greatly simplify this task, you can create an offset plane and sketch an ellipse or circle on the plane rather than using the 3D spline. The 3D spline is intended to give you the most control and flexibility.

The camera will be attached to this spline. You might also want to have a target point for the camera to follow as it goes around the path. You could place a sketch point inside the joint between the Tower and Arm parts. If the assembly or even a part origin is in a convenient location, you can also use this as a place to point the camera.

After the path exists, exit the sketch and insert a new camera. You can insert a camera by switching to the DisplayManager, the multicolored ball next to the FeatureManager and ConfigurationManager tabs. Then switch to the third icon under the top tabs, which is for lights and cameras. Now right-click the Cameras folder and select Add Camera. Figure 23.21 shows the PropertyManager for the camera.

FIGURE 23.21
The Camera
PropertyManager

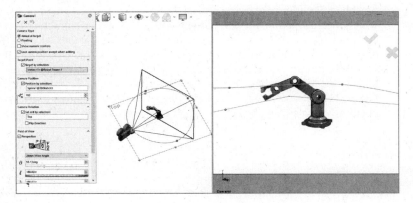

Notice that when you insert the camera, the SolidWorks graphics window splits into two viewports. The left viewport is your view of the camera, the model, and their surroundings. The right viewport is the view through the camera.

Use the Target Point selection box to aim the camera at a point on the Robot Tower part. If you aim the camera at a moving part, the motion of the camera will seem unnatural, unless the part is moving smoothly. For this assembly, you might consider aiming the camera at a dummy part in the assembly so it's moving in a jerky fashion, following a jaw, for example. You can use a part just floating in space, but generally moving left, right, up, or down as needed without being rigidly connected to any single part of the assembly.

Attach the camera to the spline by selecting the spline in the first Camera Position selection box. If you are at T=0 (the first time key point), make sure the percent position is set to 0.

To get the camera to move around the spline, move the timebar to a position such as 0.4 second, edit the Camera item in the MotionManager (right-click it inside the Lights, Cameras And Scene folder found only in the MotionManager, not in the assembly FeatureManager), and select the Properties option. Then move the Percent slider under Camera Position to about 25 percent. Do this as many times as needed to go all the way around.

If parts of the model go out of the field of view, or you feel that the camera is too far away or too close to the model, you can move the camera or change the lens. To move the camera, exit the camera PropertyManager and edit the 3D sketch.

NOTE   Remember that when you're editing unconstrained 3D sketches, it's best to do it from orthogonal views. Any points that you drag move in the plane of the screen. The best way to edit the size of the spline is to view it from the top view and drag out individual spline points.

Going Beyond 100 Percent or 360 Degrees

If you take the animation around more than 360 degrees, you must use a workaround to get it to work correctly. For example, if you use the Percent slider, and go 0-25-50-75-100 and then 25 percent, the animation will reverse direction between 100 and 25. The way to make this happen so the animation maintains continuity is to place keys at both 100 and 0 close enough to one another that the time difference is less than the frame rate of the animation. The frame rate is set in the Motion Study Properties, the icon on the far-right side of the MotionManager toolbar. For a finished animation, the frame rate could be in the neighborhood of 30 frames per second (fps), which means the time for one frame would be ⅟₃₀ second, or about 0.03 second. Therefore, if 100 percent happens at 2 seconds, you could put 0 percent at 2.01 seconds and the transition would never be seen. This workaround is used widely by people who know the software well.

The same sort of tactic works if you have to go beyond 360 degrees. You must use the zoom tools in the lower-right corner of the MotionManager to be able to see what's going on. Figure 23.22 shows two camera key points very close together in this way. To change the percent position, double-click the key point, and the Camera PropertyManager will become available.

Figure 23.22
Working around the 100 percent or 360-degree animation limitation

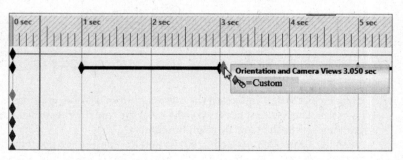

Animating with Key Points

This chapter briefly discussed key points to introduce the idea; in this section, you will learn how to use them in more detail. You can think of key points as snapshots at particular moments in time. If you say, "At the 4-second mark, the wheel must be 3 inches from the wall," this statement describes a key point for the position of the wheel. To create a key point for any property, drag the timebar to a new time and make a change to that property. Any of the animatable properties listed earlier in the chapter can create a key point.

 The Autokey button on the MotionManager toolbar does for moving components what Disable View Key Creation does for animating view changes. When you have this button pressed, moving parts with the cursor will create a new key point at the current location of the timebar.

Getting Started

Consider this easy and useful example: A customer wants you to make a little animation of a holder for a stethoscope that he will show to a potential client in PowerPoint. The holder opens, the stethoscope slides out, and then the animation reverses.

ON THE WEBSITE

The assembly with the animation saved in it is in the Animation folder labeled `scopecozy.sldasm`.

The assembly and the completed animation timeline are shown in Figure 23.23. This animation uses RealView display, which the customer has said is good enough for his purposes. Using it reduces the render time significantly when compared to using PhotoView 360 to render the animation.

FIGURE 23.23
The stethoscope
animation setup

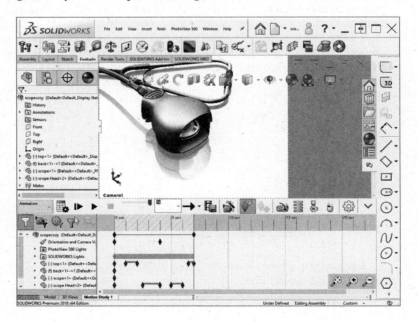

Your first task is to set up the camera. You could do this without a camera, but cameras are a convenient way to store a particular view, along with settings such as lens angle, perspective, camera position, and target. In addition, if you decide to use PhotoView 360 later, cameras are the only way to get depth of field for additional realism. Another advantage of the camera is that you can control the area in view more closely. If you don't use a camera, the area of view is just whatever is available in the viewport. With the camera, you can specify a size and aspect ratio, and the available area is cropped appropriately.

Because the stethoscope model is cut into pieces to enable different parts of it to be positioned, you must position the parts and the camera such that the break between the head and earpieces is not visible. Leave enough open area so that when the stethoscope comes out, it won't run out of the area of view.

NOTE   When adjusting the position of the camera, it's often easier to adjust the actual view than to manipulate the camera. In the Camera PropertyManager, deselecting the Lock Camera Position Except When Editing option enables you to manipulate the view directly. This setting is selected by default and will display the camera with a red X icon if you try to rotate the view when the camera view is on. Switch to camera view and deselect Disable View Key Creation.

Using the Timebar with Key Points

It's a good idea to start animations with some stillness; if you start an animation with motion, your viewer may not have time to adjust. A second is usually enough. Expand the Top part file, click the key point for the Move row at the zero (0) time mark, and Ctrl+drag it to the 1-second mark. This means that the top won't move between 0 and 1 second. Now move the timebar to 2 seconds, and open the top by dragging it up slightly. It should only open about one-half inch.

Now move the timebar to the 5-second mark. Next, you'll purposely create a mistake so you can learn how to correct it. At the 5-second mark, move the stethoscope out of the holder 3 or 4 inches. Try to make sure you don't go far enough that the rubber tube runs into the plastic parts.

Notice that this creates a change bar that shows the position of the scope head part moving continually from time 00.00.00 to time 00.00.05. The motion is supposed to start at the 3-second mark. You can see how to fix this mistake in Figure 23.24.

FIGURE 23.24
Fixing a time-line problem

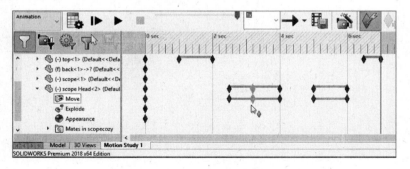

Click the key point for the motion of the scope head part. Then Ctrl+drag it from the 0-second mark to the 3-second mark.

TIP If you run the animation at this point, you may see the scope head make some unexpected movement, and a yellow line will appear to the left of the change bar for the part. To fix this, click the Calculate button next to the Play button.

Copying and Mirroring Motion

The animation is essentially done at this point, except that the stethoscope needs to go back into the holder and it must close. You don't have to manually create all the steps to close the device, although you could. It is more efficient to simply copy and reverse the paths that you have already made.

To copy both sets of motion—the top opening and the head sliding out—drag a marquee window around the key points to select them all, and then Ctrl+drag them to the 6-second mark. Notice that this creates the situation shown in Figure 23.25. If you play the animation at this point, it won't be what you want. It will simply stack the same motion on top of the original motion; you want it to be reversed.

FIGURE 23.25
Copying motion of parts

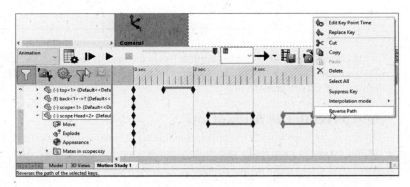

With the newly copied key points still selected, right-click one of them and select Reverse Path. Notice that this shows symmetrical key points.

Adjusting the Speed of Actions

The animation is almost complete, but it would be better if the second half of the animation went by faster than the first half. To do this, move the key points on the right side of a change bar toward the left. You may want to move both key points for the top part closing so it starts closer to the time when the scope head is back inside the holder. You could even make some of the motion overlap, so the top starts closing before the scope head is fully inside.

Again, if you see a strange effect, such as the scope head not going all the way back to where it belongs, try clicking the Calculate button again. Calculate essentially rebuilds the animation after changes.

To make the motion a little smoother, right-click in an empty space inside the timeline area and choose Select All; then right-click one of the key points and select Interpolation Mode. Click the Ease In/Ease Out option. Click Calculate again to watch the smoother animation.

If you want variable speed, say, for the scope head coming out of the holder (for example, it starts coming out slowly and then speeds up), you need to add at least one more key point. To do this, position the timebar to the left of the middle of the first scope head change bar, and click Place Key. This adds a key point in the existing change bar. This is shown in Figure 23.26. Then move the key point to the right. Make sure the new key point uses the Ease In/Ease Out Interpolation mode. Recalculate and run the animation again.

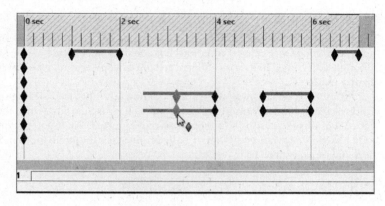

FIGURE 23.26
Adding and moving a key point in an existing change bar

If you decide that the entire animation is too fast or too slow, you can adjust this easily. Drag the right-most key point on the top row with the Alt key depressed. This will scale the entire animation up or down.

Outputting the Animation

After you're happy with the animation, click the Save Animation toolbar button. This will bring up the Save Animation To File dialog box, shown in Figure 23.27. The options for output formats are `*.avi`, or a `*.bmp` or `*.tga` series of still images. You could combine the still images to make an animated GIF to use on a website. Other types of output, such as Flash or QuickTime, are not available directly from the SolidWorks software. Movie format converters are available on the Web for this purpose.

The options for the renderer are simply the SolidWorks screen or PhotoView 360. This example uses RealView and the SolidWorks screen renderer, which provides sufficient quality for your purposes. The main advantages of PhotoView 360 over RealView are that it offers a better choice of backgrounds, anti-aliasing, and more shadow control.

LOOKING AT OTHER OPTIONS

Image Size And Aspect Ratio options are available only when you don't use a camera. Without the camera, you're at the mercy of the size and shape of the SolidWorks graphics window until you save the animation to a file.

The Schedule button enables you to schedule the output for a more convenient time. You would normally use this option when using PhotoView 360, because rendered animations can take many hours to complete, depending on render settings, length of animation, and the number of the fps.

FIGURE 23.27
Saving output data for
your animation

Frame Information enables you to set the quality of the finished rendering. Low frame rates result in choppy motion. High frame rates are much smoother, but the files may become unmanageably large. High-quality animations generally fall into the 25 to 30 fps range.

RUNNING TEST ANIMATIONS

Depending on the length of the animation and the other settings, test animations might run in the might run around 10 fps. You might also consider using a specific range of time to test just a part of the animation.

Unfortunately, many of the decisions you make regarding animation quality settings directly relate to the time you have to produce the final movie file. The biggest timesaver is to avoid PhotoView 360. If RealView suits your needs, you're well ahead on time.

SELECTING A COMPRESSOR

When you save the animation, the software prompts you to select a video compressor (codec). Typical options are the Microsoft Video and Cinepak compressors. Sometimes when you record or play back a movie with a particular compressor, you end up with lots of video noise in the movie. If this happens, try another compressor. For example, if you use Microsoft Video for an animation, and it has lots of video noise, you can switch to Cinepak to see if the results are better.

Animating with Basic Motion

Basic Motion is the functionality formerly known as Physical Simulation. It involves setting motors to turn parts, gravity to move parts and springs, and collisions to create animations that cannot be driven by mates or free motion. It uses a different solver than the rest of the animations in this chapter.

Basic Motion doesn't take into account effects such as momentum, bounce, resistance/friction, viscosity, and reaction forces. To analyze for these effects, you need to use Motion Analysis.

The Study Type selection box appears in the upper-left corner of the MotionManager. You need to use Basic Motion (refer to Figure 23.2) for this example.

Using Gravity and Contact

Figure 23.28 shows an assembly that demonstrates the gravity and contact functions of Basic Motion. The problem is easy to set up. The part that is to move (the ball) is underdefined, using only one mate to keep it in plane as it moves. The zigzag part uses a Fixed constraint.

ON THE WEBSITE

The assembly used in this example is labeled `zig zag.sldasm`.

FIGURE 23.28
Setting up contact
and gravity

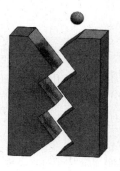

When you have added the physical simulation items, the MotionManager design tree looks like Figure 23.29. Editing items such as contact and gravity don't use the interface options that have been available in the rest of the SolidWorks software. Click (select) doesn't bring up a context toolbar; you have to right-click and access the full RMB menu.

Because this example goes by so quickly, you may want to use the Playback Speed drop-down menu to get a better look at it. You can also set playback looping options with the drop-down menu to the right of the Playback Speed.

For Contact to be successful (so two parts will not go through each other), it might be necessary to increase the fps of the animation for the Basic Motion. Also, you might have to increase the Geometry Accuracy and the 3D Contact Resolution settings. Remember that SolidWorks calculates the contact for each frame and stops the movement on interference. So, if the parts move fast, but the frames are few, a part might have already gone through the second part, with no contact registered.

FIGURE 23.29
The MotionManager design tree with added items

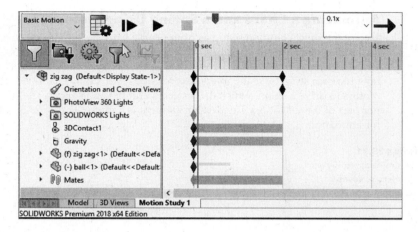

Using Motors and Springs

The use of motors doesn't necessarily require Basic Motion, but if you include springs, or contact or gravity problems, it does. Torsion springs require Motion Analysis, but linear springs require only Basic Motion. This example (available from the download materials in the Animation folder as `ratchet.SLDASM`) shows a motor driving a gear with a ratchet held to the gear teeth by a spring, as shown in Figure 23.30. A swinging ball on a spring is added to show this isn't simple 2D functionality.

FIGURE 23.30
A motor, gear, and ratchet assembly driven by Basic Motion

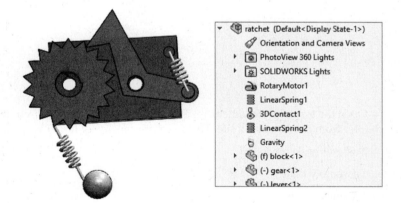

To set up this example, apply a counterclockwise motor to the inside circular edge of the gear, and select the block as the reference part. In this example, start the motor with a slow RPM (revolutions per minute), move the timebar out a few seconds, and assign a faster speed, so the motor speeds up over time.

The linear spring is easy to apply. Select the locations of both ends. This example has circular bosses on the block and the ratchet to hold the spring.

Animating a Chain and a Spring Using Motors

Two of the most common requests from people learning how to make animations in SolidWorks are animating chains and springs. This is a simple animation, but it uses a couple of tools that you should know about. Earlier in this chapter, the Yoke Link assembly was used to demonstrate how to flex a strap by using in-context relations and a loft. This chain-gear-spring example uses motors to drive a chain, which drives gears and flexes a spring. The spring is a modeled element, not part of Basic Motion. The driving element is a motor. Figure 23.31 shows the assembly ready for animation.

FIGURE 23.31
One simple assembly can demonstrate several animation ideas.

Open the assembly called `chain assembly pattern.sldasm` from the material for this chapter from the download site. The assembly consists of the following components:

2 assembly sketches

1 assembly plane

1 assembly axis

2 parts and a Chain Pattern making up the chain

2 gears

1 spring (modeled in-context, connecting the end of the chain to Plane1)

The chain is achieved with the inner and outer links and a Chain Pattern, and the spring is achieved with an in-context relation. The animation is driven by a single linear motor.

The model is created by first drawing Sketch1, which represents the path of the chain. This consists of lines and tangent arcs. Next, in order for the path to be a single smooth, continuous entity, a second sketch is created and Fit Spline is used to lay a spline over the lines and arcs. A very small tolerance value is used so the curvature comb for the spline looks as close to a line-arc combination as possible.

The interface for creating a Chain Pattern walks you through what to select, depending on what type of chain you are using, and will even locate the links on the path for you.

Without the Chain Pattern, this would require nearly 100 mates to make a functional chain. The Chain Pattern PropertyManager is shown in Figure 23.32.

FIGURE 23.32
Using the Chain Pattern to assemble a chain along a path

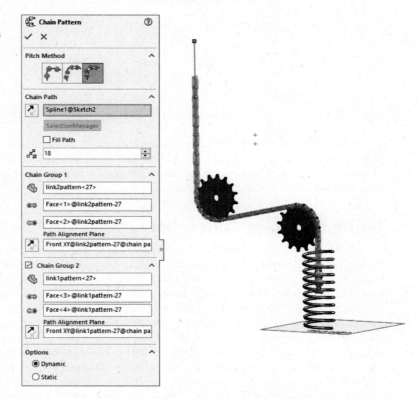

The gears are positioned at the centers of the arcs from Sketch1. The tricky part of the gears involves using the Rack-and-Pinion mate to match the linear motion of the end chain link to rotary motion of the gear. Because this is just for an animation, and not a real analysis, idealizing the assembly in this way won't have any adverse effects.

The construction of the spring is to simply use a straight line as an in-context connector between the last link of the chain and Plane1 of the assembly. This line is then used as the path of a sweep with twist enabled, which is a reasonable approximation of a spring for an animation. It doesn't flex for dynamic assembly motion, but it does for an animation.

All that remains is the motor. Figure 23.33 shows how the motor is driven. It's a linear motor, with the Oscillating motion. The Displacement Vs. Time chart shows how much the chain moves during the 6-second animation. You can also see that the chart shows how much the spring extends or retracts.

FIGURE 23.33
Charting the motion of
the assembly

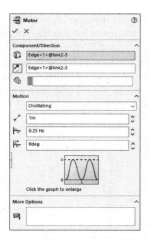

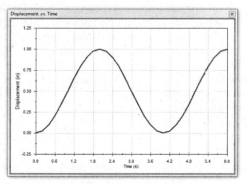

Although this assembly and the animation are simple, they demonstrate many of the techniques you need to know to make animations that are more complex. Motors with controllable output are a big part of animating automatic machinery, and making parts appear flexible adds greatly to the realism of an animation.

Using the Mate Controller

The Mate Controller is an interface that helps you drive the positions of parts through selected mates. You can use it to create configurations, but configurations are not required to use it. When using motors, it is best to work with underdefined assemblies, but the Mate Controller works best with fully defined assemblies. You can drive the mates using values, a slider, or by visually dragging parts on the screen. This is the tool that I would recommend if you have a lot of mates, a lot of possible degrees of freedom, and multiple moving parts that may not react well to manual dragging (such as an arm with a shoulder joint, elbow joint, wrist joint, and fingers). The interface enables you to lock down certain mates to control where the motion happens, even when you are visually dragging parts on the screen. This is the kind of thing you would do manually by suppressing and unsuppressing mates to enable or restrict movement.

Rather than using configurations to remember positions of the assembly, the Mate Controller allows you to specify and remember positions, which use specific values for multiple mates. This is much simpler than using configurations, and when you are done, you can save all of this information out to configurations, if you want to reuse that position data for drawings, renderings, animations, or other purposes.

It may also be a good idea to build your assembly slightly differently when you plan to use the Mate Controller. Instead of using a Concentric mate for a joint, you might consider using a Limit mate with angles. Using actual values (numbers) gives you more positive control. As usual, it is best practice to name the mates used in the Mate Controller in order to provide some clues about the functions of the mates, such as Rotate Base. If you get them in order, the Mate Controller interface will be set up logically to help you control the motion of the assembly in a certain order.

You can initiate the Mate Controller in one of several ways.

◆ Use the Mate Controller icon in the Assembly toolbar (it may not be there by default; use the Customize interface to put it there).

◆ Use the Insert menu.

◆ If you have selected one or more mates of supported types from the assembly FeatureManager, you can access the Mate Controller through an RMB menu. The supported mates are listed later in this section.

◆ Once you have used the Mate Controller and saved at least one position, there will be an entry for the Mate Controller at the bottom of the assembly FeatureManager.

The positions created by the Mate Controller can be renamed and reordered to create an animation. The Mate Controller PropertyManager has an animation interface at the bottom, as shown in Figure 23.34.

FIGURE 23.34
The Mate Controller PropertyManager interface enables you to control motion of the assembly and create animations.

The button shown to the left enables you to collect all of the *supported* mates in the assembly. The supported mate list is as follows:

- Angle and Limit Angle
- Distance and Limit Distance
- Path Mate (controls distance along path and percent along path parameters)
- Slot Mate (controls distance along slot and percent along slot parameters)
- Width Mate (dimension and percent)

If you want to create multiple animations or motion schemes, you can also create multiple Mate Controller features in the assembly.

The Bottom Line

If you keep your animation relatively simple, the MotionManager tools in SolidWorks Standard should produce adequate results in some situations. If you are using mates to drive motion, be sure to follow best practice recommendations for mates. If you are manually positioning parts, remember to place key points closer together if the motion curvature changes abruptly.

If you are making larger animations and the end product is just an AVI file, it's acceptable to break the animation into smaller bits. This makes each part of the animation much simpler to do, and work can even be delegated to other users or other machines for parallel processing. It may also be beneficial to use post-processing to add captions and narration to your movies; a few words of explanation might be valuable to viewers.

Master It   In a blank assembly, create a camera with a circular path that focuses on the origin. Save the assembly as a template, and then use that template to create an easy turntable animation of any assembly or part you put into that assembly.

Master It   Using the large dump truck, make an animation of the bucket raising and lowering, with a second before the motion, a second between raising and lowering, and a second after the lowering. Try to use the tools for mirroring the path that you learned in this chapter.

Master It   Use RealView settings if your hardware is capable. Save out an AVI movie or the previous animation. Make sure it plays back as you expect on your computer and at least one other computer.

Part IV

Creating Drawings

Chapter 24

Automating Drawings: The Basics

SolidWorks drawing templates and formats enable you to automate repetitive tasks through the reuse of data. SolidWorks can insert information about a drawing's creator and the materials to be used, and it can begin similar types of drawings from a consistent starting point. Drawing templates and formats also save settings that you may want to reuse.

IN THIS CHAPTER, YOU WILL LEARN TO:

- Understand the difference between templates and formats
- Customize drawing formats
- Create drawing templates using predefined views
- Use blocks

Comparing Templates and Formats

Templates are start documents that contain collections of document-specific settings and default views saved in the `*.prtdot` (part template), `*.asmdot` (assembly template), and `*.drwdot` (drawing template) file types. In this chapter, I will cover the `*.drwdot` file type.

Formats, more formally called *sheet formats*, are exclusive to drawing documents and contain the sheet size, the drawing borderline geometry, and the text/custom property definitions that go with the text in the drawing border. You can think of a sheet format as an underlay beneath a clear drawing sheet. Formats can also include company logo images.

You can save formats in drawing templates; in fact, this is the method that I use and recommend. Using SolidWorks' default drawing templates, the templates and formats are initially kept separate. You specify the size and the format when creating a new drawing from a blank template. However, when the format is already in the template, the size has already been determined, so the templates end up being saved as specific sizes. Of course, you can change formats later if you need to use a larger drawing sheet, but you cannot change templates.

A SolidWorks drawing template can have multiple sheets, which can be the same or different sizes. You can use a different format for each sheet. For example, if you want a default two-page drawing, you can save it as a template, with different formats for the first and second sheets.

Changing Existing Templates

After you create any kind of document from whatever kind of template, you cannot change the underlying template. However, you can change all the settings, which is the next best equivalent.

SolidWorks offers custom drafting standards, which provide some of the functionality that the ability to swap templates would achieve. You can take a drafting standard such as ISO (International Organization for Standardization) or ANSI (American National Standards Institute), make adjustments to it, and save the standard out to a file that you can distribute to other users. You can change the standard by choosing Tools ➤ Options ➤ Document Properties ➤ Drafting Standard from the menus. You can load and save standards from the same location. More details on what you can actually change within the drafting standard come later in this chapter.

While *templates* cannot be reloaded, *formats* can be. You might want to reload a format (drawing border and associated annotations) if you have made changes to the information or line geometry. You can also reload a format to change the sheet size for a drawing.

Maintaining Different Templates or Formats

Different formats must be maintained for different sheet sizes. If you do contract design or detailing work, then you may need to maintain separate formats for different customers. Some people also choose to have different formats for the first sheet of a drawing and a simplified format for the following sheets.

If you put formats on the templates, then you are making separate templates for variously sized drawings. Also, separate templates are frequently created for different units or standards because templates contain document-specific settings. I also keep a blank drawing template with a blank format on it just to do conceptual scribbles or to make an informal, scalable, and printable drawing without the baggage that typically accompanies formal drawings.

CAUTION SolidWorks can install with default document templates that use different standards. Be careful of the difference between drawings with ANSI and ISO standards or, more importantly, the use of third angle projection versus first angle projection. Figure 24.1 shows the difference between a third angle and first angle projection. Third angle is part of the ANSI standard used in the United States, whereas first angle is part of the ISO standard used in Europe and other parts of the world.

FIGURE 24.1
Third angle versus first angle projection

Third Angle   First Angle

If you work for a company that does a lot of work for manufacturing in Europe, you may have to deal with this issue more frequently. The setting that controls the projection angle is in the Sheet Properties, which you can access by right-clicking anywhere on the blank drawing sheet and selecting Properties.

Creating Custom Drafting Standards

In my experience, very few real-world companies follow any of the single drafting standards perfectly. Each company seems to have its own interpretation of, or exceptions to, the standards. SolidWorks is coming to grips with this in a practical way. In SolidWorks, you can create your own custom drafting standards, equivalent to the established ISO and ANSI standards. These standards allow you to save all the settings found in Tools ➤ Options ➤ Document Properties to a single standard that you can then transfer to other users.

To make your own custom standard, make changes to any of the items listed indented from Drafting Standard shown in Figure 24.2, and then go back to the Drafting Standard page of the Document Properties tab, rename the Overall Drafting Standard, and save the standard to a file. Once you have made a change to the default settings, the Overall Drafting Standard will be displayed as ANSI-MODIFIED, or as appropriate for your chosen initial standard. You can rename this, and SolidWorks will show which standard it was derived from, to help avoid confusion. I created a new standard, which is shown in Figure 24.2.

FIGURE 24.2
Creating a new customized drafting standard

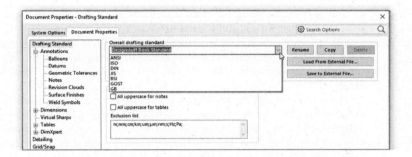

The drafting standard file type has the extension of `*.sldstd`. If someone else has sent you a standard file, you can read it into your drawing using the settings shown on the right of Figure 24.2 and assign it as the active standard; your drawing will assume all the customized properties. If you want to make new drawings with that standard, you need to create a template with that standard and use the template to create the new drawings.

ON THE WEBSITE

I have saved a custom standard file and put it in the download material for Chapter 24. You can load this file into an open drawing by choosing Tools ➤ Options ➤ Document Properties ➤ Drafting Standard and using the interface.

Creating Drawing Formats

It used to be that drawing formats were difficult to create or edit, requiring import and 2D drawing skills. With the addition in 2016 of the Sheet Format tools, this all becomes much easier.

The Sheet Format tab on the drawing adds three new tools: Edit Sheet Format, Title Block Fields, and Automatic Border. These are shown in Figure 24.3.

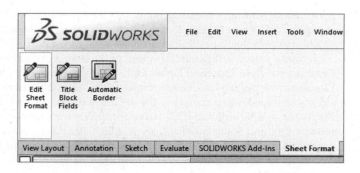

Edit Sheet Format toggles between editing the sheet (where the drawing views reside) and editing the sheet format (where the title block resides).

Title Block Fields helps you create static and linked annotations in the title block area that can be filled out automatically by custom properties in part and assembly documents. The functions of this tool are described later in this chapter under the heading "Using the Title Block Function."

The Automatic Border tool helps you place a border with zones to frame the drawing. This multistep tool walks you through deleting the existing border elements; establishing zones, margins, and line styles; and placing the new border, which is an entity that shows up in the FeatureManager for the drawing under the sheet and sheet format. You can edit these by going back to the Sheet Format tools (not by editing the 2D lines).

Customizing an Existing Format

Existing formats created manually or by importing can also be used.

The sample formats installed with SolidWorks include ANSI sizes A through E and ISO sizes A0 through A4. You can probably find enough space on the formats to place a company logo and some standard notes. Choose Tools ➤ Options ➤ File Locations to locate the path for your templates. Remember that you can use network drives for shared libraries.

You cannot open a format directly—it must be on a drawing—so to get a closer look at the format, you must make a new drawing using the format.

NOTE Templates that have been saved with a format already on them skip the step of prompting you to select a format. This enables you to create new drawings more quickly. The default SolidWorks templates don't have formats on them; if you select one of them, you'll be prompted to select a format immediately. Figure 24.4 shows the interface for selecting a format that displays after you have selected the template for a drawing.

FIGURE 24.4
Selecting a format

EDITING A FORMAT

In the drawing, whether the format has been created using new or old tools, you are either editing the sheet or editing the format. You can think of the sheet as being a piece of transparent Mylar over the top of the drawing border format. In order to get to the format, you have to peel back the Mylar. Drawing views go onto the sheet, so when you edit the format, any drawing views that may be there disappear.

To peel back the sheet and gain access to the format, right-click a blank area of the sheet and select Edit Sheet Format. Alternatively, you can access the sheet format by right-clicking the Sheet tab in the lower-left corner of the SolidWorks window. Be careful of the terms here, which include "Sheet" and "Sheet Format." The sketch lines of the format will light up like a sketch becoming active, and the "Editing Sheet Format" message will appear at the lower-right corner on the status bar.

The lines in the format border are regular SolidWorks sketch entities, but they display a little differently. Also, sketch relations are sometimes disabled in formats because solving the relations would cause the software to run slowly. Typically, the Trim, Extend, and Stretch functions are the best sketch tools for editing lines.

You can use most common image types to insert a logo or other image data onto your drawing or format by choosing Insert ➤ Picture. Not all compression styles are supported, however. I have had difficulty with compressed TIFF (Tagged Image File Format) images. Be aware of the file size of the image when you put it into the format, because images can be large, and all that extra information will travel around with each drawing that you create from the format. Figure 24.5 shows a bitmap placed in the format.

You can resize the image by dragging the handles in the corners; you can move it by simply dragging it. The image to the right in Figure 24.5 was taken from the Print Preview window. I included it here to show that the outline around the image that displays while you are working in SolidWorks does not print.

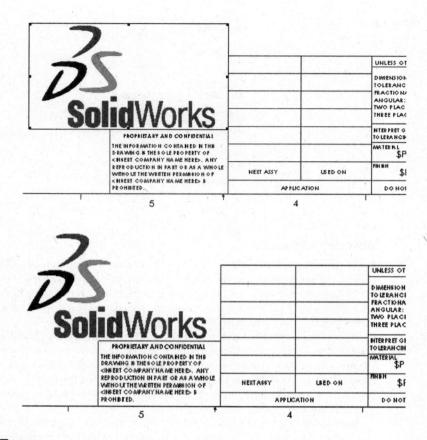

MANAGING TEXT

SolidWorks allows you to make a text box of a specific size that causes text to wrap. This is particularly useful in drawings. The upper image in Figure 24.6 shows a new annotation being added. The lower image shows the same text box after the corner has been dragged.

FIGURE 24.6
Adding an annotation
and wrapping the text

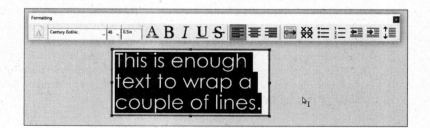

Using Custom Properties

The most important part of the drawing format is the custom properties. While the rest of the format is just for display, custom properties use automation to fill out the title block using matching custom properties in either the model or the drawing document. Custom properties can pull items such as filenames, descriptions, materials, and other properties from the model associated with the sheet, or they can pull data from the drawing itself, such as the sheet scale, filename, sheet number, and total sheets. If you are seriously looking to automate drawings, you cannot overlook custom properties.

ENTERING CUSTOM PROPERTY DATA

Custom property data is entered at the part or assembly level. This information is then reused in the drawing format and in tables such as BOMs (Bills of Materials) and revision tables, as well as searches using the FeatureManager filter. All PDM (Product Data Management) systems utilize SolidWorks custom properties. You can enter the data several ways, but the two most prominent ways are through the Summary Information dialog box and the Custom Properties tab in the Task pane.

USING THE SUMMARY INFORMATION DIALOG BOX

Figure 24.7 shows the Summary Information dialog box. This functionality has existed in SolidWorks for several releases. You can access this dialog box by choosing File ➤ Properties from the menus. You can select Property Names from a drop-down list or type your own, assign types of data, and enter a specific value for the property. The Value/Text Expression column also has a drop-down list from which you can select several preset variables, such as mass, density, and even link values used in the part.

FIGURE 24.7
The Summary
Information dialog box

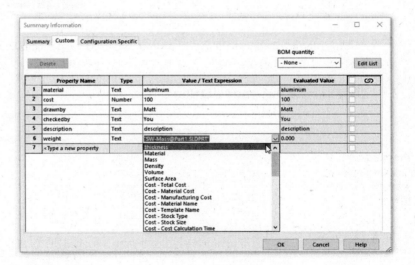

This is a perfectly functional way to enter data, but the fact that it's somewhat out of the way and hidden in the menus means that it doesn't get used as much as it should. SolidWorks came up with another way of entering data.

USING THE CUSTOM PROPERTIES TAB

The Custom Properties tab of the Task pane enables you to quickly and easily access and assign custom properties within a document. Figure 24.8 shows the process of building your own Custom Properties tab. You can start the Custom Property Tab Builder by either clicking the

Create button on the Custom Properties tab or choosing Start ➢ Programs ➢ SolidWorks ➢ SolidWorks Tools ➢ Property Tab Builder from the menus.

FIGURE 24.8
Using the Custom Properties Builder and Custom Properties tab

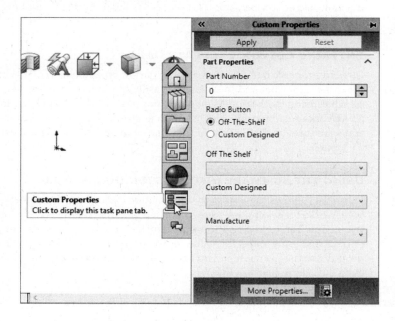

The interface enables you to add drop-down lists, toggles, and text entry boxes. This gives you lots of flexibility with custom property data entry and is a very nice addition to the software.

DISPLAYING PROPERTY LINKS

Figure 24.9 shows the existing custom property formatting in the default format being used for this example.

FIGURE 24.9
Custom property formatting in the title block

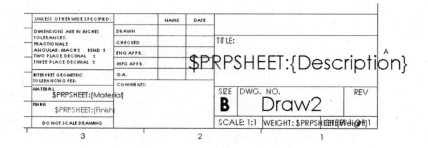

The syntax $PRP or $PRPSHEET indicates that the property that follows the syntax is to be pulled from either the current document (drawing) or from the model specified in the Sheet Properties, respectively. This is an important distinction to make. Most of the time, you can enter custom properties at the part or assembly level so you can reuse the data by drawing properties, BOM, or even design tables.

Notice that all the notes in the format that are showing raw syntax are pulling data from the model. "Draw2" and the Scale notes are driven by the drawing. When no value exists for the property to display, you have an option of what to show. The top portion of Figure 24.10 shows the settings in the View ➤ Hide/Show menu that control the display of syntax of the custom property links. In general, it is common to deselect the error display and to show the link variables.

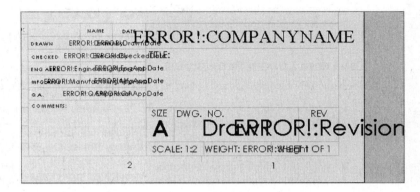

DISPLAYING ERRORS AND LINK VARIABLES

The errors in Figure 24.10 are caused by links to the local document for which there is no corresponding property. For example, the "ERROR!: COMPANYNAME" message is linked to "$PRP: COMPANYNAME," but the local custom property COMPANYNAME doesn't exist. If it existed but had a null or space value, the error would disappear.

Likewise, with the option to display link variables selected, the syntax that calls model custom properties displays until there's some value for it to pull from. If a part is put onto the drawing, then some of the properties are filled in because properties and values exist to pull from, and the rest of the properties simply disappear to make space. Notice in Figure 24.11 that the Material property has been filled in, but the Finish property has not. This is because either there's no Finish property in the part on the drawing or there's a null value in the Finish property.

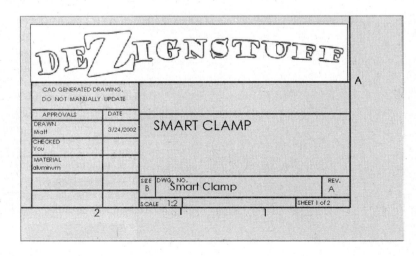

TIP   When you are initially setting up the format, it can be useful to have a dummy model already on the drawing. The dummy model should have all the custom properties that you intend to use in your drawings. This will prevent the blank fields or error messages from appearing during setup.

NOTE   If you drag and drop a part onto a drawing while editing in the sheet format, the views may appear for a split second and then disappear again. This is because you cannot display drawing views while editing the sheet format. After you exit the sheet format and go back to editing the sheet, the views can display once again.

CREATING LINKED PROPERTIES

Creating annotations that are linked to properties is easy. Begin as if you are creating a note:

1. Click the Note toolbar button on the Annotations toolbar, or choose Insert ➤ Annotations ➤ Note.

2. Place the note on the drawing. The Formatting toolbar will appear.

3. Click the Link To Property button in the Text Format pane of the Note PropertyManager. This will display the Link To Property dialog box, as shown in Figure 24.12, which gives you the option of linking to a custom property in the current (drawing) document or in the model (part or assembly) that's on the drawing.

FIGURE 24.12
The Link To Property
dialog box

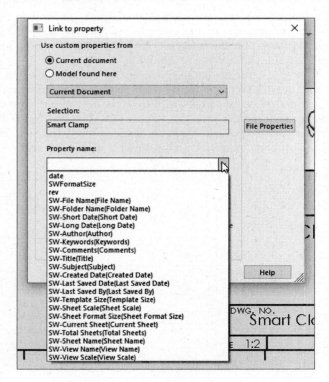

4. If the desired custom property is not in the drop-down list, you can type it into the text box or click the File Properties button to edit the properties. If the property is added to the part file or a part file with that property is used on the drawing, this linked annotation will pick it up. This button will not be available for the model if there's no model on the drawing, in which case you must type the name of the property manually.

Using the Title Block Function

The title block enables the person who sets up the sheet format to specify an area that contains notes that are easy to access without editing the format. (Many CAD administrators prefer that the users not have to deal with the details inside the sheet format.) You can even cycle through these notes in a specific order by pressing Enter or Tab. Figure 24.13 shows the resizable black border of the title block, the Title Block PropertyManager, and where the title block sits in the drawing FeatureManager.

FIGURE 24.13
Using the Title
Block Table

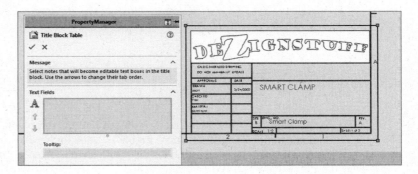

You can access the title block to edit or define it by right-clicking in the sheet format (while editing the sheet format, not the sheet) and selecting Title Block Fields, and then either edit existing notes or select new notes as the situation requires.

The title block is a resizable rectangular box. It can be any size you like, but it must remain rectangular, and you can create only one title block area per sheet format. The area bounded by the title block box is used to zoom the display to make it easier to fill in the text boxes. If you want to include areas in different corners of the drawing in the title block area, you need to make the title block box as big as the entire sheet, and the user must manually zoom to each corner.

Select each Note item to add it to the list in the PropertyManager selection box. Use the arrows to the left of the box to assign the order in which the user cycles through the boxes. You can even add a tooltip for each note. The idea is that the user clicks in a box within the title block area, fills it in, and then presses Enter or Tab to get to the next box. The order loops if the user doesn't start on the first box listed in the PropertyManager.

You cannot add notes that are already linked to properties to the title block, because they will be filled out automatically. The purpose of the title block is really to highlight and speed up manual entry.

To use an existing title block, just double-click in the title block area (designated by the resizable rectangle) from the sheet (not the sheet format), and SolidWorks will highlight the fields.

Creating a Format from an Imported DWG/DXF file

If you want to create your format from an imported DWG or DXF file, choose File ➤ Open to locate the file that you want to import and then click to open it. The DXF/DWG Import screen will appear, as shown in Figure 24.14.

FIGURE 24.14
The DXF/DWG
Import screen

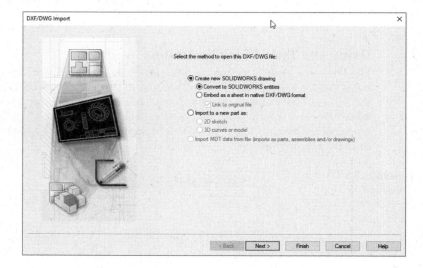

If you are interested in following along, you can find the sample files used for this example in the download data for Chapter 24. You'll find five * .dwg format files. You can use any of them to create a format, but I suggest using either the A or B size. To make a drawing format, you can select the Create New SolidWorks drawing and Convert To SolidWorks Entities options. Although one of the other options contains the word *format*, it isn't being used in the same sense, so don't be misled. When this selection is complete, click Next. Figure 24.15 shows the next screen.

FIGURE 24.15
The Drawing Layer
Mapping screen

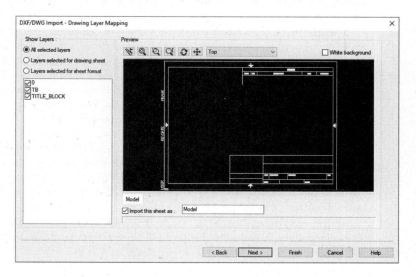

Select the Layers Selected For Sheet Format option. Select the TB layer, leaving the other layers unselected. Every imported file will be different in this respect, because layers used by title blocks vary widely. Click Next when you have made these selections. Figure 24.16 shows the Document Settings screen.

FIGURE 24.16
The Document Settings screen

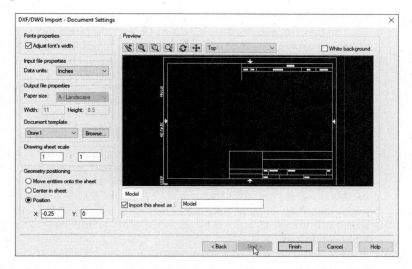

The important features in the Document Settings screen are the Document Template selection and the Geometry Positioning options.

Document Template selection is important only if you plan to save the format with a template. Be sure to select a template that doesn't already have a format saved in it. In the Geometry Positioning section, if you can get the software to center the title block for you, definitely take advantage of this functionality and use the Center In Sheet option. After you're happy with these settings, click Finish. The resulting format is shown in Figure 24.17.

FIGURE 24.17
The finished imported format

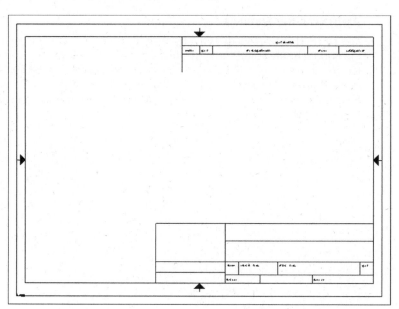

From here, you can add the links to custom properties as described earlier, as well as logo images, favorites, and blocks. You can now save the format as described in the next section.

Saving the Format

You can save drawing formats in two ways: with the template or separately from the template. You cannot edit formats separately from a template, but they do have their own file type: `*.slddrt`.

NOTE If case you are wondering how the extension `*.slddrt` relates to a sheet format, what is now known as *sheet format* used to be called a *drawing template* (thus, the *drt* of `slddrt`). What is now called a template didn't exist in 1997. The shift in architecture and, more importantly for users, the shift in terminology can still leave many people a bit confused.

Saving templates is covered in the next section. To save a format, choose File ➤ Save Sheet Format. You can do this with or without the format being active. Save the format into a location with other formats and give it a descriptive but unique name. If you haven't yet done so, this is a good opportunity to create a separate folder, outside of your SolidWorks installation folder, that contains your most frequently used files. Remember also to tell SolidWorks where this library location is by choosing Tools ➤ Options ➤ System Options ➤ File Locations ➤ Sheet Formats.

Even if you have saved a format with a template, it's a good idea to also save the format on its own. This is because you might want to use that format on an existing drawing that has a different format on it or use it on a second sheet.

Using Second Sheet Formats

When you have multi-sheet drawings, it is often important to have a simplified or specialized format for the second sheet. Figure 24.18 shows sample page-one and page-two formats side by side.

ADDING NEW SHEETS

You can add sheets to a drawing by clicking the Add Sheets icon to the right of the Sheet tabs at the bottom of the SolidWorks window or through the RMB menu of the Sheet tab at the lower-left corner of the drawing window. You can also add a sheet by RMB on the sheet or sheet format in the FeatureManager. If you right-click the first Sheet tab, the sheet that is added gets the format that is used on the first sheet. If you right-click the second Sheet tab, the added sheet gets the second sheet format.

FIGURE 24.18
First and second
sheet formats

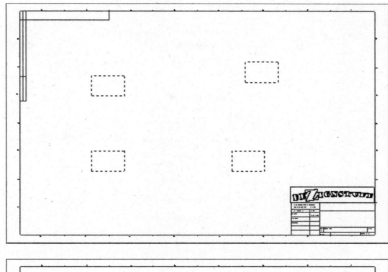

RELOADING FORMATS

If a format has been changed, and you want to update a drawing to the new format, this option is available in the Sheet Properties, as shown in Figure 24.19. Access Sheet Properties through the RMB on the sheet in the FeatureManager. The Reload button will update any changes in the separate format file.

Creating Drawing Templates

Document-specific settings are important parts of the template, and it's probably best to get one drawing size completely set up the way you want it and then create the other sizes from this drawing. This helps to ensure that the settings—such as Bent Leader Length, Font, and Line Weight—are the same for all the templates. Uniform settings on drawings give them a consistent look and make them easier to read. Drafting standards are controlled by drawing templates.

Using Predefined Views in Drawing Templates

When I use drawing templates, one of my favorite techniques to get to a multi-view drawing quickly is to put one predefined view on the template along with appropriate views projected from the predefined view. A predefined view establishes an orientation and location on the drawing sheet. You can add multiple predefined views and align them with one another on the drawing sheet so a drawing is automatically populated by the model, but this isn't recommended, because if you decide to change the orientation of the drawing, you must change each predefined view independently. If you set up a single predefined view and make the rest of the views with projected views, changing the orientation of the predefined view will cause all the projected views to update associatively. You cannot directly change the orientation of a projected view. Predefined views and views projected from predefined views appear blank until they are populated with model geometry. The *predefined* part of a predefined view is the orientation and placement of the view.

Figure 24.20 shows a template using predefined and projected views. You can access predefined views on the Drawings toolbar; although it isn't there by default, you can place it on the toolbar by choosing Tools ➤ Customize ➤ Commands and using the interface. You can also access predefined views by choosing Insert ➤ Drawing Views ➤ Predefined. Projected views can also be accessed from the Drawings toolbar.

FIGURE 24.20
Predefined views on a template

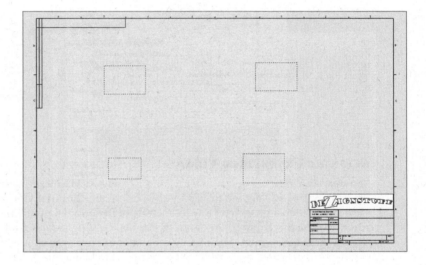

After a predefined view has been placed, you can select an orientation for it from the PropertyManager. Figure 24.21 shows the Drawing View PropertyManager. The orientation for a view is set in the top Orientation panel. In addition to orthogonal views, you can also create isometric and other custom views as predefined views.

After the view has been oriented, you may want to create more views on the drawing that also become populated by model geometry. This is where the projected views are used. Make sure that the drawing properties are set to the correct projection angle.

Because the rest of the views have been created relative to the front view, none of the views need to be rotated as they would if, for example, the top view had been placed above the back or right view.

Although it isn't on this drawing, many drawing templates include a Third Angle Projection symbol as a part of the title block, which is in the format. Figure 24.1 at the beginning of this chapter shows First Angle and Third Angle Projection symbols. They are included as blocks with the sample data in the SolidWorks installation. Blocks are discussed in more detail in Chapter 16, "Working with Assembly Sketches and Layouts."

FIGURE 24.21
The Drawing View
PropertyManager

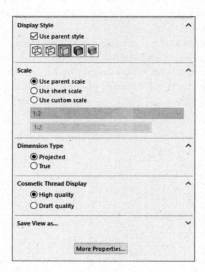

ALIGNING PREDEFINED VIEWS

You can align views to one another through a view's RMB menu, as shown in Figure 24.22. Projected views are aligned to one another automatically, but if you chose to use a predefined view rather than a projected view to one side of the original predefined view, you can use the Align Vertical By Origin or the Align Horizontal By Origin command. This ensures that the parts in each view are aligned. Aligning by center should not be used for projected views on an engineering drawing, because it isn't guaranteed to line up the edges in adjacent views.

POPULATING A DRAWING WITH PREDEFINED VIEWS

Four methods exist to populate a drawing with predefined views:

Drag-and-Drop: Drag a part or assembly from the FeatureManager and drop it in the drawing window. All predefined views are automatically populated.

Insert Model: Right-click a view and then select Insert Model. From the interface, browse for the model to be displayed in all the related (projected) views.

PropertyManager: Select a predefined view, and from the PropertyManager, select Browse in the Insert Model panel.

Make Drawing from Part/Assembly: Click the Make Drawing From Part/Assembly button in the Standard toolbar, and select a template that uses predefined views.

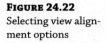

FIGURE 24.22
Selecting view alignment options

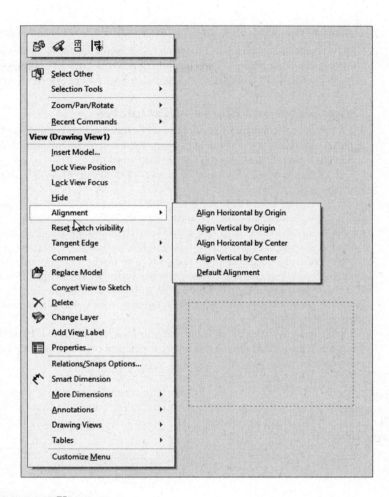

SCALING PREDEFINED VIEWS

When predefined views are created, they are set to follow the sheet scale by default; however, you can manually set them to have a custom scale. If you are using the automatic scaling option (found at Tools ➢ Options ➢ System Options ➢ Drawings ➢ Automatically Scale New Drawing Views), the sheet scale is automatically changed when the drawing views are populated to make a nice fit of the model geometry on the drawing. The scales used by the automatic feature are all standard multiples of two, so you don't have to worry about odd scale factors on your drawings.

UNDERSTANDING THE LIMITATIONS OF PREDEFINED VIEWS

The function and expectations of predefined views are fairly straightforward, although a few things could be improved. For example, SolidWorks doesn't allow you to create predefined section or detail views. Also, the View palette doesn't preview the populated predefined views.

Using Styles and Blocks in Templates

In SolidWorks, styles function like favorites for notes and dimensions. You can also think of them as working like styles and formatting in Microsoft Word, or other word-processing software, by controlling text formatting, tolerances, and symbols.

An example of a style would be to add +/-0.005" to the end of any dimension with the selected style.

Styles can be saved to files and loaded to documents. In particular, they can be loaded to documents that can be saved as templates, thereby maintaining the loaded styles. Several types of styles can be loaded into and saved with drawing templates, including dimension, note, GD&T (geometric dimensioning and tolerancing), weld, and surface finish symbols.

When a style is loaded into a template, any document that you create from that template can use any of the loaded styles. The many file types for styles exist mainly to transfer styles from one document to another, but they aren't needed after the style is loaded. As a result, before saving a template, you should gather together your styles into your library folder and load them into the template.

You can load styles by going to the interface for the type of favorite—for example, dimensions or notes. Figure 24.23 shows the top of the Note PropertyManager interface, which contains the Style panel.

FIGURE 24.23
The Style panel for the Note PropertyManager

The buttons in the Style panel of the Note PropertyManager interface have the following functions, from left to right:

- ◆ Apply the default attributes to the selected notes.
- ◆ Add or update a style.
- ◆ Delete a style.
- ◆ Save a style.
- ◆ Load a style.

This section is concerned with loading a style. After clicking this button, you can load multiple styles at once by Shift+selecting them through the Open dialog box that appears.

Even symbol types that can be applied by dragging and dropping from the Design Library can also be loaded as styles. However, I prefer dragging from the Design Library because you get a preview of the symbol; with the styles, you see only a text tag.

Blocks can also be loaded into a template or used from the Design Library as drag-and-drop items.

Using Custom Properties in Templates

Part of the usefulness of templates is that you can do work once and have it replicated many times. This is an excellent example of process automation. One of the ways that you can take advantage of this feature is by putting default custom properties in your templates. In many cases, simply having a default value for something is better than no value, and a default value may even prompt you to put a value with real significance in the property. For example, the description of a document is extremely important, especially if you're using sequential part numbers for your filenames. A custom property named Description can be added to your template, and the default value will be used unless it's changed when the template is used in a document.

You have already seen how custom properties used in parts can be instrumental in filling out a title block on a drawing. Custom properties in part and assembly documents work exactly the same as they do in drawings.

Saving a Template

To save drawing templates, choose Save As ➤ Files Of Type and then select Drawing Templates from the drop-down list. This automatically takes you to the folder for the templates, as specified in Tools ➤ Options ➤ File Locations ➤ Templates.

You may also save out the format to its own file from the edited template. Formats are needed in their own file (in addition to existing within a template) for situations when you have an existing drawing and want to change the size of the sheet and then need a format to put on the sheet. Another situation is when a drawing may come in to your organization from an outside contractor, and they have not used your format; in this case, you can simply replace their format with yours, or you can send them your format (and template, for that matter), from which the contractor can create all the drawings for you.

Separate formats are important when you have multi-sheet drawings. When adding a sheet, you also need to add a format. You can save multi-sheet drawing templates in which the first and second sheets have different formats on them.

Creating Blocks

Blocks are an important aspect of automating drawing creation. They enable you to combine text and sketch geometry and to annotate common features on drawings. Blocks are discussed in Chapter 3, "Working with Sketches and Reference Geometry," and Chapter 16, "Working with

Assembly Sketches and Layouts." Blocks can be used for many purposes, including the following:

◆ Tolerance blocks on drawings that might change with the process (if you don't have separate formats that already contain this information)

◆ Electrical or pneumatic schematic symbols that can be snapped together

◆ Flowchart type symbols

◆ Fluid flow-direction arrows

◆ Special markers calling attention to a specific detail

◆ Sheet formats that can be created as a block, enabling you to move it around as a single entity much more easily

You can create blocks by selecting a group of sketch entities, annotations, or symbols and then choosing Tools ➢ Block ➢ Make.

The Bottom Line

Getting your templates and formats correct creates an excellent opportunity to save some time with drawings by automating many of the common tasks using templates, predefined views, multiple formats, blocks, favorites, and linked custom properties. Setup becomes more important when you are administering a larger installation, but it is also important if it's just for yourself. One of the most important things you can do is to establish a file library and direct your Tools ➢ Options ➢ File Locations paths to the files. There's nothing quite as productive as having something that works right the first time and every time.

Master It Create formats for size A and B drawings. Copy them from existing DXF or DWG data, and modify them for your needs. Save as `*.SLDDRT` file type.

Use the title block functionality to create an editable block of manually filled-in annotation in the format.

Master It Set up a drawing template with the custom properties such as Revision, DrawnBy, ReleaseDate, and other properties that you can use to automatically fill out fields on your title block. Also, place one predefined view and a couple projected views.

Make sure that you save an appropriately sized format with your template, such that the template is sheet size specific.

Master It Create a second page format with simplified title block and place it in a two-page drawing template. Make sure you have stand-alone copies of the formats in case you have a situation where you need to update the formats in drawings.

Chapter 25

Working with Drawing Views

In SolidWorks drawings, the *drawing view* is a snapshot of the 3D model from a particular point of view. To change the lines on the view, you have to change the 3D model; you don't just move lines around the view.

SolidWorks automatically maintains the views better than you could do it manually. You don't have to worry about the drawing views being inconsistent or incorrect. All you have to worry about is the 3D model being correct.

SolidWorks can update any type of view from any point of view—even the most complex model or assembly geometry—perfectly.

IN THIS CHAPTER, YOU WILL LEARN TO:

◆   Use common view types

◆   Explore other view types

◆   Sketch in a view versus sketching on a sheet

Creating Common View Types

Chapter 24, "Automating Drawings: The Basics," discussed predefined views in templates. Predefined views make it faster to automatically create drawings with consistently placed, simple views. However, sometimes you may need to create views on templates that don't have predefined views, or types of view that can't be predefined, or you may need a special arrangement of views. SolidWorks has a good assortment of view types to make practically any type of view you may need.

Using the View Palette

The View palette is shown in Figure 25.1. It's activated automatically if you use the Make Drawing From Part tool, unless the drawing template that you select has predefined views on it.

NOTE   The View palette is automatically deactivated when you are using Large Assembly mode.

The View palette contains all the standard named views, the current view of the model, custom named views including saved section views, and any *annotation views* (views that the model was in when annotations were added to it). You can drag and drop these views on the drawing.

FIGURE 25.1
The View palette

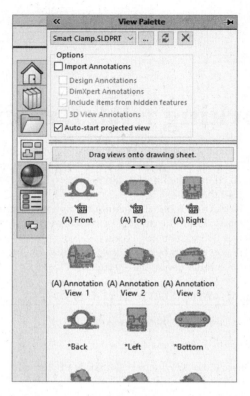

If multiple parts are available, they are listed in the drop-down list at the top of the panel. You can also browse, refresh, or cancel out of the view from this same area.

To activate the View palette without using the Make Drawing From Part tool, simply create a new drawing document, ensure that the Task pane is available, and click the View Palette tab in the Task pane. Then use the ellipsis button (. . .) to browse to a part. After you select a part, the palette window will be populated with views of the model. This method has the advantage of enabling you to see the views before you put them down. It does not link views in the same way that the predefined and projected views are linked, however.

TIP   You should be aware that it can take time to generate View Palette icons for large assemblies.

Using Model Views

Model views are one of the few types of views that are not dependent on another view. Everything has to start from somewhere, and most drawings start with either a named or predefined view. A model view starts from a named view in the model.

You can place named views by clicking the Model View button on the Drawings toolbar or by choosing Insert ➢ Drawing View ➢ Model. Using the Model View PropertyManager is a two-step process and is shown in Figure 25.2. In the first step, you select the model, and in the second step, you set the options for the view. Views dragged from the View palette are also model views.

FIGURE 25.2
The Model View
PropertyManager

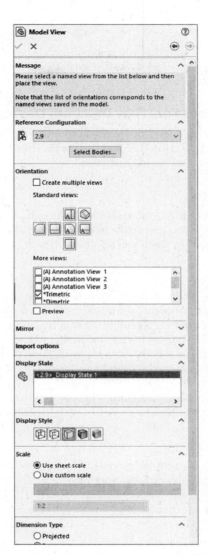

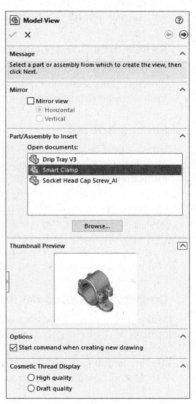

OPEN DOCUMENTS

The large selection box in the Part/Assembly To Insert panel displays any models that are open in SolidWorks at the moment. If the model that you are looking for isn't in the list, you can use the Browse button to look for it.

I typically use the Create Drawing From This Part/Assembly command if the part is open, and if not, I drag and drop the part onto a new drawing created from a template with predefined and projected views on it. This combination saves lots of extra steps.

If you click in the drawing window for some reason (for example, if you are expecting it to simply place a view), a prompt will appear, stating that you have selected a drawing document and that only parts and assemblies can be inserted into drawings.

THUMBNAIL PREVIEW

This is a nice option that shows the part that you selected in the Open Documents window. It's a useful feature, but because it's collapsed by default, it's easy to miss. After it's used the first time, it remembers the expanded setting.

START COMMAND WHEN CREATING NEW DRAWING OPTION

The Start Command When Creating New Drawing option causes this PropertyManager to open immediately when a new drawing is created. If you click in the drawing window, the prompt will appear, telling you that you're not paying attention.

REFERENCE CONFIGURATION

The Reference Configuration list enables you to select which configuration of the part to show in the view. This shows up not only when you create new views, but also in the generic Drawing View PropertyManager that shows up when you select any view.

SELECT BODIES

When a part has multiple bodies, a button called Select Bodies also shows up in this panel. If the part doesn't have multiple bodies, you won't see this button. When you click the button, it will immediately take you to another PropertyManager, the smaller one shown in Figure 25.3 called Drawing View Bodies, where you'll be sent back to the model window to select a body. Clicking the green check mark after selecting a solid body in Drawing View Bodies will then send you back to the drawing to place the view. It won't send you back to the Model View PropertyManager.

If you click the red X in the Drawing View Bodies PropertyManager, SolidWorks will leave you in the part window, and you will have to press Ctrl+Tab to get back to the drawing window.

COSMETIC THREAD DISPLAY

Make sure you read the names of the settings carefully. The Display Style panel has the same options as the Cosmetic Thread Display options, and they can easily be confused. The distinction between high and draft quality is made for performance reasons. The difference in terms of display is that in High Quality mode, hidden cosmetic threads (cosmetic threads that are behind a face) don't display in Shaded mode.

NUMBER OF VIEWS AND ORIENTATION

To create multiple views, toggle Create Multiple Views in the Orientation panel of the Model View PropertyManager. Next, select all the views from the Standard Views icons that you want to be displayed, including any choices from the More Views list, such as Current Model View and any named or annotation views that exist. These views are indicated on the drawing as boxes (representing view borders), as shown in Figure 25.3.

This is really useful functionality. It makes view selection and placement very easy and is visually clear. Unfortunately, the Single View setting is the default setting, and the PropertyManager does not remember the last setting that was used. Still, the combination of Multiple Views and Orientation is far better, in my opinion, than the View palette.

FIGURE 25.3

Placing multiple views

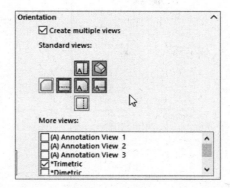

IMPORT OPTIONS

The Import Options panel is for bringing annotations into the drawing view that is being created. You should find it an advantage, being able to select these items quickly from the PropertyManager while the view is being created.

DISPLAY STATE

On the drawing, you can select the Display State. This is probably meant for situations like using Display States for hide and show operations, but remember that there is much more to Display States than just hide and show. You can also change display styles, colors, and transparency.

DISPLAY STYLE

Display Style is the selection that includes Wireframe, Shaded, Shaded With Edges, and so on. You can set the default Display Style by choosing Tools ➢ Options ➢ System Options ➢ Drawings ➢ Display Style. This panel provides an override for views being placed. This panel also enables you to control High or Draft quality views, which are described later in this chapter.

SCALE

SolidWorks drawings always default to showing views at the overall sheet scale unless the System Option on the Drawings page called Automatically Scale New Drawing Views is selected. If this setting is selected, the sheet scale saved with the drawing template is overridden. For example, a 1:1 sheet scale can be changed automatically by changing the setting to 1:4.

You can change the sheet scale through the Sheet Properties, which were discussed in Chapter 4, "Creating Simple Parts and Drawings." Controlling views with the sheet scale makes it much easier to change the size of a drawing and to scale all the views together. Individual views can be displayed at the view scale, and detail views are typically created at a different scale automatically. To locate the scale setting, choose Tools ➢ Options ➢ System Options ➢ Drawings ➢ Automatically Scale New Drawing Views. Detail Views, covered later in this chapter, automatically get a note showing the custom scale for the view.

You can automatically add a label or note to an orthogonal drawing view displayed at a scale different from the sheet scale. You access this setting at Tools ➢ Options ➢ Document Properties ➢ Views ➢ Orthographic. Enable the Show label if the view scale differs from the Sheet Scale option, and specify the rest of the settings shown in Figure 25.4 as appropriate.

FIGURE 25.4
Displaying a label to
show the view scale
when it is different from
the sheet scale

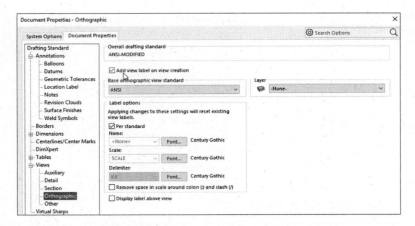

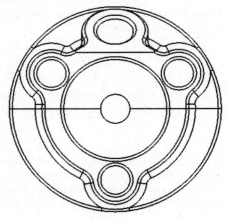

SCALE 1 : 2

DIMENSION TYPE

Even in nonorthogonal (isometric) views, true dimensions should be used for most drawing
views. Projected dimensions depend on the angle of the edge to the view plane.

Using the Projected View

The Projected View type simply makes a view that is projected in the direction that you
dragged the cursor from the selected view. For example, if you drag at a 45-degree angle, the
result is an isometric view. When placing an isometric view that you have created in this way,
SolidWorks constrains the new view to a 45-degree-angle line through the origins of the two
views. To place the view somewhere other than along this line, press the Ctrl key while placing
the view to break the alignment. The PropertyManager for the projected view is shown in
Figure 25.5.

FIGURE 25.5
The Projected View
PropertyManager

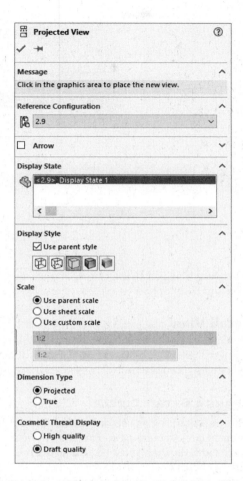

Be aware that first angle and third angle projections result in views that are opposite from one another. Third angle projection is typically ANSI standard, and first angle projection is typically ISO standard, although you often find third angle projection used in ISO as well.

When you use the pushpin on the Projected View PropertyManager, you can place multiple projected views from the originally selected view or select a new view from which to project views. Display properties and scale of the projected views are taken from the parent view.

Some views require more than one copy of the model to be loaded into RAM at once, such as views with different configurations. These views are considered high cost. Because of the extra RAM requirements, they will slow down the performance of the drawing. Projected views and model views are low cost.

Using Standard 3 View

You can access the Standard 3 View tool on the Drawings toolbar by choosing Insert ➤ Drawing View ➤ Standard 3 View. This places a front view and projects top and right views for third-angle projection drawings. Figure 25.6 shows the PropertyManager for the Standard 3 View function.

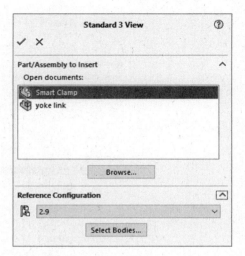

Use the PropertyManager to select open models that you want to place on the drawing. Select configuration and body or bodies to place here as well.

Using Detail View

You activate the detail view from the Drawings toolbar or by choosing Insert ➤ Drawing View ➤ Detail. Either way, you can use the function in two different ways: one that's fast and easy and the other that gives you more control but isn't quite as fast.

PRE-DRAWING A DETAIL CIRCLE

You can draw the detail "circle" before you initiate the Detail View command. When you pre-draw a detail circle, you must ensure that you're sketching in the view and not on the sheet. To draw in the view, the view must be activated. You can activate a view by clicking in the view or by bringing a sketch cursor inside the boundary of the view. When you activate a view, the status bar in the lower-right corner of the SolidWorks window displays the message "Editing Drawing View," as shown in Figure 25.7.

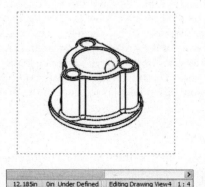

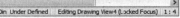

The dotted border in the image to the left shows that the view is selected, and the status bar shows that it's activated. The image to the right with the solid corners indicates that the view has Locked Focus. You can lock focus on a drawing view by double-clicking it or by right-clicking and selecting Lock View Focus from the menu.

If a view isn't activated or the focus isn't locked on the view, then any sketch elements that you draw will be placed on the drawing sheet. While sketching in a drawing view, it's a good practice to watch the status bar.

The point of all this is to sketch a closed loop in the view so it can be used for a detail view. The closed loop can be a circle, ellipse, spline, series of lines, or any other shape, as long as it's a closed loop.

A setting controls how the circle (loop) displays, in particular whether it displays as drawn or as an actual circle. This setting is found in the Detail Circle PropertyManager. If the setting is grayed out, the Style option may be set *per standard,* and the standard you are using does not allow for noncircular detail circles. You could choose With Leader instead or change the drafting standard you are using. The different results are shown in Figure 25.8.

After you create the loop, you can click the Detail View toolbar button and place the view. The view is automatically scaled by the factor set at Tools ➤ Options ➤ Drawings ➤ Detail View Scaling. By default, this scale is set to twice the parent view scale, but you can reset the default to whatever you like.

DRAWING A DETAIL CIRCLE IN-LINE

A faster way to complete the detail view is to simply click the Detail View toolbar button without preselecting or pre-drawing the loop. This activates the Circle sketch tool immediately, which activates the view as soon as you bring the cursor over the view, so that when you draw the circle, it's sure to be in the view rather than on the sheet.

Alternatively, you could swap the Circle tool for an ellipse or a spline; this works just as well, but it offers more flexibility. Regardless of the sketch tool, when you close the loop, SolidWorks prompts you to place the view. The workflow for this in-line method is better than the old-school pre-drawn loop technique.

EDITING A DETAIL VIEW

You can edit a detail view by dragging the circumference of the detail circle to a new diameter, dragging the center of the detail circle to a new location, or selecting Edit Sketch from the Detail Circle right mouse button (RMB) menu. This method enables you to edit sketch relations or otherwise edit the sketch that you used for the detail. When you are finished with the sketch, you can use the Confirmation Corner to click OK.

You can delete detail views by selecting and deleting the detail circle. Deleting the detail circle gives you the option to delete the resulting view as well as the original sketch. Also, deleting the detail view gives you the option to delete the detail circle and the original sketch.

TIP   For performance considerations, detail and cropped views are considered low-cost views, as they simply scale up a portion of an existing view.

FIGURE 25.8
Drawing a closed loop
with the Display Detail
Circle As Circles
option turned on and
turned off

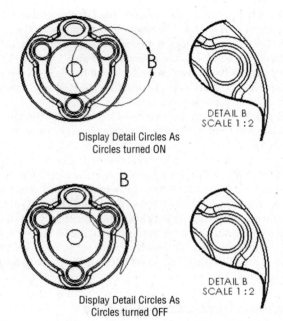

Display Detail Circles As
Circles turned ON

Display Detail Circles As
Circles turned OFF

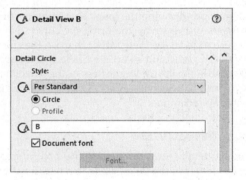

Working with Section Views

The Section View workflow goes like this:

1. Select the Section View tool.

2. Select View To Section.

3. Select the orientation. Press Tab to cycle through the options.

4. Place a section line in the view.

5. In the pop-up toolbar, click the green check mark to accept, click the curly arrow to go back a step, or click the X to cancel.

6. Place the view.

7. Double-click the section line to reverse direction.

Using the Auto-start Section View option enables you to skip the pop-up toolbar step.

Figure 25.9 shows the new Section View PropertyManager as well as the cursor interface. The lines drawn for you automatically are called Section View Assist. You can still draw the lines manually if you find it's an easier way to get the results you want.

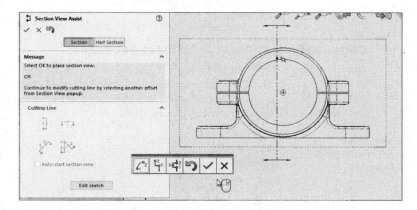

You can also use jogged section lines with the new Section tool. If you feel the need to resort to sketching the section line, the Edit Sketch option is available.

The new Section View tool borrows some skills from other areas of the software. First, the Edit Sketch option is borrowed from sheet metal functionality; it's useful if you have created a flange automatically and want to edit it manually. Second, the jogged section works much like explode lines in assemblies.

To create a jogged section, use the Vertical, Horizontal, or Auxiliary section options, as illustrated on the toolbar shown in Figure 25.10.

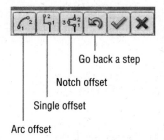

Go back a step

Notch offset

Single offset

Arc offset

You can also specify how deep you want the section view to see into the part. In the PropertyManager of the section view, you can set a depth with a number, or you can select a face, edge, or vertex to determine the depth. When you select the check box at the top of the Section Depth panel, a graphic handle becomes available on the drawing view, enabling you to visually drag the depth as well. This functionality is shown in Figure 25.11.

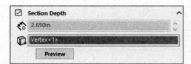

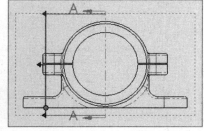

USING A HALF, PARTIAL, AND SLICE SECTIONS

A Half section is a full model view with a portion of it cut away, so it shows the sectioned and unsectioned areas. A Partial section shows only the sectioned area, with any background edges. A Slice section only shows the area that is actually cut, without any other model edges. These section types are demonstrated in Figure 25.12.

FIGURE 25.12
Comparing Partial and
Half sections

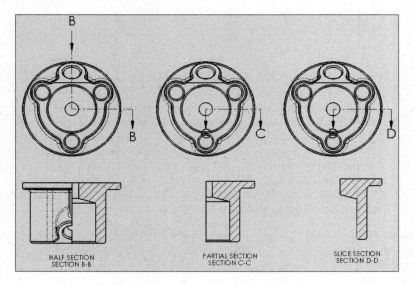

To get started with a Partial or Slice section, you can sketch a section line that doesn't go all the way through the model. To start a Half section, use the Section View Assist, as shown in Figure 25.13.

USING AN ALIGNED SECTION VIEW

The Aligned section view takes two separate sections at angles to one another and lays them out flat on the page. It is essentially two partial sections that display side by side. You can use the Section View Assist for aligned sections as well, by selecting the Aligned option in the Section View PropertyManager, as shown in Figure 25.14. Click the center of the aligned section to place the cut line in the view. You can select another centerpoint to place the angled line. The second line is vertical by default, but you can place it at any angle you choose as well.

FIGURE 25.13
Section View
PropertyManager

FIGURE 25.14
The Aligned section view

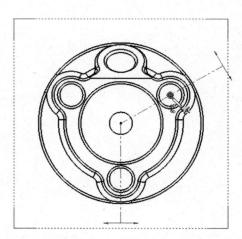

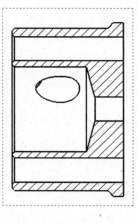

SECTION A-A
SCALE 1 : 2

EDITING A SECTION VIEW

Section views are edited in the same way as detail views. You can edit the section lines directly by dragging or by using the section line sketch through the RMB menu. You can click the RMB menu and select the Edit Sketch command to edit sketch relations, or to add to or remove sketch elements from the sketch.

Section views are also deleted in the same way as detail views, with the option to also delete the underlying sketch for the section. When you delete one segment of the section line, the resulting view, as well as the underlying sketch, is also deleted.

Section views are considered high-cost views because the computer must keep in RAM another version of the model including the section cut. However, section views also communicate the relation of the interior of an assembly to the exterior very effectively, so it may be worth the extra performance slow down.

Creating Other View Types

SolidWorks can create almost any type of view you need. You can put shaded, RealView, and transparent views on drawings. You can also put Broken, Broken-Out section, Cropped, alternate position, empty views, and even hand-drawn views.

Using a Crop View

The crop view is simply a view that looks like a detail view without requiring a parent view. This feature enables you to reduce the number of views on a sheet and save some room. However, a cropped view may be confusing if it isn't clear which area is being detailed in the cropped view.

Unlike detail views, in crop views the closed loop must be sketched in the view before you invoke the command. To make the crop view, draw the closed loop as shown in Figure 25.15 on the left, and then click the Crop View button on the Drawing toolbar or access the command by choosing Insert ➤ Drawing View ➤ Crop.

FIGURE 25.15
A sketch loop and a crop view

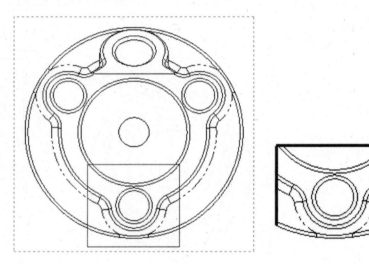

To edit a crop view, right-click the view, expand the arrow next to Crop View, and select either Edit Crop or Remove Crop. Removing the crop doesn't delete the sketch that was used to create the crop.

Again, crop views are considered low-cost views.

Using a Broken-Out Section View

The Broken-Out section view is another view type that alters an existing view rather than creating a new view. It also requires a closed-loop sketch. The Broken-Out section view is very useful in assembly views where parts are obscured by other parts—in particular, when a set of parts is inside a housing and you want to show the inside parts without hiding the housing. Of course, you can also use Broken-Out section views on parts with internal detail.

Broken-Out section views act like a cut that's created from the drawing view. Any faces created by the cut are hatched. Figure 25.16 shows a casting part view using a Broken-Out section view. You can create Broken-Out sections on parts or assemblies. You cannot create Broken-Out section views using existing detail, section, or alternate position views.

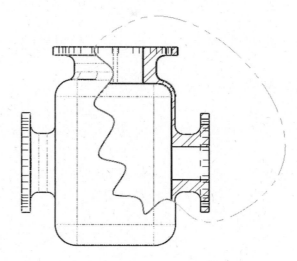

Notice that in Figure 25.16 the temporary axes for the flange holes are showing and cannot be turned off. This is probably a display bug left over from SolidWorks 2011.

The hatch pattern is associated with the materials assigned for each part. You can change the hatch scale by double-clicking a hatched region and using the settings in the dialog box shown in Figure 25.17. To change the hatch size, you must deselect the Material Crosshatch option.

Broken-Out section views require you to specify a depth for the break. You can use an edge selected from a different view or a distance to specify the depth. In the case of the Broken-Out section, the depth is into the screen, while with the regular section, the section depth is measured as a distance perpendicular to the section line.

DRAWING THE CLOSED LOOP

Broken-Out section views are initiated from an existing view either with or without a pre-drawn closed loop. If the loop is pre-drawn, you must select it before clicking the Broken-Out Section toolbar button on the Drawings toolbar or accessing the command by choosing Insert ➢ Drawing View ➢ Broken-Out Section.

If the view has no pre-drawn, preselected loop, then initiating the function activates the Spline sketch tool. It isn't necessary to use a spline as the closed loop for this view type, but Broken-Out section views are traditionally created with a freehand sort of boundary, even when drawn manually.

If the loop is closed in an uninterrupted workflow, then after the last spline point is drawn, joining the spline back to itself, the Section Scope dialog box will appear. This will enable you to select any parts that are not to be sectioned if an assembly is in the sectioned view. It's customary to avoid sectioning shafts, screws, or other cylindrical components. Figure 25.18 shows the use of the Section Scope to exclude the two shafts in the assembly from the section cut.

FIGURE 25.17
Changing the hatch
pattern on a Broken-
Out section

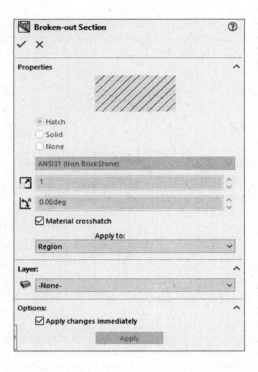

FIGURE 25.18
Using the Section Scope

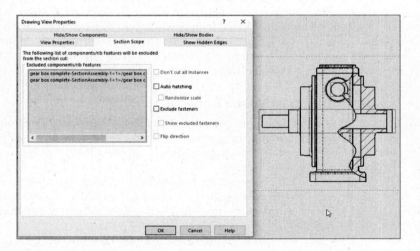

The recommended workflow is to initiate the function from the toolbar, use the spline to create the closed loop, and to not pre-draw a loop. This makes everything flow more smoothly, and you will create the view surprisingly quickly. If you must use a sketch tool other than the spline, then you must pre-draw it. Even if you simply change sketch tools when the Broken-Out section view automatically activates the spline, because the workflow has been broken, creating the closed loop won't automatically display the Section Scope interface.

SELECTING THE DEPTH

After you make the Section Scope selections, the next step is to set the depth of the cut. You can do this in several ways. Broken-Out section views are usually applied to the center of a hole if available or in other ways that show the view as cleanly as possible. If you know the depth of the cut that you want to make, you can enter it as a distance value. Of course, that raises the question, "Distance from *what*?" The answer seems to be, "From the geometry in the view that would come the farthest out of the screen toward the user." Users most often choose the distance when it doesn't matter *exactly* how deep the cut goes or exactly *where* it cuts, but it gives a relative position.

In situations when you want to cut to the center of a particular feature or up to an edge, it's far easier and less bothersome to simply select the geometry from a drawing view. For example, Figure 25.19 shows the PropertyManager interface where the depth of the cut is set. In this example, the edge of the shaft in the view to the right has been selected. This tells SolidWorks that the cut should go to the center of the shaft. Another possibility is to display the temporary axes, as shown in Figure 25.19, and to select an axis through the center of the shaft.

FIGURE 25.19

Setting the depth of the Broken-Out section view

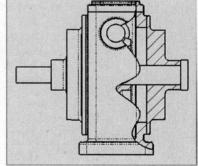

EDITING THE VIEW

At this point, the view is finished. Now you may choose to edit the view in some way, such as by changing the sketch, the depth, the section scope, and so on. Figure 25.20 shows how the Broken-Out section view is positioned in the Drawing FeatureManager. It is listed as a modification to an existing drawing view. The Broken-Out Section RMB menu is also shown. Selecting Edit Definition displays the PropertyManager (refer to Figure 25.19). Selecting Edit Sketch enables you to change the section spline shape. Selecting Properties displays the dialog box shown to the right in Figure 25.20. This contains options for the underlying original view as well as the Broken-Out section modification to the original view. Only the Section Scope tab is added by the Broken-Out section view. The rest of the options are for normal view properties.

FIGURE 25.20
Editing the Broken-Out section view

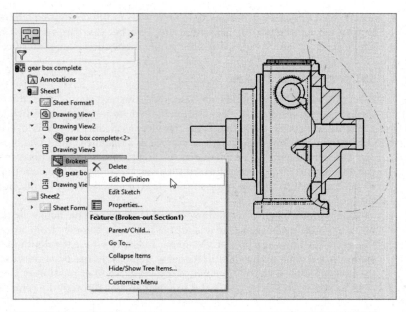

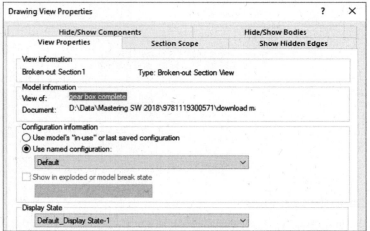

Using a Break View

Break views are typically used to display parts that are very long in one dimension on a drawing in such a way that you can see both ends or other important features. You can break views more than once in the same direction or even in opposite directions. Figure 25.21 shows the full view of a part and a view that was broken twice. Notice that the dimensions are correct, and any dimension that includes a broken length has a special dimension line.

To create a break view, click the Break toolbar button on the Drawings toolbar, or choose it at Insert ➤ Drawing View ➤ Break. You need to place break lines in pairs, and you can choose from one of five break symbol styles, as shown in Figure 25.21. You can change the style from the RMB menu or from the PropertyManager.

FIGURE 25.21
Dimensions on a
break view

FIGURE 25.21
Dimensions on a
break view

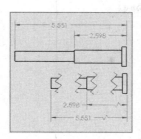

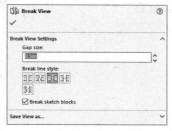

The Broken View PropertyManager also enables you to set the gap size and the style of the break. The gap refers to the gap between the break lines in the finished broken view. The setting here overrides the default for this view only. The default setting is a template setting found in Tools ➤ Options ➤ Document Properties ➤ Detailing. Other options that you can set in this location are the break line extension (the distance the lines extend past the model edges) and the break line font (on the Line Font page of the Document Properties tab). The setting that enables the broken symbol on a dimension is found on the Dimensions page and is called Show Dimensions As Broken In Broken Views.

You can remove individual breaks in a broken view by selecting one of the break lines and pressing Delete. You can add breaks by applying the Break command and adding more breaks to a view. You can alter breaks by simply dragging the break lines. In past versions, it was possible to get the view very confused by dragging one set of breaks to interfere with another set of breaks. That problem has been fixed by not allowing break lines to be dragged past one another.

Broken views enable you to dimension the break lines themselves so that when the model changes, you can control the location of the break lines relative to part geometry.

Consider using the Unbreak option from the RMB menu to temporarily unbreak a view to make dimensioning more convenient.

If you intend to create two views, one projected from the other, and you intend to break both views, create the first view and break it as desired, and then project the second. The second view will be broken in the same place as the parent view. Any projected child view will be broken in the same place. Conversely, if you create a section view from a broken view, the section view will be broken as well.

Using an Auxiliary View

An *auxiliary view* is a view that is projected from a non-orthogonal edge, intended to display edges in true length, without foreshortening. This type of view is often necessary to view features (such as holes drilled at an angle) square on, so they appear circular in the view rather than foreshortened and elliptical. An auxiliary view is shown in Figure 25.22 on the left. If the edge that the view was created from is updated, then the auxiliary view will reorient itself. The image on the right shows an auxiliary view projected from an arbitrarily drawn sketch line. The line or edge used to project an auxiliary view cannot be reselected; however, if a sketch is used to project the view, then the Edit Sketch option is available through the view arrow RMB menu.

Using an Alternate Position View

The alternate position view is available only for views of an assembly and shows the assembly in two different positions (not from different viewpoints, which requires an assembly that moves). This is another view type that doesn't create a new view but alters an existing view. Figure 25.23 shows the PropertyManager interface for the alternate position view, a sample view that it creates, and the way that it's represented in the drawing FeatureManager.

FIGURE 25.22
Two auxiliary views

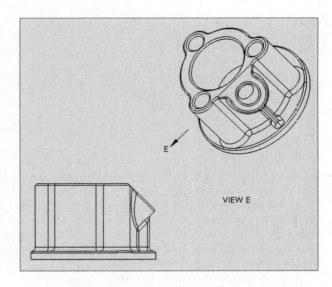

FIGURE 25.23
The alternate
position view

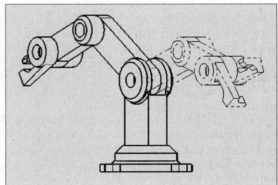

To create an alternate position view, ensure that you have an assembly on the active drawing that can have multiple positions, and click the Alternate Position View button from the Drawings toolbar, or choose Insert ➤ Drawing View ➤ Alternate Position and then select the alternate position view.

Next, click in the drawing view to which you want to add the alternate position. The PropertyManager shown in Figure 25.24 prompts you to select an existing configuration for the alternate position or to create a new configuration. If you choose to create a new config, the model window will appear, a new config will be created, and you will be required to reposition the assembly. The alternate position will be shown in a different line font on the same view, from the same orientation as the original.

TIP   The best way to create this view is to either create two configurations used exclusively for the alternate position view or to have two configurations where you know that parts won't be moved, suppressed, or hidden. The main idea is that you need to ensure that these configurations remain in the same position or are changed intentionally, knowing that it will alter this drawing view.

To delete an alternate position view, select it in the drawing FeatureManager and press Delete.

FIGURE 25.24
Using the Saved Views
command
in the model

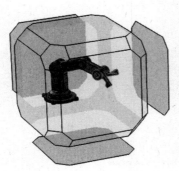

Using a Predefined View

Predefined views are discussed in depth in Chapter 24, "Automating Drawings: The Basics," and are primarily used as views on drawing templates.

Using an Empty View

Empty views are just that—empty. The reasons for creating an empty view can include making a view from a sketch, making a schematic from blocks, or combining several elements—such as blocks, sketches, imported drawing geometry, annotations, and symbols—into an entity that can be moved as a single view on a drawing.

Using a Saved View

You can create saved views by orienting the view in the model document and saving the view. Remember that views can be saved in the View Orientation window, which you can access by pressing the spacebar. Saved views are placed on the drawing using the model view functionality.

Saved views are often used with section views, to predefine the view in the model and access it quickly in the drawing.

Although not appropriate for showing dimensions, views using perspective are most useful for pictorial or illustrative views. The only way to get a perspective view on a drawing is to place a saved view in the model with Perspective turned on. You can access the Perspective option by choosing View ➤ Display ➤ Perspective, and you can edit the amount of perspective by choosing View ➤ Modify ➤ Perspective.

Access saved views in the model by pressing the spacebar and using the Saved Views flyout. Create new saved views by clicking on the Save (diskette) symbol next to the numbers under Saved Views, as shown in Figure 25.24.

To use these saved views in the drawing, place a model view on the sheet, and select the name of the saved view from the More Views list on the second page of the PropertyManager, shown in Figure 25.25.

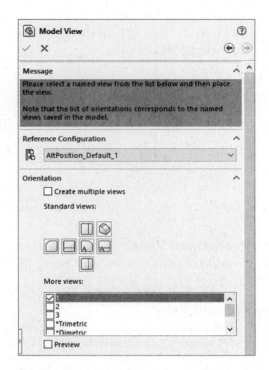

Converting a Drawing View to a Sketch

Right-click anywhere inside a view border and select Convert View To Sketch. When you do this, you will be presented with three options—replace the view with the sketch, replace the view with a block, or insert the view as a block on the drawing sheet. The second two options create the block as a copy. You might want to convert a view to a sketch if you want to make alterations to the appearance of the actual model to represent a process or illustrate something that would be difficult or impossible to model.

Saving a View to DWG/DXF

To save a view to DWG/DXF, select the view so the PropertyManager shows up, and then at the very bottom of the PropertyManager, find the panel called Save View As. This panel enables you to drag a manipulator in the view to establish the insertion point. Then click the Save icon (which looks like a diskette) to save the view as either DXF or DWG. Previously, this was available only for flat pattern views for sheet metal or for entire drawings.

Using a Relative View

The Relative View PropertyManager enables you to create a view that does not necessarily correspond to any of the standard orthogonal views or named views. Using this type of view is very similar to using the Normal To tool. First, select the face that is to be presented square to the view, and then select the face that represents the top of the view. When this view type is initiated, SolidWorks will open the 3D Model window to allow you to select the faces needed to define the view.

This type of view is particularly useful when a part has a face that's at an odd angle to the standard planes of the part. It's in some ways similar to the auxiliary view, except that in the auxiliary view, you cannot select which face is the top.

The Relative View PropertyManager has a special function that is important for drawings of multibody parts. If both faces used to establish the view are from the same body, then all the rest of the bodies in the part can be hidden with an option in the Relative View PropertyManager, which is shown in Figure 25.26. Multibody modeling is covered in Chapter 31, "Modeling Multibodies."

FIGURE 25.26
The Relative View
PropertyManager

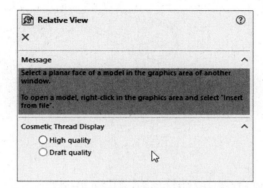

Using the 3D Drawing View Mode

The 3D Drawing View mode is not technically a drawing view type. It's a mode that enables you to select faces or edges of the model that may need to be selected for some purpose but cannot be seen from the orientation of the drawing view. You can invoke the 3D Drawing View mode from the 3D Drawing View toolbar button, which is on the View toolbar and can be accessed by choosing View ➤ Modify ➤ 3D Drawing View from the menus.

Ironically, this mode does not work for the relative view, which would be a perfect application for it. Instead, relative view makes you go to the model window. The 3D Drawing View mode is intended for views such as the Broken-Out section view, where a depth must be selected for the cut.

In Figure 25.27, notice the small toolbar above the drawing view. This toolbar is available while the 3D Drawing View mode is turned on. Clicking OK on the small toolbar turns off the mode and returns the view to its previous state.

FIGURE 25.27
The 3D Drawing
View mode

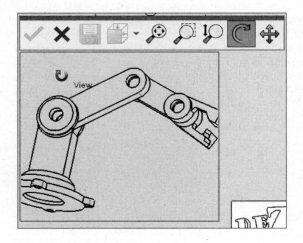

Changing View Orientation and Alignment

Although you may have selected the top view, and it displays the correct geometry, you may want to spin the view in the plane of the paper or orient it in a particular way. You can do this using two methods. The easiest way to reorient the view is to use the Rotate View tool on the Heads-Up View toolbar. This rotates the view in the plane of the paper much as it rotates the model in 3D.

Another option is to select an edge in the view and assign the edge to be either a horizontal or vertical edge. Figure 25.28 shows how a view can be reoriented using this tool, which you can locate by choosing Tools ➤ Align Drawing View ➤ Horizontal Edge or Vertical Edge.

FIGURE 25.28
Rotating a drawing view
to align an edge

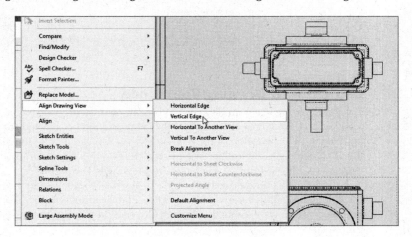

Alignment in the RMB menu refers to alignment of the entire view with other views. Align in the Tools menu refers to aligning annotations. Align Drawing View in the Tools menu is the menu you want, although it does not reference rotating the view.

Another option for view alignment is to align it relative to another view; this involves stacking one view on top of another or placing them side by side. You can do this by selecting the second pair of options in the menu shown in Figure 25.28, Horizontal To Another View and Vertical To Another View. Preselecting a linear edge will activate the Horizontal To Another View and Vertical To Another View options.

Situations may arise where a view is locked into a particular relationship to another view, and you need to disassociate the views. The Break Alignment option, which is grayed out in the menu in Figure 25.28, serves that purpose.

Using Display Options in Views

Some important display options and settings are not listed in Tools ➤ Options menu; they are available only through the menus, and in particular the View menu. You can effectively deal with most items in the View menu by assigning a hotkey that can be toggled on or off. For example, axes and temporary axes are things you often want to be visible when you're sketching something, but not visible when printing a drawing. You can easily assign the display for axes and temporary axes to hotkeys, making them ready at your fingertips. You can assign hotkeys by choosing Tools ➤ Customize ➤ Keyboard.

Using Display States

You can use display states in drawing views, but unless you are only hiding and showing parts with the display states (that is, you are not changing colors or display styles with display states), they have an effect only when a drawing view is set to Shaded Display style. You can control the display states for drawing views in the View PropertyManager. The Drawing View Properties dialog box is shown in Figure 25.29.

One of the limitations of the Display States functionality in drawing views is that when wireframe display is used, the drawing edges appear in black rather than using the color settings to show wireframe in the same color as shaded. The necessary color settings are found in two places, and you need to set both. The System Options setting is on the Colors page and is called Use Specified Color For Shaded With Edges Mode. The second setting is in the part Document Properties (not assembly), again on the Colors page, and is called Apply Same Color To Wireframe, HLR (Hidden Lines Removed), And Shaded.

Using Display Styles

The 2D drawing world is becoming less and less black and white, and SolidWorks has the capability to apply shaded views to drawings. This is probably most useful in isometric, perspective, or pictorial views on the drawings. The shading and color may be distracting for dimensioned and detailed views, but it can also be indispensable when you need to show what a part actually looks like in 3D. Not everyone can read engineering prints, and even for those who can, nothing communicates quite like a couple of shaded isometric views.

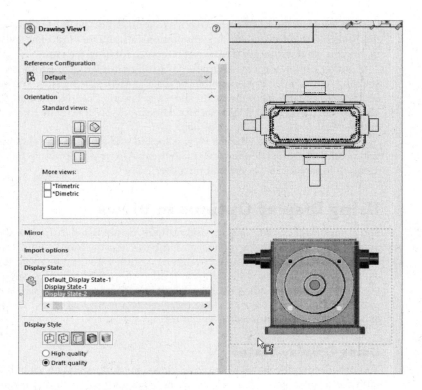

The more standard 2D drawing display modes are Wireframe, HLR, and HLV (Hidden Lines Visible), which work in the same way as they do in the model environment. Unless you override it on a per-part basis, the Display mode is set for all the components in the view.

SELECTING A COMPONENT LINE FONT

Individual components within an assembly can be shown in different fonts, similar to the display in the alternate position view. You can access this function by right-clicking the component and selecting Component Line Font. Figure 25.30 shows the Component Line Font dialog box, along with a drawing view in which a couple of part line fonts have been changed. The part can be changed only in the view where it was selected, or it can be changed across the board in all views in the active drawing where it appears. This is useful if you want to emphasize or de-emphasize certain parts in the assembly view.

USING LAYERS

Yes, SolidWorks drawings *can* use layers. You can place individual parts onto layers, and the layers can have different colors and line fonts. Most entities can be put into layers, including edges, annotations, and sketch items. Hidden layers are often used for reference information or construction entities on a drawing. Figure 25.31 shows the Layers dialog box and the Layers toolbar on a SolidWorks drawing.

FIGURE 25.30
The Component Line
Font dialog box

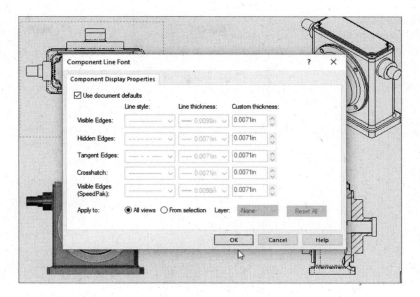

FIGURE 25.31
Using the Layers dialog
box in SolidWorks

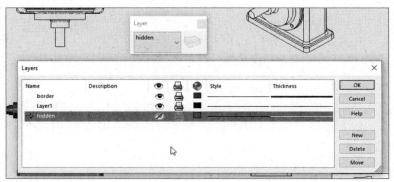

Working with Tangent Edge Display Options

SolidWorks drawings and models offer some options for displaying tangent edges. Tangent edges are the breaks between faces when the faces are tangent, such as between flat sides of a box and the fillet that comes between them. Many users find it distracting when tangent edges (which in a physical part are not edges at all) are given as much visible weight as the sharp edges of, say, a chamfer. To find the settings, shown in Figure 25.32, choose View ➤ Display or select them from the RMB menu. The Tangent Edges Removed option may be appropriate for parts with few fillets, but it causes a part to look oversimplified and makes details of the shape difficult to distinguish.

Additional options are available, including applying a color to the tangent edges by choosing Tools ➤ Options ➤ Color list for tangent edge display and the Hide/Show Edges options.

FIGURE 25.32
Edge display options

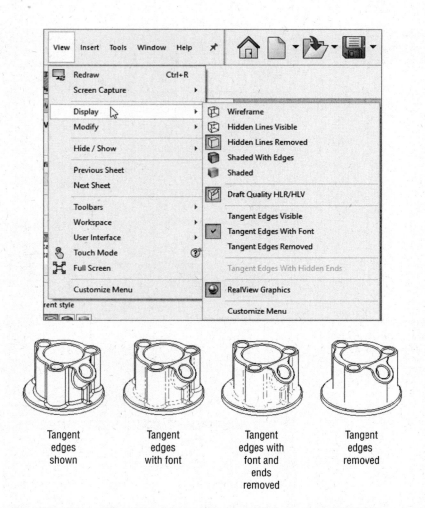

| Tangent edges shown | Tangent edges with font | Tangent edges with font and ends removed | Tangent edges removed |

You can use the Hide/Show Edges tool for specific selected edges, or just click the tool with nothing selected to activate the Hide/Show Edges PropertyManager, shown in Figure 25.33. Hide/Show Edges functionality is available only with high-quality views. View quality is addressed in the next section. Hide/Show Edges is available from the left-click context toolbar, the RMB menu, or the Line Font toolbar.

The PropertyManager indicates that Hide/Show Edges works from a selection, although it has no list box to show the edges selected. The tools offered here may not have a wide general appeal, but they probably will be the most useful to people documenting complex shapes or plastic parts. Hide Non-Planar Edges is meant to simplify the display of complex parts with lots of curvature. Hide Blend Edges limits the filtering to edges with curvature continuity across the edge, which is usually found only in more sophisticated surfaced parts. The Hide Edges Shorter Than option gives you the ability to filter the edge display again. These settings apply only to the current view, not to the entire drawing.

FIGURE 25.33
The Hide/Show Edges
PropertyManager
offers tangent edge
display options.

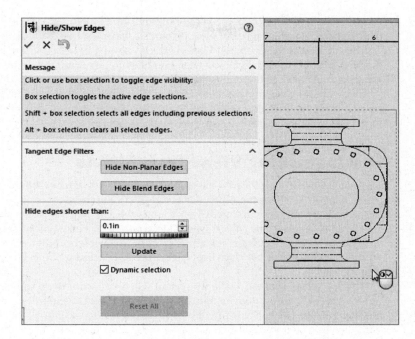

Take note of the options in the Hide/Show Edges PropertyManager message box shown in Figure 25.33:

◆ Box selection toggles the active edge selections.

◆ Shift+box selection selects all edges, including previous selections.

◆ Alt+box selection clears all selected edges.

These mass selection options can be important if you are using a command such as Tangent Edge Filters, Hide Non-Planar Edges, Hide Blend Edges, or Hide Edges Shorter Than A Given Value.

Choosing View Quality Settings

You can choose between two options for the drawing View Quality: High Quality and Draft Quality. The quality you choose influences the performance of the software. Draft Quality views are noticeably rough when viewed closely, but from a distance, they look the way they should.

All views are created as High Quality unless the View Quality setting is overridden. To find this setting, choose Tools ➤ Options ➤ System Options ➤ Drawings ➤ Display Style ➤ Display Quality For New Views. The only other way that you can create Draft Quality views is if you open a drawing from an older version of SolidWorks that used Draft Quality views.

In Figure 25.2 earlier in the chapter, the image to the right shows the Display Style pane. This PropertyManager has been taken from a High Quality view. A Draft Quality view enables you to toggle between Draft Quality and High Quality, as shown in Figure 25.33. This means that you can switch a view from Draft to High, but not from High to Draft. Also notice in Figure 25.29 that the cursor over a Draft Quality view displays a lightning bolt symbol, indicating Draft Quality.

You can access the Cosmetic Thread Display setting in both the Step 1 PropertyManager and the Step 2 PropertyManager. However, you need to be careful not to misread the interface by thinking that either of these interfaces controls the View Quality.

If you are thinking about the performance of a drawing, be aware that Draft Quality views are created from the graphics tessellation or triangle-based display information, while High Quality views are generated directly from the NURBS geometry.

Distinguishing Views from Sheets

It's sometimes difficult for new users to understand the difference between being *in* a sketch and being *out of* a sketch, or the difference between editing the *sheet* as opposed to the *sheet format*. In the same way, confusion frequently surrounds the difference between sketching in a view and sketching on a sheet. The easiest way to determine if a sketch will be associated with a view or with the drawing sheet is to look at the prompt in the lower-right corner of the SolidWorks window, on the status bar that displays the message Editing Sheet, Editing Sheet Format, or Editing View.

This issue becomes especially important when you want to do something with a sketch entity, but it's grayed out and unavailable. This means that whatever entity is active is *not* the one that the sketch entity is on. Drawing view borders expand to contain all the sketch entities associated with the view, so if you see a view that's extended on one side, larger than it should be, it could be extended to contain the grayed-out sketch entity. Activate the sheet and the suspected views; when the sketch entity turns from gray to black, you have found the place where it resides.

Tutorial: Working with View Types, Settings, and Options

This tutorial is intended to familiarize you with many of the view types, settings, and options that are involved in creating views. To begin, follow these steps:

1. From the download materials, open the part called Chapter 25 – Tutorial Part.sldprt.

2. Move the drawing template named Mastering 2pg B size.drwdot, also found in the download materials, to your Templates folder. If you do not know where your templates are located, choose Tools ➤ Options ➤ System Options ➤ File Locations ➤ Document Templates.

3. From the window with the open part, click the Make Drawing From Part button on the toolbar. The drawing will be populated with three standard views and an isometric view, as shown in Figure 25.34.

4. Click the Section View tool on the Drawings toolbar. This will activate the Section View Assist tool.

FIGURE 25.34

Using a template with
predefined views

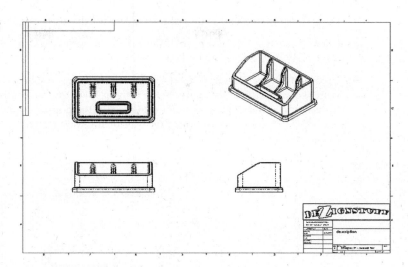

FIGURE 25.34

Using a template with
predefined views

5. In the top view (in the upper-left section of the drawing), place a vertical line that picks up
    the inference from the origin or an edge midpoint. You may have to run the cursor over
    the origin to activate the inference lines, as shown in Figure 25.35. After you place the cut
    line, click the green check on the pop-up toolbar to accept the placement. Place the section
    view to the right of the parent view. If you cannot see the origin, use the View menu
    to show it.

FIGURE 25.35

Creating a section view

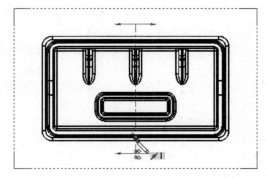

To change the letter label on the drawing, click the section line and change the label in the
top panel of the Section View PropertyManager.

NOTE   You may see a Section Scope dialog box asking you to omit the rib features. Ribs are usually not
hatched in section views.

6. Bring the cursor over the corner in the section line until the cursor looks like the image to
    the left. Double-click the cursor; the section arrows will flip to the other direction, and the
    drawing view will become cross-hatched. The cross-hatching indicates that the view needs
    to be updated.

7. Press Ctrl+Q; the view will update and remove the cross-hatching.

8. Click the section line and press Delete. Answer Yes to the prompt. You may also need to separately delete the sketched section line.

9. Create a new section view using a jogged section line, as shown in Figure 25.36. To do this with Section View Assist, activate the Section View tool, select the Vertical option, place the cut line at the origin, select Single Offset in the pop-up toolbar, (as shown in Figure 25.36), click the cut line at the origin, and then pull the jog to the right, (also shown in Figure 25.36).

FIGURE 25.36
Creating a jogged
section view

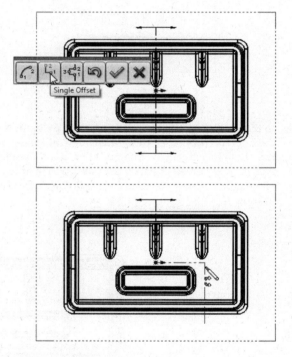

10. Click the Detail View button on the Drawings toolbar. This will activate the Circle sketch tool.

11. Sketch a circle in the front view, located in the lower-left section of the drawing. Try not to pick up any automatic relations to the center of the circle. One way to prevent this is to hold down the Ctrl key when creating the sketch.

12. Place the view when the circle is complete. Note that the view was created at a scale of 1:2. The sheet scale is 1:4, so the detail is two times the sheet scale. The detail view is shown in Figure 25.37.

13. Drag the circumference of the circle and watch the view dynamically resize.

FIGURE 25.37

Creating a detail view

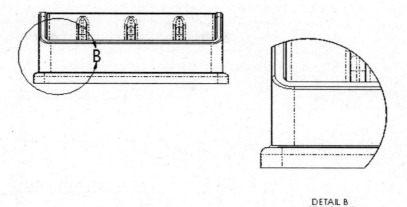

DETAIL B
SCALE 1 : 2

14. Leave the Detail circle selected so the center of the circle is highlighted. Drag the center of the circle around the view. The effect is like moving a magnifying glass over the part. If you drag the center with the Ctrl key pressed, you won't pick up any automatic sketch relations when you drop it somewhere.

15. Click the Broken-Out Section View tool on the Drawings toolbar. Draw a spline on the right view similar to the one shown in the left image in Figure 25.38. Use a section depth of 1 inch. Working with splines take a little practice.

FIGURE 25.38

Creating a Broken-Out section view

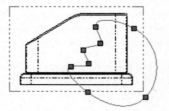 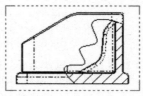

16. Click inside the view border but outside of the part in the top view (in the upper-left section of the drawing). Press Ctrl+C.

17. Click the Add Sheet icon to the right of the Sheet tab in the lower-left corner of the drawing that says Sheet1 and select Add New Sheet. If you used the template provided, a message may appear, saying that SolidWorks cannot find the format. This is because I only supplied the template file, not the format as a separate file. In any case, switch to the E size format and accept.

18. Click any spot inside the sheet and press Ctrl+V. SolidWorks will paste the copied view from the other sheet. Delete the section line. You may also need to delete the sketch lines separately.

19. Click the Projected View tool from the Drawings toolbar, and then click the pasted view. Practice making a couple of projected views, including dragging one off at a 45-degree angle to make an isometric view. Make sure one of the views is a side view showing the angled edge, as shown in Figure 25.39. After you create the views, click model edges in the views and drag them around to a better location.

FIGURE 25.39
Projecting views

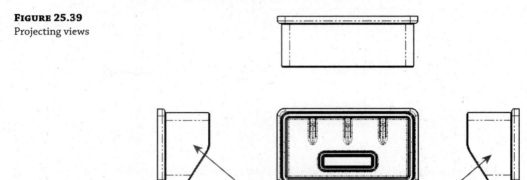

Create at least one of these views

20. Select the angled edge from one of the side views and click the Auxiliary View toolbar button. While placing the view, press and hold the Ctrl key to break the alignment. You can resize the view arrow by selecting the corners and dragging. If you drag the line itself, you can move it between the views. Alternatively, with the view arrow selected and the PropertyManager displayed, you can deselect the green checkmark icon in the Arrow panel at the top of the window to turn off the arrow.

21. Create a new drawing from the New dialog box. Select a template without predefined views on it, so the Inch B Bible Template (no Views).drwdot will work. If you select a default SolidWorks template, you need to verify that the template uses third angle rather than first angle projection. An easy way to do this is to switch the drafting standard from ISO to ANSI in Tools ➤ Options ➤ Document Properties ➤ Drafting Standard. If the automatic Model View interface appears in the PropertyManager, click the red X icon to cancel out of it.

22. Expand the Task pane and activate the View palette (the tab that looks like a Drawing icon). Click the ellipsis button (. . .) and browse for the assembly named Chapter 25 - SF casting assembly.sldasm. This is shown in Figure 25.40.

23. Drag the back view onto the drawing. Notice that when you use this technique, the views do not resize automatically, regardless of the setting at Tools ➤ Options ➤ Drawings ➤ Automatically Scale New Drawing Views.

24. Delete any view you have created using this method. Open Windows Explorer, browse to the assembly, and drag it into the drawing. The views you create using this method are equivalent to the Standard 3 View tool. This time, the views auto-size.

FIGURE 25.40

The View palette

25. Select the front view and change it to the back view. Notice that the rest of the views change to reflect the new parent view. You will get a warning about this change.

26. Zoom in on the back view. Change the view to show Tangent Edges With Font through View ➤ Display. You can also change this from the view RMB menu.

27. Click the Alternate Position View toolbar button. Type a name in the PropertyManager for a new configuration and click the green checkmark icon. SolidWorks will open the Assembly Model window.

28. Rotate the handle 90 degrees and click the green checkmark icon. SolidWorks will return to the drawing and show the new position in a dashed font, as shown in Figure 25.41.

29. Place an isometric view on the drawing. Change the Display Mode to make it a shaded view.

30. Right-click inside the view, but away from the parts, and select Properties. The dialog box will appear, as shown in Figure 25.42. Make sure that the view is set to use the default configuration, and select the Show In Exploded State option.

FIGURE 25.41
Creating an alternate
position view

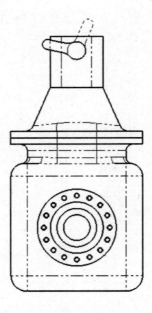

FIGURE 25.42
The Drawing View
Properties dialog box

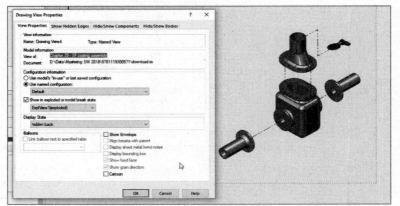

The Bottom Line

SolidWorks has the capacity to make many different types of views of parts. In addition to the tools for projecting views, custom views saved in the model document can be saved and used on the drawing. The associative nature of the drawing to the model helps ensure that drawing views, regardless of how unusual the section angle or view orientation, are displayed in the correct size, location, and geometry.

It's sometimes better to create some of the views that require sketches by pre-sketching. Utilize workflow enhancements when possible; for example, the automated workflow of the Broken-Out section works well, but forcing it to be a manual process makes it awkward to use.

Master It   Included with the downloads for Chapter 1, "Introducing SolidWorks," you will find a folder full of document (part, assembly, and drawing) templates. Using Windows Explorer, sort the templates and copy the `*.drwdot` templates into the location specified at Tools ➤ Options ➤ System Options ➤ File Locations ➤ Document Templates.

Master It   Use the Robot Arm assembly in the download data for this chapter to create a drawing that uses an alternate position view on the first page and drawing views of the individual parts on pages after the first one. Make sure to use a template with a special page 2 format.

Master It   Create a new drawing, and place two views on it using separate parts (using the Model View tool). Next, rotate one view 90 degrees and align it with the second view.

Chapter 26

Using Annotations and Symbols

Annotations and symbols are major components of communicating design through drawings. SolidWorks has several tools available to help you manage these entities to make engineering drawings look good and communicate effectively.

<u>**IN THIS CHAPTER, YOU WILL LEARN TO:**</u>

◆   Place notes

◆   Insert and create blocks

◆   Access symbols

◆   Apply center marks and centerlines

Using Notes

Notes are the workhorses of SolidWorks annotations. You can use notes in many ways and mix them with links to custom properties, hyperlinks, and text-wrapping boxes. You can also use them with styles, leaders, symbols, and balloons; you can even embed balloons into notes.

Because capitalization is such a big issue on engineering drawings, SolidWorks has added a setting to many PropertyManagers that specify text that forces all uppercase to be used. You will find this setting in the Note interface.

Setting Up a Workflow for Placing Notes

Here's an outline of the workflow to help you create annotations more efficiently.
    Follow these steps to create a note:

1.   Click the Note button on the Annotations toolbar.

2.   Click in the graphics window where you want to create the note *or* click an entity to which you want the note leader to point and *then* click where you want the note.

3.   Type the note. Press Enter at the end of a line, or if you intend to force the note to wrap later, just allow the line of text to be as long as necessary. While you create the note, the text box will expand to the right until you press Enter, and it expands down every time a line is added.

At the end of the last line of the note, *do not* press Enter again (this would create extra lines), but you may press Esc. Esc gets you out of the note and ready to place a new note. When you press Esc twice, you exit the note you were typing and then exit the Note command altogether.

4. Another way to finish the note is to click the mouse outside of the text box. After that, if you are finished, press Esc. If you want to continue with another note, click again to place it and start typing. If you want to place the same note as the first one again, the text is already there, so click a second time.

Utilizing Fonts

SolidWorks installs a font called *OLF SimpleSansOC* that works as a stick font for operations such as engraving, laser, water jet, and other CNC machine functions. Some AutoCAD monofont look-alike fonts are installed with SolidWorks that have a very narrow width and are shaped like some of the monofonts. Some of these fonts may not look good on your SolidWorks drawing,

Fonts can also be used for special characters such as mathematical symbols, Greek letters, Wingdings, and any other symbols you might find in Windows TrueType fonts.

In the Customize dialog box (Tools ➤ Customize ➤ Commands), the Formatting toolbar is not listed. The Formatting toolbar appears in the graphics area immediately over your text every time you either insert a new note or edit an existing note, unless the toolbar is already docked somewhere. You can force it to appear by right-clicking on any toolbar and selecting Formatting from the list. The Formatting toolbar controls font, size, text formatting, justification, bulleting, spacing, and indentation. These tools work on text within a small text box similar to other Windows applications such as PowerPoint. The Formatting toolbar is shown in Figure 26.1.

FIGURE 26.1
The Formatting toolbar

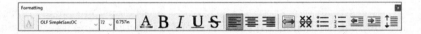

Using Text Boxes and Wrapping

Text boxes enable you to limit the size, particularly the width, that a note can occupy. This enables notes to wrap in tight spaces on title or revision blocks, as well as other places. Wrapping extends the text downward when the typical top align (justification) is used. Wrapping extends upward when bottom align is used.

You can size text boxes immediately after placement, even while they are blank; the text then wraps to fit the box width as you type it. Blank text boxes can be left on the drawing to provide a placeholder for future text. The blank text box has a rectangular border that contains an X; the border and the X are both removed when you add text. If spaces are added to a text box, the text box becomes invisible, although you can select it if you know where it is, or you can box select an area. When you move the cursor over the text box, the cursor will display the note symbol.

While typing a note, you can stretch the box larger by using any corner handle, as shown in Figure 26.2. You can make the box taller, wider, or narrower. The note box won't resize smaller if the text string it contains does not contain spaces.

You may also notice that there is a section of the Note PropertyManager called Wordwrap, which when enabled, drives the specific width of the wrapped text box. This can help you be precise or consistent if you want several notes to look the same and need something better than dragging the width of the text box visually.

FIGURE 26.2

Resizing a text box using
the lower-right
corner handle

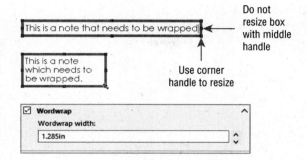

If a custom property value is used to populate a note and you select the Annotation Link Variables option in the Views dialog box, when you activate the text box to resize it, the text value goes away and the link variable is displayed. This makes it difficult to dynamically resize the box to fit the note, so it might be best to deselect the Annotation Link Variable option before placing and sizing notes.

USING FIT TEXT IN NOTES

The Text Format panel of the Note PropertyManager, shown in Figure 26.3, contains the justification buttons for note text, but it also has a Fit Text option, and some tools that aren't available on the Formatting toolbar. When the Fit Text button is depressed, changing the width of the text box changes the width of the individual characters.

FIGURE 26.3

Stretching the characters
in note text by
using Fit Text

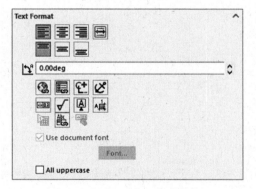

Figure 26.4 shows the Note PropertyManager when you are editing text. When you are creating the note, the vertical justification buttons (below the horizontal justification buttons) are not displayed. They are called (from left to right) Top Align, Middle Align, and Bottom Align.
Notice also the All Uppercase option, which can save a lot of time.

PATTERNING NOTES

You can pattern notes in linear and circular patterns. Figure 26.5 shows the Linear Note Pattern PropertyManager. It looks very similar to the Sketch Pattern PropertyManager.

FIGURE 26.4
Using the vertical
justification
options in a note

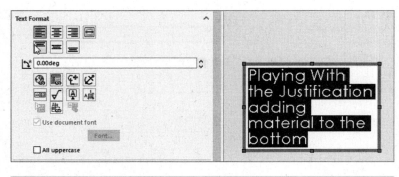

FIGURE 26.5
Patterning a note

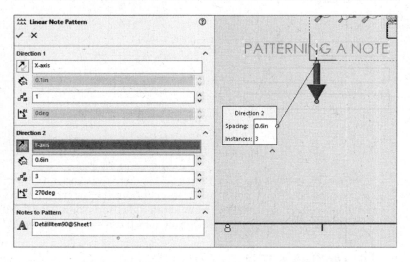

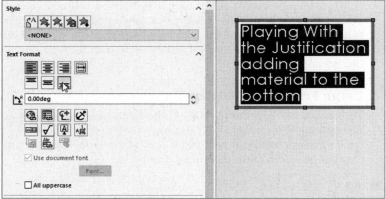

After the note is patterned, you can change individual pattern instances. Changing a patterned note doesn't work the same as changing a regular note. In a regular note, you double-click to activate it and type to replace the note contents. With a patterned note, you have to activate it, click again to deselect the text, press Delete or Back to remove the text, and then type new text.

Circular patterns work similarly to linear patterns, and they work like circular sketch patterns, with the same editing limitations.

Placing Notes and Leaders

When you start to place a note, a preview shows the text box with or without a leader, depending on the position of the cursor. If the cursor is over a blank section of the drawing, the note is placed without any leader. If the cursor is over a face, edge, or vertex, then a leader is added using the arrow found in the Attachment dialog box at Tools ➤ Options ➤ Document Properties ➤ Annotations ➤ Attachments. By default, a leader attached to a face uses a dot as an arrow, and a leader attached to an edge, sketch entity, or nothing at all uses a regular arrow. You can change these defaults at the options location mentioned previously, and you can change individual note leaders in the PropertyManager that becomes available when you select a note. These settings can also become part of a custom drafting standard.

Figure 26.6 shows the preview that displays by the cursor when you place a note over a face or blank space on the drawing.

FIGURE 26.6
Placing a note with a leader

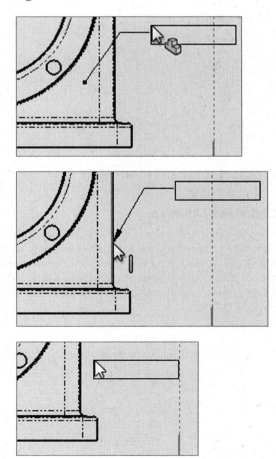

You can also change settings for bent leaders by choosing Tools ➤ Options ➤ Document Properties. You should use the same bent leader lengths for all annotations and save them in the templates that you use.

Clicking inside an active text box places the cursor between letters, as expected. Double-clicking inside an active text box selects the entire word that you click, again as expected. Ctrl+A selects all the text inside a text box. If you double-click an existing note to activate it, the entire contents will be highlighted immediately. You cannot drag and drop selected text to move it within a text box. However, you can Ctrl+C, Ctrl+X, and Ctrl+V the text.

To format the entire note, don't activate the text box; instead, select only the border of the note, and apply the setting to the entire note rather than to selected text within the note.

ADDING A LEADER TO A NOTE

To add a leader to a note that was created without a leader, click the note and select the leader options in the Leader panel of the PropertyManager, as shown in Figure 26.7. After you add the leader, you can reposition the handle at the end of the leader to attach it to an entity on the drawing.

FIGURE 26.7
Options for adding a
leader to a note

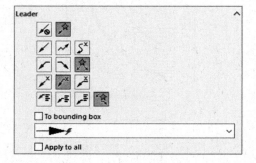

USING MULTIPLE LEADERS

You can also attach multiple leaders to notes. To create a new note with multiple leaders, preselect the entities to which the leaders are to be attached and then click the Note toolbar button.

To add a leader to an existing note, first click the note, and then Ctrl+drag the handle or small dot on the end of a leader to the second location. A note with multiple leaders is shown in Figure 26.8. To remove one of multiple leaders from a note, click the handle at the end of the arrow and press Delete.

FIGURE 26.8
A note with
multiple leaders

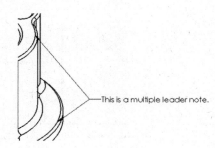

USING JOGGED LEADERS

You can switch a regular leader to a jogged leader by selecting an option in the PropertyManager shown in Figure 26.7, the second icon in the second row is the Jogged Leader icon.

After you activate the Jogged Leader option, you can add a jog point from the leader right mouse button (RMB) menu. Notice in Figure 26.9 that two options give you control over the jogged leader—Insert New Branch and Add Jog Point.

FIGURE 26.9
Jogging a leader

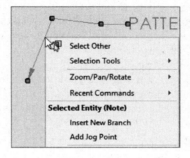

ADDING A JOG POINT OR ADDING A BRANCH

Selecting the Add Jog Point command adds a new handle to the leader that you can move around. You can add multiple jog points to the leader.

Also, you may notice that both Add Jog Point and Insert New Branch are available on regular leaders, without the Jogged Leader option enabled, although it shows up in different sections of the RMB menus. Why is this? That may be a question for your support technician.

ALIGNING NOTES AND BALLOONS

When you drag notes on a drawing, trying to align them, be aware that all the notes must be on the same level, meaning in the view, the sheet, or the format. You cannot align a note on the sheet with another note in a view.

When you select a note, nine small gray dots display around the note and in the center. They may be difficult or impossible to see, depending on the color of your sheet. The one closest to your cursor will highlight orange. When you click to drag the note, the selected dot will align with other dots in the same position from other notes. When the alignment snaps, a yellow inference line will appear, showing the relationship between the notes that are snapping to alignment. So, if you drag the center dot, you see inference lines to other center dots. If you drag the lower-left corner dot, lower-left corner dots highlight from other notes. Again, the inference lines may be difficult to see against the light-colored background of your drawing sheet.

Balloons are notes with a circular border. If you go to the Border panel in the Note PropertyManager, you can apply several types of borders to make a note into a balloon. Balloons snap to one another at quadrants, making them easy to stack horizontally and vertically.

Balloons have some additional tools for alignment, such as *magnetic lines*. Magnetic lines enable you to snap existing balloons to the lines and to space the balloons equally over the lines. Magnetic lines are hidden unless you have selected a balloon. Unfortunately, you cannot place a new balloon directly on a line. You have to place it first and then drag it onto the line. Magnetic lines are created and edited like regular sketch lines. To edit a magnetic line, select a balloon that is on the line and then drag the line or the endpoints.

To create a magnetic line, use the icon shown to the left of the previous paragraph on the Annotation toolbar (although it may not be on the toolbar by default—also be aware that the CommandManager Annotation tab does not have exactly the same tools as the Annotation toolbar), or through the menus at Insert ➤ Annotations ➤ Magnetic Line. Magnetic lines must be in the same view or sheet as the balloons that attach to them. So, if you want to align a set of balloons, create the magnetic line with the view activated (borders showing orange). If the line is on the sheet, balloons from the view will not update with the line.

Balloons also have several shapes that can be applied instead of the plain circle or circular split line. Also available are triangle (horizontal bottom), hexagon, box, diamond, pentagon, five-sided flag, triangle flag (vertical side), underline, square, square circle (circle inside a square), and inspection (hot dog shape). When a balloon uses a shape other than a circle, it is often called a *flag*. All of this functionality falls under the Balloon tool.

Balloons are covered in more depth in Chapter 30, "Creating Assembly Drawings."

Adding Styles

For notes, a style can apply a font, an underline, bold formatting, or any other setting from the Formatting toolbar, or the Text Format panel of the Annotation PropertyManager. It can even contain text, wordwrap width, or a link to a custom property. For example, you could store a commonly used note as a style, such as "DO NOT SCALE DRAWING. REFER TO SOLID MODEL FOR REFERENCE DIMENSIONS."

To create a note that uses the style setting from another existing note, preselect the style from the Style drop-down list and then place the note. To change the style of an existing note, select the note and then select the style from the drop-down list. You cannot apply more than one style at a time to a given note.

CAUTION   Sometimes, adding a style to a note can make other changes that you may not expect, such as turning off the leaders if a note has multiple leaders. In particular, if the style is made from a note with a jogged leader, then it turns off leaders for regular multiple leaders. Styles that are created from regular leader notes do not turn off jogged leaders.

Making a change to the leader of a note after you apply the style removes the style from the note, although the formatting remains. This does not apply to adding multiple leaders, only to changing the type of leader.

Applying a style may also remove the ability of the text to wrap, as well as remove any changes to the text box shape. You cannot move the corner of a text box of a note to which you have applied a style.

Styles can be saved in templates and exist only in the document in which they were created. You can share styles from one document with other documents by saving the style as a separate file. Note styles use the extension *.sldnotestl. Other annotation types use their own style file-names and can use the legacy Favorite file types as well. After you save the style, you can load it into other documents. The Style panel of the Note PropertyManager interface is shown in Figure 26.10.

FIGURE 26.10
The Style panel of the
Note PropertyManager
interface

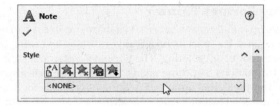

These annotation types can use styles:

◆ Note

◆ Dimension

◆ Weld Symbol

◆ Surface Finish

◆ Datum Feature

◆ Datum Target

◆ Balloon

◆ Auto Balloon

◆ Stacked Balloon

◆ Center Mark

Every type of annotation has two of its own file types for saved styles. Styles used to be called *favorites*. So, for example, notes use the two file types `*.sldnotestl` and `*.sldnotefvt`. Weld symbols similarly use `*.sldweldstl` and `*.sldweldfvt`.

Hole callouts use a different system and cannot utilize the style functionality.

The Style panel contains the following buttons:

◆ **Apply Defaults:** Removes style settings from the current interface, setting all values back to the defaults

◆ **Add or Update Styles:** Either adds a new style to the database or changes the name or other settings for an existing style

◆ **Delete Style:** Removes a style from the database

◆ **Save Style:** Saves a style to an external file, which can be loaded by other users and added to their databases

◆ **Load Style:** Loads a saved style file

Styles can be loaded into document templates so that, for every document created from the template, those styles will be available.

Using Format Painter

The Format Painter is a tool that enables you to copy visual properties between dimensions or annotations. It copies format settings such as text color, bold, and justification, but not underline, strikethrough, or bulleting. The Format Painter tool supports different properties in dimensions and annotations. For dimensions, this tool supports arrow styles, font properties, units, precision, and break line options. For annotations, this tool supports arrow styles and font properties.

To use the Format Painter, click the toolbar icon on the Annotation toolbar, and then select an annotation or dimension with formatting you would like to copy. Then either individually select or window-select annotations and dimensions to which you want the formatting applied.

Linking Notes to Custom Properties

You can link notes to custom properties. The custom properties can be from the drawing or from the model (or selected component/subassembly) that is referenced by the drawing. I mention this kind of link briefly in Chapter 20, "Modeling in Context," but discuss it more thoroughly here.

Figure 26.11 shows a note on a drawing with custom property links pulling data from the model shown on the drawing. To add these links, driven by the syntax $PRPSHEET:"material", click the icon, indicated in Figure 26.11.

FIGURE 26.11
Linking notes to custom properties

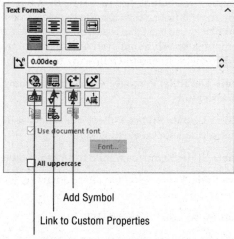

Add Symbol

Link to Custom Properties

Hyperlink text

In this case, text has been combined with custom properties, but custom properties can also appear alone. To access the Custom Properties interface, choose Tools ➤ Properties.

When you activate the note, you may want to see the syntax, or you may want to see the actual text value of the custom property. You can find the setting that controls which one is displayed by choosing View ➤ Annotation Link Variable.

Hyperlinking Text

Hyperlinking text is sometimes useful on drawings to provide a link to reference documentation, specifications, test results, and so on. The first button in the third row of the Text Format panel (refer to Figure 26.11) of the Note PropertyManager enables you to add a hyperlink to text in the note. Either copy the URL to the hyperlink dialog box that appears or browse to it from the dialog box.

Adding Notes and Symbols

Notes and symbols are regularly combined in SolidWorks. Symbols are discussed more fully later in this chapter, but they're mentioned here because of the frequency with which they're used with notes. In reference to Figure 26.11, the image of the Text PropertyManager shows the Text Format panel, which contains a button to the interface where you can add symbols.

Using Blocks in Drawings

Blocks in SolidWorks can contain sketch elements and notes. When used in drawings, blocks have several common uses, including the following:

◆ You can use standard note blocks for tolerances, disclaimers, or default requirements.

◆ You can put together a mechanism in 2D where each block represents a part.

◆ You can use flow direction for fluid systems.

◆ You can use drawing stamps such as "Not For Release," "Preliminary," "Obsolete," and so on.

◆ You can use symbols for schematics that can be snapped together.

◆ You can save drawing formats as blocks to make them easier to place as a single entity.

Like styles, blocks reside in the document in which they are created, but you can save them to a `*.sldblk` file, load them into other documents, and save them as a part of a document template.

Inserting Blocks

You can apply blocks in several ways, including by dragging from Windows Explorer and by using the Block menus (Insert ➤ Annotations ➤ Block). However, the most efficient way is to access them from the Design Library. Library folders can be established specifically for blocks. Check the setting by choosing Tools ➤ Options ➤ File Locations ➤ Blocks, and then redirect this setting to a library area outside of the SolidWorks installation directory. Figure 26.12 shows the Design Library with a folder containing blocks that are selected. The blocks do not show previews in the window, but the tool tip displays large previews. You can drag blocks from the Design Library onto the drawing sheet.

FIGURE 26.12
Blocks in the
Design Library

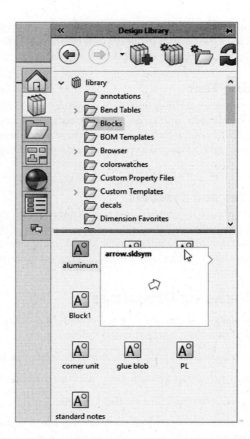

Each block has an insertion point, which snaps to any sketch entity point, even if it is in another block. This makes schematics easy to snap together. If the default insertion point is not the point that you need to snap to the other geometry, then you can place the block anywhere on the drawing and drag the point that needs to snap.

After blocks are snapped together, to detach them from one another, you can click the point at which they touch; a Coincident sketch relation will display in the PropertyManager. Deleting the sketch relation will enable you to drag the block away from the other geometry.

When blocks are inserted, you can control several options in the PropertyManager. This function may be somewhat hidden because it does not appear automatically when you place the block. After you place the block, SolidWorks wants you to place another copy of the block. If you press Esc to cancel out of placing additional blocks, the first placed block won't be selected, so the PropertyManager won't display. Figure 26.13 shows the Block PropertyManager.

FIGURE 26.13
The Block
PropertyManager

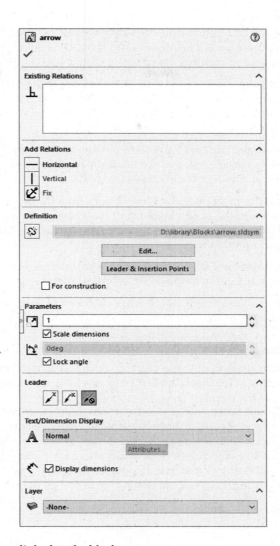

FIGURE 26.13
The Block
PropertyManager

These sketch relations are linked to the block:

Existing Relations: This panel lists the sketch relations that are linked to the block. These relations may cause the block to move improperly when you drag it. This feature is most helpful when the block is being used as a representation of a part in a simulated 2D mechanism.

Add Relations: This panel enables you to quickly select sketch relations to apply when placing blocks.

Definition: Blocks can be linked to an external file, which enables all linked instances of a block to be updated at once, even if they are being used in other drawing documents. The path box for the Link To File option displays only if you select the check box.

Edit: The Edit button refers to editing the block. A toolbar button also exists for editing blocks. Clicking the Leader & Insertion Points button enables you to edit both of the controls. You can select the For Construction option to change the entire block to construction entities.

Parameters: The top field with the two circles to the left controls the scale of the block. This number affects the entire block, including the text. You also have the option to scale dimensions so the dimension text size (not the dimension value) increases with the overall block scale.

Lock Angle: The Lock Angle option refers to the rotation of the block. If the Lock Angle option is not selected, you can rotate the block if one point on it is coincident to a stationary object, such as a vertex in a drawing view.

Leader: You will recognize these options from the Notes leaders. The leader is attached to the block where the angled black handle was placed when you created the block. You can edit the leader connection and insertion points by clicking the Leader & Insertion Points button on the Definition panel.

Text/Dimension Display: The Display Dimensions option controls whether or not any notes and dimensions in the block are displayed or hidden.

Layer: You can assign most entities on drawings to layers, which in turn have controls for items, such as line type, color, and visibility.

Creating Blocks

You can create blocks by selecting the sketch and annotation elements and clicking the Make Block button in the Blocks toolbar, or by accessing the command by choosing Tools ➤ Block ➤ Make from the menus.

By default, when you create a block, the Insertion Point panel of the PropertyManager doesn't expand. If you expand this panel, the blue Origin symbol represents the insertion point that's attached to the cursor during block insertion, as shown in Figure 26.14. The angled line hanging off the left side of the block is the leader attachment point for the block. You can also drag this line around the block and snap it to sketch geometry. By default, this block doesn't use a leader, but if one is required, you can select it when you place the block.

FIGURE 26.14
Creating a block

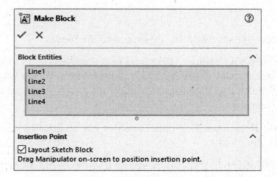

Editing Blocks

Although you have few options when creating blocks, many more options become available when you edit them. You can access editing options for a block from four locations:

- The Edit Block button on the Blocks toolbar

- The Edit button in the Block PropertyManager

- By choosing Tools ➤ Block ➤ Edit from the menus

- From the RMB menu of the block in the Blocks folder in the drawing FeatureManager

The standard edit function gives you access to the sketch and note elements that make up the block:

- **Add/Remove Entities:** While you are editing the block, the Add/Remove Entities button on the Blocks toolbar becomes available. This enables you to add or remove sketch or note entities from the block definition.

- **Rebuild:** Rebuild Blocks reapplies sketch relations within the block, without exiting Edit Block mode.

- **Explode:** Explode is available when you aren't editing the block, but when it's selected. Explode returns the contents of that particular instance of the block to the drawing, removing them from the block. This removes any leaders attached to the block, as well as sketch relations. This is not technically an edit option, but it certainly does change things.

Using Symbols

SolidWorks symbols are different than symbols that are a part of a font family. SolidWorks symbols fall into several categories, including weld, surface finish, hole, modifying symbols, GD&T (geometric dimensioning and tolerancing), and several flag symbols. You can also construct custom symbols.

Using Symbols in Notes and Dimensions

You can use symbols in notes and dimensions. They also are intrinsic parts of weld symbols and surface finish symbols. Hole Callouts use symbols extensively, as do GD&T frames.

Figure 26.15 shows the Text Format panel from the Note PropertyManager from which you can access the Symbol Library. You can also access general symbols from the Dimension PropertyManager.

More specific symbols are available in the respective PropertyManagers of Surface Finish, Weld, and Hole Callout annotation types.

FIGURE 26.15
Accessing symbols and
the Symbol Library

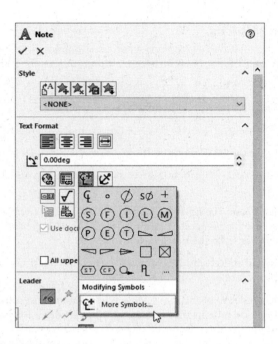

Creating Custom Symbols

You can create custom symbols in SolidWorks. In the lang\english subfolder of the SolidWorks installation directory is a file called Gtol.sym. This file stores the representations of all the SolidWorks symbols. It's also where you can create symbols of your own. You can edit the file in Notepad.

The format for creating symbols is simple enough, but it's somewhat arcane. It's effective at creating line-art symbols that can be used with text and can even be used to contain text. If you're a little inventive with this, you can create interesting shapes that integrate with your notes and dimensions.

Keep in mind that this topic does not appear in the Help files, but all the instructions you need are inside the gtol.sym file itself. You may have to experiment a little to discover what the rules are in terms of making shapes outside of the limits of the 1X1 matrix. It's probably easier to create the geometry using Blocks functionality, but blocks cannot be inserted into text notes as easily as symbols.

Also note that if you modify the gtol.sym file, anyone who uses the drawings you create must also have the same custom gtol.sym file. So, if you actually do this and work in a group environment, make sure everyone uses the same file and it's available to others. This file type cannot be shared on a network, so the gtol.sym file must be local for all users.

Using Center Marks and Centerlines

You can apply center marks either manually or automatically to edges that project as circular in the drawing view. To find the settings that control automatic insertion, choose Tools ➢ Options ➢ Document Properties ➢ Drafting Standard ➢ Centerlines/Center Marks. The size of the mark at

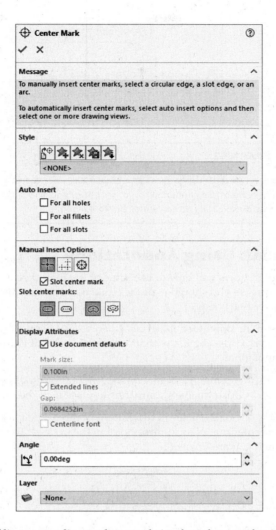

the center and the use of lines extending to the actual circular edge are also controlled on this tab, in the Center Marks section. Figure 26.16 shows some of the options available for center marks.

Center marks propagate well to patterns, and you can dimension to them individually. You can rotate center marks in views where they need to be referenced from an edge that is not horizontal. You can also place center marks into layers.

You can apply centerlines to any geometry that has a temporary axis that is perpendicular to the direction of view. Centerlines can also be placed automatically when you place the part into the drawing. You can create centerlines by selecting a face or a pair of parallel lines or concentric arcs. Centerlines may be displayed improperly on parts that are created by mirroring, as shown in Figure 26.17. This bug was originally printed in Matt Lombard's *SolidWorks 2007 Bible* (Wiley, 2008) and is still active for 2018 sp1.0.

FIGURE 26.17
Centerlines can display
improperly on a drawing
of a mirrored part.

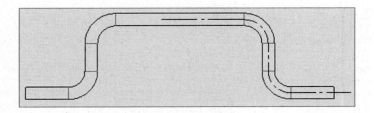

> **BEST PRACTICE**
>
> Dimensions to centerlines should be added last—or when there is no other option. Centerlines in SolidWorks have the tendency to go dangling, and when they do so, they take dimensions with them. The dimensions often cannot be reattached.

Tutorial: Using Annotations

This tutorial shows you how to use some of the tools discussed in this chapter. It doesn't cover every feature, so you should explore a little on your own and not necessarily follow the instructions exactly. Start here:

1. From the download materials, open the file named `Chapter 26 - Tutorial.slddrw`. This is a drawing file with views of the part, but it doesn't contain dimensions or annotations.

2. Click the Center Mark tool on the Annotations toolbar. If the button is not there, choose Tools ➤ Customize ➤ Commands to place it on the toolbar, along with the Centerline tool.

   Click one of the holes in the pattern of three, and click the Propagate symbol to propagate the center marks to all three holes in the pattern. The view should look like Figure 26.18 when you are finished.

FIGURE 26.18
Center marks and
centerlines on a part

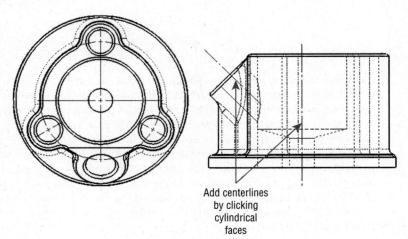

Add centerlines
by clicking
cylindrical
faces

3. Activate the Centerline tool to add two centerlines to the right view in the lower-left area. Change the view display style to Hidden Lines Visible. Select the cylindrical faces for each feature to place the centerlines. Click the vertical centerline and drag the ends past the edges of the part.

4. Select the edge indicated in Figure 26.19 and initiate a note from the Annotations toolbar. Type the text shown, all on one line. You can place the degree and diameter symbols from the Symbol Library, which you can access using the indicated button in the PropertyManager. Both symbols are in the Modifying Symbols Library, also shown in Figure 26.19. Drag the lower-right corner of the text box to make the text wrap as shown.

FIGURE 26.19
Placing symbols in an annotation

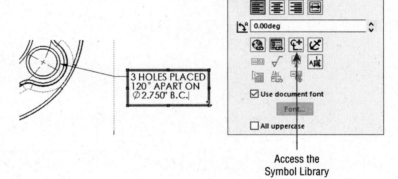

Access the
Symbol Library

5. Draw an arrow with a text note inside it, as shown in Figure 26.20. Make the sketch and text into a block by window-selecting all of it and clicking Make Block from the Blocks toolbar, or by choosing Tools ➤ Block ➤ Make. Make sure that the end of the arrow is its insertion point. You must expand the Insertion Point panel in the PropertyManager to access this option. When the block is set up, accept it by clicking the green checkmark icon. When the block is created, delete it from the drawing.

6. Place the block using the Insert Block function, so the block is to the right of the right view. After you place it, press Esc to cancel the placement of more blocks. Then select the block to activate the PropertyManager. Deselect the Lock Angle option and set the angle to 270 degrees.

FIGURE 26.20
Creating a block

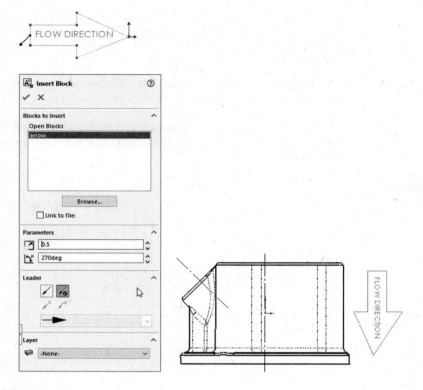

The Bottom Line

Annotations and symbols in SolidWorks have many options for connection, creation, alignment, and display. Recent releases have brought major improvements to text-box-driven annotations. Custom properties and hyperlinks enable the user to populate drawing annotations with content and links to content. Sharing styles in templates is a great idea for readily available note styles.

Blocks have several flexible uses and can be updated from external files across many documents. Their use to simulate mechanisms, piecing together schematics, and annotating drawings, in addition to the Belts functionality discussed in Chapter 3, "Working with Sketches and Reference Geometry," make blocks one of the most flexible functions available.

Master It   Create a note that is typed in with mixed case, and use a centerline symbol (the symbol, not an actual centerline) in it, and a link to a custom property from the drawing.

Master It   Create a style that simply adds bold to a note, and apply it to several notes that don't use bold. Save that style to an external file, create a new drawing using your favorite template, load the style into the template, and resave the template with the new style. Confirm that the new style has been integrated into the format by creating a new drawing with that template, creating a new note, and then applying that style to the note.

Master It

1. Create a blank drawing.

2. Create a note with 10 to 15 words, and then force it to wordwrap with a width of 2 inches.

3. Add a leader to the note.

4. Make it a jogged leader.

5. Copy the note and make multiple leaders for the copy.

6. Use the various justification or alignment options for top, middle, and bottom align, as well as left, center, and right.

Chapter 27

Dimensioning and Tolerancing

Dimensioning and tolerancing is an art form as much as a science. People become very passionate when discussing the right way to perform these tasks. In truth, the techniques are not so black and white, but are highly dependent on the industry, the means of manufacture, and the purpose of the drawing. Drawings might be used for quotes, manufacturing, inspection, assembly, testing, and so on; and the drawings, as well as the dimensioning and tolerancing used, for each purpose might need to be somewhat different in each circumstance.

Although it's important to follow standards and use drawing conventions properly, I have never seen any company follow an ANSI standard 100 percent—and this is not an argument that I want to reignite here. In this chapter, I focus on how the available tools work. You need to decide for yourself how to apply them in each situation.

IN THIS CHAPTER, YOU WILL LEARN TO:

◆ Work with dimensions on drawings

◆ Explore the Dimension PropertyManager interface

◆ Add and activate tolerances

◆ Apply items to dimensions

Putting Dimensions on Drawings

The debate on how to get the dimensions from the model to the drawing is much like the "tastes great/less filling" debate. Each side of the issue has valid points, and the question is not likely to be resolved anytime soon.

At the center of this debate is whether you should place the dimensions that you use to create the model directly on the drawing or whether you should use reference dimensions created on the drawing. In the following sections, I will examine each method for its benefits and drawbacks.

Using Insert Model Items

Insert Model Items takes dimensions, symbols, annotations, and other elements that are used to create the model and puts them onto the drawing. Because these dimensions come directly from the sketches and features of the model, they are *driving* dimensions. This means that you can double-click and change them from the drawing the same way you can change sketch and feature dimensions—and with the same effect. As a result, changing these dimensions even from the drawing causes the parts and assemblies in which they are used to be changed.

You can insert the model items in several ways: on a per-feature basis, bringing only the items that are appropriate into the current view, or bringing items into all views. Insertion can be further broken down by type of item, and it can become as specific as pattern counts, Hole Wizard items, specific symbol types, and reference geometry types. To use Insert Model Items, you can choose Insert ➤ Model Items, or you can access this command from the Annotations toolbar. The Model Items PropertyManager interface is shown in Figure 27.1.

FIGURE 27.1
The Model Items
PropertyManager
interface

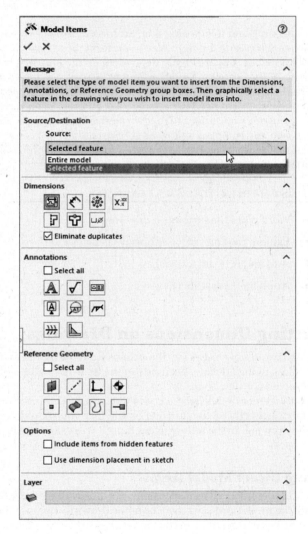

Often, the dimensions need to be rearranged to some extent, although SolidWorks does try to arrange them so they don't overlap. Figure 27.2 shows the result of bringing dimensions into all views for the part. The part is in the download materials for Chapter 27.

FIGURE 27.2

The default placement of dimensions into all views

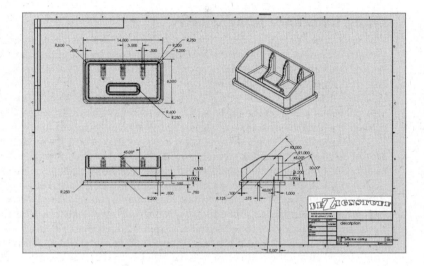

Figure 27.2 contains duplicate dimensions, overlapping dimensions, unnecessarily long leaders, radius dimensions pointing to the wrong side of the arc, dimensions for features you can't see, and lots of awkward placement. This is what you can expect from using the automatic functions. At best, these dimensions need to be rearranged, and a new view needs to be created; at worst, they probably require that you delete and replace dimensions as needed.

You can also import dimensions to specific features in specific views, in which case you would wind up going through the process several times to get the dimensions you need in the views where they are needed. If your company standards require that you must use driving dimensions on your drawings, this is probably the most successful route for you to follow.

To move a dimension to another view, you can Shift+drag it from one view to the other (make sure the dimension is appropriate in the destination view). To copy a dimension, you can Ctrl+drag it. If you cannot place the dimension in the view to which you have dragged it, the cursor will indicate this with a special cursor symbol.

If you approach this task by placing dimensions on a per-feature or per-view basis, it won't change the number of dimensions you must move; it will just mean that you will insert fewer dimensions several times. Keep in mind that if you choose this method, you must perform a significant amount of cleanup and checking. The convenience of having the dimensions put into the views for you and the ability to actually change the model from the drawing are quite useful, but you may not save very much time or effort by doing things this way.

If you design your parts with the same dimensions that will be used for the drawing, inserting model items is definitely the way to go. If your dimensions are driven by parametric or modeling needs, you may be better served by reference dimensions.

The standard ANSI Y14.41 calls for manufacturing dimensions—PMI, or product manufacturing information—to be attached directly to the 3D model. While this standard may not be evenly implemented across all industries, some manufacturers are making use of it now. 3D Views can be placed on SolidWorks drawings, and PMI information can be attached to these views. The complete functionality is found in SolidWorks MBD, which is a separate add-in package and, therefore, beyond the scope of this book.

Using Reference Dimensions

One alternative to automatically inserting all model dimensions is to manually place reference (Smart) dimensions. You create reference dimensions by using the regular Smart Dimension tool. At first, this appears to be simply re-creating work you have already done, and this is somewhat true, but there is more to the story.

These dimensions are not duplicates of the model items. In fact, the reference dimensions that you manually place on the drawing are completely different from the dimensions used in the model. The dimensions serve completely different purposes in the two settings.

When modeling, I tend to dimension in a way that is best for modeling, which is not what would be shown on a manufacturing or inspection drawing. I frequently use workarounds to avoid some special problem that would force a different model dimensioning scheme than I prefer to use. Often, a feature is located from the midpoint of an edge, which involves no dimensions whatsoever. Sketch entities may have Equal relations, which also leave sketch elements undimensioned, but still fully defined. Dimensions may lead to faces or edges that are not in the final model or to faces that are later changed by scale, draft, or fillets. Beyond that, when draft is involved, as is the case with plastic or cast parts, the dimensions of the sketch that you used to create the feature often have little to do with the geometry that is dimensioned on a print for inspection or mold building. Dimension schemes in models reflect the need for the model to react to change, while dimension schemes in drawings reflect the manufacturing or inspection methods in order to minimize tolerance stack-up and to reflect the usage of the actual part.

Although there are strictly technical reasons for dimensioning drawings independently from the way the model was dimensioned, there are other factors such as time and the neat and orderly placement of dimensions. Time is an issue because by the time you finish rearranging dimensions that were inserted automatically from the model—checking and eliminating duplicates and then manually adding dimensions that were left out or that had to be eliminated because they were inappropriate for some reason, as well as ensuring that all the necessary dimensions are on the drawing—it would have been much quicker to manually dimension the drawing correctly the first time using reference dimensions.

In most cases, inserting model dimensions into the drawing is impractical for manufacturing or inspection drawings unless you have simple plates with machined holes, or you have taken extreme care to make sure your model is dimensioned the way you would represent it on the drawing. This is because of the amount of time required to rearrange and check the dimensions, the need to ensure that you have placed the necessary dimensions and taken geometric tolerancing into account, and the simple fact that the dimensioning and sketch relations needed for efficient modeling are usually very different from the dimensioning needed for manufacturing or inspection.

I recommend that you use the manual reference dimension placement option, which works in much the same way as when dimensions are added to sketches. Dimensions that you place in the drawing in this way are called *driven*, or *reference*, dimensions. In drafting lingo, reference dimensions are usually shown with parentheses around them because they are duplicated in some way. In SolidWorks, reference dimensions are simply driven rather than driving dimensions. To find the setting that controls the parentheses around reference dimensions, choose Tools ➤ Options ➤ Document Properties ➤ Dimensions ➤ Add Parentheses By Default.

RAPID DIMENSION

Rapid Dimension offers a manipulator wheel that shows the possible locations of a dimension you are trying to place.

Rapid Dimension works for dimensions inside drawing views, not on dimensions on the sheet. It enables you to choose from either two or four options, and you can move between the options with the Tab key, making your selection with the spacebar. You can also click the manipulator to select an option. In Figure 27.3, the Rapid Dimension manipulator wheel is shown placing the diameter and linear dimensions.

FIGURE 27.3

Placing dimensions with the Rapid Dimension manipulator wheel

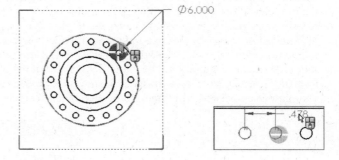

The tool does have some limitations, however. It doesn't seem to be capable of handling combined aligned dimensions or horizontal and vertical dimensions. For example, if you dimension an angled line, Rapid Dimension would only allow a dimension that's aligned to the angled line. If you dimension between the diagonal corners of a rectangle, it wouldn't allow you to place the diagonal dimension, only the horizontal and vertical dimensions.

You can disable the Rapid Dimension manipulator and control some of the other dimensioning assistance tools in the Dimension PropertyManager. This might lead to some confusion, because it seems that there are three separate Dimension PropertyManagers. The one I am talking about here is the PropertyManager that appears when the Dimension tool is active in the drawing. You see a different PropertyManager when the Dimension tool is active in the part and another one when you select an existing dimension on the drawing.

REFERENCE DIMENSIONS AND THE DIMXPERT

I've already made the case for why I think it's better to use reference dimensions on the drawing than model dimensions. This is opinion, of course, and I realize that for many simple parts, you actually *can* model them the way you would detail them, so the model items make more sense in those cases. Many respectable power users insist on using model items on drawings.

Consensus from my own experience and from users I have talked to at companies, user groups, and the forums indicate that this functionality is a work in progress (which was added over 10 years ago). Although it may offer some interesting functionality, it may not save you any time when dimensioning and tolerancing parts on a drawing. It seems that it has particular difficulty with molded or cast parts, which typically don't have parallel faces.

The DimXpert is really meant to dimension 3D parts (with nondriving dimensions), and that scheme is meant to be used as your ASME Y14.41 3D model-based definition to alleviate dependence on detailed 2D drawings and establish the 3D model through the use of 3D PDF or STEP AP 242 as a drawing standard. The use of DimXpert is, therefore, not really appropriate for 2D drawings, although SolidWorks does offer 2D DimXpert functionality. I have yet to meet any SolidWorks users, aside from SolidWorks employees, who are very enthusiastic about the current implementation of DimXpert.

Annotation Views

Annotation views are views in the model in which annotations have been added. You can access annotation views from the Annotations folder in the model FeatureManager. They are created automatically when you add dimensions or notes to the part. You can use the annotation view in the model to show the note or dimension in the view in which it was created or on the drawing to help parse the dimensions into views where they are easily read.

Annotation views can be inserted manually or automatically. You can access the settings for annotation views through the right mouse button (RMB) menu of the Annotations folder of the model, shown in Figure 27.4. The image shows part of the PropertyManager you get when inserting a named view on a drawing. It shows that the front and top views of the model have annotations associated with them (indicated by the A on the view symbol).

FIGURE 27.4
The Annotations
folder RMB menu

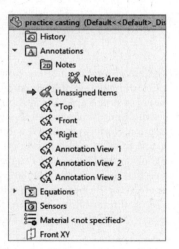

Driven Dimension Color

Driven dimensions on the drawing display in gray, and this can be a problem when the drawing is printed. You can use two methods to deal with this printing problem. The first method is to set the Page Properties of the drawing to force it to print in black and white rather than color or grayscale. To find the Page Properties, choose File ➤ Page Setup. The Page Setup dialog box is shown in Figure 27.5.

FIGURE 27.5
The Page Setup
dialog box

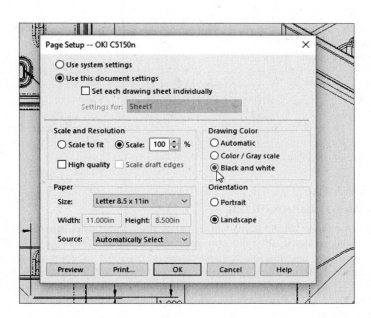

The second method is to set the color for driven dimensions to black (or another dark, saturated color such as dark blue) rather than gray. You can find this color setting by choosing Tools ➢ Options ➢ Color ➢ Dimensions Non-Imported (Driven).

ORDINATE AND BASELINE DIMENSIONS

Ordinate and baseline dimensions are appropriate for collections of linear dimensions when you have a number of items that can all be dimensioned from the same reference. Flat patterns of sheet metal parts often fall into this category. When you apply ordinate dimensions, a zero location is selected first, followed by each entity for which you want a dimension. When dimensions become too tightly packed, SolidWorks automatically jogs the witness lines to space out the dimensions adequately. You can create jogs manually by using the RMB menu. After you create a set of ordinate dimensions, you can add to the set by selecting Add To Ordinate from the RMB menu.

Baseline dimensions are normal linear dimensions that all come from the same reference and are stacked together at a defined spacing. To find the default settings for baseline dimensions, choose Tools ➢ Options ➢ Dimensions ➢ Offset Distances.

Baseline dimensions work best either when they are horizontal or when the dimension text is aligned with the dimension line (as is the default situation with the ISO, standard dimensioning). Vertical dimensions where the text is horizontal don't usually stack as neatly, because the dimension text runs over the dimension line of the adjacent dimensions. Figure 27.6 shows ordinate and baseline dimensions in the same view.

You can access ordinate and baseline dimensions from the Dimensions/Relations toolbar or by right-clicking in a blank space, selecting More Dimensions, and then selecting the type of dimension that you want to use.

FIGURE 27.6
Ordinate and baseline
dimensions in
the same view

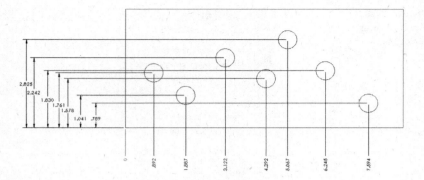

AUTODIMENSIONING

If the Insert Model Items feature is not likely to produce dimensions that are usable in a manufacturing drawing, then the Autodimension feature is even less likely to do so. However, if you use autodimensioning in a controlled way, in the right situations, it can be a valid way to create selected dimensions. The Autodimension PropertyManager is shown in Figure 27.7.

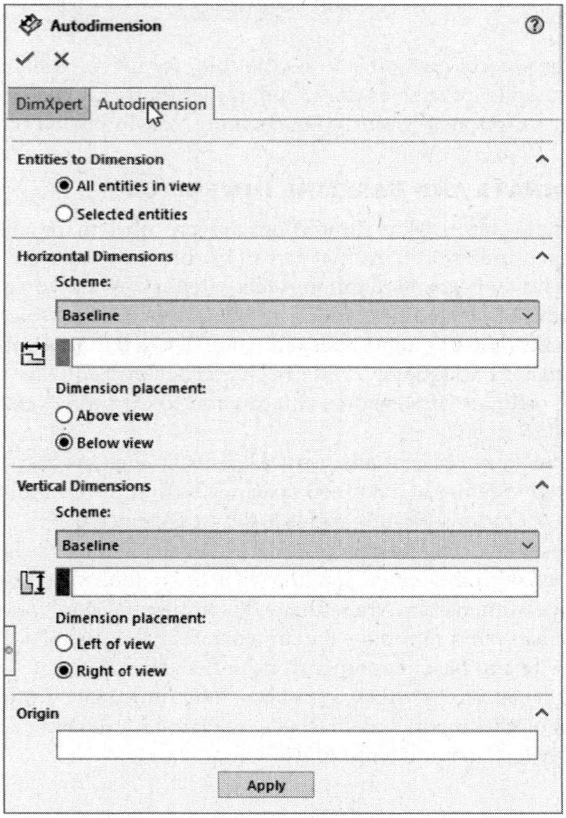

FIGURE 27.7
The Autodimension
PropertyManager
interface

Autodimension is available only in the drawing environment. In the part environment, similar functionality for sketches is part of the Fully Define Sketch tool. To access Autodimension, click the Smart Dimension toolbar icon and then click the Autodimension tab in the PropertyManager.

The Autodimension function can fully dimension the geometry in a drawing view. This is best for ordinate or baseline dimensioning where many dimensions are derived from a common reference, as is often the case with sheet metal parts or a plate with many holes drilled in it. You should limit the use of this option. Don't allow the software to dictate the dimensioning scheme for your drawing.

REFERENCE SKETCHES

For some types of dimensions, you may need to create additional reference sketch entities. For example, with angle dimensions, it may be desirable to add construction lines or points to help define the angle. You can add centerlines as separate axis-like entities, but you can also sketch in centerlines manually if needed. This type of sketch is most often attached to the view rather than the drawing sheet.

TIP Remember that, if necessary, you can create angle dimensions by selecting three points (vertex of the angle first) instead of two lines. When you do this, sketch lines are typically drawn to indicate the vertex of the angle.

You can also create an angle dimension between an angled line and the horizontal or vertical directions. To do this, use the Smart Dimension tool to select the angled line, and then select one endpoint of the angled line for the angle vertex. A set of horizontal and vertical arrows will appear, and you can select the arrow from which you want to dimension the line.

Understanding Dimension Options

The Dimension PropertyManager contains settings, default overrides, tolerances, styles, and several other important settings for use with dimensions. The PropertyManager for driven dimensions is shown in Figure 27.8. I will cover styles and tolerances specifically later in this chapter; the other tabs of the Dimension PropertyManager are discussed in this section.

DIMENSION TEXT

The Dimension Text panel enables you to add text to the dimension. You can add lines of text both above and below the dimension value itself, and you can add text before and after the DIM value on the same line. The DIM field is what places the actual value; if this syntax is somehow deleted, you can type it back in and the dimension will still work.

The Dimension Text panel includes some formatting tools, such as justification settings and a setting for the position of the dimension line. The last two rows of buttons include the more commonly used symbols, with access to the complete library, such as any custom symbols that you may have made for the library.

FIGURE 27.8
The Dimension
PropertyManager
interface

PRIMARY VALUE OVERRIDE

The most infamous habit that former AutoCAD users have is overriding dimension values. Apparently due to popular demand, the Primary Value Override is now available in SolidWorks, in the Dimension PropertyManager, as shown in Figure 27.8. This option was added to the software mainly to enable the creation of dimensions with words instead of numbers, as shown in Figure 27.9.

FIGURE 27.9
Using the Override
Dimension value

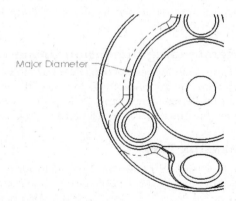

DISPLAY OPTIONS

You can control the default setting for parentheses around driven (reference) dimensions in the Add Parenthesis By Default dialog box by selecting the choosing Tools ➢ Options ➢ Document Properties ➢ Dimensions ➢ Add Parentheses By Default.

Although you can also control dual dimension defaults in the Options dialog box by choosing Tools ➢ Options, you can turn them on and off from this interface for individual dimensions. When you enable the Dual Dimension option, SolidWorks uses the settings from the Tools ➢ Options menu.

NOTE   The Display Options appear on the RMB menu. The options shown in Figure 27.8 are different depending on what type of dimension you have selected. In the images in this chapter, a diameter dimension was used.

The foreshortened radius is valid only for individual radial dimensions. A foreshortened radius is shown in Figure 27.10. Foreshortened radius dimensions are typically used for large radii when dimensions to the centerpoint are not important. The Foreshortened radius function does not work on diameter dimensions. The inspection dimension is shown in Figure 27.10 with an oval around the dimension.

You cannot foreshorten a diameter directly; however, you can create a foreshortened radius and change it to a diameter, or dimension a diameter and then hide the extension line and dimension line in one direction. This option is found by right-clicking both the extension line and dimension line. The RMB menu includes options to hide the extension line and hide the dimension line. This is useful if you have a diameter dimension in a detail view where the opposite side of the diameter is outside the detail view. This can also be used for linear dimensions that terminate to a known end outside the drawing view.

FIGURE 27.10
A foreshortened radius

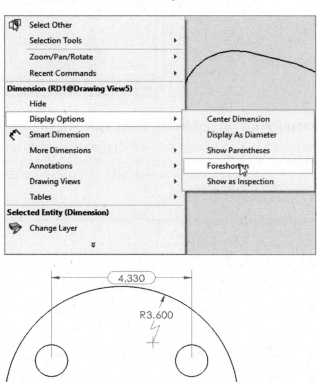

WITNESS/LEADER DISPLAY

This panel enables you to set the arrows and dimension lines to be placed inside the witness lines. You can perform this function more easily by using the handles on the arrowheads. From this panel, you can also change the display type of individual arrowheads.

BREAK LINES

When you select the Use Document Gap option in this panel, the witness, or extension, lines of the selected dimension are broken by other crossing dimension lines, witness lines, or arrows. This is shown in Figure 27.11.

FIGURE 27.11
Broken witness lines

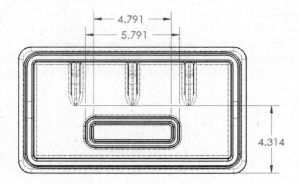

FORMATTING DIMENSIONS WITH THE DIMENSION PALETTE

When you select a dimension on a drawing (the dimension can be a model item or a reference dimension), a small symbol will appear above and to the right of the dimension. If you click the symbol, the Dimension palette will expand. The Dimension palette enables you to do the following:

- Add tolerances
- Specify dimension precision
- Assign styles (favorites)
- Apply parentheses
- Center the dimension between the witness lines
- Apply inspection dimension
- Offset the text with a leader
- Establish horizontal and vertical justification
- Add text on top of, before, after, and below the dimension value

The Dimension palette appears when you select a dimension and disappears when you move the cursor away from it. The Dimension PropertyManager still appears, but the Dimension palette pops up right next to the dimension, making it very easy to use. Figure 27.12 shows the Dimension palette.

FIGURE 27.12
Adding text and tolerances to dimensions using the Dimension palette

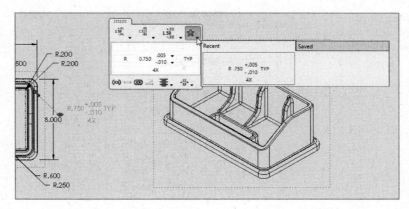

The Dimension palette seems to be the most convenient place to make these alterations to the basic dimension itself. Also, don't forget the Format Painter to copy dimension formatting to multiple other dimensions.

Adding Tolerances

You can add dimension tolerances in the Dimension PropertyManager or the Dimension palette as discussed earlier, which you can activate by selecting the dimension that you want to modify. These tolerance types are available:

♦ Basic

♦ Bilateral

♦ Limit

♦ Symmetric

♦ MIN

♦ MAX

♦ Fit

♦ Fit With Tolerance

♦ Fit (Tolerance Only)

NOTE You can also add tolerances to dimensions in models; the tolerance is brought in with the dimension if you use the Insert Model Items feature.

Refer to the Tolerance/Precision panel shown in Figure 27.8. The appropriate fields for entering numbers are activated when you assign the corresponding tolerance type to the dimension. The tolerance types that are available in SolidWorks are shown in Figure 27.13.

FIGURE 27.13
The available tolerance types in SolidWorks

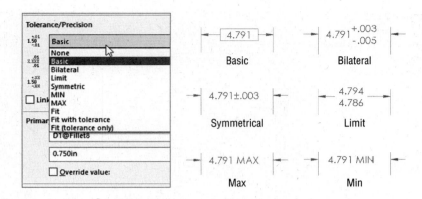

In addition to these tolerance types, SolidWorks offers a range of Fit tolerances from C8 through X7, as shown in Figure 27.14.

FIGURE 27.14
The Fit tolerances available in SolidWorks

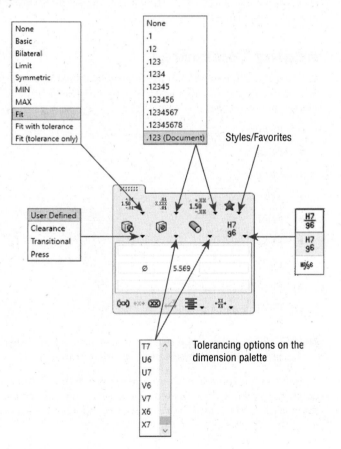

Changing Precision Values

In SolidWorks, *precision* means the number of decimal places with which dimensions are displayed. Typically, SolidWorks works to eight places with meters as the default units. You can create templates that use up to eight places as the default setting and then change the number of places for individual dimensions as necessary. The first of the two boxes under Precision is used for the dimension precision, and the second is used for tolerance precision.

You can change Precision values for individual dimensions in the PropertyManager for the dimension as well as the entire document by choosing Tools ➢ Options ➢ Document Properties ➢ Units.

Using Geometric Tolerancing Symbols

The full range of Geometric Tolerancing symbols is available for control frames, datums, datum targets, and so on. You can use the Geometric Tolerance dialog box to build control frames. This dialog box is shown in Figure 27.15. For commonly used Geometric Tolerance symbols, you may want to create and use styles.

FIGURE 27.15
The Geometric
Tolerance settings

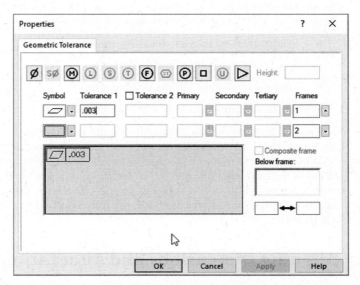

I'm not pretending to teach GD&T tolerancing in this chapter, I'm just presenting the tools SolidWorks provides to help you make it happen. The SolidWorks tools were created in step with the appropriate U.S. and international drawing standards. If your company follows somewhat different practices, or you feel you cannot meet your requirements with these tools, I can suggest a couple of things. Before you do anything drastic, you should pull together expertise on both sides of the issue. Sit down with a SolidWorks GD&T expert *and* an industry GD&T expert along with your own company's standards expert to understand where the real differences lie.

1. Get as close to your requirements as possible with the tools available.

2. Alter your requirements to match the capabilities of the tool.

3. Get another tool that meets your requirements.

Counting on SolidWorks changing the software to meet your drafting requirements is probably not going to be productive, unless you can show that SolidWorks has misinterpreted the ASME or ISO standards, and even if you can, that may take some time. Just to be practical, some flexibility may be required to keep your drawing production moving along without reinventing either your process or replacing the tools you use in your process. I have never been to a single company that really follows any of the standards 100 percent. There is always some local customization.

Using Dimension Styles

You can use dimension styles to apply many items to dimensions. Styles were formerly known as *favorites* in SolidWorks. Unlike notes, dimension styles are not limited to fonts and formatting. Here are some of the most common uses for dimension styles:

- To add standard tolerances to dimensions

- To set precision values for dimensions

- To add text, such as TYP, to a dimension

- To add a commonly used GD&T (geometric dimensioning and tolerancing) reference

You can save styles from one document and load them into another document, even between document types. For example, you can load part dimension styles into a drawing.

When a style is updated from an external file, any document that it's linked to also updates the next time it's opened. In addition, you can break links to external styles (with the appropriate button on the Styles panel). Otherwise, dimension styles have very similar functions to the other types of styles; the functions of all the buttons on the Styles panel are the same.

Aligning Dimensions and Annotations

When you place dimensions and annotations on a drawing, it is nice to have them lined up in an orderly way. Drawings contain lots of information, and that information must be easy to read. Keeping items lined up in horizontal and vertical alignment is one of the keys to making the information on a drawing easily accessible.

SolidWorks has a toolbar just for the alignment of dimensions and annotations. The toolbar is shown with labels for individual icons in Figure 27.16. To add the Align toolbar to the CommandManager, right-click one of the CommandManager tabs and select Customize CommandManager. Then click the new tab that appears and select the Align toolbar from the list.

FIGURE 27.16
Using the tools from the
Align toolbar

Using the Alignment Tools

The alignment tools are all preselect tools, so it's best to box select (or Ctrl+select) the dimensions and annotations you want to align first and then click the toolbar icon. For example, to align a set of balloons to the right, you would drag a box around the balloons, Ctrl+select any balloons you couldn't select with the box, and then click the Align Right button (although ideally with balloons, you can use Magnetic Lines). These tools work best with larger selections of dimensions or annotations. For aligning individual dimensions or pairs of dimensions, it might be better to use the drag methods discussed in the next section "Inferencing Alignment and Grid Snapping."

Using the Align Collinear/Radial and Align Parallel/Concentric alignment tools creates persistent relationships, so those dimensions aligned with the tools will maintain that alignment. The other tools on the Align toolbar don't work this way. To break an alignment created by these tools, select Break Alignment from the RMB menu.

Using the Group tool allows a set of dimensions and annotations within a single view to maintain their spatial relationships. They remain in those relative positions until they are ungrouped.

Inferencing Alignment and Grid Snapping

When you drag individual dimensions on a drawing, they are snapping to a grid. (Annotations don't snap to the grid.) This is one way that SolidWorks helps you to align them. If you drag one dimension level with another, either horizontally or vertically, a line appears and the dimension inferences the position of the other dimension, just like lines snapping in model sketches.

Annotations will inference other annotations, but they won't inference dimensions, and they won't snap to the grid.

If you want to disable both kinds of snap (grid and inference) on the fly, just hold down the Alt key while dragging, and the dimension or annotation will slide freely. To permanently disable the snapping, go to Tools ➤ Options ➤ Drawings ➤ Disable Note/Dimension Inference. To disable the snap, make sure this option is selected. You should be aware that this option controls both the snap to the grid and the inferencing of one dimension or annotation to another. You cannot separate the grid from the inferencing.

If you like the snaps and want to change the spacing, you can do that by selecting Tools ➤ Options ➤ Document Properties ➤ Dimensions ➤ Offset Distances and changing the appropriate numbers for the distance of the dimension from the edge of the part and the distance between dimensions.

If you want a group of dimensions or annotations that you have aligned to maintain their current alignment, box select them and use the Group function from the Align toolbar. All of the selected dimensions and annotations must belong to the same view.

Using Dimension Palette Alignment Options

The Dimension palette, mentioned earlier in this chapter, enables you to surround a dimension with all the necessary information, such as additional text, tolerances, symbols, justification, leader control, dual dimension display, and other useful information. It can also perform some alignment functions. If you multi-select dimensions and activate the Dimension palette, you will see what is shown in Figure 27.17. In this case, the Dimension palette is used to apply the Align Stagger function to a set of vertical dimensions to pack them close to one another. This function isn't found on the Align toolbar. However, notice that it also has some of the Align toolbar functionality, including bottom, top, left, and right justification. The functions have different names and symbols in the Dimension palette than in the Align toolbar, but they appear to do the same thing.

FIGURE 27.17
Selecting alignment options from the Dimension palette

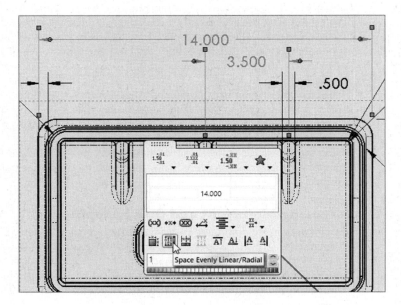

The Dimension palette is one of my favorite tools in SolidWorks drawings because it consolidates lots of functionality into a small space that's available right where you need it. When it was originally released, many users thought it got in the way, but the small activation icon solved that problem, and the functionality has only improved.

Arranging Dimensions Automatically

Every few releases, SolidWorks improves the automatic dimension-arranging tools. But to me, they have a long way to go before I will trust them to arrange dimensions on a large drawing, where they would offer the most benefit. Sometimes, they do a good job on simple rectangular parts, but they don't save much time on the complex parts.

When you put model items onto a drawing, SolidWorks automatically arranges the dimensions. The alignment option on the left side of the Dimension palette is called Auto Arrange Dimensions. Also, when you use the Autodimension function mentioned earlier in this chapter, SolidWorks automatically arranges the dimensions for you.

The best way to use these tools with dimensions and general annotations is in small, controlled situations until you learn how they react to the type of work you tend to do frequently. Selecting items in groups that are close to where they need to go will help the automatic tools do a better job.

Tutorial: Working with Dimensions and Tolerances

In this tutorial, you can use a single part in several different ways to demonstrate different dimensioning and tolerance functions. Follow these steps to learn more about these topics:

1. Open the part from the download material called `Chapter 27 Tutorial.sldprt`.

2. Open the drawing from the download material called `Chapter 27 Drawing.slddrw`

3. Tile the windows by choosing Window ➤ Tile Vertically, and drag the part from the top level of the FeatureManager into the drawing window. This will automatically populate the four drawing views.

4. Delete the top view, leaving the views as shown in Figure 27.18.

FIGURE 27.18

The drawing after step 4

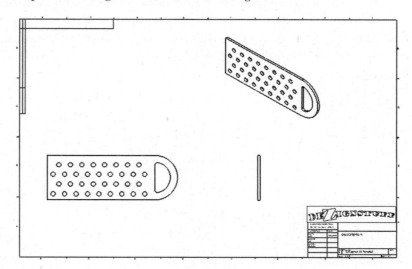

5. Choose Insert ➤ Model Items, and ensure that the Select All option is selected for Annotations and the Marked For Drawing option is selected for Dimensions. Also make sure that the Source/Destination drop-down list is set to Entire Model. Click the green checkmark icon and watch the drawing populate.

6. The resultant drawing is quite cluttered. Delete and move dimensions so the drawing looks like Figure 27.19.

FIGURE 27.19

The drawing after dimensions have been deleted and moved

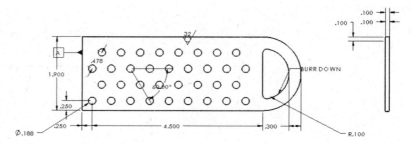

7. Shift+drag the surface finish symbol to the right view, and do the same with the 1.900-inch dimension. You may have to first Shift+drag it into the other view and then drag it again to correctly attach or position it.

8. Create a set of horizontal ordinate dimensions from the left end of the part and dimension the X position of each column of holes. Do the same for rows of holes, using the bottom edge of the front view as the zero reference. Remember that you can create ordinate dimensions by starting a normal Smart Dimension, right-clicking to display the More Dimensions list, and then selecting your choice.

9. If necessary, add center marks and centerlines to the view for clarity.

10. Select the .188 diameter dimension, and in the Dimension Text box, type **TYP** after the <DIM> text, and add a bilateral tolerance of +.003, −.005. Save this as a style by clicking the Add Style icon.

11. Apply the newly created dimension style to the R.100 dimension. The results up to this step are shown in Figure 27.20.

FIGURE 27.20

Dimensions and tolerances after step 11

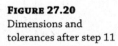
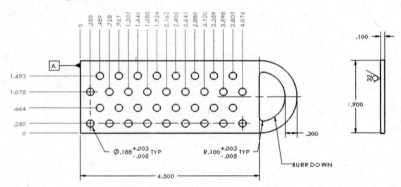

12. Make one of the dimension leaders for either the .188 or the R.100 dimension cross the extension lines of the 4.500 dimension. Then select the 4.500 dimension, and in its PropertyManager, select the Use Document Gap option in the Break Lines panel on the Leaders tab.

13. Place a B datum marker on the circumference of the smaller arc on the left end of the part. Create a Geometric Tolerance control frame, as shown in Figure 27.21.

FIGURE 27.21

Creating a Geometric Tolerance control frame

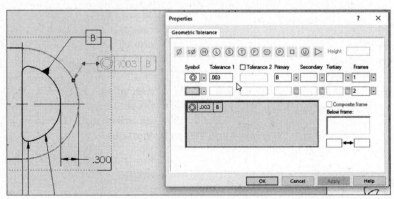

14. In the right view that shows the thickness, select the .100 dimension, and add a tolerance and a note below the text using the Dimension palette, as shown in Figure 27.22.

FIGURE 27.22
Using the
Dimension palette

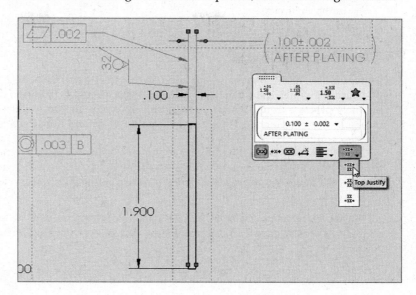

15. Delete the last two dimensions of the horizontal ordinate group (3.837 and 4.076). Start a new detail view that includes the holes those dimensions called out, as shown in Figure 27.23. Place the detail view above the main view.

FIGURE 27.23
Adding more dimensions
and annotations

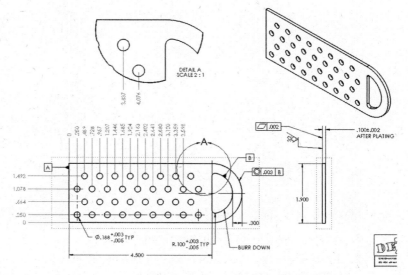

16. Right-click the zero for the horizontal ordinates, and select Add To Ordinate. Place the two ordinate dimensions in the detail view.

17. Use the Geometric Tolerance tool to make a Flatness callout of .002. Add a leader to the control using the PropertyManager and attach the leader to the .100 thickness dimension in the right view.

The Bottom Line

The argument about how to set up and use dimensions on drawings is as old as the process of creating geometrical plans from which objects are built. It's often difficult to separate fact and best practice from opinion. Although I leave it up to you to decide these issues for yourself, this chapter is intended to help you understand how to create the type of drawing you want.

The biggest conflict in this subject arises over whether to place live model dimensions on the drawing or to allow the requirements of the drawing to specify which dimensions are placed where. I am by no means impartial when it comes to this question, but again, you must choose for yourself.

Master It Create a drawing from the part called Simple Part.sldprt in the download material for this chapter. In the front view, shown here, use the DimXpert to dimension the view.

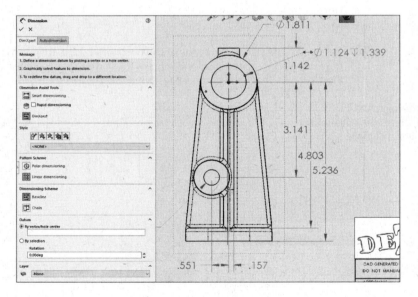

Master It Use the Dimension palette to add text and tolerances to some of the dimensions.

1. Add +/- 0.005 to the 5.236 dimension.

2. Select one of the hole callouts and replace the depth with the word **THRU**. Use the Dimension PropertyManager to do this.

3. Box select the 3.141, 4.803, and 5.236 dimensions and make them inspection dimensions.

Master It In the side view, use vertical ordinate dimensions to dimension some of the prominent features from that view.

Chapter 28

Using Layers, Line Fonts, and Colors

This chapter addresses layers, line fonts, line colors, and other strictly 2D types of functionality within SolidWorks drawings. It's never productive to try to use SolidWorks as if it were AutoCAD, but sometimes there is an overlap in functionality. If you're making the transition from 2D to 3D, you will be much further ahead if you just embrace SolidWorks for what it is and accept that it doesn't work like a 2D-only program.

IN THIS CHAPTER, YOU WILL LEARN TO:

- ◆ Use layers
- ◆ Specify line format settings
- ◆ Hide edges in drawing views

Controlling Layers

Layers are available only in SolidWorks drawing documents, not in 3D modeling or even sketching at all. Even in drawings, layers have not traditionally been used a lot in the formal SolidWorks demo or training materials.

Working with Layers in Imported 2D Data

When you import 2D data through DXF or DWG format files, the layers that exist in the original data are brought forward into SolidWorks, and you can use them in a similar way to the original AutoCAD usage. For example, you can turn layers on or off (visible or hidden), and you can change layer names, descriptions, color, line thickness, and line style.

The way you intend to use the imported data determines how you should open the file. If you only intend to view and print the drawing, then I would suggest using DraftSight, a free download from the Dassault Systèmes or SolidWorks websites. It offers a familiar interface for the AutoCAD user.

If you need to integrate data from the imported document into a native SolidWorks drawing, you can open the DWG file from the normal Open dialog box in SolidWorks.

TIP If you want to make a 3D part from the 2D data in the DWG file, you may want to import the drawing into the part sketch environment. This often leads to some speed issues, depending on the number of sketch entities in the imported file. If you prefer, sketch entities can also be copied from the drawing to the model sketch. You can even copy entities from DraftSight to the SolidWorks sketch. The sketch must be open in order to paste the sketch entities. In the case where imported 2D data is brought into the model sketch, you lose all the layer information because part and assembly documents do not allow layers.

The colors assigned to layers in data coming from AutoCAD are often based on a black background, so they can be difficult to see on a white background. SolidWorks does not have an automated tool that makes sure you have contrasting background colors. The two ways of dealing with this are to change the SolidWorks drawing sheet color to something dark or to change the individual layer colors to something dark. Both methods are easy, although if you have to send the 2D data back to its source, it might be best to temporarily change the drawing sheet color.

Figure 28.1 shows the layer interface with an imported drawing in the background. To open the Layers dialog box, click the Layer Properties button, which is found on both the Layer and Line Format toolbars.

FIGURE 28.1
The Layers dialog box and the Layer toolbar

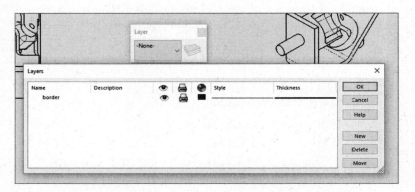

Be aware that many items in an imported drawing may come into SolidWorks as blocks. These items may need to be exploded before you can work with them. This is often the case with the drawing border, title block, or format. To explode a block, right-click the block and choose Explode.

Working with Layers on the Sheet Format

One of the most obvious uses of layers is for the drawing border sketch lines on the sheet format. The sketch lines used to create the border often have a heavier line weight and a different color that easily distinguishes them from model geometry.

You can assign layers in three ways:

◆ Select existing items, and then select a layer from the drop-down list on the Layer toolbar.

◆ Set the active layer and create new items.

◆ While creating items such as sketch entities and annotations, select the layer for the new entity directly from the PropertyManager.

To set a layer to the active layer, double-click it from the Layers dialog box (refer to Figure 28.1) or change it from the drop-down list on the Layer toolbar. When you assign an active layer, other newly created entities are also placed on the layer, not just sketch entities. Symbols, annotations, blocks, and other elements can also be put onto layers. If you're not particular about the layering scheme on a drawing, then it may be advisable to set the active layer to None, which is a valid option in the Layer toolbar drop-down list.

When you create a new layer in SolidWorks, the new layer becomes the active layer, and any new items that are added are automatically placed on that layer.

Another option when building a sheet format, or any other drawing function that requires sketching, is to use a special layer for construction geometry. This will enable you to hide the layer when it isn't being used, but it will still maintain its relations. Hidden layers can be used in several other ways (for example, as standard notes on the drawing), and they can be easily turned on or off.

Adding Dimensions and Notes to Layers

SolidWorks drawings have a tendency to be drab black-and-white drawings in contrast to AutoCAD drawings, which often seem to take on a plethora of contrasting colors. Drawings are often easier to comprehend when different types of items are colored differently, but to do this effectively, you must apply the coloring scheme consistently. Dimensions and annotations can also be placed on layers in the three ways described in the preceding section (active layer, from the PropertyManager during creation, and through the drop-down list on the Layer toolbar). However, the line styles don't affect dimensions and notes, only the color and visibility settings.

Working with Components on Layers

Assembly drawings probably suffer the most from the monochromatic nature of most SolidWorks drawings because individual components can be difficult to identify when everything is the same color. This is why SolidWorks users typically color parts in the Shaded Model assembly window. It makes sense that they would want to do the same thing on the drawing.

USING ASSEMBLY COLORS ON DRAWINGS

You can use assembly part colors on drawings. This is a document-specific setting, so it applies only to the documents where you want it to apply, not to all drawings, unless you have saved the setting in a template. If you use this setting, you may also need to be more careful in how you choose part colors in your assemblies. You will generally want to choose darker and more saturated colors, and avoid the yellows, grays, and light colors that won't contrast with the white or gray color of the default SolidWorks drawing sheet.

You can find the setting to use assembly part color on your drawing at Tools ➤ Options ➤ Document Properties ➤ Detailing ➤ Use Model Color For HLR/HLV In Drawings. HLR stands for *hidden lines removed*, and HLV stands for *hidden lines visible*. These are the two Wireframe display modes that are most frequently used on drawings. Of course, another way to display part color on drawings is to use shaded views, but for traditional drawings, shaded views are often considered nonstandard. Figure 28.2 shows the setting in the Document Properties dialog box.

FIGURE 28.2
Using assembly part
colors on your drawing

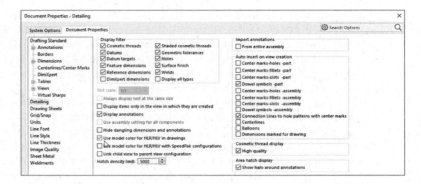

The setting mentioned for Shaded drawing views is available by selecting the view on the drawing and clicking the Shaded Display Style toolbar icon from the Heads-Up View toolbar on the drawing or from wherever the View toolbar is displayed. You could do the same thing by selecting the view and then choosing View ➤ Display ➤ Shaded or Shaded With Edges.

USING ASSEMBLY PARTS ON LAYERS

Another option to display the components of an assembly in different colors while using a Wireframe display mode that doesn't rely on colors assigned to parts in the assembly is to use the Component Line Font options. (Line fonts are covered in this chapter, in the section "Controlling Line Format.") The Component Line Font dialog box contains a Layer setting, which you can use to put a part on a layer. If the layer is set up with a color, the part will display with that color in all views of the drawing or in just the current view, depending on your settings. It takes some time to set up the individual layers for each part and then to set the parts to the layers.

You can access the Component Line Font dialog box by right-clicking a component in a drawing view. The Component Line Font dialog box is shown in Figure 28.3.

FIGURE 28.3
The Component Line
Font dialog box

In normal use, the Use Document Defaults option is selected and all the settings in the dialog box are grayed out. To gain access to these settings, you must deselect the Use Document Defaults option, as shown in Figure 28.3.

Controlling Line Format

 The Line Format toolbar contains the Layer tool and four additional tools that control lines: Line Color, Line Thickness, Line Style, and Color Display Mode. There is no actual setting or tool called *line format*. These settings can be controlled separately from layers; therefore, they can be used in model sketches as well as on drawings. In the model, the line font can be displayed only for inactive sketches. Any sketch that is both closed and shown can be displayed with the Line Format settings.

Figure 28.4 shows the Line Format toolbar along with the interfaces for Line Color, Line Thickness, and Line Style.

FIGURE 28.4
The Line Format toolbar and related interface options

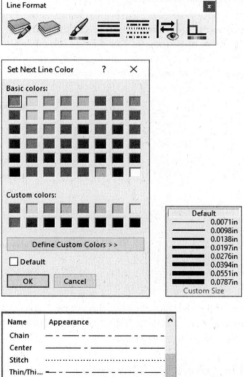

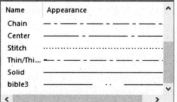

NOTE The term *line font* refers to a combination of style, end cap, and thickness. To set line fonts, choose Tools ➤ Options ➤ Document Properties ➤ Line Font and use the document-specific settings.

Using the Line Format Settings

You can specify the Line Format settings using two different methods. In the first method, you can set them with nothing selected, in which case they function like System Options (the new setting takes effect for all documents that are opened on the current computer). In the second method, if they are set with sketch entities or edges selected, then the settings apply only to the selected entities.

CAUTION If you change these settings with nothing selected, the Line Format settings for color, thickness, and style will function as system options.

Setting the End Cap Style

Another option for the Line Font settings is the End Cap Style. This offers an important option, especially for thick lines. The three options are flat, round, and square. Of these, the square style is usually most appropriate. To find this setting, choose Tools ➤ Options ➤ Document Properties ➤ Line Font. You may want to change this setting and update your drawing template files.

Figure 28.5 shows the difference between the three options of End Cap Style.

FIGURE 28.5
The End Cap Style setting options

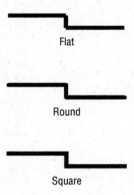

Flat

Round

Square

Notice the small notches at the sharp corners of the flat style. These can be very distracting on a drawing and, in my opinion, they don't look very professional. This notched effect is most pronounced on thicker lines.

Setting the Line Thickness

The Line Thickness settings are Default, Custom, and eight width settings. Interestingly, the different thicknesses are named in the interface where you set the actual thicknesses, but not in the interface where you set lines to thicknesses. Figure 28.6 shows the Line Thickness page (Tools ➤ Options ➤ Document Properties ➤ Line Thickness).

FIGURE 28.6
The Line Thickness settings in Tools ➤ Options

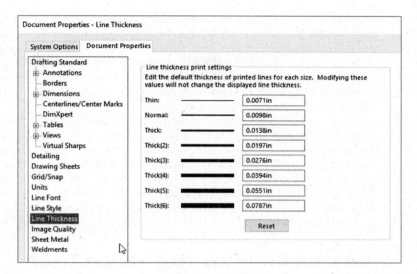

The way the line thickness is shown in the drawing has nothing to do with the numerical width that is assigned to it. For example, in Figure 28.6, notice that Thick(2) is set to 0.0197 inch, which is much wider than Thick(3), which is set to 0.0276 inch in this case. Changing the numbers affects only printed line thickness; it doesn't affect the display at all.

CAUTION The Line Thickness settings are document options, not system options. As a result, two drawings with the same line type assignments may have different numerical widths; therefore, the two drawings would print differently on the same computer. This can be a benefit or a trap, so pay attention when you change the settings.

Setting the Line Style

You can create custom line styles using the syntax shown on the Line Style page (Tools ➤ Options ➤ Document Properties ➤ Line Style). This is a document-specific setting; therefore, if you make a custom line style and want to use it in another document, you have to save it (as a *.sldlin file) and load it into the other document. Also, if you save your templates with this line style loaded, you won't have to load the styles for any document made from that template.

Changing the Color Display Mode

Color Display mode toggles between the display of assigned colors and standard sketch state colors. This is primarily used in drawings when you're making sketches where sketch relations are important. This setting is used to control the display of sketch entities only.

Hiding and Showing Edges

Sometimes, for illustrative purposes, it's desirable to hide certain edges in drawing views. The Hide/Show Edge button is on the Line Format toolbar, although it may not be on the toolbar by default. You can choose Tools ➤ Customize to put it on a toolbar. To display an edge after it has been hidden, right-click where it should be and use Hide/Show Edge from the RMB menu.

To use the Hide Edge tool, simply select the edges you would like to hide and click the Hide Edge button. To show the edges, click the Show Edge button; the hidden edges will display in orange. Selecting them at this time will display them when the command is complete.

Be aware that if your view is in Draft Quality, any edges you hide will still be shown until the view is made into a High Quality view. Also, be aware that child views may take on the display properties of their parent views, so you may have to set the main view to High Quality before the hidden edges will display (or not) properly.

You might also want to be aware of a setting under Tools ➢ Options ➢ Drawings ➢ Automatically Hide Components On View Creation. This setting hides components that are not visible in the view. Although it doesn't intuitively make sense, it allows SolidWorks to save time calculating hidden edges by simply hiding the entire component. This can save a lot of time; however, if you're not aware of what's happening and are not accustomed to looking in the Hide/Show Components area for hidden parts that were hidden automatically, it can lead to some frustration if the view changes or you add a break-out view, and the automatically hidden parts suddenly become visible. There is no automatic function to unhide these components.

Tutorial: Using Drawing Display Tools

Some of the functions described in this chapter are difficult to understand until you actually use them. This tutorial guides you through the functions step by step so you can see them in action. Start here:

1. From the download material, open the drawing called Chapter 28 - Tutorial.slddrw. Make sure that the Layer and Line Format toolbars are active and that the Hide/Show Edges buttons are available on the Line Format toolbar.

2. Right-click a blank space and select Edit Sheet Format from the menu.

3. Window+select (or Ctrl+A) everything on the format, and use the drop-down list on the Layers toolbar to assign the selection to the Border layer. Notice that this changes the color and the thickness of the sketch lines.

4. Right-click a blank space and select Edit Sheet.

5. Click the Layer Properties button on either the Layer or Line Format toolbar. Add new layers for each of the part groups, bracket, clevis, pins, and blocks, assigning different colors to each layer. Figure 28.7 shows the Layers dialog box with these layers created. Assign a different color to each new layer, preferably something that will contrast against white.

FIGURE 28.7
The Layers dialog box

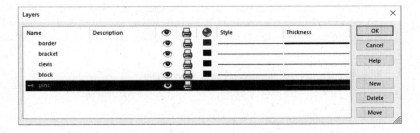

CAUTION   Be aware that creating new layers leaves the last layer that you created active, as indicated by highlighted row in Figure 28.7. You cannot set the active layer to None from the Layers dialog box; you must do this using the drop-down list in the Layer toolbar.

6. Set the active layer to None in the Layer toolbar drop-down list and exit the Layer dialog box.

7. Right-click the Bracket part in one of the views and select Component Line Font. Deselect the Use Document Defaults option and select the Bracket layer from the drop-down list in the lower-right corner of the dialog box, as shown in Figure 28.8. Make sure that the Drawing View option is set to All Views.

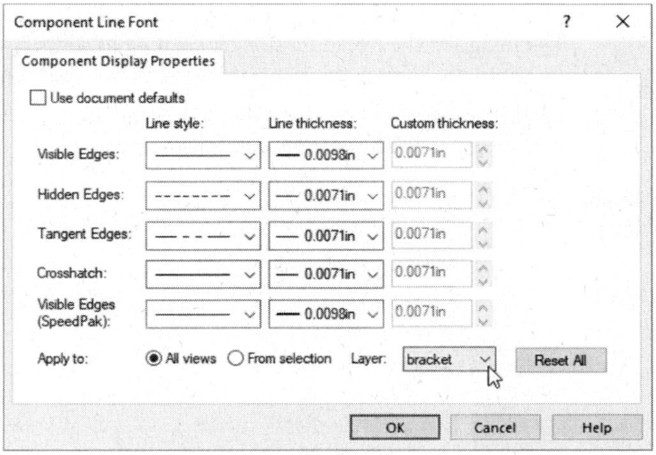

FIGURE 28.8
The Component Line
Font dialog box

8. Repeat step 7 for all the components, assigning each component to its own layer. Notice how this makes the parts easier to identify.

NOTE   Alternatively, you could simply change the line style and thickness for each component. This will save you the trouble of creating the layers, but you will lose the color settings.

9. Open the Component Line Font dialog box for the Bracket part again. This time, set the Line Thickness to 0.0787 and click OK. You may have to rebuild the drawing to show the change (Ctrl+B or Ctrl+Q). Figure 28.9 shows a detail of the corners that are created by the thick lines.

10. Notice the notches created at the corners. These notches are supposed to be fixed using the End Cap setting at Tools ➤ Options ➤ Document Properties ➤ Line Font. Set the End Cap Style to Square. Click OK to exit the Document Properties. In the drawing, select inside the view where you are working, and make sure it's set to High Quality. (The setting is found in the PropertyManager for the view in the Display Style panel. If it's already set to High Quality, there will be no other view option; if it isn't, there will be an option that is set to Draft Quality.)

FIGURE 28.9
Applying thick edges

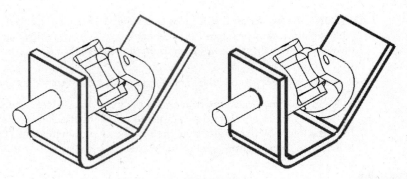

The image to the left in Figure 28.9 is the old setting with the Draft Quality view, and the image to the right is the new setting with the High Quality view.

11. In the Component Line Font dialog box, set the Line Weight setting back to Default for the Bracket part, but keep it on the Bracket layer.

FIGURE 28.10
Hiding edges

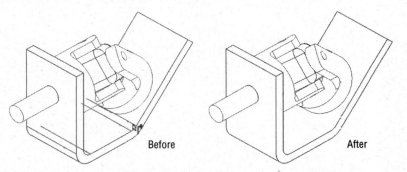

Before   After

12. In the isometric view, Ctrl+click all the tangent edges on the Bracket part, as shown in Figure 28.10. Click the Hide/Show Edges button on the Line Format toolbar.

13. Click the Hide/Show Edges button. The PropertyManager message will change to indicate that you can select Hidden Edges, and the hidden edges will display in orange. Ctrl+select the hidden edges and right-click when you are finished.

The Bottom Line

Although SolidWorks is not primarily built around the strength of its 2D drawing functionality, it offers more capabilities than most users take advantage of. Layers, colors, and line styles can make your drawings clearer and easier to read.

Master It   Create a new drawing from the part called Sample Casting.sldprt in the downloaded materials for this chapter. Make a drawing of it and import the dimensions automatically.

Create a new layer called Dimensions and move all the dimensions to it using box select or the selection filter to help.

Set the color to the new dimension layer as dark blue.

Master It   Create several new annotations and place some blocks from the library.

Create a new layer for annotations and move these entities onto it.

Change the color of the new layer to dark green.

Leave the Annotations layer as the active layer and create a new annotation.

Master It   On the Sample Casting drawing, select a couple of interior edges and hide them using the Hide/Show Edges.

Next select a couple of exterior edges and change the line font to a thicker style.

Chapter 29

Working with Tables and Drawings

SolidWorks enables you to create several types of tables on drawings. Design tables that are used in parts and assemblies can be shown on the drawing to create a tabulated type drawing. Hole tables enable you to chart the center locations and sizes of holes for easy access to manufacturing data. Revision tables help you document the revision history of a drawing. General tables are also available for any specialized items that are not covered by the other table types.

IN THIS CHAPTER, YOU WILL LEARN TO:

◆ Create the Bill of Materials

◆ Insert and display design tables

◆ Use hole tables to describe drawing details

◆ Create and control Revision Tables settings

◆ Employ general tables

◆ Use tables in models

Driving the Bill of Materials

The Bill of Materials (BOM) is one of the most frequently used types of tables that are available in SolidWorks. BOMs are intended for use with assemblies, but you can also use them with individual parts for specialized applications. The information that you can expect to see on a BOM includes item number, filename, quantity used, description, and any other custom property that you would like to add. A typical BOM is shown in Figure 29.1.

BOMs are made in one of two ways: The default BOM is made from a SolidWorks table, while an Excel-based BOM is driven by Excel. You could also create a BOM manually using a general table, but that wouldn't take advantage of any automated functions. Although Excel offers some advantages, the SolidWorks internal table type is preferred. The default Bill of Materials tool on the Drawing toolbar leads to the SolidWorks table. The Excel BOM is available by customizing the interface, but it is no longer the default. Excel and SolidWorks table-based BOMs are not interchangeable, so if you plan to customize the default templates, you need to decide which type of BOM (Excel or SolidWorks) you want to use.

SolidWorks tables are preferred over Excel for several reasons. First, Excel tables have caused a lot of crashes in the past, and removing Excel from the mix here can prevent a lot of lost data. Second, not all companies use Excel, and those who do often use very old versions. Third,

SolidWorks cannot provide enhancements to Excel functionality, especially old Excel functionality. The only way to get all of this was for the SolidWorks software designers to create their own internal tables, which has worked out pretty well. SolidWorks has also provided equivalent tools for design tables, so Excel is no longer a real requirement to get all the functionality out of SolidWorks.

FIGURE 29.1
A sample BOM

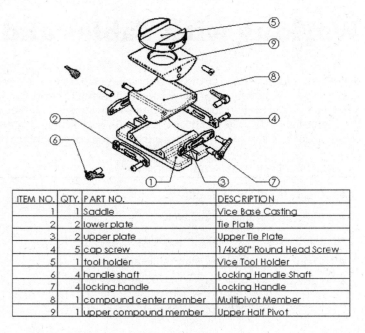

ITEM NO.	QTY.	PART NO.	DESCRIPTION
1	1	Saddle	Vice Base Casting
2	2	lower plate	Tie Plate
3	2	upper plate	Upper Tie Plate
4	5	cap screw	1/4x80" Round Head Screw
5	1	tool holder	Vice Tool Holder
6	4	handle shaft	Locking Handle Shaft
7	4	locking handle	Locking Handle
8	1	compound center member	Multipivot Member
9	1	upper compound member	Upper Half Pivot

NOTE   You can also place BOMs directly in the assembly and even in multibody part files.

Examining the SolidWorks Table-Based BOM

The BOM shown in Figure 29.1 is a default SolidWorks table-based BOM. The differences between the displays of the two types of BOMs are mainly cosmetic; the bigger difference is in the functionality. The PropertyManager interface for the SolidWorks BOM is shown in Figure 29.2.

CREATING TABLE-BASED BOM TEMPLATES

Like other types of data, the SolidWorks table-driven BOM starts from a template. The BOM in Figure 29.1 was created from the default BOM template. When a BOM is initiated, you can select the template in the Table Template panel near the top of the PropertyManager, as shown in Figure 29.2.

You create table-based BOM templates in much the same way that you create other templates:

1. Specify the settings.

2. Delete the document-specific data.

3. Save the template.

4. Access the template from a library location.

FIGURE 29.2
The PropertyManager
for a table-driven BOM

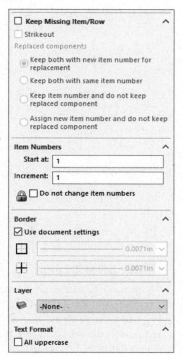

To save the template, right-click the BOM and select Save As. In the Files Of Type drop-down list, select Template (`*.sldbomtbt`). (The extension `sldbomtbt` stands for SolidWorks Bill of Materials Table Template.) Any of the settings, additional columns, links to properties, and so on are saved to the template and reused when you create a new template from it.

SETTING A TABLE ANCHOR

A table anchor locks a corner of the table to a selected point on the drawing sheet format. If you do not select a point in the format, the table is placed at a corner of the sheet. To specify a point in the format to act as the anchor, you must be editing the format. Right-click the sheet and select Edit Sheet Format. Then right-click a sketch endpoint in the format, select Set As Anchor, and specify for which type of table the anchor is intended. You can set different anchor locations for different types of tables. Figure 29.3 shows the selection and menus for this option.

TIP   You should save the format and drawing template with these table anchors specified so that you do not need to respecify them for each new document. If you want to check a sheet format to see what anchors exist, you can expand the sheet format in the FeatureManager of the drawing. The anchors will be listed under the sheet format.

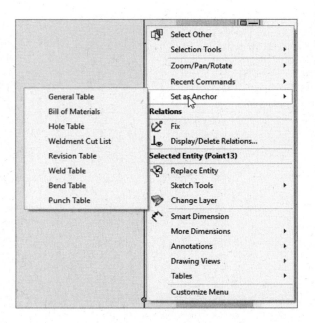

FIGURE 29.3
Setting a BOM
table anchor

USING BOM TYPES

SolidWorks has three BOM types: Top-Level Only, Parts Only, and Indented. As the name suggests, the Top-Level Only BOM shows only components on the top level. It treats subassemblies as a single entry. As a result, if the top-level assembly shown on the drawing is made up of five subassemblies and two individual parts, and you select the Top-Level Only option; then only seven items will be shown in the BOM.

The Parts Only BOM ignores subassembly structure and displays only parts in an unindented list.

The Indented BOM shows the parts of subassemblies in an indented list under the name of the subassembly. This is the most complete list of SolidWorks documents used because it includes all parts and assemblies.

The Show Numbering option for indented assemblies is activated only after you have selected the Indented option and placed the table. When you use this option, it causes subassembly parts to be numbered with an X.Y number system. For example, if item number 4 is a subassembly and it has three parts, those parts are numbered 4.1, 4.2, and 4.3.

USING CONFIGURATIONS

The Configurations panel of the BOM PropertyManager displays slightly differently for Top-Level Only BOMs compared to the other types. The Top-Level Only BOM type enables the option to show multiple assembly configurations and display the quantities for top-level components in separate columns, as shown in Figure 29.4. This figure shows that the configuration named "simplified" has some suppressed parts.

FIGURE 29.4
Configuration options
with the BOM

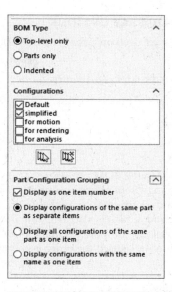

ITEM NO.	PART NUMBER	Default/ QTY.	simplified/QTY.
1	Saddle	1	1
2	lower plate	2	2
3	upper plate	2	2
4	cap screw	5	-
5	tool holder	1	1
6	handle shaft	4	-
7	locking handle	4	4
8	compound center member	1	1
9	upper compound member	1	1

LOCATING THE KEEP MISSING ITEMS OPTION

When you are making changes to a model, parts are often either suppressed or deleted altogether. Some company documentation standards require that parts that are removed from a BOM remain on the bill and appear with strikethrough formatting.

Keep Missing Items and Zero Quantity Display have both been moved to the Tools ➢ Options ➢ Document Properties ➢ Detailing ➢ Tables screen.

CHOOSING ZERO QUANTITY DISPLAY OPTIONS

The Zero Quantity Display settings are used only for configurations where a component isn't used. These three options are available:

Quantity Of Dash: Substitutes a dash for the quantity value

Quantity Of Zero: Uses a zero for the quantity value

Blank: Sets the quantity value to blank

ASSIGNING ITEM NUMBERS

Item numbers for components listed in the BOM can start at a specific number and be given a particular interval. The Do Not Change Item Numbers option means that even when rows are reordered, item numbers stay with their original components.

The Follow Assembly Order option, which is also available through the right mouse button (RMB) menu, means that the order of the components in the BOM follows the order of the components in the assembly FeatureManager. If the order is changed in the assembly, it also updates in the drawing.

EDITING THE BOM

The BOM contents can be changed on the BOM or through the RMB menu. Figure 29.5 shows a simple BOM with the RMB menu. For example, you can drag the row numbers to reorder BOM items and right-click to hide them. Row numbers are displayed only after you select the BOM table.

FIGURE 29.5
The BOM RMB interface

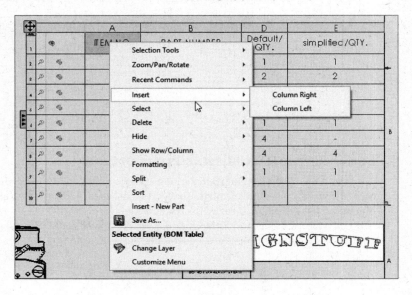

You can add columns or rows to the BOM for additional properties or manually added parts (such as items you wouldn't model, like paint or glue, although virtual components can also be used for this purpose). To change the property displayed in a column, double-click in the column

header. In previous releases, many of the settings and options now found on the RMB menu were found in a more complex Bill of Materials Properties window. The newer arrangement is more intuitive. Most SolidWorks users know to try the RMB menu if they select something and don't find the option they are looking for in the PropertyManager.

CONTROLLING THE APPEARANCE OF THE TABLE-BASED BOM

To move the table, place the mouse over the BOM and notice the border that appears around it. Drag the crossed-arrows icon in the border to move the table. When you select the table, the border will remain, enabling you to move, reorder, RMB, or respace the cells. You can change the properties of a row or a column by selecting just outside of the row or column to the top or the left.

You can establish the spacing and width of rows or columns by dragging the border on the left side of the column with the split cursor or by accessing the Column Width setting through the Formatting option in the RMB menu.

While the selection is activated, you can also expand a panel to the left and another to the top by clicking the three small arrows in the selected BOM border. Figure 29.6 shows the left panel, called the Assembly Structure panel, expanded with the cursor pointing to the three small arrows. In addition to showing the assembly structure, this panel can also show which parts are ballooned on the drawing.

FIGURE 29.6
An expanded
BOM border

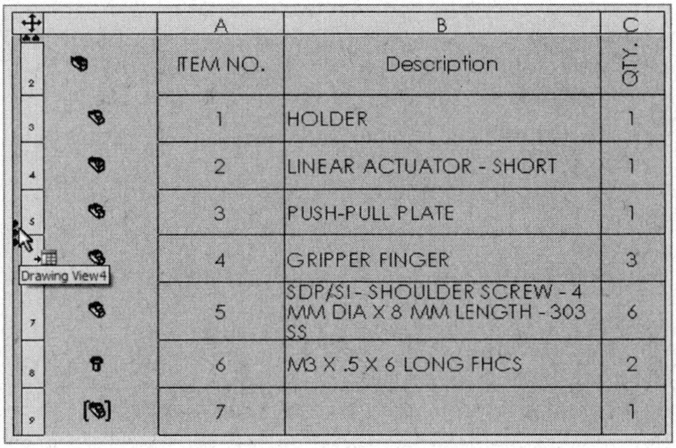

		A	B	C
		ITEM NO.	Description	QTY.
		1	HOLDER	1
		2	LINEAR ACTUATOR - SHORT	1
		3	PUSH-PULL PLATE	1
		4	GRIPPER FINGER	3
		5	SDP/SI- SHOULDER SCREW - 4 MM DIA X 8 MM LENGTH - 303 SS	6
		6	M3 X .5 X 6 LONG FHCS	2
		7		1

Notice item 7 on the BOM, which has a different symbol and no name. This is a virtual component (a component created in context but not saved to its own document file); it exists only within the assembly.

DISSOLVING, COMBINING, NUMBERING, AND RESTRUCTURING FOR INDENTED BOMS

You can dissolve an assembly in the BOM. To do this, the BOM must show an indented list. You can then access the Dissolve option from the RMB menu on the Assembly icon. You can delete any restructuring you have done to the BOM by right-clicking the Assembly icon with red arrows and selecting Restore Restructured Components.

If the BOM shows several parts that are identical, and you would like to combine them, again, you can access the option from the RMB menu.

Item numbers in indented BOMs can be flat (such as 1, 2, 3), or they can be detailed (such as 1.1, 1.2, 1.3, 2, 2.1, 2.2) to reflect parts as members of subassemblies. This formatting option is available in the BOM Type panel in the BOM PropertyManager, under the Indented option.

ADDING COLUMNS OR ROWS

To add a column, right-click near where you want to add the column and choose Insert ➤ Column Right or Column Left. Inserting rows is exactly the same. The next thing you want to do with a column is to assign what kind of data goes into it. You can use a custom property such as Part Weight or Vendor, as shown in Figure 29.7. Access this interface by double-clicking a column header and selecting Custom Property from the drop-down list.

FIGURE 29.7
Establishing the property driving the column content

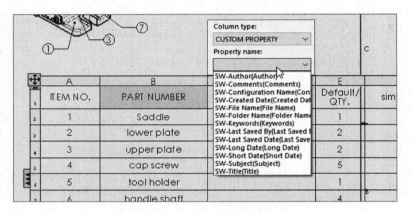

One of the really beautiful aspects of custom property management in the BOM is that if you just type text in a column that is set up to be driven by a part property, SolidWorks will automatically update the part with the property. If the property didn't exist in the part previously, SolidWorks also will create the property. You will need to select the Keep Link option in the popup when it is presented when editing a table in this way to preserve the associative link.

WARNING   To maintain the parametric link between the cell and the component, select Keep Link when the popups appear.

NOTE   If you create a BOM with the columns and properties that you like, you can save it to a template, as described earlier in this chapter.

EDITING BOMs

When you need to manually enter text in a BOM, for example in general tables or custom properties in BOMs, you can use the Tab and arrow keys to move the cursor between cells.

Here's a summary of the Navigation functionality:

Enter: Move to the next cell down.

Tab: Move to the next cell to the right.

Arrow: Move the cursor in any direction.

Shift+Arrow: Increase the selection size.

Shift+Tab: Move the cursor backward.

Shift+Enter: Move the cursor up.

Home: Move the cursor to the first column.

Ctrl+Home: Move to the upper-left corner of table.

End: In combination with the arrow keys, move to the end indicated.

Ctrl+End: Move the cursor to the bottom-right corner of the table.

Here's a summary of the Editing functionality:

F2: Edit the contents of cell.

Double-click: Edit the contents of cell.

Alt+Enter: Add multiple rows to the cell.

Delete: Delete the contents of cell without activating cell.

Backspace: Delete the contents of cell and activate cell.

Ctrl+Delete: Delete one word at a time.

Edit: Edit multiple row heights simultaneously.

Lock: Lock the row height and column width.

Copy: Copy cells from Excel to SolidWorks tables.

Retiring an Excel-Based BOM

In previous releases, Excel-based BOMs were the only way to add a BOM to a drawing. This feature has been replaced in most respects by the SolidWorks native table-driven BOM, but many people still use the Excel-based BOM either out of habit or to comply with legacy standards. Figure 29.8 shows the interface for the Excel-based BOM.

BEST PRACTICE

Unless you have a compelling reason to do otherwise, use the SolidWorks table-based BOM. This function will be best supported in future versions of SolidWorks software.

FIGURE 29.8
The interface for
Excel-based BOMs

Using Design Tables

Design tables that are used to drive the configurations of parts and assemblies can be shown on the drawing. This type of drawing is often called a *tabulated* drawing and is typical of parts that have a basic shape that is common among several sizes or versions of the part. The sizes are shown by a symbol on the drawing, with a column headed by that symbol showing the available dimensions and the corresponding size (configuration) names.

You can insert a design table into a drawing by choosing Insert ➤ Tables ➤ Design Table or by clicking the Design Table button on the Tables toolbar. In either case, you must preselect a drawing view of a part or assembly that contains a design table before the menu selection or toolbar button becomes activated.

Design tables that are displayed in this way are often formatted to some extent. You need to hide columns and rows unless you want the dimension or feature name syntax to display on the drawing as well as the values. Extra columns and rows are often added to make the design table readable.

Figure 29.9 shows the drawing with the table inserted. To display the table properly, you must edit the table in the window of the parent document and adjust the border of the table to be exactly how you want it to appear on the drawing. The adjusted table is shown in Figure 29.9.

FIGURE 29.9
A drawing with the design table inserted

	Pipe Thickness	Length	Flange Thickness	Inside Diameter	Flange Diameter	Bolt Circle Diameter	Hole Diameter
Size1	0.25	3	0.275	0.8	3.6	2.7	0.25
Size2	0.25	3.5	0.275	0.9	3.7	2.8	0.25
Size3	0.25	4	0.275	1	3.8	2.9	0.25
Size4	0.3	4	0.3	1.1	3.9	3	0.25
Size5	0.3	4.5	0.3	1.2	4	3.1	0.25
Size6	0.3	5	0.3	1.2	4.1	3.2	0.25
Size7	0.35	5	0.35	1.3	4.1	3.2	0.38
Size8	0.35	5.5	0.35	1.4	4.2	3.3	0.38
Size9	0.35	6	0.35	1.5	4.3	3.4	0.38

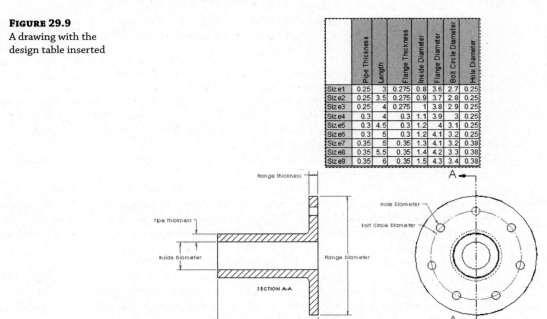

The labeled dimensions are created by simply making reference dimensions and overwriting the <DIM> value in the Dimension Text panel of the Dimension PropertyManager. If you want to examine this data more closely, the drawing and part are included in the download materials on the Wiley website. The drawing is named DT.slddrw.

This drawing uses a part design table, but you can also place assembly design tables onto the drawing. This is often called a *tabulated detail drawing*.

If you need to place something on your drawing such as a design table, but it doesn't appear that the design table will meet your needs, you can simply copy the data out of the design table and re-create it in a static Excel spreadsheet. The design table that you place on the drawing will update if it's changed in the part or assembly, just like the drawing geometry, but you must manually update an Excel spreadsheet that's created from copied data. Keep in mind that you must decide whether the automatic functions are worth the time you invest in setting them up. In many cases, they are; in other cases, they require more work than they save.

Placing Hole Tables on Drawings

You can place hole tables on drawings to include information such as the size, position, and the number of holes or slots of a given size on a drawing. Only circular holes, slots, and blind slots and counterbore slots with chamfers that were created with the Hole Wizard are recognized. You don't have to use the Hole Wizard or simple hole features to make the holes. The position is given relative to a selected reference position, and the holes are labeled. You shouldn't use a hole table for slots unless you first test to make sure you're getting correct data.

NOTE   Blind slots that were not created using the Hole Wizard are recognized as slots with width *x* length listed. Depth is not listed. You should also know that other cutouts are accepted, regardless of their shapes, but you will get a warning about the center location of such holes being approximate and unconstrained; hole sizes are not supported.

Like other table types, hole tables can use templates. As with other templates, you should store Hole Table templates in a library area outside of your local SolidWorks installation folder. You can then direct SolidWorks to this location by choosing Tools ➤ Options ➤ File Locations and specifying the path settings.

Hole tables use anchors in exactly the same way as BOMs. For more information, see the section on table anchors earlier in this chapter.

You can find the options for hole tables by choosing Tools ➤ Options ➤ Document Properties ➤ Drafting Standard ➤ Tables ➤ Hole.

Figure 29.10 shows the PropertyManager for a hole table. The left image shows the PropertyManager that appears when you create the table, and the right image shows the one that appears when you edit the table. Figure 29.11 shows the resulting hole table on a drawing with a part that contains holes. The table incorporates holes from multiple views, using a different zero reference for each view.

To initiate the Hole Table function, click Insert ➤ Table ➤ Hole Table.

To specify the datum, either select an edge in each direction to serve as the zero mark for the X and Y directions or select a vertex or point to serve as the origin in both directions.

To select the holes to be included in the table, activate the selection box in the Holes panel, and either select the hole edges directly or select the faces on which the holes are located. After you place the table, you can add holes or change the datum information. To do this, right-click the Hole Table entry in the Drawing FeatureManager and select Edit Feature. You can resize columns and rows in the same way as for BOM tables.

In the table in Figure 29.11, the Combine Same Sizes option is used, which causes several of the cells in the table to merge. This option is available from the RMB menu for the table. If you use the Combine Same Tags option, then the hole locations are not displayed—only the hole callout description and the quantity appear

You can control the hole callout description by using the file named `calloutformat.txt`, which is found in the `lang\english` subdirectory of the SolidWorks installation directory. Again, if you customize this file, you should keep it in a library external to the installation directory and list it in the Tools ➤ Options ➤ File Locations area. This text file enables you to define how hole callouts are specified for different types of holes.

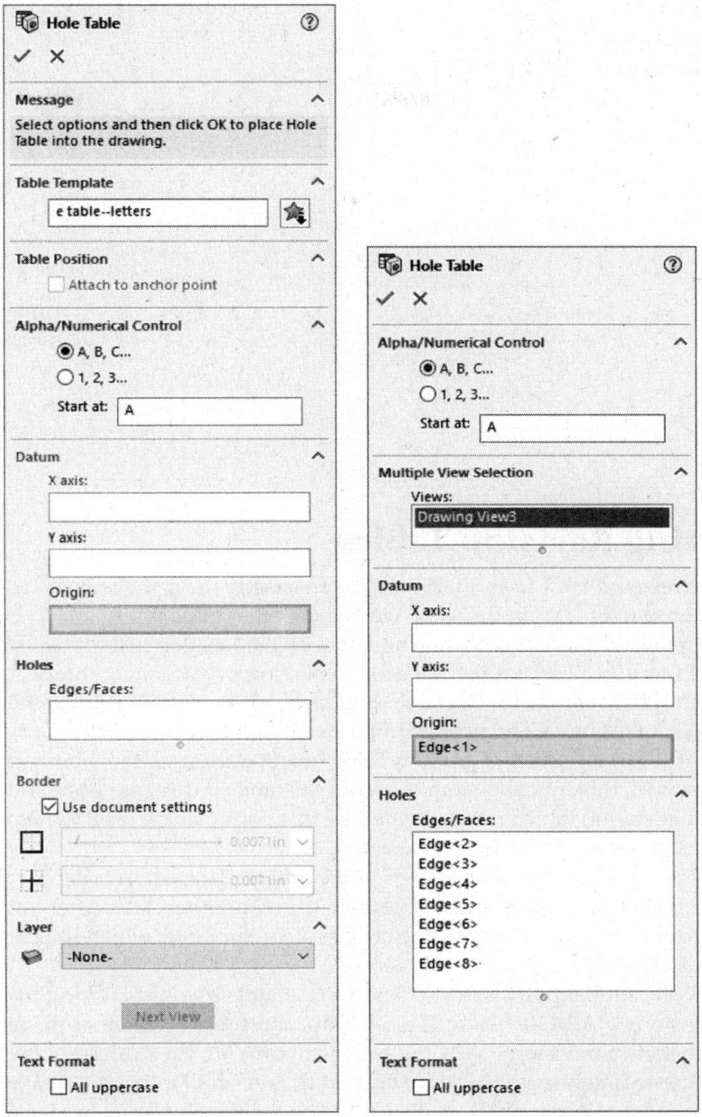

FIGURE 29.10
The PropertyManager for the hole table

FIGURE 29.11
A hole table combining
holes in different views

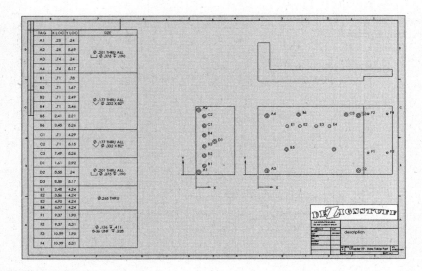

Using Revision Tables

The revision table uses a table anchor in exactly the same way as the BOM table. Revision tables also use templates in the same way as the other table types, and you should move customized templates to a library location and specify the location in Tools ➤ Options ➤ File Locations.

Figure 29.12 shows the Revision Table PropertyManager interface where you can create and control the settings for the table. You can find the default settings for revision tables by choosing Tools ➤ Options ➤ Document Properties ➤ Drafting Standard ➤ Tables ➤ Revision.

You can initiate the Revision Table function through the menus or the Tables toolbar. However, this function simply creates the table; it does not populate it. SolidWorks File Management, which is not covered by this book, can be used to help you automatically fill in the revision table as revisions are created.

You must set the table anchor in the drawing format in order for the table anchor to work. You can add or format additional columns to accept other data. After you have created the columns or formatting, you can save the changes to a template, which is also available through the RMB menu.

You can manually add a revision to the table by right-clicking the table and choosing Revisions ➤ Add Revision. This includes control over whether the revision uses numerical or alphabetical revision levels, but it doesn't provide for more complex revisioning schemes.

Immediately after you have created the revision, if the option is enabled, you will be prompted to place a balloon that contains the revision level to identify what has been changed. To finish placing symbols, you can press Esc. When you are finished placing the balloons, you can fill in the description of the revision by double-clicking in the Description cell where you want to add text. Figure 29.13 shows a revision table with balloon symbols placed on the drawing.

Revision tables work by creating a Revision custom property in the drawing document and by incrementing this revision each time a revision is added to the table. You can add more columns linked to custom properties to revision tables and Revision Table templates.

FIGURE 29.12
The Revision Table
PropertyManager
interface

FIGURE 29.13
A revision table with
balloon symbols

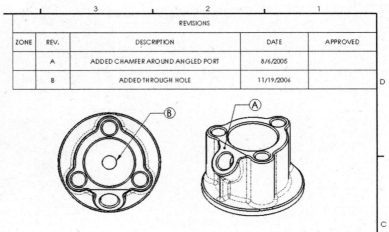

NOTE Gauge tables and bend tables are specific to sheet metal parts and are covered in detail in Chapter 34, "Using SolidWorks Sheet Metal Tools." Weldment Cut Lists are a special type of table that closely resembles a BOM table in many ways. These are discussed in Chapter 36, "Creating Weldments and Weldment Drawings".

Using General Tables

You can use general tables for any type of tabulated data. Column headers can be filled with either text labels or custom property links. You can also use regular Excel OLE objects for the same purpose, and depending on the application, you may prefer to use them.

The general table uses the filename extension `*.sldtbt`. You can create it without a template, as a simple block of four empty cells, or you can use a template that has a set of pre-created headers.

Working with Tables in Models

Proponents of solid modeling have been saying for years that 2D drawings are going to disappear. However, not everyone is convinced. Paper drawings will continue to be useful until all old manufacturing methods are abandoned, and this probably won't happen in your lifetime.

However, because some companies rely less on 2D and paper drawings, the industry is developing new ways to create 2D type documentation inside a 3D document. The ASME Y14.41 standard deals primarily with this transition.

SolidWorks is responding to this type of requirement by adding features that enable you to document the 3D data. Placing BOMs in assembly files is one way of doing this. Placing 2D type data into 3D model documents can reduce the need for paper or even electronic 2D documentation. Figure 29.14 shows a BOM inside an assembly model document.

FIGURE 29.14

Displaying BOM data inside an assembly document

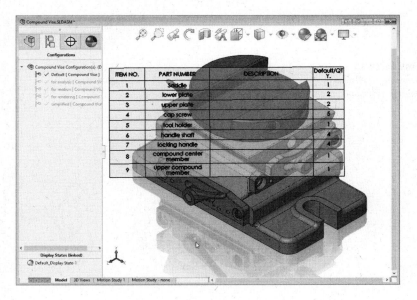

Matching the relative scale of the table to the model can be difficult. To do this, you must adjust the zoom state of the model until it's fairly small within the screen and then place the table. After you place the table, the assembly and the table will zoom together. Most users avoid this issue by viewing the table in a separate window. Alternatively, you can use the BOM Scaling box in the Bill of Materials PropertyManager that enables you to scale the BOM without using the previous method, although the previous method still works.

Items like the BOM can be placed in a Notes Area, which is defined by right-clicking on the Notes folder in the FeatureManager.

TIP Be sure to place the table in the Notes Area, so it will not spin or rotate along with the viewport.

Another type of table that you can use within a 3D model document is the title block table, which can be used inside parts and assemblies. You can use title block tables in the drawing to fill in information about the part or assembly and at the same time avoid creating a full 2D drawing.

Tutorial: Using BOMs

Rather than having tutorials for every table type, this chapter has tutorials only for the BOM, hole table, and revision table. You can transfer the skills you use with these types to the other types.

This tutorial will guide you through the steps to prepare an assembly for the drawing and BOM. Configurations and custom properties are used in this example. Remember that if a drawing view is cross-hatched and you cannot see the geometry, you may have to press Ctrl+Q to rebuild it. Follow these steps:

1. Begin this tutorial with SolidWorks closed and Windows Explorer open.

2. If you have not already done so, create a folder for a library that's not in your SolidWorks installation folder. Call it D:\Library\ or something similar. Make a folder inside this folder called Drawing Templates. Copy the files from the Chapter 29 download materials named inch B.drwdot and inch B (no views).drwdot to this new folder.

3. Launch SolidWorks and choose Tools ➤ Options ➤ File Locations ➤ Document Template. Click the Add button and add the new library path to the list. Shut down SolidWorks and restart it.

4. Open the assembly BOM Assy.sldasm from the Chapter 29 download materials.

5. Click the Make Drawing From Part/Assembly button (or select from the File menu), and make a new drawing of the assembly from the drawing template in the folder created in steps 2 and 3.

6. Delete the isometric view. Create a new view using the configuration Angle 1 and show it in the exploded state. Use the settings shown in Figure 29.16.

7. Edit the sheet format. Right-click the sketch point at the location indicated in Figure 29.15. In the pop-up menu that appears, select Set As Anchor and then select Bill Of Materials.

8. Exit Edit Sheet Format mode by selecting Edit Sheet from the RMB menu.

FIGURE 29.15
Setting the table anchor

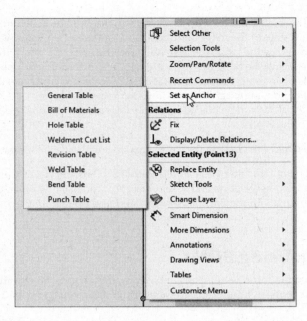

9. Select the new view and show it in the exploded state (right-click and select Properties ➤ Show In Exploded State). Then choose Insert ➤ Table ➤ Bill Of Materials or click the Bill Of Materials button in the Tables toolbar. Select the Attach To Anchor Point option, and show both configurations Angle 1 and Angle 2 in the BOM, as shown in Figure 29.16.

FIGURE 29.16
Creating an exploded view and the Bill of Materials

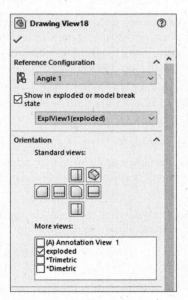

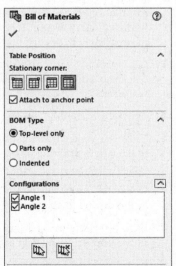

10. Click inside the exploded view, but not on any part geometry, and then select the Autoballoon tool from the Annotations toolbar. Toggle through the available options to see whether any of the possible autoballoon configurations meet your needs. If not, use the standard Balloon tool to select the part and place the balloon. This gives you more control over the attachment points and placement of the balloons.

11. Change the balloon for the short pin to be a circular split-line balloon; do this by clicking the balloon and switching the style in the PropertyManager. Notice that the quantity appears in the bottom of the balloon. The drawing view and the BOM should look like Figure 29.17.

Add a second leader to the balloon for the short pin by Ctrl+dragging the attachment point for the first leader from one pin to the other.

FIGURE 29.17

The drawing view and the BOM after step 11

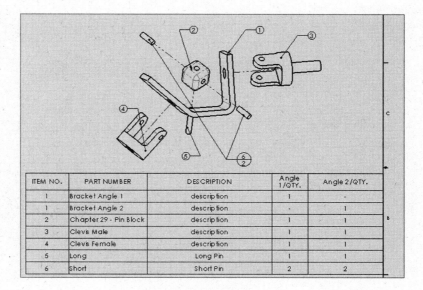

ITEM NO.	PART NUMBER	DESCRIPTION	Angle 1/QTY.	Angle 2/QTY.
1	Bracket Angle 1	description	1	-
1	Bracket Angle 2	description	-	1
2	Chapter 29 - Pin Block	description	1	1
3	Clevis Male	description	1	1
4	Clevis Female	description	1	1
5	Long	Long Pin	1	1
6	Short	Short Pin	2	2

12. Notice that several of the parts use a default description of "description." Edit each of these parts by double-clicking in the Description field for the part you want to change and changing the value right in the BOM table. This will update the part itself automatically.

13. The Bracket part is listed twice using the configuration name because of the way the configurations are set up for the parts.

Notice also that the Description field holds the configuration-specific custom property for Description, which is used in the BOM. To list the bracket only once using the filename, open the bracket, right-click one of the configuration names in the ConfigurationManager, and select Properties. In the Bill Of Materials Options panel, select Document Name from the drop-down list. Do this for the other configuration as well.

14. Notice also that the Description field holds the configuration-specific custom property for Description, which is used in the the BOM. Toggle back to the drawing (press Ctrl+Tab), select anywhere on the BOM table, and then select Table Properties from the PropertyManager. Expand the Part Configuration Grouping panel, and select the option Display All Configurations Of The Same Part As One Item. This changes how the bracket displays, as well as the pins.

15. Now add a column to the BOM that calls on an existing custom property that's already in all the parts. Place the cursor over the last column on the right, and right-click it. Choose Insert ➤ Column Right. This places a new column to the right of the last one and displays a pop-up menu that enables you to set the column to be driven by a custom property, as shown in Figure 29.18.

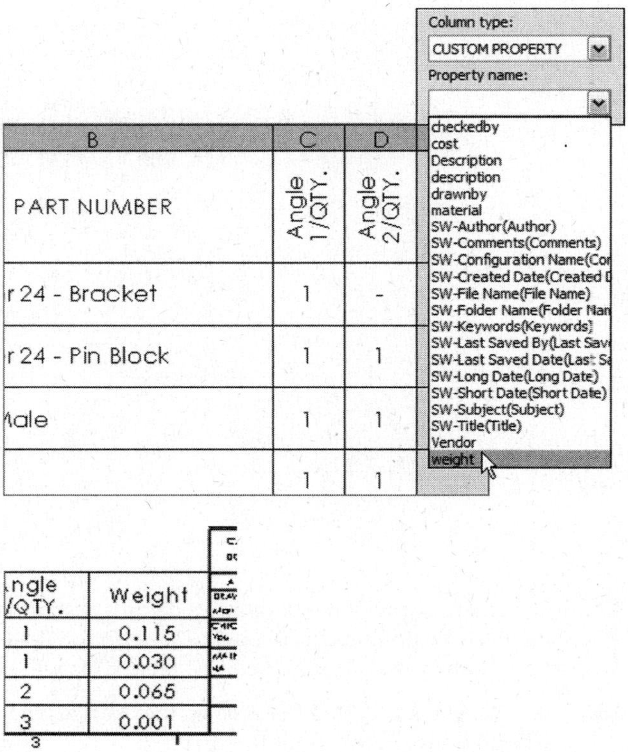

FIGURE 29.18
Adding a column
to the BOM

16. In the first drop-down selection box, select the Weight custom property. Click the green checkmark icon to accept the changes. If the pop-up menu disappears and you need to get it back, double-click the column header to redisplay it.

17. You can save the BOM with the additional column as a BOM template by right-clicking anywhere in the BOM and selecting Save As. You can then set the type to a BOM template and the directory to the library location for BOM templates.

If you want to compare your results against those in this example, check the finished drawing, which is called BOM Tutorial Finished.slddrw.

Tutorial: Using Hole Tables

This tutorial guides you through creating and changing settings that are common in SolidWorks hole tables. Follow these steps:

1. Create a new drawing from the `inch B (no views).drwdot` template. If you haven't created the BOM tutorial, move the drawing template named `inchB.drwdot` from the download materials to your library location for drawing templates. Then create the drawing from the template.

2. Click the Model View button on the Drawings toolbar and browse to the part named `Hole Table Part.sldprt`.

3. Place a front view and project a left view and an isometric view. Then press Esc to quit the command. Finally, delete the four predefined views.

4. No anchor exists in this template for a hole table, so if you want to create one, do this now. Follow the steps in the BOM tutorial for specifying the anchor point.

5. Click the Hole Table button in the Tables toolbar. Figure 29.19 shows a section of the Hole Table PropertyManager with the selections that you need to make for this hole table.

FIGURE 29.19

The Hole Table PropertyManager and selections

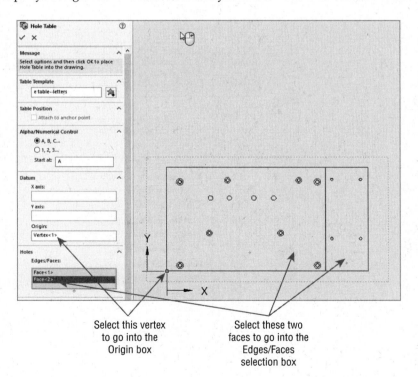

Select this vertex to go into the Origin box

Select these two faces to go into the Edges/Faces selection box

6. After you have completed the selections, click the Next View button at the bottom of the PropertyManager and make similar selections in the left view. The holes for both views are added to a single hole table.

The table is created using the default settings established in Tools ➤ Options ➤ Document Properties ➤ Tables, but you can change them here for this specific table.

7. Click anywhere in the table, and then select Table Properties at the bottom of the PropertyManager. Changing from numerical to alphabetical assigns a letter to each hole type and a number to each instance of the type. Make this change and update the table. Figure 29.20 shows the table before and after the changes.

FIGURE 29.20
Using numerical and alphabetical hole tag identification

TAG	X LOC	Y LOC	SIZE
1	.25	.24	
2	.25	5.69	
3	1.61	2.92	
4	.74	.34	Ø .201 THRU ALL
5	.74	5.17	⊔ Ø .375 ▼ .190
6	8.55	.34	
7	8.55	5.17	
8	.71	.78	
9	.71	1.67	
10	.71	2.49	
11	.71	3.46	
12	.71	4.29	Ø .177 THRU ALL
13	.71	5.15	⌄ Ø .332 X 82.00°
14	2.41	2.21	
15	3.45	5.26	
16	6.46	2.21	
17	7.49	5.26	
18	2.48	4.24	
19	3.56	4.24	Ø.265 THRU
20	4.95	4.24	
21	6.07	4.24	
22	9.37	1.90	
23	9.37	5.31	Ø .136 ▼ .411
24	10.99	1.90	8-36 UNF - 2B ▼ .328
25	10.99	5.31	

TAG	X LOC	Y LOC	SIZE
A1	.25	.24	
A2	.25	5.69	
A3	1.61	2.92	
A4	.74	.34	Ø .201 THRU ALL
A5	.74	5.17	⊔ Ø .375 ▼ .190
A6	8.55	.34	
A7	8.55	5.17	
B1	.71	.78	
B2	.71	1.67	
B3	.71	2.49	
B4	.71	3.46	
B5	.71	4.29	Ø .177 THRU ALL
B6	.71	5.15	⌄ Ø .332 X 82.00°
B7	2.41	2.21	
B8	3.45	5.26	
B9	6.46	2.21	
B10	7.49	5.26	
C1	2.48	4.24	
C2	3.56	4.24	Ø.265 THRU
C3	4.95	4.24	
C4	6.07	4.24	
D1	9.37	1.90	
D2	9.37	5.31	Ø .136 ▼ .411
D3	10.99	1.90	8-36 UNF - 2B ▼ .328
D4	10.99	5.31	

8. Change the number of decimal places used in the hole table from two places to three. You can do this in the PropertyManager.

9. Deselect the Hide Hole Centers option in the Visibility panel.

10. Select the Combine Same Sizes option in the PropertyManager.

11. Save the drawing.

Tutorial: Using Revision Tables

In this tutorial, you will create a basic revision table and make a template. Follow these steps:

1. Using a drawing that you completed in one of the previous tutorials, make sure that a Revision Table anchor has been placed in the upper-right corner of the sheet format. You must edit the sheet format to do this, by right-clicking the point that you want to use for the anchor. Remember to select Edit Sheet from the RMB menu to exit Edit Sheet Format mode.

NOTE   Ideally, the anchors for all table types should be set in templates and formats, but you'll set them up here to practice creating the anchors.

2. Click the Revision Table button on the Tables toolbar. Select the Attach To Anchor option in the PropertyManager. Click the green checkmark icon to accept the table. Figure 29.21 shows the initial stub of the revision table.

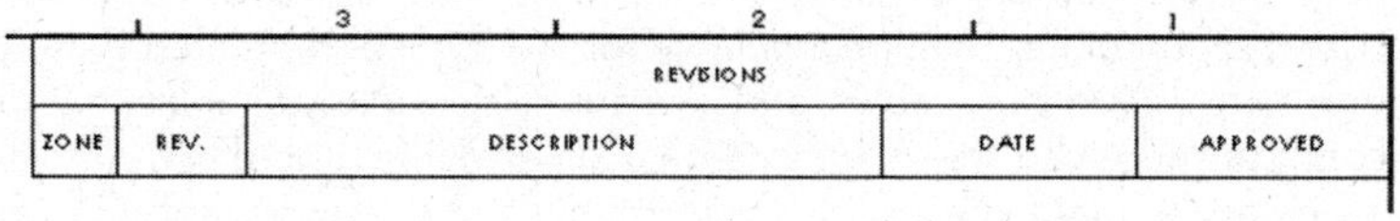

FIGURE 29.21
The initial stub of the revision table

TIP   You can save drawing templates with the Revision Table stub if it also has a format. The revision table is not saved with the format, because it has to go on the drawing sheet.

3. To initiate a new revision level in the Revision Table, right-click the table and choose Revisions ➤ Add Revision.

   Depending on the default settings in Tools ➤ Options ➤ Document Properties ➤ Drafting Standard ➤ Tables ➤ Revision, the first revision will be either A or 1. If you are using PDMWorks Workgroup, you may have other options.

   Depending on your options settings, you may immediately be prompted to place a balloon that contains the new revision level. You can place balloons with or without leaders. The balloons are meant to indicate areas of the drawing that are affected by the revision. Press Esc when you are finished placing the balloons.

NOTE   Be careful when using balloons on assembly drawings or other drawings that already have balloons on them for other purposes. It may be a good idea to use a distinctively shaped balloon for revision tables.

4. To add text to the Description field, simply click in the field and start typing. The text will automatically wrap to fit the box.

5. Practice by adding a couple of revisions, balloons, and descriptions.

6. After you have added a couple of revisions, check the custom properties by choosing File ➤ Properties ➤ Custom. Notice that a revision property has been added, and the latest revision is represented by the value of the custom property.

NOTE You cannot specify the number of revisions to be kept in the revision table as you could in previous releases. However, you can control how revision tables interact with multiple sheets, which you could not do in previous releases.

7. Add columns in the same way that you added them to the BOM. You can merge and unmerge cells, and link properties to cells. With the cursor over the last column (Approved), right-click and choose Insert ➤ Column Left. In the Column Properties, select Custom, and from the Properties drop-down menu, select DrawnBy. Accept the changes by clicking the green checkmark icon.

8. Save the template by right-clicking anywhere in the revision table and choosing Save As ➤ Rev Table Templates. Then save the template to the appropriate location outside the SolidWorks installation directory.

The Bottom Line

SolidWorks enables you to work with tables that are highly specialized for particular uses and with general tables that are available for any type of tabulated data. The most frequently used types are BOMs, hole tables, and revision tables. Design tables that drive part and assembly configurations can also be placed on a 2D drawing, but in these cases, some formatting is usually necessary to make these tables presentable and the information on it easy to read.

Master It Go through all of your drawing templates with formats, and all of your separate formats, and make sure that you have anchors for all of the table types your company creates.

Master It Take an existing assembly drawing, add a column to it, add a property, and fill out the property values in the table.

Master It Make sure the assembly has an exploded view, and make one view on the drawing show that explosion. Next, add balloons to the view, using at least two circular split-line balloons that show the item number as well as another value, such as the quantity, the weight, or a custom property value.

Chapter 30

Creating Assembly Drawings

Most of the actual tools that you might use for part drawings are the same for assembly draw-ings, with a few exceptions. This chapter covers these exceptions along with some special techniques that might make using assembly drawings easier or clearer.

IN THIS CHAPTER, YOU WILL LEARN TO:

◆ Merge parts and assemblies in one drawing

◆ Use page 2 formats

◆ Work with drawing views with special assembly functions

◆ Work with drawings of large assemblies

Combining Parts and Assemblies on the Same Drawing

Every company seems to do things differently when it comes to assembly drawings. Some use the drawings for Bill of Materials (BOM) illustration, some to manufacture assembly instructions, and some to dimension assembly-based features that are applied only after the individual components are assembled.

There is nothing to prevent you from putting parts and assemblies on the same drawing or even in the same sheet. Some users place an exploded view of the assembly on the first sheet and then start detailing each part on the same sheet, using multiple sheets, so the single drawing file documents several individual parts and the assembly. This is usually the case only for simple parts. An assembly made from several complex plastic parts couldn't be done this way, because a single complex plastic part often requires multiple sheets on its own.

Dimensioning Assembly Features

One of the more difficult questions you must answer when dimensioning assembly features on an assembly drawing is what to use as your reference. Making cuts and measuring often takes place in some kind of fixture. Fixtures make excellent references in most situations. You might consider designing the fixture in some way that enables measurement from a fixed reference either on one of the parts or on the fixture itself. This would require a drawing that acts as a qualification reference to include the fixturing reference in the drawing. This is best done as a higher-level assembly rather than adding the fixture using configurations of the product-level assembly.

Measuring to reference planes in the assembly is fine for the design, but there are no reference planes in your manufacturing floor unless they are physical faces of fixtures created for the purpose of making measurements. If your measurement spans multiple parts, keep in mind that both the individual parts and the assembly have tolerances you must consider.

Assembly cuts often are used to create 3D cutaway views. SolidWorks can't create a section view where the section cut isn't perpendicular to the sheet of paper, so the workaround is to make a cut in the assembly (as a configuration) and to display the cut assembly using an isometric view. Another method is to use the 3D Rotate function to temporarily rotate the view and select something you can't see in that view. The result remains parametric.

Assigning the Document Driving the Custom Properties

When you have a drawing with multiple parts or assemblies on it, you can control which document drives the custom properties used in the title block for that sheet. If you have multiple sheets, you can have different models driving the properties on different sheets.

To use this feature, right-click the sheet in the FeatureManager or in the graphics window (but not on other items such as the format or views) to display the RMB menu shown in Figure 30.1. Make sure the gray area on the RMB menu is labeled Sheet rather than View, and select Properties from the menu. The Sheet Properties dialog box will appear, as shown in Figure 30.1.

FIGURE 30.1
Assigning the driving document for a sheet

Click the drop-down list in the lower-left corner, labeled Use Custom Property Values From Model Shown In, and choose any view that's on the current sheet. This could be a single part or an assembly.

Remember also that when linking to a property, you can choose to link to properties of the current document (drawing), the model specified in the sheet properties, the component to which the annotation is attached, or the selected component. You can find these settings in the Link To Property dialog box, shown in Figure 30.2, by clicking the Link To Property icon in the Note PropertyManager.

FIGURE 30.2

Linking a note to a custom property from one of various documents

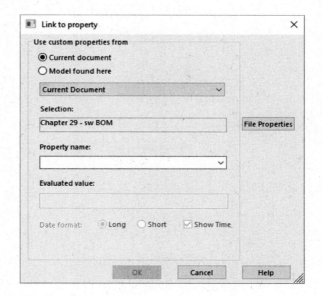

Using Multi-Page Templates

Assembly drawings often become multi-page documents. To speed up your creation of these drawings, you should have multi-page templates available to use when you need them. Most of the aspects of single-page and multi-page templates are the same, such as custom property setup and formats, but adding the page gives you some options about which you need to be aware.

ON THE WEBSITE

The two-sheet template and second-page format used in this chapter are in the Assembly Drawings folder, with the filenames Bsize 2 sheet.drwdot (template) and b sheet 2.slddrt (format).

You can use a "page 2 format" for any page other than page one. Generally, page 2 formats are just a minimal version of a page 1 format, removing information that might be considered redundant on every page of the drawing and allowing more space for drawing content. Figure 30.3 shows page 1 and page 2 formats.

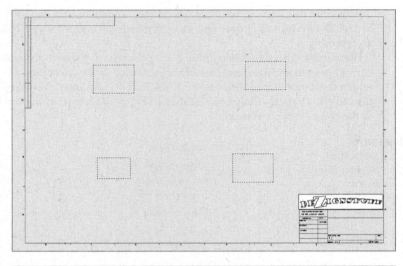

TIP Remember that to access pages of a multiple-page drawing, use the tabs under the Drawing FeatureManager area.

To make it easier to manage a large package of paper drawings, most multi-sheet drawings use the same size sheet for every sheet. However, every company has its own standards, conventions, customs, and needs.

To make a page 2 template from a page 1 template, follow these steps:

1. Open a new drawing using the sheet format that you would like to make into a page 2 format.

2. Right-click inside the sheet, but off of other items such as predefined views or the actual format, and select Edit Sheet Format from the menu.

3. Edit the format to suit your needs. This might include moving, removing, or adding lines to the border, removing linked notes, or resizing or moving a logo or other items.

4. Use a note linked on the drawing showing that the current page is Page X of Y. Both X (current sheet) and Y (total sheets) are available as properties you can link to the drawing from notes.

5. When you have the format the way you want it, save it to a special location in your library for drawing formats. You should avoid putting customized documents in folders in the SolidWorks installation directories or in default folders created by SolidWorks. For example, you can put your format documents on the D: drive (a physically separate drive from where the Windows operating system is installed) in a folder called D:\Library\ Formats\. This ensures that installing or uninstalling SolidWorks or the operating system won't delete or overwrite your customized documents.

ON THE WEBSITE

If you want to study examples of formats, refer to the downloaded material for "Assembly Drawing Formats."

Using Views with Special Assembly Functions

SolidWorks has some drawing view types that have special functionality when used with assemblies. The main ones are alternate position views, exploded views (although an exploded view is not so much a function of the drawing), Broken-Out section views, and section views with alternating hatching.

Using the Alternate Position View

The alternate position view is available only for views of an assembly and shows the assembly in two different positions (not from different viewpoints; this requires an assembly that moves). This is another view type that doesn't create a new view but alters an existing view. Figure 30.4 shows the PropertyManager interface for the alternate position view, a sample view that it creates, and the way it's represented in the drawing FeatureManager.

To create an alternate position view, ensure that you have an assembly on the active drawing that can have multiple positions, and click the Alternate Position View button on the Drawings toolbar, or choose Insert ➤ Drawing View ➤ Alternate Position and then select the alternate position view.

Next, click in the drawing view to which you want to add the alternate position. The PropertyManager shown in Figure 30.4 will prompt you to select an existing configuration for the alternate position or to create a new configuration. If you choose to create a new configuration, the model window will appear, a new configuration will be created, and you will be required to reposition parts in the assembly. The alternate position is shown in a different line font on the same view and from the same orientation as the original.

FIGURE 30.4
The alternate
position view

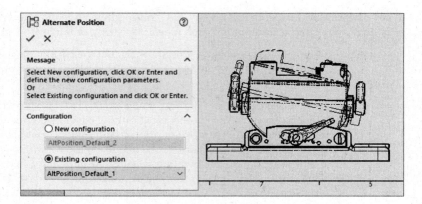

TIP The best way to create this view is to either create two configurations used exclusively for the alternate position view or to have two configurations where you know that parts won't be moved, suppressed, or hidden. The main idea is that you need to ensure that these configurations remain in the same position or are changed intentionally, knowing that it will alter this drawing view.

To delete an alternate position view, select it in the drawing FeatureManager and press Delete.

Creating Views of an Exploded Assembly

Assemblies are often depicted with the parts pulled apart in a structured way to illustrate disassembly or, more simply, the parts within the assembly. Exploded assemblies can be shown on assembly drawings using balloons with numbers corresponding to a BOM table.

Here is the workflow for creating an exploded view:

1. Open an assembly. Use the downloaded `rear derailleur.sldasm` for this example.

2. Click the ConfigurationManager tab at the top of the FeatureManager area.

3. Activate the configuration you want to explode, right-click the configuration, and select New Exploded View from the menu. You are allowed to have more than one explode feature per configuration. Figure 30.5 shows the PropertyManager for the Explode command.

4. Select a component to explode away from the rest of the parts. Usually, parts move axially if mated with a Concentric mate and perpendicularly away from the other parts if mated with a flat to flat coincident. Select the parts to be exploded together (in one move) in a group in the Settings selection box.

   Making selections in the Settings box is not as fussy as making selections for mates or other purposes. It doesn't matter if you select a face or an edge; SolidWorks understands that you want to select the part.

FIGURE 30.5
Starting to create an exploded view of an assembly

5. If you need to move the parts in a direction other than the assembly X, Y, or Z, use the Explode Direction box immediately below the bigger Components To Explode selection box in the Settings panel. In Figure 30.6, the Explode Direction box contains a temporary axis.

NOTE As an alternative, you can drag the manipulator's ball on a face or edge to redefine the exploding direction.

FIGURE 30.6
Selecting rivets
to explode

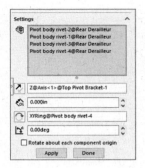

6. With the rivets selected and the direction established, drag one of the arrows on the Triad that appears in the graphics window, or type a number in the distance box in the PropertyManager. This brings up a ruler along which you can judge the explode distance.

This action produces the first explode step in the Explode Steps box in the PropertyManager. You can rename, edit, and delete the explode step.

7. To make edits, select an explode step in the assembly FeatureManager. To select a step without editing it, use Ctrl+select. This enables you to change anything you used to create the step. You can use the orange arrows to change the explode distance or rotation.

Figure 30.7 shows a completed explode for the assembly.

FIGURE 30.7
The completed explode
for this assembly

8. When you are finished with the Explode command, click the green checkmark icon to accept the results.

The completed results of an explode are displayed as an exploded view indented under the configuration from which you started the explode.

To collapse an exploded view, right-click it under the configuration and select Collapse. This will allow you to toggle back and forth between a collapsed and exploded view. Another option is Animated Explode/Collapse. This option uses the order in which the explode steps appear in the ConfigurationManager and a default speed.

NOTE After using the Animated Explode/Collapse option, make sure to turn off the Animation Controller that appears in the upper-left corner of the SolidWorks window. This controller allows you to control and save the animation, but it also blocks you from performing other actions in the assembly until you turn it off.

ADDING EXPLODE LINES

Explode lines are 3D sketch lines that show the explode path of the parts in an exploded view of an assembly. The Exploded View flyout toolbar is on the assembly toolbar by default. It includes three icons: Exploded View, Explode Line Sketch, and Insert/Edit Smart Explode Line Sketch.

To use the route line as a part of the Explode Line Sketch, you simply click the features that you want to connect with an explode line, use the arrows that appear to determine which direction the sketch should connect to the part, and then click the RMB to accept the line and move on to the next. The process is shown in Figure 30.8.

In cases where you want to move a line that the Route Line feature has created, move your cursor over the line; two small arrows will appear, as shown in Figure 30.9. They will enable you to move that line.

You might think that SolidWorks would be able to create these lines automatically from the data in the exploded view, and it can, to an extent, with Smart Explode Lines. To create Smart Explode Lines, right-click on the explode view in the ConfigurationManager and select Smart Explode Lines. This creates what is shown in Figure 30.10.

FIGURE 30.8
Drawing route lines in
an exploded view

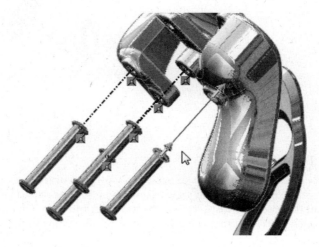

FIGURE 30.9
Moving a route line as it
is created

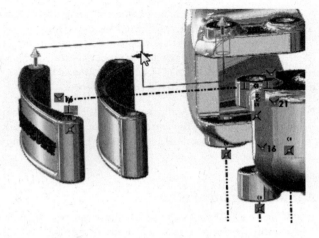

FIGURE 30.10
Adding Smart Explode
Lines to an exploded
assembly view

SHOWING EXPLODED VIEW

The best view orientation to use for an exploded view on a drawing is usually not one of the standard views. To create a custom view orientation, use the mouse to orient the view in the way that you want the assembly displayed on the drawing, and then open the assembly and press the spacebar to open the View Orientation box. Click the New View button and name the new view orientation.

Now you can place the new view on the drawing. To show the view in the exploded state, right-click inside the view (but off any part geometry), select Properties, and choose the Show In Exploded State option, as shown in Figure 30.11.

FIGURE 30.11
Showing the exploded state on the drawing

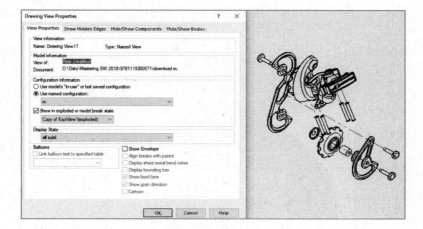

Creating Section Views

Section views are common enough in part drawings, but when you section an assembly, you must consider other things, such as not cutting fasteners and shafts. You can create assembly sections with the same options that you use for part sections, partial sections, aligned sections, and broken-out sections. Assembly sections can even be created in the model and dragged onto the drawing sheet from the View palette.

EXCLUDING PARTS FROM SECTION VIEWS

When creating a section view, you can exclude parts from being sectioned. Figure 30.12 shows the Section Scope tab of the Section View dialog box, which enables you to do this. You can also access this dialog box when editing a section view through the Section View PropertyManager by clicking the More Properties button at the bottom and then choosing the Section Scope tab.

FIGURE 30.12
Excluding bolts and pins from the section view of this assembly

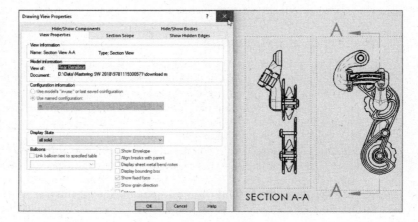

ISOMETRIC SECTION

To easily create an isometric section view, first create a regular section view, then right-click on it, select Isometric Section View from the menu, and place the new view. See Figure 30.13.

To undo this, or to set the view back to a regular section view, right-click in the view and select Remove Isometric View.

FIGURE 30.13
Isometric section

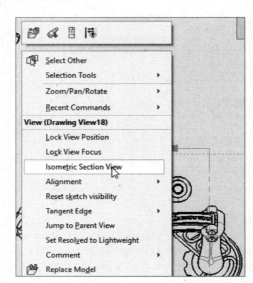
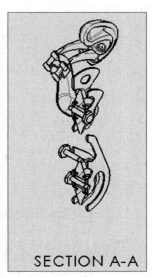

ALIGNING THE VIEW

In this case, the section line is slightly angled, and you would like to have the section view laid out straight. To orient a view in a particular way, select an edge that you want to be horizontal or vertical (assuming there is one; if not, you may have to use a sketch line or axis), and using the menus, select Tools ➤ Align Drawing View and then select either Horizontal Edge or Vertical Edge.

Remember that you can always rotate the view on the sheet with the Rotate button on the Heads-Up View toolbar on the drawing, or the 3D Rotate function. This displays a dialog box where you can type in a specific value.

ADJUSTING THE HATCHING

The default hatching may not be the right size for the parts you build. If you need to adjust the hatching—the size, the pattern, or the angle—just click the sectioned part, and the Area Hatch/Fill PropertyManager will appear. Figure 30.14 shows the PropertyManager and a hatched section view.

You can change hatching for each part (component), body, the entire view, or just the selected enclosed region. Be sure to make the right selection in the Apply To drop-down menu before you exit the Area Hatch PropertyManager.

Hatching is assigned with the material found at the top of the SolidWorks FeatureManager for each part. Each material has its own crosshatch. If a material is not formally assigned to a part, the default hatching is set in Tools ➤ Options ➤ Document Properties ➤ Material Properties settings. The default is ANSI31 (Iron BrickStone). The default can be set in part templates. This is also where the default density is established, as shown in Figure 30.15.

FIGURE 30.14
Using the Area Hatch/
Fill PropertyManager

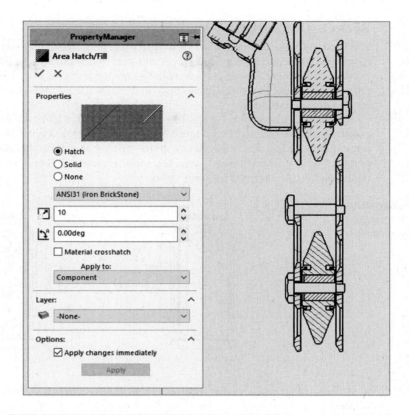

FIGURE 30.15
Changing the defaults
for density and
crosshatch

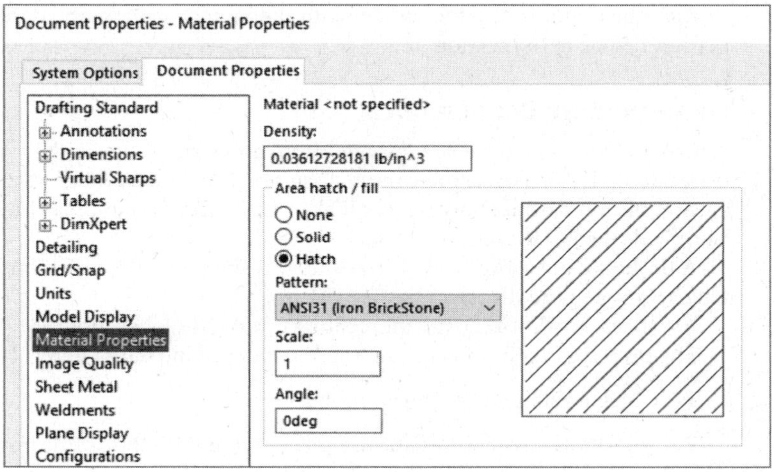

Broken-Out Section View

The Broken-Out section view is a view type that alters an existing view rather than creating a new view. It also requires a closed-loop sketch to define the section. The Broken-Out section view is very useful when a set of parts is inside a housing and you want to show the inside parts without hiding the housing. Of course, you can also use a Broken-Out section view on single parts with internal detail.

A Broken-Out section view acts like a cut that's created from the drawing view. Any faces created by the cut are hatched. Figure 30.16 shows a simple assembly view using a Broken-Out section view. On the left is the view with the driving sketch (in this case, a closed-loop spline), and on the right is the finished view. You cannot create a Broken-Out section view using existing detail, section, or alternate position views.

FIGURE 30.16
A Broken-Out
section view

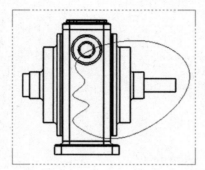 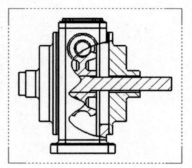

A Broken-Out section view requires you to specify a depth for the cut. You can use an edge selected from a different view or a distance to specify the depth. In the case of the broken-out section, the depth is into the screen; with the regular section, the depth is measured as a distance perpendicular to the section line.

DRAWING THE CLOSED LOOP

A Broken-Out section view is initiated from an existing view either with or without a pre-drawn closed loop. If the loop is pre-drawn, then you must select it before clicking the Broken-Out Section button on the Drawings toolbar or accessing the command by choosing Insert ➤ Drawing View ➤ Broken-Out Section.

A Broken-Out section view is traditionally created with a freehand sort of boundary, even when drawn manually.

Two basic workflows exist for creating a Broken-Out section:

The preferred method is to use a spline loop, as indicated here:

1. Click the Broken-Out Section button.

2. SolidWorks will automatically present you with the Spline sketch tool.

3. Sketch a closed-loop spline.

4. Select any excluded components (Section Scope).

5. Select the depth of cut.

The pre-selected loop method is used for nonspline cutting loops, as indicated here:

1. Sketch a loop using either spline or nonspline sketch elements

2. Select the loop using Ctrl+select, box/lasso selection, or an RMB method such as Select Chain.

3. Click the Broken-Out Section button.

4. Select any excluded components (Section Scope).

5. Select the depth of the cut.

SELECTING THE DEPTH

After you make the Section Scope selections, the next step is to set the depth of the cut. You can do this in several ways. A Broken-Out section view is usually cut to the center of a hole if a circular edge is selected. If you know the depth of the cut you want to make, you can enter it as a distance value. Of course, that raises the question, "Distance from *what*?" The answer seems to be "from the geometry in the view that is closest to the user."

In situations when you want to cut to the center of a particular feature or up to an edge, it's far easier to simply select the geometry from a drawing view. It could be the same view as the Broken-Out section or a different view of the same document (part or assembly). For example, Figure 30.17 shows the PropertyManager interface where the depth of the cut is set. In this example, the edge of the shaft in the view to the right has been selected. This tells SolidWorks that the cut should go to the center of the shaft. Another possibility is to show the temporary axes, as shown in Figure 30.17, and to select an axis through the center of the shaft.

FIGURE 30.17
Setting the depth of the Broken-Out section view

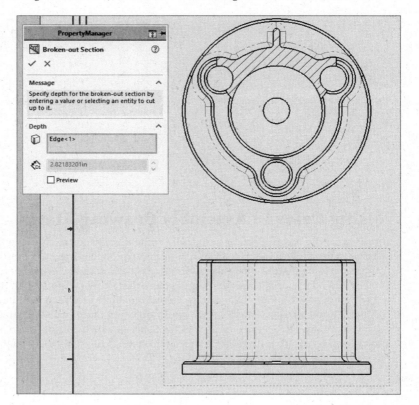

EDITING THE VIEW

At this point, the view is finished. Now you may choose to edit the view in some way, such as by changing the sketch, the depth, the section scope, and so on. Figure 30.18 shows how the Broken-Out section view is positioned in the Drawing FeatureManager. It's listed as a modification to an existing drawing view. The Broken-Out Section RMB menu is also shown. Selecting Edit Definition displays the PropertyManager (refer to Figure 30.17). Selecting Edit Sketch enables you to change the section spline shape. Selecting Properties displays the dialog box shown in Figure 30.18. This contains options for the underlying original view as well as the Broken-Out Section modification to the original view. Only the Section Scope tab is added by the Broken-Out section view. The rest of the options are for normal view properties.

FIGURE 30.18
Editing the Broken-Out section view's properties

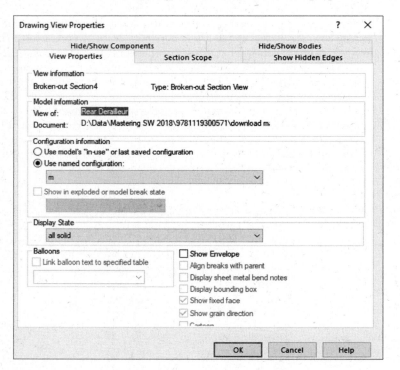

Using Color in Assembly Drawing Views

You can apply the same color to the wireframe display on the drawing that you have applied to the individual parts in the Assembly window. Colors on drawings help distinguish one part from another in assemblies, where the alternative is to look at a screenful of black lines.

On the other hand, sometimes light colors that show up well when the part is shaded on the screen don't look good when used in a wireframe line width on a white sheet. Also, with the use of part "appearances" where some people are using more realistic material displays for parts, part colors can be a range of gray to reflect surfaces such as aluminum or steel. Still, if you want to set your parts up with more abstract contrasting colors, it helps you to distinguish one part from another in the assembly model and on the drawing. Appearances, even realistic or reflective appearances, can have colors assigned to them, so you get a shiny, red steel part. The realism is far less important than the ability to tell one part from another, so the abstraction of colors that don't look realistic at all is often very helpful.

To make assembly drawings use part color, use the setting indicated by the cursor in Figure 30.19, Tools ➢ Options ➢ Document Properties ➢ Detailing ➢ Use Model Color For HLR/ HLV In Drawings. You need to specify this document property setting in the drawing. (HLR stands for *hidden lines removed*, while HLV stands for *hidden lines visible*.)

This is worth repeating: Even though this setting exists in both the assembly and the drawing,

FIGURE 30.19
The Use Model Color For HLR/HLV In Drawings option

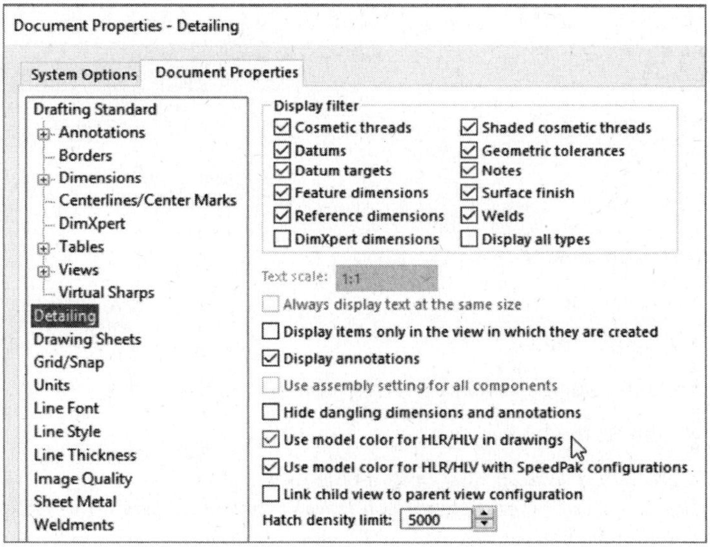

and even though there is a setting in parts that says to use the same color for shaded and wireframe, the only setting that matters in terms of getting color onto the drawing is Use Model Color Setting in the *Drawing* Document Properties.

Setting Up Drawings of Large Assemblies

You can use several tactics to try to minimize the overhead of working with large data sets in SolidWorks drawings. You have several options when working to improve the performance of large assembly drawings. Some of these options should be employed at the level of the assembly, and some you will use only in the drawing.

Using Detached Drawings

Detached drawings don't have the 3D document files loaded in memory; they just let you work with the geometry as is in the drawing. They can be beneficial in two situations: first, to speed up large assembly drawings, and second, when you have the drawing but don't have the part and assembly files. You must set up a detached drawing before deciding to open the drawing without the parts. Detached drawings use the symbol at the top of this paragraph to denote their special status both in the Windows Explorer/Open dialog and in the drawing FeatureManager.

NOTE A detached drawing is convenient when you want to send someone a SolidWorks drawing, but you don't need (or want) to give them access to the actual 3D model data. However, you first have to save it as a detached drawing.

To create a detached drawing, choose File ➤ Save As, and from the Save As Type drop-down list (shown in Figure 30.20), select Detached Drawing.

You cannot perform some drawing operations with detached drawings, including these:

FIGURE 30.20

Saving a drawing as a detached drawing

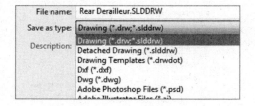

- ◆ Crop views
- ◆ Break views
- ◆ Section views
- ◆ Alternate position or relative views
- ◆ Insert model items

Detached drawings also cannot be lightweight.

Just like other operations in SolidWorks drawings, when the view needs to be updated, the view becomes hatched.

When you need to load the model to update changes or do one of the operations that require the part data to be present, right-click inside a view and select Load Model from the menu. When SolidWorks determines that you need to load the model, the software may prompt you to do this. Another option is to load the model from the File Open dialog.

You can only add certain types of views of parts—not the assembly (aux, projected, section, broken-out section), annotations, and reference dimensions to a detached drawing. So, there's a certain amount of work you can actually do with detached drawings. To remove these limitations, you can load the model.

If you save a drawing as detached, load the model, and then save the drawing and close it, the next time you open it, it will be detached. In other words, after you save a drawing as detached, it remains detached until you save it as a regular drawing. To do this, just choose File ➤ Save As, and in the File of Type drop-down list, select Drawing.

Further, be aware that Ctrl+Q (forced rebuild) will load the model without warning, while Ctrl+B (rebuild) at least gives you a warning. Also, if a drawing is linked to multiple parts, loading one will load all.

Working with Lightweight Drawings

Lightweight drawings have some similarities to lightweight assemblies. With lightweight drawings, SolidWorks loads only as much model data as it needs. If SolidWorks needs more data, it loads it. This helps assemblies and drawings to open more quickly, but some functions may be slower.

CAUTION You cannot mix the benefits of lightweight drawings with the benefits of detached drawings.

Using lightweight settings in the drawing works just like using lightweight settings in the assembly. Right-click in a view (either in the graphics window or the FeatureManager), and select Set Resolved To Lightweight, as shown in Figure 30.21. Doing this for one view sets all views to Lightweight (it is the assembly behind the view that is lightweight, not the view itself). You can resolve the assembly by choosing Set Lightweight To Resolved from the RMB menu.

FIGURE 30.21

Using lightweight settings with assembly drawings

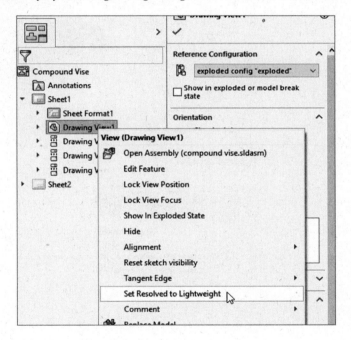

Using SpeedPak with Drawings

SpeedPak is a derived assembly configuration type that uses selected geometry to simplify the display and amount of data SolidWorks needs to load a complex assembly, with the goal of speeding up loading and work in general. To create a SpeedPak, right-click on an existing configuration in an assembly and select Add SpeedPak, and then use selection techniques to select faces, bodies, reference geometry, sketches, and curves to be displayed as part of the SpeedPak. Your selections will be displayed in assemblies and drawings in place of the full configuration geometry.

The Quick Include functionality will automatically include geometry based on your selected position on the More To Less slider. It selects more or less detail for the views you specify in the SpeedPak PropertyManager interface, shown in Figure 30.22.

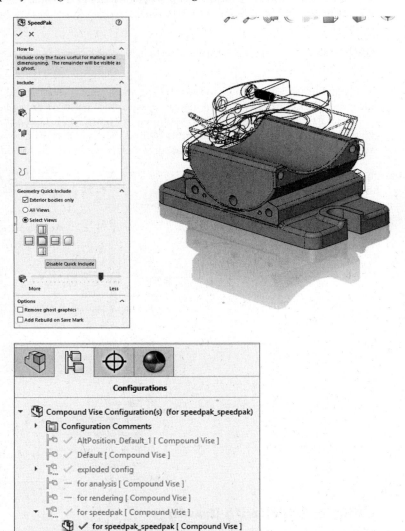

FIGURE 30.22
The SpeedPak
PropertyManager

Once created, the SpeedPak is listed in the assembly ConfigurationManager under the configuration, like a derived configuration, but with a special SpeedPak icon, shown in Figure 30.22.

Ghost graphics are anything that is not selected in the Included boxes. Ghost graphics are visible, but not selectable. If you select the Remove Ghost Graphics option in the SpeedPak PropertyManager, only the items you have included will be visible when the SpeedPak is in use (either in the assembly or the drawing). Figure 30.23 shows the model with and without the ghost graphics.

FIGURE 30.23
Model with and without
ghost graphics

If you want to use a SpeedPak in a drawing, the SpeedPak must include edges to which you want to dimension. Anything that's part of the ghost data will be shown in gray by default, but this is sometimes changed to another convenient color such as black. To use an existing SpeedPak for an assembly, right-click a view and select Properties. In the Configuration information, use the named configuration option to select the derived configuration of the SpeedPak.

Using Draft Quality Views

Draft Quality views are another way to speed up large assembly drawings. Figure 30.24 shows the difference between a Draft Quality view on the left and a High Quality view on the right. Each view starts as a Draft Quality view; however, when you change from Draft Quality to High Quality, the setting will no longer be available. You can find the Draft Quality and High Quality view settings in the view PropertyManager (just select a view, and the PropertyManager will appear on the left) in the Display Style panel. This will enable you to change from Wireframe to Shaded display modes. If the High Quality and Draft Quality toggles are not in the PropertyManager panel, then the view is already in High Quality mode. After you switch a view to High Quality, you cannot switch it back to Draft Quality.

You can change the defaults for this setting in the System Options at Tools ➤ Options ➤ Drawings ➤ Display Style ➤ Display Quality For New Views. As you might imagine, this is not a template setting; it's only a system option. To return to Draft Quality, first make sure your system is set up to create Draft Quality views, then simply switch from HLR or HLV to Shaded and back.

Keep in mind that it's easy to confuse the Cosmetic Thread Display with the Display Style. They both toggle between High Quality and Draft Quality, and when you are just looking for those features, you may settle on the first one you see with this label.

High Quality views store the detailed information (used in zoom operations) in the drawing, while Low Quality views have to go back to the model to get that data. Thus, while High Quality views take more memory, they are faster to zoom in and out. But you have to make sure your hardware can handle the extra memory requirements.

FIGURE 30.24
Comparing High Quality
and Draft Quality views

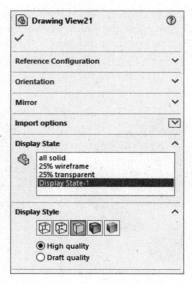

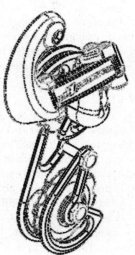
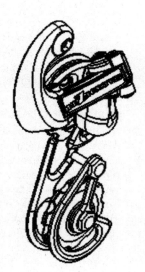

Tutorial: Creating a Simple Assembly Drawing

This tutorial guides you through creating a simple assembly drawing:

1. Create a new drawing from the New dialog box. Select Inch B Bible Template (no Views).drwdot; as the filename indicates, this template document has no predefined views. If you select a default SolidWorks template, you need to verify that the template uses third angle rather than first angle projection. An easy way to do this is to switch the drafting standard from ISO to ANSI in Tools ➤ Options ➤ Document Properties ➤ Drafting

Standard. If the automatic Model View interface appears in the PropertyManager, click the red X icon to cancel out of it.

2. Expand the Task pane and activate the View palette (the tab that looks like a drawing icon). Click the ellipsis button (. . .) and browse for the assembly named SF casting assembly.sldasm. The View palette is shown in Figure 30.25.

FIGURE 30.25
The View palette

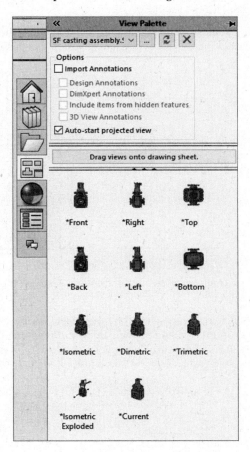

3. Drag the back view onto the drawing. Notice that when you use this technique, the views do not resize automatically, regardless of the setting at Tools ➤ Options ➤ Drawings ➤ Automatically Scale New Drawing Views.

4. Delete any view you have created using this method. Open Windows Explorer, browse to the assembly, and drag it into the drawing. The views that you create using this method are equivalent to the Standard 3 View tool. This time, the views automatically size.

5. Select the front view and change it to the back view. Use the Orientation panel of the View PropertyManager. Notice that the rest of the views change to reflect the new parent view. You will get a warning about this change.

6. Zoom in on the back view. Change the view to show Tangent Edges With Font through View ➤ Display. You can also make this change from the view RMB menu, the Tangent Edge selection.

7. Click the Alternate Position View toolbar button. Type a name in the PropertyManager for a new configuration and click the green checkmark icon. SolidWorks will open the Assembly Model window.

8. Rotate the handle 90 degrees and click the green checkmark icon. SolidWorks will return to the drawing and show the new position in a dashed font, as shown in Figure 30.26.

FIGURE 30.26
Creating an alternate
position view

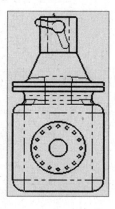

9. Place an isometric view on the drawing. Change the Display mode to make it a shaded view.

10. Right-click inside the view (but away from the parts) and select Properties. The Drawing View Properties dialog box will appear, displaying the View Properties tab, as shown in Figure 30.27. Make sure the view is set to use the Default configuration, with the Default display state, and select the Show In Exploded Or Model Break State option.

FIGURE 30.27
The Drawing View
Properties dialog box

The Bottom Line

Working with assembly drawings requires many of the same skills as working with regular drawings, but with much less dimensioning, and much more pictorial and visualization capability. Sometimes, you must use the unique tools for assembly drawings to get the job done.

Master It Create an exploded view of one of the assemblies provided with the download materials for this chapter or one of your own. Draw in the explode lines.

Master It Use a template with a second page to create a new drawing. I suggest the template called `Mastering 2pg B size`.

Create a drawing of the assembly for which you created an exploded view. The first sheet should be automatically populated with three standard views and an isometric.

Show the isometric view of the assembly in its exploded state and apply balloons to all the parts.

Place a Bill of Materials table on the drawing that shows item numbers for each balloon.

Master It Starting with the drawing from the last practice exercise, switch to the second sheet. Click on the Standard 3 View icon on the View Layout tab. Select one of the parts from the assembly. If you have not opened any parts individually, you'll have to browse for it.

Place the views on the drawing and add an isometric view.

Put some custom properties in the part and make sure that the title block on the second page format picks up some of the part information.

Part V

Using Advanced and Specialized Techniques

Chapter 31

Modeling Multibodies

SolidWorks allows multiple solid bodies within a single part at the same time. SolidWorks defines a *solid body* as a single contiguous volume. So, if you have two blocks in the same part that don't touch one another, those blocks are separate bodies. Separate bodies can intersect, and you can have copies of bodies that are exactly on top of one another. Surfaces are also bodies. While solid features by default try to form a single body if possible, surface bodies by default make separate bodies.

There are many uses for this type of functionality. At the same time, there are many ways to abuse this functionality and fall into traps. This chapter aims to help you take advantage of the benefits of multiple bodies while avoiding some of the potential traps.

IN THIS CHAPTER, YOU WILL LEARN TO:

- ◆ Create models responsibly

- ◆ Leverage multibody techniques

- ◆ Learn how to use multibodies

- ◆ Understand how to manage bodies

- ◆ Work with multibody data

You might work with SolidWorks in such a way that you would never need to use multiple bodies inside a single part, ever. Almost everything that average users normally do can be done with a single solid body per part and without any knowledge of multibody functionality whatsoever.

However, to access some more powerful functionality and options that offer more flexibility, multibody modeling is necessary. In fact, if you want to move on to surface modeling, multibody knowledge is mandatory because multibody is the default in surface modeling.

Multibody modeling is the gateway from the basic solid modeling mainly described in this book up until now into the more advanced functionality that follows. The gateway can lead in two directions: It can lead to more power, more flexibility, more options, and more advanced functionality, or it can lead to sloppy, bad habits and nasty traps. This chapter will help you tell the difference and avoid the pitfalls.

Using Powerful Tools Effectively

The SolidWorks software is so filled with powerful functionality that you'll find many ways to create any given piece of geometry. In SolidWorks, the geometry itself isn't the only measure of success. What's also important is *how* you arrived at that geometry. This isn't because some SolidWorks style police pass judgment on your technique, like a panel of judges rating an Olympic diver, but rather because your models will be passed on to other people who will need to understand how you got your results, and because your model must be able to react predictably to changes. It's not always easy to remember how you executed a particular model six months and 100 models ago. Other users may have to edit your work, and when errors appear (and they will appear), you will have to be able to navigate the design intent without destroying the relationships in the FeatureManager or completely rebuilding it. This is the reason for trying to standardize best practice issues, particularly with advanced functionality and in larger organizations where users with a wide range of abilities may work with the data.

Comparing Multibody Modeling with Assembly Modeling

Multibody modeling is one topic that bridges the worlds of part and assembly modeling. If you're a new user, you may not understand what the big deal is; after all, you just make bodies within a part, right? By the end of this chapter, you should be able to recognize that the issue is more complicated than that. If you're an experienced user, you may have already run into some problems with figuring out where to draw the line between multibody parts and assemblies. This chapter also offers you some answers.

Multibody modeling is not assembly modeling. Often, when new users are introduced to the capabilities of multibody modeling, the first thought that comes to mind is, "This is far easier than making assemblies." However, multibody modeling shouldn't be treated as a replacement for assembly modeling. There are practical reasons for the distinction.

Several assembly-type functions are missing or more difficult to obtain from multibodies. They include the following:

- Dynamic assembly motion
- Configs for separate parts and the Delete Body command
- Bounding box for separate parts and cut-list items
- Center-of-gravity calculations for individual parts
- Custom property information for individual parts and cut-list properties
- Mass property calculations for individual parts with the ability to save the results in a cut-list property or sensor
- Multibodies do not allow you to segment the rebuilds like assemblies and parts.
- Multibody troubleshooting of feature failures is far more difficult.
- Reusing commonly used parts (library parts)

I believe that the distinction between multibody and assembly modeling techniques should be kept as clear as possible. Simply because a technique appears easier at first does not make it *better*. Above all, remember that modeling multibody parts puts *all* the data for *all* the bodies in a *single* part file, in a *single* FeatureManager; there's no easy way to separate the parametric features into individual parts later, regardless of how complex the part becomes.

You may find parallels between making multibody parts and making virtual components (parts that are saved within an assembly file). Although both these techniques offer shortcuts or make some basic tasks easier, good reasons exist for being mindful of the "one part, one file" mentality, including the following:

- Segmenting rebuild times (the ability to rebuild one part instead of several)

- Segmenting large data sets (being able to work on one part at a time)

- Switching out parts

- Using multiple instances of parts

- Reusing parts

- Bills of Materials (BOMs)

- Cut lists in parts

Further, creating drawings of individual bodies of a multibody part is more difficult than creating drawings of individual parts; it can be done, but it's more difficult. Also, editing the features of individual bodies isn't as easy as if the individual body were an individual part. When you create several bodies in a single part, you constantly have to carry the feature and design intent overhead of *all* the features used to create *all* the bodies to edit any individual body. As an alternative, you can use the editing features at the end of the tree.

Using Multibody Techniques Appropriately

You may hear people recommend that at the end of the FeatureManager, only a single solid body should remain, with the rest of the bodies either consumed or deleted. On the other extreme, for some people, anything they can create is allowable. I recommend that if you decide to use multibodies, you should at least be able to articulate *why* you have chosen to do so in a way that doesn't sound like you're making excuses for careless work. Ultimately, you and your peers will be the ones to judge.

Multibody modeling is one of the areas that will induce a lot of arguments about best practices. As an example of a technique that is questionable by best practice standards but can add some capabilities to some things you do with multibody models, you can declare a multibody model as a weldment and gain certain tools such as cut lists. But if you're doing this for a plastic part, some other users may find it confusing. In the end, it is my opinion that you are best served using the available tools as they were meant to be used. The more people who are going to see your models, the more orthodox you should be with best practice rules, especially if some of the other users working with your data are less advanced.

Appropriate uses for multibody modeling include (but are not limited to) the following:

- As an intermediate step on the way to a single-body solid

- As multiple or inserted bodies for reference (reference bodies may be deleted at the bottom of the FeatureManager)

- As over-molded parts

♦ As parts that need to be assembled into a single, smooth shape, such as a computer mouse or an automobile body where the shape is impossible (or at least far more difficult) if done in-context

♦ When the end shape of the finished product is known, but the separation occurs between parts due to manufacturing methods, and materials have not been decided yet (In this case, multibody techniques can save lots of time compared to modeling an assembly.)

♦ As inseparable subassemblies (such as captive fasteners)

♦ When SolidWorks weldments result in a multibody part

♦ When features require tool bodies, such as the Indent feature

♦ When patterns are better as body patterns than as feature patterns

♦ When the Mold tools result in a single multibody part representing the plastic part and the major mold components

♦ Calculating volume of a void (cavity or hollow area)

♦ When the volume of a cavity (in a part or an assembly) needs to be computed

If you are administering a SolidWorks installation of multiple users, then you may be looking for a "bright line" test to clearly define for users which types of multibody modeling are allowable and which are not. So many possibilities exist that it's difficult to say definitively what really *should not* be done, but here's a short list that you can modify for your needs:

♦ Don't use multibody modeling simply to avoid making an assembly.

♦ Don't leave a part in a multibody state that should be joined together into a single body.

♦ Hiding a body is sometimes appropriate, and deleting a body is sometimes appropriate—understand the difference.

Okay, the lecture is over. The message that you should take from all this is not to use multibody techniques just because you can; use them when you have a solid reason to do so. This is the criterion that I use for my own modeling, what I would like to see in models that I inherit from other SolidWorks users, and a philosophy that will serve you well if you're conscientious about it.

Multibody modeling is powerful, and for complex parts, it can even increase rebuild speed compared with single-body modeling or assembly modeling. You can develop and use many powerful techniques based on multibodies, but as I mentioned earlier, sometimes you pay a price for the shortcut.

Understanding Multibody Techniques

Multibody techniques cover a wide range of functionality, and as soon as someone creates a list of what you can do with them, someone else comes up with a new technique. Still, here's a short list of techniques where multibody functionality makes things either easier or simply possible:

♦ Complex shapes across multiple parts

♦ Tool bodies and Boolean operations

◆ Local operations

◆ Patterning

◆ Simplifying very complex parts

◆ As a bridge between solids

◆ Undetermined manufacturing methods

◆ Manipulating imported geometry

In the remainder of this chapter, I will illustrate each technique using an example model and discuss the positives and negatives. As you get deeper into SolidWorks, you'll find that the more complex functions tend to come at a price. A given feature might be the only way to accomplish a particular task, but it rebuilds slowly, might work only in special conditions, might crash from time to time, or might not make sense to other users if they have to edit it.

Using Simple Methods to Create Multiple Bodies

The simplest way to create multiple bodies may also help you understand what multibody models are and how they are used. SolidWorks automatically counts the bodies in the Solid Bodies folder. For reference, the Solid and Surface Body folders are shown in Figure 31.3, along with the Display pane to aid in visualization (Color, Transparency, Hide/Show, and Display mode).

EXTRUDING MULTIPLE LOOPS

If you create two rectangles or other loops in a sketch such that the rectangles don't touch or overlap, and then extrude those rectangles, you will create a multibody part. You could also do the same with two separate features. They could be any solid features, as long as they create two separate volumes. This is demonstrated in Figure 31.1.

FIGURE 31.1
Creating multiple bodies
with a single extrusion

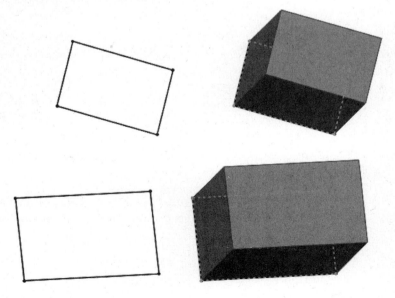

MAKING CUTS

You can also take an existing single body and cut it such that a solid chunk remains. Making a cut that severs a single solid into multiple pieces (more than two) is also possible. Sometimes you have to watch out for this, because it may not be your intention to cut off a small sliver of material, as you can wind up with multiple bodies by mistake. It's a good idea to keep an eye on the Solid Bodies folder to make sure the count doesn't change unexpectedly. However, when the part only has a single solid body, SolidWorks by default hides the Solid Body folder.

USING THE MERGE OPTION

Another easy way to create multiple bodies when you have an existing model is to start a feature connected to the rest of the model, in the normal way, but then turn off the Merge Result option. As illustrated in Figure 31.2, if you have the Merge Result option turned on, the two existing bodies and the new feature will merge into a single body. If the Merge Result option is off, the result will be three separate bodies. Solid features have the Merge Result option turned on by default. This Merge Result option is also available in revolves, lofts, sweeps, and other features that create new solid geometry.

FIGURE 31.2
Using the Merge Result option in the Extrude PropertyManager

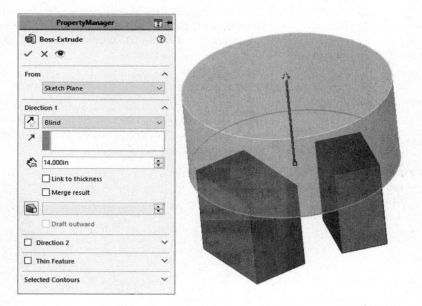

SHARING BODIES

Bodies can be imported from other SolidWorks models or through neutral file types such as Parasolid, STEP, and IGES. SolidWorks has several tools that do this, and they all function similarly with some subtle differences. These six tools are listed here:

◆ Import/Export

◆ Insert Part

◆ Insert into New Part

◆ Split

◆ Save Bodies

◆ Delete/Keep Bodies

These tools have overlapping functionality and are described in more detail in Chapter 33, "Employing Master Model Techniques." For now, it is enough to know that these functions all enable you to manage bodies in SolidWorks.

Creating Complex Shapes Across Bodies

When creating a part such as a computer mouse, you encounter complex shapes that span several individual parts. It makes the most sense to model the entire shape as a single part and then to break it up into separate bodies, making parts from the bodies, adding detail to individual piece parts, and then bringing the parts back together as an assembly.

A part that uses this technique is shown in Figure 31.3. This uses the Move/Copy Bodies feature to move bodies within the part to simulate the explode, although an exploded view can also be used in multibody parts. This function remains in the part as a history-based feature in the FeatureManager and is much more labor-intensive to create than an assembly exploded view because each body is moved by a separate feature.

FIGURE 31.3
A multibody part with a complex shape across bodies

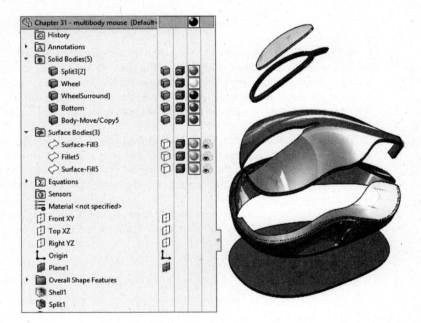

The part shown in Figure 31.1 is not complete, but the starting point for each part has been formed. The part is named Chapter 31 - multibody mouse.sldprt and is located in the materials available for download. You may find it interesting to open the part to see how it has been modeled.

From here, each body is saved to individual parts to complete the detailing, and then the parts are brought back together to create an assembly. The separate bodies in this case were created using the Split feature, which enables you to use surfaces, sketches, or planes to split a single body into multiple bodies. This is described in more detail later in this chapter.

The entire process for creating a finished assembly of finished parts is detailed in Figure 31.4. This flow chart shows conceptually how the overall shape created as a single part has moved from a single part/single body to a single part/multiple body to individual parts to an assembly of individual parts. This process is sometimes called the Master Model workflow because all of the individual parts are driven by a single master model.

FIGURE 31.4

A Master
Model workflow

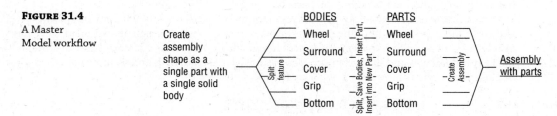

In Figure 31.5, the image to the left depicts how this part was modeled. The first step was to create the shape as a single body within the part. As shown in the FeatureManager, this is all contained inside the Overall Shape Features folder. This folder is presented here as a *black box* because surface features were used to create the part. It really doesn't matter at this point *how* the part was created, and these features are not discussed until Chapter 32, "Working with Surfaces."

The image to the right in Figure 31.5 shows transparent surface bodies that were used to split the model into separate bodies using the Split features shown in the tree. Using this technique, you can create the overall shape as a single piece and then split it into separate parts. You also can apply this technique in the context of an assembly, but this method is far more direct.

To go from the multibody part created here to a set of separate parts uses a Master Model function, which is described in more detail in Chapter 33, "Employing Master Model Techniques."

FIGURE 31.5
Splitting the part
into bodies

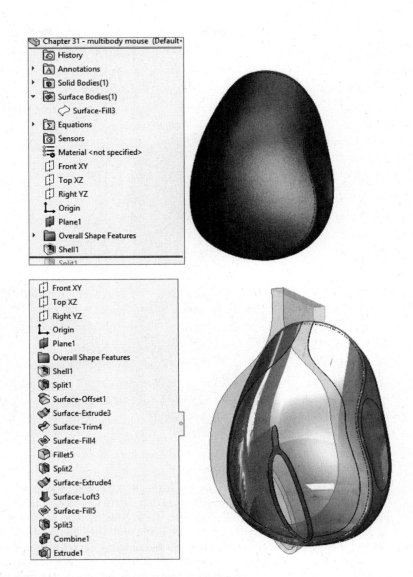

Using Tool Bodies and Boolean Operations

Some features require multiple bodies within a part, such as the Indent and Combine features, among others. Using one body to create a shape in another is a common use for bodies within a part. The body with the finished geometry is called the *target*, and the body used to create or edit the shape is called the *tool*.

FIGURE 31.6
The Indent feature using
a tool body

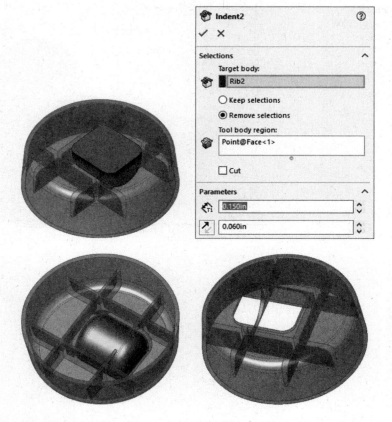

USING THE INDENT FEATURE

The Indent feature is covered briefly in Chapter 8, "Selecting Secondary Features," before multibodies are introduced, so it's fitting that I revisit it here so you can better understand the multibody aspect of its use. The Indent feature *indents* the *target* body with the *tool* body. It can also use another part in the context of an assembly as the tool. The indentation can exactly fit the form of the tool, or there can be a gap around the tool. You can also control the thickness of the material around the indent. A further option is to simply cut the target with the tool instead of indenting.

Figure 31.6 shows the target part as transparent and the tool as opaque, before and after the Indent feature has been applied. The Indent PropertyManager is also shown.

The Indent feature can be problematic if it breaks into multiple areas as it does in this part, due to the ribbing on the underside of the target body. Notice that in the PropertyManager in Figure 31.6, two selections were made in the Tool Body Region selection box. The tool body is selected on either side of the rib that bisects the tool. This concept is not very intuitive, and you may have to play with the part and the options to understand what it's doing.

FIGURE 31.7
Using the Keep
and Remove
Selections options

The Keep Selections and Remove Selections options are equally unintuitive, but they determine which side of the target body is indented. For example, if the part of the tool body that's outside of the target body (the flat side) is selected instead of the two inside regions, the resulting part looks as it does in Figure 31.7, where the tool body has been hidden. You can achieve the same result by toggling the Keep Selections and Remove Selections options. These options exist because sometimes it's difficult or impossible to select the correct areas of a body that's embedded in another body.

USING THE MOVE/COPY BODIES AND COMBINE FEATURES

The Move/Copy Bodies and Combine features can be demonstrated using the same part. The tool body that was used in the previous example to indent the main body is moved and then added to the main body in this example.

Figure 31.8 shows the starting and ending points of the process, as well as the PropertyManagers of the two features used to get from one point to the other. Keep in mind that both the Move/Copy Bodies and the Combine features are history-based features listed in the FeatureManager.

FIGURE 31.8
Using the Move/
Copy Bodies and
Combine features

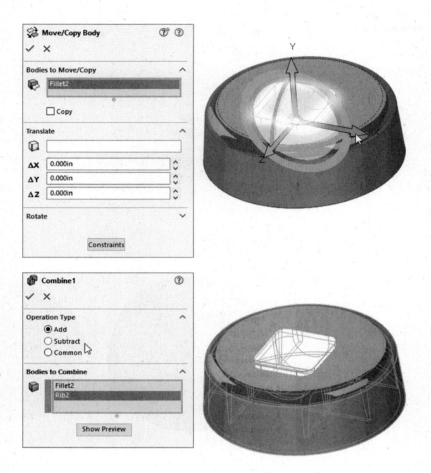

In this case, the Move or Copy Bodies feature uses distances and angles with the orange Triad. You can also use mates to move or locate the body. These mates enable you to locate bodies in a way that's similar to the way they are used in assemblies.

In the Combine PropertyManager, you'll notice that common Boolean operations—such as union (add), difference (subtract), and intersection (common)—are available through this interface.

You can use an interesting technique in this part. The features creating the smaller tool body and the Move/Copy Bodies and Combine features can be put together into a folder, and the folder itself can be reordered before the Shell feature. This means that the combined body is also shelled out, and the rib goes down inside of it. This produces an odd error message and unexpectedly places several features into the folder, but it does work.

You may want to open this part in SolidWorks to see exactly how all this was done instead of relying on the figure illustrations. The part used for Figure 31.9 is in the download material and is named Chapter 31 - rib trick.sldprt.

FIGURE 31.9
Reordering features

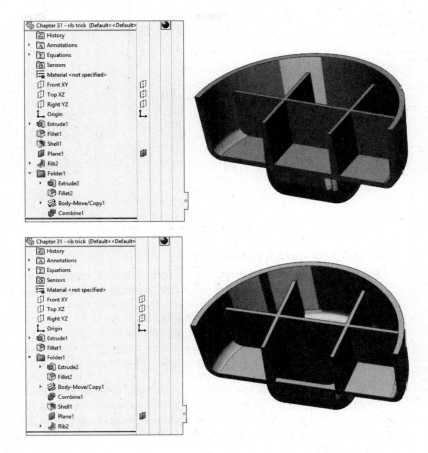

Using Local Operations

If you have ever had a modeling situation where you needed to shell out a portion of a part but not the entire part, or you had a fillet that would work only if certain geometry were not there, then you may have been able to benefit from multibody techniques to accomplish these tasks.

Using the Flex Feature

The part shown in Figure 31.10 first appeared in Chapter 8, "Selecting Secondary Features," where I demonstrated the Flex feature. This is a rubber plug for an electronic device. In order to make one side of the part flex without flexing the other side, multiple bodies were used. The part was split into two bodies using the Split feature and a plane. One side of the part was then twisted, and the two bodies were recombined. The Features folder contains the features that were used to build the original part geometry, which could just as easily have been either native or imported.

FIGURE 31.10
Splitting a part to
perform a
local operation

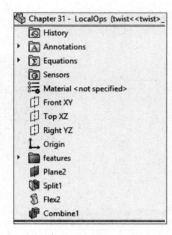

USING THE SHELL FEATURE

The Shell feature hollows out one solid body at a time, removing selected faces. If there are multiple solid bodies, you must select one to be shelled. You can select a body without selecting a face by using the small Solid Body selection box under the larger Faces To Remove selection box in the PropertyManager. If you don't select any faces to be removed, then the body is hollowed out with no external indication that the part is hollow unless you view it in section view, transparency view, or wireframe view. Single or multiple faces can be removed. This feature works by offsetting the faces of the outside of the model, and the feature may fail if this causes problems with the internal geometry.

The Multi-Thickness Shell option enables you to select faces that will have a different thickness from the overall shell thickness. This is one method that you can sometimes use to restrict the scope of the Shell feature to a certain area of a body, Multi-thickness shell is somewhat limited in that faces with different thicknesses will not shell if they are tangent or nearly tangent to one another.

Because the Shell feature works on only one body at a time, splitting a part into multiple bodies can be an effective way to limit the scope of the feature. The part shown in Figure 31.11 has been split in half, and one-half has been made transparent for visualization purposes; as a result, you can see that the part is shelled on the bottom on one end and on the top on the other end. The Shell feature has no option for doing this with existing geometry. The only ways that you can do this are either through feature order or by using multibodies. You can find the part shown in Figure 31.9 in the download material with the name Chapter 31 - LocalOps Shell.sldprt.

FIGURE 31.11
Shelling locally

To shell the part this way with feature order, you create one block and shell it, and then create the other block and shell that. In order for this technique to work, the second shell must be as big as, or bigger than, the first shell. If it's smaller, then it will (or may) hollow out areas that aren't intended to be hollow.

To shell the part with multibodies, you can use two methods. One method is to build the first block and then build the second block but turn off the Merge option. This creates bodies that are side by side. You then shell one block on the bottom and the other on the top. To avoid a double-thickness wall between them, the end face can be removed along with either the top or bottom face. If you edit the part, you may notice that one of the Shell features has two faces removed.

The second method is to build a single block and split it using a sketch line, a plane, or a surface, and then proceed in the same way as the first method.

Patterning

Patterns of bodies are fast, powerful, and commonly used alternatives to patterning features. Chapter 9, "Patterning and Mirroring," discusses feature patterns and mirroring, and it examines, at least in part, how different types of patterns affect model rebuild speeds. When appropriate, patterning bodies can also be a big rebuild timesaver. When patterning a body, none of the parametrics or intelligence is patterned with it, but you must pattern the entire body. Another odd thing about patterning bodies in SolidWorks is that there's no option to merge the bodies either to one another or to a main body. This requires an extra step that involves adding a Combine feature. Mirroring is the same, except that it has an option to merge bodies, but it only merges the original body to the mirrored body. It doesn't merge either the original or the mirrored body to a central main body.

In this example, an imported part has a "feature" that needs to be reused around the part. The technique used here is to split away the feature as a separate body and then pattern the body around the part and join it all back together. This function can be used with native geometry as well as imported. This process is shown in Figure 31.12. This function uses a simple planar surface. A plane could have been used to split off the body to be patterned, but the plane would have also split off a part of the globe at the top, so a planar surface (which can be limited in extent where a plane cannot) was used.

The image on the left in Figure 31.12 is the raw imported part. The middle image shows a planar surface created on the face of the part, where the planar surface has been used with the Split feature to cut the leg off the part. The image on the right shows the split leg patterned around an axis that was created from the intersection of two planes.

FIGURE 31.12
Splitting away a body
and patterning it

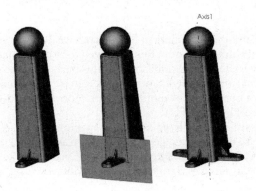

If you want to practice with this part, it's in the download material for Chapter 31; the imported Parasolid file is named Chapter 31 - Pattern import.x_t.

PERFORMANCE

In some situations, patterning bodies is a performance advantage, and in some situations, it isn't. You get an advantage from patterning bodies when the geometry used to create the pattern seed is complex, uses many features, or doesn't work well or at all for a feature pattern.

On the other hand, if you repeat the experiments from Chapter 9, "Patterning and Mirroring," using a small body with a hole in it instead of patterning a Hole feature, you will find that the body pattern is far slower than the feature patterning because of the necessary step of combining bodies.

Simplifying Very Complex Parts

Sometimes very complex parts work better when they're built in sections as separate parts than when they are built as a single feature tree. Segmenting the rebuild times for parts with hundreds of features enables you to manage how much of the tree you are willing to rebuild at one time. The example used to demonstrate this technique is a large plastic part built entirely from ribs, and making use of literally hundreds of solid bodies, and is shown in Figure 31.13.

FIGURE 31.13
A complex model created as separate parts and brought together as bodies in a single part

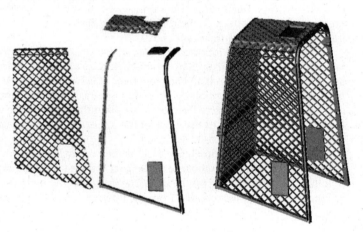

The rebuild time for a model like this can easily reach several minutes, and the feature count can be in the hundreds, or in this case, well over one thousand. To minimize the rebuild time, a different workflow was established for this part. First, the major inside and outside faces were created with surfaces. Next, the surfaces were saved into several other parts. Each of these parts represents a portion of the mold. Enough information exists in the master model to align the features in each part.

The ribs on this part were created by making a single extrusion (the Rib feature couldn't be used because there was no geometry to serve as a boundary for the ribs), and then the extrusion was patterned and the pattern was mirrored. After all the ribs were created, they had to be shaped, so the surfaces from the master model were used to cut the ribs to shape.

The ribs couldn't be extruded with a draft or with fillets, because the outer and inner surfaces were nonplanar. The draft had to be built as a Parting Line draft for the same reason, and the fillets had to be applied after the draft. Further, draft and fillets can only be applied to a single body at a time; as a result, a separate Draft feature and a separate Fillet feature had to be applied to each body, and each rib was a separate body. After the draft and fillets were applied, the bodies were joined into a single body.

I recognize that this description of how I made the part is a lot to comprehend. The point is not to show in detail how the parts were built, but to demonstrate how you can get to a part with 1,200 features or more. It's precisely on parts with this level of complexity that you need to think about modeling the part in this modular fashion—build each part separately and bring each separate section of the part together as individual bodies.

Figure 31.13 shows two of the separate pull direction parts being separated from one another in the same way that the mouse part was shown exploded in the previous example. Here the frame is also modeled as a separate part, again because it wasn't so intimately related to the other parts and was easily separated out.

After this was completed for each direction, the separate parts were put together as bodies into a single part and again joined together using the Combine feature. Having all those features in separate parts allows you to segment the rebuild time. This is the opposite of building all the parts of an assembly in a single part, where you are simply compounding your rebuild time.

This is probably a technique that you won't use very often, but when you do, it can save you lots of rebuild time. I use it whenever I have a model that takes more than 20 to 30 seconds to rebuild and I know that I'm going to be doing lots of work on it; it must also lend itself to segmenting in the way that this one did, with easily definable areas.

Bridging Between Solids

Often when modeling, you "build what you know" and "fill in as you go." An example of this would be modeling a duct between end connections that are well defined. The duct in between is defined only by the ends, which must exist first. Another example is a connecting rod where you know the diameter of each end and the distance between the ends, and the connection between them is of secondary importance.

Figure 31.14 shows a connecting rod made in this way. In this case, the bearing seat at one end was created, and the other end was created by copying the body of the first one. From there, the link between the bearing seats was created, which joined the separate bodies together into a single solid body.

This part contains some interesting features. First is the Thin Feature extrude that's used to make the first bearing seat, which is combined with a Mid plane extrude to make it symmetrical at the same time. Then comes the Move/Copy Bodies feature, which copies the body in the same way that the feature in previous examples has moved bodies. Next is the use of the Extrude From option, which extrudes from a face, and then the use of the end condition Up To Next, which ends the feature neatly. The part also incorporates fillets that use faces and features to form the selection.

If you aren't familiar with these options, I recommend that you open the part from the download materials and look at it. It's a simple part that takes advantage of nice but simple productivity-enhancing options that have been available for some time in the SolidWorks software. The part filename is `Chapter 31 - Bridge.sldprt`.

FIGURE 31.14
Connecting dis-
joint bodies

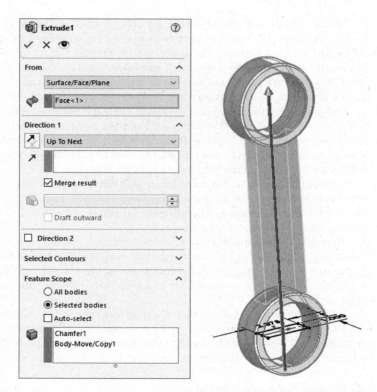

By default, Solid features have the Merge option selected, and they automatically combine with any bodies that they touch. At the same time, they don't display errors if the Merge option is selected but the new body doesn't touch any existing bodies.

Modeling for Undetermined Manufacturing Methods

Sometimes, you must start a design before you know exactly how the product will be manufactured. This is an example of where the geometry of the finished product exists first and is then broken up into manufacturable parts. The initial model, shown in the image at the top in Figure 31.15, is created as a single part as a result of input from marketing, but when it comes time for manufacturing input, the part count and processes keep changing. Where the parts break from one another keeps changing as well. When that kind of change is happening, having the parts created as individual parts is a big liability because it's difficult to change. Changing which bodies are merged together is much easier.

It's worth mentioning two potential difficulties that you may run into with methods like this. The first is that if you have people making drawings from parts that have been derived from bodies in a single part, then they are forced into the Reference Dimension scheme of dimensioning parts because the feature dimensions don't survive being moved from the multibody part. This may or may not be an issue, depending on how the people doing the drawings are accustomed to working.

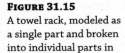

FIGURE 31.15
A towel rack, modeled as a single part and broken into individual parts in an assembly

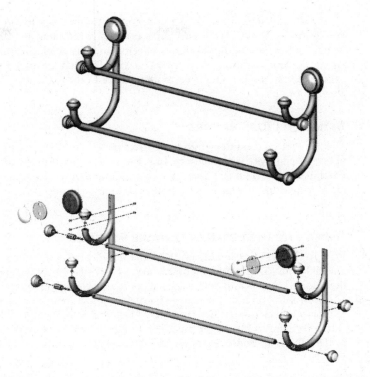

The second potential issue is what you do in situations where there are multiple instances of a part that has been modeled this way. Notice in the towel rack in Figure 31.15 that several finials, spacers, rails, and other parts are duplicated. Multibody techniques don't offer a way of dealing with this, so it requires some manual assembly modeling. You can make the assembly directly from the multibody part, but if you need make multiple instances of particular parts, you need to do this manually rather than automatically.

Applying the Feature Scope to Bodies

The Feature Scope is a panel in any feature that creates solid bodies, but it only appears when there are multiple bodies in the part. It isn't the same as the Feature Scope used for assembly features, but it functions in a similar way. In assemblies, the Feature Scope identifies which parts are affected by the current assembly feature. In parts, it applies only to bodies and can be used for features that add material as well as features that remove material (assembly features can only remove material).

The Feature Scope is a way to make the Merge Result option more selective. The Merge Result option by default doesn't discriminate; it causes the feature to merge with any other solid body that it touches. However, the Feature Scope enables the user to select which bodies to merge with or otherwise affect. Feature Scope also applies to additional feature types such as cuts. The Feature Scope becomes available in the PropertyManager whenever the part has multiple bodies and an eligible feature is used. The Feature Scope panel is shown in Figure 31.14.

The default setting for the Feature Scope is to use the Selected Bodies option with the Auto-Select option. The All Bodies option is essentially the same as using the Merge Result option. When the Selected Bodies option is selected and Auto-Select is unselected, you must select bodies for the current feature to affect them. New bodies that are added to the model are not automatically added to the list; you need to manually edit the feature and add additional bodies to the list as appropriate.

USING THE RIB FEATURE

The Rib feature used to be hypersensitive to changes to the number of bodies. When the number of bodies changed, whether more or fewer bodies, any Rib features would fail. That bug has been fixed in recent versions; however, be aware that if you are using older versions of SolidWorks, reordering or rolling back to either add or remove bodies will cause the selection of which body to effect will fail.

USING THE DELETE/KEEP BODIES FEATURE

Prior to the 2015 version of SolidWorks, the Delete/Keep Bodies feature used to be called simply Delete Bodies. Depending on how you toggle the Delete or Keep options, the feature will keep the selected bodies and delete the rest, or it will delete the selected bodies and keep the rest.

Depending on how the feature is functioning, as delete or keep, the icon in the FeatureManager will change. When it works as Delete Bodies, the block will have an X in the lower-right corner. When it is functioning as Keep Bodies, it will have a check mark. The PropertyManager for Delete/Keep Bodies is shown in Figure 31.16.

FIGURE 31.16
The Delete/Keep Bodies
PropertyManager

Managing Bodies with the Split Feature

The Split feature has essentially three functions:

- ◆ To split a single solid body into multiple solid bodies using planes, sketches, or surface bodies

- ◆ To save individual solid bodies to individual part files

- ◆ To reassemble individual part files that are saved into an assembly where the parts are all positioned in the same relative position as their corresponding bodies

The part of the Split feature that relates to this chapter is the first function mentioned, which is splitting a single solid body into multiple bodies using a sketch, a plane, or a surface body.

The Split feature cannot be used to split surface bodies. In fact, nothing in SolidWorks can split surface bodies. Only solid bodies can be split. Surface bodies can only be trimmed, so the effective workaround for not being able to split surface bodies is to copy the body, and then trim and keep one side of the copy and the other side of the original. This seems like a functionality oversight and would make a great enhancement request if you have ever come across the need for this functionality.

SPLITTING WITH A SKETCH

When you are using a sketch to split a single solid body into multiple bodies, the Split process works like this:

1. Create a sketch with an open or closed loop; even a mixture of open and closed profiles will work. If it's open, the endpoints must be on an exterior edge or hanging off into space; they cannot actually be inside the boundaries of the solid. The one restriction is that the sketch can't be already used by another feature.

2. Initiate the Split feature from the Features toolbar or from the menus by choosing Insert ➤ Features ➤ Split. You can do this with the sketch active, with the sketch inactive but selected, or with nothing selected at all.

3. Click the Cut Bodies button. This doesn't actually cut anything; it only previews the split. When this is done, the resulting bodies appear in the window below and callout flags are placed on the part in the graphics window. Figure 31.17 shows the PropertyManager and the preview.

FIGURE 31.17
Using the Split feature

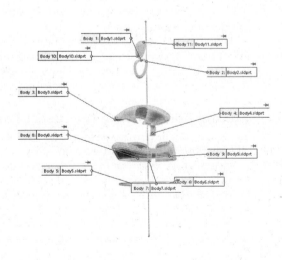

Check marks next to the body in the list indicate that the body will be saved to an external file. Using the Auto-Assign Names button will make the software assign filenames to all bodies and prepare to save them as external files, using the template information at the bottom of the PropertyManager.

The Consume Cut Bodies option removes, or consumes, any of the bodies that have a check mark.

SPLITTING WITH A PLANE

Splitting with a plane provides the same type of results and uses the same options as splitting with a sketch. However, you never have to worry about the plane being extended far enough, because the cut is made from the infinite extension of the plane. The only thing you have to worry about with a plane is whether it intersects the part.

SPLITTING WITH A SURFACE BODY

Surface bodies are used to split solid bodies for a couple of reasons. In the part shown in Figure 31.12, a surface body was used to make the split instead of a sketch or a plane, because both of those entities split everything in an infinite distance either normal to the sketch plane or in the selected plane. A surface body only splits to the extents of the splitting surface body. If you look closely at the part, you notice that a plane or sketch would lop off one side of the sphere on top of the object, but the small planar surface is limited enough in size to split only what is necessary.

Another advantage to using a surface body is that it isn't limited to a two-dimensional cut. The surface itself can be any type of surface, such as planar, extruded, revolved, lofted, or imported. Taking this a step further, the surface isn't limited to being a single face or a body resulting from a single feature; it could be made from several features that are put together as long as it's a single body and all the outer edges of the surface body are outside the solid body. If you examine the mouse part shown in Figure 31.3, you can see that it has splits made from multifeature surface bodies.

I mention splitting with surface bodies here because this is where I discuss the Split function, even though I haven't covered the surfacing functions yet. It may be useful to read parts of this book out of order; given how the topics interrelate, it's impossible to order them in such a way that some sections don't refer to a topic that hasn't yet been covered.

Adding Bodies Using the Insert Part Feature

The Insert Part button can be found on the Features toolbar, or you can access this feature by choosing Insert ➤ Part from the menus.

Insert Part enables you to insert one part into another part. When inserting the part, you have the option to insert solid bodies, axes, planes, cosmetic threads, surface bodies, and several other types of entities, including sketches and features. The PropertyManager interface for the Insert Part feature is shown in Figure 31.18.

When you use Insert Part, there's no Insert Part feature that becomes part of the tree. Instead, a Part icon is shown with the name of the part being inserted as a feature. Notice that the basket part shown in Figure 31.13 also uses Insert Part to put together bodies to form a finished part.

FIGURE 31.18
The Insert Part
PropertyManager

WORKING WITH SECONDARY OPERATIONS

One commonly used technique has to do with secondary operations. For example, you may have designed a casting that needs several machining operations after it comes from the foundry. The foundry needs a drawing to produce the raw casting, and the machine shop needs a different drawing to tap holes, spot face areas, trim flash, and so on.

You can use configurations to do this by using Insert Part in another way. This has nothing to do with multiple body techniques, but this is the only place in this book where Insert Part is covered in much detail. One of the advantages of using Insert Part is that you no longer carry around the overhead of all the features in the parent part. It's as if the inserted part were imported. The configurations method forces you to carry around much more feature overhead. Of course, the downside is that now there's an additional file to manage, but this can be an advantage because many companies assign different part numbers to parts before and after secondary operations.

STARTING POINT

Looking back to the mouse shown in Figure 31.3, the main part has been split into several bodies. You can use Insert Part to insert the whole mouse into a new part where all the bodies except one are deleted, and then the remaining body serves as the starting point for a new part. Many additional features are needed on all the bodies that make up the mouse, such as assembly features, cosmetic features, functional features, and manufacturing features.

Using Intersect to Modify Bodies

Intersect combines the capabilities of several surface and solid body tools. The tools that it combines are Split, Cut With Surface, Cut, Trim, Knit, and Thicken. Chapter 32, "Working with Surfaces," will take another look at this feature because it can use surfaces. In this chapter, we just look at its capability with solids.

Intersect can use solid bodies, surface bodies, and planes as inputs, and the output will be a number of solid or surface bodies. Based on the inputs, the Feature interface shows the possible outcomes, and you just select the body regions you want to keep. Figure 31.19 shows this feature in action. There's a block centered on the origin and a sphere inside the block, also centered on the origin.

FIGURE 31.19
Splitting a solid
with Intersect

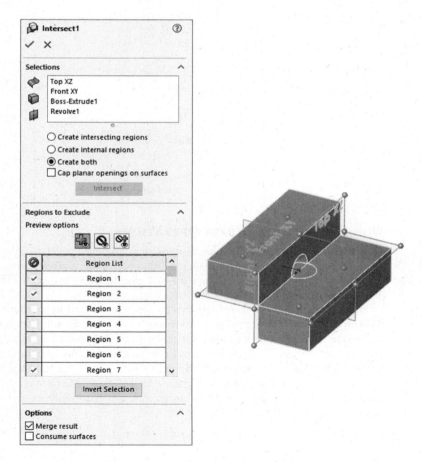

In this example, the sphere is removed from the block, which is then split by the Top and Front planes, creating four possible solid regions. By excluding the sphere and one solid region, this feature produces the result shown on the right.

This tool combines existing solid and surface functionality from features like Trim, Combine, Cut With Surface, and Knit.

It is useful for replacing many Combine Add features. It pretty much combines anything that is possible. While Combine Add outputs one body, Intersect can output multiple bodies. Is also useful for creating volumes from internal cavities, without modifying the surrounding bodies.

Managing Bodies

Managing bodies in SolidWorks isn't as clean a task as managing parts in an assembly. As you work with bodies, you may discover some surprises in how bodies are managed. Body naming and merge/split issues are among some of the behaviors you will have to learn to deal with. This section prepares you for challenges involved in managing bodies in SolidWorks.

Using Body Folders

The top of the FeatureManager includes a pair of folders—one called Solid Bodies and the other called Surface Bodies (which only exist if you have multiple solid bodies or any surface bodies). They reflect the state of the model at the current position of the Rollback bar. As a result, the folders can change and even disappear as you roll the tree back and forth in history. Figure 31.20 shows the top of a FeatureManager that has both Solid and Surface Bodies folders. Notice that the number in parentheses after the name of the folder shows how many bodies are in that particular folder.

FIGURE 31.20
Body folders in the
FeatureManager

An odd fact about these folders is that you are allowed to rename the folders, but the name changes never remain. If you go back to rename the folder again, the name that you previously assigned will display.

You may encounter another problem with the display of FeatureManager header items in general when they are set to Automatic display (which display only when they contain something). The Automatic setting for FeatureManager folder display works incorrectly from time to time. For this reason, I suggest using the Show option to display important folders. Figure 31.21 shows the Options page (Tools ➤ Options ➤ FeatureManager) that controls the visibility of folders.

FIGURE 31.21
Control the visibility of
FeatureManager items

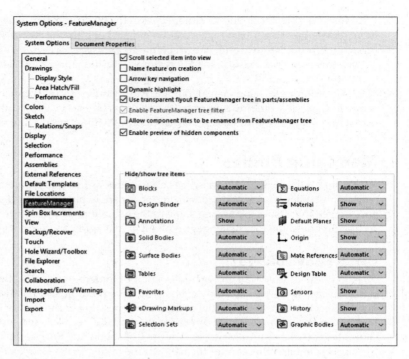

By right-clicking either of the bodies folders, you can select the Show Feature History option, which shows the features that have combined to create the bodies in an indented list under the body name. This view of the FeatureManager is shown in Figure 31.22. This option is very useful when you are editing or troubleshooting bodies.

FIGURE 31.22
Using the Show Feature
History option

Figure 31.22 also shows the other options in the right mouse button (RMB) menu. All the bodies in the folder can be alternatively shown or hidden from this menu, as well as deleted. Although the Hide or Show state of a body doesn't create a history-based feature in the tree, the Delete feature does, as discussed previously.

You can expand the Display pane in parts to show display information for bodies (see Figure 31.23). Display pane shows the colors assigned to the solid bodies, as well as the fact that several surface bodies exist but are hidden.

FIGURE 31.23

The Display pane showing information about solid and surface bodies

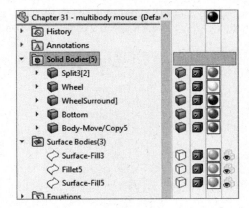

The folders also make bodies easier to identify, especially when combined with the setting found at Tools ➢ Options ➢ Display/Selection ➢ Dynamic Highlight From Graphics View. This setting quickly turns the body outline red if you move the mouse over the body in the Body folder.

Hiding or Showing Bodies

You can hide or show bodies in several ways. I've already described the method of using the bodies folders to hide or show all the bodies at once, but you can also right-click individual bodies in the folders to hide or show them using the RMB menu. Remember that with the context bars, you have the option to use them with the RMB menu as well as with left-click selections. I include all context bar options in the RMB menu generically.

If you can see a body in the graphics area, then you can right-click the body and select Hide under the Body heading. This works for both solids and surfaces. The Display pane, shown to the right of the FeatureManager in Figure 31.23, can also be used to hide or show bodies, change body transparency and appearance, and change the Display mode of bodies. Display pane is a handy tool for visualization options.

When you are hiding or showing bodies from the FeatureManager, but not using the bodies folders and using the features themselves instead, things get a little complicated. If you want to hide or show a solid body, you can use any feature that's a parent of the body to hide or show the body. For example, you can use the Shell feature in the mouse model to hide or show all the bodies of which it's a parent.

Other facts that you need to know about bodies and their hide or show states are that the Hide or Show feature is both configurable and dependent on the rollback state. As a result, if you hide a body and then roll back, it may appear again and you have to hide it again. Then, if you roll forward, the state changes again. Also, a body can be hidden in one configuration, and when you switch configurations, it remains hidden. All the unwritten rules make it rather frustrating at times to work with bodies.

Display State functionality in multibody parts is an extremely handy and a very fast way to change color, transparency, or display modes for individual bodies. The best way to handle this is to expand the Display pane and control Hide/Show, Display Mode, Appearance, and Transparency directly from the Display pane. Figure 31.24 shows the Display pane in action on a multibody part.

FIGURE 31.24
Using the Display pane to control multibody display states

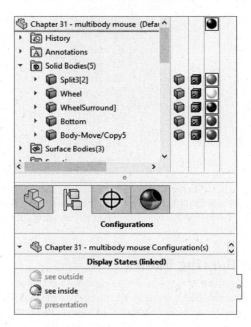

In Figure 31.24, the FeatureManager panel is split so you can see the configurations and Display State information alongside the bodies folder and Display pane. If you are familiar with display states in assemblies, it's the same as for bodies.

You can assign different materials to each body. If different parts are made of different materials, the only situations in which I would model this way would be overmolds, where multiple materials are molded onto one another, and inseparable subassemblies, like purchased components such as screws with captive washers or a circuit board with rivets. To apply materials to bodies, right-click the body in the Solid Bodies folder and select Material.

Another tool in SolidWorks is called Show Hidden Bodies. It works like its assembly equivalent Show Hidden Components. In a part with hidden bodies, right-click an empty space in the graphics window and select Show Hidden Bodies. The interface shown in Figure 31.25 is displayed, visible become hidden and hidden become visible, and the command uses a special cursor. This tool comes in handy in complex design situations where you have a large number of bodies or when you simply need to visualize existing bodies that are not shown.

FIGURE 31.25
Show Hidden Bodies
interface and cursor

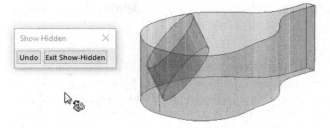

For faster (solid or surface) body visibility changes, use these shortcuts:

◆ Tab with the cursor over a body in the graphics window will hide a body.

◆ Shift+Tab with the cursor over a hidden body will show the body. (This works best with the preview techniques of selecting a body from the bodies folders or Ctrl+Shift+Tab.)

◆ Holding Ctrl+Shift+Tab previews all hidden bodies. Clicking on the temporarily shown bodies will show the selected bodies.

◆ Selecting hidden bodies in the Solid or Surface Bodies folders will preview those bodies until they are unselected. You can then press Shift+Tab with the cursor over any body to show that body.

◆ Use the Tab, Shift+Tab, and Ctrl+Shift+Tab shortcuts to hide/show bodies.

CAUTION Some features exclude bodies if the bodies are hidden when you edit the feature. Be careful of this and be sure to show all the bodies that are used in a particular function before you edit it. For example, if a body is hidden and you create a new extrude that touches the hidden body, the new body won't merge with the hidden one *even if the Merge option is on*. If the hidden body is then shown and you edit the second body, the bodies will merge upon the closing of the second body.

Deleting Bodies

I've already mentioned that you can delete bodies using the Delete/Keep Bodies feature and that this feature exists in the tree of the part. This feature previously was called Delete Bodies.

Delete/Keep Bodies doesn't affect file size or rebuild speed. In fact, I find it difficult to come up with examples of when you should use it or if a throwaway body somehow remains in the part. Some people use this feature to clean up the organization of the tree. However, all it does beyond hiding bodies is to make them inaccessible (without rolling back or editing the feature). Other users insist on keeping the tree free of extraneous bodies and immediately delete bodies that have been used. To me, this technique replaces one kind of clutter with another, and it means that tools that should be available to you (solid or surface bodies) aren't available unless you reorder the Delete Body feature down the tree and/or roll back. In any case, this is really a matter of personal working style and not of any great importance.

Some export filetypes will export all the bodies without warning. Thus, the easiest way to make sure that a file doesn't have extra bodies for the export is to just add a Delete Body feature that removes the extraneous bodies that aren't included in the final part. Also, always re-import any exported data to make sure the export worked correctly.

TIP Deleting unnecessary bodies directly reduces the number of graphics-triangles. Your large assemblies will thank you!

Renaming Bodies

Notice that the bodies that you see in the folders have been named for the last feature that touched a given body. That means that the bodies keep changing names. If you deliberately rename a body, it retains the name you give it through future changes. You should follow the same rules for naming bodies as you do for naming features. It isn't necessary to rename every body, but if you will use one body frequently and need to select it from the FeatureManager, renaming it is very useful.

Tutorials: Working with Multibodies

This section contains various short examples of multibody techniques in order from easy to more difficult.

Merging and Local Operations

This tutorial gives you some experience using the Merge Result option and using features on individual bodies to demonstrate the local operations functionality of multibody modeling. Try these steps:

1. Start a new part, and sketch a rectangle centered on the origin on the Top plane. Make the rectangle any size you like.

2. Extrude the rectangle to roughly one-third of its smaller dimension.

3. Open a second sketch on the Top plane. Hide the first solid body by right-clicking it in either the FeatureManager or the graphics window.

4. Show the sketch for the first feature, and draw a second rectangle on the far side of the rectangle from the origin. Make sure the second rectangle gets two Coincident relations to the first sketch at two corners so the rectangles are the same width. When the sketch is complete, hide the sketch that was shown.

5. Extrude the second rectangle to about two-thirds of the depth of the first rectangle.

NOTE Notice that the Merge option was not changed from the default setting (On) for the second extrude, but because the first extrude was hidden, the second extrude didn't merge with it. Be careful of subsequent edits to either of the features if the first body is shown, because this may cause the bodies to merge unexpectedly. In this tutorial, the bodies are later merged intentionally. Ideally, what you should do is deselect the Merge option of the second extrude.

6. Shell out the second extrusion by removing two adjacent sides, as shown in Figure 31.26. One of the sides is the top, and the other is the shared side with the hidden body. The body that should be hidden at this point is shown as transparent in the image for reference only. The body was made transparent to make it easier to select the face of the second body.

FIGURE 31.26
Shelling two sides
of a block

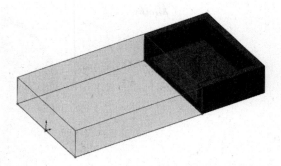

7. Show the first body either from the Solid Bodies folder at the top of the tree or from the RMB menu of the first solid feature in the tree.

8. Shell the bottom side of the first body, so the cavities in the two bodies are on opposite sides.

9. Combine the two bodies using the Combine tool you can find by choosing Insert ➤ Features ➤ Combine. This feature is also available via the RMB menu in the Solid Body folder. Select the Add option and select the two bodies. Click OK to finish the feature. Figure 31.27 shows the finished part.

FIGURE 31.27
The finished part

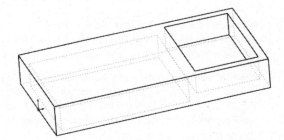

Splitting and Patterning Bodies

This tutorial guides you through the steps to delete a pattern of *features* from an imported body, separate one of the features, and then pattern it with a different number of features. This introduces some simple surface functions in preparation for Chapter 32, "Working with Surfaces." Follow these steps:

1. Open the Parasolid file from the download materials called Chapter 31 – Bonita Tutorial.x_t.

2. Using the Selection Filter set to filter the Face selection (the default hotkey for this is X), select all the faces of the leg. You can use window-selection techniques to avoid clicking each face.

3. Click the Delete Face button on the Surfaces toolbar, or access the command by choosing Insert ➤ Face ➤ Delete from the menus. Make sure that the Delete And Patch option is selected. The selected faces and the Delete Face PropertyManager should look like Figure 31.28. Click OK to accept the feature.

FIGURE 31.28
The Delete Face
PropertyManager

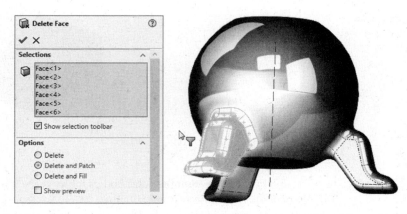

4. Repeat the process for a second leg, leaving the third leg to be separated from the rest of the part and patterned.

5. After the two legs have been removed, click the outer main spherical surface, and then choose Insert ➤ Surface ➤ Offset from the menus. Set the offset distance to zero. Notice that a Surface Bodies folder is now added to the tree, near the top.

TIP A zero distance offset surface is frequently used to copy faces.

6. Hide the solid body. You can do this from the Solid Bodies folder, from the FeatureManager, or from the graphics window. Hiding the solid leaves the offset surface, and there should be three holes in it.

7. Select one of the edges of the hole indicated in Figure 31.29 and press the Delete key. The Choose Option dialog box will appear. Select the Delete Hole option rather than the Delete Feature option. The Delete Hole operation becomes a history-based feature in the model tree. Before moving on to the next step, remember that you may need to turn off the Selection Filter for faces.

FIGURE 31.29
Using the Delete
Hole option

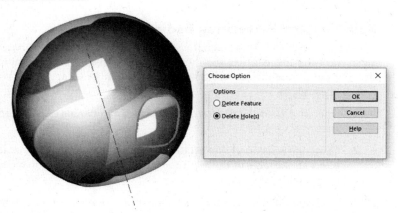

NOTE Delete Hole is really a hidden functionality of the surface feature called Untrim. Untrim is discussed more in Chapter 32, "Working with Surfaces," but you can use it to restore original boundaries to a surface.

8. After you delete the hole from the surface body, change the color of the surface body the same way you changed the colors of parts, faces, and features.

9. Click the surface body in the Surface Bodies folder, and either press the Delete key or select Delete Body from the RMB menu. Click OK to accept the feature. This will place a Delete Body feature in the tree. It will keep the body from getting in the way when it isn't needed. This isn't a necessary step, but many people choose to use it. (Suppress the Delete Body feature, because this body is needed again later.)

TIP If you delete a body in this way and then need it later down the tree, you can delete, rollback, suppress, or reorder the Delete Body feature later in the tree.

10. Now show the solid body. You'll notice that the color of the surface conflicts with the color of the solid. This mottled appearance is due to the small approximations made by the rendering and display algorithms.

11. Initiate the Split feature by choosing Insert ➤ Features ➤ Split from the menus or clicking the Features toolbar. Use the surface body to split the solid body. Click the Cut Part button, and select the check boxes in front of both bodies in the list. Click OK to accept the feature. Notice that now the Solid Bodies folder indicates that there are two solid bodies.

12. From the View menu, select the display of Temporary Axes. Initiate a Circular Pattern feature, selecting the temporary axis as the axis and the split-off leg in the Bodies To Pattern selection box. Set it to four instances, as shown in Figure 31.30.

FIGURE 31.30
Patterning a body

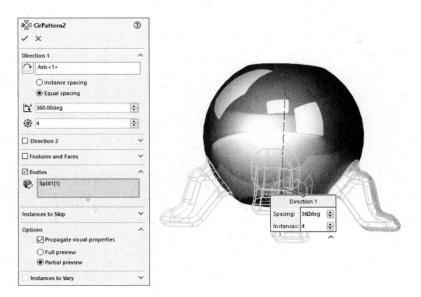

13. Use the Combine feature to add together all five bodies. You can access this feature by choosing Insert ➤ Features ➤ Combine from the menus.

The Bottom Line

Beginning to understand how to work with multiple bodies in SolidWorks opens a gateway to a new world of modeling possibilities. Like in-context design, multibody modeling is definitely something that you have to go into with your eyes open. You'll experience difficulties when using this technique, but you'll also find new possibilities that weren't available with other techniques. The key to success with multibody techniques is understanding the capabilities and limitations of the tools.

When using a model with the multibody approach, make sure you can identify a reason for doing it this way rather than using a more conventional approach. Also keep in mind the list of applications or uses for multibody modeling mentioned in this chapter. For some types of work, such as using the SolidWorks Mold tools and weldments, you cannot avoid multibody modeling.

Master It   Use the following methods to create multibodies within a part file:

◆ Multiple closed loops within a single Extrude feature

◆ Multiple disjoint features of different types within a single part

◆ Creating two solid features that merge to create a single body, then turning off the Merge Result option in the second feature to create a second body

◆ A Cut feature that separates a single body into multiple bodies

◆ Splitting a single body with a plane

Master It   Using one or more of the models created in the previous exercise, use the RMB tools from the bodies folders and the Display pane to perform the following functions to body-level geometry:

◆ Hide and Show

◆ Rename

◆ Change Color

◆ Apply Material

◆ Change Display State

◆ Make a Body Transparent

Master It   Starting with one of the parts you created in the first exercise, use Insert Part to pull one of the other multibody parts into the current one. Then use Insert Into New Part to push the current part into a new part. Notice how all the parts are listed as bodies when treated in this way. Next, use Combine to merge any bodies that are touching.

Chapter 32

Working with Surfaces

With *surface modeling*, you build a shape face by face. Faces made by surface features can be knit together to enclose a volume, which can become a solid. With solid modeling, you build many faces at once in a single feature to make the volume. In fact, *solid modeling* is really just highly automated surface modeling. Obviously, there's more detail to it than that, but this definition will get you started.

You can drive a car without knowing how the engine works, but you cannot get the most power possible out of that car by only pressing harder on the gas pedal; you have to get under the hood and make adjustments with an understanding of how it works. In a way, that is what working with surfaces is really all about—getting under the hood and tinkering with the underlying functionality.

The goal of most surface modeling is to finish with a solid. Some surface features make faces that will become faces of the solid, and some surface features only act as reference geometry. Surface modeling is inherently multibody modeling because most surface features don't merge bodies automatically.

IN THIS CHAPTER, YOU WILL LEARN TO:

◆   Understand surfacing functions

◆   Learn surfacing terminology

◆   Explore surface tools

◆   Apply surfacing techniques

Introducing Surfaces

In the end, you may never really *need* surfaces. You can perform workarounds using solids to do most of the things you need to do. However, many of these workarounds are inefficient, cumbersome, and raise as many difficulties as they solve. Although you may not view some of the typical things you now do as inefficient or cumbersome, after you see the alternatives, you may change your mind. The goal for this chapter is to introduce surfacing functions to those of you who don't typically use surfaces. I'm not showing how surfaces are used in the context of creating complex shapes—just how you can use them for various general 3D modeling tasks.

The word *surfacing* has often been used (and confused) to signify complex shapes. Not all surface work is done to create complex shapes, and many complex shapes can be made directly from solids. Many users think that because they don't make complex shapes, they never need to use surface features. This chapter shows mainly examples that don't require complex shapes, in situations where surfaces make it easier, more efficient, or simply possible to do the necessary tasks.

Although some of the uses of surfaces may not be immediately obvious, by the end of this chapter, you should have enough information and applications that you can start experimenting to increase your confidence in surfacing techniques.

Many surfacing techniques have some sort of equivalent or analog in the solid modeling world, but not all. When the analog does exist, I'll share it to help you understand the function of specific surfacing tools.

Understanding Surfacing Terminology

When dealing with surfaces, you may hear different terminology from the terminology typically used with solid modeling. This special terminology also often exists for surfaces because of important conceptual differences between how solids and surfaces are handled.

These terms are fairly universal among all surfacing software. The underlying surface and solid construction concepts are generally uniform between the major solid and surface modeling packages. What varies from software to software is how the user interacts with the geometry through the software interface. You may never see some of these terms in the SolidWorks menus, Help files, training books, or elsewhere, but as you use the software, you'll see why the concepts are relevant.

Exploring the Knit Function

The Knit function is analogous to the solid feature Combine in that it joins multiple surface bodies into a single surface body. Unlike Combine, Knit doesn't perform the subtract or intersect Boolean operations. It also has an option to create a solid if the resulting surface body meets the requirements (a fully enclosed volume without gaps or overlaps). However, unlike the solid bodies in Combine, which may overlap volumetrically, surface bodies must only intersect edge to edge, more like sketch entities that can only touch end to end.

Knit is also sometimes used in the same way that the zero-distance offset is used, to copy a set of solid faces to become a new surface body.

You can find one nice option that enables you to quickly see where the boundaries of a surface body lie by choosing Tools ➤ Options ➤ Display/Selection ➤ Show Open Edges Of Surfaces In Different Color. By default, this color is a medium blue, and you can change it by choosing Tools ➤ Options ➤ Colors ➤ Surfaces ➤ Open Edges.

Using the Trim Function

The Trim function in SolidWorks is analogous to the solid Cut. You can use sketches, planes, or other surface bodies to trim a surface body. The underlying surface is defined by a two-dimensional mesh, and for this reason, it's usually four-sided, like a woven piece of cloth, but may be other shapes. When the underlying surface is trimmed, the software still remembers the underlying original boundaries, but combines it with the new boundary, which is typically how face shapes (especially non-four-sided shapes) are created.

When you trim a surface, you can choose to delete either side of the Trim tool. With a mutual trim, both surfaces can be trimmed. A mutual trim usually leads to a corner created by the intersection of two surfaces.

Using the Untrim Function

The Untrim function is predictably the opposite of Trim. It removes the boundary from a surface. Untrim restores the natural four-sided boundary that was changed by being trimmed by adjacent surfaces. Untrim can remove the boundary selectively (one edge at a time, interior edges only, and so on) or remove all the edges at once. Untrim even works on imported geometry, as described in the tutorial in Chapter 31, "Modeling Multibodies." Figure 32.1 shows how Untrim works.

Figure 32.1
Untrimming a surface

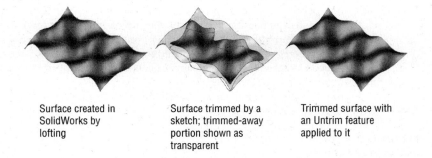

Surface created in
SolidWorks by
lofting

Surface trimmed by a
sketch; trimmed-away
portion shown as
transparent

Trimmed surface with
an Untrim feature
applied to it

Untrim works on native and imported geometry. It isn't truly like feature history in imported geometry, but it does help to uncover the underlying original shape of the face.

Hybrid Modeling

The term *hybrid* modeling can take on a lot of different connotations. You can have a mix between solid and surface, surface and subdivision, history and direct. So be careful when using the term; it means different things to different people. In this case, I'm using it to mean a combination of solid and surface modeling.

Surface modeling tends to be slower than solid modeling because you model each face individually and then manually trim and knit. Cutting a hole in a surface model is much more involved than cutting a hole in a solid. To cut a hole in a surface model, you first trim a hole on one side, then the other side, then make the cylindrical face of the hole, and then knit together the new and old faces as a single, enclosed volume.

Solid modeling is essentially highly automated surface modeling; however, as any software user knows, automation almost always comes at the expense of flexibility, and this situation is no different. Surface modeling puts the compromised power back into your hands, and that's really why we take the time to learn it.

Solid modeling strengths are predisposed to a type of part with square ends or a flat bottom because solids are creating all sides of an object at once, and capping off a solid feature with a domed shape is difficult. For example, think about an extrusion: Regardless of the shape of the sketch, you have two flat ends. Even lofts and sweeps typically end up with one or two flat ends because the section sketches are often planar. Surfaces enable you to create one side at a time. Another way of looking at it is that using surfaces *requires* you to build parts in sections.

Sometimes, you'll find that, even with prismatic modeling, surfacing functions are extremely useful. I don't propose that you dive into pure surface modeling just to benefit from a few of the advantages, but I do recommend that you consider using surface techniques to help define your solids when appropriate. This hybrid approach is sensible and opens up a whole new world of capabilities. I have heard people say after taking a SolidWorks surfacing class that they would never look at CAD geometry in the same way again.

Understanding Non-Uniform Rational B Spline

Non-Uniform Rational B Spline (NURBS) is the technology that most modern mechanical design modelers use to create 3D geometry. NURBS surfaces are defined by curves called *isoparameter lines* in perpendicular directions (referred to as U and V directions), which form a two-directional cloth-like mesh. The fact that perpendicular directions are used means that the surfaces have a tendency to be four-sided. Of course, exceptions exist, such as three-sided or even two-sided patches. Geometry of this kind is referred to as *degenerate* because one or more of the sides has been reduced to zero length. Degenerate geometry is often, but not always, the source of geometrical errors in SolidWorks and other CAD packages.

Figure 32.2 shows some surfaces with the mesh displayed on them. You can create the mesh with the Face Curves sketch tool.

FIGURE 32.2
Meshes created with the
Face Curves sketch tool

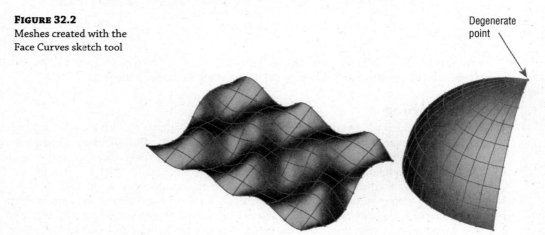

Degenerate
point

Using Developable Surfaces

Developable surfaces can be flattened without stretching. They are also surfaces that you can extend easily in one or both directions. These include planar, cylindrical, and conical shapes. It isn't a coincidence that these are the types of shapes that can be flattened by the Sheet Metal tools.

Using Ruled Surfaces

Developable surfaces are a special type of a broader range of surface called *ruled surfaces*. SolidWorks has a special tool for the creation of ruled surfaces, which is described in detail in the next section. Ruled surfaces are defined as surfaces on which a straight line can be drawn at every point. A corollary to this is that ruled surfaces may have curvature in only one direction. Ruled surfaces are far less limited than developable surfaces, but they aren't flattened as easily.

Ruled surfaces are used frequently in plastic parts and plastic mold design where draft and parting surfaces from 3D parting lines are needed.

Defining Gaussian Curvature

Gaussian curvature is not referred to directly in SolidWorks software, but you may hear the term used in more general CAD or engineering discussions. It can be defined simply as curvature in two directions. As a result, a sphere would have Gaussian curvature, but a cylinder would not.

Surfacing Tools

Surface feature equivalents are available for most solid features such as Extrude, Revolve, Sweep, Loft, Fillet, and so on. Some solid features don't have an equivalent, such as the Hole Wizard, Shell, and others. Several surface functions don't have solid equivalents, such as Trim, Untrim, Extend, Thicken, Offset, Radiate, Ruled, and Fill.

Using the Extruded Surface

The Extruded Surface feature works exactly like an extruded solid, except that the ends of the surface aren't capped. It includes all the same end conditions, draft, contour selection, sketch rules, and so on that you're already familiar with. Figure 32.3 shows the PropertyManager for the extruded surface.

FIGURE 32.3
The Extruded Surface PropertyManager

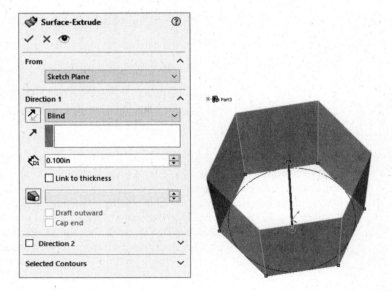

You can create extruded surfaces from open or closed sketches, with open probably being the most popular type.

When two nonparallel lines are joined end to end in the same sketch, the result of extruding the sketch is a single surface body that's made of two faces with a hard edge between them. If the sketch lines were disjointed, the extrude would result in disjoint surface bodies. If the sketch lines were again made end to end, but done in separate sketches, the resulting surface bodies would be separate bodies; the second body would not be automatically knit to the first one as happens with the way solid features merge. This is an important quality of surfaces to keep in mind. If you create surfaces in different features and want them knitted into a single body, then you have to do that manually.

If you have a split line on a surface, you can select the surface and start the Extruded Surface command. You will then need to select a plane or axis to define the extrusion direction, and specify the depth of the extrusion. Figure 32.4 shows the PropertyManager and result of this function.

FIGURE 32.4
Extruding a 3D surface

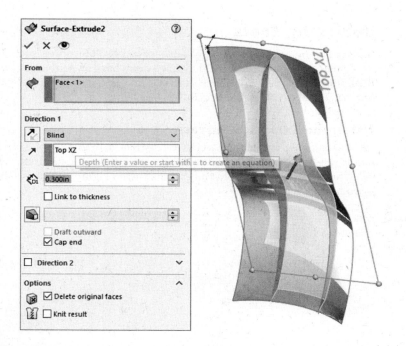

This technique is special because of the additional options: Cap End, Delete Original Faces, and Knit Result. It would be nice for these functions to exist with regular sketch-based extrudes and other surface features as well.

You can find a similar function in the Surface Extrude's ability to extrude a 3D sketch. You can also use a regular Solid Extrude to extrude a 3D sketch, and it will cap the ends for you. I find all these extrude options interesting, but I have yet to find an application for them. The ability to extrude a 3D surface duplicates the Ruled Surface, although the additional options must be selected manually.

Using Boundary Surface

The Boundary Surface feature was created as a higher-quality replacement for the Loft feature, but certain limitations mean that Loft has not been removed from the feature list. The Boundary Surface feature most resembles a loft, but it has elements of the sweep and fill. Loft also does a few things that Boundary cannot, such as a closed loop loft without a direction 2 curve, and most importantly, a centerline loft. Boundary Surface can use sketches, curves, or edges in several arrangements, such as curves arranged in an X, F, E, T, L, and other shapes. Figure 32.5 shows some of these shapes.

FIGURE 32.5
Using different curve arrangements with the Boundary Surface feature

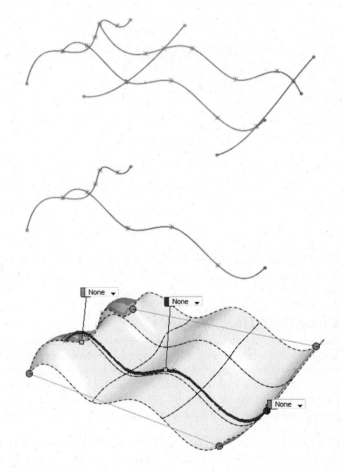

If several edge or sketch segments combine to form a curve in one direction, then you must use the SelectionManager to form the edge segments into a group. SelectionManager enables you to select portions of a single sketch or to combine elements such as Sketch, Edge, and Curve into a single selection for use as a profile or guide curve for Boundary or Loft features.

The interface for the Boundary Surface is shown in Figure 32.6.

FIGURE 32.6
The Boundary Surface
PropertyManager

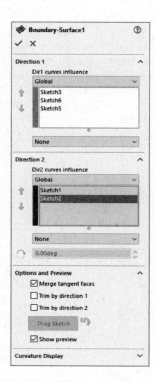

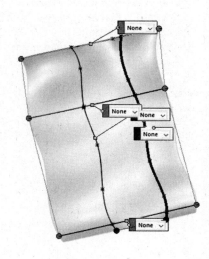

The main advantage of Boundary Surface over Loft is that Boundary Surface can apply a curvature boundary condition all the way around, while Loft cannot apply curvature continuity across the guide curves. I default to Boundary Surfaces when possible. Boundary Solid features are also available.

Using the Offset Surface

The Offset Surface feature's closest relatives are the Thicken feature and the Sketch Offset. It may also fail for the same reasons. For example, if you offset a .25-inch radius arc by .3 inches to the inside, it will fail because it cannot be offset up to or past a zero radius. The same is true of offsetting surfaces. Complex surfaces don't have a constant curvature; they're more like a spline by having a constantly changing curvature. If the offset is going in the direction of decreasing radius and is more than the minimum radius on the face or faces being offset, then the Offset Surface feature will fail.

One of the ways to troubleshoot a failing Offset Surface is to use the Check tool to check for minimum radius. Remember that the area with the minimum radius is a problem only if the curvature is in the same direction as the offset. If a small radius will increase when it's offset, then that small radius isn't the problem. The problem comes from the other direction where you are offsetting to the inside of a small radius.

Unlike the Sketch Offset function—and as shown in Chapter 31—you can offset surfaces by a zero distance. This is usually done to copy either solid or surface faces to make a new surface body. Zero-distance offset and Knit are sometimes used interchangeably, although Knit causes a problem if you are selecting a surface body that's composed of a single face. Knit assumes that you're trying to knit one body to another, so by default, it selects the body and then fails with the message that you cannot knit a body to itself. Because Knit has this limitation, and Offset doesn't, I prefer the Offset tool when copying faces to make a new surface body. You may also notice that when you enter a zero for the offset distance, the Offset PropertyManager name changes automatically to Copy Surface.

Knit does have two functions that Sketch Offset does not. One of them is the option to create a solid from the knit body if it forms a closed body. The second option is somewhat more obscure, offering the ability to select all faces on one side of a Radiate Surface. I discuss this option in more depth later in this chapter in the "Using Knit Surface" section.

When talking about copying surface bodies, you must also consider the Move/Copy Bodies feature, described in Chapter 31. When you're simply copying a body without also moving it, this feature issues a warning that asks whether you really intend to copy the body without moving it. This is an annoying and pointless message. Also, the Move/Copy Bodies feature doesn't enable you to copy only a part of a body (selected faces) or to merge multiple bodies into one like the Knit and Offset Surface features.

All things considered, I recommend using the zero-distance Surface Offset feature to copy bodies or parts of bodies unless your goal is to immediately make a solid out of it (in which case, you should use the Knit feature) or when using a Radiated Surface (typically in a mold-building application).

Using Radiate Surface

The Radiate Surface feature isn't one of the more commonly used surface features. It has been largely superseded by the Ruled Surface. This is because Ruled Surface does the same sort of thing that Radiate Surface does—and more. Radiate works from an edge selection, a reference plane, and a distance. The newly created surface is perpendicular to the selected edge and parallel to the selected plane and is the set distance wide. It's probably most commonly used in creating molds or other net shape tooling such as dies for stamping and forging, blanks for thermoforming, and so on. Figure 32.7 shows the PropertyManager and selection for creating a Radiate Surface.

The one application where the Radiate Surface has a very interesting usage is when you combine it with the Knit function. Figure 32.8 shows a part surrounded by a Radiate Surface (shown here in wireframe) in which the Knit feature is being used to select all the faces to one side of the radiated surface. The second smaller selection box in the PropertyManager that contains Face<1> is called a *seed face* and causes the Knit to automatically select all the faces on the same side of the model as the selected seed face. The requirement here is that the Radiate goes completely around the model and separates the faces into faces on one side of the Radiate and faces on the other side of the Radiate. The use of the Radiate with the Seed Face selection is extremely useful for mold creation.

FIGURE 32.7
The Radiate Surface
PropertyManager

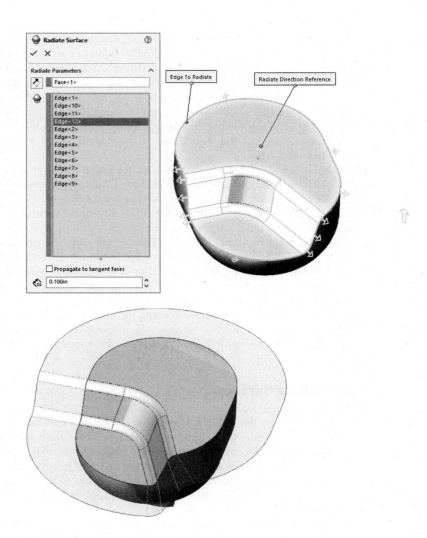

FIGURE 32.8
Using Radiate
Surface with Knit

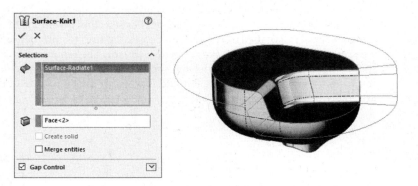

Using Knit Surface

The Knit Surface functionality was discussed previously in the "Understanding Surfacing Terminology" section as well as in the "Using Radiate Surface" section.

If the knit operation results in a watertight volume, the Try To Form Solid option turns the volume into a solid. You can also make a solid from a surface using three other functions. The Fill Surface feature has an option to merge the fill with a solid or to knit it into a surface body; if the knit surface body is closed, then it gives you the option to make it a solid. This is a very nice, complete interface design, with options that save you many steps. The Fill Surface feature is described in more detail later in this chapter.

Create Solid is available only when you use Knit Surface or Fill Surface. Whenever you want the surface to become a solid body using Fill or Knit Surface, Create Solid highlights but remains inactive until all the surfaces are merged together and create a closed volume. Create Solid only highlights when you check Merge Result.

The Gap Control panel, shown in Figure 32.9, shows the gap between the edges of surfaces to be knit and enables you to see the gaps in a certain range and force gaps of less than a specified tolerance value, called the Knitting Tolerance, to knit.

FIGURE 32.9

Knitting surfaces with gaps using tolerances

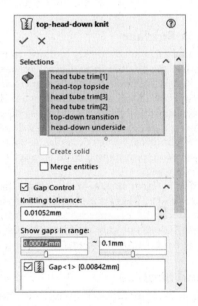

With all powerful tools, the possibility of misusing those tools always exists. The ability to play with tolerances is a double-edged sword. On one hand, it gives you the ability to force surfaces to knit that may have otherwise not knit at all, by making the model tolerate larger gaps in defining solids or knitting surfaces. SolidWorks may force together surfaces or edges that have problems that should be solved in other ways, such as removal and remodeling. Gap tolerances can cause problems during import operations to other software that doesn't have the capability to adjust tolerances. You should definitely use the Gap Control options, but also be aware of the potential problems you might see with data downstream.

Using Thicken Surface

The other function that also creates a solid from a surface is the Thicken feature. If a surface body that encloses a volume is selected, then the option Create Solid From Enclosed Volume appears on the Thicken PropertyManager, as shown in Figure 32.10. You can access the Thicken feature by choosing Insert ➤ Boss/Base ➤ Thicken from the menus.

FIGURE 32.10
The Thicken
PropertyManager

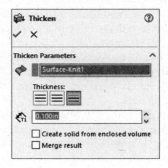

Using Planar Surface

Planar surfaces can be created quickly and are useful in many situations, not just for surfacing work. Because they are by definition *planar*, you can use them to sketch on and for other purposes that you may use a plane for, such as mirroring, cutting, or dimensioning.

However, more commonly, planar surfaces are created from a closed sketch such as a rectangle. You can create multiple planar surfaces at once, and the surfaces don't need to all be on the same plane or even parallel. This is commonly done to close up holes in a surface model, such as at the bottom of cylindrical bosses on a plastic part, using a planar circular edge. A good example of this is the bike frame part named `bike frame.sldprt` in the Chapter 32 download materials from the Wiley website.

Remember that a planar surface was used in Chapter 31 with the Split feature to split the leg off of an imported part. This was more effective than a sketch or a plane because the split was limited to the bounds of the planar surface, not infinite like the sketch or the plane.

A planar surface does not knit itself into the rest of the surface bodies around it automatically; you must use the Knit feature to do this.

Using Extend Surface

The Extend Surface feature functions in much the same way that the Extend function works in sketches. However, spline-based surfaces are more difficult to extend than sketch entities. Figure 32.11 shows the PropertyManager interface and an example of the feature at work.

The only item here that requires explanation is the Extension Type panel. The Same Surface option means that the extended surface will simply be extrapolated in the selected direction. A planar surface is the easiest to extend because it can go on indefinitely without running into problems. A cylindrical surface can be extended only until it runs into itself. Complex lofted or swept surfaces are often difficult to extend. Extrapolating a complex surface isn't easy to do and often results in self-intersecting faces, which will cause the feature to fail.

FIGURE 32.11

The Extend Surface
PropertyManager

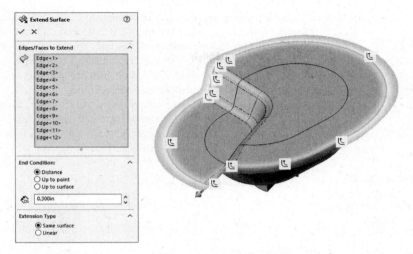

When the Same Surface setting works, it creates a nice result because it doesn't create an edge where the extension begins; it smoothly extends the existing face.

The Linear option is more reliable than the Same Surface option because it starts tangent to the existing surface and keeps going in that direction, working much like a Ruled Surface. It doesn't rely on extending the existing surface. This option creates an edge at the starting point of the new geometry.

Using Trim Surface

The Trim Surface feature was described briefly earlier in this chapter, but it warrants a more complete description here. Surfaces can be trimmed by three types of entities:

◆ Sketches

◆ Planes

◆ Other surfaces

When you use surface bodies to trim one another, you have two options: Standard or Mutual Trim. The Standard option causes one surface to act as the Trim tool and the other surface to be trimmed by the Trim tool. When you select the Mutual Trim option, both surfaces act as the Trim tool, and both surfaces are trimmed.

For an example of trimmed surfaces, open the mouse example from Chapter 31 and step through the tree. This shows a couple of types of trimmed surfaces, as well as extended surfaces and others.

Many people overlook the ability to trim a surface with a plane, which can be very handy sometimes. Planes are infinite, which means you have less to worry about when it comes to changes that affect features rebuilding correctly.

Finally, the ability to trim with 2D sketches is well known, but trimming with 3D sketches is less known. A 3D sketch tool called Spline On Surface enables you to draw a spline directly on any surface body. An option exists in the Trim Surface PropertyManager to trim a surface with this type of sketch. This is very useful in many situations if you can remember that it's available.

The trimming interface can sometimes be visually confusing. When your mouse moves over a section of the surface that will be either kept or removed, that portion of the surface will change colors. Whether it is kept or removed depends on which option is selected in the PropertyManager: Keep Selections or Remove Selections.

For example, Figure 32.12 shows a portion of the `bike frame.sldprt` that is provided with the download material for this chapter. The vertical and horizontal tubes are being trimmed with the C-shaped and straight-line sketches, respectively. The selected portions of the tubes are set to be kept using the Keep Selections option.

FIGURE 32.12
Trimming sections of bike frame tubing, and the Trim PropertyManager

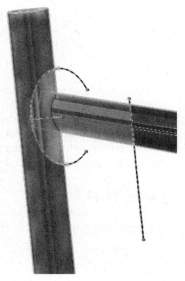

Using Fill Surface

The Fill Surface feature is referred to by the SolidWorks interface and documentation as either Fill or Filled, depending on where the reference is made. In my opinion, it is one of the most powerful tools in the surface modeler's toolbox. It is sometimes amazing what this feature can do. The Fill Surface feature is intended to create oddly shaped holes between surface bodies. You can use constraint curves to drive the shape of the fill between the existing boundaries. It can even knit a surface body together into a solid, all-in-one step. Beyond this, you can use Fill Surface directly on solid models and integrate it directly into the solid automatically (much like the Replace Face function, which is described later in this chapter). While in development, it was referred to as an N-sided patch.

Several rather complex examples of Fill Surface are found in the bike frame example. One of these fills is shown in Figure 32.13.

FIGURE 32.13
The Fill Surface
PropertyManager and
the results of
applying it

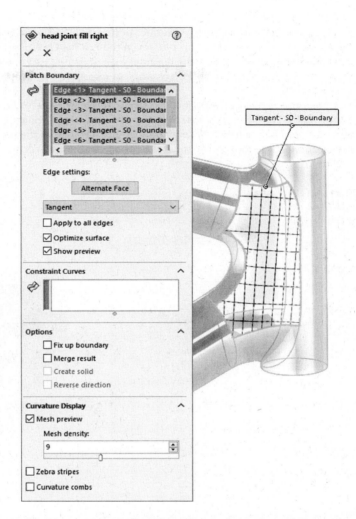

The first thing you should notice about the Fill Surface is that it created an oversized, four-sided patch and trimmed it to fit into the available space.

When using the Fill Surface, you'll want to have a patch completely bounded by other surfaces, as shown in Figure 32.11. Fill Surface can work with a boundary that isn't enclosed, but it works better with a closed boundary.

You can set boundary conditions as Contact, Tangent, or Curvature. *Contact* simply means that the faces touch at an edge. *Tangent* means that the slopes of the faces on either side of the edge match at all points along the edge. *Curvature* means curvature continuous (or C2), where the Fill Surface matches not only tangency, but also the curvature of the face on the other side of the boundary edge. This results in a smoother transition than a transition that's simply tangent.

When you select the Optimize Surface option, SolidWorks tries to fit the four-sided patch into the boundary. Notice that on this part, even though the Optimize Surface option is selected, it's clearly being ignored because the boundary is a six-sided gap and cannot be patched smoothly with a four-sided patch. It isn't necessarily an improvement to optimize a fill surface, even when it works.

Constraint curves can influence the shape of the fill surface. An example of this is shown in Figure 32.14. This screen shot is from the mouse example, controlling the shape of the thumb indentation. The construction splines shown on the faces of the part were created by the Intersection Curve tool and enabled the spline used for the constraint curve to be made tangent to the surface.

FIGURE 32.14
The Fill Surface feature with constraint curves

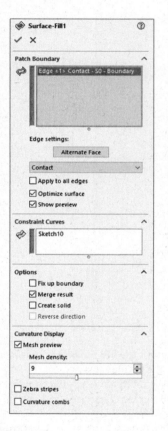

Using MidSurface

The MidSurface feature is intended to be used in conjunction with analysis tools to create plate elements for thin-walled structures, or midplanes for flow scenarios. It works on parallel or offset faces, creating a surface midway between the faces. If the faces have opposing draft (symmetrical, such that a wall is wider at the bottom than at the top), then the MidSurface feature won't work. It works on linear walls and cylindrical walls, but not on elliptical or spline-based shapes. The PropertyManager for the MidSurface is shown in Figure 32.15.

FIGURE 32.15

FIGURE 32.15
The MidSurface
PropertyManager

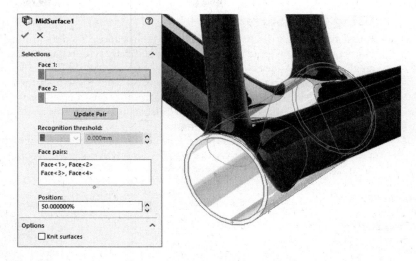

The percentage of distance between face pairs can be adjusted from the default 50 percent, and if possible, resulting faces can be knit into a single body.

Using Replace Face

The Replace Face feature doesn't create new surface geometry, but it does integrate existing surface geometry into the solid. It replaces selected faces of a solid or surface body with a selected surface body. Replace Face is one of the few tools that can add and remove material with a single feature.

If you were to manually perform the functions that are done by Replace Face, you would start by deleting several faces of the solid, then extending faces, and then trimming surface bodies, and finish by knitting all the trimmed and extended faces back into a single solid body.

This is a very powerful and useful tool, although it's sometimes difficult to tell in which situations it will work. Figure 32.16 shows a part after a Replace Face feature has been performed. The surface used to replace the flat face of the solid has been turned transparent. The first selection box is for the original face or faces, and the second selection box is for the surface body with the new faces. The tool tips for each of the boxes are Target Faces For Replacement and Replacement Surface(s), which seem a little ambiguous. I like to think of them as Old (top) and New (bottom).

FIGURE 32.16
Using Replace Face

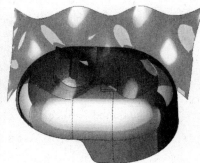

Using Ruled Surface

Ruled surfaces are discussed in general in the section "Understanding Surfacing Terminology." Here, I discuss the topic in more detail, specifically with regard to the SolidWorks interface for creating ruled surfaces.

The Ruled Surface feature in SolidWorks is one of those features that you may never miss until you see it in action. It's extremely useful for constructing faces with draft, extending faces tangent to a direction, making Radiate Surface types, building molds, and many other applications. It can also be frustratingly unreliable.

A ruled surface requires a model (surface or solid) edge from which to start. You cannot create a ruled surface from a sketch or curve. The icon will not even become active until you have solid or surface geometry in the graphics window.

FIGURE 32.17
The Ruled
Surface Property-
Manager interface

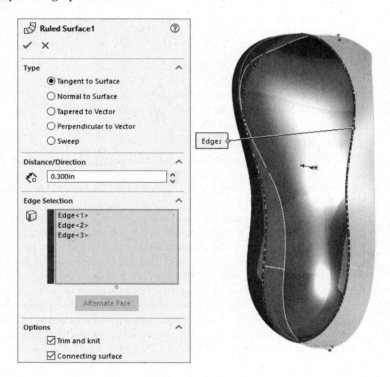

Figure 32.17 shows the PropertyManager interface for the Ruled Surface.

The Ruled Surface feature works from the edge of a solid or surface body. The feature has five basic types of operations that it can perform:

◆ Tangent To Surface

◆ Normal To Surface

◆ Tapered To Vector

◆ Perpendicular To Vector

◆ Sweep

The Tangent To Surface setting creates a surface that is tangent to the surface of the selected edge. The Alternate Face option would be available if the base shape had been a solid, with a face filling the big elliptical hole. This would make the ruled surface tangent to the bottom face instead of the side.

With the Normal To Surface setting, it tilts up 5 degrees from the horizontal because the surface is lofted with a 5-degree draft angle at the big end, making a ruled surface that's normal.

The Tapered To Vector setting needs a plane or axis selection to establish a direction, and then the ruled surface is created from that reference at the angle that you set. With a combination of the Alternate Side button and the arrow-direction toggle button next to the plane selection, you can adjust the cone created by this setting. The interface to make the changes isn't exactly clear unless you use this function often, but it does work.

The Perpendicular To Vector setting is a better option than the Normal To Surface setting when the surface has been created with some sort of built-in draft angle. This is also the setting that looks most like the Radiate Surface feature, although it works much better than Radiate Surface.

The Sweep setting makes a face that's perpendicular to the surface created by Perpendicular To Vector. It's as if a straight line were swept around the edge. This is actually a great way to offset an edge or 3D sketch: using the edge of the surface as the offset of the original.

Using Intersect

The Intersect feature is not strictly surface-based. Its solids functions are covered in Chapter 31. Its primary purpose is to take several entities such as solid and surface bodies, faces, and planes, and create new solid bodies from combinations of those. One of the best usages of this feature is finding fill levels for liquid in a container. For example, Figure 32.18 shows a watering can with a solid block of water and then, after the Intersect feature has been applied, the volume of water that was inside the watering can.

FIGURE 32.18
Using Intersect to fill a watering bucket with liquid

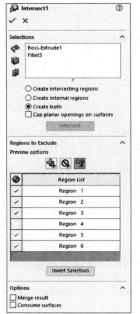

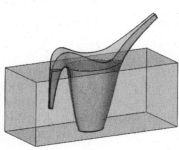

If you would try to do this same example and keep the watering can intact, that would be more challenging. It might require different settings such as Invert Selection or the preview options available at the top of the region list, unless you use the Create Internal Regions option. The Intersect feature is not an easy-to-use function, mainly because the results can be tough to visualize, or select, and there are a lot of ways to use and visualize the results. The ability to turn on or off the pieces that will be kept or removed is helpful, but selecting body parts that are inside two volumes is just plain hard to do. You might want to make a copy of the watering can body and use that to be consumed in the feature, or you could do a Boolean subtract and delete the body of water that winds up outside the watering can. I recommend that you take some time to play with the sample files if you think you may have use for this particular feature.

Other nice usages for this feature include creating molds and breaking a single solid into manufacturable bodies.

Here are some of the unique capabilities of the Intersect tool:

- Can add and subtract material in the same feature

- Can later completely change methods without needing to delete and re-create the feature

- Can add surfaces and planes to combine feature options

- Can make bodies from the empty spaces that are fully enclosed

- Can consume bodies (or not) as you wish

- Can output multiple solid bodies (imagine combining several bodies when some of them are not touching at all)

NOTE I'd like to thank Dwight Livingston from the SolidWorks Forum for the previous list of Intersect capabilities.

Tutorial: Working with Surfaces

The best way to learn about surfaces is to experiment. I recommend that you closely follow the tutorial steps once, and then when you understand the concepts involved, you can go back and experiment.

Using Cut With Surface

Follow these steps to gain some experience with the Cut With Surface feature:

1. Create a new part, and draw a rectangle on the Top plane, centered on the origin, about 4 inches by 6 inches, with the 4-inch dimension in the vertical direction.

2. Extrude the rectangle mid-plane, by 2 inches.

3. From the Surface toolbar, select Lofted Surface, and select one 4-inch edge as a loft profile. Then select a second 4-inch edge diagonal from the first one. This is shown in Figure 32.19.

4. Expand the Start/End Constraints panel and set both ends to use the Direction Vector setting, selecting the plane in the middle of the long direction in each case. In the part shown, the Right plane is used. Click OK to accept the feature. This is shown in Figure 32.19.

FIGURE 32.19
Lofting a surface from
the edges of a solid

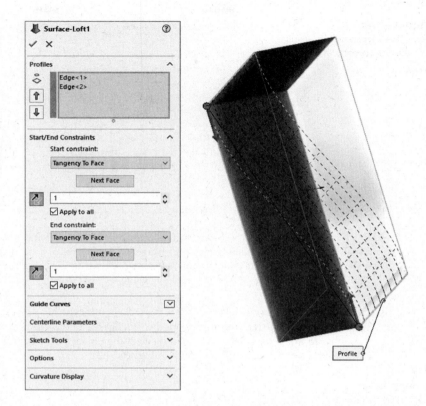

5. From the menus, choose Insert ➤ Cut ➤ With Surface. Select the surface from the flyout FeatureManager, and toggle the arrow direction so that the top is cut off. (The arrow points to the side that's cut off.)

Using Offset Surface

Follow these steps to gain some experience with the Offset Surface command:

1. Open the part called Offset Tutorial.sldprt from the download materials.

2. Right-click a curved face of the part and click Select Tangency in the menu.

3. With the faces still selected, from the Surfaces toolbar, click Offset Surface and set the surface to offset to the outside of the part by .060 inches. You can tell when the surface is offsetting to the outside when the transparent preview appears. If you don't see the transparent preview, toggle the Flip Offset Direction arrow button. Click OK to accept the feature when you're satisfied.

4. Look in the Surface Bodies folder at the top of the FeatureManager tree, expand the folder, use the Display pane (F8) to change the transparency, as shown in Figure 32.20. This is done so you can see the part underneath the surface, without mistaking the surface for the actual part.

FIGURE 32.20
Using the Display pane
to change transparency

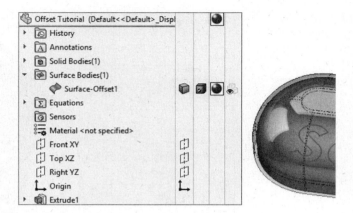

TIP A common practice is to change surface colors to something that contrasts with the part color. I usually use a color like yellow, which suggests temporary status or construction. Some users take this a step further and set the template colors for surface types by choosing Tools ➤ Options ➤ Document Properties ➤ Colors.

5. Select Sketch2 and select Extruded Boss/Base from the Features toolbar. Don't mistake the extruded surface for an extruded solid. Set the end condition to Up To Body, activate the Body Selection box, and select the Offset Surface body from the Surface Bodies folder. The result is shown in Figure 32.21.

FIGURE 32.21
Extruding with the Up
To Body setting

TIP It's preferable to select the surface from the Surface Bodies folder, rather than the feature list or the graphics window. In this case, you want to extrude up to a body. If you make the selection from the feature list, then you're likely to select a feature (which is okay in this situation, but not in all situations). If you make the selection from the graphics window, the selection is likely to be interpreted as a face. It's best to be as explicit as possible when making selections because SolidWorks may interpret your selection literally. In this case, it's probably a better idea to use Up To Body for the end condition than Up To Surface, because the goal is really to use the surface body as the end of the feature.

6. To invert the lettering so it sits below the surface rather than above the surface, you can make a few simple changes. Edit the Offset Surface feature and flip the direction of the offset so the surface is inside the solid rather than outside the solid. You can't see it unless the solid is either transparent or in Wireframe mode.

7. Delete the extrude that you created to extrude the text. There's no way to change an extrude into a cut in this context.

8. Re-create the extrude as an extruded cut. Use the From settings at the top of the PropertyManager window. The settings and results are shown in Figure 32.22.

FIGURE 32.22
An extruded cut

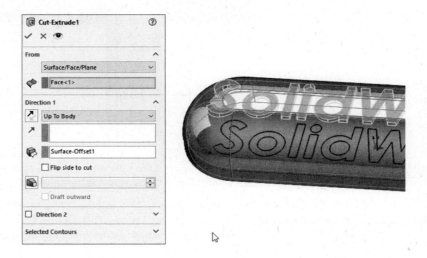

Another way to accomplish this is to use the Move Face tool, select the faces of the letters, and move them .120 of an inch into the solid.

Using Fill Surface Blend

Sometimes, fillets don't meet your needs. Blends, such as those shown in the bike frame example, are smoother and can blend just about anything. However, the technique is not exactly straightforward. Follow these steps to gain familiarity with this technique:

1. Open the part called Blend.SLDPRT from the download data for Chapter 32. Box select all the features from the DeleteFace1 to the Shell and suppress them.

2. On the Top plane, draw a square 2 inches on a side and centered on the origin.

3. Use the Split Entities tool found on the Sketch toolbar, or choose Tools ➤ Sketch Tools ➤ Split Entities from the menus. Divide each line of the rectangle into three pieces, with the

two outer pieces of each line being .6 inches (use an Equal sketch relation). The sketch should be fully defined when you're finished. This arrangement is shown in Figure 32.23. This is done because the edges of the tubes need to be broken into sections.

With the lines split, now use the Split Line tool at Insert ➤ Curves ➤ Split Line to split the faces of all tubes.

FIGURE 32.23
Using split entities to
split lines

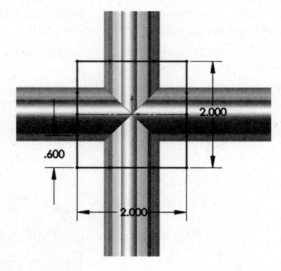

4. Use Delete Face to delete the ends of the four tubes. Set the option to Delete, not the default option of Delete And Patch. This converts the solid into a surface body.

5. Use the sketch with the split entities to trim out the center section of the tubes, keeping the outer section and leaving four surface bodies. This divides each tube end into four segments where they have been trimmed, as shown in Figure 32.24.

FIGURE 32.24
Split ends
after trimming

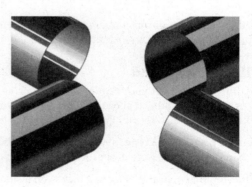

6. Initiate the Lofted Surface feature and select the nearest edge segments from adjacent tubes. If the loft preview twists, use the light-blue handles to straighten it out or deselect and reselect one of the edges in approximately the same location as the other edge was selected. Expand the End Conditions panel and set each edge to use the Curvature setting. You may adjust the End Tangent Length option if you want, but keep in mind that this may make the part asymmetrical.

   As a note, you may choose to use the Boundary Surface feature in the place of the Loft feature. For this function, the two are similar enough.

7. Create lofted surfaces all the way around the part, linking all the tubes. Figure 32.25 shows the part with three of the lofts already completed and the last one in progress.

FIGURE 32.25
Adding lofted surfaces

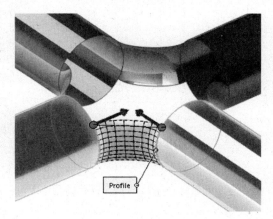

8. Start a Planar Surface feature and select the open ends of each tube where the faces were deleted in step 4.

NOTE   Not all features allow you to operate from multiple bodies, but the Loft and Planar Surface features do. Features such as Fillet and Draft restrict you to creating features that are associated with one body at a time.

9. Start a Knit Surface feature and Shift+select all the bodies in the Surface Bodies folder (select the first body in the list and Shift+select the last body). When you click OK to accept the feature, notice that the number of surface bodies changes to one. Selecting bodies in this way is much faster for large numbers of bodies than selecting them one at a time from the graphics window.

NOTE   Notice that the open edges of the surface body are shown in a different color. At this point, there are two open edges around the holes at the intersection of the tubes.

10. Right-click any of the open edges and choose Select Open Loop. Initiate the Fill Surface. Change the Edge setting option to Tangent and make sure that the Apply To All Edges option is selected. Select the Merge Result option, but leave the Try To Form Solid option

unselected. The model at this point is shown in Figure 32.26, along with the PropertyManager settings that are used.

This is the type of situation for which the Fill Surface is really meant. In fact, this technique was created specifically to take advantage of the Fill Surface capabilities.

FIGURE 32.26
Creating a Fill
Surface patch

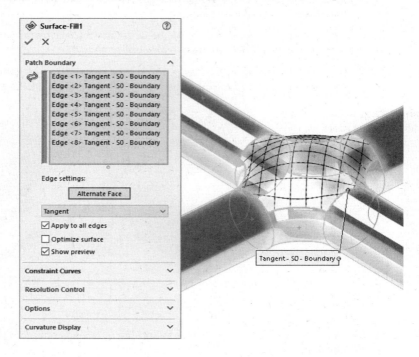

11. Click OK to accept the feature.

12. Start another Fill Surface feature, turning the part over to use the same selection on the back and the same settings as the first fill. However, on this one, also use the Try To Form Solid option. Click OK when the selections and settings are complete.

13. For the last feature, apply a Shell feature, selecting the flat ends of the tubes and shelling to .100 inches. The final state of the model is shown in Figure 32.27.

FIGURE 32.27
The finished model

The Bottom Line

Surface functions have a wide range of uses other than for complex shape parts, but thinking about your models in terms of surface features requires a slightly different approach. Becoming comfortable with the terminology, and the similarities and differences between solids and surfaces, is the first step toward embracing surfacing tools for everyday work.

You can think of surfaces as being reference geometry—stand-alone faces that you can use to complete various tasks.

Master It   Sketch a rectangle and extrude it as a surface. Then close one of the open sides with a planar surface and knit together the two surface bodies. Next, use the Thicken tool to thicken the surface into a hollow box.

Notice the change from the count in the Surface Bodies folder to the Solid Bodies folder. Save the part.

Master It   Open the part saved in the previous exercise, and use Save As to make a copy of it with a new name.

Delete the Thicken feature.

Use a Fill feature to close the open side in the box, and use the options in the Fill feature to knit the part into a single surface body and make it solid.

Master It   Open the part used in the previous exercise and use Save As to save it with a new name.

Use the Move Copy Bodies command to make a copy of the solid body, and move the copy to one side so it does not touch the original.

Use Delete Face to delete one face of the new body. Notice that the solid body changes to a surface body.

Use a Loft surface to again close up the missing face, use Knit to knit it into a single surface body, and use Thicken to make it a solid body again.

Finally, use the solid Loft feature to loft between the two faces of the solid bodies that are closest to one another, and merge the result so there is a single solid body in the part.

Chapter 33

Employing Master Model Techniques

In this book, the term *master model* refers to a technique where an entire assembly is laid out or has its major faces constructed in a single part, and that part—or elements of it—is then placed into other files from which the individual parts are created. As such, the major faces and major relationships are created in a single file, while all of the details are created in the individual files. Master model techniques are generally used in situations that in-context design cannot deal with or where in-context design is cumbersome.

IN THIS CHAPTER, YOU WILL LEARN TO:

◆ Define the master model

◆ Apply Pull functions

◆ Apply Push functions

Master Model Tools and Techniques

Master model techniques comprise four separate features or functions that have some similarities, and they rely heavily on the knowledge of parent/child concepts and multiple bodies. These four features are Split, Save Bodies, Insert Part, and Insert Into New Part.

As an example of a master model technique, consider the mouse model shown in Figure 33.1. The overall shape is modeled as a single part and then split into several bodies using multibody methods. Then, using the four master model features, the individual bodies are used to create individual part files, where detail features are added.

Understanding the concepts of *parent* and *child* relationships between documents is key to understanding how master model techniques work. A parent document is always the driving document—the one that existed first—so changes to the parent propagate to the child. The child document is always dependent on the parent. In these master model schemes, it isn't always possible to find the child document from the parent, but you can always find the parent from the child.

FIGURE 33.1
A mouse master model

The concepts of Push and Pull type functions were developed for this book, so you may not find them in other documentation. Classifying the techniques can be helpful in understanding which tool is best for various situations. *Push* simply means that the relationship is defined in the parent document, and data is pushed out. *Pull* means that the relationship is defined in the child document, and data is pulled in.

Here's a quick summary of the four master model tools that this chapter covers:

- ◆ **Insert Part:** This function enables you to pull all the solid and surface bodies, sketches, reference geometry, and even features from an existing part into the current part. It's available as a toolbar icon and from the Insert menu.

- ◆ **Insert Into New Part:** This function enables you to insert a selection of solid and surface bodies from the current part into a brand-new part. Even though this function is initiated from the parent document, it's classified as a Pull function because it doesn't leave a feature in the parent but does leave one in the child. This function doesn't have an icon.

- ◆ **Split:** This function enables you to split a single solid body into multiple solid bodies and save (push) each body to a separate part file. This function is available as a toolbar icon and a menu entry in the Insert ➤ Features menu. It creates a feature in the FeatureManager of the originating (parent) part file.

- ◆ **Save Bodies:** This function enables you to save (push) all the solid bodies from a part out to separate part files. This function is available only through the RMB menu on the Solid Bodies folder. It creates a feature in the FeatureManager of the parent part. This is different from Keep/Delete Bodies.

The one common weakness of all these tools is on the file management side, or more precisely, the body management side. It comes down to a question of what happens to the child document if you rearrange the bodies in the parent document. Body management issues can arise in a number of ways. The Insert Part feature is the one that has received the most development attention from SolidWorks when it comes to the robustness of file and body management issues, but Insert Part still doesn't cover all the functionality. (You cannot insert selective bodies; you must insert all solids or all surface bodies.)

Using Pull Functions

Pull functions are initiated from the child document and pull data from the master model (parent document) into the child document. These functions insert a feature into the child that points to the parent, but they don't insert a feature into the parent that points to the child. The features that fall into this category are Insert Part and Insert Into New Part.

Understanding the Insert Part Feature

You initiate Insert Part from the child document by choosing Insert ➤ Part from the menus or by clicking the Insert Part button in the Features toolbar (which may not be on your toolbar by default). As the name suggests, this feature pulls one part into another. Insert Part gives you the option to bring forward all solid and surface bodies, planes, axes, and sketches in addition to other options. You can even break the link between the inserted part and the parent data. This simply copies all the sketch and feature data into the current part. The Mirror Part feature also uses this same PropertyManager with the same options. The Insert Part PropertyManager interface is shown in Figure 33.2.

FIGURE 33.2
The Insert Part
PropertyManager

Figure 33.3 shows the FeatureManager of a part where the only feature is an Insert Part feature. All the solid bodies are listed under the normal Solid Bodies folder as well as under a second Solid Bodies folder under the inserted-part icon. Other inserted items—such as surface bodies, planes, sketches, and axes—are also listed in folders under the inserted-part icon.

FIGURE 33.3
The FeatureManager showing items inserted with an inserted part

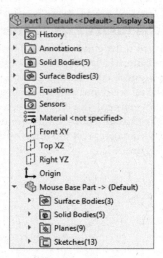

You cannot be selective about which bodies are pulled forward—solids or surfaces—but you can delete unwanted bodies after you have brought them all in (using Delete/Keep body). If you are trying to handle data efficiently, this may not be the best option for you. Because you must first bring forward all the bodies and then delete those you don't want, the body data is still stored inside the part. Remember that the Delete/Keep bodies is a history-based feature and doesn't actually delete; it suppresses the body and simply makes it inaccessible in the part history. If you are inserting a part with many complex bodies, you may want to use a more selective method such as Insert Into New Part or Save Bodies, each of which is described in more detail later in this chapter.

One of the advantages of using Insert Part is that you can insert the part at any point in the child part's feature history. Using configurations, you can also insert the parent part at any point along the parent's feature history. Using part history is one of the trickiest aspects of working with multiple models, whether you are working in the context of an assembly or using a master model technique.

For the inserted part, you can set configurations of the parent document in the External References dialog box, which is available through the RMB menu of the feature that is inserted into the child document FeatureManager. The External References dialog box is shown in Figure 33.4. If the overhead of bringing many bodies forward only to be deleted is an issue for you, then you can use parent part configurations to delete the bodies first; then you can select which configuration to insert by using List External References from the child document.

As the original inserted bodies are modified by additional features in the child document, the names change, and they are removed from the folder under the inserted part and appear only in the Body folders under the top level.

FIGURE 33.4
The External References
dialog box

FIGURE 33.4
The External References
dialog box

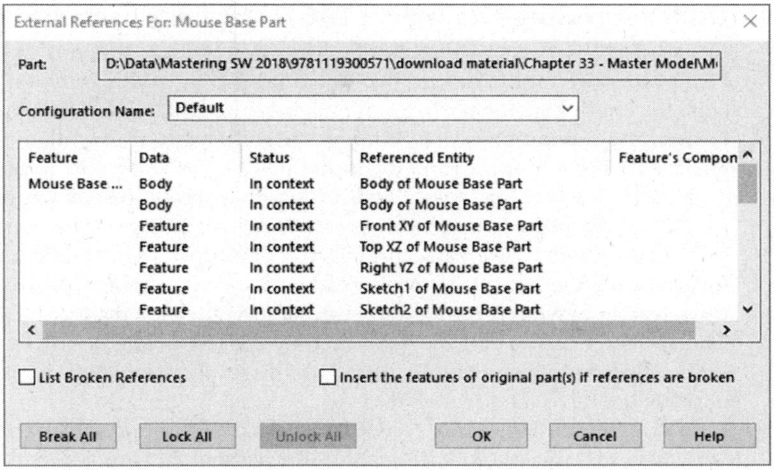

File management is a real issue with all these master model functions; in fact, it may be the *biggest* problem that arises with them, although you could say the same thing about overall body management. It's safe to say that you should be careful and follow file management best practice recommendations when performing name changes for documents with external references, especially if they use any of these features.

If you want to get a little practice with the Insert Part feature, follow this workflow:

1. Open a new part. Call this the child part.

2. Identify an existing part from which you want to make some references. Call this the parent part. Examples of the kinds of references that you might want to make between parts in an in-context assembly include matching a size or location of a feature on the parent part. To make it most interesting for experimentation, the parent part should have multiple solid or surface bodies.

3. With the child part open, click Insert ➤ Part.

4. In the PropertyManager that appears (refer to Figure 33.2), select the entities that you want to bring forward from the parent to the child.

5. Experiment with making relations between new geometry and the inserted geometry. Use multibody techniques to manage the visibility and access to the inserted bodies.

The Insert Part feature has received lots of attention from SolidWorks developers. For this reason, Insert Part in more recent versions of SolidWorks is most resilient to changes and is the most flexible when allowing the user to make changes.

For example, if the name of the parent file changes, you can edit Insert Part to recover from that error. If the number of bodies in the parent part changes, you can edit the results in the child part to prevent more downstream errors.

Unfortunately, this feature is also inefficient for inserting parts with large numbers of bodies. You may want to choose one of the following techniques for using a single body from a part with a large number of bodies. Insert Into New Part would be a good function for this because it allows you to be more selective about which body is brought forward from the parent to the child.

Understanding the Insert Into New Part Feature

Insert Into New Part qualifies as a Pull function because it doesn't create a feature in the FeatureManager of the parent file, even though it's actually initiated from the parent rather than from the child. This function doesn't have a drop-down menu location, nor does it have a toolbar button. You can initiate it only through the RMB menu from either the FeatureManager Solid or Surface Bodies folders or from the individual bodies within the folders.

This gives Insert Into New Part both advantages and disadvantages when compared to Insert Part. One advantage is that it can selectively insert either solid or surface bodies, or even selections of both types. You can Ctrl+select multiple bodies (solid and/or surface) to bring forward only the bodies you need. However, it cannot bring forward planes or axes, or change the selection of what is brought forward after you create the feature. You also cannot use it to add a body to an existing part file; you can only use it to create new documents. This is definitely a good news/bad news situation, but with this information, you can make a more informed decision about which function to use.

When you use Insert Into New Part to place bodies into a part, the bodies are not shown in the same way that the Insert Part function shows them. In Figure 33.5, the Stock feature symbols are used rather than the Inserted Part symbol.

FIGURE 33.5

Bodies placed in a part using Insert Into New Part

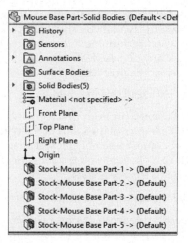

Keep in mind that if this feature loses its referenced bodies, they cannot be reattached. This means that you cannot intentionally replace a body. For most users, neither situation (lost references or the need to replace bodies) should arise often, if at all, but it may still be a roadblock when implementing this function.

Using Push Functions

Push functions are initiated from the master model (parent document) and push data from the parent part out to a child part. A feature in the tree of the parent identifies the point at which the model is pushed out to the child, and the child file can be found from the parent. These options combine to give the Push functions better overall control than the Pull functions; however, there might be other factors that are more important.

The first feature in the child part is a Stock feature, which contains a reference back to the parent, so the parent can be found from the child. The features that fall into this category are Split and Save Bodies. The bidirectional identification of the source (parent) and target (child) of the feature offers a distinct advantage over the Pull functions, which don't allow you to identify the child from the parent document.

Working with the Split Feature

The Split feature has three functions, two of which are plainly visible and one that's hidden. Its main function is, of course, to split a body into multiple bodies. It can also save the bodies to individual parts. The hidden function is that it can then create an assembly and reassemble the individual parts back into a complete assembly where all the parts are placed in their original relationships to one another. The Split PropertyManager is shown in Figure 33.6.

FIGURE 33.6
The Split
PropertyManager

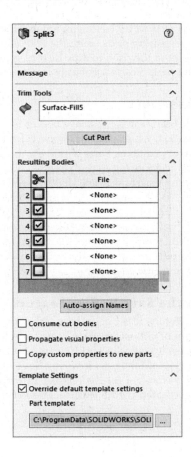

SPLITTING A BODY

The primary function of the Split feature is to split a single solid body into multiple bodies. You do this with sketches, planes, or surface bodies. The Split feature can save both the preexisting bodies and any bodies that result from the split as individual part files using the Stock feature as the initial feature in the part.

ASSIGNING NAMES AUTOMATICALLY

The ability to save solid bodies out to part files directly from the lower half of the Split Property-Manager caused some serious file management problems in earlier versions of SolidWorks. Fortunately, recent versions of SolidWorks have removed most of the bugs from this complex feature.

When you save the bodies to individual part files, SolidWorks automatically assigns names for the parts. These names take the form of `<Body1>.sldprt`. You can manually assign names either in the lower half of the Split PropertyManager or in callouts on the screen. You can change the names later if necessary. Features added to the parts created from the Split feature should update correctly when you rename the parts in the Split feature.

One drawback of creating parts using the Split feature is that you cannot insert the body geometry at any point in the child feature history. It goes only at the top. You cannot insert the data into an existing part; it can be put only into a new part.

CREATING AN ASSEMBLY

After you create the Split feature and save bodies to new parts, the RMB menu displays the Create Assembly option, which puts all the parts from the bodies in the original part back together in the correct positions. Parts within the assemblies that you create this way are fixed in space with the same relationship to the assembly origin that they originally had as bodies to the part origin. Although this arrangement doesn't need mates to be properly positioned, it doesn't easily allow motion. To allow motion, you must mate the parts using more traditional assembly methods.

Create Assembly is also a separate feature, found in the Insert ➤ Features menu. It uses the same icon as the Split feature. It will not allow you to put the bodies into an existing assembly, you have to create a new one. It will allow you to combine the body results from multiple Split features, to allow some efficiency.

Working with the Save Bodies Feature

To access the Save Bodies feature, you can either right-click the Bodies folder and select it from the RMB menu or choose Insert ➤ Features ➤ Save Bodies from the menu options. Save Bodies works by displaying path and filename information in the Resulting Bodies selection box of the Split PropertyManager. However, Save Bodies enables you to create an assembly right in the PropertyManager for the feature, rather than as a hidden feature with no record of the assembly name created by the feature. The PropertyManager for Save Bodies is shown in Figure 33.7.

FIGURE 33.7
The Save Bodies
PropertyManager

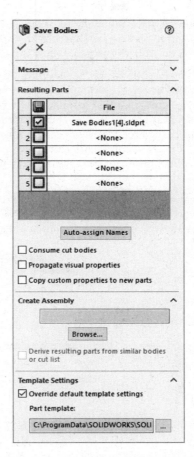

FIGURE 33.7
The Save Bodies
PropertyManager

Save Bodies is found in the Solid Bodies folder RMB menu and the lower half of the Split feature PropertyManager. You can use it to save bodies to parts if the bodies already exist. Save Bodies also has the Create Assembly functionality built right into the PropertyManager.

In both the Split and Save Bodies PropertyManagers, the Consume Cut Bodies option means that if a body is saved to a part, it is removed from the parent part. So, if you saved all the bodies to files, the parent part would be empty after the Split or Save Bodies feature in the FeatureManager.

Tutorial: Working with Master Model Techniques

Some of the concepts presented in this chapter may not make much sense until you apply them to a specific situation. The goal of this tutorial is to demonstrate the strengths and weaknesses of the various functions, as well as to give you some practical experience with the file management issues you'll encounter. In the following tutorials, you will use each of the four tools with the mouse multibody part to become familiar with their different functions.

To work with the Insert Part function, follow these steps:

1. Make sure you have access to the files from the download materials for Chapter 33. Create a new part, and insert the part named `Mouse Base Part.sldprt`. You can access Insert Part by choosing Insert ➤ Part from the menu options. After you issue the command, SolidWorks will attach the part to your cursor and prompt you to specify a location for the inserted part in the PropertyManager. Drop the part at the origin of the child part, or simply click the green checkmark icon to accept the part. There is no need to use the Move dialog box; if it appears, deselect the option that enables it. For this part, don't transfer any of the optional items, only the solid bodies.

2. After the feature is accepted and appears in the feature tree, right-click it and select List External Refs from the menu. The External References dialog box will appear with the list of configurations displayed, as shown in Figure 33.8.

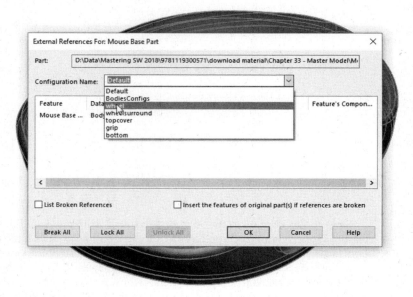

FIGURE 33.8
The External References dialog box

3. Select the Wheel configuration from the list.

4. Save and name the part file in such a way that it has the name of the technique used to create it (Insert Part) and the name of the body that it represents (such as Wheel).

NOTE This tutorial has been prepared to flow smoothly. If you ever choose to do modeling in this way, then you will need to know what this preparation work entails. In the mouse master model, you should make a separate configuration for each body, and in that configuration create a Delete Body feature that deletes all the bodies except one. The alternative to this approach is to bring all the bodies into each new part, and use a Delete Body feature in each child part that deletes all but the one body that is needed. The advantage to using configurations is that bringing in a single body theoretically decreases the overhead (memory and file size) for the individual part files.

5. Repeat steps 1 through 4 for each of the five bodies in the master model.

6. If the mouse master model (Mouse Base Part.sldprt) is open, close it. In any of the child parts, the inserted-part feature shown in the tree should display the Out Of Context symbol (–> ?). Right-click the inserted-part feature and select Edit In Context; this will open the master model.

Notice that from the master model, you have no way of knowing where the child parts are or even *if* any child parts exist. Notice also that there's no easy way to create an assembly.

7. Create a new assembly document.

8. Drop all the individually created parts into the assembly by selecting them in Windows Explorer and dragging them onto the assembly origin. This is probably the easiest way to create an assembly using the Insert Part feature.

NOTE There's no link from the parent to the child; if you rename the child part, the parent won't lose track of it. However, there's a link from the child to the parent; if you rename the parent without the child being open at the same time, the child will lose track of the parent. If you change the parent, the child won't update unless the arrow symbol (–>) shows In-Context. If it is out of context, broken, or locked, the child won't update with the parent. Both documents must be open at the same time to make the update happen (although they don't both need to be open when the original edit happens to the parent master model).

9. Save and close all the parts and assemblies.

To work with the Insert Into New Part function, follow these steps:

1. For this feature, start from the master model; open the part Mouse Base Part.sldprt. Make sure the part is set to the Default configuration. If it's set to a different configuration, inserting bodies will require an extra step of assigning which part configuration to use in the assembly.

2. Expand the Solid Bodies folder in the FeatureManager. Right-click the first body in the list (Wheel) and select Insert Into New Part from the menu.

NOTE You could select multiple bodies and even combine solid and surface bodies to insert using this technique.

3. When prompted, name the new part using the same convention used in the previous tutorial, which was to use the name of the technique (Insert Into New Part) and the name of the body. In this part, leave the configuration setting in the External References dialog box to the Default configuration.

4. Repeat steps 1 through 3 for each of the bodies.

5. Right-click the Stock feature in the tree and select Edit In Context. SolidWorks will open the master model part.

NOTE Again, there's no way back to the child document from the master model using the Insert Into New Part feature.

6. Create a new assembly document and use the same technique from the previous tutorial to put all the parts in the assembly located from the origin. Again, no automated assembly creation tool exists for this method.

7. Save all the documents and close them.

To work with the Split function, follow these steps:

1. This time, start from a copy of the master model part. The Split feature makes additions to the model, and because you have already created assemblies based on the original, you should create any additional features using a copy of the part rather than the original. Copy it using the Copy and Paste feature in Windows Explorer and rename the copy as **Split Tutorial**.

NOTE   It's best to copy and rename this document before continuing with the rest of the tutorial. Otherwise, you may encounter problems with the file references, from which it will be difficult to recover.

2. With the newly copied and renamed document open, initiate the Split feature by choosing Insert ➤ Features ➤ Split.

3. Because the bodies already exist, there's no need for the Trim tools or Cut Part functions in the Split feature, only for the resulting bodies. To save the bodies to individual files, you must give each one a unique name. You can click the Auto-Assign Names button to automatically name them with the existing names of the bodies. It might be difficult to discern where the callout flags are pointing. After all the names are satisfactory, click OK to accept the feature.

NOTE   The Consume Cut Bodies option deletes any bodies involved in the Split feature. For most purposes, you should deselect this option. Deselecting the option makes sure that the bodies are still available after the Split feature. If you want to eliminate the bodies after they are saved, you should select the Consume Cut Bodies option.

4. To automatically create an assembly with all the components located in the proper location, right-click the Split feature in the Master Model FeatureManager and select Create Assembly. Multiple Split features can be included in this command if bodies have been created by multiple Split features. Click the Browse button to locate and name the new assembly. Click OK when you are finished. Completing this step opens the assembly that you just named and located. When you create the assembly, the parts appear but may not be displayed in the FeatureManager until you have saved and reopened the assembly file. You should still have access to the data through the RMB menu from the graphics window.

5. Right-click one of the parts in the assembly to open it. Notice that a Stock feature is used in the tree, so you can access the parent part and change the parent part configuration used in the current part. Right-click the Stock feature and select Edit In Context.

6. With the master model open, right-click the Split feature and select Edit Feature. From here, you can see where each of the child parts is located.

7. If you rename any of the documents, you should do this by using either SolidWorks Explorer or the Save As command with the other documents open as well. If you want to rename the parent part (master model), make sure that all the child parts are open as well. (You can easily do this by opening the assembly; although the assembly was created from the master model, there's no direct link between the Split feature and the assembly.)

8. Save and close all the files before proceeding.

To work with the Save Bodies function, follow these steps:

1. As before, create a copy of the original master model part, and rename the copy **Save Bodies Tutorial**.

2. Open the renamed copy and right-click the Solid Bodies folder. Select Save Bodies from the menu. (Save Bodies has its own icon, which looks like the Split icon and is used to denote the placeholder feature in the FeatureManager.)

3. Use the Save Bodies PropertyManager to save the solid bodies to separate files. (This interface is nearly identical to the lower section of the Split PropertyManager.) The major addition in the Save Bodies dialog box is that the Create Assembly function is directly within the PropertyManager. The primary benefit of this addition is that it retains the name and path of the assembly in this interface so you can look it up later if necessary.

NOTE In both the Split/Create Assembly and Save Bodies features, when you create an assembly, SolidWorks may rebuild the tree of the part as many times as you have bodies to save. This may take some time for a complex model with lots of bodies.

4. Open the reconstructed assembly. Right-click one of the parts and select Open Part to open it in its own window. Notice that the Stock feature has again been used to push a single body into the part.

5. Right-click the Stock feature and select Edit In Context, which will take you back to the master model.

6. Save and close all the files.

The Bottom Line

Each of the four functions covered in this chapter has strengths and weaknesses. The Insert Part feature is probably the most flexible of them, mainly because of the additional items you can bring forward from the parent document, and the fact that it can handle both solid and surface bodies. The Split feature also has unique strengths because of its ability to split bodies, save multiple bodies to files, and reassemble the parts as an assembly.

If you are working with surface bodies, you must use Insert Part or Insert Into New Part. Another important strength can be found in the Save Bodies feature, which makes the child accessible from the parent and identifies the assembly in the parent.

Master It Leading up to master model techniques, you need to be proficient with body management. Master model is really just moving the body conversation to external files.

- Name the four Master Model tools.

- Name three body management tools.

Master It Follow these steps:

1. Open a new part, draw a centered rectangle centered on the origin, and extrude it mid-plane to make a block.

2. Use the Split command and the three default planes to split the part into eight bodies. (Click the scissors to automatically select all the bodies for saving to parts.)

3. Use Auto-Assign Names within the Split command to make parts for each body.

4. Use the Create Assembly command (Insert ➤ Features) to create an assembly from the bodies created by the Split Command.

5. Assign different appearance properties to each part in the assembly.

6. Open the List External References for one of the bodies and locate the path to the original part.

7. Use the Lock All button to lock references for this body. Notice that only the references for this body are locked. The rest of the external references are still functional.

8. The locked external reference symbol –> * shows up on the locked part, but the rest of the parts still use the active external reference symbol –> . Check this by editing the Stock feature for both locked and unlocked parts.

Master It Go back to the master model (the original part where the block was created) and follow these steps:

1. Close all parts and assemblies other than the original master model.

2. Using the Save As Copy and Continue option, save the master model with a new name. Then close the master model. Everything should be closed at this point.

3. Open the new master model.

4. Roll back before the Split feature and add fillets to all the corners of the part, and then roll back down after the Split feature. (The Split feature fails.)

5. Edit the Split feature, recut the part with the three planes, and reassign names to all the bodies. Notice that SolidWorks avoids the previously created filenames. Make sure the Propagate Visual Properties option is selected. Exit the feature.

6. Assign the colors in the part to the bodies this time, and the colors will propagate to the parts.

7. Execute the Create Assembly step again, making a new assembly with the new master model.

8. Use Isolate to edit each body in the new assembly and add a Shell feature that removes the inside faces. Do this for at least three of the parts.

9. Change the size of the second master model, save it, and then switch to the assembly, which will update.

Chapter 34

Using SolidWorks Sheet Metal Tools

SolidWorks contains two completely separate methods for working in sheet metal, and they both use regular SolidWorks parts (*.sldprt). In one method, you can use dedicated Sheet Metal features from the start, and in the other method, you build a part using thin features and other generic modeling tools, and then convert it to sheet metal so you can flatten it.

The reason for two methods is that the generic modeling method came first, and then SolidWorks introduced a more powerful set of dedicated Sheet Metal features. You can use these tools together or separately, and either way you get an accurately flattened part at the end. Situations where you might want to use one or the other are covered in this chapter.

Sheet metal tools don't always represent real-world sheet metal manufacturing processes 100 percent accurately, because some shapes that result from bending processes are too complex to easily represent in a CAD model. Sometimes you still have to use your imagination, particularly where bends intersect or overlap.

It is assumed that any cuts to a sheet metal part are sheared normal to the face of the part, unless otherwise specified.

IN THIS CHAPTER, YOU WILL LEARN TO:

- ◆ Use the Base Flange controls
- ◆ Use generic models to make sheet metal parts
- ◆ Work with imported geometry
- ◆ Make rolled conical parts

Using the Base Flange Features

The features used in the Base Flange method are easy to grasp conceptually, and they have many individual controls. These are the tools that represent the newer method of building sheet metal parts from dedicated Sheet Metal features. You can edit many of the features by pulling handles, by using spin arrows, or by entering specific numbers or dimensions. Maybe best of all, SolidWorks knows to change the thickness for the entire part at once.

The SolidWorks sheet metal Base Flange method works on a straight brake-press basis. This means that you can place straight bends of a constant radius. The software doesn't behave well when bends intersect, and it doesn't allow bends to cross. SolidWorks doesn't flatten anything where the material deforms or do anything other than a straight bend. The exceptions to this are the lofted bends, swept flanges, and edge flange on a curved edge. You should use these three features sparingly, and you should always verify the results before depending on the flat patterns you get from these features.

You will most often design a part in 3D and then flatten it for manufacturing, but SolidWorks also offers a workflow where you start with a flat pattern and add bend lines to it. Both methods work, but designing in 3D is most effective when you are trying to make a sheet metal part fit together with other parts.

Understanding sheet metal manufacturing processes is very helpful for using SolidWorks sheet metal tools to design functional and manufacturable parts. SolidWorks helps you by not allowing you to create a part that cannot be flattened, but it's still easy enough to model a part that cannot be manufactured or cannot be manufactured economically. You may find it useful to rely on the expertise of either designers with experience or shop personnel to help you learn how to design for sheet metal processes.

You can access the Sheet Metal features by clicking the tool you need in the Sheet Metal tab of the CommandManager or by choosing Insert ➤ Sheet Metal from the menus and selecting the appropriate tool.

Using the Base Flange/Tab Feature

The first feature you add to a sheet metal part is the Base Flange feature. In addition to letting SolidWorks know that the part is a dedicated sheet metal part, the Base Flange/Tab tool has three functions:

◆ By drawing an open contour in the first feature, the Base Flange tool creates a thin feature-like extrusion that includes the rounded corners of the bends.

◆ By drawing a closed contour in the first feature, the Base Flange tool creates a flat pattern sheet that is shaped like your sketch so you can start.

◆ When the Base Flange tool is used at any time other than the first feature, it functions as a tab.

Figure 34.1 shows these three functions of the Base Flange/Tab feature.

FIGURE 34.1
The three functions of the Base Flange/Tab feature

Notice that the sketch of the part shown in preview in Figure 34.1 has all sharp corners and that the bend radius is automatically added to each corner by the software. SolidWorks automatically adjusts when bend directions are combined to make sure that the inside radius is always the same, regardless of bend direction.

The bends are shown as BaseBend features in the FeatureManager. You can change individual bend radii from the default setting by editing the BaseBend feature, as well as by assigning custom bend allowances on a per-bend basis. You cannot change the bend angle for these particular bends because the angle is controlled through the sketch. However, for other types of bends (such as those created by edge flanges), you can adjust the bend angle through the feature PropertyManager.

If you need to, you can reorder all the bends from a list that you can access from the right mouse button (RMB) menu selection Reorder Bends on the flat pattern. This dialog box is shown in Figure 34.2.

FIGURE 34.2
The Reorder Bends
dialog box

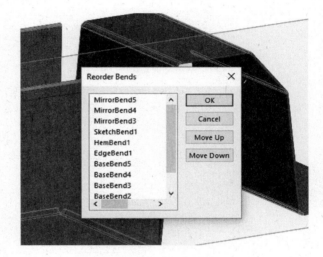

The BaseBend features can be suppressed, but the only effect this has is to prevent the associated bend from flattening when the Flat Pattern feature is unsuppressed.

Using the Sheet Metal Feature

The FeatureManager is shown for the Base Flange with all the bends in Figure 34.3. The Sheet-Metal1 feature is automatically added to sheet metal parts as a placeholder for default Sheet Metal settings such as Material Thickness, default Bend Allowance settings, and Auto Relief options, as well as the default Inside Bend Radius.

GAUGE TABLE

Gauge tables are a legacy table type, which is simply an Excel spreadsheet. The data from gauge tables was consolidated with other types of flat pattern calculation into what are now called *bend calculation tables*, which are described in more detail later in this chapter.

Gauge tables enable you to assign a thickness and available inside-bend radii, which limits the choices that the user has for those settings in the table. Each K-Factor has a separate table, and the choices listed in the table appear in the drop-down lists in the Sheet Metal PropertyManager. Figure 34.4 shows the top few lines of a sample gauge table and a Sheet Metal PropertyManager when a gauge table is used.

FIGURE 34.3
The FeatureManager
after the base
flange is added

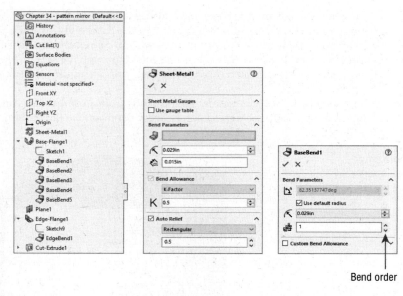

Bend order

FIGURE 34.4
A sample gauge table
and the Sheet Metal
PropertyManager

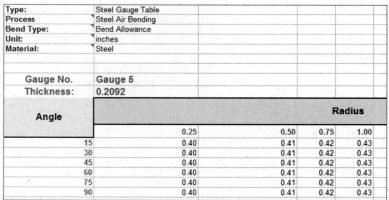

Type:	Steel Gauge Table		
Process	Steel Air Bending		
Bend Type:	Bend Allowance		
Unit:	inches		
Material:	Steel		
Gauge No.	Gauge 5		
Thickness:	0.2092		
Angle			**Radius**
	0.25	0.50	0.75	1.00
15	0.40	0.41	0.42	0.43
30	0.40	0.41	0.42	0.43
45	0.40	0.41	0.42	0.43
60	0.40	0.41	0.42	0.43
75	0.40	0.41	0.42	0.43
90	0.40	0.41	0.42	0.43

If necessary, you can override the values that are used in the gauge table by using the override options in the thickness, bend radius, and K-Factor fields of the PropertyManager.

The Bend Allowance options (Allowance, Deduction, and K-Factor) are explained in more detail later in this chapter.

ON THE WEBSITE

Sample tables with both gauge and bend data are provided in the download material for this chapter.

BEND RADIUS

This option specifies the default Inside Bend Radius for all bends in the part. You can override the values for individual bends or individual features.

THICKNESS

The Part Thickness is grayed out in the Sheet Metal PropertyManager. You can change the value by double-clicking any face of the model and then double-clicking the thickness dimension displayed in the graphics area. The thickness displays as a blue dimension rather than a black dimension. It's easier to identify if you have dimension names selected, because it's assigned the link value name Thickness and has a red link symbol to the left of the dimension value.

All features in sheet metal parts that use the thickness value use a link value to link all the feature thicknesses. This makes it easy to globally change the thickness of every feature in the entire sheet metal part.

To save these settings to a template file, you can create a Sheet Metal feature, specify the settings, delete the Sheet Metal features, and then save the file to a template with a special name that represents the settings that you used.

TIP When a link value is named Thickness, the Extrude dialog box always shows a Link To Thickness option to link the depth of an extrusion to the Thickness link value. If you save a template where Thickness has been created as a link value, then the option is always available to you, regardless of whether you're making sheet metal parts.

BEND ALLOWANCE

You can control the Bend Allowance by using four options:

- Bend Table
- K-Factor
- Bend Allowance
- Bend Deduction

Bend Table

Two general types of bend tables are available: text-based and Excel-based. The first few rows of each type of table are shown in Figure 34.5. Each table can use K-Factor, Bend Allowance, or Bend Deduction.

FIGURE 34.5

Sample text-based and Excel-based bend tables

```
Bend Allowance Tables
-----------------------
# Available types are Bend Allowance/Bend Deduction/K-Factor
# Keywords (Type:, Unit:, ...) must start at the beginning of the line.
Type: Bend Allowance
Material: Steel
Unit:   meters


Thickness: 0.0005
Bend Radius (read across)    0.0000  0.0005  0.0010  0.0015  0.0020  0.0025  0.0030  0.0040  0.0050
Opening Angle (read down)
                       5    0.0002  0.0002  0.0002  0.0002  0.0002  0.0002  0.0002  0.0002  0.0002
                      10    0.0002  0.0002  0.0002  0.0002  0.0002  0.0002  0.0002  0.0002  0.0002
                      20    0.0002  0.0002  0.0002  0.0002  0.0002  0.0002  0.0002  0.0002  0.0002
```

Unit:	Inches												
Type:	Bend Allowance												
Material:	**Soft Copper and Soft Brass**												
Comment:	Values specified are for 90-degree bends												
Radius	**Thickness**												
	1/64	1/32	3/64	1/16	5/64	3/32	1/8	5/32	3/16	7/32	1/4	9/32	5/16
1/32	0.058	0.066	0.075	0.083	0.092	0.101	0.118	0.135	0.152	0.169	0.187	0.204	0.221
3/64	0.083	0.091	0.1	0.108	0.117	0.126	0.143	0.16	0.177	0.194	0.212	0.229	0.246
1/16	0.107	0.115	0.124	0.132	0.141	0.15	0.167	0.184	0.201	0.218	0.236	0.253	0.27

Sample bend tables can be found in the lang\english\Sheetmetal Bend Tables subdirectory of the SolidWorks installation directory. Although the values may not be what you need, the syntax and organization are correct. You may want to contact your sheet metal fabrication shop to see what they are using for a table or equations.

NOTE Data from gauge tables and bend tables have been consolidated, but both legacy types can still be read.

K-Factor

When sheet metal is formed from a flat sheet, bending the metal causes it to stretch slightly on the outside part of the bend and to compress slightly on the inside part of the bend. Somewhere across the thickness of the sheet is the *neutral plane,* where there is no stretching or compression. This neutral plane can be at various places across the thickness, depending on the material, tooling, and process. The ratio of the distance from the inside bend surface to the neutral plane to the thickness is identified as the K-Factor, where 0.5 means halfway, 0 means on the inside face, and 1 means on the outside face. Typically, you can expect values between 0.5 and 0.3.

Bend Allowance and Bend Deduction

Bend Allowance and Bend Deduction are specific length values, not a ratio like the K-Factor. The Bend Allowance is essentially the arc length of the neutral plane through the bend region. The Bend Deduction is the length difference between a sharp corner and the radius corner, as expressed by the formula in Figure 34.6.

The three values are related, as shown in Figure 34.6. The dark rectangle represents the bend area. Material outside of the bend area really doesn't matter, although it's usually shown and used in the generally accepted formulas about bend calculations for sheet metal.

You usually use a ratio t/T (the K-Factor) from a published table or by asking your sheet metal vendor what values they typically use. The values from the tables have been developed experimentally by bending a piece of metal of known length and then measuring the arc length of the inside of the bend and the arc length of the outside of the bend. By comparing these numbers to the original linear length of the bent area, you can find the t value and thus the K value. From the K value, the BA (Bend Allowance) value can be calculated, and from that, the BD (Bend Deduction) value is easy to find.

FIGURE 34.6

Calculating the Bend
Deduction from the
Bend Allowance
and K-Factor

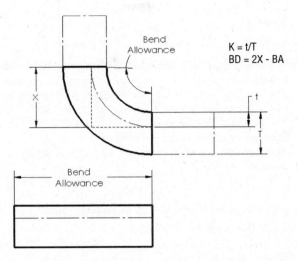

The specific formulas for finding these numbers aren't as important as an intuitive grasp of what the numbers mean and how they are used, at least in relation to using SolidWorks to model sheet metal parts. The numbers used to fill out bend tables using *K*, *BA*, or *BD* values are typically taken from experimentally developed tables.

Bend Calculation Tables

Bend calculation tables are Excel spreadsheets that enable you to divide bend angles into ranges and assign flat (also referred to as developed) length equations for each range. You can also assign an equation for the K-Factor.

The Excel table must be set up like the example shown in Figure 34.7 in several respects.

FIGURE 34.7

Setting up the bend
calculation table

	A	B	C
1	bend type:	bend calculation	
2	unit:	inches	
3	material thickness:	t	
4	radius	r	
5	k-factor	0.65+0.5*lg(r/t)	
6	bend angle	180-a	
7			
8	**Angular Range**	**Equation**	**Use Tangent Length**
9	0<=b<=90	v=pi*((180-b)/180)*(r+((t/2)*k))-2*(r+t)	yes
10	90<b<=165	v=pi*((180-b)/180)*(r+((t/2)*k))-2*(r+t)*tan((180-b)/2)	no
11	165<b<=180	v=0	no

The declarations in the first several rows must include the following items in the first column (capitalization is not important, but the colon must be as shown). Although the first column may also contain other declarations, it must have at least the ones shown here:

bend type:

unit:

material thickness:

radius

k-factor

bend angle

The available options for Bend Type are Bend Allowance, Bend Deduction, K-Factor, and Bend Calculation.

The available options for Unit are Inch, Millimeter, Meter, and Centimeter (although it looks like plurals are also allowed, such as *inches*, but abbreviations, such as *in*, are not).

The Material Thickness can be any variable letter you choose. The Radius can also be any variable letter you choose.

The K-Factor can be an equation or a specific value. In the SolidWorks Web Help, the equation shown as a sample is

$$k = 0.65 + 0.5 * lg(r / t)$$

The *lg* in this case is assumed to mean logarithm. I found that the DIN 6935 standard says that the formula for the K-Factor is

$$k = (0.65 + \log(r / t) / 2) / 2$$

This differs from the SolidWorks-provided equation by a /2 term. *K* is sometimes approximated as $0.44 * T$. You should note that K-Factors are usually determined experimentally, and designers who are not intimately familiar with the process details should work with a manufacturing expert to learn the ropes of calculating sheet metal flat patterns.

The headers shown in Row 8 of the Excel spreadsheet in Figure 34.7 must be spelled as shown without embellishment.

The equations in cells B9 to B11 can use the variables for thickness and radius from the parameters specified in the declarations at the top of the table. It may seem odd, but the equations are just entered as text into the cells of the spreadsheets. They are not active Excel equations. They must be read into SolidWorks and evaluated there, not in Excel. I haven't verified these equations for accuracy. As demonstrated with the K-Factor equation, you should verify the equations yourself or with help before depending on them for production data.

The variable v used on the left side of the equations represents the length of the flattened (developed) bend area. The Web Help (which is the most complete source of information available for this feature as of this writing) refers to a β (beta) variable, which in the equations appears to be replaced with the letter b.

So, you must assume that b stands for bend angle, and the equation for bend angle $(180 - a)$ includes the variable a, which is shown in the Help diagrams as a linear dimension, but which you must assume is the angle through which the sheet metal must bend. So, when a is 45, b is 135, which corresponds to bending the sheet metal 45 degrees, but the bend angle is 135 degrees. Figure 34.8 shows how these variables relate to actual geometry.

Notice that the Tangent Length option can apply only when the bend angle is 90 degrees or less. For more than 90 degrees, you must use the Virtual Sharp method.

Also, be aware that the angles here are measured in degrees. In design tables, you have the option to use degrees or radians.

AUTO RELIEF

When a bend doesn't go all the way across a part, some sort of feature is needed at the end of the bend. In real manufacturing processes, the metal may just transition smoothly from the bent area to the flat area; however, in SolidWorks, the software cannot create that smooth transition—or it could, but it would add significantly to sheet metal rebuild times. For this reason, all bends in SolidWorks sheet metal must terminate cleanly, with some sort of a cut, or as they are called here, a *relief*. SolidWorks allows three kinds of reliefs: Rectangular, Tear, and Obround.

FIGURE 34.8
Assigning variables to geometry in bend calculation tables

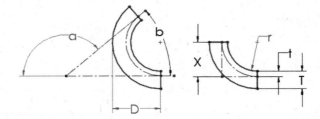

Auto reliefs were formerly called Bend reliefs. You can specify three different Auto Relief options to be applied automatically to bends that end in the middle of material. These options are illustrated in Figure 34.9.

FIGURE 34.9
The three Auto Relief configurations: Rectangular, Tear, and Obround

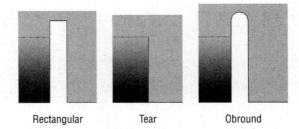

For the Rectangular and Obround types, you can control the width and the distance past the tangent line of the bend through the Relief Ratio selection box, which is immediately below the Type selection box in the Sheet Metal PropertyManager. This ratio is the width of the relief divided by the part thickness. For the Rectangular relief, a ratio of 0.5 and a thickness of .050 inches means that the relief is 0.025 inches wide and that it goes 0.025 inches deeper into the part beyond the tangent line of the bend. The Obround relief goes slightly deeper because it has a full radius after the distance past the tangent line of the bend, so it essentially goes a total of one full material thickness past the tangent line.

The Tear relief is simply a face-to-face shear of the material with no gap.

Using the Flat Pattern Feature

The Flat Pattern feature is added automatically to the end of the tree when the Base Flange feature is added. This feature is used to flatten the sheet metal part when the feature is unsuppressed. The Flatten toolbar button acts as a toggle to unsuppress or suppress the Flat Pattern feature in the tree. It may be a little confusing, but the Flatten toolbar button and the Flat Pattern feature in the FeatureManager refer to the same functionality. As mentioned earlier, the Flat Pattern feature has a couple of special properties that aren't seen in other features. The first is that it remains at the *bottom* of the FeatureManager when other Sheet Metal features are added.

The second property of the Flat Pattern feature is that it's added in the *suppressed* state. When it's unsuppressed, it flattens out the sheet metal bends.

Notice also that the Flat Pattern PropertyManager allows you to select an edge, axis, or sketch line to denote the grain of the material.

By editing the Flat Pattern feature, you can set a few options. The Flat Pattern PropertyManager is shown in Figure 34.10.

FIGURE 34.10
The Flat Pattern
PropertyManager

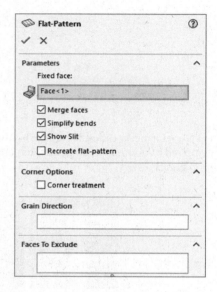

The Fixed Face parameter determines which face remains stationary when the part is flattened out. Generally, the largest face available is selected automatically, but if you want to specify a different face to remain stationary, you can do that here.

When the Merge Faces option is selected, it causes the flat pattern to form a single face rather than being broken up by the tangent lines around the bends. This does a few things:

◆ Selecting the face of the flattened part and clicking Convert Entities (found on the Sketch toolbar) makes an outline of the entire flattened part, which is easier to use for certain programming applications.

◆ The edges around the outside aren't broken up.

◆ The tangent edges around the bends aren't shown.

The differences between flat patterns with this option selected and unselected are shown in Figure 34.11.

Bend lines are shown in both examples in Figure 34.11.

When you turn on the Simplify Bends option, it simplifies curved edges that are caused by flattening bends to straight lines from arcs or splines. When the option is off, the complex edges remain complex. Simple edges can be cut by standard punches and don't require Computer Numerical Control (CNC)–controlled lasers or abrasive water jets.

The Corner Treatment option controls whether a corner treatment is applied to the flat pattern of a part. The corner treatment is illustrated in Figure 34.12. I created this corner using a model that had a miter flange around the edges of a rectangular sheet.

FIGURE 34.11
The Merge Faces option showing on and off

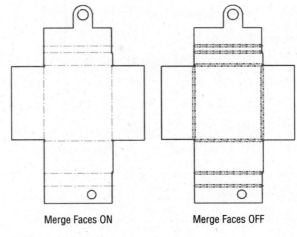

Merge Faces ON   Merge Faces OFF

FIGURE 34.12
Using the Corner Treatment setting in the Flat Pattern PropertyManager

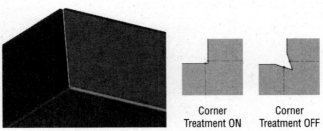

Corner   Corner
Treatment ON   Treatment OFF

NOTE   You can export a `*.dxf` file of the flat pattern directly from the model without creating a drawing by right-clicking the Flat Pattern feature and selecting Export To DXF/DWG.

Using the Edge Flange Feature

The Edge Flange feature is intended to turn a 90-degree (the default) flange from a selected straight edge in the direction and distance specified using the default thickness for the part. The default workflow for this feature is that you select the tool, select the edge, and then drag the distance, clicking a distance reference such as a vertex at the end of another flange of equal length or typing a distance value manually. You can select multiple edges from a part that don't necessarily need to touch one another. That's all there is to a simple default flange, although several options give you some additional methods for angle, length, and so on. Figure 34.13 shows the Edge Flange PropertyManager, as well as a simple flange.

EDIT FLANGE PROFILE

The Edit Flange Profile button in the Edge Flange PropertyManager enables you to edit a sketch to shape the flange in some way other than rectangular or to otherwise edit the shape of the flange. Notice in Figure 34.13 that both of the flanges made by a single Flange feature have been edited. You can do this by selecting the flange for which you want to edit the profile before clicking the Edit Flange Profile button.

FIGURE 34.13
The Edge Flange
PropertyManager and
a simple flange

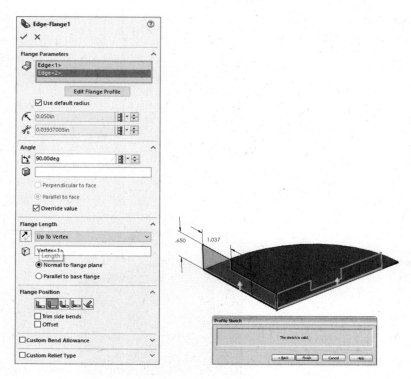

NOTE If you have added dimensions to the sketch, as shown in Figure 34.13, then you can no longer use the arrow to drag the length of the flange. To edit the length, you must edit the sketch or double-click the feature and then double-click the dimensions that you want to change.

You can add holes to the flange profile as nested loops. This enables you to avoid creating additional hole features but doesn't enable you to control the suppression state independently from the Flange feature.

By pulling one of the end lines back from the edge (or past the edge to make it longer), you can make flanges go only part of the way along an edge. This works even though the end lines appear black and fully defined. A situation where the sketch has been edited this way is shown in the image to the right in Figure 34.13.

Use Default Radius

This option enables you to override the default Inside Bend Radius that is set for the entire part for this feature. The bend radii for individual bends within an edge flange that has multiple flanges cannot be set; the only override is at the feature level. If you need individual bends to have different bend radii, you must do this using multiple Edge Flange features.

Gap Distance

The gap distance is illustrated in Figure 34.14. The Gap Distance selection box is active only when you have selected multiple edges in the main selection box for this feature. The *gap* refers to the space between the inside corners of the perpendicular flanges.

FIGURE 34.14
Specifying the
gap distance

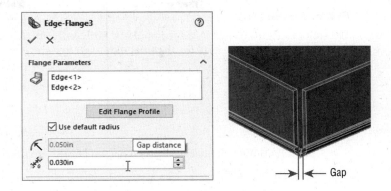

ANGLE

Because the edge flange isn't dependent on a sketch for its angle like the base flange is, you can set the angle in the Angle panel of the PropertyManager. The values that this selection box can accept range from any value larger than zero to any value smaller than 180. Of course, each flange has practical limits. In the flange shown in Figure 34.15, the limitation is reached when the bend radius runs into the rectangular notch in the middle of the flange to the right, at about 158 degrees. The angle affects all the flanges that are made with the feature. To create a situation where different flanges have different angles, you must create separate flange features.

FIGURE 34.15
Establishing the limit of
the flange angle

FLANGE LENGTH

As mentioned earlier, if you have edited the Flange profile sketch and a Flange Length dimension is applied in the sketch, then the flange length is taken from that sketch dimension. If this dimension has not been added to the profile sketch, the options for this setting in the PropertyManager Flange Length panel are Blind, Merge, Up To Edge, and Up To Vertex. Using Up To Vertex is a nice way to link the lengths of several flanges.

In the Flange Length panel of the Edge Flange PropertyManager, there are options shown on icons for the start reference of how the Blind length of the flange is measured. These icons should be self-explanatory. They are Outer Virtual Sharp, Inner Virtual Sharp, and Tangent Bend.

FLANGE POSITION

The small icons for Flange Position should be fairly self-explanatory, with the dotted lines indicating the existing end of the material. From left to right, here are the names for these options:

- Material Inside
- Material Outside
- Bend Outside
- Bend From Virtual Sharp (for use when an angle is involved)
- Tangent to Bend

TRIM SIDE BENDS

In situations where a new flange is created next to an existing flange, and a relief must be made in the existing flange to accommodate the new flange, you can select the Trim Side Bends option to trim back the existing flange. Leaving this option unselected simply creates a relief cut, as shown in Figure 34.16. This functionality requires some imagination from the user. A real sheet metal part manufactured like this would have a deformed area in the corner where the bends that are going in different directions overlap. This overlapping bend geometry is too complex for SolidWorks to create automatically, so it offers you a couple of options for how you would like to visually represent the corner. The Flat Pattern is correct, but the formed model requires some imagination.

FIGURE 34.16
Using the Trim Side
Bends option

Trim Side Bends OFF   Trim Side Bends ON

CURVED EDGES

Edge flanges can be created on curved edges, but the curved edge must be on a planar face. For example, if the part were the top of a mailbox, then an edge flange could not be put on the curve on the top of the mailbox. The flange would have to be made as a part of the flat end of the mailbox, instead.

Figure 34.17 shows edge flanges used on a part. Notice that reliefs are added to the ends of the bends, although they are not really needed.

FIGURE 34.17
Curved edge
flanges on a part

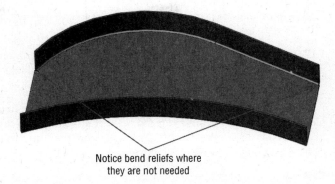

Notice bend reliefs where
they are not needed

All the edges that you select to be used with a curved edge flange must be tangent. This means that in Figure 34.17, neither of the edge flanges could have been extended around the ends of the part. You would need to create separate Edge Flange features for those edges.

Because these edge flanges are made in such a way that they are developable surfaces, they can be (and are) flattened in such a way that they don't stretch the material of the flange when the flat is compared to the formed shape. Doubtless, there's some deformation between the two states in the actual forming of this flange, so its manufacturing accuracy may not be completely reliable.

You may also want to examine the Swept Flange feature introduced later in this chapter, as it does some of the same things as curved edge flanges.

Using the Miter Flange Feature

The Miter Flange feature can create picture-frame-like miters around corners of parts; it correctly recognizes the difference between mitered inside corners and mitered outside corners. The PropertyManager and a sample miter flange are shown in Figure 34.18.

FIGURE 34.18
The Miter Flange
PropertyManager and
a sample part

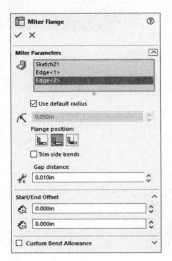

A Miter Flange feature starts off with a sketch that's perpendicular to the starting edge of the Miter Flange feature.

TIP A quick way to start a sketch for a miter flange that's on a plane perpendicular to a selected edge is to select the edge and then click a sketch tool. This automatically creates a plane perpendicular to the edge at the nearest endpoint.

Miter Flange sketches can have single lines or multiple lines. They can even have arcs. Still, remember that just because you can make it in SolidWorks doesn't mean the manufacturer can make it. Check with the manufacturer to ensure that the part can be made. Also, you usually will learn something from the experience.

TIP When you're selecting edges for the miter flange to go on, be sure to remain consistent in your selection. If you start by selecting an edge on the top of the part, you should continue selecting edges on the top of the part. If you don't, SolidWorks will prompt you with a warning message in a tool tip that says that the edge is on the wrong face.

Some of the controls in the Miter Flange PropertyManager should be familiar by now, such as Use Default Radius, Flange Position, Trim Side Bends, and Gap Distance. You have seen these controls before in the Edge Flange PropertyManager.

The Start/End Offset panel enables you to pull a miter flange back from an edge without using a cut. If you need an intermittent flange, you may need to use cuts or multiple Miter Flange features, as shown in Figure 34.19.

FIGURE 34.19
The Start/End Offset settings for a miter flange

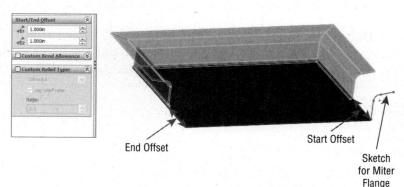

End Offset

Start Offset

Sketch
for Miter
Flange

You may find some similarities between functions of the Miter Flange feature and the Swept Flange feature, introduced later in this chapter.

Using the Hem Feature

The Hem feature is used to roll over the edge of a sheet metal part. This feature is often used to smooth over a sharp edge or to add strength to the edge. You can also use it for other purposes, such as to capture a pin for a hinge. SolidWorks offers four different hem styles—Closed, Open, Tear Drop, and Rolled—which are shown as icons on the Hem PropertyManager. The PropertyManager for the Hem feature is shown in Figure 34.20.

FIGURE 34.20
The Hem
PropertyManager and
a sample hem

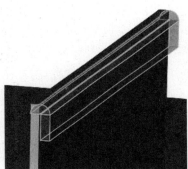

One of the limitations to keep in mind with regard to hems is that SolidWorks cannot fold over a part so the faces touch perfectly line on line. Doing this would cause the two sections of the part to merge into a larger piece, thereby removing the coincident faces. SolidWorks, computers, and mathematics in general don't always handle the number zero very well. In reality, you can often see light through these hems, so a perfectly flush hem may not be as accurate as it seems.

You can edit the profile of the Hem, like an edge flange, to control the length of the edge that's hemmed. To do this, click the Edit Hem Width button below the Edges selection box in the Hem PropertyManager, shown in Figure 34.20.

Using the Jog Feature

The Jog feature puts a pair of opposing bends on a flange so the end of the flange is parallel to, but offset from, the face where the jog started. The Jog PropertyManager and a sample jog are shown in Figure 34.21.

The Jog feature is created from a single sketch line on the face of a sheet metal part. The geometry to be jogged should have no side bends; it should be a simple tab-like flange (refer to Figure 34.21). The line to create the jog can be drawn at an angle, causing the jog to also be angled.

The three icons on the Jog Offset panel illustrate what dimension is being controlled by that setting.

FIGURE 34.21
The Jog
PropertyManager and a
sample jog

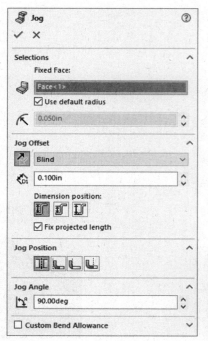

FIXED FACE

Like most Sheet Metal features, the Jog feature bends faces on the part; when it does so, although it may be obvious to you as the user, it isn't obvious to the software which face should remain stationary and which faces should be moved by the bend. The Fixed Face selection box enables you to select a face, or in this case, a part of a face, that you want to remain stationary as the rest of the faces move. The black dot on the face identifies it as stationary.

TIP Problems can sometimes arise when you are using configurations that change sizes, because these markers for fixed faces can be pushed onto other faces. This can cause problems with assemblies and drawings and, in general, makes visualization difficult. In cases like this, it may be advisable to select a larger face or one that has fewer changes, if possible, to be used as the fixed face.

JOG OFFSET

You can control the direction of the jog by using the arrow button to the left of the End Condition selection box. You can control the jog distance by selecting the end condition Up To Surface, Up To Vertex, or Offset From Surface. The default setting is Blind, in which you simply enter a distance for the offset, in exactly the same way that end conditions are controlled for features such as extrudes.

FIX PROJECTED LENGTH

One setting that may not be obvious is the Fix Projected Length. This refers to the length of the flange that the jog is altering. In Figure 34.21, you can see that the height of the jogged feature is shorter than the length of the original tab. The jog obviously requires more material than the original, but the Fix Projected Length option is selected, so the height is maintained. If you deselected this option, the finished height of the flange after the jog is added would be shorter, because the material is used by the jog, and additional material is not added. For comparison, the image to the right in Figure 34.21 shows this situation.

JOG POSITION

The Jog Position selection establishes the relationship between the sketched line and the first bend tangent line. The Jog Position icons have tool tips with the following names, from left to right: Bend Centerline, Material Inside, Material Outside, and Bend Outside.

JOG ANGLE

The Jog Angle selection enables you to change the angle of the short perpendicular section of the jog. You can angle it to smooth out the jog (angles of less than 90 degrees) or to curl back on itself (angles of more than 90 degrees). Again, be sure to check your manufacturer's capabilities.

Using the Sketched Bend Feature

Sketched Bend works in some respects like half of a jog. It requires the sketch line and the Fixed Face selection. You define a bend position with the same set of icons that you used in the jog, and you assign a bend angle in the same way.

TIP　You can use the Sketched Bend feature to "dog ear" corners. You do this by drawing a line across the corner at an angle, setting the angle to 180 degrees, and overriding the default radius with a much smaller one, such as .001 inches.

Unlike Jog, the Sketched Bend feature doesn't show you a preview. The Sketched Bend PropertyManager is shown in Figure 34.22.

FIGURE 34.22
The Sketched Bend
PropertyManager

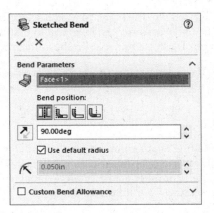

Using the Closed Corner Feature

The Closed Corner feature extends flanges on the sides to meet with other flanges. It's typically used when corners leave big open gaps in order to create a corner that's more easily welded shut. Figure 34.23 shows a part where angled flanges have been applied. This creates big gaps in the corners. Although a miter flange may have been better, these were created using regular edge flanges.

FIGURE 34.23
Applying the Closed
Corner feature

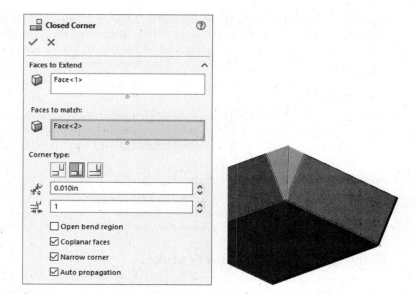

FACES TO EXTEND

You must select the thickness face of one of the flanges in order to extend it. Selecting one face automatically selects the matching face from the other flange that you also want to extend. The Corner Type selection icons depict the selected face as red, and the three icons display tool tips: Butt, Overlap, and Underlap.

FACES TO MATCH

The faces selected in the Faces To Match selection box act as an Up To end condition for the faces to extend. SolidWorks 2013 enables you to manually select matching faces in the Faces To Match selection box for those times when the automatic selection does not work.

NOTE If you deselect faces in the Faces To Extend or the Faces To Match selection boxes, the Auto Propagation option toggles off to enable you to make selections manually.

GAP

The Gap setting enables you to specify how close you want the closed corner to be. Keep in mind that you cannot use the number zero in this field. If you do, SolidWorks will remind you to "Please enter a number greater than or equal to 0.00003937 and less than or equal to 0.86388126." It's good to know your limits.

OVERLAP/UNDERLAP RATIO

The Overlap/Underlap Ratio setting controls how far across the overlapped face the overlapping flange reaches. Full overlap is a ratio of 1, and a Butt condition is (roughly) a ratio of zero. This ratio is available only when you have specified Overlap or Underlap for the corner type.

OPEN BEND REGION

The Open Bend Region option affects how the finished corner looks in the bend area. If Open Bend Region is selected, then a small gap is created at the end of the bend. If the option is deselected, then SolidWorks fills this area with geometry. Figure 34.24 shows the finished model with this option selected and unselected, as well as the resulting Flat Patterns for each setting.

FIGURE 34.24
The Open Bend Region option, both selected and unselected, and the resulting flat patterns

Open Bend
Region ON

Open Bend
Region ON -
Flat Pattern

Open Bend
Region OFF

Open Bend
Region OFF -
Flat Pattern

CORNER TRIM AND BREAK CORNER FEATURES

When the Coplanar option is selected, any faces that are coplanar with any selected faces are also selected Corner Trim and Break Corner features. The Corner Trim feature is available only when the sheet metal part is in its flattened state. The Corner Trim PropertyManager also has the Break Corner Options interface built right into it. However, the Break Corner feature is available only when the sheet metal part is in its folded state. Figure 34.25 shows the combined interface. Both functions are included here, and SolidWorks treats them as if they are part of a single function.

CAUTION The corresponding function in 3D Formed Shape is Corner Relief. If you use one, don't use the other.

When finished, the Corner Trim feature places itself after the Flat Pattern feature in the FeatureManager. It similarly follows the suppress/unsuppress state of the Flat Pattern feature. When the Break Corner feature is used on its own, it's placed before the Flat Pattern feature. With this in mind, it seems best to use Break Corner as a separate feature unless it's being used specifically to alter the flat pattern in a way that cannot be done from the folded state.

Break Corner on its own is primarily used to remove sharp corners using either a chamfer or a rounded corner. This tool is set up to filter edges on the thickness of sheet metal parts, which is useful, because these edges are otherwise difficult to select without lots of zooming. Break Corner can also break interior corners.

One of the main functions of the Corner Trim feature is to apply bend relief geometry to the flat pattern. The three available options are Circular, Square, and Bend Waist. These options are shown in Figure 34.26.

FIGURE 34.25
The Corner Trim
PropertyManager,
including the Break
Corner Options panel

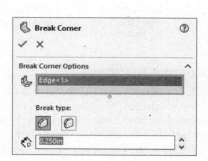

FIGURE 34.26
Applying the Corner
Trim Relief options

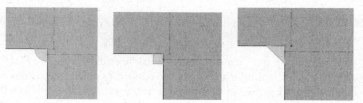

Using the Corner Relief Feature

SolidWorks also has a Corner Relief feature, which applies corner reliefs in the 3D model. The bend relief in the Corner Trim feature is displayed only in the 2D model.

You can manually select corners or allow the software to collect them all for you. You can select from Rectangular, Circular, Obround, Tear, and Constant Width reliefs. Figure 34.27 shows the reliefs previewed on the 3D model, and these carry through to the flat pattern. If you use the Corner Relief feature, you don't need to use the Bend Relief option in the Corner Trim feature.

TIP Corner Relief is a computationally expensive feature, so you should evaluate whether you really need to show this type of feature on the 3D model, or if the 2D corner trims will be enough.

FIGURE 34.27
Selecting options with
the Corner Relief feature

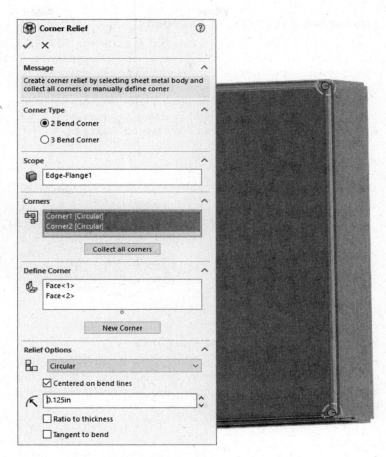

Mirroring and Patterning in Sheet Metal

Most Sheet Metal features can be patterned or mirrored following the same logic as normal SolidWorks parts. Figure 34.28 shows a part with some features mirrored.

FIGURE 34.28
Mirroring some features
on a sheet metal part

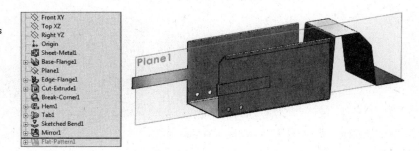

MIRRORING SHEET METAL FEATURES

Notice that not all the features are mirrored. In particular, the Corner Break and the Sketched Bend features wouldn't mirror. When you get into a situation where individual features don't mirror, you have two options, just as you do when mirroring a normal SolidWorks part: you can re-create the features on the other side manually or mirror the body rather than the features.

Figure 34.29 shows the same part from Figure 34.28 but modeled by mirroring the body instead of just the features, so all the geometry is symmetrical. You can use this technique along with changing the feature order to make asymmetrical parts when the need arises.

FIGURE 34.29
Mirroring the entire sheet metal body

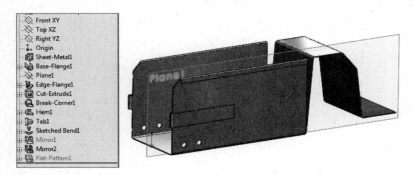

PATTERNING SHEET METAL FEATURES

Patterning also works for multiple Sheet Metal features. Figure 34.30 shows the patterned tabs with holes and hems. Controlling the bend placement of the first feature changes all the patterned instances. This works nicely, especially because most patterns in sheet metal are less demanding than general patterns.

FIGURE 34.30
Patterning multiple features in sheet metal

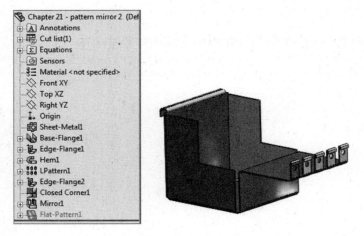

If you examine the part shown in Figure 34.29 (Chapter 34 - pattern mirror 2.sldprt from the download materials), you'll see that it also contains a mirror feature that mirrors a Closed Corner feature. To me, this is very reasonable pattern/mirror functionality from SolidWorks.

Forming Tool Feature

SolidWorks has created two methods for applying forming tools. One is to save the forming tool to the Design Library as an `*.sldFTP` file type in a generic Library Area folder. The other way is to put a regular `*.sldPRT` file into a folder specially intended for forming tools. (The words *form* and *forming* seem to be used interchangeably, without a discernable difference in what they mean, so I assume they mean the same thing.)

In this chapter, I generally assume to use the method with the special folder, but other than the special folder and the file extensions, I don't see any difference between the two methods for applying forming tools to sheet metal parts in SolidWorks. You should note that the SolidWorks documentation refers to certain forming tools that have been placed in a part before SolidWorks 2012 that may have a lock symbol on them, signifying that they cannot be edited.

Forming tools in SolidWorks enable you to place features that aren't formed on a brake press. These features aren't straight-line bends but rather punched, drawn, formed, lanced, sheared, or otherwise deformed material. One of the important things to understand about forming tools is that they don't stretch the material in the SolidWorks part in the same way that happens in a real-life forming operation. In real life, material is thinned when it is punched, stamped, or drawn. In SolidWorks, the thickness of a sheet metal part remains the same, regardless of what happens to it. For this reason, you need to be careful when using mass properties of sheet metal parts or doing stress analysis of parts that have formed features. You might consider taking your part weight from the flat pattern rather than from the formed sheet metal.

SolidWorks installs with a library of fairly simple forming tools that you can use as a starting point for your own personal customized library. You can also examine some of these tools to see how they create particular effects. You find this library in your Design Library in the Task pane. Some of the more interesting forming tools are the lances and louvers.

NOTE   It is worth specifying that there are two types of forming tools: The `*.sldprt` files that require a specially designated folder are called "forming tools," and the files with the special extension `*.sldftp` are called Form Tools.

CREATING FORMING TOOLS

Current versions of SolidWorks use library features as tools to form another part. For older versions, the forming tools are essentially a part used as a tool to form another part. One flat face of the forming tool part is designated as a *stopping face,* which is placed flush with the top face of the sheet metal part. You can move and rotate the tool with the Modify Sketch tool, and you can use dimensions or sketch relations to locate it.

To create a forming tool, click the Forming Tool button on the Sheet Metal toolbar. Figure 34.31 shows the PropertyManager interface for this tool.

FIGURE 34.31
The Form Tool PropertyManager and a sample tool with an orientation sketch

The stopping face turns a special color, and so do any faces that are selected in the Faces To Remove selection box. Faces To Remove means that those faces will be cutouts in the sheet metal part.

Another aspect of the forming tool is the orientation sketch. Create the orientation sketch by using Convert Entities on the Stopping Face. The orientation sketch cannot be manually edited; so for forming tools where *footprints* are symmetrical but other features in the tool are not, you cannot tell from the sketch which direction the forming tool should face.

When creating a forming tool, you must remember to build in generous draft and fillets, and not to build undercuts into the tool. Also keep in mind that when you have a concave fillet face on the tool, the radius becomes smaller by the thickness of the sheet metal; as a result, you must be careful about minimum radius values on forming tools. If a concave face on the tool has a 0.060-inch radius and the tool is applied to a part with a 0.060-inch thickness, the tool will cause an error because it forms a zero-radius fillet, which is not allowed. Errors in applied Forming Tool features cannot be edited or repaired, except by changing forming tool dimensions.

After the forming tool is created, special colors are used for every face on the part. For example, the stopping face is light blue, the faces to remove are red, and all the other faces are yellow. Figure 34.32 shows the small addition made to the FeatureManager when you make a part into a forming tool. This feature didn't exist in older versions of the tool.

FIGURE 34.32
The FeatureManager of a forming tool part

FORMING TOOL LIBRARY

The folder that the forming tools are placed into in the Design Library must be designated as a Forming Tool folder. To do this, right-click the folder that contains the forming tools and select Forming Tool Folder (a check mark appears next to this option). As I mentioned at the top of this section, this specially designated folder in the Design Library is one of two methods to use forming tools. The other is to place the forming tools in any library folder and use the `*.sldFTP` extension.

PLACING A FORMING TOOL

To place a forming tool on a sheet metal part (forming tools are allowed to be used only on parts with sheet metal features), you can drag the tool from the library and drop it on the face of the sheet metal part. Forming tools are limited to being used on flat faces.

To position the tool, use the Position tab in the Form Tool Feature PropertyManager, as shown in Figure 34.32. With this tab active, you can create or move sketch points to locate the reference point for the tool. You can also use the properties in the PropertyManager to rotate and even configure the forming tool.

By default, forming tools create external references to the Forming Tool library file. You can turn this off in the PropertyManager. You can also change the tool to reference another file by right-clicking on the tool in the FeatureManager and selecting Replace Form Tool.

SPECIAL TECHNIQUES WITH FORMING TOOLS

One application of forming tools that is asked for frequently is the cross break to stiffen a large, flat sheet metal face. SolidWorks has a cosmetic cross break, which I discuss next. Cross breaks are clearly not something that SolidWorks can do using straight bends, but a forming tool can do it.

You can create the forming tool by lofting a rectangle to a sketch point on a plane slightly offset from the plane of the rectangle. This creates a shallow pyramid shape. Open the part from the material on the website for Chapter 34 called `Chapter 34 - Cross Break Sheet Metal .sldprt` to examine how this part was made. Figure 34.33 shows the Cross Break forming tool applied to a sheet metal part.

FIGURE 34.33
The Cross Break forming tool applied to a part

Cross Breaks

Using a forming tool to create a cross break is overkill for most situations. You may need to do it if you need to actually show the indented geometry. The Cross Break feature is essentially a *cosmetic* cross break, and it enables you to specify the radius, angle, and direction used to create the cross break. It doesn't actually change the part geometry at all, but it does add two curve-like display entities.

When you place a Cross Break feature, you have the option to edit the sketch profile that creates the cross. This sketch has two intersecting lines. You cannot add more lines; the feature fails if you have more than two lines in the sketch. (For example, if you wanted to put three breaks across a hexagonal face, the software wouldn't allow this.) The lines don't have to end at a corner, but they do have to end at an edge. If the lines extend past or fall short of an edge, the feature displays a red X error icon, but it still creates the break lines where the sketch lines are.

Figure 34.34 shows the Cross Break PropertyManager and a part to which a cross break was applied. Notice that you can see the break lines through the solid, much like curves or cosmetic threads.

FIGURE 34.34
Creating a cross break

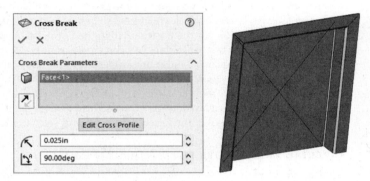

The Cross Break feature shows up in the FeatureManager just like any other feature, not like a cosmetic thread, which is the only other entity in the software that the cross break resembles.

Form Across Bends

A second special technique is a *gusset* or a form that goes across bends. This can be adapted in many ways, but it's shown here going across two bends. I cannot confirm the practicality of actually manufacturing something like this, but I have seen it done.

The technique used here is to call the single, long flat face of the forming tool the stopping face. The vertical faces on the ends and the fillet faces must be selected in the Faces To Remove selection box. The fillets of the outside of the forming tool also must exactly match the bends of the sheet metal part. You may need to edit this part each time you use it, unless you apply it to parts with bends of the same size and separated by the same distance.

When you place the tool on the sheet metal part, you must place it accurately from side to side to get everything to work out properly. This part is in the same location as the Cross Break file and is called Chapter 34 - Form Across Bends Sheet Metal.sldprt. Figure 34.35 shows the tool and a part to which it has been applied.

You may also want to look at the Gusset feature, which is introduced later in this chapter, and is a more conventional way to create gusset geometry.

FIGURE 34.35
Forming across bends

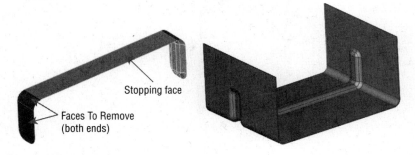

Using the Lofted Bends Feature

The Lofted Bends feature enables you to create transitions between two profiles. The range of functionality available through the Loft feature isn't available with Lofted Bends; it's limited to two profiles with no end conditions or guide curves. Both profiles also must be open contours in order to allow the sheet metal to unfold.

The Lofted Bends feature isn't part of the Base Flange method, but it's part of the newer set of sheet metal tools available in SolidWorks. Figure 34.36 shows what is probably the most common application of this feature. The bend lines shown must be established in the PropertyManager when you create or edit the feature. The Bend Lines option is available only if both profiles have the same number of straight lines. For example, if one of the profiles is a circle instead of a rectangle with very large fillets, then the Bend Lines options aren't available in the PropertyManager.

FIGURE 34.36
The Lofted Bends
PropertyManager, a
sample, and a flat
pattern with
bend lines

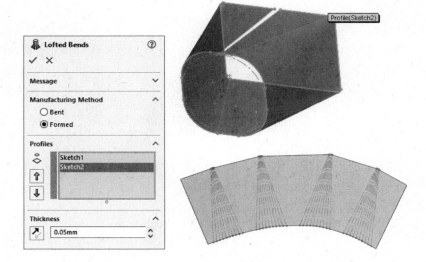

Like the forming tools, you can also use lofted bends in situations for which they were probably not intended. Figure 34.37 shows how lofting between 3D curves can also create shapes that can be flattened in SolidWorks. In this case, a couple of intermediate steps were required to get to the 3D curves, which involve surface features.

FIGURE 34.37
Using 3D curves with
the Lofted Bends feature
to create flattened
complex shapes

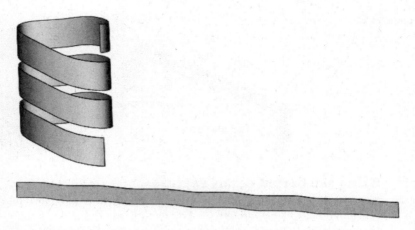

The Lofted Bends feature has two methods of working, as shown in Figure 34.37 and Figure 34.38. Bent and Formed on the Manufacturing Method panel are these two choices. A lofted bend with the Bent option will show straight, brake-press-type bends and flat panels of the sheet metal part used to create the shape. A formed bend will show a curved part. Figure 34.38 shows a part using the Bent option on the left and a part using the Formed option on the right. These parts are in the downloads for this chapter. You don't have to use parallel planes or rounded corners in the sketches, but rounded corners make getting the model correct much easier.

FIGURE 34.38
Lofted bends, bent
and formed

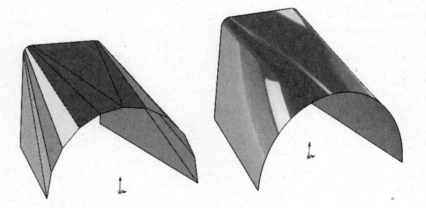

Using the Unfold and Fold Features

Unfold is a feature that unfolds selected bends temporarily. It's typically used in conjunction with a Fold feature to refold the bends. This combination is used to apply a feature that must be applied to the flat pattern—for example, a hole that spans across a bend.

Figure 34.39 shows the FeatureManager of a part where this combination has been applied, as well as the part itself, showing the bend across a hole, and the PropertyManager, which is the same for both features.

FIGURE 34.39
Applying the Unfold and
Fold features

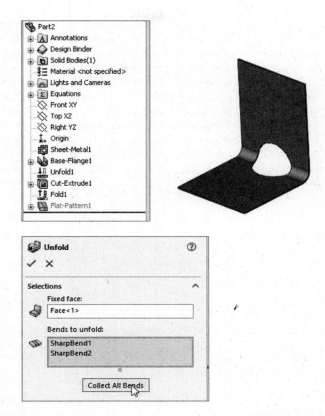

Both the Unfold and Fold features make it easy to select the bends without zooming in, even for small bends. A filter is placed on the cursor when the command is active, which allows only bends to be selected. The Collect All Bends option also becomes available. This feature also requires that you select a stationary face to hold still while the rest of the model moves during the unfolding and folding process.

Using the Swept Flange Feature

The Swept Flange feature is similar to the Miter Flange, with the main difference being that Swept Flange is used to create a new sheet metal part, while the Miter Flange is used in an existing sheet metal part. Also, the Miter Flange feature will add reliefs along the way, and the Swept Flange feature will not. This implies that the two features will probably be used in different types of manufacturing processes; Miter Flange looks more like a straight, brake-press-type operation, and Swept Flange has elements of a die rolling process, stamping, or possibly progressive die.

Like any sweep, the Swept Flange feature requires a path (curve, sketch, edges, Selection Manager selection) and a profile sketch to drive along that path. Both selections must be open profiles, since the part is made from flat (probably roll) stock, not tube.

NOTE   Remember that just because you can draw it and show it in 3D on the SolidWorks screen doesn't mean it is realistic and can be manufactured.

Figure 34.40 shows the sketches used to create the example and the PropertyManager of the Swept Flange feature, as well as the resulting FeatureManager. This feature can be flattened by the software—but again, remember, you have to apply your knowledge of the limits of material processing to know what is possible to manufacture and what is not.

A swept flange is typically flattened as if it were formed from a roll of material, like a rain gutter on the side of a house (see Figure 38.41). This means the profile is flattened, and the path is straightened out as well, making a rectangular blank. When the Flatten Along Path option is checked, the profile is flattened, but the path is not straightened, giving a blank roughly the shape of the path. The Material Inside option will change the neutral plane and may fail on one side or another, according to self-intersection issues with the flattening (if it doesn't work when it's on, try turning it off).

FIGURE 34.40
Creating a swept flange

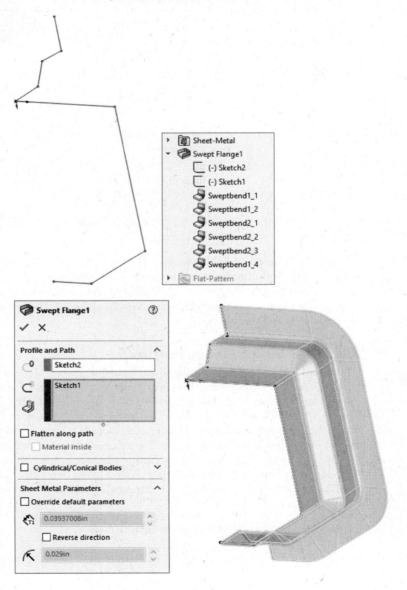

FIGURE 34.41
Flattening a swept flange

Using the Gusset Feature

The Gusset feature enables you to place a stiffening gusset on your part quickly and easily. On an existing sheet metal part, initiate the Gusset feature and select a location on a bend. The default gusset is 45 degrees and rounded, but you can create flat-top gussets, add side draft, change the angle and width, as well as fillet dimensions.

Figure 34.42 shows the Sheet Metal Gusset PropertyManager (in two parts), along with a preview of the feature. Since this is sheet metal, remember that the material is a constant thickness (although in reality there will be some variation of thickness when you deform a part like this).

If you need a shape other than the one provided by the Gusset feature, you may have to resort to the technique demonstrated in the earlier section "Form Across Bends."

Using the Tab and Slot Feature

The Tab and Slot feature is meant to create geometry to help physically assemble your product. It can be used in a single part, a multibody part, or an assembly. This is a Sheet Metal feature, but it can also be used in weldments and general parts for woodworking joints and other processes or materials.

Let's start with an example where a single part is formed that uses a tab and slot to give it more rigidity. The first time you work through this feature, the PropertyManager may look intimidating, but with some practice (and after reading the tool tips), you will become familiar with the workflow.

1. Select edge on which the tab(s) will be created.

2. Select the face to which the tab will extend.

3. Select two points that will serve as the limits of the tab area. By default, these are the ends of the first edge you selected. If you want something more specific, it might be a good idea to sketch it in and use the end points of the sketch to limit the tab.

   The Offset panel refers to the width of the tab, and the offset will be measured from the points you specified in the previous step.

   Spacing enables you have a pattern of tabs or just a single tab.

   Length enables you to specify how long or how long in relation to the face you selected in the second step that tab sho0uld be. For example, if the tab is to be welded, it should be flush with the surface, but if it is to be peened, bent with hand tools, or crushed into place, it should protrude out beyond the surface.

   The Slot panel enables you to specify how much bigger the slot is than the tab, for ease of assembly.

FIGURE 34.42
Creating a gus-
set on a bend

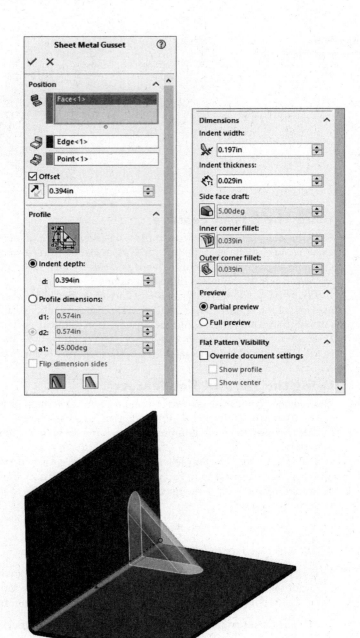

You can create multiple sets of tabs and slots by using the New Group feature to start a second set.

Figure 34.43 shows a strip of sheet metal formed into a box for extra rigidity, using three tabs and slots to join together the box.

FIGURE 34.43
Creating joining tabs
and slots to form a box

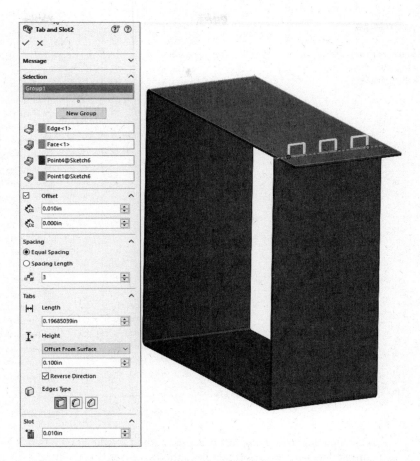

The sample part for this screen capture is named `Chapter 34 - Tab and Slot.slprt` and included with the download materials for this chapter.

Making Sheet Metal Parts from Generic Models

SolidWorks can also convert generic constant-thickness models into sheet metal parts that flatten and on which any of the dedicated Sheet Metal features can be used. You can make models from Thin Feature extrudes or regular extrudes with Shell features and then use the Insert Bends feature to make them sheet metal parts. The structure of parts created with the Insert Bends feature is somewhat different. Figure 34.44 shows a comparison of the two methods' FeatureManagers for simple parts.

The most notable difference is that the Insert Bends part starts off with non–Sheet Metal features. The Rip feature also stands out, but the Rip feature is not exclusive to sheet metal. Although you can use Rip on any model, it's found only on the Sheet Metal toolbar.

The Sheet Metal feature is found in both the Base Flange and Insert Bends methods and has the same PropertyManager function in both methods.

FIGURE 34.44

Comparing the default
features for the Base
Flange and Insert
Bends features

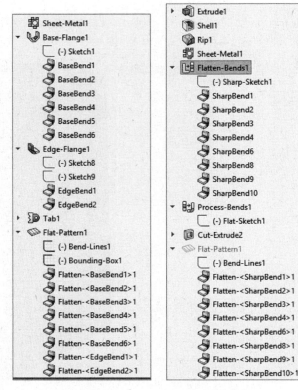

Base Flange method   Insert Bends method

The new features in the Insert Bends method are the Flatten Bends and Process Bends features. The way the Insert Bends method works is that the model that's built with the sharp-cornered non–Sheet Metal feature is flattened by the Flatten Bends feature. The model is then reconstructed with bends by the Process Bends feature.

The main rule that SolidWorks enforces on sheet metal models regardless of how they came to be sheet metal is that the parts should have a consistent wall thickness. When all the geometry is made from the beginning as a sheet metal part (using the Base Flange method), there's never a problem with this. However, when the part is modeled from thin features, cuts, shells, and so on, there's no telling what may happen to the model.

If you perform an Insert Bends operation on a model that doesn't have a consistent wall thickness, then the Flatten Bends and Process Bends features fail. If a thickness face isn't perpendicular to the main face of the part, then the software simply forces the situation, making the face perpendicular to the main face.

Using the Normal Cut Feature

If a Cut feature is placed before the Sheet Metal feature, then as far as SolidWorks is concerned, the part is not a sheet metal part. However, if the Cut feature is created after the Sheet Metal feature, the model must follow a different set of rules. The "normal shear" mentioned previously is one of those rules. In Figure 34.45, the sketch for a cut is on a plane that isn't perpendicular to the face into which the cut is being made. Under a normal modeling situation, the cut would just go through the part at an angle. However, in SolidWorks sheet metal, an option is added to the PropertyManager for the cut. This is the Normal Cut option, and it's selected by default. You could be modeling and never even notice this option, but it's important because it affects the geometrical results of the feature. It is also a stand-alone feature that can be applied to the model after abnormal cuts have been made.

As shown in Figure 34.45, when the Normal Cut option is selected, the thickness faces of the cut are turned perpendicular (or *normal*) to the face of the sheet metal. This is also important because if the angle between the angled face and the sketch changes, the geometry of the cutout can also change. This setting becomes more important as the material becomes thicker and as the angle between the sketch and the sheet metal face becomes shallower.

FIGURE 34.45
Using the Normal
Cut option

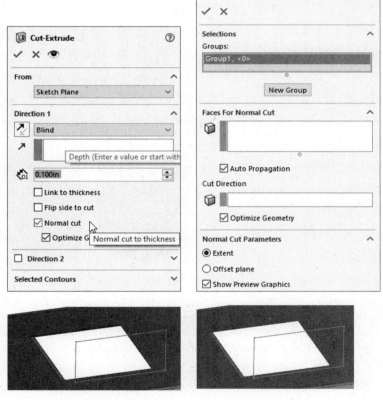

Normal Cut OFF   Normal Cut ON

SolidWorks allows you to have angled faces on side edges and maintains the angle when it flattens the part. A cut that doesn't use the Normal Cut option and creates faces that aren't perpendicular to the main face of the part doesn't cause the Flat Pattern feature to fail.

Using the Rip Feature

When someone is building a sheet metal part from a generic model, a common technique that is used to achieve consistent wall thicknesses is to build the outer shape as a solid and then shell the part. The only problem with this method is that it leaves corners joined in a way that cannot be flattened. You can solve this problem by using the Rip feature. Rip breaks out the corner in one or both directions in such a way that it can be unfolded. Bend reliefs are later added automatically by the Process Bends feature.

Figure 34.46 shows the Rip PropertyManager and the results of using this feature. The model was created to look like a Miter Flange part.

FIGURE 34.46

Using the Rip feature

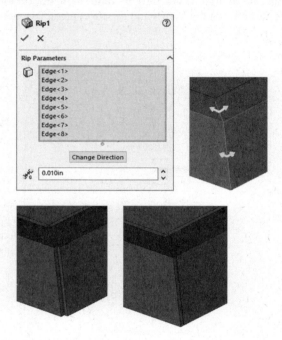

Notice also in Figure 34.46 that after the Rip, the edges of the material are still sheared at an angle. Because the top of the part was shelled, the thickness of the part is not normal to the main face of the sheet metal. You can fix this by using the Flatten Bends feature, which lays the entire part out flat, calculates the bend areas, and corrects any discrepancies at the edges of the part.

NOTE   Rip functionality is included in the Insert Bends Sheet Metal PropertyManager when it's first initiated, although it's no longer there when you edit the part later. If you use it, the Rip data becomes a feature of its own and is placed before the Sheet Metal feature in the FeatureManager. Be aware that there are slight differences between using the Rip function as an independent feature and using it as a part of the Insert Bends feature. You may want to check this on a part you're working with to verify which method best suits your needs.

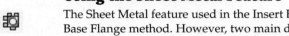

Using the Sheet Metal Feature

The Sheet Metal feature used in the Insert Bends method is very similar to the one used in the Base Flange method. However, two main differences exist: Insert Bends Sheet Metal requires the user to select a fixed face, and Base Flange Sheet Metal allows the use of gauge tables. Both features function as placeholders and otherwise contain the same information, use the same name and icon, and are inserted automatically when a different feature is created.

Using the Flatten Bends Feature

The Flatten Bends feature is added automatically by the Insert Bends tool. As mentioned earlier, it takes the model with sharp corners and lays it flat, adjusting the material in the bend area and normalizing the thickness faces around the flat pattern. The Merge Faces option is available in the Flat Pattern feature in the Insert Bends method; therefore, the flat pattern created by the Flatten Bends feature always has edges created by the tangent lines of the bends.

Notice in Figure 34.47 that the Flatten Bends feature has a sketch and several Sharp Bend features under it. The Sharp Sketch is simply an account of the bend lines, and you cannot edit it manually. The Sharp Bend features can be suppressed, in which case they aren't reformed in the Process Bends feature. You can also edit Sharp Bend features to change the default radius, bend allowance, and relief type.

FIGURE 34.47
Using the Flatten
Bends feature

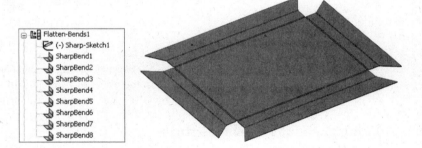

Using the Process Bends Feature

The Process Bends feature takes all the flat pattern information, the bend information, and entities in the flat sketch and rebuilds the model with the formed bends. The flat sketch under the Process Bends feature is the Insert Bends method version of a sketched bend. You can add sketch lines here to bend panels of the part. After you add lines to this sketch, exiting the sketch will cause the part to be created with a default 90-degree bend corresponding to the line. Of course, all the Sketched Bend rules exist, such as that the line has to extend at least up to the edges of the part, the lines cannot extend across multiple faces, and construction lines are ignored.

For every bend created by a sketch line in the Process Bends Flat Sketch feature, a Flat Bend feature is added to the list under Process Bends. You can control the angle and radius of each of these flat bends by editing the Flat Bend feature. This is all illustrated in Figure 34.48.

FIGURE 34.48
Using the Process
Bends feature

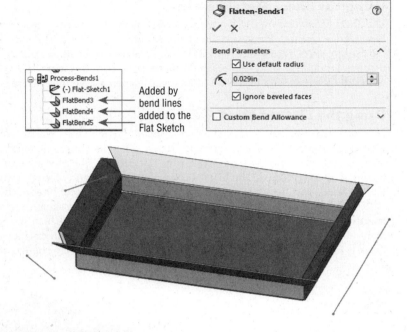

Process-Bends1
  (-) Flat-Sketch1
  FlatBend3 ← Added by bend lines
  FlatBend4 ← added to the
  FlatBend5 ← Flat Sketch

Flatten-Bends1

Bend Parameters
☑ Use default radius
0.029in
☑ Ignore beveled faces
☐ Custom Bend Allowance

Using the No Bends Feature

With a single button click, you can use the No Bends tool on the Sheet Metal toolbar to roll back the model before the Flatten Bends feature in the tree. This is used primarily to add new geometry that is turned into bends through the Flatten and Process Bends features.

Using the Flat Pattern Feature

The Insert Bends method uses the Flat Pattern feature as well as the Base Flange method. However, it wasn't part of the original scheme and was added at some point after the new tools had proved their value. This enables you to utilize the new features as well, as discussed later in this chapter in the section on Mixing Methods, page 988.

Using the Convert To Sheet Metal Feature

The Convert To Sheet Metal feature can use either SolidWorks native data or imported data. It can also use solids as well as surfaces. The model can be shelled or not shelled and have filleted edges or not. This feature enables you to identify which edges will become bends and automatically identifies the edges to rip. See Figure 34.49.

This tool is very useful for imported geometry and for parts with tricky shapes. Although the PropertyManager interface looks complex, it's fairly straightforward to use. Your first selection in the top Fixed Entity box should be a stable face, preferably an outer face on the bottom or the top. Inner faces generally don't work.

FIGURE 34.49

Using the Convert To Sheet Metal feature

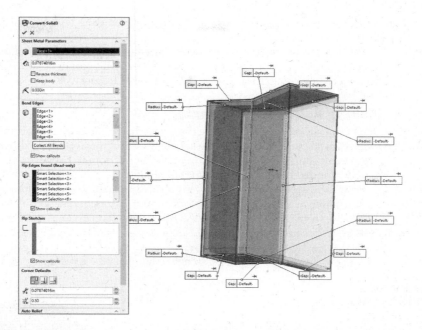

Note that you can reverse the thickness of the sheet metal, so the solid that you start with can be treated as the volume inside the sheet metal enclosure, or the outer faces of the initial solid turn out to be the inner faces of the sheet metal part. Use the Reverse Thickness option to accomplish this.

Selecting Bend Edges is the next step, with the implication that any edge that isn't a bend will be ripped. Also note that three bend edges cannot intersect at a point, and one bend edge cannot intersect at the middle of another edge.

The default Bend Radius, Thickness, and Auto Relief options are set the same way as in other Sheet Metal functions.

Using Other Methods

The sheet metal tools have been available in SolidWorks for quite some time and have had some time to mature and for users to become well acquainted with them and develop effective techniques using them.

Working with Imported Geometry

Working with imported geometry starts at the point where you use the Rip feature. Although imported geometry can be geometrically manipulated to some extent in SolidWorks, this is beyond the scope of this chapter. The need for a model with walls of constant thickness still exists, even if the imported model has filleted edges showing bend geometry already in the model.

FeatureWorks can be used to recognize Sheet Metal features or to fully or partially deconstruct the model by removing bend faces as fillets. Although FeatureWorks is not covered in this book, the technique may be useful when editing imported parts with overall prismatic geometry that is common to sheet metal parts.

When a sheet metal part is imported, whether it meets the requirements immediately or must be edited in one way or another to make a sheet metal part of it, you can simply use the Insert Bends feature or even the Convert To Sheet Metal feature.

Making Rolled Conical Parts

One of the reasons for maintaining the legacy Insert Bends method is to have a way of creating rolled conical parts. You can create cylindrical sheet metal parts by drawing an arc that almost closes to an entire circle and creating a base flange from it. However, you can also use swept flanges or lofted bends for these types of models.

With the Insert Bends method, a revolved thin feature does the job nicely. You simply revolve a straight line at an angle to the centerline, so the straight line doesn't touch or cross the centerline; the revolve cannot go around the full 360 degrees, because there must be a gap. Sheet metal parts aren't created by stretching the material (except for forming tools).

When creating a rolled sheet metal part, you cannot select a flat face to remain fixed when the part is flattened. Instead, you can use a straight edge along the revolve gap, as shown in Figure 34.50.

FIGURE 34.50
Selecting a straight edge for a conical part

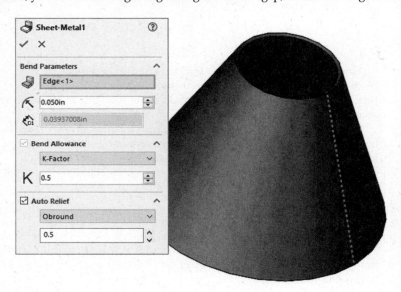

NOTE When a conical sheet metal part is created, it doesn't receive the Flat Pattern feature at the end of the FeatureManager. This is because none of the Base Flange method features are allowed on this type of part.

Mixing Methods

If you use the Insert Bend tool on a part, you can still use the more advanced tools available through the Base Flange method, unless it's a cylindrical or conical part. A Flat Pattern feature is added to the bottom of most Sheet Metal feature trees, and the presence of this feature is what signifies that the current part has now become a sheet metal part to the Base Flange features.

However, I recommend that you avoid mixing the different techniques to flatten parts—for example, suppressing bends under Flatten and Process bends, as well as using the flat pattern.

Using Multibody Techniques with Sheet Metal

You can use multibody techniques with sheet metal models. For many of the same reasons you might want to make any other kind of model using multibody techniques, you may also want to make sheet metal parts using similar techniques. When you create parts using multibody techniques, you can have multiple Base Flange features. With those multiple Base Flange features, you also get multiple Flat Pattern features. Also, you can use the Split feature to create multiple sheet metal bodies. The rules laid out for multibody parts are generally also going to apply for multibody sheet metal parts and have several implications for limitations of sheet metal parts, such as the following:

- If you have multiple bent bodies, you can show only one body flattened at a time.

- By merging sheet metal bodies, you eliminate both Flat Pattern features of the old bodies and create a brand new Flat Pattern feature for the new body.

These commands can create new bodies in sheet metal parts:

- Convert To Sheet Metal

- Lofted Bend

- Insert Bends

- Base Flange

- Insert Part

- Split

These commands can merge bodies in sheet metal parts:

- Edge Flange

- Combine

The Mirror function enables you to mirror bodies, but the new bodies must to be merged manually with the existing body.

A multibody sheet metal part has a Cut List folder, which acts like a Solid Bodies folder and lists each sheet metal body. Each cut-list item lists the sheet metal body and, under that, the features associated with each body. The part also has a Sheet Metal folder with a Sheet Metal feature for each body. The Sheet Metal features for each body hold the defaults for each body, such as thickness and bend radius. The Flat Pattern folder includes a Flat Pattern feature for each body. Each body can be flattened individually, but not at the same time.

Using Insert Part

Using the Insert Part feature inserts an existing part as a new body inside a sheet metal part, but even if the inserted part had been a sheet metal part initially, it wouldn't show up as sheet metal after being inserted in the other part.

You can join the inserted part to the local sheet metal body by using the Combine feature, but not by using the Merge option in an edge flange as you can to merge two bodies modeled within a single part. When the Combine feature is used, any sharp intersection between the parts is left sharp and won't flatten unless you use the Insert Bends feature to convert the sharp into a bend. This is an odd twist on combining the old (Insert Bends) method with the new (Base Flange) method.

Using Multiple Base Flanges

Another method to get multiple bodies inside a sheet metal part is to start from disjoint Base Flange features. You cannot have multiple open profiles in your first feature, but you can have multiple Base Flange features. From there, you can build flanges toward one another until flanges touch. Figure 34.51 illustrates a situation where a disjoint flange created by a Base Flange feature is connected to the main part using an Edge Flange feature with the Up To Edge And Merge option selected in the Flange Length section.

FIGURE 34.51
Using an edge flange to connect disjoint bodies in a sheet metal part

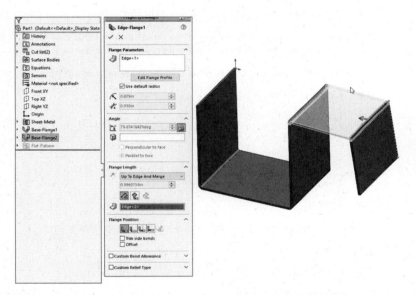

Tutorial: Working with the Insert Bends Method for Sheet Metal Parts

The Insert Bends method has been relegated to duty mainly for specialty functions. To gain an understanding of how this method works, follow these steps:

1. Create a new blank part.

2. On the Top plane, open a sketch and sketch a rectangle centered on the origin 12 inches in the horizontal direction and 8 inches in the vertical direction.

3. Extrude the rectangle 1 inch with 45 degrees of draft, Draft Outward, in Direction 1, and extrude 1 inch with no draft in Direction 2. The two directions should be opposite from one another.

4. Shell out the part to .050 inches, selecting the large face on the side where the draft has been applied. The part should now look like Figure 34.52.

FIGURE 34.52
The part as of step 4

5. Use the Rip feature to rip out the four corners. Allow the Rip to rip all corners in both directions. The part should look like Figure 34.53.

FIGURE 34.53
Ripping the corners

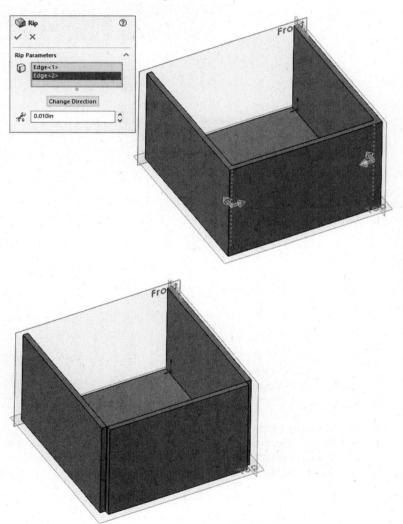

Completed rip

6. Create an Insert Bends feature, accepting the default values and picking the middle of the base of the part for the fixed face.

7. Draw a rectangle on one of the vertical faces of the part, as shown in Figure 34.54.

FIGURE 34.54
Adding a sketch
for the cut

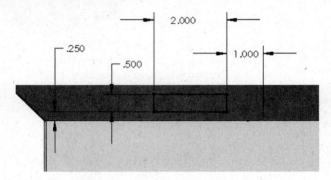

8. Use the sketch to create a Through All cut in one direction. Notice that the Normal Cut option is on by default. Examine the finished cut closely; notice that it's different from the default type of cut because it's not made in a direction normal to the sketch but rather in a direction normal to the face of the part. Details of this are shown in Figure 34.55.

FIGURE 34.55
Using the Normal
Cut option

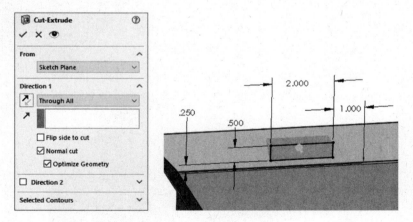

9. Click the Flatten button on the Sheet Metal toolbar. Notice that the Flat Pattern feature becomes unsuppressed and that the Bend Lines sketch under it is shown. This works just as it did in the Base Flange method. The finished part is shown in Figure 34.56.

FIGURE 34.56
The finished part with
the Flat Pattern feature
unsuppressed

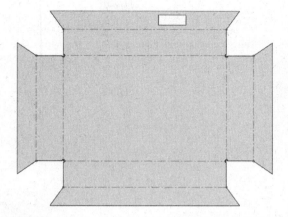

Tutorial: Using the Base Flange Sheet Metal Method

SolidWorks Base Flange method for sheet metal is fun and easy to use, as you'll see in
this tutorial:

1. Open a new part using a special Sheet Metal template if one is available.

2. On the Top plane, draw a rectangle centered on the origin, 14 inches in X by 12 inches
   in Y (or Z).

3. Initiate the Base Flange tool, set the thickness to 0.029 inches, and change the K-Factor to
   .43. Notice that the default Inside Bend Radius is not shown. This setting is made in the
   Sheet Metal feature that's placed before the Base Flange feature in the FeatureManager.

4. After the base flange has been created, edit the Sheet Metal feature and change the default
   bend radius to 0.050 inches.

5. Click one of the 14-inch edges and then select the Line tool from the Sketch toolbar. This is
   a shortcut to creating a plane perpendicular to the end of the edge and opening a new
   sketch on the plane. This is useful in other situations in addition to working with sheet
   metal. Draw a sketch similar to the one that's shown in Figure 34.57. The arc overrides the
   default Inside Bend Radius setting and directly controls that particular bend.

FIGURE 34.57
The sketch to start a
miter flange

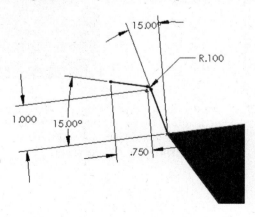

6. With the sketch still active, click the Miter Flange button on the Sheet Metal toolbar. Use the settings shown in the image to the right in Figure 34.58. Select three edges as shown. Remember to select the edges on the same side of the base flange. In particular, notice the Start/End Offset settings. Click OK when you are satisfied with the settings.

FIGURE 34.58
Specifying the Miter Flange settings

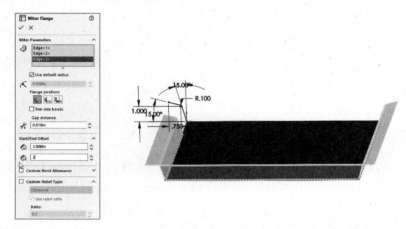

7. Select the remaining edge that isn't touched by the miter flange, and click the Edge Flange tool on the Sheet Metal toolbar. Click the top point of one end of the miter flange to establish the flange length using the Up To Vertex end condition.

8. Click the Edit Flange Profile button in the PropertyManager, and manually pull the sketch back from the ends of the flange. Add dimensions to make the flange 3 inches from the corner on the left side, and 5 inches from the corner on the right side, as shown in Figure 34.59; otherwise, use the default settings for the flange. Click OK to accept the feature when you are satisfied with the settings.

FIGURE 34.59
Creating an edge flange

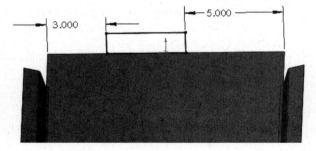

9. Select the inside edge of the top of the edge flange that you have just created and initiate a Hem feature. Use the settings Material Inside, Closed Hem, with a length of 0.25 inches, and make the material go toward the inside of the box. The settings and preview of the feature are shown in Figure 34.60.

FIGURE 34.60

Creating a hem

10. Create a second edge flange the same height as the first, just to the right of the first flange. Edit the Flange profile, and pull the new flange away from the existing flange. Add a dimension to make the new flange 2 inches wide. Click OK when you are satisfied with the settings.

11. Open a sketch on the inside face of the new edge flange and draw a line across the flange 0.75 inches from the end.

12. Create a Jog feature with the settings shown in Figure 34.61. Make sure to set a custom bend radius by deselecting the Use Default Radius option and entering **0.025 inches**. If you don't set the custom radius, you may get a warning that the jog distance is less than a minimum jog value. When you're selecting the fixed face, be careful to select the side of the line with the largest area or the face you want to remain where it is while the rest of the part bends and moves around it.

13. From the website, in the download materials for Chapter 34, find the part named Chapter 34 - Cross Break.sldprt. Copy this file to a folder in the library that you have established outside of your SolidWorks installation folder, called Forming Tools.

14. Make sure this folder appears in the Design Library. You may have to press F5 or click the Refresh button at the top of the Task pane. When the folder appears, right-click the folder and select the check mark next to Forming Tools folder.

15. When the file has been copied and the folder has been assigned as a Forming Tool folder, drag the Chapter 34 - Cross Break part from the folder and onto the big flat face of the sheet metal part. It will be put into a sketch that looks like Figure 34.62.

FIGURE 34.61
Creating a jog

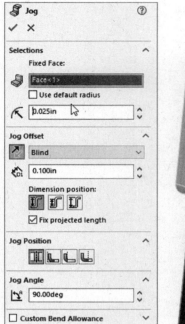

FIGURE 34.62
Placing a forming tool

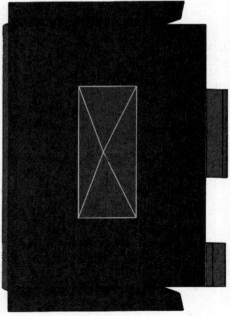

16. After you have dropped the feature into the sketch, drag the origin of the sketch onto the origin of the part and click Finish. Notice that the cross break is in the middle of the part, but it's too small.

17. Double-click the new feature in the FeatureManager; a set of dimensions will appear on the screen. Change the 4-inch dimension to 13.9 inches and the 6-inch dimension to 11.9 inches. The cross break should look like Figure 34.63.

FIGURE 34.63
Resizing the cross break
to 13.9 inches

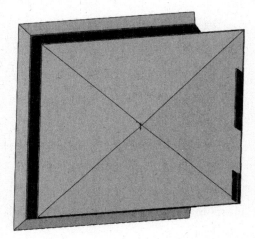

18. Create a new configuration named Flat. In this configuration, suppress the forming tool that you just placed, and unsuppress the Flat Pattern feature at the bottom of the tree.

The Bottom Line

SolidWorks offers a broad range of sheet metal tools to tackle most of your modeling situations. Some of the tools still require a little imagination to visualize real-world results because the complex shapes created in the real world where bends intersect are problems for such highly automated software. The tools are able to deal with imported or generically modeled geometry as well as parts created using the dedicated sheet metal tools.

Master It There are three basic methods for working with sheet metal in SolidWorks: Base Flange, Insert Bends, and Convert Entities. We'll have one exercise for each method.
Follow these steps to build a basic Base Flange type part:

1. Create a sketch like the one shown here.

2. Use the Base Flange tool on the Sheet Metal toolbar to extrude the sketch midplane 4 inches, with a thickness of 0.025 inch.

3. Add a flange to one of the open sides that matches the height of the tallest flange (use Up To Vertex). The defaults are an Inside Bend Radius of 0.029 inches, an angle of 90 degrees, and the flange position set to Inside. Turn on Custom Relief and use the Tear type.

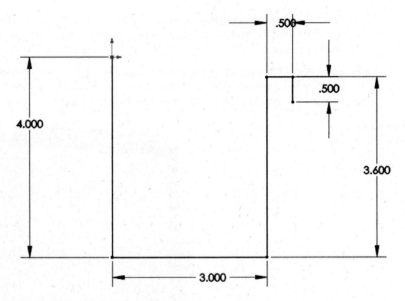

4. Put a Sheet Metal Gusset feature in the middle of the newly created bend. Here are the settings:

   Offset = 1.5"

   Indent Depth = 0.375"

   Flat Gusset, Edge fillet = 0.1"

   Indent Width = 0.500"

   Corner Fillets = 0.2"

   Toggle between the partial and full preview to see the effect of the fillets to make sure everything works before committing to the settings. Turn on all the options under Flat Pattern Visibility so the gusset is located on the flat, even though it won't actually be there. Your model should now look like the one shown here.

5. Flatten the part to see the result.

Master It   The second Sheet Metal method uses Insert Bends. Let's make a part with that method.

1. Copy the initial sketch from the last part and paste it on the Front plane of a new part. Edit the sketch and drag the point that appears to be at the origin away from the origin, and then drop it back onto the origin to make sure it picks up that relation. The sketch will turn from blue (underdefined) to black (fully defined).

2. Extrude the sketch *using the regular Extrude command (not the Sheet Metal Base Flange)* using midplane, 4 inches, thickness 0.025 inch, material to the inside.

3. Open a sketch on the base inside face of the part and convert entities on one of the edges at an open end. Drag the ends back and dimension them 0.125 inch from the edges.

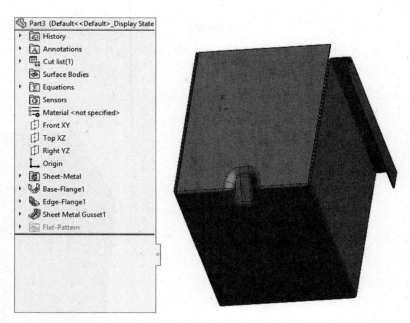

4. Extrude the open sketch up to the vertex of the *shorter* flange as shown in the following graphic. Set the thickness to 0.025 inch, and the material to the inside. (If the material goes to the outside, you will have edge-to-edge contact between the existing body and the new feature, which constitutes a zero-thickness edge and thereby produces a new body rather than merging with the existing body.)

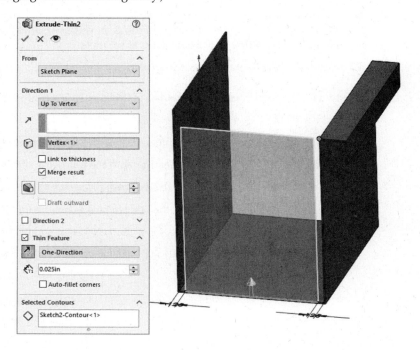

5. Use the Convert Insert Bends feature (this may not be on the toolbar by default, so use Insert ➤ Sheet Metal ➤ Bends if necessary). Set the Bend Radius to 0.30 inch and the Auto Relief to 0.50 inch. Accept the feature. This will give you the situation shown shown here.

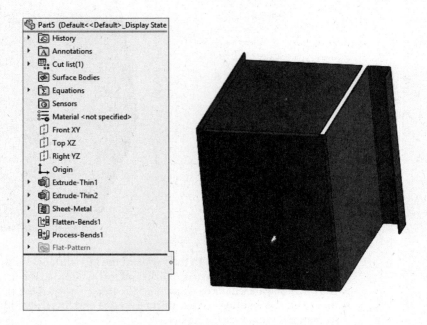

6. Use the edge flange to add a new flange on the remaining open end of the box. This doesn't seem like a big deal, but it combines new (Base Flange) and old (Insert Bends) methods for working with SolidWorks sheet metal.

7. Flatten the part to make sure it is correct.

Master It The final Sheet Metal method is Convert To Sheet Metal. Follow these steps:

1. Make a 3D box, 3 × 4 × 6 inches.

2. Use the Shell feature to make it into a 0.025-inch thin wall part and remove one 6 × 4 face.

3. Use the Convert To Sheet Metal feature with the following settings:

   ◆ Select the bottom face as the fixed entity.

   ◆ Select the four edges around the bottom face as bend edges.

   ◆ Under Corner Defaults, select Open Butt, 0.05″ gap and 0.5 overlap ratio.

   ◆ For Auto Relief, use Tear with a 0.5 relief ratio.

4. Initiate a Corner Relief feature, as in the following graphic, with the following settings:

   ◆ Two bend corners

   ◆ Rectangular relief for all corners

   ◆ 0.1″ slot length

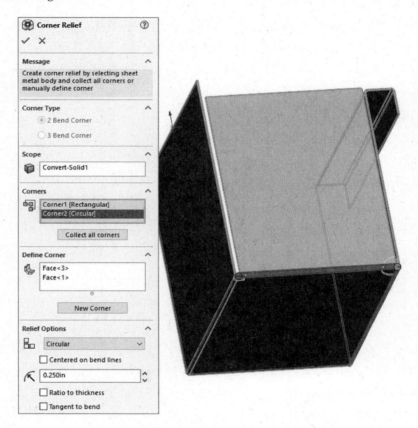

5. Flatten the part to make sure it is correct.

Chapter 35

Creating Sheet Metal Drawings

After you create your sheet metal models, you will need to make drawings to use to get them manufactured. Fortunately, SolidWorks provides some nice tools to document, dimension, and annotate your parts in 2D.

Depending on whether your company does its own sheet metal manufacturing, you may or may not actually make flat pattern drawings. Many companies that use outside manufacturing for their sheet metal parts may just send their suppliers a drawing with views of a dimensioned part in the folded state. This is because the final formed dimensions are what you want the shop to be responsible for, and if they use different flat dimensions to achieve that, it doesn't really matter.

Many users may think that providing a fully dimensioned flat pattern is very valuable to the sheet metal shop. If your sheet metal shop is a professional outfit, they probably have their own software and their own way of doing things; in which case, a flat pattern is redundant information and may create more confusion than clarity.

On the other hand, if you are the sheet metal shop, or you specifically create drawings for the sheet metal shop, then creating the flat pattern is actually your business. This chapter gives you all the information you need to know to make sheet metal drawings, regardless of your role and without trying to tell you how to do your job. It's best to work out with the shop what data will make the process the fastest and cheapest with the fewest errors.

IN THIS CHAPTER, YOU WILL LEARN TO:

- ◆ Work with flat patterns
- ◆ Make special sheet metal drawing templates

Making Sheet Metal Drawings

Sheet metal drawings can take on various roles in your product development process—anything from general "make me a part that looks like this" to actually specifying how the work is to be done. Some drawings may need only the flat pattern or only the formed part. Here I'll assume that a sheet metal drawing requires both the formed and flat part, just to cover as much ground as possible.

If you need a drawing with both formed and flat geometry, you might consider making a two-page drawing—one page with the flat pattern and the other page with views of the 3D part. You might use one drawing sheet for the press operator and the other sheet for inspection. If you need only the flat pattern, you might consider using an isometric view of the part just for reference.

If your sheet metal parts are welded together with other sheet metal, structural, cast, stamped, or plate parts, you might want to refer to the section later in this chapter on multibody sheet metal drawings. You can accomplish the same things with an assembly (and in some cases, the assembly will be the better option), but many people think that modeling in multibodies is easier. Sheet metal multibody techniques are a little different—and in my opinion, they don't offer as many advantages as normal multibody techniques. If you must work in this mode, be careful to leave room on your drawing for exploded views and a weld list. Flat patterns require some extra thought if you have multiple sheet metal bodies in a single part.

You may also want to make a special drawing template for sheet metal drawings. The special template can contain custom blocks, title blocks, or table anchors.

Getting the Flat Pattern

When you need to make a drawing to use for building a sheet metal part, getting the flat pattern is an essential part of the process. SolidWorks provides several ways to develop the flattened bend sections in the K-Factor, bend allowance, bend deduction, and bend calculation tables. Getting these values or equations correct is key in making the flat pattern the correct size to produce the finished part accurately. Chapter 34, "Using SolidWorks Sheet Metal Tools," covers how to use these methods, but you should obtain the actual values from your sheet metal shop.

You create the drawing of a sheet metal part in the same way that you would create one for any other type of part. You can use one of several methods, including using the Create Drawing From Part command or dragging and dropping the part onto a drawing. Sheet metal drawings may serve different purposes. Usually, a sheet metal drawing requires dimensioned orthogonal views of the finished part, and sometimes, it also requires a flat pattern describing the blank from which the finished part is to be formed.

To show a view of the flat pattern on a drawing where you already have a sheet metal part, select the view from the FeatureManager or the graphics window, and in the list of views below the Standard Views area of the Orientation panel of the PropertyManager, select Flat Pattern from the list. The Drawing View PropertyManager is shown in Figure 35.1.

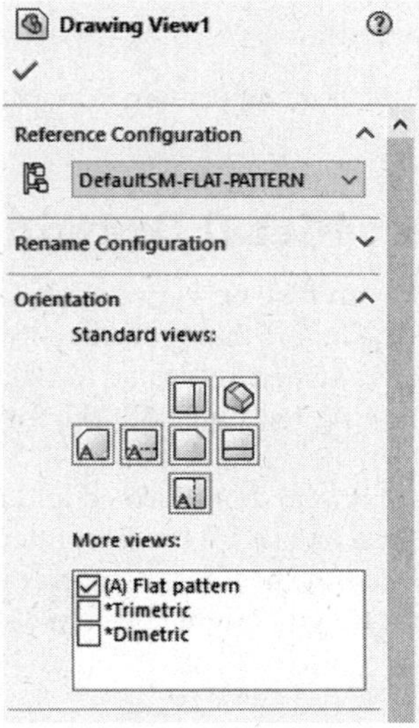

FIGURE 35.1
Converting a view of a
sheet metal part to a
flat pattern

This won't work from a projected view, and if you have placed a named view, SolidWorks may change the view of the part to lay the flat pattern down on the sheet.

Understanding Flat Patterns and Configurations

When a sheet metal part is put onto a drawing, SolidWorks automatically creates a derived configuration called SM-FLAT-PATTERN. The configuration doesn't exist until the part is put onto a drawing. For a part made with the Base Flange Sheet Metal method, the derived configuration in Figure 35.2 shows the default arrangement.

FIGURE 35.2

Automatically created derived configuration for the flat pattern

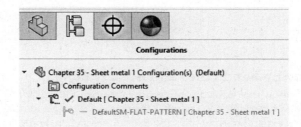

If your part already had multiple configurations, only the configuration that's shown on the drawing would display a derived flat pattern. If you later show another configuration on the drawing, the derived flat pattern won't automatically be created until you show a flat pattern of that configuration.

> **BEST PRACTICE**
>
> Be careful if you plan to make sheet metal parts with derived configurations for reasons other than the flat pattern. The automatic, derived-flat-pattern configuration functionality may or may not be able to work with your manual or design-table-driven derived configuration scheme.

There's a second way to get a flat pattern of a sheet metal part on the drawing. If you use the drop-down list in the Reference Configuration panel of the Drawing View PropertyManager, you can select the derived-flat-pattern configuration from there. The flat patterns that you get using these two methods may be oriented differently, and if you use the Flat Pattern selection from the More Views options, you also will get bend lines and annotations marking the direction, angle, and inside radius of the bend. The difference between the resulting views of these two methods is illustrated in Figure 35.3.

The PropertyManager for the flat pattern view contains many settings that are not shown or discussed here. You may find it useful to explore the entire contents of the PropertyManager for the view to see other items you can control, which include rotation of view, scale, quality of view and cosmetic threads, and many others.

FIGURE 35.3
Comparing flat pattern
views placed by using
the More Views options
or by showing the
derived-flat-pattern
configuration

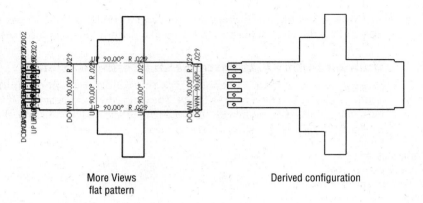

More Views
flat pattern

Derived configuration

Showing Bend Lines and Bend Notes

If you show the derived configuration, the bend lines are not included in that view. To turn on the bend lines, you need to go to the FeatureManager for that view, scroll to the Flat Pattern feature, expand it, right-click the Bend Lines sketch, and select Show.

Figure 35.4 shows the Drawing FeatureManager with the Bend Lines sketch highlighted.

FIGURE 35.4
Turning on the bend
lines for a flat
pattern view

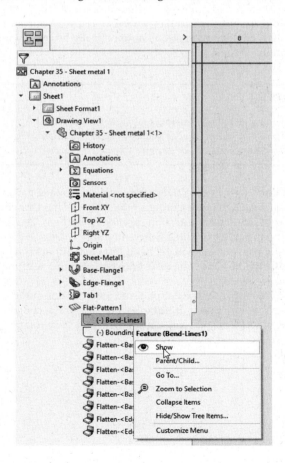

To get the bend notes to show up, you need to use the Drawing View PropertyManager Bend Notes panel, shown in Figure 35.5.

FIGURE 35.5
Showing the bend notes
for a flat pattern

You can configure the content of the bend notes using the Text Box and the Syntax buttons. These buttons, located at the bottom of the screen, represent, in order from left to right:

- Bend Direction
- Supplementary Angle
- Complementary Angle
- Bend Radius
- Bend Order
- Bend Allowance

Other options for the display of bend notes are also available. Select Tools ➤ Options ➤ Document Properties ➤ Sheet Metal ➤ Bend Notes ➤ Style, and you can choose from the following options:

- Above Bend Line
- Below Bend Line
- With Leader

When the notes are above or below the bend lines, they are aligned with the bend line, so the notes could be horizontal, vertical, or angled. If there's a succession of bends, interrupted in some way but close to one another, these notes can be on top of one another and difficult to read.

If you use the With Leader option, all notes are horizontal with respect to the drawing sheet, and a leader points to the bend line.

You should explore the settings at the above-mentioned Tools ➤ Options location, as there are several in this location that can help you control the appearance of the bend notes, including Layer, Color, Line Type, Font, Border, and so on. Notice, too, that you have the powerful functionality that covers the insertion of Cut List Properties in the drawing.

Showing the Bounding Box for the Flat Pattern

SolidWorks automatically calculates a bounding box for your sheet metal flat pattern. This is the smallest rectangle into which the flat pattern will fit. This can be useful if your manufacturing process cuts the flat pattern from individual blanks rather than a bigger sheet with nested flat patterns. Generally, the bigger sheet allows you greater material efficiency, but it may also be difficult to manage if you don't have the equipment, and it may be unnecessary if you are making low volumes of certain parts.

The bounding box may not be aligned the way you might expect, but it represents the smallest rectangle that SolidWorks calculates will include your flat pattern. Many shops have separate nesting software that may allow for custom fits or some additional options. If you're not sure if your shop would benefit from a bounding box on the drawing, you may want to ask directly.

You can have some control over the bounding box. If you specify a grain direction in the Flat Pattern PropertyManager, the bounding box will align with the grain direction. You can use an edge, an axis, or a sketch to define the grain direction. The grain direction is the pattern of streaks on the face of the sheet metal that indicates the direction the sheets were processed in fabrication. Sheet metal properties can vary somewhat if measured with and against the grain. Sometimes, the grain is specified in a certain orientation for aesthetic reasons.

The bounding box is stored in the sheet metal part as a sketch, which you can see right below the Bend Lines sketch shown in Figure 35.4. You can show this sketch, and the drawing will display it as a construction line. Figure 35.6 shows a flat pattern with a bounding box.

Showing Bend Areas on the Part

If you want to show or hide the bend areas for all bends on the flattened part, open the part in its own window and edit the Flat Pattern feature. You cannot edit the feature from the drawing; you must do it from the part's own window. In the Flat Pattern PropertyManager, make sure the Merge Faces option is turned off.

Figure 35.6 shows the bend lines (Merge Faces) turned off, and Figure 35.7 shows the bend lines (Merge Faces) turned on. Figure 35.7 also shows the Bend Area setting that's available from the model. In Figure 35.7, the Tangent Edges are set to use a font. You can find this setting at View ➤ Display ➤ Tangent Edges With Font or on the RMB menu for the view.

As a note, when showing a flat pattern of a part using welded corners, the welded corners must be suppressed before the flat pattern can be shown. This is the case with the part used in the Figure 35.7.

FIGURE 35.6
Showing a bounding box
on a drawing

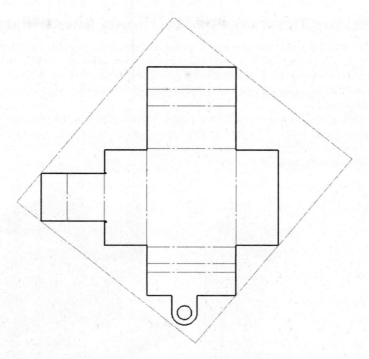

FIGURE 35.7
Showing the tangent
bend lines on a
flat pattern

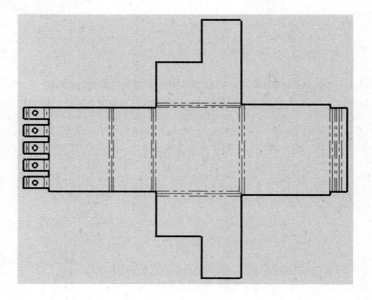

Making Drawings of Multibody Sheet Metal Parts

You cannot flatten multiple sheet metal bodies simultaneously within a single sheet metal part. However, SolidWorks is adding more capabilities for drawings of multibody parts. You might do best to use them as a bridge to a single body, or when other parts such as small welded bits or PEM fasteners are pressed into a sheet metal part, creating an inseparable subassembly.

Figure 35.8 shows two different part scenarios that this chapter addresses. The part on the left is a simple sheet metal part with PEM standoffs from the SolidWorks Toolbox pressed into holes. The part on the right is a sheet metal part with multiple sheet metal parts and a simple plate, intended to be welded together.

FIGURE 35.8
Two multibody sheet
metal scenarios

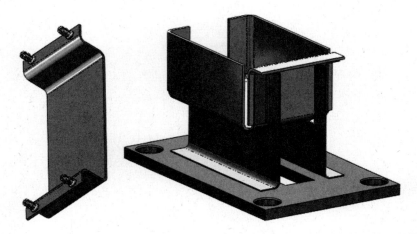

Both methods are valid uses of multibody sheet metal parts.

Displaying Bodies on the Sheet Metal Drawing

SolidWorks allows you to hide bodies within a drawing view. To do this, click inside the view. At the top of the PropertyManager for the view in the Reference Configuration panel is a button labeled Select Bodies; use this button to change the bodies that are visible in the drawing view. The Select Bodies button and the Body Selection list are shown in Figure 35.9.

FIGURE 35.9
Selecting the bodies to
show on the drawing

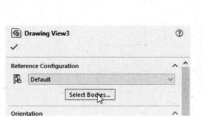

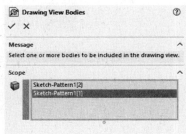

CAUTION   Use the Select Bodies button in the Reference Configurations panel of the View Property-Manager to hide bodies in views. If you use another method, you may not be able to control which bodies are shown in a particular view. Whether this is a bug or by design is unclear, but the functionality doesn't appear to be consistent.

The functionality that allows you to use the part color on the drawing doesn't apply to bodies. If you use this setting, all the bodies use the part color. If your part uses an appearance, a color is always part of the appearance assignment, although the part may not display the color. For example, a steel appearance may still have a blue color assigned. You will see the texture-like appearance when the part is shaded, but you will see the associated color when the part is shown in Wireframe mode.

Using a Cut List in a Sheet Metal Part

When you create a new sheet metal part, the FeatureManager automatically gets a new item called a cut list. The cut list is technically called a "Weldment Cut List," but it's used in sheet metal as well as in weldments to keep track of the parts modeled as bodies. The cut list is not very interesting until you have multiple pieces to list, and this happens in a part file only when you have multiple bodies. Beyond using multibodies as an interim condition where you're bridging between bodies, the cut list is used when the final model is intended to have multiple bodies. The real use of the cut list is to list on the drawing each of the individual pieces that go together to make the finished part. These pieces can be purchased hardware, other sheet metal parts, or welded plate parts, among other items.

You can add several types of values to the cut list. It's essentially a Bill of Materials for welded assemblies. To access the interface for Cut List Properties, right-click the Cut List folder and select Properties. Figure 35.10 shows a default Cut List Properties table.

FIGURE 35.10

Managing the properties for a sheet metal cut list

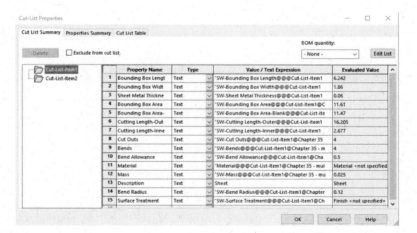

Managing Cut List Properties

To fill out the Cut List Properties, use the Cut List Summary the same way that you would use the Custom Properties data entry. Notice also that several properties already exist for the cut list. These include sheet metal–specific items like Bounding Box Length, Sheet Metal Thickness, the number of bends, material, or a special cut-list-specific description. You can add more custom properties as well.

Notice that on the left in Figure 35.10 is a list of all the cut-list items. This enables you to set the properties for each item. Although most of the values use automated syntax, others, like the Description or any custom properties you might add, require manual data entry.

The next step after arranging all your Cut List Properties is to create a drawing and add the cut list to a view.

When you create a drawing of a multibody sheet metal part, you can place the cut list on the drawing.

Placing the Cut List on the Drawing

After you create the multibody sheet metal part, filled out the Cut List Properties, and created at least one drawing view of the part (flat or formed), you'll be ready to put a cut list on the drawing. I will assume you're placing a default cut list and then need to create a customized one later. The next section also describes how to create a cut list template after you have made one to suit your needs.

With the multibody sheet metal drawing active, select Insert ➤ Tables ➤ Weldment Cut List. The Weldment Cut List PropertyManager is shown in Figure 35.11.

FIGURE 35.11
Configuring a Weldment Cut List for a multibody sheet metal part

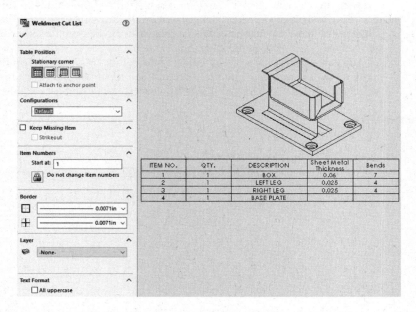

The first option in the Weldment Cut List PropertyManager is to select the template. By default, there's only the single sample table, which you probably need to customize somewhat to suit your needs. You'll do that shortly.

After you have set the options to your satisfaction, place the cut list on the drawing by clicking where you want to place the table. Notice that as you drag the table around, it snaps to the drawing format border. You can place it at one of these snap locations or just place it in a blank area on the drawing.

When you select a column header (labeled with a letter), a Column PropertyManager will appear, along with a text-formatting bar. This is all shown in Figure 35.12.

FIGURE 35.12
Customizing the Cut List column

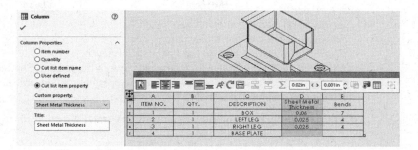

From there, you can change the information in the selected column. The first three column properties are built-in properties: Item Number, Quantity, and Description (cut-list item name). The User Defined option lets you manually enter whatever text you want. The Cut List Item Property option allows you to select from a list of automated values, shown in Figure 35.12.

You can add additional columns by right-clicking a column and selecting Insert ➢ Column Right or Column Left. The additional columns can be formatted like the others.

Saving a Cut List Template

After you have customized the cut list the way you like it—with the automated or manual entry fields set up to save you time the next time you need to use a similar table—you can save the table as a template. Right-click the table and choose the Save As option. The file type that is assigned is *.sldwldtbt. This long-file extension presumably stands for "Weld Table Template." Although a weld table and a cut list are not necessarily the same thing, they do use the same templates.

Save the template file in the location established for your Weldment Table templates. You can find them at Tools ➢ Options ➢ File Locations ➢ Weldment Cut List Templates, which by default points to C:\Program Files\SolidWorks Corp\SolidWorks\lang\english, but you can (and should) keep all your custom templates in a path that won't be overwritten by reinstalling or uninstalling the software—and a place that multiple users can share if necessary.

The next time you need to use this template, you can select it using the Table Template drop-down list in the Weldment Cut List PropertyManager.

The Bottom Line

SolidWorks has lots of special drawing functionality built around sheet metal parts. You may want to create a special template or format for sheet metal drawings or even use multipage drawings for including both flat and formed views of the part.

Multibody modeling in sheet metal opens another range of possibilities in documenting inseparable subassemblies and small weldments using sheet metal parts. The use of a cut list is similar to the use of a BOM, and though originally intended for weldments, it's also useful for sheet metal parts.

Master It   Create a blank drawing using a B-size template that has a second page (for example, the Mastering 2pg B size.drwdot). Remove any predefined views.

Create a flat-pattern-drawing view of the part Chapter 35 - Master It 1 start.sldprt.

Apply bend notes to the view.

Show bend lines without bend areas,

Show the bounding box on the flat pattern view.

On the second page, place an isometric view of the part, in Shaded With Edges mode.

Make sure the custom properties from the part have filled out the title block information.

Scale the isometric view at 2:1.

Master It   Apply ordinate dimensions in horizontal direction for the major edges and baseline dimensions vertically.

Master It   On the second page, place an isometric view of the part, in Shaded With Edges mode.

Make sure the custom properties from the part have filled out the title block information.

Scale the isometric view at 2:1.

Chapter 36

Creating Weldments and Weldment Drawings

Weldments are specialized parts that are similar in some ways to sheet metal parts. They are identified as a special kind of part by a Weldment feature in the FeatureManager, and you use a special set of tools to create and edit them. The specialized part enables specialized functionality such as cut lists, special body trimming functions, and gap creation between bodies.

IN THIS CHAPTER, YOU WILL LEARN TO:

- ◆ Use 3D sketching techniques
- ◆ Create weldment-specific features
- ◆ Add nonstructural components
- ◆ Create sub-weldments
- ◆ Understand cut lists
- ◆ Place the Weldment Cut List on a drawing

Weldments in SolidWorks are built on structural profiles along sketch entities in a multibody part environment. Weldment members can be straight or curved, you can make them using standard or custom profiles, and you can build them from both 2D and 3D sketches. A cut list within the multibody part keeps track of the length of each profile that is needed to fabricate the weldment.

You can use weldments for round or rectangular tubular structures, structures made from channels, flanged sections, standard or custom shapes, gussets, and end caps. They can also represent weld beads in the part. You can also use weldments to create structures that are bolted together, structural aluminum extrusion frames, vinyl window frames, and wooden frames and structures, and you can put them into assemblies with other parts such as castings, sheet metal, and fabricated plates.

Sketching in 3D

The 3D sketch is an important tool for creating weldments (and many other features) in SolidWorks. Structural frames are a large part of the work that's typically done using weldment functionality, and frames are often represented as 3D wireframes. You can represent 3D wireframes with a combination of 2D sketches on different planes, with a single 3D sketch, or with a combination of 2D and 3D sketches. If you have confidence in your ability to use 3D sketches, then that's the best way to go. 3D sketches can be challenging, but they're manageable if you know what to expect from them.

Navigating in 3D Space

When drawing a line in a 3D sketch, the cursor and origin initially look like those shown in Figure 36.1. The large red origin is called the *space handle*, with the red legs indicating the active sketching plane. Any sketch entities that you draw lie on this plane. The cursor also indicates the plane to which the active sketching plane is parallel. The XY graphic shown in Figure 36.1 doesn't mean that the sketch is going to be *on* the XY plane, just parallel to it.

FIGURE 36.1
The space handle and the
3D sketch cursor

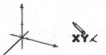

Pressing the Tab key causes the active sketching plane to toggle between XY, YZ, and ZX. The active sketching plane indication doesn't create any sketch relations; it just lets you know the orientation of the sketch entities that are being placed. If you want to create a skew line that isn't parallel to any standard plane, you can do this by sketching to available endpoints, vertices, origins, and so on. If there are no entities to snap to, then you need to accept the planar placement, turn off the Line tool, remove any automatic relations, rotate the view, and move one end of the sketch entity in a different plane.

An excellent tool to help you visualize what's happening in a 3D sketch is the Four Viewport view. This view divides the screen into four quadrants, displaying the front, top, and right views in addition to the trimetric or isometric view. You can sketch in any of the viewports, and the sketch updates live in all the viewports simultaneously. This arrangement is shown in Figure 36.2. You can easily access the divided viewport screen by clicking buttons on the Standard Views toolbar. You can also manually split the screen by using the splitter bars at the lower-left and upper-right ends of the scroll bar areas around the graphics window.

FIGURE 36.2
The Four Viewport view

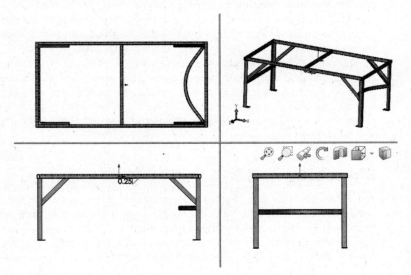

When you move unconstrained entities in a 3D sketch, they move in the plane of the screen. You can use this to your advantage to create or edit lines in 3D space, but it can also lead to unexpected results. When you view the sketch at an angle, move it, and then rotate the view, you may notice that the sketch has shot off into deep interplanetary space. This is another reason for using the Four Viewport view, which enables you to see what's going on from all points of view at once, thereby avoiding any surprises.

Understanding Sketch Relations in 3D Sketches

Several relations are available in 3D sketches that aren't found in 2D sketches, such as AlongX, AlongY, AlongZ (which act as replacements for horizontal and vertical), and OnSurface.

Relations in 3D sketches are not projected as they are in 2D sketches. For example, an entity in a 2D sketch can be made coincident to an entity that's out of plane. This is because to make the relation, the out-of-plane entity is projected into the sketch plane, and the relation is made to the projection. In a 3D sketch, "coincident" means coincident, with no projection.

Keep in mind that solving sketches in 3D is more difficult than it is in 2D. You'll see more situations where sketch relations fail or flip in the wrong direction. Angle dimensions are particularly notorious in 3D sketches for flipping direction if they change and go across the 180-degree mark. When possible, you should work with fully defined sketches and be careful (and conservative) with sketch relations.

For example, the sketch shown in Figure 36.3 cannot be fully defined without also overdefining the sketch. The main difficulty is that the combination of the tangent arc and the symmetric legs of the end brace cannot be located rotationally, even using the questionable reliability of 3D planes that are discussed next. The only workable answer to this problem is to create a separate 2D sketch on a real 2D sketch plane, where the plane is defined by the elements of the 3D sketch.

FIGURE 36.3
Three-dimensional sketches may be difficult to fully define.

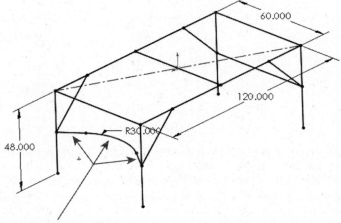

This set of sketch entities cannot be located rotationally within the 3D sketch

Creating Planes in Space

It's possible to create planes directly inside 3D sketches. These planes are defined by constraints and selections rather than selecting a type of method to define a plane. Sketches can be created on these planes and move with the planes. Having planes in the sketch also enables planar sketch entities such as arcs and circles in 3D sketches.

Unfortunately, you must watch out for many things with 3D planes. Be aware that they don't follow their original definition like normal reference-geometry-type planes. Planes inside 3D sketches act more like sketch entities in that if they are underdefined, they can move around inside the sketch. Watching sketch planes move in a sketch is very unsettling for most SolidWorks users. Figure 36.4 shows the PropertyManager interface for creating 3D planes; however, keep in mind that the plane doesn't maintain the original relation to these initial references. The parent-and-child relations that SolidWorks users are used to are suspended for this one function, or they work in the reverse from what you normally expect.

FIGURE 36.4
The PropertyManager for creating 3D planes

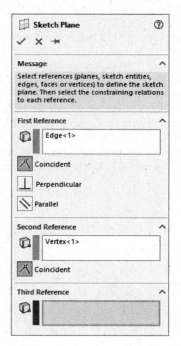

A 3D plane cannot be fully defined unless some sketch geometry on the plane is in turn related to something else. Limited types of sketch relations can be applied directly to the actual plane. Horizontal and vertical relations cannot be applied directly to the plane to orient it. Horizontal and vertical relations of entities on the plane are relative only to the plane and not to the rest of the part; therefore, making a line horizontal on the plane doesn't mean anything when the plane rotates (which it's free to do until it's somehow constrained to prevent this).

Beyond this, when a plane violates a sketch relation, the error isn't reported, which severely limits the amount of confidence that you can place in planes that are created in this way.

The biggest danger is in the plane rotating, because that's the direction in which it is most difficult to fully lock down. The best recommendation here is to create reference sketch lines with relations to something stable, preferably outside of the 3D sketch.

If you choose to use 3D planes, you can activate them for sketching by double-clicking a plane. The plane is activated when it displays a grid. You can double-click in an empty space to deactivate the plane and return to regular 3D Sketch mode. The main thing that you give up when abandoning 3D sketch planes is the ability to use the Dynamic Drag options when all loft or boundary sketches are made in a single 3D sketch.

Limiting Path Segments

Some of the path segments that are allowed in 3D sketches can be used only if you sketch them on a plane. These entities include circles and arcs, and can include splines, although splines aren't required to be on a plane. To sketch on a 3D plane (a plane created within the 3D sketch), you can simply double-click the plane.

Some sketch entities and tools exist that you cannot create or use inside a 3D sketch, even if a sketch plane is activated. They include the following:

◆ Autodimension

◆ Fully Define Sketch

◆ Modify Sketch

◆ Sketch Slot

◆ Ellipse

◆ Polygon

◆ Dynamic Mirror

◆ Offset Entities

◆ Sketch text

◆ Sketch Picture

To sketch on a standard plane, planar face, or reference geometry plane, you can Ctrl+click the border of the plane with the Sketch Entity icon active or double-click the plane. The space handle will move, indicating that newly created sketch entities will lie in the selected plane.

Using Dimensions in 3D Sketches

Dimensions in 2D sketches can represent the straight-line distance between two points, or they can represent the horizontal or vertical distance, depending on the position of the cursor when you place the dimension. In 3D sketches, dimensions between points are *always* the straight-line distance. If you want to get a dimension that's horizontal or vertical, you should create the dimension between a plane and a point (the dimension is always measured normal to the plane) or between a line and a point (the dimension is always measured perpendicular to the line). For this reason, reference sketch geometry is often used freely in 3D sketches, in part to support dimensioning.

This is one of the differences between 2D and 3D sketches that users find difficult to manage. If you're used to visualizing dimensions within 2D sketches, direction-controlled dimensions in 3D sketches can be difficult to visualize and even more difficult to create.

Using the Weldment Tools

Like the Sheet Metal tools, the Weldment tools in SolidWorks are specialized to enable you to create weldment-specific features in a dedicated environment. Everything starts from a sketch or set of sketches representing the wireframe of the welded structural members.

Using the Weldment Feature

The Weldment button on the Weldment toolbar simply places a weldment placeholder in the FeatureManager. This placeholder tells SolidWorks that this part is a special weldment part—much in the way that the Sheet Metal feature in sheet metal parts is a placeholder—and denotes a special part type. The Weldment feature moves to the top of the tree, regardless of when you create it in the part history. If you don't create a Weldment feature manually, then one is automatically created for you and placed at the top of the tree when the first Structural Member feature is created. Structural members are discussed in the next section.

This feature offers only a few special default settings: You can set custom properties that transfer to all cut-list items that are created in the current part, and the Merge Result option is deselected by default in weldment parts. The ability to set custom properties is important when multiple weldments go together to make an assembly. To access the Custom Properties interface, shown in Figure 36.5, select the Properties option on the Weldment feature RMB menu.

FIGURE 36.5
The Weldment
Properties interface

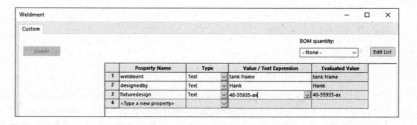

The general workflow for creating weldment parts is as follows:

1. Create a new part and insert a Weldment feature.

2. Create a structural layout of 2D sketches, 3D sketches, or a combination of 2D and 3D sketches to represent a structure to be fabricated by cutting and welding structural shape stock.

3. Ensure that you have a library with appropriate structural shape sketches, properties, materials, and so on.

4. Make sure that you have allowed for sketch lines in the structural layout to represent a corner, centerline, or some other reference in the library structural shape sketch. This can greatly affect intersections between structural members.

5. Assign structural shapes to individual lines in the structural layout. Be sure you understand the rules on using groups.

6. Trim and miter intersections between structural members to suit your design.

7. Add plate entities such as end caps and gussets.

8. Add weld beads as needed.

9. Place the weldment into an assembly, and add castings and sheet metal parts, as well as holes and fasteners to attach nonwelded components.

Introducing the Structural Member Feature

A *structural member* is the basic building unit of weldments in SolidWorks. You can create a structural member by extruding or sweeping a profile along one or more path segments, and it may result in a single body or multiple bodies. The path segments may be in the form of 2D or 3D sketches.

NOTE   A single Structural Member feature can create multiple bodies, with each body corresponding to a single cut length of stock. In other words, the feature name "structural member" doesn't necessarily refer to a single piece of the weldment, although it may.

When creating the sketch for the weldment, it's important to decide what the sketch represents. For example, does it represent the centerline of the structural elements or does it represent a corner? You can orient and position structural shape profiles relative to the frame sketch in several ways, with positioning at the shape centroid being probably the most intuitive for closed shapes and a corner being most intuitive for angle channels.

Figure 36.6 shows a single 3D sketch of a simple frame and a Structural Member feature in the process of creation. You must select the standard first, then the type, and finally the size. A limited number of profiles come with the software, and although you'll probably need to create some custom profiles, they're fortunately very easy to create.

To access a large number of weldment profiles in various standards, open the Design Library and click the SolidWorks Content icon. Under that, the Weldments folder has several zip files containing weldment profiles. Ctrl+click an icon to download the file, and then extract the contents of the zip file to the library location you have established for your weldment profiles.

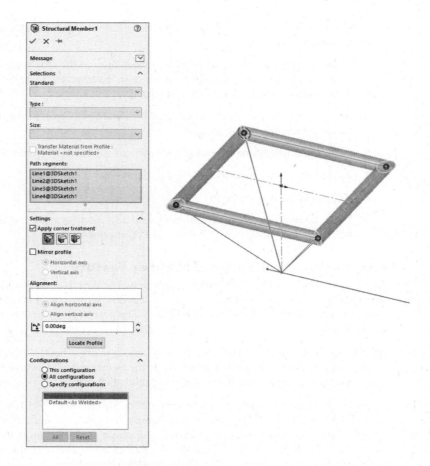

GROUPING SELECTED PATH SEGMENTS

The concept of *groups* is simple. You can organize selected path segments within a structural member feature into two kinds of groups: parallel or contiguous. A single structural member may have multiple groups.

Parallel groups contain parallel path segments that don't touch. Parallel groups also require that you select the structural profile before you can select more than one path segment.

Contiguous groups contain path segments that touch end to end, two segments at a time. A contiguous group cannot have one path segment intersect in the middle of another or more than two path segments intersecting at a corner.

Each group can have only a single orientation of the structural profile. For example, if each frame leg needs the profile rotated to a different orientation, you need to rotate the legs in four separate groups instead of all in a single group.

Given those requirements, if the frame shown in Figure 36.6 were to be created entirely from the same structural profile—say, ANSI (American National Standards Institute) inch, square tube, 3 × 3 × 0.025—it would require a minimum of five groups, as shown in exploded form in Figure 36.7. The file used to create this image is included in the download materials from the website under the name Weldment groups.sldprt.

The main advantages of the groups functionality are that each member within the group is automatically trimmed to other members of the group, and you can control gaps within or between groups. The only trimming you need to take care of separately is the trimming between members of different groups.

FIGURE 36.7

Using groups to create the welded frame

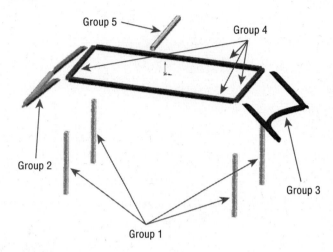

Group 5

Group 4

Group 2

Group 3

Group 1

LOCATING AND ORIENTING THE PROFILE

When you apply a profile to a path segment in a Structural Member feature, the profile must have some relationship to the path segment. The default point where the path "pierces" the profile is at the sketch origin. To change the pierce point, you can click the Locate Profile button at the bottom of the Structural Member PropertyManager, which zooms the view to present the profile sketch so you can select another sketch point to use as the pierce point. You can select any sketch point on the profile, including endpoints, sketch points, and virtual sharp points if they are present in the sketch.

Profile sketches are generally surrounded by several sketch points, which may seem unnecessary until you consider that you can use any of the points to position the profile. The Settings panel at the bottom of the Structural Member PropertyManager is shown in Figure 36.8 and displays a profile sketch with the interface.

In addition to locating the profile sketch, you can also rotate the profile using the Angle field in the Settings panel. This rotates all the bodies that are created by the Structural Member feature at the same time. In the example of the four-legged frame, if the legs are rectangular or circular, they can all be created in the same Structural Member feature because they're all rotated in the same way. However, if the legs are made from an asymmetrical shape such as an angle, then each leg needs to be made using a separate Structural Member feature, with each leg rotated differently.

USING DISJOINT SKETCH SEGMENTS

You can select disjoint sketch segments in a single Structural Member feature if they're parallel to the first segment and use the same profile height location and orientation. For example, in Figure 36.7, notice the four angled supports in the corners attaching to the legs. Because they're parallel in pairs, all four of these supports could not be made in a single group. Later in this section, when those path segments are actually used to place structural members, the additional requirement of using an angle profile will mean that each profile needs to be rotated differently from the other profiles and, as such, cannot be used in a single group.

FIGURE 36.8

Locating the profile

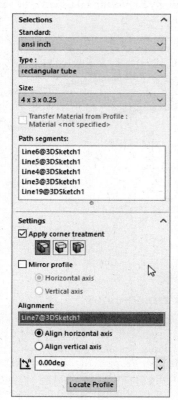

USING CUSTOM PROFILES

Most of the custom profiles that you will need may be simply new sizes of existing profiles. You can easily create a custom profile by opening an existing profile, editing it, and saving it under a different name using the Save As command. You can also use configurations in the library part to create multiple sizes of the profiles, which can then be selected for use in weldment parts.

Other sources for custom profiles include 3D Content Central, which has a large number of erector-set aluminum extrusion profiles and the accessory hardware for those systems. Toolbox also has a Structural Steel sketch generator, shown in Figure 36.9, which enables you to generate most standard shapes. If you have Toolbox installed on your system, you can find this tool in the Toolbox menu.

Weldment profiles are great candidates for storing in your special library folder, separate from the SolidWorks installation directory. To establish this library location, you can choose Tools ➤ Options ➤ File Locations ➤ Weldment Profiles. Also keep in mind that if you share design duties with other users, either the library location should be shared among users on a network or the libraries should be copied to each user's local library. You can also share library data through a Product Data Management, or PDM, program.

If you are creating completely new custom profiles, remember that when locating the profile relative to the path segments, you can use any sketch point. As a result, you should provide ample selections for pierce points. Virtual sharps function well around filleted corners, as well as sketch points at the centroid of a shape.

FIGURE 36.9
The Structural Steel sketch generator interface

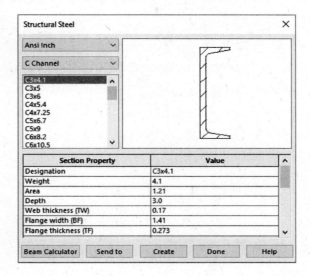

In addition to sketch geometry, the library part files should also contain custom property information about the structural shape, such as part number, supplier, material, and so on. This information propagates to the cut list.

ADDING CORNER TREATMENTS

Any intersection of sketch lines at mutual endpoints within a single group, except as noted in this section, creates a situation that requires that the corners be cut to match. Figure 36.10 shows an example of the options available when lines meet at right angles. Notice that within a group, you have the option to set a weld gap at the intersections.

To access the toolbar with the Corner Treatment options, you can click the pink dot at the intersection of the path segments. The default Corner Treatment settings are found in the Structural Member PropertyManager, but you may need to adjust them individually.

Two situations don't require corner treatments. The first situation is when a line intersects another line at some location *other* than an endpoint in the same Structural Member feature— for example, a support meeting the main member in the middle. In this situation, the member that ends in the middle of the other member is trimmed to a butt joint. The second situation is when an intersecting member is created by a later Structural Member feature. You deal with this situation by using the Trim/Extend function, which is described later in this chapter.

NOTE   You may encounter a situation where it seems like a good idea to create collinear sketch segments. In a typical extrusion, the faces created from collinear lines are simply merged together as one. However, in a weldment, this doesn't work when it's done in a single feature. In order to create structural members on collinear sketch lines, you must either extend one line to encompass the length of both lines or do the work in two separate Structural Member features.

FIGURE 36.10
Corner Treatment
options

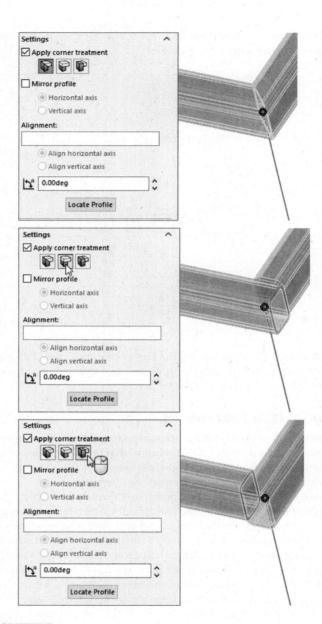

USING ARC SEGMENTS

When arc sketch segments are part of the selection for a Structural Member, a Merge Arc Segment Bodies option appears after the selection box in the Selections panel. This means that any *tangent* arc segment will be joined to the entities to which it's tangent, but any nontangent entities will create separate bodies.

Figure 36.11 shows a tangent arc in the curved leg brace, along with the Merge Arc Segment Bodies option in the PropertyManager.

FIGURE 36.11
A tangent arc segment
used in a Structural
Member feature

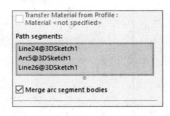

If the Merge Arc Segment Bodies option isn't selected, then a separate body is created for arc segments. The Merge Arc Segment Bodies option applies to the whole feature and cannot be set selectively for individual arc segments within the selected sketch entities; it's either selected for all or deselected for all. If some arc segment bodies are merged and others are not, then you should create separate Structural Member features.

It's also a curious limitation that only one arc may be selected if the selected path segments are disjointed. For example, you cannot select the two arcs for two J-shapes that don't touch in the same Structural Member feature. The obvious workaround is to create two separate groups.

PATTERNING BODIES AND SKETCHING WITH SYMMETRY

Bodies created by the Structural Member feature can be patterned and mirrored. Remember that there's a difference between patterning *features* and patterning *bodies*. The Move/Copy Bodies feature is also appropriate for creating bodies to be used in the weldment, although the Structural Member feature doesn't create them directly.

This is mentioned here to emphasize the point that sketching with symmetry is still important, although it's more difficult with 3D sketches than with conventional 2D sketches. Symmetry in a 3D sketch can be used only when a plane is activated, and you can activate regular reference geometry planes, not just 3D sketch planes. This is also mentioned because in larger weldments (or when using slower computers), performance may be an issue, and mirroring or patterning bodies is certainly a performance enhancement over building parametric features.

CREATING CONFIGURATIONS

When you start creating a weldment, SolidWorks may automatically create a derived configuration, depending on the setting at Tools ➤ Options ➤ Document Properties ➤ Weldments ➤ Create Derived Configurations. Both configurations are named Default, but they have different descriptions. The parent configuration description is As Machined, and the derived, or indented, configuration description is As Welded.

This arrangement holds true for any additional top-level configurations that you create in the part—they will all get the description As Machined and inherit an identically named derived configuration with the description As Welded. These configurations are meant to help you create drawings where the raw weldment is distinguished from the weldment after it has been machined, ground, and drilled.

Using the Trim/Extend Feature

In situations where you must create multiple Structural Member features, thereby creating intersecting bodies, you must deal with the interferences using the Trim/Extend feature. An example of this is shown in Figure 36.12. The legs and braces shown are all being trimmed by a single face on the bottom side of the rectangular section of the frame, where a small arrow will appear.

FIGURE 36.12
Using the Trim/
Extend feature

Bodies can be trimmed by planar faces or other bodies. Bodies can also be trimmed before they are mirrored or patterned. Although trimming with faces is faster, it may not give the same geometrical results.

The Extend option enables either trimming or extending, as appropriate. If the Extend option isn't selected, then trimming is the only action available.

Using the End Cap Feature

The End Cap feature closes off an open-ended structural member. You can add multiple end caps in a single End Cap feature. The PropertyManager and the end product are shown in Figure 36.13.

The end cap using the Outward option sits on the outside face of the member and overlaps the thickness of the member by the inverse of the thickness ratio that's applied in the Offset panel. If the Use Thickness Ratio option is turned off, it functions as an offset from the outer faces of the member from which it is created. When this option is turned on, the thickness ratio can range from zero to one. For a value of zero, it's flush with the outer faces of the member, and for a value of one, it's flush with the inner faces of the member. Using the Inward option, the cap fits inside the hole in the member.

Working with the Gusset Feature

The Gusset feature creates a three-, four-, or five-sided gusset in a corner between structural members, as shown in Figure 36.14. You can place the gusset at specific locations along the edge in the corner, or you can offset it by a specific dimension in a specific direction by using the settings in the Parameters panel. You can control the size and thickness of the gusset in the Profile panel. There's no sketch for this feature type; it's simply created from the parameters that you enter in the PropertyManager interface. Again, if you need to make multiple Gusset features in succession, you can use the pushpin icon to keep the interface displayed until you close it by clicking the red X icon.

FIGURE 36.13
Using the End
Cap feature

FIGURE 36.14
Using the Gusset feature

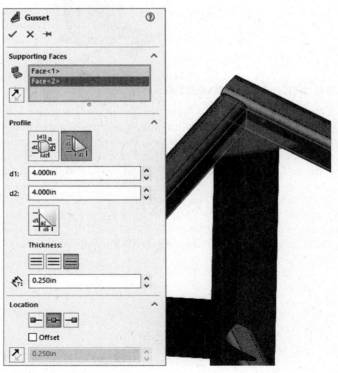

Using Nonstructural Components

Nonstructural components are frequently needed in weldments and include items such as feet, plates, brackets, mounting pads, and castings. Simpler items that can be easily modeled in place can be modeled directly into the weldment part. You can also insert parts into the weldment using the Insert Part feature and move them into place by using dimensions or mates. In general, if any item is actually welded into the weldment, you should place it in the weldment part; however, items that are bolted on should probably be placed into an assembly. Of course, this probably depends more on your company's documentation standards, part-numbering standards, and assembly processes than on software capabilities.

When you're modeling a plate using the standard Extrude feature, except that the Merge option is deselected by default. This ensures that nonstructural components that are manually modeled, such as this part, are created as separate bodies and not merged together with the existing structural items.

FIGURE 36.15
A footplate added to the weldment

Using Sub-Weldments

From a modeling point of view, sub-weldments are generally used for either organizational or performance reasons to group together elements of a weldment or to break a larger weldment into more manageable pieces. This is in much the same way that subassemblies are created for the same purposes within larger assemblies. From a fabrication point of view, sub-weldments are also used to break a large weldment into pieces that can be transported or handled.

To create a sub-weldment, you can select several bodies from the cut list and then select Create Sub-Weldment from the RMB menu. (You can also select the bodies from the graphics window if you use the Select Bodies selection filter.) This creates a separate folder for the sub-weldment bodies. You can then right-click the Sub-Weldment folder and select Insert Into New Part.

Working with Cut Lists

The cut list that's maintained in the model FeatureManager is simply a replacement for the Solid Bodies folder. It has most of the same functionality as the Solid Bodies folder, as well as a few additional items. The Cut List folder symbol in the FeatureManager can appear in two potential states; these symbols are shown in the left margin. When the cut list requires an update, the top image is shown; and after the update has been performed, the bottom image is shown. Cut lists are updated automatically when you access a drawing that uses the cut list, but you can also update them manually through an RMB option or by the forced rebuild, Ctrl+Q.

You can access the Update command by right-clicking the Cut List folder and selecting it from the RMB menu. Figure 36.16 shows the result of the update. The weldment solid bodies are broken down further into subfolders that reflect quantities of identical bodies. Notice that the weld beads at the bottom of the list are not in a folder.

FIGURE 36.16

The cut list in the model FeatureManager

NOTE You can assign different materials to bodies within a part in SolidWorks. SolidWorks doesn't account for the weldability of different materials.

Using Cut-List Properties

In addition to the custom properties for the document, SolidWorks weldments also utilize Cut-List Properties. You can access Cut-List Properties by right-clicking a Cut List Item folder (other than the top-level Cut List folder) at the top of the FeatureManager and selecting Properties. The Cut-List Properties may not be available for a newly created weldment until you have updated the cut list (right-click the top-level Cut List icon and select Update).

Figure 36.17 shows the Cut-List Properties dialog box, which allows users to enter data such as length and material for BOMs and cut lists.

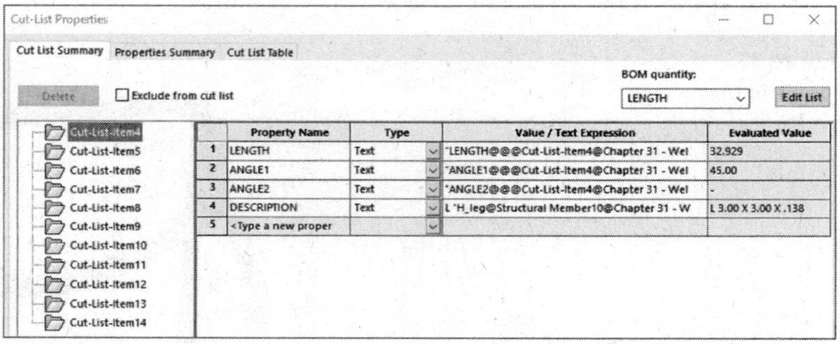

FIGURE 36.17
Use the Cut-List Properties dialog box to enter relevant data for BOMs and cut lists.

Notice the Properties Summary tab, which enables you to look at each property and see the value for each cut-list item. This is where you would select a property such as Description, assign descriptions for each cut-list item, and then go on to the next property—say, Material—and assign values for that property.

The Cut List Table tab shows you a preview of the cut list and enables you to use cut-list templates that might have different default columns established. Figure 36.18 shows the Cut List Table tab of the Cut List Properties dialog box.

As Figure 36.18 shows, you may need to enter information for items added to the weldment such as end caps or gussets. Cut-list properties are also added when you insert a bounding box for nonstructural members.

Excluding and Reordering Cut-List Items

To exclude a feature in the FeatureManager from the cut list, you can select Exclude From Cut List from the feature's RMB menu. The next time the cut list is updated, the members that were created by that feature will be listed at the bottom of the Cut List folder with the weld beads. To include the item again in the cut list, select Include In Cut List from the feature's RMB menu and update the cut list again. Figure 36.19 shows a folder that has been excluded from the cut list.

FIGURE 36.18
The Cut List Table tab previews the cut list for you and gives you the opportunity to edit values in the table.

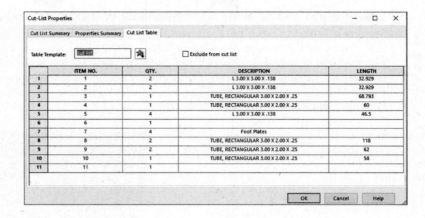

Cut-List Properties

Cut List Summary Properties Summary **Cut List Table**

Table Template: cut list ☐ Exclude from cut list

	ITEM NO.	QTY.	DESCRIPTION	LENGTH
1	1	2	L 3.00 X 3.00 X .138	32.929
2	2	2	L 3.00 X 3.00 X .138	32.929
3	3	1	TUBE, RECTANGULAR 3.00 X 2.00 X .25	68.793
4	4	1	TUBE, RECTANGULAR 3.00 X 2.00 X .25	60
5	5	4	L 3.00 X 3.00 X .138	46.5
6	6	1		
7	7	4	Foot Plates	
8	8	2	TUBE, RECTANGULAR 3.00 X 2.00 X .25	118
9	9	2	TUBE, RECTANGULAR 3.00 X 2.00 X .25	62
10	10	1	TUBE, RECTANGULAR 3.00 X 2.00 X .25	58
11	11	1		

OK   Cancel   Help

FIGURE 36.19
Excluding an item from a cut list

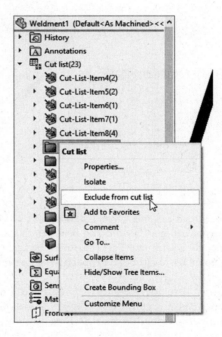

Only entire Cut List folders can be eliminated from the cut list, not individual bodies. To reorder items in the cut list, just drag and drop the folder to where you want it to be in the list.

Using Weld Beads and Fillet Beads in Weldments and Assemblies

Weldment

Fillet Bead

Weld Bead

The icons for Weldment, Fillet Bead, and Weld Bead look very similar. The Weldment tool is used to proclaim the part as a Weldment part. The difference between a fillet bead and a weld bead is that the Fillet Bead feature creates actual solid geometry, which shows up in a weldment part as a feature, while the Weld Bead feature creates a cosmetic representation of a weld bead. Figure 36.20 shows the Fillet Bead features in the FeatureManager and the actual fillet bead between a plate and a structural member.

FIGURE 36.20
The Fillet Bead feature in the FeatureManager and on the part

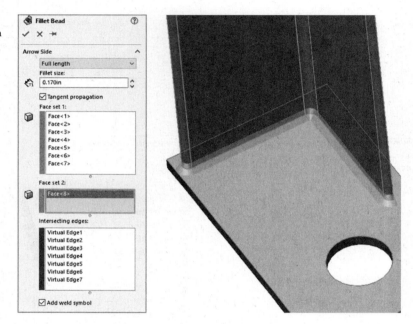

To create a weld in an assembly, you still use the Weld Bead tool. The Weld Bead feature produces a cosmetic display of a weld and keeps track of it in a folder at the top of the assembly FeatureManager or the Weldment Part FeatureManager.

Figure 36.21 shows the Weld Bead PropertyManager and the preview it applies to a weldment part.

The Weld Bead feature doesn't show up in the part or assembly FeatureManager as a feature (even though you access the command at Insert ➤ Assembly Feature ➤ Weld Bead), and it doesn't create geometry that adds mass. It does produce a cosmetic weld bead on the part, and it creates a new folder in the FeatureManager right below the Annotations folder. The entries in the folder show how many weld beads of what length are applied to the entire weldment. Fillet beads add nothing to the Weld folder. As a result, the type of information you need to have in your model will help you determine if you want to use the Fillet Bead or Weld Bead feature. If you need to show welds in an assembly, you have to use the cosmetic display of weld beads.

FIGURE 36.21
The Weld Bead feature shows up in the Weld folder and as a cosmetic display on the part.

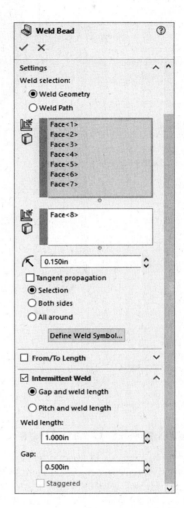

The Weld Bead PropertyManager also gives you the option to define the ANSI weld symbol before the feature is complete. The interface for defining the weld symbol is shown in Figure 36.22. Use the Define Weld Symbol button in the Settings panel of the Weld Bead PropertyManager to access this interface.

FIGURE 36.22
Assigning a weld symbol
in the Weld Bead feature

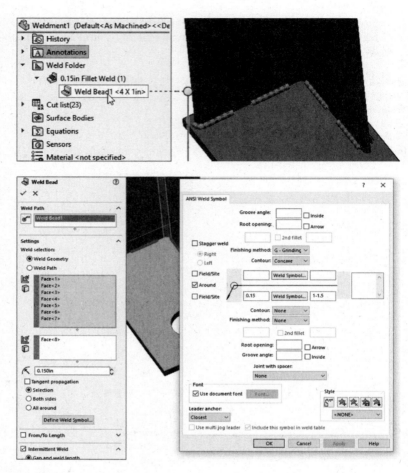

Creating Weldment Drawings

Weldment drawings have a couple of special features that distinguish them from normal part drawings. The first is obviously the cut list. Like a BOM in an assembly, you can place the Weldment Cut List on a drawing by choosing Insert ➤ Table ➤ Weldment Cut List. Figure 36.23 shows a sample cut list on a drawing. In this case, the blank rows represent nonstructural components: the footplates and the gusset. You can manually add data for these parts either directly into the table or by adding it to the properties of the corresponding folder in the cut list in the model document.

Figure 36.23 also shows an auto-ballooned isometric view of the entire weldment. This works the same way that assembly auto-ballooning works, and it corresponds to the cut list in the same way that the assembly corresponds to the BOM.

FIGURE 36.23

A cut list on a drawing

ITEM NO.	QTY.	DESCRIPTION	LENGTH
1	2	L 3.00 X 3.00 X .138	32.929
2	2	L 3.00 X 3.00 X .138	32.929
3	1	TUBE, RECTANGULAR 3.00 X 2.00 X .25	68.793
4	1	TUBE, RECTANGULAR 3.00 X 2.00 X .25	60
5	4	L 3.00 X 3.00 X .138	46.5
6	1		
7	4		
8	2	TUBE, RECTANGULAR 3.00 X 2.00 X .25	118
9	2	TUBE, RECTANGULAR 3.00 X 2.00 X .25	62
10	1	TUBE, RECTANGULAR 3.00 X 2.00 X .25	58

Weldment drawings can also include views of individual bodies. You can do this by making a relative view, selecting both faces from the same body, and then using the PropertyManager of the relative view in the window of the solid model to control whether the view shows the entire part or just selected bodies. The Relative View PropertyManager is shown in Figure 36.24.

FIGURE 36.24

The Relative View PropertyManager

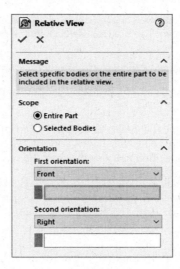

When you place a drawing view of a weldment, you can also link a cut list to a particular view. This might help you with putting multiple weldments on a drawing or laying out the process for fabricating a weldment, showing the weldment in various stages of completion.

To access the Relative View PropertyManager interface, follow these steps:

1. Click the Relative View button on the Drawings toolbar, or choose Insert ➤ Drawing View ➤ Relative To Model.

2. Right-click a blank space on the drawing sheet and select Insert From File. Browse to the part file.

3. Identify the faces to be shown in the particular orientations, and specify whether the entire part or the selected bodies should be shown in the view.

Tutorial: Working with Weldments

This tutorial guides you through building a section of a tubular truss support. You can create many different types of weldments, from simple small-gauge frames to large architectural designs such as this one. This tutorial also helps you to navigate successfully through some 3D sketch functionality for creating fully defined sketches.

Follow these steps to learn about working with weldments:

1. Open a new part. If you have Toolbox, activate it by choosing Tools ➤ Add-Ins ➤ SolidWorks Toolbox. If you don't have Toolbox, simply draw two concentric circles on the Front plane of a new part. The circles should have diameters of 10.02 inches and 10.75 inches. Alternatively, you can copy the library feature from the download material to a path such as `D:\Library\Weldment Profiles\Custom\Pipe\P-Pipe10in .sldlfp`.

2. If you have Toolbox, choose Tools ➤ Add-ins ➤ SolidWorks Toolbox ➤ Structural Steel. If you don't have Toolbox, just select a shape from the installed SolidWorks library.

3. Select ANSI Inch, P Pipe, P10. This profile has an inside diameter of 10.02 inches and an outside diameter of 10.75 inches. Click the Create button and then click Done.

4. Use Custom Properties to add any properties that you want to have automatically added to the cut list.

5. Remembering the techniques on library features, first close any open sketches, select the sketch from the FeatureManager, and then save the part as a Library Feature Part file to the location specified at the end of step 1.

NOTE The Custom folder (located in the first level under Weldment Profiles) is recognized as the Standard, similar to ANSI or ISO (International Organization for Standardization). The next folder down, Pipe, is recognized as the Type, and the name of the file is recognized as the Size, in the same way as shown.

6. Choose Tools ➤ Options ➤ File Locations ➤ Weldment Profiles, and add your non-installation directory location to the list of folders. Alternatively, you can remove the Program Files location from the list and copy the files from that location to your own library location.

7. Open another new part and open a new 3D sketch in the part. Double-click the Top (ZX) plane to activate it and click the Center Rectangle sketch entity.

8. Draw a rectangle around the origin. The sketch should look like Figure 36.25. Apply an Equal relation to two adjacent sides of the rectangle, and dimension any of the lines as 120 inches.

9. Turn off the rectangle and double-click in a blank space to deactivate sketching on the Top plane.

10. Activate the Line sketch tool and press Tab until the cursor indicates the XY plane.

FIGURE 36.25
FIGURE 36.25
A centered rectangle in
a 3D sketch

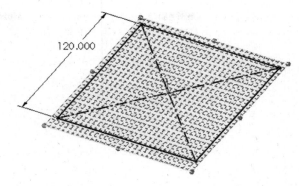

11. Draw a line from one corner of the square down, trying to avoid any automatic relations such as Coincident relations to other points and any AlongX, AlongY, or AlongZ relations. Connect the other three corners of the square with the free endpoint of the new line, as shown in Figure 36.26.

FIGURE 36.26
Adding lines

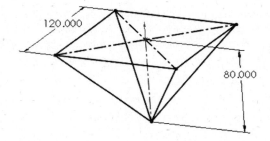

12. Rotate the view slightly. Notice that the first line that you drew in step 10 and one other line are on a plane. Drag a right-to-left selection box around the point where the four lines converge, and assign an Equal relation to all the lines. This makes the shape into an upside-down pyramid.

13. Drag the point. Notice that it moves up and down, although it seems a little erratic. Place a dimension between the point and the part origin. Notice that the sketch becomes overdefined and turns red and yellow. Theoretically, this combination should work, but SolidWorks doesn't accept it.

14. Using the Display/Delete Relations tool, delete all the Equal relations that you just added to the part. It may be faster to select Undo from the File menu or to press Ctrl+Z.

15. Draw a vertical construction line from the part origin to the point where the four lines meet, and assign this line an AlongY relation. Notice that the point drags much more smoothly. This is a good reason for using simpler relation schemes when possible. In this case, the four equal relations that had to be solved simultaneously are now replaced by a single relation that's easier to solve when you drag the sketch. Apply a dimension of 80 inches to the new construction line.

16. Draw a new line from the point where the four lines come together AlongX in the positive X direction. Dimension this new line as 120 inches. The sketch should look like Figure 36.27.

FIGURE 36.27
The sketch after step 16

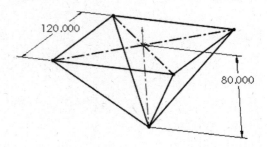

17. Exit the sketch. Click the Structural Member toolbar button on the Weldments toolbar. In the Standard drop-down list in the Structural Member PropertyManager, select Custom. In the Type drop-down list, select Pipe. In the Size drop-down list, select P-Pipe10in. This is the name that corresponds to the way you saved the library feature part in step 5.

18. In the Path Segments selection box, select the original four sides of the rectangle. In the Settings panel, make sure that the Apply Corner Treatment option is selected and that the End Miter icon is selected. This is shown in Figure 36.28. Accept the command when you are finished.

FIGURE 36.28
The Structural Member PropertyManager and the sketch after step 18

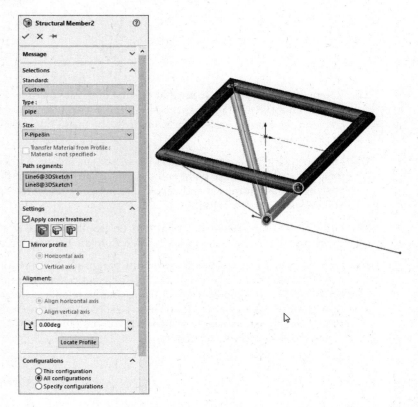

19. Expand the Structural Member feature. Notice that the four bodies are listed under it. Click the Cut List folder to expand it. The bodies should also be listed there.

20. Open the 10-inch Pipe library feature that you created at the beginning of this tutorial. Edit the two dimensions to subtract 2 inches from each dimension, and add a custom property description called Support Leg. Choose File ➢ Save As to save the library feature to the same location as the original, but with the filename `P-Pipe8in.sldlfp`.

21. Initiate another Structural Member feature, this time selecting the 8-inch size of pipe from the Custom folder. In the Path Segments selection box, select two of the angled lines that go to opposite corners. Keep the feature open for the next step.

NOTE   Remember that you cannot create three intersecting structural members with a single group. To create material on all four lines, you need two separate groups within the Structural Member feature.

22. Make a second group with the other pair of angled lines. Accept the feature when you are satisfied. The model should look like Figure 36.29.

FIGURE 36.29
The model showing the features accepted in step 22

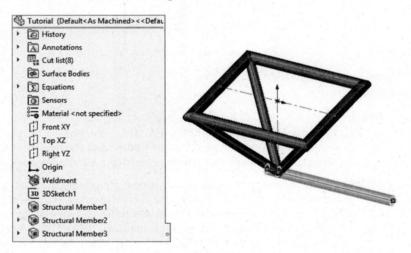

23. Apply another Structural Member feature to the 10-foot (120-inch) section, again using the 10-inch-diameter pipe. Notice that this member isn't long enough to cut through the peak of the pyramid.

24. Edit the 3D sketch and draw a 12-inch extension to the original line past the peak of the pyramid. Use an additional line rather than extending the existing one. Exit the sketch.

25. Edit the Structural Member feature to add the new line.

NOTE   You have to deselect the Apply Corner Treatment option to get this technique to work. If this option is selected, SolidWorks will try to miter or otherwise create a corner treatment between the bodies, which will fail when the parts are parallel.

26. The four angled members need to be trimmed on both ends because they extend to the ends of the sketch entities rather than stopping at intersecting members. Initiate the Trim/Extend feature. Select the four angled members in the Bodies To Be Trimmed selection box. Select the four members created by the original rectangle as the Trimming Boundary, and make sure that the Bodies option is selected (as opposed to Face/Planar), as shown in Figure 36.30. Accept the feature when you are finished.

FIGURE 36.30
The model after step 26

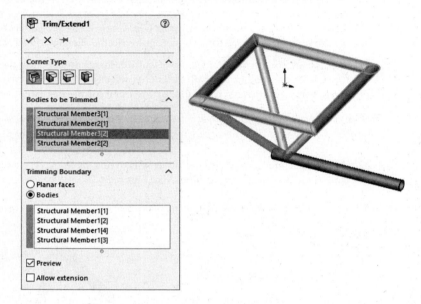

27. Create another Trim/Extend feature. This time, trim off the point end of the four angled members using the 10-inch horizontal pipe and the small segment as the trimming boundary. Half of the support structure has been modeled to this point.

28. Create the rest of the support structure by mirroring the existing bodies. Create a Mirror feature using the free end of the 10-foot-long member as the mirror plane and selecting all the bodies in the Bodies To Mirror selection box. Don't select the Merge Solids option, because you'll need to merge solids manually. Click OK to accept the feature when it's set up properly. The PropertyManager for the Mirror feature is shown in Figure 36.31.

NOTE An easy way to select all the bodies is to use the flyout FeatureManager; select the first body in the list, and Shift+select the last body.

29. Select the Combine feature (Insert ➤ Feature ➤ Combine), and set it to Add. Select the two 10-foot sections and the two smaller 1-foot sections to combine them into a single continuous body. Click OK to accept the feature. Also hide the 3D sketch.

30. Right-click the Cut List folder and select Update. Figure 36.32 shows before and after images of the Cut List folder.

31. Right-click the folder for the large-diameter cross member and select Properties. Change the Description field to read **Support Pod Members**.

FIGURE 36.31
The PropertyManager for the Mirror feature in step 28

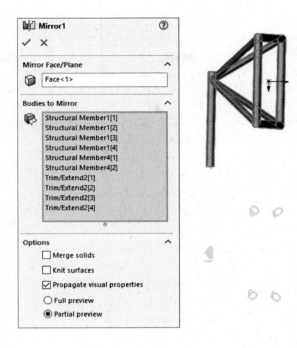

FIGURE 36.32
The Cut List folder in step 30

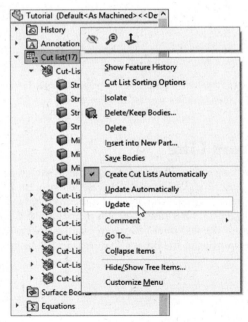

32. Use the Create Drawing From Part/Assembly button on the standard toolbar to make a drawing. Place the front, bottom, and isometric views, and then press the Esc key to quit placing views.

33. Select one of the views and choose Insert ➤ Table ➤ Weldment Cut List. When the PropertyManager displays, select the options that you want and click OK. Then place the table.

34. Click inside the bottom view, and from the Annotations toolbar, click Auto-Balloon. The finished drawing looks like Figure 36.33.

FIGURE 36.33
The finished drawing

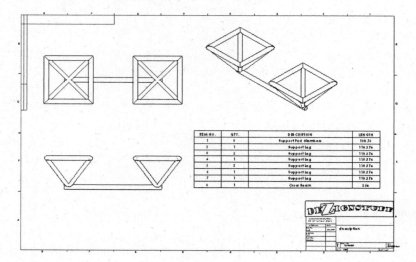

NOTE Relative views are difficult to create with a round pipe rather than a rectangular tube, although you can use planes as references for relative views.

The Bottom Line

Weldments are based on either a single 3D frame sketch or a set of 2D sketches, usually denoting the centerlines or edges of the various structural elements. This creates a special type of part in the same way that the Sheet Metal commands create a special type of part. Structural profiles are placed on the frame sketch to propagate and create individual bodies for the separate pieces of the weldment. Custom profiles are easily created as library features; you can add custom properties to the library features, and then the custom properties will propagate to the cut lists.

Master It   The first step in being able to model welded structures effectively is to have access to good libraries of structural section shapes. Whether you use the default installed libraries, use Toolbox libraries, or download individual structural shapes, building your library is key.

Move all of your library data into an area that is not affected by SolidWorks uninstalls or reinstalls—ideally, some location that would even survive an OS reinstall (i.e., not on your C: drive). You may want to have it on a network drive to share it with others. Hint: don't use mapped drives, instead use a UNC path such as \computer_name\shared_folder.

Redirect SolidWorks to look for Weldment Profiles in the local or network location you have specified.

Master It   Build a picnic table using a custom profile (1.5 × 5.5).

Master It   Create a drawing of the picnic table and add a cut list.

Chapter 37

Using Imported Geometry and Direct-Editing Techniques

Dealing with geometry imported from other CAD systems is often difficult, particularly in history-based systems. Imports aren't always clean, meaning they often need repairs. Sometimes, you might want to change it. Imported data is often called "dumb geometry" because it has no features. Imported data can be edited using Direct Editing tools and techniques.

The Direct Editing tools in SolidWorks enable you to change a part without having access to the history of features that created the part; however, they do create history-based features in SolidWorks. Direct editing works on both native and imported geometry either by simply moving faces or by editing the geometry directly rather than indirectly through feature definitions or sketches.

This chapter looks at the Import and Export tools available in SolidWorks and the Direct Editing tools that can be used to manipulate imported or native geometry.

IN THIS CHAPTER, YOU WILL LEARN TO:

- ◆ Understand how imported geometry works
- ◆ Examine the traditional role of Direct Editing tools
- ◆ Benefit from Direct Editing tools
- ◆ Import and repair solid geometry

Understanding the Basics of Imported Geometry

Geometry that's transferred between CAD packages is called *imported* geometry. The transfer usually happens through IGES (Initial Graphics Exchange Specification; pronounced *eye-jess*), STEP (Standard for the Exchange of Product), Parasolid, or ACIS (named for the initials of three people who created the standard: Alan, Charles, and Ian's System) formats. SolidWorks also reads some native CAD data directly. For example, SolidWorks can read data directly from versions of Pro/ENGINEER, Unigraphics/SDRC (NX), Inventor, Solid Edge, CADKEY, and Rhino, as Figure 37.1 shows. In most cases, features aren't transferred between CAD packages. The geometry that you wind up with is called "dumb" geometry because the list of features that the model had in its parent software is no longer there.

You can import data in two ways. The most common way is to use the Open dialog box and switch the Files Of Type to an imported file format. The other way is to use the Imported

Geometry feature by choosing Insert ➤ Features ➤ Imported Geometry from the menus. The Open dialog box creates a new part with the imported feature at the top of the FeatureManager, as shown in Figure 37.2. Using the Imported Geometry feature enables you to insert imported geometry anywhere you like within the FeatureManager, even after other features have been added.

FIGURE 37.1
SolidWorks opens neutral format files as well as several native formats.

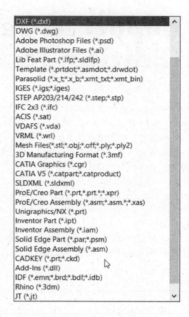

DXF (*.dxf)
DWG (*.dwg)
Adobe Photoshop Files (*.psd)
Adobe Illustrator Files (*.ai)
Lib Feat Part (*.lfp;*.sldlfp)
Template (*.prtdot;*.asmdot;*.drwdot)
Parasolid (*.x_t;*.x_b;*.xmt_txt;*.xmt_bin)
IGES (*.igs;*.iges)
STEP AP203/214/242 (*.step;*.stp)
IFC 2x3 (*.ifc)
ACIS (*.sat)
VDAFS (*.vda)
VRML (*.wrl)
Mesh Files(*.stl;*.obj;*.off;*.ply;*.ply2)
3D Manufacturing Format (*.3mf)
CATIA Graphics (*.cgr)
CATIA V5 (*.catpart;*.catproduct)
SLDXML (*.sldxml)
ProE/Creo Part (*.prt,*.prt.*;*.xpr)
ProE/Creo Assembly (*.asm;*.asm.*;*.xas)
Unigraphics/NX (*.prt)
Inventor Part (*.ipt)
Inventor Assembly (*.iam)
Solid Edge Part (*.par;*.psm)
Solid Edge Assembly (*.asm)
CADKEY (*.prt;*.ckd)
Add-Ins (*.dll)
IDF (*.emn;*.brd;*.bdf;*.idb)
Rhino (*.3dm)
JT (*.jt)

FIGURE 37.2
Imported geometry comes in without any feature history.

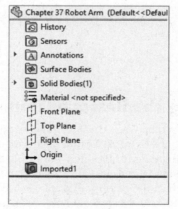

Chapter 37 Robot Arm (Default<<Defaul
- History
- Sensors
- ▸ Annotations
- Surface Bodies
- ▸ Solid Bodies(1)
- Material <not specified>
- Front Plane
- Top Plane
- Right Plane
- Origin
- Imported1

You can use the Data Migration tab in the CommandManager to find tasks that support imported geometry. The tools on this tab are shown in Figure 37.3.

Many of these tools aren't directly related to imports but may be frequently used with imported bodies. FeatureWorks is a part of the SolidWorks Professional bundle and is beyond the scope of this book; however, it's mentioned as one possible workflow for editing imported geometry toward the end of this chapter.

FIGURE 37.3
The SolidWorks Data Migration tab on the CommandManager helps you find Import tools.

Using SolidWorks 3D Interconnect

SolidWorks 3D Interconnect enables you to treat imported documents as (one-directionally inbound) associative to the original native format files. This means that if you import an Autodesk Inventor file using 3D Interconnect, and then change that file in Inventor, you can update the imported geometry in SolidWorks. Changes to the part in SolidWorks cannot be sent back through the link to the original native Inventor part. 3D Interconnect functionality is supported for the following systems:

◆ **CATIA V5:** .CATPart, .CATProduct for V5R8 – 5–6R2016

◆ **Autodesk Inventor:** .ipt for V6 – V2016, .iam for V11 – V2016

◆ **PTC:** .prt, .prt.*, .asm, .asm.* for Pro/ENGINEER 16 – Creo 3.0

◆ **Solid Edge:** .par, .asm, .psm for V18 – ST8

◆ **NX software:** .prt for UG 11 – NX 10

This functionality is turned on by default starting in SolidWorks 2017. You can control the settings for 3D Interconnect at Tools ➢ Options ➢ Import.

When a part is imported using 3D Interconnect, it comes in with the -> symbol that connotes external links. The external link works by first importing the "dumb" body geometry from the native file (much in the way the Parasolid body is stored within a SolidWorks part), and then reimporting the body from a changed file. It is better to get body data directly from the native file than it is to get it from a translated format such as IGES or even STEP—and in my opinion, this is the biggest advantage of using 3D Interconnect.

The claimed associative link is somewhat dubious. Primarily, the SolidWorks imported data is being saved internally as a Parasolid body in a separate SolidWorks part. There is no real link to the native format file in the sense that you are used to native SolidWorks parts being actively open and linked to a SolidWorks assembly.

Secondly, you are able (and have been able for some time) to do this reimport without using 3D Interconnect by simply using the Edit Definition function for an imported body. After all, it is this functionality that SolidWorks is using behind the scenes, automating it somewhat and giving it a fancy name. Whether this is more or less work than using the so-called associative nature of 3D Interconnect is for you to decide.

Again, my opinion is that because some direct modeling CAD packages are able to import data and directly edit that data (and SolidWorks is not able to do that, as you will see later in this chapter), SolidWorks probably felt as if they needed to answer this lack of functionality, even though the answer is predominantly smoke and mirrors.

Anyone with a little practical experience knows that importing data from CATIA can be challenging. Using 3D Interconnect to extract solid body data and convert it to Parasolid is likely the most reliable way to convert CATIA V5 data.

The rest of this chapter is written with the assumption that 3D Interconnect has been disabled. To work through the exercises as intended, I recommend that you turn 3D Interconnect off until you think you need it.

Gaining Experience with Imports

When SolidWorks imports data from another CAD program, the result is an imported feature in the FeatureManager. The example shown in Figure 37.2 is the situation you're typically looking for: the result is a single solid body. Frequently, imports don't come in this clean. When imports start giving you trouble, you'll see errors on a single body, or possibly multiple bodies, or even surface bodies. SolidWorks can address some types of errors automatically, and you can address some manually. From time to time and for various reasons, you might get such a messy part that you just want to try a different method to import it (for example, different import or export settings, or a different file type).

The best way to start to feel comfortable with imported data is to be exposed to a wide range of files—some that work and some that don't. This chapter isn't intended to be a short course on import repair, but repair is certainly part of the reality of working with imported data.

Understanding the Results of Imports

When you import geometrical data into SolidWorks, you can get several different types of results:

- Single solid body in a part file
- Assembly of multiple parts
- Multiple solid bodies in a part file
- Surface bodies in a part file
- Combination of solid and surface bodies in a part file

When you get an assembly of parts, SolidWorks uses the default template that you have designated in Tools ➤ Options ➤ Default Templates, creates new parts, and saves them to your hard drive automatically.

Some imports also create a report file with the extension *.rpt or *.err. This file includes statistics about the entities and precision of the data, filename, units, the originating system, and some information about errors that occurred during the import.

Figure 37.4 shows the first section of a report written for the import of an IGES file.

FIGURE 37.4

Report files can help you understand the contents of the imported file.

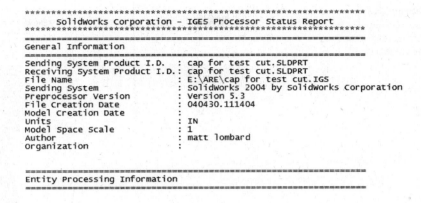

```
************************************************************
        Solidworks Corporation - IGES Processor Status Report
************************************************************
==========================================================
General Information
==========================================================
Sending System Product I.D.   : cap for test cut.SLDPRT
Receiving System Product I.D. : cap for test cut.SLDPRT
File Name                     : E:\ARE\cap for test cut.IGS
Sending System                : Solidworks 2004 by Solidworks Corporation
Preprocessor Version          : Version 5.3
File Creation Date            : 040430.111404
Model Creation Date           :
Units                         : IN
Model Space Scale             : 1
Author                        : matt lombard
Organization                  :


==========================================================
Entity Processing Information
==========================================================
```

DEMONSTRATING SOME DATA IMPORT

I'm going to import a few parts that don't come in perfectly and ask you to follow along with the files in the materials you downloaded from the website. This isn't so much a click-by-click tutorial as a "watch over my shoulder" demonstration with commentary.

Starting with a Parasolid import because Parasolids are the fastest and easiest, open the part called Chapter 37 Robot Arm.x_t from the download material for Chapter 37. You can open translated format files in a couple of ways. Many people look for an Import or Translate option in the File menu, but it's not there. You can use the Open command and select Parasolid from the Files Of Type drop-down list, but that's the slow way. I prefer to open a translated file using Windows Explorer, and drag and drop the file onto the SolidWorks window.

After you open the file, you'll notice a couple of things. The first thing that stands out to me is that the model displays in Shaded mode, regardless of how you have the display set. For example, I like to use Shaded With Edges, but imports always set it back to Shaded.

The next thing to notice is the Imported1 feature in the FeatureManager. In this case, the import was clean, so there are no warnings (yellow triangles) or errors (red circles). This isn't always a good indication of the state of the part, though, because some errors that SolidWorks knows about aren't displayed on the Imported Feature icon. To investigate closer, right-click the Imported1 feature and select Import Diagnosis, or click Import Diagnosis from the Evaluate tab of the CommandManager.

In this case, the model really is clean. Running Import Diagnosis is the only way you can really know this. Figure 37.5 shows the FeatureManager, the Import Diagnosis, and the part itself.

Next, open the Parasolid file called bad face.x_b. This one also imports without an error or warning on the Import feature, but there's clearly a missing face. It's easier to visualize the separate faces of the part if you change the Display mode to Shaded With Edges. If you examine the part closely, you can see that several faces aren't lined up square with the rest of the part. Notice also that there are small sliver faces. This may be intentional, or it may be part of the problem. Triangular faces and sliver faces (with very sharp corners, usually long and narrow) are often the source of errors in translated parts.

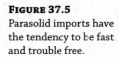

FIGURE 37.5
Parasolid imports have the tendency to be fast and trouble free.

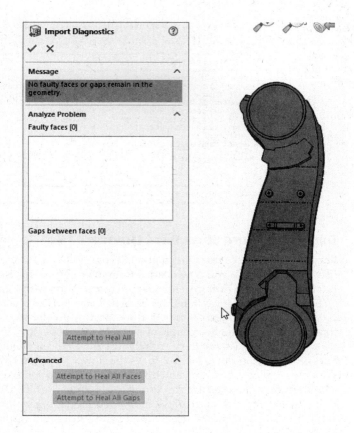

Right-click the Import feature and run the Import Diagnosis; you'll see the faulty face listed. Click the Attempt To Heal All button to fix the faulty face. Figure 37.6 shows the part with the faulty face.

Now open the Pro/ENGINEER file called bad face 2.prt.29. Pro/ENGINEER files often end with version numbers as their extensions. You need to be careful if you see a file that looks like a Pro/ENGINEER file with no version extension. SolidWorks used the *.prt extension for the first couple of years, and it still opens this type of file as a native file. You may still find some of those parts in circulation.

Open the file using the Import Geometry Directly option, switch the display to Shaded With Edges, and run an Import Diagnosis. The part has a bad face. If you click the face in the Faulty Faces list, you can see that the face is next to a small, pointy triangular face, shown in Figure 37.7. The Attempt To Heal All option takes care of it.

Import the same file, but this time choose the Analyze The Model Completely option. It should tell you that it recognizes 13 out of 13 features. Click the Features button and watch the part rebuild. Notice that this time the part comes up with a feature error. The error is on a fillet. It isn't an accident that the previous error was on a face next to a fillet face.

Notice that the Parasolid parts came up almost immediately, but the Pro/ENGINEER parts take several seconds to process the data. As the imported files become larger and larger and branch into assemblies, this difference in processing time becomes more and more pronounced.

FIGURE 37.6
Three-sided and sliver faces are often the sources of errors with imported parts.

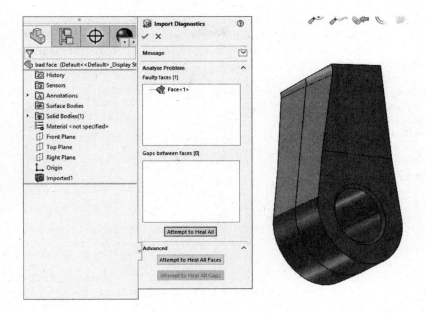

FIGURE 37.7
Importing the same data in different ways can give you different results.

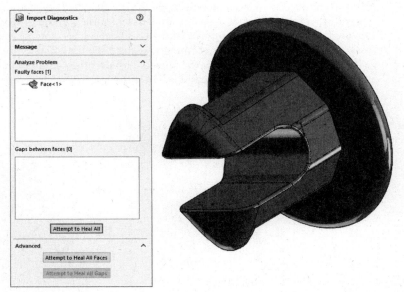

Next is a sheet metal part. Open sheet metal.x_t. Change the display to Shaded With Edges. The part looks good, and Import Diagnosis says that it's okay. Because this is a sheet metal part, and it appears to have a consistent thickness, you'll try to flatten it. Click the Sheet Metal CommandManager tab and click the Insert Bends icon (on the far-right side). Select the big flat face as the face to remain stationary (the top selection box), and click the green checkmark button to accept the result.

The sheet metal features are added to the part, but notice in Figure 37.8 that they have failed. A close inspection of the part reveals that there's a small ledge between the big flat face and the inside bend on both ends. This was probably a modeling error rather than a translation error. You may be able to fix this to make it usable as a sheet metal part; but for imported geometry editing, you'll need to go to the end of this chapter. Here, I cover the results of attempting to repair this model.

FIGURE 37.8
Very small errors can cause special functionality in SolidWorks not to work. Repairing those errors isn't always straightforward.

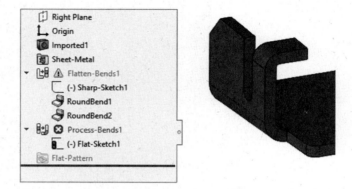

The last part I want to show in this "watch over my shoulder" demonstration is a part that I consider to be a complete loss. This is an IGES file that came from an Autodesk Mechanical product. In the download materials, open the file called valve body.igs. This part takes several seconds to import. When it does import, it has 10 surface bodies, dozens of face errors, and some obvious problems with a couple of faces that somehow became out of control. This is one of the reasons so many users do not recommend using IGES files. This type of error is more prevalent with IGES files than other formats. Figure 37.9 shows the FeatureManager and the part on the screen. Again, notice that the locations where the huge problem faces come off the model are pointy triangular faces.

FIGURE 37.9
Some parts are simply beyond repair.

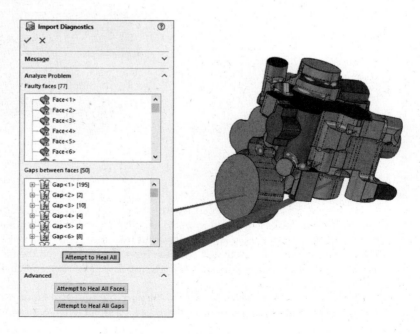

Very often you will find that the import results between versions of SolidWorks differ. For example, in SolidWorks 2018, this valve body imports with enough success that you might be able to model over the surface bodies and eventually piece together the original model. Earlier versions didn't get that close.

NOTE If you get an error that says "There are no points that exist in this file" when you import an IGES file, it's probably because you have Scan To 3D selected in your add-ins list. IGES is one of the accepted file types for bringing in point cloud data, and Scan To 3D assumes you are trying to use the IGES for that. Scan To 3D is an add-in that comes with SolidWorks Professional, not with SolidWorks Standard, so it's beyond the scope of this book. To disable it, choose Tools ➤ Add-ins and deselect the check mark in the box next to Scan To 3D.

If you get a part that's this bad, your first move should be to try to get better data from the source. If that isn't available, you'll have an uphill battle trying to make this part work. Automatic healing with the Import Diagnosis isn't going to touch this part. The repair is going to be an exercise in manual surface modeling. If you don't have the patience for that, you could try solid modeling from the reference faces on the part. If you look closely at the interaction of some of the fillets, it won't be a surprise that the translation failed so badly. Many of the fillets are badly hacked together. In addition, if this is a casting, someone is going to need to apply draft to the part, and with all the fillets on it, this part isn't going to lend itself to that very well.

Handling Import Errors

Import errors are usually caused by differences between the exporting and importing CAD software vendors. Some imports are more prone to errors than others. For example, the IGES format is interpreted different ways by different software vendors, so it's very prone to errors.

Another type of error is due to tolerance or accuracy issues. CATIA is notorious for having very large tolerances on exported data. This enables CATIA to work with large data sets more easily, but it means that when the geometry is read into SolidWorks, which typically requires more accurate data, you can see a lot of errors. The fact that the CATIA-to-SolidWorks translation is one of the most problematic in the CAD industry seems odd because SolidWorks and CATIA are both owned by Dassault Systèmes, but the difficulties have persisted for more than a decade, so it isn't a technological difficulty; it's a business decision.

Repairing Import Errors Automatically

SolidWorks has a tool called Import Diagnostics. Import Diagnostics can run automatically or manually to find the errors in imported data and to make repairs if possible. You can access Import Diagnostics by right-clicking an imported feature in the FeatureManager, as long as there are no native SolidWorks features that follow the imported feature. Figure 37.10 shows typical results from a faulty import.

Sometimes, the errors that Import Diagnostics finds are things you can see, such as missing faces, and sometimes, they are things you can't see, like the edges of a face that don't intersect or inconsistent face normals. When errors can be found and repaired by Import Diagnostics, that's the best way to go.

FIGURE 37.10
Import Diagnostics helps you find and repair errors in imported data.

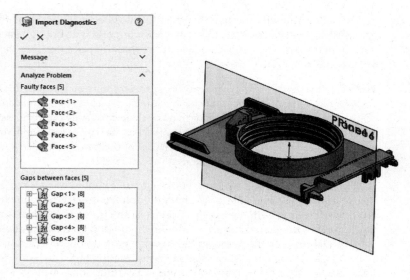

REPAIRING IMPORT ERRORS MANUALLY

Some errors are so big that the Import Diagnostics cannot fix them. An example of this type of error is when a face is missing altogether from the imported data. When something like this happens, the only thing you can do is resort to surface modeling. If the import leaves you with surface bodies, and it cannot repair them automatically, you must be able to remove the bad faces and replace them with new faces that you construct. This is all about using Surface tools to create the new face, extending and possibly trimming the new face to fit into the gap caused by the bad face or faces, and then knitting everything together back into a solid. This may be an oversimplification of the workflow for manual import repair, but it's essentially the big-picture steps that you must go through to get the task done.

Some models are so bad that you can't fix them, or they wouldn't be worth your time to fix. If automatic repairs don't work and simple manual repairs don't work, the next thing to do is to go back to the source of the file and ask for better data.

> **BEST PRACTICE**
>
> Whenever you export data to another CAD system, it's considered best practice (and professional courtesy) to *round trip* (save out, then read back in) the data to make sure you can accurately read the data you saved out.

If you get bad data, you don't have access to the source, and automatic and manual errors prevent you from using the data, then the next best thing is to rebuild the part using the error-filled data as a reference. This is never a pretty thing, but if you really need the data to be clean, and there is no other way, this is what you need to do.

You can take measurements in one file and build a new part in another file, build one file in the context of an assembly directly over the problem file, or even rebuild it as a multibody part.

TRICKING DATA INTO WORKING

Occasionally, you can employ tricks to heal problem imports. Simply saving out of SolidWorks as Parasolid and reading back in repeatedly can sometimes heal troublesome imported geometry. I frequently use Rhino to import problem files and then export from Rhino as a Parasolid. Rhino is an inexpensive surfacing application. You can read more about it at www.rhino3d.com. You can download and install a trial version that allows you to save 25 times. Rhino works great as a translator because it reads and writes many file types that SolidWorks doesn't read. Sometimes, when I get a very bad IGES file, I read it into Rhino, save it out as Parasolid, and then read the Parasolid into SolidWorks. Sometimes, this repairs the data to the point that SolidWorks can deal with it more effectively.

This isn't to say that Rhino is a better file translator than SolidWorks, because this workaround doesn't always improve things. It's sometimes effective, and because it's free, the only thing that trying it costs you is time.

ENSURING GOOD DATA

If you can't get a SolidWorks file from someone who needs to send you data, the type of translation file that you do get has a huge influence on the likelihood that your translation will be successful. Ask for data in this order:

1. **Parasolid (including native formats that use Parasolid, such as NX, Unigraphics, and Solid Edge).** Parasolid can come in text format (*.x_t) or binary format (*.x_b). You may also see file extensions such as .xmttxt from older versions of Unigraphics. Of these, the binaries are smaller, but the text files have WordPad readable and editable headers that can be useful in various situations, such as correcting units or part scaling, as well as telling what the parent CAD program was.

TIP CATIA does not export to Parasolid. CATIA users must save to STEP, and then download and install a free STEP-to-Parasolid convertor to generate a Parasolid file.

2. **STEP (AP 214 or AP 203).** The AP stands for application protocol. Most mechanical CAD programs use these two protocols, which were developed for automotive and configuration-controlled design (read more at www.steptools.com/library/standard/step_2.html).

3. **ACIS.** ACIS creates *.sat files.

4. ***.VDAFS, *.VDA ().** This is a German automotive geometry transfer format.

5. **IGES.** Because of the age and lack of clear definition in the IGES format, little about it is truly standard anymore, and many geometry-creation-software packages export data that SolidWorks cannot read correctly. Although this format is a standard for old-timers, it's one you probably want to avoid unless you're getting data from someone you know will give you something usable.

Another advantage of the Parasolid data is that SolidWorks reads it so quickly. A large IGES or STEP file can take minutes to read in, where SolidWorks can read equivalent Parasolid data in a couple of seconds. After the data is read into SolidWorks, it should all be the same, with no difference between data from Parasolid and any other source, because it's all converted to Parasolid to be stored inside the SolidWorks file. Parasolid reads in very quickly, so it saves time.

Whether or not the data you receive is of value to you depends in part on what you want to do with it. If your data is for a visual representation and not a CAD-accurate NURBS (Non-Uniform Rational B-Spline) model, you may be able to accept a wider range of data types. If you're looking for manufacturing quality data, dealing with some formats is simply not worth your time. The following file types are mesh data that SolidWorks can read and are useful for visual data, but useless for clean NURBS data:

*.stl: Stereolithography, typically used for rapid prototypes

*.vrml: Virtual reality markup language, typically used for games; an old format that allowed color to be transmitted with the mesh geometry

*.cgr: CATIA graphics

Converting Point Cloud Data

One of the most common import questions is how to import data from file formats such as *.obj or *.3ds, among others. These file types are mesh files, which means they are simply point cloud data. SolidWorks and most other CAD programs create geometry that's based on NURBS data, where the surfaces are represented by very accurate mathematics. Mesh data is represented by points in space, which is much faster to work with because it's similar to the data used by graphics cards and drivers to display curvy shapes. Mesh data is used by Hollywood, video game developers, and computer graphics studios; NURBS data is used in engineering and manufacturing. It's easy to convert NURBS to mesh, but it is more difficult to convert mesh to NURBS. The mesh-to-NURBS conversion can be done, but complex software and specialized expertise is needed for it to happen correctly.

NOTE   SolidWorks can make the mesh-to-NURBS conversion with the Scan To 3D software. Because this isn't included in the Standard package, it's beyond the scope of this book and isn't covered here.

Understanding the Traditional Role of Direct Editing Tools

Traditionally, direct-editing CAD software has lived by the rule that how you create geometry shouldn't affect how you edit the geometry. Therefore, direct-editing CAD packages still use functions like Extrude and Revolve to build parts, but they won't return to those functions to edit the part; instead, they directly manipulate faces of the part by moving, offsetting, and rotating.

CAD software that depends on Direct Editing tools has existed for a long time. Some direct-editing CAD products have appeared on the scene and have renewed an interest in direct-editing techniques. Until this recent resurgence, the direct-editing programs were seen as old-fashioned and inferior to parametric history-based programs.

One way to think of direct editing is that it leaves the intelligence in the software. In history-based techniques, you put the intelligence in the data.

Technically, what SolidWorks does when it works with imported featureless geometry is not direct editing, because it leaves a trail of history-based features behind, which is very much opposed to most of the benefits you get from true Direct Editing tools, such as lack of rebuild time, lack of a history tree, and so on. If you want to research direct editing in the form of synchronous technology developed by Siemens PLM, you can find a free, short book that I wrote on that topic at `https://www.plm.automation.siemens.com/en/campaigns/single_topic.cfm?Component=247520&ComponentTemplate=186312`

History-based modelers are still popular with users who design things. There must be more to this story, because the direct-editing scheme has some weaknesses. There are situations in which certain edits cannot be made in a straightforward way or reversing a set of edits doesn't result in the original configuration.

This background information is important as a part of the overall discussion of the place these tools have in the SolidWorks software. Adding Direct Editing tools to SolidWorks isn't an earth-shattering change, but it's of secondary importance. The Direct Editing tools in SolidWorks are a bit odd because direct editing stands as an opposite to history-based techniques. In SolidWorks, the Direct Editing tools are *within* history-based software. You don't really get all of the available benefit from direct editing when it's done inside of the history-based method.

Understanding the Strengths and Limitations of Direct Editing Tools in SolidWorks

Some of the selling points for the direct-editing CAD tools are that you don't have to worry about how a part was made (you just make the changes you want to make) and that feature trees with "history" always include feature rebuilds (and users tend to complain about these rebuilds taking a long time, especially for large parts and assemblies).

Without a doubt, grappling with feature order and feature rebuild times are problems that SolidWorks users face daily and often complain about.

These are direct-editing strengths:

◆ Feature order problems are avoided.

◆ Rebuild time is avoided.

◆ Changes are more intuitive, being geometry-based rather than logic-based.

◆ How something was made doesn't matter.

Probably the most serious limitation of the Direct Editing tools is that after a face has been eliminated from the model, you cannot bring it back using more Direct Editing tools. For example, consider the part in Figure 37.11.

If you change the bottom square area such that the flat face between the bottom square and the arc disappears, you cannot get it back by just moving the face back to where it was; you would have to move the face and then make a cut to reinstate the flat face. This limitation is less serious when the Direct Editing tool is just another tool within a history-based modeler, because you can resort to the more powerful history-based tools to compensate, but with a dedicated direct-editing-only tool, you'll be up against a more difficult task.

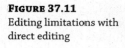

FIGURE 37.11
Editing limitations with
direct editing

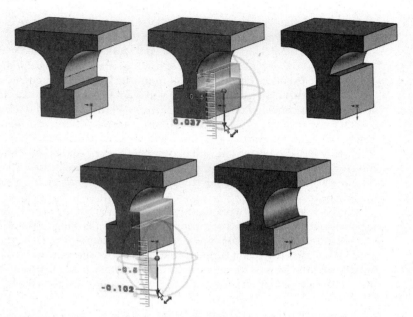

Other limitations of direct-editing-only CAD software "have to do with" or "are related to" features that themselves are some sort of process, such as fillets or shells or extruded sketch text. Although fillets and shells are two of the most problematic features for history-based modeling, they are also two features that create the biggest limitations for direct-editing software.

Using SolidWorks Direct Editing Tools

So how does SolidWorks, a history-based system, incorporate the advantages of direct-editing techniques, which are *not* typically thought of as history-based? What does it look like when contradictory regimes collide and start sharing ideas? SolidWorks has taken ideas from a history-free scheme and incorporated them into a history-based scheme.

First, I'll show you how this works in a simple example. Using the part from Figure 37.11, Figure 37.12 shows the FeatureManager and the original sketch. Notice that the original sketch hasn't changed, but the part itself has. Rolling back eliminates the Move Face features, and making changes to the original sketch changes the starting points for the Move Face features when they are unrolled.

You may be able to imagine that in a part with a much longer feature tree, where the relationships between the faces and the features are more complex, overriding that complexity by editing a face directly could have some appeal.

FIGURE 37.12
Direct edits in a
history-based part

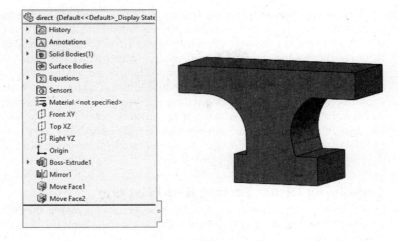

Using Move Face

When it comes down to it, the direct-editing capabilities in SolidWorks are primarily represented by the Move Face feature. There are other features like Delete Face, and some of the body transformation tools, but Move Face is the primary tool.

Move Face enables you to move (offset, rotate or translate) a selection of faces that does not have to correspond to any features. They don't even have to connect. As long as translating or rotating the selected faces can work by extending or trimming neighboring faces, Move Face will probably work. The limitations that most often cause Move Face edits to fail are tangencies that can't be extended or situations that require a new face to be created.

For example, Figure 37.13 shows the top section of the imported rivet being moved by the Move Face tool. It required the selection of 48 faces to do this, dragging along the graphical interface.

FIGURE 37.13
The Move Face
tool in action

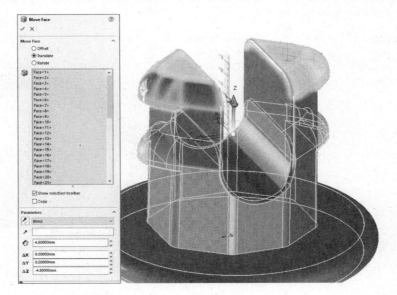

Because this is imported geometry, and the edit is something other than a cut or added geometry, Move Face and direct edit are really something different and extremely powerful. To work this way, you need to have an intuitive grasp of the NURBS or BREP model. You don't have to worry about which faces are controlled by which features, or which sketch drives which feature; you just select the faces you want to change and tell the software how you want to change them. At least that is the concept in traditional direct-editing software. But as I mentioned earlier, SolidWorks is not traditional direct-editing software; it's a history-based modeler. SolidWorks can still do this edit, but in true history-based modeling fashion, it has to record the edit as a feature, which a true direct editor would not do. This is the main conflict when it comes to SolidWorks and direct editing. SolidWorks can do some of the direct-editing functions, but it does so in a very nondirect-edit sort of way.

Combining Direct Editing with History

SolidWorks has several features that don't create new geometry; they edit existing geometry only, whether it's native or imported. These include the tools from the Direct Editing tab of the CommandManager, shown in Figure 37.14.

FIGURE 37.14
The tools from the Direct Editing tab of the CommandManager

I'll show you a slightly more complex example. In traditional SolidWorks usage, if you wanted to move the face indicated in Figure 37.15, you would go back and edit the sketch or feature that was used to create it. That would be easy enough, and the fillets would update to match the new geometry.

FIGURE 37.15
Fillets greatly complicate direct-editing schemes.

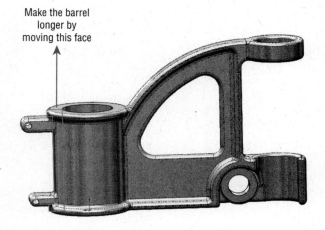

Make the barrel longer by moving this face

A proponent of direct-editing software would say that first finding the feature you need to change is difficult, and then waiting to unbuild the model back to that sketch, then waiting for the change to rebuild all the features after the sketch is complete, and finally dealing with the downstream features like fillets that might fail due to the changes is frustrating—and he would be right. (You can find a feature in the tree by right-clicking geometry in the graphics window and selecting Go To Feature In Tree.) The problem is that the part, as shown in Figure 37.15, cannot be changed at all in the traditional direct-editing scheme. In the direct-editing scheme, the fillets are just faces; they aren't intelligent features. If you move faces they are attached to, you have to also explicitly tell the fillet faces what to do.

While the direct-editing implementation in software such as Solid Edge is smart enough to make changes to models with fillets on them, the Direct Editing tools in SolidWorks are less sophisticated and cannot deal with the fillets at all.

Here's how to simplify the part by suppressing fillets and using the Move Face feature to change the part (see Figure 37.16). In order to do this, you will have had to make sure that no fillet features have children other than other fillet features. Here, I've suppressed the fillets and moved the ring around the top of the barrel as well as the mounting boss.

FIGURE 37.16

Using Move Face to extend the length of the barrel of the cast part after the fillets have been removed

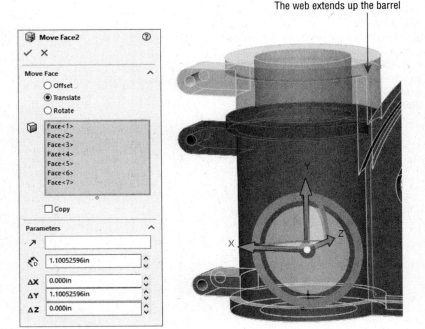

In order to make this move, I had to select seven faces:

- Top of the ring
- Bottom of the ring on the left
- Bottom of the ring on the right

◆ Top of the boss

◆ Bottom of the boss

◆ Full round on the end of the boss

◆ Hole in the mounting boss

Notice how the web now extends up the side of the barrel. This is the type of edit that would be clumsy in SolidWorks history-based tools if it were what you wanted to do. In direct edit, it's the kind of edit that would be clumsy if it were *not* what you wanted to do.

This is one of the limitations of direct-editing techniques in general—not a limitation of SolidWorks, but a limitation of the concept as implemented in SolidWorks.

Figure 37.17 shows where the weakness of using the Direct Editing tools within SolidWorks begins to show up. The first feature in the part is a revolve that uses a sketch. The last feature in the part is a Move Face feature that moves the faces created by the revolve. So, if you want to change the geometry of the barrel, it's controlled by two different features. If you make the sketch a specific size, the Move Face feature changes it. Move Face can change only relative to a starting point; it cannot make something a specific dimension.

FIGURE 37.17
The Move Face features put some geometry in double jeopardy because it can be changed from two different places.

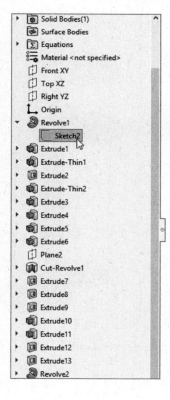

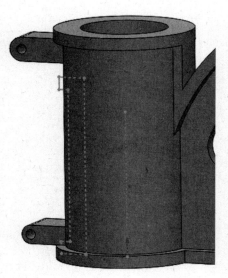

Some SolidWorks power users consider this double-jeopardy condition sloppy design or bad practice. You can make a strong case that the Direct Editing tools should not be used on native SolidWorks parts and that you should edit the feature the way it was created. There is certainly a place for that argument. But I know from my own modeling work that sometimes changing a feature way back in the tree can have unintended repercussions later in the tree, just due to the limitations of history-based modeling. Using a Move Face feature late in the tree avoids fixing lots of propagated errors. Is that a cheap, sleazy cheat? You will have to decide that for yourself.

Combining Direct Editing with Imported Geometry

Regardless of any argument against using Direct Editing tools on native SolidWorks data, there can be no such argument against using them on imported data. Direct Editing tools may have their limitations, but when dealing with imported geometry in SolidWorks, your choices are limited, as you see from the following:

- Direct Editing tools
- Cut and add modeling
- Manual Surfacing tools
- FeatureWorks deconstruction

When faced with these options, Direct Editing tools look like the safe choice. The big problem is that, if the part is covered with fillets, you may not be able to change much. In cases like that, you might use a combination of tools, such as FeatureWorks to remove fillets, and then directly edit to make changes.

Tutorial: Importing and Repairing Solid Geometry

This tutorial walks you through the button clicks to import CAD data from IGES and make some edits:

1. From the download data, open the file called cover.igs. You can open this file by selecting it in the Open dialog box (File ➤ Open) or by dragging and dropping it from Windows Explorer.

2. Right-click the Imported1 feature and run Import Diagnosis. Notice that Import Diagnosis finds no errors on the part.

3. Look at the inside of the part, in the area near the part origin, and notice that, on one end of the tab, all the fillets come to a point, as shown in Figure 37.18. This is clearly not right, although Import Diagnosis didn't identify it as a problem.

FIGURE 37.18
A corner where three fillets come together isn't correct.

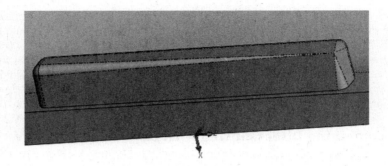

4. Open a sketch on the flat face from which the tab protrudes. Right-click any edge where the tab intersects the sketch face and select Select Tangency. Then click the Convert Entities toolbar button, click the green checkmark icon to accept the result, and exit the sketch.

5. Right-click one of the long faces of the tab and select Select Tangency. This selects all but two faces of the tab. There are 16 faces altogether. Activate the Delete Face feature, select the Delete and Patch option, select the two remaining faces of the tab, and accept the result. The model should remain a solid model, and the tab should be replaced by a smooth face.

6. Select the sketch created in step 4 and extrude it to a blind depth of 0.050 inch. Apply a fillet around the end face with a radius of 0.010 inch.

7. Activate the Move Face feature. Select all the faces of the two side tabs and the Snap feature on the end. Use the Translate option and the Right (YZ) plane as the direction and use a distance of 0.25 inch. You should have no less than 21 faces selected. Faces that are parallel to the translate direction don't need to be selected, because they're automatically extended or trimmed to fit. If you're having trouble selecting the right faces, refer to Figure 37.19 and open the finished part from the download materials on the website called `Tutorial1finished.sldprt`.

FIGURE 37.19
Moving tabs and Snap in a single Move Face feature

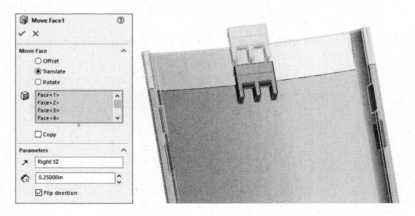

8. Save the part under a different name and exit.

Tutorial: Flex and Freeform

This tutorial steps you through importing and editing geometry using the Move Face, Flex, and Freeform features in SolidWorks:

1. Open the Parasolid file from the Wiley website called `ellipse.x_t`.

2. Increase the size of the part by using the Move Face feature with the Offset option. You can enter the offset distance in the appropriate field of the PropertyManager. Use an offset distance of about 0.08 inch. Make sure only the elliptical face of the model is selected.

3. Activate the Flex feature and use the following settings (as shown in Figure 37.20):

    ◆ Select the body in the graphics window in the top selection box.

    ◆ Select the Bending option in the Flex Input section.

    ◆ Select Hard Edges in the Flex Input section.

FIGURE 37.20
Using Flex Bending to bend an imported part

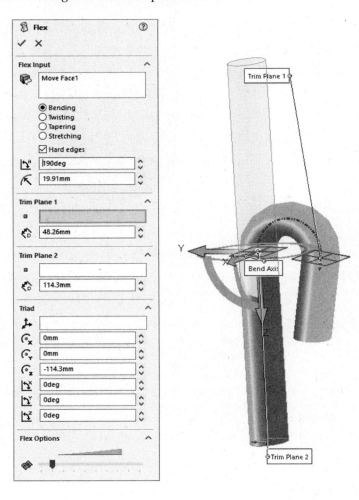

♦ Select 190deg for the angle.

♦ In Trim Plane 1, set the distance to 48.26 millimeters (or 1.9 inches).

♦ In Trim Plane 2, set the distance to 114.3 millimeters (or 4.5 inches).

Accept the feature when you are finished.

4. Open a sketch on the Front (XY) plane, orient the view normal to it, and then sketch an ellipse with one end of the major axis at the origin and the rest dimensioned, as shown in Figure 37.21.

FIGURE 37.21
Sketching an ellipse

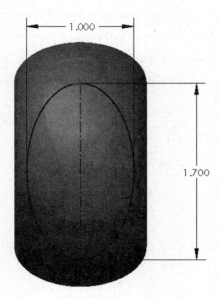

5. Initiate a split line (Insert ➤ Curves ➤ Split Line) and select the bent face of the part. Accept the feature when you are finished.

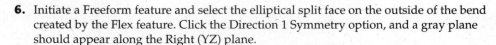

NOTE The Split Line option splits the outside and the inside of the curved face. If you select Shaded With Edges, you can see the split on both sides.

6. Initiate a Freeform feature and select the elliptical split face on the outside of the bend created by the Flex feature. Click the Direction 1 Symmetry option, and a gray plane should appear along the Right (YZ) plane.

7. Click the Add Curves button, snap the cursor to the Symmetry plane and click to add a curve. The Symmetry plane will highlight orange when it's selected. Add a second curve parallel to the first one about one-third of the way from the Symmetry plane to the edge of the split.

8. Click the Add Points button and place a point approximately as shown in Figure 37.22. Place a point on the second curve in approximately the same location as the first point. Figure 37.22 shows one point on each curve. Click the Add Points button to deselect it when you are finished.

FIGURE 37.22
Locating a point

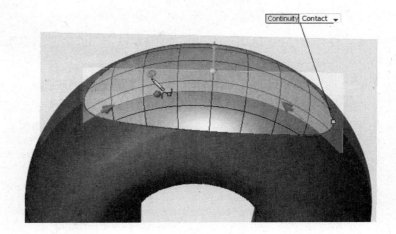

9. Change the Continuity flag pointing to the edge of the split from Contact to Curvature.

10. Click the curve on the Symmetry plane, and then click the point on that curve. Drag the arrow handle to pull the point away from the part approximately as shown in Figure 37.23.

FIGURE 37.23
Pulling the point to create a freeform shape from the existing face

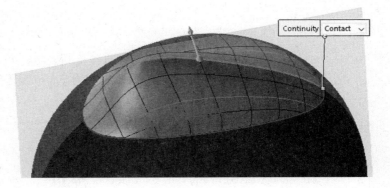

11. Click the second curve, and then click and move the second point in a way similar to the first point. When you are finished, the part should look similar to Figure 37.24.

12. Save the file using a different name.

FIGURE 37.24
The finished free-
form surface

The Bottom Line

In recent years, Direct Editing tools have received lots of hyped press and marketing attention. However, CAD tools dedicated to working primarily as Direct Editing tools aren't going to overtake the tools used by professionals who design and model for production. If anything, they'll be used primarily by non-CAD specialists for simple editing and simple concept development, and possibly by downstream data consumers such as FEA analysts or CNC (Computer Numerical Control) machinists.

The Direct Editing tools available within SolidWorks are powerful and are becoming more powerful with each release. Although they may be best applied to imported data, they can also be applied to native SolidWorks data. This brings up questions of best practice and duplication of effort. Sometimes, the changes involved in editing a feature near the top of a long feature tree can be time-consuming compared to simply moving a couple of faces.

Master It   Familiarize yourself with existing import and export options. Use a model without errors for practice. If you have another CAD package available to you, use that for practice as well.

Master It   Open an assembly from one of the chapters on assemblies and export it. Then import it to see how it behaves and what you get. The practice of export/import is called a *round trip*. It is one way you can verify that the software has written good output data.

Be aware that importing an assembly will save automatically named part files on your hard drive. Make sure that the filenames are not overwriting or causing conflicts with other part files.

Master It   The direct editing features are

◆   Move Face

◆   Delete Face

You can also perform any function that affects bodies rather than features.

Take the `Chapter 37 - casting direct edit.sldprt` part and practice removing fillets (using the Delete Face feature with the Delete and Patch option) without using any history-based tricks like rolling back or suppressing. Start with a simple loop like the filleted edges of the pie-shaped cut out in the web of the part.

Remember that unlike true direct-editing CAD tools, SolidWorks leaves a history-based feature every time you use the Delete Face.

Chapter 38

Using Plastic Features

SolidWorks has several tools that were specifically designed to model and evaluate plastic parts. These tools can help simplify and standardize some of the complex repetitive tasks involved with plastic part design.

You can manually do all the work that these tools automate, which is useful when the automated tools don't provide the necessary options or flexibility. The more complex your models, the more comfortable you need to be with workaround techniques.

Because of the specific needs of plastic part modelers SolidWorks also has a set of powerful evaluation tools that help you examine your models to check the amount of draft, thickness, and location of undercuts. Finding design-related manufacturability problems in manufacturing is expensive. Finding them in the design office is far less expensive and conserves time. Having a good grasp of the evaluation tools is an important component of good plastic part and mold modeling practice.

This chapter is written for those of you who are already experienced in plastics practice and terminology, but who need to understand the SolidWorks tools used with the plastic and mold features. In this chapter, I assume that you already have a grasp of basic plastics and mold design and terminology.

IN THIS CHAPTER, YOU WILL LEARN TO:

◆   Explore Plastic features

◆   Use plastic evaluation tools

Using Plastic Features

The Plastic features available in SolidWorks are Mounting Boss, Snap Hook, Snap Groove, Vent, Lip/Groove, and Indent, as well as the more standard Draft and Shell. These features offer standardized but flexible geometry to help you make more consistent models more quickly and with less tiresome repetition. You can find most of the features discussed in this section on the Fastening Features toolbar. The remaining features are on the Features toolbar.

Some of these features have applications beyond just molded plastic parts. Many molding, casting, or *net shape* processes exist in plastic materials, as well as metals, ceramics, and composites.

Using the Mounting Boss

The Mounting Boss feature enables you to place a boss with fins and either a hole or a pin on the end. It doesn't enable you to place a counterbored hole or a through hole to facilitate screw bosses. It's aimed primarily at press pins rather than screw bosses.

Figure 38.1 shows the Mounting Boss PropertyManager along with the preview of the boss in progress. The part used in this figure is in the download materials available from the Wiley website, with the filename Chapter 38 - right frame.sldprt.

FIGURE 38.1
A mounting boss in progress

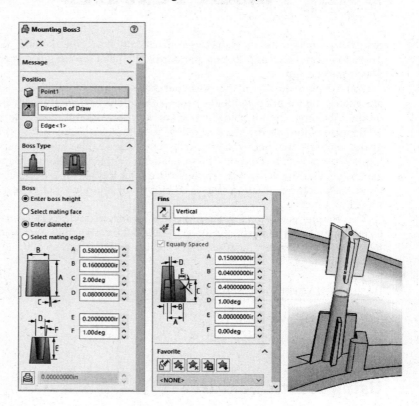

The workflow for the Mounting Boss feature is as follows:

1. Select a spot on the part that represents where the boss will attach to the part. This can be either a flat or curved face. In the example in Figure 38.1, because I selected a curved face, it's necessary to also supply a direction of pull. If you select a flat face, the Direction selection box in the next step won't be available.

2. Select a plane, planar face, edge, or axis to establish the axis of the boss. This is usually the direction of draw. Notice in the part shown in Figure 38.1 that an axis established early in the part is named as the Direction Of Draw. This step is optional. The default is the direction normal to the face selected in step 1.

3. Select an existing circular edge to align the boss. The new boss is concentric with the circular edge. This step is also optional. You can choose to use dimensions to locate the boss *after the feature is created*. If you use dimensions, you cannot locate the boss while the PropertyManager is active.

4. The Boss panel of the Mounting Boss PropertyManager is used to establish the height and other dimensions of the central boss. Diameter and draft dimensions are obvious. You can establish height by a dimension or by an "up to" face using the Select Mating Face option. There's no option for an "offset from face" end condition.

5. The Fins panel of the Mounting Boss PropertyManager is used to control the alignment, draft, height, width, and patterning of the ribs around the boss. The first box is for a direction vector such as a plane, edge, or axis to establish the rotational orientation of the ribs. You cannot use a sketch for this. The significance of the dimensional values is obvious. The Fin Pattern function is also obvious except for the Equally Spaced option, which is available only when the number selected is 2. Then you must select a vector to establish the orientation of the fins, which form a right angle for a corner.

6. The Mounting Hole/Pin panel enables you to specify a pin or hole boss and the associated sizes. It's interesting to me that it doesn't enable through holes or counterbore holes from the outside of the part, along with associated screw sizes for clearance.

7. SolidWorks has renamed Favorites in the rest of the software to Styles; however, in the Mounting Boss and the Lip/Groove, it's still called Favorites, and it saves settings like other Favorites/Styles functionality.

8. After you have successfully accepted the creation of the boss, if you didn't use a circular edge to locate the boss (step 3), you can expand the Mounting Boss feature in the FeatureManager and edit the 3D sketch under the boss. Inside this sketch is a point, which you can dimension to locate precisely. Remember that dimensions in 3D sketches follow some special rules. To get orthogonal dimensions parallel to X, Y, or Z axes, you'll need to dimension from planes. Three-dimensional sketch dimensions don't snap to horizontal or vertical orientations like 2D sketches.

   If you select a flat face for the initial position of the boss, you get a 2D sketch instead of a 3D sketch.

The features created by this tool aren't manually editable. They aren't made of extrudes and Rib features that are accessible behind the Mounting Boss interface. You must go through the Mounting Boss PropertyManager to edit the features, and you cannot edit sketches used to make the features. You can use Move Face to change sizes if you need to make something asymmetrical. As with any SolidWorks feature, you can access dimensions by double-clicking the feature in the FeatureManager or in the graphics window.

To make a screw boss instead of a pin boss, use the optional setting for Hardware Boss in the Mounting Boss PropertyManager, shown in Figure 38.2.

An effective way to pattern a single Mounting Boss feature around a part is to use the Sketch Driven Pattern feature. This feature uses a sketch with a set of points where each point represents the center of a patterned instance. Refer to the model in the download materials and examine the Sketch Driven Pattern option at the bottom of the FeatureManager. Use the Chapter 38 - right frame.sldprt file and change to the "nonmirror" configuration if it isn't already there.

FIGURE 38.2
Using the Hardware
Boss option

Using the Snap Hook and Snap Hook Groove

Snap Hook and Snap Hook Groove are two separate features. Lip/Groove combines both functions into a single PropertyManager to help you get results that work together more easily. Figure 38.3 shows the PropertyManager for the Snap Hook feature, along with a completed hook.

FIGURE 38.3
The Snap Hook
PropertyManager
with a completed
Hook feature

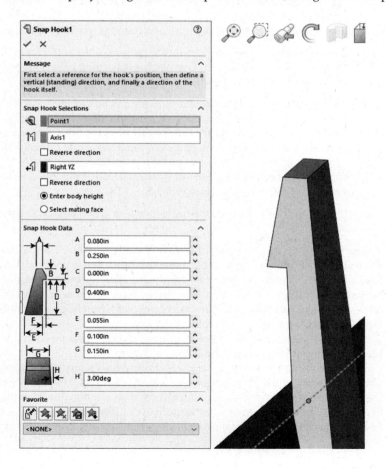

The workflow for the Snap Hook feature goes like this:

1. Select a spot on the model that corresponds to the center of the undercut edge where the hook intersects the part. It looks like you can select a face or an edge when you first create the feature, but the software always converts the selection to a 3D sketch point when the feature is accepted.

2. Select a vector (face, edge, or axis, not a sketch) to set the vertical orientation of the hook, or the "top."

3. Select another vector to define the "front" of the hook (the undercut side).

4. Choose to select a mating face or enter a number to define the height of the hook.

This feature uses a 3D sketch point where you made the selection in step 1. You cannot dimension this point while setting up the feature; you can dimension this point only by creating the feature and then going back and editing the 3D sketch absorbed under the feature. This is also the arrangement with the Lip/Groove feature. Remember that you cannot dimension 3D sketches the same way that you dimension 2D sketches. You may need to dimension to planes rather than edges or points to get the dimensions you really want.

The Snap Groove PropertyManager interface is shown in Figure 38.4, along with a cross section of a finished Snap Hook and a Snap Hook Groove. To use the Snap Hook Groove feature, you must have already created a Snap Hook feature. The interface seems to imply that the body that the groove goes into must be in the same part as the body of the Hook feature, but this isn't the case. You can create this feature in-context between a part with a hook and the part to receive the groove, or in a multibody part.

FIGURE 38.4
The Snap Hook Groove
PropertyManager
with a completed hook
and groove

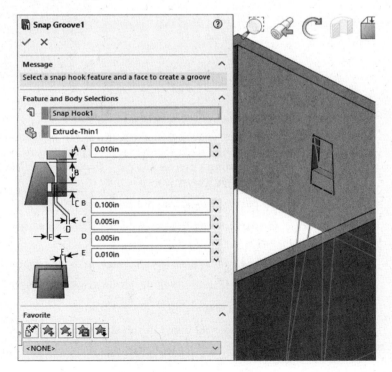

NOTE   Before designing extensive undercuts into a plastic part, talk to the mold builder if possible. The builder may have either limited or special capabilities that could impact the practicality of one approach as opposed to another. I find it beneficial to work closely with a mold designer or builder on plastic part projects.

When I model plastic parts, rarely do situations call for a generic Snap feature. Usually, situations require more inventiveness due to space restrictions or curvature or material thickness considerations. The Snap Hook and Snap Hook Groove features are reasonably easy to use, but they may not have the flexibility for application in all situations.

FIGURE 38.5
Using the Lip/
Groove feature

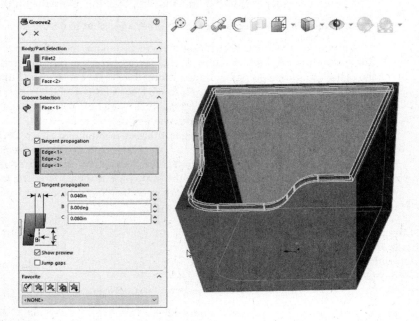

Using Lip/Groove

The Lip/Groove feature enables you to create a matching lip and groove in either a pair of parts in an assembly or a pair of bodies within a single part. Figure 38.5 shows the Lip/Groove PropertyManager creating a groove in a part. The same interface also creates the Lip feature.

The workflow for this feature goes like this:

1. Select the part or body to receive the groove.

2. Select the part or body to receive the lip. If you only want to create a groove, you can skip the lip steps.

3. Select a plane, planar face, straight edge, or axis to establish the direction of pull.

4. Select the faces that represent the parting surface along the area to get the lip/groove.

5. Select the edges that the lip/groove will affect.

6. Set the dimensions for both Lip and Groove features.

In some cases, the automated tools may not be able to create what you need. You can employ one of several manual workarounds to make lips and grooves:

◆ On a planar parting line, you can use sketches offset from the edges and then extrude either a boss or a cut.

◆ Using a Thin Feature extrude (boss or cut) can also be effective on planar parting lines.

◆ Using trimmed and thickened (again, boss or cut) surfaces can be effective but may also be more difficult.

◆ One of my favorite methods, especially for nonplanar parting lines, is to combine a thin feature with an extrude up to an offset surface body.

◆ Using a sweep to cut or add material can be effective on either planar or nonplanar parting lines.

Each of these is really a workaround technique and not a specific plastic modeling tool. I won't go into depth on these techniques here. In the download material for this chapter, you'll find example parts that demonstrate each technique.

Using the Rib Feature

The Rib feature is a flexible tool for creating ribs in a number of different situations. Ribs can be drawn in two different orientations, which the SolidWorks interface calls Parallel To Sketch and Normal To Sketch. The names appear on tool tips only when the cursor is hovering over the icons. To be more precise, what they really mean is that the rib will be created either parallel or normal to the sketch *plane*. If the sketch is a single line, it can be very difficult to tell the difference between parallel and normal.

To me, these names aren't very descriptive. I call the two orientations *plan view* (view from the top, looking in the direction of draw, normal to the sketch plane) and *skyline* (looking from the side, perpendicular to the direction of draw, rib is parallel to the sketch plane). To me, these names are more intuitively descriptive and better reflect the function of the rib.

Ribs can incorporate draft, extend or trim the feature beyond the sketch automatically, and break normal sketch rules (plan-view ribs only).

Figure 38.6 shows a plan-view rib that violates normal sketch rules. Also shown is the Rib PropertyManager. Several models in the download material show examples of various rib techniques.

The Rib feature workflow should be self-explanatory:

1. Draw the sketch, either the plan view or skyline. The sketch represents the top of the rib. Material can only be added between the sketch and the rest of the part. Remember that the sketch plane direction makes a difference.

2. Initiate the feature and set the type of rib and the direction. Use the Flip Material Side toggle to change the direction of the gray arrow, which should point from the top of the rib toward the part.

3. Set the thickness and draft amount and direction.

FIGURE 38.6
The Rib
PropertyManager and
a Rib feature

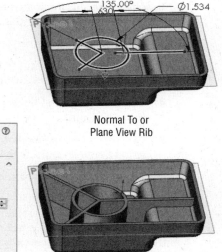

Normal To or
Plane View Rib

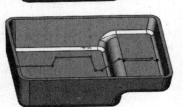

Parallel To Sketch
or Skyline Rib

USING DRAFT IN THE RIB FEATURE

When you create ribs, you almost always apply draft to them. You can apply draft as a separate feature, or you can apply draft as a part of the Rib feature. It's often easier to just do it as part of the Rib feature, but some people like to make all their drafts as separate Draft features to keep the part faces orthogonal for as long as possible, or they just like to organize all the Draft features into a folder at the end of the FeatureManager so that there's never any question about which feature controls the draft.

By default, when you apply draft as a part of the Rib feature, the draft is applied from the sketch end of the rib. This can cause rib thickness problems if you have created a skyline rib where the rib may have various heights. In this case, the top of the rib will vary in thickness, and it may cause the base of the rib to be too thick. When you work this way, sometimes you have to experiment with the proper thickness at the top of the rib in order to get a thickness at the bottom of the rib that doesn't cause sink marks on the outside face of the part. A solution to this is to use the At Wall Interface option, which appears only after you enable Draft in the PropertyManager. Then you can specify the thickness and draft so that the base of the rib maintains a specified thickness.

Using Intersection Curves as References

Ribs are features that typically go inside hollowed-out parts. For that reason, they're often difficult to visualize, especially when they're on a plane that is deep down inside a part. You may find it useful to use some sort of a reference that shows where the current sketch plane intersects the wall of the part. For this, I typically use intersection curves. This technique can be used in either plan view or skyline-type ribs.

The Intersection Curve tool is on the Sketch toolbar. While in a 2D sketch, activate the tool and then select faces that intersect the current sketch plane. Deactivate the tool when you're finished. You may want to select all the lines selected by the Intersection Curve tool and turn them into construction geometry. This provides a good reference for the rib sketch without interfering with the Rib feature.

Figure 38.7 shows an example of using an intersection curve as a reference for setting up a rib sketch. The construction lines at the ends and below the right end of the skyline rib sketch are *intersection curves*.

Figure 38.7
Using intersection curves as references

At the ends of the shell, the intersection curves serve to give the sketch a reference point to be fully defined. Under the right end of the rib sketch, the intersection curve gives you a reference to dimension the height of the rib in the shallower section of the part. The part shown in Figure 38.7 is in the download material, with the filename Chapter 38 - skyline.sldprt.

Terminating Ribs

The Rib feature automatically extends and trims ribs based on your rib sketch. This is a great ease-of-use function, but it tends to lead to sloppy sketching for Rib features. If you sketch a rib and the sketch doesn't lead all the way to the wall of the part, SolidWorks extends it. If your sketch line goes past the wall, SolidWorks trims the rib so that it only goes up to the wall of the part. Figure 38.8 shows how the two straight ribs are extended from the existing sketches on a pair of plan view ribs.

FIGURE 38.8
Extending ribs

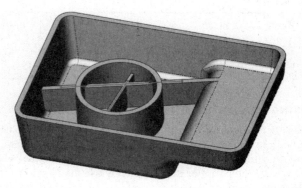

Sometimes, you don't want a rib extended to the wall of the part. You may want to terminate a rib at a specific location in the middle of the part. The way to do this is to use a skyline rib and end the skyline sketch with a vertical (plus or minus draft) line that points to the base of the part. Figure 38.9 shows how to accomplish this. Notice that on the left end of the rib, it's extended straight down to the bottom of the part, and on the right side of the rib, it's extended up to the next wall.

FIGURE 38.9
Terminating a skyline rib

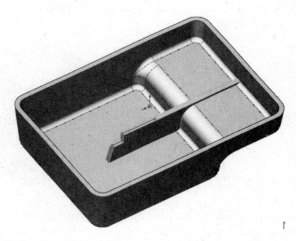

A final termination situation I want to mention is one that can sometimes happen at curved edges. If the extension of the rib cannot be contained by the model, the rib will fail. This situation isn't always as obvious as you might think. When a nonhorizontal rib intersects a curved edge, it usually forces you to fake something a little. Figure 38.10 shows an example of why this happens.

The reason for the error shown in Figure 38.10 is that even though the rib sketch intersects the edge of the part, the width of the top of the rib would go past the edge and not intersect anything. One way to deal with this is to make the sketch intersect the part a little closer to the center of the part from the edge.

FIGURE 38.10
The part wall doesn't terminate the rib.

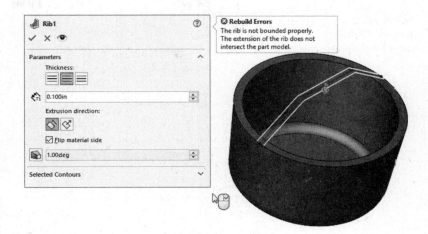

USING THIN FEATURES

Thin Feature extrusions are sometimes used in place of ribs. Thin features don't have all the specialized options available with the Rib feature, but they do offer simplicity as the main attraction. Thin features can substitute for Rib features when the rib is a stand-alone rib that doesn't touch the side walls of the part. They can be used to sketch and extrude from the bottom of the rib or from the top. When extruding a thin feature with draft, the end (thickness) faces get drafted as well, which might cause a problem if you are trying to attach the rib to a wall. Extruding a thin feature down from the top of the rib can replace a plan-view rib, but it won't enable you to break sketch rules like the plan-view rib.

I personally prefer to use Rib features, except for freestanding ribs where you don't want the sides extended up to the next wall.

Using Draft

SolidWorks Draft is surprisingly powerful for all its simplicity. All the aspects of working with Draft could take up an entire chapter on its own. I'll try to hit the most important points in this brief synopsis. The Draft feature creates three types of draft:

◆ **Neutral Plane Draft:** This feature drafts faces from a plane or planar face where the intersection of the drafted face and the neutral plane is what the draft pivots about.

◆ **Parting Line Draft:** This feature drafts faces from a pivot edge on selected edges.

◆ **Step Draft:** This feature drafts faces from parting line edges and can create a step at the parting line (similar to pivot draft in other software).

Figure 38.11 shows the PropertyManager of the Draft feature, including the DraftXpert, which is mentioned later in this section.

FIGURE 38.11
Draft and DraftXpert
PropertyManagers

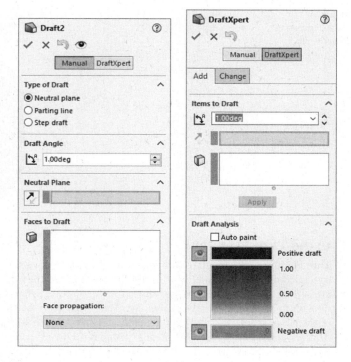

NEUTRAL PLANE DRAFT

The workflow for Neutral Plane draft is as follows:

1. Select Neutral Plane (the plane or planar face at which the intersection of the drafted face doesn't move). The direction of pull is always normal to the neutral plane.

2. Set the draft angle (how many degrees from the direction of pull vector the selected faces should be tilted). This is not a cumulative angle, so applying 3 degrees of draft to a face that is already drafted 5 degrees results in 3 degrees rather than 8 degrees.

3. Select the Direction (one side or the other side of the neutral plane). The arrow points in the direction of decreasing material. If you're drafting a surface body, the "decreasing material" concept doesn't apply, so you just have to experiment to see which direction is the one you intend. The Draft feature doesn't have a preview option.

4. Select the faces to draft using Face Propagation options. Inner/Outer faces refer to inside or outside loops around the Neutral Plane face. All means that all faces that have an edge on the Neutral Plane face.

PARTING LINE DRAFT

The workflow for Parting Line draft is as follows:

1. Select a direction of pull. This can be an edge, axis, sketch line, plane, or planar face. You also have to set the direction to positive or negative along the selected direction.

2. Select the parting lines. These are edges of the faces you want to draft. The parting line edges remain stationary while the rest of the face tilts. Along with the parting line selection, you may also need to use the Other Face option. Every edge is adjacent to two different faces. The Draft feature automatically selects the face it thinks you want to draft, but it doesn't always get it right. The Other Face option enables you to intervene when the automatic selection is incorrect.

3. Set the draft angle. Remember that you can use the Allow Reduced Angle option if necessary.

STEP DRAFT

The most complex type of draft that SolidWorks creates is the Step draft. Step draft is used on nonplanar parting lines when Parting Line draft would cause the drafted faces to be split into multiple faces.

The word "step" can be said to refer to two different aspects of this feature. First, the parting line can be said to be a "stepped" parting line because it's nonplanar and at two different levels. Second, the draft actually steps out the drafted face at one level of the parting line. Step draft keeps the face intact and introduces an intentional mismatch ledge (step) at the parting line.

Figure 38.12 shows the difference between Parting Line draft and Step draft on a simplified part. The image on the left is the Parting Line draft. The middle image is Step draft, where a ledge is created only on one side of the parting line. The image to the right is essentially double Step draft, where the total step size is minimized by distributing it across both sides of the stepped parting line. The draft in these images is slightly exaggerated to make it easier to see.

FIGURE 38.12
Comparing Parting Line draft to Step draft

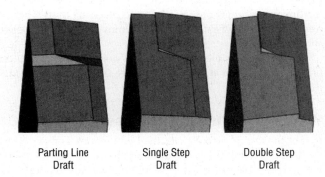

| Parting Line Draft | Single Step Draft | Double Step Draft |

The workflow for Step draft is as follows:

1. Start with a part that has a stepped split line, where the angled line makes angles of more than 90 degrees rather than less than 90 degrees.

2. Create a plane that defines the direction of pull and is located at the level of one of the split lines (for single Step draft) or at the midpoint of the angled line (for double Step draft). The location of the plane will determine the "pivot" point for the drafted faces.

Essentially, the line of intersection between this plane and the drafted face will remain stationary and the rest of face will pivot around it.

3. Initiate the Draft feature and set the option to Step Draft. Consult your tooling people about whether to use tapered or perpendicular steps. Perpendicular steps are probably the easiest to tool.

4. Select the edges of the parting line. Make sure that the yellow arrows indicate the faces to which you want to apply draft.

The Step Draft feature can draft faces only on one side of the parting line at a time. Drafting the faces on the other side of the parting line doesn't require another Step Draft feature. You can use a Neutral Plane feature, using the plane created in step 2 as the neutral plane. It maintains the steps created by the Step Draft feature.

SOME DRAFT LIMITATIONS

One important limitation of draft in SolidWorks is that it cannot draft faces in both directions in the same feature. For example, if you have a parting line on a part, you must first draft the faces on one side of the parting line and then the faces on the other side of the parting line. This results in two separate Draft features rather than one and is simply an inconvenience.

Another inconvenience that affects many features in addition to draft is that you can only draft faces from a single body at a time—an understandable limitation, but annoying and inconvenient.

The biggest limitation is that you can't draft a face if it has a fillet on one of its edges that runs perpendicular to the direction of pull. To get around this, you usually have to tinker with the feature order, or use the DraftXpert to place the draft where it should be. On imported parts, you might have to use FeatureWorks to remove the fillet or Delete Face to reintroduce the sharp corner.

You may sometimes find that draft doesn't work if you don't draft all faces that are tangent to one another. This is the situation where the fillet is on an edge that is roughly parallel to the direction of pull.

WHAT TO DO WHEN DRAFT FAILS

Part of the key to success with the Draft feature is that you have your expectations aligned with the actual capabilities of the software. If you recognize a situation where the draft cannot work, you may be able to correct the situation by changing feature order, combining Draft features into a single feature, breaking the draft into multiple features, or changing the geometry to be more "draft friendly."

Sometimes, the Allow Reduced Angle option can be used for Parting Line draft. If you use this, follow it up with a draft analysis to make sure that you have sufficient draft in all areas of the model. This option enables the software to cheat somewhat in order to make the Draft feature work. The SolidWorks Help documentation actually has a more detailed explanation of when to use this option. I tend to just select it if a draft fails, particularly if the parting line used becomes parallel or nearly parallel to the direction of pull.

Draft can fail for a number of reasons, including tangent faces, small sliver faces, complex adjacent faces that cannot be extended, or faces with geometry errors. When modeling, it's best to minimize the number of breaks between faces. This is especially true if the faces will be drafted later. Generally, the faces you apply draft to are either flat faces or faces with single-direction curvature. You can't expect SolidWorks to draft anything you throw at it; you should try to give it good, clean geometry.

When Draft does fail for a reason that doesn't seem obvious to you, you should use the Check utility under the Tools menu and also try a forced rebuild (Ctrl+Q) with Verification On Rebuild turned on. The Check utility checks the model for geometry errors. Verification On Rebuild checks more rigorously for features intersecting the model incorrectly. Some features may fail with the option on that would not fail with it off. When this happens, there's something wrong with that feature that the simplified default error checking didn't catch.

DRAFTXPERT

DraftXpert is a tool used to create multiple Neutral Plane Draft features quickly. You can also use it to edit multiple drafted faces without regard for which features go to which faces.

Using Indent

Indent is a feature that uses a solid body as a tool and indents a thin-walled area in the target part around the tool. For example, if you're building a plastic housing around a small electric motor, then the Indent feature shapes the housing and creates a gap between the housing and the motor. Figure 38.13 shows the PropertyManager interface for the Indent feature, as well as the geometry created by Indent.

FIGURE 38.13
Using the Indent feature

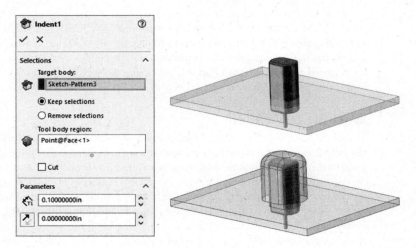

In this case, the small motor is placed where it needs to be, but there's a wall in the way. Indent is used to create an indentation in the wall by using the same wall thickness and placing a gap of .010 inch around the motor. The motor is brought into the wall part using the Insert ➤ Part command. This is a multibody technique. (Multibodies are examined in detail in Chapter 31, "Modeling Multibodies.")

The workflow for Indent is as follows:

1. Open or create a thin-walled part (plastic, sheet metal, machined, and so on) in which you want to create an indentation.

2. Create a new body that will be the positive shape of the negative indentation. You can use Insert ➤ Part to insert an external preexisting part if you want.

3. Start the Indent command by choosing Insert ➤ Features ➤ Indent.

4. Select the thin-walled part into which you want to put the indentation (as Target Body).

5. Click an area on the tool body and change the Keep or Remove option as necessary. Use Keep when you select a location on the tool body where you want to create a thin-walled area; use Remove if you want the selected area to be free of material.

6. Set the Thickness for the material thickness and the Clearance for free space between the tool body and the new thin-walled material.

The Indent feature is particularly effective if you have a part that is nearly finished with lots of detail on it that might be lost by rolling back and making drastic changes to the feature history. (It also works in assemblies, where a part can be the Tool in an Indent feature to modify the Edited part.)

The Cut option is good for non-thin features, where you want an offset cut-with-body. It's just like the Combine (subtract) tool, but with the ability to add an offset.

Anecdotally, the Indent feature is one of those tools that I can say has really saved me a lot of time. I had a customer ask for a major redesign on a plastic assembly that would have meant redoing all the work I had done up to that point. Instead, I was able to create a tool body, use it to indent the master model with a constant wall thickness, and proceed like nothing had happened. So, it saved me tens of hours on this particular project. Keep an open mind about unfamiliar tools. You may get an idea some day and save yourself a lot of time.

Working with Shell

The Shell feature is a powerful yet sometimes tricky feature to work with in SolidWorks. Many users just expect it to work regardless of the condition of the geometry, but it requires that some simple conditions be met. In general, to allow the Shell feature to work, you must have a model where the minimum outside curvature (convex) is greater than the shell thickness. Shell works in 3D much like the offset sketch works in 2D. If the curvature is too small, you cannot offset an arc to the inside. The same applies to Shell; the thinner the shell, the more likely it is to work.

Also, generally speaking, if the body you are shelling doesn't have faces that are tangent to one another, you'll have fewer problems, although faces that are nearly tangent or very pointy can sometimes cause problems.

You can use Shell to hollow out a solid, such as a bottle, as shown in Figure 38.14. You can also use the Shell feature to "shell to outside," which adds material to the outside and removes the original solid.

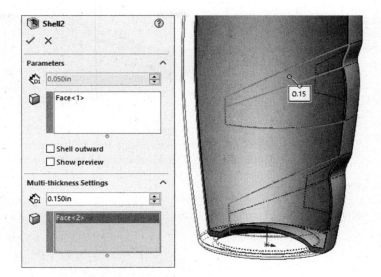

FIGURE 38.14
The Shell feature can create multi-thickness shells.

USING MULTI-THICKNESS SHELL

Figure 38.14 shows the PropertyManager set up for a multi-thickness shell. In this case, the bottom of the bottle is 0.150-inches thick, while the rest of the bottle is 0.050-inches thick. The top of the bottle is selected so that it's open. If you don't select a face to be open, the bottle will simply be hollow with no openings. The image on the right in Figure 38.14 shows half of the bottle in Wireframe display to help you visualize the thickness differences. To get a better view of this model, you can find it in the download materials, with the filename Chapter 38 - creased bottle.SLDPRT.

An important part of using the Multi-Thickness settings is to remember that SolidWorks can't assign different thicknesses to faces that are connected by tangency. All the adjacent tangent faces must have the same thickness. Another way to say this is that adjacent faces that are to have different thicknesses must not be tangent to one another. The reason for this is that SolidWorks cannot transition between two thicknesses when the two faces are tangent.

USING SHELL OUTWARD

Shell Outward is another option, and it is especially useful for bottles. You may be more interested in modeling the contents of a container than the actual container. To help you visualize this idea, think of modeling a liter of frozen water—not the bottle, just water frozen in the shape of the inside of the bottle. Now that you have the contents, you want to create the bottle. This is what the Shell Outward option is meant to do. Figure 38.15 shows the result, where the inside is the original modeled shape and the bottle shown on the outside was "grown" by the Shell Outward option.

Figure 38.16 shows one of the trickier usages of the Shell feature. This figure shows a planter tray that's manufactured by thermoforming. It may be difficult to tell how to model a part like this, because it could be shelled from either side—the top or the bottom.

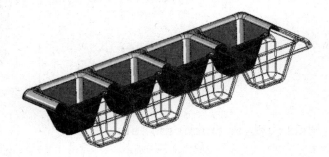

In this part, several faces were removed in the Shell feature, which you may not think of doing with the conventional examples used to show this function, but it works very well for cases like this, especially thermoformed type parts.

Open the file called Chapter 38 - potting tray.SLDPRT from the download materials. The final feature is used to allow you to better visualize the effects of the shell.

UNDERSTANDING THE SHELL WORKFLOW

The workflow for using the Shell feature to produce the potting tray part goes like this:

1. Create a solid part where one side of the solid represents the faces of the finished model. The other side may be a simple block. Figure 38.17 shows the model before applying the Shell feature.

2. Initiate the Shell command. In the Faces To Remove selection box, select all the faces that should be removed or that will become thickness faces. This should amount to the six faces of the block sitting on top of the tray.

3. Use the Show Preview option if you are having difficulty visualizing the result. Be aware that this option may slow down the operation of the software while the Shell PropertyManager is open, but it will help you see the result based on your current selection.

TIP The Shell command has superior troubleshooting functionality when compared to Offset Surface. For more information, go to `https://www.javelin-tech.com/blog/2012/05/offset-thicken-commands/`.

Using the Vent Feature

The Vent feature is highly specialized and is intended for both sheet metal and plastic parts. Figure 38.18 shows examples of vents.

The part used in Figure 38.18 can be found in the download materials in the file called `Chapter 38 - Vents.SLDPRT`.

A Vent feature has four main components:

◆ Boundary

◆ Ribs

◆ Spars

◆ Fill-In Boundary

Figure 38.19 shows the PropertyManager of the Vent feature. This is represented as a single column in the PropertyManager, but here it's split into two columns to fit the format of this book.

FIGURE 38.19
The Vent PropertyManager is used to specify the geometry of the feature.

The Vent feature also has several rules, most of which aren't explained by the Help feature or the interface:

- All of the sketch elements must be in the same sketch.

- The entire feature must exist on a single face.

- No sketch elements can hang off of the face.

- The Fill-In Boundary may not have a nested contour.

- You must have one rib before you can create any spars.

- Spars and Ribs can be interchangeable as long as at least one sketch element in the Rib selection crosses the boundary.

- If Ribs or Spars have sketch elements that aren't tangent (lines meet at an angle), the intersections will have notches on the ends, as if each sketch line were extruded individually (see the circular and triangular examples in Figure 38.18). As a workaround, you can remove the notches by using the Delete Face feature with the Delete and Patch option, selecting the two flat faces of the notch to be deleted.

The Boundary is the outline of the cutout. In Figure 38.20, the Boundary is the elements of the rectangle. The Ribs are the concentric circles, and the Spars are the radial lines.

FIGURE 38.20

Identifying the components of a Vent feature

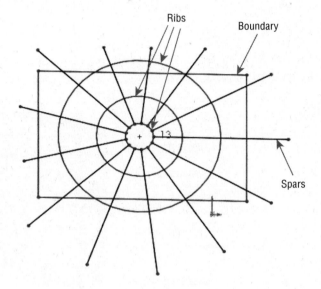

The workflow for a Vent feature is as follows:

1. Create a sketch that contains the Boundary, Ribs, Spars, and Fill-In Boundary. Rib and Spar sketch elements represent the mid-line of the feature.

2. Select each element of each Boundary, Rib, Spar, and Fill-In Boundary in its respective selection box.

3. Set the widths and thicknesses of each item.

4. (Optional) Change the Radius For The Fillets option in the Geometry Properties panel to add fillets to all sharp corners of the feature. If a fillet fails, it won't identify which corner failed; the whole feature will fail.

5. Use the Flow Area panel to calculate the open space of the vent.

6. Use the Favorite panel of the Vent PropertyManager to store commonly used settings. Favorites can be saved externally and shared with other users.

Using Plastic Evaluation Tools

The plastic evaluation tools in SolidWorks enable you to automatically check the model for manufacturability issues such as draft, undercuts, thickness, and curvature. The tools used to do this are the Draft Analysis, Thickness Analysis, Undercut Checker, and Curvature tools.

Using Draft Analysis

The SolidWorks Draft Analysis tool is a must when you're working with plastic parts. The part shown in Figure 38.21 has many of the situations that you are going to encounter in analyzing plastic parts. The Draft Analysis tool has four major modes of display:

- ◆ Basic
- ◆ Gradual Transition
- ◆ Face Classification
- ◆ Find Steep Faces

FIGURE 38.21
Basic draft analysis results

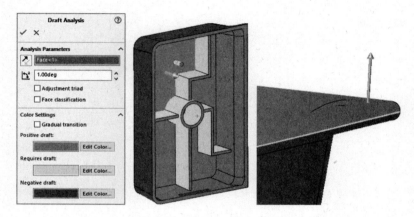

Draft Analysis is found in the View ➤ Display menu and, like the Section View tool, is either on or off. This is beneficial because it updates face colors dynamically as you model. It also has some drawbacks. The display method for the tool leaves the colors looking very flat, without highlights on curved faces, which makes parts—especially curved parts—very difficult to visualize.

BASIC

The Basic draft analysis (with no options selected) simply colors faces red, green, or yellow. Colors may display transitioning if the draft shifts between two classifications. This transition type is shown in Figure 38.21 in the image to the right. For a clearer view of this method, look at the Chapter 38 Draft Analysis.sldprt part in the download materials.

You can perform all types of draft analysis in SolidWorks by selecting a reference flat face or plane and setting a minimum allowable angle. In Figure 38.21, all walls have at least a 1-degree draft, except for the rounded edge shown in the image to the right and the dome. Both of these shapes transition from an angle less than 1 degree to an angle greater than 1 degree.

This basic analysis is good for visualizing changes in draft angle, but it also has some less desirable properties, which become apparent as you study the other types of draft.

GRADUAL TRANSITION

Although the Basic draft analysis can show a transitioning draft, the Gradual Transition draft analysis takes it a step further. With the Gradual Transition draft, you can specify the colors. It's also useful because it can distinguish drafts of different amounts by color. It may be difficult to tell in the grayscale image in Figure 38.22, but the ribs, which were created at 1 degree, have a slightly different color than the floor of the part, and the walls also have a different color. Notice that cavity and core directions have different colors as well (called Positive and Negative draft in the draft analysis). You may want to open this part in SolidWorks, re-create the settings, and run the analysis so you can see the actual colors.

FIGURE 38.22
The Gradual Transition draft analysis

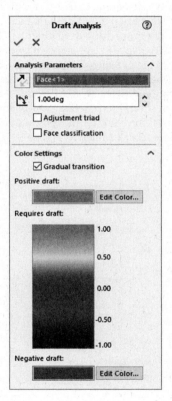

Some problems arise when you use this Display mode, the first being the flat, non-OpenGL face shading that's used to achieve the transitioning colors. This often makes it difficult to distinguish curved faces and faces that face different directions. The second problem is that you cannot tell that the boss on top of the dome has absolutely no draft. In fact, there's no way to distinguish between faces that lean slightly toward the cavity and faces that lean slightly toward the core. The third problem is the strange effect that appears on the filleted corners. The corners were filleted after you applied the draft and before the shell, so the filleted corners should have exactly the same draft as the sides; however, from the color plot, it looks to be a few degrees more.

CAUTION   Gradual Transition gives an interesting effect, but it isn't a reliable tool for determining on its own whether a part can be manufactured.

FACE CLASSIFICATION

Face Classification draft analysis groups the faces into classifications using solid, nontransitioning colors. You'll notice a big difference between the coloration of the Face Classification draft analysis faces and of the Basic or Gradual Transition faces. Face Classification uses OpenGL face shading, which is the same as that used by SolidWorks by default. This allows for better shading and differentiation between faces that face different directions. The Basic Analysis coloration looks like all the faces are painted the same flat hue, regardless of which direction they are facing, which makes shapes more difficult to identify. The non-OpenGL alternative shading method makes it possible to display a transition in color. SolidWorks OpenGL shading cannot do this.

Another advantage of using the OpenGL shading is that the face colors can remain on the part after you have closed the Draft Analysis PropertyManager.

Face Classification draft analysis also adds a classification that isn't used by the Basic draft analysis. The term *straddle faces* refers to faces that straddle the parting line, or faces that, due to their curvature, pull from both directions of the mold. These are faces that need to be split. On this part, a straddle face is shown in Figure 38.23.

FIGURE 38.23
Face Classification draft analysis and a straddle face

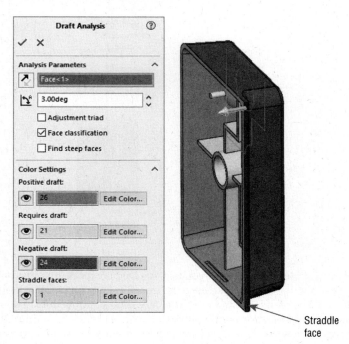

Straddle face

The light bulb icons to the left of the color swatches enable you to hide faces by classification. This is useful when you're trying to isolate certain faces or visualize a group of faces in a certain way. This can be an extremely useful feature, especially when you have a very complex part with a large number of faces, some of which may be small and easily lost in the mix with other larger faces.

The face counts that appear in the color swatches are very helpful features that are absent from the Basic draft analysis. Consider using DraftXpress for situations where you have to add draft to models, as it has built-in draft analysis.

BEST PRACTICE

I prefer Face Classification draft analysis because it's the clearest. If I need additional detail regarding other types of faces, I may run a Steep Face draft analysis as a supplement. The best practice here isn't that you follow my favorite type of draft analysis, but that you understand what you need to know and then use the appropriate tools to find this information. This may include running multiple analyses to collect all the necessary information.

FIND STEEP FACES

A *steep face* is defined as a face that transitions from less than the minimum angle to more than the minimum angle. Steep faces are different from straddle faces in that straddle faces are actually positive *and* negative, while steep faces are either entirely positive or entirely negative. On this part, the dome inside the part is classified as a steep face, as shown in Figure 38.24.

FIGURE 38.24
A steep face

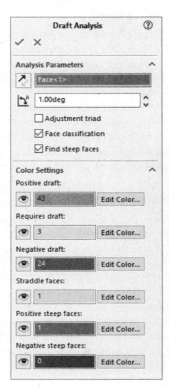

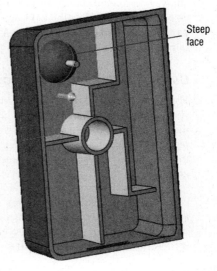

UNDERSTANDING THE DRAFT ANALYSIS WORKFLOW

The workflow for the Draft Analysis tool is as follows:

1. Open a part for which you want to analyze the draft.

2. Select View ➤ Display ➤ Draft Analysis, or select it from the Evaluate tab of the CommandManager.

3. Select a plane or planar face for the direction of pull, and then set the options you want to use to visualize the draft on your part. The draft colors display immediately after you select the direction of pull.

4. If you want to keep the colors on while you work, click the green checkmark icon. The Draft Analysis icon on the toolbar and menu will display as selected. If you don't want to see the colors anymore, click the red X icon. If you click the green checkmark icon and then later want to turn off the Draft Analysis display colors, you must deselect the Draft Analysis icon in the toolbar or menu.

Using Thickness Analysis

You can run Thickness Analysis in two modes: Show Thin Regions and Show Thick Regions. Of these, Show Thick Regions is the most versatile.

USING THE SHOW THIN REGIONS OPTION

The Show Thin Regions option, or the *Thinness* Analysis, requires you to input a minimum acceptable thickness. Every face with a thickness above this value is turned a neutral gray, and every face with a thickness below this value is displayed on a graduated scale.

Figure 38.25 shows the PropertyManager for this analysis and its result on the same part used for the draft work in the preceding sections.

One of the things to watch out for here is that some anomalies occur when you apply this analysis to filleted faces. The faces shown as colored were created by the Shell feature and should be exactly 0.100 inches thick. However, it does correctly represent the undercut on the end of the part and the thickness of the ribs. A nice addition to this tool would be the identification of minimum thickness faces. Perhaps you can submit an enhancement request.

USING THE SHOW THICK REGIONS OPTION

The Show Thick Regions option works a little differently from Show Thin Regions. You need to specify an upper-thickness limit value, beyond which everything is identified as too thick. In these examples, the nominal wall thickness of the part is shown as .100 inches, and the thick region limit is set to .120 inches. For this type of analysis, the color gradient represents the thicknesses between .100 inches and .120 inches, while in the Thinness Analysis, the color gradient represents the values between .100 inches and 0 inches.

The analysis can produce some anomalous results, especially at the corners and also in the middle. Again, this is a useful tool, if not completely accurate. You can use it to find problem areas that you may not have considered, but you should certainly examine the results critically.

This feature can generate a report, which to some extent answers questions about how or why it classifies faces in the way it does. To get a complete picture of the situation, it may be useful to

FIGURE 38.25
Results of the Thinness
Analysis option

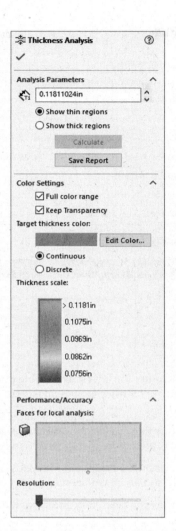

look at the report when you are using the results to make design or manufacturing decisions. A sample of the report is shown in Figure 38.26.

UNDERSTANDING THE THICKNESS ANALYSIS WORKFLOW

The workflow for the Thickness Analysis tool is as follows:

1. Open a thin-walled part with some variations in thickness.

2. Start the Thickness Analysis tool by selecting Tools ➤ Thickness Analysis or by clicking the icon on the Evaluate tab of the CommandManager.

3. Select the Thin or Thick Regions option, depending on what you are most concerned about.

FIGURE 38.26

A sample of a Thickness Analysis report

Summary

Total surface area analyzed	66.739in^2
Critical surface area(% of analyzed area)	1.533in^2 (2.30%)
Maximum deviation from target thickness	0.064in
Average weighted thickness on critical area	0.145in
Average weighted thickness on analyzed area	0.098in
Number of critical faces	6 Face(s)
Number of critical features	5
Minimum thickness on analyzed area	0.001in
Maximum thickness on analyzed area	0.182in

Analysis Details

Thickness range	Number of faces	Surface area	% of analyzed area
0.118in to 0.134in	4	0.57in^2	0.85%
0.134in to 0.15in	0	0.329in^2	0.49%
0.15in to 0.166in	0	0.359in^2	0.54%
0.166in to 0.182in	2	0.275in^2	0.41%

4. For a Thin Region analysis, enter the lowest acceptable thickness. For a Thick Region analysis, enter the low and the high acceptable thickness values.

5. (Optional) Select individual faces for local analysis in the Performance/Accuracy panel. This will also give you the option to get a more accurate display. The default is the least accurate option. Accuracy comes at the cost of longer analysis time.

6. Click Calculate. This calculation may take a few seconds or longer, depending on the complexity of your part. It isn't an instantaneous display.

7. Observe the color gradient on the faces. Blue indicates that the wall is too thin, and red indicates that it's too thick.

Undercut Analysis

The Undercut Analysis tool is in the View ➤ Display menu and on the Evaluate tab of the CommandManager. It is also an on or off display tool, which changes dynamically as you change the model. Undercut Analysis is conceptually flawed in that it gives incorrect results every time. However, if you think of the labels as being changed slightly, the results become partially usable.

Even if you and your mold builder know that a part has absolutely *no* undercuts, the Undercut Analysis tool nonetheless always identifies *all* the faces to be undercut. In fact, the only faces that this tool identifies as *not* undercut are faces that have no draft on them (even if they are in fact undercut). The only time it correctly identifies an undercut is when it classifies the undercut as Occluded Undercut. Faces that have no draft and are occluded undercut are improperly identified as simply No Undercut.

You may want to avoid this tool because too much interpretation of incorrect results is necessary; however, if you still want to use it, here is a translation guide that may help:

◆ **Direction 1 Undercut:** Should read Pull from Direction 2

◆ **Direction 2 Undercut:** Should read Pull from Direction 1

◆ **Straddle Undercut:** Should read Straddle Faces

◆ **No Undercut:** Should read No Draft in the Primary Draft Direction, but may be Occluded Undercut Faces

◆ **Occluded Undercut:** Should read Occluded Undercut Faces that have draft in the completely irrelevant primary draft directions; doesn't include occluded undercut faces that have no draft in the primary direction

Figure 38.27 shows the PropertyManager for this function and the results. If you want to test it for yourself, the part is in the download material with the filename `Chapter 38 Draft Analysis.sldprt`.

FIGURE 38.27
The results of the Undercut Detection tool

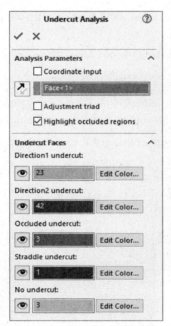

Understanding the Undercut Analysis Workflow

The workflow for the Undercut Analysis tool is as follows:

1. Open a plastic part model in which you want to find undercuts.

2. Open the Undercut Analysis tool from View ➤ Display or using the icon on the Evaluate tab of the CommandManager.

3. Select an axis, flat face, or plane to establish the direction of pull of the mold.

4. Interpret the results using the suggested labels listed earlier.

5. If you want to keep the colored display, click the green checkmark icon. If you want the model to display with the normal model colors, click the red X icon. If you chose the green checkmark icon but want to turn off the color display, turn off the Undercut Detection tool by clicking on it again on the toolbar or in the menu.

The Bottom Line

SolidWorks provides a vast amount of plastics functionality. The more you use these features, the more power you'll find in them. They'll become second nature after you've used them for a while. The power and flexibility are amazing when you think of the incredible range of parts that you can make and evaluate with these features. Automated functions aren't the answer to all problems, however. You need to be well versed in workaround techniques for more complex situations.

Master It   Follow these steps to create matching mounting bosses:

1. Create a new part, and extrude a solid box using the Midplane option, with the size of the box at least 4 × 4 × 4.

2. Use the Shell feature to hollow the box out with a wall thickness of 0.1″, without selecting a face to remove.

3. Use the Intersect feature and select the solid body and the original sketch plane to create two separate bodies. Make sure to turn off the Merge Result option. You want to keep the outer two shelled bodies so you are left with two halves of an open box.

4. Sketch a circle on a face of the block parallel to the split plane, as shown here.

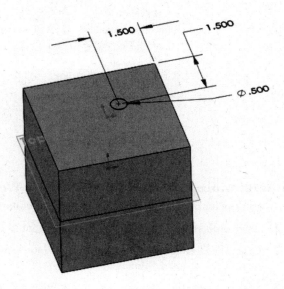

5. Initiate a mounting boss, using the circle to locate the boss, and an edge perpendicular to the split as the direction.

6. Select Hardware Boss type and the Head option. Other options are shown in the following graphic. You cannot go back to change the boss from Hardware Boss to Pin Boss later.

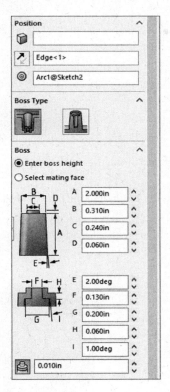

7. Use the settings in the preceding graphic for the fins. Make sure you use a model edge to fix the direction of the fins.

8. Accept the Mounting Boss options.

9. Apply a section view so you can see the inside of the boxes and still see the mounting boss.

10. Start the Mounting Boss feature again. Select the face opposite the original mounting boss face to put the new boss on. Select a circular edge of the first boss to locate the new boss. Select the Hardware Boss, Thread type as shown in the following graphic. Use a flat mating face to specify the length.

11. Determine the direction of the fins of the second boss and accept the second Boss feature.

12. Save the part.

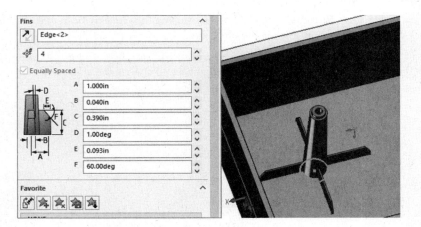

Master It Open the part you created in the previous Master It exercise and prepare to add a Lip/Groove feature to it.

1. Use the Save As functionality to rename the part to **Master It Lip-Groove.sldprt**.

2. Use the tool tips in the Lip/Groove Property Manager shown here for each selection box to make proper selections for the lip (add material) and groove (remove material).

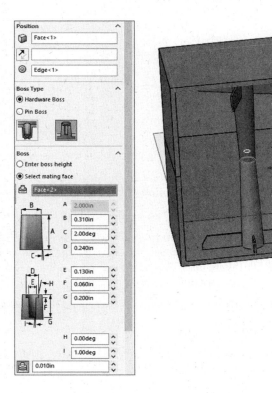

3. The visualization may be difficult for this feature, but with a multibody part, SolidWorks temporarily hides the appropriate body at the appropriate time to allow you to make the selections.

Master It   The Undercut Analysis tool has been incorrect since it was added to the software. It's a little embarrassing considering the fact that the rest of the software is generally pretty good. It's like it was developed by someone who didn't understand the concept at all. Your mission, should you choose to accept it, is to write an enhancement request to SolidWorks to get them to fix this tool using either my suggestions earlier in the chapter or your own suggestions.

Chapter 39

Using Mold Tools

The SolidWorks Mold tools give you a process by which you can take parts designed for the injection molding process and split cavity and core blocks for them, as well as additional core pins or slides. This process often requires manual intervention.

To work with the tools in this chapter, you must understand how surfaces work. Features such as the Boundary Surface, Knit, Trim, and others are covered in Chapter 32, "Working with Surfaces."

This chapter introduces you to both the formal Mold Tools process and the less-formal manual Mold Splitting methods used in the industry.

IN THIS CHAPTER, YOU WILL LEARN TO:

- ◆ Understand SolidWorks' capabilities with mold geometry
- ◆ Use Mold tools manually

Working with the Mold Tools Process

The goal of the Mold Tools process is to start with the CAD data of a part engineered for molding, and from that data, produce geometry that can be used to create the cavity and core for injection molding that part. Figure 39.1 shows a solid block with a cavity and a parting surface, along with the individual blocks created by the split.

The tools and process are generic enough that you could use them to create casts, forging dies, powder metal dies, and tooling for most plastic forming processes. SolidWorks doesn't provide libraries or functionality for building the entire mold or mold components. Mold tools require you to follow a semiautomatic process, with the tools appearing on the toolbar in the order in which they are intended to be used, from left to right.

Mold tools rely heavily on surfacing and require a fair amount of manual intervention for certain types of parts. The first half of this chapter deals with the semiautomatic process—the way it is *supposed* to work. The last half of the chapter deals with the manual side of the process—the way things really work with day-to-day models.

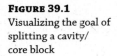

FIGURE 39.1
Visualizing the goal of
splitting a cavity/
core block

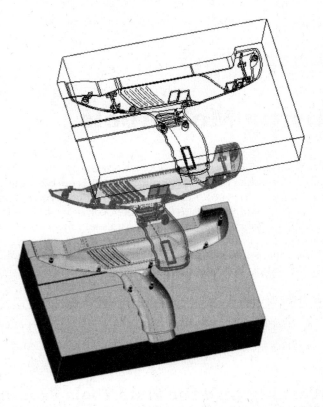

The general workflow for using Mold tools to create cavity and core blocks for a mold is as follows:

1. Create split lines on the as-designed plastic part to add draft where needed.

2. Create draft as needed.

NOTE The Parting Line tool can do automatic face splitting at +/- draft transition.

3. Scale the part up to compensate for shrinkage during molding.

4. Identify the parting lines that separate cavity faces from core faces.

5. Create *shut-off faces,* which are surfaces that close any through holes in the part and represent places where the steel from the cavity side of the mold directly touches steel from the core side of the mold. These openings in the part are capped by Surface features.

6. Create parting surfaces. These are the faces outside the part where the steel from opposite sides of the mold touch.

7. Create the tooling split. The Tooling Split feature uses the faces of the shut-offs and parting surfaces and the faces of either the cavity or the core side to split a block into two sides.

8. Create any core features. In SolidWorks, the word *core* refers to the material used to make core pins, side action, slide, lifter, or pull in a mold.

With the formal SolidWorks process, you start in the part file with just the final plastic part in it and then build both the cavity and core blocks around the plastic part. You also build any side actions or core pins within the part file. This uses a master model approach.

Figure 39.2 shows the part of the Mold Tools toolbar that identifies the process. This toolbar also includes many surfacing and plastics analysis tools, but only the tools directly related to the Mold Tools process are shown in Figure 39.2.

FIGURE 39.2

The Mold tools

Mold tools are really meant for tooling engineers, but part designers often use the first part of the process to apply draft to parts. Tooling engineers often need to add or correct draft to the plastic parts they receive from part designers when these parts are without draft or aren't designed with any process in mind.

If you were to create a mold with manual modeling functions, you might go through roughly the same steps in the same order. The SolidWorks process often runs into problems in the automated surface modeling areas, such as shut-offs and parting surfaces. You may need to intervene in the process manually for these steps. Fortunately, the SolidWorks process is flexible enough to allow manual modeling as needed.

Each of these process steps may have several steps of its own. The process of creating a cavity and core is far from a push-button operation, but when you understand the overall process, the detailed steps become clearer.

Preparing the Plastic Part for Mold Tools

The Mold Tools process formally starts with identifying edges as parting lines. Before you get to that point, you must do some things to the plastic part model, such as shelling the part, creating draft, and accounting for shrinkage.

For this example, you'll use a part, shown in Figure 39.3, from the download files. This part uses a master model technique to create multiple parts from a single surface model, and then it's inserted into a new part for the Mold Tools process, so three levels exist for the part. The one you're concerned with in this example is called `Mold Tools medical device.sldprt`, which contains a single feature: an inserted part called `Medical Device Frame.sldprt`.

SHELLING THE PART AND APPLYING DRAFT

Shelling and applying draft to a plastic part isn't something you can cover in a couple of paragraphs. Shell and Draft features, including the evaluation techniques to determine the wall thickness, direction, and amount of the draft that was applied, are covered in detail in Chapter 38, "Using Plastic Features."

FIGURE 39.3
The plastic part for the
example in
this chapter

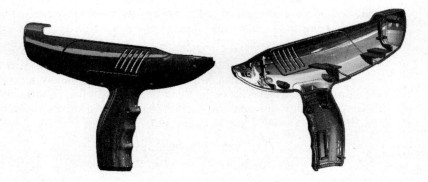

ADDING THE PLASTIC PART TO A BLANK PART

The Mold Tools process works in Multibody mode rather than in Assembly mode. This makes sense as long as you don't start by putting all the Mold Tools features into the same file that contains all the Plastic Part features. This would make a single part with many features that exist for different purposes.

When you're preparing a part for Mold tools, the best practice to follow is to insert the designed plastic part into a new part using the Insert Part feature at the top of an empty new part. This does a couple of things. First, it separates the rebuild time for the Mold Tools from the rebuild time for the plastic part. In addition, if you're just working on the plastic part, you don't want to have to worry about the Mold Tools features. Second, it separates the features of the Mold tools so you're not working with the live plastic part data when all you need is the final geometry.

This step is just a recommended part of the process that has been added; it isn't part of the process that SolidWorks has established for the tools, but you'll probably find it useful.

USING THE SCALE FEATURE

The Scale feature is used to make the plastic part slightly larger to compensate for plastic shrinkage during molding. Scale is driven by a multiplier value, so a part that's twice as big gets a scale factor of 2, and one that's half as big gets a scale factor of 0.5. Plastic materials have a shrink rate that's usually measured in thousandths of an inch of shrink per inch of part. Five thousandths inch per inch is equal to a 1.005 scale factor. If the part is 4 inches long, the mold cavity to produce it must be 4.020 inches with that material.

Some materials have *anisotropic* shrink rates, meaning they shrink different amounts in different directions, with the primary direction being considered the direction of the molten plastic through the mold cavity. SolidWorks has a means to compensate for this, although it may not always be practical. Usually the shrink directions are identified as *in the direction of flow* or *across the direction of flow*, and the direction of flow of molten plastic inside a mold cavity isn't always a straight line. Any anisotropic shrink applied to a part in SolidWorks is an approximation at best. If you deselect the Uniform Scaling option in the Scale feature, SolidWorks enables you to set different scale factors for X, Y, and Z directions. The Scale PropertyManager is shown in Figure 39.4.

FIGURE 39.4
The Scale
PropertyManager

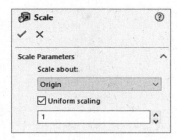

Where you should put the Scale feature is debatable. Some people argue that it should be placed in the plastic part file, so it's ready to create the mold geometry. Others believe it should be placed in the part file in which the Mold tools are created, because you might design a mold for polypropylene differently from a mold for 20 percent glass-filled nylon—so the mold is at least in some ways specific to the material.

This is where the story begins for the medical device example. Follow these steps to scale the part:

1. Start a new part, and as the first feature, create an Insert Part feature. Use the `Chapter 39 - Handle Main Body.sldprt` file in the download materials.

2. Delete the top and bottom bodies from the inserted part.

3. Scale the part about the origin. Figure 39.5 shows the FeatureManager and PropertyManager for the new feature.

Inserting Mold Folders

The first step in the process of using SolidWorks Mold tools is to insert Mold folders. Mold folders are subfolders in the FeatureManager that the Mold tools add under the Surface Bodies folders. You can add these folders manually using the Insert Mold Folders button on the Mold Tools toolbar. They are used to organize the different groups of faces used in separating the cavity and core solid bodies. The folders that are added are shown in Figure 39.6.

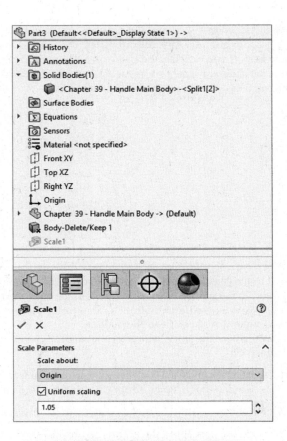

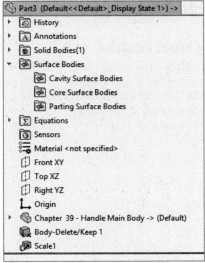

Parting Lines

The Parting Lines feature identifies (semiautomatically or manually) the edges that separate the cavity faces from the core faces. Follow these steps to establish the parting line around the part.

1. Click the Parting Lines toolbar icon in the Mold Tools toolbar.

2. With the first selection box in the Mold Parameters panel active, select the Right (YZ) plane and make sure the arrow is pointing in the direction of pull for the inside of the part, as shown in Figure 39.7.

FIGURE 39.7
Setting the Mold Parameters for the parting lines

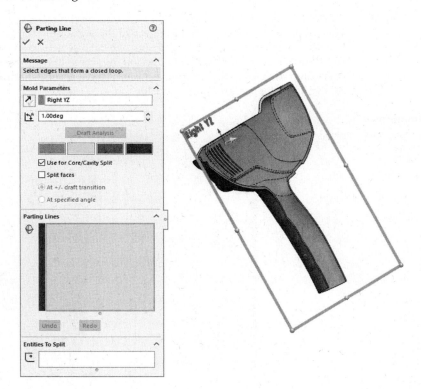

3. Set the draft angle to 1 degree, which is the minimum angle allowed for this mold. In practice, the minimum draft applied to this mold is 1 degree, so you could use .5 degrees here.

   You should have done the draft analysis before getting to this point so that you aren't depending on this analysis to make sure everything is okay. For example, this draft analysis inside the Parting Line PropertyManager cannot tell you how many faces need draft.

4. Select an edge that is between a green and red face. The wavy edge along the finger grip area is a good one. SolidWorks cannot identify the parting line as the set of all edges that share green and red faces, so you'll perform this step semiautomatically.

   The easiest way to do this is to click the wavy edge and then click the Propagate tag that appears as shown in Figure 39.8.

FIGURE 39.8
Propagating the
parting-line
edge selection

This propagating selection should select all the parting-line edges automatically, and it does, but in the example shown in Figure 39.9, it also selects some redundant edges. SolidWorks labels the redundant edges on the screen to help you see which ones need to be deselected. Notice that the message box at the top of the Parting Line PropertyManager tells you that the feature is not yet ready.

FIGURE 39.9
Correcting redundant
selections

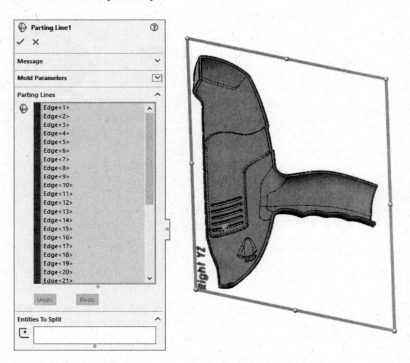

After deselecting the redundant edges, the message box in the PropertyManager turns yellow, because the Parting Line feature doesn't split the mold. In this case, the part has screw holes that go through the part, so you need to create shut-off surfaces to close them. However, you're now done with the Parting Line feature. Remember the tools to select edges; manual selection, Propagate, the Yes/No toggles, and so on. You may have to use one or more of these tools to complete the task.

5. Click the green checkmark icon to accept the feature.

Thirty-five edges should be selected in the Parting Lines selection box.

Initiating the Shut-Off Surfaces

The mold industry is full of terminology that may not be familiar to some designers. *Shut-offs*, in mold lingo, are just locations inside the mold where the two sides of the mold dies touch one another. Shut-offs in the mold usually create holes within a plastic part. The shut-off surface—where the steel from one side of the mold touches the steel from the other side of the mold—is usually flat. Shut-off faces touch each other with significant pressure, so they are usually flat and perpendicular to the clamp force so they don't induce lateral forces. However, angled shut-offs can exist, and passing shut-offs are highly angled—as much as 80 degrees or so.

The screw holes that go through the plastic part require shut-off faces in order to create the mold cavity and core. You can't just seal off any end of the holes; you must pay attention to which end of the hole is where the drafts in opposite directions meet. In this case, the counter-bored holes from the outside must be drafted from the outside, so they must be sealed or shut off from the inside.

When you initiate the Shut-Off Surfaces feature, SolidWorks identifies some of the necessary shut-offs for you, as shown in Figure 39.10.

FIGURE 39.10

Creating shut-offs

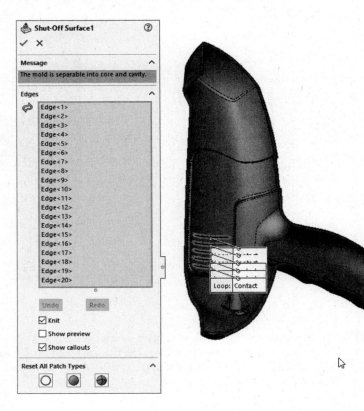

To use the Shut-off Surfaces feature, follow these steps:

1. Click the Shut-Off Surfaces toolbar icon on the Mold Tools toolbar. SolidWorks should automatically select the inside edges of any screw holes, but there aren't any in this part.

2. Locate the slanted ventilation slots in the plastic part, right-click the edge of one of them, and choose Select Tangency from the RMB menu. Four edges are added to the list box for each slot, and there are five slots.

   When all 27 edges are selected, the message box at the top of the Shut-Off Surface PropertyManager turns green, as indicated in Figure 39.10.

3. Ensure that the center option (All Contact) is selected in the Reset All Patch Types section before you finish.

4. When you are satisfied with the results, make sure the settings match those in Figure 39.11, and click the green checkmark icon to accept the feature.

FIGURE 39.11
The default parting surface on the medical device part

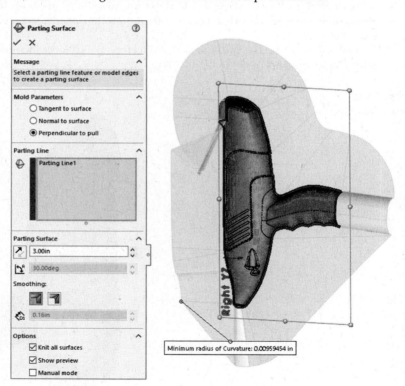

NOTE If the feature doesn't work and displays an error message stating that it cannot knit, deselect the Knit option. Although this isn't ideal, you can troubleshoot later, because the automated Shut-Off feature doesn't allow you to troubleshoot in the middle of the command.

If you must disable the Knit option, and the feature works, you may notice that some of the shut-off surfaces turn red and some turn green. This is just because SolidWorks actually creates one red and one green shut-off surface for each location. The red surfaces are knit together into the Cavity Surface body, and the green surfaces are knit together into the Core Surface body.

When all the appropriate edges around all the holes and slots are selected, the Shut-Off Surfaces PropertyManager message window turns green and displays the message, "The mold is separable into core and cavity."

The tags on the loops in the graphics window display the text "No Fill," "Contact," and "Tangent." The No Fill condition means that you do not want SolidWorks to create the shut-off surfaces. You'll do these manually. Sometimes shut-off surfaces require complex or multifeature shut-offs, which you must do manually. The Contact condition means that the shut-off surface just needs to touch the edges, usually at a right angle. The Tangent option creates a surface that's tangent to the surrounding faces all the way around.

Sometimes you need a combination of conditions in a single shut-off, in which case you must finish the feature manually. When the parting line and shut-off surfaces are complete, SolidWorks automatically knits together all the surfaces in each Cavity and Core folder into a single surface body.

Parting Surface

The Parting Surface feature in SolidWorks Mold tools works best on planar parting lines that are convex all the way around. On the sample medical device part used in this chapter, Figure 39.11 shows what SolidWorks makes of the parting surface.

It's a mess. Therefore, SolidWorks isn't going to create the entire parting surface for this part automatically.

USING THE MANUAL OPTIONS

From the disappointing result shown in Figure 39.11, you can just change to Manual mode and change the Parting Surface distance to 1 inch.

In Manual mode, you drag the pink dots around the black rectangle until the resulting surface makes sense. The pink dots are like connectors in a Loft feature. At some point, SolidWorks will display a black dot on the black rectangle, which is where the pink dot should snap. Why the software knows this now and not before is a little baffling, but at least it gives you the option to semiautomatically fix this surface.

To get this to work, you must arrange the pink dots around the perimeter such that none of the black lines overlap one another or the part to be molded. In the area where the inset face curls around the bottom of the part, this becomes difficult and causes SolidWorks to create bad faces. If you are doing this exercise on your own, try to arrange the pink dots as shown in Figure 39.12. If you see a gap in the surface along the edge or a place where it appears to overlap itself, this will cause an error in the finished surface. This isn't an ideal method for creating tooling surfaces, but it does work.

There are still some things to change here, and every mold designer might do this differently. You can even stop using the SolidWorks process and create the surface using your own methods if you choose.

FIGURE 39.12
Using Manual mode

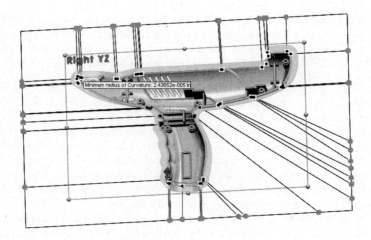

REPAIRING THE MANUAL MODE PARTING SURFACE

To repair the surface made in the previous procedure, follow these steps:

1. Use Delete Face (with the Delete option) to delete portions of the parting surface that will not work to split the mold. Delete Face can be found on the Surfaces toolbar or through the menus at Insert ➤ Face ➤ Delete.

2. When you delete the face, right-click the Parting Line feature in the FeatureManager and hide it.

3. Start the boundary surface from the Surfaces toolbar and fill in the missing gaps in the parting surface with Boundary, Loft, or Planar Surface features.

4. You should finish with a surface as shown in Figure 39.13.

FIGURE 39.13
The completed boundary surface

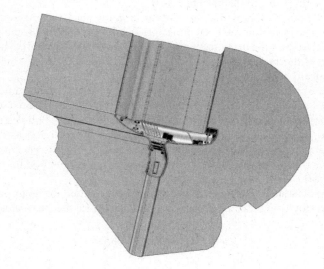

The last thing that needs to be done to the parting surface is to knit it together into the core surface and the cavity surface. Follow these steps to accomplish this:

1. Use Knit to knit together the boundary surface and the parting surface body resulting from the Manual Mode process.

2. Make sure this knit surface goes into the Parting Surface Bodies folder, as shown in Figure 39.14.

FIGURE 39.14
The completed parting surface and feature tree

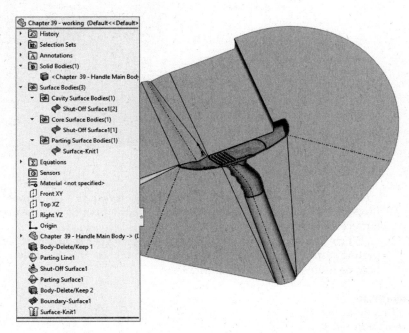

The parting surface is larger than you need it to be, and it's not a pretty shape, but neither of those issues matters.

Tooling Split

Assuming you have completed the parting surface either manually or through the SolidWorks Mold tools, the next step is the tooling split. If you complete the parting surface manually, make sure it's knit together as a single surface body, and then in the Surface Bodies folder, drag the knit surface into the Parting Surface folder. The Tooling Split feature doesn't work unless all the surface bodies are in their correct folders.

Initiate the Tooling Split feature and select a planar face, approximately the parting plane. SolidWorks doesn't give you very good instructions about what it expects, but next you should sketch the mold insert block, which is typically rectangular, square, or circular, and centered on the molded piece. If this is a multicavity mold, make something you can pattern later. Once you have created and exited the sketch, the software will start to extrude it and send you to the Tooling Split PropertyManager, shown in Figure 39.15, where you can preview the feature. The feature produces two solid bodies, representing the cavity and core blocks of the mold. This model is included in the download material for this chapter.

FIGURE 39.15
The Tooling Split
PropertyManager and
the finished product

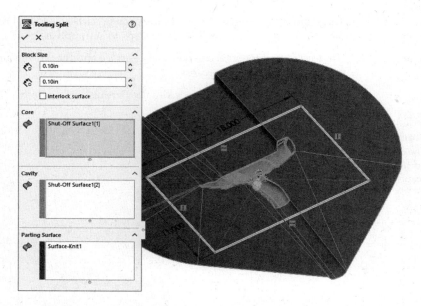

Make the block size approximately 4 inches on each side of the mold. Notice how the PropertyManager has picked up the surface bodies from each of the Core, Cavity, and Parting Surface folders.

When you accept the feature, SolidWorks splits your solid mold block into two using the parting surface. This is where some of your multibody and assembly visualization skills will become useful, as shown in Figure 39.16.

FIGURE 39.16
Visualizing the cavity
between blocks and the
parting surface

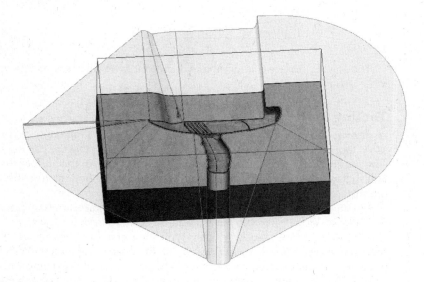

A tooling engineer would certainly change a few things about the layout of this split, but for learning how the tools work, this is sufficient. From here, you might want to continue to add gates, runners, sprue, and so on. To send the cavity and core blocks to a shop for mold building, you probably want to separate the multibody part into individual part files.

NOTE   To check the cavity and core blocks to ensure that they make the desired shape, make a new block that's larger than the original part, ensuring that the Merge Result option is deselected. Then use the Combine tool to subtract the mold parts from the new block. Finally, use the inverse scale to shrink it back down to the finished part size.

Using the Core Feature

The following example is a version of the previous example that included the screw bosses. It uses the Core feature to create a set of core pins. All the standing steel that creates the counter-bores for the screw bosses is made from separate replaceable pins. You can use many techniques to locate pins rotationally. This isn't a lesson in mold design—only in mold modeling techniques.

NOTE   It is interesting to consider the Core feature as a Split using a closed contour sketch, with a Blind condition.

You can either create a sketch beforehand or just make a sketch when the Core feature asks you for it. The Core feature is looking for a sketch that will cut out the block of mold material from which you want to make a core. Again, you can use this for side cores or core pins. In this case, you'll make several core pins.

To start, activate the Core feature; then sketch circles centered on each of the screw boss cores in the cavity body. When you exit the sketch using the Confirmation Corner, SolidWorks will prompt you for an extrusion depth for the sketch to create the feature. The Core PropertyManager and the feature preview are shown in Figure 39.17.

FIGURE 39.17
The Core feature

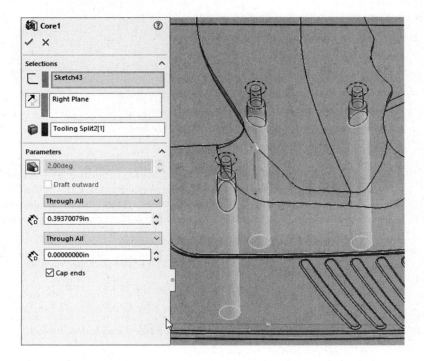

Again, you can save these core pins as individual part files. You can use similar techniques to create side cores, lifters, or other types of side actions.

Working Manually with Mold Tools

You can conduct the entire mold modeling process manually, without using any of the semiauto-mated tools from Mold tools. You may even come across situations where you don't need to use surface modeling at all. These situations will often involve parts with a planar parting line, with no shut-offs or cores.

Experienced mold designers tend to use different techniques, from cutting away chunks with solids to using all manual surfacing methods to using about 80 percent Mold Tools techniques and manual surfacing for the other 20 percent.

You'll next run through two examples of manually intervening in the Mold Tools process. In the first, you will learn how to create a passing shut-off, and in the second, you will learn how to create the parting surface.

Passing Shut-Offs

Plastic Snap features are often created in molds by using passing shut-offs rather than some sort of lifter or horn pin slide. Eliminating actions from a mold can be economical, as long as the passing shut-off doesn't introduce wear or alignment problems. When you're creating parts that require this sort of feature in the mold, consult your mold builder.

Passing shut-offs can be difficult to visualize. It might be helpful to open the part `passing shut off.sldprt` shown in Figure 39.18 and study the geometry.

FIGURE 39.18
A part that requires passing shut-offs

Two pairs of passing shut-offs are modeled in this part.

Using the Part Reviewer (Tools ➤ SolidWorks Applications) is probably the best way to see what's going on with this part. You will also need to use Ctrl+Shift+Tab and Tab to hide/show solid and surface bodies. Looking at the part and studying the steps involved will help you learn and understand. The basic steps to create the surface body called Shut-off 1 are as follows:

1. Create a ruled surface for the planar edges.

2. Loft surfaces between the parting line edges and the ruled surface.

3. Extrude a flat shut-off face at the parting line of the Snap feature.

4. Use the cavity or core knitted body to trim the extruded surface.

5. Use the extruded surface to trim the ruled and lofted surfaces.

6. Knit the surface bodies together.

The hardest part of creating this passing shut-off is visualizing what the interface between the steel from opposite sides is going to look like. Keep it as simple as possible. Tool builders request a wide range of angles for the passing shut-off (mold steel touching at steeply angled faces). The minimum draft they can possibly stand ranges from 5 to 15 degrees of draft. You should try to give at least 8 degrees and more if you can. The tool builder also looks for a minimum land (flat steel making contact from either side) on the top of the shut-off boss, generally not less than 1 mm, or approximately 0.050 inches, to work with round numbers.

Don't be discouraged if you don't completely understand this the first time around. The concept itself is difficult, and visualizing the geometry is even more difficult.

Creating Nonplanar Parting Surfaces

The method SolidWorks uses to create the parting surface is adequate for simple tasks, such as molding a Frisbee or dinner plate, but it won't work well for more complex projects such as handheld medical devices. Figure 39.19 shows the part in the download material named `frame parting surface.sldprt`. The result is entirely unacceptable for several reasons, including big gaps in the parting surface and unnecessarily complex parting surface (which in practice have to perfectly seal off against one another under pressure).

FIGURE 39.19
An automatically created parting surface for the handheld medical device

From the examples shown here, you can see that the SolidWorks Mold tools are not entirely reliable for nonplanar parting lines. Flat parting-line disks and boxes work well. Beyond that, you should expect to do some manual surface modeling.

NOTE If you want software that will create automatic parting surfaces for you, consider MoldWorks and SplitWorks from R&B Mold and Die Design Solutions (`www.RnBUSA.com`). This software also includes highly automated mold libraries and aids to help you model and document every aspect of mold hardware.

To manually create the parting surfaces for this part, you'll tackle the difficult step first, which turns out to be easy after you know a couple of tricks. The first step is to create a sketch and use it to lay out directions that you can pull off the nonplanar sections of the parting line. Figure 39.20 shows three lines that identify the nonplanar top, base of grip, and trigger areas.

FIGURE 39.20
Projecting nonpla-
nar sections

The sketch lines lead in directions where those edges can be projected without running into other geometry.

Then the edges of each nonplanar portion of the parting line can be converted into sketch entities in a 3D sketch and extruded as a surface along each of these three directions. From there, it's simple to create planar surfaces between the nonplanar sections. This technique may not work for all nonplanar parting lines, but it does work for this one.

The Bottom Line

SolidWorks Mold tools establish a method you can use for the semiautomated tasks involved in creating parting line, cavity, core, and parting surface entities and even pins, pulls, and slides. For more involved nonplanar parting lines, you will probably want to intervene manually, which will call on your skills with surfaces, bodies, and visualization.

Master It   Understanding the draft analysis is the first real skill you need to have to create mold geometry in SolidWorks—aside from being able to create drafted parts, of course.

1. Open the downloaded part named Chapter 39 - Master It start 1.sldprt.

2. Run a draft analysis on it with the draft angle set to 1 degree and using the Face Classification setting. Face Classification counts the numbers of each type of face (positive, negative, requires draft and straddle—needs to be split). The Draft Analysis button stays depressed after you exit the command so that it retains the colors (rather than actually changing face colors). While in this mode, you can still work on the model, and additional features will be draft analyzed as well.

3. To exit this mode and set the colors back to model color, turn off the Draft Analysis icon in the Mold Tools toolbar. Save the model.

Master It Starting from where you left off in the previous exercise, follow these steps:

1. Use the SolidWorks Mold tools to add the Mold folders to the FeatureManager.

2. Expand the Surface Bodies folder to make sure it has subfolders called Cavity Surface Bodies, Core Surface Bodies, and Parting Surface Bodies.

3. Initiate the Parting Line command and use the same Pull Direction reference as you did for the draft analysis previously. Set the draft angle to 1 degree and click the Draft Analysis button.

4. Examine the part to make sure that the face coloring hasn't changed.

5. Notice that SolidWorks has identified a parting line with 13 entities, and that the message at the top of the PropertyManager is yellow (the warning is shown in the following graphic.

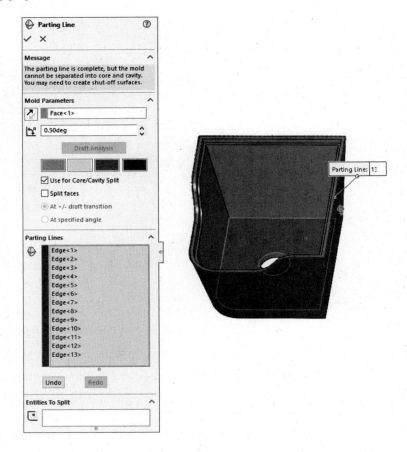

6. Accept the feature and initiate the Shut Off tool.

7. The shut-off may identify both the top and the bottom of the hole as shut-offs, but they will be identified as redundant. You need only one shut-off for this part. The

shut-off edge needs to have all red faces on one side and all green faces on the other. So, you should delete the edge that has the same color on both sides. The PropertyManager message should read "The mold is separable into core and cavity" and be in a green field.

8. Accept the feature and save your model.

Master It   To finish this simple mold, you need to create a parting surface and split the cavity/core block.

1. Initiate the Parting Surface tool. Set the Distance to 4 inches. Your model should look like the following graphic. This is a relatively simple nonplanar parting line, and SolidWorks gets this one correct.

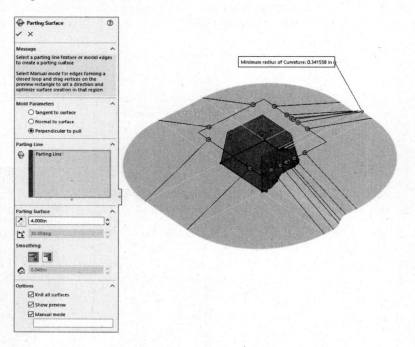

2. Initiate the Tooling Split tool and select the big flat face of the parting surface.

3. Sketch a square centered on the hole, 6 inches on each side, and exit the sketch.

4. Set the block size to 4 inches, and do not use the Interlock option.

5. Use F8 to show the Display pane, and expand the Solid Bodies folder and the Parting Surface Bodies folder.

6. Make sure to turn off the Draft Analysis mode at this point.

7. Designate the top mold as Insert Body and the parting surface as Wireframe, and hide the cavity and core surface bodies as well as the original part.

Appendix A

The Bottom Line

Chapter 1: Introducing SolidWorks

Easy access to your tools cuts just seconds out of your work time every day, but a good habit will cut minutes, and several good habits can cut hours.

Master It   After SolidWorks has been installed as shown in this chapter, find the desktop icon, and put it on your taskbar or other easy-to-access interface element.

Solution   If SolidWorks is going to be part of your everyday tools, make sure it is easy to access.

File organization is one of the keys to a successful SolidWorks implementation. While I don't expect you to have everything figured out at this stage in your learning, you need to start thinking about how to manage your SolidWorks libraries of templates and key features as well as your project data.

Master It   Make sure you know where the settings in Tools ➤ Options are located for identifying the locations for templates, and change this location if necessary.

Solution   You may need to specify a network drive if you are sharing templates with other users. You may also need to customize some templates for your company's particular needs. Make sure you are also familiar with the specific file extensions that SolidWorks uses.

One of the key concepts of managing SolidWorks is associativity. Data created in one file can be shown in another file. For example, part data is shown in both assemblies and drawings.

Master It   Open a SolidWorks drawing (`*.slddrw`) and drag a SolidWorks part (`*.sldprt`) onto it. Make a change to the part and watch it update on the drawing.

Solution   The easiest way to make a simple change is to double-click on the part shown in the drawing, and then double-click on a dimension. Change it by a small amount to try to avoid rebuild errors.

Chapter 2: Navigating the SolidWorks Interface

Learn the different parts.   The SolidWorks interface has many elements because SolidWorks has so much functionality. You can access most elements multiple ways, which can be liberating because it offers options, but it also can add to the confusion because there is so much to know. You do not need to know every way to do everything; you only need to know the best way for you.

Master It Identify each area around the SolidWorks window.

Solution Use Figure 2.1 and tool tips to go around the interface and name each area.

Customization is key. Customization opportunities in SolidWorks are vast. Everyone has different tastes and preferences when it comes to running the interface. Some prefer the keyboard, some the mouse. Some prefer the touch interface. There are different strategies that depend on your specific situation—for example, saving space, saving mouse travel, or saving mouse/keyboard clicks. SolidWorks has touch interface options, as well as various accessibility tools intended to accommodate special needs such as different input devices or color blindness.

Master It Create some simple keyboard shortcuts (hotkeys) for the functions you think you will use the most.

Solution Start from the sample Excel list of existing hotkeys, and add some of your own for things like Tools ➤ Options or Tools ➤ Evaluate ➤ Measure.

Manipulate multiple windows. Manipulating multiple windows is important in all computer use, but especially in CAD, where you work with enormous amounts of data and numbers of documents that surpass other types of programs.

Master It Open several sample documents from the Wiley download data and practice manipulating the windows.

Solution Use the window controls in the upper-right corner of the SolidWorks application to span multiple displays. Use Ctrl+Tab to cycle through open SolidWorks documents and Alt+Tab to cycle through open Windows applications. Use the R key to see the Recent File list.

After using this chapter to find the various ways of using the interface, you can develop the way that is most comfortable for you and stick with it. Save the settings and share them with other users or move them to other computers where you work.

Chapter 3: Working with Sketches and Reference Geometry

Create new sketches and edit existing ones. In SolidWorks, each sketch is named and must be on a plane or planar face. You can edit only one sketch at a time, and there are things you cannot do while in a sketch.

Master It Practice creating new sketches and using the various sketch entities on the Sketch toolbar to familiarize yourself with the range of tools that are available and how they work.

Solution   Practice working with dimensions and sketch relations. Use the Smart Dimensions tool to create dimensions on line and arc geometry. Use relations to control how dimensions move and change sketches when the dimensions increase or decrease in value.

Create new reference geometry and use the planes to create new sketches.   As you get deeper into this book, you will learn more uses for the Reference Geometry tools. For now, the primary function is to establish planes for sketches without relying on adding relationships to solid geometry.

Master It   Practice moving or redefining planes to see how the change affects the resulting 3D geometry. Also build your skills by creating planes using the available options. If you can imagine a way to define a plane, use the three selection boxes and available constraints to see how many different types you can create.

Solution   Use the Plane Wizard to create new planes. Ctrl+drag a plane to make an offset plane. Rename planes to denote their purpose. Start sketches on a couple of planes.

Use a range of sketch entities.   While you can often get by using just lines and arcs, there are times when more advanced sketch entities are more appropriate. Ellipses, parabolas, conics, splines, even slots, polygons, and sketch text are all valid sketch entities that are very useful in certain situations.

Master It   Practice using some of the more advanced sketch entities on the Sketch toolbar.

Solution   Remember that you can use either the Click+click or click-and-drag method to create sketch entities. Follow the prompts in the lower-left area of the SolidWorks window.

Chapter 4: Creating Simple Parts and Drawings

SolidWorks data is made of parts, assemblies, and drawings. In this chapter, you learned how to create simple examples of each type.

Master It   Create a simple block with holes in it, where every item is dimensioned fully. Use an existing SolidWorks template.

Solution   *Fully dimensioned* means that all the sketch elements are black and cannot be dragged. Use the sample part from the download material for this chapter called `Sample Solution Simple Block.sldprt`.

Master It   Create a simple assembly where you bring together some of the parts that you created or worked with in this chapter, and use mates to locate them with respect to one another.

Solution   Remember that the first part you bring into an assembly will be locked in place. Other parts will be able to move around until you mate them into place. Work with mates to mate flat faces and/or holes. Refer to the `Sample Assembly Solution.sldasm` in the downloadable material.

Master It   Create a simple drawing of a single part you made earlier in this chapter. Fill in some custom properties, and make sure the properties propagate over to fill out the title block on the drawing. Use various types of views, annotations, symbols, and dimensions.

Solution   Drag the part onto the drawing sheet. Use Insert ➤ Model Items to place dimensions from the model into the drawing. Use the file `Sample Solution Simple Block.slddrw` as a reference.

Chapter 5: Using Visualization Techniques

Visualization is one of the most important tools in SolidWorks.   Visualization is a key function of the SolidWorks software. You will use these tools multiple times an hour and, in some cases, constantly throughout the day. Visualization can be an end to itself if you are showing a design to a vendor or client, or it can be a means to an end if you are using visualization techniques to analyze or evaluate the model. In both cases, SolidWorks presents you with an astounding list of tools to accomplish the task. The tools range from the analytical to the cosmetic, and some of the tools have multiple uses.

Master It   Practice using the keyboard and mouse display controls, including the arrows and modifier keys. Access the Orientation box with Ctrl+spacebar and manipulate the view using each of these tools.

To become acquainted with the names of all the tools on toolbar, use the mouse to hover over the Heads-Up View toolbar. Make sure to look at all the drop-downs and flyouts.

Solution   The middle mouse button is frequently used in SolidWorks.

Master It   Use the DisplayManager and the Task pane to access all of the information and tools to apply appearances and visual properties to your model. Make sure to use the DisplayPane flyout from the FeatureManger to have quick access to appearances applied to your part.

Solution   SolidWorks did not make this part of the interface simple or compact, so it may take some extra time to understand and remember where all of the various controls and information are located.

Master It   Acquaint yourself with all of the settings available in Tools ➤ Options ➤ Colors and ➤ Display. Don't forget the settings under Tools ➤ Options ➤ Document Properties ➤ Model Display. Create templates with the background and visual properties you want to use.

Solution   You may have to refer back to this chapter to make sure you understand some of the settings and options available for backgrounds, colors, and templates. Compare templates with your coworkers.

Chapter 6: Getting More from Your Sketches

Edit sketch relations.   Effectively using sketch relations is a fundamental skill that you need to have to be successful with SolidWorks. You will use them constantly to make sure your models behave predictably to change.

Master It   Open one of the sample parts from this chapter, show the flat tree, and edit each sketch. Make sure you understand what each sketch relation is doing.

Solution   You will create each feature once, but you will edit features many times. Editing skills are actually more important than creation skills, because you will spend more time editing.

Reverse engineer a simple part using digital images.   Take pictures from at least two sides of a simple object you can model using simple extrude features, trying to make the photos look like drawing views. Use the images as sketch pictures, align the edges on the photo with the X and Y of the sketch, and sketch over them.

Master It   Insert the photos into sketches and model with the image as a reference.

Solution   It is often useful to have a ruler in the image, or to have an accurate measurement of an edge that you can identify in the image.

Create a wireframe representation of a chair from 3D sketches.   3D sketches are frequently used in many types of design. Getting some practice drawing lines in 3D space will help you gain command of these tools.

Master It   Start by creating the centerlines of the square members of a simple wooden chair.

Solution   It will be easier if you start from the origin or create construction geometry connected to the origin. Make sure you have a plan for which part of the chair is in positive X territory, and so on. Use multiple viewports and a rotated view. Use dimensions and sketch relations to make everything update together when the sketch is changed.

Chapter 7: Modeling with Primary Features

SolidWorks has a wide selection of feature types to choose from, ranging from simple extrudes and revolves to more complex lofts and sweeps. Some features have so many options that it may be difficult to take them all in at once. You should browse through the models from the downloads for this chapter and use the Rollback bar (described in detail in Chapter 2, "Navigating the SolidWorks Interface") to examine how the parts were built. Then you can try to create a few on your own. The best way to learn these features is to use them on practice parts and through experimentation. Curiosity is your greatest teacher.

Master It   Copy the part (remodel it from scratch) called `LowerLinkBibleBike ch7.sldprt` from the download material. Use the Measure tool under Tools ➤ Evaluate ➤ Measure.

Solution   If you're having trouble getting the information you need from the Measure tool, use the Rollback bar ➤ Tiled windows ➤ Edit Feature and double-click to find dimensions.

Depending on the type of work you do, Fillet features can be an important part of your job. Work through this exercise to get some practice with fillets.

Master It   Open the part `Chapter 7 fillet example.sldprt` from the download materials for this chapter. Add fillets to all edges except the outer edges on the Top plane. Remove existing fillets where necessary.

Solution As a hint, try to work through the fillets in order from the largest to the smallest. Remember this part will have draft on it. There is already some draft. Remember also that there are a couple of aids for applying a lot of fillets at once—selecting faces or features and using the FilletXpert selection toolbar.

Whether you create a lot of complex shapes or do machine design at your job, sweeps can be important features to master. Open the part Chapter 7 Curves.sldprt and examine how each feature was made. use the Rollback bar, expand all features, and use the Flatten Tree option (RMB on name of part in FeatureManager, or use Ctrl+T) to try to understand as much as you can about how it was made.

Master It The curves are the tricky part to this one. You have a 3D sketch, a helix, a projected curve (one sketch projected onto another), and a composite curve (two curves added together end to end). Re-create Chapter 7 Curves.sldprt using your own dimensions.

Solution Remember, SolidWorks does not always display the features in the same order in which they were created, so you may have to use the Flatten Tree (Ctrl+T) command to understand how each curve came to be through multiple other items.

Chapter 8: Selecting Secondary Features

SolidWorks has a wide range of features beyond the basic extrudes and revolves. You saw the depth of the standard features in Chapter 7; now in Chapter 8, you have seen the breadth of some of the less-used, but still useful operations. You won't use each of these secondary features every day, but it is nice to know that if you need to show a model in a flexed in-use state, you at least don't have to directly model the deformed part manually.

Springs are very commonly needed to be custom designed in small mechanisms that you might be called upon to create. The ability to model these items is a valuable skill.

Master It Use a Helix and a 3D sketch to create a sweep path for a spring with elongated ends for use in a light mechanism.

Solution Remember that you can convert the helix into a 3D sketch entity to make it easier to connect to in the 3D sketch.

Packaging and fixturing are additional types of design and modeling that are important for an engineer to master. Create a cavity such that the file named Chapter 8 Bottle.sldprt can nest into it.

Master It Use the Indent feature to create the cavity in a thin sheet of material.

Solution In the Chapter 8 Bottle part file, create a rectangular extrusion larger than the bottle, but only 1 mm or .0.025 inches thick. Make the new extrusion a different color to differentiate it from the bottle. Use the following graphic as a reference.

When you extrude the thin sheet, make sure the Merge option is turned off.

Use Indent, selecting the thin sheet as the Target, and select the half of the bottle that you want to be inside the cavity as the Tool body. Use the following graphic as a reference.

Make the thickness of the cavity 0.015″ to account for stretch, and leave a gap of 0.005″

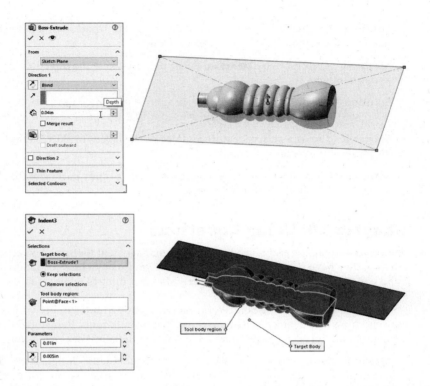

Text often has to go on irregular surfaces. Work through this example to gain some experience putting it there.

Master It   In the downloadable file Chapter 8 Tutorial Bracket Casting.sldprt, some text is wrapped onto one of the cylindrical bosses. Put a model number on the second boss using the same process.

Solution   For this task, you need the sketch text and Wrap feature. Examine the existing Wrap feature to see how it was done, and repeat it with a six-digit model number on the other side.

Chapter 9: Patterning and Mirroring

Feature patterns and mirrors are powerful tools, but you must have some discipline to benefit from their usefulness. Patterns in particular are extremely flexible, with many types of functions and options available. You should avoid sketch patterns if possible, not only because of performance considerations, but also because complex sketches (sketches with lots of entities and relations) tend to fail more often than simple sketches.

Master It   Create an irregular sketch region on a flat face of a solid part of your choosing, add a hole inside the irregular region, and then use the Fill Pattern feature to fill the region with patterned holes.

Solution   Use the Reference Fill Pattern.sldprt part from the download material as a reference to examine how a fill pattern is made.

Master It   Create a two directional linear pattern where the directions are not perpendicular to one another.

Solution   Use the Reference Curve Driven Pattern Direction 2.sldprt file as a reference to make sure you know how to control this type of pattern feature.

Master It   Create a pattern feature and use the Instances to Skip to remove a couple of instances of the patterned feature.

Solution   Check the Chapter 9 Solution Skip.sldprt part from the download material for hints at the solution for this exercise.

Chapter 10: Using Equations

SolidWorks equations and related dimension-management tools are powerful. In the last several releases, they have been vastly updated. Even if you're not a huge equation user, the ability to build equations in the Modify and PropertyManager dimension boxes is a great convenience for such a powerful function.

Be careful about crossing SolidWorks native equation functionality with configurations; you may end up with dimensions that are controlled by both tools. Remember that the calculation capability of Excel is far greater than what is found in SolidWorks equations.

Master It   Equations and variables are keys to parametric design. Start simple by creating a rectangle with sides made equal by using the same variable name for vertical and horizontal dimensions.

Solution   Chapter 10 Solution 1.sldprt holds the key. Edit the sketch and show the dimensions. You can enter the variable name right in the Modify box. To make the second one equal, type an equal sign where you would normally put the dimension value, and click the other dimension. This automatically makes an equation where the second dimension equals the first one.

Master It   After you have created the rectangular sketch with equal sides, make the extrusion depth also equal so that no matter what size it is, the solid will always be a cube.

Solution   To do this, type an equal sign where you would normally type the extrusion depth in the PropertyManager, and then click the first dimension to which you assigned a variable; SolidWorks automatically makes the assignment.

Test this a couple of times by changing a dimension and watching the solid rebuild. Remember, you cannot change a dimension that is driven by an equation.

Master It   One of the most common situations in design is needing to spread out holes. Equations are a great way to do this. Study the part named Chapter 10 Equations.sldprt and re-create it on your own.

Solution   The key to this part is getting the pattern of holes correct, and then writing an equation that evenly spaces the holes, taking the end spacing into account.

Chapter 11: Working with Part Configurations

Configurations are a powerful way to control variations of a design within a single part file. Many aspects of a part can be configured, although a few cannot. Manually created configurations are useful for making a small number of variations and a small number of configurations, but they become unwieldy when you need to make more than a few variations of either type.

Using design tables to control design variations is recommended because you will be able to see more clearly all the changes you have made to all the configurations. Additionally, by having the power of Excel available, you will be able to access many functions that are not shown here, such as using lookup tables and Concatenate functions to build descriptions or configuration names.

Master It   Create a simple block from a fully dimensioned sketch, name all of the dimensions, and create three configurations such that each configuration changes one of the dimensions. Show all the dimensions on the screen.

Solution   Compare your part against the download file named `Chapter 11 Solution 1.sldprt`.

Master It   Take the part from the previous exercise and auto-create a design table, add 10 more configurations, with different dimensions in each, and configure a custom property called Vendor to have a different value in each configuration.

Solution   Compare your part against the download file named `Chapter 11 Solution 2.sldprt`.

Master It   Take the part from the previous exercise and add a feature to it. Use the design table to turn the feature on or off (unsuppressed or suppressed) in each configuration. Also change the part color in several configurations.

Solution   Compare your part against the download file named `Chapter 11 Solution 3.sldprt`.

Chapter 12: Editing, Evaluating, and Troubleshooting

Working effectively with feature history, even in complex models, is a requirement for working with parts that others have created. When I get a part from someone else, I usually look first at the FeatureManager and roll it back if possible to get an idea of how the part was modeled. Looking at sketches, relations, feature order, symmetry, redundancy, sketch reuse, and so on are important steps in being able to repair or edit any part. Using modeling best practice techniques helps to ensure that when edits have to be done, they are easy to accomplish, even if they are done by someone who did not build the part.

Evaluation techniques are really the heart of editing, as you should not make too many changes without a basic evaluation of the strengths and weaknesses of the current model. SolidWorks provides a wide array of evaluation tools. Time spent learning how to use the tools and interpret the results is time well spent.

Master It   Set and test the following ease-of-use settings. Set and test the following settings to make sure you know where to find them and what they do:

◆ Arrow Key Navigation for the FeatureManager

◆ Flyout FeatureManager

- Selection Breadcrumbs
- Dynamic Reference Visualization
- Show Flat Tree

Solution

- Tools ➤ Options ➤ FeatureManager ➤ Arrow Key Navigation
- Flyout FeatureManager is available when the PropertyManager obscures the regular FeatureManager
- Breadcrumbs display in upper-left of graphics window or at the cursor with the D hotkey.
- View ➤ User Interface ➤ Dynamic Reference Visualization
- RMB on the name of the part in the FeatureManager, and select flyout for Tree Display ➤ Show Flat Free

Master It   Use the part from the download material called `Horizontal.sldprt`. This part uses several sketches to drive the entire part. Take a look through this part, and try to re-create one that is similar.

Solution   Use the Rollback bar, Edit Feature, and Edit Sketch to compare your work against mine. Also use the Part Reviewer and Dynamic Reference Visualization.

Master It   Edit the previous part to see if you can make features fail. In particular, reorder some fillets. Next, try the same thing with the part called `Vertical.sldprt`, which is provided with the download material. Examine the Vertical part and try to figure out why reordering the fillets causes so many failures.

Solution   The Horizontal part will not allow you to edit it in such a way that it will fail. The Vertical part will fail when fillets are reordered, because so many dimensions and sketch relations are made from edges created by the fillets—hence, they have formed parent/child relations.

Chapter 13: Building Efficient Assemblies

Assemblies are more than simply parts and subassemblies put together with mate relationships; several other types of features and placeholders can also exist in the assembly FeatureManager. Organizing assembly components is fairly straightforward and can offer benefits for finding parts as well as controlling suppression and display states globally.

The assembly FeatureManager contains several options for the data to display for subassemblies, parts, configurations, metadata, and features within. Remember that all the data that you include in your SolidWorks documents can be accessed and reused later, so it's worth the effort to name it properly. Descriptions can be very important, both at the part level and also for features and configs.

Master It   Use SolidWorks Treehouse to establish the framework for a simple product with two layers of subassemblies. Add some custom properties to the documents that you might want to use to fill in a BOM. Use appropriate templates and save the documents to a special folder.

Solution   Use the data in the Solution1 folder contained in the download data to compare to your solution. You can use SolidWorks or Treehouse to open the existing files.

Master It   Speed is a huge part of building an efficient assembly. You measure speed with the Tools ➤ Evaluate ➤ Performance Evaluation tool. Open the Performance Evaluation tool while looking at an assembly (for example, the Bike Finished.sldasm) and learn what you can about what types of features and techniques cost you the most rebuild or display regeneration time.

Solution   The number of shaded triangles goes up for curved parts or parts with a lot of small detail. Your graphics card calculates display based on triangles. Settings such as Verification On Rebuild and Large Assembly Mode also influence rebuild times. Overall assembly statistics also have an effect, including total components, unique parts, number of bodies, subassemblies, number of mates, and so on.

Master It   Use the Assembly Visualization tool to sort the parts according to various criteria, and become more familiar with the information presented by Performance Evaluation.

Solution   Expand the PropertyManager area so you can see the names of all the parts, and then click on the column headers to sort the list by Rebuild Time and Open Time. Examine the similarities and differences between the order of parts. Also sort by Graphics Triangles, and notice the effect of Quantity. What would you have done differently in this assembly to make it open faster and take less time to rebuild?

Chapter 14: Getting More from Mates

A thorough understanding of mates (and their editing and troubleshooting techniques in particular) makes the difference between a real assembly artist and a user who struggles through or avoids certain tasks. Much about mates is not straightforward, but with practice you can understand and master them. You can put assemblies together quickly, with a focus on rebuild performance and Dynamic Assembly Motion.

Although best practice concepts should not dominate your designs, they are great guidelines from which to start. To avoid making big mistakes, watch out for the pitfalls outlined in the section in this chapter that summarizes mate best practices to follow.

Master It   SmartMates are a key to putting assemblies together quickly in SolidWorks. Practice using SmartMates in a single assembly window, and also between a part and assembly in tiled windows. Practice using the Tab key to flip the orientation of the mate.

Solution   Successful SmartMates will get a Coincident and a Concentric mate. Make sure you are getting the mates you intend, and use the cursor icons to convey that information.

Master It   Make sure you understand the function of mates. Go through a sample assembly and sort through the mates that prevent motion and the mates that enable motion. Put these mates into separate folders.

Solution The mates shown with the ground symbol in the Mate folders under the parts are the ones that ground the parts. This is shown in the following graphic, and you can see them in action in the assembly named `Robot Assembly ground.sldasm`.

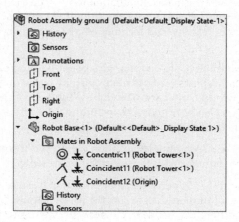

Master It Work through several of the specialized mechanical mates and make sure you can use the sample assemblies to re-create the motion. Use the parts from the sample assemblies for each of the mates and reassemble the parts to have the intended motion.

Solution Use the assemblies for Hinge, GearMates, CamMultipleFace, CamSingleFace, and LinearCoupler for this practice exercise.

Chapter 15: Patterning and Mirroring Components

Performance and best practice are both issues that require compromise. Patterns can cause a performance reduction because of the nature of the references. However, they can also improve performance because the need for extra mates is reduced, and it is easier to simplify the assembly by suppressing the pattern feature.

Feature-driven patterns are driven by feature patterns and transgress best practice suggestions, but they also add a parametric link, which updates the component pattern automatically. In addition, they offer many more options that are driven by the pattern options available to features in a part.

Master It Create a new part with a feature pattern, then put that part in an assembly, and use the `Patterned Part.sldprt` from this chapter and pattern it using a pattern-driven pattern.

Solution The solution should look like the tutorial example from this chapter.

Master It Create a new assembly from a template that uses axes for the main X-, Y- and Z-directions. There is one called `AxesAssembly.asldot` in the MBD template folder. Insert an assembly such as one of the sample bicycle wheel assemblies, and pattern it in three directions.

Solution   You will have to use two separate Component Pattern features to accomplish this. The result (depending on how many patterns you make) may tax the display on your computer. Part of what you should learn from this chapter is that just because you can do something is not enough reason to do it. You need to consider performance when assemblies and patterns start to become large. The definition of "large" will be whatever number of components starts to tax your computer.

Master It   Create a new assembly, and open a new sketch in the assembly. Create a closed-loop sketch that is bigger than 6 inches on a side where all of the elements are tangent (no small fillets or tangent arcs between lines).

Create a curve-driven pattern that uses the `Patterned Part.sldprt` to be patterned in two directions based on elements in the sketch.

Copy the sketch to a perpendicular plane in the assembly and create a chain pattern using the same part and the Distance Pitch method in the Chain Pattern PropertyManager.

Solution   See the solution in the `Solution 3 pattern assembly.sldasm` file.

Chapter 16: Working with Assembly Sketches and Layouts

Laying out an assembly with reference sketches is a more disciplined way of working that can help you avoid some of the complications of external references and in-context design work. It is up to you to decide whether the informal 2D layout sketches are preferable to the formal 3D sketch-based Layout feature. Both offer tools to control positions of parts and even features of parts within an assembly.

Traditional assembly-modeling methods where each part is located by mates from another part do not stand up well against changes in the parts themselves. The main goals of the layout methods are centralization of control and stability of changes. I invite you to explore some of these methods using the tools you have learned in this chapter.

Master It   Use an assembly Layout to create a four-bar link and assign parts to the blocks in the Layout sketch. To remind you, the workflow for Layout is like this:

1. Open the assembly.

2. Click the Layout tool.

3. Sketch three bars of differing lengths.

4. Create three separate sketch blocks, one using each bar.

5. Assemble the bars to create a four-bar link mechanism. (Yes, a four-bar link can have only three bars, the fourth bar is ground.) If you cannot see how to do this in a 3D sketch, refer to the downloaded example for this chapter for hints.

6. Test the motion of the assembled link blocks.

7. Exit the Layout.

8. Create parts on each of the blocks.

9. Use the sketches in the parts to create solid geometry for the bars.

10. In the assembly, test the motion using dynamic assembly motion (dragging parts).

Solution Refer to the 4-bar Link Layout solution.sldasm assembly in the download material for a working Layout assembly using a four-bar link.

Master It Use the assembly you created (or the downloaded example named 4-bar Link Layout solution.sldasm) to first rename and then save out the internal virtual parts so they are external, stand-alone parts.

Solution Rename the parts by right-clicking on that part and selecting Rename. To save the part to an external part file, use the RMB menu and click Rename, which is the next option down the list.

Master It Edit the Layout from the previous exercise. Change the length of one of the links. This will involve first clicking the Layout tool, and then editing one of the blocks. When you exit the block, the layout sketch and then the solid geometry should both update. Perform a test by exiting the layout and making sure the motion is still correct.

Solution Refer to the downloaded example file named 4-bar Link Layout solution.sldasm to confirm that you have done the work correctly.

Chapter 17: Using Assembly Tools

SolidWorks packs lots of powerful and useful tools into the assemblies environment. Even if you are an experienced user, it pays to look through the list now and then because new functions are added frequently, or you may have a new use for an old tool.

Master It Open the assembly called Bike.sldasm from the downloaded materials for this chapter. Use each of the tools in the Tools ➤ Component Selection list to practice selecting parts in the assembly:

◆ Volume Select—Drag a rectangle and then drag it to create a solid volume.

◆ Select Suppressed

◆ Select Hidden

◆ Select Mated To

◆ Select Identical Components

◆ Select Internal Components

◆ Select By Size

Solution Selected components are displayed in blue and shown in the Breadcrumb display and the FeatureManager.

Master It Use Advanced Select to select any components where the configuration name is *not* Default. Then invert the selection (RMB on a highlighted item, and it should be the first selection in the list), and then suppress all of the nonconfigured items.

Solution You could do this more easily if you changed the initial conditions of the select, but using Invert Selection is good practice. Notice that this suppresses all the instances of the chain pattern, so you will have to manually suppress the Chain Pattern feature separately.

Master It Use one of the selection methods of your choice to select multiple components. Save the selection as a Selection Set.

Solution With the components selected, right-click and select Save Selection from the list. This will add a folder to the Folder list at the top of the FeatureManager. If you clear the selection by clicking in blank space and then click the newly created Selection Set, the previously highlighted parts will be reselected.

Chapter 18: Using Libraries, Assembly Features, and Hole Wizard

Assembly features can be quirky and are often used for specialized or niche applications. Having this functionality available gives you another tool in your toolbox for solving design and documentation problems.

The Hole Wizard can be a useful tool for placing machined holes through multiple parts. Automation is a great thing, and you should utilize it where it helps your process.

Master It The most basic step in reusing data in the form of libraries is establishing the location of your libraries. Use the settings at Tools ➤ Options ➤ File Locations to do this. First, determine if you need local (on your computer) or network locations for these libraries.

Solution Settings can be copied to multiple machines via the Registry or the SolidWorks Settings Wizard. Select a location for your libraries where it won't be overwritten by SolidWorks while installing, reinstalling, or updating the software. It is also a good idea to keep the libraries off of the drives where the operating system is installed, so your computer can be recovered without losing any saved data if there is a crash.

Master It Make sure you know where in your interface to find the Design Library and how to navigate its various elements.

Solution Refer to Chapter 2, "Navigating the SolidWorks Interface," to see how to access the Design Library.

Master It Toolbox can be an integral part of using libraries with SolidWorks. Learning to manage Toolbox, however, may drive you to make the decision to create and manage your own library of standard parts. Make sure you have learned where the weaknesses of Toolbox are and how to work around those weaknesses.

Solution   Toolbox's main weakness is when you have multiple users or share Toolbox data with people who don't all have the same parts built. Because Toolbox builds parts as they are needed, some users may have parts that others do not. Also, one Toolbox user can have customizations that others with whom he or she shares data does not. Toolbox is a brilliant idea, but its ability to work around differences is limited. Make sure that you have your file management issues worked out, and that everyone works from the same libraries. The potential problem is that Toolbox will suppress hardware for which it does not have a match. You may even save assemblies in a state where your Toolbox data cannot be retrieved. Many companies use Toolbox to create the parts, but then rename them and store them separately in libraries. Using Toolbox with configurations can add to the confusion if you are not careful.

Chapter 19: Controlling Assembly Configurations and Display States

Display states in the assembly can save you lots of time because they change faster than configurations and offer more options for visualization, including mixed display modes. Assembly design tables can select display states and drive many other parameters in assemblies. Remember also that Modify Configurations and the Configuration Publisher work in assemblies as well as in parts. Assembly configurations are very powerful tools for product variations and performance, especially when combined with a SpeedPak.

Master It   List at least three of the reasons or conditions under which to use display states instead of configurations.

Solution

◆ Display states should be used in assemblies instead of assembly configurations when you are controlling the visibility or appearance of components.

◆ Display states allow you to change between states more quickly than you can change between configurations. Display states also involve much less data than configurations.

◆ Display states can be linked to configurations.

Master It   List at least three reasons to use design tables when you're working with assembly configurations.

Solution

◆ Design tables are an organized way to keep track of the contents of multiple configurations.

◆ Design tables centralize the control of configurations, which can sometimes be confusing because of all the different ways of driving them.

◆ Design tables also give you all of the automation, organization, and analytical power of Excel to arrange and drive the data being fed to your model.

Master It   Explain the difference between Hidden and Lightweight model states.

Solution   With a hidden model, there is no visual data, but all the parametrics are active. With lightweight, only the visual data is loaded, with no parametrics.

Chapter 20: Modeling in Context

Although in-context functions are powerful and seductive, you should use them sparingly. In particular, be careful about file management issues such as renaming parts and assemblies. The best approach is to use SolidWorks Explorer or the Save As command with both the parts and assemblies open.

In-context techniques, including the Layout feature, are the pinnacle of true parametric practice and enable you to take the concepts of design intent and design for change to an entirely new level.

Master It   The first step in being able to work fluently with external references is to be able to recognize, identify, and edit them. Select a part from the download materials for this chapter with external references, and use the skills you developed in this chapter and others to remove all of the external references without deleting sketches or features.

Solution   The tools used to edit external references are the Hide/Show Relations in sketches, the Edit Feature tools that show end conditions for features, and the List External Relations tools. You may also need to Edit Sketch Plane to accomplish this. As always, look for the -> symbol.

Master It   Sometimes mixing advanced techniques can lead to undesirable results. Name a couple of advanced techniques you need to be careful of when combining with in-context.

Solution   Motion, multiple contexts, configurations, multiple instances, circular references, etc.

Master It   Describe the differences and similarities between a broken reference and a frozen reference.

Solution   A broken reference cannot be fixed other than by deleting it. Broken references are created with the List External References box. Frozen features are created with the Freeze bar, similar to the Rollback bar. The similarity is that neither a broken or a frozen reference will update.

Chapter 21: Editing, Evaluating, and Troubleshooting Assemblies

You might create your work once in SolidWorks, but you are almost guaranteed to spend more time editing it than you did creating it. Because of that, you need to be even more adept at editing and evaluating your SolidWorks assembly than you are at creating it. SolidWorks has lots of tools to help you do this.

Master It   File management is one skill that doesn't relate to engineering or design, but all CAD operators must be experts. Mismanaging the file can mean you lose a lot of work—or worse yet, by mismanaging, you can create problems with the work that you don't realize until it's too late.

As an exercise, use the SolidWorks Pack And Go to make a zipped copy of an assembly that has in-context references. If possible, take the zip file to another computer with SolidWorks on it and open it up. Check to make sure all of the in-context references are still in-context (and not out of context).

Solution   Use the Performance Evaluation tool to look at the assembly before and after transfer to make sure all the external references are intact.

Master It   Sometimes it's easier to look at the big picture and the small detail separately. When you are working on getting Fillet34 to work just right, it's not always a convenient time to also be changing the overall structure of your product's assemblies and subassemblies.

To get some practice, use the SolidWorks Treehouse tool to create the assembly structure for one of your company's products or an automobile if you need a different idea. Get as detailed with it as you can with the time you have available.

Solution   Getting organized at the beginning of a project is often a key to success later. Organization helps you plan for various types of work that you know are coming. For example, you can't do stress analysis until all the components exist in CAD. You need drawings to get quotes from vendors.

Make sure that your Treehouse structure is detailed and accurate.

Master It   Efficiency is one of the most important qualities of processes, workers, and tools. Use the SolidWorks Performance Evaluation tools to look at the Bike assembly to evaluate which parts are costing you the most to open on your computer. Cost is often measured by rebuild time. Make a set of recommendations for remodeling the bike so that the design costs are lower.

Solution   For this exercise, design costs are measured by rebuild and editing time. Other factors such as open time, errors, display performance, and overall statistics must also come in to play.

Chapter 22: Working with Large Scale Design

SolidWorks has long been used for the design of equipment and components that go into buildings. With Large Scale Design, the software also works for the design of small plants and gridded structures. Walk-through capabilities give Large Scale Design users some animation capabilities, and the *.IFC export options allow users to share SolidWorks Large Scale Designs with other BIM software users.

Master It   Use Large Design Review to examine the dump truck.sldasm model that is included with the download materials for this chapter. Also open the same model in standard SolidWorks and familiarize yourself with the differences between the two.

Solution   Large Design Review or LDR is primarily a viewer that looks at SolidWorks assembly data in lightweight mode.

Master It   Again, use the dump truck model to make a walk-through. Use either the manual controls or the 3D sketch path to direct the walk-through.

Solution   Create a movie to finish the walk-through project.

Master It Start a new part and open a new GridSystem feature. Lay out a three-story structure to hold processing equipment, where the spacing between the first two floors is 10 feet and the spacing between Floors 2 and 3 is 12 feet.

Solution Save the end product and examine it with the View Grid Components tool.

Chapter 23: Animating with the MotionManager

If you keep your animation relatively simple, the MotionManager tools in SolidWorks Standard should produce adequate results in some situations. If you are using mates to drive motion, be sure to follow best practice recommendations for mates. If you are manually positioning parts, remember to place key points closer together if the motion curvature changes abruptly.

If you are making larger animations and the end product is just an AVI file, it's acceptable to break the animation into smaller bits. This makes each part of the animation much simpler to do, and work can even be delegated to other users or other machines for parallel processing. It may also be beneficial to use post-processing to add captions and narration to your movies; a few words of explanation might be valuable to viewers.

Master It In a blank assembly, create a camera with a circular path that focuses on the origin. Save the assembly as a template, and then use that template to create an easy turntable animation of any assembly or part you put into that assembly.

Solution Test this by making new assemblies with a single part or another assembly inserted into it. Yes, they will all be the same aside from the geometry of the part/assembly, but they can be created in seconds.

Master It Using the large dump truck, make an animation of the bucket raising and lowering, with a second before the motion, a second between raising and lowering, and a second after the lowering. Try to use the tools for mirroring the path that you learned in this chapter.

Solution Getting practice with the simple tasks will get you going on more interesting animations.

Master It Use RealView settings if your hardware is capable. Save out an AVI movie or the previous animation. Make sure it plays back as you expect on your computer and at least one other computer.

Solution Sometimes getting the video codecs straight on your computer is the key to viewing movies you have created in SolidWorks.

Chapter 24: Automating Drawings: The Basics

Getting your templates and formats correct creates an excellent opportunity to save some time with drawings by automating many of the common tasks using templates, predefined views, multiple formats, blocks, favorites, and linked custom properties. Setup becomes more important when you are administering a larger installation, but it is also important if it's just for yourself. One of the most important things you can do is to establish a file library and direct your Tools ➤ Options ➤ File Locations paths to the files. There's nothing quite as productive as having something that works right the first time and every time.

Master It   Create formats for size A and B drawings. Copy them from existing DXF or DWG data, and modify them for your needs. Save as `*.SLDDRT` file type.

Use the title block functionality to create an editable block of manually filled-in annotation in the format.

Solution   Formats should have a border around the outside of the drawing area and a title block with text annotations.

Master It   Set up a drawing template with the custom properties such as Revision, DrawnBy, ReleaseDate, and other properties that you can use to automatically fill out fields on your title block. Also, place one predefined view and a couple projected views.

Make sure that you save an appropriately sized format with your template, such that the template is sheet size specific.

Solution   Test your template by putting a part onto it, to make sure it populates all the views and all the fields in the title block.

Master It   Create a second page format with simplified title block and place it in a two-page drawing template. Make sure you have stand-alone copies of the formats in case you have a situation where you need to update the formats in drawings.

Solution   Second drawing pages are often useful in assembly drawings, or package or process drawings where you have a large number of views or large-scale views.

Chapter 25: Working with Drawing Views

SolidWorks has the capacity to make many different types of views of parts. In addition to the tools for projecting views, custom views saved in the model document can be saved and used on the drawing. The associative nature of the drawing to the model helps ensure that drawing views, regardless of how unusual the section angle or view orientation, are displayed in the correct size, location, and geometry.

It's sometimes better to create some of the views that require sketches by pre-sketching. Utilize workflow enhancements when possible; for example, the automated workflow of the Broken-Out section works well, but forcing it to be a manual process makes it awkward to use.

Master It   Included with the downloads for Chapter 1, "Introducing SolidWorks," you will find a folder full of document (part, assembly, and drawing) templates. Using Windows Explorer, sort the templates and copy the `*.drwdot` templates into the location specified at Tools ➤ Options ➤ System Options ➤ File Locations ➤ Document Templates.

Solution   This should have been done already, but the need for templates in the correct location should be clearer now that you've made a lot of drawings in this chapter.

Master It   Use the Robot Arm assembly in the download data for this chapter to create a drawing that uses an alternate position view on the first page and drawing views of the individual parts on pages after the first one. Make sure to use a template with a special page 2 format.

Solution   There are a couple templates provided with second pages, and at least one template contains a stand-alone second page, in case it needs to be added at some point.

Master It   Create a new drawing, and place two views on it using separate parts (using the Model View tool). Next, rotate one view 90 degrees and align it with the second view.

Solution   There are two ways to rotate the view: one way would be to make a horizontal edge vertical, and the second way would be to use the Rotate View tool on the Heads-Up View toolbar. To align views, right-click inside the view border, select Alignment, select a method, and then click the view to which you want to align the first view.

Chapter 26: Using Annotations and Symbols

Annotations and symbols in SolidWorks have many options for connection, creation, alignment, and display. Recent releases have brought major improvements to text-box-driven annotations. Custom properties and hyperlinks enable the user to populate drawing annotations with content and links to content. Sharing styles in templates is a great idea for readily available note styles.

Blocks have several flexible uses and can be updated from external files across many documents. Their use to simulate mechanisms, piecing together schematics, and annotating drawings, in addition to the Belts functionality discussed in Chapter 3, "Working with Sketches and Reference Geometry," make blocks one of the most flexible functions available.

Master It   Create a note that is typed in with mixed case, and use a centerline symbol (the symbol, not an actual centerline) in it, and a link to a custom property from the drawing.

Solution   The All Uppercase option can be found in the Note PropertyManager. The Symbol Library is also in the Note Text Format panel (behind the centerline symbol), and you can link to Properties from the icon to the left of the Symbol Library.

Master It   Create a style that simply adds bold to a note, and apply it to several notes that don't use bold. Save that style to an external file, create a new drawing using your favorite template, load the style into the template, and resave the template with the new style. Confirm that the new style has been integrated into the format by creating a new drawing with that template, creating a new note, and then applying that style to the note.

Solution   The steps for this should be self-evident, just going through the steps in a self-directed way should help solidify awareness of this functionality for the reader.

Master It

1. Create a blank drawing.

2. Create a note with 10 to 15 words, and then force it to wordwrap with a width of 2 inches.

3. Add a leader to the note.

4. Make it a jogged leader.

5. Copy the note and make multiple leaders for the copy.

6. Use the various justification or alignment options for top, middle, and bottom align, as well as left, center, and right.

Solution   The point here is to gain a little dexterity with adding enhancements onto notes and getting them formatted the way you need to for local company drafting standards.

Chapter 27: Dimensioning and Tolerancing

The argument about how to set up and use dimensions on drawings is as old as the process of creating geometrical plans from which objects are built. It's often difficult to separate fact and best practice from opinion. Although I leave it up to you to decide these issues for yourself, this chapter is intended to help you understand how to create the type of drawing you want.

The biggest conflict in this subject arises over whether to place live model dimensions on the drawing or to allow the requirements of the drawing to specify which dimensions are placed where. I am by no means impartial when it comes to this question, but again, you must choose for yourself.

Master It Create a drawing from the part called `Simple Part.sldprt` in the download material for this chapter. In the front view, shown here, use the DimXpert to dimension the view.

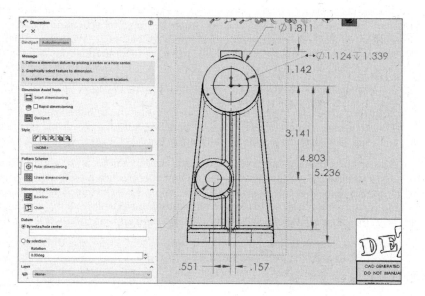

Solution Initiate the DimXpert by clicking the Smart Dimension icon in the sketch or Annotation toolbar. Then follow these steps:

1. Click the DimXpert button on the Dimension Assist Tools panel.

2. On the Datum panel, click in the By Vertex/Hole Center box, and select the circumference of the big cylindrical boss at the top of the view. The green arrows should appear.

3. Start clicking on features/edges of the part, and the DimXpert will add dimensions.

Master It Use the Dimension palette to add text and tolerances to some of the dimensions.

1. Add +/- 0.005 to the 5.236 dimension.

2. Select one of the hole callouts and replace the depth with the word **THRU**. Use the Dimension PropertyManager to do this.

3. Box select the 3.141, 4.803, and 5.236 dimensions and make them inspection dimensions.

Solution   The saved drawing `Simple Part Solution.slddrw` shows the result.

Master It   In the side view, use vertical ordinate dimensions to dimension some of the prominent features from that view.

Solution   It is best to turn on temporary axes or draw in axes for the cylindrical features to get started. To start the vertical ordinate dimensioning, click the Smart Dimension tool and make sure the Smart Dimension option is selected in the PropertyManager. Next, right-click, and under the More Dimensions flyout, select Vertical Ordinate. Select the bottom edge first, which will assign 0.

Chapter 28: Using Layers, Line Fonts, and Colors

Although SolidWorks is not primarily built around the strength of its 2D drawing functionality, it offers more capabilities than most users take advantage of. Layers, colors, and line styles can make your drawings clearer and easier to read.

Master It   Create a new drawing from the part called `Sample Casting.sldprt` in the downloaded materials for this chapter. Make a drawing of it and import the dimensions automatically.

Create a new layer called Dimensions and move all the dimensions to it using box select or the selection filter to help.

Set the color to the new dimension layer as dark blue.

Solution   You are starting to string together several automatic functions in SolidWorks. See how fast you can move through all of this data, and then imagine how long it would have taken on the drafting board.

Master It   Create several new annotations and place some blocks from the library.

Create a new layer for annotations and move these entities onto it.

Change the color of the new layer to dark green.

Leave the Annotations layer as the active layer and create a new annotation.

Solution   As you practice these workflows, the new tools will become second nature to you.

Master It   On the Sample Casting drawing, select a couple of interior edges and hide them using the Hide/Show Edges.

Next select a couple of exterior edges and change the line font to a thicker style.

Solution   Drawings give you the opportunity to communicate, and communication sometimes requires drawing someone's attention to a particular area. Using color and heavier lines are good ways to do that. With some of these new capabilities you have learned, you might consider using them to see if they help you make clearer drawings.

Chapter 29: Working with Tables and Drawings

SolidWorks enables you to work with tables that are highly specialized for particular uses and with general tables that are available for any type of tabulated data. The most frequently used types are BOMs, hole tables, and revision tables. Design tables that drive part and assembly configurations can also be placed on a 2D drawing, but in these cases, some formatting is usually necessary to make these tables presentable and the information on it easy to read.

Master It   Go through all of your drawing templates with formats, and all of your separate formats, and make sure that you have anchors for all of the table types your company creates.

Solution   The way to test this is to make new drawings with each template and place tables on them. Doing work ahead of time makes it so much more rewarding when the automatic setup pays a benefit.

Master It   Take an existing assembly drawing, add a column to it, add a property, and fill out the property values in the table.

Solution   Open one of the parts and check to see that the properties have been added.

Master It   Make sure the assembly has an exploded view, and make one view on the drawing show that explosion. Next, add balloons to the view, using at least two circular split-line balloons that show the item number as well as another value, such as the quantity, the weight, or a custom property value.

Solution   Attaching text (meta) information to graphical/geometric information is a great way to communicate quickly with people reading your drawings. Automatically supplying as much information in your drawings as possible will save you time and money, and it will help ensure that necessary information is on the drawing.

Chapter 30: Creating Assembly Drawings

Working with assembly drawings requires many of the same skills as working with regular drawings, but with much less dimensioning, and much more pictorial and visualization capability. Sometimes, you must use the unique tools for assembly drawings to get the job done.

Master It   Create an exploded view of one of the assemblies provided with the download materials for this chapter or one of your own. Draw in the explode lines.

Solution   The explode should show how the parts or subassemblies go together, and the explode lines should graphically connect corresponding points on mating parts.

Master It   Use a template with a second page to create a new drawing. I suggest the template called Mastering 2pg B size.

Create a drawing of the assembly for which you created an exploded view. The first sheet should be automatically populated with three standard views and an isometric.

Show the isometric view of the assembly in its exploded state and apply balloons to all the parts.

Place a Bill of Materials table on the drawing that shows item numbers for each balloon.

Solution   It should be self-evident if each of these steps is correct. If you are having problems figuring out where to find something, or how to make something happen, refer back to this chapter. Remember, a lot of tools can be found on the right mouse button menu, and SolidWorks is very context-sensitive, so having the right thing selected is important (view versus sheet versus geometry).

Master It   Starting with the drawing from the last practice exercise, switch to the second sheet. Click on the Standard 3 View icon on the View Layout tab. Select one of the parts from the assembly. If you have not opened any parts individually, you'll have to browse for it.

Place the views on the drawing and add an isometric view.

Put some custom properties in the part and make sure that the title block on the second page format picks up some of the part information.

Solution   Automation becomes its own reward when you start getting more out of it than you have to put into it. Learning some of the more advanced features in the software also pays off when you are able to accomplish more and more impressive tasks with a minimum of ongoing effort.

Chapter 31: Modeling Multibodies

Beginning to understand how to work with multiple bodies in SolidWorks opens a gateway to a new world of modeling possibilities. Like in-context design, multibody modeling is definitely something that you have to go into with your eyes open. You'll experience difficulties when using this technique, but you'll also find new possibilities that weren't available with other techniques. The key to success with multibody techniques is understanding the capabilities and limitations of the tools.

When using a model with the multibody approach, make sure you can identify a reason for doing it this way rather than using a more conventional approach. Also keep in mind the list of applications or uses for multibody modeling mentioned in this chapter. For some types of work, such as using the SolidWorks Mold tools and weldments, you cannot avoid multibody modeling.

Master It   Use the following methods to create multibodies within a part file:

◆   Multiple closed loops within a single Extrude feature

◆   Multiple disjoint features of different types within a single part

◆   Creating two solid features that merge to create a single body, then turning off the Merge Result option in the second feature to create a second body

◆   A Cut feature that separates a single body into multiple bodies

◆   Splitting a single body with a plane

Solution   The steps to perform each of these types of body creation are self-explanatory, but the real value here is just getting used to going through the steps and seeing the result.

Master It   Using one or more of the models created in the previous exercise, use the RMB tools from the bodies folders and the Display pane to perform the following functions to body-level geometry:

◆   Hide and Show

◆   Rename

- ◆ Change Color
- ◆ Apply Material
- ◆ Change Display State
- ◆ Make a Body Transparent

Solution The steps to perform each of these types of body creation are self-explanatory, but the real value here is just getting used to going through the steps and seeing the result.

Master It Starting with one of the parts you created in the first exercise, use Insert Part to pull one of the other multibody parts into the current one. Then use Insert Into New Part to push the current part into a new part. Notice how all the parts are listed as bodies when treated in this way. Next, use Combine to merge any bodies that are touching.

Solution One way to run an interference check on bodies is to put the part into an assembly, and in the Interference Check, make sure the option is active to Include Multibody Part Interferences.

Chapter 32: Working with Surfaces

Surface functions have a wide range of uses other than for complex shape parts, but thinking about your models in terms of surface features requires a slightly different approach. Becoming comfortable with the terminology, and the similarities and differences between solids and surfaces, is the first step toward embracing surfacing tools for everyday work.

You can think of surfaces as being reference geometry—stand-alone faces that you can use to complete various tasks.

Master It Sketch a rectangle and extrude it as a surface. Then close one of the open sides with a planar surface and knit together the two surface bodies. Next, use the Thicken tool to thicken the surface into a hollow box.

Notice the change from the count in the Surface Bodies folder to the Solid Bodies folder. Save the part.

Solution A part created with these instructions can be found in the downloaded data for this chapter named master it exercise 1.sldprt.

Master It Open the part saved in the previous exercise, and use Save As to make a copy of it with a new name.

Delete the Thicken feature.

Use a Fill feature to close the open side in the box, and use the options in the Fill feature to knit the part into a single surface body and make it solid.

Solution A part created with these instructions can be found in the downloaded data for this chapter named master it exercise 2.sldprt.

Master It Open the part used in the previous exercise and use Save As to save it with a new name.

Use the Move Copy Bodies command to make a copy of the solid body, and move the copy to one side so it does not touch the original.

Use Delete Face to delete one face of the new body. Notice that the solid body changes to a surface body.

Use a Loft surface to again close up the missing face, use Knit to knit it into a single surface body, and use Thicken to make it a solid body again.

Finally, use the solid Loft feature to loft between the two faces of the solid bodies that are closest to one another, and merge the result so there is a single solid body in the part.

Solution A part created with these instructions can be found in the downloaded data for this chapter named `master it exercise 3.sldprt`.

Chapter 33: Employing Master Model Techniques

Each of the four functions has strengths and weaknesses. The Insert Part feature is probably the most flexible of them, mainly because of the additional items you can bring forward from the parent document, and the fact that it can handle both solid and surface bodies. The Split feature also has unique strengths because of its ability to split bodies, save multiple bodies to files, and reassemble the parts as an assembly.

If you are working with surface bodies, you must use Insert Part or Insert Into New Part. Another important strength can be found in the Save Bodies feature, which makes the child accessible from the parent and identifies the assembly in the parent.

Master It Leading up to master model techniques, you need to be proficient with body management. Master model is really just moving the body conversation to external files.

Name the four Master Model tools.

Name three body management tools.

Solution The four Master Model tools are as follows:

◆ Insert Part

◆ Insert Into New Part

◆ Save Bodies

◆ Split/Create Assembly

The body management tools are as follows:

◆ Keep/Delete Bodies

◆ Rename Bodies

◆ Move Bodies

◆ Body folders

◆ Body appearances/materials/display style

◆ Feature Scope (list of bodies a feature affects)

- Show Feature History (for bodies)
- Merge Result
- Combine/Join/Cavity
- Intersect

Master It Follow these steps:

1. Open a new part, draw a centered rectangle centered on the origin, and extrude it mid-plane to make a block.

2. Use the Split command and the three default planes to split the part into eight bodies. (Click the scissors to automatically select all the bodies for saving to parts.)

3. Use Auto-Assign Names within the Split command to make parts for each body.

4. Use the Create Assembly command (Insert ➤ Features) to create an assembly from the bodies created by the Split Command.

5. Assign different appearance properties to each part in the assembly.

6. Open the List External References for one of the bodies and locate the path to the original part.

7. Use the Lock All button to lock references for this body. Notice that only the references for this body are locked. The rest of the external references are still functional.

8. The locked external reference symbol –> * shows up on the locked part, but the rest of the parts still use the active external reference symbol –> . Check this by editing the Stock feature for both locked and unlocked parts.

Solution Compare your results to the master it exercise assembly.sldasm file included with the download material for this chapter.

Master It Go back to the master model (the original part where the block was created) and follow these steps:

1. Close all parts and assemblies other than the original master model.

2. Using the Save As Copy and Continue option, save the master model with a new name. Then close the master model. Everything should be closed at this point.

3. Open the new master model.

4. Roll back before the Split feature and add fillets to all the corners of the part, and then roll back down after the Split feature. (The Split feature fails.)

5. Edit the Split feature, recut the part with the three planes, and reassign names to all the bodies. Notice that SolidWorks avoids the previously created filenames. Make sure the Propagate Visual Properties option is selected. Exit the feature.

6. Assign the colors in the part to the bodies this time, and the colors will propagate to the parts.

7. Execute the Create Assembly step again, making a new assembly with the new master model.

8. Use Isolate to edit each body in the new assembly and add a Shell feature that removes the inside faces. Do this for at least three of the parts.

9. Change the size of the second master model, save it, and then switch to the assembly, which will update.

Solution Compare your results to the `master it exercise assembly 2.sldasm` file included with the download material for this chapter.

Chapter 34: Using SolidWorks Sheet Metal Tools

SolidWorks offers a broad range of sheet metal tools to tackle most of your modeling situations. Some of the tools still require a little imagination to visualize real-world results because the complex shapes created in the real world where bends intersect are problems for such highly automated software. The tools are able to deal with imported or generically modeled geometry as well as parts created using the dedicated sheet metal tools.

Master It There are three basic methods for working with sheet metal in SolidWorks: Base Flange, Insert Bends, and Convert Entities. We'll have one exercise for each method.

Follow these steps to build a basic Base Flange type part:

1. Create a sketch like the one shown here.

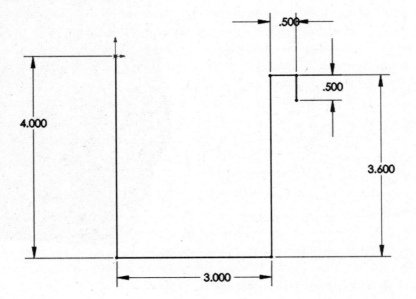

2. Use the Base Flange tool on the Sheet Metal toolbar to extrude the sketch midplane 4 inches, with a thickness of 0.025 inch.

3. Add a flange to one of the open sides that matches the height of the tallest flange (use Up To Vertex). The defaults are an Inside Bend Radius of 0.029 inches, an angle of 90 degrees, and the flange position set to Inside. Turn on Custom Relief and use the Tear type.

4. Put a Sheet Metal Gusset feature in the middle of the newly created bend. Here are the settings:

   Offset = 1.5″

   Indent Depth = 0.375″

   Flat Gusset, Edge fillet = 0.1″

   Indent Width = 0.500″

   Corner Fillets = 0.2″

Toggle between the partial and full preview to see the effect of the fillets to make sure everything works before committing to the settings. Turn on all the options under Flat Pattern Visibility so the gusset is located on the flat, even though it won't actually be there. Your model should now look like the one shown here.

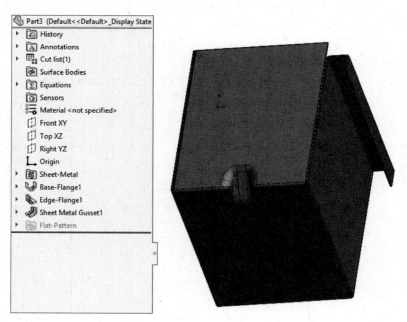

5. Flatten the part to see the result.

Solution Check your completed part against the one in the download material for this chapter named Chapter 34 - Master It 1.sldprt.

Master It The second Sheet Metal method uses Insert Bends. Let's make a part with that method.

1. Copy the initial sketch from the last part and paste it on the Front plane of a new part. Edit the sketch and drag the point that appears to be at the origin away from the origin, and then drop it back onto the origin to make sure it picks up that relation. The sketch will turn from blue (underdefined) to black (fully defined).

2. Extrude the sketch *using the regular Extrude command (not the Sheet Metal Base Flange)* using midplane, 4 inches, thickness 0.025 inch, material to the inside.

3. Open a sketch on the base inside face of the part and convert entities on one of the edges at an open end. Drag the ends back and dimension them 0.125 inch from the edges.

4. Extrude the open sketch up to the vertex of the *shorter* flange as shown in the following graphic. Set the thickness to 0.025 inch, and the material to the inside. (If the material goes to the outside, you will have edge-to-edge contact between the existing body and the new feature, which constitutes a zero-thickness edge and thereby produces a new body rather than merging with the existing body.)

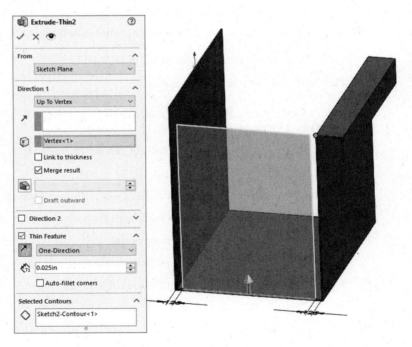

5. Use the Convert Insert Bends feature (this may not be on the toolbar by default, so use Insert ➤ Sheet Metal ➤ Bends if necessary). Set the Bend Radius to 0.30 inch and the Auto Relief to 0.50 inch. Accept the feature. This will give you the situation shown here.

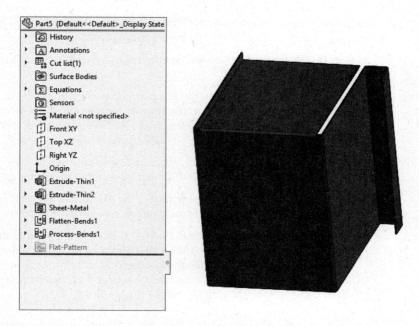

6. Use the edge flange to add a new flange on the remaining open end of the box. This doesn't seem like a big deal, but it combines new (Base Flange) and old (Insert Bends) methods for working with SolidWorks sheet metal.

7. Flatten the part to make sure it is correct.

Solution   Check your completed part against the one in the download material for this chapter named Chapter 34 - Master It 2.sldprt.

Master It   The final Sheet Metal method is Convert To Sheet Metal. Follow these steps:

1. Make a 3D box, 3 × 4 × 6 inches.

2. Use the Shell feature to make it into a 0.025-inch thin wall part and remove one 6 × 4 face.

3. Use the Convert To Sheet Metal feature with the following settings:

   ◆ Select the bottom face as the fixed entity.

   ◆ Select the four edges around the bottom face as bend edges.

   ◆ Under Corner Defaults, select Open Butt,0.05″ gap and 0.5 overlap ratio.

   ◆ For Auto Relief, use Tear with a 0.5 relief ratio.

4. Initiate a Corner Relief feature, as in the following graphic, with the following settings:

   ◆ Two bend corners

◆ Rectangular relief for all corners

◆ 0.1″ slot length

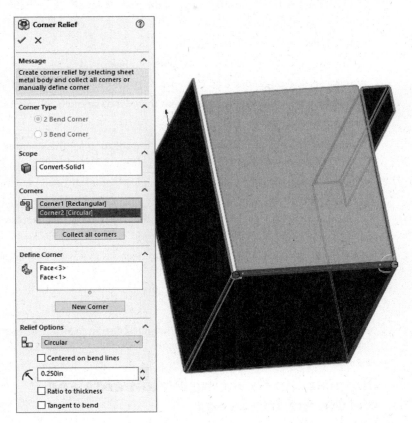

5. Flatten the part to make sure it is correct.

Solution   Check your part against the completed part to check yours against is in the download material for this chapter named `Chapter 34 - Master It 3.sldprt`.

Chapter 35: Creating Sheet Metal Drawings

SolidWorks has lots of special drawing functionality built around sheet metal parts. You may want to create a special template or format for sheet metal drawings or even use multipage drawings for including both flat and formed views of the part.

Multibody modeling in sheet metal opens another range of possibilities in documenting inseparable subassemblies and small weldments using sheet metal parts. The use of a cut list is similar to the use of a BOM, and though originally intended for weldments, it's also useful for sheet metal parts.

Master It   Create a blank drawing using a B-size template that has a second page (for example, the `Mastering 2pg B size.drwdot`). Remove any predefined views.

Create a flat-pattern-drawing view of the part `Chapter 35 - Master It 1 start.sldprt`.

Apply bend notes to the view.

Show bend lines without bend areas,

Show the bounding box on the flat pattern view.

On the second page, place an isometric view of the part, in Shaded With Edges mode.

Make sure the custom properties from the part have filled out the title block information.

Scale the isometric view at 2:1.

Solution   Check your drawing against the solution for this exercise in the download materials for this chapter called `Master It 1 finish.sldprt`.

Master It   Apply ordinate dimensions in horizontal direction for the major edges and baseline dimensions vertically.

Solution   Check your drawing against the solution for this exercise in the download materials for this chapter called `Master It 1 finish.sldprt`.

Master It   On the second page, place an isometric view of the part, in Shaded With Edges mode.

Make sure the custom properties from the part have filled out the title block information.

Scale the isometric view at 2:1.

Solution   Check your drawing against the solution for this exercise in the download materials for this chapter called `Master It 1 finish.sldprt`.

Chapter 36: Creating Weldments and Weldment Drawings

Weldments are based on either a single 3D frame sketch or a set of 2D sketches, usually denoting the centerlines or edges of the various structural elements. This creates a special type of part in the same way that the Sheet Metal commands create a special type of part. Structural profiles are placed on the frame sketch to propagate and create individual bodies for the separate pieces of the weldment. Custom profiles are easily created as library features; you can add custom properties to the library features, and then the custom properties will propagate to the cut lists.

Master It   The first step in being able to model welded structures effectively is to have access to good libraries of structural section shapes. Whether you use the default installed libraries, use Toolbox libraries, or download individual structural shapes, building your library is key.

Move all of your library data into an area that is not affected by SolidWorks uninstalls or reinstalls—ideally, some location that would even survive an OS reinstall (i.e., not on your C: drive). You may want to have it on a network drive to share it with others. Hint: don't use mapped drives, instead use a UNC path such as `\computer_name\shared_folder`.

Redirect SolidWorks to look for Weldment Profiles in the local or network location you have specified.

Solution   The file locations are set at Tools ➤ Options ➤ File Locations ➤ Weldment Profiles. Ideally, you should remove the old location and add the new location. You can add paths manually rather than by browsing by using the Edit All button, which enables text editing, so you can copy and paste paths from a list. These settings can also be copied through the Copy Settings Wizard and by editing the Windows Registry.

Master It   Build a picnic table using a custom profile (1.5 × 5.5).

Solution   Check your work against the model in the download material for this chapter called `Master It picnic Solution.sldprt`.

Master It   Create a drawing of the picnic table and add a cut list.

Solution   Check your work against the model in the download material for this chapter called `Master It Solution.slddrw`.

Chapter 37: Using Imported Geometry and Direct-Editing Techniques

In recent years, Direct Editing tools have received lots of hyped press and marketing attention. However, CAD tools dedicated to working primarily as Direct Editing tools aren't going to overtake the tools used by professionals who design and model for production. If anything, they'll be used primarily by non-CAD specialists for simple editing and simple concept development, and possibly by downstream data consumers such as FEA analysts or CNC (Computer Numerical Control) machinists.

The Direct Editing tools available within SolidWorks are powerful and are becoming more powerful with each release. Although they may be best applied to imported data, they can also be applied to native SolidWorks data. This brings up questions of best practice and duplication of effort. Sometimes, the changes involved in editing a feature near the top of a long feature tree can be time-consuming compared to simply moving a couple of faces.

Master It   Familiarize yourself with existing import and export options. Use a model without errors for practice. If you have another CAD package available to you, use that for practice as well.

Solution   Export options are available at Tools ➤ Options ➤ Import/Export. Set the File Format to each type and examine the options available with each.

Master It   Open an assembly from one of the chapters on assemblies and export it. Then import it to see how it behaves and what you get. The practice of export/import is called a *round trip*. It is one way you can verify that the software has written good output data.

Be aware that importing an assembly will save automatically named part files on your hard drive. Make sure that the filenames are not overwriting or causing conflicts with other part files.

Solution You must develop good file management practices with importing assemblies. Overwriting data is a danger of the automatic saving of parts.

Master It The direct editing features are

◆ Move Face

◆ Delete Face

You can also perform any function that affects bodies rather than features.

Take the Chapter 37 - casting direct edit.sldprt part and practice removing fillets (using the Delete Face feature with the Delete and Patch option) without using any history-based tricks like rolling back or suppressing. Start with a simple loop like the filleted edges of the pie-shaped cut out in the web of the part.

Remember that unlike true direct-editing CAD tools, SolidWorks leaves a history-based feature every time you use the Delete Face.

Solution Use the example saved in the download materials as Master It Solution Fillet.sldprt for reference.

Chapter 38: Using Plastic Features

SolidWorks provides a vast amount of plastics functionality. The more you use these features, the more power you'll find in them. They'll become second nature after you've used them for a while. The power and flexibility are amazing when you think of the incredible range of parts that you can make and evaluate with these features. Automated functions aren't the answer to all problems, however. You need to be well versed in workaround techniques for more complex situations.

Master It Follow these steps to create matching mounting bosses:

1. Create a new part, and extrude a solid box using the Midplane option, with the size of the box at least 4 × 4 × 4.

2. Use the Shell feature to hollow the box out with a wall thickness of 0.1″, without selecting a face to remove.

3. Use the Intersect feature and select the solid body and the original sketch plane to create two separate bodies. Make sure to turn off the Merge Result option. You want to keep the outer two shelled bodies so you are left with two halves of an open box.

4. Sketch a circle on a face of the block parallel to the split plane, as shown here.

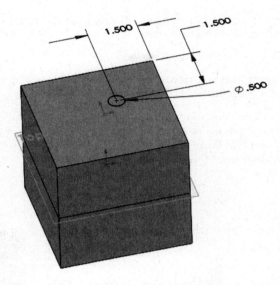

5. Initiate a mounting boss, using the circle to locate the boss, and an edge perpendicular to the split as the direction.

6. Select Hardware Boss type and the Head option. Other options are shown in the following graphic. You cannot go back to change the boss from Hardware Boss to Pin Boss later.

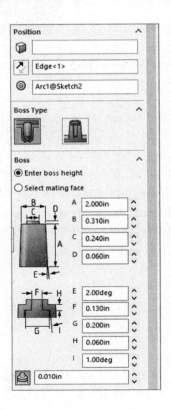

7. Use the settings in the preceding graphic for the fins. Make sure you use a model edge to fix the direction of the fins.

8. Accept the Mounting Boss options.

9. Apply a section view so you can see the inside of the boxes and still see the mounting boss.

10. Start the Mounting Boss feature again. Select the face opposite the original mounting boss face to put the new boss on. Select a circular edge of the first boss to locate the new boss. Select the Hardware Boss, Thread type as shown in the following graphic. Use a flat mating face to specify the length.

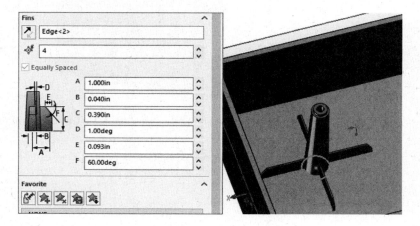

11. Determine the direction of the fins of the second boss and accept the second Boss feature.

12. Save the part.

Solution You can use the part called `Master It Boss.sldprt` in the download data for this chapter to check your work.

Master It Open the part you created in the previous Master It exercise and prepare to add a Lip/Groove feature to it.

1. Use the Save As functionality to rename the part to **Master It Lip-Groove.sldprt**.

2. Use the tool tips in the Lip/Groove Property Manager shown here for each selection box to make proper selections for the lip (add material) and groove (remove material).

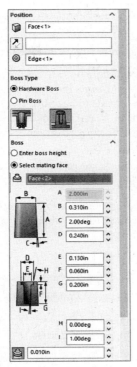

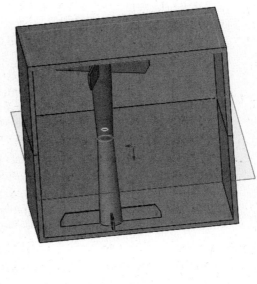

3. The visualization may be difficult for this feature, but with a multibody part, SolidWorks temporarily hides the appropriate body at the appropriate time to allow you to make the selections.

Solution Examine the part in the download materials for this chapter to check your work.

Master It The Undercut Analysis tool has been incorrect since it was added to the software. It's a little embarrassing considering the fact that the rest of the software is generally pretty good. It's like it was developed by someone who didn't understand the concept at all. Your mission, should you choose to accept it, is to write an enhancement request to SolidWorks to get them to fix this tool using either my suggestions earlier in the chapter or your own suggestions.

Solution Submit your enhancement requests to the following website:

```
https://customerportal.solidworks.com/SWSearch/search
.aspx?src=er&SRN=
```

Chapter 39: Using Mold Tools

SolidWorks Mold tools establish a method you can use for the semiautomated tasks involved in creating parting line, cavity, core, and parting surface entities and even pins, pulls and slides. For more involved nonplanar parting lines, you will probably want to intervene manually, which will call on your skills with surfaces, bodies, and visualization.

Master It   Understanding the draft analysis is the first real skill you need to have to create mold geometry in SolidWorks—aside from being able to create drafted parts, of course.

1. Open the downloaded part named Chapter 39 - Master It start 1.sldprt.

2. Run a draft analysis on it with the draft angle set to 1 degree and using the Face Classification setting. Face Classification counts the numbers of each type of face (positive, negative, requires draft and straddle—needs to be split). The Draft Analysis button stays depressed after you exit the command so that it retains the colors (rather than actually changing face colors). While in this mode, you can still work on the model, and additional features will be draft analyzed as well.

3. To exit this mode and set the colors back to model color, turn off the Draft Analysis icon in the Mold Tools toolbar. Save the model.

Solution   The positive or negative is determined by what you select as the direction of pull reference. In this case, 6 faces are drafted in a positive direction, 40 in a negative, and 0 each in the Requires and Straddle Faces classifications.

Open the part Chapter 39 - Master It draft analysis.sldprt to check your results.

Master It   Starting from where you left off in the previous exercise, follow these steps:

1. Use the SolidWorks Mold tools to add the Mold folders to the FeatureManager.

2. Expand the Surface Bodies folder to make sure it has subfolders called Cavity Surface Bodies, Core Surface Bodies, and Parting Surface Bodies.

3. Initiate the Parting Line command and use the same Pull Direction reference as you did for the draft analysis previously. Set the draft angle to 1 degree and click the Draft Analysis button.

4. Examine the part to make sure that the face coloring hasn't changed.

5. Notice that SolidWorks has identified a parting line with 13 entities, and that the message at the top of the PropertyManager is yellow (the warning is shown in the following graphic).

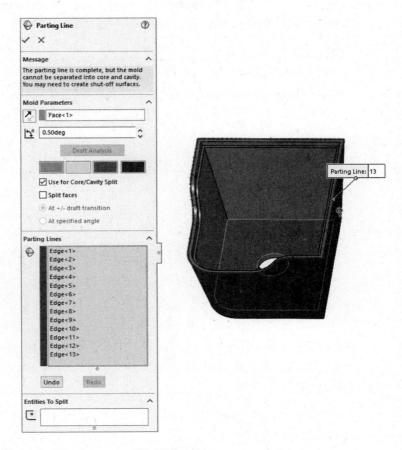

6. Accept the feature and initiate the Shut Off tool.

7. The shut-off may identify both the top and the bottom of the hole as shut-offs, but they will be identified as redundant. You need only one shut-off for this part. The shut-off edge needs to have all red faces on one side and all green faces on the other. So, you should delete the edge that has the same color on both sides. The PropertyManager message should read "The mold is separable into core and cavity" and be in a green field.

8. Accept the feature and save your model.

Solution Compare your model against Chapter 39 - Master It shut off.sldprt to check your results.

Master It To finish this simple mold, you need to create a parting surface and split the cavity/core block.

1. Initiate the Parting Surface tool. Set the Distance to 4 inches. Your model should look like the following graphic. This is a relatively simple nonplanar parting line, and SolidWorks gets this one correct.

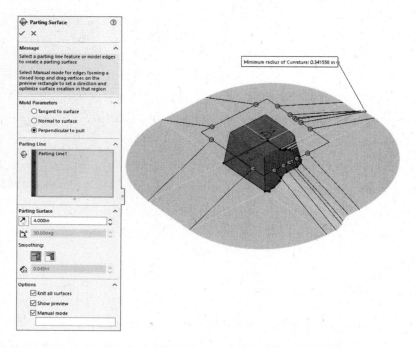

2. Initiate the Tooling Split tool and select the big flat face of the parting surface.

3. Sketch a square centered on the hole, 6 inches on each side, and exit the sketch.

4. Set the block size to 4 inches, and do not use the Interlock option.

5. Use F8 to show the Display pane, and expand the Solid Bodies folder and the Parting Surface Bodies folder.

6. Make sure to turn off the Draft Analysis mode at this point.

7. Designate the top mold as Insert Body and the parting surface as Wireframe, and hide the cavity and core surface bodies as well as the original part.

Solution Compare your model against Chapter 39 - Master It split.sldprt to check your results.

Appendix B

Finding Help

SolidWorks software has been around for more than 23 years now. In that time, the resources available to users seeking help have increased dramatically. These resources take many forms, from personal websites with information from individual experience to commercial online magazines or forums with advanced interfaces. In this appendix, I have assembled some of the worthier sources of quality information.

The goal of this book is not to endorse any commercial sites or services, but some of the listed resources are commercial in nature and may feature advertisements, logins, or paid subscriptions.

SolidWorks Help

The SolidWorks Help is irregular in the quality of information of various topics. For some topics, it is very thorough, and you can learn a lot by reading it. For other topics, you will be left wondering what the main topic being discussed was, where you might find the function in question, and what you might use it for, among other things. This book points out some naming irregularities, which also make searching difficult. Any search for help should include the official help files, but also the web. It shouldn't need to be said, but be careful when searching the Internet for information, as there is no guarantee the information will be reliable.

Some functions, such as Sheet Metal Bend Allowances and the Referenced Documents Search Routine, are extraordinarily well documented. Isolated topics are surprisingly thorough and extremely helpful.

SolidWorks Help is available in traditional Help files on the computer, as well as web-based help. SolidWorks Web Help was created because it is relatively easy for SolidWorks to keep a website up to date. You can access the Web Help by turning on the Use SolidWorks Web Help option in the Help menu in SolidWorks or at http://help.solidworks.com.

SolidWorks Web Help

Web Help was introduced to help SolidWorks keep the Help files updated without having to send out help updates in the service packs. It also enables the use of other search tools and links to online data sources to make finding help that much easier.

You can access SolidWorks Web Help through the Help ➤ SolidWorks Help menu selection as usual, but you need to make sure that the Use SolidWorks Web Help option (also in the Help menu) is activated. The following three sections pertain only to the traditional (non-Web) Help.

Contents

SolidWorks terminology has been a sticking point at times in the writing of this book because terms are either unclear or overlap. Still, it is difficult for two people to talk about the software if they are not using the same terminology. The Glossary, found at the bottom of the Help Contents list, is one of the most useful and yet most underused portions of the Help files. Often when a new user asks me a question, it can be impossible to discern what the user is talking about because he is not familiar with the SolidWorks terminology, is substituting AutoCAD or Inventor terminology, or is assuming all modeling terminology is universal. As dull as it may be, this Glossary should be required reading for all new users. Simply understanding the language being used by the training materials, Help files, and other users can give you a big head start when it comes to learning the software. Look through it. I promise you'll learn something useful.

Search

Many users overlook the three options at the bottom of the Search window: Search Previous Results, Match Similar Words, and Search Titles Only. All three are useful in narrowing your search. With the new Web Help, Search is improved, includes a section that allows you to further narrow the search results, and works like a guided search. Guided search provides a list of results, but also provides an index-like set of topics (in the upper-right corner) that you can use to narrow the search further.

Additionally, most of the Help linked to from the search results has a link to search the Knowledge Base (KB) on a related phrase. This search of the KB may or may not include any results. I have seen several links from the Help to the KB that were empty.

SolidWorks Website

Most of the valuable information on the SolidWorks website (www.solidworks.com) is behind the subscription login, but some free information is also available. It may be worthwhile to explore the SolidWorks site a bit, because it includes a large amount of information ranging from graphics cards evaluations to training files.

Graphics Cards

To get to the SolidWorks website Graphics Card information, go to the main SolidWorks page, click the Support link, click the System Requirements link, and finally the Graphics Card Drivers link. SolidWorks has tested the range of most popular graphics cards and drivers for compatibility with various versions of SolidWorks and has rated them at various levels.

Customer Portal

The SolidWorks Customer Portal is full of useful information. It requires a login, and you can find it at https://customerportal.solidworks.com. Portions of the portal, such as the SolidWorks Forums, are available to anyone with or without a subscription. Other areas, such as the service pack downloads, are available only to subscription customers.

SolidWorks Forums

The SolidWorks Forums have areas of wide interest for most users. They include about 40 different topic areas, each with a constant flow of information. SolidWorks employees sometimes answer questions, and knowledgeable users often give good answers and invaluable perspectives on not just modeling and CAD admin topics but also general mechanical engineering or materials sourcing.

You can read the forums without an account, but you need an account to post messages. Accounts can be granted to anyone even if you are not on maintenance. You can find the forums at http://forum.solidworks.com.

Make sure to read the Terms of Use available at the bottom of every Forum page. The moderators do not usually apply the rules strictly, but I have seen posts removed that should have been allowed and posts allowed that should have been removed. Generally, if you ask, answer, or comment in good faith, you will not have any problems.

Knowledge Base

If you have used the Knowledge Base before and found it less than satisfying, you owe it to yourself to try it again. The KB is constantly updated with new information, which comes from several sources, including general technical support results and the Help documentation. Searches actually turn up a lot of useful information. Results may include tech support responses to customer issues, SPRs (software performance reports—also known as bug reports), white papers, articles, and so on. In addition, you can look up SPR numbers you have received from tech support to check the reports' statuses. I consulted the KB several times while writing this book. It has been built from vast amounts of internal SolidWorks corporate support documentation, as well as the support database. I give it very high usability marks!

Software Downloads

Manually downloading and installing software and upgrades for SolidWorks is becoming outdated, although you can still do it. The SolidWorks Installation Manager works much like Microsoft Automatic Update. It downloads and even installs updates for you automatically. There is also a new Background Downloader that will download service packs while your Internet connection is otherwise idle, so they will be available to you when you want to use them. You can also work with automated administrative image installations. I particularly like that Background Downloader can download service packs before the links on the SolidWorks website are active. Of course, if you need or simply want to download service packs manually, this option is also available.

Release Notes

All the Release Notes for all the service packs of the current version are also available from the main Customer Portal window. This is essential information for CAD administrators. Technical Alerts, changes to the System Requirements (www.solidworks.com/sw/support/SystemRequirements.html), and new installation details are listed here.

Even if you think you do not need to know any of this information, it still makes for interesting (and at times alarming) reading. The Technical Alerts typically warn of severe bugs or other problems and how to work around or fix them.

What's New

What's New is a great document to refer to when you are learning a new version of SolidWorks. The What's New document comes in HTML and PDF formats. I find the PDF to be easier to access and read, but possibly less up-to-date than the HTML version. What's New is an important document to read before considering installing a new version, or if you have skipped versions. If you are looking for a What's New document from a version that you do not have installed, you can find all of the What's New documents on Ricky Jordan's blog (`www.rickyjordan.com/whats-new-guides`).

Installation and Administration Guides

Installation and administration guides are available for SolidWorks, eDrawings, and SolidWorks Simulation. They contain the basics about the topics and are not as detailed as other sources of information.

CAD Admin Dashboard

The CAD Admin Dashboard allows an administrator to view hardware, benchmarks, and settings for various machines under his or her control. This information is all stored in a SolidWorks database, which you can access from the website with a sign-in.

Some of the information listed here appears to be incorrect—in particular, all of the video cards on my computers are listed as "Not Supported," even though I'm using drivers downloaded from the SolidWorks website. The Windows Experience Index is also listed, but it is rounded to one digit. So just approach this with that in mind.

Online Forums

There are many types of online forums for SolidWorks. I have already discussed the forum on the SolidWorks website. Other forums are not directly sponsored by SolidWorks Corporation, and they may vary in quality. Your reseller may have available resources, so ask.

Blogs

Blogs for SolidWorks and related topics cover everything from opinion-based essays to speculation about future products, tips and tricks, or CAD industry news. Most are written by SolidWorks users rather than journalists, so you'll get specifics about a tool that you actually use.

I write a blog, which you can find at `http://dezignstuff.com/`. It covers many SolidWorks subjects that you may not find elsewhere, including CAD Administration topics, and articles on competing products and technologies. I also provide links to many other SolidWorks-related blogs, forums, and websites.

My blog has updates to books, notices of new books, lists of errors found in books, and a lot of other content. I deal with philosophical and ethical questions related to product design and CAD in general. I post advanced tips and sometimes excerpts from books. I also post questions for readers and polls where readers can express their opinions.

Many other blogs exist, including very good general CAD or other non-SolidWorks topics, and you should be able to find most of them from the links on my blog and the others listed here. These blogs do not all fit the same mold. Some are highly optimistic; others focus on tech gadgets, social networking, tech tips, or CAD news; some simply parrot press releases; and so on. For the best list of other CAD, design, 3D, rendering, and engineering blogs, view the blog roll in the right column of my blog.

Forums

Some forums are commercial, which means they are likely to contain advertising. These forums include:

- `https://forums.solidworks.com`. This is SolidWorks' site with official forums. The forums are very active in a wide range of topics and lightly moderated. This requires a login but does not require a current SolidWorks subscription.

- `https://my.solidworks.com/mylearning`. This site contains a lot of free self-directed training information.

- `www.productdesignhub.com`. This site is aimed at both industrial and product designers. It has an active forum for sharing ideas as well as a lot of great articles, videos, and other useful content.

- `www.core77.com`. This is probably the premier industrial design website available.

- `www.mcadforums.com`. This site has a lot of traffic and content, but it also uses Flash advertisements.

- `www.eng-tips.com`. This forum receives plenty of traffic, has a sign-in popup, and is highly censored.

- `www.3dcadtips.com`. This site is run by the owners of the *Design World* magazine, and it has a lot of information on general engineering topics as well as CAD.

Appendix C

What's on the Website

You can find and download the companion files from the Wiley website at www.wiley.com/go/mastersolidworks. The download materials consist of single zip files, one for each chapter. You will also find video tutorials, but I'll tell you more about them later in this appendix.

Extract the contents of the file to your hard drive in a location that is easy to access. The download material contains examples and tutorial parts, assemblies, and drawings, as well as templates, macros, and tables as appropriate for each chapter. The files are organized within folders for each chapter and are named for the chapter and the function they demonstrate. Some of the files are starting points for tutorials, and some are finished models meant to be examined.

If you make changes to files, I recommend that you use the Save As command (File ➤ Save As) and rename the altered file to keep the original file intact. You also can retrieve originals from the original downloaded files again if needed.

The download material also includes video tutorials for each chapter. The videos are narrated and offer another learning option to the print-only tutorials found in the book. The videos do not duplicate the print-only tutorials.

CAUTION I do not recommend that you open files directly from the zip files, because SolidWorks will respond with messages about read-only files.

System Requirements

Make sure that your computer meets the minimum system requirements listed in this section. If your computer doesn't match up to these requirements, you may have a problem using the contents of the download site.

Because of the changing nature of hardware and software requirements, please refer to the SolidWorks website for the latest in system requirements:

https://www.solidworks.com/sw/support/SystemRequirements.html

SolidWorks Versions

Files created in SolidWorks 2018 are not compatible with older versions of SolidWorks. So, if you have a version of SolidWorks older than 2018, you will have difficulty reading most of the files on the accompanying downloaded files. You may find some files that came from older versions in the downloaded data, but this only happens where the files have not been updated for new versions. Most if not all of the files are updated between versions of the book.

As a matter of policy, SolidWorks software does not open up future-version files. So, if you have SolidWorks 2015 installed, you cannot read files saved in SolidWorks 2018. If you have a question about this policy of the Dassault Corporation, you should contact your SolidWorks reseller. The author of this book does not have the ability to save 2018 files to previous versions.

This book was written using the SolidWorks 2018 version software, and while some of it may be applicable to previous versions, some of it may not due to annual changes that happen in the course of software development. This book was based on an earlier SolidWorks Bible I wrote. Earlier versions of the *SolidWorks Bible* do exist (2011, 2010, 2009, 2007, and 2013) and are still available—although some may only be available used or from third-party sellers, not from Wiley (the publisher of these books).

Troubleshooting

If you have difficulty installing or using any of the material in the companion downloads, try the following solutions:

♦ **Turn off any antivirus software that you may have running.** Installers sometimes mimic virus activity and can make your computer incorrectly believe that it is being infected by a virus. (Be sure to turn the antivirus software back on later.)

♦ **Close all running programs.** The more programs you're running, the less memory is available to other programs. Installers also typically update files and programs; if you keep other programs running, installation may not work properly.

♦ **Contact the author.** For problems with the content of the download data, visit my website (www.dezignstuff.com) or blog (www.dezignstuff.com/blog), or send me an e-mail (matt@dezignstuff.com).

♦ **See the ReadMe file.** Refer to the ReadMe file located at the root of the download website for the latest product information at the time of publication.

If you have trouble viewing the downloaded videos, please install the TechSmith video codec.

Customer Care

If you still have trouble with the download data, contact Wiley Product Technical Support at http://support.wiley.com. John Wiley & Sons will provide technical support only for installation and other general quality control items. For technical support on the applications themselves, consult the program's vendor or author.

To place orders or to request information about other Wiley products, you can call:

Americas: +1 877 762 2974

Asia: +65 6643 8333

Australia and New Zealand: +61 7 3859 9611

Germany (DEU), AUT, CHE, LUX, LIE: +49 6201 606 400

All other EMEA: +44 (0) 1243 843291

Index

M

X

Z